FREEDOM AND CRISIS

An American History

Second Edition

FREEDOM AND CRISIS

An American History

Generously Donated to
The Frederick Douglass Institute
By Professor Jesse Moore
Fall 2000

ALLEN WEINSTEIN
SMITH COLLEGE

R. JACKSON WILSON
SMITH COLLEGE

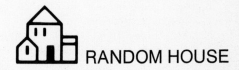 RANDOM HOUSE

To Andrew and David with love
Allen Weinstein

To Ann and Mary Corley, and all their generations
R. Jackson Wilson

Second Edition
98765432
Copyright © 1974, 1978 by Random House, Inc.

Library of Congress Cataloging in Publication Data

Weinstein, Allen.
  Freedom and crisis.

  Includes bibliographies and index.
  CONTENTS: v. 1. To 1877.—v. 2. Since 1860.
  1. United States—History.   I. Wilson, Raymond
Jackson, joint author. II. Title.
E178.1.W395 1978   973   77–17298
ISBN 0–394–31217–1

Text design: William Frost, Dimensions

Manufactured in the United States of America

Grateful acknowledgment is extended to the following for permission to reprint previously published material:

Joan Daves:—From "I Have a Dream" by Martin Luther King, Jr. Copyright © 1963 by Martin Luther King, Jr.
Doubleday & Co., Inc.:—From *Six Crises* by Richard Nixon. Copyright © 1962 by Richard M. Nixon.
Alfred A. Knopf, Inc.:—From *In the Court of Public Opinion* by Alger Hiss. Copyright © 1957 by Alger Hiss.
Random House, Inc.:—From *Witness* by Whittaker Chambers. Copyright 1952 by Whittaker Chambers.
Charles Scribner's Sons:—From *The Spirit of St. Louis* by Charles A. Lindbergh. Copyright 1953 by Charles Scribner's Sons.

CONTENTS

UNIT FOUR

DIVIDED AMERICA   304

UNIT SEVEN

MODERN AMERICA   708

UNIT EIGHT

CONTEMPORARY AMERICA 816

AUTHORS' INTRODUCTION

Freedom and Crisis is a book of discovery about the American past. The reader will quickly recognize, by glancing at the table of contents or by flipping through the pages, that this book is different from the ordinary "text." The difference is embodied in the way that *Freedom and Crisis* organizes the American experience.

Units are arranged in pairs of chapters. Every pair opens with a dramatic narrative of a significant episode in the American past. Each episode was chosen not only because it conveys an exciting story but also because it introduces many aspects of American life during the period under investigation. The chapter that follows then locates the episode within its appropriate historical context, interpreting the major forces that shaped the actions described in the episode.

This remains the book's basic format: a narrative chapter on a single episode, based on fresh documentary research, followed by an explanatory chapter linking historical fact and interpretation to the episode itself. The account of

Bacon's Rebellion in Chapter 3, for example, is followed by a chapter on seventeenth-century plantation colonies. Similarly, Charles Lindbergh's exciting trans-Atlantic flight serves as the basis for a chapter on technological changes in twentieth-century America.

We have employed this novel approach to an introductory book on American history for one very good reason. Our primary concern from the start has been to write a book that would hold the interest of today's students, perhaps the most inquisitive but skeptical generation of students ever. To do this, we felt that a book had to be readable and realistic. *Freedom and Crisis* is both. The book dramatizes critical moments in the American democratic experience and deals candidly with both the extension and the denial of liberty at those times.

Freedom and Crisis is not a traditional book on United States history, then. Often such traditional books are written in the belief that there exists a certain body of data (election results, dates and outcomes of wars, treaties, major laws, and so forth) that comprises American history. We accept this idea only to the extent that most of the data of conventional texts can be found somewhere in this book. Sometimes, however, the information is located in maps, charts, and special features rather than in the text itself.

Frequently overlooked by students (and even by some teachers) is the point that this central body of data, the "facts," emerges only after a certain selection on the part of historians. There exists, after all, an almost infinite number of facts that could be chosen to represent the history of the human experience. In writing this book, we simply carried the usual selection process a step farther. Half the book is devoted to selected dramatic episodes. When linked to the accompanying chapters, the episodes form our bedrock of factual material. Using this foundation, students can then inquire into the fundamental questions of American history.

Most episodes can be read simply as absorbing stories. Thus readers will discover much about the country's past merely by studying such vivid incidents as the Boston Massacre, the Aaron Burr conspiracy, the Nat Turner revolt, the Wounded Knee massacre, the Triangle fire, the Philippines revolt, the Bonus March, the attack on Pearl Harbor, and Watergate. But by using the interpretative chapter accompanying each episode, students will develop the ability to extract greater meaning from the facts in these dramas and, at the same time, acquire an understanding of related historical events.

Freedom and Crises moves chronologically through the American experience, but certain themes recur and receive particular attention. The book devotes several episodes, for example, to patterns of race and ethnic relations, especially the treatment of blacks, Indians, immigrants, and other oppressed minorities. The struggle for political liberties and economic betterment, class conflicts, territorial expansion, technological change, and basic ideological and cultural disputes are also treated.

The constant interplay of factual drama and careful interpretation is the book's distinctive feature. Facts and concepts cross paths on each page, thereby avoiding the usual unhappy classroom extremes of concentrating either on what happened or on why it happened. *Freedom and Crisis* has no room for empty historical abstractions that leave students without a factual anchor. Nor does an uncontrolled flood of rampaging facts lacking solid conceptual boundaries spill endlessly off the printed pages. The paired chapter format, we believe, avoids both these extremes.

The episode-explanatory chapter pairs present a concise but comprehensive introduction to the history of the United States. Yet although the book covers the American experience, we wrote with less direct concern for coverage than for concreteness, drama, and interpretive depth. Almost every detail included in the narrative episodes has a larger meaning, so that students and instructors must work outward in this text from concrete detail to generalized understanding.

We make no apologies for this approach to studying and learning history, since professional historians use it daily. History as an act of inquiry involves putting great questions to small data, discovering general significance in particular events. *Freedom and Crisis* evolved from our belief that students are both willing and able to engage in the same process of inquiry as professional historians. In this manner each incident in the American odyssey, from the earliest European discoveries to our generation's exploration of the moon, can become a personal act of discovery for the reader, risky but rewarding.

The chapters that follow chart our personal roadmap through the American experience. The book will achieve its purpose only if it stirs the reader into beginning his or her own private journey through the past.

Second Edition

FREEDOM AND CRISIS

An American History

UNIT ONE

COLONIAL AMERICA

The European conquest of the American continents was, like most momentous events in human history, a confused and complicated experience punctuated by a measure of greed, cruelty, and violence. The first pair of chapters in this unit of *Freedom and Crisis*, second edition, deals in general with the initial European discoveries, explorations, and attempts at colonization. For its specific example, it focuses in detail on the Spanish conquest of the elaborate and advanced Aztec civilization in Mexico.

From a modern perspective, the European triumph seems to have been an inevitable result of superior technology. But from the perspective of the sixteenth and seventeenth centuries, the European foothold in the New World appears to have been the precarious result of advantages won through daring exercises in ruthless desperation.

When the English managed to establish their first successful settlement in North America, they did not encounter Native American civilizations as advanced as those the Spanish found in Latin America. Nor did they find gold and silver. What they found was land — land that sometimes seemed impossible to conquer.

The early English settlements held on by a thread just as thinly stretched as the one that enabled Cortez and his men to survive in Mexico. They, too, encountered blood and suffering. Gradually, in the course of the seventeenth century, two successful centers of colonization developed, one in Virginia and the other in Massachusetts. Then, from these initial centers, English settlement fanned out into Maryland and the Carolinas, into Connecticut and Rhode Island, and into New York and Pennsylvania.

The two initial areas of English success—Virginia and Massachusetts—were alike in many ways. Their colonists faced the same basic problems of getting food, building shelters, and dealing with the native Americans they were trying to displace. And, at first, colonists in both regions tried to fulfill similar ideas about how a colony should work and be governed.

But, in the end, deep and important differences developed between the plantation colonies in the South and those of New England. Differences in climate and soil meant differences in the economic basis of colonization. Southern agriculture could use slaves imported from Africa. Another difference stemmed from Massachusetts being settled initially by the members of an intensely religious movement known as Puritanism, a movement characterized by some more or less radical ideas about how society ought to be reformed.

The second pair of chapters in this unit covers the political uprising in Virginia known as Bacon's Rebellion and a general study of the plantation colonies in the South. Chapter 5 of the third pair of chapters is about the witchcraft scare in the town of Salem, Massachusetts. This chapter is followed by a general discussion of the nature of the English colonies in New England.

Both stories—Bacon's Rebellion and Salem Witchcraft—like the episode on Spanish conquest of Mexico, reveal essential facts about the men and women of those times, and tell us much about the nature of the European experience in the New World.

1
CORTEZ AND MONTEZUMA

A. W.

For days Emperor Montezuma had eaten and slept badly, for he feared for the safety of his kingdom. Strange ships had been sighted on the coast, and Montezuma anxiously awaited the return of messengers he had sent to greet the strangers, to present them with gifts of gold and precious jewels, and to urge them to leave Mexico at once. Montezuma believed the newcomers might be ancient Aztec gods, returning—as a prophecy foretold—to claim his empire for their own. Both a deeply religious man and a cautious ruler, the emperor wished neither to offend his gods nor to lose his throne.

Following Aztec religious practice at times of great crisis, the emperor ordered that upon the messengers' return, two Indian captives be brought to the city's largest temple and sacrificed to the supreme Aztec god, Huitzilopochtli. Montezuma's priests tore open the breasts of the captives, and the messengers were sprinkled with their blood. This was necessary because the messengers had completed a dangerous and difficult mission: their eyes had looked upon the gods' faces. They had even conversed with the gods!

On the coast of the Gulf of Mexico, the messengers had sighted the white sails of gigantic ships. Armed strangers had led them before a light-skinned but sunburnt man, stocky and heavily bearded, who wore the armor of a warrior. This was the "god" himself, the returning Aztec deity Quetzalcoatl, god of learning and of the wind, whose sign was that of a serpent.

The messengers told the god that his vassal Montezuma was guarding his kingdom for him and had sent them to pay him homage. They dressed the god in Quetzalcoatl's vestments: a serpent's mask, armor, and other "divine adornments" heavy with jewels and gold. The other strangers—also light-skinned and bearded like the god himself, armor-clad and armed with swords—crowded around Montezuma's brown-skinned, clean-shaven envoys. Only when the messengers had completed their ceremonial presentation did the god finally speak: "And is this all? Is this your gift of welcome? Is this how you greet people?"[1]

The god ordered them chained by the neck and feet. The frightened messengers submitted without protest. They then watched several of the strangers walk toward a long iron cylinder tipped upward near the ship's edge. At the god's command, his men lit the cylinder with burning sticks, and the noise of the explosion that followed sent the messengers fainting onto the deck.

When they recovered, they were unchained, and once again the god spoke: "I have heard that you Mexicans are very great warriors, very brave and terrible. Supposedly one Mexican can pursue, overpower, conquer, and rout ten, even twenty, of his foes. I want to find out if you are truly that strong and brave."

The god next handed them swords, spears, and leather shields, ordering them to return at daybreak to fight his own men. The envoys protested strongly. If they fought with the strangers, Montezuma would surely put them to death. The god seemed amused by the frightened Aztecs. "No," he said, "it must take place. I want to see for myself." He dismissed the messengers and sent them back to their canoes. They paddled furiously away from the ship, some with oars and others with only their hands, fleeing from the god's command.

The messengers did not return. Instead, they hurried westward from the coast to report to Montezuma in the Aztec capital, Tenochtitlán

An Indian view of Cortez on his march to Mexico City. The eagle perched on the cactus, at right, was the Aztec national symbol and today forms the Mexican coat of arms.

---

[1]During his travels Cortez acquired several "interpreters." One such person was Jerónimo de Aquilar, a Spanish castaway who lived among the natives of Cozumel—an island of Mexico's Yucantan coast. The 'god's' other chief interpreter was an Indian women whom the Spaniards named Doña Marina. She was a 'gift' from one of the first Indian tribes he and his men conquered. Doña Marina became Cortez's main interpreter with Indian messengers such as those from Montezuma.

Deferential Aztec ambassadors present an angry Cortez with tokens of Montezuma's friendship and fealty in this sketch of a dramatic early moment in the conquest of Mexico.

(now Mexico City). From time to time they paused for food and water in villages or cities inhabited by Indians previously conquered by the Aztecs. Thus Montezuma's own messengers spread word among the conquered tribes about the arrival of strangers more powerful than the Aztecs themselves!

Once they had washed in the blood of the two sacrificed captives, the messengers told the emperor all about "Quetzalcoatl." Montezuma listened with fright, especially when they mentioned the explosive weapon: "If the cannon is aimed against a mountain, the mountain splits and cracks open." But their description of the god and his followers was no less fearful:

> How fearsome, for example, did the god's companions dress!: Their trappings and arms are all made of iron. They dress in iron and wear iron coverings on their head. Their swords are iron; their spears are iron. Their deer carry them on their backs wherever they wish to go.
>
> And how strange their appearance!
>
> Their skin is white, as if it were made of lime. They have yellow hair, although some of them have black. Their beards are long and yellow, and their moustaches are also yellow.

Montezuma hung on the messengers' every word. They confirmed all the earlier omens and signs, all the predictions of Aztec priests and magicians. His own messengers testified to the emperor's greatest fear: the return of Quetzalcoatl himself.

At once the emperor began preparing himself for the arrival of Quetzalcoatl, much as one of Montezuma's own fearful vassals would prepare himself for the emperor's arrival. The sacred Aztec texts stated clearly that Quetzalcoatl's return meant the end of Montezuma's reign and the destruction of the Aztec Empire. It had taken several hundred years for Montezuma's ancestors to extend their control from their original home on the small island fortress of Tenochtitlán in the great inte-

A sixteenth-century map presents a stylized view of Tenochtitlán. At the center stands the plaza with a great pyramid temple where important sacrifices took place. Causeways lead across Lake Texcoco to "suburbs"—here depicted as European fortresses. One Spaniard wrote on entering the city: "Gazing on such wonderful sights, we did not know what to say. Some of our soldiers even asked whether the things we saw were not a dream."

rior Lake Texcoco until they ruled all of Mexico. Most of the other tribes feared them. The few villages or cities that continued to resist had to fight constant and generally losing battles against the Aztecs, battles aimed not at killing the enemy but at taking as many prisoners as possible: a constant supply of human sacrifices for the insatiable Aztec gods.

Now in their calendar year "13-Rabbit" (A.D. 1518), Aztec dominance over Mexico faced its major challenge. Montezuma brooded:

> What will happen to us? Who will outlive it? Ah, in other times I was contented, but now I have death in my heart! Will our lord Quetzalcoatl come here?

At the same time, Montezuma began to search for means of determining whether or not the strangers were *truly* gods. "Strangers as powerful as gods" might be disposed of or dealt with more easily than Quetzalcoatl himself.

First, in the usual fashion of Aztec diplomacy, he sent magicians, along with his own personal wizards, to confront the strangers. He provided them with food for the strangers and with "captives to be sacrificed, because the strangers might wish to drink their blood." Traveling east, his magicians linked up with the gods moving westward from the coast. Immediately they began to sacrifice the captives, but as the strangers watched the Aztec ritual,

An artist's later conception of the Aztec emperor Montezuma, which contrasts the monarch's jewelry and plumage with a set of piercing eyes and a calm, dignified—but expressive face. Contemporary accounts of Montezuma do not necessarily conflict with the portrayal.

they were filled with disgust and loathing. They spat on the ground, or wiped away their tears, or closed their eyes and shook their heads in abhorrence. They refused to eat the food that was sprinkled with blood, because it reeked of it; it sickened them, as if the blood were rotted.

Montezuma's wizards had failed him: they had no magic powerful enough to turn the strangers back. And all along the route to Tenochtitlán, scores of Indians paid homage to the god and his few hundred companions. Thousands joined the march, until it stretched out for miles along the royal road. Several times, the strangers fought against hostile tribes whom they encountered along the way. Each time, the god and his men triumphed. One tribe in particular resisted ferociously. The Tlaxcalans, whose lands were to the east of those controlled by Montezuma and the Aztecs (see map, p. 7), had alternately fought with the Aztecs or lived in a state of uneasy alliance with them. Now, they battled the strangers three times before finally surrendering and pledging their friendship and alliance. After defeating the Tlaxcalans, the strangers marched on towards the Aztec capital, stopping at the town of Cholula. The Cholulans feigned friendship but planned to attack the strangers (acting at the direct orders of Montezuma). Through Doña Marina, the god learned of this plan and launched an attack of his own. The Cholulans were defeated and, like the Tlaxcalans, joined the ranks of Indian tribes supporting the strangers' march toward Tenochtitlán.

One final time the emperor tried to appease the approaching strangers and to induce them to depart. He sent Aztec war chiefs rather than wizards this time, warriors who presented them with golden feathers and necklaces, at which point the "gods" began grinning.

They picked up the gold and fingered it like monkeys; they seemed to be transported by joy. . . . For in truth they lusted for gold. Their bodies swelled with greed, and they hungered like pigs for that gold.

The strangers asked through their Indian interpreters whether the leading Aztec envoy was the emperor himself, to which that man replied, "I am your servant. I am Montezuma." The Indians who accompanied the strangers knew better. When they informed the gods of this lie, Quetzalcoatl himself shouted at the Aztec impersonator:

You fool! Why try to deceive us? Who do you take us for? You can not fool, nor mock us, nor deceive us, nor flatter us, nor trick us, nor misguide us, nor turn us back, nor destroy us, nor dazzle us, nor throw dust in our eyes! You are not Montezuma, but he cannot hide from us either. Where can he go? . . . We are coming to see him, to meet him face to face.

As the god drew ever closer to the city, Montezuma abandoned all efforts to halt his progress. Many Indians were eager for the god's arrival, especially tribes like the Tlaxcalans, who had chafed under Aztec rule for two centuries. One such Indian was the prince of the city of Texcoco, who led his people not only in joining the strangers' army but in accepting their religion as well. Although the prince did not understand why Quetzalcoatl pretended to worship an even greater god, he listened as the god explained that "the emperor of the Christians had sent him here, so far away, in order that he might instruct them in the law of Christ." Upon hearing Quetzalcoatl describe the mysteries of this "Christ," the Texcocoan prince and most of his noblemen asked to be converted to the new religion. Thus the two strongest subject tribes of the Aztecs, the Texcocoans and the Tlaxcalans, had joined the strangers' small band.

The strangers and their sprawling columns of Indian allies strode across one of the three causeways that led over the lake to the Aztec capital. They found this normally bustling and noisy thoroughfare almost deserted. On most days, tens of thousands of tradesmen, nobles, priests, and ordinary people used the causeway. That day, however, "all lay quiet: the people did not go out or venture forth. . . . The people retired to their houses . . . and the common folk said: '. . . Now we shall die; we shall perish.' "

Across this deserted, water-borne highway walked a remarkable caravan: the pale-skinned strangers themselves—armed, iron-clad, many riding their strange "deerlike" animals, some carrying iron crossbows; still others pulling the dreaded cannon; the thousands of Indians who had joined the procession during its trip across Mexico; and the god himself, Quetzalcoatl, directing the entire operation from a position between his own companions and his Indian subjects.

When the god and his huge army entered Tenochtitlán, they were the first armed and possibly hostile force in centuries to walk unopposed through the elaborate and complex defenses that the Aztecs had thrown around their capital. "We entered Tenochtitlán," one of the soldiers later wrote, over a causeway wide enough for three or four or more horsemen to ride comfortably abreast. The causeway was built across the lake and had wooden bridges that could be raised or removed. The water was [so] full of canoes loaded with people who were watching us that it was frightening to see such multitudes.

As we approached the city we could see great towers and churches of the kind they build, and large palaces and dwellings. There were over one hundred thousand houses in this city, each house built over the water on wooden piles, with nothing but a beam connecting one house to another, so that each one was a fortress in itself.

Montezuma, dressed in his imperial finery and attended by scores of Aztec princes, chieftains, and knights, awaited the god. The emperor himself presented gifts of flowers and precious ornaments to the visitors. Finally the god spoke: "Are you Montezuma? Are you the king?" The emperor replied that he was, and then came forward, head bowed low, and made a welcoming speech:

Our lord, you are weary. The journey has tired you, but now you . . . have come to your city, Mexico. No, it is not a dream. . . . I have seen you at last! I was in agony . . . [but] now you have come out of the clouds and mists to sit on your throne again.

This was foretold by the kings who governed your city. . . . You have come back to us; you have come down from the sky. Rest now, and take possession of your royal houses. Welcome to your land, my lords!

The god ordered his Indian translator to respond to the emperor:

Tell Montezuma that we are his friends. There is nothing to fear. We have wanted to see him for a long time, and now we have seen his face and heard his words.

This woodcut reconstruction of the great temple at Tenochtitlán and surrounding area suggests the extraordinary achievement of Aztec architecture, building design, and decorative arts. The great pyramid temple, site of Aztec human sacrifices, towers over the various subsidiary temples, government buildings, and fortress walls suggesting the gigantic scale of Montezuma's capital city.

Turning to Montezuma directly, Quetzalcoatl continued:

We have come to your home in Mexico as friends. There is nothing to fear.

The strangers then took Montezuma by the hand and patted him on the back to demonstrate their affection. Dismounting from their horses, they strode into the royal palace, accompanied by Montezuma and his chiefs. Within a week, Montezuma was to be their prisoner, and his chief nobles would flee into hiding.

"Quetzalcoatl" was known to his troops as Hernando Cortez. The "god" was a Spanish soldier and adventurer who had sailed to the Mexican coast from Cuba with a small fleet. Cortez had been ordered by Cuba's Spanish governor Velazquez to explore for precious metal, which would then be divided among the king of Spain, the Cuban governor, Cortez, and his men.

Cortez learned from the coastal Indians that the many tribes of the Mexican peninsula had been formed into an empire by the Aztecs. The process resembled the recent Christian reconquest of Spain itself. But the Aztecs worshiped natural forces that the Spaniard and his men considered pagan deities. Cortez was particularly offended by the Aztec ritual of human sacrifice. From the moment he first learned of these Indian religious practices, Cortez determined not only to search for treasure, but to substitute Christian rituals for the Aztec forms of placating the gods.

Very early in the expedition, Cortez decided *not* to share any of the Aztec gold, silver, or precious stones with Governor Velazquez. He would deal directly with the king of Spain in soliciting royal honors and in dividing up wealth and a new territory. Most of his men agreed. To keep those who remained loyal to the Cuban governor from returning to Havana and disclosing his treachery, Cortez resorted to a simple but drastic expedient. Once he and his men landed on the shores of Mexico, he burned his ships. From that moment on, he was legally a traitor to the Spanish king's representative, the governor of Cuba. Cortez realized that if he failed to stuff the king's coffers with Aztec gold, he would return to Spain in chains, if at all.

Although his troops did not consider their captain a god, as Montezuma did, they rallied to Cortez's almost godlike self-confidence. The Spaniards fought few battles before reaching the halls of Montezuma, yet they managed to force most of the Indian towns and villages they passed into submission. And upon their arrival in Tenochtitlán, they were welcomed as gods and escorted into the palace.

Although Montezuma soon realized that the strange warriors were not gods, the Aztec emperor continued to believe the ancient prophecies concerning the destruction of his kingdom. He became a prisoner in his own palace, and his power over the people of Mexico weakened at once. The Aztecs had offered no resistance to the white-skinned visitors, partly because of their own fears and partly because of Montezuma's commands. Their fears increased as they watched their own leaders either

Ornate Aztec carvings.

hiding from or bowing to "Quetzalcoatl." For several months the strangers ruled Mexico City by issuing their orders through Montezuma. Thus without shedding any Mexican blood, a mere three hundred heavily armed soldiers gained temporary control over an empire of millions.

When the Spaniards retired to their quarters on their first evening in the emperor's palace, they accidently discovered the main Aztec treasure room, filled (as one Spaniard later wrote) with "a large quantity of idols, featherwork, jewels, precious stones, silver, and an astonishing amount of gold, as well as so many lovely things that I was amazed." For the moment Cortez decided to leave the treasure undisturbed, and he ordered the secret room sealed. One of Montezuma's servants, who had watched the scene, reported to the emperor that "the Spaniards grinned like little beasts and patted each other in delight. When they entered the hall of treasures, it was if they had arrived in Paradise."

Montezuma informed Cortez that he offered the contents of the room to the Spanish king, along with whatever else remained of his own personal treasure. Cortez and his men, "amazed at the great liberality of Montezuma," proceeded to divide the gold according to the custom of such expeditions: one-fifth for King Charles; one-fifth for Cortez, "captain general" of the band; a large portion to cover the expenses of mounting the expedition in Cuba, and another substantial sum to pay for Governor Velazquez's destroyed ships; smaller shares for the various captains and officers who served under Cortez; and finally, shares for the ordinary troops, which were "so little that many of the soldiers did not want to take it and Cortez was left with it all."

At first, Cortez was less successful in swaying Aztec religious practice than he was in gold hunting. During his early days in Tenochtitlán, he urged Montezuma several times to forbid human sacrifice in the Aztec temples, but to no avail. Montezuma did grant Cortez's "request" for permission to erect a separate Christian place of worship, with a cross and a statue of Christ and the Virgin Mary, but he refused to abandon his own gods. Because the Spanish captain general hoped to dominate the Aztecs by using Montezuma as a figurehead emperor, he compromised for the moment. After all, an all out fight within Tenochtitlán would find three hundred Spaniards and their Indian allies surrounded by three million Aztecs.

Some time after Montezuma had been placed under "house arrest," his Aztec nobles began plotting to drive out the Spaniards. The emperor, however, observed his pledge of loyalty to Cortez and revealed their schemes. Montezuma even ordered the chief Aztec plotter, his nephew Cacama, seized and delivered to Cortez. Next Montezuma called a council of Aztec nobles, priests, and chief vassals, urging them all to submit to Cortez and to the Spanish king. Although they protested, the nobles obeyed, at least verbally, and pledged their loyalty.

Cortez by this time was so confident of Montezuma's continued influence over his people that he ordered the closing of Aztec religious shrines. For days thereafter, the Spaniards and their Indian converts to Christianity destroyed statues of Aztec gods, drove the native priests from their temples, cleansed the altars used for human sacrifices, and erected Christian shrines throughout Tenochtitlán.

Finally, the captain general apparently decided to increase his authority over the Mexicans by completing the humiliation of Montezuma. First, Cortez displayed before the emperor two Aztec nobles who, he said, had confessed that Montezuma had ordered them to lead a revolt against the Spaniards. Then he ordered Montezuma placed in irons. He forced the emperor to watch as the two Aztec prisoners were burned to death before his eyes.

If Cortez hoped to make the Aztecs and Montezuma even more fearful by this action, he miscalculated badly. Even Montezuma now threw his support behind the secret plans of Aztec nobles and priests to organize armed resistance to the Spaniards. The emperor no longer seemed uncertain and frightened; he began to recover his strength and resolve. At a private meeting, he warned the captain general to leave Mexico immediately because "the gods are very angry with me for entertaining you here." Montezuma indicated clearly to Cortez that he could no longer guarantee the Spaniards' safety against an Aztec attack.

Cortez stalled for time. For several weeks, Montezuma, reconfirmed in his authority, and Cortez, quietly encircled by hostile Aztecs, skirted each other uneasily. Both men waited for some decisive break in this contest of wills. The "break," like Cortez himself, came from the coast. A new expedition of nineteen ships arrived at Vera Cruz, a small settlement Cortez had founded. These ships brought soldiers from Cuba, sent by Governor Velazquez to destroy Cortez and his party. "Now you will not need to build ships," Montezuma told Cortez blandly. The emperor's agents had been in touch with the expedition's commander, Pánfilo de Narváez, and knew of its purpose.

Cortez left Tenochtitlán within days, taking most of his soldiers and Indian allies to confront Narváez. He left behind a small Spanish contingent under the command of one of his captains, Pedro de Alvarado. Montezuma remained a hostage, and most Aztecs seemed willing to wait, hoping that the soldiers of Cortez and Narváez would destroy one another. Then there would be time to deal with Alvarado's small rear guard.

But Alvarado proved restless as the appointed caretaker of Tenochtitlán; shortly after Cortez departed, the pent-up conflict between Spaniard and Aztec, which seemed almost like a struggle between a bee and an elephant, broke into warfare. It was the bee that went on the attack.

The occasion for battle came when Aztec priests requested Montezuma's permission to celebrate the feast of their chief god, Huitzilopochtli. This major harvest festival in Aztec religious life included an elaborate, exhausting dance-and-song ceremony which Aztec warriors performed at night in the temple courtyard. Alvarado heard rumors that the Aztecs planned to attack his troops once the dance ended. The hostility that the Spaniards were now encountering throughout Tenochtitlán, combined with the drum beatings, trumpet blarings, and frenzied dancing of the festival, struck fear in the Spaniards. Alvarado lacked Cortez's cool composure at such moments, and he misunderstood the ceremonial nature of the occasion.

Alvarado ordered his men to block the temple's entrances. Then the Spaniards moved into the courtyard and massacred all those within. An Aztec narrative described the scene:

> They attacked all the celebrants, stabbing them, spearing them, striking them with their swords. They attacked some of them from behind, and these fell instantly to the ground with their entrails hanging out. Others they beheaded: they cut off their heads, or split their heads in pieces. . . . No matter how they tried to save themselves, they could find no escape.

When news of the slaughter spread through Tenochtitlán, the entire community exploded in anger and grief. Montezuma's captains assembled thousands of warriors within hours, and armed with only spears and javelins, they attacked. Alvarado and his men immediately took refuge in the palace. The first siege of Tenochtitlán had begun.

Alvarado ordered Montezuma shackled again, and his soldiers opened fire with cannon and muskets to defend themselves against the thousands of Aztec spears. The Aztecs, enraged at the unprovoked slaughter of their temple dancers, scorned an emissary from Montezuma, who pleaded with them to return to their homes. "Who is Montezuma to give us orders?" they shouted at the envoy. "We are no longer his slaves!" Aztec captains and warriors denounced Montezuma himself for collaboration with their enemies. They put the emperor's servants to death, prevented food and supplies from entering the palace, and seized anyone attempting to enter. At the same time they watched closely the roads and causeways leading to the city, to guard against Cortez's return.

While Alvarado brought war to Tenochtitlán, Cortez managed to capture Narváez's expedition with a minimum of bloodshed. He first

A European woodcut portraying a somewhat benign looking group of male and female Aztecs paying homage in a may pole-like circle dance to carved images of their gods.

sent gifts of gold to Narváez's men and promised them more treasures if they joined him. Then he led his forces in a night attack on Narváez's camp. After some brief, half-hearted resistance, most of the eight hundred soldiers (Cortez had half that number) surrendered and swore loyalty to Cortez. Twelve days later, Cortez received a message from Alvarado describing his desperate situation. Cortez and his soldiers, now numbering perhaps a thousand, began a second march on the Aztec capital.

The Mexican siege had proved effective. By the time Cortez arrived in Tenochtitlán, Alvarado's men had almost exhausted their food and water. Cortez's column entered the city without resistance; the Mexicans apparently hoped to trap *all* the Spaniards inside the royal palace. By this time, the Aztec nobles had deposed Montezuma as emperor in favor of his brother Cuitlahuac, a man long committed to total destruction of the Spaniards. The Aztecs renewed their attack on the palace, opening a raging, four-day battle.

During this time, while still a Spanish captive, Montezuma died. The Spaniards later claimed that he had been fatally wounded by rocks thrown by his own people while pleading for peace from the palace roof. Aztecs insisted that he had been killed by the Spaniards.

With the battle going badly for the Spaniards, the royal palace, no longer a fortress, was fast becoming a death trap. Cortez decided to abandon Tenochtitlán and withdraw at night. By the time he fled the city, only four of the eight bridges on the causeway that led to safety were still in Spanish hands. All of these were under attack by Aztec warriors.

The captain general apparently hoped to surprise his opponents, but it proved impossible to hide from Aztec sentries the movement of a thousand Spaniards, several thousand "loyal" Indians, horses, cannon, and baggage. Cortez and his men also tried to cart away the *entire* Aztec treasure horde, most of it by then melted into ingot bars—a total of eight tons in gold. By the time this procession reached the causeway's second bridge, the alarm had been sounded; thousands of Aztec warriors encircled the fleeing Spaniards. The lake was thick with canoes full of Indians, who swarmed over Cortez's retreating company. "The canal was soon choked with the bodies of men and horses" ran one Aztec account of the episode. "They filled the gap in the causeway with their own drowning bodies."

When the armies had finished hacking and slashing at one another in the dark, at least six hundred of Cortez's thousand men had been killed, while his Indian allies (chiefly the Tlaxcalans) counted over two thousand dead. At least that number of Aztecs also perished in the battle, an episode that Cortez's men referred to later as *la noche triste*, the night of sorrows.

The remnants of Cortez's Spanish and Tlaxcalan army found itself harried mercilessly during the retreat that followed. Thousands of Aztec warriors remained behind in Tenochtitlán, many of them scouring the canals for gold and equipment abandoned by the Spaniards, but an even greater number marched north on Cortez's trail. They massed for a final attack, which occurred the following day (July 7, 1520) on a plain outside the village of Otumba. The battle ended indecisively, with the Spanish and Tlaxcalan contingents still intact. The next day they reached the safety of the Tlaxcalans' own territory. The Aztecs pursued them but did not attack again, and for the moment "Quetzalcoatl" and his depleted company could rest.

"When the Spaniards left Tenochtitlán," wrote a Mexican chronicler, "the Aztecs thought they had departed for good and would never return. Therefore they repaired and decorated the temple of their god" and began again to hold traditional Aztec religious celebrations. Yet life in Tenochtitlán never returned to normal, for Cortez was a persistent individual. He sent immediately to the coastal settlement at Vera Cruz for additional powder, weapons, and soldiers. Even more important, he managed to persuade his dispirited band of 400 survivors that they could reconquer the Aztecs and regain their gold.

The captain general and his men, several badly wounded (Cortez himself had lost two fingers on his left hand), marched after only three weeks' rest against the nearby Mexican town of Tepeaca. The defenders were easily overcome and most of them sold into slavery, a fate that Cortez decreed would await any Indian allies of the Spaniards who reneged on their promises of loyalty. The victory at Tepeaca had its desired effect. Indian tribes that had deserted the Spaniards after their flight from Tenochtitlán quickly rejoined their ranks, especially once they saw that Cortez was willing to allow his allies to continue their religious practice of ritual sacrifice.

Cortez began to prepare methodically for the assault on Tenochtitlán. He spent months gathering his Indian forces while constructing thirteen fortified sloops, known as brigantines, for use on Lake Texcoco during the coming battle against the Aztecs. Events in Tenochtitlán itself during this period worked to his advantage. Smallpox, a disease new to Mexico, spread quickly through the city, killing thousands (a fair return, one Spanish writer insisted, for the syphilis that the Indians had first transmitted to the Spaniards). Among those who died was the Aztec emperor, Cuitlahuac, who was replaced by one of Montezuma's sons-in-law, Cuauhtemoc. In the months from August 1520 to April 1521, the Spaniards and their Tlaxcalan allies raided a number of Mexican garrisons surrounding Lake Texcoco, seeking mainly gold and slaves while awaiting Cortez's order to begin the main assault.

By May 1521, Cortez's preparations were complete. He launched his brigantines on Lake Texcoco and sent messengers to his various Indian allies summoning them to battle. That month his entire force moved out, an impressive contrast to the scruffy band of stragglers that had taken refuge in Tláxcala territory the previous year. Now, with new recruits from ships that had landed on the coast, Cortez had again managed to muster almost a thousand Spaniards, as well as eighty-six horses and plenty of powder for his cannon. Marching alongside the Spaniards were more than seventy-five thousand Indian soldiers. Now a naval commander, Cortez directed the battles that followed from the deck of a brigantine, dividing the land forces into mixed Spanish-Indian units, each commanded by a Spanish captain. Soon after arriving at Lake Texcoco, his ships destroyed more than a thousand Aztec canoes. "We killed and drowned many of the enemy—the greatest sight to see in the world," Cortez later wrote to the Spanish king. More important, this early victory over the Aztecs assured the Spaniards control of the lake itself and thus helped seal the Aztecs inside Tenochtitlán, away from their allies and sources of supply across the lake.

The Aztecs, now encircled, were forced into an unfamiliar defensive role. The defenders of Tenochtitlán fought as bravely and ferociously to *preserve* their city as the Spaniards had fought the previous year to *leave* it. Several times Cortez himself nearly lost his life. He probably would have been killed if his Aztec pursuers had not been trying to capture him alive for use as a sacrifice.

The Spaniards, while waging continuous battle against the warriors of Tenochtitlán, at the same time attempted to starve out the city. Cortez's forces blockaded all the land and canal approaches to Tenochtitlán and seized relief supplies. For every Spaniard or Indian sacrificed to the Aztec gods, a thousand Mexicans perished through a longer, although not less painful, process, as the Aztec chronicles describe:

> The only food was lizards, swallows, corncobs, and the salt grasses of the lake. The people also ate water lilies and seeds, and chewed on deerhides and pieces of leather. . . . They ate the bitterest weeds and even dirt.

Several times the new Aztec emperor Cuauhtemoc and his chief nobles rejected Spanish demands for the city's surrender, while day by day Cortez and his army fought closer and closer toward the center of

Tenochtitlán. At Cortez's orders, his Indian vassals systematically destroyed every building and structure they captured, choking off all possibility of Aztec ambush and escape. They leveled entire streets, until the lake city of Tenochtitlán—only months before, the most majestic city in the Western Hemisphere—had become a desolate island wilderness. In the last days of the battle, Cortez's forces slaughtered thousands of Mexico's army, now penned into less than one-eighth the city's area at its very center.

The battle ended on August 13, 1521, almost two years to the day since Cortez had begun his original march from the coast to Tenochtitlán. That day, over 15,000 Mexicans perished during a final assault by Cortez's troops. The remaining Aztec troops and nobles, including the emperor, fled by canoe into the city's maze of canals, but Cuauhtemoc was captured by a brigantine crew. With his formal surrender, the independence and empire of the Aztecs ended.

A desolate peace settled upon Tenochtitlán:

> We found the houses full of corpses [wrote the Spaniard Bernal Diaz], and some poor Mexicans still in them who could not move away. Their excretions were the sort of filth that thin swine pass which have been fed on nothing but grass. The city looked as if it had been ploughed up. . . .

The essential bloodiness and confusion of Cortez's final assault on Tenochtitlán emerges clearly from this nineteenth-century portrayal of the scene. Attacked on all sides by Aztec warriors—and themselves attacking at the same time—both sides fought an acknowledged war to the death for possession of the city.

Of the 300,000 Aztec warriors who had begun the defense of Tenochtitlán, only 60,000 remained. Still the Spaniards' Indian allies continued killing indiscriminately, looting for gold, and taking Aztec captives, either as slaves or as victims for eventual sacrifice. Cortez took many Aztec nobles as his personal prisoners and ordered the entire city—which was strewn with unburied corpses—cleansed by fire.

Within days after his victory, Cortez exchanged gifts with his Indian allies, and the bulk of their 200,000 troops marched homeward from Tenochtitlán, laden with gold and captives. His own Spaniards, after celebrating a Thanksgiving Mass, began a relentless search for the Aztec gold lost during *la noche triste*. Despite the torture to which they subjected Aztec captives, however, they recovered only two of the original eight tons of gold. Much of that had to be sent to the coast for shipment to Spain as "the royal fifth," the share owed to King Charles.

Once the pillage and slaughter in Tenochtitlán ended, many of Cortez's men received not gold but Aztec slaves as compensation. Those Mexicans who managed to survive the destruction of their nation faced a future as slaves, either to the Spaniards or to their Indian allies. Cortez appointed himself the governor of all Mexico. With Tenochtitlán destroyed and its population made homeless, the last expression of Aztec culture came from the poems written to mourn this misfortune. Part of one such poem reads:

> Broken spears lie in the roads,
> we have torn our hair in our grief.
> The houses are roofless now, and their walls
> are red with blood. . . .
>
> We have pounded our hands in despair
> against the adobe walls,
> for our inheritance, our city, is lost and dead.
> The shields of our warriors were its defense,
> but they could not save it. . . .
>
> Weep, my people; know that with these disasters
> we have lost the Mexican nation.
> The water has turned bitter, our food is bitter!
> These are the acts of the Giver of Life. . . .

Three ships left Vera Cruz for Spain in December 1522. Their cargo consisted of gold—"the royal fifth"—and of exquisite Aztec jewelry sent by the acting governor of Mexico, Hernando Cortez, to His Most Catholic Majesty, King Charles V. The ships never reached Spain. They were attacked and seized by a French privateer, who delivered their contents to his own sovereign, Francis I. But the real prize—the Aztec Empire, not the remnants of Montezuma's treasure house—would remain in Spanish hands for almost three centuries after the first sighting of the returning "Quetzalcoatl."

2
EXPLORING AND CONQUERING AMERICA

A. W.

Cortez arrived in the New World more than twenty thousand years after the North American Indians. For hundreds of years, European scholars expended considerable effort and ingenuity in demonstrating that the Indians were the survivors of the sunken continent of Atlantis or the ten lost tribes of Israel. But nothing so spectacular had happened. Instead, roving Mongolian hunters had slowly wandered through Siberia, across the prehistoric land bridge of the Bering Strait, and into Alaska.

It took several thousand years for them to spread throughout the entire Western Hemisphere—past the Mississippi and the Great Lakes, down along the Rockies and the Andes, and on to the islands of the Caribbean.

Only when they had settled at various points did these nomads begin acquiring traits linked with a sedentary life, such as agriculture and domestication of animals. They then slowly developed complex civilizations varying in sophistication and size from the Aztecs to the Patagonians. None of them, however, could withstand the onslaught of the Europeans. Not all Indian states fell as quickly or as painfully as Montezuma's, and some would not have to contend with the whites for many years. But the Indians' control of the continents they had discovered had passed. Within two centuries of the first landing, the newcomers had divided up nearly fifteen million square miles among themselves.

DEVELOPMENT OF THE AZTEC EMPIRE

Since the Aztecs were perhaps as highly organized as any society the Europeans encountered, the building of their civilization deserves examination. The Aztecs borrowed freely from earlier cultures in the area. First came the people of Teotihuacán, who constructed a great city near the later site of Tenochtitlán. Teotihuacán flourished during the fourth and fifth centuries A.D. Here the Indians built pyramids, palaces, and religious temples.

A later people in the Valley of Mexico, the Toltecs, built another great city, Tula, just north of Teotihuacán. Under the leadership of a strong king named Quetzalcoatl, the Toltecs conquered a sizable territory, built beautiful palaces, and erected huge stone sculptures. Although Toltec rule collapsed, Indians in the Valley of Mexico retained Toltec cultural patterns. For example, they began worshiping Quetzalcoatl as a god. They believed that he had departed to the East, abandoning his people, but that one day he would return by ship from the other end of the world. This legend was the basis for Montezuma's initial fear that Cortez and his men were returning deities.

The Aztecs, a group of simple warriors, came into the Valley of Mexico from the north around 1215. Neighboring peoples helped to educate them in the fine arts and skills that had been handed down from the Toltecs. The Aztecs needed little training in the art of warfare, however. Within decades of their arrival in the valley, they had conquered every major city-state in the area.

The new overlords built upon the achievements not only of local peoples, but also of those in nearby regions, notably the Mayas. Mayan culture surpassed that of both the Aztecs and the Toltecs. Mayan civilization reached its height between A.D. 200 and 700. The people were not united under one government, but they lived clustered around such ceremonial cities as Tikal and Palenque.

THE FIRST AMERICANS

THE INCAS

Because of their cultural achievements, the Mayas have sometimes been thought of as the Greeks of pre-Columbian America. Similarly, the Incas have been compared to the Romans because of their imperial political and administrative organization. The Inca Empire sprawled over the western part of South America. It covered large portions of modern Ecuador, Peru, Bolivia, and Chile—in other words, most of the land available for cultivation on the Andean Plateau. In the eleventh century, at roughly the same time the Toltecs were invading the Mayan region, the Incas began ex-

tending their control along the Pacific slope of the southern continent. At its peak in the sixteenth century, the Inca Empire stretched 1500 miles down the coast and 300 miles inland. It surpassed the Aztec state in communications and organization, as well as in size.

The Incas considered their emperor, known himself as "the Inca," to be divine. He ruled from the capital city of Cuzco, high in the Andes Mountains. An excellent system of roads and runners connected Cuzco to every part of the empire.

The good Inca roads made it easy to move troops. "Not an insurrectionary movement could occur, not an invasion on the remotest frontier," wrote an American historian, "before the tidings were conveyed to the capital, and the imperial

Latin American artists and craftsmen produced works of outstanding quality. The great stone head at left, which stands eight feet high and weighs twenty tons, was carved by the Olmec people of Mexico, forerunners of the Toltecs. Another early culture—the Chavin of Peru—specialized in fine metalwork. The hammered silver object at top left represents the head of a puma. The Mayan stone relief above depicts a god receiving offerings from a priest, with writing overhead. This sculpture is known as the Panel of the Slaves because of the figure upon which the god sits.

armies were on the march along the magnificent roads of the country to suppress it."

The Incas had a more efficient war machine than the Aztecs, but it could not resist the Europeans either. An adventurer named Francisco Pizarro had first heard of a rich inland kingdom while voyaging along the Pacific coast during the 1520s. In 1531 he led a group of Spaniards into the Inca domain. They found the empire in the throes of a civil war between two sons of the previous emperor. The more successful imperial contender, Atahualpa, had recently won control.

Because of this civil war, Inca forces were weakened and divided. They could not muster effective resistance when Pizarro attacked. The climax of Pizarro's campaign came in a scene resembling the episode in Tenochtitlán, when the Spaniards slaughtered peaceful Aztecs at wor-

The Mayan buildings above are among several at Chichén Itzá. At left is a temple to Kulkulcan, the Mayan counterpart of Quetzalcoatl. The round structure at right is an astronomical observatory.

High in the Andes lies the Inca town of Macchu Picchu, below. Undiscovered by Spanish conquerors, it remained hidden in the mountains until an American explorer stumbled across it in 1911.

ship. Pizarro lured Atahualpa to a meeting, where he ordered Spanish troops to cut down thousands of poorly armed, unsuspecting Inca soldiers. Pizarro promised to release the Inca emperor after payment of a fantastic ransom in gold and silver worth an estimated ten million dollars. Once the Indians had delivered the ransom, Pizarro had Atahualpa executed.

NORTH AMERICAN CULTURES

The complex societies developed by the Aztecs, Mayas, and Incas contrasted with the simpler cultures of most North American Indians at the time of the European influx. On the one hand, the Indian population in Latin America was large; there were probably over fifteen million Indians south of the Rio Grande when the whites came. Societies were stable; people built cities and made a living by farming settled areas. Corn, the staple crop for almost all American Indians, was probably first cultivated in Mexico.

On the other hand, probably no more than a million Indians lived in what eventually became the United States and Canada. Instead of large civilizations like the Aztecs or the Incas, North American Indians formed small tribal groupings. Tribal societies in North America reflected the wide variety of climates and geographic features of the world's third largest continent. Alaska, Florida, the Great Plains, and the Rockies produced a striking diversity of lifestyles.

Remnants of some relatively advanced Indian cultures still exist in several regions of North America. One such culture flourished in southern Arizona, where an Indian-built complex of irrigation canals dating to the eighth century suggests highly sophisticated farming techniques. The Pueblos, the oldest inhabitants of the Southwest, lived in adobe villages built on high mesas. More warlike and nomadic tribes like the Navajos and the Apaches moved into the region later.

In the Mississippi Valley, early Indians known as Mound Builders heaped earth and rubble into pyramids and other structures used as temples or burial mounds; these have yielded many beautiful works of art.

In the large area to the north between the Rockies and the Mississippi River lived the Plains Indians: the Cheyenne, the Pawnee, and the

The European explorers of North America discover, often to their surprise, that the local Indian nations not only fought bravely and roamed their lands as hunters but also were skilled farmers, who introduced a number of crops—including the popular varieties of local corn—to the strangers from across the ocean, as in this ritualized sketch of an encounter between the two cultures.

Sioux. Although these tribes did some farming, hunting was the main source of their livelihood and the basis of their social organization. After the coming of the whites—and with them the horse—the Plains Indians happily gave up farming altogether and lived entirely by hunting the buffalo, which roamed the plains in vast numbers.

Small tribes like the Shoshoni and the Ute roamed the bleak lands between the Rockies and the Pacific Ocean. They made a poor living gathering wild plants and eating small animals such as rabbits and snakes. In California—home of the Pomos, Hupas, and others—acorns were a staple food. Life was easier there, and people had time to make some of the finest basketwork in the world.

Tribes such as the Kwakiutl, Nootka, and Tlingit lived in what is now Oregon, Washington, and British Columbia. They based their society on salmon and other fish available in the rivers, and on lumber from the great forests of cedars, using the wood to created handsome canoes and totem poles (many of which survive today).

Explorers landing on the east coast encountered more settled tribes living by a combination of fishing and hunting. Most of them dressed in deerskin and lived in bark-covered wigwams. The famous Iroquois confederacy occupied the New York State region. This league of five tribes consisted of the Mohawks, Oneidas, Onondagas, Cayugas, and Senecas. In the Southeast, Seminoles, Cherokees, and Creeks greeted the Spaniards coming up through Florida.

THE INDIAN WAY

Clearly, Indian life differed a great deal from group to group and place to place. But certain traits were common to almost all Indians and set them apart from other peoples—especially from the Europeans who settled in America. One of these characteristics was the Indian attitude toward land. A tribe might have hunting rights to a certain territory, but its members no more owned this territory than the sky above it. Even among the complex farming societies of Latin America, land generally belonged to the community or per-

Indians of a vanished era scratched these mysterious figures on a cliff wall in Wyoming. They may represent priests or perhaps gods held sacred by the tribe.

haps to a god or spirit. Indians had a different concept of land ownership than did the Spanish invaders.

Indians also had different attitudes about warfare. For them it was as much a ceremony as a conflict. Even in the Aztec Empire, where territory and tribute were important, the basic goal of war was to capture prisoners for a religious purpose. To many North American tribes, war was almost a game. Plains fighters, for example, achieved as much glory for touching an enemy in battle as for killing him.

The first Europeans who came to America were accustomed to monarchs, and to strong monarchs at that. But even a ruler of Montezuma's importance did not possess absolute power. He was in fact elected to his post, and many of his duties were merely ceremonial. Few chiefs of North American tribes had the authority to rule by themselves. When there was an issue to be decided, all the respected elders of a band would gather together and, after lengthy deliberations, reach a unanimous decision.

In America north of the Rio Grande, Indians created a number of distinctive styles. Typical of the Mound Builder culture is the kneeling stone figure at left, found in Tennessee. From New York State is the Cayuga Iroquois mask above, braided from corn husks. Masks like this were worn by members of the so-called False Face Societies—secret organizations whose members performed dances and other rituals to heal the sick. Below is a slate canoe sculpted by a Haida Indian of the Northwest. The figure in front is a shaman, or medicine man. He wears a crown of bear claws set in a rope of twisted cedar bark. The reclining figure at the back, with closed eyes, probably represents a dead person.

Indian religious concepts differed greatly from those of Christianity. The idea of an afterlife was, at most, vague. They prayed to no one God, but often to a multitude of gods or spirits. (The Aztecs worshiped more than 300 deities.) Indians were believed to have their own guardian spirits that helped them through life. Such spirits were also thought to inhabit trees, animals, rivers, and mountains. The Indians trusted in what we would call magic, but they soon found out that their magic could not make the white man disappear.

FIRST CONTACTS

Five hundred years before Cortez, in the far northeastern corner of the New World, Indians had in fact driven off the first European settlers. After raiding Ireland, France, and Italy, the red-bearded Vikings (or Norsemen) from Scandinavia also sailed far out into the North Atlantic. In the ninth

Navajo Indians of the Southwest are noted for their sand paintings, like the one above. Each one, combining sacred symbols and used as part of a healing ceremony, is formed by a priest in the morning and destroyed before nightfall. At right above are blanket bands woven by the Sioux Indians of the Great Plains. These were made after the white man came with beads for trade; in the early days, women fashioned similar designs using dyed porcupine quills or wampum (beads drilled from clam shells). The whale statuette at right was carved by a Chumash Indian of California.

century they established a settlement in Iceland. From this base of operations they conducted daring voyages of exploration farther westward.

Vikings led by Eric the Red discovered and settled Greenland during the tenth century. Around the year 1000, Eric's son Leif anchored his ship off the coast of what is now Newfoundland. He called the place Vineland the Good, and he and his men spent the winter there before returning to Greenland. A decade later, other Vikings sailed from Iceland to found a colony of farmers and tradesmen in Vineland. After spending two or three years fighting hostile Indians, however, they abandoned their settlement and returned to their Greenland base.

Cortez knew as little of his Scandinavian predecessors as Montezuma did. His knowledge that a New World existed came, of course, from the reports of an Italian, Christopher Columbus, exploring under the Spanish flag. In 1492 Columbus, with ninety men in three small ships, landed on a small island in the Caribbean, and promptly returned to Spain to announce that he had found China.

SPANISH AND PORTUGUESE EXPLORATION

Lacking the Vikings' pure thirst for adventure, the Spanish had a specific reason for sending out Columbus and the many Spanish explorers who followed him. For centuries, luxury products such as spices, jewels, and silk had come from Asia overland or across the Indian Ocean. In either case, the Italian middlemen transported the goods from the eastern end of the Mediterranean into western Europe. They had a monopoly on the trade, so they charged high prices. Nations on the Atlantic—Portugal and Spain, for example—decided to bypass the Mediterranean (and the Italians) and do their own trading with the East.

The Portuguese concentrated mainly on finding a route around Africa and then eastward to India and China. In the early fifteenth century, Prince Henry the Navigator sponsored a school of navigation on his country's southwestern coast. He devoted his life to sending out fleets of ships to explore the west coast of Africa. Year by year the Portuguese sailed farther south along the African coast. In 1488 Bartholomew Diaz voyaged as far as the Cape of Good Hope, at the tip of Africa. Vasco da Gama sailed around the cape and reached India in 1498, returning to Portugal with a rich cargo the following year. In 1500 Pedro Cabral, headed for India, was blown off course by trade winds and landed in what is now Brazil. This region of South America, claimed by Portugal, was the only area in the Western Hemisphere that the Portuguese exploited.

The Spanish, pursuing a different strategy, sent Columbus west to reach Asia. Although the admiral found only a scraggly village of naked Indians, he remained convinced that he had reached, if not China, certainly the outlying areas of Asia. On Columbus's three subsequent voyages, mainly to the Caribbean islands of Cuba and Hispaniola, the Spanish monarchs Ferdinand and Isabella sent along everybody needed to duplicate Spanish society in the New World. The ships carried missionaries, artisans, knights, soldiers, and

Christopher Columbus, by the Italian artist Sebastiano del Piombo. This portrait was not painted from life; no one is sure what the great explorer looked like.

field laborers. Unfortunately, even all this support could not establish a successful colony when the expected riches of the East failed to materialize. At one point the impatient Spanish rulers had Columbus brought back to Madrid in chains. Despite Columbus's lack of material success, he did set a pattern for future settlers.

The honor of having two continents named after him went not to Columbus but to a Florentine bank manager, Amerigo Vespucci. He claimed to have sailed to America several times. In widely read letters, he described his experiences in what he called the New World. In 1507 a geographer named Martin Waldseemüller suggested naming the new land "America, because Americus discovered it." (*Americus* is the Latin form of Vespucci's first name.)

In 1519 the Portuguese explorer Ferdinand Magellan, with Spanish backing, sailed around the southern tip of South America. He crossed the Pacific and thus found the westward route to the East. Magellan was killed by natives in the Philippine Islands. But his navigator, Sebastian del Cano, continued westward in the only ship that remained of the original five. He returned to Lisbon in 1522, having completed the first voyage around the world. The people of Europe than realized what many scholars had already known—namely, that the world is round. And they realized, too, that a whole "New World" lay to the west between Europe and Asia.

EARLY SPANISH EXPLORERS

In the fifty years after Columbus's first voyage, a host of Spanish explorers and conquerors performed incredibly daring and profitable feats all over America. Like Columbus, they dreamed of fame, of winning converts to the Christian faith, and of wealth; Spanish goals have been described as "glory, God, and gold."

For every Cortez or Pizarro who found the riches he had dreamed of, there were many who discovered only dusty, impoverished villages, bitter disappointment, and sometimes violent death. No Spaniard appears to have gotten rich

The many sides and interests of fifteenth-century Prince Henry the Navigator of Portugal, notably his military exploits and his scientific school of navigation at Cueta received sympathetic representation in this later rendering.

exploring what is now the United States. Juan Ponce de León (who sailed to America on Columbus's second voyage) failed to find either gold or the legendary fountain of youth when he explored Florida in 1513. After trying unsuccessfully to found a settlement on the peninsula in 1521, he was wounded by Indians and died on his return voyage to Cuba. Searching for the legendary "Seven Cities of Cibola," said to be full of riches, Francisco Vasquez de Coronado explored much of the Southwest in 1540–1542. When found, the "Seven Cities" turned out to be nothing more fabulous than the simple adobe villages of the Pueblo Indians. Hernando de Soto, leading a large military expedition from Cuba, wandered from Florida and the Carolinas to Texas and became the first white man to look upon the Mississippi. After finding only bloody battles with Indians, he died of disease and disappointment in Louisiana. Not wanting the Indians to find a white body, his men wrapped and weighted his corpse and threw it into the river he had discovered.

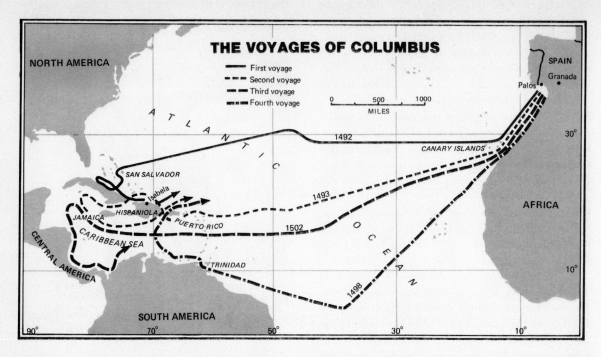

THE VOYAGES OF COLUMBUS

First voyage
Second voyage
Third voyage
Fourth voyage

NORTH AMERICA

ATLANTIC

SPAIN
Granada
Palos

1492

CANARY ISLANDS

30°

AFRICA

SAN SALVADOR

Isabela

HISPANIOLA
JAMAICA
PUERTO RICO
CARIBBEAN SEA
CENTRAL AMERICA

1493

1502

OCEAN

10°

TRINIDAD

1498

SOUTH AMERICA

MILES
0   500   1000

CREATING AN EMPIRE

In spite of all these setbacks, the Spanish continued to come to the New World in tremendous numbers. They formed political units and appointed Spanish rulers. They built missions, military outposts, and towns. In short, they created an overseas empire.

By 1600, a quarter of a million Spaniards had settled in the Western hemisphere. Here they introduced crops previously unknown in America—among them wheat, rye, oats, and barley. They found that bananas, peaches, and citrus fruits would grow well in America, too. Sugar cane became an especially important crop in tropical regions. The Spanish also brought draft animals—horses, mules, and oxen—and livestock, including cattle, hogs, and sheep. And the newcomers quickly learned to grow native American crops: corn, tomatoes, potatoes, beans, cacao, and tobacco.

Spanish civilization in the Americas prospered on gold and silver acquired from the Aztec and Inca empires. Fabulously rich silver mines were discovered in Mexico and Peru in 1545. Silver and to a lesser extent gold were for many decades Spain's chief exports from the New World.

SPANIARDS, INDIANS, AND AFRICANS

After the Spanish conquests of America, those Indians who survived war and epidemic diseases were virtually enslaved by their conquerors. Thousands labored in the mines digging and smelting silver and gold; others farmed and tended livestock.

Some Spanish friars and priests protested against mistreatment of the Indians. In time, the Spanish crown passed laws designed to limit the abuse of native labor. These efforts, however, were not notably successful in preventing cruelty and exploitation. Cortez, Pizarro, de Soto, and other Europeans of that time regarded Indians as barely human. After a century of Spanish rule, the Indian population of Mexico, through maltreatment and white men's diseases, had been reduced

Hernando de Soto's stark encounter with one of the Indian nations along his march of conquest receives vivid—and perhaps exaggerated—portrayal in this scene. The various symbols of Spanish presence: the horses, artillery, gold-hunger, and efforts at conversion to Christianity all find their place in the picture.

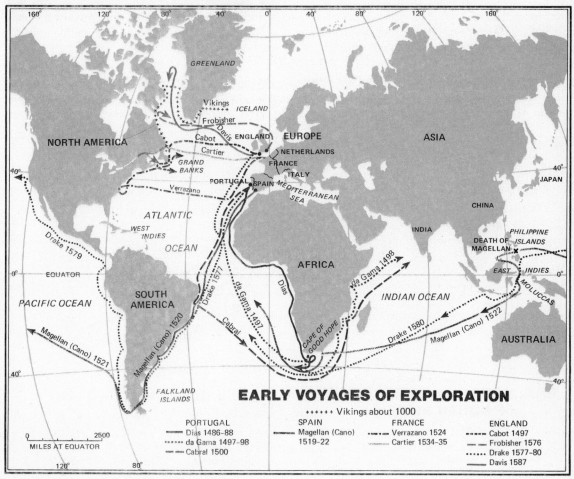

EARLY VOYAGES OF EXPLORATION

++++++ Vikings about 1000

PORTUGAL	SPAIN	FRANCE	ENGLAND
Dias 1486–88	Magellan (Cano)	Verrazano 1524	Cabot 1497
da Gama 1497–98	1519–22	Cartier 1534–35	Frobisher 1576
Cabral 1500			Drake 1577–80
			Davis 1587

MILES AT EQUATOR
0   2500

from five million to one million. The Mexican experience was not unique. Elsewhere in the New World—in Peru and on the Caribbean islands, for example—the Indian population decreased at comparable rates and for similar reasons.

As many Indians died or fled beyond the range of Spanish settlements, another steady source of cheap labor was necessary, since raising crops like sugar cane required a large labor force, so the Spanish began importing black slaves from Africa. The first slaves came as early as 1510. In later years Europeans kidnapped and bought hundreds of thousands more Africans to ship to the New World.

Packed tightly into cramped cargo spaces, on ships called "floating coffins," some blacks preferred to jump overboard than accept slavery. Many more died of disease on board. Only a fraction of the slaves survived the journey, but enough reached America to make the trade profitable, and their numbers increased. They were more resistant to the diseases of the whites than the Indians were, since they had already been exposed to them in Africa. Due to their previous experience

with agriculture, the blacks also proved to be better at it than the Indians, many of whom—especially those in the Caribbean and in North America—had done relatively little farming.

THE SPANISH EMPIRE: THEORY AND REALITY

Spain dominated sixteenth-century European politics, diplomacy, warfare, and economic life as gold and silver flowed in from its American possessions. This vast influx of precious metals had serious consequences for the Spanish economy. It caused an enormous rise in prices—that is, inflation. Prices rose about 400 percent in Spain during the sixteenth century—a tremendously high rate of inflation for those times. The Spanish government often found it impossible to collect enough tax revenue to pay its debts.

Furthermore, inflation made it difficult for Spanish farm or manufactured goods to compete with cheaper foreign imports. Thus the same harvest of gold and silver that gave Spain temporary

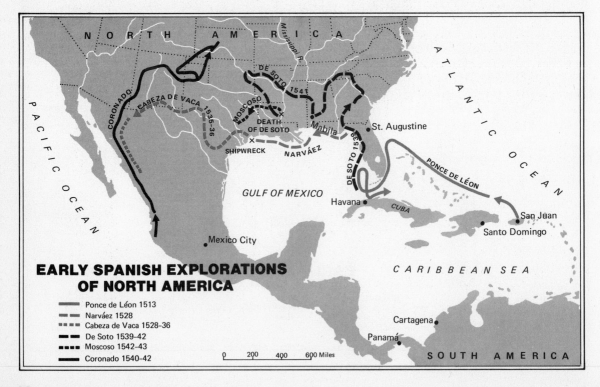

EARLY SPANISH EXPLORATIONS OF NORTH AMERICA

——— Ponce de Léon 1513
– – – Narváez 1528
▪▪▪▪ Cabeza de Vaca 1528–36
▬ ▬ ▬ De Soto 1539–42
■■■■ Moscoso 1542–43
——— Coronado 1540–42

0   200   400   600 Miles

THE LAND THE EXPLORERS FOUND

The first Europeans who came to America were not literary men, but adventurers with a purpose—to discover routes to the East, or gold, or land for settlement. Still, they were curious and observant, and kept good records of what they saw. Coming from a populated land of cities and farms, they were struck by America's seeming emptiness, its great forests, its plentiful wild game and fruits.

One of the oldest accounts of America was written by an anonymous Viking chronicler about land not unlike this shoreline at Mt. Desert, Maine: "They found it a fair, well-wooded country. It was but a short distance from the woods to the sea, and there were white sands, as well as great numbers of islands. They found neither dwelling of man nor lair of beast."

*For further information on the foreign observers quoted in this essay, see "Notes on

Whoso maketh navigations to those countries hath not only extreme winds and furious seas to encounter, but also many monstrous and great islands of ice—a thing both rare, wonderful, and greatly to be regarded.

We were forced sundry times, while the ship did ride here at anchor, to have continual watch, with boats and men ready with hawsers to fasten onto ice that was tossed to and fro in the harbor with the ebb and flood. The men would haul the ice away with force of oars so that it would not endanger our ship.

[DIONISE SETTLE, WITH MARTIN FROBISHER, 1577]

Ice floes near Baffin Island

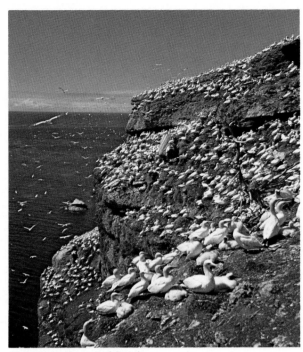

Gannets near the coast of Canada

Newfoundland we found very subject to fogs and mists. The ground of it is very rocky, and upon it there is great store of fir trees, and in some places red. About the shore it hath great abundance of codfish.

The three Islands of Birds are sandy red, but with the multitude of birds upon them they look white. The birds sit there as thick as stones lie in a paved street. The greatest of the islands is about a mile in compass. The second is a little less. The third is a very little one, like a small rock. At the second of these three lay on the shore in the sunshine about thirty or forty walruses which, when our boat came near them, presently made into the sea, and swam after the boat.

[CHARLES LEIGH, 1597]

Along the shore, Cape Cod

Near this cape we came to anchor in fifteen fathoms, where we took great store of codfish, for which we called it Cape Cod. Here we saw schools of herrings, mackerels, and other small fish in great abundance. This is a low sandy shore, but without danger. We came to anchor again in sixteen fathoms. This cape is well near a mild broad, and lieth north-east east. The captain went here ashore and found the ground to be full of peas, strawberries, huckleberries, etc., then unripe.

[BARTHOLOMEW GOSNOLD AND BARTHOLOMEW GILBERT, 1602]

Adirondack Mountains, New York State

This region is almost an island, surrounded by the great river Saint Lawrence, which passes through several lakes of great extent. On the shore of this great river there are very high mountains, and the air is temperate. All these places abound in game. Fishing is abundant, there being many varieties, both those which we have in France, as also others which we have not. There are likewise many birds in their time and season. The country is traversed by numerous rivers, brooks, and ponds, connecting with each other and finally emptying into the river St. Lawrence and the lakes through which it passes. The country is very pleasant in spring, is covered with extensive and lofty forests, and filled with wood similar to that which we have in France.

[SAMUEL DE CHAMPLAIN, 1615]

Wild grapes

We saw in this country many vines growing naturally, which growing up, took hold of the trees as they do in Lombardy. If they were tended in good order by husbandmen, without all doubt they would yield excellent wines. Having oftentimes seen the fruit thereof dried, which was sweet and pleasant and not differing from ours, we think those here do esteem the same, because in every place where they grow, they take away the under branches growing round about, that the fruit thereof may ripen better.

[GIOVANNI DA VERRAZANO, 1524]

Southern forest and underbrush

The Indians led us into a country difficult to traverse and strange to look at, for it had very great forests, the trees being wonderfully tall and so many of them fallen that they obstructed our way so that we had to make long detours and with great trouble. Of the trees standing many were rent from top to bottom by thunderbolts, which strike very often in that country, where storms and tempests are always frequent.

[ÁLVAR NÚÑEZ CABEZA DE VACA, 1528]

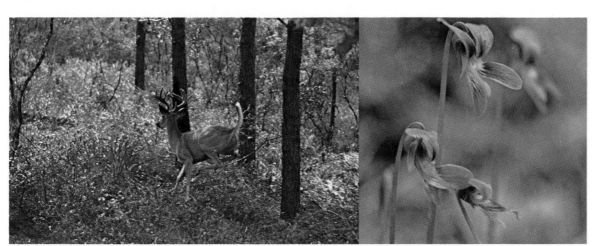
White-tailed deer   Wild violets

Deer in some places there are in great store. Near unto the seacoast they are of the ordinary bigness of ours in England, and some less, but further up into the country, where there is better food, they are greater. They differ from ours only in this: their tails are longer, and the snags of their horns look backward.

[THOMAS HERIOT, 1585]

Mother opossum with young

Trees and swampland, Florida

The animals we saw included one that carries its young in a pouch on its belly as long as the young are small, until they are able to look for their sustenance. Even then, when they are out after food and people come, the mother does not move until her little ones are in the pouch again.

[ÁLVAR NÚÑEZ CABEZA DE VACA, 1528]

An Indian guided them through an immense pathless thicket of wilderness for seven days, where they slept continually in ponds and shallow puddles. Fish were so plentiful in them that they were killed with blows of cudgels.

["A FIDALGO OF ELVAS," WITH HERNANDO DE SOTO, 1541]

Countryside around Jamestown

Island in the Caribbean

All this coast, and the part of the island which I saw, is mainly a beach. The island is the loveliest thing that I have seen, for, if the others are very lovely, this is more so. It has many trees, very green and tall. The singing of little birds is such that it seems that a man could never wish to leave this place. The flocks of parrots darken the sun, and there are large and small birds of so many different kinds and so unlike ours, that it is a marvel. There are, moreover, trees of a thousand types, all with their various fruits and all scented, so that it is a wonder. I am the saddest man in the world because I do not recognize them.

[CHRISTOPHER COLUMBUS, 1492]

Parrot fish from the Bahamas

Cuban parrot

←The territory for pleasantness of seat, for temperature of climate, for fertility of soil, and for the commodity of the sea, besides multitude of bears (being an excellent good victual), was not to be excelled by any other whatsoever. To the northwest the farthest place of our discovery was distant from Roanoke about 130 miles. Our passage thither lay through a broad sound, but all fresh water. The channel was of a great depth, navigable for good shipping, but outside the channel the sound was full of shoals.

[RALPH LANE, 1585]

In this river we saw many crocodiles of sundry bignesses, but some as big as a boat, with four feet, a long broad mouth, and a long tail, whose skin is so hard that a sword will not pierce it. His nature is to live out of the water as a frog doth, but he is a great devourer, and spareth neither fish, which is his common food, nor beasts, nor man.

[JOHN HAWKINS, 1564]

A crocodile, from an early engraving

Grasslands on the Great Plains

Now we will speak of the plains. The country is spacious and level. No settlements were seen anywhere. In traversing 250 leagues, the other mountain range was not seen, nor a hill nor a hillock which was three times as high as a man. The country is like a bowl, so that when a man sits down, the horizon surrounds him all around at the distance of a musket shot. There are no groves of trees except at the rivers.

[PEDRO DE CASTAÑEDA, WITH FRANCISCO VÁSQUEZ DE CORONADO, 1541-42]

One of the earliest depictions of the buffalo, 1558

The buffalo's shape and form are so marvelous and laughable, or frightful, that the more one sees it the more one desires to see it, and no one could be so melancholy that if he were to see it a hundred times a day he could keep from laughing heartily as many times, or could fail to marvel at the sight of so ferocious an animal. They are so thickly covered with wool that it covers their eyes and face, and the forelock nearly envelops their horns. This wool, which is long and very soft, extends almost to the middle of the body, but from there on the hair is shorter.

[JUAN DE OÑATE, 1598]

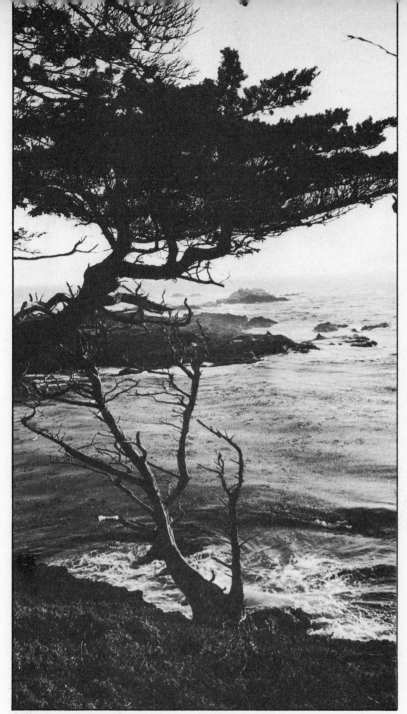
California coastline near Monterey

We arrived at Monterey in the evening. The next day the men landed. Mass having been said and the day having cleared, there having been much fog, we found ourselves to be in the best port that could be desired. Besides being sheltered from all the winds, it has many pines for masts and yards, and live oaks and white oaks, and water in great quantity, all near the shore.

[SEBASTIÁN VIZCAÍNO, 1602]

One of the richest sources of silver in the world was a mountain known as Cerro Rico, at Potosi, Bolivia. In this 1584 painting, Indian laborers using llamas struggle up and down the hillside while other workers sort and stack the ore for shipment to Spain.

dominance in Europe also helped cripple her long-range chances as a food-producing, manufacturing nation.

Spain's overwhelming desire for precious metals grew out of a certain view of economic life held by most European governments. According to this view, the true measure of any nation's economic prosperity and power was the amount of gold and silver it controlled. Later economic writers gave the name *mercantilism* to this set of ideas, which has generally governed the economic behavior of European nations since the fifteenth century. Spain's New World possessions, and the gold and silver found there, allowed Madrid to put such ideas into practice.

Spain alone had the mines from which to acquire gold and silver directly. Every other European power turned to foreign commerce to increase its stock of precious metals. The goal was to maximize exports and minimize imports from other countries; this was known as a favorable *balance of trade*. Mercantilists believed that gold and silver could best be kept within a country by achieving such a favorable balance of trade. To this end, the ships of Portugal, Holland, England, France, and other European nations crossed and recrossed the oceans in search of new opportunities for trade. Spain, in contrast, never developed a strong commerce, partly because of her smug certainty that New World mines would eternally provide all the gold and silver she needed.

Unfortunately for Spain, those sources ran dry in the seventeenth century. Her great period of national prosperity waned. So did her political and military influence in Europe. What endured from decades of Spanish conquest and exploita-

ATLANTIC TRADE ROUTES

NORTH AMERICA

ENGLAND

Glasgow
Bristol
London

EUROPE

Lisbon
Cadiz

AFRICA

SOUTH AMERICA

Boston
Newport
New York
Philadelphia
Charleston

Intercoastal Trade

Cuba
Jamaica
Hispaniola
Puerto Rico

WEST INDIES

Horses

Textiles, hardware

Naval stores, whale oil, potash, lumber, furs, naval stores

Tobacco, rice, indigo, furs, naval stores

Meat, fish, lumber, grain, rum

Textiles, hardware

Wine, fruit, salt

Wine, fruit

Wine

Madeira Is.

Sugar, molasses, fruit

Manufactured goods

Slaves

Rum, iron

Slaves, gold
"Middle Passage"

Ivory, gold, slave coasts

Grain, fish, cattle, lumber

Slaves, molasses

Slaves, sugar, molasses, coin, slaves

Slaves

African Slave Trading

0   600
Miles

tion was not the treasure itself. Instead, there remained a vast imperial domain studded with great plantations, ranches, and orchards. Through it ran an equally impressive network of Catholic missions and churches, strung like rosary beads along the Spanish-American countryside. And over all lay the veneer of Spanish language and culture.

FRANCE IN THE NEW WORLD

King Ferdinand of Spain, the patron of Columbus, called himself "His Most Catholic Majesty." Therefore, when he wished to have his claims to the new discoveries made legitimate, he knew exactly whom to consult. In 1494, Pope John II, strongly influenced by the Spanish and Austrian ruling family of Hapsburg, drew a line down the Atlantic from north to south, cutting through Brazil, with all of North America to the west of it. He proclaimed that all new lands east of the line belonged to Portugal; west of it, to His Most Catholic Majesty of Spain.

Predictably, other European nations did not accept this division as happily as Spain and Portugal did. Francis I, who became king of France in 1515, reacted strongly. "Show me the will of Adam," he demanded, "dividing the world between Spain and Portugal." In challenging Spain's claim to the New World, Francis was only opening a new front in his European war with the Hapsburgs. From 1521 to 1559, France fought a perpetual battle with Charles V and his heirs. In hopes of bringing in some badly needed revenue, Francis sent Giovanni de Verrazano, a Florentine navigator, across the ocean in 1523. He told Verrazano to find a water route through North America to China. This idea of a "northwest passage" would fascinate explorers for the next century.

Unlike the first Spanish explorer, Verrazano had a fairly good idea of what he would find. For twenty years, French fishermen had sailed to Newfoundland to gather codfish. Verrazano navigated along the eastern coast of the continent from the Carolinas to Newfoundland, establishing a French claim to North America, but he found no route to China.

Distracted by civil war, France did not attempt to develop her claim for sixty-five years; then Henry IV sent out his friend Samuel de Champlain. Champlain founded Quebec and reached the Great Lakes, but he failed to establish anything comparable to Spanish colonization in Mexico or Peru. Instead, French exploration continued at a leisurely pace. It was not until almost the end of the seventeenth century that René Robert Cavelier, sieur de La Salle, reached the foot of Lake Michigan and then journeyed down the length of the Mississippi to New Orleans. After one hundred and fifty years of fitful efforts, with long periods of neglect, France could claim an enormous North American empire—half of modern Canada plus the valley of the Mississippi.

The society of New France differed greatly from that of New Spain. The Spanish took the Aztecs' gold and land, destroying the Indians in the process. The French never found gold, and very few Frenchmen wanted to come to Canada to take the Indians' land. Thirty years after Champlain had founded Quebec, only two French farmers had immigrated. The only economic value Canada had for the French was the fur trade, which required amicable relations with the Indians.

THE PROTESTANT POWERS IN AMERICA

After the Protestant Reformation had swept across Europe in the first half of the sixteenth century, Spain and France, the western European superpowers, remained Catholic. But other nations that had adopted various types of Protestantism now had new reason to challenge the Spanish domination of the New World. As would often happen in the future, European conflicts extended overseas.

After a long and hard-fought war of rebellion, the Netherlands by 1600 had won their independence from Spain. During the struggle, the Spanish had attempted to destroy the Dutch Reformed Church. The Dutch, who had won largely by virtue of their superior seamanship, preyed profitably upon Spanish shipping before actually attempting their own overseas colonization.

In 1609 the Dutch sent an Englishman named Henry Hudson to try to reach Asia over the top of Europe. Turned back by ice, Hudson instead sailed to America, up the New York river that now bears his name. His sailors brought back the story of a rich land to the Netherlands. A dozen years later, the Dutch founded the Dutch West India Company, largely as a weapon against the Spanish. While concentrating on the plunder of the Spanish and Portuguese colonies, the company established a small colony on Manhattan Island, as well as some nearby forts.

But Dutch farmers proved no more eager to cross the Atlantic than French farmers. New Amsterdam rapidly became a polyglot colony with residents from all nations, especially after the Dutch annexed a small Swedish colony on Delaware Bay. The company lost interest, and the colonists exhausted themselves in a long war with the Algonquin Indians. Forty years after its founding, New Amsterdam was itself annexed by the greatest Protestant power, England.

BACKGROUND OF ENGLISH COLONIZATION

As early as 1497, the English crown had sent an exploratory expedition to the New World. Henry VII sent John Cabot, a Genoese born Giovanni Caboto, to discover an English northwest passage. A second voyage by Cabot in 1498 confirmed both the presence of fish and the absence of Chinese. Given these discoveries, Henry VII, a tight man with a shilling, refused to finance future voyages.

His son, Henry VIII, was too busy getting married and unmarried, and forming a new Protestant Church of England, to support colonial ventures. Eventually the English Reformation would serve to populate Massachusetts, but under Henry it prevented any colonization at all. Henry's elder daughter, Queen Mary, was a Catholic who had married King Philip II of Spain and had no interest in encroaching upon her husband's domains. She channeled English adventuring around the top of Europe, and chartered the Muscovy Company to trade with Russia in 1555. Although English

merchants and sailors profited from such dealings, they hungered for the richer (and warmer) trade with America.

Their opportunity came with the succession to the throne of Henry's younger daughter, Elizabeth I, one of the most remarkable women of history. The red-haired Virgin Queen was as strong a Protestant as her sister had been a Catholic, and had little respect for the claims or property of Spain. She also cared little for the division of the New World by Pope John II, whose successor had declared her illegitimate and an illegal occupant of the English throne. Soon after she became queen in 1558, English ships again turned west and once more began to make voyages across the Atlantic.

In some ways England seemed an unlikely candidate to challenge Spain's power in the New World. A relatively small country on the fringes of Europe, England did not even control the entire island of Great Britain (Scotland remained independent until 1603). England had about as many people as the Netherlands, half as many as Spain, and one-quarter as many as France. Finally, parliamentary control of the purse strings greatly limited the moneys available to Elizabeth, preventing the kind of explorations that kings of Spain had financed personally.

Hundreds of thousands of black-faced sheep grazing quietly in the English countryside lay behind the largest European migration to America. For centuries English merchants had carried on a large and lucrative trade in wool across the Channel. Consequently, private citizens, when gathered together in joint stock companies (the forerunners of modern corporations), possessed enough capital to underwrite settlements in Massachusetts and Virginia.

The sheep had also helped produce settlers for the new land. For several decades, landowners had been involved in the process of *enclosure* — fencing in what had been common farmland — in order to raise more sheep, a more profitable endeavor than simple crop growing. The process forced many farm laborers off the land, resulting in an extremely high rate of unemployment in sixteenth-century England. In some places, as much as one-third of the population lived on poor relief.

Finally, England's long history of shipping wool to Europe involved the development of a large fleet of ships and men who knew how to sail them. In what would essentially be a naval contest with Spain in the Atlantic, England's skilled and experienced — is somewhat informal — navy might prevail even over Spain's greater resources in gold and population.

EARLY ELIZABETHAN EXPLORATION

The idea of a northwest passage to the Orient fascinated Elizabeth as much as it had her grandfather Henry VII. Starting in 1576, she dispatched Martin Frobisher on three voyages over the top of Canada. Frobisher explored Labrador and became the first European to encounter the Eskimos, but found no Chinese shortcut.

Some English sailors set their goals beyond the ice floes of Hudson's Bay. Although England had not officially declared war against Spain, the rich Spanish treasure fleets were tempting targets. English captains also kidnapped slaves from Africa and smuggled them into Spanish America, which tried to limit the number of slaves brought in. Elizabeth's sailors believed strongly in an aggressive Protestantism, which allowed them to rationalize dealing in slaves as a means of Christianizing blacks, and permitted them to justify anything done against Catholic Spain.

Queen Elizabeth supported and encouraged this slave dealing and semiofficial piracy. She hoped to add funds to her royal coffers while reducing Spanish power. From 1562 to 1568, Sir John Hawkins made three voyages, smuggling slaves from Sierra Leone and returning to England with ginger, sugar, and pearls. In 1570 Elizabeth commissioned Hawkins's cousin, Sir Francis Drake, as a *privateer* — essentially a pirate who split his booty with the crown. The following year Drake led a group of seventy sailors in an ambush of a Spanish mule train lumbering across the Isthmus of Panama with a cargo of silver from Peru. After pillaging a Spanish town on the Panama coast in mid-1573, Drake returned safely to England with his prizes.

Queen Elizabeth ruled England, in her words, with the body of a woman "but the heart and stomach of a king."

DRAKE SAILS AROUND THE WORLD

In 1577 Drake set out with five ships and 164 officers and men to break Spain's monopoly in the Pacific. His squadron sailed near the Cape Verde Islands, where he captured Spanish and Portuguese ships. Proceeding southward along the east coast of South America, Drake beat back an attempted mutiny, losing ships and men along the way. He rounded Cape Horn and reached the Pacific in September 1578 with only one remaining vessel, the *Pelican* (later renamed the *Golden Hind*).

Drake then turned north, seizing treasure and provisions from Spanish ships and towns along the way. To escape enemy attack, he kept heading north — sailing, he wrote, "on the backside of America." Along the coast of California he stopped at a "fair and good bay" — what may be the San Francisco Bay of today. Finding no northwest passage to take him back to England, he crossed the Pacific (taking on a valuable cargo of pepper in

Sir Francis Drake was described by a Spainard as "of medium stature, blonde, rather heavy than slender, merry, careful." The portrait comes from a contemporary painting of Drake.

what is now Indonesia), rounded the Cape of Good Hope, and sailed up the west coast of Africa to reach Plymouth in September 1580.

Drake reached England uncertain of his reception. Spain was demanding the return of Drake's booty and his execution as a pirate, and hinted at war if Elizabeth refused. After a time of uncertainty, the queen, influenced by Drake's new status as a popular hero (and the estimated twenty-five-million-dollar value of his prizes), knighted Drake and allowed him to continue his raids on Spanish America.

Roanoke—the island at center—was protected from the sea by the Outer Banks, including Hatteras (here called "hatorasck"). Sunken ships lie in the foreground.

ENGLISH VENTURES

The voyages of her "sea dogs" made the New World appear so attractive to Elizabeth that she took yet another step. In the 1580s she began to authorize other English adventurers—not pirates this time, but enterprising businessmen among the nobility—to explore and to found settlements.

Sir Humphrey Gilbert, attracted by the profits and glory of dealing with the New World, now persuaded Elizabeth to give him a charter to discover and settle such lands. Gilbert made two attempts at colonization. In 1578 he was either forced back by bad weather or diverted by the more attractive possibilities of piracy (historical accounts differ on this point). He tried again in 1583 with a larger expedition. This time he reached Newfoundland and took possession of a surprised international colony of summer fishermen. Soon afterward, however, he perished in a storm.

The dream of an English colony in America was carried further by Gilbert's half brother, Sir Walter Raleigh. He took over Gilbert's charter in

JOHN CABOT

With a little luck, John Cabot might have discovered America. Like Columbus, Caboto had kept company with a wide circle of Italian geographers and sought support from foreign rulers for his curious notion that Asia could be reached by sailing west across the Atlantic. Caboto, however, could not gain backing for his expedition until several years after Columbus, when King Henry VII of England and the merchants of Bristol sent him across the Atlantic on a route well north of that taken by his fellow Genoese.

Cabot (he had Anglicized his name after reaching England), shrewdly suspected, from his study of the expeditions of Marco Polo, that whatever Columbus might claim, Cuba was not part of the Asian mainland. He combined this conclusion with something long known by the English fishermen who regularly sailed to Iceland. There they had heard of a large continent west of Greenland, once colonized by the Norsemen but since abandoned.

Cabot put the two facts together and reached his own erroneous conclusion: the Vikings had reached the northeast coast of Asia, which then stretched off the the southwest, eventually lying far to the west of Columbus's discovery. By sailing over the old Norse route, and then following the coast south, Cabot expected to establish the precise location of China and Japan. In 1497, with a royal patent, he set out on that mission.

Henry VII realized that whatever Columbus had discovered now belonged to Spain. But if Cabot actually found something new, England could also establish claims.

With an agreement giving King Henry one-fifth of whatever he brought back, Cabot sailed across the Atlantic, probably landing somewhere in Newfoundland or Canada's Maritime Provinces. He coasted for several hundred miles along the shoreline, not far enough to find China, but enough to convince him that he had reached the Asian mainland. Cabot then turned around and returned to Bristol, convinced that one more voyage would do it. He wanted a larger and stronger expedition with him when he actually reached the empire of China.

In May 1498, John Cabot departed Bristol harbor with five ships, including one directly provided by the usually tight-fisted King Henry. Merchants of London and Bristol had competed with one another in assembling Cabot's cargo for trading with the Asians. Adventurers had fought to get on the ships, to get a share in the wealth the "great admiral" had been openly promising since his return from the previous voyage. Shortly after the ships put to sea, some of the hopefuls were disappointed; one of the ships had to put in at Ireland for repairs.

All that is known for certain about the other four is that they did not find China. History does not record their return to Bristol, but the inglorious return of a failed expedition might not have caused much of a stir. Cabot himself may have drowned or been killed by Indians, or he may even have found his way back to England, a defeated and inconsequential person. It is probable that some of the ships did manage to return to England. In 1501 the king of Spain granted an explorer's patent to a Spaniard who had apparently accompanied Cabot. There is also an even stronger bit of evidence; after 1500, English maps no longer showed Asia on the other side of the Atlantic; instead they portrayed a large area labeled "New Found Land." It remained for other explorers (including John Cabot's son, Sebastian), to provide the details that would enable map makers to draw that part of the New World with some confidence, and it would be many years before they could draw it with precision.

Drake's campaign of the 1580s was his first act of open warfare against the Spanish. He commanded a fleet of twenty-nine ships. One successful episode was the sack of Santo Domingo, above. While the fleet lay at anchor, foot soldiers — their ranks bristling with spears — attacked the walled city from the left. Drake was a daring man who much enjoyed what the English of his day called "singeing the king of Spain's beard."

1584 on even more favorable terms than those granted his relative. Raleigh sent out an advance party that year to search for a suitable site. After Gilbert's misadventures in the chilly climate of Newfoundland, Raleigh decided to look further south. His scouting party found a promising site, which it called Roanoke Island, along the Atlantic coast south of Chesapeake Bay. Raleigh named the entire coastal region Virginia, in honor of

Elizabeth, England's Virgin Queen.

In 1585 Raleigh dispatched an expedition of settlers to Roanoke Island. They spent most of their time roaming through the countryside searching for gold. They also explored nearby rivers looking for the Pacific Ocean. In other words, they did everything but colonize. The entire settlement returned the following year.

In 1587 Raleigh sponsored yet a third expe-

The mysterious end of the Roanoake or "lost" colony reached the awareness of other British explorers only in 1591, when they returned to the settlement fo find all of its inhabitants missing without having left any indication of their whereabouts except for the word "CROATOAN" (the name given to a nearby island) carved on a doorpost. This later sketch shifts the location to a tree.

dition, this time commanded by an artist, John White. This group contained the first English women and children to come to America, and Raleigh hoped to duplicate faithfully the society of England in the wilderness. White helped the 118 settlers organize their colony but soon had to return to England for supplies. European war prevented his return for four years.

White finally sailed back to America in 1591. When he reached Roanoke, he found the settlement in ruins. The entire colony had vanished without a trace, except for the single word CROATOAN — the name of a nearby island — carved on a doorpost. White's own daughter and granddaughter, the first English child born in America, were among the missing.

THE INVINCIBLE ARMADA

Spain, the most powerful nation in Europe, would not tolerate activities like Raleigh's — or like Drake's — forever. In 1588 King Philip II of Spain, hoping to ensure Spanish control of the Americas and the Atlantic, and to reclaim England for the Catholic Church, sent a large fleet against his sister-in-law Elizabeth. Hundreds of ships departed from the same port Columbus had used, carrying soldiers for invasion and priests for reconversion.

The sailors who had ravaged Spain on the oceans now rallied to the defense of their homeland. Drake, Hawkins, Frobisher, and other veteran captains moved their ships into the Channel, bringing a new idea of naval warfare. According to the traditional strategy, as used by the Spanish, ships were mainly transportation for soldiers, who would capture enemy ships by hand-to-hand fighting. Accordingly, the Spanish galleys were large and cumbersome, and were propelled largely by oarsmen. Expertly sailing their smaller ships in and out of the Armada, Drake and the English destroyed many of the invading ships. Others, heading northward, went down in a series of furious storms off the Scottish and Irish coasts.

Although the Armada came to grief thousands of miles from America, the battle proved crucial for the English settlements. England now controlled the Atlantic and could establish and supply her colonies without fear of Spanish blockades.

Soon after the defeat of the Armada, England established its first permanent colonies in the New World. "He who rules the sea," proclaimed Raleigh jubilantly, "rules the commerce of the world, and to him that rules the commerce of the world belongs the treasure of the world and indeed the world itself." If England did not yet rule the world, it would soon rule a large part of North America.

SUGGESTED READINGS—CHAPTERS 1-2

Cortez and Montezuma

Charles Gibson, *The Aztecs Under Spanish Rule* (1964); Miguel Leon-Portilla, *Broken Spears: The Aztec Account of the Conquest of Mexico* (1962); Hammond Innes, *The Conquistadors.*

Discoveries and Explorations

John B. Brebner, *The Explorers of North America;* Samuel Eliot Morison, *Admiral of the Ocean Sea* (1942), *The European Discovery of America: The Northern Voyages, A.D. 500–1600* (1971), and *The European Discovery of America: The Southern Voyages: A.D. 1492–1616* (1974); John H. Parry, *The Age of Reconnaissance* (1963).

Indian Cultures

Woodrow Borah, and Sherburne F. Cook, *The Aboriginal Population of Central Mexico on the Eve of the Spanish Conquest* (1963); H. E. Driver, *Indians of North America* (2nd ed., 1970); Alvin M. Josephy Jr., *The Indian Heritage of America* (1969); J. A. Hester, Jr. and Kenneth MacGawan, *Early Man in the New World;* G. R. Nash, *Red, White and Black: The Peoples of Early America* (1974); Carl O. Sauer, *Sixteenth-Century North America: The Land and People As Seen by Europeans* (1971);

George C. Vaillant, *Aztecs of Mexico;* W. E. Washburn, *The Indian in America* (1975).

Spanish America

C. R. Boxer, *The Portuguese Seaborne Empire* (1969); A. W. Crosby Jr., *The Columbian Exchange: Biological and Cultural Consequences of 1492* (1972); Charles Gibson, *Spain in America* (1966); Lewis Hanke, *The Struggle for Justice in the Conquest of America* (1949); Clarence H. Haring, *The Spanish Empire in America* (1947); James Lang, *Conquest and Commerce: Spain and England in the Americas* (1975); James Lockhart, *Spanish Peru, 1532–1560* (1968); John H. Parry, *The Spanish Seaborne Empire* (1966).

England and the New World

Wallace Notestein, *The English People on the Eve of Colonization, 1603–1630* (1954); David B. Quinn, *England and the Discovery of America, 1481–1620* (1974) and *Roanoke Voyages, 1584–1590* (1955); A. L. Rowse, *The Elizabethans and America* (1959) and *The Expansion of Elizabethan England* (1955); J. A. Williamson, *Voyages of the Cabots and the English Discovery of North America Under Henry 7th and Henry 8th* (1929).

3 BACON'S REBELLION

R. J. W.

In their calendar year "12-House" the Aztecs began to notice terrible omens—a comet, a flood, strange birds, a fire—omens that seemed to be signals of a great disaster. But the Aztecs were not the only early Americans to take omens seriously. Almost two hundred years later, and thousands of miles to the north and east, others watched the skies and became afraid. The new omens appeared in Virginia, where about thirty thousand English people lived on the shores and riverbanks of England's first successful colony in the New World. And the English took the omens about as seriously as the Aztecs had.

The year was 1675. Thomas Mathew, a Virginia tobacco planter on the south bank of the Potomac River, observed three strange and ominous signs. First there was a large comet, "streaming like a horse tail, until it reached almost the horizon." The other two signs were even more unusual. Flights of pigeons that filled a quarter of the sky came into Virginia from the interior. When they roosted at night, their weight broke even large tree limbs. According to Mathew: "This sight put the old planters under portentous apprehensions, because the like was seen when the Indians committed the last massacre." The third "strange appearance" was "swarms of flies about an inch long and big as the top of a man's little finger, rising out of spigot holes in the earth, which ate the new-sprouted leaves from the tops of the trees, and in a month left us."

As Thomas Mathew tried to interpret the meaning of the three omens, he might have thought of the hurricane that had recently devastated the colony. Or he might have remembered a drought that had spoiled almost an entire year's tobacco crop—the English planters' most important economic asset. More than likely, however, Mathew and his neighbors thought of Indians. There had been problems recently with a tribe of friendly Doeg Indians, who lived just across the Potomac River in Maryland. Mathew himself had neglected to pay for some goods he had bought from the Doegs. In retaliation, the Doegs had tried to steal some of Mathew's hogs, but a band of Englishmen had traced the Indians down and killed one or two of them. Mathew also knew that a band of Susquehannah Indians, much more warlike than the Doegs, had moved down from farther north to the Maryland side of the Potomac. Technically, both the Doegs and the Susquehannahs were friendly and lived under Maryland's protection. But the Potomac region was crowded — with Virginians, Marylanders, Doegs, and Susquehannahs. All the English who had lived through or even heard about earlier Indian wars expected trouble.

Trouble came to Mathew's door. He owned another plantation several miles up the Potomac, run by an overseer and a herdsman named Robert Hen. On a Sunday morning in July 1675 some people on their way to church passed near Hen's house and saw him lying in his doorway, hurt. An Indian lay nearby. Both men had been "chopped on their heads, arms and other parts, as if done with Indian hatchets." The Indian was already dead, and Hen was dying. But he had time to gasp, "Doegs! Doegs!" before he died. Then a boy who had been hiding under a bed in the house came out and told the people that "Indians had come at the break of day and done these murders."

Stealing hogs was one thing, but the death of an Englishman was much more serious. The Virginians had a militia to deal with such matters, and the local leaders called the farmers to arms. Years later, Mathew recalled what happened:

> Of this horrid action, Colonel Mason, who commanded the militia regiment of foot, and Captain Brent, the troop of horses in that county, having speedy notice, raised thirty or more men. They pursued the Indians twenty miles up and four miles over the river into Maryland. Landing at the dawn of day, they found two small paths. Each leader took a separate path, and either found a cabin, which they silently surrounded.

The English were not nearly so skilled at forest warfare as the Indians. But this time they were able to catch their enemy by surprise — probably because the Indians knew that it was against English law for Virginia militia to cross into Maryland.

> Captain Brent went to the Doegs' cabin. Speaking the Indian tongue, he called to have a *Matchacomicha Weewhip*, a Council, such being the usual manner with Indians. The king came trembling forth, and would have fled, when Captain Brent, catching hold of his twisted lock (which was all the hair he wore), told him he was come for the murderer of Robert Hen. The king pleaded ignorance, and slipped loose. Brent shot him dead with his pitol. The Indians shot two or three guns out of the cabin; the English shot into it. The Indians thronged out at the door and fled. The English shot as many as they could, so that they killed ten, and brought away the king's son of about eight years old.

So far, the Virginians' mission of revenge had been successful, at least by their own standards. They had taken ten Indian lives for one English life. And at this point they were not troubled by the fact that they had illegally invaded a sister colony. They did not even mind the fact that they had no way of knowing whether or not these particular Indians had actually been involved in the murder of Hen. But the other half of the company of militia was about to make a very costly mistake.

> The noise of the shooting awakened the Indians in the cabin which Colonel Mason had encompassed. They likewise rushed out and fled. The company shot fourteen before an Indian came and with both hands shook Colonel Mason (in a friendly way) by one arm, saying "*Susquehanougs Netoughs!* Susquehannah friends!" and fled. Whereupon Colonel Mason ran among his men, crying out, "For the Lord's sake, shoot no more! These are our friends, the Susquehannahs!"

Mason and Brent took their militia back to the Virginia side of the Potomac. They had won a military victory, in which thirty Virginians had killed almost as many Indians. They had punished the Doegs. But in doing so, they had caused more problems than they had solved, for the Susquehannahs would want revenge.

The Susquehannahs who escaped Colonel Mason's troops went upriver to a fort their tribe had built on the Maryland side. The main body of the tribe had about a hundred warriors, plus their wives and children. They had built an English-style fortress with walls made of tree trunks sunk into the ground. At the corners were firing platforms, and the square was surrounded by a ditch.

With the Susquehannahs safely inside their fort, the English had time to stop and think. The governor of Maryland sent a protest to the Virginia captial at Jamestown concerning the Virginians' illegal invasion

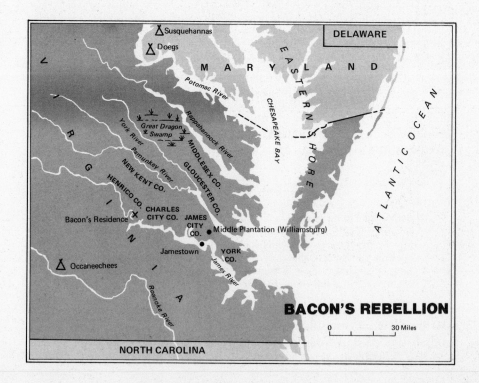

BACON'S REBELLION

0   30 Miles

of Maryland territory. A month passed without any serious trouble, and the governor of Virginia, Sir William Berkeley, ordered an investigation. He told two militia leaders to call together all the officers in the northern area of Virginia to conduct an inquiry. Berkeley wanted to move cautiously. He had kept peace with the Indians for over thirty years, and he did not want an Indian war now. But the militia leaders violated their orders. Instead of calling out the officers of the militia to make an investigation, they called out the troops. And, without authority, they asked for help from Maryland. Altogether, about a thousand men were quickly assembled from the two colonies. Before Governor Berkeley knew what was happening, they set out up the Potomac to attack the Susquehannah fort.

The English arrived at the Indian fort in late September 1675, about two months after the murder of Robert Hen. The commanders asked the Indians for a council, just as they had done at the Doeg cabin. The Indians sent out four of their "great men." The English betrayed the truce by axing the Susquehannah chiefs to death; then they attacked the fort.

The Susquehannahs were ready, however. They resisted the English successfully for several weeks, "shooting many of our men, and making frequent, fierce and bloody sallies. And when they were called to, or offered parley, they gave no other answer than 'Where are our four *Cockarouses* (Great Men)?'"

The Indians kept themselves from starving by stealing English horses for food. But finally they had to escape. Seventy-five braves crept out of the fort at night, with their families, and killed ten sleeping English sentries in the process. In the morning the English militia awoke to find only three or four old people left in the fort. The Susquehannahs, bitter at the murders of their chiefs, broke up into small bands of roving warriors, determined to take revenge. In a body, contained within their fort, they could have been controlled by the English. Now there was no way to keep track of them.

So far, every move the English had made was wrong. Governor Berkeley was outraged by the open murder of the Susquehannah chiefs. At the next meeting of the House of Burgesses (the lower house of the Virginia legislature) he declared: "If they had killed my grandfather and grandmother, my father and mother and all my friends, yet if they had come to treat of peace, they ought to have gone in peace!"

But more than the governor's sense of honor had been damaged. The militia had lost fifty men in its siege of the Susquehannah fort. (This loss in a colony of 30,000 inhabitants is comparable to the loss of more than 20,000 soldiers in twentieth-century America.) Moreover, the roaming Susquehannahs soon began to make themselves felt. In January 1676 they raided some settlements on the upper Rappahannock and Potomac rivers and killed or captured thirty-six people.

Then the Indians surprised Berkeley by sending him a proposal of peace. The Susquehannahs, too, had their idea of justice. The Susquehannah chief told the governor that since the Indians had now killed ten

English settlers for every one of the murdered "great men," they were satisfied. There need be no more war. But if the English wanted war, the chief concluded, his people were ready to fight to the last man.

The "Indian troubles" had reached a critical point, and a policy decision had to be made. The murder of Hen, the attacks on the Doeg and Susquehannah cabins, the disastrous campaign against the Susquehannah fort, and the Susquehannah attacks of January could all be regarded as a series of small incidents. They grew out of a misunderstanding between Thomas Mathew and the Doegs. All in all, about an equal number of Indians and whites had been killed. And the Susquehannahs seemed ready to call off the fighting. Thus Governor Berkeley replied to them in a peaceful way, and during April and May the Susquehannahs killed no whites, though they did steal some livestock.

There were really two conflicts in Virginia. The first, obviously, was between whites and Indians. The second was between small, frontier planters and the royal government. The small planters, like other frontiersmen throughout American history, believed that the solution to the first conflict was simply to wipe out all the Indians. Good land was already becoming scarce in the settled areas of Virginia, and whites were crowding north and west. The tobacco planters on the frontier had a very simple program. Every Virginian was armed, and most had horses. So volunteers would gather wherever there was the slightest hint of trouble, and would kill as many Indians as they could find.

One difficulty with this policy was that it offered no real way of dealing with the many small tribes of friendly Indians that lived on permanent "plantations" (reservations) among the whites. These friendly tribes, such as the Doegs of Maryland, had technically become subjects of the English ruler may years earlier. They had a legal right to their lands, under English law, and they were a valuable source of beaver skins—a commodity second only to tobacco in economic importance in Virginia.

Governor Berkeley, as head of the royal establishment, wanted a policy of peace and order that would protect the friendly tribes and the beaver trade. He also wanted Indian policy to rest in the hands of the government at Jamestown, not in the hands of hundreds of small planters scattered along the edges of the wilderness. Berkeley's Indian policy, in other words, was generally defensive, while that of the small planters was offensive. The government's policy, which was slow and cautious, conflicted with the farmers' wish for drastic and immediate action.

The governor made the next move. He called the Virginia legislature into session in early March and had an act passed that declared war on the Indians and provided for defense against them. The colony would build a fort at the falls of each river and create a permanent army of approximately 500 men. Parties of horsemen would conduct regular patrols between the forts. To prevent a repetition of the murders of Indians that had occurred the preceding winter, the act provided that the governor's personal permission would be necessary for any attack on an Indian fort or village—a permission that might take days to obtain.

To the planters on the frontier, Governor Berkeley's plans made very little sense. The English forts would be separated by miles of forest, through which the Indians could move at will. The forts, with their permanent garrisons, would be expensive. Tobacco prices were very low, and many planters could hardly make ends meet. Paying taxes to support a useless military policy would only add to their economic troubles. Furthermore, it would not provide them with any real security from the Indians.

According to the report of a royal commission that later investigated the episode, the "vulgar sort" began to protest the governor's policy. Berkeley himself summed up the situation with classic simplicity and accuracy: "How miserable the man is," he wrote home to England, "that governs a people where six parts of seven at least are poor, indebted, discontended, and armed."

According to the report of the royal commission, the plain people of Virginia were near rebellion:

> The unsatisfied people finding themselves still liable to the Indian cruelties, and the cries of their wives and children growing grievous and intolerable to them, gave out in speeches that they were resolved to plant tobacco rather than pay the tax for maintaining the forts; that the erecting of the forts was a great grievance and cheat, and of no more use than another plantation with men at it; and that it was merely a design of the grandees [wealthy planters] to take all the tobacco into their own hands.

One group of angry planters from Charles City County went so far as to send out a call to arms against the Indians. When they brought a petition to the governor asking him to support an attack on the Indians, Berkeley angrily sent the petitioners away and "bid a pox take" them. The Charles City County men decided to gather in arms anyway, and they set up a camp on the James River, where they were joined by men from Henrico County. They were now in open rebellion against the royal government. According to the report of the royal commission sent to investigate:

> The rout [the "giddy-headed multitude"] being got together now, wanted nor waited for nothing but one to head and lead them out on their design. It so happened that one Nathaniel Bacon, Jr., a person whose lost and desperate fortunes had thrown him into that remote part of the world about fourteen months before, was fit for such a purpose.

After months of trying to restore peace and maintain a cautious Indian policy, Governor Berkeley was faced with a collective force of about 300 rebellious men ready to defy his orders and follow a young and vigorous leader. In the weeks that followed, concern about the Indians became almost irrelevant, or at least secondary. Nathaniel Bacon and Governor Berkeley conducted a bitter and violent personal contest for control of Virginia, a contest known as Bacon's Rebellion.

Sir William Berkeley, the governor, and Nathaniel Bacon, Jr., the rebel, were in many ways very much alike. In fact they were even cous-

The royal commissioners sent to investigate Bacon's Rebellion included this plan of the Susquehanna fort in their report to the king. The square fort, top, is surrounded by swamps (marked "x") Below are the tents of the English. At left ("o") is "the Virginians main Garde." At right ("n") is "the Merrylanders main Garde."

ins by marriage. Both came from wealthy English families. Each held a degree of Master of Arts from a great English university — Berkeley from Oxford and Bacon from Cambridge — in a day when most people could not even read. In addition, Bacon had traveled across Europe in the company of a tutor, and he had studied law in London for two years. Governor Berkeley, who had even written a play while still in England, was something of an amateur scholar and scientist. Most important, both men were enormously proud and quick to anger.

The two crucial differences between Berkeley and Bacon were age and position. Sir William Berkeley was almost seventy years old when the Indian troubles erupted. He had been governor of Virginia off and on since the early 1640s. In his youth, he had gained fame as a vigorous leader in the English wars against the Indians. Now he was tired. He wrote home to his king saying that his bones could not bear another six months in office. His age had also made him extremely irritable.

Nathaniel Bacon, on the other hand, was only in his twenties. According to contemporary accounts, he was extremely vain and ambitious, and he had a fortune and a career to make. The governor had an office: he was the king's principal servant in the largest and most profitable English colony in America. Bacon was a young planter with two plantations near the frontier, a born leader without an official position and without a following.

When the men of Charles City and Henrico counties gathered on the James River, Bacon had been in Virginia only a little over a year. But he had a great deal of money, and he was quite dashing. As soon as Bacon had come to Virginia, Berkeley had appointed him to the Governor's Council, the upper house of the Virginia legislature. His fortune, his dash, and his position—together with the fact that he lived near the western frontier—made him a ripe candidate for the leadership of the rebellious planters camped near his home. As the royal commission of investigation described him:

> He was said to be indifferent tall but slender, blackhaired and of an ominous, pensive, melancholy aspect, not given to much talk, or to make sudden replies, of a most imperious and dangerous hidden pride of heart, despising the wisest of his neighbors for their ignorance, and very ambitious and arrogant. But all these things lay hidden in him until he became powerful and popular.

This description, recorded after Bacon was dead, was written by the commissioners of a king whose authority Bacon had defied. The people whom Bacon led had kinder words for him, but both his friends and enemies agreed that Nathaniel Bacon was a man of hot temper and quick to violence.

According to the report of the royal commission, Bacon was mildly tricked into taking command of the rebel army. He was:

> in company of one Crews, Isham, and Bird, growing to a height of drinking, and making the sadness of the times their discourse. Crews and the rest persuaded Mr. Bacon to go over and see the soldiers on the other side of the James River, and to take a quantity of rum with them to give the men to drink. And (as Crews and others had before laid the plot with the soldiers) they all one once in the field shouted and cried out "Bacon! Bacon! Bacon!"—which, taking fire with his ambition, easily prevailed on him to head them.

After this staged and somewhat alcoholic demonstration, Bacon and his "soldiers" made a decision. They would ask the governor once more for a commission to go to war with the Indians. If Berkeley refused again, they would fight anyway.

> Bacon's friends told him they would go along with him to take revenge on the Indians, and drink damnation to their souls to be true to him. And, if he could not obtain a commission, they would assist him as well and as much as if he had one. He boasted what great service he would do for the country, and subtly and secretly seduced the vulgar and most ignorant people (two-thirds of each county being of that sort) so that their whole hearts and hopes were set now upon Bacon. Thus Bacon encouraged the tumult. And as the unquiet crowd followed him, he listed them upon a large paper, writing their names circular-wise, so that the ringleaders might not be found out.

Sir William Berkeley— shown here before the time of Bacon's Rebellion—was not always a harsh ruler. But after his bloody revenge on the insurgents, King Charles II remarked, "The old fool has killed more people in that naked country than I have done for the murder of my father."

During the next few days Bacon recruited about 300 men to his cause. When Governor Berkeley angrily refused him the commission, Bacon led his troops into the forest. Berkeley rode out from Jamestown with a troop of "gentlemen" to try to stop Bacon, but he was too late. All he could do was to proclaim Bacon and his followers "rebels and mutineers."

In the meantime, Bacon and his men had marched off to the southwest. They found no Susquehannahs. Gradually, as provisions ran low, the force dwindled away to about fifty men, tired, restless, and hungry. Finally, they came upon a well-built fort belonging to a tribe of Indians called Occaneechees. The Occaneechees were friendly. In fact, they made their living partly by serving as middlemen in the beaver trade between the English and Indians who lived farther south and west. Their fort was many miles from the nearest English plantation, on an island in the Roanoke River. There was no evidence that they had been involved in the recent troubles.

The Occaneechees greeted Bacon and his followers warmly, sending out canoes to bring them to the island fort. Bacon explained that he was hunting Susquehannahs. The Occaneechee chief informed him that there was a band of Susquehannahs nearby and that, as a gesture of good will, the Occaneechees would wipe them out. Bacon agreed, and remained safe at the Occaneechee fort with his men while the small Susquehannah party was destroyed. A few prisoners were brought back to the Occaneechee fort and tortured to "entertain" the English.

Eyewitness accounts of what happened next are confused. For some reason Bacon ordered his men to surround the Occaneechee fort and keep as many Indian women and children outside as possible. This tense situation was broken by a shot that killed one of Bacon's men. But the English were already at the fort walls, ready to fire in through the portholes. For a day and a half they poured shot in on the Indians. They also "fell upon the women and children without, disarmed and destroyed them all," according to a version of the event written by one of Bacon's own followers. When the battle was over, the Occaneechees had been destroyed. Bacon felt no need to justify the attack or make any distinctions between Indian friends and enemies. He said simply: "We fell upon a town of Indians, beginning our fight after midnight close at their portholes."

Bacon had not fired a shot at the Susquehannahs. Instead, he had destroyed a friendly tribe—men, women, and children. But, like most of his followers, his aim was to kill Indians, not to conduct careful negotiations or make fine distinctions between friends and foes. He rode with his band of Indian fighters back to Henrico County, boasting of a great victory.

While Bacon was killing Occaneechees on the far-off Roanoke, Governor Berkeley was busily trying to repair his collapsing political popularity. He had not called for the election of a new House of Burgesses in more than fifteen years. So he called for a new election, and he even provided that all freemen could vote (the vote was normally restricted to property owners). This move was designed to appeal to the "rabble" who supported Bacon.

The governor also offered to pardon Bacon, if Bacon would apologize. But Bacon refused, saying that "Indians in general were all enemies," and that he would not stop warring against them. The governor's policy backfired. In the new election the House of Burgesses was packed with Bacon men. The two commanders who had attacked the Susquehannah fort in the fall of 1675 were elected. Bacon himself was voted a burgess from Henrico County.

The new assembly opened on June 5, 1676. Bacon came cautiously down the river to Jamestown in a sloop with thirty armed men. He anchored out of gunshot range of Jamestown and waited to see what the governor would do. Berkeley, now angry and bitter, reacted in a way that Bacon might easily have anticipated. He sent a visiting ship, the *Adam and Eve*, to capture Bacon's little sloop. Bacon, the rebel, the wealthy young planter, and a recently elected member of the House of Burgesses, was taken into Jamestown as a military prisoner.

The governor now had Bacon in his power, but he also had to face the people of Virginia and their elected legislators. Berkeley's concern for order and calm won out over his anger: he decided to liberate Bacon and return him to his place on the Governor's Council. He also promised him a commission to fight the Indians. Bacon, in return, agreed at last to humble himself.

In a dramatic gesture Berkeley stood stiffly before the House of Burgesses and said, "If there be joy in the presence of the angels over one sinner that repenteth, there is now. For we have a repentant sinner before us. Call Mr. Bacon!" Bacon entered the chamber and knelt before Berkeley, begging the pardon of God, the king, and the governor. Berkeley paused for a moment and then said three times, "God forgive you; I forgive you!"

Both Berkeley and Bacon were probably just acting. Berkeley was not really interested in angelic rejoicing over a repentant sinner. He was trying chiefly to maintain peace and order until he became powerful enough to subdue Bacon for good. Bacon, on his part, was interested only in the commission that would officially make him "General of Virginia."

Neither man got what he wanted. Berkeley delayed the commission, and after a few days Bacon suddenly disappeared from Jamestown. For ten days rumors about his activites filled the air. Then, on June 23, Bacon reappeared, this time at the head of an army of about 400 men, all armed, with more than a hundred on horseback. He had not come to beg the governor's pardon this time. He had come instead to demand his commission, and to take it by force if necessary.

The scene that followed was partly drama, partly farce. Bacon approached the little statehouse between two files of his own foot soldiers. The governor, with his council, came out to meet him. Berkeley

A contemporary mural depicts Jamestown in the early years. In the foreground is the James River. Farmers beyond the town would take refuge inside the palisade in case of attack.

opened his coat and shirt and pointed to his chest, offering Bacon a coward's chance: "Here! Shoot me! Before God, a fair mark! Shoot!" The governor repeated this insulting invitation several times. Bacon, with equal sarcasm, made a gentle reply: "No, may it please your honor, we will not hurt a hair on your head—nor of any other man's. We are come for a commission to save our lives from the Indians. You have so often promised it, and now we will have it before we go."

Berkeley once more refused to give him the commission; and turning his back on Bacon, he began to walk toward his office at the other end of the statehouse. The members of the House of Burgesses, meeting inside, had all crowded to the windows to watch. Bacon followed the governor, shouting and waving his arms, and then suddenly commanded his men to aim their cocked flintlocks at the burgesses in the windows.

"God damn my blood!" Bacon swore. "I'll kill governor, council assembly and all, and then I'll sheath my sword in my own heart's blood!"

The burgesses were terrified. Bacon gave an order for his men to fire if he drew his sword. Bacon's men were shouting, "We will have it! We will have it!"

Then one of the frightened burgesses waved a handkerchief from the window, shouting back, "You shall have it! You shall have it!"

Bacon had won in this showdown, simply by commanding a superior armed force. The governor had no alternative but to give in or lose his office, perhaps even his life, to the rebels. The assembly made Bacon "General of the Virginia War." A day or two later, the burgesses adjourned to go to their plantations. Berkeley went home to sulk. Bacon led his troops back west, this time with an official commission in his hands. He quickly set about appointing junior officers, to whom he gave the power to take horses, ammunition, and other goods from the plantations of Virginia for the Indian war he planned to wage. It was rumored that he was preparing to fight any royal troops that might be sent over from England to put down his rebellion. For the time being, Bacon was in control of Virginia.

For the next few weeks Berkeley did nothing. Nor did Bacon seem to do much besides getting his army organized. Probably a few scouting parties searched for Indians, but there was no action. Bacon had become more interested in his rebellion than in fighting Indians. At the end of July he assembled all his forces at Middle Plantation, the future site of Williamsburg, a few miles from Jamestown. Berkeley, in despair, fled across the Chesapeake to a plantation on the Eastern shore, abandoning the government.

At Middle Plantation, Bacon held what amounted to a political convention. He sent out an oath for all Virginians to swear, promising they would be loyal to him and even fight royal soldiers in his defense. On August 3 he also issued a "Manifesto and Declaration of the People." It stated the rebels' case against the Indians very clearly. All Indians were enemies and outlaws and ought to be wiped out. The governor had treated them as "darling and protected" subjects, as "quiet and honest neighbors." And, according to the manifesto, the governor had used the beaver trade solely to enrich himself and a small group of friends. This trade had enabled the Indians to arm and murder English settlers. Bacon's solution was simply to put an end to the trade by putting an end to both groups of traders. He ordered the arrest of Berkeley and his associates and promised death to all the Indians.

Bacon's manifesto also introduced a new element into the rebellion. At Middle Plantation, for the first time, Bacon's movement took on a tone of a political revolution. Everyone who wrote about the rebellion at the time agreed on one fact—that Bacon's followers were of the "poorer sort," whereas Berkeley's were "gentlemen" or "grandees." The manifesto recognized this apparent class division for the first time.

The manifesto was full of brilliant political rhetoric, the product of Bacon's excellent education. "If virtue be a sin," Bacon began, then he and his followers were guilty. But, he continued, "we cannot in our hearts find one single spot of rebellion or treason." Instead, Bacon ap-

After signing a treaty with the Potomac Indians in 1677, the English presented their chief with this silver medal, inscribed—somewhat carelessly—"Patomeck."

pealed "to the country" to examine its rulers, not its rebels. Over the years Governor Berkeley had gathered around him the wealthiest planters of the colony. These Virginians were a ruling elite—or so Bacon's rebels thought. This elite were men of "vile" education and background, Bacon charged. But they had been suddenly made into "grandees" by "mysterious wiles." Altogether, they were nothing but "sponges who have soaked up the public treasure, unworthy favorites and juggling parasites, whose tottering fortunes have been supported at the public charge."

Bacon marshaled the "people" against these so-called grandees. He insisted that the king would finally side with the people, once the political corruption of the ruling planters was exposed. Bacon demanded the surrender of Berkeley and nineteen of his "wicked counselors" within four days. After that time, he declared, anyone who hid or protected any of the "oppressors" would be considered "traitors to the people." Bacon signed the manifesto: "Nath. Bacon, Gen'l. by the Consent of the People."

Up to now, Bacon had been declared a "rebel and mutineer" by proclamation of the governor. But by marching back to Middle Plantation, sending out "Bacon's oaths" to all the counties of the colony, and issuing the manifesto and declaration, Bacon had become a rebel by even his own definition. In a conversation with John Goode, a Henrico County neighbor, Bacon tried to work out a strategy for resisting England and liberating the colony:

In this early English drawing, Virginia Indians feast on fish and corn. When the colonists were hungry, the Indians gave them grain. Later, when the Indians were starving, the whites traded them 400 bushels for "a mortgage on their whole countries."

BACON: There is a report that Berkeley has sent to the king for two thousand redcoats.[1] Tell me your opinion. May not five hundred Virginians beat them, we having the same advantages against them the Indians have against us?

GOODE: On the contrary, I think five hundred redcoats may either subject or ruin Virginia.

BACON: You talk strangely. Are we not acquainted with the country, so that we can lay ambushes? Can we not hide behind trees? Are we not as good or better shots than they?

But Goode pointed out to Bacon that with their fleet the English could easily win.

GOODE: They can accomplish what I have said without hazard by landing where there is no opposition, firing our houses and fences, destroying our cattle, preventing trade and cutting off imports.

BACON: I am confident that it is the mind of this colony, and of Maryland as well as Carolina, to cast off their governors. And if we cannot prevail by arms, we may retire to the Roanoke [River] and establish our own government there.

By this time, both Bacon and Goode were becoming angry.

GOODE: Sir, this design will produce utter ruin. I hope you will excuse me from having any part in it.

BACON: I am glad to know your mind, but I think this proceeds from mere cowardice.

---

[1]English troops were given this name because of their scarlet uniforms.

At any rate, if a revolution was part of Bacon's plan, he seemed to have won easily. Berkeley had abandoned most of Virginia, and many of the planters appeared ready to follow Bacon. Without any real authority Bacon ordered the election of a new House of Burgesses to meet in Jamestown on September 4.

When he had completed all these successful but dangerous political actions, Bacon gathered his troops and set out west in search of the Indians. They were still supposed to be his principal concern. Once again, he did not pursue the Susquehannahs, the real "enemy." Instead, he plunged his army into the Great Dragon Swamp to search for the village of a small, friendly tribe, the Pamunkeys. (Some suspected them, wrongly, of planning opposition to the English.) The swamp was a difficult place for Indians to maneuver in; it was nearly impossible for armed Englishmen. Bacon's army, which at first probably numbered a thousand, gradually dwindled down to about 150 wet, tired men who were running low on food. Several times, Bacon had to make fiery speeches to whip up the falling spirits of his men:

Dancing in a circle, Indians brandish bunches of leaves and other religious symbols. When left alone, the tribes of Virginia were usually industrious and peaceable.

> I would rather my carcass should lie rotting in the woods, than miss doing the service the country expects from me. All you gentlemen that intend to abide with me must resolve to undergo all the hardship this wild can afford, and if need be to eat chestnuts and horseflesh before you return.

Finally, after days of marching back and forth across the swamp, Bacon stumbled on the Pamunkey village. His men immediately charged and opened fire. The Indians did not resist but simply ran. The English killed eight Pamunkeys, and captured forty-five more. This was Bacon's second "victory" over the Indians. He stumbled out of the swamp toward Jamestown (expecting to find the new House of Burgesses ready to meet). He had the captured Pamunkeys tied in a row as evidence of his success as an Indian fighter.

When Bacon emerged from the swamp, instead of finding a victory celebration, he was confronted with the shocking news that Berkeley had somehow managed to occupy Jamestown again. The governor had a thousand troops. Moored on the James were several large English ships with heavy guns, ready to defend the capital.

The shrewd old governor had played a sly trick. He had won control of Virginia's waterways. The colony in 1676 was as much water as land. The Chesapeake Bay and rivers like the James, the York, and the Potomac led everywhere into the settled areas of the colony. Bacon too had realized this early in the rebellion, and he had taken over two or three large merchant ships and armed them with cannon from Jamestown's fort. It was hoped that these ships could capture any other vessels that might sail from England, including warships of the royal navy.

Early in September, while Bacon was hunting Indians in the Great Dragon Swamp, his little fleet sailed the thirty miles across the Chesapeake to attack Berkeley on the Eastern shore. The rebel "navy" had 300 men, more than enough to capture Berkeley. But the governor

An Indian watchman crouches in a small hut in the midst of a corn field. As a sort of living scarecrow, he frightens away birds and other animals that might destroy the Indians' crop.

shrewdly sent word to the captain of the fleet that he wanted to negotiate. The captain went ashore and unfortunately accepted too much of Berkeley's wine. While Bacon's captain drank, a small boatload of men loyal to Berkeley rowed out to the largest ship. With the help of the English sailors on board—who had been forced to join Bacon's forces against their will—Berkeley's men quickly captured the ship and disarmed Bacon's troops. By threats and promises Berkeley quickly raised an army and sailed back to Jamestown. The detachment of men Bacon had left there abandoned the town, and Berkeley went ashore and fell to his knees to praise God for his mercy and help.

This was the situation Bacon confronted when he marched out of the Great Dragon Swamp. In bitter anger he led his troops on a forced march toward Jamestown, picking up recruits along the way. Finally, after a march of forty miles in one day, the men reached the outskirts of Jamestown. Bacon kept his tired men up all night, cutting down trees and digging a trench by moonlight, ready for the charge he was certain would come from the town and the cannon that would be trained on him from the ships in the river.

The next day, however, when no attack came, Bacon decided to move up heavy cannon of his own to fire at Jamestown's fortifications. To cover his men while they put the guns in place, Bacon sent scouts out to bring in the wives of some of Berkeley's leading supporters. He forced the women to stand between his men and Berkeley's guns while places were dug for the guns. Then they were released.

Finally, Berkeley decided to attack. Bacon described the battle this way:

> Yesterday, they made a sally, with horse and foot in the van [the front]. The forlorn [the lead] was made up of such men as they had compelled to serve. They came up with a narrow front, pressing very close upon one another's shoulders, so that the forlorn might be their shelter. Our men received them so warmly that they retired in great disorder, throwing down their arms, as also their drums and dead men. They show themselves such pitiful cowards.

Bacon was right. Even the governor's supporters agreed that their men went out "like scholars going to school, with heavy hearts; but they returned home with light heels."

Once Berkeley's heavy-hearted "scholars" were safely back inside Jamestown, they began to mutter of mutiny. Even the governor's officers encouraged the talk of desertion. Finally, Berkeley had no more than twenty men on whom he could rely. Under the safety of nightfall, he loaded his ineffective troops once more on to the ships and slipped off down the James.

Bacon had won again, or so it seemed. But all of his victories added together meant nothing. He was finally forced to realize that, in the long run, his situation was hopeless. In the first place, the governor still had the only useful ships in the colony, and he could take control of every other ship that sailed into Virginia from the Atlantic. This meant that Berkeley could land forces anywhere in the colony. Bacon had taught

Berkeley a difficult lesson: controlling the statehouse was not the same thing as controlling the colony.

Now Bacon had to learn the same lesson. For him, occupying Jamestown was worthless as long as Berkeley was armed with ships and the title of royal governor. More important, Bacon realized that Berkeley would certainly have already sent home to England for help. Any morning tide might bring in royal warships and the king's redcoats to occupy the colony. Bacon might kill Pamunkeys. He might even drive the governor again and again to the Eastern Shore. But the entire colony of Virginia had fewer people than the city of London alone. And the English king had the world's greatest navy to pit against Bacon's army.

So despite his dramatic capture of Jamestown, Bacon was doomed. There would be no time to unite the people against Berkeley's supporters. The new House of Burgesses Bacon had ordered would never meet. Sooner or later, Bacon and his officers would either have to die in battle or be hanged as traitors. There was no way out. After occupying Jamestown, Bacon waited until night and then burned down every building in the town, even the church. From their ships down river Berkeley and his troops could see the fires light the harvest sky.

Over the next few weeks Bacon tried to strengthen his position by issuing new oaths of loyalty and enlisting new recruits. But because Berkeley did not venture off the Eastern Shore, Bacon's men could do nothing. They grew disorderly and began to loot plantations, much to their general's dismay.

But Bacon faced an even more serious problem. In either the Great Dragon Swamp or the trenches outside Jamestown, he had become ill with dysentery—the "bloody flux," as it was called then. He had also become so infested with lice that his clothes had to be frequently burned. On October 26 he died.

Bacon's death brought about the quick collapse of his rebellion. While he was alive, it had no real chance of success, but with him dead, it simply did not exist. When Berkeley received the welcome news that his enemy had died, he began to attack the remainder of Bacon's followers with his ships. Here and there, small groups of rebels fought back. In one such battle a dozen or so rebels were killed. But on the whole, the rebels did not resist. But between the time of Bacon's death and March of 1677 the governor had twenty-three rebels hanged.

Finally, when it was no longer needed, help came from England. News of Bacon's Rebellion had caused great concern in London, and the king had sent over several warships, a thousand redcoats, and a royal commission of investigation. The English expected to find Bacon in command and Berkeley either dead or imprisoned. What they found instead was the governor securely in control and Bacon dead. Still, their instructions provided that if Berkeley was still alive, he should return to England as soon as possible. The governor delayed returning in order to hang rebels. but he finally set sail for London in March. He never returned to America. He reached London in June and died in July, without ever seeing the king to explain what had happened.

4 THE PLANTATION COLONIES

R. J. W.

William Berkeley never stopped complaining that Nathaniel Bacon was a recent immigrant, a man who had been in Virginia for less than two years, when he became a rebel and mutineer. But the governor himself was an immigrant, as were most of the planters. Virginia was an immigrant society. The colony had existed for only about seventy years when Bacon's Rebellion occurred. Probably a majority of the people in the colony had been born not in Virginia but in England, not in the New World but in the Old. This fact, though obvious, is sometimes too easily forgotten, and it helps explain not only Bacon's Rebellion but much of the history of early America.

Like the first immigrants, the Indians, and like earlier Europeans before them, the English came to Virginia and the other colonies for one basic reason: to improve their lives. And, like the earlier immigrants, the English came without any real plans or much information. They had hopes instead: hopes of finding gold and silver as the Spanish had done in Mexico and Peru; and, like many explorers, hopes of finding a northwest passage to the wealth of the East. Some English people hoped to convert the Indians to Christianity. Then, too, the desire to make England a great and powerful nation moved many of the English either to become immigrants or to give money and support to colonization. A straightforward itch to travel, to see new sights, was sometimes as important as any other motive for colonization.

All these motives—the desire for wealth, the missionary spirit, patriotism, adventure—were present, sometimes in the same person. But underlying them all, from the beginning of English colonization to the American Revolution—and probably to the present—was the idea that the New World meant wealth. To most Europeans, America meant gold, land, or profitable trade. Almost all the immigrants who came voluntarily thought of the New World as a place where they could improve their fortunes.

The problem that brought on Bacon's Rebellion was no different from the problem that existed in every part of America: *Whose* fortune was going to be improved first and most? And who was going to pay the price? There was an almost comic character to Bacon's marches to the west and back to the east, his inability to decide whether to fight Indians or his own government. But all the marching and countermarching grew out of one crucial fact. In Virginia, and all the other English colonies, there were three principal groups of factors: Indians, English colonists, and England herself. Obviously, each had different ideas about how to divide the natural wealth of the New World. Bacon and the colonists stood literally between the Indians on the one side and England on the other. The curious fact that Bacon destroyed both Indian forts and his own capital city is a pointed illustration of the colonists' dilemma.

In 1676 the 30,000 English of Virginia thought of themselves as a small, weak group, virtually at the mercy of both the Indians and the English crown. The people who followed Bacon into his rebellion were lashing out blindly at both opponents, without much hope of real success on either front. To understand what made Bacon's followers act the way they did, their rebellion must be seen as one chapter in the story of the English conquest of North America.

THE FOUNDING OF VIRGINIA

The history of Virginia began with a document issued by the English king, James I, on April 10, 1606. Since the 1580s, Englishmen had been making unsuccessful stabs at colonization. Now a new group of "knights, gentlemen, merchants, and

This many-chimneyed house in Surrey County, Virginia, was supposedly fortified as a stronghold by Nathaniel Bacon. It comes complete with ghosts.

other adventurers" was ready for another try. They petitioned the crown for the right to create a colony. The king granted the petition by issuing the charter of 1606, which marks a kind of official beginning of the history of not only Virginia but of the United States.

The charter first asserted the king's claim to most of North America—"that part of America, commonly called Virginia," between 34 and 45 degrees north latitude. This included everything from Cape Fear in North Carolina to what is now Bangor, Maine—a total of about 2 million square miles of land. Then, the charter granted the right to plant colonies to two groups of "loving subjects." There would be two trading companies, one based in London and the other in the town of

Plymouth. Each company could begin by creating one colony. The London Company could settle anywhere between 34 and 41 degrees north latitude, an area extending from Cape Fear to what is now New York City. The Plymouth Company could establish its colony anywhere between 38 and 45 degrees, which included the coast between approximately Washington, D.C., and Bangor. If both companies decided to found their colonies in the overlapping area, they had to settle at least a hundred miles apart.

The king did not grant all of his 2 million square miles in America to the two Virginia companies. Far from it. Each company got control of only 10,000 square miles of land. From their "first seats" the London and Plymouth companies were

VIRGINIA LAND GRANTS, 1606 - 1620

—— 1606 grant to Virginia Company of London
- - - 1606 grant to Virginia Company of Plymouth
▬▬ 1606 grant to the Council for New England

any gold or silver, furthermore, they would have to pay a fifth of it to the crown.

Within these limits the merchants of the London and Plymouth companies had the right to send over colonists (called planters) and to develop trade, agriculture, and industry. The charter of 1606 said nothing about self-government or freedom of religion. The merchants who financed the colonies were interested primarily in making money. It cost a great deal to outfit ships and buy tools, seed, and livestock for the first settlers. The shareholders who put up the money to back these ventures expected to have it returned with a reasonable margin of profit.

The first settlers might find gold. They could trade with the Indians. They could cut lumber for shipment back to England. Most important, they could try raising a cash crop that was not grown in England—rice, for example, or sugar or citrus fruit. The merchants at home in England could then import the crop at a profit. The colonists (and the Indians) would, in turn, buy from the merchants such necessities as cloth, tools, nails, and furniture. If their colony worked out as the merchants of the London Company hoped, it would be the perfect mercantilist dream: a source of imports and a market for manufactured goods that would free England from dependence on Spanish, French, or Dutch markets. England could take a giant step toward becoming a self-sufficient kingdom, to the profit of her merchants and her government.

Settling Jamestown Such were the ideas and expectations of the merchants. The 120 Englishmen who sailed in three ships for Virginia in December 1606 probably had the same kind of ideas in mind. After a long voyage, 104 of them reached the entrance to Chesapeake Bay on April 29, 1607. For two weeks they explored the bay and some of its rivers. Finally, they chose a point of land situated about thirty miles up the river that they had already named after King James. They landed and unloaded their supplies. Their settlement, too, they named after the king: James Fort, or Jamestown.

Things went smoothly at first, and after about seven weeks the leaders of the colony sent

given control of the coastlines for fifty miles north and south and of the land a hundred miles inland. They could also control the ocean for a hundred miles out to sea.

The rest of America, however, remained firmly in the king's hands. More important, the government of the companies would be in the hands of a Royal Council of thirteen men appointed by the king. These appointees were responsible directly to the king. If the colonists discovered back their first report to the Royal Council for Virginia. The report included some complaints, but it presented a generally optimistic picture—the kind that was to lure thousands of other Englishmen over the Atlantic in the coming years.

In this pleasant land, the colonists reported, they had already accomplished the first tasks of planting: "Within less than seven weeks, we are fortified well against the Indians. We have sown good store of wheat. We have sent you a taste of clapboard.[1] We have built some houses." The only note of caution in the first report was a request that new supplies and people be sent as quickly as possible, lest the "devouring Spaniard lay his ravenous hands upon these gold-showing mountains."

This was the Englishmen's "Virginia." For the king, it was a vast region with enormous possibilities for the crown and the nation. For the merchants, it was an investment that could pay off handsomely. For the colonists, it was a fair land with great rivers, rich soil, and "gold-showing mountains." No one, neither the king nor the merchants nor the settlers, could see Jamestown for what it really was—a death trap.

Hardship and Disease The land called Virginia had already claimed the lives of the entire Roanoke settlement. It also killed hundreds of the people who came to Jamestown. In 1607 the 104 "first planters" came. In the next year and a half, two groups of reinforcements totaled almost 200. Out of this group of 300, only 80 men were left alive in the summer of 1609—about one out of four.

The first really large "supply," as it was called, arrived in 1609. This group of 600 included women and children for the first time. But, by the next summer, only 60 people were left alive. This meant that, in the first three years, the odds of staying alive in the new settlement were only about one in twelve. Nor did things get much better as time passed. In the first seventeen years of settlement, about 10,000 Englishmen sailed to Jamestown. But the surviving population in 1624 was only 1,275.

At the beginning, Virginia colonists spent too much time looking for gold and not enough growing crops. This was partly the fault of the English shareholders, who wanted a quick return on their investment. Even after the settlers began farming more extensively, they underwent some lean years because they had to rely for many of their supplies on imports from England.

In the next fifty years, up to the time of Bacon's Rebellion, survival became easier, and the population of Virginia[2] grew to about 30,000. But it grew slowly, and Bacon's followers could remember how difficult and dangerous settling the colony had been. Nearly everyone had a friend or a relative who had died as a result of one of the dangers of the place: Indians, starvation, or disease. Despite their success, Virginians in 1676 still regarded their hold on the New World as weak and uncertain. The possibility of death and failure still seemed to lurk around every corner. Life was full of risks—a fact that helps explain the willingness of Bacon's followers to take up arms against both the Indians and the government for reasons that might seem petty today. The experience of colonization in the seventeeth century was one that combined hope and optimism with danger and death.

Of the three dangers, disease was the greatest. The town was located on marshy ground where mosquitoes flourished during the summer, and a hundred of the first settlers died from malaria. (At that time, of course, no one knew of the connection between mosquitoes and malaria.) Probably even more settlers died from diseases brought over from England—mainly the plagues that were simultaneously killing Europeans by the hundreds of thousands. The ships that came to Virginia in the early years were terribly overcrowded, like immigrant ships throughout most of American history. Disease spread quickly and easily among the passengers. One ship, one of the unluckiest on record, lost about 130 out of 180 passengers before even sighting Virginia. Then

---

[1]By "a taste of clapboard," the writer meant a small amount of split oak (used for making barrels).

[2]As other colonies were established along the Atlantic coast in what had originally been known as Virginia, the term became restricted in meaning. By the time of Bacon's Rebellion, "Virginia" referred to the colony only.

there was dysentery (the "bloody flux" that had killed Bacon).

It took an English immigrant about two years to develop immunities to the unfamiliar bacteria in his new homeland—to become "seasoned," as the Virginians put it. Many died before they could attain immunity. Even in Bacon's day the chances of surviving the first two years were probably not much better than two out of three.

One of the early records of Jamestown summed up the horrors of the situation this way:

> There were never Englishmen left in a foreign country in such misery as we were in this new-discovered Virginia. If there were any conscience in men, it would make their hearts bleed to hear the pitiful murmurings and outcries of our sick men, every night and day. In the mornings, their bodies were trailed out of their cabins like dogs to be buried.

Relations with the Indians For those who managed to stay on their feet, there was the problem of the Indians, who wasted little time in making their first attack. Just six days after the landing at Jamestown, several hundred Indians rushed out of the woods at the men planting their first crop of wheat. The English, having an enormous advantage in weapons, defeated their attackers. The Indians very quickly learned that they could not win large battles, and they began ambushing individuals and small groups that wandered too far from the fort.

The English found their Indian neighbors utterly unpredictable. The Indians were usually willing to trade. They sold beaver hides cheaply enough. They also helped the English plant their first crops of corn. But it was difficult to work out long-range, overall policies. The Indians of the area were broken up into many small tribes and clans, each of which had its own ideas of how to deal with the strangers.

Fortunately, there was a loose confederation among the tribes in the area under a ruler named Powhatan. The English decided to "crown" Powhatan with a copper crown sent from England. In English theory the ceremony made Powhatan and all his people subjects of James I. This move, combined with the Indians' real desire to trade what they thought were worthless beaver skins to the foolish whites, kept an unsteady peace, as long as the English stayed close to their fort and muskets. Even this uneasy truce kept the English hemmed inside the unhealthy Jamestown settlement. They were so crowded that at one point they were even planting in the streets of their little town.

Finally, in 1613, the English won a long peace with Powhatan by the simple tactic of kidnapping his daughter Pocahontas and holding her as a hostage. They converted her to Christianity, and one Englishman, John Rolfe, married her and took her to England. There she became the central attraction of an otherwise dull London social season. The English colonists had first seen Pocahontas as a naked girl doing cartwheels in front of her father's lodge. Seven years later, she was being introduced at the court of King James. (And a year after that, she was dead of smallpox.)

Thus by trickery and trade the English managed to live among the Indians for the first fifteen years of Virginia history. However, Indian resentment was growing because of white inroads on their lands. In 1622, with Powhatan dead and Pocahontas all but forgotten, the Indians massacred some 400 whites—almost a fourth of the total population. The English had spread up and down the James in the ten years of peace that followed the marriage of Rolfe and Pocahontas. On their isolated plantations they were easy targets for the Indians. But when they recovered from the Indian attack, the colonists were just as angry as Bacon's followers would be fifty years later. They attacked the Indians' villages and adopted a new policy of destroying their enemy's corn crops in order to starve them out. In a few years the Indians were beaten and stopped fighting.

Once more there was an uneasy truce, this time for almost twenty years. Then, in 1644, there was another massacre, in which the Indians took about 500 lives. The whites' new counterattack was led by Sir William Berkeley, who personally captured the Indians' chief. The peace that Berkeley made lasted a generation—until Bacon's Rebellion. Berkeley's success made him proud of his record in dealing with the "Indian problem." This pride helps account for his bitterly angry response to the young upstart Bacon in 1676.

Ironically, Berkeley had little reason to be proud, and Bacon had just as little reason for attempting to wipe out the Indians by force. They were just two men in a massive flow of white Europeans into North America, a flow that would soon reach into the millions. In the long run, the Indians were certain to lose their continent, and nothing that people like Berkeley or Bacon did was likely to change the result. No matter how many thousands died of malaria and dysentery at Jamestown, thousands of others kept coming to the New World.

In 1607 there were about 10,000 Indians in Virginia ready to oppose the 104 white men who sailed up the James. By 1670 there were about 30,000 whites and only 4,000 Indians. Few of the "missing" 6,000 Indians were combat casualties. They had died of European diseases to which they had no inherited immunities. Some had been starved out by the collapse of their economy and their way of life. Others had moved west to escape the whites.

There was a profound difference in the relationship to the environment of the Indians and the Europeans. The Indians lived *in* nature. They farmed in small areas and hunted only for food. Left to themselves, they would probably have kept a stable population for centuries. The whites, in contrast, used up the environment. They took unlimited quantities of beaver, for example, not for food but for skins to make into hats. And they needed ever more and larger fields for their tobacco. The landscape of Virginia, which could have supported 10,000 Indians forever, was literally transformed into hats and tobacco smoke for Europeans thousands of miles away.

At first, the Indians cooperated. They loved the white man's cheap jewelry, his cloth, and his tools. For these things they could trade beaver skins. The white man's demand for beaver was practically unlimited, and the Indians were skillful hunters and trappers. The only difficulty was that the slow, exposed beaver was a very vulnerable prey. In the space of one man's lifetime, beaver would become scarce in areas near white settlements. This meant that the Indians had lost their "cash crop" for trade with the whites.

The Indians were then doomed. They might lash out blindly, as in the attacks of 1622 and 1644 in Virginia. But one by one the tribes of Powhatan became dependent on the whites. Tribes like the Doegs and the Pamunkeys were put on their own reservations under the so-called protection of colonial governments in Virginia and Maryland. Ironically, it was against these already beaten and ruined tribes that Bacon and his followers aimed their cruel and useless attacks.

PROBLEMS OF GOVERNMENT

In some ways Bacon's Rebellion was only one episode in a long conflict between the Indians and the English. But the rebellion involved more than the "Indian problem"—or, from the Indians' viewpoint, the "white problem." Bacon and the planters who sided with him also were interested in the way Virginia ought to be governed. The problem of the colony's government was as old as Jamestown. During the seventy years before Bacon's Rebellion, Virginia had never really developed a stable system of government, and Bacon's mutiny occurred within a tradition of political instability and unrest.

The trouble had begun even before the first ships entered Chesapeake Bay. The charter of 1606 provided that the Royal Council in England would appoint a local council to govern the colony. There were six councillors aboard the first fleet. During the first two years, while the planters died by the dozen, the councillors argued among themselves, chiefly over matters of rank. Of the first ten men appointed to the Jamestown council, one was tried for mutiny and executed in Virginia. Two died. Two others went back to England voluntarily, and four were sent back to London under arrest. The tenth and probably the luckiest man was a sea captain who spent almost no time in Jamestown. By 1609 it was clear that the system of council government would not work. The colony obviously needed a single governor with broad powers.

In the meantime, the London Company was having its problems. The Jamestown colony was

The 1622 Indian attack on Virginians, as imagined by an artist. Gory pictures of Indian atrocities appealed to Europeans, who held contradictory views of native Americans as either violent brutes or noble savages untouched by the vices of civilization.

not making a profit, and the first two years of settlement had cost a great deal of money. So the company petitioned King James for a new charter granting more generous terms. The new charter of 1609 eliminated the Plymouth Company entirely. It vastly increased the size of the land grant to the other company, now known as the Virginia Company. This company now owned a strip of land 400 miles wide and extending "up into the land from sea to sea." The new charter also gave control of the company to its investors, the stockholders.

Any person could become a stockholder by buying a share for about £12[3] or by becoming a settler in the colony. At the end of seven years the company would divide whatever profits there were. At the same time each stockholder would receive land — 100 acres for each share he owned.

The new charter greatly strengthened the Virginia Company. It could now raise money by selling stock. And it now owned an enormous area of land. For the colonists, however, the new charter had other effects. It replaced the old governing council with a single governor. Appointed by the company for a life term, he had almost absolute power over the colony. For nine years Jamestown was ruled by a set of very harsh laws. They

[3]It is difficult to work out present-day equivalents for seventeeth-century money. This figure might be roughly estimated as equal to $1,000 today.

may have saved the colony, because its death-trap atmosphere made strong discipline necessary. But these laws were made in the interests not of the colonists but of the company in England. In early Jamestown, as in Bacon's time, there was an inevitable conflict of interest between those who actually went to Virginia and those who stayed behind in England.

The charter was revised again slightly in 1612, mainly because the Virginia Company was going bankrupt and needed a new source of money. This time, the king gave the company the right to conduct a lottery. From then on gambling was the main source of the English capital invested in Virginia. Over the long run, the company spent about £200,000 — an enormous sum of money in that day — on settlement. It made no profit at all. As a business venture, Virginia was a total failure.

Land Allocation   In 1618 it was time to divide lands and profits under the charters of 1609 and 1612. There were no profits, but the Virginia Company did grant 100 acres to every colonist who had paid his way to Virginia since 1607. At the same time, the company made a very important change in the land system. Before 1618 all the land had belonged to the company and had been farmed for it by the colonists. A new company charter ruled that every new Virginia settler would get 50 acres of land for himself and 50 acres for every member of his family over fifteen. The colonist would also receive 50 acres for each servant brought or sent over. This meant that an Englishman with a wife, two grown children, and three servants would own 400 acres of land as soon as he reached Virginia.

Prospective settlers who could not afford to pay for their passage to Virginia could come over as servants. A man or woman signed a bond called an indenture, promising to work for a specified master for a period of years, usually seven. At the end of the period the indentured servant gained his or her freedom. At the same time, the former servant received farmland in the usual way — 50 acres for himself or herself and 50 acres each for a spouse or a grown child.

Much of Virginia was settled under the rules of 1618. Together they became known as the head-right system, since a colonist was entitled to a certain amount of land for each "head" he brought to Virginia. At the same time, the company also made huge grants of free land to various people — some as large as 200,000 acres.

From 1618 on, Virginia was really not much more than a focus of speculation in real estate. In fact, much of American history has been a story of land sales, grants, and speculation. In 1676 the people who followed Bacon into rebellion were interested in opening up new land. They were ready to wipe out any Indians who stood in their way. The English had moved into the Indians' "neighborhood," just as later groups of immigrants would move into English neighborhoods. The result, both in 1676 and later, was conflict between old settlers and new ones that often led to violence.

Governors and Assemblies   The new land policy of 1618 changed the character of Virginia. It made the colonists much more independent of the Virginia Company, since they now owned their land directly. But they were still ruled by a governor who was appointed in England and who served for life. The company tried to soften this contradiction by allowing the settlers to elect representatives to pass some of their own laws.

In 1619 the first elected legislature in America met in Jamestown. The governor was present. So were the appointed members of his council, which still existed as an upper house of the legislature to give advice to the governor. There were also twenty-two elected burgesses, two from each of the eleven regions into which the colony was divided. This House of Burgesses formed the lower house of the Virginia legislature. Their first meeting lasted only six days. But the burgesses passed a number of laws and helped to establish a principle that the colonists would be governed partly by their own elected representatives, not just by men appointed in England.

Gradually, during the next hundred years, Virginia's political system became a model for many of the other colonies being settled by the English: a governor appointed in England; an upper house or council, also appointed; and an elected lower house. A regular pattern developed in colonial politics. Any conflict of interest between the Americans and the English became contests between the governors and the assemblies. Only when this system broke down, as it did under Governor Berkeley, did the colonists resort to force.

The changes of 1618 might have brought stability to Virginia. The colony seemed to be a safer place (at least until the Indian attack of 1622). The land system was fair. The House of Burgesses was functioning. But, back in London, the Virginia Company was in trouble. The king took away its privilege of holding a lottery, and it went bankrupt. In 1624 the government abolished the company, and the king took over control of Virginia, making it a royal colony. From then on the monarch appointed the governors—as he did Berkeley in 1642, for example. The royal governor, in turn, appointed members of the Governor's Council—as when Berkeley appointed Bacon in 1674. But the king did allow the settlers to continue to elect their own burgesses—and one of the burgesses they elected in 1676 was Nathaniel Bacon.

A GROWING ECONOMY

Thus the settlers coped in various ways with the problems of disease, Indians, and government. Another crucial problem was that of earning a living. The colonists could grow enough to feed themselves during most years. What they needed was a crop that they could sell in England to obtain the money to buy tools, clothing, furniture, and other manufactured articles. Without a cash crop their lives would remain primitive and their progress slow.

The Virginians experimented with grapes and olives, oranges and lemons, silkworms, and a dozen other possibilities. They finally settled on tobacco. John Rolfe made one great contribution to Virginia by marrying Powhatan's daughter. But an even greater contribution was his successful cultivation of the first smokable tobacco in 1612.[4]

Tobacco From 1612 on, tobacco growing was like a fever in Virginia. Tobacco was even planted

---

[4]The tobacco grown by Indians in North America was too harsh for European tastes. Rolfe introduced a different species, that grown by Indians in Latin America.

This plain but stately building, the so-called Capitol, housed the Virginia legislature after the capital was moved to Williamsburg in 1699. The Governor's Council met in one wing, while the House of Burgesses met in the other.

in the streets of Jamestown. The Virginians used it instead of money. They paid taxes with it, and used it to pay their public servants, soldiers, and preachers. Most important of all, they loaded it on ships to sell in England and the Netherlands. In 1617 they managed to load about 20,000 pounds of tobacco. Two years later, the quantity had already tripled. By 1700, production had gone up to 20 million pounds a year. This total had increased to 50 million pounds by the time of the American Revolution. Tobacco was the staff of life in Virginia.

Tobacco was, in some ways, the perfect colonial crop. It was not grown in England, so Virginia was not competing at home with any English product. Tobacco was also profitable. One man's labor in a tobacco field earned as much as the work of six men in a wheat field. A tobacco planter did not have to clear much land; one man could farm only about one-and-a-half acres of tobacco, but his yield would be about 1,500 pounds of tobacco a year.

Furthermore, there was a ready market for tobacco all over Europe, and, per pound, it brought more income than wheat or timber. When prices were good, the Virginia or Maryland planter would get enough to buy all the tools or furniture or clothing his family needed for the year. He might also clear enough money to pay the passage of an indentured servant, who was worth another 50 acres of land under the head-right system and who would produce another 1,500 pounds of tobacco each year for the next seven years.

But there were problems, of course. Tobacco wore out land very rapidly. Newly cleared woodlands were good for only four or five years. After this period the crop yield thinned, and the planter had to clear more land. Soon good land was scarce. Virginia became, in an odd way, crowded. Finding additional good land meant moving farther and farther up the rivers—the James and the York first, then the Rappahannock, the Potomac, and others. This migration brought the planters into continuous conflict with the Indians, and helped cause the attacks of 1644 and 1676. Most of Bacon's rebels were planters who had moved out into the new areas and wanted even more land for their tobacco.

A second problem with tobacco was that it made the planters dependent on prices in the London market, a market over which they had no control. No one knew, when he planted tobacco in the spring, whether the price in the fall would be enough to meet his expenses. During a bad year the planter still had to have tools and clothing. Then he had to buy on credit. Tobacco planters all over Virginia gradually accumulated debts to the English merchants who supplied them with manufactured goods. These debts were passed on from father to son, from generation to generation, as part of the plantation estate. The size of the annual crop and tobacco prices on the London market were the most important facts in the life of any Virginian or Marylander.

In 1619 the English government required that all Virginia tobacco would from then on have to be shipped to England for the benefit of the mother country. If the English price happened to be low, the planters could not sell to the Dutch or anyone else in order to get higher prices. They were at the mercy of the English traders. This restriction angered many planters, especially during bad years.

All these problems came to a head in the years just before Bacon's Rebellion. Tobacco prices fell, and Bacon's indebted followers were in deep trouble. Part of the answer, to some Virginians, lay in the direction of independence from the English market and perhaps even from English political control. And, logically enough, access to an expanded European market—especially to the Dutch tobacco trade—might go hand in hand with new political involvements. It was no accident, then, that part of Bacon's somewhat vague scheme for independence involved the hope that Dutch ships might help protect Virginia from English naval attack. In return, of course, Dutch merchants could expect to profit from a larger share of the colonists' tobacco crops. Bacon's plan was premature. It was never spelled out in any detail. In fact, it was a scheme hatched in the heat of rebellion and in the despair of impending defeat and capture. But Bacon's ideas actually included the main elements that would enter the minds of Virginia revolutionaries a century later. The rebels of 1776 would still be worried about

Tobacco—here shown in an English book of 1596—had its enemies. King James called smoking "loathesome to the eye, hateful to the nose, harmful to the brain."

commercial dependence on England, about debts, and about the arrogance of English power. And those rebels, too, would look to other European countries (including the Dutch) for help. In the end, it would be French ships that would help produce the final, crushing defeat of British power in Virginia.

The Founding of Maryland Neither Bacon's nor Berkeley's followers had any way of knowing what would come to pass a hundred years later. They could only look back at their own past and around at their present. And what they saw was a success story. Despite their problems and their hardships, the English had managed to plant themselves and their tobacco in the New World. And they had already begun to expand their new society. In fact, by the time of Bacon's Rebellion, there were not one but two successful English colonies in the Chesapeake Bay area. In an action that disturbed many Virginia speculators, Charles I had given away about 10 million acres of Virginia to a Catholic friend and supporter named

George Calvert. Calvert was an aggressive man. He had been a member of the London Company that founded Jamestown, and he never had given up the dream of making a fortune out of the New World. He was also a convert to Catholicism, and he hoped to found a colony in the New World that might serve as a haven for other Catholics, who were never quite safe in Protestant England.

The Stuart kings, James I and Charles I, both smiled on Calvert. (Their royal mother, a Catholic, had been deprived of her head on the orders of her Protestant half-sister, Elizabeth I.) They ennobled Calvert as the first "Lord Baltimore," and they helped him in his efforts to promote a colony in America. James I gave Calvert a grant in Newfoundland, but a winter's experience convinced him that it was not a suitable place. Then, in 1632, Charles I gave Calvert an even more attractive grant in Virginia: all the land on the eastern shore of Chesapeake Bay, plus a curious strip north of the Potomac River, running west toward the unexplored Appalachians. The charter of 1632 was quite different from the original Virginia grant. It did not create a modern commercial enterprise. Instead, it seemed to look back to an older, feudal England. It made Calvert and his heirs "absolute lords and proprietaries" of their new colony. This meant, in effect, that they had the same kinds of powers in Maryland that the king himself had in England. They could grant large tracts of land to anyone they chose, making the grantees their "vassals." The only restrictions were that their laws had to conform to English laws, that they had to have the consent of the "freemen" or their representatives (just as the king had to have the consent of Parliament), and that they must pay the English crown each year a token of two arrowheads, plus a fifth of any gold or silver they discovered.

The new colony, which was named after Charles I's French Catholic wife, Maria, got off to a slow start. The old London company, which still claimed some of its rights in Virginia, put legal obstacles in the way. George Calvert died before the grant even became effective. It then passed to his son Cecil; but he had to stay on in England to protect his rights. So it was not until 1634 that the first settlement of Maryland was made. Two ships,

THE PHASES OF COLONIZATION

Colony	First Phase 1607–1640	Second Phase 1640–1675	Third Phase 1675–1735
Conneticut	Windsor, 1633 Wethersfield, 1634 Hartford, 1636 New Haven, 1638		
Delaware	Zwaanedael (Lewes) (settled by Dutch), 1631 Fort Christina (Wilmington) (settled by Swedes), 1638		
Georgia			Darien, 1721 Savannah, 1733 Augusta, 1735
Maryland	St. Mary's, 1634	Annapolis, 1648	
Massachusetts	Plymouth, 1620 Gloucester, 1623 Salem, 1626 Boston, 1630		
New Hampshire	Rye, 1623 Portsmouth, 1624		
New Jersey	Gloucester, 1624 Hoboken, 1630 Hackensack, 1639	Swedesboro, 1641 Elizabeth, 1664	
New York	Kingston (settled by Dutch), 1615 Fort Orange (Albany) (settled by Dutch), 1623 New Amsterdam (New York) (settled by Dutch), 1624		
North Carolina		Edenton, 1658 Currituck, 1672	Bath, 1705 New Bern, 1710
Pennsylvania	Marcus Hook (settled by Swedes), 1640		Bristol, 1681 Philadelphia, 1682 Germantown, 1683
Rhode Island	Providence, 1636 Portsmouth, 1638 Newport, 1639	Warwick, 1643	
South Carolina		Charleston, 1670	Beaufort, 1711
Virginia	Jamestown, 1607 Hampton, 1610 Newport News, 1611		

bearing the gentle kind of names that seem to have been common among English colonizing vessels, the *Ark* and the *Dove,* hove into the Chesapeake with about 250 settlers aboard. Once in Maryland, however, the colonists planted themselves without the horrors of massacre, starvation, and disease that had plagued the Jamestown settlement. Within a few years, the little town of St. Mary's, the "first seat" of Maryland, was the center of a thriving tobacco culture very much like that of Virginia.

Despite the Calverts' hopes, most of the new settlers were Protestants, not Catholics. Maryland also copied the Virginia system of land grants to induce settlement. Very little of the feudal vision of the charter was ever to find concrete expression in practice. In fact, the most unique aspect of the new colony—and the thing for which colonial Maryland is still most famous—was not "feudal" at all, but rather modern in style. In 1649, Cecil Calvert prepared a law guaranteeing religious freedom to all Christians. The Maryland legislature, the House of Delegates, passed it as the Toleration Act. But the law did not grow out of Calvert's modernity or liberalism, or out of the enlightened principles of the colonists. Instead, it was the result of a fact of life: the colony was settled mainly by Protestants, who were fearful of their Catholic proprietor's power over them. The Toleration Act in fact made little difference in the patterns of immigration or religious practice. In the main, Maryland developed into a tobacco colony very much along Virginian lines, with the same economic, social, and political structures and the same kinds of anxieties and unrest that motivated Bacon and Berkeley and their respective supporters.

Slavery One difficulty with the tobacco economy was that it required a good deal of labor. Crops like wheat or corn needed more land, but they did not demand much handwork. Tobacco was (and still is) a crop requiring careful tending, from the first planting to the packing of the cured leaves almost a year later.

Virginia and Maryland were in a mixed situation. In one sense they were crowded, because fresh new land was becoming more and more scarce. But in another sense they were underpopulated, because there was a shortage of labor needed to tend the expanding tobacco crops. During most of the years before Bacon's Rebellion this problem was met by importing white indentured servants from England, at the rate of about a hundred a month up to 1690. The servants did not acquire their own land for seven years, and in the meantime they worked in existing tobacco fields.

There was, however, another source of cheap labor, one that did not use up land and that eventually made Virginia and the other Southern colonies very different from the rest of the country: black people from Africa. The first "Negars," as they were called, came to Virginia in 1619. They came not as slaves but as indentured servants. They did not come in large numbers until about the time of Bacon's Rebellion. In 1650 there were still only 300 blacks in Virginia. By 1671 the number had risen to 2,000. Ten years later, in 1681, there were 3,000.

At about the same time, the legal status of the blacks as slaves for life was spelled out. In 1670 the House of Burgesses passed a law that sealed the fate of black people, though it did not refer to them by race directly: "All servants not being Christians [that is, not being white Europeans] imported into this colony by shipping shall be slaves for their lives."

PLANTATION SOCIETY

Slavery did not become basic to Virginia until the eighteenth century. But already the way was being prepared for the kind of society Americans associate with the word *plantation:* a society of vast estates, in which the planter lived like a great lord (a "grandee," Bacon's men would have said), supported by the labor of blacks whom he owned and bred as he did his horses or cattle. Virginia eventually became such a plantation society, as did Maryland, the Carolinas, and Georgia. By the middle of the eighteenth century all the Southern colonies were basically alike, with large plantations involved in staple farming that used slave labor.

Slaves gather for festivities on a Carolina plantation. According to one expert, both the drum and the dance depicted are of Yoruba origin. (Many American slaves were descended from the Yoruba people, whose home is near the coast of West Africa.)

Bacon's Rebellion took place during the early stages of the change. Before 1670 or so, Virginia was still a region of small farms. Settlers usually owned a few hundred acres and still worked the land themselves with the help of their sons and perhaps one or two servants. The servants themselves would soon be free, and they would, in turn, become small planters. After approximately 1700, Virginia was controlled by a growing class of great planters, whose estates consisted of thousands of acres and whose great fortunes (and debts) rested squarely on the shoulders of black men and women.

Bacon's Rebellion can be explained, in part, as a personality conflict between the governor and the young revolutionary. It can also be understood as the outcome of troubles between the Indians and the white settlers. But it did have a political content, too. Whenever the rebels and the government talked about this political content, both always referred to the battle between the "poorer

sort" and the "grandees." The rebellion took place during the first years of the expansion of slavery. Bacon's followers—some of them, at least—probably sensed the new kind of society growing up around them. They feared the growth of an aristocracy that would control local governments and also enlist the power of the royal governor most of the time. Those who supported Berkeley probably looked forward to the creation of just such a planter aristocracy.

In 1676 the two groups—the rebels and the government—were in fact roughly equal economically. Where they differed was essentially in their way of looking into the political future, of interpreting the kinds of changes that were occurring. Virginia, Maryland, the Carolinas, and Georgia grew into the kind of society that Berkeley would have favored. The colonies were loyal to the king and his governors most of the time—at least until the 1770s, when planter-aristocrats like Thomas Jefferson and George Washington finally felt able to throw off English support, protection, and control.

Washington and Jefferson were great patriots, political leaders, and statesmen. But whatever else they were, Bacon's men would have recognized them as slaveholding "grandees." It is odd in some ways that Jefferson—a wealthy Virginian with slaves—should have written "All men are created equal." But the contradiction was not new; it lay at the heart of Virginia's history. An immigrant in Virginia could easily obtain a plantation of 150 acres of tobacco land. He could elect his own representatives—even a rebel like Bacon—to the House of Burgesses. These conditions might make it seem that all men (at least all *white men*) were in fact equal.

But these democratic realities existed in an economy of tobacco and of slavery, an economy that tended to produce, inevitably, an aristocratic social structure. The contradiction was personified in Bacon. He was a wealthy man, a member of the Governor's Council, and the son of an aristocrat— but still the enemy of the "grandees." The same kind of contradiction existed in Thomas Jefferson a century later.

THE CAROLINAS AND GEORGIA

At the height of his rebellious career, Nathaniel Bacon told a neighbor that he believed "Virginia and Maryland as well as Carolina" were all ready to "cast off their governors." And, he thought, if his rebellion failed, he and his followers might "retire to the Roanoke" and establish their own government there, safe from Berkeley and safe, for a while, from English power. Bacon's ideas were vague and half-formed, and it is difficult to know what he meant exactly. But to "retire to the Roanoke" probably meant to move into the area around Albemarle Sound, where the Roanoke empties into the Atlantic.

In 1675, a motley group of Virginians were settled there, occupying what amounted to Virginia's southern frontier. They were a lawless lot, and were regarded by people like Berkeley as a band of thieves and ne'er-do-wells. In fact, when Bacon's Rebellion finally collapsed, one of Bacon's chief lieutenants, John Culpeper, did flee to the Albemarle frontier and lead a brief "revolution" there. Eventually, Culpeper was taken to England and tried for treason. But he was acquitted on the curious ground that there was no settled government in Carolina against which a man *could* commit meaningful treason, no matter how hard he might try. What Bacon referred to as "Carolina" was a subject of considerable confusion. The colony had existed on paper for a long time, but it was not until the decades after Bacon's Rebellion that this paper existence was translated into another successful colonial experience.

The Carolina Proprietary On paper, Carolina was older than Maryland. In 1629, Charles I had granted the colony to his attorney general on more or less the same terms as his grant of Maryland to Calvert three years later. For twenty years, no settlements were made. And, in the 1650s, only a few hundred Virginians and a small group of migrants from Massachusetts tried to found communities. After his restoration to the throne in 1660, Charles II revoked the grant of 1629 and, in 1663, created a group of eight powerful proprietors, granting them an even larger territory. The grant included, approximately, what today comprises North and South Carolina, and Georgia.

The Carolina proprietors, whose ranks included Governor Berkeley, were enormously powerful men. In fact, William Berkeley was very much the smallest fish in the pond. One of the eight was Edward Hyde, an earl and lord high chancellor. He also happened to be the father-in-law of James, duke of York, soon to be King James II. Another proprietor was General George Monck, the most important military figure in Charles II's England. A third was George Carteret, widely regarded as the richest man in England. Perhaps the most active proprietor of all was Anthony Ashley Cooper. In 1663, Cooper was on his way toward enormous fame, fame that made him eventually the Earl of Shaftesbury and founder of what was to become England's most important political party—the Whigs. In 1663, Cooper was already chancellor of the Exchequer—a post roughly comparable to that of secretary of the Treasury in the modern United States.

In the 1660s, then, the entity known as "Carolina" was a very curious thing. At one end of it stood a stunning representation of English power, wealth, and office. At the other end were a few hundred Virginians hanging on to some rather poor land in the northeastern corner of the vast,

vacant colony. Between these two sets of people, there was litte or no common ground. The proprietors' plans were aimed at making large amounts of money for themselves, primarily from the disposal of their only real asset, the land itself. But they also had other purposes. For one thing, they were committed to slavery (several of them had investments in the African slave trade), and, from the

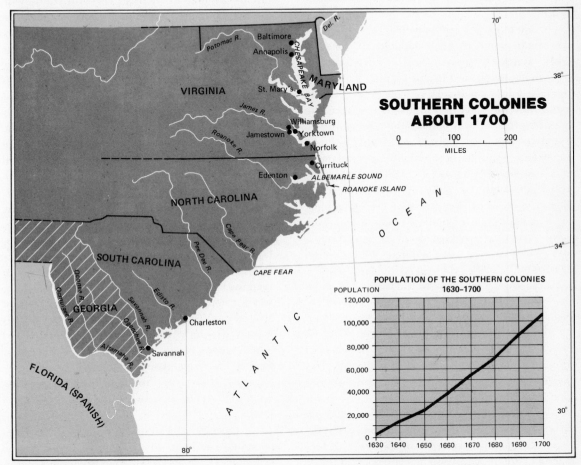

Permanent English settlement in the Southern colonies began after the Virginia grant of 1606. From then on, English kings carved big chunks of land out of Virginia to form the four other Southern colonies.

Land north of the Potomac River was given in proprietorship to Lord Baltimore in 1634. Land south was given to eight noblemen as proprietors by King Charles II in two separate grants in 1663 and 1665. The king hoped that this new colony, Carolina, would serve as a buffer state, protecting Virginia from Indian and Spanish attack. The first settlers to Carolina came in 1653 from Virginia. They settled in the northeast, along Albemarle Sound. Carolina was treated as

one colony until 1712, when it became known as North Carolina and South Carolina.

The last mainland colony to be claimed was the land southwest of Carolina, between the Savannah and Altamaha rivers. Georgia was founded not as a proprietory nor as a corporate colony, but rather under the trusteeship of a group of Englishmen. The most famous of these trustees was James Oglethorpe. Oglethorpe's goal was to create a refuge for worthy Englishmen imprisoned for debt. The founding of this new colony was greeted with delight by South Carolinians, who saw Georgia as a bulwark against the Spanish in Florida. By 1700 the population of the Southern colonies (excluding Georgia) was 104,588. Virginia was the most populous.

beginning they rewarded those settlers who brought slaves to the colony. For another thing, the proprietors had a philosophical commitment in common: they were deeply opposed to the development of a "numerous democracy" of the sort that Bacon's Rebellion represented. The Carolina proprietors tried to make their colony into a fortress of traditional "feudalism" against what they perceived as dangerous democratic tendencies in English life.

Their chosen instrument was a curious document known as the "Fundamental Constitutions." It was drawn up by John Locke, who was to be famous, later, as the philosopher of natural rights. But Locke was very far from being a democrat at this early stage of his life, and the "constitution" he proposed was perhaps the most conservative document to grow out of the English colonial experience. Carolina, according to the Fundamental Constitutions as issued in 1665, was to be governed ultimately by the proprietors. The chief among them would be known as the "palatine," the remainder as "seigneurs." Below them, there would be a class of nobles known as "landgraves," and below them, a class of minor nobles called "caciques." Finally, the rest of the free population, known as "leet-men" would live and labor on the estates of the nobility. At the bottom, of course, would be slaves. Along with titles would go grants of land and political power. The net result, the proprietors hoped, would be a feudal utopia—a much neater version of feudalism than had ever existed in actual fact in medieval England.

In practice, the settlers never accepted the basic ideas behind the Fundamental Constitutions—except for the practice of slavery. The proprietors kept the constitution suspended much of the time, and actually made most of their land grants according to the Virginia pattern rather than according to their own visionary scheme. Northern Carolina, especially, attracted a variety of colonists—English Quakers, French Protestant refugees known as Huguenots, Swiss and German immigrants, and the sort of Virginia immigrants that caused the Albemarle settlement to become known as "Rogues Harbor." For various reasons, none of these groups cared a whit for the proprie-

tors' vision. It was no accident, therefore, that when John Culpeper fled to Albemarle, he found supporters who were quite ready to "cast off their governors" (as Bacon had put it). In general, northern Carolina developed as a poor extension of Virginia tobacco society, kept from rapid development by the lack of good harbors.

The situation in southern Carolina was different—for reasons that had very little to do with the Fundamental Constitutions. After some delay, a successful colony was planted at Charleston in the 1670s. Charleston quickly grew into a trading town, with an excellent harbor, a fort, and a very modern street plan—in fact, the only real town in the southern colonies. But the city depended on a staple agriculture, employing slave labor, every bit as much as did the Virginia economy to the north. There was a ready market for agricultural goods in the nearby British West Indies, and South Carolina soon developed a busy trade with the islands, consisting mainly of food exports. More important for the long run, however, was the successful experiment with rice as a cash crop. Soil and climate combined to create the conditions favorable for this difficult crop, and slave labor was available to carry out the arduous work of planting, cultivating, and harvesting. Soon there was a plantation elite in southern Carolina that rivaled the Virginia elite in its pretensions to aristocracy. The only real difference was that the Carolina planters tended to live in Charleston rather than on their own plantations. Leaving that difference aside, however, the life styles of the wealthy elite in the two colonies were very much the same.

Carolina also developed (despite the Fundamental Constitutions) a "normal" type of government. There was a governor appointed by the proprietors, a council, and an assembly. The council in time came to function as the upper house of the legislature, and was appointed by the governor. The lower house was composed of the "representatives of the people"—representing, in practice, the landowners of the colony. In the 1690s, Charleston became the capital of the colony. The governor resided there, and a deputy was appointed to govern the northern part of the colony. Finally, in 1712, the two colonies were separated, and

JAMES EDWARD OGLETHORPE

James Edward Oglethorpe, the founder of Georgia, was born into a world dominated by seventeenth-century conflicts and antagonisms. He died after the American Revolution at the age of 89. Across this turbulent span of almost a century, he typified many of the main preoccupations — and some of the curious eccentricities — of eighteenth-century British colonialism and imperialism.

The life of Oglethorpe's family was dominated by their loyalty to James II and the Stuart monarchy. When James was deposed by the Glorious Revolution of 1688–89 and replaced by a new "constitutional" monarch, Sir Theophilus Oglethorpe remained stubbornly loyal to the old king. James Edward inherited this loyalty and spent much of his youth on the Continent, living as a free-lance soldier and a member of the Stuart court-in-exile in France and Italy. Finally, even the most ardent supporters of James ("Jacobites," they were called) gave up. Oglethorpe drifted home in 1722, at the age of twenty-six, to take control of the family manor and to enter Parliament, as his father and older brothers had done before him.

In politics, Oglethorpe was a Tory, an opponent of the Whig party that had come to power after the Glorious Revolution and that dominated Parliament during the eighteenth century. But Oglethorpe's "conservatism" was much more than an echo of his family's Jacobitism. He, like many of the Tories, was also a reformer. He opposed slavery, rum, the impressment of sailors, and the mistreatment of convicts. He was also an ardent supporter of a strong military policy — chiefly against Spain; and he wanted an expansion of the empire — chiefly at the expense of Spain.

All these concerns came conveniently together in the late 1720s when Oglethorpe became interested in Georgia. The colony could serve as a refuge for ex-convicts, he hoped, and also as a model society without rum or slaves. Incidentally, it could welcome religious dissenters from both England and the Continent. Most important of all, it would be an outpost of the empire against the Spanish in Florida. Oglethorpe's interests were very different, then, from the commercial ones of the Virginia Company, or the proprietary ones of the Calverts.

Oglethorpe came to Georgia with the first colonists in 1733. For the next ten years, he attempted to realize his vision, to combine social reform and military effectiveness. But he was exposed, all along, to difficulties. The settlers refused to cooperate, and often threatened rebellion. The Spanish kept military pressure on Georgia, and diplomatic pressure on London. Carolinians objected to Georgia's invasion of the profitable Indian trade. Even Oglethorpe's fellow "trustees" complained about his sloppy accounts and his failure to file adequate reports with them. In the seventeenth century, these difficulties might not have been serious, but the administration of the empire was becoming more and more organized and public. Finally, after several crossings of the Atlantic, Oglethorpe was pushed into resigning. He was even subjected to a court-martial trial — though he was quickly acquitted of all charges.

After his resignation, Oglethorpe married an heiress and settled into a genteel life. He was promoted in military rank several times, finally becoming an inactive general. He lived much of the time in London, where he was part of the most sophisticated social and literary circles of the period. As for his colony, it also went very much its own way, almost unmarked by Oglethorpe's philanthropic vision and his unwanted reforms.

each was given its own government. Then, in 1729, in keeping with its colonial policies in all of North America, the crown revoked the proprietary charter, and both North and South Carolina became royal colonies like Virginia, with governors, councils, and other officials appointed by the crown.

Georgia One of the lessons that could be drawn from the experiences of Maryland and the Carolina proprietorship was that the realities of the situation in each case turned out to matter more than the abstract aims and goals of English promoters and proprietors. Calvert's purpose may have been, in part, to create a refuge for Catholics and a quasi-feudal society; but, in practice, other forces prevailed over these goals. The Carolina proprietors' Fundamental Constitutions was blown aside by the winds of actual experience, too, and their colony developed into a "normal" plantation society with a "normal" governmental structure. This relationship between founders' visions and actuality was even more true in Georgia, the last British colony to be established on the mainland of North America.

Originally, Georgia was part of the Carolina grant of 1663. But the Carolinians failed to settle the area. Since both Spain and England claimed the land, and since the two nations were at war much of the time, it was inevitable that the English government would eventually encourage settlement there—for military reasons in addition to the usual economic motives for colonization. In fact, the individual chiefly responsible for the colonization of Georgia was a military man, General James Oglethorpe (see p. 77). Oglethorpe was also a politician, however, and his most telling political experience was as a member of a parliamentary commission investigating English prisons. Oglethorpe became convinced in the 1720s that simple poverty led too many Englishmen to prison, many of them because they could not pay their debts. The solution to the problem, Oglethorpe and several wealthy friends believed, might lie in colonization. The result of their efforts was a unique charter issued by George II in 1732. The charter carved a new colony (named after the king) out of the Carolina grant. But the charter did not create either proprietors, like those of Maryland and Carolina, or a commercial company, like that of the original Virginia charter. Instead, the king named a board of "trustees" who would be in charge of the settlement of the colony for twenty-one years. They could make no money for themselves, and, after the period of trusteeship, the colony would automatically revert to the crown, to be added to the growing list of royal colonies. In the meantime, the trustees were not required to create a colonial legislature; they could make laws themselves and could appoint a governor and other officials.

The enterprise got off to a quick start. In the fall of 1732, the first 130 settlers left England—so well provisioned by the trustees that only two of them died at sea. The immigrants who followed were of three main types. Some were free Englishmen, who were given grants of farms on the Virginia pattern of 50-acre head-rights. Many others were poor Englishpeople (though very few were actually convicts), who came as indentured servants and were promised 20-acre grants after serving out their terms. Several hundred others were Protestant refugees from the Continent—most of them Germans. The trustees forbade Catholic immigration, for fear that Catholics would harbor secret sympathies for Spain.

The fear of Spain was also behind a number of the trustees' policies. First, they wanted to make Georgia a colony of small farms, since this would provide the most militarily efficient population. So they restricted the size of individual grants to 500 acres, and promised most immigrants only 20 or 50 acres of land. Second, they forbade slavery, not because they were opposed to it in principle, but because they believed a slave population would be militarily unsafe from Spanish subversion. They even forbade the importation of rum, not because they opposed drinking, but because rum might well mean unnecessary Indian troubles, and Indian troubles could expose the colony to Spanish intrigue or attack. In short, the trustees tried to create a disciplined military colony of sober, white, Protestant farmers.

The difficulty was that the interests of the colonists ran against those of the trustees. For one thing, the only profitable agriculture that seemed possible was rice farming on the model of Southern Carolina. But rice lands were also malarial lands. And this, in the eyes of Englishmen, meant that only black slaves were a suitable labor force. The colonists also understood that quick money lay in the fur trade, and this required a much freer hand with the Indians than the trustees were ready to allow. In addition, the colonists wanted a voice in the lawmaking process, they wanted larger farms, and they wanted rum. Several years before the expiration of the trustees' control, frustration among the colonists finally forced the trustees to relinquish control of Georgia. The forces of actual experience triumphed over the trustees' vision: Georgia began to develop the plantation agriculture, capitalist economy, slave labor, and mixed royal government that prevailed in all the other southern colonies.

SUGGESTED READINGS-CHAPTERS 3-4

Bacon and Bacon's Rebellion

T. J. Wertenbaker, *Torchbearer of the Revolution* (1940); W. E. Washburn, *The Governor and the Rebel* (1957).

Colonial Virginia

Edmund S. Morgan, *American Slavery, American Freedom* (1975); W. F. Craven, *The Southern Colonies in the Seventeenth Century, 1607–1689* (1949).

Indians and the Indian "Problem"

W. T. Hagan, *American Indians* (1961); W. R. Jacobs, *Dispossessing the American Indian: Indians and Whites on the Colonial Frontier* (1972).

Slavery and Racism

W. D. Jordan, *White Over Black: American Attitude toward the Negro, 1550–1812* (1968); M. W. Jernegan, *Laboring and Dependent Classes in Colonial America, 1607–1783* .

Southern Society and the Southern Myth

Carl Bridenbaugh, *Myths and Realities: Societies of the Colonial South* (1952); W. R. Taylor, *Cavalier and Yankee: The Old South and American National Character* (1969); L. C. Gray, *History of Agriculture in the Southern United States to 1860* (2 vols., 1933).

5 WITCHCRAFT AT SALEM VILLAGE

R. J. W.

The two girls were strangely sick. Betty Parris, who was nine years old, and her cousin, eleven-year-old Abigail Williams, often stared dully into space. Sometimes they went down on their hands and knees and made hoarse, choking sounds. At other times they simply fell to the floor and screamed. The girls lived in the house of Betty Parris's father, Samuel, a minister. The house stood in the center of a small settlement called Salem Village, Massachusetts. It was January 1692.

At first Samuel Parris kept quiet about the girls' behavior. But, as the minister of the town, he was more carefully watched by his neighbors than any other man. His house stood at the center of the village. It was just down a dirt road from the tavern and not far from the only meeting house, or church. Something had to be done, so Samuel Parris sent for the village doctor. Since the minister's family was considered the most important family in the village, the doctor proceeded seriously and carefully. He examined the girls, consulted his medical books, and tried various medicines. Nothing worked, and his books gave him no clue. Finally, he gave up. The girls, he told the Reverend Parris, were not physically sick at all, but they had been touched by "the evil hand."

No one in Massachusetts in 1692 needed to be reminded that the doctor was talking about witchcraft. Four years earlier, in Boston, an Irish woman called Witch Glover had been hanged for bewitching four children. One of Boston's most famous ministers, Cotton Mather, had taken one of the bewitched children into his own house to try to cure her. Mather had then published a book on witchcraft, a book read in every town of the Massachusetts Bay Colony. (Samuel Parris had a copy.)

Practically every citizen of the colony believed that the devil actually did visit the earth, persuading men and women to join him, and giving them a witch's power to torment innocent people. All over Europe at this time, witches were being accused, convicted, and hanged or burned at the stake. The people of Salem Village were just as superstitious as Europeans and other Americans. Cotton Mather was one of the best-educated men in the colony. Samuel Parris had attended Harvard College. The doctor who first examined Betty Parris and Abigail Williams was an educated scientist. All of these men believed in witchcraft. If such educated community leaders accepted the idea that an evil hand was at work, what could be expected of the plain farmers of Salem Village?

As soon as gossip leaked out about Betty Parris and Abigail Williams, their young friends began to have similar fits. Between January and September of 1692 a group of about a dozen girls steadily acted bewitched. Betty Parris was the youngest of the afflicted children; the oldest of the group were two young women of twenty. Today they would probably all be called teen-agers. This group of teen-aged girls was joined from time to time by other afflicted persons, some of them adults, but most of them young people. A few adults argued that the girls were only pretending and that a good spanking would cure them. But most of the people of Salem Village, of nearby Salem Town, and of the whole Massachusetts Bay Colony took the girls' fits seriously.

At first the girls did not name anyone as their tormentors. All over Salem Village parents and other relatives prayed and fasted. Samuel Parris called in the ministers of several neighboring towns, and they too prayed and fasted. The questions in their minds were: Who was bewitching the girls? Whom had the devil persuaded to join him in witchcraft? Finally, on February 25, some of the girls called out three names. Whether the afflicted children had a plan or not, they were very shrewd. They named three women who were, for different reasons, not respected in the community.

The first was Tituba, a slave in the house of Samuel Parris. Tituba was from one of the islands of the West Indies, where Samuel Parris had worked as a merchant before coming to Salem to preach in 1689. She probably was part black and part Indian. Tituba was married to another slave, John Indian, who also belonged to Parris. During dark winter afternoons in the Parris kitchen, Tituba had no doubt told weird stories of the islands to Betty and Abigail. She had also shown magic tricks to the village girls who were now afflicted.

The second person identified by the afflicted girls was Sarah Good. In her own way Sarah Good was even more vulnerable than Tituba. Her husband was a laborer who had never held a job for long. Sarah herself was something of a hag. She smoked a pipe, muttered to herself, and often went begging from door to door in the village.

The third supposed witch was a prosperous old woman named Sarah Osburne. After her husband had died, she had offended the town by living with an overseer on her farm. Although she had eventually married the man, she had stopped going to church. Thus she had developed a bad reputation generally.

In 1692 there were no regular judges in Massachusetts. Court

Cotton Mather did not speak out against the witch trials at the time, but later stated that he thought they had been unfair. He himself believed in "curing" witches through fasting and prayer.

cases were presided over by members of the colonial legislature known as assistants. So the parents and relatives of some of the afflicted children went to the two assistants of Salem Town and asked for the arrest of Tituba, Sarah Good, and Sarah Osburne.

March 1 was an exciting day for the village. The constables and uniformed military guard went out with drums to meet the two assistants coming from Salem Town. With this military escort the assistants marched into the meeting house, which had been converted into a courtroom. The assistants took their seats on a platform at the front of the church, with the afflicted girls facing them in the front pew. Almost everyone else in the village crowded in. Sarah Good was then brought forward for preliminary questioning.

One of the assistants, John Hathorne, was a stern, dark man who took his work very seriously. He leaned forward toward cranky old Sarah Good and began to question her:

> HATHORNE: Sarah Good, what evil spirit have you familiarity with?
> SARAH GOOD: None.
> HATHORNE: Have you made no contract with the devil?
> SARAH GOOD: No.
> HATHORNE: Why do you hurt these children?
> SARAH GOOD: I do not hurt them. I scorn it.
> HATHORNE: Who do you employ, then, to do it?
> SARAH GOOD: I employ nobody.
> HATHORNE: What *creature* do you employ, then?
> SARAH GOOD: No creature. But I am falsely accused.
> HATHORNE: Have you made no contract with the devil?
> SARAH GOOD: No.

Up to this point, Hathorne had not shaken this stubborn woman. She simply denied everything, saying in a tough old voice, "I scorn it!"

But Hathorne and the other assistant, Jonathan Corwin, had made a decision before opening the court. They would accept the testimony of the afflicted children about who it was that tormented them. According to this decision, even if Sarah Good were standing innocently before the judges, her "shape," or spirit, might attack the girls. If the afflicted girls said that Sarah Good's shape was pinching or hurting them, then she would be put in jail for a full-scale witch trial and possible hanging.

According to the legal procedures of the day, Sarah Good was not told of this decision in advance. Nor was she represented by a lawyer. Hathorne's next move was very important. It established the pattern for all the hearings that would follow. The clerk's record of the testimony continued:

> Hathorne desired the children all of them to look upon her and see if this were the person that had hurt them. And so they all did look upon her, and said this was one of the persons that did torment them. Presently they were all tormented.

Here was the key to Hathorne's prosecution of the witches: "Presently they were all tormented." Here, for the first time, the afflicted girls learned that their moaning and screaming could attract attention. After a short time the girls quieted down. They said that they were being tor-

Known as the Witch House, this gabled building in Salem dates back to 1675. It received its name because it was once the home of Jonathan Corwin. Some preliminary hearings in the witchcraft trials took place here.

mented by the shape of Sarah Good, the cranky old woman who, at that moment, was standing so still in the meeting house. Hathorne returned to the attack. Sarah Good held her ground for a moment, but then she began to break down:

> HATHORNE: Sarah Good, do you not see now what you have done? Why do you not tell us the truth? Why do you thus torment these poor children?
> SARAH GOOD: I do not torment them.
> HATHORNE: Who was it, then, that tormented the children?
> SARAH GOOD: It was Osburne.

In her panic Sarah Good tried to save herself by pointing an accusing finger at Sarah Osburne. But in doing so she sealed her own fate. Hathorne and Corwin reasoned this way: Sarah Good was not afflicted. Therefore, unless she were a witch, how could she know that Sarah Osburne attacked the children? Hathorne could see that the hag was going to pieces, and he hurried the process:

> HATHORNE: What is it you say when you go muttering away from persons' houses?
> SARAH GOOD: If I must tell, I will tell.
> HATHORNE: Do tell us then.
> SARAH GOOD: If I must tell, I will tell. It is the commandments.

Hathorne sensed that she was lying. Sarah Good might still have saved herself if she could have repeated even some of the Old Testament commandments. But when Hathorne asked her to name one, she hedged:

> HATHORNE: What commandment is it?
> SARAH GOOD: If I must tell, I will tell. It is a psalm.
> HATHORNE: What psalm?

As the clerk of the court recorded, "After a long time, she muttered over some part of a psalm." He also recorded: "Her answers were given in a very wicked, spiteful manner, with base and abusive words and many lies." Sarah Good was taken away, and her husband was questioned briefly. The clerk recorded this curious testimony:

> It was here said that her husband had said that he was afraid that she either was a witch or would be one very quickly. The worthy Mr. Hathorne asked him his reason why he said so of her. He anwered that it was her bad carriage [attitude] to him, and indeed, said he, I may say with tears that she is an enemy to all good.

Once finished with questioning Sarah Good, Hathorne and Corwin then called Sarah Osburne, who quickly panicked. She tried to claim that she herself had been bewitched. To save herself, she tried to throw suspicion on Tituba's husband, John Indian, by claiming that she had been attacked by a "thing like an Indian, all black." But the afflicted girls would not let her join their circle. They accused her just as they had Sarah Good, and she was taken away. The assistants then sent for Tituba, who was to be the star of the day.

Tituba's situation was frightening. Samuel Parris owned her as a slave. As the village minister, he claimed to own her soul. Between the time little Betty Parris first accused Tituba until she testified, Parris had sometimes beaten her and sometimes prayed for her. By March 1 she had worked out a shrewd plan. She would confess. But she would also save herself by throwing greater suspicion on others and by claiming that she was no longer working with the devil. Once more Hathorne took the lead in the questioning. At first, Tituba's answers sounded like Sarah Good's and the afflicted girls behaved the same way:

> HATHORNE: Tituba, what evil spirit have you familiarity with?
> TITUBA: None.
> HATHORNE: Why do you hurt these children?
> TITUBA: I do not hurt them.
> HATHORNE: Who is it then?
> TITUBA: The devil for aught I know.

But then Tituba began to execute her plan. As soon as she began to confess, the afflicted girls calmed down. It was as though Tituba's confession released them from their spells for the time being.

> HATHORNE: Did you ever see the devil?
> TITUBA: The devil came to me and bid me serve him.
> HATHORNE: Who have you seen?
> TITUBA: Four women sometimes hurt the children.
> HATHORNE: Who were they?

At this point Tituba had to be careful. The children were cooperating by not acting tormented. But she had to name names that the assistants and the village farmers would accept. She also had to try to protect her husband, John Indian. Sarah Osburne had testified that she was bewitched by "a thing like an Indian, all black." Tituba invented a "tall man from

Boston," dressed in black, to throw suspicion off John Indian. When she named Sarah Osburne and Sarah Good as witches, Tituba called them Goody. (This was an abbreviation of "Goodwife," a common way of addressing married women.) But she claimed that she did not know who the other witches were.

Then Tituba began to weave a tale of witches, devils, and strange animals. The citizens of the village listened in fascinated horror.

> TITUBA: There is four women and one man. They hurt the children. And they lay all upon me and they tell me if I will not hurt the children, they will hurt me.
> HATHORNE: What also have you seen?
> TITUBA: Two rats, a red rat and a black rat.
> HATHORNE: What did they say to you?
> TITUBA: They said serve me.
> HATHORNE: Why did you not tell your master?
> TITUBA: I was afraid they would cut off my head if I told.
> HATHORNE: What attendants hath Sarah Good?
> TITUBA: A yellow bird. And she would have given me one.
> HATHORNE: What meat did she give it?
> TITUBA: It did suck her between her fingers.
> HATHORNE: What hath Sarah Osburne?
> TITUBA: A yellow dog. She had a thing with a head like a woman, with two legs and wings.
> HATHORNE: What else have you seen with Osburne?
> TITUBA: Another thing. Hairy. It goes upright like a man. It hath only two legs.
> HATHORNE: What clothes doth the man [the "tall man from Boston"] go in?
> TITUBA: He goes in black clothes. A tall man with white hair, I think.

At the mention of these creatures, the afflicted girls began to behave strangely again. The timing was perfect. Hathorne had to ask Tituba who was bewitching the girls. His question gave Tituba a chance to end her testimony in a helpful way. She could again throw suspicion on someone else. Doing so would prove that she wanted to help hunt down the witches. But then she could claim that she could no longer "see." This would prove that she was free from the devil's spell herself. Things worked out perfectly:

> HATHORNE: Do you see who it is that torments these children now?
> TITUBA: Yes, it is Goody Good. She hurts them in her own shape.
> HATHORNE: And who is it that hurts them *now?*
> TITUBA: I am blind. I cannot see.

Tituba, Sarah Good, and Sarah Osburne were questioned several more times during the next few days. On March 7 they were sent to jail in Boston to await a full trial. Sarah Osburne fell ill and died on May 10 without a trial. Sarah Good had a baby in jail, who died—confirming everyone's suspicions that she was an evil woman.

With the three witches in jail, Salem Village might have calmed down. But Tituba had said that four women, plus the tall man from Boston, were tormenting the afflicted girls. And the girls continued to be afflicted. This meant that more witches were on the loose.

Shortly after Tituba, Sarah Good, and Sarah Osburne had been taken away, Salem Village had a day of fasting and prayer. Once more the ministers of the neighboring towns came to meet with Parris. Once more the girls were watched, prayed over, and questioned. Finally, they called out a name, a name that shocked everyone and started the trials off in a new direction. The girls named Martha Cory, who was not a slave like Tituba, not a hag like Goody Good, and not a sinner like Goody Osburne. Martha Cory was an upstanding member of the village congregation. For the first time the girls had accused an adult with a solid reputation. If Martha Cory could be successfully attacked, then no woman in Salem Village would be safe.

The warrant for Martha Cory's arrest was dated March 19. But because that day was a Saturday, she was not to be arrested until the following Monday, March 21. On the Sunday between she bravely showed up at church, where a visiting minister, Deodat Lawson, was to conduct the church service. Lawson had once been the minister of Salem Village and was now living in Boston. He came to Salem to witness the witchcraft proceedings, and he had spent the night in Parris's house, where he watched Abigail Williams go through a violent fit of hysteria. The next morning, Lawson went to the meeting house to preach.

It was no ordinary Sunday service. Goodwife Cory herself came bravely to church, and there, during prayers and the sermon, the afflicted girls had fits. Ordinarily, it was a serious offense to whisper, doze off, or even look out the window during church services. In the meeting houses men were assigned the job of patrolling the aisles during the sermon — which might last several hours — to prod or even hit people who misbehaved or did not pay attention. But the afflicted girls broke all the usual rules. Abigail Williams yelled out at the minister, and she was imitated by several of the other girls. Finally, Abigail pointed to an exposed beam above the head of Martha Cory and called out, "Look where Goody Cory sits on the beam, suckling her yellow bird betwixt her fingers."

The girls had learned Tituba's lessons well. From the time of her confession to the end of the trials, they often mentioned strange animals, especially the yellow bird. Martha Cory, of course, was simply sitting in her pew. But when the girls cried out, all eyes looked overhead to the beam where her shape was supposed to be sitting with its sinister yellow bird. When Martha Cory came before the assistants the next day, most of the villagers had already made up their minds that she was guilty.

The visiting minister, Deodat Lawson, wrote an account of Martha Cory's examination by Hathorne and Corwin:

> On Monday the 21st of March, the magistrates of Salem were appointed to come to the examination of Goodwife Cory. And about twelve of the clock, they went into the meeting house, which was thronged with spectators. Mr. Noyes [a minister from Salem Town] began with a very pathetic prayer. Goodwife Cory, being called to answer what was alleged against her, desired to go to prayer. This was much wondered at, in the presence of so many people.

Martha Cory was a very proud and rugged woman. When two officers of the town had first come to her farm to ask her about the charges of witchcraft, she had laughed at them. Now, in her examination, she was trying to beat the village at its own game. If they could pray, then she would pray herself. But Hathorne refused:

> The magistrates told her they would not admit it. They came not there to hear her pray, but to examine her in what was alleged against her. The worshipful Mr. Hathorne asked her why she afflicted these children. She said she did not afflict them. He asked her who did, then? She said, "I do not know. How should I know?"

Hathorne began with the same questions he had put to Sarah Good and Sarah Osburne. Once more, the suspected witch denied everything. Once more, the afflicted girls involved the suspect more deeply by having fits. This time, however, they refined their techniques. Every time Martha Cory moved an arm or bit her lip, the girls acted afflicted in exactly the same parts of their bodies:

> The number of afflicted persons were about that time ten. Those were most of them at Goodwife Cory's examination, and did vehemently accuse her in the assembly of afflicting them, by biting, pinching, strangling, etc. And that they did in their fit see her likeness coming to them, and bringing a book to them. She said she had no book. They affirmed that she had a yellow bird that used to suck betwixt her fingers. Being asked about it, she said she had no familiarity with any such thing. She was a Gospel woman, which title she called herself by. And the afflicted persons told her, Ah! She was a Gospel witch.
>
> It was observed several times that if she did but bite her under lip in time of examination, the persons afflicted were bitten on their arms and wrists and produced the marks before the magistrates, ministers, and others. If she did but pinch her finger, or grasp one hand hard in the other, they were pinched and produced the marks before the magistrates and spectators.

Then the afflicted girls threw terror into the entire audience by saying that there was a gathering of witches that very moment in front of the meeting house!

> The afflicted persons asked her [Martha Cory] why she did not go to the company of witches which were before the meeting house mustering? Did she not hear the drumbeat? They accused her of familiarity with the devil, in the shape of a black man whispering in her ear. They affirmed that her yellow bird sucked betwixt her fingers in the assembly.
>
> She denied all that was charged upon her, and said they could not prove a witch. She was that afternoon committed to Salem prison.

Martha Cory was the first respectable woman to be accused of being a witch. Once the afflicted girls had succeeded in their attack on her, they were able to accuse anyone in the village. During the last week of March and the first days of April, several women with sound reputations were arrested and brought before the assistants. The village was in a deepening panic. Neighbors began to suspect each other, and people quickly forgot the difference between evidence and common gossip.

The panic spread from Salem Village to Salem Town, and then to the rest of the Massachusetts Bay Colony. By April 11 the examinations had to be moved to the larger meeting house in Salem Town. The deputy governor and several other leading citizens of the colony came up from

Boston to observe the proceedings. The afflicted girls were no longer a local phenomenon. Now they were watched and wondered at by people from all parts of Massachusetts.

In the middle of April, with spring well on its way, the first break showed in the ranks of the afflicted girls. One of the women identified as a witch in early April was Elizabeth Proctor, whose husband owned a large farm in the southern part of the village. The Proctors' maid, Mary Warren, was one of the afflicted girls. But the Proctors did not believe in witchcraft at all, and, furthermore, they had the courage to say so in public. At Elizabeth Proctor's examination some of the girls had screamed out that her husband, John, was also a witch—or a wizard, as male witches were called. This accusation alarmed Mary Warren. She did not like Mrs. Proctor at all, but she seems to have had a twenty-year-old's crush on John Proctor, who was a middle-aged man. Outside the meeting house, she began to admit that the afflictions were all a sport, that John Proctor was not a wizard at all.

When the other afflicted girls found out about Mary Warren's betrayal, they accused *her* of being a witch. So, on April 18, she was arrest-

SALEM IN 1692

── Boundaries of Salem Village   ☐ House
LOCATIONS IN SALEM TOWN

1 Courthouse	6 Bishop
2 Prison	7 Corwin
3 Meeting house	8 Hathorne
4 Place of execution	9 Gedney
5 English	

ed and brought before the assistants. Suddenly, she had moved from the favored pew of the afflicted girls into the seat of fear where she had watched grown men and women collapse in panic. This was a crucial point in the trials. If Mary Warren could hold her ground against the screams of the afflicted girls, the stares of the audience, and the sternness of Hathorne, then the trials might come to a halt.

Samuel Parris himself kept the official record of the scene:

[As soon as she was coming toward the bar, the afflicted fell into fits.]

HATHORNE: Mary Warren, you stand here charged with sundry acts of witchcraft. What do you say for yourself? Are you guilty or not?
MARY WARREN: I am innocent.
HATHORNE: Hath she hurt you (speaking to the sufferers)?

Some were dumb. Betty Hubbard [one of the afflicted girls] testified against her, and then said Hubbard fell into a violent fit.

HATHORNE: You were a little while ago an afflicted person. Now you are an afflictor. How comes this to pass?
MARY WARREN: I look up to God and take it to be a great mercy of God.
HATHORNE: What? Do you take it to be a great mercy to afflict others?

This trick question of Hathorne's took Mary Warren by surprise. At the same time, all the afflicted girls began to howl. It was too much for the young woman to bear. She broke down and became incoherent. She struggled from time to time to regain control of herself, but it was no use. By now the fits may have become real hysteria, which Mary Warren and some of the other girls could no longer start or stop at will.

Now Mary Warren fell into a fit, and some of the afflicted cried out that Goody Cory and Proctor and his wife came in their apparition [shape] and struck her down.

Mary Warren continued a good space in a fit, and she did neither see, nor hear, nor speak.

Afterwards, she started up, and said, "I will speak," and cried out, "Oh I am sorry for it. I am sorry for it," and wringed her hands, and fell a little while into a fit again. And then she came to speak, but immediately her teeth were set, and then she fell into a violent fit, and cried out, "Oh, Lord, help me! Oh, Good Lord, save me!"

And then afterwards she cried again, "I will tell! I will tell!" And then she fell into a dead fit again.

The afflicted girls had won. Mary Warren was taken to Salem to jail, where she was questioned again and again by the assistants and ministers. Finally, on May 12, she admitted that both the Proctors were witches. By then, she was probably completely out of touch with reality. She confessed that she herself had "signed the devil's book," and she wildly accused several other people of witchcraft.

What happened in Massachusetts in 1692 was really quite simple. A group of teen-aged girls caused a brief revolution. In January they were ordinary girls, taking orders from adults, working very hard in their homes, listening to long sermons in church on Sundays and other days. By the spring of 1692 they held an enormous amount of power—even the power of life and death—over a large number of the adult citizens of

Massachusetts. They had begun by accusing poor old women and slaves. But within a few weeks they were charging ministers, merchants, and other solid citizens. The girls probably had no plan, at least not at the beginning. Still, they were able to terrify tough old pioneer farmers. They were also able to use the power of the Massachusetts government to send innocent men and women to the gallows.

As panic gripped Salem and the rest of the colony during the summer of 1692, displays of both courage and cowardice could be seen, sometimes in the same family or individual. One such mixture of responses occurred in the case of George Jacobs, a toothless village elder who shuffled about with the aid of two canes. Jacobs's household included his son and daughter-in-law — "a woman crazy in her senses who had been so several years," according to local gossips. There were four grandchildren, the eldest a teen-ager named Margaret. Jacobs's servant, Sarah Churchill, was one of the afflicted girls.

Old Jacobs, like John Proctor, had scoffed openly at the girls' claims that they were possessed by witches. He even went so far as to mock his own servant, Sarah, as a "witch bitch." Unfortunately for Jacobs, no one in Salem in 1692 could make such remarks and escape reprisal. On May 10, Jacobs was summoned to answer to charges of being a wizard. Jacobs, like John Proctor and Martha Cory, was crisp and caustic in his examination, because he considered the accusation completely ridiculous:

> HATHORNE: Here are them that accuse you of acts of witchcraft.
> JACOBS: Well, let us hear who they are and what they are.
> HATHORNE: Abigail Williams.
> JACOBS: (Laughing) I am falsely accused. Your worships, all of you, do you think this is true?
> HATHORNE: Nay, what do you think?
> JACOBS: I never did it.
> HATHORNE: Who did it?
> JACOBS: Don't ask me. I am as innocent as the child born tonight. You tax me for a wizard. You may as well tax me for a buzzard.

But it was no use. Old Jacobs was sent away to the Boston jail. His son and namesake, George, Jr., did not wait to undergo a similar examination. Instead, he fled the colony, leaving not only his crazed wife but also their four children to face alone the consequences of having had a close relative declared a wizard. The consequences were not long in coming. The town officers soon dragged Mrs. Jacobs before the afflicted ones. At first the girls did not recognize her. Then one of them, probably her former servant, Sarah Churchill, cried: "Don't you know the old witch? And then they cried out at her, and fell down in their fits." Mrs. Jacobs spent the next ten months in prison as a suspected witch, with her three youngest children left to the care of sympathetic neighbors.

Margaret, the eldest child, had even worse luck. She was brought in to give testimony against her grandfather. Afraid that she would be denounced herself as a witch, Margaret confessed in order to save her life, accusing both her grandfather and the Reverend George Burroughs, a former village minister, of being wizards. Only after her grandfather and Burroughs had been put in prison did Margaret finally summon the courage to recant her confession. She wrote from prison, denying her previous accusations against Old Jacobs and Burroughs, but the court ignored this statement and Margaret remained in jail for another year, where she wrote this confession:

> The humble declaration of Margaret Jacobs unto the Honored Court now sitting at Salem:
> I was cried out upon by some of the possessed persons. The Lord above knows I knew nothing. They told me if I would not confess, I should be put down into the dungeon and would be hanged. But if I would confess, I should have my life. This did so afright me, with my own vile, wicked heart, to save my life made me make the confession I did, which confession is altogether false and untrue. What I said was altogether false, against my grandfather, and Mr. Burroughs, which I did to save my life and to have my liberty. But the Lord, charging it to my conscience, made me in so much horror that I could not contain myself before I had denied my confession, which I did, though I saw nothing but death before me, choosing death with a quiet conscience than to live in such horror.
> Margaret Jacobs.

The girl managed to visit Reverend Burroughs before his execution in August, however, and received his forgiveness. Old Jacobs was also told of her recantation before his own execution and, although his property had already been confiscated, he showed his pleasure at Margaret's brave act of conscience by including her in his will. After her grandfather's death, Margaret wrote from prison to her vanished father describing her experiences. She ended her letter by stating simply: "My Mother poor Woman is very Crazy, and remembers her kind love to you." Since Margaret's letter was placed later in the Salem Court records, it probably never reached her father.

By this time, almost two dozen more people had been arrested, and many more were being accused every day. By the last week of May, nearly fifty people had been sent to the dark, crowded Boston jail, waiting for their final trials. The accused were no longer outcasts or simple local farmers. One of those arrested in May, for example, was Philip English, the foremost shipowner of Salem. (He later escaped from jail and fled to New York.)

At last, on May 28, the afflicted girls named the Master Wizard. They had been questioned for weeks by the assistants and ministers about the "tall man from Boston" whom Tituba had first mentioned on March 1. Everyone presumed that he was the guiding hand behind the entire witches' plot. The magistrates summoned him to court, and on May 31 a tall man from Boston walked into the Salem meeting house. His name was John Alden. He was the son of the Plymouth Colony's famous lovers, John and Priscilla Alden. This John Alden was more famous as a soldier than a lover, for he was a sea captain who had fought bravely in recent battles with the Indians.

Alden would never have come to Salem by his own choice, since he thought that the accusation of witchcraft was insanely foolish. But the

Judge William Stoughton was a stubborn and overbearing magistrate. But he donated generously to Harvard College, which named Stoughton Hall in his honor.

deputy governor of the colony, William Stoughton, ordered him to appear for questioning. So Alden marched into court to face his accusers. Later, writing in the third person, he gave an angry description of what took place:

> John Alden was sent for by the Magistrates of Salem upon the accusation of a company of poor, distracted, or possessed creatures or witches. And being sent by Mr. Stoughton, arrived there the 31st of May, and appeared at Salem Village before Mr. Gedney [a third assistant], Mr. Hathorne, and Mr. Corwin.
>
> Those wenches being present, who played their juggling tricks, falling down, crying out, and staring in people's faces, the Magistrates demanded of them several times who it was of all the people in the room that hurt them?

Could the girls identify a man they had never seen before—except for his shape? For a moment the girls were helpless.

> One of these accusers pointed several times at one Captain Hill, there present, but spoke nothing. The same accuser had a man standing at her back to hold her up. He stooped down to her ear. Then she cried out Alden, Alden, afflicted her. One of the Magistrates asked her if she ever had seen Alden. She answered, "No." He asked her how she knew it was Alden. She said the man had told her so.

The assistants had to be careful, for Alden was an important man and a war hero. They ordered a ring of men to stand in the street; then they took the girls outside to see whether they could pick Alden out of the ring. Somehow, the girls immediately selected him, and the assistants ordered him arrested. His sword was taken from him, and he was brought back inside. But Alden was no poor slave or hag of Salem Village. He stood his ground to the end:

> Mr. Gedney bid Alden confess, and give glory to God. Alden said he hoped he would give glory to God, but appealed to all that ever knew him, and challenged any one that could bring in anything that might give suspicion of his being such a one [a wizard]. They bid Alden look upon the accusers, which he did, and then they fell down. Alden asked Mr. Gedney, what reason could be given why Alden looking upon *him* did not strike *him* down as well? But no reason was given that I heard.
>
> Alden told Mr. Gedney that there was a lying spirit in them [the afflicted girls], for I can assure you that there is not a word of truth in all these say of me. But Alden was again committed to the marshal.

Alden spent the next fifteen weeks awaiting trial, not in prison but under guard at his Boston home. This special treatment was due to his friendship with the colony's leading ministers—men like Cotton Mather of Boston—and with crown officials like the governor himself. These ministers met with Alden from time to time in order to pray and fast for his deliverance, but whether they meant "deliverance" from the charge itself or from being a wizard was uncertain.

Although Alden was a strong and self-assured man, he began to doubt his chances of escaping trial. Finally, in September 1692, after several witches had been hanged, he fled to friends in neighboring Duxbury and pounded on their door at midnight, shouting: "The devil is after me!" His friends smuggled Alden to safety in New York. There he joined other well-to-do or prominent individuals who had left Massachusetts rather than face the Salem court. There was no democracy among witches in the Bay Colony. With wealth or influence one had a far better chance of reaching safety in colonies like New York than did the ordinary citizen accused of witchcraft. The following year, Alden was declared innocent by special proclamation, and the tall man from Boston returned to Massachusetts, his person and property untouched.

Meanwhile, during the storm of arrests and imprisonments, a ship from England was bringing the man who would eventually control the outcome of events — Sir William Phips. He had recently been appointed the first royal governor of the Massachusetts Bay Colony.

Sir William Phips was born in New England, the son of a poor farmer in Maine. He had made a fortune in Boston. He had added to it in the Caribbean Islands, not far from where Samuel Parris had worked as a merchant and had bought Tituba and John Indian. Phips found a sunken Spanish ship near Haiti and raised a treasure in gold worth well over a million dollars. England's king at the time, James II, had knighted Phips as a reward. Sir William was also the hero of several battles against the Indians and the French in America. After a trip to England he was returning home as a wealthy hero and the governor of Massachusetts.

When Sir William's ship sailed into Boston harbor in May 1692, he knew nothing of the witchcraft trials because he had been at sea for weeks. He was horrified at the news. Like almost everyone else at the time, Phips believed in witchcraft. But he was determined to get to the bottom of things. Dozens of suspected witches were in Boston jail awaiting trial. At the end of May, Phips appointed a special court to try the prisoners. He named seven judges, with his deputy governor, William Stoughton, as the chief justice. The court was called a Court of Oyer and Terminer.[1] Verdicts of innocent or guilty were to be handed down by a jury picked from the men of Salem Town, where the trials were to take place.

The prisoners had to put their faith in the court. The judges were men of high standing in the colony. They would probably be very careful about hanging men and women who had been accused by a group of hysterical young girls. What the prisoners did not know, at first, was that most of the judges were just as severe as Hathorne.

Before they opened the Court of Oyer and Terminer, the judges made several decisions that were harmful to the suspected witches. First, they decided that the records of the earliest examinations before Hathorne and Corwin would be admitted as evidence. The new court would, therefore, hear only testimony gathered since the first examinations. Second, the judges decided to accept the testimony of the afflicted girls about the shape of the witches. Third, the court would not punish any witch who confessed. This meant that confessions were rewarded, and it encouraged some, like Tituba, to name innocent suspects in their

---

[1]This old English term was derived from French words meaning "to hear" and "to determine."

A crude English drawing of 1655 shows the hanging of witches. A hangman climbs up to check the bodies. Below stand three condemned women and various officers of the law.

confessions. All these rules meant that the accused witches hardly had a chance for a fair trial.

On June 2 the judges first tried a woman named Bridget Bishop. Stoughton probably chose her because the case against her was strong. She was the wife of a tavern keeper in Salem Town and she had a very bad reputation. Also, several confessing witches had said that she was one of their leaders. The jury quickly found her guilty, and the judges sentenced her to death. She was given a few extra days of life by an embarrassing discovery. There was no Massachusetts law providing the dealth penalty for witches. The colonial legislature, known as the General Court, quickly passed such a law. On June 10 the sheriff took Bridget in a cart to the top of Gallows Hill, where she was hanged. The first witch was gone.

But many more suspects were waiting, and Hathorne and Corwin were still conducting examinations in the village. Sometimes as many as fifty new witches were accused in a single day, no longer just in Salem Village but all over eastern Massachusetts. One week, then two weeks passed after the hanging of Bridget Bishop. But still the judges did not meet again. They were quarreling among themselves about the meaning of the afflicted girls' testimony concerning shapes. This kind of evidence, which was called spectral evidence (from "specter," meaning "ghost"), was considered all-important. Without it there would not be a case against a single suspected witch. The quarreling judges turned to the ministers of Boston and nearby towns to decide the question. The ministers finally decided that spectral evidence should be used, as long as the judges and jury were careful with it.

On June 28 the court met again, to try Rebecca Nurse. Goodwife Nurse was from a large and prosperous farm family of Salem Village. She was an old woman and nearly deaf. But she was a member of the church, and before the witchcraft panic she had been a respected old grandmother. The jury took the ministers' advice about being careful in admitting spectral evidence. This time, they ignored the shrieking, afflicted girls and brought back a verdict of not guilty. Chief Justice Stoughton quickly bullied the jury into reversing its verdict, however. Then Rebecca Nurse's relatives went to Governor Phips and persuaded him to stop the hanging. But it was no use. When Stoughton and others heard about Phips's action, they insisted that he change his mind.

Neither the jury nor the governor could save Rebecca Nurse, and on Tuesday, July 19, she was hanged. Four other women were hanged on the same day. One was the old hag of Salem Village, Sarah Good. When she was about to die, one of the ministers tried to persuade her to confess. Goody Good might well have done so. She had spent months in prison. One child had died there with her. A second child had been arrested as a witch, though she was only five years old. But these things had only toughened the old hag's will. "You are a liar," she spat back at the preacher. "I am no more a witch than you are a wizard. If you take my life away, God will give you blood to drink." With that, she went up the ladder to the waiting rope.

At the September meeting of the Court of Oyer and Terminer, one man refused to plead either innocent or guilty. He was Giles Cory, the husband of Martha Cory, who had already been condemned. Under an old English law, Cory was taken into a vacant field beside the prison in Salem Town and tortured. Heavy stones were piled on his chest, but he would not surrender and say either "innocent" or "guilty." Instead (according to legend), he said only "More weight!" By afternoon he had been crushed to death. Three days later, on September 22, the sheriff hauled eight more convicted witches to the top of Gallows Hill to die, bringing the total dead to twenty—not counting the several who had already died in prison.

After the hangings of September 22, as suddenly as it had begun, the panic was over. The afflicted girls had gone too far. In the early fall of 1692 they began to accuse almost everyone, including the pious wives of well-known ministers. One girl even claimed that Cotton Mather, the colony's leading minister, was a wizard. Several of the girls began to see the shape of Lady Mary Phips, the governor's wife! These charges simply could not be accepted.

The trials that began in Salem Village were stopped by some of the leading citizens of the colony. They had finally become convinced that the entire affair had been a terrible mistake. On October 26, before the Court of Oyer and Terminer opened again, the General Court ordered a new meeting of ministers to consider the problem. Three days later, the General Court dismissed the trial court, and Governor Phips began releasing prisoners on bond. In November, following the advice of the ministers, the governor established a new court, with new rules. In the new trials spectral evidence would not be accepted. And, just as

Margaret Sewall, a sister-in-law of judge Samuel Sewall, lived in Salem at the time of the trials. Her dignified appearance was the ideal of New England Puritans.

Samuel Sewall, of the Court of Oyer and Terminer, was the only witch-trial judge to admit error. In 1697 he made a public confession at the Old South Church in Boston.

In 1711 the legislature of Massachusetts Bay passed an act to reverse the attainders of those executed for "a horrible witchcraft" in 1692. This meant mainly that lands and other property they had forfeited could be restored to their heirs.

important, confessing witches would be hanged. Under these new rules there could be almost no convictions. One by one, the prisoners were tried and found innocent. Five still insisted on confessing, and they were sentenced to hang; but Phips overruled the court and allowed even these five to live. It was too late for Sarah Good, Martha Cory, John Proctor, Old Jacobs, and the rest who had died. But the Salem witch trials were over at last.

Salem and the rest of the colony then started the impossible task of settling accounts. The released prisoners were required to pay for food and time in prison. Some remained in jail for several months until these charges were paid. Samuel Parris's congregation voted to dismiss him, and he left Salem Village in disgrace. No one knows what happened to little Betty Parris, but her younger brother went insane and died a young man.

In January 1697, five years after Betty Parris and Abigail Williams had first been afflicted, the General Court voted a fund of £598 (worth about $30,000) to be distributed among the relatives of the dead and the surviving witches. The money proved small compensation for the terrible anguish endured. When it was divided up, the lives of Martha Cory and Giles Cory turned out to have been worth about fifty dollars.

After any tragedy, people's minds eventually turn to other matters. In Salem Village the families of the dead gradually and painfully made peace with the families of the afflicted girls. By 1706 the little town was calm. But on August 25 of that year, the meeting house was once more filled to overflowing. A young woman named Anne Putnam had come to ask for admission to membership in the church. According to New England church custom, she had to make a public confession, after which the members of the church would vote on whether to accept her.

As a young girl of twelve, Anne Putnam had been one of the most active of the afflicted girls. Now, at the age of twenty-six, she was asking for full admission into the adult community. The congregation was seated while the new minister read her confession:

> I desire to be humbled before God for that sad providence in the year about '92. I, then being in my childhood, was made an instrument for the accusing of several persons of a grievous crime, whereby their lives were taken away from them. I now have good reason to believe they were innocent persons. What was said or done by me against any person, I can truly say I did not out of any anger, malice, or ill-will. What I did was done ignorantly, being deluded by Satan. I desire to lie in the dust, and to be humbled for it, and earnestly beg forgiveness of God, and from all those unto whom I have given just cause of sorrow and offence.

The minister finished reading, and he then asked the congregation to vote. Sitting in the meeting house were many relatives of the innocent men and women whom Anne Putnam had helped to imprison and hang. They must have frowned and clenched their hard farmers' fists. But they voted along with the rest of the congregation, unanimously, to accept Anne Putnam's plea for forgiveness. Shakily, she sat down. The story of the Salem witches had finally ended.

GAINING A FOOTHOLD IN THE NEW WORLD

After some shaky beginnings, the English colonies in North America took root and flourished. The land soon boasted farms, towns, and busy harbors. (The South Carolina plantation shown here, built in the early eighteenth century, exported rice and indigo.) Foreigners who traveled to the country during its early days were interested in the economic reasons for its success. How did people make a living? Were Americans better off than their counterparts in other countries? What were a newcomer's chances of prospering?

Henry Wansey, an English visitor, thought that the keys were freedom and hard work. He wrote: ''Everyone is at full liberty to follow the bent of his genius. Three fourths of the people are actively employed in either agriculture, trade, or commerce. There are but few idle drones in the hive, and, with all these advantages, their rapid progress to wealth and improvement is certain, and must be great beyond conception.''

[For further information on the foreign observers quoted in this essay, see ''Notes on Sources.'']

PICTORIAL ESSAY 2

A view of early Baltimore, with tobacco growing on the hill at right

All of Maryland that we have seen is high land, with few or no meadows, but possessing such a rich and fertile soil, as persons living there assured me, that they had raised tobacco off the same piece of land for thirty consecutive years. The inhabitants, who are generally English, are mostly engaged in this production. It is their chief staple, and the means with which they must purchase everything they require.

[JASPAR DANCKAERTS, 1679]

The Blue Mountains, [the Catskills] which reared their towering summits above all the other mountains, were now seen before us towards the north, but at a great distance. The farms became very numerous, and we had a view of many grain fields between the hills.

[PETER KALM, 1748]

A New York farm, with the Catskills in the background

Swedes trading with the Indians

In dealing with the Indians, you must be positive and keep to your word, for if they persuade you to lower your price, they will spend time in higgling for further reductions, and seldom conclude any bargain. Sometimes you may with brandy or strong liquor dispose them to give you ten times the value of your commodity. At other times they are so stubborn that they will not offer half the market price, especially if they are aware that you plan to influence them with drink, or that they think you have a desire for their goods, which you must appear to slight and disparage.

[JOHN LEDERER, 1669]

Sawmill operated by water power

New England produces very good timber. The firs are of an extraordinary growth, for masts, yards, and planks. The sumac is much used by the tanners and dyers. The cedar produces sweet gums, besides being extremely useful in making shingles for coverings for their dwellings, as being the most durable and least injured by the weather. But the treasure and glory of the woods are the monarch oak, the spruce, and fir trees, which are in such abundance that the navy of England might be supplied with all sorts of naval stores at a cheaper rate than from the Baltic.

[THOMAS ANBUREY, 1778]

The fishermen take yearly upon the coasts many tons of cod, hake, haddock, and pollack, which they split, salt, and dry at their stages, making three voyages in a year. When they share their fish at the end of every voyage, they separate the best from the worst. The first they call merchantable fish. These they sell to the Massachusetts merchants, who send them to Lisbon, Bilbao, Bordeaux, Marseilles, and other cities of France. The refuse fish they sell to the Caribbean islanders of Barbados, Jamaica, and so on, who feed their Negroes with it.

To every shallop belong four fishermen—a master or steersman, a midshipman, a foremastman, and a shore man who washes the fish, dries it, and tends their cookery. These often get in one voyage £8 or £9 a man for their shares, but it does some of them little good. For the merchant at the end comes in with a traveling tavern—a boat laden with the legitimate blood of the rich grape, and with brandy, rum, and tobacco. Coming ashore, he gives them a taste or two, which so charms them that for no persuasions that their employers can use will they go out to sea for two or three days, nay sometimes a whole week, till they are wearied with drinking. If a man of quality chance to come where they are roistering, he must be sociable and rolypoly with them or else be gone. For when wine in their guts is at full tide, they quarrel, fight, and do one another mischief.

[JOHN JOSSELYN, 1674]

Unloading and drying fish at Newfoundland

Launching the ship *Fame* at Salem, Massachusetts, 1802

*The principal branch of American
manufacture is the building of vessels. The
Americans excel in naval architecture,
and in this particular point certainly rival
the most industrious people of Europe.
The annual tonnage of vessels built in the
different yards is estimated at about
100,000 tons.*

[FELIX DE BEAUJOUR, 1810]

Trade card of a manufacturer of spermaceti (whale oil) candles

*In Rhode Island and particularly in the small town of
Nantucket, famed for its fisheries, spermaceti candles are
made, which in whiteness rival those of wax, but they
do not give so pure and equal a light.*

[FELIX DE BEAUJOUR, 1810]

PE 2–6 /

Wasteland, unhealthy climate, poor people, ragged clothing—such is approximately the general idea of this continent in Europe. But oh how far from the truth is this! The land requires too little work to remain uncultivated. The robustness of the men and the fine color of the women attest to the healthiness of the climate. Not only the abundance, but also the luxury in which people live belies their reputed poverty. And the pleasure which everyone who is introduced to their society experiences is incontestable evidence of their gracious manner of living. The [American] peasant does not know what misery is; he eats meat four times a day and drinks tea twice a day. If money is scarce, everything is cheap. At present such is the compeition here among ships from Europe (where perhaps they imagined that the Americans were all naked) that they are obliged to sell their merchandise at a loss. The quantity of all kinds of lumber, fish, oil, blubber, material for soap, flour, and salt meat will, before long, bring to this continent enough money to enable it to be recognized as a wealthy country.

[FRANCESCO DAL VERME, 1783]

Elijah Boardman, a wealthy Connecticut merchant

In the heart of New York City's commercial district, 1797

Merchants' counting house in Philadelphia

Table for converting currency

Philadelphia, if we consider that not eighty years ago the place where it now stands was a wild and uncultivated desert, inhabited by nothing but ravenous beasts and a savage people, must certainly be the object of everyone's wonder and admiration. It contains about 3,000 houses, and 18 or 20,000 inhabitants.

The Pennsylvanians, as to character, are a frugal and industrious people: not remarkably courteous and hospitable to strangers, unless particularly recommended to them; but rather, like the inhabitants of most commercial cities, the reverse. They are by far the most enterprising people upon the continent. As they consist of several nations, and talk several languages, they are aliens in some respect to Great Britain: nor can it be expected that they should have the same filial attachment to her which her own immediate offspring have. However, they are quiet, and concern themselves but little, except about getting money.

[ANDREW BURNABY, 1760]

Forges are established in New Jersey, Pennsylvania, Maryland, and Virginia. In several states, particularly the northern ones, utensils of iron the most necessary for agriculture and building are manufactured.

[FELIX DE BEAUJOUR, 1810]

Air furnace for casting iron, from an early advertisement

Went with a party to see Dickson's cotton manufactory. There are two large buildings four stories high and eighty feet long. Twelve or fourteen workmen from Manchester. All the machinery in wood, steel, and brass was made on the spot from models brought from England and Scotland. They are training up women and children to the business, of whom I saw twenty or thirty at work. They give the women two dollars a week, as well as board and lodging. The children are bound apprentice till twenty-one years of age, with an engagement to board, clothe, and educate them.

[HENRY WANSEY, 1794]

Early American flask, decorated with an eagle

Carding machine constructed by English immigrant Samuel Slater in 1790

6 PURITAN NEW ENGLAND

R. J. W.

The governor kept a careful journal, beginning in late March while his ship still rode at anchor in England. Now, more than two months later, his little fleet of four vessels was getting close to that part of America that John Smith had named New England. On the fifth of June, 1630, the ship's crew took a sounding and found the ocean's bottom at about eighty fathoms (less than 500 feet). The governor, the seamen, and the other passengers peered anxiously ahead, straining for their first sight of America. But, even though it was summer, the weather was still chilly and foggy on the North Atlantic. Only in the afternoon did the mists clear and permit the governor that moment of excitement that had come to Columbus, to Cortez, to the Jamestown settlers—to all Europeans catching their first sight of a new coast. On the horizon, the governor could just make out the shoreline of Maine. (He sketched it carefully into his journal, of course.)

The fleet continued on course. The next day, still a good distance from the coast, the ships slowed and the men fished. The governor, always a student of practical details, noted that they took sixty-seven large cod in less than two hours. Only on June 11 did the lead ship, the *Arbella*, finally turn south and begin the search for the final destination, described in the royal charter the governor kept below decks as "a certain bay there, commonly called Massachusetts, alias Mattachusetts alias Massatusetts Bay." The entry in the governor's journal was more relaxed than usual:

Then we tacked and stood west-southwest. We had now fair, sunshine weather, and so pleasant a sweet air as did much refresh us. And there came a smell off the shore like the smell of a garden. There came a wild pigeon into the ship, and another small land bird.

A few days of careful sailing brought the *Arbella* to anchor at a tiny English settlement called Nahumkeck (which would soon be renamed Salem).

The governor was John Winthrop. The *Arbella* was the lead ship of a fleet bringing about 1,000 English colonists to New England. And this fleet was only the vanguard of a migration that would bring about 20,000 more over the next ten years. Winthrop and most of these immigrants were part of a political and religious movement known as Puritanism. They shared some of the motives that had led English colonists to Virginia or Spaniards to Mexico. But the Puritan colonists of New England were different. They were embarked, as they saw it, on a mission much more important than colonization. They were chosen, they believed, to perform a special "errand" for God: the creation in the new world of a purified Christian commonwealth. By the 1640s, they had succeeded in building a series of distinctive communities, clustering around Massachusetts Bay but reaching north into Maine and New Hampshire and west and south into Rhode Island, Connecticut, and Long Island. It was this Puritan world that would eventually become the setting for the witchcraft episode of 1692.

PURITANISM

To be a Puritan in the sixteenth and seventeenth century was not a simple, clear-cut thing. There was no formal organization, no political party, not even a church called "Puritan." There was only a social movement—a movement that was often underground and revolutionary. And like most social movements, Puritanism was never clearly defined. The leaders of the movement themselves almost never used the term. "Puritan," in fact, was a word used most often by the enemies of the movement, a term of criticism or insult.

For many modern Americans, "puritanical" means nothing more than prudish, priggish, and repressive, especially in matters of sex. The concept of Puritanism has been so murky, ill-defined, and emotionally loaded that many historians have urged that it be abandoned. The history of New England might best be understood as just another episode in the colonization of North America, not fundamentally different from the history of Virginia, or Georgia, or Pennsylvania.

The problem with such a strategy is that the men who led and controlled society in New England in the seventeenth century did most certainly *believe* they were doing something different and special. From John Winthrop to Cotton Mather, several generations of religious and political leaders labored to keep alive a heightened consciousness of special purpose, mission, and divine errand. Samuel Parris still had some of it, and so did men like Hathorne, Sewall, and Stoughton. The ways that people think about their lives are as much a part of their history as the things they actually do. The history of New England in its first century was very much the history of a set of ideas and attitudes—an ideology—that can still usefully be labeled "Puritan."

The Puritan Sensibility Puritan ideology contained complex ideas about religion, politics, family and social life, economics, art, and science—indeed about every aspect of human life. But somewhere near the center of all these ideas lay a relatively simple attitude toward the world—an emotional stance, a sensibility that in some way governed what the Puritan thought about everything else. The Puritan was a man distressed by what he saw happening in his world. To him, England during the reigns of Elizabeth I, James I, and Charles I was a profoundly disturbing place and time. And the sense of disturbance went much deeper than the usual human grumbling about "the times." A few Englishmen at first, and then growing numbers, began to feel basically detached and alienated from their own society. But gradually others—merchants, tradesmen, lawyers, country squires, workers in the small industries of the day—began to share the deep conviction that something had gone fundamentally wrong. The typical candidate for involvement in the Puritan movement was literate and industrious, neither noble nor peasant. He had a sense of himself as sober, hard-working, and responsible—or, as he would have put it, "godly." Such men (and a few women, too) felt trapped in a nation that was becoming every year more corrupt, disordered, and

John Winthrop was a man of refinement and sensitivity. Though some questioned his arbitrary rulings (he had no faith in democracy), none doubted his integrity.

sinful. By the end of the sixteenth century, there was an identifiable style of writing and preaching, a style governed by the central feeling of dismay, a style that was already being called Puritan.

This sense of embattled dismay had a historical dimension. Puritan preachers and writers gradually invented a contrast between what England had once been and what it was becoming. The old England, in their mythology, had been a land of simplicity, homely virtue, and order. The new society had corrupted these old values in every way. Even in matters as minor as dress or hair styles, the Puritan saw only decline.

Part of the problem, the typical Puritan felt, was that foreign influence had crept into English life. From France, Spain, and Italy had come habits, styles of dress, manners, and morals that were both corrupt and alien. These countries were the strongholds of Catholicism in Europe, so every influence from them was part of a vast intrigue to undermine Protestantism in England. And if the government itself fell under foreign influence, as it seemed to do under James I and Charles I, then the Puritan had to contemplate drastic action—such as emigrating or making a revolution.

Such attitudes marked the Puritan as a radical. This led many of the critics and enemies of Puritanism into the fatal error of viewing the Puritan as an agent of disorder and anarchy, an opponent of authority. In truth, however, the Puritan felt that there was not *enough* order, not enough law, not enough discipline. To Puritan eyes, the rich, the powerful, and the noble had developed a contempt for law and tradition. On the other side, the poor had lost their ancient ways of simplicity and deference and were leaving their ancestral plots and villages in alarming numbers to wander about the countryside or cluster in the slums of London. The net effect was that there seemed to be neither governors nor governed. In every area of life, the normal lines of authority and order seemed to have collapsed.

The Puritan solution to the problem was discipline. But (and here, again, the opponents of Puritanism often failed to grasp the point) discipline was not to be imposed by force. Instead, true order had to grow out of the free, voluntary decision of individuals to live "godly" lives. For cor-

rupted people in a corrupted society, forceful control might be necessary. But the ultimate goal was to reform society, to create a purified commonwealth in which order would flow naturally from the will of the citizens. There would be no contradiction, in such a society, between freedom and order. (Here is an important clue to the odd decision in 1692 to send no confessed witch to the gallows. When even a slave like Tituba confessed, she signaled that she had regained her capacity for freedom and could now make a voluntary choice. A witch who refused to confess was still in the grip of the devil, still not free to rejoin the disciplined community.)

Puritanism as a Religious Experience The Puritans' distress and their yearning for discipline and order were almost as much emotions as ideas. Something more was required: a theory about nature and human society that would give coherent form to emotions. Fear and anger had to be translated into a more formal language. For any European of the period, the most obvious and easily available language was religion.

For the most part, Puritan religious ideas were the ideas of the Protestant Reformation. Puritans pictured their age as one of climactic struggle between the old, Catholic order and a new, Protestant one. To them, the sins and errors of Catholicism were obvious. Like most other Protestants, they believed that many of the popes, bishops, and priests had fallen into sinful habits of luxury, cruelty, and corruption. The errors of Catholicism, which were even more numerous than the sins, could be classified under one main heading. For centuries, the Church had been undermining the relationship between God and the individual. The Church had, in fact, tried to stand between God and humanity—first as a bridge, but then as a barrier. As Puritans and other Protestants saw it, the Church's multiplicity of rituals and sacraments, its complicated hierarchy, its insistence on the use of Latin as the only language of religion, had removed God from individual human experience. God could be reached, it seemed, only through the Church—through the imposing cathedrals, the mysterious music, the use of Latin, the darkened confessional.

In general, the Protestant formula was to simplify the religious life and make it more accessible to the individual. The Puritans wanted to go further in this direction than most other Protestants. To them, religious experience ought to be as opposite to Catholic practice as possible.

The Puritan began with one of the most common Christian doctrines. An enormous gulf existed between God and humanity. God was all-powerful and all-perfect. Men and women were sinful, weak, and vile. But God, in his mercy and in the distant stretches of his own eternal time, had decided to save a fraction of the race. The others he had damned forever. No one deserved salvation. No one could earn it—not by any amount of prayer or good works. Salvation was the free gift of God's grace. And this gift of grace came directly, not through an institutional church, not through any process of confession and absolution.

Because of God's merciful decision, those living at any given time included a number of the saved. These "elect," who were predestined for heaven, were the true church. They might not be organized, they might not have buildings and ministers. But they were the only real church, the church "invisible," as Puritans and other Protestants liked to call it. The error of Catholicism had been to ignore this invisible church of the true elect and to concentrate instead on building and maintaining the "visible," institutional church.

The Puritans' dream was to gather as many of the English "elect" as possible into congregations, to exclude all others from membership. These purified churches could then work to gain power in the world, to get the largest possible measure of control over society. For the Puritans, the only authentic religious institution was such a church of elected "saints." They did not admit the authority of any other religious power—neither bishops nor archbishops, popes nor kings. The congregations of the elect, they thought, should have the power to admit new members, choose and dismiss their own ministers, hear confessions, and excommunicate sinners. (It was the Salem Village congregation that hired Parris, and it was they who fired him. And it was the whole membership of the church that heard Anne Putnam's confession and voted whether to accept it or not.)

The Puritans' ideal of congregation, then, was the basis for their religious life. Ordinary people, sinful and damned, should be required to attend church and should be forced by law to obey God's commandments, even though they could not be members. The elect *were* the church. They would "gather" themselves, sign their own compacts or covenants, and thus create their own religious institutions. After that, they would settle all important questions by vote. And they would recognize no other religious power on earth.

Theoretically, each congregation was free to go its own way. But there were certain principles upon which all the Puritans were agreed. Religion should be simple and comprehensible, stripped of mystery and confusion. There should be no instrumental music, and the hymns should be simple. The Bible should be read in English (not Latin) and by everyone. There should be no holy days, not even Christmas. Ministers should dress like everyone else and should marry like everyone else. Nothing—no stained glass or art, no stone arches, carved pews, or organs—should distract the congregation from the direct worship of God.

The English Reformation The political-religious condition of England was a dreadful tangle for the Puritan. England was supposedly a Protestant nation. But the motives of the English monarchs who had created English Protestantism were more political than religious. Henry VIII and his daughter, Elizabeth, would have been content with a "reformation" in which the only real change was that the king or queen replaced the pope as head of the church. For the rest, the Church of England was a compromise between Catholic and radical Protestant ideas. The hierarchy remained intact, with its bishops and archbishops. Prayers were still prescribed, not made up by individual ministers. Congregations still knelt in churches ornamented with stained glass before priests wearing elaborate robes.

In institutional terms, the Puritan was a person who wanted to "purify" this Church of England of its remaining "papist" practices. But the Puritans' insistence on the ultimate power of the individual congregation was, ultimately, a threat to the crown itself, since the king was the final religious authority. It was this fact that placed the Puritans in conflict with their own government. Elizabeth and James I regarded them as dangerous and annoying fanatics, and harassed them with fines and imprisonment. Charles I, who became king in 1625, carried the persecution further. He appointed William Laud archbishop, and Laud proceeded to dismiss ministers he suspected of Puritan leanings. In one famous case, a Puritan who published a book attacking Laud was fined and imprisoned and had his ears cut off as punishment.

The Laudian "persecution" (as the Puritans thought of it) only seemed to strengthen the movement. More Puritan books appeared, more and more Anglican priests were converted, new converts and allies were found in merchant groups and among lawyers and politicians. Finally, Charles I made a fateful mistake. He challenged the power of Parliament. This move created an alliance between the king's Puritan opponents and those who, for other reasons, wanted a strong Parliament able to resist royal authority. In 1629 — just before Winthrop set sail on the *Arbella* — Charles I finally dissolved Parliament and declared that he would rule England alone. The stage was set for a civil war between the king's forces and the supporters of Parliament. And this crisis, in turn, made even more converts to Puritanism.

CITY UPON A HILL

A Charter In March of 1629, Charles I overcame his fears and suspicions long enough to give Massachusetts to a group of Puritan gentlemen. The old Plymouth Company that had originally been given the northern part of "Virginia" had been dissolved. Subsequent attempts to colonize New England had achieved only small successes. Now, Charles I granted the right to settle an area almost the width of modern Massachusetts to a new company "by the name of the Governor and Company of the Mattachusettes Bay in Newe England."

The Massachusetts Bay Company was, in structure, a regular joint-stock corporation, with shareholders (called, in the language of the day, freemen) and officers. The king appointed the first governor, but thereafter he was to be elected each year by the stockholders. These freemen, according to the charter, were to meet four times a year in a "general court" to vote on officers and policies for their business.

By some stroke of luck, oversight, or genius, however, the charter omitted one normal provision. The *place* of the General Court meetings was not specified. This meant that the company could take its charter anywhere and hold meetings anywhere. It was this lapse that made it possible for Winthrop, the second governor of the company, to bring the charter to America on the *Arbella*. This done, he and his colleagues could transform a trading company charter into what amounted to a political constitution.

Fewer than ten of the migrants of 1630 were stockholders of the Massachusetts Bay Company, and, technically, only they had the power to vote laws and elect their governor. Winthrop and the other stockholders quickly decided to do something that went far beyond the normal practice of English joint-stock corporations. They admitted all the adult male church members — the religious "elect" — to the status of freemen, or stockholders. This meant that all men admitted to full membership by a gathered congregation could vote for representatives to the General Court. By this stroke, the Massachusetts Bay Company was transformed from a corporation into a commonwealth.

Political participation in the new commonwealth was restricted to the saints elect. Thus the "invisible church" was made visible not only in congregations but in the political structure of the colony as well. Church and state were technically separate, but the same individuals would control each, and for the same goals and purposes. The stockholders' meetings in a General Court were transformed into a legislature of "Assistants" — the position held by Hathorne and Corwin when they came out to Salem Village to hold hearings in 1692. Since the charter specified only a few small obligations to the king, the Bay Company was practically independent of England. The wide North Atlantic insulated the colonists from English failings and corruptions. No wonder, for a man like John Winthrop, the breeze off the Maine coast would seem "so pleasant a sweet air as did much refresh us."

A Model The transformed charter provided the Puritan migrants with a political structure. But they all were deeply convinced that *no* political structure would work without an emotional commitment to the community on the part of each of its members. It was just as important to spell out this commitment as it was to have a government. In midpassage, with the charter safely locked below, Winthrop gathered his "company" on the deck of the *Arbella* and delivered a lecture about their mission. His title was "Christian Charitie: a Modell Hereof." His purpose was to remind the settlers of the supreme importance of their mission and of the kinds of "charity" or love that mission would require of them.

In his lecture, Winthrop distinguished between two kinds of human situations. People live most of their lives in ordinary times he said, but they also pass through extraordinary "seasons and occasions." In ordinary times, the main cement of society is status or class. Some people are rich and powerful, some poor and weak; and everyone is "knit together" by relationships of dependence, protection, charity, and law. Such is God's "providence." But extraordinary times and seasons, according to Winthrop, bring a suspension of God's normal providence. Familiar and comfortable lines of class and status fade or break down, encouraging anarchy. This was what he and the other Puritans thought had happened in old England. The only way to avoid such an outcome, to restore order and make society work again was to find a different way of binding people together. Winthrop's solution was demanding but simple. In extraordinary seasons of crisis, Christians should be bound by love: the love of the Christian individual for the Christian community.

Of course, no "season" could be more extraordinary than the one the colonists were experiencing. They were a godly company chosen by God to perform a special work. This was their

"commission." And it placed them under heavy obligations. They must abandon their normal concerns with their own private welfare and place their love of the community uppermost:

> We must be knit together in this work as one man. We must delight in each other, make others' conditions our own, rejoice together, mourn together, labor and suffer together—always having before our eyes our Commission and Community in the work, our Community as members of the same body.

If such a community of Christian love could be created, the bare skeleton of the charter would come to life.

Towns and Congregations Armed with their charter, and with their ideal of Christian charity, the Puritan migrants set about building godly communities in the wilderness. The 20,000 or 30,000 settlers who belonged to Winthrop's generation came remarkably close to realizing their dream of a City upon a Hill. There was never enough "love," to be sure; but there was a good deal of luck and quite enough pious determination. Around Massachusetts Bay, and then outward into Connecticut, Long Island, Western Massachusetts, New Hampshire, and even Maine, a society of Puritan towns was planted. These towns were highly integrated and disciplined communal units. In them, two public institutions functioned in close, almost drilled order: the town government and the congregation. For the individual, life was defined and regulated by these closely related public bodies.

In New England, as in all the English colonies, the primary economic resource was the land itself. But the Puritans devised their own curious system for parceling out the land. They did not make grants or sales to individual "planters." Instead, the General Court granted land to towns. The towns could then grant the land to individual heads of families, but they could also hold much of it in "common," as a reserve for the future. Each individual family, then, was ultimately dependent on its town. Town government, like church government, was a kind of democracy of the elect. Freemen gathered in town meetings to elect officers, vote on ordinances and taxes, and make decisions about roads, bridges, and similar details so important in any agricultural community. The towns also became the basic political unit of the colonies, since they elected the members of legislatures everywhere in New England.

Town government was, in effect, an extension of church government. The same "freemen"—adult male church members, usually the heads of families—ruled both in church meetings and in town meetings. The first-generation congregations were created with a great deal of care and deliberation. In some cases, the potential members would meet together each week for as long as a year, examining each other's spiritual state with what they called "loving" intensity. Only after this process did they decide who might be a member of the new church, a "visible saint." Then, with great deliberation, these saints, or the adult males among them, would draw up a "covenant" or compact, creating their church. After the church had been carefully "gathered," new applicants for membership had to undergo a searching public examination before they could be voted into membership. And any member could be disciplined and even excommunicated if his fellow members decided he was a "hypocrite inwardly."

Between them, the town and the congregation reached very far into the lives of every colonist in New England. Life had, by modern standards, an extraordinarily public character. And what was not touched and controlled by towns and congregations was often regulated by legislation in the General Court. Massachusetts, Connecticut, and Rhode Island all had laws governing such things as the prices of nails, the amount of flour to be used in bread, the amount of thread that each household had to spin every year. In the towns, there were numerous sets of rules and requirements: for church attendance, fence maintenance, the management of livestock, the number of days that men had to work on public roads, bridges, and dams. Blasphemy, Sabbath-breaking, fornication, and adultery were viewed not only as sins but as crimes, and perpetrators were prosecuted.

All this communal regulation of life is what gave the Puritans their later reputation for being authoritarian and repressive. They had no interest whatever in religious toleration or individual freedom. The idea that there was room for more than one opinion on any important question seemed foolish to them. There was only one true and godly answer to any question, and it would be a sin to "tolerate" any point of view or mode of behavior that was not God's way.

In their town meetings and church votes, the Puritans did not practice majority rule but

An old sketch depicts the plymouth meeting house, built in 1683. In the early days, the Pilgrims met for services in the lower story of the fort that stood at one end of their settlement.

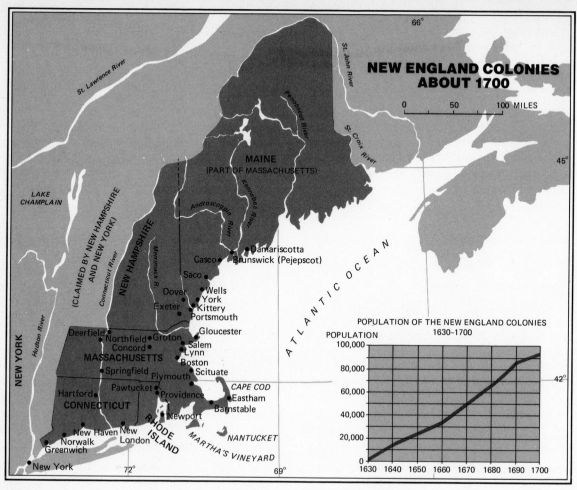

NEW ENGLAND COLONIES ABOUT 1700

0   50   100 MILES

MAINE
(PART OF MASSACHUSETTS)

LAKE CHAMPLAIN

(CLAIMED BY NEW HAMPSHIRE AND NEW YORK)

NEW HAMPSHIRE

St. Lawrence River

St. John River

St. Croix River

Penobscot River

Kennebec River

Andrascoggin River

Merrimack R.

Connecticut River

Hudson River

Damariscotta
Casco ● Brunswick (Pejepscot)
Saco
Wells
Dover ● York
Exeter ● Kittery
Portsmouth
Gloucester
Deerfield ● Groton
Northfield ● Concord
MASSACHUSETTS ● Salem
Lynn
Springfield ● Boston
Plymouth ● Scituate
Hartford ● Pawtucket
CONNECTICUT ● Providence
Newport
New Haven ● New London
Norwalk
Greenwich
New York

NEW YORK

RHODE ISLAND

CAPE COD
Eastham
Barnstable

MARTHA'S VINEYARD

NANTUCKET

ATLANTIC OCEAN

66°
45°
42°
72°   69°

POPULATION OF THE NEW ENGLAND COLONIES 1630–1700

POPULATION

100,000
80,000
60,000
40,000
20,000
0
1630 1640 1650 1660 1670 1680 1690 1700

By 1700, the New England colonies had a population of 92,763. Over three fourths of this total lived in Massachusetts and Connecticut. Northern New England, as can be seen, had not yet taken on the form familiar to us today.

Maine's English beginnings went back to a grant to proprietors Sir Ferdinando Gorges and John Mason. In 1622 they received the land between the Merrimac and Kennebec rivers. They did little to build up a colony. Most early settlers came from Massachusetts, and the region remained part of that state until 1820.

In 1629 Gorges and Mason divided their lands. Mason received the region between the Piscataqua and Merrimack rivers, which he named New Hampshire. Like Maine, it had many ties to Massachusetts. The colony became a separate royal province in 1679. Both New Hampshire and New York claimed it, but there were no English settlements in the region until the eighteenth century.

argued and sweated their way toward a consensus. They hated the idea of factions or parties. They had been a faction in England, to be sure, but their hope had been to win out completely and to establish their way as the only allowable way. The very point behind the migration had been to win this kind of total victory in the new world. And, once it was won, the victory had to be protected by the most careful regulation of the details of life.

Families and Farms The Puritans of seventeenth-century New England wasted little or no time discussing such issues as "democracy" or religious "freedom." What they were interested in was the creation of a society that was closely knit and well regulated. They were operating within a set of myths about traditional English agricultural villages. In these old peasant communities, the Puritans believed, life had been tightly integrated and harmonious, simple and well ordered. The typical Puritan town patterned itself accordingly. The families clustered in houses at the town center. The fields and pastures lay scattered in small plots throughout the town. Life was stable and closely controlled. Very few people came into the village or left it. In some ways, the situation was ludicrous. New Englanders were perched on the edge of a vast and tempting continent. But instead of expanding rapidly into it on individual terms — as Virginians and others did — they huddled together in communities that soon looked almost crowded, their version of the peasant villages in the worn world they had left behind.

Puritanism was in many ways a movement aimed at recovering a "lost" way of life. And, for a generation or two in America, it succeeded. The irony was that the idea of the old English way of life was almost as much an invention as it was a memory. Agricultural villages in England were not nearly as stable as Puritan towns. Despite the vast area of free land around them, the Puritans managed to hold their communities so tightly together that only about one person out of every 100 would leave their town in any given year. English villages, by contrast, lost about 5 people out of every 100 each year.

In the striking degree of cohesion they managed to maintain, Puritan towns went well beyond "traditional" English villages. The Puritans were in a curious position. They were deliberately *trying* to act out a traditional script. But when tradition becomes conscious effort, it is no longer tradition at all. Traditional English villages were not planned and "gathered" under covenants. They just happened. Puritan towns were deliberate, artificial creations — conscious choices. They did not grow "naturally" out of the environment; they were attempts to *defy* the environment, to create closed communities in a wide-open frontier setting. So long as men like Winthrop had their way, individuals were forbidden to strike out on their own into the wilderness as the Virginians did.

The Puritans' remarkable success at maintaining their communal towns for three or four generations was, partly, a result of pious determination. But determination was helped along by plain good luck. A civil war in England kept other, non-Puritan Englishmen from emmigrating to New England, where they might have disturbed the towns. Soil and climate ruled out a staple crop like tobacco that might have encouraged a large-scale, individualistic, plantation-type agriculture.

Most important of all, they were able to maintain large families dominated by the original "saints" for unusually long periods of time. The original "elect" had another virtue: they lived a long time. The life expectancy of men and women in the first generation of Massachusetts settlers was about what it is today — seventy years or so. By comparison, life expectancy in England was only about fifty years. In New England, marriages occurred a little earlier in life, too, so women could expect to bear about twice as many children as their English sisters. In England, a man married at

The town of Boston (shown here in the 1640s) was founded in 1630, when Winthrop and others moved there from Charlestown, across the harbor. They named their settlement after Boston, England. The name is a shortened version of St. Botolph's Town.

Even in the early days, New England was noted for commerce and manufacturing. Here workers—including a smith, a tailor, and a shoemaker—ply their trades.

about thirty and died at about fifty. The odds were high that he would not live to see his grandchildren. John Winthrop's godly company married at a somewhat younger age and, by living to a ripe seventy, could expect not only to see their grandchildren, but to see them grow up and marry.

In New England—and this was not true anywhere in the European world—the three-generation family became "normal." Sons and grandsons remained in their towns, waiting to inherit their share of the family land. And while they waited, they were very much under the authority of the original settlers, the old saints. By the 1660s, these aging saints had become surrounded by their own legendary past—the heroic past of migration and settlement. On their farms, in their churches, at their town meetings, they were the force that preserved the astonishing stability of their communities. They were what made the towns seem "knit together as one man."

A Praise and Glory For about thirty years, Winthrop's prediction seemed to come true. The Lord did seem to "dwell among us as his own people." There were problems, of course. About 200 people died the first winter. And, after a few years of uneasy peace, the Pequot Indians of the Bay area finally lost patience with the encroachment of the growing settlements in the western part of the colony and made war. But problems

like these could be solved. Even the "starving time" of the first winter was nothing compared to the Jamestown experience, and by the second year survival was not an important issue in New England. As for the Pequots, they could be dealt with, too. An angry Puritan army surrounded the main camp of the Indians, set it afire, and killed about 400 of their enemy. The few Indians who survived were hunted down efficiently and either killed or sold as slaves. All the while, the preachers sang their thanksgivings that the Lord had lent his strength in battle.

Even the most severe economic problem, the lack of a staple crop, could be overcome. Colonists all over the New World were finding gold or silver or a crop they could send back to Europe. The Puritans found nothing of the sort. But they made ends meet from the start by trading in furs, taking wood from the forests, and, above all, fishing for the cod that Governor Winthrop had so carefully noted in his *Arbella* journal.

Even though the agriculture of New England was primarily one of subsistence, there were small surpluses of beef, pork, and beans almost from the beginning. And the New Englanders began almost at once to do something no other seventeeth-century colonists were able to do. They began to engage in trade, carried in their own small ships, instead of depending on English merchants and shipping. Within a half century, merchants from Boston and Salem were shipping New England goods to Europe and the West Indies, bringing slaves from Africa to Virginia and the Indies, bringing sugar from the islands to be distilled into rum and reexported or consumed, carrying tobacco from Virginia to England. The Puritans also launched into manufacturing, with a state-supported iron furnace and foundry; and they minted their own coin, a "pine-tree shilling." All this—the shipbuilding, the trade, the manufacturing—was aimed toward making New England as economically separate from the mother country as possible.

In other respects, too, the colony matured rapidly. In 1636, Harvard College was established, primarily to train new ministers. In 1647, the General Court created a public school system. Each town with fifty or more families was required to support a teacher, and each town of 100 or more families had to have a Latin grammar school to prepare young men for the college. Connecticut had a similar law, and from the 1640s on, New England had probably the most literate population in the western world. No aristocrats came to New England—and none were wanted. But some quite well-to-do immigrants were attracted to the colony, as were some scholars with solid public reputations in England, like the minister John Cotton—especially as civil war between Puritans and Royalists drew nearer.

Expansion was another sign of success and maturity. In 1635 and 1636, settlers under the leadership of another distinguished minister, Thomas Hooker, moved to the Connecticut Valley and established Hartford, then two other towns nearby. Another group settled around New Haven, on Long Island Sound. The dissenters expelled by the Puritans also established new settlements—in Rhode Island, New Hampshire, and Maine—and the Bay Colony claimed jurisdiction over these new colonies, too, despite the fact that they were founded by men and women who disagreed with the established government of Massachusetts. The disagreements usually were on minor points of theology, and the new colonies were, for all practical purposes, Puritan.

The English authorities were in no position to oppose this expansion. In the late 1630s, the struggle between Charles I and Parliament broke into open war, with the Puritans gradually gaining control of the parliamentary side. Eventually, the royalists were beaten and the king beheaded, and from 1649 to 1660 a Puritan leader, Oliver Cromwell, governed England as "Protector" of the realm. During the first thirty years of settlement, then, the New England colonists created a mature, practically independent commonwealth.

DISSENT, DECLINE, DOMINION

The City upon a Hill did not last. It may have been doomed from the beginning, despite its early successes and inherent good luck. But after about 1660, the godly commonwealth fell prey to three related enemies. The first was dissent within the community. The second was what the ministers called declension or decline—an apparent failing of the original piety and energy that had created the commonwealth. The third, and probably the most important, was a reassertion of English authority after the Stuart monarchy was restored in 1660. These three problems came finally to a head in the 1680s and 1690s and helped set the stage for the Salem witchcraft hysteria of 1692.

Roger Williams and Anne Hutchinson There was no simple Puritan creed. The members of the movement shared a general set of beliefs, but there were shades of opinion on a number of religious questions. The pressures of persecution and civil war in England demanded unity, and disputes there were usually covered over by a relaxed policy of "toleration" within the movement. In America, these pressures were absent and disagreement even over very narrow points of theology divided the towns from time to time. In a way, the Puritans were the victims of their own sophistication. Even a layman could follow theological arguments and see their implications. So a challenge as to the precise nature of "grace" might suddenly threaten to tear the commonwealth apart. The cases of Roger Williams and Anne Hutchinson illustrate this point precisely.

Roger Williams, everyone said, was a gentle man, a learned minister, and a devout Puritan. The problem was that he was almost too devout. When he came to Salem as minister, he began to fret publicly that the churches were "impure," even in the City upon a Hill. He argued, for example, that requiring the saints and the damned to attend church meetings together was corrupting. And he wanted the churches to declare themselves formally separated from the Church of England, to give up even the pretence of wanting to purify the established church. He insisted on a total separation of church and state—not to protect the government from religious influences, but to protect the church from the "worldly" influences of government. So, he argued, religious offences ought not to be punished by civil authorities. From his Salem pulpit, he even began to suggest that there was something illegal about the Massa-

ANNE HUTCHINSON

The Puritan communities around Massachusetts Bay were, by modern standards, strikingly homogeneous. The first generation of settlers were all English. They were all Protestants, of course, and almost all were serious in their piety. Still, there were some fundamental intellectual tensions in Puritanism that produced dissent even in such a homogeneous social order.

From time to time these ideological tensions found a concrete focus in an individual, as they did in the curious and precarious life of Anne Hutchinson. On the surface there was nothing in Anne Hutchinson's experience to set her apart from her fellow-New Englanders. When she immigrated to Boston in 1634, she appeared to be a perfectly typical, middle-aged Puritan wife.

Anne Hutchinson took her own religious experience very seriously. She actually felt, she thought, an "indwelling" of the Holy Spirit, a kind of inward voice that made her certain that she was one of God's elect. And she was just as certain that her salvation had been a result of God's pure grace, not of any of her own efforts or "works."

Anne Hutchinson was a fiercely committed woman with a quick mind. She began to attract not only attention but followers, and soon the Boston congregation was split into two factions. On one side, there were Hutchinson's disciples with their sweet slogans like "free grace," "gospel truth," and "glorious light." On the other side, there were her own minister, the preachers from neighboring congregations, and the colony's governor, John Winthrop, with their concern for unity and order.

At first the authorities tried to reason with Mrs. Hutchinson. But she persisted stubbornly. Gradually, people like Winthrop began to see her as a truly dangerous adversary—"a woman of haughty and fierce carriage, of a nimble wit and active spirit, and a very voluble tongue." Eventually, in November of 1837, she was charged with blasphemy and summoned before the General Court to be tried.

She defended herself skillfully, citing scripture passage for passage against her chief prosecutor, Governor Winthrop. But then she made a fatal error. She admitted that she believed not only that the Holy Spirit dwelt within her, but that she actually experienced mystical revelations. Her fate was sealed, for the doctrine of free grace combined with the idea of personal revelations was too great a threat to social order. Winthrop personally delivered the sentence of the court: "Mrs. Hutchinson, the sentence of the court you hear is that you are banished from out of our jurisdiction as being a woman not fit for our society."

Roger Williams, that other thorn in the side of the Massachusetts establishment, offered Mrs. Hutchinson sanctuary in Rhode Island. She and some of her followers moved there to found the town of Portsmouth. Four years later, after her husband had died, Anne Hutchinson migrated again, to New York, near Pelham Bay. In August of 1643, she and five of her children were killed by Indians—an event hailed by some in Massachusetts as a divine providence.

chusetts charter. The king had no right to give away Indian lands, he said, and the English would never really own their homes and fields until they bought them from the native Americans in fair bargaining.

Such talk threatened the entire basis of the commonwealth: the power of the saints to hold their land and to control the public lives of the nonsaints. Even John Winthrop liked Williams; he was, Winthrop said, "sweet and amiable." But by 1635 the Massachusetts authorities had realized that he was also dangerous, and they decided to send him back to England. Williams, however, sneaked out of Boston during the winter and went to Rhode Island. He bought land from some Narragansett Indians and established the town of Providence in 1636.

Williams was a Puritan. His disagreements with the Massachusetts establishment were caused by his demand that the Puritans' own churches be "purified" further. His principle was that the saintly should worship together, in seclusion from the rest of the world. In fact, later in his life, he reached the point where he could worship comfortably only when he was completely alone. The incidental result was a commitment on the part of Williams to religious "freedom." It ought not to matter, he thought, what the ungodly did. So, at Providence, the rule was that any religious beliefs that did not disturb public order would be allowed. Paradoxically, a piety as deep and demanding as Williams's left the door open to a relaxed diversity.

No sooner had Roger Williams fled to Rhode Island than another dispute erupted in Boston. The cause this time was another gentle and devout person, Anne Hutchinson. She had come to Massachusetts in 1634 with her large family, a 43-year-old woman who was eventually to have fifteen children. Her husband was a well-to-do merchant. To all appearances, she should have been a model citizen. She was a friend of John Cotton and other ministers, and she read the Scriptures avidly.

Like Roger Williams, Anne Hutchinson's problem was that she insisted too much on certain items of the Puritans' own faith. Specifically, she was preoccupied with the idea of people being saved by the free gift of God's grace, without any effort or "exertion" on their part. She began to accuse even ministers like John Cotton of deserting this principle and falling into a gospel of "works." The problem was aggravated by the fact that Anne Hutchinson did not keep her ideas to herself. She began to hold meetings, to examine sermons, and to attract a following that included many of the richest merchants in Boston.

The actual differences in theology between Anne Hutchinson and the Massachusetts establishment were very narrow. They too believed in "free grace." But it was important to them to be able to control social behavior, so they insisted, somewhat illogically, that everyone had obligations to God, even if fulfilling those obligations did not necessarily earn salvation. In a series of meetings with Anne Hutchinson, several ministers tried to get her to see her "errors." She seemed to soften, sometimes, but then harden again.

Finally, the religious leaders declared the problem to be a governmental one, and Anne Hutchinson was brought before Winthrop and some of the other magistrates in Boston for a public trial. There she presented a skillful scriptural defense of her views. She might even have won, had she not lapsed into a dangerous claim. The holy spirit actually dwelt within the heart of a saint, she said, revealing itself directly, not through scripture or miracles, but as a personal revelation.

This was too much. The image of a group of saints running loose, listening to their own private spiritual voices, alarmed men like Winthrop, who were committed above all to order. Mrs. Hutchinson and a number of her supporters were banished in 1637. She found a haven in Providence, and then, with a small group of family and supporters, went on to New York and settled near Pelham Bay. In 1643, she and five of her children were killed by Indians.

Baptists and Quakers The Church of England represented the most conservative wing of the Protestant Reformation in England. Most Puritans were somewhere near the center of the Protestant movement. But there were numerous other sects, most of them small, who wanted reforms that were more radical than most Puritans could accept. The two most important for the New England experience were the Baptists and the Friends, or Quakers.

The issue between Baptists and other Protestants was, as their name suggests, the rite of baptism. Anglicans, like Catholics, baptized the children of church members. Baptists wanted to reserve baptism for adults who had undergone conversion. There should be no halfway members of the church, they argued, no people who had been baptized but not converted. The Baptists, like Roger Williams, also wanted a much clearer separation of church and state than the Puritans practiced. In 1651, three Baptist preachers came into Massachusetts from Rhode Island. They made public attacks on the Puritans' standing order, and for their trouble were arrested and tried. They were found guilty, fined, and ordered to leave the colony. One of them refused to pay the fine, and he was publicly whipped.

The Quakers were even more dangerous. They denied the need for *any* churchly discipline. They insisted that the state had no authority over individual religious beliefs. They even denied the need for ministers and sermons. And, like Anne Hutchinson, they preached that the holy spirit entered the soul of a converted Christian and dwelt there as an "inner light." During the 1650s and 1660s, Quaker missionaries, some of them women, began to come into Massachusetts to challenge the authority of ministers and magistrates. They refused to be silent during sermons and spoke out as they were inspired by their individual inner lights. When ordered to behave, they refused. When arrested and taken before assistants for trial, they would not take oaths and even refused to take off their hats in court. Their obstinacy was met with threats, banishment, imprisonment, and public whippings. As time passed, the punishments became more severe, and eventually the Massachusetts authorities resorted to mutilation. Cutting off an ear was a favorite device. Nothing seemed to work, however. Finally, in 1659, a Quaker named Mary Dyer was sentenced to be hanged. She was freed at the last moment, as she waited at the gallows, and ordered out of Massa-chusetts. But she returned the next year and this time *was* hanged, earning something like a sainthood among her fellow Quakers because of what they called her "double death."

The "witches" of Salem were not dissenters in the normal sense. They were not anything in particular but victims. But they were *seen* as the servants of an alien faith, as an organized group of spiritual servants of the devil. And this was precisely the way the Puritans had looked on Baptists and Quakers. The occasional hanging of a witch was not unusual in Massachusetts—or in England or Virginia, for that matter. What was unusual at Salem was the fear that a large number of people had joined together in an organized conspiracy to undermine the peace and spiritual security of the commonwealth. In that sense, the witchcraft trials represent an extension of the Puritan experience in dealing with dissenters of all sorts—an experience that seems to progress step by step from reprimand and banishment to mutilation and hanging.

Declension   Almost from the beginning, ministers and other leaders would complain from time to time that piety was waning, that the spirit of New England was declining. But after about 1660, this kind of complaint became a steady chorus. Ministers, especially, began to preach over and over again on the ways that New England had faltered, had forgotten its divine errand. God's special care seemed to have been withdrawn from the commonwealth, and new troubles tumbled one after another into the picture.

The ministers had a lot to complain about— or so it seemed to them. New conversions were few. The restoration of the Stuarts in 1660 threatened interference from outside. The invasion of Baptists and Quakers seemed to signal trouble. Even the Indians had become a major source of trouble. In 1675, under the leadership of a chief known as King Philip, they mounted a really serious war against the colonists and destroyed about twenty towns. In the process, they killed off about one white male out of every sixteen. This time, the New Englanders had to use friendly "praying" Indians to help defeat their enemies. And it took three years of dark terror to complete the process—a far cry from the quick, unaided victory of 1637 over the Pequots.

All these specific troubles might have been seen as divine tests designed to strengthen the godly in their faith. However, the real issue was not the troubles themselves but what the ministers and other leaders thought lay behind them. The secret, they thought, was in the growing "worldliness" of the descendants of the founders of the City. Worldliness meant sin, of course, but it meant more. To the Puritans, worldliness had one underlying cause: a concern for the self as against the community. Any sort of self-seeking ambition or individualism was a betrayal of the spiritual welfare of the community. And there were many signs that individualism was gaining the upper hand.

For one thing, as the New England colonies prospered, more and more individuals tried to break out of the communal discipline of their towns and churches. The old practice of clustering a town's houses at its center gradually gave way to the building of farmhouses on the fields of individual families—the pattern displayed in the map of Salem Village on page 88. Carpenters, shoemakers, and other artisans often were restless under the rigid control of wages and prices. Land speculation by individuals developed into a common practice, especially after the reassertion of royal authority that followed the Restoration. Perhaps most important of all, the rise of a merchant class threatened the spiritual integrity that the ministers believed so important.

There was a built-in tension between the desires and practices of merchant capitalism and on the Puritans' concept of a controlled society. Merchant capitalism was a form of individualism; Puritanism was a communal ideology. It was no accident that Anne Hutchinson's supporters were drawn mainly from the ranks of the better-off merchants of Boston, whereas John Winthrop's support came mostly from the farmers of the outlying towns. It was no accident, either, that it was individual merchants who were often severely disciplined by their churches and even by the General Court—for their attempts to get the highest prices the market would bear. As Boston and Salem and other towns along the coast came to have larger and richer classes of merchant-shipowners, it became clear that the old Puritanism would eventu-

This engraving of 1651 is the earliest known view of Manhattan when, as New Amsterdam, it still belonged to the Dutch. In 1664 the English sailed into this harbor, took the fort, and seized the colony, renaming it New York.

ally give way to a new, more relaxed and liberal form of Protestantism with which the new capitalists could feel comfortable.

By the 1690s, this process of accommodation was well under way. But in outlying agricultural communities like Salem Village, the resentment of townsmen and traders was festering just below the surface. One of the most startling facts about the witchcraft episodes of 1692 is that so many of the accused lived near or had strong connections with Salem Town. The afflicted girls had no knowledge of sociology or economic theory. But they did seem to have an instinctive sense that they could tap village resentment of the larger, more progressive, wealthier town. Samuel Parris often preached sermons against "worldliness,"

and no one could doubt that he meant economic self-seeking. He was, after all, a failed merchant himself. In this important sense, the witchcraft hysteria was an episode in the process of "declension"—easily its most violent episode, to be sure, but part of the larger process all the same.

The ministers presented declension as a general social problem. But in a special way, it was their own narrow, professional problem. The question for them was would they be able to maintain their position of profound authority as the colony became more and more "modern" and less and less a series of agrarian villages. In the long run, the answer was no. But the Puritan clergymen and their many supporters did not give up easily. Samuel Parris was an unusual man in a bi-

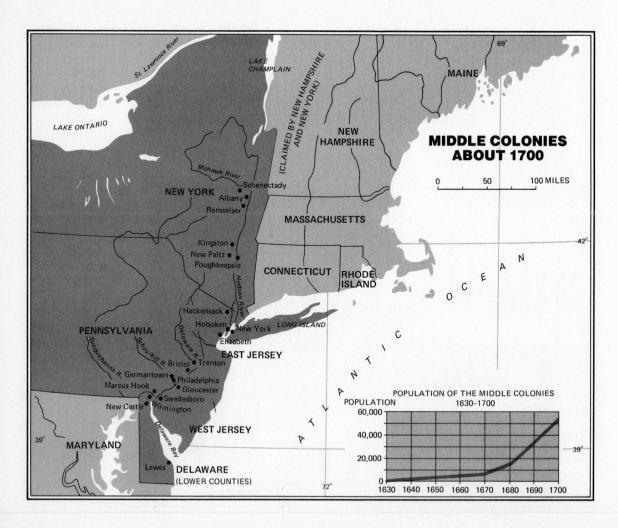

MIDDLE COLONIES ABOUT 1700

0   50   100 MILES

POPULATION OF THE MIDDLE COLONIES 1630–1700

zarre situation. But, in effect, he was able to use the village hysteria for a brief time to assert his authority over the rest of the village.

The irony is, of course, that the key to Parris's efforts were children—his own Betty and the rest of the "afflicted." But even this was not unusual, for the ministers' preoccupation with declension had been focusing attention on New England's children for more than 30 years before 1692.

By the 1660s, it had become clear that many of the children of the first generation settlers were not having their own conversion experiences. They were baptized but not converted. This created a new difficulty when they had children of their own—the grandchildren of the original saints. Could these children be baptized? Theoretically, each congregation could make up its own mind. But the problem was so universal that the ministers of the colony tried to find a common solution. They devised what became known as the Half-Way Covenant of 1662.

The Half-Way Covenant recommended that the churches baptize any child descended from a church member—even a grandparent or great-grandparent. Since there were four grandparents and eight great-grandparents, this meant that almost every infant had some claim to be baptized. The ministers' motives were obvious: They wanted to bring as many people under the umbrella of the church as possible. If they could not do it through conversion, they would accept baptism as a halfway measure. But most of the churches of Massachusetts and Connecticut refused to go along. There was a rift—the first one, really—between the ministers as a group and the churches. And it took thirty more years, until the end of the century, to heal it.

Gradually, reluctantly, the churches gave in, but only after a generation of quarreling. Little wonder that it seemed to the preachers that "the heart of New England is lost, even in New England." To ministers like Cotton Mather it seemed that the Puritans had been able to brave every danger—the wilderness, the Indians, the Church of England, and the king—only to lose out because they could not conquer their own faintness of spirit. To the aging saints in their churches, the solution was not to make membership easier but to hold the line. Only after the 1690s did the min-

---

The land between the Southern colonies and the New England colonies was known as the Middle Colonies. This region early attracted settlers from many different countries in Europe, and from other colonies.

The Dutch staked one of the first claims in the Middle Colonies on the basis of explorations by Henry Hudson in 1609. Dutch merchants established fur trading posts at Fort Orange (Albany), on the Connecticut River, and on the Delaware River. They called the land they claimed New Netherland. Dutch merchants negotiated a famous real estate deal with the Indians. They purchased Manhattan Island for twenty-four dollars' worth of goods, and changed its name to New Amsterdam.

The Dutch were also responsible for the settlement of Delaware. A Dutchman obtained a charter that organized a company headed by Swedes and Dutchmen. Fifty Swedes sailed up the Delaware River in 1638 and established Fort Christina, on the site of present-day Wilmington. Several Finnish families joined them later. The colony was called New Sweden.

In 1655 the Dutch strengthened their hold on this region by seizing Fort Christina. But New Sweden did not remain in Dutch hands long. King Charles II of England did not like having Dutch settlements wedged in between the English colonies. In 1664 he declared that all the territory between the Connecticut and Delaware rivers belonged to this brother James, the Duke of York. The Dutch, realizing they were in no position to fight, surrendered when an English fleet sailed into New Amsterdam. Thus ended Dutch colonial power in mainland America. The new proprietor, the Duke of York, promptly renamed the colony New York.

Included in James' grant was the region of New Jersey, which had been settled by Swedish and Dutch pioneers. James gave the land to two of his friends, Lord John Berkeley and Sir George Carteret. The province was soon divided into East Jersey and West Jersey. In 1702 England claimed all New Jersey as a royal colony. There is still a Board of Proprietors for East Jersey and one for West Jersey.

The most successful of the Middle Colonies was Pennsylvania. William Penn, a Quaker, received the land from Charles II in 1681. He envisioned his colony as a refuge for fellow Quakers. Arriving in Pennsylvania in 1682, he carefully studied his property before selecting the site of Philadelphia. Attracted by the prospect of good land, political liberty, and religious toleration, people flocked to Pennsylvania. By 1700 Philadelphia had 10,000 people. It would eventually outstrip Boston as the largest city in colonial America.

In 1682 Penn convinced the Duke of York to grant him control of the southern portion of the Delaware River. This area, already inhabited by Swedes and Dutch, was known as "the lower counties." It became the colony of Delaware in 1704.

isters win out, but most of the meaning had gone out of their victory. The City upon a Hill had died.

English Dominion No matter how much the ministers might complain about internal spiritual decline, the most serious assault on the City came from the outside. In 1660, the Puritan colonies were the only English settlements north of Virginia. And they were almost free of London's control. Forty years later, there were English colonies all down the coast—in New York, New Jersey, and Pennsylvania. And the royal government had reasserted its authority in ways that staggered the independent New Englanders.

At first, all that the home government tried to do was to control trade with the colonies in a series of laws called Navigation Acts. The first, passed in 1660, closed the colonial trade to all foreign ships—which did not bother New Englanders very much, since their ships qualified as English. But the law also listed certain "enumerated" articles that could be exported from the colonies *only* to England. If enforced, this provision would drastically interfere with the New Englanders' trading patterns with Europe and the West Indies. A second exertion of English power came in 1663, with an act providing that all goods imported into the colonies from any European country had first to be shipped into England and then reexported to America. The third Navigation Act, passed in 1673, imposed taxes (duties) on goods shipped from one colony to another—a serious threat to New England merchants, who carried on a lively trade with the British colonies in the West Indies. This law also provided for customs officers stationed in the colonies to collect the duties—the first royal officials to be stationed in New England, symbols of the power of the Stuart monarchy.

Much more serious and direct, however, was the king's assault on the charter. In 1660, the crown had the right to appoint a governor in only one American colony—Virginia. The first serious signal that all this would change came in 1679, when Charles II denied Massachusetts' claim to New Hampshire and established a separate, royal colony there. Soon after, Charles began the legal proceedings necessary to revoke the Massachu-setts Bay Company's charter. The crown won its case, and in 1684 Massachusetts lost its separate existence as a corporate colony.

One year later, Charles died and James II became king. James was an ardent imperialist, having been heavily involved in taking New Netherlands from the Dutch and turning it into the royal colony of New York just a few years earlier. To the horror of the Puritans in all the New England colonies, he decided to create something called the Dominion of New England, including all the colonies east of New York. As royal governor of the dominion (to which New York and New Jersey were eventually added), James appointed Sir Edmund Andros. Andros was an Anglican, and, having set up his headquarters in Boston, he ordered regular services held for loyal members of the Church of England. He also tried to levy taxes on the colonists and denied their right to legislate freely in the General Court. He even threatened the validity of all the General Court's grants of land to the towns, thus calling into question the right of almost every farmer to his land.

Luckily for New England, James II was overthrown in the bloodless Glorious Revolution of 1688 and replaced by William and Mary, the new monarchs chosen by Parliament. Hearing the news, the citizens of Boston mobbed Andros and threw him into prison. For a brief moment, it looked as though the Lord had intervened. Cotton Mather's father, Increase, was despatched to England to plead for the restoration of the old charter.

Mather failed. The ship that brought him back to Massachusetts in 1692 also brought the new, royally appointed Governor Phips and a new charter declaring Masschusetts a royal colony.

The new charter was better than Andros and the Dominion. It confirmed the powers of the General Court and secured the land titles that derived from the old charter. But William and Mary cut into the heart of the Puritans' commonwealth by replacing the religious qualification for suffrage with the usual English property qualification. No longer could the saints rule their towns without opposition from the unconverted. The new charter also required religious toleration, not only for the Church of England, but for Baptists, Quakers, and others. On paper, at least, Massachusetts could no longer be distinguished from Virginia. Phips began a process of "royalization" in Massachusetts that lasted until the 1760s. And the process succeeded. It had taken the colonists less than a day to carry out the little revolution against Andros. When the next revolutionary movement against England began, in 1765, it took 10 years to reach the point of open resistance to England and a long and difficult war to complete.

Neighbors The Puritans of the 1630s and 1640s had hoped that they could dominate not only New England but perhaps even most of "northern Virginia." Small bands of Puritans had settled on Lond Island and even in Maryland, Virginia, and finally in the Carolinas. But by the 1690s, this hope of expansion was dead. The Puritans had been beaten in England, and they were about to be swallowed up in a burst of English colonization in New York, New Jersey, and Pennsylvania—which soon were being called the "middle colonies." New York was Dutch and Anglican. Pennsylvania had its beginnings as a Quaker colony. New Jersey was a mixture of Swedes, Anglicans, Puritans, and Quakers. But all these colonies had one thing in common: They had no interest in the Puritans' old dream of a City upon a Hill.

The middle colonies came into separate existence as a paper reality in 1664, a few years after the Restoration, when Charles II gave to his brother James, duke of York, all the lands between the Delaware and Connecticut rivers. Since 1609, the area had been claimed by both England and Holland. There were also a few Swedes and Finns settled on the Delaware. But the only important colony was New Netherlands, whose main center was on Manhattan Island, near the mouth of the Hudson. From this center, the Dutch exercised a weak control over the Delaware and competed with English colonists for the Connecticut Valley and Long Island. During the 1650s and 1660s, England and Holland fought a series of wars, and New Netherlands was one of the prizes. The English captured it easily in 1664. The Dutch won it back in 1673. But they lost it again the next year, this time for good.

The duke of York owned New York outright, as a proprietor. But when the duke of York became King James II, New York immediately became "royal." James, however, proceeded cautiously. He recognized the title to their lands of the Dutch colonists, even though some of them owned vast personal estates, some as large as 700,000 acres. Though himself a Catholic, James recognized the fact that New York was peopled by a mixture of Dutch Calvinists, Anglicans, Puritans, and others. To encourage settlement, he decreed religious toleration and issued a Charter of Liberties and Privileges extending limited self-government to the colonists. At first, growth was slow. But by 1685, when New York became a part of the Dominion of New England, about 30,000 colonists lived there. It was clear that the colony would grow quickly and might well surpass Massachusetts as a trading and shipping center.

While still duke of York, James granted New Jersey to two tireless imperialists, Sir George Carteret and Sir John Berkeley, both of whom were also Carolina proprietors. Berkeley, in turn, sold off his half of New Jersey to two wealthy Quakers. The duke, meantime, had given what was to become Delaware to another Quaker, William Penn, in 1682, who was tireless in his attempt to create a haven for Quakers on both sides of the Delaware River.

Like the Calverts, Penn belonged to a religious minority that was often harassed. But, again like the Calverts, he belonged also to a distinguished family that often benefited from royal whims. Penn's father, Sir William, was an admiral and a great landholder in Ireland. Before his conversion to Quakerism, Penn himself had been educated as a typical landed gentleman. But from the time of his conversion he was an active and controversial promoter of the Quaker cause—even if he sometimes had to promote it from within prison.

Charles II was indebted to Admiral Sir William Penn, both financially and as an ally in the quest for the restoration of the crown. When Sir William forgave his son for becoming a Quaker, William Penn inherited the debt, and Charles II found it easier to pay off in land than in cash. He granted Penn the land west of the Delaware River

William Penn, the Quaker who founded Pennsylvania, maintained excellent relations with the Indians. This romanticized painting by Benjamin West portrays Penn (center) signing a treaty with the Delawares in 1682.

in 1681. The duke of York had cooperated by tossing Delaware colony into the bargain in 1682. And, in the same year, Penn and some fellow Quakers succeeded in buying the remaining half of New Jersey. A cluster of Quaker colonies had been inserted between New York and the Chesapeake colonies.

Penn took Pennsylvania (it had been named by Charles II in honor of the old admiral, not the Quaker son) seriously. He came to the colony in 1682 and personally laid out the plan for Philadelphia. He was as much a utopian as the Puritans (the name Philadelphia means "City of Brotherly Love"). But, like other Quakers, he did not believe the state should interfere in religion. So he drew up a tolerant Frame of Government that guaranteed a measure of self-government and religious freedom.

Like Roger Williams, Penn also took the Indians seriously, and he bargained fairly (though always successfully) with them for land. As a result, during his lifetime at least, the colony enjoyed a unique immunity from Indian troubles.

The Quaker colonies easily absorbed the Finns and Swedes already settled in the Delaware Valley. They absorbed the equally large number of Puritans who had settled in New Jersey. Within 15 years, Philadelphia had grown to a city of 10,000 people, and a shrewd observer might already have guessed that in the space of a lifetime it would surpass Boston as the largest and most successful American city.

SUGGESTED READINGS-CHAPTERS 5-6

Salem Witchcraft

Paul Boyer and Stephen Nissenbaum, *Salem Possessed: The Social Origins of Witchcraft* (1974); Marion L. Starkey, *The Devil in Massachusetts* (1949); David Levin, *What Happened in Salem?* (1960); Paul Boyer and Stephen Nissenbaum, *Salem-Village Witchcraft: A Documentary History of Local Conflict in Colonial New England* (1972).

Puritanism

Alan Simpson, *Puritanism in Old and New England* (1955); Edmund S. Morgan, *The Puritan Dilemma* (1958); Perry Miller, *Orthodoxy in Massachusetts* (1959), *The New England Mind: The Seventeenth Century* (1954), *The New England Mind: From Colony to Province* (1953), and *Errand into the Wilderness* (1956); Charles Grant, *Democracy in the Connecticut Frontier Town of Kent* (1961); Sumner C. Powell, *Puritan Village* (1963); John Demos, *The Little Commonwealth* (1965); Michael Zuckerman, *Peaceable Kingdoms: New England Towns in the Eighteenth Century* (1970); S. H. Brockunier, *The Irrepressible Democrat: Roger Williams* (1940); Emery Battis, *Saints and Sectaries: Anne Hutchinson and the Antinomian Controversy in the Massachusetts Bay Colony* (1962).

UNIT TWO
REVOLUTIONARY AMERICA

The British colonies in North America at the time of Bacon's Rebellion and the Salem trials had been little more than a series of isolated settlements scattered along the eastern coast. The planters of Virginia and the Puritans of Massachusetts, like other early colonists, were still basically Europeans. They continued to identify with the European concepts of home, family, culture, and government. Royal authority remained almost unchallenged, and when social crises occurred, more often than not, they were resolved by the exercise of British power. Thus Governor Berkeley in Virginia, backed by English soldiers, put an end to Bacon's rebels, and in similar fashion, Governor Phips in Massachusetts clamped a final lid on the Salem hysteria.

By the mid-eighteenth century, two generations after the fateful events described in the previous episodes, all this had changed. With remarkable speed, the British colonists and other settlers in English North America had created a distinctly new and American society. From Georgia to Maine, the settlement line was almost solid, as population expanded along with agriculture and commerce. Cities like Boston, Philadelphia, and New York became almost as large and as wealthy as many European urban centers.

Culturally, the new society remained mostly British, while it absorbed large clusters of German, Dutch, and Swedish immigrants (among others) who settled along the seaboard. But as it grew, British North America became increasingly conscious of its identity and style as distinctly American rather than English. The events that moved the thirteen colonies toward their fateful decision to break with England in the mid-1770s came at the end of two decades during which a multiplicity of actions had engraved American patterns of family life, religious and cultural values, economic behavior, and—most importantly—political autonomy upon the older British fabric of this society. The chapters

CHAPTER 7
THE BOSTON MASSACRE

CHAPTER 8
THE COMING OF INDEPENDENCE

CHAPTER 9
GEORGE WASHINGTON AND THE TRANSITION
  TO NATIONHOOD

CHAPTER 10
CREATING A NEW GOVERNMENT

that follow describe this process of "Americanization," the political strife that ensued from it, and the creation of a new nation from the turmoil of revolution.

Chapter 7 describes the background and drama of that March 5, 1770 event that occurred in Boston when a squad of British soldiers fired their weapons into a noisy and threatening crowd of Bostonians. One of a series of such conflicts that grew during the 1760s and 1770s between the American colonies and British authorities, the Boston Massacre symbolized the evolving separation of mother country and colonies. Chapter 8 details the chain of events leading to American independence.

But the winning of independence and the creation of a loosely-connected confederation of thirteen distinct "nation-states" proved only the first part in a two-phase drama of nation building. To the surprise of many, including a number of their own leaders and citizens, the Americans managed to win the Revolutionary War. The hero of that war, General George Washington, retired to his Virginia plantation after directing American military efforts. Soon, he and many of his revolutionary associates came to believe that the new government they had brought into existence had not succeeded in consolidating the political society for which they had fought. After long and thoughtful deliberation, Washington concluded that the Confederation had to be replaced. The slow, painful, and concrete process by which Washington—and, by extension, other revolutionary leaders—reached this conclusion forms the subject of Chapter 9. The creation of a new constitution and frame of government for the United States of America is described in Chapter 10. Having entered the eighteenth century a small, weak, European, and divided people, Americans began their first century as an independent people in 1800 with a host of problems but, also, with resources as a new country born of their three-decade long struggle for survival, independence, and nationhood.

7 THE BOSTON MASSACRE

A. W.

Some called the eleven-year-old boy Christopher Seider, others, Christian Snider. Whatever his real name, Christopher Seider (let us call him that) stood in a crowd outside Ebenezer Richardson's home in Boston's North End on the windy morning of February 22, 1770. Seider was one of several hundred Bostonians gathered there, many of them youngsters like himself. They had penned Richardson and his family inside, and now they pelted the house with eggs, fruit peelings, sticks, and stones. The crowd broke most of the house's glass windowpanes. One rock struck Richardson's wife. Others barely missed his two daughters. Richardson took an unloaded musket to the window and aimed it at the mob outside. The crowd broke down his front door, but continued to stand outside— probably because of its healthy respect for the gun—and bombard the house with stones.

Richardson then loaded his musket with small birdshot pellets. He fired and hit several members of the crowd, some of whom were injured slightly. Christopher Seider, less fortunate than others, fell to the ground with eleven pellets in his chest and abdomen. He died that evening.

The angry crowd surged into the house after the boy fell. It cornered Richardson, who surrendered without further resistance. The mob prepared to lynch Richardson, and doubtless would have except for the timely appearance of William Molineux, one of Boston's leading "radical" opponents of British authority. Molineux persuaded the angry crowd to turn Richardson over to the law officials. Within the hour Richardson appeared before four justices of the peace and a thousand onlookers in Faneuil Hall. Witnesses were heard at the open hearing, and Richarson was held in jail until the next session of the Massachusetts Superior Court, charged with "giving Christopher Seider a very dangerous wound." After Seider died, the charge became murder.

Before his death Seider had been unknown to most of Boston's 16,000 residents. On February 26, however, he received the "largest funeral perhaps ever known in America" up to that time. Several thousand Bostonians braved snow-clogged streets to pay tribute to his memory. The funeral was organized by one of Boston's leading radicals, Samuel Adams, a lawyer and former town official with a reputation as an effective political agitator.

Seider's death provided Adams, and the cause of colonial resistance, with a ready-made juvenile martyr to British "tyranny." It was disclosed that Richardson had served in previous years as an informer for the British customs commissioners. These commissioners had been sent to Boston in 1767 to collect duties on colonial imports set by Parliament in the Townshend Acts.

A few days later, after Christopher Seider's death, Boston's townspeople poured into the streets again, this time not as a mob but as a funeral procession. The following opinion appeared in the *Gazette*, the unofficial newspaper of the Sons of Liberty: "Young as he was, [Seider] died in his Country's Cause, by the Hand of an execrable Villain, directed by others, who could not bear to see the enemies of America made the Ridicule of Boys."

Boston merchants, along with merchant groups throughout the North American colonies of Great Britain,[1] viewed the taxes imposed upon them by Parliament as both unfair and illegal. In an attempt to force Parliament to repeal the Townshend Acts, they organized a boycott of all British manufactured goods, which was referred to as the nonimportation agreement. Those merchants and other colonists who protested against the taxes levied upon them by the king and Parliament came to be known as Whigs (a term used earlier for *English* opponents of royal tyranny) or Patriots; the more militant among them organized themselves into the Sons of Liberty. Their opponents, those colonists who believed Great Britain did have the right to tax them, were known as Loyalists or Tories.

After passage of the Townshend Acts, increasingly large and unruly crowds of Patriots began to roam the streets of Boston at night, intimidating Tories or crown officials with threats of violence—and with violence itself. British officials claimed that such mobs were directed by radical leaders like Samuel Adams and William Molineux, and some of them were. On occasion, a town meeting[2] could transform itself into a mob simply by moving from its usual meeting place in Faneuil Hall into the streets, where it had been summoned to help enforce the decisions of the town leaders, most of whom were Patriots. Crowds like these often included the city's most respectable merchants and politicians. Mobs also gathered spontaneously, their numbers swelled by the presence in

---

[1]In 1707 England was united with Scotland. After this date the governmental unit as a whole is usually referred to as Great Britain. Its overseas possessions together became known as the British Empire.
[2]Boston was governed by a town meeting consisting mostly of voters. It met whenever the need arose. It could bring as many as 3,000 people together for several days running.

that port city of sailors, itinerant workers and artisans, jobless teenagers, and local bullyboys. More often than not, the more spontaneous crowds were dominated by those with powerful lungs or muscles. The mob that stormed Ebenezer Richardson's house had gathered in this spontaneous fashion. They were reacting to Richardson's attempt, that same night, to keep another, more organized mob from interfering with a merchant who was reported to be violating the nonimportation agreement.

During the two years preceding this incident, the Patriots and the colony's royal government had struggled bitterly to control Boston's economic and political life. Patriots like Samuel Adams used the easily aroused mobs to pressure even Tory merchants into endorsing the non-importation agreement. The royal governor of Massachusetts, Francis Bernard, troubled by the Patriots' effective economic boycott and their control of the city's streets, encouraged the British Army Commander in North America, Major General Thomas Gage, to send troops from the large garrison at Halifax, Nova Scotia, to help restore the authority of the crown in Boston. But Bernard himself could not directly request troops. He had first to secure the consent of the Governor's Council, the upper house of the Massachusetts legislature. This council, which was elected by the citizens, generally sided with the opponents of British taxation and control. Bernard outlined his dilemma, one shared in some measure by most royal governors in the American mainland colonies, in a letter written in July 1768 to an official in Great Britain:

> General Gage has now informed me that his orders to Halifax are that the Troops shall be collected & kept in readiness, but are not to move till I require them. I answer that then they will never move: for I shall not make such a requisition without the Advice of Council; & I never expect to obtain that: neither their popular Constitution nor the present intimidation will permit it. . . . In short, my Lord, Troops are not wanted here to quell a Riot or a Tumult, but to rescue the Government out of the hands of a trained mob & to restore the activity of the Civil Power, which is now entirely obstructed. And if an open Defiance of the Authority of Great Britain: a persecution of all those who are supposed to be maintainers of that authority . . . are not sufficient to show the Expedience of quartering Troops at Boston, we must wait till it becomes more apparent.

But if Bernard could not order troops, the authorities in London could. In October 1768 Boston witnessed the arrival of the first redcoats from the two regiments to be stationed there—the Fourteenth and the Twenty-ninth. After a lengthy struggle with Boston's local officials to secure adequate quarters for the soldiers (one regiment spent its first night in Faneuil Hall), the troops began regular patrols. Overnight, Boston became a garrisoned town; the center of colonial opposition to parliamentary and royal authority had been "occupied." But the presence of troops failed to check the townspeople's "mobbish disposition"; it succeeded only in helping to unify the various local factions that opposed British attempts to tax and govern. Before the soldiers came, these factions had few visible symbols of British authority to complain about. Neither the ineffective Governor Bernard, nor the talented but unpopular Lieutenant Governor Thomas Hutchinson—not even the customs commissioners themselves—had rallied patriotic sentiment among the people as intensely as did the presence of the British troops, whose numbers ranged from 600 to 1,000 men. In the months between the arrival of the troops and the death of Christopher Seider, tempers flared frequently on both sides.

During these months the troops controlled their sentry posts. The Patriots controlled the merchants and the town meeting. Crown officials controlled Boston by day. The mobs, when they appeared, controlled the streets at night. The royal governor controlled only his temper. He resigned in 1770 in favor of Thomas Hutchinson, who became lieutenant governor. As far as anyone could judge, however, none of the authorities controlled Boston itself with any certainty. Both royal officials and Patriot leaders freely predicted that any major incident could trigger an open rebellion against British authority in that edgy community.

Relations between Bostonians and the British troops were sometimes friendly, sometimes hostile. Two groups among the unwanted soldiers made them even less welcome than they would otherwise have been. These were the many Irish Catholics, whose presence offended the town's Protestant citizens, and the number of black troops, an affront to those Bostonians who kept black slaves or servants.

Any occupying army, of course, must expect hostility from those whose territory it controls. The British army was no exception. From the moment the troops arrived, the town's Patriot newspapers filled their columns with accounts of friction involving townspeople.

British soldiers disembark at Boston's Long Wharf in October 1768. According to engraver Revere's caption, the troops then marched up King Street "with insolent parade."

Thomas Hutchinson, a loyal servant of the crown, moved to England in 1774 and never returned to America. But he loved Boston and was homesick for it until he died in 1780.

There were numerous fights (always begun by the soldiers, according to townspeople), many minor acts of harassment, and endless arguments as the redcoats attempted to patrol the community. Soldiers who looked for quarters in the town for their families were overcharged shamelessly, if they managed to secure quarters at all, and few Boston merchants resisted the temptation to raise their normal prices for these unwanted British customers. But what proved particularly galling to the troops and their officers was not the understandable bitterness of private citizens, it was the crippling hostility of public officials, especially the magistrates of Boston's court system. For example, sentries who were instructed to challenge passers-by at fixed guard posts throughout Boston, especially after dark, found that civilians could and often did swear out warrants against the sentries themselves for disturbing the peace! The civil magistrates generally fined harshly any soldiers on guard duty whom townspeople accused of rude behavior. "We are in a pleasing Situation," wrote one British officer, "who are ordered here to Aid & assist the Civil Magistrate in preserving the peace & protecting his Majesty's subjects, when those very magistrates are our Oppressors." Ordinary soldiers complained about unfair treatment at the hands of American justices of the peace with the same kind of outrage voiced by colonial merchants at their treatment by British customs commissioners. Each side believed that justice could never be secured in the other's courts, and there was much truth to these notions.

By late 1769 it had become clear that both the Townshend Acts and the dispatch of troops to Boston had failed to enforce British taxation. The struggle to assert royal authority in Boston had ended in a political stalemate between crown officials and the city's Patriot leadership — neither the troops nor the mobs managed to control the streets unopposed. Bernard and Hutchinson were reluctant to risk a general uprising by trying to enforce the customs laws, which merchant signers of the nonimportation agreement continued to ignore. Samuel Adams and his fellow radical Patriots, for their part, proved equally reluctant to provoke outright rebellion against all British authority. However, British officials and most American Tories believed that the Patriots wanted not only to abolish the onerous customs duties but to end British rule entirely. They viewed the Patriots, in General Gage's words, as "an illegal combination of people" conspiring to stir popular feeling against Britain as a first step along the road to revolution. The Patriots, for their part, did not consider themselves conspirators. But they did view the British authorities and Tories in this light — as schemers trying to deprive provincial America both of its traditional liberties and of its hard-earned income. "There was a cursed cabal [group of plotters], principally residing in this town," Samuel Adams wrote in 1769 of Boston's Loyalists, "who . . . were perpetually intriguing to bring about another parliamentary tax act; for no other purpose than that they might feast and fatten themselves upon the spoils and plunder of the people." Adams added:

One man has as good reason to affirm that a few, in calling for a military force under pretense of supporting civil authority, secretly intended to introduce a general massacre, as another has to assert, that a number of loyal subjects, by calling upon one another to be provided with arms, according to law, intended to bring on an insurrection.

Although Adams argues the existence of a British-Tory conspiracy in this passage, he also acknowledges his opponents' belief in a comparable Bostonian plot against British rule. That the 600 harassed British soldiers who occupied Boston in early 1770 "secretly intended to introduce a general massacre" against Boston's 16,000 residents may seem improbable today. But at the time many Bostonians believed it, and they acted accordingly. Tensions ran high in the early months of 1770. Each group feared an attack that it believed its opponents had plotted well in advance. More often than not, however, the violence that actually flared up was unplanned and disorganized.

The British troops recognized by 1770 that their role in Boston had little to commend it. The job was lonely. The soldiers were shunned by the town's Patriot majority, abused in the courts, challenged boldly on the streets, and threatened regularly by mobs. Further, their wages were small. Many soldiers braved local hostility and sought jobs during their off-duty hours. Unfortunately, there were few part-time jobs available in Boston; there had been a grave depression in local commerce because of the enforcement of the nonimportation agreement. Bostonians were worried about their own unemployed, whose numbers increased daily. Competition between off-duty soldiers and unemployed townsmen for the few available jobs provoked a number of noisy arguments and minor fights.

One such incident took place on March 2, 1770, only four days after Christopher Seider's funeral. With emotions still running high in the town, this minor battle brought Bostonians and redcoats to the brink of major civil conflict. The trouble began at John Gray's "ropewalk,"[3] a large plant where a number of workers produced rope and cable. Temporary laborers' jobs were often available there. These attracted unemployed townspeople and British troops, who frequently needed extra money. On this particular day a British soldier named Thomas Walker of the Twenty-ninth Regiment entered the plant and asked for work. Ropemaker William Green, a Bostonian, asked him: "Soldier, do you want work?" "Yes, I do," replied Walker. Green responded with an amused smirk, "Well, then go and clean my outhouse." The other ropemakers roared with laughter, but Walker's face turned red with fury. "Empty it yourself!" he shouted at Green. After the pair exchangèd hard words for a moment longer, the fight began.

The ropemakers pounced on Walker and pummeled the unfortunate soldier badly before he managed to get away. He returned shortly with eight or nine other redcoats, and the slugfest resumed. Both sides fought mainly with wooden clubs, although the soldiers also slashed

---

[3]At this time rope was made in a long, low building. A ropemaker walked backward from one end to the other, paying out fiber from a bundle at his waist and braiding it as he walked.

away at times with their swords. The Bostonians managed to chase Walker and his cohorts from the ropeworks, but the soldiers returned within minutes, bringing with them nearly thirty reinforcements. But the number of civilians had also grown. Soon Gray's ropewalk was jammed with troops and ropeworkers, cracking their clubs against all comers. Both sides suffered casualties, some quite severe, until the soldiers were once more driven from the factory.

The following day, Saturday, March 3, a trio of redcoats returned to the ropewalk, where they renewed the battle against workers on the scene. This time, one of the soldiers suffered a fractured skull and arm before he and his friends withdrew. Sunday, March 4, seemed more peaceful, although a group of British officers visited the ropewalk searching for a missing British sergeant, whose comrades had reported him killed by the townspeople.

Although the sergeant's body was never found, rumors spread among the troops that the Bostonians planned some larger dramatic gesture of revenge against the British soldiers. One private "remembered some ropemakers asking where the Twenty-ninth [Regiment] planned to bury its dead." A Bostonian later swore that he heard four soldiers from the regiment say that "there were a great many townspeople who would eat their dinners on Monday next [March 5], who would not eat any on Tuesday."

The day of Monday, March 5, passed without incident. A foot of snow covered the ground. Bostonians who braved the cold, windswept city walked cautiously over the ice sheets that covered most of the streets. Boston had no street lamps then. As darkness fell, people had only a first-quarter moon to light their way. Snow covered King Street, where stood both the Custom House and the Main Guard, British army headquarters.

No one in Boston knew that in London, earlier in the day, the British Parliament had repealed most of the controversial Townshend Acts (all but the one on tea). This was a stunning victory for colonial protesters. The news of the repeal, though, reached Boston only in late April. And by that time Bostonians were preoccupied with the events that took place on King Street on the bitter cold evening of March 5. It was then that the fragile structure of civic peace in Boston finally collapsed.

The incident began as had similar ones in the past—with a soldier, a sharp-tongued young Bostonian, and a fight. The soldier, Private Hugh White of the Twenty-ninth Regiment, was on guard duty at a sentry box on the corner of King Street and Shrimton's Lane, down the street from both the Main Guard and the Custom House. Along came a young wigmaker's apprentice named Edward Garrick. Garrick spotted a British officer named Goldfinch, and shouted within earshot of Private White: "There goes the fellow that won't pay my master for dressing his hair." Joined by another apprentice, Garrick strolled through the King Street area, later returning to White's sentry post, where he resumed his criticism of Captain Goldfinch. At this point, Private White defended the officer as a gentleman who would pay all his debts. "There are no gentlemen in the 29th Regiment," shouted Garrick, whereupon White left his post and joined Garrick in the street.

"Let me see your face," ordered White. Garrick obliged, and White immediately smashed his musket into the young wigmaker's head. Garrick cried out in pain, and his companion began exchanging curses with the angry sentry. Within minutes a crowd of some fifty townspeople had gathered in the street, surrounding the lone sentry, shouting at him to stand and fight them. White loaded his musket, retreated down the block to the steps of the Custom House, fixed his bayonet, and faced the angry crowd.

The mob began throwing large chunks of ice at White, screaming as they flung the missiles: "Kill him, kill him, knock him down. Fire, damn you, fire, you dare not fire." The town watchman suddenly appeared on the scene and urged the sentry to restrain himself, pleading that most people in the mob were youths who would not hurt him. As the crowd continued nevertheless to pelt him with ice, White responded: "Damn them; if they molest me I will fire." Finally, he shouted for assistance from the nearby regimental headquarters: "Turn out, Main Guard!"

Meanwhile, similar mobs had gathered elsewhere in Boston. Just a few blocks from King Street, soldiers strolled along Brattle Street carrying clubs, bayonets, and other weapons, while a solitary Bostonian ran up and down the immediate area shouting the usual call for a mob to gather: "Town born, turn out! Town born, turn out!" A crowd collected quickly at a regimental encampment called Murray's Barracks near Brattle Street. Soon volleys of snowballs hurled at the soldiers accompanied the shouts of bystanders. Several British officers, including Captain Goldfinch, ordered the soldiers back into the barracks to forestall bloodshed. More than once, officers knocked their own troops to the ground to prevent them from shooting into the onrushing crowd.

Another throng gathered in Dock Square, only two blocks from Private White's sentry post on King Street. Several hundred townspeople poured into the empty stalls of Boston's town market. They ripped the legs off produce and butcher tables and shouted "Fire!" to attract additional recruits from the neighborhood.

The cry of "Fire!" repeated endlessly through the dark Boston streets attracted a number of sleepy townspeople. Boston depended on volunteer firefighting companies. So groups of such firefighters carrying buckets joined the three separate crowds of agitated Bostonians spoiling for a fight with the soldiers. At some point, church bells began tolling an additional call for firefighters.

Bostonians of all ages converged on King Street—some with buckets, others with sticks. Many ran from the Dock Square and Murray's Barracks fracases once those incidents had quieted down. The crowd in King Street varied in size from several dozen to several hundred over the next hour, as men and boys moved along the town's cramped lanes and alleys. "There is no fire," shouted one youth to a bystander. "It is the soldiers fighting." "Damn it, I am glad of it," came the response. "I will knock some of them on the head." A number of Bostonians left the sidewalks to join the unruly scene in the streets.

The mob that gathered in King Street surrounded White's sentry post but made no immediate attempt to overwhelm him. Meanwhile, the British officer of the guard that evening, Captain Thomas Preston, had been summoned from his dinner table by White's urgent request for reinforcements. He went to the Main Guard on King Street, and he surveyed the crowd. By now it had grown to at least several hundred (accurate estimates were difficult). After deciding to help the beleaguered White, Preston ordered up a relief party of sentries—six privates and a corporal. This group then marched toward the menacing crowd, their muskets empty and shouldered but their bayonets fixed.

Preston's few soldiers managed to push through the crowd, loading their muskets after reaching White's empty sentry box. White still confronted the large throng from a position on the Custom House steps. At Preston's orders and without interference from the bystanders, he joined the other soldiers.

Preston had ordered the sentries out primarily to relieve White. Having done so, the captain tried to march his soldiers back toward the Main Guard. The surrounding mob either would not or could not allow the troops through, so great was the press of bodies. Some people in the throng began shouting at the redcoats: "Damn you, fire. You can't kill us all." Within moments Preston found himself and his men cut off from assistance. He ordered his soldiers to form a curved line with their backs to the Custom House. Although they tried to keep the crowd from encircling them, some Bostonians managed to slip behind the soldiers.

The crowd, obviously leaderless, shuffled angrily yet uneasily around the nervous redcoats, uncertain whether to attack or withdraw. To add to the confusion, the church bells kept tolling. Every few moments, more bucket-carrying Bostonians arrived at the scene. Many exchanged their buckets quickly for clubs or ice chunks when they understood the situation. Preston shouted for the crowd to disperse, but received in return only laughter, hooting, and a pelting with snowballs. The crowd taunted the soldiers to shoot, and the small company of British troops clenched their weapons tightly.

The only town official to brave the mob scene was one James Murray, a Tory justice of the peace, who arrived at King Street to read the Riot Act. By law, the statute forbidding riotous gatherings had to be read to a mob before it took effect. The crowd knew this. They knew, therefore, that Preston and his men would be on questionable legal ground if they fired without having first ordered the mob to disperse by a reading of the Riot Act.

The mob wanted to prevent the reading . A volley of snowballs and ice chunks soon sent Murray scurrying toward safety. The mob's anger increased when some of its members recognized at least two of the sentries, Privates Matthew Kilroy and William Warren, as participants in the battle at the ropewalk four days earlier. At the same time, Private White himself spotted a familiar face in the crowd, a young woman named Jane Whitehouse, whose home was near his own Boston living quarters. "Go home," he cried, taking her arm and pushing her toward the corner. "Go home, or you'll be killed."

The mob soon abandoned all restraint short of directly assaulting the soldiers. Individuals began pushing forcefully against Preston's troops, daring them to fire, denouncing them as cowards and scoundrels, challenging them to fistfights. "Why do you not fire? Damn you, you dare not fire. Fire and be damned," they continued to shout. There were small duels, as townsmen carrying clubs beat them against the guardsmen's musket barrels and bayonets. Preston continued to shout demands that the crowd disperse, at the same time restraining his frightened band of soldiers from opening fire. Several times the captain was approached by Patriot leaders in the crowd who asked whether he intended to fire. Each time he responded, "By no means, by no means."

A Tory dignitary urged the captain to disperse the unruly rioters with a warning volley of musket shot. At this, stressing his desire to prevent bloodshed, Preston placed himself directly in front of the muskets so that he would be the first victim of any shooting. The crowd cheered at Preston's predicament, which at the moment seemed an almost perfect reflection of the overall British situation in Boston—the inability to either maintain public order or withdraw gracefully.

No more than a foot or two separated the line of soldiers from the nearest rioters. Suddenly a club went sailing from the midst of the crowd into the dimly lit street, hitting Private Hugh Montgomery. The private fell to the ground and dropped his musket on the ice. No one knows what triggered that particular act of violence, or what emotions Private Montgomery felt as he staggered to his feet and recovered his musket. However, matters were at the breaking point. Montgomery shouted, "Damn you, fire," and proceeded to pull his trigger. Within seconds, members of the crowd lunged at Preston and his troops, swinging their clubs wildly. The soldiers managed to fight off these blows, but in an interval of from fifteen seconds to two minutes (the exact time remains unclear), the other troops also fired their weapons.

Preston neither ordered the shooting, nor did he—stunned at Montgomery's impulsive action—order it to stop. When the shooting stopped, the crowd continued to advance on the small group of soldiers, although few people got close enough to swing their clubs. The soldiers parried blows while reloading their muskets. They fired another round. Again the firing took place sporadically, with single shots being fired over a period of minutes. This time, several people in the crowd were wounded, and some fell to the ground. Finally, the crowd began to disperse, although it regrouped quickly when the firing had stopped, this time to recover the bodies of those who lay dead or wounded. The soldiers, fearing another attack, raised their muskets to fire a third round. By now, Preston had regained his composure and personally shoved down his soldiers' gun barrels before they could shoot, shouting, "Stop firing! Do not fire!"

The mob drew back for the moment, carrying the bodies of those hit by the troops. Preston's soldiers began to explain to their agitated captain that they had fired after hearing what they believed to be *his* command. While emergency hospitals for the wounded were being set up in nearby homes, Preston marched his company back to the Main Guard. He then turned out the entire guard and placed it in formation on King Street between the Main Guard and Boston's Town House (the Old State House). The troops were drawn up in street-firing position, an eighteenth-century tactic for controlling urban riots in narrow streets. Rows of soldiers stood in single-file formation. The man at the head of the line would shoot, then move to the back of the line. There he reloaded and waited his turn to shoot once more.

In front of the Custom House, small groups of Bostonians passed grimly along King Street and stared at the bloodstains splattered on the

A plan of the scene of the Boston Massacre was drawn by Paul Revere for use at the trial of Preston's men. More accurate than his engraving of the event, it shows the location of the chief buildings nearby and the places where four of the dead fell.

icy thoroughfare. Word had spread quickly through town that, as a result of the shooting, five men lay dead or dying. Among the dead was one who would soon become the most famous martyr of the evening's bloodshed, Crispus Attucks. (Accounts differ as to whether he was a free black, a runaway slave, or an Indian of the Natick tribe.) Four others also died—an Irish Catholic immigrant named Patrick Carr; Samuel Gray, the son of the ropewalk owner; seventeen-year-old Samuel Maverick; and a young apprentice sailor named James Caldwell.

The withdrawal of Preston's men did not dispel the threat of further bloodshed that very night, as angry Bostonians filled the streets, hurling curses at the British troops and crying "To arms!" Every church

Although only a mediocre artist, Paul Revere was a fine silversmith in addition to being an ardent Patriot. As a skilled craftsman, he cast cannon for the army, printed the first Continental money, and designed the state seal still used by Massachusetts.

bell in Boston began pealing. Even the town's official drums—which generally summoned the militia to combat—beat solemnly to announce the tragedy. Within an hour after the so-called massacre itself, more than a thousand citizens crowded King Street. Rumors spread quickly among the townspeople that the soldiers planned a wholesale slaughter of the inhabitants. Local Tories were attacked and beaten in the streets. British officers and soldiers also found it dangerous to walk through Boston without armed escorts that night.

Moderate Patriot leaders pleaded with Lieutenant Governor Hutchinson, the leading civil official in town, to remove Preston's troops from King Street before their presence provoked further retaliation from the crowd. Hutchinson approached the troops and exchanged some harsh words with Preston. But he declined to order the soldiers back to quarters. Instead, he addressed the people from a balcony of the Town House. He urged them to retire peacefully, promising that he would do everything possible to ensure a full inquiry into the shooting. "The law shall have its course," he shouted. "I will live and die by the law." Apparently, this was also the view of the many Bostonians in the crowd who left quietly. Hundreds remained, however. They demanded both immediate action against the British soldiers and removal of the troops from Boston's streets. Preston's superior officer, Lieutenant Colonel Maurice Carr, feared a renewed confrontation between the crowd and the troops. He ordered the soldiers on King Street to abandon street-firing formation and return to their barracks. As the troops marched off, the crowd—now silent and somber—dispersed.

At 2 A.M. on March 6 the town sheriff served a warrant on Captain Preston for his role in the episode. Preston surrendered an hour later. A few hours afterward, the eight redcoats in Preston's sentry party were also imprisoned. All nine were charged with murder.

After the arrest of Preston and his men, Boston drew back from the brink of civil disorder. Hutchinson and Carr were not the only ones who feared a bloodbath. Most responsible Patriot leaders shared their anxieties. They believed that the continued presence of troops among angry townspeople would only provoke violence on an uncontrollable scale. So they urged the removal of British troops from the town itself to Castle William, an island fort in Boston harbor.

Bostonians were still outraged over the massacre. At a town meeting on March 6, which was dominated by Samuel Adams and other Patriots, the people demanded removal of the British troops. Hutchinson tried to compromise between his loyalty to the crown and his recognition of the town's anger. He ordered only Preston's regiment, the Twenty-ninth, to Castle William.

The town meeting remained dissatisfied. On March 10 it sent a committee led by Samuel Adams to see Hutchinson. The group demanded that the remaining British regiment be ordered out of town. Hutchinson and his advisers had no choice but to submit. They ordered the Fourteenth Regiment, the last British troops in Boston, to depart the following day for Castle William. Boston now returned to the control of its own, Patriot-dominated town meeting. The remaining royal dignitaries—Hutchinson, the customs commissioners, and lesser officials—could not direct the course of events without assistance from troops. The Patriots had no further need for nightly mobs to confront crown authority. Thus the immediate threat of civil disorder ended.

With the troops gone from Boston, the Patriots turned their attention to settling accounts with the imprisoned soldiers. On March 12 the *Gazette* employed the term "massacre" in connection with the events of March 5. This was the first public use of the term. A week later, on March 19, Boston's town meeting approved printing a version of the events that justified the behavior of the rioters and condemned the British soldiers. Entitled *A Short History of the Horrid Massacre at Boston*, the pamphlet was dispatched on fast ships to England to soften British anger at the Bostonians' conduct toward the troops. The Patriots decided not to distribute the pamphlet in Boston itself, lest it prejudice the soldiers' trials.

Also on March 19, the town meeting petitioned Hutchinson for an early trial of the prisoners. The lieutenant governor and other Loyalists resisted, considering the aroused state of emotions in Boston regarding Preston and his men. "I have assurances from the court," Preston wrote General Gage on April 1, "that they will continue [postpone] the trial . . . until the last week in May [although] great pain is being taken to intimidate the judges and compel them to bring it on sooner." Hutchinson's concern for a fair trial seemed even more understandable after the conclusion of Ebenezer Richardson's trial. On April 21 a Boston jury found Richardson guilty of the murder of Christopher Seider. They did so despite the judge's instruction from the bench that Richardson had clearly committed justifiable homicide in self-defense.

Soon after the massacre, both Tories and Patriots began arguing that the incident had been part of a prearranged scheme of wholesale murder on the part of their opponents. Such assertions appeared in versions of the incident prepared by the British military authorities and in the town meeting's *Short History*. A town meeting on May 15 issued statements that referred to "a deep-laid and desperate plan of imperial despotism . . . for the extinction of all civil liberty" in the American colonies. On the other hand, Hutchinson viewed the behavior of Adams and the Patriots as simply the "designs of particular persons to bring about a revolution, and to attain to independency." In the aftermath of the massacre, belief in conspiratorial plots hardened into obsessions on both sides. Loyalists and Patriots seemed worlds apart, and Boston was split irrevocably into two camps. "They call me a brainless Tory," said one local gentleman. "But tell me . . . which is better—to be ruled by one tyrant three thousand miles away, or by three thousand tyrants not one mile away?" Aware of this tension, Hutchinson and other crown dignitaries employed various legal devices to delay proceedings against Preston and his soldiers. They were finally indicted in September.

Preston's trial began on October 24. Ironically, one of his prosecu-

Samual Adams, a major orator and activist in the independence movement from his Boston base, devoted his life to the revolutionary movement. Friends helped support him and his family for much of the period, and he lived his last years in a state he chose to describe as "honorable poverty."

tors was a well-known Tory, Samuel Quincy. And his defense was under-taken by two of the colony's leading Patriot lawyers, John Adams (Samuel Adams's cousin) and Josiah Quincy (Samuel Quincy's brother). There is some evidence that Samuel Adams and other Patriot leaders encouraged John Adams and Josiah Quincy to act as defense counsel, not wishing the British government or public to feel that Boston had failed to provide a fair trial.

Whatever their motives, Adams and Quincy performed brilliantly. Actually, Preston's chances for acquittal seemed good from the start, especially since five acknowledged Tories were among the jury. The failure or inability of Patriot leaders to pack the jury with hostile Bosto-nians suggests that the Patriots were less concerned with convicting Preston and his men than with exploiting the trial as propaganda.

A parade of prosecution and defense witnesses testified to the different British and Bostonian versions of the events on King Street. James Brewer's testimony for the prosecution summarized the claim that the soldiers had lacked sufficient provocation to fire into the crowd.

> Q. Did you see anything thrown at the soldiers?
> A. No.
> Q. Did you hear anybody call them names?
> A. No.
> Q. Did you hear any threatening speeches?
> A. No, except that the people cried "Fire! Fire!" The word "fire" was on every-body's mouth.
> Q. Did you take that to be the cry of fire, or bidding the soldiers fire?
> A. I cannot tell now what I thought then.
> Q. Did you see anything extraordinary, to induce them to fire that gun?
> A. Nothing, but a short stick was thrown, which seemed to go clear over all [the soldiers'] heads.

A typical statement for the defense came in the testimony of New-ton Prince:

> I ran to the door [of my house] and heard the cry of fire. I went out and asked where the fire was; somebody said it was something better than fire. I met some with clubs, some with buckets and bags, and some running before me with sticks in their hands . . . there were a number of people by the west door of the Town-house; they said let's go and attack the main guard. . . . After a while they huz-zaed and went down King Street; they went down to the Custom-house, and I went down . . . There were people all round the soldiers . . . I saw people with sticks striking on the guns.
> Q. Did you hear at that time they were striking, the cry of fire, fire?
> A. Yes, [the crowd] said fire, fire, damn you, fire, fire you lobsters,[4] fire you dare not fire.

At several points during Captain Preston's trial — and later during the other soldiers' trial — John Adams threatened to resign as defense at-torney because his co-counsel, Josiah Quincy, wished to introduce evi-dence that Bostonians had triggered the violence. Adams felt that the

---

[4]"Lobsters" was a slang term for British soldiers because of the red coats they wore.

British soldiers could be acquitted without putting Boston and the Patriot cause itself on trial.

From the manner in which they dealt with Boston itself, the closing arguments by prosecution and defense lawyers used at the soldiers' trial illustrated the basic issues of Preston's case as well. The chief prosecutor, Robert Treat Paine, tried to absolve the mob itself of blame for the shooting. He answered "yes" to his own questions: "Was it lawful for the inhabitants of Boston to walk the streets that evening with sticks? Was it lawful for them to run on the cry of 'fire!'?" And he responded "no" to this critical question: "Must they be answerable for the rude speech of every person that happens to be near them, when it does not appear they assented to them and joined in putting them in execution?" In other words, Paine thundered, Preston's company of sentries had no lawful right to fire into the crowd. They were therefore, guilty of murder.

While Paine defended the radical mob's behavior, lawyer Josiah Quincy (defense lawyer for the sentries as well as for Preston) denied the importance, perhaps even the existence, of such a mob. He insisted that

> Boston and its inhabitants have no more to do with this cause than you or any other two members of the community. . . . The inhabitants of Boston, by no rules of law, justice, or common sense, can be supposed answerable for the unjustifiable conduct of a few individuals hastily assembled in the streets.

In other words, Quincy argued that the crowd's responsibility for provoking the incident was essentially different from the soldiers' guilt or innocence of the murder charge itself. Yet Quincy went on to defend the soldiers' innocence of murder, at the same time defending Boston against those who would criticize it.

Who, then, was to blame for the massacre? The prosecutor pointed to outside agitators who had provoked the violence, and he mentioned two such groups in his summation. One was "sailors and foreigners of the lower Class . . . who are fond of mingling with such Commotions and pushing on a disorder of which they feel not the Consequences." The other was the British army. The crowd's threatening words and hostile stirrings were only natural "among a free People Oppressed and galled with the ravagings of an ungoverned Soldiery [and were not] to be construed as Evidence of an Insurrection or a design to put in Execution the Supposed threats." John Adams picked up the outsider theme and made it the pivotal argument of his defense summation. Although the British did not come out unscathed, the soldiers' defender obviously directed his eloquence against the mob itself. But *what* mob? Composed of *whom*?

> The plain English is, gentlemen [that] most [of the mob] was probably a motley rabble of saucy boys, Negroes and mulattoes, Irish teagues,[5] and outlandish jack tarrs [sailors]. . . . There was a mob in Boston on the 5th of March that attacked a

John Adams was forty-one when this drawing was made, in 1776. His grandson later described him as "grave and imposing, but not unbending" and as one who "delighted in social conversation."

---

[5]"Teague," from the Irish name "Tadhg," was a nickname for an Irishman.

party of soldiers. . . . And indeed, from the nature of things, soldiers quartered in a populous town will always occasion two mobs where they prevent one. They are wretched conservators of the peace!

As for the role of Boston's citizens in the episode, Adams continued:

A <u>Carr</u> from <u>Ireland</u>, and an <u>Attucks</u> from Framingham, happening to be here, shall sally out upon their thoughtless enterprises, at the head of such a rabble . . . as they could collect together, and then there are not wanting, persons to ascribe all their doings to the good people of the town.

Judge Edmund Trowbridge, shrewdest of the three-judge panel that presided at both trials, told the jury that if they were satisfied "that the sentinel was insulted and that Captain Preston and his party went to assist him, it was doubtless excusable homicide, if not justifiable." Trowbridge went on to deny the conspiracy theories of the massacre. He stated that there had been "no concerted plan on either side," only the provocative actions of an angry crowd and the nervous reaction of frightened soldiers. In that situation "any little spark would kindle a great fire—and five lives were sacrificed to a squabble between the sentry [Private White] and Piemont's barber's boy [Edward Garrick]." The jury at Preston's trial appeared to agree with the judge. On October 30 it found the officer not guilty.

The second trial began on November 27 and ended on December 5. Six of the eight soldiers were also found not guilty. The two others, Matthew Kilroy and Hugh Montgomery, were found guilty of manslaughter. Both soldiers later used a legal technicality to avoid imprisonment. Nine months from the day of the massacre itself, the eight men who had fired their weapons into the King Street crowd had all returned to their military posts. As for the massacre, its fame was only beginning.

Boston was peaceful for a brief period after repeal of the Townshend Acts. In colony after colony during 1770 merchants repudiated their nonimportation agreements. They swiftly resumed trade with Great Britain so that competitors from other provinces would not take over their business. In the rush to resume business as usual, only Boston held firm, demanding that England repeal the remaining duty on tea and renounce similar taxes in the future. Finally, Boston too had to accept the inevitable and abandon nonimportation.

By the end of 1770 the Patriot movement had lost momentum throughout British North America. The spark of rebellion that had flared momentarily at the time of the massacre now flickered low. Samuel Adams confessed in a letter of April 1771:

The Generality are necessarily engaged in Application to private Business for the Support of their own families, and when at a lucky Season the publick are awakened to a Sense of Danger [and] a manly resentment is enkindled, it is difficult, for so many separate Communities as there are in all the colonies, to agree in one consistent plan of Opposition.

Boston, as Samuel Adams recognized, was the symbol and center of colonial resistance. The game of rebellion would continue to be played first in that throbbing seaport town, where so many prominent political, economic, and intellectual leaders resided. As part of their campaign to rekindle colonial resistance to Great Britain, Boston's Patriots produced a number of posters, pamphlets, engravings, and poems. Many of them dealt with the massacre. The events of March 5 began filtering into the daily language of patriotic protest as American Patriots reviewed for their audiences the major lessons of the massacre — namely, that the proper response to tyranny was resistance, and that true resistance usually meant the sacrifice of life as well as property. The following appeared in the Boston *Gazette:*

Let THESE Things be told to Posterity!

And handed down
From Generation to Generation
'Til time shall be no more!
Forever may AMERICA be preserved,
From weak and wicked monarchs,
Tyrannical Ministers,
Abandoned Governors,
Their Underlings and Hirelings!
And may the
Machinations of artful, designing wretches,
Who would ENSLAVE THIS People
Come to an end.

Every March 5, in the years that followed the King Street killings, Boston remembered. On that anniversary day a major speech was given to commemorate the five martyrs. The speeches were highly emotional in tone. They were concerned more with evoking the images of blood-stained streets and dying victims than with asserting political and constitutional arguments for freedom. Leading Patriots delivered the orations. For example, John Hancock spoke in 1774. The 1775 oration was given by Joseph Warren, whose heated remarks stirred a large audience in Faneuil Hall. When Warren cried out the words "Bloody Massacre" for the first time, an irreverent listener, presumably a Tory, shouted back, "Oh fie!" Many of those in the gallery, believing that the speaker had shouted "Fire!" began jumping out of the windows. They collided on the ground with a passing regiment of parading British soldiers, whose fife and drum contingent blared so noisily that some of those inside the hall began to suspect another massacre. The incident amused bystanders and participants alike. But New England had no further humorous moments in connection with the annual observances of the massacre. On March 5 of the following year, Peter Thatcher addressed the gathering with a passionate plea for American independence. It concluded simply: "O God, let America be free!"

8 THE COMING OF INDEPENDENCE
A. W.

In many ways, there was nothing new about the crisis of the 1770s in Massachusetts. The troubles of Governors Bernard and Hutchinson had been experienced earlier by many other royal officials in other colonies. At least as far back as the days of Sir William Berkeley in Virginia, the relationship between American colonists and royal officials had been a troubled one. Powerful stresses and strains were built into the very structure of the British Empire. Many royal governors had complained about how the colonists tried to escape, bypass, or limit British control of colonial life and trade.

What had changed in the years since Berkeley had less to do with the type of quarrel between governors and colonists than with the context of their argument. Conflicts in Boston and elsewhere grew heated in the 1760s. They stemmed from rapidly changing views on both sides of the Atlantic as to the rights and obligations of American subjects under the British crown.

The situation of the colonists before the 1760s had seemed obvious. They swore — and felt — loyalty to the British crown. But they gave their own colony first allegiance. Politically, a colonial American's "country" was his province, and his public life centered in the towns, counties, and cities of that province. Intercolonial political contacts were rare before the 1760s. Within each province, colonists had always taken certain rights and privileges for granted. Among these were the common law, the protection of private property, the right to representative legislatures, and the privilege of trial by jury.

Colonial obligations to the mother country seemed equally clear. Many of these involved trade and its regulation.

A CENTURY OF "SALUTARY NEGLECT"

In general, the British government followed a mercantilist policy in relation to its American colonies. The British believed that all their colonies existed mainly to bring benefits to the mother country. Mercantilism, in theory, represented a reasonable division of economic labor between colonies and mother country. The mother country would produce most of the manufactured goods needed by the empire. The colonies would produce raw materials. In some cases Britain even paid bounties (for example, on naval stores[1] and indigo) to encourage colonial production. With other products, such as tobacco, Englishmen living at home were forbidden to compete with colonial producers.

In carrying out its mercantilist policies, England passed a number of trade regulations known as the Navigation Acts. Their purpose was to ensure that American commerce would "terminate in the advantage of the Mother State, unto whom it owes its being and protection." Another purpose was to limit the amount of colonial produce carried to Europe in foreign ships, especially those of the Dutch.

The Navigation Act of 1660 was a major trade law affecting the American colonies. It declared that goods from the American colonies could be transported in English ships only. The English crown also wanted to limit profits made by colonial shippers from the sale of American produce. So the 1660 Navigation Act enumerated certain commodities such as tobacco, sugar, indigo, and cotton (most of English America's leading exports). These commodities could be shipped to points outside the empire only from England.

---

[1]Naval stores were certain products needed to operate British navy and merchant ships; they included hemp, tar, and resin.

British restrictions on colonial commerce were a basic source of American discontent, and a major cause of the revolution. In this Virginia dockside scene, tobacco—a popular commodity throughout England and Europe—is being loaded for export by slaves.

Later acts added to the enumerated list new sources of trade almost as fast as Americans developed them—molasses, naval stores, rice, and furs.

It was easier to pass such laws than to enforce them. Smuggling was common. It was not difficult for a colonial merchant to ship enumerated goods to French colonies in America or even to mainland Europe. Breaking the law was all the easier because British colonial administration during the seventeenth and eighteenth centuries was very disorganized. Several different royal agencies in the British government helped to set early policies for the mainland colonies.[2] In 1696 an

agency known as the Board of Trade was created to bring some degree of order to colonial administration. Throughout the eighteenth century the Board of Trade had primary responsibility for shaping royal policy in America. (It was the Board of Trade, for example, that approved the dispatch of troops to Boston in 1768.)

Administrative reorganization did not solve all Britain's colonial problems. For one thing, political conflicts, both internal and external, often preoccupied the mother country. Those responsible for colonial regulation were generally too busy with other concerns to worry about widespread smuggling in America. Even if British officials had wished to enforce the laws more rigorously, they had few customs officers and few ships for coastal patrol. Thus, from the viewpoint of British imperi-

[2]That is, British North American colonies other than those in the West Indies.

al control, the century after 1660 was accurately called a period of "salutary neglect."

As far as the colonists were concerned, they had relatively few complaints about the imperial system during this period. It seemed to meet the needs of a largely undeveloped, labor-starved group of provinces that specialized in producing raw materials. Colonial commerce and agriculture matured under mild royal supervision. Successive Board of Trade members rarely interfered when American merchants violated the Navigation Acts with regularity.

Colonial Government From his distant London office, a British administrator may easily have winked at American violations of the law. It was much more difficult, however, for a royal governor stationed in one of the colonies to keep his good humor.

By 1760, eight of the thirteen colonies were under direct royal control. In these colonies, governors like Francis Bernard or Thomas Hutchinson received their appointments directly from the king. In every royal colony except Massachusetts (where the council was elective), the governor appointed a council, which usually included the wealthiest and most distinguished citizens in the colony.

On paper a royal governor looked unbeatable. His duties were numerous. He enforced royal legislation. He summoned and adjourned colonial assemblies—or dissolved them whenever their actions threatened royal authority. He vetoed colonial statutes if they conflicted with British law. He also commanded the provincial militia and appointed local judges. Despite these impressive powers, the governors often found themselves isolated among unfriendly colonists and lacking the means to enforce royal authority against colonial assemblies.

In a way, the colonial assemblies were the key. For although the king appointed the colonial governors, the assemblies paid their salaries. And they did so irritably, ungenerously, and on a year-to-year basis. Each mainland British colony had an assembly that controlled the colony's purse strings. The assemblies had the right to initiate legislation, levy taxes, and appropriate money—including the governor's salary—on a yearly basis. Except for Pennsylvania, all the colonies had two-house (bicameral) assemblies. The elected lower house passed laws, assessed taxes, and dispensed funds. The upper house, appointed by the king in royal colonies, advised the governor.

By passing tax measures that had only limited duration, the colonial assembly ensured that it would be called into session regularly by any royal governor who needed more revenue quickly. By stating how money raised by specific taxes should be spent, an assembly limited the governor's freedom of action. In extreme cases of conflict with crown officials, the assembly resorted to the effective practice of withholding salaries. The assembly was powerful not only because it was elected by the people. Voters and nonvoters alike were kept aware of its actions by means of newspapers, political meetings, and even sermons.

Estimates differ concerning the number of colonists who met the requirements for voting in the mid-eighteenth century. Voters had to be Christians, though not of any particular religious denomination. They were required to own a certain amount of property, but the amount of land or its monetary equivalent required was not unreasonably high. In almost every colony property qualifications for voting were met by a large majority of the *white, free, male* population. (These were, of course, important restrictions, since they excluded free blacks, slaves, and women.) The exact proportion of voters probably ranged from 50 to 75 percent in most colonies. In Massachusetts, for example—a colony composed mainly of small, family-owned farms—more than 80 percent of the male population could have voted at the time of the Revolution.

Whatever royal governors or imperial legislation might have said on the matter, every colonial assembly already exercised the functions of local self-government by 1750. The assemblies had a strong tradition of victory in asserting their claims for colonial autonomy. Supporting the assemblies' actions were majorities of each colony's qualified voters. Even most leading Tories—men such as Thomas Hutchinson, for example—argued for a greater measure of internal self-government in the American provinces.

BENJAMIN FRANKLIN

"Americans do not inquire concerning a stranger, *What is he?* but, *What can he do?*" So Benjamin Franklin commented on the opportunities available to anyone in colonial America. In America, he observed, any industrious young man could become "self-made," rising from poverty and obscurity to fame and wealth. One such individual was Franklin himself. On his deathbed in 1790, he could claim to have been a printer, author, scientist, inventor, philanthropist, and diplomat.

Franklin was born in Boston in 1706, the fifteenth child and youngest son of a family of seventeen children. He left school at the age of ten. First he was an apprentice to his father, a candle- and soapmaker, and then to his brother, a printer. At the age of seventeen he ran away to Philadelphia, with one Dutch dollar and a copper shilling in his pocket. He found employment in a print-shop, and soon demonstrated his ability. Through his brother-in-law, Robert Holmes, he met the eccentric Governor Keith, who sent Franklin off to London, where Franklin found work at Palmer's printing house. After two years in London, he returned to Philadelphia in 1726 and worked as a shop clerk, learning accounts and becoming an "expert in selling."

Within seven years Franklin had bought the weekly newspaper, the *Pennsylvania Gazette*, rescuing it from near bankruptcy. It ran profitably for the next thirty-six years. During these same years Franklin created the overwhelming popular *Poor Richard's Almanack*, published yearly from 1732 to 1757. It contained local information for all the colonies, and sayings on the virtues of thrift and hard work. It was "Poor Richard" who said that "A penny saved is a penny earned," "Time is money," and "Little strokes fell great oaks." The *Almanack* sold thousands of copies in America every year and was translated and reprinted in many European countries.

Franklin grew wealthy. He devoted much of his energy to making Philadelphia a better city. He initiated street lighting, police and fire protection, and a colonywide militia. He helped establish a circulating library—the first in the United States—the American Philosophical Society, and the University of Pennsylvania. His scientific and inventive genius, typically American in its practical outlook, produced bifocal eyeglasses, the Franklin stove, a stool that opened up into a ladder, and a rocking chair that fanned the sitter while rocking. By the age of forty Franklin was a distinctly successful man. But, he wrote his mother, he would rather have it said that "he lived usefully," than that "he died rich."

Unquestionably Philadelphia's most prominent citizen, Franklin was sent to London in 1767 to act as agent for Pennsylvania. He emerged as a spokesman for American independence. When he returned home, the Revolution had already broken out. He served in the Second Continental Congress and in 1775 went to France to negotiate for financial and military aid. Franklin charmed the French with his wit, wisdom, and kindness. His personal popularity added much to the success of his diplomatic mission.

When Franklin returned to his beloved Philadelphia, he received a hero's welcome. He was elected president (mayor) of the city. And at the age of eighty-one he became a delegate to the Constitutional Convention in 1787. His interest in the welfare of mankind prompted him to sign a petition to Congress calling for the abolition of slavery. Death claimed him three months later in April 1790. Philadelphia lost its most famous citizen, and the young nation lost a man who embodied its very spirit.

CONFLICT WITH FRANCE

From their earliest days, the mainland English settlements had waged almost continuous warfare against the Indian tribes and European settlements along their borders. As the seventeenth century drew to a close, the chief European rival for control of North America was France. Her trading posts and fortified settlements ringed the British colonies like a vise from the eastern tip of Canada to the mouth of the Mississippi River. Aiding the French were thousands of Indians—great tribes like the Algonquins and the Hurons—with whom they traded furs. The powerful tribes of the Iroquois Confederation, however, were allies of the British.

France and Britain fought a series of four wars between 1689 and 1763. At stake were territories in Europe and possessions throughout the overseas empires of the two nations. In America, British troops were aided by American militia and their Indian allies in their fight against combined French and Indian forces.

The first of these wars, known in America as King William's War (1689–1697), ended inconclusively. In the next war, Queen Anne's War (1702–1713), the British won most of the battles, both in Europe and America. As a result, Britain acquired Nova Scotia, Newfoundland, and the Hudson Bay region of Canada. The third conflict, called King George's War (1740–1748) in America, ended as indecisively as King William's War. But the French and Indian War, the fourth and last round of fighting, was much more decisive. It began in the spring of 1754.

The Albany Congress As war began, the American colonies displayed in dramatic fashion their divided condition and mutual suspiciousness. What made the display even more striking was the fact that the first attempt to achieve intercolonial unity was organized by none other than the British Board of Trade.

The Board of Trade wanted the colonists to meet with Britain's Iroquois allies. The purpose of the meeting was to discuss defense measures to be taken against the French and their Indian allies. The British also wanted to encourage cooperation among the various colonial militias, which had been sadly lacking up to this time. The result was the Albany Congress, which met in June and July of 1754. Seven colonies sent delegates. Among them were Thomas Hutchinson of Massachusetts and Benjamin Franklin of Pennsylvania (see page 141).

Once the meeting began, Franklin went beyond the British agenda and proposed instead a general plan of intercolonial union. According to Franklin's plan of union, the king would appoint a president-general, a kind of supergovernor, presumably with the usual lack of enforcement authority. The provincial assemblies would be represented in proportion to their tax payments in a grand council, a kind of superassembly somewhat like our present-day Congress. Taxes on each colony would support the grand council's control of intercolonial defense, Indian relations, and westward expansion. The central body would be allowed to raise an army and navy and build forts and settlements. The president-general, however (like the royal governors), could veto any laws in the king's name.

The Albany Congress approved the essential outlines of Franklin's plan and submitted it to the colonial assemblies. Three of these simply ignored the proposal. The other four rejected it, agreeing with the Boston town meeting that the Albany Plan endangered popular liberties. Throughout the French and Indian War, each colony preferred to protect itself. Whatever common defense did exist in British North America was led and staffed largely by regular units of the British Army. None of the colonial assemblies was willing to surrender its taxing powers; nor, for that matter, did any assembly wish to allow any "grand council" to divide the unclaimed lands in the interior that some colonies hoped to acquire by driving out the French.

The French and Indian War In the beginning, this conflict (also known as the Seven Years' War) went badly for the British. Colonial assemblies were reluctant to contribute men and money to the fight. The result was a series of British defeats along the frontier line with French Canada.[3] Not until William Pitt became prime minister in 1757 did the British war effort begin to take shape. For one thing, Pitt shifted the war's main emphasis from Europe (on which it had been centered during the earlier three Anglo-French conflicts) to the empire. Here Pitt assigned most of Britain's military strength. Pitt bankrupted the national treasury to pay for additional regiments of British troops to send to America.

In order to win over the colonial assemblies, Pitt directed British military officials to assume the cost of feeding and arming colonial militia. The British also promised to repay the assemblies for money they spent to supply and pay addi-

---

[3]One American who got his first taste of battle in this conflict was George Washington. As a young officer with British general Edward Braddock, he took part in an unsuccessful campaign against the French near what is now Pittsburgh.

tional volunteers. Such generosity swelled the ranks of colonial regiments that fought alongside British redcoats in subduing the French.

The British won a series of military victories under aggressive new commanders such as James Wolfe and Jeffrey Amherst. In 1759 they captured Quebec from the French, who were led by the Marquis de Montcalm. Within a year all of French Canada lay in British hands. In the Treaty of Paris in 1763, France surrendered all of her North American possessions east of the Mississippi from Canada to Florida. The exception was Louisiana, which France had earlier ceded to its ally Spain.

During the war all did not go smoothly between Britain and her colonies. For one thing, Pitt insisted on rigorously enforcing the Navigation Acts in America. British warships patrolled in force to choke off trade with the enemy.

Northern colonial merchants were also out-

British General Braddock was ambushed by French and Indians near Fort Duquesne (the site of Pittsburgh). After having five horses shot from under him, he was mortally wounded.

raged by Britain's intensified hunt for smuggled goods through the use of so-called general writs of assistance. These were unlimited search warrants good for the entire period of a king's reign. They allowed customs officers to enter and search any building in daytime, without having prior knowledge of allegedly imported goods.

After the death of King George II in 1760, Boston merchants (many of whom later led the nonimportation campaign) retained James Otis, one of the colony's best lawyers, to argue the illegality of the writs in order to prevent their renewal under the new king, George III. Otis lost his case, and the writs were upheld. Often during the following decade, royal customs officials barged unannounced into Boston warehouses and homes searching for smuggled goods.

INCREASED BRITISH CONTROL

After the French and Indian War, it became clear that the British intended to regulate their American provinces much more closely and thoroughly in the future than they had in the past. One important decision involved the new trans-Appalachian territories recently acquired from the French. Even before 1754, settlers had begun moving into the rich Ohio Valley. Land companies were organized to take control of the region's fur trade and to explore other opportunities. Then the British government issued the Proclamation of 1763, banning, for an indefinite time, settlement and land grants beyond the crest of the Appalachian Mountains. Land speculators (among them George Washington) denounced British efforts to close off the West. American settlement and land speculation continued.

Another problem was financial. Who would pick up the tab for Britain's costly victory over France? Pitt's war strategy had succeeded, but in the process England had spent £82 million. Despite heavy wartime taxation, the British national debt had run up to £130 million by 1764. Every leading British minister during the 1760s and 1770s agreed that it was only fair for the American

colonies to share in paying off the war debts. After all, they reasoned, the mainland provinces had achieved virtually complete security on their borders at almost no cost to themselves.

Americans disagreed with the British argument that Parliament had the right to tax colonists along with other British subjects. This dispute over taxation, brought on by the British government's search for revenue, quickly became the major source of colonial unrest during the 1760s. Throughout the eighteenth century most Americans had accepted Parliament's right to legislate for the colonies. But they denied its right to tax them. Most Americans would probably have agreed with the Virginia legislature that, "Laws imposing taxes on the People ought not to be made without the Consent of Representatives chosen by themselves." Colonial assemblies believed that they had won the exclusive right to initiate taxes

George III, long thought to have become insane in later life, probably suffered from a rare inherited disease.

within their own provinces. Yet in April 1764, George Grenville, Britain's first lord of the treasury, steered through Parliament a law that challenged this right and, in the process, stirred up colonial resistance from New England to Georgia.

The Sugar Act When George Grenville became British finance minister in 1763, he made an embarrassing discovery: the customs service in America cost the British government four times as much in salaries as it collected in revenues! Grenville's solution was a revenue-raising bill that came to be known as the Sugar Act.

Earlier in the century the British had taxed foreign molasses at the rate of sixpence a gallon in order to encourage colonials to purchase this product from the British West Indies. The regulation was largely ignored. American rum distillers found it much cheaper to bribe customs officials (at a penny a gallon) so they could smuggle in cheaper molasses from the French West Indies. Grenville's Sugar Act of 1764 was designed to eliminate such colonial trading freedom.

The new statute lowered the molasses duty from six to three pence. The new duty applied to both British and foreign molasses entering the colonies. This provision transformed a trade-regulating device into a revenue-producing tax. The Sugar Act also placed new tax duties on such commodities as sugar, indigo, wine, and textiles.

More upsetting to the colonists than the taxes themselves was Parliament's obvious determination to enforce their collection. Colonial shipowners now had to file official papers for every vessel leaving and entering American harbors. Moreover, accused violators of the Sugar Act would be tried in admiralty (naval) courts distant from their hometowns or cities. Such courts operated without juries and under rules according to which a defendant was considered guilty until proved innocent. Provincial merchant smugglers had come to depend on sympathetic local juries or judges (men like Boston's justice of the peace William Molineux, who had persuaded a mob to surrender Ebenezer Richardson). Local jurors and judges generally gave violators of British trade regulations what the defendants wished—freedom, not justice.

A storm of protest over the Sugar Act spread quickly through the colonies. It was sparked by commercial cities like Boston, which reminded their rural countrymen of the stake all Americans had in the new British policies. "If our Trade may be taxed, why not our Lands?" asked the Boston town meeting in a thumping denunciation of the Sugar Act. "Why not the produce of our Lands and every Thing we possess or make use of?" Similar complaints filled newspapers from Massachusetts to the Carolinas. Widespread smuggling continued. Yearly collections of revenue from the Sugar Act averaged a ridiculously small £20,000.

Grenville (and many other British officials) failed to realize that, to provincial Americans, their freedom as British subjects involved the right of their assemblies alone to levy taxes over them. Americans were as much concerned with the precedent set by the Sugar Act as with its actual enforcement. The rights of Englishmen, colonists argued, depended upon a person's right—as James Otis put it—to be "free from all taxes but what he consents to in person, or by his representative." Actually, the colonists did lack representation in Parliament; by and large, however, they did not want it. They recognized shrewdly that this would lead to tighter English control of provincial affairs.

Additional Regulations Colonial protests over the Sugar Act did not lessen Grenville's interest in squeezing additional revenue out of North America. In March 1765 Parliament passed the Stamp Act. It required Americans to buy tax stamps for newspapers, legal documents, and other types of printed matter. Englishmen had paid such a tax for decades. Grenville made certain to mention that revenues raised from the new tax, which was to take effect in November 1765, would be applied entirely to "the Defense of the Colonies."

A related measure also sponsored by Grenville was the Quartering Act, passed by Parliament in March 1765. It obliged colonial assemblies to furnish British troops stationed in their colonies with adequate living quarters and provisions. Many colonists considered the timing strange. Britain had kept almost no royal troops garrisoned in America when the French, the Spanish, and the

NORTH AMERICA IN 1754

NORTH AMERICA IN 1763

INDIAN RESERVE

HUDSON'S BAY COMPANY

PROCLAMATION LINE

INDIAN RESERVE

SPANISH LOUISIANA

EAST FLORIDA

WEST FLORIDA

British
French
Spanish
Russian
Unexplored or disputed

Indians menaced the western borders of almost every colony. Now, after this threat had been removed, she planned to station soldiers in America. Americans realized that the troops were actually being sent to enforce royal authority—which they did with such mixed results in Boston three years later.

The Stamp Act and the Quartering Act fed the growing suspicion of Britain among knowledgeable Americans. Had the British government deliberately set out to deny them freedoms they had previously exercised? Some of these might be called negative freedoms—the absence of British taxation, the lack of a British army in their midst, lax enforcement of the Navigation Acts. Others were positive—trial by local juries, the liberty to expand westward.

None of the king's ministers would have denied that Britain meant to change its permissive ways in North America. They would have argued, though, that Parliament did not wish to deny legitimate colonial rights. It wanted only to remind the mainland colonies of their equally legitimate responsibilities toward the mother country. In practice, however, Britain's sudden effort to tighten

the parental screws triggered an immediate protest from her fully grown New World children.

American Opposition   The Stamp Act generated the first successfully organized intercolonial opposition to British policy. It took the form of almost complete resistance to buying the required stamps. For a lawyer, merchant, newspaper editor, small businessman, or even a planter, the stamps represented both a costly expense and an illegal parliamentary attack on colonial liberties. As usual, resistance centered in the commercial cities and towns, to which Britain had sent most of the stamps and tax collectors. For the first (but hardly the last) time in the struggle, Boston became the center of both legal and violent protest.

The Massachusetts assembly took the lead in June 1765, when it proposed an intercolonial meeting to unify opposition to parliamentary taxation. Boston mobs—often organized by the same Sons of Liberty who would prove so effective later in the decade—ransacked the homes of several British officials, including the chief royal stamp collector. The mobs also burned Lieutenant Governor Thomas Hutchinson's elegant mansion to the ground, destroyed important government records, and forced several stamp distributors to resign their offices. Riotous Sons of Liberty played a similar role in New York City and elsewhere.

Meanwhile, peaceful forms of protest were having an even more unsettling effect on British policy. As early as May 1765, a young lawyer named Patrick Henry introduced a series of resolutions in the Virginia House of Burgesses. They asserted that this body alone had the right to tax Virginians. The House of Burgesses adopted the more moderate of Henry's resolutions, but it rejected his call for outright resistance to collection of stamp taxes. Most other colonial assemblies followed Virginia's lead and passed similar resolutions, all of which Parliament ignored.

But the British government could hardly overlook the resolutions passed by an intercolonial Stamp Act Congress, first proposed by Massachusetts. The assemblies of nine colonies were represented when this congress convened in October 1765 in New York City. Although the congress assured Parliament of "all due subordination," it denied that Britain had the right either to tax the colonists or to try Americans in admiralty courts. Furthermore, the delegates demanded immediate repeal of both the Sugar Act and the Stamp Act.

In order to put teeth into these demands, more than a thousand colonial merchants from all the major trading cities quickly organized an effective boycott of British manufactured goods. This was the first of several times that colonial economic pressures through such nonimportation agreements were to force changes in British policy. The merchants played a crucial role in the struggle with Britain—so crucial that the strength of colonial resistance at any given moment depended to a large degree on the extent of merchant support.

American colonists sometimes used violent methods to intimidate those who were supposed to collect Stamp Act taxes. With the tax collector looking on in dismay, a New Hampshire mob stones his effigy and carries a coffin through the streets.

The most important long-term result of the Stamp Act protests was that Americans of all classes and backgrounds began to learn the habit of resistance. Some Americans—including militants like Samuel Adams—even began to advocate independence and revolution. They argued that a people had the right to change or overthrow a government that systematically violated people's rights and exceeded its authority. Such opinions frightened members of Parliament. William Pitt urged repeal of the Stamp Act on the grounds that doing so would restore the loyalty of most moderate Americans and isolate the minority of radicals: "If we repeal the Act, we shall have all the sober part of America on our side, and we shall easily be able to chastize the few hot-headed republicans among them." Pitt might also have reminded his colleagues that the Stamp Act had proved a total failure. It earned no revenue, since no Americans could be found who were brave enough to collect the tax. American business continued as usual, while British manufacturers suffered from the boycott of their goods in America. Responding finally to economic and political pressures, Parliament repealed the Stamp Act in March 1766.

A DEEPENING CRISIS

Americans might have celebrated the repeal of the Stamp Act a bit more heartily had not Parliament coupled its repeal with passage of another measure. This was the Declaratory Act, which reaffirmed colonial subordination. It also asserted Parliament's right to pass any law it wished (presumably, therefore, any *tax* law), "to bind the colonies and people of America."

In 1767 a new British finance minister, Charles Townshend, exercised this option. He secured a new program of colonial duties, to be placed on imports of items such as paper, tea, lead, paint, and glass. Townshend believed somewhat naïvely, that his move would produce much-needed revenue. Instead, he succeeded only in raising again the unsettled issues of the Stamp Act crisis.

Once more, Massachusetts led intercolonial resistance. Its assembly sent a Circular Letter to the other colonial legislatures urging some form of united opposition similar to the Stamp Act Congress. The Circular Letter denied that Massachusetts advocated independence. Still, the British government considered the letter dangerous enough to demand that the assembly rescind it. When the assembly refused, Governor Bernard, on orders from London, prevented the legislators from meeting in 1768. Special town meetings summoned delegates to an extralegal convention to discuss the matter. It was at this point that two regiments of British troops were sent to occupy Boston and protect the unpopular customs commissioners.

The civic turmoil during the next two years was to lead directly to the Boston Massacre. New York City was also the scene of protests and mob violence after Parliament had dissolved the New York assembly for refusing to obey the Quartering Act.

As with the Stamp Act, however, the peaceful boycott of British goods by colonial merchants proved more effective with Parliament than threats or violence. Boston's nonimportation agreement was followed by other cities, among them Providence, Newport, and New York. In the Virginia assembly a set of resolutions sponsored by George Washington supported Massachusetts' Circular Letter. When the royal governor dissolved the assembly, its leaders regrouped informally and endorsed a nonimportation campaign. Throughout the colonies unrest died down only after Parliament had repealed all the Townshend duties except the tax on tea. The king's new prime minister, Lord North, had insisted that this tax remain in order to uphold the "supremacy of Parliament" in America.

Lacking a dramatic rallying point against Britain, many American Patriots lapsed back easily into provincial loyalties. Even dogged fighters like Samuel Adams were hard-pressed to keep alive much bitterness toward royal authority during the few relatively quiet years that followed repeal of the Townshend Acts. Customs commissioners went about their business. British troops remained quartered in the colonies. And royal governors began to act more confidently.

"GIVE ME LIBERTY, OR GIVE ME DEATH!" This 1870 rendering of Patrick Henry's March 23, 1775 oration to the Virginia assembly shows vividly how later Americans viewed his famous "war cry of the Revolution."

To counteract this apathy, Samuel Adams and other Sons of Liberty in Boston created a Committee of Correspondence to publicize complaints against the British. The idea spread throughout the colonies and revived intercolonial cooperation. The committees found something juicy to write about when Rhode Islanders burned a British customs patrol boat, the *Gaspée*, after it ran aground in Narragansett Bay. The incident, which occurred in June 1772, led to a royal investigation. To the Patriots' delight, the investigators could find no sign of the culprits. The incident also probably served as a model for another one, involving a shipload of tea, which took place in Boston harbor in December 1773.

The Boston Tea Party Tea was the colonists'

most popular beverage. Few Americans liked Lord North's decision in May 1773 to aid the financially ailing British East India Company by granting it a monopoly in America. Previously, the company had sold its tea to British wholesalers. They in turn sold to American wholesalers, who distributed the tea to local merchants. The British government now proposed to allow the East India Company to sell tea directly through its own agents in America. This step would eliminate both British and colonial middlemen.

The immediate effect was to reduce the retail price of tea considerably. But Americans grasped almost immediately the long-term effect of this action. In return for cheaper tea, they were being asked to accept a new royal interference in normal patterns of colonial commerce. If Parliament could so easily dispose of a profitable, long-standing colonial tea trade, then no portion of America's commerce would be safe from British interference.

Public protests against the Tea Act spread quickly throughout the colonies. They were fueled by passionate letters exchanged by the Committees of Correspondence and by the almost unanimous opposition of colonial newpapers. Once again the British government had unintentionally revived the colonial resistance movement. In New York and Philadelphia royal authorities, fearing violence, ordered the first East India Company tea ships back to Britain without attempting to unload them. In Charleston the tea was simply locked in a warehouse and not offered for sale.

Bostonians, as usual, thought of a more effective way to rally patriotic sentiment and provoke royal anger. On December 16, 1773, a ship called the *Dartmouth* lay at dockside waiting for her captain to decide whether to try to unload her cargo of tea. That night, led by the Sons of Liberty, a band of townspeople disguised as Indians boarded the *Dartmouth*. A huge crowd of Bostonians cheered as the "Indians" dumped the cargo overboard.

Aftermath: The Intolerable Acts Parliament responded to this "tea party" by passing a series of laws designed to punish Boston. These so-called Coercive Acts took away the city's liberties. One of them closed the port to all commerce until its residents had paid for the spoiled tea. Another authorized the transfer of cases involving British officals from Massachusetts to England in order to escape the hostility of local judges and juries. A third act revised the fundamental structure of Massachusetts' government to strengthen royal authority in the colony. The upper house (Governor's Council) would now be appointed by the king and no longer elected. Town meetings, in which the Sons of Liberty engaged in their most effective organizing, could be held only once a year. Once more British troops appeared in Boston. General Gage, commander-in-chief of all British troops in America, became military governor of Massachusetts. For Bostonians, British occupation

and interference with normal political and economic life was far more sweeping than it had been during the controversy over the Townshend duties.

Another statute passed by Parliament at this time was the Quebec Act, which applied to the recently conquered French territory that Americans had already begun settling. The law recognized the practice of Roman Catholicism and French civil law in that area—both unpopular with the largely Protestant and largely English colonists of the thriteen colonies. They dubbed the Coercive Acts and the Quebec Act the Intolerable Acts.

Supplies and pledges of support from all over the provinces flowed into Boston. The Intolerable Acts achieved something that had previously eluded Samuel Adams and the Sons of Liberty—the unification of colonial resistance to Britain.

OUTBREAK OF THE REVOLUTION

In June 1774 the Massachusetts assembly asked other colonies to send delegates to a congress where they could agree on common action against the Intolerable Acts. Fifty-five delegates from twelve colonies attended the First Continental Congress, which met at Philadelphia in September. (Georgia was unrepresented at this time, but later sent delegates.) The Congress rejected by one vote a compromise proposal for a new scheme of colonial government similar to Franklin's 1754 Albany Plan. The Congress then endorsed a set of resolutions proposed originally by a convention in Suffolk County, Massachusetts. These Suffolk Resolves demanded direct resistance to the Intolerable Acts. The Congress also adopted John Adams' Declaration of Rights and Resolves, a statement of the colonists' constitutional arguments.

The most practical step taken by the Continental Congress was to create an association to enforce a complete boycott against Britain. Delegates vowed not to import, export, or consume

British goods until the crisis had been settled. Before adjourning in October 1774, the delegates also decided to meet again in May 1775.

King George and his ministers had erroneously believed that colonial resistance was confined to Massachusetts, and their reaction to the First Continental Congress reflected this mistaken judgment. They convinced themselves that stern measures in that colony would dampen unrest elsewhere. "The New England governments are in a state of Rebellion," George III remarked in November 1774. "Blows must decide whether they are to be subject to this country or independent."

General Gage, ordinarily as stubborn as George III himself about punishing colonial resistance, had been sobered by his new role as governor of Massachusetts. He tried to warn London of what lay ahead. The provincial militia was then gathering on the outskirts of Boston. To subdue it and reassert parliamentary authority in Massachusetts, Gage wrote Lord North, would require 20,000 additional troops. Until their arrival, Gage recommended that Britain suspend the Coercive Acts in order to reduce tensions in America. But his superiors responded by declaring Massachusetts to be in a state of rebellion. They sent Gage an additional 3,500 men. And they directed the general to suppress the rebellion and arrest "the principal actors in the provincial Congress." Gage attempted to obey this order on April 19, 1775, and, in the process, began the American Revolution.

Open Hostilities in Massachusetts Not surprisingly, the conflict began in Boston. Massachusetts Patriots had been drilling for months, organized into extralegal militia companies sometimes called Minutemen. Gage had been informed that the Patriots were storing arms at Concord, west of Boston, and that Samuel Adams and John Hancock were also in the vicinity. The British general sent a force of some 700 regulars to confiscate the arms and arrest the Patriot leaders.

On April 19, arriving at Lexington on their way to Concord, the British found about seventy Minutemen assembled on the town common. The British commander ordered the Americans to disperse. Then someone—whether British or American remains unclear—fired a shot. Just as had happened six years earlier during the Boston Massacre, a single shot led to additional firing and a state of general confusion. When the smoke cleared, the Minutemen had fled, leaving eight dead and ten wounded. The British continued to Concord only to find that most of the colonial arms stored there had already been removed. The British destroyed what supplies they could find and fought several skirmishes with small groups of Minutemen.

Meanwhile, colonial militia had converged on Lexington and Concord throughout the day, the alarm having been spread the previous night by a few Boston Sons of Liberty, including Paul Revere. Some 900 British reinforcements joined the first detachment at Lexington for the march back to Boston. But they found themselves outnumbered and outvolleyed by more than 4,000 colonial marksmen, who fired from behind stone walls and other cover. The colonists peppered the British troops with musket fire along their twenty-mile retreat. Even the 1,500 additional redcoats sent by Gage to protect the retreat failed to prevent it from turning into a chaotic stampede.

By the time the British straggled back to safety in Boston, they had lost 73 men and suffered 149 wounded, compared to American casualties of 49 killed and 39 wounded. More ominously still, the Minutemen did not return to their homes. They began instead to surround Boston, and their ranks grew. First they came from other Massachusetts towns. Then, within days, volunteers began arriving from other colonies as well. Gage and his undermanned British garrison now found themselves under siege from all sides.

Two months later, reinforced by only 1,100 troops, Gage attempted to break the colonial lines ringing Boston. He fought colonial militia entrenched on two strategic high points, Breed's Hill and Bunker Hill. After a furious day's fighting, on June 17, the British cleared both hills of American soldiers. The cost was high. The British suffered more than 1,000 killed or wounded out of an attacking force of 2,000 men. The Americans counted fewer than 450 men killed, wounded, or captured. As one of Gage's officers aptly remarked, "another such victory would have ruined us."

In a contemporary British cartoon, Father Time displays a lantern slide to Britannia (the personification of Britain). At center is an exploding teapot—symbolizing the Boston tea party—with victorious American troops at right and defeated redcoats at left.

The Second Continental Congress In May 1775, while 16,000 colonial militia penned the British garrison in its uncomfortable quarters among Boston's hostile townspeople, the Second Continental Congress met at Philadelphia. Its members now confronted not merely colonial protests but also the newer reality of armed revolt. After the British "victory" at Bunker Hill, George III had relieved Gage of his command and formally declared the colonies to be "in open rebellion." The Continental Congress accepted the description and began the difficult job of trying to make the rebellion succeed.

One of the first acts of the Congress was to appoint one of the delegates, George Washington of Virginia, as commander-in-chief of Continental forces. Delegates also prepared to requisition men and supplies for the new army.

Some of the men at Philadelphia still considered the revolt a temporary break with Britain. They believed that the grievances that had inspired it could be resolved by compromise. In deference to these moderates, the Continental Congress, in July 1775, adopted a conciliatory document that came to be known as the Olive Branch Petition. The delegates, "as faithful subjects," requested the repeal of all oppressive legislation and an end to tyranny.

The Second Continental Congress also passed a Declaration of the Causes and Necessities of Taking up Arms. This document was drafted by John Dickinson of Pennsylvania and a new delegate from Virgina, Thomas Jefferson. It defended colonial resistance as the only alternative to "unconditional submission to the tyranny of irritated ministers." It also denied that the Ameri-

CANADA AND ITS NEIGHBORS

The original European settlers in Canada were the French, who first came in the early seventeenth century. Like the English in Virginia, these colonists were sent by a trading company operating under royal charter. The stockholders were allowed to set up a fur trade, but they were also committed to establish colonies in Canada.

Once in Canada, however, men were lured from the stern task of hacking out pioneer farms by the free life of the forest and by dreams of a quick fortune made in the fur trade. They became hunters and trappers—often living with the Indians—rather than settling down to raise large broods of children. By 1660 there were only 2,000 inhabitants in New France, compared with 75,000 in the thirteen English colonies. This scant population did not produce enough food to support itself, nor was it a match for hostile Indians. The French government took over the colony in 1663.

During the next hundred years the government made a systematic effort to peo-ple New France. Population did increase, but in 1760 the colony fell to the British in the French and Indian War. By 1763, the British controlled the four chief regions of Canada—Quebec, Nova Scotia, Newfoundland, and Rupert's Land. These provinces, along with the thirteen colonies and British possessions in the Caribbean, formed Britain's American empire.

Renewed imperial controls, which followed the British victory of 1763, ran counter to a rising desire for independence in the thirteen colonies. Americans hoped that Nova Scotia and Quebec would sympathize with their grievances against Britain. (They did not consider Newfoundland or Rupert's Land, as they were too far away.)

Although part of the same empire, Nova Scotia and Quebec did not cast their lot with the thirteen colonies. Few of the American protests applied to Nova Scotia. The closing of the western lands did not affect the colony, which had many empty acres of its own. Nor was Nova Scotia a Massachusetts, ready to stand on its own feet in world trade.

In Quebec support for the colonies to the south was not forthcoming either. The Catholic Canadians had little love for the Protestant Americans, nor much interest in English traditions of government. In Quebec the French were a majority. But if Quebec combined with the other colonies, the French would be a minority. In addition, because of decades of warfare, the colonists of France and those of Britain still regarded each other more as enemies than as friends.

Despite Canadian neutrality, the American Revolution had a profound influence on Canada. She became a refuge for supporters of the crown—Tories to the Americans, United Empire Loyalists to the British. Over 40,000 moved north to Canada. Their descendants live there still.

Quebec in 1758

can aim was complete independence and promised to lay down arms once Britain ceased its abusive behavior.

The declaration was a response to the so-called Conciliatory Act, passed by Parliament the previous February. The act had promised to exempt from British taxes those colonies that paid for royal expenses voluntarily. The declaration rejected this idea and signaled the colonists' continued opposition to British policies.

SEVERING TIES WITH BRITAIN

All the actions taken to strengthen intercolonial resistance reinforced Lord North's belief, shared by George III, that the Americans wanted complete independence. Various proposals for compromise were defeated by Parliament. The British government's answer to the Olive Branch Petition was to send 25,000 additional troops to America. Britain also began to hire foreign mercenary soldiers. In August 1775 the king had declared the colonies to be in rebellion. In December Parliament outlawed trade with the colonies and declared American ships and cargoes subject to confiscation.

As far as Britain was concerned, she was at war with rebellious subjects in a conflict that permitted only one solution: the colonists' submission as dutiful children to the mother country and the king. As far as a growing number of Americans were concerned, the colonies had no choice left but to fight. This involved taking a more serious step toward independence: repudiating the basic symbol of British power—the British monarchy—and colonial allegiance to it.

People do not usually surrender their customary loyalties easily or without overwhelming reasons. Many of the delegates at Philadelphia shrank from defying the king himself. To strike such a blow at the symbol of monarchy required someone who hated both the British crown and the ruler on whose head it now rested. The man who struck the blow was a recently arrived immigrant from England named Thomas Paine.

Thomas Paine left England in 1774 for the colonies. He was a failure in marriage and a failure in business. More important, however, he was an ardent republican who believed in rule by the people rather than by a monarch. He made an enormous impact in America with his anonymously printed pamphlet, *Common Sense*, which first appeared in January 1776. Paine's pamphlet sold 150,000 copies in the critical months from January to July 1776.

Common Sense contained outspoken attacks on George III as "the royal brute of Britain." Paine also assailed the idea of monarchy itself. He wrote: "Of more worth is one honest man to society and in the sight of God, than all the crowned ruffians that ever lived." Under Paine's influence enthusiasm for republican government spread quickly throughout the colonies.

In May 1776 the Continental Congress adopted John Adams's proposal urging all provincial assemblies to suppress any remaining vestiges of royal government, to establish constitutions, and to create new state governments based upon popular consent. Royal authority had already collapsed throughout the colonies by this time, as British officials fled to safety and American Tories retreated into silence. Colonial assemblies began functioning as independent, provisional state legislatures.

The Second Continental Congress had already begun acting like a provisional national government. It sought diplomatic and military assistance abroad. It authorized Americans to attack English shipping retaliation for the British embargo on American trade. In addition, it opened American ports to foreign shipping, thus formally ending any further pretense at recognizing England's right to regulate American trade.

The decisive step in the move toward independence came on May 15. Virginia's new revolutionary legislature instructed its delegates to the Congress to introduce a resolution proposing both independence and an intercolonial confederation. Many Virginians were already convinced that Britain was indifferent to colonial interests. This belief grew stronger after the efforts made by Virginia's last royal governor, Lord Dunmore, to recruit slaves into the British army by promising them freedom. Rumors of a British scheme to stir up a slave rebellion swept the South in 1776. Such rumors probably helped some fearful Southerners to overcome their reluctance and endorse a complete break with the mother country.

The Declaration of Independence On June 7 Richard Henry Lee introduced Virginia's independence resolution into the Congress. A five-man committee was assigned the task of preparing an appropriate document defending colonial actions. The committee consisted of John Adams, Benjamin Franklin, Thomas Jefferson, Roger Sherman of Connecticut, and Robert Livingston of New York. The thirty-three-year-old Jefferson, the youngest man in the Congress, became chairman of the committee. Adams and Franklin made suggestions, but the draft was largely Jefferson's.

By late June more moderates had accepted the idea of a complete break. On July 2 Congress finally voted to approve Richard Henry Lee's earlier motion "that these united colonies are, and of right ought to be, free and independent states." Jefferson's Declaration of Independence was then submitted to the full membership of the Congress.

Delegates altered some of the wording, but they made few substantial changes except to strike out a rather questionable passage blaming George III for the existence of slavery in America.

Most of Jeffersons's draft had a familiar ring to the delegates. Perhaps most original was its attempt to attribute colonial oppression to royal rather than parliamentary tyranny. Much of the Declaration consisted of a list of the alleged "injuries and usurpations" by George III that had forced America to resort to rebellion. Some of the complaints were reasonable: the king's interference with representative assemblies, his abuses of civil rights, his use of an army of occupation without colonial consent, and his allowing Parliament to tax the colonies and restrain their trade. Other grievances had plainly been designed to arouse American fears, not to gain foreign support. Of such a nature were charges that the king had incited slave and Indian insurrections, "plundered our seas, ravaged our coasts, burnt our towns, and destroyed the lives of our people."

Jefferson's preamble to the Declaration attempted to justify a people's right to rebel and to alter their form of government. He employed con-

An American cartoon satirizes the British retreat from Concord. British troops, portrayed with jackass heads, stop to burn and plunder in this distorted but lively drawing.

The Declaration of Independence, as seen by a Chinese craftsman. Porcelain platters like this were made for the export trade in the nineteenth century. It is difficult to identify any particular signer since they look so much alike—and so remarkably Chinese!

cepts that were thoroughly familiar to his associates in Congress and to his American readers. They included (1) the duty of a government to protect a people's unalienable "natural rights"—among which are "Life, Liberty, and the Pursuit of Happiness"; and (2) government's origin in the consent of those governed. The preamble also spoke of the obligation of a people to alter or abolish their government whenever their rights were persistently violated—in other words, it defended their right to revolution. (For the complete text of the Declaration of Independence, see the back of this volume.)

John Adams later said that there was "nothing new" in Jefferson's Declaration. Its author would have agreed. Most of these ideas had been included in earlier statements of independence. What was new about the Declaration, which Congress adopted on July 4, 1776, was its suggestion that Americans had become a single, separate people, and the "united colonies" a single, separate nation. The president of the Continental Congress, John Hancock, reportedly said as he signed the Declaration (the first to do so): "We must be unanimous; there must be no pulling different ways; we must all hang together." To which Benjamin Franklin supposedly replied: "Yes, we must indeed all hang together, or most assuredly we shall all hang separately." The exchange probably never occurred. But it suggests an important symbolic truth. During the previous decade, colonists had come to think of their loyalties as national. They had begun to see themselves as Americans, not just as Massachusetts people, New Yorkers, or Virginians.

From a sense of shared grievances and efforts at common action, a broader definition of national loyalty had begun to evolve. This pattern of allegiance would be strengthened immeasurably in the revolutionary struggle that loomed ahead. Even for many of those who had hoped for a compromise settlement, there seemed to be no choice but to acknowledge their mutual peril as *Americans* in revolt.

SUGGESTED READINGS-CHAPTERS 7-8

Boston Massacre

Richard B. Morris, *Government and Labor in Early America* (1946); Carl Bridenbaugh, *Cities in Revolt, 1743–1776* (1955) and *Mitre and Sceptre* (1962); Edmund S. Morgan, *Birth of the Republic, 1763–1789* (1956); Edmund S. Morgan and Helen M. Morgan, *The Stamp Act Crisis* (1953); Hiller B. Zobel, *Boston Massacre* (1976).

Economic Life

Lewis C. Gray, *History of Agriculture in the Southern United States to 1860* (2 vols., 1933); Arthur L. Jensen, *Maritime Commerce of Colonial Philadelphia* (1963); Richard Pares, *Yankees and Creoles* (1950).

Social and Cultural Life

J. T. Adams, *Provincial Society, 1690–1763* (1927); Bernard Bailyn, *Education in the Forming of American Society* (1960); Sacvan Berkovitch, *The Puritan Origins of the American Self* (1975); Daniel J. Boorstin, *The Americans: The Colonial Experience* (1958); Carl Bridenbaugh, *Cities in the Wilderness, 1625–1742* (1938) and *Myths and Realities: Societies of the Colonial South* (1952); J. M. Bumsted, and John E. Van de Wetering, *What Must I Do To Be Saved?* (1976); Lawrence A. Cremin, *American Education: The Colonial Experience, 1607–1783* (1970); Alan Heimert, *Religion and the American Mind From the Great Awakening to the Revolution* (1966); James A. Henretta, *The Evolution of American Society, 1700–1815* (1973); Michael Kraus, *The Atlantic Civilization: Eighteenth Century Origins* (1949); Ernest May, *The Enlightenment in America* (1976); Richard Slotkin, *Regeneration Through Violence* (1973); R. P. Stearns, *Science in the British Colonies of America* (1970); Louis B. Wright, *The Cultural Life of the American Colonies, 1607–1763* (1957); Michael Zuckerman, *Peaceable Kingdoms* (1970).

Politics and Government

Charles M. Andrews, *The Colonial Period in American History,* (vol. IV, 1938); Bernard Bailyn, *Origins of American Politics* (1968); Lawrence H. Gipson, *The British Empire Before the American Revolution,* (15 vols., 1936–1970); Jack P. Greene, *The Quest For Power* (1963); Michael Kammen, *Empire and Interest* (1969); Leonard W. Labaree, *Royal Government in America* (1930); Howard H. Peckham, *The Colonial Wars, 1689–1762* (1964).

Origins of the Revolution

John R. Alden, *The American Revolution, 1775–1783* (1969); Charles M. Andrews, *Colonial Background of the American Revolution* (1924, rev. ed., 1931); Bernard Bailyn, *Ideological Origins of the American Revolution* (1967) and *The Ordeal of Thomas Hutchinson* (1974); Thomas C. Barrow, *Trade and Empire: The British Customs Service in Colonial America, 1660–1775* (1967); John Brooke, *King George III* (1972); Robert M. Calhoon, *The Loyalists in Revolutionary America* (1973); Ian R. Christie and Benjamin W. Labaree, *Empire or Independence, 1760–1776* (1976); Oliver M. Dickerson, *The Navigation Acts and The American Revolution* (1951); Lawrence H. Gipson, *The Coming of the Revolution* (1954); Jack P. Greene, ed., *The Reinterpretation of the American Revolution, 1763–1789* (1968); George H. Guttridge, *English Whiggism and the American Revolution* (1972); Merrill Jensen, *Founding of a Nation* (1968); Stephen G. Kurtz and James H. Hutson, eds., *Essays on the American Revolution* (1973); Pauline Maier, *From Resistance to Revolution* (1972); Jackson T. Main, *The Social Structure of Revolutionary America* (1965); Richard Merritt, *Symbols of American Community, 1735–1775* (1966); William H. Nelson, *The American Tory* (1961); R. R. Palmer, *The Age of the Democratic Revolution,* (2 vols., 1955–1964); J. R. Pole, *Political Representation in England and the Origins of the American Republic* (1966); John Shy, *A People Numerous and Armed: Reflections on the Military Struggle for American Independence* (1976) and *Toward Lexington: The Role of the British Army in the Coming of the American Revolution* (1965); Willard Wallace, *Appeal to Arms* (1951); Chilton Williamson, *American Suffrage from Property to Democracy, 1760–1860* (1960); Esmond Wright, ed., *Causes and Consequences of the American Revolution* (1966); Alfred Young, ed., *The American Revolutionary* (1976).

9 GEORGE WASHINGTON AND THE TRANSITION TO NATIONHOOD

R. J. W.

Friday, October 19, 1781. A bright sun makes the weather warm for mid-autumn. A sense of expectancy hangs over the small Virginia hamlet of Yorktown, which stands on a low cliff above the York River, just a few miles from Jamestown. Inside Yorktown are about 7,000 British troops, commanded by Charles, Lord Cornwallis, the best of King George's generals in America. Facing Yorktown on the south and east are American and French armies under the command of George Washington. They have been digging trenches, mostly at night, edging closer and closer to the British lines. The Americans have some brass cannon advanced to within a few hundred feet of Cornwallis's defenses. The cannon will not be fired. Beyond the town, down the York River toward Chesapeake Bay, lies a fleet of French warships, preventing a British retreat by sea. The password of the day for Washington's troops: "Independence." The order of the day for Cornwallis's army: "Surrender."

At about two o'clock in the afternoon, along a road leading south out of Yorktown, the American and French armies lined up in formation, the Americans on one side of the road, the French on the other. Finally, the British came marching down the road. Their fife and drum corps played a melancholy tune entitled "The World Turned Upside Down." Cornwallis was "indisposed," so at the head of the British troops came an Irish brigadier, Charles O'Hara, Cornwallis's second in command.

He rode up to the French commander, the Comte de Rochambeau, who sat on horseback among a group of American and French officers. O'Hara offered to surrender his sword. Rochambeau refused it, and pointed silently toward Washington, the commander of the joint French-American force.

There was a moment of painful formality. Since Cornwallis himself had not approached the American commander, Washington refused to accept the sword from a second in command. The honor, he said, belonged to his second in command, Major General Benjamin Lincoln of Massachusetts.

Down the road from Yorktown came the tough, veteran British regiments. These were troops that had fought the Americans from New York to Charleston, year in and year out since 1776. General Lincoln directed them into a field encircled by French soldiers. One regiment after

York, Virginia 17th Octr. 1781

Sir

I propose a Cessation of Hostilities for Twenty four hours, and that two Officers may be appointed by each side to meet at Mr. Moore's house to settle terms for the surrender of the Posts of York & Gloucester. I have the honour to be

Sir

Your most obedient & most humble Servant

Cornwallis

His Excellency
General Washington
&c. &c. &c.

Lord Cornwallis asked for a meeting with the Americans at Yorktown four years to the day after Burgoyne's capitulation at Saratoga. Afterward, Cornwallis served as governor general of India and, later, as viceroy of Ireland.

another formed in the surrender field, saluted, laid down its weapons, and then marched out again. Some of the British troops were drunk, some cried, others cursed. Some marched quietly, probably glad that they no longer had to endure the American and French artillery bombardment of the past several days. But drunk or sober, cursing or quiet, they were prisoners, all 7,000 of them. No one knew it then — and a peace treaty would not come for two more years — but the War for American Independence was over.

For Washington it had been a difficult, sometimes bitter, six years since he had taken command of the militia that surrounded Gage's force in Boston. There had been times when he had rubbed his neck nervously and wondered whether it had been made for a noose. At one time or another, the British had managed to occupy Boston, New York, Philadelphia, and Charleston — all the important coastal cities. In the summer and fall of 1776, the British had landed a huge army of 20,000 men on Staten Island, in New York harbor. This force had methodically driven Washington out of Long Island, then off Manhattan and down into New Jersey. Washington's troops did not fight well, and their weapons were poor. The Americans ran away so fast that at one point the British buglers ridiculed them by blowing a fox-hunting call to signal a charge.

Gradually, Washington had to learn a hard lesson. He was involved in a type of guerrilla warfare. The enemy used larger and better-trained armies in the field. Thus the Americans, without a well-organized force, could pursue only a hit-and-run strategy. Washington had to learn, too, that the British could afford to lose major battles, but that he could not. One smashing defeat and the movement for independence would be lost. The men whom Americans now celebrate as the Founding Fathers — the Adamses, Jefferson, Franklin, Washington, and the others — would simply be hanged as traitors. The British, on the other hand, could afford to lose one army after another until their people and politicians back home grew tired of the war.

Washington learned these lessons. He kept his army on the move. Sometimes he surprised the enemy. This happened with a force of German mercenaries at Trenton on the morning after Christmas in 1776, when he crossed the half-frozen Delaware River to wake the enemy to the sound of his guns. But every time large numbers of British made an important move near the coast, Washington was practically helpless. In the summer of 1777, the year after he had chased Washington out of New York, the British General Sir William Howe decided to take Philadelphia. Washington resisted at Brandywine, just south of the city. But the British overcame his force and ran the Continental Congress out of Philadelphia. Washington tried to make another stand at Germantown but was unsuccessful. He then retired to Valley Forge, between Philadelphia and Trenton, to spend a cold and hungry winter. Washington's steadiness of purpose encouraged the small band of soldiers whose sufferings he shared.

The Americans had a real chance only when the British marched inland from the coast. Then their huge fleet gave them no protection, and

Life and Leisure in the Young Republic

''The eighteenth century's greatest epoch was undeniably the time when long-oppressed and devastated America appeared on the world theater and presented herself before amazed Europe in full youthful power as a separate self-governing state.'' So wrote Axel Klinkowström, who visited the new nation shortly after its birth, and commented favorably on the American people. (Those shown here are strolling past a town house in Philadelphia.) Indeed, the Revolutionary period was an exciting time for the United States. But Americans continued to savor the pleasures of home and the world around them. Having ensured their economic survival and political independence, they were now creating a distinctive life of their own.

[For further information on the foreign observers quoted in this essay, see ''Notes on Sources.'']

PICTORIAL ESSAY 3

Mary Lightfoot of Virginia, age seven

The European instructors brought to teach in America have always admired the docility and modesty with which girls behave whenever they find themselves in a school with a regular discipline, at least if they are not spoiled to begin with. These qualities are united to a certain freeness and maturity of judgment rarely found elsewhere.

[GIOVANNI GRASSI, 1810-17]

Pennsylvania Germans singing a birthday song

At Bethlehem, I went to the house of the "single men." I entered the manager's apartment, and found him busy copying music. He had in his room a piano, made in Germany. I talked music with him, and discovered that he was not only a performer but a composer as well. When we went into the chapel together, I asked him to play the organ. He played some improvisations, into which he introduced a great deal of harmony and chords in the bass.

[MARQUIS DE CHASTELLUX, 1782]

In the United States on the seventh day of every week, the trading and working life of the nation seems suspended. All noises cease. A deep tranquillity, say rather the solemn calm of meditation, succeeds the turmoil of the week, and the soul resumes possession and contemplation of itself. Laying aside for a while the petty passions which agitate life and the fleeting interests which engross it, the American strays into an ideal world, where all is great, eternal, and pure.

[ALEXIS DE TOCQUEVILLE, 1835]

"The First, Second, and Last Scene of Mortality," needlework by Prudence Punderson of Connecticut

At about seven or eight o'clock of the evenings when there are no formal dinners they have tea. At tea the whole family is reunited and friends, acquaintances, and even strangers are invited. Tea in the evening is accompanied by a boring and dull etiquette. The mistress of the house serves, and passes the cups around. Until you turn over the cup and put the spoon on top they will keep bringing you fresh cups. There are a thousand stories, true or false, of Frenchmen, ignorant of this customary signal, who were drowned with that beverage.

[M.-L.-E. MOREAU DE SAINT-MÉRY, 1794-98]

A Rhode Island family at tea

*The theater is on the southeast side of the park, and is a
large, commodious building. The interior is handsomely
decorated and fitted up in as good style as the London
theaters, upon a scale suitable to the population of the city.
The scenes are well painted and numerous. The machinery,
dresses, and decorations are elegant and appropriate to the
performances, which consist of all the new pieces that
appear in London, and several of Shakespeare's best plays.*

[JOHN LAMBERT, 1806]

Playgoers watching an English farce at the Park Theater, New York City

Shopping at the furniture store of Duncan Phyfe, New York City

Blindfold an Englishman and convey him to New York, unbind his eyes, and he will think himself in an English city. The same sort of streets; shops precisely the same; the same beautiful and modest women crowding in and out of them; the same play-houses; the same men, same dress, same language. He will miss by day only the nobility and the beggars, and by night only the streetwalkers and pickpockets.

[WILLIAM COBBETT, 1817-19]

An English fashion plate of the late eighteenth century

The taste in dress is chiefly English, extremely simple, neat, and elegant. The finest cloth and the finest linen are the greatest adornment. The women (as everywhere), seeking to please, allow themselves more variety of ornament than the men. Every year dressed dolls are brought from Europe, which, silent, give the law of the mode. However, distinction of rank among the feminine half is not striking as a result of any distinct costume. In the item of dress, each selects according to her taste, means, and circumstances.

[JOHANN DAVID SCHOEPF, 1783]

The dinner was served in the American, or, if you will, in the English, fashion. It consisted of two courses. One included the entrées, roast, and warm side dishes, the other, the sweet pastries and preserves. When the second course is removed, the cloth is taken off, and apples, walnuts, and chestnuts are served. It is then that healths are drunk; the coffee which comes afterwards serves as a signal to rise from table.

[MARQUIS DE CHASTELLUX, 1780]

A dinner party in Boston

The crafts are greatly respected in this country. They have taken on a different character than in Europe. The rich merchant continues, in spite of his success and the public offices he may have held, to put his hands to his own work.

[AXEL KLINKOWSTRÖM, 1820]

A quilting bee in the South

Dancing, for the inhabitants of the United States, is less a matter of self-display than it is of true enjoyment. At the same dance you will see a grandfather, his son and his grandson, but more often still the grandmother, her daughter, and her granddaughter. If a Frenchman comments upon this with surprise, he is told that each one dances for his own amusement, and not because it's the thing to do.

[M.-L.-E. MOREAU DE SAINT-MÉRY, 1794-98]

Merrymaking at a Wayside Inn, by Paul Svinin

The End of the Hunt, artist unknown

Hunting in Virginia was a far different thing from its English original. The meaning of the latter is simple and explicit. A party of horsemen meet at an appointed spot and hour, to turn up or turn out a deer or a fox, and pursue him to a standstill. Here a local peculiarity—the abundance of game—upsets all system. The practice seemed to be for the company to enter the wood, beat up the quarters of anything from a stag to a snake, and take their chance for a chase. If the game went off well and it was possible to follow it through the thickets and morasses, ten to one that at every hundred yards up sprung so many rivals that horses and hunters were puzzled which to select. Every man, if he chose, could have a deer to himself—an arrangement, I was told, that proved generally satisfactory, since it enabled the worst rider, when all was over, to talk about as many difficulties surmounted as the best.

[JOHN BERNARD, 1799]

Tombstone of a minister, from a New England graveyard

The inhabitants of Marlborough [Massachusetts] are nearly all Congregationalists. The prayers of those Congregational ministers whom I have heard have been of a general and tolerant nature which embraces all sects and denominations of Christians, beseeching the safety and welfare of all men without respect of persons. Their sermons were generally zealous, but devoid of all absurd tenets, dogmas, and denunciations. Faith was earnestly recommended, but the necessity of good works was strenuously enforced.

[JOHN LAMBERT, 1808]

Princeton is a college built by the state of Jersey some years before the war. I dismounted to visit this vast edifice for a moment. I was almost immediately joined by Mr. Witherspoon, the president. From him I learned that this college is a complete university and that it can contain two hundred students and more. There is only one class of the humanities. Two others are devoted to perfecting the young men in the study of Latin and Greek, a fourth to natural philosophy, mathematics, astronomy, etc., and a fifth to moral philosophy.

[MARQUIS DE CHASTELLUX, 1782]

Nassau Hall at the time of the Revolution

their lines of supply and reinforcement were stretched too far. In the summer of 1777, while Howe was capturing Philadelphia, British General John Burgoyne pushed down from Canada toward Albany, a long and difficult overland march. Burgoyne was met at Saratoga in September by several American forces. There he was beaten into surrender. This defeat saved the Revolution by encouraging the French to enter the war on the side of the Americans. In the South, the British were able to take Charleston easily enough. But again, when they went inland during 1780 and 1781, the Americans turned them back time after time.

Finally, at Yorktown, Cornwallis's army was cornered. The British force had fought its way in a twisting path up from Charleston, across South Carolina, North Carolina, and half of Virginia. During this campaign, Cornwallis had been able to move through the country almost at will. But he had not been able to control the countryside or defeat the Americans. At last, in October 1781, Washington put together a superior force outside Yorktown. It consisted of his own Continental army, some militia units, and some French troops. In the Chesapeake, giving decisive help, was the French fleet.

After Cornwallis surrendered, the British could have continued the war. They might have sent another army, and yet another, and then a new fleet. But the French were tying the British down in the West Indies and in Europe, and the British were tired of the American war. When Lord North, the prime minister, received the news of Yorktown on a Sunday in November, he exclaimed wildly, "It's all over!" He soon resigned, and the British evacuated Charleston. Peace negotiations opened in Paris in April 1782 among British, French, and American commissioners. Their dealings were lengthy, but it gradually became clear that the fighting was over.

After Yorktown, General Washington rested for a week at Mount Vernon—his first time there in six years. Then he moved his army to Newburgh, New York, to await the outcome of peace negotiations. The American Congress ratified the peace treaty, the Treaty of Paris, in April 1783. But the British did not evacuate New York until November. At last, early in December of 1783, Washington decided that his war was over. He asked his officers to meet him at an inn to say goodbye. One of them, a member of Washington's staff, wrote a moving account of the scene:

> The time now drew near when the Commander-in-Chief intended to leave for his beloved retreat at Mount Vernon. On Tuesday, the fourth of December, it was made known to the officers then in New York that General Washington intended to commence his journey on that day.
> At twelve o'clock the officers repaired to Fraunces' Tavern in Pearl Street, where General Washington had appointed to meet them and to take his final leave of them. We had been assembled but a few moments when His Excellency entered the room. His emotion, too strong to be concealed, seemed to be reciprocated by every officer present.
> After partaking of a slight refreshment, in almost breathless silence, the General filled his glass with wine, and turning to his officers, he said, "With a heart full of love and gratitude, I now take leave of you. I most devoutly wish that your

War broke out in April **1775**, with clashes at Lexington and Concord. In May, Ethan Allan and his "Green Mountain Boys," a small colonial force from what is now Vermont, captured Fort Ticonderoga and Crown Point. In the fall, Americans led by Richard Montgomery and Benedict Arnold launched an unsuccessful assault against Canada in an effort to get Quebec to join the rebellion.

The next year, **1776**, saw action in both South and North. At Moore's Creek Bridge, Patriots were victorious against a group of Loyalists. Americans also repulsed a British naval attack on Charleston. The British were forced to evacuate Boston in March. However, they defeated the Americans decisively at the Battle of Long Island (August 27) and the Battle of White Plains (October 28). Washington retreated southward, but on December 26 routed German mercenaries at Trenton. Eight days later he defeated Cornwallis at Princeton.

The two chief campaigns of **1777** took place in the North. In June Burgoyne invaded the United States from Quebec. He took Fort Ticonderoga, but was stopped at Bennington on August 16 by New Hampshire militiamen. After defeats at Saratoga in September and October, he surrendered on October 19 — a loss that led to the alliance between the United States and France. Meanwhile, Howe left New York for Philadelphia. Washington failed to stop him at Brandywine (September 11) and Germantown (October 5), and went into winter quarters at nearby Valley Forge.

In **1778**, the British, now led by Sir Henry Clinton, evacuated Philadelphia. That summer, George Rogers Clark, a Kentucky militiaman under orders from Virginia, led 175 men into the west and succeeded in seizing the British forts at Kaskaskia, Cahokia, and Vincennes. A setback to the American cause was Clinton's capture of Savannah in December.

After an indecisive period throughout **1779**, the year **1780** brought increased conflict. Clinton took Charleston in the spring and Cornwallis defeated an American force at Camden on August 16. But an American victory at King's Mountain (October 7) kept Cornwallis from progressing farther.

In **1781**, Cornwallis was victorious at Guilford Courthouse (March 15). Heavy losses followed, however, and he was forced to retreat to Wilmington. Late in the summer he made his way to Yorktown. There he was trapped by land forces under Washington and Rochambeau and a fleet under the Comte de Grasse. Cornwallis' surrender on October 19 ended the war.

---

latter days may be as prosperous and happy as your former ones have been glorious and honorable."

After the officers had taken a glass of wine, General Washington said, "I cannot come to each of you, but shall feel obliged if each of you will come and take me by the hand."

General Knox, being nearest to him, turned to the Commander-in-Chief, who, suffused in tears, was incapable of utterance, but grasped his hand, when they embraced each other in silence. In the same affectionate manner, every officer in the room marched up to, kissed, and parted with his General-in-Chief.

Such a scene of sorrow and weeping I had never before witnessed, and hope I may never be called upon to witness again.

But the time of separation had come, and waving his hand to his grieving children around him, he left the room, and passing through a corps of Light Infantry that had been paraded to receive him, he walked silently on to Whitehall, where a barge was waiting. We all followed in mournful silence to the wharf, where a prodigious crowd had assembled to witness the departure of the man who, under God, had been the great agent in establishing the glory and independence of these United States. As soon as he was seated, the barge put off into the river, and the great and beloved General waved his hat and bid us a silent adieu.

From the New Jersey shore Washington rode south to Philadelphia, then on to Annapolis, Maryland, where Congress was in session.[1] The "General-in-Chief" was by far the most popular and respected man in America. The new nation had a weak government, few traditions, and almost no leaders of national stature. Washington could easily and quickly have claimed political powers equal to his military powers. But he chose to resign. He went to Annapolis to turn in his commission as general of all Continental forces. In a draft of a speech to Congress, he spoke

---

[1] After the Continental Congress was forced to leave Philadelphia, it met in several towns for varying lengths of time. It held sessions in Annapolis for a year, beginning in November 1783.

THE REVOLUTIONARY WAR

U.S. moves
British moves
★ Battle

MILES
0   200

of an "affectionate and final farewell" and of taking "ultimate leave" of
public office.

For some reason, though, when Washington actually delivered
the speech to Congress on December 23, he struck out the words "final"
and "ultimate." At the end of his address Washington said only that he

was taking "leave of all public employments." His farewell was only "affectionate," not "final."

The General Washington who resigned his commission was in many ways the simplest and most straightforward of men. Even his very few enemies recognized his almost perfect honesty and forthrightness. But Washington also embodied some important paradoxes of the American Revolution and the American situation in general. He was, to begin with, an aristrocrat who (along with other aristocrats) had somehow led the first modern revolution, a revolution with many democratic overtones. Furthermore, history had placed Washington at the absolute center of the revolutionary stage. It is probably true that if he had been killed or captured or become ill, the Revolution would have collapsed very quickly. But Washington was not, at heart, a dedicated revolutionary. He had been involved in the movement for revolution in Virginia from almost the beginnings in the 1760s. But he did not have the flaming philosophical dedication of the men whose words and ideas had been so important: Thomas Jefferson, Thomas Paine, Samuel Adams, and others like them. Before 1776, Washington had been a minor figure in the Virginia movement. Even during the war, he was often dismayed to find himself so constantly at center stage. And when the war was over, he appeared to want nothing more than to return to Mount Vernon by Christmas Day 1783, and to stay there.

These paradoxes in Washington point to some larger problems of his country. In the last analysis, his power and influence had been military. He was not a great general in the tactical sense. But he was the only general, over the long haul from 1775 to 1783, whom everyone could trust. And, as a general, he had maintained the only real unity and sense of nationality the Americans had. Now the fighting was over, the army broken up, and Washington back at Mount Vernon. Could Americans create a political unity to replace the military one that had won the Revolution? Would political leaders come forward who could unify the former colonies the way Washington had managed to hold the Continental army together at Valley Forge? And would political institutions be developed to replace the war as a means of making Virginians and New Yorkers into one people? These were the questions that were raised, indirectly, by Washington's retirement to Mount Vernon. And the indirect questions soon became more tangible.

When Washington rode home at the end of 1783, he had no wish to raise any such questions. Indirect or direct, they simply were not much on his mind. He was a public figure, and he knew it. From the time of the Revolution on, his life would always be full of public affairs. His days would be taken up with receiving distinguished visitors in his Virginia home. And an incredible amount of his time would always be absorbed with writing to important political figures, in both Europe and America. (His letters fill thirty-nine thick volumes.) But thinking about public affairs, entertaining important visitors, and keeping up a steady correspondence on the issues of the day—all these did not necessarily

NORTH AMERICA IN 1783

CLAIMED BY
RUSSIA, SPAIN,
AND BRITAIN

CLAIMED BY U.S.
AND BRITAIN

CLAIMED BY U.S.
AND BRITAIN

UNITED
STATES

CLAIMED BY U.S.
AND SPAIN

British
French
Spanish
Russian
Unexplored or disputed

involve a direct participation in politics and government. What Washington wanted in 1783 was time—time to rest, time to build his plantation and attend to the thousands of acres of land he owned in the west. He wanted time for his wife, Martha, and the rest of his family, time for riding, foxhunting, and the other preoccupations of a leisured Virginia planter.

At first it seemed to work. Washington enjoyed his self-imposed retirement. Since it was winter, there was little farm work to supervise. The roads were bad, and not very many visitors came. The general seemed to believe he could turn himself into a gentleman planter again. To old military comrades he wrote: "The tranquil walks of domestic life are now beginning to unfold themselves. I am retiring within myself." He described himself as a "wearied traveller," home at last "after treading many a painful step with a heavy burden on his shoulders."

Turning inward for Washington had always meant Mount Vernon. This great estate was the center of Washington's conception of himself as a private man. Mount Vernon always represented the opposite of his public life. It was his refuge and sanctuary.

Mount Vernon was indeed a comfortable sanctuary. The great mansion that is now an American landmark was not yet finished, but it was rich, large, and beautiful. It stood on the Potomac River, about fifteen miles south of present-day Washington, D.C. Around the house lay the plantation, some 8,000 acres of land, covering four full miles along one bank of the river. The plantation was built and sustained by about 200 slaves. Everything about it was on a grand scale. The working land was divided into several different farms, with names like "River Farm" and "Muddy Hole Farm." From these farms came huge quantities of food. The plantation as a whole produced eight tons of pork every year for the slaves and the rest of Washington's "family." Other items of food—including enormous quantities of fish from the Potomac—were produced by the wagonload or barrelful.

And so, in Washington's heart, Mount Vernon was the visible, touchable focus of his private life. Another focus—that of politics, revolution, war—always pulled him away from Mount Vernon, out into the world of Virginia and American politics. When Washington resigned his commission in 1783, not only had he just left the army, but he had also returned home in a very special sense. He was fifty-one years old. He was healthy (except for the bad teeth that bothered him all his life). Yet he was a healthy man on the downhill side of middle age. For all he or anyone else could tell, he had already reached his peak of fame, public service, and involvement in politics. If he had never again left Mount Vernon, he probably would still have been known as the Father of His Country.

Mount Vernon in 1790. On the lawn stroll Washington and his wife, arm in arm. With them are her two children—Nelly Custis at left and George Custis (with his tutor) at right.

There were two flaws, however, in the picture Washington had of himself. More than any other man in the country, he *was* the American cause. In an almost unique way, vanity and patriotism were the same emotion in him. He was so closely identified with his new country that any ambition for it almost amounted to an ambition for himself—and vice versa. In an odd sense, Washington could actually have no private life. The second flaw was that he was in some ways a poor man. He would have to build his fortune rather than retire on a fortune ready-made. The war had been expensive for him and his plantation. Slaves had been sold and crops had spoiled. Also, Washington had accepted no salary during his years as commanding general—though he had been reimbursed for his actual expenses.

As Washington added up his accounts in 1784, he found himself short of money. At the end of the year he could not have put his hands on more than £86 in cash (about $500). In land he was rich—at least on paper. Besides Mount Vernon, he owned well over 30,000 acres in the West, which he had bought before the war. Some of this land was just west of Pittsburgh. More was farther down the Ohio River near the present city of Cincinnati. The land was a speculation, however, only a potential source of wealth. It was worth very little at this time. Mount Vernon with its slaves was a great plantation, but the land had become too poor for successful tobacco agriculture. (From Berkeley's time on, tobacco had been a great depleter of soil.) The plantation was simply not a paying proposition in any substantial way.

Washington's wealth made him one of the richest men in America. But it was an odd form of wealth. Either it was impossible to turn into ready cash, like Mount Vernon itself, or it was potential wealth, like the western lands. Washington's other assets—fine horses, clothes, furniture, and dogs—were all luxuries, not real wealth.

In many respects, Washinton's financial future rested on the lands in the West. The value of those lands, in turn, depended on getting settlers to the West, improving road and water transportation, and extending orderly government into the Ohio Valley. In a very concrete way, then, Washington's future was tied to the nation's. He was not a narrow man, and he was certainly not selfish. But it was clear to him that he had a great stake in the new Republic. If it prospered, so would he. And if it became a respectable nation among nations, his work in shaping it would have been worthwhile and his reputation and honor secure.

These kinds of concerns and reflections drew the retired general back toward public life. Mount Vernon could not be walled off from the world, nor could Washington daydream for long on "the tranquil walks of domestic life." He had too much energy and too much of the habit of participation and power. These traits were reinforced by his great pride in himself and his country. When Washington's economic circumstances were added to such a picture, almost anyone could easily have predicted that his retirement would be either very short or very incomplete.

The most direct temptation to involvement beyond Mount Vernon led west, to the Ohio Valley lands. Several issues were on Washington's mind. He was angry that land speculators were illegally offering his Ohio land for sale in Philadelphia and New York markets. Trespassers, or "squatters," were living on his land near Pittsburgh, without paying rent or recognizing Washington's title. Also, several Virginians, including Thomas Jefferson, were talking about opening up a trade route from the Chesapeake Bay area to the West. They planned to use the Potomac River and some of the branches of the Ohio for water transportation, possibly building canals or new roads across the short stretches between the eastern and western rivers. Washington was very interested in such schemes. They would help his state and the nation. And, obviously, opening the West for settlement and trade would also be to his own economic advantage.

All these concerns put Washington on horseback in early September 1784 for a trip west. He was accompanied by his nephew, and an old friend and his son, plus three servants. The group started northwest along the Potomac toward the Allegheny Mountains and Pittsburgh. From there they planned to go by boat to the lands down the Ohio. On the way, Washington traveled over what was known as Braddock's Road, through territory he had scouted, surveyed, and fought in as a young soldier thirty years earlier in the French and Indian War. Now the French were gone, the country was filling with farmers, and the British were surrendering the entire Ohio Valley to the Americans.

Washington traveled as the first citizen of the United States. But he traveled to argue with plain farmers who were living on his land and who were not ready to surrender what they thought of as their rights, even to the Revolutionary General-in-Chief. Trying to maintain a pace of five miles an hour, he finally reached his land on September 18. In his diary, he kept a running account of his encounter with the squatter famers:

> September 19th: Being Sunday, and the people living on my land *apparently* very religious, it was thought best to postpone going among them till tomorrow.
> 20th: Went early this morning to view my land, and to receive the final determination of those who live upon it. Dined at David Reed's, after which Mr. James Scot and Reed began to inquire whether I would part with the land, and upon what terms. They did not conceive they could be dispossessed, but to avoid contention they would buy if my terms were moderate. I told them I had no inclination to sell. However, after hearing a great deal of their hardships, their religious principles, and unwillingness to separate or remove, I told them I would make a last offer: the whole tract at 25 shillings per acre. Or they could become tenants upon leases of 999 years.

The "tenants" discussed the question among themselves for a long time, while Washington sat gravely to one side. Then they turned back to him and said that they would not buy, move off, or pay rent. Washington would have to sue them:

> They had a long consultation. They then determined to stand suit for the land. I told them I would receive their answers individually, and accordingly I called

them by name as they stood. They severally answered that they meant to stand suit, and abide the issue of the law.

Washington probably saw cabins like this one on his trip west. The chimney was a refinement; many such buildings had only a hole in the roof for escaping smoke.

Washington had come face to face, on a very practical level, with a problem that was worrying many wealthy Americans who lived in the East: Would the settlers in the new lands beyond the mountains be subject to rules and laws made in the East? Could the frontier be governed? Or would the new areas be lawless and separate from the United States? Theoretically, as educated Americans looked toward the Mississippi River, the wilderness seemed to be both a tremendous opportunity and a tremendous problem. But Washington did not have to think on a theoretical level. (He was not much of a philosopher by nature, anyway.) He had already encountered the problem, and it had the most direct and worrisome kinds of consequences for him. If the time came for using governmental power to deal with such problems, he would be ready to see that power put to use.

The question of power and the western lands presented itself in yet another way on Washington's trip. The general had planned to go down the Ohio to his other lands, but every traveler he met coming east advised him to stay away. The Indians, they said, were on the warpath. He was told over and over that it would be dangerous to travel much farther into the Ohio country. He decided to head for home, having accomplished almost nothing. Some day, he thought to himself and later wrote to his friends, the United States would have to deal aggressively with the Indians. The government would have to buy land, make treaties, and, if necessary, use force. The problems and opportunities of westward expansion seemed always to demand more power and stronger government.

So far, Washington had met only disappointment. But his return trip had its rewards. He decided to head for home by a southern route up the Cheat River, a tributary of the Monongahela that cuts south into what is now West Virginia (see map, page 208). From there he would cross the mountains to the upper reaches of the Potomac, looking for places to build connecting roads between the two rivers. If such roads were possible, all the future produce of the Ohio Valley could come down the Potomac to Virginia instead of going north and east to New York or down the Mississippi to New Orleans. Virginia could become the commercial center of the new nation.

Washington headed up the Cheat on September 23. His trip took eleven days. Along the way he carefully noted every twist and turn of the rivers, every rapids, every stretch along which roads might be built. The going was rough. The discomfort, however, had been worth it. For Washington believed that this part of the trip was a success. He felt that he had found the key to the future of the West, of his own lands, of Virginia, and of the struggling economy of his young nation.

When Washington reached Mount Vernon on October 4, he went to work on a series of detailed reflections about his trip:

4th: Reached home before sundown, having travelled on the same horses since the first day of September, by the computed distances, 680 miles.

And, 'tho I was disappointed in one of the objects, namely to examine the land I hold on the Ohio and Kanawha, and rescuing them from the hands of land jobbers and speculators, I say notwithstanding this disappointment, I am well pleased with my journey.

Page after page in his diary he filled with his thoughts and calculations—detailed estimates of distance, of what rivers were navigable and how far, and where the lines of trade might eventually run. He began with an analysis of river transportation in northern Virginia. All the rivers, taken as a network, "could afford water transportation for all that fertile country between the Blue Ridge and the Allegheny Mountains." This filled Washington with proud confidence about the economic future of Virginia. But his thoughts ran well beyond the boundaries of his state, far to the west. The trade of western Virginia, great as it might become, was still "trifling, when viewed upon that immeasurable scale which is inviting our attention!"

Here was the key to Washington and to many others like him in the new nation. They had won independence. Now their minds were free to concentrate on the richest kinds of visions about the future of their country—especially, a new empire to the west! Part of Washington's mind may have been tied to Mount Vernon and visions of retirement. But now he was thinking of expansion.

Nor were his reflections vague and abstract. Washington rummaged among all the maps and papers in his possession and worked out in surprising detail a scheme for connecting the Ohio Valley to the Atlantic, perferably through Virginia—past his own great mansion, in fact, down the Potomac to Chesapeake Bay. Detroit, he calculated, would be the critical point in the Ohio Valley. It would control all the commerce of the Great Lakes region—as far west, Washington figured, as the Lake of the Woods in northern Minnesota! According to Washington's estimates, the total distance from Detroit to Alexandria, Virginia, was only a little over 600 miles. The distances from Detroit to Philadelphia and New York were over 700 and 900 miles, respectively. So Virginia had the advantage. It would not be Philadelphia, New York, or Boston that would become the economic and commercial capitals of the Republic. It would be Alexandria. (This city is just across the river from Washington, D.C., today—though Washington had no idea in 1784 that the federal capital would ever be created.)

All these calcuations were of great importance for Washington. His mind ran in large strategic channels:

Hitherto, the people of the western country have had no excitements to industry; they labor very little. But let us open a good communication with the settlements west of us, and see how astonishingly our exports will be increased.

No well-informed mind need be told that the flanks and rear of the united territory are possessed by other powers, and formidable ones too. It is necessary to apply the cement of interest to bind all the parts of the country together by one indissoluble band, particularly the Middle States and country back of them.

After Washington returned from his trip west, he had this map printed on the basis of his sketches. Cumberland, lower right, is on the Potomac River in Maryland. The land to the north ("Glades of Great Yough") is part of Pennsylvania.

Washington had focused on a problem that would occupy him for a long time to come: how to apply the "cement" of economic interest—trade—to hold the nation together and make it powerful. If the United States failed to achieve this unity and power, the West might very soon form a new nation and separate from the United States, or it might even join with Spain or Great Britain.

As a result of his trip, Washington could see more clearly than before just how closely his own life was related to such large questions. His patriotism, which was intense and powerful, was not merely a notion or an ideal. It was also directly tied to his own stake in the future of the Republic that he had done so much to bring into existence.

All these reflections led to a simple set of questions: Would Americans have the good sense to see how much was at stake and what had to be done? Would the governments of Virginia and the other states support projects to make the new commerce come to life? Would the central government be stable and powerful enough to maintain the unity of the nation and hold the West in line? The symbolic questions that had ridden with Washington from New York to Virginia in 1783 were gradually becoming more and more real.

For Washington himself, a chain of events had begun that was to lead him eventually to join in overthrowing the existing government of the United States, creating a new constitution and government, and becoming the nation's first President. The chain ran clearly from his farmhouse confrontation with his Pennsylvania squatters in 1784 to the presidency four years later. One link in the chain was the observations he had made on the trip home. Another was his careful reflection on western trade. Now came the next link: an attempt to get Maryland and Virginia to cooperate in opening up the Potomac to trade.

When Washington reached home in October 1784, he moved quickly from reflections on the west to practical politics. He traveled to the new capital of Virginia at Richmond to lobby for his Potomac project. It was clear that Maryland would have to cooperate, since the Potomac formed the border between the two states. So Washington was appointed commissioner to arrange for similar legislation in the two states. It took him only three days to hurry to Maryland's capital, Annapolis, even though it meant missing his second Christmas at home since the war. Mount Vernon suddenly became a political clearing house. Washington was acting the politician in ways he had not practiced since he was a young man. He drafted laws, and copies passed through his home on their way to and from Richmond and Annapolis.

By the end of December everything was falling into place. Washington worked far past his usual nine o'clock bedtime on the project. As he wrote to his young friend James Madison on December 28, 1784: "It is now near 12 at night, and I am writing with an aching head, having been constantly employed in this business since the 22nd without assistance." His eyes and hand were tired, and the letter was messy: "I am ashamed to send such a letter, but cannot give you a fairer one." But the work was worth it.

Everything was complete by the first week in January. The legislatures of both Maryland and Virginia had appropriated money and joined in creating a joint-stock company to open up river transportation to the west. Washington was soon named president of the Potomac River Company, as it was called. Throughout the next two years he paid very close attention to its affairs. He fussed over the details of planning and surveying and suffered through all the delays. He went about the project with such energy that Madison made a very shrewd observation about him: "The earnestness shows that a mind like his, capable of grand views, and which has long been occupied with them, cannot bear a vacancy."

Commissioners from Maryland and Virginia met several times, at least once at Mount Vernon itself. Then, in January 1786, just a year after the Potomac Company was formed, the Virginia legislature took a surprising step that would soon have even more surprising consequences. The legislature suggested that delegates from all the states meet at Annapolis to discuss trade, taxes, and other matters of common concern. Such a meeting seemed innocent enough, but in fact it by-passed the existing central government completely. Washington thought carefully about the proposal. In many ways, it had grown directly out of his own work on the Potomac Company. But it raised large questions about the political future.

Washington was optimistic. He wrote a French friend:

> The country is recovering rapidly from the ravages of war. The seeds of population are scattered far in the wilderness. Agriculture is prosecuted with industry. The works of peace, such as opening rivers, building bridges, etc., are carried on with spirit.

Despite the apparent prosperity, there was a problem of government, a problem that made Washington and many of his friends increasingly uneasy. During the Revolution the states had written a consitution, the Articles of Confederation, to bring a central government into being. This government was weak, Washington thought, too weak to fulfill the vision of empire he believed in. If the central government was weak, the states would constantly quarrel with one another. All during 1785 Washington's letters were filled with complaints:

> Contracted ideas and absurd jealousy are leading us from those great principles which are characteristic of wise and powerful nations, and without which we are no more than a rope of sand. The Confederation appears to me to be little more than a shadow without the substance. If we are afraid to trust one another, there is an end of the Union. We are either a united people, or we are not. If we are not, let us no longer act a farce by pretending to it.

Because of these fears and doubts, Washington was concerned about the meeting at Annapolis, which was finally scheduled for September 1786. But the result of the meeting was only more anxiety. Only five states sent delegates. None at all came from New England. Here lay one source of Washington's frustrations. Out in the country, there was activity and opportunity. A great nation was waiting to be built, as it had waited in 1775 to be born. But the state governments, Washington felt, seemed to care nothing for the opportunity. Still, the few delegates who did come to Annapolis accomplished one thing. They recommended another meeting—a convention to begin in Philadelphia in May 1787—to consider what ought to be done to strengthen the Articles of Confederation.

Washington's reaction to the Annapolis Convention was a mixture of frustration and hope—frustration because more had not been accomplished and hope for a more promising meeting to be held in Philadelphia the following year. Other news soon burst in to trouble him further. An armed rebellion of some kind was under way in Massachusetts. Most of the rebels were farmers. They seemed to come mainly from the western part of the state. (They probably were men much like the tenants on Washington's Pennsylvania lands.) In September, bands of these men had kept courts from sitting in many sections of Massachusetts. Memories of 1776 crowded in on Washington. This time, however, it was an *American* government that was being threatened by mobs.

Friends sent Washington warped reports of the rebellion. It had a leader, a Revolutionary War captain named Daniel Shays. It was well organized and might even have foreign support (from old Tories, probably). Shays and his followers believed in some kind of radical division of all private property. They wanted all debts canceled, all taxes abolished. They were threatening to raid the federal arsenal at Springfield. Then they planned to march on Boston and bring down the established government.

These reports were wildly exaggerated, though Washington had no way of knowing it. Daniel Shays was not so much a leader of an organized movement as a surprised farmer who somehow found himself signing statements drawn up by the rebels. The rebels did not believe in abolishing private property, debts, or taxes. They were protesting more personal economic difficulties—namely, the seizure of their farms to pay their debts. The only time they threatened the Springfield arsenal, in January 1787, they were fired on by government cannon and ran away without returning a single shot. Once it reached the Springfield area, the Massachusetts militia (led by Benjamin Lincoln of Yorktown fame) easily put the rebellion down without a real battle.

To Washington, however, and to most men of wealth all along the eastern coast, Shays's Rebellion was like a sudden thunderclap. Washington's informants were in near panic, and he shared their fears. The leaders of the Revolutionary movement in the 1770s had always wildly exaggerated the dangers of British actions, as though every new tax meant tyranny or slavery. Now Washington and many of his friends exaggerated the significance of Shays's Rebellion. A few hundred farmers turning out to close some county courts seemed to spell the eventual downfall of the whole federal Republic.

On the last day of October, Washington sat at his writing table working on two long and important letters. The first was addressed to an organization of former Continental officers, the Society of the Cincinnati. Washington had been president of the Cincinnati for three years. They were scheduled to hold a general meeting and elect a president in May 1787 at Philadelphia. The time and place were exactly those chosen for the new convention to revise the Articles of Confederation. Washington's letter was a careful defense of his decision not to attend the meeting and not to serve again as president. He cited his heavy correspondence, his work on the Potomac Company, and problems with his health. All these increased his determination to pass the rest of his days "in a state of retirement." More than anything else, the general said, he wanted "tranquility and relaxation."

Washington's second letter was about Shays's Rebellion. It seemed to say that no matter how much he wanted retirement, Washington would not be able to stay away from politics:

> I am mortified beyond expression when I view the clouds that have spread over the brightest morn that ever dawned upon any country. You talk of employing influence to appease the present tumults in Massachusetts. Influence is no government. Let us have a government by which our lives, liberties and properties will be secured; or let us know the worst at once.

These are my sentiments. Let the reins of government be braced and held with a steady hand. If the Constitution is defective, let it be amended, but not trampled upon whilst it has an existence.

Washington's canal project, and his hopes for the West, had made it clear to him that the Confederation had its problems. Shays's Rebellion pushed him over the line. To him, the rebellion proved that even in the older states the Confederation could not guarantee public order. How could such a government hope to make western expansion orderly and secure? Washington was now convinced that the Articles of Confederation were not workable. The central government was almost bankrupt, barely able to meet its current obligations. More importantly, it could not even begin to pay off the huge debts that Congress had run up while fighting the war—debts owed to foreign governments as well as American citizens. And there was little hope that the debts would ever be paid, since the Articles did not give the central government the power to tax. It was very unlikely that this lack of taxing power would be remedied, either, since the Articles could be amended only with the agreement of every state.

There was another side to things, of course. Many political leaders believed that the problems of the Confederation would work themselves out in time. The west would be settled, the canals built, the debts somehow paid off. After all, even in a moment of crisis, Massachusetts had been able to handle Shays's Rebellion with ease. In any case, people's first loyalties belonged to their state and local governments, not to any central government, strong or weak. And there was always the gloomy possibility that a strengthened central government might turn out to behave like a king and a parliament. Washington, however, thought otherwise. All his experience, his ambitions, his interests, and his beliefs conspired to convince him that nationalism was the solution.

During the winter and early spring of 1786–1787, questions about the nation's future began to focus on Washington himself. He had more prestige than any man in America. No one else had a reputation approaching his as a man of honor, good sense, and character. If he wanted a stronger national government, how could he hold back from sharing in the movement to abandon the old constitution and write a new one?

The Virginia legislature nominated Washington as a delegate to the Philadelphia Convention. Some of his most faithful young followers, among them James Madison and Alexander Hamilton, kept urging him to join the movement. Others advised him to hold back, not to risk his flawless reputation on a venture that might prove to be an embarrassing failure. Month after month, Washington made excuses. Some were valid. He did have an aching rheumatism that forced him to go around the Mount Vernon farms with one arm in a sling. There were deaths in the family, financial troubles, and even a brief quarrel by letter with his mother. All these things reminded him that his life was full enough without involving himself in the creation of a new constitution.

In the end, though, Washington had no choice. The pressure from his friends was too powerful. His fears for his country were too strong. And, in the last analysis, he wanted to be part of a great event, to stand somewhere near the center of activity. In his letters of the spring, Washington referred often to his reputation. He was as close to being vain as he had been in twenty years. It may have been this vanity that provided the final tiny weight needed to tip the balance toward Philadelphia and away from Mount Vernon—though his rheumatism was better, too.

Philadelphia was miserable in May. It rained day after day. Most of the delegates were late in arriving. On the day the convention was set to open, only Virginia and Pennsylvania were represented. Gradually, enough delegates drifted into town to conduct business. To no one's surprise, Washington was unamimously elected president of the Convention. Week after week he sat in the chair, listening and wondering whether or not a new government could be created. Would the people accept this new Constitution? Would it work?

When the sections of the Constitution outlining the powers of the new office of President of the United States were being discussed, Washington must have listened with special care. Not a man in the room doubted that the office would belong to him if he would have it.

During the whole Convention Washington made only one speech. He had a talent for knowing when to be quiet and follow the lead of others who were quicker with words and ideas than he could ever be. Washington was always alert. He could follow a point in political theory or philosophy very well. But he made few. If he was a leader in Philadelphia, it was because other people trusted in his character, not because he led the way toward the new frame of government.

After the new Constitution had been created, Washington hoped for its ratification. Once more he did not actually lead. Younger men with more interesting minds—especially men like Madison and Hamilton—carried the burden of trying to explain the Constitution to an extremely suspicious public.

After a precarious struggle, the Constitution was ratified by the required number of states. The Articles of Confederation were set aside. A presidential election was held, and Washington was, almost inevitably, given all the electoral votes.

The new President left Mount Vernon for New York[2] in mid-April 1789. From town to town—Alexandria, Wilmington, Philadelphia, Princeton—the citizens and the militia turned out for ceremonies. The trip took seven days. Finally, on April 23, Washington took a barge across the Hudson to Manhattan. There were more salutes, bells, and cheers as he reentered the city he had left from Fraunces' Tavern. A week later, Washington was inaugurated on an open porch that looked down on a crowd in Wall Street. The judge who administered the oath turned to the cheering crowd and shouted, "Long live George Washington, President of the United States!"

---

[2]New York City was the capital of the United States until June 1790.

10
CREATING A NEW GOVERNMENT

R. J. W.

Late in the year 1799, George Washington died. It was the middle of December, cold and wet, but he was back home, at Mount Vernon. For eight years he had served as first President of the new Republic, and then had come a brief and final period of retirement. Washington's health had been good almost to the end, and he died gently. "I am just going," he said to a friend. "Have me decently buried and do not let my body be put into a vault in less than two days after I am dead. Do you understand me?" "Yes, sir," answered the friend. "'Tis well," said Washington, and soon he was dead. His body had to be measured for the coffin, and the doctor recorded that he was "in length, six feet, three-and-one-half inches, exact."

The measurement of Washington's "length" and his last words are interesting. His height, which was extraordinary in a day when most men were much shorter than they are today, was in keeping with the almost gigantic reputation he had acquired. There have been times, during his lifetime and the centuries since, when he seemed more than human, when he seemed to rise above his surroundings just as his enormous monument does today. Washington's last statement, "'Tis well," says a good deal about the kind of philosophical calm he seems to have won for himself during the long, difficult period between the Revolution and his death. About a month before he died, Washington heard from a friend about recent political troubles in the nation's capital. He would say nothing, Washington replied, because "the vessel is afloat, or very nearly so, and

considering myself as a passenger only, I shall trust to the mariners whose duty it is to watch, to steer it into a safe port."

Washington had come a long way since he took command of the straggling little army outside Boston in 1775. Now, at the end of the century, the "vessel was afloat." The Revolution had been won, difficult times had been endured, and the country had a government that looked promising. Washington had survived two presidential terms. John Adams, the second President, was now completing his term. The next year, the first year of the new century, a third President would be chosen. There had been two constitutions. There had been times when war with either Britain, France, or Spain looked inevitable. But somehow the "vessel" had stayed afloat. And the man who had stood so near the center of the stage in the turbulent quarter-century was indeed entitled to congratulations at the end.

It had not been easy. There were times when it had seemed impossible. Every single year of the twenty-five years between Lexington and Washington's death had held out hope and fear. Washington and his fellow Americans had acquired what amounted to a habit—hoping for the best and fearing the worst at the same time.

There was plenty to fear. The Revolution might be lost, and its leaders might, as Franklin had joked, "hang separately." Or the Americans might win the Revolution only to lose their country. They might not be able to create a stable national government to hold the old colonies together. Or the new nation might be carved up by hungry European powers, just as North America had earlier been divided among several empires.

But the sense of opportunity was just as intense as the sense of danger. If Americans could bring it off—that is, if they could make the Revolution work and their government survive—then they had a chance to create a nation built on principles of liberty. With half a huge continent in which to expand, this nation might break down the corruptions, the inequalities, the tyrannies that had ruined people's lives in Europe. A new kind of nation, a republic, with a new kind of citizen, might grow in prosperity, power, and peace.

In 1787 the first covered wagon left Ipswich, Massachusetts, for new land near Marietta, Ohio. Settlement of the west was a continuing problem for the confederation.

In the minds of most Americans, confidence and doubt lived together. They provided the backdrop against which a critical period of history was being acted out. There seemed to be only one real certainty in Washington's mind and in the minds of his countrymen: the fate of America was being decided in the years after 1775. Some held an even more extravagant opinion: that it was not just the fate of America but the fate of humanity that somehow hung in the balance.

Against such a backdrop every incident loomed as critical. Every issue seemed final.

Every hint of success or failure was read with the anxiety of a frightened fortuneteller. In taverns and town meetings citizens debated the issues of the day. They were likely to be poorly informed by a bad press and by rumor. But of one thing they were certain: one false move and they were finished. Even this "certainty" may have been incorrect. The history of the nation might well have taken the course it did no matter what short-run decisions people made.

Still, debate was the pastime of an entire generation during and after the Revolution. Gradually, in Congress, state legislatures, and conventions at Annapolis and Philadelphia, debates grew more and more skillful. Painfully, Americans piled up a mountain of experience in political theory. Their leaders became as sophisticated and adept as any generation of politicians in any nation's history. The questions were simple and classic: What form of government best preserves the liberties of its citizens? Can a national government exist without destroying individual states? How are powers to be split among legislative bodies, executive officers, and courts? What is the relationship between a national constitution and the laws of the states?

The real problems may have been practical ones, such as Washington's problem with his western lands. But American political leaders earned a generation's experience at translating practical problems into political theory and then retranslating the theory into practice through consitutions and legislation. If Washington could relax somewhat at the end, it was because he and his generation of Americans had survived a revolutionary quarter-century with an astonishing mixture of stubbornness, skill, and plain luck.

THE CONFEDERATION PERIOD

The First and Second Continental Congresses were revolutionary governing bodies. They had no real legal standing. To the British, especially, they were little more than collections of outlaws and traitors. They were engaged in an act of frightening significance—making a government where none had existed before. They exercised powers, such as making war, that usually belong only to established governments. Even before the Declaration of Independence was drawn up, the Second Continental Congress appointed a committee to draft a new consitution in order to give the government legitimacy. Congress debated the draft constitution until November 1777, when it agreed on the new Articles of Confederation. Another year passed before a majority of the states accepted the Articles.

In the meantime, the revolutionary government, the Continental Congress, simply kept on exercising power the way it had from the beginning. The arrangement was quite undemocratic in a way. Congress had no direct "consent" from the people. But there was a war on, and politics had to be adjusted to reality. At last, in the spring of 1781, Maryland, the last state, finally ratified—five years after the original committee had been appointed. The Articles were official. They created a new national government, bearing the name "The United States of America."

Government Under the Articles In most ways the new Articles simply confirmed the practices of the old Congress. The constitution created a confederation of states, each of which was to retain its "sovereignty, freedom and independence." The states were the real political entities. The Articles created a government that was somewhat like a national government but also somewhat like a treaty relationship among sovereign powers. The legislatures of the states chose delegates to the Congress. In Congress, voting was by states, with each state having one vote regardless of its population. Small states like Rhode Island and Delaware had as much legislative power as large states such as Virginia and Massachusetts. A state might choose to send as few as two delegates to Congress or as many as seven. No matter how many delegates it had, each state had an equal vote.

Congress had some of the powers that normally belong to national governments. It could declare war and raise armies and navies. It could borrow funds. It could coin money, issue paper money, and operate a post office. It could send ambassadors to and negotiate treaties with foreign nations. In essence, the states gave Congress the power to do all the things they had willingly allowed the king and Parliament to do before the Revolution.

But the states kept for themselves powers they had refused to allow the king and Parliament: regulating commerce and raising money through taxes. Congress could not control the conditions of trade among the states or with foreign nations. And when the United States needed money, as every government does, it had to ask the states for it in a request called a "requisition." If a state did not pay its requisition, Congress was powerless to enforce the issue.

It seems obvious today that a government that has no source of revenues is no government at all. But the states had recently been in the midst of a revolution against the central authority of Parliament and the crown. They did not want to create a new central government that might subvert their liberties the way the British had tried to do. To the average American his or her "country" still meant Virginia or Pennsylvania or Massachusetts. So Americans were ready to face the peace with the same kind of government that had conducted the war. This meant a government of states. They would work together to solve problems after they arose, but not before.

There was no federal judiciary under the Articles and no Supreme Court to make final decisions about constitutional questions. Congress had the power to settle disputes among states. This power was to work through a complicated system of arbitration, however, not through a national court. The state courts were expected to enforce federal law at the local level. There was no executive, either, although the Articles did provide for a number of secretaries that might eventually develop into a cabinet system like that of the British.

Obviously, there could be no separation of powers among legislative, judicial, and executive branches under the Articles. The colonists had long been familiar with the idea of separation of powers, for they had had ample experience in the conflicts between governors and assemblies. In all the state constitutions there were elaborate schemes of checks and balances—that is, the executive, legislative, and judicial departments were separated in function but balanced in power. At this time, though, the states thought of the national government as an instrument to be used only for certain very limited purposes.

Even the limited powers of the Congress were difficult to exercise. On all important questions nine votes out of thirteen were necessary for passage of a bill. This meant that a few small states could block any piece of legislation. It was almost impossible to amend the Articles. An amendment had to have the consent of every state. It was obvious that new states would soon be admitted to the Confederation. This would make it even more difficult to ratify amendments.

The Confederation had one excellent chance of surviving: a proposal to allow Congress to charge a tariff of 5 percent on all imports from abroad. An amendment providing for such a tariff was passed by every state but Rhode Island. But since amendments had to be unanimous, Rhode Island's refusal was enough to kill the proposal. The smallest state was able to block the Confederation's best hope of generating a steady source of revenue; and this, in turn, probably sealed the fate of the Articles.

Achievements Under the Articles Political leaders and historians have often dismissed the Articles of Confederation as a weak and ineffectual frame of government. After all, from Maryland's ratification in 1782 to the Philadelphia Convention, the Articles lasted only five years. And, in retrospect, it seems obvious that the Articles had so many flaws that a new constitution was almost inevitable.

But when the question is put into proper perspective, and when the partisan opinions of victorious nationalists like Washington are set aside, it is equally obvious that the confederation system made some remarkable achievements. For one thing, the Confederation was not born in 1782 but in 1775, with the Second Continental Congress. This means that Americans were able, within the framework of a confederation, to declare their independence and conduct the war. They made a major alliance with France and wrote a treaty of peace with Britain. For a dozen violent and eventful years, internal peace and a reasonable level of cooperation among the states was maintained.

Most important of all, the Confederation was able to take control of the vast territory between the Appalachians and the Mississippi and to provide for orderly settlement and government there. In a series of laws, climaxed by the Ordinance of 1787—the so-called "Northwest Ordinance"—Congress established the basic set of rules under which new land could be organized

NOAH WEBSTER

The efforts of men like Washington to forge a more independent and secure political structure for the new nation were paralleled by similar preoccupations in every area of life. Poets and novelists set out to create a new, "American" literature. Others attempted to create an "American" style in religion or dress or manners or even diet. Noah Webster—whose name became almost synonymous with "dictionary"—tried to devise an American *language* as different as possible from the English language of England.

Webster's efforts began when he was a modest schoolteacher in the tiny town of Goshen, New York. In 1782 (the year the British and Americans began to negotiate the peace treaty), Webster published a little spelling book. The title eventually became *The American Spelling Book*, but for several generations of Americans who learned from it, it was known universally as "the Blue-backed Speller." Together with a grammar book he wrote in 1784 and a reader of 1785, Webster's speller created a common language for a society with the world's highest literacy rate.

Webster's purposes were mixed, but all of them were common to his age. He believed that literacy was closely tied to character. In fact, a common slogan about the Blue-backed Speller was that it "taught millions to read and not one to sin." But virtue, for Webster as much as for Washington, was closely tied to nationality. He was not interested solely in creating virtuous character, but virtuous national character. This, he thought, required a language that was uniform, that cut across regional lines and class differences.

The main principle behind Webster's speller was simplicity. He changed British endings like "-our" in such words as "honour" or "labour" to the "-or" in "honor" and "labor." The mysterious "-re" in British words like "theatre" or "centre" became "er" for Webster's generations of pupils. The double middle consonants in British words like "waggon" became single, as in "wagon." Ambiguous spellings like "gaol" became phonetically recognizable as "jail." Similarly, "plow" replaced "plough." (There were limits to reform, however, and some of Webster's proposals—like "wurd" for "word" or "iz" for "is"—did not catch on.)

After the successes of his speller, Webster was preoccupied with two grand projects. The first was his dictionary. He spent years collecting notes on the ways in which Americans spoke and wrote English. In 1828, he finally published the result, his famous dictionary. It was in two volumes and included about 12,000 "new" words—words, that is, that had not appeared in any English dictionary published previously.

Webster's second great preoccupation was reminiscent of Washington's ambition to build a canal system connecting Virginia to the West. Webster wanted a national copyright law to protect the interests of authors by preventing printers from simply copying books without paying authors any royalties. Webster was not a nationalist *because* of his concern for the economic interests of writers—any more than Washington was a nationalist merely because he owned Western lands. But, in both cases, there was an intimate connection between ideas and interests, a harmony of ideological and practical concerns, that made a strong nationalism seem the only appropriate option.

into territories and finally become new states. A clear cut survey system was created. Land in the territories—one thirty-sixth of the whole—was set aside for the support of a public school system. A General Land Office was formed to sell the remaining land. Finally, in what may have been its most significant action, Congress prohibited slavery in the Northwest Territory—the area that eventually became the states of Ohio, Indiana, Michigan, Illinois, and Wisconsin.

Any assessment of the Articles of Confederation must take into account the fact that the Articles were a product of history, not just of abstract political theory. For two centuries, each of the colonies had strained for a larger and larger degree of independence. Only when there was trouble—war with France, or with Indians, or with Britain—did the colonies admit their dependence on each other or on a national government. All this experience taught the same lesson: the real, day-to-day business of governing was a matter for the individual states.

Within the states, in fact, political leaders displayed great legislative and constitutional skill. Between 1776 and 1780, with no real help from Congress, eleven of the thirteen states wrote new constitutions. (Rhode Island and Connecticut kept their old colonial charters with a few changes.) The methods varied from state to state, but some common characteristics emerged in all the constitutions. In every state, the powers of government were divided among executive, legislative, and judicial branches. All the constitutions put explicit limits on the powers of government. They all contained some kind of listing of the rights of citizens. And they all recognized the consent of the people as the only ultimate source of governmental authority.

All in all, then—despite the restless impatience of critics like Washington—the period of confederation was one of rather spectacular accomplishment, both at the national level and within the states. A revolution had been won, and some of its principal results had been written into constitutions and laws. And all this had been gained despite almost overwhelming odds. Men like Washington might be shocked and frightened by something like Shays's Rebellion. But any partisan of the Confederation could point to the other side of the coin: the Rebellion had been brief, and Massachusetts *was* able to restore order without the help of any powerful central government.

Five Major Problems of the Confederation   The Articles of Confederation created a government that was equal to its immediate tasks. But there were other problems and opportunities that the Confederation could not handle efficiently. These were the problems and opportunities that had disturbed Washington and many of his fellow participants in the Revolution—especially younger figures like Madison and Hamilton.

The first, and in a way the most severe, problem was public finance. During the Revolution the Continental Congress had issued mountains of paper money. This paper currency was really a debt. It amounted to a vast number of promises by the government to pay off, at some future time and in "real" money, the dollar value of each bill. The states followed the same practice, so the country was flooded with paper money of all types. The real value of this paper money depended on the hope that the national or state government would eventually be able to pay off all or part of the debt.

Congress simply could not meet its obligations. This meant that the paper money of the United States was practically worthless. In 1783 and 1784, a United States dollar could buy about fifteen cents' worth of goods. The government was nearly bankrupt. There was no effective national currency in circulation. The states paid only about a sixth of the requisitions made by Congress. They were trying to pay off their own individual debts by buying back state-issued paper money. The result was a shortage of cash. People found it difficult to conduct ordinary business.

Only a stronger government, with the power to raise money through taxes, could solve this problem. It was this realization, as much as any other, that moved political leaders in the various states to think of revising the Articles. The movement that led to the Annapolis Convention, the Philadelphia Convention, and eventually to a new government was fed by fear of financial anarchy and bankruptcy.

A second problem involved commerce. Under the Articles, the states were free to make their own trade regulations, both with foreign nations and other states. Foreign trade, always extremely important in the American economy, depended, of course, on relations with foreign nations. The Revolution had not altered the basic economic relationship between America and Europe. Europe was still the principal market and manufacturing center. But the Revolution had removed the British government from the picture. Now the Americans were free from British restrictions; but they were also "free" from British protection.

Sensing American weakness at the national level, the British put restrictions on American trade that were more severe than those of the old colonial system. For example, they barred American ships from other British colonies in the New World. Old patterns of trade were completely broken. New avenues of direct trade with nations like France and Spain did not take up the slack—at least not fast enough.

To those concerned about the nation's future, it seemed clear that the national government would have to be made strong enough to write new treaties of commerce with European nations. Otherwise, Americans would be ruined. They had to depend on European markets in which to sell their tobacco and other agricultural products. And they had to be able to buy European manufactured goods on a reasonable basis in order to survive.

A third difficulty was political stability. This was what people like Washington wanted most of all. If stability could be achieved, then Americans could seize the opportunities open to a new nation. The western lands furnished an important example. A stable political situation would allow people to move west, create new states, grow more crops, and import new quantities of manufactured goods. In doing so, they would be building a great new empire. But if stability was not gained, then the British would refuse to evacuate their military posts in the Ohio Valley (which they did). The Spanish would try to break up American control of the Southwest by closing the Mississippi to American traffic (which they did). The frontier settlers would feel no loyalty to the nation, would grow lawless, and would refuse to pay debts and recognize eastern law and control (which they did).

Still another troublesome problem was the possibility of quarrels among individual states or different geographic regions of the country. Already New York and New Jersey had experienced a bitter dispute, when each tried to tax the other's goods as "imports." And boundary quarrels had produced scattered armed conflicts between citizens of different states. Almost any law or treaty would have different effects on the North and the South, since one section depended heavily on commerce and the other was almost purely agricultural. Unless the states surrendered their sovereignty, sooner or later some issue would cause the nation to fly apart into competing regions.

Within the individual states, too, there were potential conflicts among groups that could tear state governments apart. Washington felt that Shays's Rebellion was frightening. It was even more frightening as an indication of what might happen in other states. There might be disputes between western farmers and eastern merchants or between religious groups or between political factions. If the country was to survive, it seemed essential to create a national government with enough power to settle problems among and within states.

Added to all these issues, in the minds of many political leaders, was what might be called the "problem" of democracy. The leaders of the Revolution were not democratic in ways that we would recognize. That is, they did not believe that everyone should participate directly in government. All the states had some kind of property or taxpaying qualification for voting. Only people with an economic stake in society could take part in government (and of these, only free white males). All the states had complicated barriers to popular control of any branch of the government. The political theory held by almost all the Founding Fathers taught that the people are sovereign only in an abstract sense; individuals are equal only in theory. In practice, they believed that government ought to be in the hands of men of education and property.

An American ship, the *Argo,* sails homeward after a trading voyage to France.

In almost every state, however, there was a political faction that wanted more democracy—a broader suffrage, more frequent elections, shorter terms of office for leaders. Such factions demanded laws that would protect debtors from their creditors. They tried to get the states to print more, not less, paper money. With more money the farmers could pay off their debts to bankers and merchants in cheap, almost worthless, currency. These factions demanded equal representation in the legislatures for the farming areas outside cities like New York, Boston, and Philadelphia. They talked, in other words, of what Washington would have scorned as "democratical" government. To Washington—and to most of the wealthy, educated leaders who came from the eastern seaboard—such talk could lead only to anarchy. The inherent danger· in the Articles was that in any given state the "democratic" faction might get control of the government. If this happened, there would be no national power to intervene in behalf of the state's republican government. There would be no national constitution forbidding the states to abolish debts, private property, and political privilege.

During the few years between the peace of 1783 and the Philadelphia Convention, all these problems, domestic and foreign, gradually came together. The concerns might differ from person to person. John Adams might fear democracy more than Thomas Jefferson. Washington might be more concerned with western lands than Alexander Hamilton, whose principal worry was public finance. But sooner or later, in much the same way that the Revolutionary movement had built up in the colonies, the movement to revise or repudiate the Articles of Confederation grew. People in one state corresponded with their friends and relatives in another. Soon most of those who had led the Revolution were involved in a movement to make a second, peaceful revolution. They would throw off their government, just as they had done in 1776, and replace it with another.

Washington's interests, plans, and fears led him to Philadelphia in exactly the same way that dozens of other people were led by their interests,

Independence Hall (then called the Philadelphia State House) was the meeting place of the Continental Congress and the Constitutional Convention. This view, dating from about 1778, shows a cobbled street and the water pumps that served the neighborhood.

plans, and fears. All the delegates went to Philadelphia sharing the conviction that something had to be done. The Articles had to be drastically altered or else thrown out. If the Articles could have been amended more easily, the Philadelphia Convention might well have simply changed them, leaving the government basically intact. As it was, there seemed to be no option but to start fresh, to draw on the experience of making state constitutions, and to build a new United States.

THE PHILADELPHIA CONVENTION

The fifty-five delegates who straggled into Philadelphia in the summer of 1787 were an extremely interesting group of politicians. As statesmen go, they were young. More were under thirty than over sixty. Together they represented an enormous amount of experience—in war, in Congress, on foreign missions, and in state governments. Thirty-one had college educations—at a time when most people could not read, and only a tiny fraction of the population went to school for more than a few years. If fact, every delegate who spoke in the convention was college educated. Most of them were wealthy men who were as interested in maintaining social order as they were in experimenting with political forms. They were, in short, a political, economic, and social elite.

Perhaps the most interesting fact about the Convention was that almost all its delegates had decided the main question before coming to Philadelphia. They were already committed to building a national government to replace the old Confederation. Before the first hour of debate in the hot hall where they met, most of them had agreed on another point: their essential goal was to create a government that would operate directly on *citizens of the United States*, rather than on the *states* as the old Congress had done. Since this goal was more or less taken for granted, the real questions involved methods. How would the interests of the small states and large states by reconciled? How would power be divided among various branches of government? How would the question of slavery be handled, if at all?

For all its importance in our history, the Constitutional Convention spent much of its time in what might be called tinkering. The delegates' work was a kind of political carpentry, in which they arranged and rearranged parts to satisfy the most people. There was very little discussion of high-flown political theory. Whenever a word like "democracy" was mentioned, it was used as a scare word, to provoke fear.

All the tinkering had one objective. Delegates wanted to create a political structure that would not frighten the people, who were very much afraid of strong central government. They also wanted to avoid putting any particular state or geographic section of the country at a disadvantage. The Founding Fathers needed a consensus, a common acceptance of what they had accomplished.

The Virginia and New Jersey Plans The Convention spent much of its time discussing the virtues and faults of two different plans. The first, called the Virginia Plan (which was drafted by Virginian James Madison), would have made voting in the national legislature dependent on population. Thus Virginia or Massachusetts, for example, would have had more votes than Rhode Island or Delaware. The second plan, the New Jersey Plan (proposed by delegate William Patterson of New Jersey), would have continued the system used in the Articles, giving each state the same number of votes.

There were several other important differences between the Virginia and New Jersey plans.

James Madison has been called the "master builder of the Constitution." His journals are the main source for later knowledge of proceedings of the Convention.

The Virginia Plan provided for an executive with a veto power over acts of Congress. In other words, it proposed creating a strong executive, with power balancing that of the legislature. The New Jersey Plan proposed an executive, too. But it would have been composed of several people elected by the legislature, like a cabinet. And it would have had no veto power.

Both the Virginia Plan and the New Jersey Plan provided for a national judiciary, separated from and working in balance with the executive and the legislature. But there was an important difference. According to the Virginia Plan, there would be both a national supreme court and other, lower federal courts. The New Jersey Plan, in contrast, provided for a supreme court only. Under this plan, therefore, the national court in most cases could only act on appeals from the state courts. Thus the Virginia Plan would have called for a judiciary whose powers might balance those of the executive and legislature. Under this plan the judiciary would be more independent of the state courts, too.

Though there were some exceptions, gener-

William Paterson held several important posts after the Convention—senator, governor of New Jersey, and associate justice of the Supreme Court.

ally the delegates from the small states supported the New Jersey proposal, while those from large states favored the Virginia Plan. The reasons were obvious. The Virginia Plan would give the large states almost complete control of the national government. The New Jersey Plan would have made the states equal in Congress; it would have made Congress much more powerful than the other branches of government. No great principles of liberty or democracy were involved in this conflict. The issue was simple and practical. How could the new constitution be adjusted to give equal protection to the interests of both the large and the small states?

THE NEW CONSTITUTION

Out of the debate over the Virginia and New Jersey plans came a series of compromises, sometimes known as the Great Compromise. As with many compromises, the solution to the main problem was really very simple. The Convention dele-gates created a Congress consisting of two houses. The upper house, which they named the Senate, would have equal representation, with each state sending two senators. In the lower house, the House of Representatives, representation would be apportioned according to population.

The Senate was essentially the kind of legislature proposed in the New Jersey Plan. It protected the interests of the small states. In fact, the Convention provided that this feature of the Constitution could never be amended unless every state consented to have the number of its senators reduced. The House of Representatives, on the other hand, was a reflection of the large-state bias of the Virginia Plan.

As a concession to some of the smaller states and to states where slavery was not common, the South agreed to count a slave as only three-fifths of a person. This meant that the number of representatives for a state like Virginia or South Carolina would not be so large as originally suggested by the Virginia Plan. (Slaves are not mentioned as such anywhere in the Constitution. Instead, they are referred to as "other persons" or "such persons."

Powers of the Federal Government   The powers given to Congress were about the same as those exercised by the old Congress under the Articles. Congress could wage war, conduct diplomatic relations, and coin and borrow money. Two important new powers were added, powers whose absence had crippled the old Congress. The new Congress could raise revenues through taxation. Furthermore, it could regulate commerce with foreign nations and among the states.

A more significant revision of the old Articles was the creation of an executive branch, independent of Congress and on an equal footing with it. The chief executive would be called the President. (Everyone in the Convention assumed, as they drew up the article on executive powers, that the first President would be Washington.) The President's principal duty was to execute the laws passed by Congress, but he was also given some of the powers that the British king exercised—being commander-in-chief, for example, and conducting foreign policy.

The Constitution also provided for a judicial branch. There would be a Supreme Court with final power to enforce federal laws and interpret the Constitution whenever legal questions arose. In addition, Congress had the power to create other federal courts to ensure that federal law and the Constitution remained what the Constitution said they should be — the "supreme law of the land."

Checks and Balances Among these three branches of the new government, there was to be a complicated system of relationships. Each branch was to have some independence from the others. That is, there was to be a separation of powers. The judges of the federal courts would serve for life. This would presumably make them independent. The President would owe his office to no other branch of the federal government but to the electors of the electoral college. Senators would be elected by and therefore responsible to state legislatures. Congressmen would answer to their constituents. All the officers of the new government, in other words, would have separate bases of power and support.

These separations were far from complete, however. Judges were to be nominated by the President and approved by the Senate. They could be removed from office through the process of impeachment by Congress. Nor was the presidency altogether separate. Obviously, presidential programs of almost every type would eventually require money. Funds would have to be voted by Congress. Also, presidential appointees, such as ambassadors or cabinet officers, would have to be approved by the Senate. Finally, as a last resort, a President could be removed from office through impeachment.

Despite the creation of the executive and judicial branches, the framers' minds were still dominated by their own experience. The legislature was, for most of them, still the basic, lawmaking centerpiece of the new government — as it had been in the states and in the Confederation. The powers of Congress were subjected to new checks. The President was given the power to veto any law unless a two-thirds majority in Congress overturned his vetoes. And the members of

the Convention assumed in their debates that the courts, especially the Supreme Court, would have the power to declare any act of Congress unconstitutional. (In the end, the Constitution did not explicitly give the courts this right, and a good deal of argument was to take place on the question of whether the courts actually had this ultimate power. In practice, however, no Congress and no President every defied a Supreme Court ruling — at least not for long.) Still, within the constitutional limits of its powers, a two-thirds majority in Congress was given about as much freedom of action as Parliament had ever had in England.

In these and other ways, the powers of government were separate yet interdependent through a system of checks and balances. The idea behind this system was that no part of the government ought to become powerful enough to override the other branches or violate the Constitution. At any one time a strong President, a runaway Congress, or a determined Supreme Court might take the initiative on a policy question. But the other two branches would always be watching carefully — at least in theory. Each would thus protect its own powers and defend the basic structure of government as laid down in the Constitution.

Federalism The Constitution created a federal system of government — that is, one in which power is divided between the national government and state governments. In keeping with their general approach, Convention delegates wanted this division of powers and responsibilities to be a balanced one. On the one hand, the Constitution itself limited the powers that the national government could exercise. And the states were protected by retaining control over the processes of electing senators and congressmen.

On the other hand, nothing was said about state sovereignty in this new Constitution. The states were forbidden to do two very important things. No state could issue paper money. Nor could any state "impair the obligation of contract." This meant that no state legislature could pass any law that significantly altered existing property relationships. The specter of Shays's Rebellion lay behind these two provisions.

In this engraving of 1788, Washington and Franklin ride in a chariot, carrying the Constitution and a liberty cap (a popular symbol based on the cap a Roman slave received when he was freed). The two statesmen are drawn by thirteen men, representing the original states.

Attitudes Toward Democracy The Constitution that came out of Philadelphia contained a few guarantees of individual liberties. The states and the federal government were forbidden to create titles of nobility. The federal government was forbidden to set up any religious qualifications for holding office. Except for these provisions and one or two others, the Constitution was remarkably silent about the great question of liberty, the question that had rung out so loudly in 1776.

As for democracy, the Constitution had nothing at all to say. Only one group of officials in the new government would be elected by the people directly—members of the House of Representatives. Even in this case the states were given complete control of property or religious qualifications for voting. Senators were to be chosen by the state legislatures. And the President would be selected by the electoral college. Justices of the Supreme Court and other federal judges would be appointed by the President (who had been chosen by the electors). Then judges would be confirmed by the Senate (chosen by the state legislatures).

Every member of the Convention would have agreed that these provisions were much better than direct popular election. The people might rule, in theory. But they would be allowed to rule only at a distance and through machinery complicated enough to slow down or stop any movement toward popular democracy at the national level. Furthermore, the federal government guaranteed each state a republican form of government. This meant that any move toward anarchy—like Shays's Rebellion—could be met by federal force.

No state could fail to protect the defenders of order and property.

Was there, then, no genius to the Constitution? Was it nothing more than political tinkering resulting from a desire to protect order from the "democratical" elements in society? Many of the delegates would probably have answered no. They were practical, hard-bitten men who had been burned more than once by popular movements that threatened to get out of hand.

But for a few others, notably Madison, there was another aspect to the Constitution that not many people noticed at the time. The opening words of the document are "We the People." This Constitution, unlike the Articles and many of the state constitutions, would rest, in some sense or other, on the popular will. And it would operate directly on the people, with no intervention of state power.

The government could tax individual citizens. It could try them in its own courts under its own laws. The federal courts might even declare state or local laws unconstitutional—though this possibility was hardly discussed at all in Philadelphia. Finally (the most inspired maneuver of all), the Constitution would be ratified by specially chosen conventions in the states, not by the state legislatures. Thus the new government would be created not by the states but by "We the People."

THE STRUGGLE FOR RATIFICATION

The new Constitution was drafted and approved by a majority of delegates by mid-September. (For the complete text, see the back of this volume.) At this point, the delegates at Philadelphia must have felt somewhat uneasy. They had been told by their state legislatures to amend the Articles of Confederation. But they had scarcely considered this as a possibility. Instead, they had created a new government. They had held secret debates about a scheme that amounted to a coup d'état. They knew they had very little chance of getting all the states to accept the new government, at least not for several years. So they proposed their

Alexander Hamilton wrote at least fifty-one of the eighty-five essays in *The Federalist*. All were signed with the pen-name "Publius."

most radical idea of all: the new Constitution would go into effect as soon as nine state conventions had accepted it.

The Founding Fathers had some important advantages. For one thing, almost everyone agreed that something had to be done about the Articles. Another advantage was the prestige of men like Washington and Franklin. A third was the method of ratification. The state legislatures might have rejected the document in order to preserve their own powers. But a series of conventions elected for the specific purpose of judging the plan would give it a better chance of adoption. As for the document itself, delegates argued that their complicated structure of checks and balances left little to fear from the new central government. Finally, they promised to write a Bill of Rights to protect the citizens, just as soon as the new government went into effect.

Despite all these advantages, ratification was an uphill fight. A shrewd observer of American politics in 1787 would probably have predicted that the Constitution would be rejected. There was opposition in Congress. Why, some of its members argued, should that body roll over and

John Jay—like Hamilton—distrusted the common people, and believed that government should be controlled by men of means and education.

play dead? Some members of the Constitutional Convention itself, frightened by the final result, had refused to sign the document and were ready to mount opposition. Finally, there were the old traditional state loyalties to overcome. The Constitution, much more than Patriot leaders of the Revolution, much more than the Articles, asked people to think of themselves as Americans, not solely as citizens of a state.

Generally, those who favored the Constitution were more aggressive than its opponents. They wrote more, spoke more, and lobbied more. Three young men—Madison, Hamilton, and John Jay of New York—produced a remarkable series of newspaper essays in favor of the Constitution. (The essays were later published as a book, *The Federalist*.) They have become so much a part of our history that they have even been cited as evidence in Supreme Court opinions. Madison, Hamilton, and Jay also managed to acquire the name "Federalist" for their political faction. ("Nationalist" would have been more accurate.) This seemed to leave no name for the opposition but the clumsy and empty title "Antifederalist."

The first state convention to act, that of Delaware, did so swiftly. After that the fight for ratification was close, tough, and full of bargaining. The decisions of the four largest states—Massachusetts, New York, Pennsylvania, and Virginia—were crucial. Theoretically, the Constitution could have been ratified without the participation of any of them. Actually, however, the new government would have been crippled without all of them. Pennsylvania fell into line in December 1787. But when the Massachusetts convention first met, the vote on the Constitution was 192 against, 144 in favor. The situation was as bad or worse in Virginia and New York. Eventually, in February 1788, the Federalists managed to win over Massachusetts, which voted 187 to 168 in favor of the Constitution. In Virginia the convention ended by supporting the Constitution 89 to 79 at the end of June 1788. Meanwhile, New Hampshire ratified on June 21, becoming the ninth state to do so and thus officially putting the Constitution into effect. Five other states had also ratified by the end of June. But New York still stood outside, along with North Carolina and Rhode Island.

The Antifederalists were very strong in New York. But Virginia's ratification helped turn the tide. With it, ten states had already ratified. It looked as if New York, the only large state not to do so, might stand alone. The essays of *The Federalist* also had a strong impact. New York ratified on July 26, a month after Virginia's vote. North Carolina and Rhode Island hung back until 1789 and 1790, respectively, but there was no need to wait. The old Congress simply shut up shop and ordered new elections for early in 1789.

THINGS LEFT UNSAID AND UNDONE

To Washington, Madison, Hamilton, and the other Federalists, it was clear that a crisis had been averted. They had acted with care and energy, they believed, and saved the nation from itself. The uphill struggle for ratification had been the final critical stage, but they had won. To many Antifederalists, however, a world had been lost. Now they could only engage in opposition politics in the new Congress when it finally met. Regarding the choice of President there was no question; Washington was the only conceivable man for the job. But the fight over ratification had caused men to band together into factions, with the beginnings of platforms or programs.

The Constitution said nothing at all about political parties. In fact, most of the delegates at Philadelphia said they despised the spirit of faction. But Americans had been busily organizing what amounted to political parties since at least the 1760s. In retrospect, the rise of distinct political parties in the early years of the Republic seems logical and natural.

The Constitution said nothing about another important feature of national life. Except for the so-called three-fifths clause and provisions relating to the slave trade and fugitive slaves, it was silent on the issue of slavery. During the decades after 1787 the two most prominent features of American history were the rise of political parties and a series of crises involving slavery. The Founding Fathers were great political leaders. But they were not prophets. If they were trying to guess at the future, they badly misjudged what it held.

In the final analysis, the Constitution represented only a political structure, a kind of skeleton on which history would have to build a political and social body. The "vessel was afloat," as Washington said. But only experience would tell whether its compass, sails, and other equipment would be able to provide the order and stability that the Philadelphia Convention wanted so badly. Soon, challenges would come from directions and from people that the delegates at Philadelphia could hardly have imagined, much less prepared for.

The Bill of Rights   Another subject on which the Constitution was almost silent was "liberty"—all those rights that individuals have *against* governments. This question was fiercely debated during the ratification process, and the Federalists responded by promising to add amendments spelling out the rights of citizens under the new government. The result of this promise was a series of amendments—twelve, at first, but reduced to ten—that came quickly to be known as the Bill of Rights.

The task of drawing up the amendments fell to James Madison. He sifted through a large number of recommendations, some proposing as many as forty different provisions. He also worked through precedents in the state constitutions, particularly the Declaration of Rights adopted in Virginia in the first year of the Revolution. Finally, Madison boiled the proposals down to the now-familiar guarantees of freedom of speech, press, religion, assembly, trial by jury, the right to bear arms, and so forth, plus a general amendment stressing that the federal government had *only* those powers explicitly granted in the Constitution. (Two other proposals, concerning the proportioning of representation and the salaries of members of Congress, were quietly dropped.)

The amendments were quickly ratified—though three of the original states did not get around to doing so until 1941—150 years later. One of the main objections of the Antifederalists had been met, and the Constitution had at last some genuine claim to originality and historic significance.

SUGGESTED READINGS–CHAPTERS 9-10

George Washington

Douglass Southall Freeman, *George Washington* (7 vols., 1948–1959); Marcus Cunliffe, *George Washington, Man and Monument* (1958); Bernard Knollenberg, *Washington and the Revolution* (1940); Esmond Wright, *Washington and the American Revolution* (1957).

Confederation Government

Merrill Jensen, *The Articles of Confederation* (1940) and *The New Nation: A History of the United States during the Confederation, 1781– 1789* (1950); Clinton Rossiter, *1787: The Grand Convention* (1966).

The Significance of the West

B. H. Hibbard, *A History of the Public Land Policies* (1924); R. M. Robbins, *Our Landed Heritage* (1942).

The Nature and Meaning of the Constitution

Charles Beard, *An Economic Interpretation of the Constitution of the United States* (1913); R. E. Brown, *Charles Beard and the Constitution* (1956); Forrest McDonald, *We, the People: The Economic Origins of the Constitution* (1958); Jackson T. Main, *The Antifederalists: Critics of the Constitution, 1781–1788* (1961); R. A. Rutland, *The Ordeal of the Constitution: the Antifederalists and the Ratification Struggle of 1787–1788* (1966); Gordon Wood, *The Creation of the American Republic, 1776–1787* (1969); E. S. Morgan, *The Birth of the Republic, Seventeen Sixty Three–Eighty Nine* (1956); J. R. Alden, *The American Revolution, 1775–1783* (1954).

Experience on the State Level

E. P. Douglass, *Rebels and Democrats: The Struggle for Equal Political Rights and Majority Rule During the American Revolution* (1955); Marion Starkey, *A Little Rebellion* (1955).

UNIT THREE

EXPANDING AMERICA

The first decades of the American nation proved to be a formidable testing time for the new republic. Although Americans took pride in their newly established frame of government, and although they quickly accepted the Constitution's basic principles, the national government had to be put into practice. Its future, especially in the earliest years, was by no means assured. Many Americans—and our enemies abroad—asked themselves: Can the new and unique federal republic survive in a world of monarchies, most of them autocratic and unfriendly?

A major threat to domestic tranquility involved the possibility that the nation might split apart. In 1806 a former Vice President, Aaron Burr, planned a conspiracy intending to create a new republic in the Mississippi Valley. Burr's conspiracy, which forms the subject of Chapter 11, failed. The United

States survived this crisis and many others in the post-Revolutionary era. Chapter 12 follows the most important of these crises in describing "The Republic on Trial." Among the most significant episodes during this testing time were the fierce political battles of the 1790s, which pitted Federalists against Jeffersonian Republicans. Jefferson's election to the presidency cooled political tempers somewhat, but he and his successor, James Madison, faced international disputes during the Napoleonic period that ultimately led to a second war with Britain in 1812. Jefferson's purchase of Louisiana created still other difficulties: Could such a dispersed nation be held together as it began expanding relentlessly westward?

In the 1820s, after a so-called Era of Good Feelings that followed the decline of Federalist-Jeffersonian arguments, a new brand of politics emerged. First in the states and

CAPITOL, WASHINGTON.

then in the federal government, "the people" became supreme through universal white manhood suffrage and through a host of practical and symbolic changes. Symbolizing this process was the emergence of Andrew Jackson, a "common man" by birth and upbringing, as President in 1828. Chapter 13 describes Jackson's "Road to the White House"—his dramatic life from earliest days and military career to the presidency. Chapter 14 explores the nature of Jackson's political world. It examines the emergence of mass political parties, the growth of the presidency as an institution, and the key issues of this Second Party System.

The first half of the nineteenth century proved to be not only a period of political innovation but also a period of massive economic, social, and cultural change for the United States. The creation of a new factory system and an urban working class, expansion into farming areas of the Southwest and Northwest, and the evolution of a modern commercial capitalist economy were accompanied by a host of parallel developments outside the economic realm. Foremost among these developments involved the spread of new religious groups and the revival of religious activity among older churches—a phenomenon that ranged from the sedate emergence of rational sects such as the Unitarians to the more emotional millenial beliefs of groups such as the Millerites, described in Chapter 15. The religious developments of this era had a decided and complex impact upon the growth of reform movements such as education, woman's rights, temperance, pacifism, and antislavery. The entire reform impulse and some of its leading manifestations—along with the major patterns of religious development in the first half of the nineteenth century—form the subject of Chapter 16.

11
AARON BURR, CONSPIRATOR

R. J. W.

Early on the morning of July 11, 1804, a pair of small barges carried two duelists across the Hudson River from New York to the New Jersey town of Weehawken. The two seconds for the duel, and the usual doctor, were also aboard. The two parties in the duel went to a level spot along the river, cleared away some of the summer brush, and carefully loaded the pistols. After the two men took up positions ten paces apart, one of the seconds called out "Present!" Each man raised his pistol in a salute similar to a fencer's "En Garde!" Without any further ceremony or signal the two men fired, one a little after the other. One of the men spun partly around and fell forward. The small, round shot had lodged in his spine, and he was bleeding internally. The other man started to rush forward as if to help or offer a gentleman's apology. But he was pulled away by his second and taken quickly back across the river to New York. The wounded man went home more slowly, lapsing in and out of consciousness. He lived with pain, doses of opium, and a grieving family, into the next afternoon. Then he died.

The dead man was Alexander Hamilton, a hero of the Revolution. He had been first secretary of the Treasury, and he was a leader of the Federalist party. He had achieved a remarkable career in his forty-nine years. As he lay dying, his doctor released frequent public bulletins on his condition. After his death, the city of New York went into official mourning. Mass meetings demanded the arrest of the "murderer," who escaped from the city after a few days. Finally, in New York and New Jersey Hamilton's opponent was indicted for murder. He fled first to Philadelphia and then south to Georgia and out of the country to Florida (still a Spanish possession). Much of the time, he traveled under an assumed name, like any ordinary fugitive from justice.

Sooner or later, however, this particular outlaw had to come out of hiding. For he was, in fact, the Vice President of the United States, Aaron Burr. He could afford to spend the late summer and early fall in the South. But Congress would soon go into session, and it was his constitutional duty to preside over the Senate. He was fairly certain that the murder charges would eventually be dropped. In the meantime, he would not be arrested if he stayed out of New York and New Jersey. Even though New York was his home, he had no reason to go there. His handsome house had been sold at auction to pay off some of his debts, and his other creditors were howling for the rest of his money. So, on November 4, the Vice President, over his head in debt and wanted for murder, took his seat as the president of the Senate. One senator, shocked at Burr's display of nerve, wrote angrily to a friend that "We are indeed fallen on evil times!"

It was not really the Senate that had fallen on evil times. The main victim (aside from the dead Hamilton, of course), was Burr himself. He was a gentleman and had fought an honorable duel—still the custom among gentlemen of the day. He had won. But he had lost, too.

Burr had enjoyed as spectacular a career as Hamilton. Like Hamilton, he had been one of the young heroes of the Revolution. A brilliant lawyer, he was said never to have lost a case. He was also a very shrewd and successful politician. He had already been a senator from New York, and in 1800 he had narrowly missed becoming President.

Now, in the fall of 1804, Burr was in disgrace because of the duel and his debts. His term as Vice President was expiring. He had just been defeated in an attempt to become governor of New York—a defeat that Hamilton had helped bring about and that was the cause of their duel. Hamilton had been criticizing Burr privately for many years. During the

Richmond Hill, Aaron Burr's New York home, stood in what is now lower Manhattan. At the time this engraving was made, in 1790, the house was occupied by John Adams. Burr moved here in 1797, but sold the house in 1803 to pay off some of his debts.

campaign for governor, letters of Hamilton were released publicly. They referred to Burr as "a dangerous man and one who ought not to be trusted with the reins of government." When Hamilton refused to apologize, Burr challenged him to a duel. Burr was still in his forties, but is seemed that his career might be ruined.

Burr, who never allowed himself to become publicly flustered, kept up an appearance of calm. In a letter to his married daughter, Theodosia, he even made a joke of the entire affair:

> You have doubtless heard that there has subsisted for some time a contention of a very singular nature between the states of New York and New Jersey. The subject in dispute is which shall have the honor of hanging the Vice President. A paper received this morning asserts, but without authority, that he has determined in favor of New York. You shall have due notice of the time and place. Whenever it may be you may rely on a great company, much gayety, and many rare sights, such as the lion, the elephant, etc.

To his daughter's husband, Burr hinted that the situation was more serious. The duel would not cost him his life, to be sure. But his career was a shambles, and so he wrote, "I shall seek another country."

One thing was certain. During that winter the Vice President's mind was not on Senate business. He was busy instead with mysterious maps and a dangerous partnership. An old friend of Burr's was in Washington that winter. He was James Wilkinson, the highest ranking general in the army of the United States. The general he also happened to be a spy. For years he had been Agent 13 on the Spanish espionage rolls. He was very much interested in the same sorts of maps and plans as Burr.

The Vice President who was wanted for murder and the general who was a spy had known each other for many years. In fact, they had been twenty-year-old captains together during the first year of the Revolution. Under the command of Benedict Arnold, who became the most famous traitor in American history, the two men had served on an unsuccessful American invasion of Canada. Their paths parted when Wilkinson was forced to leave the army after joining a plot against George Washington. Burr went on to become a major on Washington's staff.

Like many others in trouble, Wilkinson had gone west. He made a career in politics in western Pennsylvania and Kentucky, and he began his secret occupation as a Spanish agent. In 1791, Wilkinson was able to reenter the army and fight against the Indians in the Ohio Valley. He rose rapidly in rank, and by 1796 was the highest ranking general in the army.

From about 1794 on, Burr and Wilkinson had carried on a secret, coded correspondence. Now, together again in Washington in the winter of 1804–1805, they made new plans and copied maps of Spanish possessions in the Southwest and of the western territories of the United States.

At this time, Spain still ruled the American West and Southwest, as well as Mexico. (The term "Mexico" was often used to refer to all of these North American regions.) The Spanish also owned East Florida—

the peninsula itself—and what was called West Florida—the area west of the peninsula, north of the Gulf of Mexico. The United States had just purchased the territory known as Louisiana, the vast region between the Mississippi River and the Rocky Mountains (see map, page 228).

In the area between the Mississippi and the Appalachians, change was the order of the day. So far, only Tennessee, Ohio, and Kentucky had been admitted to statehood. But from Michigan to Mississippi, settlers were on the move, driving out Indians and clearing land. If these western states and territories decided to secede from the Union, there was little chance that the federal government could use force to hold them.

Two very dangerous but exciting possibilities occupied the imaginations of Burr and Wilkinson. One was an invasion of Spanish territory. The other was an attempt to separate America's western lands from the rest of the Union. Involvement with Spain meant preparing for a military conquest, which was a crime under American law. Separation of the West from the rest of the country meant treason. If only one of the plans worked at first, then Burr and Wilkinson might try to combine the two. The result could be magnificent—a new nation stretching all the way from Ohio to Panama. The two plans had one very practical advantage. They required the same kind of preparation. If money could be found for it, a private army might be raised in the West. This army would travel down river by way of the Ohio, the Cumberland, the Tennessee, and the Mississippi to New Orleans. Only then would a final choice have to be made between the conquest of Spanish possessions and the separation of the West.

These schemes made a great deal of sense in 1805. After all, the United States was a small and relatively weak nation. The government exerted little control over the states and territories west of the Appalachians. It had no control at all over the new lands west of the Mississippi. It seemed only a matter of time before Mexico and the Southwest broke away from Spain in a revolution such as the Americans had recently fought against Britain. The United States and Spain had been on the verge of war for some time. If war came, the conquest of Mexico and the Southwest would become a patriotic duty. Burr and Wilkinson had influence and friends in high places. Some friends could be brought into the plan, and others could be tricked into helping. There was little need to fear the American army, even if Wilkinson had not been in command. Its strength consisted only of about 3,000 troops scattered along the Atlantic coast and through the West. Burr and Wilkinson had every reason to believe that one scheme or the other, conquest or secession, would work. It was just possible that both plans might succeed, with thorough preparation, careful timing, and a run of good luck.

The first step was to obtain money and military support from some foreign power. When Burr fled New York after the duel with Hamilton, he visited the British minister, Anthony Merry. Merry reported to his government that Burr had made an astonishing proposal.

I have just received an offer from Mr. Burr to lend his assistance to his majesty's government in any manner in which they may think fit to employ him, particularly

Wilkinson, who denounced Burr, was never fully trusted by the prosecution, either. He performed poorly in the War of 1812 and retired to write three dull and pompous volumes of memoirs.

in endeavoring to effect a separation of the western part of the United States in its whole extent.

In late March of 1805, after a winter of planning with Wilkinson, Burr went to Merry again. This time he had a more detailed scheme. Merry reported home in a dispatch marked "Most Secret":

> Mr. Burr has mentioned to me that the inhabitants of Louisiana seem determined to render themselves independent of the United States, and that the execution of their design is only delayed by the difficulty of obtaining assurance of protection from some foreign power.

Burr wanted the British to station a squadron of ships at the mouth of the Mississippi in order to immobilize the American navy. And he wanted a "loan" of half a million dollars. Merry was hooked. His secret dispatch ended by recommending Burr in the most favorable terms:

> He certainly possesses, perhaps in a much greater degree than any other individual in this country, all the talents, energy, intrepidity, and firmness which are required for such an enterprise.

The response from England was painfully slow, so Wilkinson and Burr went ahead on their own. They managed to persuade President Jefferson to appoint Wilkinson governor of the Territory of Louisiana, which was created in 1805. Wilkinson would make his headquarters in St. Louis. Burr, meanwhile, would take a tour down the Ohio River and travel for several weeks in Kentucky and Tennessee. Then he would go down the Mississippi to New Orleans, making plans and enlisting support along the way.

Burr left Washington on horseback on April 10, 1805. Three weeks later he arrived in Pittsburgh to begin his work. He embarked on the Ohio River in style. He wrote to his daughter, Theodosia, on April 30:

> Arrived in good order yesterday. Find my boat and hands ready. My boat is, properly speaking, a floating house, sixty feet by fourteen, containing dining room, kitchen with fireplace, and two bedrooms; roofed from stem to stern; steps to go up, and a walk on the top of the whole length; glass windows, etc. This edifice costs one hundred and thirty-three dollars.

On this elaborate "ark," as he called it, Burr went everywhere and saw everyone of any importance. He visited the senators and congressmen he knew from Washington. He stopped at plantations and country houses. Everywhere he was treated as a celebrity. At each stop, the story was the same. There might be a concert or a traveling play. There was certain to be a dinner or two with the leading citizens. Most important, there would be at least one long and guarded conversation among the men only, flavored with whiskey, secrecy, and cigars. Then Burr would hint at his plans and sound out his hosts for their possible future support.

Burr left the Ohio River at Louisville, Kentucky. Then he rode south across the state and into Tennessee. He visited Andrew Jackson at his plantation, The Hermitage. For four days he filled Jackson with the exciting prospect of a war against Spain, in which Jackson's hill-country militia could help drive the Spanish out of Florida and then off the entire continent. From Nashville, Burr went down the Cumberland on one of Jackson's boats to rejoin his own great houseboat. He met Wilkinson at a small fort where the Ohio empties into the Mississippi.

Wilkinson gave Burr a military escort (even though Burr was no longer the Vice President) and an "elegant barge" for the trip down river to Natchez and New Orleans. In New Orleans Burr continued to hint at his purposes and find potential supporters. Then he headed north on horseback, through Nashville for another visit with Jackson. In St. Louis, Wilkinson's headquarters, Burr reported on his trip. Then he made the hard, slow journey back east, arriving in Washington in November. Though only a little over a year had passed since Burr's duel with Hamilton, his life had taken on a new direction, a new style, and new goals.

The next year was frustrating. Minister Merry's appeal to the British government for funds got nowhere. With a new collaborator—Jonathan Dayton, a senator from New Jersey—Burr tried to trick the Spanish themselves into financing the secession of the West. But the Spanish minister was cautious and would provide only $1,500, hardly enough to finance an army. Wilkinson was strangely silent, perhaps sensing that the time was not ripe. Burr began to suspect his colleague of being faint-hearted. Worst of all, both Spain and the United States were doing everything possible to avoid a war. Against such obstacles, no amount of preparation, cunning, or timing could win out. Burr wrote Wilkinson a coded letter complaining that "Nothing has been heard from Brigadier [Wilkinson] since October." The bad news, Burr said, was that the "execution of our project is postponed till December; want of water in Ohio renders movement impracticable."

"Want of water in Ohio" was the plotters' code phrase for "lack of necessary money." Without money they had no chance unless there was a war with Spain. Unfortunately for the conspiracy, the administration of President Jefferson grounded its foreign policy on the simple principle that "Peace is our policy." Then, just at the moment when everything looked hopeless, the Spanish made a curious decision that almost led to the war Burr wanted so much.

When the United States bought Louisiana from France in 1803, its western boundary was left undefined. Technically, the United States could have claimed everything east of the Rio Grande. But the Spanish claimed the Texas region and sent in about 1,500 troops to occupy the almost empty area. Since Jefferson believed that Americans might never settle west of the Mississippi, he decided not to quarrel over Texas. Instead, he set the border with Mexico at the Sabine River. But the Spanish placed the border east of the Sabine, at a small stream named the Arroyo Hondo (see map, page 208). In the fall of 1805, after Burr had returned east from his trip to New Orleans, the Spanish moved a few troops— twenty-nine men and one officer—across the Sabine. In February 1806 an American force of sixty soldiers forced the Spanish to evacuate their post and return across the Sabine. These border incidents were small and not very dangerous, and Burr probably did not know about them. In fact, it took the government about six weeks to receive emergency messages from the border.

The country between the Sabine and the Arroyo Hondo was virtually uninhabited and either the United States or Spain could have given it up with no loss to national interest or security. But both sides were stubborn. Jefferson, when he finally learned of the problem, announced that he intended to hold the Sabine line. The Spanish authorities in Mexico then reinforced their garrison and once more crossed the Sabine. The American commander in the area reported to his government that the situation was desperate. He had only 200 men fit for duty, six old guns, and a shabby fort. The Spanish refused to answer his request to withdraw.

Jefferson was determined. He ordered the frontier reinforced. Early in May the President told Wilkinson himself to move his headquarters to New Orleans and take personal command of the troops in the disputed area. Now the general was in an awkward position. All along, he had been trying to juggle three roles: commanding general of the army, spy for Spain, and plotter with Burr. The problems on the border brought the three roles into painful conflict and put him in a predicament.

In a crisis, Wilkinson could choose to combine any two of his three roles, but at least one of them had to be dropped. In case of war with Spain, he could be both commanding general and Burr's collaborator in the conquest of Mexico. The roles of spy for Spain and collaborator with Burr could work together if the goal were the secession of the West. Wilkinson's third option was to remain commanding general and spy for Spain. This would require him to keep peace with Spain along the Sabine but also to desert Burr and thus prevent either the conquest of Mexico or the secession of the West. The choices were extremely difficult. They depended on circumstances that Wilkinson could not completely control, such as the movements of Spanish troops and the agressiveness of Jefferson. Like many men confronting hard choices, Wilkinson moved slowly. Jefferson ordered him to leave St. Louis in May. The general hung back until August, when he finally started down river to New Orleans.

Burr's problem, as he fretted through the spring of 1806, was just the opposite of Wilkinson's. Wilkinson had too many roles to juggle; Burr had no role and was trying to find one. During the months when it seemed that there would be no war with Spain, Burr had been raising money among his friends and relatives. He had also decided to buy part of a huge land grant on the Ouachita River in what is now the state of Louisiana. If nothing else worked, he could bring in settlers and become a private prince. The preparations for the Ouachita plan—boats and armed men—were exactly the same as for the conquest of Mexico or the secession of the West.

When Burr heard the news of the border incidents on the Sabine River and that Jefferson had ordered Wilkinson to go to New Orleans, he made a fateful decision. On July 24, he sent a messenger west with a secret letter to Wilkinson written by Senator Jonathan Dayton. Dayton began by trying to convince Wilkinson that Jefferson was about to replace him as governor of Louisiana Territory. He ended by urging Wilkinson to act:

> It is now well ascertained that you are to be displaced in the next session [of Congress]. Prepare yourself, therefore, for it. You know the rest. You are not a man to despair, especially when such prospects offer in another quarter. Are you ready? Are your numerous associates ready? Wealth and glory! Louisiana and Mexico!

Jonathan Dayton (after whom Dayton, Ohio is named) was indicted for treason in 1807, but his case was never tried.

The message was almost clear. Burr and Dayton were trying to get Wilkinson to commit himself. But to what? Dayton's words (which Burr probably dictated)—"You know the rest. . . . Louisiana and Mexico!"—left all the options open.

Burr himself wrote a letter on July 29 in the code he and Wilkinson had always used. It was much more elaborate, but it still left the choice of destinations open. Whereas Dayton's letter tried to frighten Wilkinson, Burr's tried to trick him by falsely claiming that all the pieces had fallen into place and by implying that success was certain:

> Your letter postmarked 13th May is received. I have at length obtained funds and have actually commenced. The eastern detachments from different points and under different pretences, will rendezvous on the Ohio, 1st of November.

Burr was exaggerating. The "eastern detachments" did not exist on July 29, except perhaps in his imagination. This exaggeration was small, however, compared the the lies that followed immediately:

> Every thing internal and external favors our views. Naval protection of England is secured. It [an English naval force] will meet us at the Mississippi.

The promise of English naval support was simply a lie. Minister Merry had not succeeded in getting a promise of help from London. In fact, he had been discharged by his government for his role in Burr's proposed intrigue. Burr continued trying to excite Wilkinson's imagination:

> It will be a host of choice spirits. Wilkinson shall be second to Burr only, and Wilkinson shall dictate the rank and promotion of his officers. Burr will proceed westward 1st August, never to return. Our object, my dear friend, is brought to a point so long desired. Burr guarantees the result with his life and honor, with the lives, and honor, and the fortunes of hundreds of the best blood of our country.

Then Burr gave a few details of his planned movements:

> Burr's plan of operation is to move down rapidly from the Falls [of the Ohio—that is, Louisville], on the 15th of November, with the first 500 or 1,000 men, in light boats now constructing for that purpose, to be at Natchez between the 5th and 15th of December, there to meet you, there to determine whether it will be expedient to seize on, or pass by, Baton Rouge [still a Spanish possession].

Burr's famous letter of July 29 to Wilkinson was written in a combination of English words and a numbered code. (The code numbers were page-and-entry references to a dictionary that both men owned.) The opening paragraphs of the letter are quoted on the previous page. The third paragraph reads: "Burr will proceed westward 1st August, never to return. With him goes his daughter; her husband will follow in October, with a corps of worthies." (The three did meet with Blennerhassett at Lexington in October.) The next paragraph goes on to other practical details of the negotiations: "Send forthwith an intelligent and confidential friend with whom Burr may confer; he shall return immediately with further interesting details; this is essential to concert and harmony of movement. Send a list of all persons known to Wilkinson west of the mountains who could be useful, with a note delineating their characters." The letter continues on a second page and is followed by a note from Wilkinson, added when the letter was submitted as trial evidence. He denies any recollection of the May 13th letter, but supposes "it was one of Several Short notes written to him with the design to extract from him the particulars of Some grand Project."

After setting down these details, Burr wrote a sentence that may have contained the key to entire scheme:

> The people of the country to which we are going are prepared to receive us; their agents, now with Burr, say that if we will protect their religion, and will not subject them to a foreign power, that in three weeks all will be settled.

What "country" did Burr have in mind? The Louisiana Territory or Mexico? There probably were no agents of either Louisiana or Mexico with him at the time. Both areas were Catholic, so the protection of their religion would be a problem in one as well as the other. The most important clue may be the timetable of three weeks. Burr could hardly have hoped to put together a fleet, sail across the Gulf of Mexico to Veracruz, and conquer Mexico in such a short time. On the other hand, capturing New Orleans and proclaiming a new western nation probably could be done in three weeks, with Wilkinson's help. What Burr probably planned to do was to gather his forces, meet Wilkinson at Natchez, and then decide whether to invade Mexico, take over New Orleans, or peacefully settle the Ouachita lands. The simple fact was that his future was in Wilkinson's hands, and those hands became more unsteady every day.

Burr closed his letter with a last attempt to coax Wilkinson into action: "The gods invite us to glory and fortune; it remains to be seen whether we deserve the boon." A few days after he had sent messengers west with the letter, Burr set out for the Ohio, never to return—or so he believed.

Shortly after Burr left for the West, Wilkinson started down river from St. Louis. He reached Natchez early in September and started up the Red River to the main American fort at Natchitoches. He arrived there on September 22 to find a small, unprepared garrison, with no cannon or horses ready for duty. For thirty hot, frustrating days the general bargained and hesitated and tried to reinforce his little army. At first he was tough. He wrote the Spanish military commander of Texas that his orders were "absolute." The border was the Sabine River, and the Spanish must withdraw or face the consequences. But the Spaniard was just as tough. His orders were to enforce the Spanish claim east to the Arroyo Hondo, he said, and the choice of peace or war rested with Wilkinson.

While Wilkinson carried on his correspondence with the Spanish officials, he wrote very excited letters to his American friends. For a crucial two weeks at the end of September and the beginning of October, he became convinced that war with Spain was certain. He was ready for much more than a squabble over the border between Texas and Louisiana. At last, his dream of conquering Spanish Mexico seemed about to come true. On September 26 he wrote to a friend, Senator John Smith of Ohio:

> I have made the last effort of conciliation. I shall be obliged to fight and flog them. Five thousand mounted infantry may suffice to carry us forward as far as the Grand River [the Rio Grande]. There we shall require 5,000 more to conduct us to Monterrey [Mexico], and from 20,000 to 30,000 will be necessary to carry our conquests to California and the Isthmus of Darien [Panama].

To another friend Wilkinson exclaimed, "a blow once struck, and away we go!"

It was at this critical point—with the Spanish refusing to retreat and war seemingly certain—that Wilkinson finally received Burr's coded letter of July 29. The letter had taken two months to catch up with him, and it hit him at an awkward moment. If a war did begin, Wilkinson would be pinned down in a land action in Texas. There was no way to control what Burr might do in New Orleans. If Burr were telling the truth, if he did have a thousand men and a British fleet, he could undoubtedly have his way in New Orleans. Then he could probably invade Mexico by sea before Wilkinson could get his troops assembled, much less advance to the Rio Grande. The moment had finally come when Wilkinson must choose. He received Burr's letter on October 8. He waited and thought for two agonizing weeks. He also drank more whiskey than was his usual custom, for his situation was difficult indeed.

Meanwhile, Burr was traveling in the Ohio country, having boats built and recruiting volunteers. Sometimes he said that he was going to settle the Ouachita land grant. At other times he talked of raising a force of volunteers for the war with Spain that was sure to begin soon. He visited Cincinnati, Frankfort, Lexington, Nashville, and all the settlements in between.

Burr also established a base of operations. In the Ohio River near Cincinnati was an island owned by a wealthy Irish immigrant named Harman Blennerhassett. Blennerhassett had become involved with Burr during the winter of 1805–1806. He seems to have had a vision of himself as minister to England in the new government of Mexico that Burr would establish. Whatever the vision, Blennerhassett was willing to put himself into debt and danger to help Burr. According to the timetable, boats would be built at Blennerhassett Island and at other points along the river. From the island, at around the beginning of December, the fleet and the volunteers would start south.

All during September and October, preparations went fairly smoothly. Many boats were completed. Dozens of volunteers were recruited, many of them the young sons of leading planters, politicians, and military men. In Kentucky, Ohio, and Tennessee, Burr's expedition — whatever its destination — was the main subject of gossip and speculation.

Some talk was good for Burr. Like any enterprise, his needed advertising. But the talk began to filter back to Washington. Jefferson's administration became first suspicious and then alarmed. Early in November a Kentucky district attorney even attempted to have Burr arrested on the grounds that he was planning an invasion of Mexico. Most Kentuckians interpreted this action as a political move. The district attorney was a member of the Federalist party, and Burr was a Republican. In addition, the district attorney had so admired Hamilton that he had taken the name as his own legal middle name. Two sympathetic juries, one in November and another in December, found Burr innocent of any crime.

Blennerhassett's mansion boasted paintings and furniture imported from Paris and London. He too was taken to Richmond for trial, but not prosecuted. Blennerhassett died in poverty in Europe, and his island home fell into ruins.

Still, it was clear that Burr's preparations could not go on much longer without forcing the government into some kind of response.

Burr did not know as he completed his preparations that he had already been betrayed. Wilkinson had made his decision. He would do whatever was necessary to make peace with the Spanish on the border, and then he would turn against Burr. He could then gain credit with the Spanish for protecting their interests. At home he could claim that he had saved his country from Burr's intrigues.

On October 20 Wilkinson put his plan in motion. He wrote President Jefferson two very strange letters. In the first, he enclosed an "anonymous" document—which he actually wrote himself. In it Wilkinson sounded an alarm against "a numerous and powerful association" illegally organized for the invasion of Mexico. The general had to be careful not to appear involved. He claimed:

> It is unknown under what auspices this enterprise has been projected, from whence the means of its support are derived, or what may be the intentions of its leaders.

In his second letter Wilkinson again warned the President. Again he tried to appear innocent and confused:

> The magnitude of the enterprise staggers my belief. I have never in my whole life found myself in such perplexity. I am not only uninformed of the prime mover and ultimate objects of this daring enterprise, but am ignorant of the foundation on which it rests.

Wilkinson knew that when the President received these letters, he would have no choice but to move against Burr. This left only one nagging problem. If the Spanish insisted on starting a war, then Burr and his force might suddenly appear to be heroes on their way to fight the enemy. To cover this possibility, Wilkinson added an incredible postscript to his second letter to Jefferson:

> Should Spain be disposed to war seriously with us, might not some plan be adopted to correct the delirium of the associates, and by a suitable appeal to their patriotism engage them in the service of their country? I do believe that I could accomplish the object.

Here was Wilkinson's escape hatch in case something went wrong. If war with Spain did come, he would simply rejoin Burr in the plan to conquer Mexico.

Now everything depended on the Spanish, and on this front Wilkinson had extraordinary luck. On October 23, three days after he wrote Jefferson, he mounted his troops to begin a slow, tense march toward the Sabine. He did not know at the time that the small Spanish force had already withdrawn west of the river. When he met no resistance, Wilkinson proposed a neutral zone between the Sabine and the Arroyo Hondo. No Spanish forces would cross the Sabine, and no American troops would cross the Arroyo Hondo. The Spanish accepted the agreement,

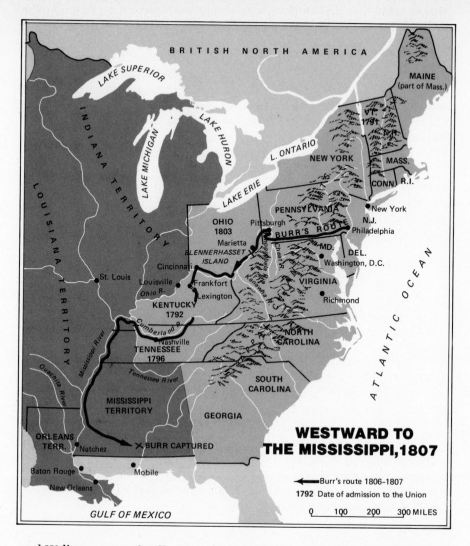

WESTWARD TO THE MISSISSIPPI, 1807

← Burr's route 1806–1807

1792 Date of admission to the Union

0 100 200 300 MILES

and Wilkinson was finally free to confront Burr. He immediately headed east for Natchez and New Orleans.

Before marching east, Wilkinson sent a messenger to the Spanish authorities in Mexico asking for a payment to Agent No. 13 for keeping peace and stopping Burr's plan to conquer Mexico! The Spanish government refused to pay this particular bill. But the resourceful Wilkinson did finally manage to get Jefferson to pay the messenger $1,500 in "expenses" for the trip.

Burr was now in deep trouble, though he did not know it. There was still a slender chance that he might salvage something, but only if he moved quickly. Even by fast express Wilkinson's letters would take six weeks to get to Washington. Burr thus had until early December before the federal government could act. Wilkinson would also need several weeks to travel to New Orleans and put the city's defenses in any kind of order. If Burr could get to Natchez by his original deadline of December 15, he might still have a chance to trick or surprise Wilkinson. This meant that Burr and his collaborators had to get their boats into the water by the middle of November. Any delay would give the government time to act and Wilkinson time to prepare. News that there was to be no war with Spain would soon reach Ohio and Kentucky, and this would threaten every version of Burr's scheme; he did not know that Wilkinson had written to Jefferson, made peace with Spain, and turned for New Orleans.

Burr's plans were certainly ambitious enough to attract intense suspicion. He was having fifteen boats built at Marietta, Ohio, near Blennerhassett Island. Andrew Jackson was building five more at Nashville on the Cumberland River. At least eight others were being bought or built in Pittsburgh and other settlements on the Ohio. These twenty-eight boats could carry at least a thousand men and their supplies—a force several times larger than the army Wilkinson would command in New Orleans. But the boatbuilding went more slowly than Burr had planned, and he showed no hurry to get into action.

The first four boats were launched in Pittsburgh on December 4. By this time any hope Burr might have had was gone. Ohio officials had been watching preparations at Marietta for many weeks, and they now knew of Wilkinson's treaty with the Spanish. On December 9 they seized the fifteen boats at Marietta. Harman Blennerhassett and a few other men got away down the Ohio in the four boats that had just arrived from Pittsburgh.

Burr knew nothing about these events. After his second trial in Kentucky he went to Nashville. He did not start down the Cumberland until December 22. By that time it was already much too late. Burr finally made his rendezvous with Blennerhassett and the others on December 27, at the junction of the Cumberland and Ohio rivers. There were only ten boats and less than a hundred men.

Burr would surely have quit at this point if he had known of Wilkinson's betrayal. But he still believed that a small force at New Orleans could accomplish a great deal, if Wilkinson helped. Burr had learned that Wilkinson had made peace with the Spanish. He must have thought that either the peace would be temporary or he and Wilkinson would capture New Orleans instead of Mexico. In any case, he went on down the river, completely out of communication with the rest of the world. On January 10, 1807, he pulled to shore at a small settlement just north of Natchez. A man quickly showed him a newspaper that told the story of Wilkinson's treachery. He also learned that President Jefferson had ordered his arrest. The former Vice President was once more a fugitive from justice.

General Wilkinson had already declared martial law in New Orleans and had begun to arrest Burr's friends there. Burr decided to take his chances with civilian courts in Mississippi Territory. There he hoped to be out of Wilkinson's grasp. But after a few weeks of legal maneuvering, Burr learned that Wilkinson had sent troops north to arrest him. He fled and hid with friends for about two weeks. Finally, on February 19, he was surprised and captured near Mobile. He was then taken east under military arrest for trial in Richmond, Virginia.

Burr's trial began on March 30, 1807. It lasted five months and caused more attention than any other criminal trial in America up to that time. Some of this attention was simply a result of Burr's high political position and the fact that he was charged with one of the worst of all crimes, high treason. But his trial also had great political significance. President Jefferson committed himself actively to prosecuting Burr, and so he became almost a party to the trial. Many Federalists, on the other hand, became partisans of Burr in order to align themselves against the President (who was a Republican). The trial was presided over by none other than the Chief Justice of the United States, John Marshall. He was a Federalist and a bitter enemy of the President (see page 219). Jefferson, Burr, and Marshall had last been together on March 4, 1800. Then Marshall has administered the oaths of office to President Jefferson and Vice President Burr. Now all three were locked together in an ugly and curious political combat over whether the President's legal staff could force the Chief Justice to convict the former Vice President of treason.

Almost everyone believed that Burr was guilty of *something*. The President had publicly declared that Burr was guilty before the trial even began. The question was, however, guilty of what? Before the Revolution, British law had made conviction in treason cases fairly easy. The framers of the Constitution, in order to protect citizens from the power of the federal government, had defined treason quite narrowly. Only two things, the Constitution clearly said, were treasonable. One was giving "aid and comfort" to enemies of the United States. The other was "levying war" against the United States. Since the country was at peace, it technically had no enemies. So Burr had to be convicted of "levying war." (What the term "levying" actually means was one of the main issues of the trial.)

The Constitution contained another important provision. There had to be two witnesses to an overt act of treason. The government would have to prove that Burr had actually participated in an act of war against the United States—not just that he plotted or encouraged it. And the government would also have to have at least two eyewitnesses to the specific act.

Jefferson anxiously ordered the government's lawyers to do everything necessary to get a conviction. Still the prosecution had trouble putting a case together. At first, Marshall refused to even to begin a trial for treason because the government could produce so few witnesses. The strongest witness would probably be Wilkinson, but weeks passed and he did not show up. One of Burr's lawyers pointed out that "In Europe, a general had been known to march the same distance at the head of his *army* in a shorter time than General Wilkinson has had to pass from New Orleans to this place." The court recessed, one hot June day after another, to wait for the general. Washington Irving, who was covering the trial for a New York newspaper, commented sarcastically on the delay. Members of the court, he wrote, used the opportunity to go home, see their wives, have their clothes washed, and "flog their Negroes."

However the citizens of Richmond may have passed the time they finally were treated to a sight of the general. On June 15 Wilkinson strode into court, as Irving described him, "booted to the middle, sashed to the chin, collared to the ears, and whiskered to the teeth." Wilkinson described his own courtroom appearance in a letter to Jefferson:

> I saluted the bench and my eyes darted a flash of indignation at the little traitor. This lionhearted hero, with haggard eye, made an effort to meet the indignant salutation. But it was in vain. He averted his face, grew pale, and affected passion.

Irving's newspaper story of the same meeting was a bit different:

> Wilkinson strutted into court and took his stand, swelling like a turkey-cock and bracing himself for the encounter of Burr's eye. Burr turned his head, looked him full in the face, and then cooly resumed his position. The whole look was over in an instant, but it was an admirable one.

Whoever won the exchange of looks, Wilkinson's pretrial testimony was enough—barely enough—to have Burr indicted for treason. The trial began on August 3.

The first task was the selection of a jury. Virginia was Jefferson country, and it was difficult, if not impossible, to get an unbiased jury. Even the ghost of Hamilton rose up to haunt Burr. Burr and his lawyers questioned one juror very closely, and the man turned to the courtroom and said, "I am surprised that they should be in such terror of me. Perhaps my name may be the terror, for my first name is Hamilton." (He was excused.) Finally, Burr accepted an obviously biased jury, since he hoped to win on questions of procedure and law. These would be decided by the judge, not the jury.

The government lawyers received instructions directly from the President almost every day. Determined to prove that Burr had intended to make war, they held that he had assembled an armed force at Blennerhassett Island for this purpose. According to the prosecutors, his action was what the Constitution meant by "levying war."

The strategy of Burr's defense was to make the prosecution prove its accusation. As Burr sarcastically observed, Mr. Jefferson was having a great deal of trouble even *finding* a war:

> Our President is a lawyer, and a great one, too. He certainly ought to know what it is that constitutes a war. Six months ago he proclaimed that there was a civil war [between Burr's forces and the government]. And yet, for six months have they been hunting for it, and still cannot find one spot where it existed. There was, to be sure, a terrible war in the newspapers, but nowhere else.

Day after day, Burr and his lawyers tore holes in the government's case. The prosecution had proved only that thirty or forty men congregat-

Burr was sketched at the time of his trial by a French artist. Most of the audience was hostile to him. After his acquittal, a Baltimore mob hanged him in effigy, along with his chief defender, Marshall, and Blennerhassett.

ed at Blennerhassett Island in early December of 1806. But Burr was not even present on the island at the time.

Burr's lawyers were brilliant and cutting in their cross-examination of government witnesses. Burr, acting as his own lawyer, was even more brilliant and more cutting. One by one, the prosecution witnesses were broken. One had to admit, under Burr's questioning, that he had just been paid $10,000 by the government. Another ended by testifying *for* Burr; he admitted that, as far as he knew, Burr's force had been gathered for use only in a war against Spain. A third testified against Burr, only to have his own son follow him to the stand to swear that his father was "old and infirm, and like other old men, told long stories and was apt to forget his repetitions." Another witness, who knew Blennerhassett well, revealed that the latter was so nearsighted that it was ridiculous to imagine his participating in a military action.

The outcome depended on how Chief Justice Marshall defined treason. If he ruled that treason could mean participating in a *plan* that eventually led to treason, then the jury might find Burr guilty. But Burr's lawyers argued that the government would have to prove that Burr had been personally present and had participated in the act of levying war. For days lawyers for the government and for Burr argued the point. On the last day of August, Marshall made his ruling. He decided in favor of Burr. To prove treason, he said, the government would have to prove by two eyewitnesses that Burr had been present and taken part in a specific act of war against the United States. Since the government had not made such a case, the jury had to deliberate only briefly. On September 1, Burr was found not guilty.

Burr had won the case, just as he had won his duel with Hamilton. But he always seemed to lose in winning. He was still in legal trouble in several states, and he was now more deeply in debt than ever. Also, much of the public was convinced that Marshall, the Federalist, had let Burr go free just to embarrass the Republican administration. Burr's career was finished. Once more, he decided to "seek another country," and he went to Europe in a self-imposed exile that lasted four years. In 1812 he came home to practice law in New York. At the age of seventy-seven he married a wealthy widow; she soon sued him for divorce (charging him with adultery!). The divorce became final on September 14, 1836. Burr died the same day, at the age of eighty.

12 THE REPUBLIC ON TRIAL

R.J.W.

The career of Aaron Burr was a strange one. In many ways his life was an expression of a unique, ambitious, and unpredictable personality. But when Burr's duel with Hamilton, his Western scheme, and his trial for treason are considered today, they make almost perfect sense as part of the larger history of the United States. The generation that made the Revolution and the Constitution continued to govern the United States until the 1820s. The lives of this generation were controlled by four main tendencies. Each of them was very much present in the life of Burr.

First, the development of party politics and the first two-party system occupied the minds and energies of just about every important American during the period after 1789. Burr was, first and last, a politician. He was deeply involved in almost every political battle until his duel with Hamilton. In fact, political conflict between the two men was a major factor behind the duel.

Second, the history of the United States during the decades after Washington's inauguration was tied very closely to foreign affairs. Relations with France, Spain, and Britian tended to dominate national and even local politics. Many leading politicians and military figures were involved in secret intrigues with one foreign power or another. Burr sensed this situation clearly, especially after his duel. His mind was controlled by thoughts of war with Spain and secret arrangements with Britain.

Third, the years between 1789 and the 1820s were marked by rapid expansion of territory and population. During this period the territory of the United States doubled. Thousands of pioneer settlers pushed over the Appalachian Mountains into the valleys of the Ohio, the Tennessee, and the Mississippi rivers. Burr's thoughts ran west with this expansion.

Fourth, the United States was involved in a serious test of whether the federal system would work. Each section of the country had its own special interests and institutions. It was not clear whether the nation could survive. Would the Western farmers secede? Would the question of slavery divide the North from the South? Would New England leave the Union and try to go it alone? These questions were quite real and important, not just to Burr but to other leaders.

THE DEVELOPMENT OF PARTY POLITICS

The two-party system is such a familiar feature of our national government that it is difficult for us to realize that the men who made the Constitution did not plan for it. In fact, almost all of the framers despised the idea of "factions." In the Constitution they tried to create a government that would discourage the formation of national parties.

The framers of the Constitution knew that conflict between organized groups was bound to occur. Farmers would be pitted against merchants, slaveholders against nonslaveholders, the rich against the poor. Such divisions in society were bound to lead to factions, which would struggle for domination of state governments. These struggles would bring out people's worst failings: selfishness, intrigue, ambition, and deceit. In order to gain the advantage, political parties and their leaders might stop at nothing. They might mobilize their supporters by appeals to fear and greed. And people's loyalties would not be to their country but to their party.

To try to prevent the rise of parties, the authors of the Constitution tried to frame a government that would be beyond the reach of factions and interests. They believed that the system of checks and balances would make it impossible for any group to gain control of the whole federal structure. The President would not be the tool of a political party, because he was elected by the electoral college, not the people. Since federal judges were to be appointed for life, they would not depend on party support for their offices. If a party formed in the popularly elected House of Representatives, then surely the Senate would counteract it. (Senators, elected for long terms of six years, would be more independent than members of the House, who had to run for election every two years.) The Constitution forbade the states to do certain things, such as coin money and regulate interstate commerce. So the worst effects of party politics in the states could be controlled from the national capital.

The political history of the first forty years of the United States is, among other things, the story of the failure of these hopes. The national government did not prove to be above party. Political parties did emerge. The presidency did become a party office. Control of the national government became the highest prize in the conflict between one party and another. Supreme Court justices, senators, and congressmen did become party men with party loyalties. In fact, the very men who had written the Constitution to guard against parties became partisan leaders themselves. Even Washington, who had seemed in 1789 to stand loftily above all conflict and ambition, was drawn into the struggle and made a symbol of party conflict.

At first, Washington's dignity was his greatest asset. The friends of the new government knew that only he could be the first President. Only he could convince the people that the power of the central government would be fairly and evenly used. It would not operate in favor of any section or class, but in a generous and truly national way. Washington strained to create an appearance of majesty. He rode a white horse with a striking saddlecloth made from a leopard skin. He also had an elegant coach, bearing his crest and drawn by a matched team of six cream-colored horses. His house in New York was one of the grandest in the city, and it was fully staffed with servants. Almost everything Washington did was calculated to give an impression of an almost regal stateliness, far above ambition and partisanship.

Some men in Congress wanted to put an official seal upon Washington's kingly manner. Just after the first inauguration, Washington's friends in Congress drew up a message of congratulations. There was a debate over how to address the President. One of Washington's admirers went so far as to propose the title "His Highness, the President of the United States and Protector of Their Liberties." After a heated debate, men of simpler taste won the day, and the letter was addressed to "George Washington, President of the United States."

In his appointments, Washington tried to fill federal offices with people from different states and with different interests. He hoped that his administration could be representative of the country at large. His secretary of the Treasury, Alexander Hamilton, was from New York. The Secretary of State and the Attorney General, Thomas Jefferson and Edmund Randolph, were both planters from Virginia. The fourth member of what finally became known as the cabinet was Henry Knox of Massachusetts, secretary of war.[1]

Hamilton's Financial Program   The only man in the new government who had a clear political program was Alexander Hamilton. When he took office as secretary of the Treasury, his job was to try to make some sense out of a confused financial situation. The United States was more than $54 million in debt. It could not operate effectively until it could pay off what it owed.

Most of the debt was in the form of certificates, like the United States savings bonds that are sold today. They had been printed during the 1770s and 1780s to finance the Revolution. Many of them had gone to soldiers of the Continental army as pay for their services. The certificates were promises that the government would someday, somehow, pay back in real money what it owed private citizens and foreign governments.

_____

[1]Although Washington did consult with the heads of his executive departments, they did not hold regular meetings. The Cabinet as a formal institution did not develop until the Administration of Thomas Jefferson.

This anti-Republican cartoon was published in 1795. A dignified Washington leads his troops out to meet the French "cannibals." Jefferson, clutching at a chariot wheel, shouts at his followers (in a French accent), "Stop de wheels of de gouvernement."

No one expected the federal government to able to pay back the entire debt, so the worth of the certificates declined. Speculators bought them for a fraction of their face value. For example, a soldier who held a certificate worth ten dollars might sell it to a speculator for one dollar, on the theory that a dollar in the hand is better than ten in an uncertain future. All over the country millions of dollars in certificates had been bought up or taken in trade. The government theoretically owed the entire $54 million. But no one expected it to pay back more than a few cents on the dollar.

Individual states had also printed certificates, and they were in debt, too. Some states were paying off what they owed. Others had little money with which to do so.

Hamilton made two unexpected proposals. One, known as "funding," called for the government to pay off the entire federal debt at its full, or par, value. The other proposal was termed "assumption." The federal government would take over (assume) the states' debts and pay them off at par. The money would be paid to whoever actually held the certificates at the time. The original holders, many of them ordinary farmers who had fought in the Continental army and the state militias during the Revolution, would get nothing. The effect would be to create, by government power, a class of very rich men, men who had bought federal or state certificates for as little as a few cents on the dollar.

Hamilton did not propose to pay off federal and state debts with cash. Instead, holders of certificates would receive newly issued government bonds. Funding and assumption, plus interest on bonds, would cost a great deal of money. Hamilton called for two new taxes. One was a tax to be paid by distillers of alcoholic beverages. The other was a tariff on imports, which would not only raise money but also encourage American manufactures. The secretary of the Treasury also proposed a national bank to help the government make all its financial transactions.

Some parts of Hamilton's program were acceptable to most people. Others aroused opposition. One group of congressmen, led by Madison, attacked the funding plan. Madison believed that speculators who had bought federal certificates should be paid half their value. He felt that the original holders should get the other half. Madison also opposed the assumption plan. Virginia had been paying off its own debt, while some other states had not. Why should Virginians be taxed to pay off the debts of other states?

Madison's congressional opposition to Hamilton's plan was powerful. He was soon joined by Jefferson, the secretary of state. But Hamilton had strong backing, too. The disagreement over funding and assumption was settled by a classic political bargain. Madison and Jefferson promised to deliver enough votes in Congress to pass Hamilton's proposal. In return, Hamilton would deliver the votes of *his* followers for a measure providing that a new national capital would be created in the South rather than the North. The city would be called Washington, and it would be located on the Potomac River in a district that would bear the name "Columbia." The measures were passed in July 1790 and were soon signed by Washington.

Republicans Versus Federalists Within two years, Hamilton had also succeeded in getting the new taxes he wanted and in establishing a national bank. But the groundwork had been laid for organized conflict between two major factions on the national level. From 1790 on, every major decision on domestic and foreign policy caused a quarrel. Jefferson and Madison, year after year, organized their forces. Slowly, almost against their wills, they formed a political party. They studied local and state elections throughout the country. They supported candidates for Congress and the Senate who they thought would be sympathetic to their views.

The followers of Jefferson and Madison were mostly small farmers and debtors. Many of them were former Antifederalists who thought Hamilton's program was a scheme to create a powerful federal government at the expense of states' rights. Gradually, this group adopted the name Republicans (or Democratic-Republicans). This term emphasized their avowed dedication to the interests of the people at large.

Hamilton's followers were mainly merchants, bankers, and speculators. They gradually began to call themselves Federalists. This name was derived, of course, from the term for supporters of the Constitution in 1788.

The support for both Hamilton's group and Jefferson's group was mixed. Only a small minority of Americans voted, anyway, so both parties' claims to represent "the people" were false. In general, Jefferson and Madison aimed their arguments toward small farmers, Southern planters, and old Antifederalists. They even adopted the name "Democratic-Republican"—though it was "Republican" that eventually stuck. Hamilton and his supporters, on the other hand, were much more frank in their appeal to the "better sort"— including merchants, bankers, and speculators. In practice, voting support for the Republicans was only slightly more "democratic" than for the Federalists. But Jefferson was successful in creating the lasting myth that his was the party of the "people" against the rich and the well-born. Every new party created since has tried to lay claim to the same myth.

In 1792, Washington still stood "above party," and both sides joined in reelecting him.

In 1798 Congress was the scene of a brawl between Republican Matthew Lyon, left, and Federalist Roger Griswold, right. In the Speaker's chair sits an amused Jonathan Dayton.

During his second term, he gradually identified himself with the Federalists. He still talked of standing above party and of disliking parties more than any feature of government. But he was under constant pressure from Hamilton and his friends to support their positions. Bit by bit, Washington's second term took on the appearance of a real administration—that is, it was staffed by members of one party whose goal was achieving a specific political program.

Yet, when Washington finally gained his longed-for retirement, he wrote a farewell address whose main theme was a condemnation of party politics. The address was not published until September 1796. The Republicans claimed that Washington had waited until then so that they would not have time to mount a presidential campaign before the elections in November. So the address was, in its way, a political gesture, especially because of its timing. In its content, however, Washington's farewell address was a bitter and eloquent condemnation of political parties.

Let me warn you in the most solemn manner against the baneful effects of the spirit of party. This spirit serves always to distract the public councils and to enfeeble the public administration. It agitates the community with ill-founded jealousies and false alarms; kindles the animosity of one part against another; foments riot and insurrection. It opens the door to foreign influence and corruption.

In theory, at least, Madison and Jefferson might still have agreed. But by 1796 they had had six years of experience in opposition politics. And they had formed, like it or not, a party. The Republicans nominated Jefferson for the presidency, to run against Federalist John Adams. Despite the short time available to run a campaign, Jefferson was a close second in the electoral college. According to the awkward provisions of the Constitution, the runner-up in the electoral vote was to become Vice President. So for the next four years the United States was governed by a Federalist President and a Republican Vice President.

During Adams's term of office, party conflict reached a high pitch. Everywhere, Republicans were organizing for the election of 1800. The Federalists could sense the tide running toward Jefferson. In anger and desperation they managed to ram through Congress a series of laws designed to stifle political opposition. Three of these Alien and Sedition Acts were directed against new immigrants from Europe, most of whom became Republican voters. (One of them, for example, increased the period of residence from five to fourteen years before an alien could become a citizen.) The fourth was a law making it illegal to "oppose any measure of the government of the United States." This Sedition Act of 1798 in addition made it a crime to publish any "false, scandalous and malicious writing against the government of the United States or either house of the Congress or the President." Under the Sedition Act federal judges (appointed by a Federalist President) attempted to silence Republican criticism. One Republican candidate for Congress was even sent to prison for speeches made against Adams during the campaign of 1798.

Madison and Jefferson were able to use the Sedition Act as a means of trying to unite their party and the state governments against the Adams administration. Madison wrote a resolution for Virginia and Jefferson one for Kentucky. These so-called Virginia and Kentucky Resolutions de-

nounced the law as unconstitutional. They held, too, that the states could resist any federal law that they judged to be a violation of the Constitution. These resolutions drew the lines very clearly for the election of 1800, and they put the Republicans firmly on the side of states' rights against federal power.

The Election of 1800 The Republicans organized an intense campaign in the summer and fall of 1800. New York was a typical and important state. The Republicans had to win it if they were to take the presidency from Adams and the Federalists. New York political affairs were in the hands of none other than Alexander Hamilton for the Federalists and Aaron Burr for the Republicans. In the state elections of 1799 Hamilton's party had won an impressive victory. But Burr, Jefferson's candidate for the vice presidency, now went to work in the city of New York. He got Republicans to the polls by every means possible, and the result was a victory in the state legislature. Since the legislature in New York chose presidential electors, New York delivered all its electoral votes to Jefferson. Virginia, the largest state, also went to Jefferson. Although Adams held all the New England states, the Jeffersonians got more than half the votes in Pennsylvania.

The outcome was a narrow victory for Jefferson: seventy-three electoral votes to Adams' sixty-five. The presidency had changed hands, and political power had moved from one organized party to another. Burr's strategy had been crucial. New York's twelve electoral votes would have saved the presidency for Adams and the Federalists. Through hard work and careful maneuvering Burr had beaten Hamilton in New York City, and he had won the vice presidency for himself.

The result should have been clear, but it was confused by an odd provision of the Constitution. The document recognized no distinction between presidential and vice presidential candidates. It simply provided that the person having the most electoral votes would be President and the runner-up Vice President. However, all the electors who had voted for Jefferson also voted for Burr, so there was a tie vote. This meant that the

JOHN MARSHALL

For thirty-four years, from 1801 until his death at the age of eighty, John Marshall was chief justice of the United States Supreme Court. He was a firm nationalist, a Federalist in politics, and a rigorous and skillful interpreter of law and the Constitution. More than any other single individual, he managed to give shape and meaning to the Constitution.

Marshall was born on the Virginia frontier in 1755. Like Hamilton, Jefferson, and Burr, he grew up just in time to serve in the Revolutionary War. He then became a lawyer (after only six weeks of formal training), and almost as quickly got himself elected to the Virginia legislature. He also became a leading champion of the Federalist cause in the Virginia fight over ratification. In 1800, he was appointed, in quick succession, secretary of state in the Adams administration and then chief justice.

Three decisions of outstanding importance decided by Marshall and his fellow justices were: *Marbury* v. *Madison* (1803), *McCulloch* v. *Maryland* (1819), and *Gibbons* v. *Ogden* (1824). The first, *Marbury* v. *Madison*, grew out of some last-minute appointments of justices of the peace for the District of Columbia, made as final patronage gestures by the

by Adams, and even sealed by the acting secretary of state—none other than John Marshall. But, in the hectic transfer of power to the Republican victors of 1800, a few of the commissions were not delivered. One belonged to William Marbury, who sued the new secretary of state, James Madison, for his commission. The suit went directly to the Supreme Court under a provision of the Judiciary Act of 1789, giving the court the power to issue orders to federal officials to carry out their legal duties.

Marshall's problem was acute, but his strategy was brilliant. He ruled that Marbury *did* have a legal right to his commission, but that the Supreme Court should not issue the order. The Constitution gave the Court original jurisdiction in a number of specific types of cases. Therefore, the section of the Judiciary Act that added to the Court's original jurisdiction was unconstitutional. Marbury would have to go to another court, first. Marshall had thus laid out the principle that the Supreme Court could rule on the constitutionality of acts of Congress.

McCulloch v. *Maryland* (1819) set forth a parallel principle with respect to state laws. The state of Maryland passed a measure that threatened to tax a federal agency, the Bank of the United States, out of existence. The bank refused to pay, and Maryland sued James McCulloch, a bank officer. When the case reached the Supreme Court, Marshall declared that any state law that was in conflict with a federal law was null and void.

Gibbons v. *Ogden* (1824) gave broad meaning to the commerce clause of the Constitution. New York State had granted a monopoly of steamboat commerce on the Hudson River to the steamboat's inventor, Robert Fulton, and his associates. Aaron Ogden had eventually acquired the monopoly. Thomas Gibbons challenged the state's power to grant such a monopoly. The Hudson River steamboat trade involved a great deal of interstate commerce, Gibbons argued, and the Constitution gave Congress, not the states, power to regulate interstate commerce. Marshall accepted Gibbons's arguments and ruled that the monopoly was unconstitutional.

election would have to be decided by the House of Representatives.

Once the election was thrown into the House, the situation was even more confused. In the first place, voting was by states and each state was allowed one vote, no matter what its population. In the second place, the House was free to choose *any* of the candidates, even though Jefferson and Burr had both beaten Adams in the electoral college. The voting quickly settled down to a contest between Jefferson and Adams. Burr stood rather coyly to one side, refusing to shift his political support to Jefferson. Thirty-five ballots were cast before Hamilton threw *his* support to Jefferson. Hamilton did this because, although he disliked Jefferson, he hated Burr. His action settled the election. It also made the relationship between Burr and Hamilton impossible, and, together with events in New York, led the two men finally to the dueling ground at Weehawken.

Jefferson, a Man of New Ideas   After the election, Jefferson tried to soften party divisions, as Washington had always done. He announced that "We are all Federalists; we are all Republicans." But nothing could hide the fact that a political changeover had taken place. Jefferson himself called it the revolution of 1800. He believed that the victory of his party over Hamilton, Adams, and the Federalists would cause a basic reversal in the direction of American history. His principles were different from theirs. And his party had committed itself to ideas of liberty and democracy that probably did have a profound and long-term effect on the lives of ordinary Americans.

Jefferson's conception of the good society rested on one fundamental opinion. As he put it, "Those who labor in the earth are the chosen people of God." Plain farmers, he felt, ought to be the backbone of any society. And the plain farmers of the Republic ought to have as much political power as they had virtue. They ought to control the government in a more or less direct and democratic way.

The central government ought to be devoted above all to republican simplicity. It should be small and relatively weak, so that it could not interfere with the liberties of the people. Power

Jefferson's greatest personal attraction, according to one admirer, was "a countenance beaming with benevolence and intelligence."

should be decentralized—that is, divided up among smaller authorities such as state and local governments. Then people could keep a close eye on their elected representatives.

It sometimes seemed that Jefferson's political philosophy was based on a conflict between two simple ideas: power and the people. Whatever contributed to governmental power injured people's control over their own private lives. Jefferson wanted a "government which shall restrain men from injuring one another." But government should do no more than this. It should leave men "otherwise free to regulate their own pursuits of industry and improvement."

Such a government ought to practice the strictest economy. The number of federal offices should be cut to the bare minimum. The national debt should be quickly liquidated. (It had ballooned from $54 million to about $83 million as a result of Hamilton's program of funding and assumption.) In fact, Jefferson promised to pay off the entire debt within sixteen years. To save on expenses, Jefferson reduced the army from 4,000 to 2,500 men. He cut the navy back sharply to a defensive force of coastal guns and small gunboats.

In his own life, too, the new President practiced his principles of simplicity and economy. He reduced the amount of formal entertaining at the White House. He dressed and lived quietly and simply in comparison to the aristocratic elegance of Washington. In fact, Jefferson embarrassed some Americans by receiving visitors while wearing threadbare clothes and tattered bedroom slippers.

Jefferson's was a political program that promised *not* to do things: not to maintain a powerful government with a large standing army and a powerful navy; not to allow the federal government to become powerful at the expense of the rights of the states and the people; not to pursue a financial policy that would benefit only a small class of merchants, bankers, and speculators. The heart of Jefferson's idea of government was his belief that the American people—most of whom really were plain farmers—could build a great nation if only they were let alone. Jefferson himself was a cultivated aristocrat, a highly educated man, and a wealthy slaveholding planter. But his political philosophy was one of democratic simplicity and an almost religious faith in the good sense of the people.

In the long run, Jefferson and the other Republican Presidents who followed him were the captives of history. They were forced to expand, not contract, federal power in order to meet emergencies and opportunities that came their way. But their revolution was one of ideas, not acts. Jefferson and his successors made words like "liberty" and "democracy" the most important words in the political language of Americans. And, after 1800, a democratic faith in the people became the most prominent and unique feature of American political life.

Jefferson continued to believe that political parties were evil. True, he had helped build a party that had turned the Federalists out of office. But he had done so because he believed that the Federalists were a bad party and the Republicans were a good one.

After 1800 the Republicans were committed to making their party the only party, to driving the Federalists out of existence altogether. Jefferson was elected easily for a second term in 1804. Madison won the presidency in 1808 and 1812, and he was followed into office by another Virginian, James Monroe, in 1816. By this time the Federalist party had collapsed and did not even run a candidate. Monroe won again in 1820. By 1824 the fall of the Federalists was so complete that the son of John Adams, John Quincy Adams, won the presidency as a Republican.

After 1824 a new party structure would emerge, with two new parties replacing the Republicans and the Federalists. But, for the time being, it appeared that the Republicans had actually realized the hopes of the Founding Fathers by creating a unified government.

FOREIGN AFFAIRS

During most of the twenty-five years after Washington's first inauguration, Europe was at war. Britain and France fought everywhere in Europe, around the Mediterranean, and in almost every other corner of the world. In the process, other European nations and the United States were drawn into the conflict.

Events in Europe had a profound effect on the United States in two fields. One was the economy. Americans imported most of their manufactured goods from England, and they in turn sold many agricultural products—like tobacco and cotton—in Europe. This transatlantic trade was crucial to farmers in the southern and western states. Merchants in eastern cities also depended heavily on a brisk trade across the Atlantic. European nations at war needed the American trade, but at the same time they tried to cut their enemies off from American shipping. By turns, the English and the

French attacked American ships. They even kidnapped American seamen for service in their own navies and merchant marine, a practice known as impressment.

The other field affected by European affairs was American politics. The conflict between Britain and France was an old one, going well back into the eighteenth century. Indeed, the Americans had fought their Revolution against the British with French help. But there was a new element in the conflict after 1789. In that year the French began a revolution against their monarchy. They proclaimed France a republic in 1792, and from then on they fought their wars for ideological reasons, as well as for the more traditional military, political, and economic ones. In fact, the French thought of themselves as the agents of "a war of all peoples against all kings."

In the beginning, many Americans favored the French Revolution. To them it meant another monarch deposed, another republic created. America's old ally, the Marquis de Lafayette, even sent Washington the key to the Bastille—a notorious Parisian prison whose capture was one of the opening events of the Revolution.

Gradually, though, the French Revolution seemed to take a dangerous turn. At the height of revolutionary fervor, in 1793 and 1794, thousands of Frenchmen, including the king and queen, were guillotined. To many Americans (especially those with Federalist sympathies) this experience was a lesson in the excesses of democracy. But others—the political disciples of Jefferson—followed their leader in stubborn sympathy with the French Revolution and its democratic changes. Thus, politics in America felt the impact of politics in Europe.

Out of this situation arose a crucial question: Could the United States remain neutral, since her trade and her politics were tied so closely to events in Paris and London? From George Washington to John Quincy Adams, American Presidents and their administrations had to devote at least as much attention to foreign as to domestic questions. In fact, much of the time, it was impossible to draw a line between the two.

This long episode in foreign policy involved almost every American political leader, from Washington, Hamilton, and Jefferson to men like Burr and Wilkinson. Burr's plans and intrigues were not the schemes of an isolated individual. Instead, he could claim the company of dozens of other public figures, all constantly involved in speculation, secret plans, and even spying. In the 1790s at least two Cabinet officers were actively working for European governments. Many senators, congressmen, and lesser politicians were so sympathetic to one European side or the other that they lost sight of American purposes and goals.

For almost twenty-five years, Americans had no real independence of Europe. They were tied to France, Spain, and Britain by every ship that left America for Europe, by developing systems of party loyalty, and by tough, troublesome issues of war and peace. Only after 1815, with peace in Europe, did Americans find release from European entanglements.

A Shaky Neutrality Several forces pushed the United States toward a new war with Britain during the 1790s. Ill feeling still lingered after the Revolutionary War. The British refused to evacuate their military posts in the Northwest Territory. They also refused to return American slaves whom they had seized during the Revolution. Many Americans sympathized with the French because of their aid during the war. In addition, there was the treaty of 1778, in which the United States pledged to come to the aid of France in case of conflict with Britain.

When France and Britain went to war in 1793, Washington's administration faced its first difficult decision in foreign policy. Partly under the influence of Hamilton, who despised the French for their democratic republicanism, Washington decided to ignore the alliance of 1778 and remain neutral. But the British made it very difficult for him. They used their position in Canada to stir up hostile Indians against American settlers. And British warships began to stop and even seize American merchant vessels trading with French islands in the West Indies.

At the same time, the French lost a chance to cement their relations with Americans by sending over a blundering diplomat, Edmont Genêt.

Genêt made the mistake of acting as though France and the United States were already allies. He did things that no representative of a foreign government can get away with for long. He set up French courts to take charge of captured English ships. He tried to talk a group of Americans into an armed attack on New Orleans (since Spain sided with Britain at the time). Worst of all, he interfered in domestic political matters. Even Jefferson, the ardent supporter of the French Revolution, could not stomach such behavior. Washington ended by demanding Genêt's recall to Paris.

In the meantime, despite Genêt's clumsiness, anti-British feeling was running high in America. There was real danger of war. Washington wanted to avoid it and settle old questions. He sent John Jay, a Federalist leader and a close friend of Hamilton, to London to negotiate a treaty.

Jay returned home in 1794 bearing a document that became known as the Jay Treaty. The British agreed to give up their Northwest posts. They made a few other concessions of a minor nature. In general, though, the treaty was unfavorable to the United States and offered no real protection to American shipping. It immediately became a political issue. Republicans opposed it and Federalists supported it. Even Washington, who wanted desperately to avoid a war, was reluctant to sign it, but he finally did so.

Negotiations With France The Jay Treaty made American relations with France more difficult, since the French believed that anything that helped the British hurt them. Late in Washington's administration and in the early months of Adams's presidency, the French began to intercept American shipping. Furthermore, they treated American sailors serving on British ships as pirates to be hanged. Like Washington, Adams tried to meet the crisis by insisting on neutrality and opening negotiations. He sent a team of three negotiators to Paris to try to arrange a treaty recognizing American trading rights and somehow putting an end to the embarrassing alliance of 1778.

The American mission failed. The French foreign minister, a shrewd and corrupt man named Charles Talleyrand, demanded a bribe of $250,000 for himself. He never met the Americans. Instead, he communicated with them through three anonymous go-betweens known only as X, Y, and Z. Through these agents Talleyrand also demanded that the Americans pay the government of France several million dollars as the price of peace and a treaty. Two of the three American commissioners returned angrily to America to report to a shocked President and Congress. For a time, war seemed inevitable.

Adams's position was delicate. Many members of his party wanted war with France—partly to discredit the Republicans and partly to solidify their own hold on the national government. Adams moved considerably in their direction. He called for a stronger navy, better coastal defenses, and the arming of American merchant ships. He also gave in to Hamilton's demands that the army be strengthened. The retired Washington even agreed to take charge of the army in case of war, with Hamilton as his second in command. For several years American and French ships fought an undeclared war in the Atlantic.

But Adams was determined to avoid an unnecessary war, even if it hurt his position among the Federalists. In 1799 he sent another American mission to France with orders to negotiate an agreement. There the Americans found a new government in control. Its leader, Napoleon, was anxious to establish good relations with the United States. He agreed to scrap the 1778 alliance and also to end French interference with American shipping. For the time being, Adams had preserved American neutrality once more.

Trouble With Britain After his victory in the presidential election of 1800, Jefferson began to dismantle the army and navy that Washington and Adams had expanded. Europe was temporarily at peace, and it looked as if the United States could achieve the promises of independence, freed from foreign involvements. In 1803, however, Europe again donned the familiar mask of war. The major player this time was the commanding figure of Napoleon. Over the next dozen years Napoleon's incredible ambition sent French armies all over Europe and as far from France as Egypt and Russia.

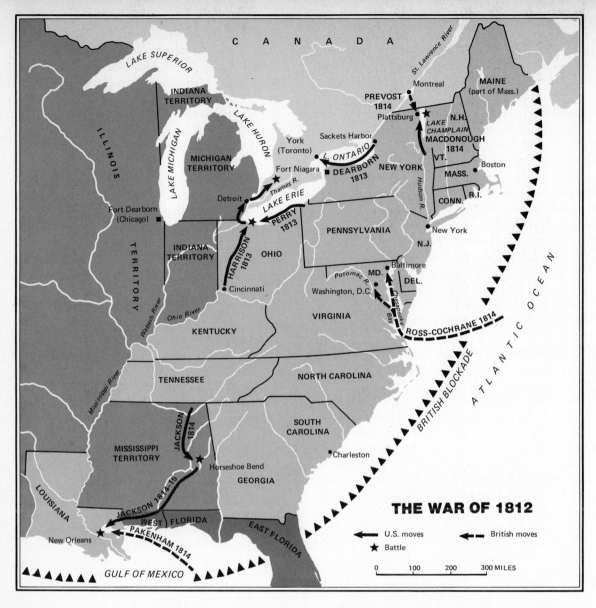

The American plan called for attacks against the British from Detroit, Fort Niagara, and Plattsburg, New York. In **1812** William Hull marched from Detroit into Canada. Fearing trouble from Indians on his flank, however, he retreated and surrendered Detroit without a shot. In August the American garrison at Fort Dearborn was wiped out.

In **1813** Americans were more successful. In April Henry Dearborn sailed from Sackets Harbor, New York, across Lake Ontario and burned York (now Toronto). Oliver Hazard Perry's September victory on Lake Erie forced the British to abandon Detroit. William Henry Harrison, who had moved north from Cincinnati, pursued the retreating British into Canada and defeated them at the Battle of the Thames in October.

In **1814** the Creek Indians, allied with the British, attacked Americans along the frontier. Andrew Jackson, moving south through Mississippi Territory, dealt the Creeks a heavy defeat at the Battle of Horseshoe Bend. In September British troops under Robert Ross and Alexander Cochrane sailed up Chesapeake Bay. They burned Washington, D. C., but failed to take Baltimore. That same month a British force under George Prevost moved south from Montreal. Americans led by Thomas Macdonough went north to meet them and won an important victory at the Battle of Lake Champlain. Late in the Year a large British fleet commanded by Edward Pakenham moved north from Jamaica. In **1815,** in the most spectacular battle of the war, Jackson defeated them at New Orleans.

The French emperor contemplated an invasion of England, and he even thought of moving some of his armies into North America. The British were locked in what they regarded as a deadly struggle for survival. For Americans the questions were the same old ones: Would they be able to carry on their vitally necessary trade with Europe? Would they be able to preserve their precious neutrality?

Beginning in 1805 British and French warships both began to intercept American merchant shipping again. The British controlled the seas, so they stopped more vessels. The British followed one practice that the French did not. They would board American vessels, pick out men whom they suspected of being British subjects, and force them into service in the royal navy. This practice of impressment, which to most Americans seemed little short of kidnapping, added to the fury that gradually built up in the United States.

Jefferson was committed to peace, to a small army and navy, and to a policy of negotiation rather than threat and bluster. But between 1805 and 1807 the British seized about a thousand American ships, and the French about five hundred. No administration, no matter how devoted to peace, could permit American ships and sailors to be treated like this.

Another crisis occurred in the summer of 1807. A British warship fired on an American vessel within view of the Virginia shore. The British ship, the *Leopard,* fired three broadsides into the American frigate, the *Chesapeake.* The *Chesapeake's* guns were out of order, and she could return only one cannon shot. Three Americans were killed and eighteen wounded before the *Chesapeake* limped home in an odd mixture of pride and disgrace.

Facing an aroused nation, Jefferson tried to ward off a war with Britain by a device used in pre-Revolutionary days. He asked Congress for a law, the Embargo Act, which simply prohibited Americans from exporting *anything* to foreign countries. It also forbade all ships to leave American ports bound for any other nation. In short, the embargo was designed simply to halt foreign trade altogether. Jefferson hoped that the British need for American markets, plus the French desire to import American goods, would force the two nations to behave more respectfully toward American commerce.

The embargo failed. It hurt Americans more than it hurt either the British or the French, because American farmers could not export their products. The law lasted until the end of Jefferson's second administration, when he happily left Washington for his plantation, Monticello. His successor, James Madison, then had to grapple with the problem. Madison's efforts at first were only modifications of Jefferson's policy. For the embargo Madison substituted a modified policy of trade restriction with the Non-Intercourse Act of 1809. He reopened foreign trade with all nations *except* Britain and France. And he promised to resume commerce with either country if only it would respect American rights on the seas.

The War of 1812 The Madison administration experimented with one form of trade restriction or another for more than three years. Finally, Madison asked for a declaration of war, citing impressment and trade interference. Congress responded on June 18, 1812. Just two days earlier, the British had announced a favorable change in policy. But it was too late.

The Americans were involved in a war that was almost impossible for them to fight. They had little or no way of attacking the British directly. Canada was vulnerable to invasion, or so it appeared. But the United States was afraid that Britain would defeat Napoleon quickly and then turn the full power of her army and navy on North America. In such a contest the small American defense forces would have had little chance.

The first months of the war passed without much significant action. The Americans planned a three-pronged attack on Canada through Lake Champlain and the Great Lakes, but all three attempts failed. The British took Detroit, and their Indian allies massacred the Americans at Fort Dearborn (the site of Chicago).

The United States did better on water than on land, at least during the first year of the war. On the Atlantic, American vessels were able to capture several British ships. Later, however, a British blockade restricted American actions. On Lake

The British bombarded Fort McHenry, near Baltimore, throughout the night of September 13–14, 1814. The successful resistance of the Americans inspired a bystander, lawyer Francis Scott Key, to write the verses of "The Star Spangled Banner."

Erie, Captain Oliver Hazard Perry smashed a British fleet in September 1813, restoring American control of this region.

Early in 1814 the British and their allies crushed Napoleon's armies and exiled him.[2] Britain was now free to devote more attention to the war with the United States. In August a British fleet, with troops aboard, sailed into Chesapeake Bay. Memories of the hard days of the Revolution must have been reawakened in every American old enough to recall the loss of Philadelphia, New York, and Charleston. On August 24, British troops landed, captured Washington, and burned the Capitol and the White House.

The British planned another major invasion through New Orleans. They knew—just as Burr and Wilkinson had—the strategic value of the city and its river to the United States. Their invading force was met by Americans under the command of an old friend of Burr's, General Andrew Jackson of Tennessee. In January of 1815, Jackson met the British in a battle that soon became legendary. His riflemen and artillery, firing from carefully placed positions, tore into a rigid British formation and killed or wounded over 2,000 of the enemy. Jackson's force suffered only a dozen casualties. At last, after three years of frustration, the United States had a genuine victory and a genuine military hero.

[2]Napoleon escaped from exile a year later, in March 1815. After collecting another army, he was decisively defeated near Brussels at the Battle of Waterloo, in June.

The Battle of New Orleans took place on the east bank of the Mississippi about five miles south of the city. In the main skirmish, January 8, three British generals were killed.

The only problem about the great victory at New Orleans was that the war was already over. For several months a group of American commissioners had been carrying on peace negotiations with the British at Ghent, Belgium. In December 1814, less than two weeks before the Battle of New Orleans, the two sides had agreed on a treaty and the war ended. The Treaty of Ghent provided only that the situation between Britain and America would remain just as it was in June of 1812. No concessions or promises were made, and no territory changed hands.

The War of 1812 made little sense at the time, and it settled no real problems. Three years after it began came Waterloo. From that time on Britain was not involved in a war with any Continental nation for a hundred years. If the Ameri-

cans could have held out for three more years, British harassment of their trade would probably have stopped, and the war could have been avoided.

But at least the war was over, and the United States had not lost. In fact, many Americans, encouraged by Jackson's victory, thought of the war as a successful defense of American independence and neutral rights. They called it a Second War for Independence.

TERRITORIAL EXPANSION

One of the most obvious facts of life for the generation of Americans who lived after the making of

THE TRANS-MISSISSIPPI WEST, 1807

———— Lewis and Clark 1804–1806
– – – – Pike 1806–1807
⚲ Spanish missions

0   100   200   300 MILES

the Constitution was growth. In 1790, at the time of the first census, there were fewer than 4 million Americans, and most of them lived on the eastern seaboard. Only about one person in every twenty-five lived over the mountains in Kentucky, Tennessee, and Ohio. But the spirit of expansion was everywhere. Every year thousands of families set out for the Ohio Valley to make new homes. This

growth and movement were very much on the minds of American political leaders. Washington felt that strenuous efforts would have to be made to tie eastern and western peoples together. Burr, on the other hand, believed that the federal government could not hold the loyalty of the western settlers.

By 1810 the population of the United States

had almost doubled, to over 7 million. And by 1820 it was almost 10 million. As it grew, the population shifted steadily westward. In 1820 one of every ten citizens of the United States lived west of the Appalachian Mountains.

Everyone who looked carefully at the United States in the 1790s knew that the future lay in the West. Franklin's calculations for the future always took for granted that the Ohio and Mississippi valleys held the key to the nation's destiny. Washington thought along similar lines, and so did Jefferson. When Hamilton's death had disgraced Burr, he simply followed an American reflex: when in trouble or in doubt, look to the West for new opportunities and answers.

The Louisiana Purchase   According to the peace treaty of 1783, the western boundary of the United States was to be the Mississippi River. This seemed to provide enough land to absorb the people and energies of the infant nation for decades to come. There was only one sore point. Spain still held most of the western half of the continent— and she controlled the Mississippi River and its outlet at New Orleans. The farmers west of the Appalachians depended almost entirely on the river as an outlet for their crops. (It was this traffic that Washington had wanted to divert to the East, through Virginia.)

It came as a bitter shock when the United States learned in 1801 that Spain had given Louisiana to France in a secret treaty. Now New Orleans and the vast Mississippi Valley would be in the hands not of weak Spain but of powerful and

Even before the purchase of Louisiana, Jefferson began planning for its exploration. To lead the first expedition, he chose his private secretary, Meriwether Lewis (shown at left in Indian garb). He and William Clark—the younger brother of George Rogers Clark—spent two years gathering facts on the geography and peoples of the region. Their notebooks included the drawing of a Flathead Indian woman, right above. Another explorer sent out by Jefferson was Zebulon Pike, above left. He discovered, but failed to climb, the mountain peak in Colorado that bears his name. When he was in Mexican territory, his papers were taken from him. They remained in the Mexican archives until discovered by an American scholar a hundred years later.

ambitious Napoleon. In 1802 the Spanish—still theoretically in control of New Orleans—caused another shock when they declared that Americans would no longer have the right to use New Orleans as a port.

Jefferson summed up the horror of most Americans when he said that there was "on the globe one single spot, the possessor of which is our natural and habitual enemy. It is New Orleans." As was his custom, Jefferson turned immediately to negotiation. He made Napoleon an offer to purchase New Orleans from France for $2 million. The American negotiator, James Monroe, was greatly surprised and pleased when the French offered to sell not just New Orleans but the entire territory of Louisiana—about 800,000 square miles of lush but practically uninhabited country—at least as whites defined "uninhabited."

In April 1803 the Americans closed the deal. They bought all of Louisiana for $15 million—a price that averaged out at about $2 per square mile for one of the richest unsettled areas in the world.

The purchase created some problems for Jefferson. He believed in what is called strict construction—a strict interpretation of the Constitution. Basic to his theory of government was the idea that the President and Congress could do only those things that the Constitution expressly gave them power to do. The Constitution nowhere gave the President the power to acquire new territory. In contrast to Jefferson's position was loose construction, favored by the Federalists. They felt that the government could do not only the things mentioned specifically by the Constitution but also other things that were merely implied. Thus, they would have argued, the power to make treaties implied the power to acquire territory, since acquisition was in the nature of a new treaty arrangement.[3] After some quarreling, mainly with himself, Jefferson gave up on what he called "metaphysical" questions. He asked Congress to

appropriate the $15 million. The United States took formal possession of New Orleans in December of 1803, just seven months before the duel between Hamilton and Burr.

SECTIONAL STRAINS IN A GROWING NATION

The Louisiana Purchase was approved in the Senate by a wide margin, twenty-four votes to seven. But the opposition was significant because it pointed toward a powerful and underlying problem in American life. Most of the opponents were from New England. People there realized that the westward movement would sooner or later result in a basic shift of people, economic power, and political control away from the East to the western territories and states. The Founding Fathers had worried about whether one government could control a nation as large as the United States. The years between 1790 and 1815 were full of tests of the American motto, *e pluribus unum*—"out of many, one."

One of the fundamental purposes of the authors of the Constitution had been to control local and sectional interests and prevent uprisings like Shays's Rebellion of 1786. Between 1789 and 1815, the nation passed through several similar tests, each of which seemed to challenge national authority over the states and sections on a very fundamental level.

The Whiskey Rebellion During Washington's first administration, farmers in western Pennsylvania provoked the first major challenge to federal power. These were farmers like those who had refused to move off Washington's land and like those whom Burr would later try to recruit to his cause.

One part of Hamilton's financial program had been a tax on distilled liquor, which meant mainly whiskey. At this time the cheapest and most economical way for most western farmers to transport their grain crops to the East was to turn

---

[3]This difference of interpretation first came up when President Washington was deciding whether to sign Hamilton's bank bill in 1791. Jefferson, a strict constructionist, argued against it; Hamilton's loose constructionist views carried the day.

the grain into whiskey. So the Congress was taxing not a luxury but a basic economic product.

Many farmers resisted the tax. In the summer of 1794 they even mobbed tax collectors, much as Americans had attacked Stamp Act tax collectors a generation before. The rebellion was small, much smaller than Shays's uprising had been eight years earlier. But President Washington reacted with a series of steps that went well beyond what was needed. He called out 15,000 militiamen and marched them west toward Pittsburgh with himself at their head. This excessive display of federal military power worked immediately, of course. The rebels were totally intimidated. In his zeal Washington revealed the depth of his old concern about maintaining law and order in the West.

After the rebellion had been suppressed, Washington delivered an address to Congress in which he condemned not only the rebels but national political clubs called Democratic Societies. The societies had been formed in enthusiastic support of the French Revolution. Most of them were the local bases of Republican political strength. But to Washington's mind the sectional question of East versus West was closely tied to the question of Republican opposition. Anything that threatened national unity, whether it was a sectional uprising or an opposition political group, was an evil to be dealt with quickly.

The Hartford Convention During the administration of John Adams, sectional stress focused heavily on the Alien and Sedition Acts. Organized opposition came primarily from Virginia and Kentucky, in the resolutions written by Madison and Jefferson. It looked for a time as though the Republican party might become a sectional party, with strength only in the South and the West, while Federalists held complete power in the North and the East. Through the efforts of men like Burr, this split was avoided, and the Republicans built strong organizations in New York and Pennsylvania. New England continued to be the only true Federalist stronghold. It was from New England that the main opposition to the Louisiana Purchase was voiced in 1803. Whenever there was a possibility of war with Britain or France, the Republicans leaned toward war with Britain, while the Federalists leaned toward war with France.

Before the War of 1812, the New England states, which were tied closely to Britain by trade, had bitterly opposed Jefferson's embargo. New England opposed the war even more. In Congress the strongest voices for war had been those of the so-called War Hawks—congressmen from the frontier regions who wanted to invade and annex Canada, adding even more land to the western domain at the expense of the East. Politicians and businessmen all over New England felt that the government had betrayed them and was willing to sacrifice their interests to the war fever of the rest of the country.

In opposition to the war, New England resisted militia calls and wartime taxes and continued to trade with the enemy in Canada. In 1814 the New England governors called a convention in Hartford, Connecticut, to raise the same kinds of questions that the Annapolis Convention had raised about the Articles of Confederation. In calling the convention, the governors asserted that the Constitution had failed, that the New England states were not receiving "equal rights and benefits," and that the frame of government would have to be seriously revised. A few members of the convention demanded immediate secession from the Union. The convention drafted a series of proposed amendments to the Constitution—all of which would have weakened the federal government—and sent them to Washington to the next Congress.

Time, however, cured problems that might not have been solved otherwise. When the Hartford Convention proposal reached Washington, news of Jackson's victory had just arrived, and the news of the peace treaty was not far behind. As was to happen so often in American history, sectional crisis had been resolved by events and not by statesmanship. Despite its lack of positive results, the Hartford Convention had raised what was to become the basic political question for the next generation: Would the United States be able to resolve sectional differences, or would some crisis sooner or later divide one part of the country from the other?

SUGGESTED READINGS—CHAPTERS 11-12

Aaron Burr, Conspirator

T. P. Abernethy, *The Burr Conspiracy* (1954); Nathan Schachner, *Aaron Burr* (1937); J. R. Jacobs, *Tarnished Warrior* (1938); M. R. Werner, *The Admirable Trumpeter* (1941); V. B. Reed and J. D. Williams, eds., *The Case of Aaron Burr* (1960).

Jefferson and Colleagues

Henry Adams, *A History of the United States During the Administrations of Jefferson and Madison* (9 vols., 1889–1891); Marcus Cunliffe, *The Nation Takes Shape, 1789–1837* (1959).

A Systematic Introduction to the 1790s

J. C. Miller, *The Federalist Era, 1789–1801* (1960); William Nisbet Chamers, *Political Parties in a New Nation: The American Experience, 1776–1809* (1963); Joseph Charles, *The Origins of the American Party System* (1956); Noble Cunningham, *The Jeffersonian Republicans* (1957); Richard Hofstadter, *The Idea of a Party System* (1973).

Civil Liberties

Irving Brant, *The Bill of Rights* (1965); L. W. Levy, *Legacy of Suppression: Freedom of Speech and Press in Early American History* (1960).

From Independence to the War of 1812

S. F. Bemis, *Jay's Treaty* (1923); Felix Gilbert, *To the Farewell Address* (1961); J. W. Pratt, *The Expansionists of 1812* (1925); L. S. Kaplan, *Jefferson and France* (1967); Reginald Horsman, *The Causes of the War of 1812* (1962).

13
ANDREW JACKSON: THE ROAD TO THE WHITE HOUSE

A. W.

The Seminole Indian chiefs stood on the shore and watched the soldiers hang the old man. Almost alone among white men, Alexander Arbuthnot had cared about them and had tried to help them. For his pains, the Scottish trader's body now dangled limply from the yardarm of his own schooner, under the hot Florida sun in the spring of 1818.

Arbuthnot had been caught up in a war between the United States and the Seminoles, an offshoot of the Creek Indian confederacy who lived mostly in Spanish Florida and occasionally crossed the border to raid American settlements in Georgia and Alabama. The U.S. government, eager to stop the raids and anxious to acquire Florida, sent Major General Andrew Jackson and several thousand men into Spanish Florida. Jackson's forces found few Indians willing to fight, but after several skirmishes he did capture two Seminole leaders, whom he promptly hanged in April 1818. He also ran across two Britons. "My love," the general wrote to his wife Rachel, "I entered the Town of St. marks on yesterday. I found in St. Marks the noted Scotch villain Arbuthnot . . . I hold him for trial." Further to the east, American forces encountered Lieutenant Robert C. Armbrister, formerly of His Britannic Majesty's Royal Marines. Both Britons were jailed as allies of the Seminoles.

The War of 1812 had ended only three years earlier, and Americans still imagined that the British were a malignant force causing the Creeks and Seminoles to raid into the United States. Jackson, acting as commanding general, ordered a court martial for Arbuthnot and Armbrister. His legal basis for trying two British subjects on Spanish soil in an

American military court was shaky at best. But when Andrew Jackson felt he was right, technicalities rarely impressed or stopped him.

The case against Arbuthnot, a tall, white-haired, carefully dressed man in his seventies, consisted of one letter, a bill of sale, and two witnesses. Arbuthnot had written the letter to his friend, the Seminole leader Bolecks ("Bowlegs" the American dubbed him), warning him to avoid battle with Jackson's powerful army. Jackson insisted, however, that the letter contained military information and provided advice to the Indian enemy. The bill of sale listed ten kegs of powder Arbuthnot had sold to the Indians. The witnesses, both personal enemies of the Scotsman, testified to having seen a letter he had written to the Seminoles urging them to attack the Americans. The letter itself was not produced.

Arbuthnot defended himself in a simple but eloquent speech to the court. He denied advising the Seminoles to go to war, since he wished to avoid bloodshed. The sale of a few powder barrels to be used in hunting was, he pointed out, a normal part of a trader's business. How long, after-all, would ten kegs have lasted in a war? Arbuthnot pointed to the flimsy nature of the documentary evidence and the hearsay nature of the oral testimony. He swore that he was no agent of the British government.

The case against Armbrister *appeared* to be more serious, though it showed him as pathetic rather than malevolent. The young Royal Marine had been removed from his regiment for dueling with another British officer and had gone to stay with his uncle, the British governor of the Bahama Islands. Armbrister came to Florida on a holiday. To impress the Indians, he said that he was a British agent and that his uncle would be sending them arms and other supplies to use against the Americans. Armbrister was all talk—but the talk was to cost him his life. The very manner of his capture revealed how unthreatening he was. Wandering through the night with an attendant and two slaves, he simply stumbled across the American army!

Armbrister confidently threw himself on the mercy of the court. "I should have no fears, as I am in the hands of Christians," he told his captors. "I know they will not murder me." The tribunal, headed by Jackson's second-in-command, Major General Edmund Gaines, consisted of fourteen American officers. They decided the case rapidly. Alexander Arbuthnot would be hanged as a spy; Lieutenant Robert Armbrister would be shot as a spy. But the court then reconsidered and commuted the young, bumbling Armbrister's sentence to fifty lashes and a year at hard labor.

A courier brought news of the sentences to Jackson for approval. The general, who was with his troops in the field, quickly signed Arbuthnot's death warrant—but he rejected the court's clemency for Armbrister. Instead, he scribbled out an order restoring the original sentence. The ex-Marine would be shot.

Jackson, as major general of the United States Army of the South, had bigger things to do than watch the execution of two spies. He marched his army off toward Pensacola, the capital of Spanish Florida. Jackson's aim was to seize the principal Spanish forts and to ship the colonial governor off to Havana, Cuba. He believed (and so, he thought, did President Monroe) that the Seminole threat could never be ended while Spain kept Florida.

Armbrister still could not believe that he was to die. Frantically, he demanded to know whether Jackson had left a pardon before marching away. He had not. Still, it took the dread music of fife and drum summoning the firing squad to convince the ebullient Armbrister of his doom. "I have heard that sound in every corner of the globe," he reflected quietly, "and now I hear it for the last time." The shots rang out a few minutes later, Armbrister collapsed in the dirt, and several soldiers rowed Arbuthnot out to his ship. As the rope went around his neck, the Scotsman swore that Great Britain would avenge his death. The Americans let his body hang for about twenty minutes before cutting it down.

Arbuthnot's threat almost came true. London exploded with anger at the news of the executions. In the streets and in newspaper columns, Jackson and other Americans were damned as murderers. War would have been declared, admitted the foreign secretary, "if the Ministry had but held up a finger." But the British then had more than enough problems in Europe to keep them occupied, and a third war with America was out of the question.

Jackson had more to fear from his own government. When word of the executions, and of his occupation of Spanish Florida, reached Washington, President Monroe and all but one cabinet member favored relieving Jackson of his command immediately. Fortunately for the general, the lone dissenter, Secretary of State John Quincy Adams, persuaded the others not to admit American fault. Adams, a leading authority on international law (among other things), promised his colleagues that he could justify Jackson's activities and defend the United States position.

"It is an established principle of the laws of nations," Jackson had argued in ordering the executions, "that any individual of a nation making war against the citizens of another nation, they being at peace, forfeits his allegiance, and becomes an outlaw and a pirate." Unfortunately, nobody but Jackson had heard of any such "principle." So Adams's defense had to be a masterpiece of legal distortions and diversions. Rather than defend the lawfulness of Jackson's actions themselves, Adams (like Jackson) went on the attack. He denounced Arbuthnot as a "pretended trader" and argued that anyone who aided "savages" to fight civilized nations could not claim protection under the rules of war. Furthermore, while agreeing in principle that all occupied territory in Florida should be returned to Spain (Adams was then negotiating for American purchase of the territory), the secretary refused to admit that Jackson had been wrong to seize the Spanish forts.

After defeating the Seminoles and the Spaniards in Forida, Jackson had returned to the Hermitage, his plantation manor house outside Nashville, Tennessee. There he learned that opponents of the Monroe Administration, led by the ambitious Speaker of the House of Representatives, Kentucky's Henry Clay, planned a thorough investigation. Jackson decided to make the long ride to Washington to defend his actions.

He had no intention of answering to Congress for his behavior or of letting rival politicians in the capital bandy his name about. If Congress insisted on stirring up the issue, Jackson would make them answer directly to him. This was hardly an idle boast, considering his character, his ambitions, and — especially — his past.

In 1788, Andrew Jackson had crossed the Appalachian Mountains into Tennessee (then part of North Carolina) with a horse, a slave girl he had bought for $200, and a commission as traveling prosecutor. The twenty-one-year-old lawyer was accompanying a friend to a new town called Nashville. The friend had been lucky enough to obtain appointment as a judge in the new community, and Jackson tagged along, hoping to secure a good position there also.

His legal training and knowledge were decidedly limited. Jackson had experienced one personal tragedy after another from his earliest days (his father had died shortly before his birth in 1767; his two brothers and his mother had all died of war wounds or epidemic diseases during the Revolution), and he had attended school only irregularly. To the end of his long life — he died in 1845 — Jackson might spell a word two or three different ways in the same document or letter. The best that any well-disposed friend could claim for him was that at least he spelled better than either Washington or Napoleon. Jackson had gathered his scant store of legal knowledge by reading law in an attorney's office in western North Carolina for two years. But a good deal of that time had been spent not at study but in taverns and at racetracks; and very early in his young manhood, Jackson had fought the first of his several duels.

Still, to impose the law upon a frontier territory such as Tennessee, determination and physical courage were often more important than legal acumen. Jackson and his fellow lawyers traveled the state with knife and rifle close at hand. And if, at times, he had to *catch* a suspected criminal before he could prosecute, Jackson could handle that as well.

His tall, lanky figure, topped with a shock of red hair and blazing blue eyes, became well known throughout the new state. Men feared his temper but, at the same time, respected his courage and honesty. When Tennessee entered the Union in 1796, Jackson, then a twenty-nine-year-old prosecutor (and protégé of the state's first governor, William Blount), served as delegate to the convention that wrote the Tennessee constitution. He soon became the state's first member of the House of Representatives, a passionate supporter of Jefferson's Democratic-Republican party.

Philadelphia, then the nation's capital, failed to charm the new congressman, and, in turn, even a leader of his own party found him an "uncouth-looking personage, with manners of a rough backwoodsman." An extreme anti-Federalist, Jackson opposed a resolution praising the previous Administration and wishing ex-President Washington a pleasant retirement. Jackson also refused to wear a powdered wig, then the fashion, and instead wrapped his long hair in an eel skin. Nor did he care much for all the talk and paperwork of Congress. He soon resigned his House seat, but political duty then dictated that he accept a promotion to the United States Senate. Blount, his benefactor, had been expelled from that body in 1797, so Jackson went back to serve during one Senate session. Again, he resigned as soon as Congress adjourned.

By that time Jackson's personal affairs, both financial and domestic, required his full attention. Although he had rapidly grown wealthy in land speculation, a panic in 1795 had wiped away most of his gains and left Jackson with an abiding suspicion of banks and paper money. It would take him nearly nineteen years to climb out of debt.

Jackson had also acquired a wife, in 1791. Rachel Donelson Robards, recalled one contemporary, was "irresistible to men." They admired her figure and her dark eyes, and even forgave her addiction to smoking a corncob pipe. At first meeting, Jackson found her enchanting. He also found her married, although she and her husband, Lewis Robards, already lived apart. Jackson clearly played an important role in making the couple's separation permanent. On hearing that Rachel's husband was approaching Nashville in an unpleasant frame of mind, Jackson escorted Rachel out of danger and down to the Mississippi River port town of Natchez. Frontier social mores were reasonably permissive for their day, but Jackson's 300-mile, unchaperoned trip with another man's wife raised eyebrows and caused gossip. Upon reaching Natchez, the couple heard that Robards had obtained a divorce. Andrew and Rachel were promptly and happily married.

Too promptly, as it turned out. For Rachel's first husband had not yet obtained a final divorce decree; he had only started proceedings for one. For two years before the true situation was uncovered, the Jacksons unwittingly lived in adultery and bigamy. When they discovered the confusion, and after Rachel's divorce from Robards had finally taken effect, Andrew and Rachel went through another marriage ceremony. But even this did not prevent the tangled episode from plaguing the Jacksons for the rest of their lives.

Tennesseans, however, rarely discussed Jackson's marital affairs in public, since the duel still settled many personal disputes in that day. Even the most amusing bit of gossip at Andrew Jackson's expense seemed too costly if it meant a challenge from the hot-tempered Jackson to meet over pistols. Nashville's lack of interest was even more pronounced after Charles Dickinson's experience in 1806.

Jackson's quarrel with Dickinson began over a horse race. But it assumed an uglier dimension when the latter made disparaging allusions to Rachel Jackson. Jackson's second son called on Dickinson and arranged a meeting over pistols at dawn across the border in Kentucky. According to the rules of the dueling code, combatants faced each other twenty-four paces apart and fired once upon command. The seconds then reloaded pistols for another exchange—if necessary.

Charles Dickinson was an accomplished marksman; his seconds rarely had to reload. Dickinson had a reputation as a sure shot and boasted that he would kill Jackson with his first bullet. Jackson, not a quick shooter, decided to let Dickinson fire first. Even if hit, he reasoned, his

Rachel Donelson Robards Jackson, born in Virginia in 1767, migrated with her family to a frontier Kentucky farm and later to Tennessee. After her turbulent early marriage to Lewis Robards, and her two weddings to Andrew Jackson (both before and after her divorce), she managed the Hermitage, from which Jackson was frequently absent, and raised a dozen foster children, mainly the sons of relatives.

willpower would sustain him until he had killed the man who had maligned his wife.

The opponents stood and awaited the signal. On the cry of "Fire!" Dickinson's arm flashed out and a gunshot pierced the early morning silence. But Jackson did not fall. He did not even move. His second saw only a puff of dust arise from his jacket.

"Oh God!" cried the horrified Dickinson, stumbling backward. "Can I have missed him?" For answer, he heard only Jackson's second say sharply, "Back to the mark, sir!" Dickinson returned to his position. Jackson carefully sighted along the barrel of his gun and shot his enemy down. The bullet split an artery and Dickinson died that evening.

Only after Dickinson had been carried off to bleed to death did a servant boy notice that Jackson's right boot was full of blood. The victor now opened his coat, and his second saw for the first time where Dickinson's bullet had lodged. It had missed Jackson's heart by inches, breaking two ribs. But Jackson had refused to give his opponent the satisfaction of knowing that he had been hit. "I would have killed him," Jackson swore later, "even if he had shot me through the brain."

Charles Dickinson had many friends and influential allies, so Jackson's revenge proved costly at first to his political ambitions. For the next six years he lived quietly on his cotton plantation. When Congress declared war on Britain in 1812, however, Jackson soon regained his old rank (acquired years earlier) as major general of the Tennessee militia. Although as untrained in war as he had been when starting out as a lawyer, Jackson led three expeditions during the war.

The first campaign, though aborted, helped build his public reputation. Residents of Tennessee and Georgia liked the idea of acquiring Florida from Spain—by force if necessary—and Jackson shared their goal. He assured the secretary of war that his men, unlike certain militia units from Northern states who had refused to cross into Canada, had "no constitutional scruples, and, if the Government orders, will rejoice at the opportunity of placing the American eagle on the ramparts" of Spain's Florida forts.

Thus, by early 1813, Jackson had marched with several thousand volunteer soldiers to Natchez and stood poised to invade eastern Florida. President Madison and Congress decided otherwise. The military authorities in Washington ordered Jackson to dismiss his troops and thank them but said nothing about pay, provisions, or transport for their return home. Jackson was furious and reassured his men that, if necessary, he would march them back "on my own means and responsibility." Although the general's worth as a military strategist was still untested, the combination of devotion to his men with stern enforcement of discipline among them had earned Jackson the affectionate yet appropriate nickname "Old Hickory" (a wood noted for its toughness).

In his second campaign, the quarrelsome major general fought Indians and not American bureaucrats, building a personal legend. Jackson was recovering from wounds received in a brawl with Thomas Hart

Benton (later a senator from Missouri) and his brother Jesse. One of the Bentons had put a bullet in Jackson's shoulder, where it remained when Jackson set out in 1813 to fight the Creeks, the only major group of Southern Indians actively hostile to the United States during the War of 1812. On the way into Creek territory (in what is Alabama today) Jackson had to threaten personally to shoot those militiamen whose one-year enlistment period had expired and who wished to return to Tennessee. In March 1814 his troops won a decisive victory over the Creeks at Horseshoe Bend on the Tallapoosa River. More than ten times as many Indians as whites died in the battle, and the surviving Creeks fled into Spanish territory.

Jackson's third campaign of the war, against the British at New Orleans, assured him lasting fame. When Andrew Jackson arrived in New Orleans in December 1814 with only two thousand troops, chances for additional victories appeared remote. Despite his victory over the Creeks and his commission as a major general in the regular army, many felt that he did not fit the part of a great general. Certainly he did not look it. An aristocratic Creole lady caught one glimpse of Jackson and winced; he resembled a "Kaintuck flatboatman." Worried residents of New Orleans had further cause for complaint: Jackson had divided his forces. The latest messages from Washington had warned the general of a possible British attack at either Mobile or New Orleans. Jackson accepted that estimate until very late in 1814 and, therefore, divided his men between a force at Mobile, and one upriver at Baton Rouge, where they could move toward New Orleans *or* Mobile, depending upon where the British attacked.

Meanwhile, a thousand miles to the southeast, the British had assembled their assault fleet off the West Indian island of Jamaica. Ten thousand sailors manned the ships that would carry almost eleven thousand fighting men, veteran soldiers and marines, many of whom had taken part either in the Napoleonic Wars or in the capture and burning of Washington that spring. Jackson's uncertainty over the scene of battle was realistic, since the British did not decide on New Orleans until late November, a decision made by the admiral of the fleet, not the commanding general, who had not yet arrived. (In matters of mismanagement, disorganization, and upset timetables, the professional British military proved every bit as adept as the amateur Americans.)

The enemy's army commander, Major General Sir Edward Pakenham, had served ably against the French forces in Spain. When he caught up with his armada, he agreed that New Orleans, near the mouth of the Mississippi, represented a far more valuable prize than Mobile. The British also hoped that the French residents of Louisiana, who had been Americans for only a dozen years—that is, since the Louisiana Purchase—would refuse to fight for the Stars and Stripes (the same mistake made by Americans invading Canada in 1812, who had convinced themselves that French Canadians would turn on the British and help the invaders). Pakenham carried with him a royal commission as governor of Louisiana. Once he had pushed out the Americans, he would rule, in

Andrew Jackson's victory over the Creeks at Horseshoe Bend, when he was 46, not only established his national reputation as an Indian fighter, but resulted in his promotion from a Tennessee militia General to commander of the southern division of the regular army. In this climactic battle of the long Creek War, 800 out of 1000 Creek warriors were killed, the greatest number in any Indian battle, although there were few casualties among Jackson's troops and Indian allies. A year before, after the first battle of the war, Jackson adopted a three-year-old Indian boy, Lincoyer, whose parents had been killed, and who remained in the Jackson household until his death at 16.

trust for Spain, all the territory "fraudulently conveyd by [Napoleon] Bonaparte to the United States."

The British hoped to improve their chances still more by enlisting the help of the pirates of Barataria Bay for the invasion. From this inlet one hundred miles south of New Orleans, Jean Lafitte, himself a land-loving businessman (although many called him a "pirate"), directed a very profitable operation against all sorts of shipping. Louisiana's Creole leaders regarded the Baratarians tolerantly, and Lafitte was willing to dicker with all sides. Britain offered him cash (something he always needed), plus amnesty and a Royal Navy commission (neither of which he needed), if he would fight against the Americans.

To make the most of a tangled situation, Lafitte now wrote to the governor of Louisiana. The governor had recently put a $500 price on Lafitte's head—the pirate had responded by offering a $30,000 reward for the governor's. But such acrimony was now behind him. Calling himself "a lost sheep who desires to return to the fold," Lafitte promised, if not to reform, at least to fight the British. When Jackson heard this, he ignored his previous description of the Baratarians as "hellish banditti" in the pay of the British and graciously accepted the pirates as allies. Soon afterward, Lafitte's brother managed somehow to escape from jail.

The general's quick and positive response to Lafitte showed his awareness of his side's weakness. Even with his Tennesseans, the Baratarians, Creole businessmen of the city militia, the Kentucky sharpshooters, and a group of friendly Choctaw Indians, Jackson needed more troops. He agreed to use two batallions of New Orleans free blacks, already organized, as well as a third batallion which was quickly shaped up, to form a regiment. Jackson appointed white officers for the unit, but let the soldiers select their own noncommissioned officers. To an army paymaster reluctant to disburse wages to the new regiment, Jackson sent a curt note: "Be pleased to keep to yourself your opinions upon the policy of making payments to particular corps."

Earlier, Jackson had been undecided about which city the British would attack. Now he faltered briefly in guarding against their invasion route. Although all approaches to New Orleans had been ordered blocked, the Tennessean had not ensured that the job was actually done. Nor had he acquired sufficient supplies for his troops. Two days before Christmas, he first learned that the enemy was encamped nine miles from the city. They had moved two thousand men up through an unguarded bayou. A prudent (and less effective) general might have immediately concentrated on his fortifications. "Gentlemen, the British are below," Jackson announced to his officers. "We will fight them tonight." The ensuing battle, a night attack by the Americans, was a standoff, with about equal casualties on both sides—but it saved New Orleans. Reasoning that Jackson must command overpowering force (fifteen thousand men at least) to come out and attack in that risky fashion, the British commander decided to advance no further. That gave Jackson two vital weeks to organize his forces.

Preparations for battle continued on both sides over the Christmas holidays. Pakenham brought seventeen heavy cannon from his ships. But he never established superiority in artillery, a mistake that would cost him dearly. On January 4, 1815, a large Kentucky militia contingent marched into the American camp, but few of the men even had rifles. "I don't believe it," Jackson supposedly complained. "I have never seen a Kentuckian without a gun and a pack of cards and a bottle of whiskey in my life." As Jackson rode off to the front line, a New Orleans resident asked him if the women should leave the city. "Say to the ladies not to be uneasy," answered the general. "No British soldier shall enter this city unless over my dead body." The remark seemed, at that moment, as much a prediction of things to come as a promise of safety.

At six o'clock on the morning of January 8, the Americans saw two red rockets streak up from the British lines. This, they knew, signaled an attack. The band of Battalion d'Orleans struck up "Yankee Doodle," as the Americans waited. Except for the artillery, Jackson's troops would hold their fire until the British came within 200 yards. In the heavy fog and early-morning semidarkness, the defenders, four deep behind their mud and timber wall, could hear the bagpipes of the Ninety-third Highlanders before they could see anything. When the breeze cleared patches in the fog, they began to distinguish the many lines of British troops still off in the distance but approaching at a measured pace. The red-coated British infantry had pushed the French out of North America, twice driven back American invasions of Canada, and just defeated Napoleon. Awaiting the nine thousand advancing Britishers were half as many backwoods farmers, New Orleans businessmen, newly organized free blacks, pirates, Indians, and a very few American army regulars.

Only when Jackson was sure that the redcoats were within range of his men's muskets did he give the command to fire. The American artillery, already very effective, had stopped to let some of the smoke clear from the field. Hundreds of rifles barked out as one, and as the front rank dropped behind to reload, the second came forward to fire. By ranging his troops in four lines, Jackson could maintain a constant wall of flame in the face of the invaders. The Baratarians, the only nonregulars on the American side who could handle cannon, helped blow great holes in the enemy lines.

Soon the advancing British had to step over the bodies of dead and wounded comrades. Their red lines first buckled and then broke under a "leaden torrent no man on earth could face," in the words of one British officer who watched the carnage. There was no lack of valor on the attackers' part, officers or enlisted men. But Jackson held a superb defensive position, with the river on one flank and a swamp on the other. When a British flanking maneuver on the Mississippi's west bank produced no real results, the frontal attack then under way became suicidal. Pakenham, trying desperately to rally his men, caught two bullets and died on the field, as did the handful of attackers who reached the American parapet. As the troops retreated, some in panic, others more slowly, the commander of the British reserve units saw no point in continuing the slaughter, and he ordered the attack ended.

It all took less than half an hour. Two thousand British soldiers lay on the battlefield, dead or dying. The defending Americans had seven killed and six wounded. Four of the casualties were black soldiers, so eager for battle that they had left their lines to chase the retreating British. Shattered in spirit, the British invaders sailed away eleven days later, after burying their dead. They had time to dig only shallow graves, and that summer the stench of death hovered over New Orleans. The body of Pakenham, who had expected to become His Britannic Majesty's Royal Governor of Louisiana, was returned to London preserved in a barrel of rum.

In mid-February, Jackson, still governing New Orleans under martial law, finally received news from Washington. The British and American governments had signed a peace treaty at Ghent, Belgium, on December 24. The Battle of New Orleans, in short, had been fought fifteen days after the war's end.

But the two-month lag in communications was to prove of enormous benefit to the United States. By January 1815, the Americans were still mired in the war's bad news. The British burning of Washington only confirmed their military dominance in the conflict. True, a few naval victories had interrupted the parade of American defeats, but New England was demanding an end to the war at almost any cost, and talk of secession ran through Massachusetts and Connecticut. When Northerners heard nothing from New Orleans, newspapers accused President Madison of concealing the city's loss. "If an attack has been made on Orleans," despondently reasoned the New York *Post*, "the city has fallen."

Word of Jackson's victory burst upon this gloomy atmosphere, and the country went wild. "GLORIOUS!!! UNPARALLELLED VICTO-

Andrew Jackson's "almost incredible victory" at the Battle of New Orleans in January, 1815, was one of the rare American triumphs in an otherwise bleak war record. Jackson's assortment of nonregulars fired at close range upon successive waves of the attacking British troops, who became sitting ducks for the American artillery. After a short time, many lay strewn across the battle field of the British along with their commander, Sir Edward Pakenham. Ignoring strategic reasons for the defeat of the more numerous British veterans, grateful Americans credited Jackson's energy, courage, and power, as well as providential intervention.

RY!" screamed the headlines. Jackson immediately became the nation's hero and made a triumphant return from New Orleans to Nashville. Every state legislature passed a resolution of gratitude. New York's tribute, written by a young state senator named Martin Van Buren, called Jackson's triumph "an event surpassing the most heroic and wonderful achievements which adorn the annals of mankind."

The Battle of New Orleans, by removing the sting from a stalemated, often humiliating war, caught the popular imagination. Volunteers, mainly farmer-soldiers, had routed England's professional troops, a fact that seemed to confirm everything Americans liked to believe about republics and democracy. (The country quickly forgot the many times during the War of 1812 when royal forces had smashed republican militiamen.) In the popular mind, Jackson's victory had proved American freemen invincible and, therefore, had demonstrated our national supe-

JACKSON'S MILITARY CAMPAIGNS

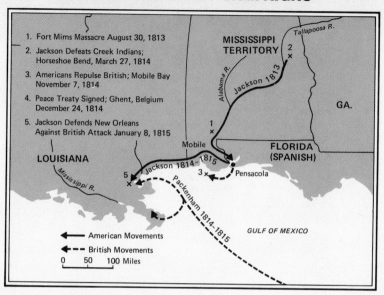

1. Fort Mims Massacre August 30, 1813
2. Jackson Defeats Creek Indians; Horseshoe Bend, March 27, 1814
3. Americans Repulse British; Mobile Bay November 7, 1814
4. Peace Treaty Signed; Ghent, Belgium December 24, 1814
5. Jackson Defends New Orleans Against British Attack January 8, 1815

MISSISSIPPI TERRITORY

Tallapoosa R.

Alabama R.

Jackson 1813

GA.

LOUISIANA

Mississippi R.

Mobile

FLORIDA (SPANISH)

Jackson 1814–1815

Pensacola

Packenham 1814–1815

GULF OF MEXICO

← American Movements
◄-- British Movements

0   50   100 Miles

riòrity. "The Hunters of Kentucky," a minstrel show ballad about the battle, swept the country, becoming perhaps the nation's first number one hit song.

That a nonprofessional soldier had led the army helped swell the legend considerably. All Americans soon knew the story of Andrew Jackson, a poor orphan who had achieved wealth and influence through his own efforts. It helped considerably that Jackson was a product of the frontier, where American society seemed to be functioning in its most classless and democratic form. That Jackson had come to own a large plantation with many slaves indicated to his many enthusiasts only the extent of opportunity in America.

Jackson's friends in Tennessee watched with great interest the national wave of adulation. The country had once made a military hero President; might it not be persuaded to do so again? Their thoughts ran not to 1816, when Secretary of State James Monroe would probably run for the White House, but to 1824, by which time Monroe would have completed two terms and Jackson would still be only fifty-seven. In 1815, Jackson responded publicly to the proposal with appropriate modesty: "No sir, I know what I am fit for. I can command a body of men in a rough way, but I am not fit to be President." But while Jackson, with decreasing sincerity, told this to visitors, two of his close friends published a popular biography of the hero. The Jackson legend grew still further with his conquest of Spanish Florida three years later.

Thus, the angry Jackson who approached Washington in 1819 to face official censure for his high-handed conduct in Florida bore the strengths of a popular idol and the potential of a long-shot presidential candidate. The capital was full of other hopefuls who wanted to see Jackson eliminated. Two of them, Secretary of the Treasury William Crawford and Secretary of War John C. Calhoun, had just voted in the cabinet to recall Jackson in disgrace from Florida. A third, Speaker of the House Henry Clay, would now have his turn.

The House Military Committee, which Clay controlled, had voted without dissent to recommend censure of Jackson, both for hanging Arbuthnot and shooting Armbrister and for seizing Spanish Florida. The House had then begun a twenty-seven day debate of the censure move. During its deliberations, Jackson arrived in Washington.

The general refused to appear in public at first, remaining in his hotel until the House had voted. Jackson boiled with rage at his accusers, feeling that he had not only done nothing wrong but had carried out the accepted policy of the Monroe Administration. Secretary of State Adams tried to calm Jackson, assuring the general that his conduct could be justified by the great theoreticians of international law, Grotius, Vattel, and Puffendorf. "Damn Grotius! Damn Vattel! Damn Puffendorf!" exploded Jackson. "This is a matter between Jim Monroe and myself."

Clay led off the House debate with a long warning of the danger military heroes posed to democracies. He later denied implying that he meant to indict Jackson as a threat to the government, but if Clay's speech did not mean that, it meant nothing. Jackson believed deeply in the Constitution and in democratic civil government. No accusation could have infuriated him more, and from that day Jackson, a relentless hater, hated Henry Clay.

But Jackson also had brilliant defenders in the House, led by the Tennessee delegation. The representatives of the Southwest believed, as Jackson did, that only firm action could deal with the Indian menace to settlements on the frontier. On the final vote, the House not only refused, by a vote of 90 to 54, to condemn Jackson for the executions, but, by a 91-to-65 tally, it endorsed his seizure of Florida.

Vindicated, the hero of New Orleans now emerged from his hotel in triumph and journeyed to celebrations in his honor held at Philadelphia and New York. On these occasions, only once did anyone have the temerity to raise the subject of Arbuthnot and Armbrister. "They were spies," answered Jackson coldly. "They ought to have been executed. And I tell you, sir, that I would do the same thing again."

Jackson returned to Washington to find that the Senate had launched its own investigation of his conduct in Florida. But, for whatever reason, the Senate soon lost interest, and when the United States finally bought Florida from Spain two years later, Monroe sent Jackson there as territorial governor. Jackson accepted the job for a short time — as a symbol of vindication rather than for any real interest in the post. He returned to Tennessee within a year.

A very different Andrew Jackson appeared in Washington in December 1823 as United States senator and candidate for President. Since spring, he and his friends had been writing amiable, fence-mending letters to political figures in all parts of the country, and Jackson now even spoke and wrote an occasional kind word or two about his old enemies.

"General Jackson's manners," admitted an opponent, "are now more presidential than those of any of the candidates." But such niceties were soon forgotten when Jackson suddenly indulged himself in one of those outbursts of temper for which he was famous. The cause this time was political.

Four rivals for the White House, all more experienced in politics than he, faced the new senator, however. William Crawford claimed the support of the old Republicans, including Jefferson himself. John Quincy Adams, son of the only Northern President, counted on the united vote of New England. John C. Calhoun, younger than the rest, would become a major candidate if, as he expected, Pennsylvania lined up with the South on his behalf. Clay of Kentucky represented the young West and a program of high tariffs and government aid to economic development. None of the four professional politicians considered Jackson, although a national hero, to be a major threat. Adams indirectly offered him the vice-presidency, which, Adams suggested, "would offer an easy and dignified retirement to his old age." (The considerate Adams was exactly 118 days younger than Jackson.)

Two events swiftly altered the situation. Crawford, considered to be the front-runner, suffered a stroke. Although his supporters gamely predicted recovery, they found it difficult to press the claims of a man who could neither move nor speak. Then, several months later, a Calhoun meeting in Pennsylvania overruled its chairman and endorsed Jackson. The secretary of war now shelved his dreams of the presidency and announced himself as a vice-presidential candidate under Jackson.

Thus, the hero of New Orleans, without having taken a public stand on any major issue, now became almost overnight the leading candidate for the White House. Professional politicians could not understand the man's popular appeal. But many ordinary Americans saw Jackson as a simple and able person who had already served his country well and now asked only for the chance to serve again—a man of action, not words, who scorned the tangled political world of party machines, caucuses, and Eastern business interests. When skeptics asked where Jackson stood on the issues of the day, his followers replied with rapturous descriptions of the Battle of New Orleans.

In 1824, the states of the Union chose presidential electors on different days and by various methods. But long before the last returns reached Washington from Louisiana (by this time a state), it became clear that no candidate had won a majority. Adams's strength was concentrated in the Northeast; Crawford's in three Southern states; and Clay's in the West. Only Jackson could point to national support, having won eleven states from New Jersey to Illinois and southward to Calhoun's South Carolina. But even with his ninety-nine electoral votes, Jackson had still finished thirty-two short of victory. The House of Representatives would choose the new President.

This should have worked to the advantage of Clay, Speaker and virtual boss of the House. But the Constitution states that the House can choose only among the top three contenders, and Clay had finished fourth, a few votes behind Crawford. The other candidates quickly recognized that Clay, although he could not himself attain the presidency, would probably determine who among them would gain the office. Emissaries of Adams, Jackson, and Crawford soon besieged the Speaker. Clay enjoyed the attention, but he had vowed that, having missed the presidency this time, he would negotiate primarily with a view to improving his chances for the future.

Every political reason led him to support Adams. Both Clay and Jackson came from the Southwest, but Clay would be more likely to succeed a New Englander like Adams. Even were Jackson, if acclaimed President, to name Clay secretary of state, Calhoun, who had been elected Vice President, would surely press his prior claim to be Jackson's heir. Also, although this probably did not influence the Speaker too much, his political stance corresponded closely with Adams's beliefs. Finally, Clay did not think that Jackson would make much of a President. "I cannot believe," he wrote a friend, "that killing two thousand five hundred Englishmen at New Orleans qualifies a man for the various difficult and complicated duties of the Chief Magistracy."

Clay met with Adams on January 9, 1825. Communications between cities were slow at the time, but news traveled fast through Washington—then, as it does today. Within hours, the capital knew that Speaker Clay had joined with Secretary of State Adams. Jacksonians fumed indignantly, still hoping that Adams could be stopped. Each state would cast one vote in the House, and Adams needed thirteen for victory. New York, still in doubt, could provide the thirteenth vote. For a month, pro- and anti-Jackson forces worked to gain the New York vote. It boiled down to the decision of a vacillating and aged New York Dutch aristocrat, Steven Van Rensselaer. First Clay and Daniel Webster, then Jackson's supporter Martin Van Buren, extracted promises of support from the eighty-one-year-old congressman. On election day, February 9, Van Rensselaer, confused and undecided, tottered onto the House floor. As tellers passed the ballot box around, he looked upward for heavenly guidance. Receiving none, he hung his head and saw an Adams ballot at his feet. Convinced that the Almighty works in mysterious ways, Van Rensselaer picked up the slip and put it in the box. John Quincy Adams would be President of the United States.

For the second time, the House of Representatives—as in 1800— had chosen the President. The process, though constitutionally correct, produced a national uproar. Jackson and his followers felt deprived, if not defrauded outright. When Adams named Clay his secretary of state, they unleashed a storm of protest. "The Judas of the West has closed the contract," raged Jackson, "and will receive the thirty pieces of silver." Jackson, offended but hardly Christlike, was playing sarcastically upon one of Henry Clay's nicknames, "Harry of the West." In the Senate, Jackson and fourteen others voted unsuccessfully to block Clay's confirmation.

Soon after Adams's inauguration, Jackson resigned from the Senate. The Tennessee legislature had again nominated him for President. Jacksonians in all parts of the country, convinced that their man had been cheated out of the White House, now impatiently awaited the 1828 rematch. While they still boasted of New Orleans, they now also denounced the Adams-Clay "corrupt bargain," in which the presidency had been bought and sold. "Why is Adams on shaky ground?" ran a popular riddle spread by Jackson's friends. The answer: "Because he stands on slippery Clay." Administration members tried vainly to deny the charges—and their denials only gave more currency to the accusation. Politically the issue ruined Clay for years.

Jacksonians received additonal assistance from Adams's policy proposals. The President sent to Congress an ambitious national economic program, one calling for a higher tariff, government sponsorship of road and canal construction, and even a national university. Adams even recommended that the federal government operate a chain of observatories, or what he called "lighthouses of the skies." Old-line Jeffersonians, who still believed in limiting the powers and activities of the federal government, reacted in horror. The younger Adams seemed to them as much a Federalist as his father, and in 1828 many of the Old Republicans took shelter in Jackson's camp.

The Jackson forces organized efficiently for the next presidential election. They established hard-hitting, sometimes slanderous, newspapers across the country. By denouncing Adams and Clay at countless rallies and ridiculing the President's call for astronomical "lighthouses," they gave a decided anti-intellectual tone to the Democratic campaign. In Congress, led by Martin Van Buren of New York, Jackson men obstructed most Administration moves. Many federal officeholders, from the postmaster general on down, worked openly for Jackson, and Adams refused to stop them. The upright New Englander did not believe in firing government officials for political reasons.

But, as the election approached, Clay rallied the Administration (National Republican) forces into a semblance of a counterattack. They circulated thousands of copies of the "Coffin Handbill"—a campaign document charging Jackson with the unjust and merciless hanging of six militiamen in 1815. They raked up the story of his duels with Charles Dickinson and others and invented many more incidents of Jackson's mayhem. Worst of all, at least in the candidate's mind, they reopened the subject of Jackson's marriage. "Ought a convicted adulteress," inquired one editor unctuously, "and her paramour husband to be placed in the highest office of this free and Chistian land?"

On this subject, Jackson did not have control over his rage. He considered Clay responsible for the attacks and called the secretary of state "the basest, meanest scoundrel that ever disgraced the image of his God." Jackson's advisers kept him, with difficulty, from challenging Clay to a duel, and they lived in fear that Jackson would do something to ruin their carefully planned campaign. "For Heaven's sake, for your country's sake," warned one friend, "do remember that but one man can write you down—and his name is Andrew Jackson."

Politicians who thought they had seen everything watched the campaign of 1828 in shock. Torchlight parades and libelous attacks on opponents would apparently decide the next President. From a thousand stumps and platforms, the Jacksonians denounced the "corrupt bargain" and the "lighthouses of the skies." The old general, they cried, was a man of the people; Adams was a Boston aristocrat who had installed a billiard table in the White House! The supporters of Adams dismissed Jackson as an illiterate and an adulterer, a military chieftain who endangered the liberties of all Americans. Supporters of Jackson retaliated by suggesting that Adams, a former Harvard College professor and professional diplomat, had acted as a pimp for the czar of Russia while serving as minister to St. Petersburg! Both sides resorted time and again to such vile and unjust charges.

Except perhaps for the size of Jackson's majority, the election result surprised few people. The military hero and uncertain speller had swept the West and the South, while also taking Pennsylvania. Adams won only New England, New Jersey, and half of the New York vote. And, in a statistic now calculated for the first time—the popular vote—Jackson led Adams by 150,000. Four times as many men voted in 1828 as had voted four years before, slightly more than half of all those eligible.

But at the peak of Jackson's triumph, Rachel Jackson died. Her husband refused to accept that fact and spent an entire night sitting beside her lifeless body. For the rest of his life, Jackson believed that campaign slander had killed his wife. As he had done in 1819 and again in 1823, Jackson began the long trip by horse and flatboat from Nashville to Washington. But the President-elect now journeyed in sorrow. "May God forgive her traducers," he told a friend. "I know that I never shall."

Meanwhile, Washington nervously awaited the coming of its new leader. The capital had known its past Presidents well—they had lived there, holding high political offices before moving into the White House. But, except for his brief service in House and Senate, Jackson had not. Washingtonians knew of him mainly by rumors, most of which they hoped were untrue. As one uneasy resident wrote: "General Jackson will be here [about] 15. of Feb—Nobody knows what he will do. My opinion is that when he comes he will bring a breeze with him. Which way it will blow I cannot tell."

14
THE JACKSONIAN ERA
A. W.

Andrew Jackson, the first President to be born in a log cabin.

Jackson did indeed bring a breeze with him; within weeks his political enemies were calling it a hurricane. In the eight years before Old Hickory returned to his home at the Hermitage, he permanently remodeled and strengthened the office of the presidency. Moreover, he helped to create a new political party system and to recast the electorate's ideas of what it expected from government. Well after he left the presidency, even after his death in 1845, Americans knew that they had lived in the Age of Jackson.

Before the 1820s, politics in the United States had worked in a relatively genteel fashion. Most states had limited the right to vote to male property owners, and in both the North and the South, wealthy merchants or large landowners had dominated public affairs. Many states had come so thoroughly under control by one party—the Federalist or the Jeffersonian Republican party—that competition hardly existed. Presidential elections in those times were very different from the bitter Jackson-Adams contest of 1828.

This genteel state of affairs had begun to change long before Jackson entered the White House, but the country's first frontier President clearly helped to speed up the process.

THE ERA OF GOOD FEELINGS

At the time that Jackson threw back the British at New Orleans, American politics had already begun to change. The declining Federalists were further weakened by charges of wartime disloyalty because of the Hartford Convention, and by 1820 they had all but disappeared. For nearly ten years a so-called Era of Good Feelings characterized the political scene, with political competition occurring mainly among groups within the all-powerful Republican party.

This all-inclusive Republican party was not the same one that Jefferson had fashioned. When the war ended, Republicans adopted some of the same measures that they had condemned in the past. This proved especially true with regard to the national bank and the tariff.

The Second Bank of the United States, a corporation with both private and public directors, chartered in 1816, had branches in the major cities and provided most of what little regulation existed of the American financial system. As Jackson rose steadily to power in the 1820s, so did the bank, on a collision course that would provoke the most spectacular political confrontation of the 1830s.

The same war that had made a hero of Jackson had caused the creation of his eventual adversary. The federal government had gone deeply into debt during the war, and it needed more revenue. Dozens of new banks had sprung up after the expiration of the charter of Hamilton's Bank of the United States in 1811. The state banks had operated poorly during the war, and the country now clearly needed a better financial system. The government had to pay off its debts. Moreover, there was growing pressure on it to take a more active role in promoting economic growth. Many Americans wanted federal money to be spent on building a network of roads and canals—internal improvement, as it was then called—especially west of the Appalachian Mountains.

Swallowing pride and party principles, Republicans responded to these pressures by chartering a second national bank. President Madison overcame his previous objections to such a bank. A young South Carolina representative of the Southern planter interest, John C. Calhoun, introduced the bank recharter bill. It passed in 1816, providing for a bank to run until 1836.

Next came the tariff. Like the bank issue, debate on the tariff in 1816 began with patriotic statements and a nationwide agreement, but it ended before long in fierce political squabbling. American manufacturers, located mainly in New England, were just then getting started. They wanted higher tariff duties so that Americans would buy fewer foreign goods and more of their own products. They wanted not just a revenue tariff, to bring in funds, but a protective tariff—one set high enough to protect American producers from foreign competition.

In 1816, Calhoun and many other Southerners voted in favor of a higher, protective tariff. They did so not to enrich the New England manufacturers but to bring in the additional revenue then needed by the federal government. National security was one of their primary concerns at the time. Southerners—like Americans in all sections—feared the outbreak of yet another war with Britain, since the War of 1812, a standoff, had settled none of the disputed issues. The United States must be better prepared, militarily and financially, argued Southerners, than it had been in 1812.

There was less agreement on internal improvements. The country did need a better transportation system, and Congress passed a bill authorizing national funds. But here, Madison's constitutional conservatism stood in the way. Despite his lapses from Jeffersonianism on the tariff and the bank, Madison could not convince himself that the federal government had the right to spend money in this way. The President vetoed the bill, and for the next two generations each state had to build its own roads and canals.

The Federalists offered little opposition to the candidacy of Secretary of State James Monroe to be Madison's successor. And again, four years later, Monroe received every electoral vote but one for reelection. Throughout his administration, Monroe issued soothing calls for an end to all party divisions. The composition of his cabinet—with the ex-Federalist Adams in the State Department, the Old Jeffersonian Crawford of Georgia in the Treasury, and the Southern nationalist Calhoun as secretary of war—showed that all elements of the political spectrum now coexisted within the Republican party. Harmony had indeed been established in national politics—for a while.

The Panic of 1819 But trouble was already brewing. The first sign was a financial panic. Since the War of 1812, people had been speculating heavily in foreign trade and Western lands. They bought on credit, hoping to reap a large profit before having to pay off their debts. Then, in 1819, the Second Bank—under new management—began calling in loans. As a result, many state banks stopped paying hard money for their notes or closed, and numerous investors went bankrupt.

The Panic of 1818—the first of a series of economic downturns that would continue to occur in the United States at approximately twenty-year intervals until 1929—affected the whole nation, although Western states were the hardest hit.

The national bank, then just three years old, was widely blamed for the hard times. Many Americans attacked the bank as a corrupting agent of aristocracy and privilege, and several state legislatures tried to tax its branches out of existence. The Supreme Court ruled such laws unconstitutional (see page 219). But the strong antibank feelings that had surfaced never really disappeared. Politicians would capitalize on them throughout the 1820s, and Jackson would find in such feelings a reservoir of political support during the 1830s.

Americans had distrusted banks even during the colonial period—often with good reason, given the high rate of bank failures. In the 1820s, Kentucky and Tennessee witnessed "relief wars," during which debtors organized against creditors. Everywhere, private banking interests were on the defensive. These struggles were a prelude to the Jacksonian battles of the 1830s. They also provided a training ground for several important politicians who would later join Jackson's antibank crusade.

The Missouri Compromise Another sign that the short-lived Era of Good Feelings (1816–1824) had its own tensions came when the always troublesome problem of slavery surfaced again. In the same year as the panic, the issue of statehood for Missouri came to a head. The Missouri Territory was part of the original Louisiana Purchase. Its residents had applied for admission to the Union in 1817. But, at the time, a congressman from New York had demanded that slavery be prohibited in the state as the price of admission. The uneasy sectional truce on the question of slavery quickly evaporated. Congress was deadlocked on the issue for over a year. Southerners had equal voting strength in the Senate, since the nation then had the same number of slave states and free states. Northerners controlled the House of Representatives, however, because the North had acquired a larger population since 1789. Antislavery representatives argued that Congress could and should make prohibition of slavery a condition for admitting new states. Southerners retorted that all states, old or new, were sovereign and could decide the matter of slavery for themselves.

The very mention of the slavery question in Congress terrorized Southerners. As the struggle went on in Congress, Richmond, Virginia, was said to be as "agitated as if affected by all the Volcanic Eruptions of Vesuvius." Southerners, who always suspected that the North wanted to destroy their "peculiar institution" of slavery, now felt their suspicions confirmed. They readied themselves for a long fight on what they considered a life-or-death issue. "To compromise is to acknowledge the right of Congress to interfere and to legislate on the subject," wrote one prominent Southern politician; "this would be acknowledging too much."

Yet compromise they did, when Maine, then a district of Massachusetts, petitioned Congress to become a separate state. Southerners would not admit Maine as a free state unless Missouri joined the Union with the right to permit slavery. Henry Clay, Speaker of the House and a Kentucky slaveholder more identified with the West than with the South, now piloted a three-part compromise through Congress, with a different coalition backing each part. Maine would be admitted as a free state, Missouri as a slave state, and slavery would be banned in the remaining areas of the Louisiana Purchase and in future acquisitions above 36°30′ latitude.

The Missouri crisis frightened Americans in the North and West as well as in the South, and with good reason. They knew that truly national politics and parties could not exist if slavery became an active issue bitterly dividing the sections of the country. This "momentous question, like a fire-bell in the night, awakened and filled me with terror," wrote Jefferson, in retirement at Monticello. "I considered it once as the knell of the Union . . . this is a reprieve only, not a final sentence." Many other anxious politicians agreed with this analysis, although few were willing to admit it publicly.

The South in particular regarded the compromise uneasily, especially its limitation on the future expansion of slavery. "Instead of joy," one Southern editor mourned, "we scarcely ever recollect to have tasted of a bitterer cup." All three Southerners in Monroe's cabinet advised him that the restriction of slavery was unconstitutional. Sixty percent of the Southern congressmen who voted for the compromise were not returned to the next Congress.

Both Southerners and Northerners now hoped that the slavery issue could be kept quietly localized. The Missouri debates had exposed the deep division between supporters and opponents of slavery. Clearly, these sectional issues and attitudes had the power to rip the Union apart. Throughout the Age of Jackson, however, politicians would strive to keep the slavery genie bottled up.

A RETURN TO PARTY POLITICS

As we have seen, the election of 1824 emphatically closed out the Era of Good Feelings. It also destroyed the method that Americans had first used to select presidential candidates, the congressional caucus or party meeting. The caucus had often been denounced as aristocratic and undemocratic. After Crawford, who was nominated by caucus in 1824, lost the election, nobody suggested holding another one in the future. Politicians had to find a new process, one that at least seemed more democratic.

They found the answer during the next few years in a new nominating device, the convention. Conventions were supposed to be more representative of a party's membership and thus more democratic than the caucus. Only members of the national or state legislature could attend a legislative party caucus. But, in theory, any party member could become a convention delegate. Grassroots political elements could be represented at a convention, as could groups or factions that had not been able to elect their leaders to Congress.

This change reflected the general movement toward increasing popular participation in the governmental process. Throughout the 1820s, state constitutional conventions revised the old Revolutionary constitutions, lowering or abolishing the property qualifications for voting. More offices were now filled by direct vote of the people; in some states even presidential electors were now chosen by direct vote.

At first, old-line politicians resisted the changeover to conventions. Yet they had little to worry about. Party bosses found that it was not difficult to manipulate convention delegates. On the other hand, conventions did provide excellent window dressing. Most important, they gave the appearance of equality in an age when political operations were becoming more and more democratized.

A Second Adams For the presidential election that followed the Adams-Clay victory in the House of Representatives, Americans required neither caucus nor convention to indicate the candidates. Jacksonians hungered for their next electoral bout with John Quincy Adams. Only with a brilliantly successful Administration could the President hope to fend off their challenge, and, for that, Adams was the wrong man at the wrong time.

Like his father, John Adams—another crusty, stubborn, and inflexible man—John Quincy Adams believed in government by the most able and talented. Also like his father, John Quincy Adams learned quickly that such a belief did not make him popular with the majority of his fellow Americans. Adams had been preparing for the presidency all his life, but once in the White House, he found that his hands were tied. He became a minority President, without any real control over Congress. He also lacked the ability to make either himself or his programs popular with the public. Adams was bound to fail, and fail he did.

Voting day in Philadelphia, as elsewhere in the Jacksonian era, occasioned much rowdy excitement. During this period the number of voters increased, not only because suffrage requirements were eased but also because people took more interest in politics.

For four distressing years this very capable individual fussed and floundered. The job called for talents Adams did not possess and could not acquire. He was reserved—a "cold fish" to most people who met him. He was short-tempered with any person he considered a fool, and he claimed to have met many—especially in politics. And he was totally unwilling to compromise.

President Adams's expansive first message to Congress, calling for "lighthouses of the skies," ended whatever survival chances his Administration might have had. It especially shocked Martin Van Buren, opposition Senate leader, political boss of New York's Albany Regency, and a confirmed Jeffersonian. Van Buren now traveled to Virginia to confer with leaders of the so-called Richmond Junto, the clique that dominated the politics of the state. Van Buren proposed a North-South Republican alliance that would not only oust Adams but prevent Adams's ideas from gaining power in the future.

Jackson, Van Buren argued, could accomplish the first end and would be a reasonable President. He was already very popular. He did not support the extreme states' rights position, but neither did he favor a strong national government. Furthermore, Van Buren promised that his Northerners would see that slavery was kept out of national politics. The Southern states would thus be free from antislavery attacks during Jackson's presidency, and hopefully afterward as well. In short, after Jackson's victory in 1828, Van Buren wanted to revive the coalition originally formed by Burr of New York and Jefferson and Madison of Virginia. Both the original Jeffersonian group and the new Jacksonian alliance were known as Dem-

THE MONROE DOCTRINE

James Monroe

In President James Monroe's annual message to Congress on December 2, 1823, he included the principles of foreign policy later known as the Monroe Doctrine. Monroe and his Secretary of State, John Quincy Adams, wanted to clarify the American position in two specific problem areas. They succeeded in a wider sense, as one historian states, by planting their principles "firmly in the national consciousness."

The first problem area was the Northwest. Since 1821 Russia had been encroaching on the Oregon Country, claimed jointly by Britain and the United States. In October 1823, Adams stated bluntly that "the American continents are no longer subjects for any new European establishments." This principle was repeated in Monroe's speech.

South America was the second problem area. Eight new republics had declared their independence from Spain, but their existence was precarious. Despotic regimes in Europe were successfully crushing revolutions on the Continent, and it was no secret that Spain was eager to regain her lost colonies. In August 1823 the English foreign secretary proposed a joint British-American manifesto to warn Europe against intervention. British merchants wanted to retain their profitable new markets in South America, now open to them after the breakup of the Spanish monopoly. And Britain could back up a threat with the power of its navy.

Adams, however, did not want the United States to be "a cockboat in the wake of the British man-of-war." He suspected that the British might restrict American expansion in some way as a price for their support. Also, Britain had not officially recognized the new republics, as the United States was doing. So Adams suggested an independent course of action. Monroe agreed and decided to include a warning in his message to Congress.

Monroe declared that intervention by European monarchies in the democracies of the New World would be judged as "the manifestation of an unfriendly disposition toward the United States." He pledged the United States not to interfere with any existing European colonies in the New World and to keep out of the "internal concerns" of Europe.

The speech was acclaimed at home but viewed abroad as "arrogant." Yet the European powers took no action. Why? Two months earlier, unknown to Adams and Monroe, the English had pressured France to agree not to assist Spain in any invasion of her ex-colonies. Thus the issue had already been defused. Russia, unable to gain support for intervention, withdrew its claims to the Pacific Northwest early in 1824. The South American republics seemed indifferent to the speech. They were more impressed with "the oaken fleets of Britain" than with "the paper shield of Monroe."

So the significance of Monroe's declaration was discounted at first. In years to come, however, his principles were invoked with great reverence. The strength of the nation lent weight to his ideas.

ocratic-Republicans. But the Jeffersonians were more generally referred to as Republicans, while the Jacksonians called themselves Democrats. Anti-Jackson Republicans were first known as National Republicans, later as Whigs.

JACKSON AS PRESIDENT

Few people knew what would happen when Jackson took office. He had been deliberately vague about issues while campaigning, and the Jacksonian Democrats were then more of a faction gathered about a leader than a party with a platform. His inaugural address revealed little except a call for "reform." This word was political shorthand, an indication that Jackson intended to reward his friends and punish his enemies. During the previous generation of one-party, Republican rule, turnover among public officeholders had not been great. The last large-scale shift in government employees had occurred when Jefferson had become President and removed a good many Federalists from office. Since that time a Republican elite, many of them anti-Jackson, had settled cozily into federal jobs, some for a quarter century. Jacksonians understandably demanded that the new President replace these older officials with loyal Jackson supporters.

Jackson went about as far as Jefferson had, but he and his supporters made more noise about it. He removed about 10 percent of the federal officeholders during his first year as President, and a total of about 20 percent in eight years. It was not the clean sweep hoped for by the Democratic politicos. But the Jacksonians did radically change the nature of federal patronage, in the sense that Jackson openly defended the principle of rotation in office — what came to be known as the spoils system. He agreed with Senator William L. Marcy of New York—an associate of Van Buren—that "to the victor belong the spoils." Jackson acted on the theory (if not always the practice) that, in a democracy, persons of normal intelligence could capably fill most public offices. To Jackson's political opponents this view seemed dangerous. Yet rotation in office, at all levels of American government, became the standard practice after Jackson and lasted for decades.

Strengthening the Office Jackson's opponents saw him as a tyrant, an uncouth military man from the West. Needless to say, this opinion did not conform to Jackson's vision of himself as an "Old Republican," a true Jeffersonian. But Republicanism had changed significantly since Jefferson's presidency. Jackson hoped to revive what he called the "Republican principles of [17]98." He did not want national power to increase at the expense of the states. Yet his role as a strong President and his ability to dramatize political issues for ordinary people in every section stimulated the growth of national power. Just as Jefferson had strained his principles to purchase Louisiana, Jackson would sometimes find his ideas fairly elastic when put to the test.

Old Hickory's "Old Republicanism" took several forms. In his first annual message, the President criticized the national bank. He also rejected the idea of a high, protective tariff. (Unlike some Southerners, however, he did not deny the tariff's constitutionality.) On the issue of internal improvements, Jackson held views like those of the Republican Presidents prior to John Quincy Adams. In 1830 he vetoed the Maysville Road Bill, which would have involved the federal government in a road-building project in the state of Kentucky. He argued that such matters should be left in local hands. He believed, though, that the national government could contribute to interstate projects. This is why he favored national support for the Cumberland Road, and east-west improvement that passed through several states. Jackson received firm support on this question from Martin Van Buren, who was his secretary of state from 1829 to 1831. Van Buren's state, New York, had completed the Erie Canal in 1825 without federal money, and further major internal improvements in the state were unlikely.

Jackson did much to strengthen the American presidency. He was by far the strongest Chief Executive up to his time and one of the most forceful in American history. Since Jefferson's first term, power had been steadily slipping out of

AN EXPANDING FRONTIER

One of the most important features of the national experience has been the steady movement westward of the American people. They traveled through tangled forests, down rivers, and on pathways like the Allegheny road shown here, well worn by the 1830s. Americans overcame obstacles with amazing energy. In a few years they had not only tamed the wilderness, but also created whole new cities, among them Cincinnati, Louisville, Chicago, and St. Paul.

Alexis de Tocqueville praised the fearlessness of the pioneers: "Millions of people are marching at once toward the same horizon. Their language, their religion, their manners differ; their object is the same. Fortune has been promised to them somewhere in the West, and to the West they go to find it."

[For further information on the foreign observers quoted in this essay, see "Notes on Sources."]

PICTORIAL ESSAY 4

The Squatters, by George Caleb Bingham

A squatter is a person who, without any title to the land, or leave asked or granted, squats himself down and declares himself the lord and master of the soil for the time being. There is nobody to question his right. These hardy fellows are sometimes called the pioneers of the wilderness—and justly so—for they go ahead of the more orderly and civilized population and clear away the grounds in the line of march.

[BASIL HALL, 1828]

Engraving of Daniel Boone, said to be the earliest print made west of the Mississippi

On our way to Pittsburgh we met with various specimens of the backwoodsman, and I must say that, when clad in their green hunting shirts, with deerskin caps and leggings, their muscular attitude fully displayed in the free handling of their long rifles, they presented the most picturesque appearance I had ever seen. They had a way of leaning on their guns and surveying a stranger which struck me as singularly intelligent. It implied conviction, not inquiry. It was a look that said, not "Who are you?" but "I know you."

[JOHN BERNARD, 1800]

*From camp all the trappers—
some on foot, some on horseback, according to the distance
they have to go—start every
morning in small parties in all
directions ranging the distance
of some twenty miles around.
There is much anxiety and
danger in going through the
ordinary routine of a trapper's
duty. For as the enemy is generally lurking about among the
rocks and hiding places, watching an opportunity, the hunter
has to keep a constant lookout,
and the gun is often in one hand
while the trap is in the other.*

[ALEXANDER ROSS, 1810-25]

Setting Traps for Beaver, by Alfred Jacob Miller

*The driver stopped and came to tell us ladies that he was sorry to trouble us to get out,
but that an emigrant's wagon had blocked up the ford of a creek which we had to
cross. It must not be supposed a common circumstance that an emigrant's wagon was
left in a creek. The "camping out" is usually done in a sheltered, dry spot in the
woods, not far from some little stream, where the kettle may be filled and where the
dusty children may be washed.*

[HARRIET MARTINEAU, 1835]

Emigrating westward, a family camps beside a stream

Methodist missionary on his way west

Indiana housewife outside her log cabin

A lively scene from Davy Crockett's Almanac

At one lone dwelling we found a neat, respectable-looking female, spinning under the little piazza at one side of the cabin, which shaded her from the sun. Her husband was absent on business. She had no family, and no companion but her husband's faithful dog, which usually attended him in his bear hunting in the winter. She was quite overcome with "lone," she said, and hoped we would tie our horses in the wood and sit awhile with her during the heat of the day. We did so, and she rewarded us with a basin of coffee. Her husband was kind and good to her, and never left her without necessity, but a true lover of bear hunting—which he pursued alone, taking only his dog with him, though it is common for hunters to go in parties to attack this dangerous animal.

[MORRIS BIRKBECK, 1818]

Pioneers cutting trees in a clearing

At intervals a log cabin, with its little space of cleared land about it, nestles under a rising ground and sends its thread of blue smoke curling up into the sky. Sometimes the ground is only just now cleared, the felled trees lying yet upon the soil and the log house only this morning begun. As we pass this clearing, the settler leans upon his axe or hammer and looks wistfully at the people from the world.

[CHARLES DICKENS, 1842]

The Mill Boy, by George Caleb Bingham

These lonely settlers are poorly off. Their corn for bread must be ground thirty miles off, requiring three days to carry to the mill and bring back the small load of three bushels. Articles of family manufacture are very scanty, and what they purchase is of the meanest quality and excessively dear. Yet the people are friendly and willing to share their simple fare.

[MORRIS BIRKBECK, 1818]

A squatter came splashing through the mud to the spot where I was and begged me to take a paddle with him in his canoe, hollowed out, as he told me, by his own hands from the trunk of a cypress. I went along with him and found his wife seated in a very nice, clean, roomy cottage made of logs, with a large fireplace lined with mud on one side, the whole whitewashed and very neat. An air of comfort pervaded the whole establishment, which I had not expected. The squatter was really quite active in his hospitality.

[BASIL HALL, 1828]

Inside a backwoodsman's home

Chippewa chieftain with a white trader

Pushed by the European population toward the northwest of North America, the Indians come, by a strange destiny, to die on the very shores where they landed in unknown centuries to take possession of America. In the Iroquois language, the Indians call themselves the "men of forever" —Ongoue-onoue. These "men of forever" have gone, and foreigners will soon leave to the heirs of a whole world only the earth of their tombs.

[FRANÇOIS-RENÉ DE CHATEAUBRIAND, 1791]

Frontier neighbors at a community scutching (beating flax to separate the fibers)

When several families settle at the same time and place, the colonists do not become brutalized as easily as the solitary settler. When he is surrounded by gloomy woods and closed horizons, cut off from association with his fellows, he soon loses those civilized habits that a community develops.

[AXEL KLINKOWSTRÖM, 1820]

Every boy, as soon as he can lift a rifle, is constantly practicing with it, and thus becomes an astonishingly expert marksman. When I was in Kentucky, a hunter offered to fire twenty times at a dollar at a distance of 100 yards, on condition that I should give him a dollar every time he struck it and that he would give me one every time he missed it. But I had seen such specimens of their rifle-shooting that I did not choose to accept his offer.

[WILLIAM BLANE, 1822-23]

Shooting for the Beef, by George Caleb Bingham. (The cow at left goes to the winner.)

It is a peculiarly happy feature of the Constitution of the United States that every state has itself an independent government. The western states of America are each a nursery of freedom. Every new settlement is already a republic in embryo. They extend political life in every direction. Every new state, therefore, is a fresh guarantee for the continuance of the American Constitution and directs the attention of the people to new sources of happiness and wealth. It increases the interest of all in upholding the general government and makes individual success dependent on national prosperity.

[FRANCIS J. GRUND, 1837]

Stump Speaking, by George Caleb Bingham

St. Paul, Minnesota, in 1856

The next moment St. Paul was before us, standing upon a high bluff on the eastern bank of the Mississippi. The town is one of the youngest infants of the Great West, scarcely eighteen months old, and yet it has in this short time increased to a population of two thousand persons. In a very few years it will certainly be possessed of twenty-two thousand, for its situation is as remarkable for beauty and healthiness as it is advantageous for trade.

[FREDRIKA BREMER, 1850]

Whatever may be the talents of the persons who meet together in society, the very shape, form, and arrangement of the meeting is sufficient to paralyze conversation. The women invariably herd together at one part of the room, and the men at the other. In justice to Cincinnati, I must acknowledge that this arrangement is by no means peculiar to that city, or to the western side of the Alleghenies. The gentlemen spit, talk of elections and the price of produce, and spit again. The ladies look at each other's dresses till they know every pin by heart, and talk of Parson Some-body's last sermon on the day of judgment or Dr. T'otherbody's new pills for dyspepsia. When the "tea" is announced, they all console themselves together for whatever they may have suffered in keeping awake.

[FRANCES TROLLOPE, 1828]

In a Cincinnati ballroom

presidential hands and into those of the Congress. Jackson, however, reversed the process.

During his eight years as President, Jackson restored the White House as the focal point of national politics. Where Congress had largely dictated to the last three Presidents, Jackson now set out to manage Congress. Working closely with loyal Jacksonians like House Speaker Andrew Stevenson and Senator Thomas Hart Benton—whose bullet the President still carried in his shoulder— he tried to get Congress to support his policies and defeat bills he did not like. And anti-Administration congressmen soon found it difficult to get presidential patronage for constituents hungry for jobs. But when his policies failed with Congress, Jackson had no hesitation about vetoing bills. Twelve times he refused his assent to a bill passed by both houses of Congress—three times more than his five predecessors combined. A favorite device of his was the pocket veto—delay in signing a bill until Congress adjourned. Perhaps most important, Jackson vetoed some bills just because he thought them unwise, not necessarily because he regarded them as unconstitutional.

Jackson introduced another innovation into his conduct of the office. Previously, Presidents had relied for advice on their cabinets, often consisting of politicians as interested in their own careers as in the nation's problems. Jackson now assembled around him his own personal advisers—a so-called kitchen cabinet that included Van Buren and two newspapermen, Francis Prescott Blair and Amos Kendall. Blair edited the Administration newspaper, the Washington *Globe,* and Kendall held a minor job in the Treasury Department, but both were available to advise Jackson on strategy, to consult with party leaders, or to draft Jackson's messages to Congress.

Finally, Jackson was the undisputed head of his party, as well as leader of the government. His power in each role strengthened him in the other, and his extraordinary personal popularity helped him in both. Democrats all over the country followed the Administration line as it appeared in the *Globe,* or they soon ceased to be Democrats.

Jackson brought a new concept of the presidency to the White House. Some previous occupants, as well as his political opponents, saw the President's duty as only to administer the government, while Congress, representing the people, made the laws. But Jackson saw himself as the direct representative of the American people, elected by the entire nation, while each congressman represented only a small part of it.

The "Eaton Affair" Dramatizing Jackson's concept of the presidency was an intensely personal issue that frayed relations between himself and his Vice-President, John C. Calhoun, whose support had helped gain Jackson victory in 1828. Embittered by Jackson's evident preference in assigning cabinet posts for Van Buren and his political allies, Calhoun lost most of his remaining influence in the Administration as a result of an episode that came to be known as the "Peggy Eaton affair."

Jackson enjoyed the social company of Peggy O'Neill Eaton, wife of his friend, Tennessee Senator John H. Eaton, whom the President appointed secretary of war. Daughter of a tavern keeper and a widow at the time she married Eaton, other Washington wives gossiped incessantly about Mrs. Eaton's morals while spreading rumors that she had engaged in a love affair with John Eaton while her former husband still lived. Once Eaton joined the cabinet, Mrs. Calhoun and other wives of leading Jackson Administration officials refused all social contact with the Eatons while continuing their slander-mongering.

Nothing could have guaranteed Jackson's anger toward the gossips more easily than what he treated as an obvious comparison to his political enemies' earlier slanders about his beloved dead wife Rachel. The President turned this social flap into a test of political loyalty and insisted that cabinet members deal respectfully with Mrs. Eaton. Caught between their wives and their President, most—including Calhoun—stood ground and continued to question Peggy Eaton's virtue (and virtues). Martin Van Buren, however, a widower, found it easier—and politically useful—to cultivate the Eatons' friendship, something that did not pass unnoticed by Jackson. After many months of battling within the Administration over the "Eaton affair," Jackson (with the approval of Van Buren) finally forced the resignation of his entire cabinet in 1831 as a means of reorganizing it with friendlier—and more compliant—figures. Van Buren went to England as American minister where he remained until the Senate voted against his confirmation by a single vote—Calhoun's, casting a tie-breaking ballot as vice-president. The entire episode strengthened Van Buren's claims on Jackson while rupturing the President's personal links to Calhoun.

Nullification In the crisis over nullification, Jackson most strongly demonstrated his forcefulness and his claim to represent all the American people. Trouble had been brewing over the federal tariff law for many years. In 1828 the South Carolina legislature published an *Exposition and Protest*. It branded protective tariffs as unjust and unconstitutional and termed the 1828 version, supported by Jackson, the Tariff of Abominations. Changes must come, the *Exposition* warned, or South Carolina would act.

Improbably, the man behind the *Exposition* was the Vice President of the United States, John C. Calhoun. Brilliant, ambitious, and totally humorless, Calhoun had begun his political career as a strong nationalist, favoring both a national bank and a protective tariff. But the shifting political sands of South Carolina could no longer support such a stand, and Calhoun now attempted to devise means of protecting his and other states from the national government. Like the rest of the South, he had been profoundly impressed by the Missouri crisis and felt the slave states required strong defenses against a potentially hostile national government. Explained Calhoun, "I consider the Tariff but as the occasion, rather than the real cause of the present state of things."

Calhoun thought he had found a solution in the Virginia and Kentucky resolutions, written by Madison and Jefferson in the late 1790s. He now interpreted them to mean that a state could nullify (refuse to enforce) an act of Congress that it considered unconstitutional. Obviously, the South would find Calhoun's solution extremely useful against any antislavery laws passed by Congress. The aging Madison denied that the resolutions carried Calhoun's interpretation, but South Carolina accepted it.

As Southern complaints about the tariff continued, Jackson tried to arrange for a compromise bill to lower import duties. But he never lost sight of the fundamental issue, state defiance of federal law. Jackson rejected nullification totally, vowing to preserve the union by any means necessary. He applied all the power of the presidency and all the force of his personality to block nullification and denounce John Calhoun.

Nevertheless, South Carolinians went ahead and declared the 1828 tariff "null and void" in their state. What would Jackson do? Though he might compromise on tariff rates, he would not compromise federal authority. "I consider . . . the power to annul a law of the United States, assumed by one state, incompatible with the existence of the Union," he proclaimed in December 1832. South Carolina should not think that it could nullify the Constitution peacefully, and, he warned: "Disunion by armed force is treason." Jackson got Congress to pass a Force Bill reaffirming the President's right to use troops to put down rebellion and enforce the laws. In fifteen days, he wrote a South Carolina Unionist, he could send forty thousand armed troops to South Carolina to put down rebellion; in forty days, two hundred thousand. The Hero of New Orleans would not look far for a general to command them. "I repeat to the Union men, fear not, *the union will* be preserved."

Meanwhile, South Carolina had received no substantial support from other Southern states. The state's isolation left it no real hope of defending itself or nullification. Early in 1833, Clay and Calhoun worked out a compromise bill reducing tariff rates over the next ten years to an acceptable level. The nullification issue collapsed, though to save face South Carolina declared the Force Bill unconstitutional. An armed clash had been avoided. The Union stood firm. Jackson emerged from the struggle with more strength and greater prestige than before. The President had shown character, political skill, and moral courage—all of which he would need in his next major campaign, the war against the Second Bank of the United States.

The Bank War—and After Why did Jackson oppose the Second Bank of the United States and

PETER COOPER

As an old man looking backward, Peter Cooper said that his life had fallen into three parts—thirty years to get started, thirty years to gain a fortune, and thirty years to distribute it wisely. As inventor, manufacturer, and philanthropist, Cooper became a legendary figure. One historian called him "as distinctly an American type as Benjamin Franklin, and as quickly taken to the American heart."

Born in 1791 in New York City, the young Cooper revealed a restless nature and a talent for tinkering. As a boy, he made shoes and hats and even a simple washing machine. For his first child he devised a mechanically rocked cradle attached to a musical instrument, patented as a "Pendulous and Musical Cradle." Some of his ambitious projects, such as propelling ferryboats by compressed air, were grotesque failures. Others, such as an endless chain to haul canal boats, went unrecognized. "I was always fussing and contriving," he wrote, "and was never satisfied unless I was doing something difficult—something that had never been done before, if possible."

He came to a turning point in 1821, when he bought a glue factory in New York. It became the foundation of his fortune. In a few years he had a monopoly in the field and was able to pursue other interests. Cooper invested in real estate and railroads. In 1830, for the Baltimore and Ohio Railroad, he built and piloted the first steam locomotive in the United States, nicknamed "Tom Thumb." With a good sense of the demand for iron in an increasingly industrialized economy, he bought iron mines and ironworks, producing the first structural iron for fireproof buildings. As president of the giant North American Telegraph Company, he supported Cyrus Field in his project for laying the Atlantic cable.

In 1856 Peter Cooper calculated that he was a millionaire. So he turned to the realization of his long-held dream: a workingman's institute in New York City for "the advancement of science and art." He was painfully aware of his own lack of formal education, and yet he was distrustful of much "book learning." Thus he wanted to develop a school "so that the boys and girls of this city who had no better opportunity than I had to enjoy means of information would be enabled to better their condition." Cooper Union opened in 1859, offering free courses in science, technology, art, and design, as well as a library and a museum.

Cooper's public career included reform politics. Some of his ideas were far in advance of his time—controlled currencies, unemployment relief works programs, and government regulation of railroads. In his last years, according to one writer, he became "an unwearied figure for social justice."

Cooper's personal qualities explain the esteem in which the public held him. He had the self-confidence and optimism of the master craftsman. Though hard working, he was never ruthless. At his funeral in 1883, this tribute was paid: "Here lies a man who never owned a dollar he could not take up to the Great White Throne."

A cartoon version of the Bank War portrays Jackson as a donkey trampling on branch banks. Van Buren, as a sly fox, goes after the U. S. Bank. In the background are chained dogs, representing administration newpapers, baying their approval of Jackson's antics.

come to hate its president, Nicholas Biddle? As an investor, Jackson had lost money in a panic in the 1790s, and he had distrusted banks ever since. As a Jeffersonian, he regarded the bank as a dangerous institution. He thought it was too large and too national in scope. To him, it represented a concentration of economic power, created by the federal government, that endangered states' rights and thus endangered the rights of the people. The Supreme Court declared the Second Bank of the United States constitutional, but Jackson felt that the President had as much right as the Court to interpret the Constitution.

The existence of the Bank became the primary issue in the election of 1832. Although the Bank's twenty-year charter did not lapse until 1836, Biddle took the advice of Henry Clay and asked for a twenty-year recharter four years early. Clay, running for President as the National Republican candidate, needed an issue on which to challenge Jackson. Clay identified himself totally with the bank, and even took on one of its attorneys as his running mate.

Jackson was never one to refuse a challenge. After Congress had passed the bank recharter bill, the President vetoed it in a stinging message drafted by Amos Kendall. The powers of the bank, he charged, were "unauthorized by the Constitution, subversive of the rights of the states, and dangerous to the liberties of the people." He called the bank an instrument used by wealthy merchants to oppress the workers and farmers. "It is to be regretted," he warned, with at least one eye on the fall elections, "that the rich and powerful too often bend the acts of government for their own purposes."

The election of 1832 transformed the Jacksonian party of 1828 into the Democratic party, a coalition with party issues and a party constituency. The cementing issue was the Bank of the United States, which symbolized Democratic objections to many other kinds of concentrated government power, such as a high protective tariff and internal improvements.

The Democratic constituency largely reflected the Van Buren-Ritchie agreement of the previous decade, including most of the South and most urban workers in the North. The latter Democratic constituency was steadily increasing: Between 1820 and 1860, three million Irish and two million Germans streamed into the United States, most of them into the ranks of the Democratic party. The Democrats could also count on the support of many backwoods farmers of the West, who supported Jackson and disliked the Eastern bank.

In 1832, workers and farmers both saw the bank as a tool of the rich; they wanted to be paid for their labor and their crops in gold and silver, rather than in banknotes. But Jackson's supporters also included many who disliked the Bank for exactly the opposite reason. They felt it was restricting the flow of paper money too tightly, keeping other banks from issuing their own banknotes freely enough to encourage economic growth. But they joined with the other Jacksonians in alleging that the bank only helped to make the rich richer.

Jackson's opposition had an issue and a leader—but not much else. Henry Clay, with only the limited and ineffectual organization of the National Republican party, counted on the bank issue to provide the rest of his votes. For Clay and the National Republicans, the bank stood for many other issues. It was part of Clay's "American system," a plan of positive government action to encourage manufacturing and tie the country together. The system consisted of the bank, a high protective tariff, and extensive internal improvements. For the system, swore Clay, he "would defy the South, the President and the Devil."

The South and the President, at least, defeated Clay roundly in 1832. Whether the bank issue helped or hurt Jackson's campaign is difficult to judge. Although he improved his showing in the electoral college, he was less popular with the voters than when he had run as a fresh and untried candidate in 1828, and his percentage of the popular vote declined. Some Southerners reacted unfavorably to his antinullification stand, and a new party in the North called the Anti-Masons siphoned off additional votes. In fighting the bank, Jackson had seemingly raised the threat of class war. Many of his opponents, including wealthy businessmen in New York City and elsewhere, thought that he was trying to set the poor against the rich. All this was more than offset, however, by the incredibly bungled campaign waged by Clay and the National Republicans.

Having gained another four years in the White House, Jackson was convinced that the American people wished him to crush the bank forever. He was also sure that anyone who attacked the bank was for him, and anyone who supported it was against him. Those who wanted to remain Jacksonian Democrats in good standing had to join the antibank crusade. Those who felt they could not support Jackson on this issue switched over completely to the opposition. But Jackson was not a man to let such defections bother him. He would now begin the second battle of the Bank War.

Distrusting Biddle, Jackson now wished to remove all government deposits from the bank, to weaken it, and perhaps kill it. By law, only the secretary of the Treasury could order the removal of deposits. Jackson found it necessary to replace two men before he found a secretary who would remove the deposits—future Supreme Court Chief Justice Roger B. Taney. The government would now put its money into selected state banks, many of them controlled by Democrats eager to obtain interest-free government deposits. These favored institutions soon acquired the nickname of "pet banks."

Biddle now counterattacked. The Philadelphia banker, a man of considerable talent and arrogance, liked to boast that he wielded, as president of the bank, more power than the President of the United States. He would not see that power destroyed without a struggle. He stopped issuing new loans and called in many that the bank had previously granted. The nation immediately plunged into a serious recession. Biddle watched the situation with satisfaction, hoping that he might yet get his recharter. "Nothing but the evidence of suffering," he explained coolly, "will produce any effect on Congress."

Many people felt that Jackson had gone too far and that both the party and the economy had been permanently damaged. Petitions poured into Congress asking for recharter of the bank. Among the thousands of signatures were the names of prominent Democratic merchants, including a sizable number from Northern cities. Some merchants, perhaps a bit braver than the rest, actually went to see Jackson to plead their case. "What do you come to me for?" asked the President, enjoying himself greatly. "Go to Nicholas Biddle. We have no money here, gentlemen. Biddle has all the money."

As calmly as he had taken aim at Charles Dickinson, Jackson had taken aim at Nicholas Biddle. Any plan aimed at breaking Jackson's will was doomed to failure. Before he would recharter the bank, the President told Van Buren, "I would cut off my right hand from my body."

But would the issue be decided over Jackson's head? Both sides recognized that the congressional elections of 1834 would have an important influence on the outcome of the Bank War. To fight those contests, Jackson's opponents now created a new party, the Whigs. They took their name from the British party that usually opposed the king. After all, they explained, they opposed "King Andrew I." The party consisted mostly of the National Republicans, plus Democrats who had left the party over the bank issue. Apparently, however, not enough had defected. Despite the economic hardships of the winter and spring, Jackson's candidates did well at the polls that year. They even made slight gains in the fall elections for Congress.

Jackson had won the Bank War. The Second Bank of the United States was dead. Biddle later obtained a charter for his bank from the Pennsylvania legislature. But the institution was no longer a national bank, thus it was no longer as powerful

as it had been. In 1839 Biddle resigned, and two years later his bank went bankrupt. Biddle died soon afterward.

Since the mid-1820s the nation had once more prospered, and in the early 1830s the economy began to boom. The government was taking in far more money than it spent. In fact, the national debt completely disappeared during Jackson's tenure—one of the few times in American history that it did so. Speculation in Western lands had become almost a mania. American capitalists were heavily involved, as were European investors. Since the United States was still an underdeveloped, credit-hungry nation, there was a demand for additional capital. Many new banks were chartered. Their promissory notes (written promises to pay a specified sum of money, either on demand or at a certain time) circulated as unofficial paper money.

The speculative boom worried Jackson. In 1836 he issued the Specie Circular, an executive order directing government land agents to accept only gold and silver specie (hard money) as payment. The Deposit Act of that same year included the first federal regulation of the pet banks. But the Whigs added a rider providing that the federal government's surplus revenues should be distributed among the states. This money, in state hands, caused more inflation. Thus it worked against Jackson's Specie Circular.

JACKSON AND THE SUPREME COURT

After the Bank War, Jackson enjoyed one more triumph before leaving the White House. Since 1801, Jeffersonians and Jacksonians had unhappily regarded the Supreme Court under Chief Justice Marshall constantly upholding the power of the federal government and the sanctity of contract. Attempts by anti-Marshall Presidents to outnumber Chief Justice Marshall with their own appointments had failed to affect the decisions of the Court.

Jackson had had one serious run-in with

Marshall, over a subject to which the President was highly sensitive—Indian policy. The Cherokee Indians in Georgia had developed a modern farming society, with their own written language and their own elected government, based on an 1827 constitution in which the tribe declared itself an independent Cherokee Nation. Georgia officials, anxious to open Cherokee lands to white settlers, in turn declared state authority over the Indians and ordered the seizure of Cherokee land. White Georgians planned to ship the Cherokees across the Mississippi, as they had done earlier in the case of the Creeks, a course of action approved by Jackson. The Cherokee Nation brought suit, claiming that their treaty with the United States government allowed them to remain unhindered where they were. Marshall spoke for a majority of the Supreme Court in upholding the Cherokees in two cases—*Cherokee Nation v. Georgia* (1831) and *Worcester v. Georgia* (1832)—directing Georgia state officials to allow the Cherokees to continue running their own affairs and on their own territory. According to Marshall, Georgia's laws did not apply to the Cherokees and white settlers. Even state officials could not enter the Indians' lands without permission from the Cherokees. Georgia ignored the order and proceeded to seize Cherokee lands, while Jackson, for his part, did nothing to compel state obedience to federal law. "John Marshall has made his decision," he is reputed to have said; "now let him enforce it."

Several years after a small handful of renegade Cherokees signed an 1835 treaty ceding its Georgia lands in exchange for an Indian Territory (later Oklahoma) reservation and a $5 million settlement, Jackson sent an army led by General Winfield Scott to direct the removal of 16,000 Cherokees from Georgia. Unwilling to leave their homes, the Cherokees, along with remnants of other tribes, were forced, at rifle and bayonet point, on the arduous trek west during the winter of 1838. Bitter frosts, starvation, and disease took

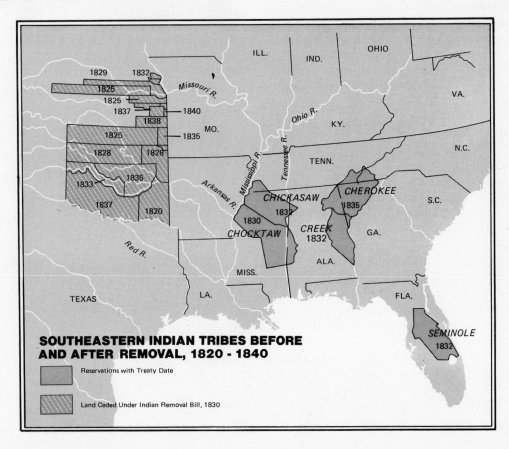

SOUTHEASTERN INDIAN TRIBES BEFORE AND AFTER REMOVAL, 1820 - 1840

Reservations with Treaty Date

Land Ceded Under Indian Removal Bill, 1830

the lives of several thousand Indians before they arrived in the dry wasteland of "Indian Territory." The march became known afterwards among American Indians as "the trail of tears." While Jackson's Indian policy led to the removal of most Cherokees, Creeks, Seminoles, Choctaws, and Chickasaws from the South, similar efforts in the new northwestern states had decimated – and expelled – tribes like the Fox and Sac Indians who stood in the way of white settlement in Illinois and Wisconsin. By the 1840s, most Indian tribes east of the Mississippi River had lost complete control of tribal lands and lapsed into the status of federal (or state) wards, where they had not been physically removed to desolate and unpopulated areas west of the Mississippi.

Several tribes resisted removal forcibly, the most notable instance being the Seminoles led by Chief Osceola in Florida. Pressured to leave for western "Indian Territory" in compliance with an 1833 treaty, the Seminoles revolted, supported by a number of runaway black slaves who had joined the tribe in preceding years. Fighting, for a time, a successful guerrilla-style war against federal troops sent by Jackson, the Seminoles and blacks held out in the Everglade jungles for several years before their eventual defeat (their leader, Osceola, had been seized deceptively under a flag of truce and shipped off to prison where he died). But whether through actual battle, as in the Seminole War, or through his contemptuous dismissal of Marshall's Supreme Court decisions, Jackson displayed a marked contempt for the rights of Indian Nations. But Jackson was not unique in this view. Rather, he held the attitude toward Indians – that they could not coexist with an expanding white settler civilization – that characterized most of his contemporaries and guided the actions of most nineteenth-century Presidents.

In 1835, Marshall died, just in time for Jackson to name his successor. Jackson chose Roger B. Taney, the secretary of the Treasury who had finally removed the deposits. He soon saw a difference in the court's rulings. In the *Charles River Bridge* case (1837), Taney ruled that a state charter, in this case for a bridge, did not constitute an unbreakable monopoly if a second bridge was required by traffic. Property rights were impor-

tant; but the public, too, had rights. The states must use their powers, ruled Taney, "to promote the happiness and prosperity of the community."

VAN BUREN'S UNHAPPY REIGN

Jackson had been a towering figure as President. But his stature appeared even greater in comparison with the President who preceded him and the one who followed him – both of whom had unfortunate administrations. John Quincy Adams, returning to national politics in the 1830s and 1840s as an antislavery congressman from Massachusetts, must have felt some satisfaction over the

Van Buren's shrewd manipulations gained him such nicknames as the "Little Magician" and the "Red Fox of Kinderhook" (his home in New York). But his wit and cheerful disposition won him many friends.

trials of Martin Van Buren, or the Little Magician, as he was called.

Martin Van Buren was Jackson's hand-picked choice for the Democratic nomination in the 1836 presidental election. The Whigs could not muster a single strong candidate, and Van Buren won easily over several regional candidates. But even during the campaign, it became clear that economic problems would soon loom large. No sooner had Van Buren been inaugurated in the spring of 1837 than he faced an economic panic, the worst the country had ever known. There were several causes. One was the Specie Circular, which had made much paper money worthless. Another was the fact that British banks raised interest rates and called in loans. In May 1837, New York banks suspended specie payments, that is, they refused to pay out hard cash in exchange for paper money. Other banks soon followed.

All parts of the American business system suffered in the Panic of 1837 and the depression that followed. The price of cotton, America's chief export item, tumbled. Land sales fell from 20 million to 3 1/2 million acres in a year. Merchants found that they could not sell their goods. When sales dropped, factory owners laid off workers. Debtors could not make payments and went bankrupt.

Van Buren responded to the panic by asking Congress to create an independent Treasury system. Like many other Democrats he had, by then, come to associate the economic crisis with banking itself, whether in the form of a national bank or the pet banks. Van Buren proposed that the United States should simply deposit its funds in "subtreasuries," owned and managed by the government itself. Thus public funds would be separated completely from the private banking structure. Despite three years of successful resistance by Whigs and conservative Democrats, Congress finally enacted the subtreasury plan in 1840. But it did not seriously affect the nation's economic growth, either favorably or otherwise.

The Locofocos Jacksonian Democrats had attacked the Second Bank of the United States as an undemocratic institution. These attacks went too far for Whig businessmen and politicians, who saw a threat to their economic and political freedom. But they did not go far enough for a small group of radical Democrats called Locofocos, who hated the bank in particular and the wealthy in general.

Most of the Locofocos were artisans, workers, and small businessmen in the urban East. Many had lost their jobs in the Panic of 1837, displaced by new manufacturing techniques that were part of the growing factory system. They had previously organized themselves into early trade union and local workingmen's parties, many of which achieved some success in winning reforms from state legislatures. Ardently supporting political and economic equality, they hoped to turn the Democratic party into an even more strongly anti-bank and proworkingman's party than it was under Jackson and Van Buren. Van Buren's own anti-bank policies had already led many Whigs to brand the entire Democratic party as Locofoco.

Specifically, the Locofocos wanted to prevent private banks from issuing too much paper money and engaging in speculation. Such activities, they felt, had led to the financial panics of 1819 and 1837. Many Jacksonians—workers, farmers, and middle-class Americans—were still reeling from the effects of the recent economic crisis. They hoped to restore a currency system based almost entirely on gold and silver. Some of them even wanted to eliminate paper money altogether.

A HIGH POINT FOR WHIGS

As Van Buren's first term drew to a close, the Whigs marshaled their forces to unseat the Democrats. They had the support of most wealthy Americans, and had recently received a new influx of Democrats who had swallowed Jackson's bank policy but could not endorse Van Buren's. The Whigs also held some appeal for voters among the middle class and working people. Some working people voted Whig out of fear and hatred of the (largely Democratic) immigrants. They found support in the South among the wealthiest planters, those who had heavy dealings with Eastern businessmen and thus identified with their financial interests. The Whigs also had a hard core of support in the West, among recent settlers from New England, the party's stronghold.

In addition, the Whigs attracted business interests concerned with economic and social expansion. Rejecting Jacksonian fears about panics and paper money, these Whigs argued that the country needed *more* economic development. They wanted more roads, canals, and railroads, and more credit for investors. Government, including the federal government, should play a more active role in spurring development for the benefit of all.

The Whigs smelled victory in the presidential election of 1840. Their factions seemed united at last. Besides, Van Buren, as the President in office, shouldered responsibility for the depression. He had warned that "all communities are apt to look for government for too much." This negative attitude toward federal power did not help in his search for votes.

Van Buren had other problems as the election approached. The "Little Magician" could not make the slavery issue disappear. Continuing his policy of trying to keep slavery out of national politics, he was losing votes on both sides. Many Southerners attacked him for refusing to annex Texas after American settlers there had set up an independent republic (see Chapter 20). Many Northerners regarded him as "soft" on slavery and attacked him for refusing to support abolition in the District of Columbia. People like Calhoun and Adams were beginning to destroy the North-South gentleman's agreement.

Taking advantage of the anti–Van Buren feeling, Whigs decided to mute their own differences. Party managers turned their backs on the Whigs' leading politicians and chose, instead, a candidate with a popular Jacksonian image. He was a military hero and a Westerner, General William Henry Harrison of Ohio.

When a Democratic editor unwisely tried to discredit Harrison as a man content to sit in front of a log cabin drinking hard cider, Whigs turned the slur into a boast. They decorated their floats with log cabins and dispensed hard cider at rallies. They rarely mentioned that Harrison was

A Harrison campaign poster features a trumpeting angel, and includes as well a cheering crowd and the inevitable log cabin and cider barrel.

born in a Virginia mansion belonging to his father, a signer of the Declaration of Independence. Campaigning for Harrison, Daniel Webster actually apologized: "Gentlemen, it did not happen to me to be born in a log cabin; but my elder brothers and sisters were born in a log cabin. Its remains still exist. I make to it an annual visit. I weep."

At the same time, Whigs depicted Van Buren, the son of a small-town tavern keeper, as an overdressed, would-be aristocrat. They said he lived in luxury, perhaps on dishonestly acquired money. The charges were nonsense, for Van Buren was too smart to be dishonest. Yet, the President's earlier reputation as Jackson's political wirepuller and party chieftain did him no good.

In 1840, the Whigs came of age as a popular party. The National Republicans had previously presented a faintly aristocratic image that was politically damaging. But the new Whig coalition of 1840, which now included hard-fighting political pros from both the Democratic and Anti-Masonic parties, changed all that. The party launched a typically Democratic campaign, with the issues drowned out by songs, rallies, and torchlight parades. One Democratic politician remarked bleakly, "We have taught them to beat us."

The Whigs had learned the lesson well and piled up a Whig landslide. Many states went Whig for the first (and last) time. A record number of Americans—almost 80 percent of those eligible to vote—participated in this national election.

The Whig party had finally arrived, but for how long? When Harrison took over in March 1841, it appeared that the Whigs would remain in power for many years, and that a real two-party system had been established. Even the Whig leaders bypassed as presidential candidates had cause for satisfaction. Daniel Webster became secretary of state. Clay intended to run the administration from the Senate, where he was the most influential Whig, especially since Harrison's inaugural address promised that Congress, not the White House, would lead the way in national affairs. Harrison regarded the veto—so often used by Jackson to browbeat Congress—as a last resort, to be used sparingly, if at all.

But Whiggery's triumph lasted exactly twenty-nine days. Harrison caught cold during his inaugural and died. John Tyler of Virginia became the first Vice President to succeed to the presidency. Tyler won a crucial point at the outset. He quickly rejected the suggestion that decisions be made by majority vote of the cabinet. This change — one that Harrison apparently had been considering favorably — would have permanently crippled presidential power. Though not elected to the presidency (his opponents called him His Accidency), Tyler made a vital contribution to maintaining the prestige and power of the office. He established the precedent that a Vice President would inherit the full power of the office, rejecting all attempts to call him "Acting President."

Tyler scored lower as a party leader and as a direct representative of the people. A states' rights Southerner, he had been put on the ticket to broaden its appeal. He now demonstrated the dangers of such a policy, infuriating Whig leaders (and damaging the party permanently) by his ve-

Tyler, photographed some ten years after he served as President, lived the life of a Virginia country gentleman after his term of office expired.

toes of legislation that would have carried out their program. Two national bank bills met with vetoes at Tyler's hands. All of the cabinet except Webster resigned, and the President was officially read out of the Whig party. For a while Tyler hoped he might be vindicated by winning the election of 1844. He tried to build his own organization by offering jobs to cooperative politicians. Except for fellow Virginians and a few hungry office seekers, however, Tyler did not win over many regular Whig party members.

Instead, Tyler devoted much of his "accidental" presidency to foreign affairs. Webster negotiated a treaty with Britain over the boundary between Canada and the northeastern United States. Tyler himself became obsessed with annexing Texas. He ignored warnings that such a move would shatter the fragile sectional truce on slavery. In 1844 he appointed the Democrat John C. Calhoun as secretary of state and ordered the negotiation of a Texas annexation treaty. The Senate rejected the treaty, partly because the South Carolinian had urged it as necessary for the defense of slavery. Calhoun's undiplomatic statement underlined what everyone knew. Slavery, by then, had replaced the Second Bank and related financial concerns as the single most important issue in American political life.

SUGGESTED READINGS – CHAPTERS 13-14

Andrew Jackson: The Road to the White House

James C. Curtis, *Andrew Jackson and the Search for Vindication* (1976); Marquis James, *Andrew Jackson: The Border Captain* (2 vols., 1977); Robert V. Remini, *Andrew Jackson and the Bank War* (1967) and *The Election of Andrew Jackson* (1963).

A Return to Party Politics

James S. Chase, *The Rise of the Presidential Nominating Convention* (1973); Robert G. Gunderson, *The Log-Cabin Campaign* (1957).

Jackson As President

Lee Benson, *The Concept of Jacksonian Democracy: New York As a Test Case* (1961); George Dangerfield, *The Awakening of American Nationalism, 1815–1828* (1965); William W. Freehling, *Prelude to Civil War: The Nullification Controversy in South Carolina, 1816–1836* (1966); Thomas P. Govan, *Nicholas Biddle* (1959); Bray Hammond, *Banks and Politics in America from the Revolution to the Civil War* (1957); Richard M. McCormick, *The Second American Party System* (1966); Marvin Myers, *The Jacksonian Persuasion* (1957); Sydney Nathans, *Daniel Webster and American Democracy* (1973); Edward Pessen, *Jacksonian America* (1969); Leonard L. Richards, *The Advent of American Democracy, 1815–1848* (1977); Arthur M. Schlesinger, Jr., *The Age of Jackson* (1945); Glyndon G. Van Deusen, *The Jacksonian Era* (1959); John W. Ward, *Andrew Jackson: Symbol for an Age* (1955); Leonard D. White, *Jacksonians: A Study in Administrative History, 1829–1861* (1954).

Jackson and The Supreme Court

Stanley I. Kutler, *Privilege and Creative Destruction: The Charles River Bridge Case* (1971); Michael Paul Rogin, *Fathers and Children: Andrew Jackson and the Subjugation of the American Indian* (1975); Malcolm Rohrbaugh, *The Land Office Business* (1968); Ronald N. Satz, *American Indian Policy in the Jacksonian Era* (1975).

15
THE MIDNIGHT CRY: THE MILLERITES AND THE SECOND COMING

A.W.

The brightest comet of the century hung in the night sky for a month. Its brilliance was visible even in daytime. Scientists would later calculate that the Great Comet's tail had stretched for 108 million miles, but Americans in the year 1843 knew only that they had never seen anything like it. Citizens of the young republic liked to think of themselves as practical and rational people, and of their nation as having left behind not only the tyranny of the Old World but also its superstitions. Even American self-confidence and patriotism, however, could not contain a spreading feeling of uneasiness when the heavens seemed aflame.

But one small group of Americans remained cool and confident. The big comet did not perplex or surprise them. They had studied their Bible lore carefully—even painstakingly—and, though not claiming to have foreseen this specific heavenly display, they did expect to witness many wonders before the year ended. And why not? A close reading of the Scriptures assured these Americans that Jesus Christ would return to earth during 1843, after which the heavens would roll together like a scroll as the final trumpet sounded.

When the Great Comet appeared in 1843, coincidental with Millerite predictions of the Second Coming, thousands of believers were alerted to Christ's impending reappearance on earth. With its huge, brilliant tail overshadowing a less visible head, the comet hovered in the sky for a month, only eighty million miles away from earth.

"Christ was coming—the Bridegroom Cometh." During the first half of the 1840s more than a hundred preachers of this biblical interpretation of "Adventism" crisscrossed the Northeastern United States, from the Canadian border down to Maryland, from Massachusetts to Ohio. Many thousands attended huge outdoor meetings at camp sites, or in large urban tabernacles, listening breathlessly to descriptions of the Last Judgment and the punishment of sinners, trying hard to understand the elaborate calculations of itinerant preachers that placed such events just a few months away. Between fifty and a hundred thousand Americans embraced the Adventist doctrine of Christ's Second Coming, additional thousands read illustrated pamphlets or Adventist newspapers, and as many as a million people may have been sufficiently influenced to feel either relief or regret in 1843 and 1844, when the heavens stayed put, "normal" time continued, and Christ declined to appear.

Believers in the doctrine kept themselves in a state of readiness, despite the scoffing of non-Adventist Americans. Many paid off their debts and some disposed of their worldly possessions to do so. Some of them, thinking that Christ would come before harvest time, neglected spring planting. They spent a good deal of time gathered together in prayer. They withstood the taunts and mockery of neighbors by trying to explain the deadly peril facing nonbelievers. "Here are thousands in this city of *brotherly love*," deplored one second advent lecturer from Philadelphia, "who do not so much as dream that they are on the brink of eternity, who will soon by the trumpet of God be awakened to the horrors of their situation."

The Second Coming, proclaimed the movement's founder, would occur between March 21, 1843, and March 21, 1844. And just as that fateful period began, the Great Comet suddenly flared across the southwestern sky.

"You are gazing along the sky—you see a lightning light along it— *it is the Lord!*" explained a pamphlet entitled *Letters to Everybody*. "You go to the door to meet a mother, a brother, or a friend—you meet the *Lord! . . .* Prepare to meet your God! Prepare to meet His day! Prepare to meet His judgment! Prepare! Prepare!"

Adventism in America began, like many offshoots of Christianity, with a devout person reading the Bible. On an autumn day in 1816, in the state of New York, a farmer in his mid-thirties named William Miller withdrew into his study with a copy of the Bible. He meant to read it, Miller later wrote, until he understood it thoroughly. To help him comprehend some of the biblical language, Miller had with him only a single popular guide to the Bible.

Miller lived in the town of Low Hampton in northeastern New York, near the Vermont border. During the early nineteenth century, waves of religious enthusiasm, often triggered by traveling preachers, periodically swept through the towns and cities of northern New England and upstate New York. Because of its receptivity to fire-and-brimstone evangelical preaching, central and western New York became known as "the burned-over district." The greatest revival preacher of the

Reverend Charles G. Finney, the most successful revivalist of the antebellum era, was less than pious as a youth. He spent his twenties working in a law office, until a religious conversion led him into theological studies.

era, Charles G. Finney, got his start "burning-over" west-central New York. And it was there that a young man named Joseph Smith saw visions, received *The Book of Mormon* from the angel Moroni, and founded the Church of Jesus Christ of the Latter-Day Saints. William Miller's town, Low Hampton, had also seen its share of fiery revivalism.

Still, William Miller seemed an unlikely candidate to be swept up in this emotional religious crusade. The son of a poor farmer, Miller was the only one of sixteen children to be interested in books—an interest that he pursued by drawing on the libraries of neighbors. In the home of Matthew Lyon, a radical Jeffersonian congressman, he had read the anticlerical writings of Voltaire and Tom Paine. Miller became a deist, a believer in God but not in organized religion. He also developed an interest in politics and became a town constable, or deputy sheriff. He seemed destined to become no more than a prominent citizen of Low Hampton, the village skeptic, and perhaps to serve a term or two in the state legislature.

But Miller, like many other men, had his life rearranged by a war. In 1814, as Captain Miller of the 30th Volunteer Infantry, he waited with fifteen hundred other Americans for an attack by a far larger force of British regulars at Plattsburgh, New York. Miller expected the American defenders to be brushed aside, leaving all New York open to a British drive. It might mean defeat in the struggle that many Americans considered a second war of independence.

The attack never came. Just offshore, on Lake Champlain, an outnumbered and outgunned American naval squadron defeated the British invasion fleet. A day-long artillery exchange followed, but, lacking naval support, the British army had to pack up and march back to Canada. The unexpected withdrawal stunned Miller, causing him to reexamine old beliefs. "It seemed to be that a Supreme Being must have watched over the interests of this country in a special manner, and delivered us from the hands of our enemies," he later said.

Returning to Low Hampton, Miller could neither resume his skeptical ways nor rid himself of them entirely. About a year after the war, he stood in the pulpit of the town's Baptist church (where he had become the reader) and experienced the vision that altered his life completely. "Suddenly," he recalled," the character of a Saviour was vividly impressed upon my mind. . . . I was constrained to admit that the Scriptures must be a revelation from God." A few days later, Miller launched on his long and exhaustive study of the Bible.

Within two years, Miller was satisfied he understood the Good Book, thereby joining the countless thousands of Americans of that era who underwent personal conversion experiences. But he had also decided on another far less widely held conclusion. After studying the Book of Daniel and the Book of Revelations closely, Miller had emerged certain that he knew when Christ would reappear on earth, when the Second Coming would take place.

The Book of Daniel purports to relate the divine visions of a Hebrew courtier in Babylon during the sixth century B.C.—visions expressed in highly allegorical and symbolic terms.[1] The second text, the Book of Revelations, is a Christain vision of the end of the world. Ostensibly written around 100 A.D. by St. John, it is even more cryptic and obscure than the work of Daniel. Long before William Miller, many students of the Bible, including the English scientist-philosopher, Isaac Newton, had striven to comprehend the hidden meanings of the two mysterious books.

William Miller, shown as severe and determined in this contemporary lithograph, used complex calculations based on scripture to point to 1843 as target date for the Second Coming.

"And from the time . . . that the detestable thing that causeth appalment is set up, there shall be a thousand two hundred and ninety days," read Miller in the small study of his wooden frame house. "Happy is he that waiteth, and cometh to the thousand three hundred and five and thirty days."

What did this mean? Days, Miller decided from other biblical references, should be interpreted as years; and as a devout nineteenth-century American Protestant, he recognized immediately "the detestable thing." It must be the Roman Catholic church, which remained anathema to American Protestants of almost all denominations—anti-Catholicism often extending from a dislike for the church's religious doctrines to overt hostility toward Irish and German Catholic immigrants in the 1840s. The Catholic church figured prominently in William Miller's calculus of the Second Coming, which moved back and forth through history along the following general line in an effort to understand the biblical prophecies of a Second Coming: French revolutionary troops had invaded Italy in 1798, captured Rome, and taken the Pope prisoner. Going back in time 1,290 years, Miller arrived at 508 A.D., when the Christianized Roman Empire had stopped offering daily sacrifices to the pagan god Jupiter. Miller's chart moved forward 1335 years from then, thereby arriving at the year 1843. "Unto two thousand three hundred evenings and mornings," Miller read in another passage from the Book of Daniel, "then shall the sanctuary be victorious." Dating this prophecy from 457 B.C., when the Jews had returned from their "captivity" in Babylon to rebuild their temple (which Miller believed had been the "sanctuary" mentioned in Daniel), Miller again arrived at 1843.

Cross-checking with Revelations, Miller found an account of "the great whore that sitteth upon many waters, with whom the kings of the earth had committed fornication." According to St. John, "the holy city shall they tread underfoot forty and two months. And I will give power unto my two witnesses, and they shall prophesy a thousand two hundred and three score days, clothed in sackcloth." Again going back from 1798, Miller reached 538 A.D., when Rome had begun to enforce the decree making Christianity the only legal religion. Adding to 1798 the forty-five years from Daniel, he again reached the year 1843. Miller performed other calculations, from less obvious predictions, and constantly arrived at 1843.

[1] Modern biblical scholarship has placed the book's authorship in the second century B.C., which may account for the accuracy of some of its predictions up to that date.

"I was thus brought," Miller explained, "in 1818, at the close of my two years study of the Scriptures, to the solemn conclusion, that in about twenty-five years from that time all the affairs of our present state would be wound up."

For the next five years, Miller kept silent, while he meticulously checked and rechecked the calculations. But when he began to explain his findings to friends and neighbors, he found to his astonishment that people did not accept them. He had anticipated a joyful eagerness to believe and a grateful expectancy over Christ's coming. Disappointed, Miller returned to tilling his fields and to ensuring that at least he and his family prepared adequately for the event.

One August morning in 1831, William Miller, still guarding his secret from strangers, came down to breakfast. Suddenly, he was to recall in later years, he heard a loud voice ordering him, "Go tell it to the world!" Miller was nearly fifty at the time, and not a picture of robust health. Old war wounds bothered him. Daily work on the farm, along with his nighttime labors on the calculations, had worn him down. For a time, Miller resisted obeying the voice and its message, but decided, finally, that if an opportunity to spread the word came, he would take it. To judge by his previous experience, Miller concluded, he risked nothing more than some harmless derision.

The same day that Miller made this decision, he received an invitation to speak to a neighboring Baptist congregation. Miller went and explained his second advent timetable. Surprisingly, both speaker and theory were warmly received. Miller began receiving more invitations. He was ordained a Baptist minister and was soon speaking throughout northeastern New York, western Vermont, and even nearby Canada.

Miller's preaching was based largely on his comprehensive knowledge of the Bible painstakingly acquired over the years. "Where your hearers are not well indoctrinated," he counseled minister friends, "you must preach *Bible;* you must exhort *Bible;* you must pray *Bible;* and love *Bible;* and do all in your power to make others love *Bible* too."

But Miller brought more than just scriptural learning to his mission. He quickly developed an acute sense of the dramatic. Speaking mainly in small rural churches to audiences who were barely literate but deeply religious, he communed easily with those who, like himself, spent six long days a week in hard, monotonous farm labor—people who had rarely been in a large-sized town, much less a city. His listeners would sit in stunned awe while the white-haired, ailing man, aflame with the glory of his idea, roared out over the wooden pews: "At this dread moment, look! The clouds have burst asunder; the heavens appear; the great white throne is in sight! Amazement fills the Universe with awe! He comes! He comes! Behold the Saviour comes! Lift up your heads, ye saints! He comes! He comes! He comes!"

Shortly after embarking on the crusade, Miller got some powerful aid in enlarging his circle of followers (now beginning to be called Millerites). In November 1833 much of the United States Northeast wit-

1843 MILLERITE CHART

nessed meteor showers of enormous proportions—a "rain of fire" that turned the night sky almost white. A Yale professor pronounced the phenomenon "probably the greatest display of celestial fireworks since the creation of the world." Less learned persons were even more impressed by the implications of the sight. "I called to my wife to behold," wrote a man who later became a Millerite leader, "and while robing she exclaimed, 'See how the stars fall!'—and we felt in our hearts that it was a sign of the last days."

In 1837, when dozens of converted preachers were already sounding the Millerite "midnight cry" in northern New England and upstate New York, Miller perceived a more earthly, less spectacular, but equally convincing sign of the impending spiritual crisis. The Panic of 1837 ushered in a serious *economic* crisis in the United States, a depression that was to last four years. In a county near Miller's home, by one report, "nearly half of our population [lack] bread. What grain there is cannot be had without money, and that is not to be had. Such things will be in the latter days."

During the second half of the 1830s, Miller delivered over eight hundred lectures to packed churches, often evoking from his listeners emotional repentance for past sins and demands for their immediate baptism. His church lectures, when published, quickly sold thousands of copies. Yet, at first sight, Miller was a singularly unimpressive figure. One church elder who had invited him to speak was alarmed to meet a "white-haired old man, shaking with the palsy" and dressed in an old cloak and beaver hat. But the frail visitor soon converted both the elder and a large part of his congregation. Miller's lectures made believers out of thousands. In 1839 he made his most important convert, a minister named Himes.

The Reverend Joshua V. Himes was twenty-three years younger than William Miller. Himes's father, a prosperous merchant, had wished to educate his gifted son for the ministry at Brown University, but financial reverses forced a major change in plans and Joshua became instead a cabinetmaker's apprentice. Woodworking proved dull, however, and the lure of a religious profession proved irresistible. Joshua Himes worked hard at his chosen vocation, first as a rural exhorter and itinerant preacher, until he managed to secure a post in a large urban Baptist congregation.

When Himes met Miller, the younger cleric was serving as minister of the Chardon Street Church in Boston. Himes's interests went beyond the formal bounds of religion and into social reform. He favored the abolition of slavery and maintained a friendly acquaintance with the radical abolitionist William Lloyd Garrison. He supported the prohibition movement and other reform crusades of the era.

Himes traveled up to New Hampshire with a group of ministers to listen to William Miller preach the imminent Second Coming. He was enraptured by Miller's prophecies and sought out the older man after his lecture. "What are you doing," Himes asked, "to spread or diffuse this doctrine throughout the world?" Miller explained apologetically that he was an old man; he did what little he could, went where he was invited to speak, and answered letters of inquiry. "I then told him," said the convert, "that he might prepare for the campaign, for doors should be opened in every city in the Union, and the warning should go to the ends of the earth!"

As his first energizing step, Himes brought Miller to Boston. It was the older preacher's first appearance in a major city. Himes had provided a widespread advertising campaign for Miller's full week of lecture-sermons at Chardon Street. "I am now in this place," Miller wrote his son, "lecturing, twice a day, to large audiences. Many, very many, go away unable to gain admittance. . . . I hope God will work in this city." Thanks to Himes, Millerism had become an *urban* crusade as well.

Miller soon expanded his mission. He spoke in many parts of Massachusetts and Connecticut. In Maine, he enjoyed great success during two weeks at Portland. A local editor described him, now almost sixty, as "self-possessed and ready, distinct in his utterance, and frequently quaint in his expressions." In May 1840 it was New York City's turn to hear Miller for the first time.

Innovative techniques, most of them the work of Himes, accompanied the movement's geographical expansion. Himes began the first Millerite newspaper, the Boston *Signs of the Times.* He acquired the publishing rights to Miller's lectures and sold or distributed many thousands of copies. He organized, in October 1840, a convocation of Millerite leaders and ministers.

But Miller himself was unable to attend the meeting. The aging man had pushed his limited strength to the breaking point and now lay stricken with typhoid fever. As he tossed fretfully on his bed in Low Hampton, Miller, ever given to calculating, figured that in the past year he had traveled 4,500 miles and delivered 627 lectures. But so much remained to be done. "Why was I deprived of meeting those congenial minds in this good, this glorious cause of light and truth?" he cried out in a letter. "Here I am, a weak, feeble, toil-worn old man, upon a bed of sickness, with feeble nerves and, worse than all, a heart, I fear, in part unreconciled to God. But bless the Lord; O my soul!"

Throughout 1841 and 1842, under the active guidance of Joshua Himes, Millerism continued to gain strength in the Northeast. To proclaim further the Adventist promise and warning, additional newspapers appeared: in New York the *Midnight Cry,* in Philadelphia the *Alarm.* Joshua Litch, a Methodist minister, left his own denomination to preach Millerism in Philadelphia. Charles Fitch abandoned a Boston pulpit to go out to Ohio. He found a receptive audience among the Western farmers, many of them having already heard of Millerism from recent New England settlers. Fitch helped establish Millerite newspapers in Cincinnati and Cleveland. The enterprising Himes even put batches of Millerite literature on ships leaving Boston for Europe, for South America, for Asia. Inquiries from overseas slowly filtered into Boston and Low Hampton.

The center of the movement, however, remained in New England

and upstate New York, where Himes employed the old and tested practice of the Baptists and Methodists—the camp meeting. Several Millerite preachers, together with local assistants and volunteers, would move into an open area and set up tents. Then they would erect wooden platforms upon which to display the giant charts and illustrations of Miller's arguments. Such camp meetings lasted one or even two weeks, all day and into the night, with preachers steadily expounding William Miller's complex but compelling interpretations of Revelations and Daniel, usually under a huge tent seating thousands. Bed and board were available for $2 a week. Beginning in 1842, Millerites from Maine to Lake Erie held close to 125 such camp meetings.

The Boston poet and author, John Greenleaf Whittier, overcome with curiosity (and perhaps even a touch of anxiety), traveled to a great Millerite camp meeting in nearby New Hampshire. "Drawn about in a circle, forming a background of snowy whiteness to the dark masses of men and foliage, were the white tents, and back of them the provision-stalls and cook-shops," reported Whittier. "The preachers were placed in a rude pulpit of rough boards, carpeted only by dead forest leaves and flowers, and tasseled, not with silk and velvet, but with the green boughs of the somber hemlocks around it."

Yet it was the people, not the camp's design, that impressed the poet most. "Here," marveled Whittier,

> were sober, intelligent men, gentle and pious women, who verily believing the end to be close at hand, had left their counting-rooms, and workshops, and household cares to publish the great news, and to startle, if possible, a careless and unbelieving generation into preparation for the day of the Lord.

THE MILLERITES MOVEMENT, 1843–1848*

*Larger dots indicate greater intensity.

But Whittier did not stay a week, nor did he become a convert. "I find it extremely difficult to comprehend how it is that this goodly, green sunlit home of ours is resting under a curse."

At such meetings, Miller (restored to good health), Himes, and the rest of a growing corps of Millerite preachers would dwell on the positive glories of the Lord's coming and explain carefully and rationally the biblical prophecies that foretold the imminent arrival of Jesus. But some of the Millerites used different, more standard, evangelical approaches. One, according to a not-too-friendly observer:

> excels in terrific descriptions of hell and torture. He opens the abyss, and his graphic language points the mind's eye to material torments and their infliction by the Devil, who, with his horn, hoof, and tail, rises to their terrified view.

This sort of hellfire and damnation preaching, though it bore little relation to Miller's own method, aided in convincing many who would never otherwise have understood the significance of his complex arithmetical calculations of the Second Coming.

Joshua Himes's brilliance at organizing and publicizing the Millerite movement brought great success, but it also provoked criticism that often became abusive. Orthodox clergymen and most of the press reacted to the growth of this strange movement with alarm. They ridiculed its beliefs and impugned its leaders' good faith. "If the Almighty intended to give due notice of the world's destruction," commented a New York paper, "He would not do it by sending a fat, illiterate old fellow to preach bad grammar and worse sense." And John G. Whittier, despite some sympathy, had come away from that camp meeting feeling that Millerism was "acting upon a class of uncultivated and, in some cases, gross minds."

Scoffers and detractors far outnumbered the movement's adherents in the country. These critics charged that Millerism was causing suicides and insanity throughout New England and the Middle Atlantic states. Such charges hurt Miller's cause the most. Some people felt that belief in Miller's theory was cause enough for commitment to an insane asylum. Wild reports circulated: Millerites were allegedly wearing "ascension robes" for their rise to heaven, supposedly climbing to the tops of trees to be closer to the celestial sphere, and jumping off in the hope of being in midair when the Lord arrived. Not surprisingly, the ordinary American's equation of Millerite Adventism with lunacy led to burlesque criticism. One paper mocked Miller's calculations with this fable: "We saw a dog with his tail curled up to form the figure 3, and inasmuch as he was going on 4 legs, making 43, and looked to be 18 years old . . . the wonderful coincidence in the matter [produced] the prophetic period of 1843." A Massachusetts editor contributed *his* little joke: "Married folks with small families must make the best Millerites, as they are most seriously disturbed by the 'Midnight Cry'."

Many people charged that Miller himself did not believe his predictions, but profited financially from the movement. "Miller makes plenty of (sic) $ by his speculations on the future," the Westfield (Massachusetts) *News Letter* assured its readers. "Of all millers, we know of no miller who brings more grist to his mill than Miller the prophet." In 1842, the Philadelphia *Ledger* proclaimed that Miller's hypocrisy had been exposed beyond all denial: he had refused an offer of $2,000 for his farm, even though the prospective buyer was willing to delay taking possession until after 1843. The *Ledger's* editor seems not to have wondered what a man who expected the world to end momentarily would want with $2,000.

Even those nonbelievers who conceded Miller's sincerity zeroed in on Himes, the organizer-promoter, denouncing him as a hypocrite and a thief. "We can hardly conceive of a character more completely lost to every obligation of virtue and honesty, to say nothing of religion [than Joshua Himes]," fulminated one Boston paper. When Himes opened an 8,000-seat tabernacle in Boston in May 1843, local newspapers reported—falsely—that he had taken out fire insurance for seven years, though claiming to expect the Second Coming any day.

Himes was also having problems within his own church at the time. Miller had never tried to exercise control over those preaching his

The fervor of the Millerites, as they prepared for the Second Coming, aroused ridicule and hostility, as shown in this cartoon of a smug and maniacal Miller (well-provisioned for the world's end).

doctrines, and some had added refinements. John Starkweather, for example, an assistant preacher at Himes's Chardon Street Church, decided that true participation in God's work involved physical as well as mental commitment. When Himes, returning from an organizing trip, found most of his congregation shaking their bodies or rolling on the floor, he reacted strongly. Accused by a Starkweather supporter of throwing cold water on the joyous enthusiasm, Himes retorted, "I would throw on the Atlantic Ocean before I would be identified with such abominations as these."

Besides press hostility, Millerites faced more direct and severe problems. Rowdies sometimes broke up their meetings, shouting insults, throwing rotten eggs and vegetables, and provoking fights. When Miller visited Philadelphia in February 1843, he attracted large crowds day after day. But when ruffians joined the crowds and started a riot, the visit was cut short by three days. Shortly after the prophet's departure, a theater in the city began staging a farce called *Miller, Or the End of the World*. The object of all this scorn knew perfectly well where the criticism originated. The inhospitable Philadelphians were "engaged in the work of their master, the devil."

But none of this could matter much, with the day of the Lord so close at hand. As Miller proclaimed on January 1, 1843:

> This year—O blessed year!—the captive will be released, the prison door will be opened, death will have no more dominion over us, and life, eternal life, will be our everlasting reward.

Millerites were ready.

Even as they rejoiced and reflected upon the life to come, Millerites were determined to use what time remained to alert the rest of the world to its state of danger. The *Voice of Truth and Glad Tidings of the Kingdom at Hand*, a Millerite paper in western New York, instructed the faithful: "Dispose of *all* you have which you do not actually need for the present wants of yourself and family, and for the prosecution of your lawful business, to aid in sending out the truth to the perishing."

Such fervor could be found throughout the movement, and no one felt the responsibility it created more keenly than William Miller. His flock had grown large. Tending it proved a continuous strain on his mind and body. In the spring of 1843 he lay ill once more in Low Hampton. A few months earlier, he had admitted to Himes, "I find that as I grow old, I grow more peevish and cannot bear so much contradiction. Therefore I am called uncharitable and severe. No matter, this frail life will soon be over." But until then, Miller would work.

The movement faced a major problem in the growing desire among the faithful to set a precise date in order to anticipate the Coming. Early in April 1843, a rumor spread that the 23rd of that month was *the* day. The Millerite leaders never endorsed the idea, but nevertheless it caught on, particularly in Philadelphia, where believers left their labors and gathered that day at their tabernacle. On the 24th the unbelieving *Ledger,* ever caustic, crowed: "Some of our readers may doubtless experience a little surprise at waking up this morning and finding themselves alive and kicking, instead of being as crisp and as shrivelled as an old boot or a burnt cornfield."

Undaunted, though surely disappointed, Millerites continued as before. In June, they set up a giant tent in Rochester, New York. As with previous camp meetings, local exhorters had prepared the ground with preachments and pamphlets. "Our anticipated convention may, after all be held on the '*new* earth'," one organizer had written to Miller. "But we feel bound to work '*till* the trumpet of Gabriel shall summon us away."

Thousands streamed into Rochester from the countryside to hear Himes, Fitch, and others. The convention ran for two weeks, with prayer meetings and Bible classes. Halfway through, the wind blew the great tent down. Millerites interpreted the fact that no one had been injured in the mishap as a good omen, and local merchants—perhaps recognizing the financial benefits of a tourist attraction—contributed $100 to help reraise the tent.

Many others, however, especially orthodox Protestant clergymen, displayed little Christian charity. The attempt "to fix the day or the year of our Lord's coming [is] full of presumption and peril," declared one Vermont cleric. Many ministers of varied denominations agreed. Adventists began to talk of leaving their old churches, and setting up their own. "If you are a Christian, come out of Babylon [out of captivity and sin]," demanded Fitch. "If you intend to be found a Christian when Christ appears, *come out of Babylon,* and come out now."

As 1843 turned into 1844, and the days of the "given" year began to run out, anticipation and excitement again rose to a peak. On March 21 the Adventists gathered at their meeting places once more to await the Lord. "The time, as I have calculated it, is now filled up," confided Miller, "and I expect every moment to see the Saviour descend from Heaven." Within a few weeks the founder had to "confess my error, and acknowledge my disappointment"; but neither Miller nor his followers abandoned their conviction of an imminent coming.

Incredibly, the disappointment of early spring 1844 only intensified the Millerites' commitment. Convinced that they had erred by mere days or weeks or months, they redoubled their preaching and printing. Throughout 1844, while most Americans concerned themselves with a hard-fought presidential campaign, Millerites worked toward a more significant, cosmic victory. One Western paper quoted an Indiana Millerite as predicting that "none of you will see either Clay or Polk elected. Christ will be our next President, and will rule over us all." (A Hoosier skeptic was willing to bet, however, that "He won't carry Indiana, no how.")

Miller taxed his failing strength in a final effort to rally supporters. In August he went out to Ohio with Himes. Miller spoke to enormous crowds in Cincinnati and in Cleveland—where the tabernacle had been built with a glass skylight, expected to roll back on Judgment Day. The

Cleveland *Plain Dealer* reported that Miller was "a very honest appearing gentleman for one who has deceived so many, and none worse than himself."

Although still confident that the advent of Christ was at hand, Millerites understandably renewed their inquiries regarding the timing. One Bostonian, Samuel S. Snow, thought he knew. The logical time, he argued, would be the tenth day of the seventh month of the Jewish year, the day of atonement and purification. That would be October 22, 1844. This belief spread quickly through Millerite circles, and in early October, Miller himself accepted it. "If Christ does not come within twenty or twenty-five days," he wrote on October 6, "I shall feel twice the disappointment I did in the spring."

The leader had allowed himself to be led. Miller now reflected the beliefs of his followers, whose sense of urgency for the Second Coming was intense. Once again, Millerites paid their debts, and loaned money to indebted fellow believers. They swarmed in from the Massachusetts countryside and slept in the Boston tabernacle. The councilmen of Meredith, New Hampshire, ordered Millerites to work, or be "taken care of as idlers and spendthrifts are"—in other words, arrested as vagrants. In Baltimore, a woman took her Millerite husband to court, demanding that he be made to work. A Philadelphia shoemaker hung out a sign, "This shop is closed in honor of the King of Kings, who will appear about the 23rd of October. Get ready, friends, to crown him Lord of all."

Millerite leaders braced for the event. Joshua Himes journeyed to Miller's village, Low Hampton, to be with his spiritual teacher at the end. Litch wrote of his "joyful expectation of seeing the King of Kings within ten days." The October 12 issue of the *Midnight Cry* editorialized serenely, "We believe this to be our LAST paper," and it found a further good omen in an earthquake near Rome. The editor's farewell commended his readers to God's grace.

> Philadelphia
> October 24, 1844
>
> Dear Bro. Miller, and Himes if with you.
>
> It is a cloudy and dark day—the sheep are scattered—and the Lord has not come yet. Dr. Gorgas, in spite of all I could do, led off about one hundred and fifty to flee from the city on Monday morning. Most have returned. . . . But the brethren here are firm as a rock—they hope to see the Lord yet before the feast of Tabernacles ends. I hope so too. Be of good courage, Brother Miller. In a little while he that shall come, will come and will not tarry. All our public meetings have ceased and we feel as though there was silence in heaven for half an hour. What we shall do if the Lord does not come I cannot tell.
>
> I want to hear from you very much. If Bro. Himes is with you I want him to write and let me know what he thinks of doing if time continues after a week from Sabbath. I think by that time, we will be able to gather again—but still I hope we shall be gathered by the great Trumpet.
>
> J. Litch

October 22 was the last precise date set by the second advent Millerites. The idea of expecting the Lord at a definite, arithmetically determined time was discredited by the failures of 1843–1844. Adventism did not die, however, and even during the shock of October 1844 (as one correspondent assured Miller) the Millerites "never loved each other so well as now in this hour of furnace trial." For the remainder of the nineteenth century, however, Adventist believers who discussed the Second Coming generally disclaimed any connection with Millerism or similar calculations of exact dates for Christ's appearance.

Understandably, the failure of the predicted October 1844 Second Coming hit the Millerites with greater force than their previous disappointments. "Our fondest hopes were blasted, and such a spirit of weeping came over us as I never experienced before," remembered Hiram Edson. "It seemed that the loss of all earthly friends could have been no comparison. We wept and wept. . . . Has the Bible proved a failure? Is there no God, no heaven, no golden home city, no paradise?"

Troubled as he was, Edson did not surrender to despair but helped salvage something from the disaster. In the midst of his anguish, Edson had a vision, seeing Christ enter an inner sanctuary within heaven in the skies. The Millerites, decided Edson, had been right about the date, but they wrongly interpreted its significance. Christ was not scheduled to *appear* on that day but to begin *preparations* for the Second Coming, which could now be expected at any time. Edson's vision became the basis of a *new* religious movement, the Seventh-Day Adventists, which soon numbered a half million adherents in the United States and several million in other countries.

But William Miller did not live to see the Adventist movement and spirit continued in this manner by Edson and others. Miller died in 1849, five years after he had led his followers in the final preparations for the Second Coming—which never occurred. Not only did this failure discredit Miller with many of his former supporters, but—although an ordained minister—he was excommunicated from his local Baptist church. Yet Miller's spirit never broke and, as he lay dying, Joshua Himes appeared in Low Hampton one final time to be at his side. As Miller and Himes, the prophet and his spokesman, prayed together in Low Hampton, they still expected Christ's appearance at any moment.

16
RELIGION AND REFORM IN ANTEBELLUM AMERICA

A. W.

Most Americans considered the Millerites deluded, not merely mistaken. Yet Adventism, the belief that God's perfection was close at hand, was not nearly so foreign to the experience of ordinary Americans in that era as those who taunted William Miller and his followers seemed to believe. Miller, it should be remembered, was an ordained Baptist minister and did most of his preaching in "regular" denominational churches. His interpretation may have been unique, but he used as text the Bible, the book that the great majority of Americans still professed to consult as their most important moral guide. During the first half of the nineteenth century, Americans paid more serious attention to religion than at any other time in their history except, possibly, in seventeenth-century Puritan New England. Between the Revolution and the Civil War, while American nationality was shaped and institutionalized, Americans (which at the time meant primarily Protestants) grappled with problems of God and country. For many, those problems were inseparable.

As the eighteenth century ended, American religiosity seemed on the wane. Many of the nation's leaders (Jefferson and Franklin, among others), had embraced the religion of Reason.

Deism represented an attempt to bypass orthodox forms of religion. It substituted, instead, belief in an imprecise God who had created a very precise universe. To orthodox Christians—whether Congregationalists in New England, or Episcopalians in the South—deism meant little more than atheism sugar-coated with spirituality. During the election of 1800, Jefferson's religion (or lack of it) became a campaign issue, though not enough of a negative factor to cost him the presidency.

THE SECOND GREAT AWAKENING

Americans in that era were experiencing a remarkable and wide-ranging religious experience called the Great Revival (or the Second Great Awakening). Beginning in the late 1790s, a wave of religious enthusiasm swept most of the country. Revival meetings, especially those in the frontier states west of the Appalachian Mountains, converted thousands and attracted much attention. In the West, as open a society as then existed in the United States, older, more established religious customs and doctrines gave way to an exuberant religiosity. Preachers stressed a gospel of salvation, and thousands responded with conversions and commitments that, although sometimes short-lived, were nonetheless sincere.

The Great Revival fundamentally altered American Protestantism. Whereas, sixty years earlier (during the First Great Awakening) itinerant preachers in countryside and city had been able to rekindle some of the fire of Calvinism (with its doctrine of election and predestination), by the time of the Great Revival, American Calvinists (found mainly in the Congregationalist and Presbyterian churches by this time) saw doctrinal purity replaced for many of their number by the happier promise of eternal life. Denominations such as the Baptists and Methodists offered salvation. No longer need one live with the terrible uncertainties of Calvinist damnation hanging over one's head. A positive commitment to God could bring, if not the certainty, then at least the probability of salvation. Men and women could become active instruments of their own salvation. Works, not

This decorous Methodist Camp Meeting under the trees, with parasoled ladies and frock-coated gentlemen, reflects the sect's high-toned aspirations rather than the usual ambiance of revivalist gatherings in the antebellum era. The "getting" of religion, exhortations, and mass conversions that typified evangelical crusades often involved a great deal more emotion and commotion than is evident above. The great revivals of the early nineteenth century decreased the influence of the conservative clergy but increased the number of conversions and the membership of newer sects.

faith alone, counted for something in the great scoreboard in the sky.

Even more startling, preachers began telling Americans that God *wanted* them to be saved, that God meant love. Hellfire and damnation preaching did not become outdated, as evidenced by the conduct of some Millerite preachers who warned of terrible things in store for those resisting God's message. But, though hell still existed and eternal damnation still threatened, believers also knew that God was in heaven, gladly awaiting the arrival of the saints.

Unitarianism The replacement of the Puritan God of wrath by a gentler God of love also helped create several new sects. Though hardly a mass movement, Unitarianism was one of the most important. It began late in the 1700s, in Boston and in outlying Congregationalist churches, and won many followers among well-educated middle-class New Englanders early in the nineteenth century. In 1803 a Unitarian gained appointment to the professorship of divinity at Harvard College. The struggle for the post clearly revealed the split between religious reformers and the more orthodox Calvinists in New England. Unitarianism included several beliefs that more orthodox Protestants could not accept. First, as their name indicates, Unitarians rejected the Trinity, believing Jesus to be a great religious teacher but not the son of God. Unitarians denied original sin, insisting on mankind's innate goodness and stressing the human capacity for moral improvement. Their most prominent leader, William Ellery Channing of Boston, preached the Unitarian message with a clarity and benevolence that made him a national figure. He was also involved in a variety of reform activities, as were many of the leading Unitarian preachers.

Transcendentalism The best known of these preachers, Ralph Waldo Emerson, went beyond Unitarianism to expound a transcendental philosophy that made him *the* popular philosopher of nineteenth-century America. Unitarians fostered a belief in the potentially divine character of human life. Beginning with this conviction, Emerson and a number of intellectuals in the Boston area developed the philosophy called transcendentalism, forming a Transcendental Club that remained small in numbers but culturally influential. During the early 1840s—the years that Miller's calculations had indicated would be the last—Emerson, Margaret Fuller, Henry David Thoreau, and other transcendentalists published a journal of literature and the arts, The *Dial*, that offered an effective sounding board for these religious and philosophical rebels.

Transcendentalists believed in mankind's natural goodness and perfectability, and in the active presence of a divine spirit within each human being. God lived within each individual. This meant that everyone remained open to direct moral guidance. In effect, each person became his or her own church. There was no need for actual churches or ministers to mediate in the search for God. "Why should not we enjoy an original relation to the universe?" Emerson wrote in his book, *Nature*, published in 1836. "There are new lands, new men, new thoughts. Let us demand our own works and laws and worship." According to transcendentalist doctrines, each person possessed an "oversoul," an inner soul or spirit, which, when correctly instructed by divine insight, would point the way to perfection and salvation.

Yet, Unitarianism was too geographically restricted and transcendentalism too highbrow to affect the lives of most Americans. Emerson became a successful lecturer and a nationally known personality, but probably no more than a handful of his listeners understood his explanations of the oversoul. What many more Americans responded to was what today would be labeled "old-time religion"—a blend of evangelical fervor and strenuous piety, of joyous commitment combined with intolerance toward sin and sinners.

Revivalism Nowhere did these religious currents converge with such spectacular results as in New York State's "burned-over district." There, in central and western New York, evangelical American Protestantism flowered as never before. Starting in the early years of the nineteenth century, when the region was still sparsely settled, revivalism steadily gathered strength. By the 1830s it had peaked in new cities of the area, such as Rochester and Buffalo. The religious ferment of the burned-over district involved a diluting, almost a breaking down, of older organizational forms. In "the district," Presbyterians and Congregationalists joined together in a short-lived merger, and the denominational label of a revivalist preacher counted for less than the force of his message (sometimes *her* message—since a few women were able to break through the sex barrier and do some of the preaching). A Baptist might exhort in a Presbyterian church, and vice versa. Although conservative clergymen were less than happy when the revivalists came to their areas, there was no way to contain the enthusiasm of their congregations.

New York's burned-over district produced the greatest revival preacher of his day, a man named Charles G. Finney. Like William Miller, Finney was originally a skeptic. He had decided to study law. But a pious fiancée and a gnawing belief that "lawyering" was not an *honest* profession turned him toward the ministry. He began preaching in the small towns of central and northern New York, riding circuit, just as lawyers did. Finney attracted larger and larger audiences and won many converts. Finney became pastor of the Second Free Presbyterian Church of New York City in 1832 and ran it successfully—gaining many converts—until he withdrew in 1836. The following year, he helped establish a theological

Ordained in 1824, Finney began an evangelical career in western New York and "awakened" new converts with unparalleled vigor for the rest of his life. Using the tactics of the itinerant revivalist, Finney preached a doctrine of salvation and reform that inspired a generation.

department at the antislavery college newly founded at Oberlin, Ohio, where he remained for more than three decades. His was not a fire-and-brimstone approach; it was a hopeful message, though not a simple-minded one. Finney, like many other clerics of his day, tried to retain the pious intensity of Calvinism while discarding some of its more rigid theological doctrines. The attempt was doomed, but the effort shaped the contours of much of modern American Protestantism.

Finney, along with many other evangelical ministers of the nineteenth century, stressed the importance, for churches and their members, of good works and constant involvement in practical morality. Finney himself, like the more decorous Bostonian, Reverend Channing, ended his days as a strong antislavery reformer. One of Finney's many converts, Theodore Weld, became a leading abolitionist.

Mormonism Charles Finney was thoroughly conventional when compared with William Miller or with Joseph Smith, founder of the Mormon church—another product of the burned-over district. Young Smith, born in 1805, unlike William Miller, had no taste for farming. He became instead a part-time gold digger, one who could supposedly divine the location of buried gold. Soon, Smith struck it rich beyond his wildest dream. An angel appeared to reveal the location of a book written on gold pages and in a strange script. In the late 1820s Smith, the only person who could read the book (he used magic spectacles), translated the text, while fellow believers transcribed what he dictated.

The result, the Book of Mormon, is today the sacred text for the Church of Jesus Christ of the Latter-Day Saints, founded in 1830 in Seneca County, New York. Mormons, like the Millerites, had to withstand the scorn of unbelievers; but in the case of Smith and his followers, opposition was much more extreme. The Mormons left New York in 1831 and, like many thousands of others, went west, first to Ohio, then to Missouri, and, in 1839, establishing the Mormon town of Nauvoo in Illinois. But there would be no peace even there. With economic rivalry as an underlying cause, and opposition to Smith's next major revelation (polygamy) as the stated objection, an Illinois mob set upon and murdered Smith in 1844. The Mormons, now led by Brigham Young, then pushed still further westward and settled in Utah near the Great Salt Lake.

Anti-Catholic Nativism Mormons were not the only religious minority to fall victim to violence at the hands of rejuvenated, militant Protestant America. Although the United States legally proclaimed religious freedom, and although church and state had been separated, toleration did not imply acceptance. At times, even toleration was lacking. The status of Catholics had always been uneasy in America, since colonial times. As more and more Catholic immigrants arrived in the early nineteenth century, Protestants (who, often as not, fought the good fight against one another) could unite temporarily in opposition to Catholics. The

Increasing hostility in New York State drove the Mormons west to Missouri and Ohio, where local opposition was expressed by the tarring and feathering of Prophet Joseph Smith. The next Mormon settlement, at Nauvoo, Illinois, was more successful, but there, too, the Saints soon aroused opposition. After Smith was murdered, the majority of Mormons decided to follow Brigham Young further west to a New Zion near the Great Salt Lake in Utah.

idea of a vast Papist conspiracy against Protestant America, which had strong roots in colonial era anti-Catholicism, began to spread. During the 1830s, small but insistent "nativist" movements sprang up in Eastern cities. The groups denounced Catholicism as un-American, criticized unrestricted immigration from Catholic countries, and were particularly angry over the ease with which immigrant Americans could gain the vote. Samuel F. B. Morse, better known as the inventor of the telegraph than as a nativist, led one such group in New York City.

For the most part, anti-Catholicism during the 1830s kept within nonviolent bounds, with one notable exception: In 1834, the good citizens of the Boston area burned down a Catholic convent in Charlestown. No lives were lost, but the crowd's murderous fury demonstrated yet again that religious passion can often overcome religious principles. And the Charlestown outrage pointed ahead to the much stronger nativism that would visit America in the 1850s, following the massive Irish and German Catholic immigration of 1847–1856. A relatively minor Catholic population in the U.S. of slightly over 300,000 in 1830 had grown to more than 3 million by 1860, most of the newcomers impoverished and uneducated Irish and Germans who settled in the cities.

Conflicts between the largely working-class Catholic population of the urban North during the 1830–1860 period and the Protestant native-born majority focused often on the question of public school education. In state after state, Protestant nativists fought successfully to deny public funding to Catholic denominational schools. These victories had the effect of leaving the public schools nominally nonsectarian but, in fact, strongly Protestant (often evangelical) in moral orientation in such practices, for example, as regular study of and readings from the King James Bible. Catholics proved less successful in gaining a share of tax revenues for schools in which their doctrines would be taught with public funds. Instead, a number of states during the 1840s embarked on a program of developing a privately-financed system of parochial school education (based on tuition payments and the contributions of the faithful). This program would provide religious training along with secular teaching—but within schools run by the Catholic church, so that American-born Catholic youths could be shielded in their formative years from the educational influences of the predominately Protestant culture.

SOCIAL CRUSADES OF ANTEBELLUM AMERICA

Background and Motivation of Reformers What led people to try to change so many of their society's customs and institutions? One important fac-

tor was the widespread belief in progress. Many Americans during the antebellum decades came to feel that progress was apparent in all areas of national life. They believed that rapid economic growth could be matched by steady improvement in society and values.

The belief in a divine mission for America had been understood in religious terms by seventeenth-century Puritans. Eighteenth-century American leaders had thought of it largely in political terms. Now it was seen in social terms by nineteenth-century antebellum reformers. They wanted to liberate Americans by correcting personal defects and eliminating social wrongs. They aimed at achieving *worldly* perfection within the nation itself (not the celestial perfection of the Millerites' Judgment Day)—and in their own lifetimes. Most reformers believed that, in the struggle to perfect American life, they would achieve their own moral perfection as well.

This dream was certainly not confined to the United States at this time. American reformers borrowed ideas from (and corresponded regularly with) their counterparts in Europe. For example, American abolitionists learned much from the British movement to abolish slavery. Many American reformers, especially the Utopians, were influenced by French socialist-communitarian thinkers. Generally, though, the American reformers resembled religious crusaders more than their European counterparts did. American reform was closely connected to the evangelical Protestant movements of the day. Nevertheless, although religion and reform were indeed linked, antebellum reform had a distinctly *this*-worldly tone, an almost secular concentration on the alteration of existing human institutions or the creation of new ones.

Many Americans lent part-time support to one or another reform activity; but a small number of people devoted their entire lives to the task of achieving social perfection. The dedicated reformer emerged during the 1830s and 1840s as a distinct social type in the United States. Men and women pursued reform as a vocation, especially in New England (no longer Puritan but still puritanical) and to a lesser extent in the Middle Atlantic and Middle Western states. The novelist Nathan-

RALPH WALDO EMERSON

In the history of American writing, the Jacksonian period was a very special moment. In the life span of a single generation, a dazzling new literature burst suddenly into view. The novels of James Fenimore Cooper, Nathaniel Hawthorne, and Herman Melville constituted as fine a body of fiction as was being produced in any nation in the world. Henry David Thoreau's *Walden* and Walt Whitman's *Leaves of Grass* took their places among the most imposing works of art in the English language. Indeed, what Noah Webster and other intellectuals had yearned for so much at the beginning of the century—a new, authentic, and distinctive American culture—was, by mid-century, a flourishing reality.

At the center of this exciting phenomenon stood a quiet, even shy, former Unitarian minister, Ralph Waldo Emerson. He was not as popular a writer as was Cooper. He produced no work of art as lastingly important as the *Leaves of Grass*. But Emerson had a very special kind of significance. In his lectures, his essays, and his poems, he brought together all the principal themes and questions that preoccupied the major intellectuals of the period. And because of this, some of his essays became a Bible of sorts for young Americans who decided to pursue careers as writers, poets, reformers, or philosophers. Emerson's life—first as a Boston minister, then as a freelance writer and lecturer living in Concord—was extremely quiet. But he carried on an intense internal struggle—a struggle of ideas and symbols. And out of this struggle, and out of the famous *Journals* where he recorded it, came radical positions on the primary issues of the century—radical positions that soon became a new orthodoxy among writers and artists.

Emerson's radicalism, which he announced in controversial lectures and essays in the 1830s and 1840s, was primarily a radicalism of celebration. He celebrated "Nature" as against "civilization." He was the philosopher and the poet of the "self-reliant" individual. And against the legitimate needs of such an individual, Emerson counted the requirements of society very little. He praised instinct, intuition, experiment, and freedom. He condemned dry logic, routine, and law. He wrote excitedly about whatever was new and young, and he talked constantly of escape from the "sepulchres of the fathers" and the "dry bones of the past." And these commitments led directly and obviously to a celebration of what was "American," and to the repudiation of much of what was "European."

From all this, Emerson's readers could draw a clear and somewhat radical picture of an ideal "American scholar"—as Emerson called the writer. He should plant himself firmly on his own private instincts. He should have no reverence for established customs, and no patience with law. He should be young, and if he could not be young, he should side with the young in almost everything. He should ruthlessly question every rule and institution to see whether they were in tune with "Nature." He should be innovative and daring, always ready to risk public criticism and rejection. And the scholar should do all these things in an acute and continuing consciousness of his identity as an American.

As Emerson put it in his most popular lecture, "Trust thyself: every heart vibrates to that iron string. Whoso would be a man, must be a non-conformist. A foolish consistency is the hobgoblin of little minds, adored by little statesmen and philosophers and divines."

iel Hawthorne was once such a reformer. He wrote:

> We were of all creeds and opinions, and generally tolerant of all, on every imaginable subject. Our bond, it seems to me, was not affirmative, but negative. We had individually found one thing or another to quarrel with in our past life, and were pretty well agreed on the futility of lumbering along with the old system any further. As for what should be substituted, there was much less agreement.

Hawthorne raised a question that many have asked about American reformers: Why did some people try to change society while most of their countrymen remained content to tolerate existing conditions? What were the reformers' motives? The answers have been as varied as the reform activities themselves. Unfriendly observers and skeptical historians have identified antebellum reform with the personal frustrations or unfulfilled ambitions of the reformers, with psychological or emotional disturbance, even with derangement. Enthusiasts have responded that intense commitment, even fanaticism, is a praiseworthy reaction in the face of evil or in response to obvious social problems.

Clearly, the motivation of each individual reformer can be judged only on its own merits. But it is helpful to remember that the antebellum American reform movements occurred during an unsettled period. The economy was undergoing rapid change. A new transportation network of roads, canals, and, later, railroads was opening up the American West to mass settlement. This meant that Western farmers could have access to Eastern or even overseas markets—markets that offered tremendous opportunities for economic growth, but also dangers, as when the economy plummeted downward in the panics of 1837 and 1857. At the same time industry grew, and that growth created demands for cheap, reliable labor in the new factories.

At first, Americans naively thought that industrialism could be fostered in a happy, benign atmosphere, free from the horrors of the Industrial Revolution in Britain: the New World would, in this as in other ways, instruct the Old. The capitalists who owned the textile mills in Lowell,

Massachusetts, thought (like Voltaire's Dr. Pangloss) that theirs was the "best of all possible worlds," with happy young female workers making cotton cloth and happy factory owners making money. It worked for a while, from the 1820s to about the mid-1830s. But economic downturn, wage cuts, strikes, and the replacement of Yankee mill hands with more easily bossed Irish immigrants put an end to the Lowell dream—though not to the growth of industry or profit making.

Antebellum America was a society in motion. Thousands of people were moving westward. Many hundreds of thousands were moving into the fast-growing cities, where social problems, being more concentrated, were also becoming more visible. Boatloads of immigrants, expectant and exploitable, arrived daily during the 1840s and 1850s. Whatever the personal factors involved, whatever the motivation—philanthropy or arrogance—no reforming spirit could remain unaffected by at least some of these developments.

The Cold Water Army On the night of April 2, 1840, six friends met at a Baltimore tavern, as was their custom, and prepared for a night of hard drinking. Nearby, at a local church, a temperance advocate prepared to deliver a sermon on the evils of alcohol. As a lark, the six decided to attend the lecture—and these sinners who came to scoff remained to pray. Afterward, they organized the Washington Temperance Society, the parent organization of a loose-knit network of prohibition societies that spread to most parts of the country and almost did away with "demon rum" eighty years before the prohibition era of the Roaring Twenties.

The fervor of the Protestant crusade of 1800–1860, and its potential both as a reforming factor and as a method of social control, is amply illustrated in the crusade for temperance. At first, "temperance" did not necessarily mean prohibition. For one thing, Americans of the colonial and early national periods were a hard-drinking lot. Wheat and rye were plentiful and cheap. So was corn. And rather than let those crops rot once their normal markets had been exhausted, American farmers generally turned them into liquor. The home still was as much a part of a well-run Ameri-

DEVELOPMENTS IN TECHNOLOGY, 1750–1860

(DATES REFER TO PATENT OR FIRST SUCCESSFUL USE)

YEAR		CONTRIBUTION	IMPORTANCE/DESCRIPTION
1750	Benjamin Franklin	LIGHTNING ROD	Protected buildings against damage from electrical storms.
1775	David Bushnell	SUBMARINE	First American submarine; submerged by taking water into tanks and surfaced when water was pumped out.
1787	John Fitch	STEAMBOAT	First successful American steamboat.
1793	Eli Whitney	COTTON GIN	Simplified process of separating fiber from seeds; helped make cotton a profitable staple of Southern agriculture.
1798	Eli Whitney	JIG FOR GUIDING TOOLS	Facilitated manufacture of interchangeable parts.
1802	Oliver Evans	STEAM ENGINE	First American steam engine; led to manufacture of high-pressure engines used throughout eastern United States.
1813	Richard B. Chenaworth	CAST-IRON PLOW	First iron plow to be made in three separate pieces, thus making possible replacement of parts.
1830	Peter Cooper	RAILROAD LOCOMOTIVE	First steam locomotive built in America.
1831	Cyrus McCormick	REAPER	Mechanized harvesting; early model could cut six acres of grain a day.
1836	Samuel Colt	REVOLVER	First successful repeating pistol.
1837	John Deere	STEEL PLOW	Steel surface kept soil from sticking; farming thus made easier on rich prairies of Middle West.
1839	Charles Goodyear	VULCANIZATION OF RUBBER	Made rubber much more useful by preventing it from sticking and melting in hot weather.
1842	Crawford W. Long	FIRST ADMINISTERED ETHER IN SURGERY	Reduced pain and risk of shock during operations.
1844	Samuel F. B. Morse	TELEGRAPH	Made long-distance communication almost instantaneous.
1846	Elias Howe	SEWING MACHINE	First practical machine for automatic sewing.
1846	Norbert Rillieux	VACUUM EVAPORATOR	Improved method of removing water from sugar cane; revolutionized sugar industry and was later applied to many other products.
1847	Richard M. Hoe	ROTARY PRINTING PRESS	Printed an entire sheet in one motion, vastly speeding up printing process.
1851	William Kelly	"AIR-BOILING PROCESS"	Improved method of converting iron into steel (usually known as Bessemer process because English inventor had more advantageous patent and financial arrangements).
1853	Elisha G. Otis	PASSENGER ELEVATOR	Improved movement in buildings; when later electrified, stimulated development of skyscrapers.
1859	Edwin L. Drake	FIRST AMERICAN OIL WELL	Initiated oil industry in United States.
1859	George M. Pullman	PULLMAN CAR	First sleeping-car suitable for long-distance travel.

can farm as the grist mill. Anyone seeking to control or limit the production and consumption of alcoholic beverages in America obviously would have a difficult task.

Early temperance advocates hoped to rely on persuasion, and they made limited demands. Hard liquor became the prime culprit, with beer and wine apparently exempt from the temperance injunction. Neither high taxes nor horror stories on the evil effects of drink seemed to work, however, so the temperance forces shifted their line of appeal. The citizens of a godly republic, they argued, must be prepared to discharge their civic and religious duties. But how could a drunken sot vote intelligently for political representatives or pay due homage to God? Obviously, he or she could not.

The American Society for the Promotion of Temperance (founded in 1826) and allied groups, working especially through the churches, urged people to sign a pledge of total abstinence. Many thousands did, and often signing the pledge formed part of a religious conversion. By the mid-1830s the society could claim over a million persons on the temperance (total abstinence) wagon. Still the evils of drink would not go away. Those who refused to give up alcohol, and who thereby polluted society, might have to be coerced into godly behavior.

After the start of the Washington movement in 1840, demands for legal action through state prohibition laws—forbidding the sale of alcoholic beverages—became the hallmark of the antiliquor campaign. But laws must to some extent reflect public opinion; to influence the public, to educate it to the need for prohibition laws, temperance men and women mounted a tremendous publicity campaign—one that resembled in many ways the organized enthusiasm of Harrison's concurrent Whig presidential campaign in 1840.

Rallies, parades, picnics, mass meetings—all marked the efforts of the so-called cold water army. Writers and poets poured (to overfilling) their talents into the crusade. Miss C. B. Porter's *The Silver Cup of Sparkling Drops* included the lines:

I gazed upon his pallid cheek
And asked him how his cares begun—

He sighed, and thus essayed to speak,
"The cause of all my grief is *rum*."

Timothy Shay Arthur, a writer who specialized in rum demonology, produced a best seller, *Ten Nights in a Bar Room.* But the heaviest guns of the cold water army were the preachers who inveighed against drink as strenuously and as sincerely as they fought against the devil.

Temperance became a political force to be reckoned with, especially in the Northeast. But its advocates may have overreached themselves and become overconfident on the basis of a few legislative victories. In 1838, Massachusetts had passed a "fifteen gallon" law, stipulating that sales of liquor had to be in amounts of fifteen gallons or more. This obvious discrimination against the poor had one unexpected but understandable effect: a Democrat was elected governor of Massachusetts for the first time. The law was then repealed. Nearby, the state of Maine made legislative history in 1846 by becoming the first state to ban alcoholic beverages altogether. Other states, including some in the West, followed suit; when New York (which had adopted local option in 1845) went for prohibition in 1854, the victory of the temperance advocates seemed an accomplished fact.

It was not. First, the rest of the nation did not rush to emulate Maine's example. Much of the South pretended to be blissfully unaware of the crusade, and the Middle Atlantic states remained ambivalent. Second, some of the prohibition laws had been badly drafted, opening them up to lawsuits. Pre–Civil War temperance suffered perhaps its most severe setback in 1856, when the New York courts ruled that state's prohibition law unconstitutional because it deprived citizens of vested rights in property (their liquor) without due process of law.

Education Although the movements urging the spread of educational facilities—especially tax-supported primary schooling for all—were not so directly a part of the Protestant crusade as was the temperance movement, the religious factor was present nevertheless. The free primary school—what came to be called "the little red schoolhouse"—was, at first, very definitely a Protestant schoolhouse. Catholics objected that, when public school instruction included Bible readings using the Protestant, King James version of the Bible, then public institutions were being used to serve sectarian purposes. (This was long before anyone in authority paid much attention to the few who objected to having any Bible readings in the public schools at all.)

Diffusion of schooling, it was felt, would wipe out illiteracy, a scourge as bad as alcoholism; at the same time the school system would instill in pupils proper moral attitudes and values. In short, along with its altruistic and humanitarian purposes, advocates of the public school argued that it would provide a superb agency for social control in a society that was becoming increasingly individualistic, harder to manage, and downright "licentious."

Whatever their definition of "progress," most reformers agreed that the surest road to progress in the United States was through education. They worked to reduce illiteracy. (Although literacy in America was relatively high in comparison to other societies of that time, it is probable that before the Civil War a majority of Americans could not read or write.) The reformers also tried to improve educational opportunities in a variety of ways. Outside of the South, belief in state-supported primary education for every child became widespread. Public school systems were established throughout the North. In the South, a more limited number of children—mainly from the wealthier classes—continued to attend private academies or to receive instruction from tutors.

The leader of the Northern public school movement was Horace Mann of Massachusetts,

The movement for educational reform in the 1830s and 1840s attempted to remedy a nationwide neglect of schooling and a degenerating educational situation. Where schools existed at all, localities kept funding low by providing minimal facilities, inadequate equipment, short terms, and teachers, who were often untrained and incompetent. State-supported public school systems, it was hoped, would be an improvement over the makeshift one-room schoolhouse depicted here— where one unfortunate student appears to have fallen asleep on his backless bench.

ably seconded by Henry Barnard in neighboring Connecticut. The New England common school system, established in colonial times and calling for state aid to towns that established primary schools, had fallen into decay. Many economy-minded small towns had no schools at all; others had ramshackle schoolhouses with poorly paid teachers (mostly males at that time). During the 1830s and 1840s, Horace Mann worked to reorganize his state's school system, raise teacher salaries, and upgrade teacher training. Massachusetts, which doubled its educational budget under Mann's prodding, established the first teacher training institution in 1839. Formal education at the secondary school level also grew in importance. A number of progressive schools—primary

In 1837, Horace Mann dropped a promising career as lawyer and state legislator to become the first State Superintendent of Education in Massachusetts. During his twelve-year tenure, the state's public schools were impressively reformed: teaching standards were raised, the school year was lengthened, state appropriations were doubled, and "Normal Schools" were established for the training of teachers.

and secondary—opened in New England. But it should be stressed that, in the pre–Civil War period, secondary education remained far out of reach of the vast majority of young people, and even primary education was by no means universally available.

Horace Mann, as state secretary of education in Massachusetts, stated his case for education in well-publicized annual reports. Appropriations time brought this warning from Mann:

> In a republic, ignorance is crime. . . . If we do not prepare our children to become good citizens, if we do not develop their capacities, if we do not enrich their minds with knowledge, imbue their hearts with the love of truth and duty, and a reverence for all things sacred and holy, then our republic must go down to destruction.

Mann's well-publicized twelve annual reports (1837–1848) as secretary of the state board of education in Massachusetts brought to the attention of reformers and officials throughout the country not only the specific problems of Massachusetts schools but the more general concerns and issues of public education. In 1838, he began editing a magazine called the *Common School Journal* devoted to spreading the gospel—and highlighting the problems—of public school education. Under Mann's leadership in Massachusetts, the salaries of teachers improved significantly and the number of children enrolled in public schools increased yearly. Elementary school curriculums were modernized, and new methods of teaching reading to the young or the illiterate received his special attention. Mann resigned as secretary in 1848 after being elected to Congress as an antislavery Whig, although not an abolitionist, and in 1852, he became the first president of the newly-founded Antioch College at Yellow Springs, Ohio, where he taught and administered until his retirement in 1859. Only weeks after retiring, Mann died, still the most influential leader of public education in his generation.

Higher education expanded, too. State universities were established in several Southern and Midwestern states. New private colleges and universities also sprang up. Oberlin College in Ohio, founded in 1833, was the first coeducational col-

Oberlin College, founded on the Ohio frontier, became a hotbed of antislavery activism in the decades following 1833, as well as a station on the Underground Railroad. The Oberlin Theological School was heavily supported by prominent eastern abolitionists and the student body of the college recruited from reform-minded New England and New York.

Schoolteacher Mary Lyon raised the funds to establish Mount Holyoke College by soliciting contributions, door-to-door, from other Massachusetts women. Although the "Seminary" for girls that she founded in South Hadley, Massachusetts, in 1837 was not chartered as a college until 1886, after her death, the level of instruction and entrance requirements from the outset were on a par with those at men's colleges. The pious Miss Lyon also insisted upon a religious atmosphere and, since she believed in the virtue of manual labor, required all students to assist with the housework.

lege in the country. It was also one of the few schools to admit blacks, and it became a center of antislavery agitation. Horace Mann spent the final years of his life at Antioch College, another Ohio antislavery and coeducational institution.

Mount Holyoke in Massachusetts, founded in 1837 as Mary Lyon's Female Seminary, was the first to offer women advanced education. During the period, such opportunities for women increased but at a pitifully slow pace. Women were different, mentally as well as physically, argued the men who dominated American society and who had as little sympathy for the idea of formal education for women as they did for the notion of allowing women to vote. While men like Horace Mann and Henry Barnard had no easy time of it, the women who fought for educational reform—Emma Willard, who started a "female seminary" in Troy, New York; Mary Lyon, who did likewise in Massachusetts; and Elizabeth Blackwell, who earned and insisted on receiving the first medical degree awarded an American woman—had the hardest fight against prevailing sex prejudice.

Mass education of a more informal kind also flourished in the antebellum period. Breakthroughs in machine technology had resulted in a "printing revolution" that permitted the low-cost production of reading material by steam-powered rotary presses. Hundreds of mass circulation newspapers and magazines, catering to almost

Educator Emma Hart Willard, who was determined to improve women's education—and to prove that women could master as difficult subjects as men—campaigned in New York (unsuccessfully) for the state funding of girls' schools. In 1821, she established the Troy Female Seminary, with financial support from the town, and introduced an advanced curriculum that included math, history, geography, and a wide range of sciences—rather than the hodge-podge of handicrafts usually offered at girls' schools. Mrs. Willard was particularly devoted to teacher preparation and trained two hundred of her graduates to enter the teaching profession.

every segment of public taste, made their appearance. The famous "penny press" dated from 1833. In that year, the New York *Sun* demonstrated the possibility of profitably increasing readership by cutting its price to one cent. Weekly editions of such leading papers as Horace Greeley's New York *Tribune* (founded in the early 1840s) became the equivalent of the first national magazines for a mass audience. Periodicals such as *Harper's Weekly* and *Godey's Lady's Book* were only two of many serving the apparently insatiable reading appetite of an increasingly literate America.

The most influential form of adult education in this period—again outside the South—was the lyceum movement. It originated in New England in 1826. Lyceums were established by the hundreds throughout the North and Middle West. They were basically lecture halls with small libraries and facilities for discussion and study groups. Lyceums drew a steady stream of well-paid lecturers on regional and even national tours. No better device existed for mass education in a country that still lacked universal literacy but which valued the arts of public speaking and debating.

Almost any cause could gain an attentive audience (and perhaps some converts) simply by sending a speaker to tour the lyceums. Hundreds of reformers—ranging from such rarified philosophers as Emerson to the more down-to-earth men arguing simple nostrums guaranteed to elevate mankind—all followed the lyceum circuit hoping to arouse America to the need for change.

There proved to be no shortage of causes to expound. In addition to temperance and education through formal schooling, reformers called for the end of capital punishment; some demanded changes in the prison system through the establishment of penitentiaries that would rehabilitate and not merely punish; others lectured on spiritualism or the principles of phrenology (character analysis by measuring the contours of the head); still others urged the total renunciation of war; some wanted the few Jews then living in America converted to Christianity; many demanded equal rights for women; still more demanded the abolition of slavery. Lyceum lectures were not exclusively reform platforms, but the lecture-study circuit never lacked for reformers—those who saw and fretted about the imperfections of a society that they thought should be constantly striving to improve itself.

Treatment of the Handicapped One cause that received a great deal of attention for the first time during the antebellum decades was the manner in which Americans treated the mentally ill. Foremost among those responsible for changing public attitudes on this controversial question was Dorothea Dix, a Boston schoolteacher, who spent years studying conditions in the country's insane asylums. Dix found most inmates "confined in cages, closets, cellars, stalls, and pens, where they were chained, naked, beaten with rods, and lashed into obedience." When she exposed these inhuman conditions, all of which she had seen personally, some critics denounced her agitating; but with the help of people like Horace Mann and the young politician Charles Sumner, Dix persisted. Her detailed reports to state legislatures on the hideous conditions, and her long campaign for public recognition of the problem, in and outside of Massachusetts, led to many improvements in state-supported mental hospitals.

One of those who helped Dorothea Dix in her campaign to ease the sufferings of mental patients was Dr. Samuel Gridley Howe. A romantic figure, who had fought in the Greek war for independence, Howe was also a very practical reformer. He had concentrated on the education of the deaf and the blind and had succeeded in educating a young woman named Laura Bridgman, a blind deaf-mute. His "feat" in so doing, which attracted a great deal of curiosity and attention, greatly aided Howe in raising money for his Perkins Institute for the Blind. Before he opened his school for the blind, Howe spent several days blindfolded so that he might gain a better understanding of the problems faced by his future pupils.

Other reformers, forerunners of the modern social worker, helped the "neglected poor," the unemployed, the newly arrived immigrant. The work of such individuals as Joseph Tuckerman of Boston and Charles Loring Brace of New York called attention to poverty amidst the plenty of the nation's developing cities.

Pacifism The peace movement gained many followers in the early nineteenth century. A Maine merchant named William Ladd founded the American Peace Society in 1828. It was weakened after a few years, however, when it split into warring factions over the question of whether nations might use force to defend themselves. Some pacifists condemned the use of force under any circumstances, arguing that there was no such thing as a "just" war. Among their leaders was abolitionist William Lloyd Garrison. He led those who believed in absolute pacifism into a much smaller

society, the New England Non-Resistance Society, which condemned violence even in self-defense.

While pacifism gradually lost followers as the slavery controversy heated up during the 1840s and 1850s, the Mexican War of 1846–1848 created a second convulsion within the American Peace Society. A group of dissidents, led by Elihu Burritt, wanted the war condemned. Failing in that, they founded the League of Universal Brotherhood. But the "war" that did the most to undermine organized pacifism was the "war against the slave power." Many of the leading pacifists, like Garrison and Burritt, were also abolitionists. When faced with the choice of fighting or of giving in to slavery, such men renounced pacifism. Thus Garrison ended by praising John Brown's raid on Harper's Ferry and supporting the Civil War.

Woman's Rights Women were active in almost every progressive cause in antebellum America. In the process of trying to improve conditions for others, they came to recognize the degree to which they themselves were deprived of equal citizenship. They had no political rights, and, upon marriage, they lost some of their civil rights, in particular, control over whatever property they had owned. Most of all, women suffered from limited professional and social opportunities. They were refused admission to most secondary schools and universities. Practically all careers but marriage were considered "unfeminine." Yet women were expected to work. And on the nation's farms and in the small towns, where a majority of Americans then lived, women did their share of the work—perhaps more than their share, since they also did most of the work involved in child rearing. But women working outside the home, rural or urban, and their participation in public activity, if not actually forbidden, was frowned upon.

The movement for woman's rights began in earnest in 1840. That year, an antislavery meeting in London refused to admit women delegates. Two Americans—Lucretia Mott and Elizabeth Cady Stanton—met in the balcony, where they had been forced to sit as passive spectators, while the male delegates conferred below in the main hall. Their humiliation by fellow abolitionists was not a situation that sat well with the talented and strong-willed Mott and Stanton. The women began discussions that continued (by letter) after their return to the United States.

In 1848, Mott and Stanton were among the organizers of the first Woman's Rights Convention, at Seneca Falls, New York. The delegates issued a manifesto paraphrasing the Declaration of Independence. It stated that "all men and women are created equal" and it demanded that women be allowed "immediate admission to all the rights and privileges which belong to them as citizens of the United States."

The woman's rights movement, next to abolitionism,[1] was the most controversial of antebellum reform crusades. Some male reformers, notably Garrison, Wendell Phillips, and Samuel Gridley Howe, actively supported the feminists. Others, especially clergymen worried about conventional morality and journalists looking for a good story, attacked or ridiculed the movement. On one point both clergy and press were united: that the "Bloomer-style" of dress temporarily adopted by leading feminists was shocking. Actually, it was only different, since it consisted of a knee-length jacket over a pair of "Turkish" trousers that were not form-fitting. The costume as a whole was no more revealing or provocative than conventional dress. But Bloomerism proved such a handicap to feminism, it evoked so much criticism, that feminists reluctantly returned to less comfortable petticoats and gowns.

Nevertheless, American women made some progress during the pre–Civil War years. Women were allowed to become elementary and then high school teachers. State legislatures began to award married women control over their own property; Mississippi was the first, in 1839; New York followed in 1848. Girls began attending secondary schools in small numbers, and a few colleges offered higher education to women.

Probably the most important breakthroughs, however, were stubbornly personal. Distinguished careers pursued by individual reformers and intellectuals—such as Blackwell, Dix, Mott, and Stanton—dented the dominant image of

woman's mental and emotional unfitness for serious vocations outside the home. In educational institutions like Willard's Female Seminary, which taught mathematics, history, and philosophy, a small percentage of American women began to find themselves intellectually. These reforms came at a time when women were thought incapable of learning much besides singing and embroidery, and when most women seemed permanently imprisoned by their "circumstance." Susan B. Anthony, an ardent feminist (and abolitionist) who worked to gain the vote for women, once declared that she "would ignore all law to help the slave, and ignore it all to protect an enslaved woman."

Utopian Communities The idealism and social unrest of the period were perhaps best symbolized by the Utopian communities that sprang up mushroomlike in the antebellum era. From the 1820s through the 1840s more than a hundred colonies were set up. Most were inspired by one or another religious belief, although some were secular, established as proving grounds for new economic or social theories.

The purpose of New Harmony, Indiana, according to its founder, was "to introduce an entire new system of society." He was a successful Scottish industrialist named Robert Owen, who believed that capitalism represented selfishness and that only socialism (communitarian socialism) could bring harmony to society. In 1825 Owen purchased a ready-made colony of 30,000 acres from a German religious group. Within six weeks he had brought together 800 colonists. But New Harmony also attracted its share of crackpots and loafers. Quarrels broke out over major and minor issues. And Owen's frequent absences left the group without strong guidance. Within two years, New Harmony was disbanded.

Brook Farm, a few miles west of Boston, operated on a smaller scale but with a more distinguished group of adherents. It began in 1841 as a progressive prep school and cooperative farm, with all pupils and group members sharing daily chores. Its leader, George Ripley, former Unitarian minister and sometime member of the Transcendental Club, believed in "plain living and high

[1]For a full account of abolitionism, see Chapter 22.

The Oneida Community's sexual practices created much controversy. Here, the Oneidans vote on whether to allow the union of two members under their highly regulated scheme of "complex marriage."

thinking." He thought that people could develop more fully when freed from competition. Many intellectuals were associated with Brook Farm. Emerson considered it a nice place to visit, but he did not want to live there. Nathaniel Hawthorne was a group member. (He later satirized the experiment in his novel *The Blithedale Romance*.) When a highly structured, more impersonal working and living system was introduced in 1845 (in other words, when it became more regimented), the farm lost its appeal for many supporters. A fire in 1846 destroyed the main building and brought the experiment to an end. Brook Farm, according to transcendentalist Orestes Brownson, had been "half a charming adventure, half a solemn experiment."

Less intellectual, and unconcerned with charm, was the Oneida Community in upstate New York, started by John Humphrey Noyes in 1848. Noyes believed that small industry provided a better economic base for a colony than did agriculture. So the community produced and marketed animal traps, furniture, and other consumer goods. Property was owned jointly and distributed equally. Conventional marriage was replaced by "complex marriage," a system in which all group members were considered married to each other. Noyes and his followers believed that no man-made laws could separate them and that they belonged to one another. These doctrines were criticized severely by the outside world. The Oneida Community, like the Mormons, paid the price for their sexual unorthodoxy and financial success. The group finally abolished complex marriage in 1879. Soon afterward, the community itself was dissolved, becoming a joint stock company that specialized in manufacturing silverware.

Most American Utopian communities were

unable to become truly self-sufficient or to maintain their cherished isolation from the outside world. Many floundered when it came to putting their high ideals into practice. Yet a few made noteworthy contributions. New Harmony sponsored some important educational innovations—the kindergarten and the trade school. Brook Farm's combination of work and culture was highly praised, and its school was much admired. As for Oneida, its members pioneered in eugenics and in what, today, would be called encounter sessions.

Most Americans knew about the Utopian communities, but few approved of them and even fewer actually participated in these early American experiments in communitarianism. Utopian withdrawal offered no solution to a mass society, innovative though some communities might be. To outsiders they appeared, at best, as exotic retreats. Most Americans still believed that piecemeal reform—working to correct gradually the abuses in society as a whole, rather than creating new mini-societies—offered greater hope. Some approached the task of reform with the sour anxiety of a Lyman Beecher, orthodox Congregationalist from Connecticut; others were blessed with the cheerful and optimistic spirit of a William Ellery Channing, the Boston Unitarian. Yet both were clergymen imbued with the belief that mankind could and should better its lot on earth, and approach closer to moral perfection. Such attitudes made the starburst of American reform in the antebellum years a reality and offered a more certain prospect for the future than did the Adventist hopes of William Miller and his followers.

Origins of the Abolition Movement Of all the reforms influenced by religion, the one with the closest connections was abolitionism. Certain religious groups had been particularly active in the antislavery movement from its beginning in the eighteenth century. These included the Methodists, Episopalians, and, particularly, the Quakers. Ethical opposition to slavery inspired many leading figures of the Revolutionary period to free their slaves. It also influenced Northern states to abolish slavery gradually by the 1820s.

A leading antislavery organization of the early nineteenth century was the American Colonization Society, founded in 1817. It worked to obtain gradual, compensated emancipation of slaves. After being freed, slaves were to be transported immediately elsewhere, preferably to Africa. The society actually colonized very few blacks. But it did help found Liberia in 1822 as a refuge for ex-slaves. Many Southerners joined the American Colonization Society in an effort to resolve their moral doubts over slavery, but the Society lost most of its support in the South after a Virginia slave insurrection in 1831 that would help shape attitudes toward slavery in both sections for the next three decades—the Nat Turner Revolt.

SUGGESTED READINGS—CHAPTERS 15–16

The Coming of the Millerites

Clara E. Sears, *Days of Delusion* (1924); Francis D. Nichol, *Midnight Cry: A Defense of William Miller and the Millerites* (1944); Whitney R. Cross, *The Burned-Over District: Enthusiastic Religion in Western New York, 1800–1850* (1950); Bernard A. Weisberger, *They Gathered at the River: The Story of the Great Revivalists and Their Impact upon Religion in America* (1958); Fawn M. Brodie, *No Man Knows My History: The Life of Joseph Smith* (1971).

Religious Reforms

Thomas F. O'Dea, *The Mormons* (1964); William W. Sweet, *Religion in American Culture, 1765–1840* (1952); Ray A. Billington, *The Protestant Crusade, 1800–1860* (1938); Timothy L. Smith, *Revivalism and Social Reform in Mid-Nineteenth Century America* (1965); Daniel W. Howe, *The Unitarian Conscience: Harvard Moral Philosophy, 1805–1861* (1970); Sydney E. Ahlstrom, *A Religious History of the American People* (1972); Carl Bode, *The American*

Lyceum (1956); Ralph L. Lusk, *The Life of Ralph Waldo Emerson* (1949); Perry Miller, ed., *Transcendentalists: An Anthology* (1950); Mark Holloway, *Heavens on Earth* (1951).

Social Crusades

William G. McLoughlin, *The Meaning of Henry Ward Beecher* (1970); John A. Krout, *The Origins of Prohibition* (1925); Harold Schwartz, *Samuel Gridley Howe, Social Reformer* (1956); Rush Welter, *Popular Education and Democratic Thought* (1962); Michael Katz, *The Irony of Early School Reform: Educational Innovation in Mid-Nineteenth Century Massachusetts* (1968); W. David Lewis, *From Newgate to Dannemora: The Rise of the Penitentiary in New York, 1796–1848* (1965); Arthur E. Bestor, Jr., *Backwoods Utopias: The Sectarian Origins and the Owenite Phase of Communitarian Socialism in America: 1623–1829* (1950); Jonathan Messerli, *Horace Mann* (1971); David S. Rothman, *The Discovery of the Asylum* (1971); Gerald N. Grob, *Mental Institutions in America: Social Policy to 1875* (1973); Peter Brock, *Pacifism in the United States: From the Colonial Era to the First World War* (1968); Michael Fellman, *The Unbounded Frame: Freedom and Community in Nineteenth Century American Utopianism* (1973).

Change in American Thought

Ernest L. Tuveson, *Redeemer Nation: The Idea of America's Millenial Role* (1968); Alice Felt Tyler, *Freedom's Ferment: Phases of American Social History from the Revolution to the Outbreak of the Civil War* (1964); Clifford S. Griffin, *The Ferment of Reform, 1830–1860* (1967); F. O. Mathiessen, *American Renaissance: Art and Expression in the Age of Emerson and Whitman* (1941); Daniel Boorstin, *The Americans: The National Experience* (1965); Rowland Berthoff, *An Unsettled People: Social Order and Disorder in American History* (1971); Perry Miller, *The Life of the Mind in America* (1965); Oliver W. Larkin, *Art and Life in America* (1949); Clifford S. Griffin, *Their Brothers' Keepers: Moral Stewardship in the United States* (1960); Neil Harris, *The Artist in American Society: The Formative Years, 1790–1860* (1966).

UNIT FOUR

DIVIDED AMERICA

Shortly after the Missouri Compromise of 1820, Thomas Jefferson and John Adams, aging patriots, exchanged letters on the one remaining major problem that seemed to threaten the nation's stability. "The real question, as seen in the states afflicted with this unfortunate population," wrote Jefferson in 1821, "is, Are our slaves to be presented with freedom and therefore a dagger? Are we then to see again Athenian and Spartan confederacies? To wage another Peloponnesian War to settle the ascendancy between them?" Adams was equally skeptical. "Slavery in this country," he responded, "I have seen hanging over it like a black cloud for half a century." The "black cloud" was still there when the two Founding Fathers died, in an awesome coincidence, on the same day — July 4, 1826, the fortieth anniversary of American independence.

During the 1820s and 1830s economic issues such as the Bank War and land policy deflected popular attention from the "black cloud." Only in the 1840s did the landscape once more become overcast with the problem, as Americans grappled with the question of slavery's expansion. Even then, slavery did not completely preoccupy the American people. The nation doubled its population between 1830 and 1850. An industrial factory system began to develop in the North and Middle West. Millions of European immigrants landed on American shores. The country fought a war with Mexico and gained huge new territories in the West. Yet all these events occurred within a society torn by a fundamental and unresolved social problem — the place of blacks and slavery in American life.

The four pairs of chapters that follow examine various phases of the American experience from the 1830s to the 1870s, with special emphasis on changing reactions to the problems of slavery and race. Chapter 17 tells the story of the most important slave revolt in United States history, led by Nat Turner. It serves as a focal point for the discussion of slavery in Chapter 18 which portrays the patterns of Southern society as they affected both slaves and their masters. Chapter 19 deals with the drama of congressional efforts to achieve a compromise over the issue of slavery in the Western territories. The resultant Compromise of 1850 and surrounding events serve as a vehicle for the exploration, in Chapter 20, of three dominant themes of the 1840s and 1850s: Northern economic growth, westward expansion, and the politics of sectional conflict.

John Brown's raid, the subject of Chapter 21, triggered extreme sectional hysteria in both South and North. It can also be seen in relation to a general climate of reform, described in Chapter 22, that characterized the antebellum period. Sectional differences in the United States culminated in civil war and continued in the bitter Reconstruction era that followed. The meaning of the Civil War in human terms is dramatized in Chapter 23 through an account of Sherman's devastating march through Georgia. Chapter 24 describes the major events of the Civil War and Reconstruction—the climactic struggles of a tragic and tortured period in our national past.

17 THE NAT TURNER REVOLT

A. W.

Six poorly clad black men huddled around their campfire in the woods drinking brandy and barbecuing a pig. They had arrived at this meeting place about noon, started the fire, and waited in silence. Toward midafternoon another black man suddenly emerged from the surrounding trees. The six turned to greet him. It was this short and stocky figure for whom they had been waiting. His name was Nat Turner. A later description of him reads:

> Five feet 6 or 8 inches high, weighs between 150 and 160 pounds, rather bright complexion, but not a mulatto. Broad shoulders, large flat nose, large eyes. Broad flat feet, rather knockkneed, walks brisk and active. Hair on the top of the head very thin, no beard, except on the upper lip and the top of the chin. A scar on one of his temples, also one on the back of his neck. A large knot on one of the bones of his right arm, near his wrist, produced [by] a blow.

Turner greeted the other blacks and joined them around the campfire. We know his companions only by their first names—Sam, Nelson, Hark, Will, Henry, and Jack.

Turner sat down, stared directly at Will, and demanded to know something he already knew quite well. Why had Will come to this rendezvous? According to Turner's later account, Will replied that "his life was worth no more than others and his liberty was as dear to him." Turner continued the questioning: "I asked him if he thought to obtain his freedom. He said he would, or lose his life."

The seven men spoke further about their plans until some time after sunset. Then, at a command from Turner, they trudged back out of the woods and through ripe tobacco fields to a clearing. Here stood a large, handsome frame house. It belonged to a white man named Joseph Travis, who happened to own Nat Turner. An eighth black, Austin, joined them at the Travis home. Then, as Turner later recounted, "they all went to the cider press and drank, except myself."

About midnight the group gathered in front of the house. Turner climbed through a window, opened the doors to his men, and gave them guns that had been stored inside. His men now insisted that he "spill the first blood." Armed with a hatchet and accompanied by Will, Turner entered Travis's bedroom and swung wildly at the sleeping man. The blow merely grazed Travis's skull, and he jumped out of bed screaming for his wife. A second later, Will bashed his head in with an ax. Within moments, wielding his ax, Will also killed Mrs. Travis and their three oldest children, none of whom ever awoke.

The band of black men then searched the house for arms, collecting a half-dozen rifles and several pounds of gunpowder. They left soon afterward and started walking down a road that led to the town of Jerusalem (now Courtland), some fifteen miles away. They had gone only a short distance when someone remembered that the Travises had a fourth child, a baby who slept in a cradle near its parents' bed. "Henry and Will returned and killed it," Nat Turner later observed. He formed the others "in a line as soldiers" and marched his seven-man "army" down the road. With the murder of this one family began the greatest slave revolt in the history of the United States. It started on Sunday, August 21, 1831, in the sleepy Virginia county known as Southampton.

Southampton County, in southeastern Virginia, was an important agricultural area. It had several large farms that employed slave labor and might have been called plantations. Such was the Travis homestead. More common were small farms tilled by poor whites who owned no slaves. The federal census in 1830 showed that Southampton was second among Virginia counties in growing rice and potatoes. A decade later, it led the state in cotton production.

Southampton County's planters might have felt an occasional twinge of concern over their safety. Blacks in the area (most of them slaves) outnumbered whites by almost two to one. Among the 9,501 Southampton blacks counted by the 1830 census takers was a thirty-year-old, Bible-reading, visionary slave preacher named Nat Turner.

Turner was born in Southampton County on October 2, 1800. At the time, members of his family were slaves of a man named Benjamin Turner. (It was common for slaves to be given the last name of their master.) When Nat was only three or four years old, he already felt that he had been singled out by God to achieve some great work. As he said later, he thought he "surely would be a prophet." Young Nat certainly seemed a prodigy to his elders. His upbringing was unusual for a slave child, in several ways. At an early age he was taught to read and write by his parents. As a youth, he spent much time at prayer. Also, he was apparently spared much physical labor. Instead, he had free time when he could study schoolbooks belonging to his master's children or simply be alone with his thoughts. He remembered other slaves turning to him for help because of his "superior judgment."

At a very early age, Turner decided to pursue a lonely, almost friendless, life while awaiting the great works for which he believed

God had prepared him. "Having soon discovered myself to be great, I must appear so, and therefore studiously avoided mixing in society, and wrapped myself in mystery, devoting my time to fasting and prayer."

Several times as a young man in his twenties, Turner claimed to have divine visions. His reputation as a preacher spread among whites as well as blacks in Southampton County. Yet he appeared aloof and puzzling to most of his fellow slaves. One time he escaped. But, instead of trying to reach shelter in the Great Dismal Swamp—some twenty-five miles away—he stayed in the woods for thirty days. Then he casually returned to his owner. "The Negroes found fault, and murmured against me," Nat later remarked, "saying that if they had my sense they would not serve any master in the world." By this time, however, Nat Turner believed himself destined for a greater role than that of an escaped slave, skulking in swamplands to avoid recapture. "I now withdrew myself as much as my situation would permit, from the intercourse of my fellow slaves, for the avowed purpose of serving the Spirit more fully."

Turner's vision of a divinely inspired slave revolt came to him in 1828, according to his account. "The Spirit instantly appeared to me," he said, and told him of the task ahead: "I should arise and prepare myself, and slay my enemies with their own weapons." A heavenly sign would instruct him when to begin. The signal that triggered his actual plan to revolt was an eclipse of the sun in February 1831. That month, Turner outlined his general scheme to Henry, Hark, Nelson, and Sam, who later brought in Will and Jack. Turner's men began to call him the Prophet because of his mystical statements. The small band of plotters could gather easily at church meetings or barbecues to plan the rebellion, since few whites in the Jerusalem area had the slightest suspicion of an impending uprising.

Nat Turner's master in 1831, Joseph Travis, had acquired him in 1830 after marrying the widow of his former owner. Turner remembered Travis as "a kind master, [who] placed the greatest confidence in me; in fact, I had no cause to complain of his treatment to me." But Travis was a slaveholder. As such, he was marked by "the Prophet" for destruction.

To the very moment of revolt Nat Turner spoke more easily with the God whose commands he believed he was obeying than with his own black followers. After agreeing to meet his six companions in the woods at noon on the fateful Sunday, he joined them instead hours later, for "the same reason that had caused me not to mix with them for years before." However, once the Travis family had been chopped to pieces and the revolt was underway, Turner's aloofness no longer affected them. The killing began in earnest.

Some 600 yards from the Travis house lived Salathiel Francis. His home was the rebels' next stop as they obeyed Turner's command to "carry terror and devastation" along the road to Jerusalem. Their work was aided by the fact that the rebellious slaves knew most of the families in the neighborhood. When they arrived at the Francis house, Sam knocked at the door and shouted that he had a letter to deliver. It was

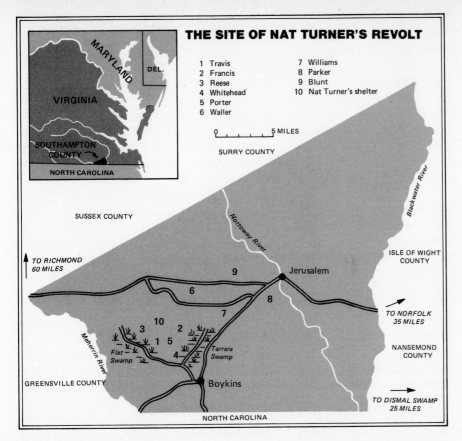

THE SITE OF NAT TURNER'S REVOLT

1 Travis
2 Francis
3 Reese
4 Whitehead
5 Porter
6 Waller
7 Williams
8 Parker
9 Blunt
10 Nat Turner's shelter

0 _____ 5 MILES

after midnight. Yet the unsuspecting planter opened the door immediately, only to be dragged outside and beaten to death. No one else was home, so Turner and his men marched on the the home of a Mrs. Reese, whose door they found unlocked. They murdered Mrs. Reese in her bed.

By sunrise on Monday other slaves had joined the group. They now numbered fifteen, with nine mounted on horses. Monday morning they arrived at the house of Elizabeth Turner, whom Will killed, along with Sarah Newsome. No woman was raped either then or at any point during Nat Turner's march of destruction. At each stop along they way, however, the rebels destroyed whatever valuable property they found, and they seized money, guns, and ammunition.

From the Turner residence the blacks on horseback rode on to the home of Richard Whitehead, while the others detoured to kill a slave-holding family named Bryant. As the nine armed blacks rode onto his property, Richard Whitehead stared unbelievingly from a nearby cotton patch. The blacks called him, and, as he walked toward them, Will's ax dropped him in his tracks. Dismounting, the slaves tore through the house, putting to death the entire family. Here occurred the only murder Nat Turner acknowledged having committed personally during the entire uprising—that of Whitehead's daughter Margaret. Margaret "had concealed herself in the corner. On my approach she fled, but was soon overtaken, and after repeated blows with a sword, I killed her by a blow on the head, with a fence rail."

By then the six blacks who had detoured to the Bryant home returned, having "done the work of death assigned them." The entire party moved on toward Jerusalem. The mutinous slaves again broke into small bands, since several scattered slaveholding families lay in their path. The main group, led by Turner himself, rode on to Richard Porter's home, only to discover that Porter had escaped with his family. "I understood there," Nat later acknowledged, "that the alarm had already spread, and I immediately returned to bring up those sent to other plantations."

Richard Porter's family was not alone in escaping from Nat Turner's wrath. By dawn on Monday, August 22—less than twelve hours after the revolt began—small numbers of whites began straggling into Jerusalem from the direction of the killings, rousing the town to the threatened black invasion. Within hours, a rider left Jerusalem and headed north for the state capital at Richmond, about seventy miles away. He carried an urgent letter appealing for military help.

Wild rumors spread quickly across the state. In the absence of more accurate information from Southampton, the rumors threw white Virginians into a panic. Thousands of angry slaves, it was said, had banded together to take over the state. According to reports, the rebels were well armed and commanded by soldiers from Haiti.[1] Rumor had it that Northern abolitionists (supporters of immediate freedom for the slaves) had helped incite the insurrection.

Whole companies of the state militia were hastily called up, and they headed for Jerusalem. By the time the first outside help had arrived, however, the uprising had already been crushed by Southampton County's own militia groups and armed white farmers. They had begun riding out after the small band of black rebels shortly after Richard Porter and others first sounded the alarm.

When he found Porter's family missing, Nat Turner realized the importance of marching as quickly as possible to seize Jerusalem. He knew, too, that he should keep his band together at full strength in the event of an attack. At each house along the way the rebels slaughtered the white inhabitants and urged nearby slaves to join them. By the time Turner and his men reached the home of a Captain Harris, who had also fled with his family, their ranks numbered about forty. Most seemed untroubled by Harris's absence, as they jubilantly destroyed his valuables, drank his liquor, collected his rifles, and rode on.

By this time "General Nat"—as his men reportedly started calling him—had decided on his tactics. He ordered those on horseback to ride ahead, killing whomever they met along the way. This would frighten the remaining whites in the area so that they would flee from their

This crude drawing appeared in a tract called "Horrid Massacre in Virginia," published in 1831. A mother begs one of Turner's men to spare the lives of her children.

---

[1]In 1794 blacks in Haiti—led by Toussaint L'Ouverture—had overthrown French rule there. Although the French captured Toussaint, they failed to retake the colony. The success of the black revolt in Haiti frightened American slaveholders for years afterward.

homes and even abandon Jerusalem to his men. Turner himself remained at the rear, directing his foot soldiers while coaxing the slaves he met to join the rebellion. When General Nat reached a house, its occupants had usually been killed, although he later commented: "I sometimes got in sight in time to see the work of death completed, viewed the mangled bodies as they lay, in silent satisfaction, and immediately started in quest of other victims." In this way, Mrs. Levi Waller and her ten children were killed, then William Williams and his two small boys. Mrs. Williams was caught running away and brought back to her dead husband's side. The rebels ordered her to lie down beside him and shot her. Several other families perished as well. By Monday afternoon the rebel band numbered between fifty and sixty, "all mounted and armed with guns, axes, swords, and clubs." They were only three miles from Jerusalem. Their leader urged them to press on into the town, but several of them insisted on stopping at the plantation of James Parker, where they had relatives. Most of Turner's men rode across the fields toward Parker's house to collect their kinfolk (the Parker family had already escaped) but Turner himself remained at the roadside with seven or eight of his soldiers. This delay proved fatal for the rebels.

A local militia captain, Alexander Peete, had ridden out from Jerusalem at the head of eighteen volunteers. He was probably as startled to find Nat Turner and his small band of blacks in front of the Parker plantation as Turner was to see Peete. Turner coolly ordered his handful of followers to form ranks and prepare to fire. Shots rang out on both sides, and the white militiamen fled. The black insurgents pursued Peete's men until the retreating militiamen ran headlong into another party of armed whites who had left Jerusalem to hunt down the rebels. Turner's small band, now heavily outnumbered, scattered into the surrounding woods. Most of them were wounded. For the rest of Monday afternoon, General Nat backtracked across much of the area of his earlier march. He combed the woods for his men while evading the growing numbers of militiamen who searched for him. By evening he had collected almost forty men, including several new slave recruits. He placed guards around his camp and rested for the night. But the men on patrol panicked, believing the camp under attack. When order was restored, Turner's "army" had been reduced to about twenty.

"The Prophet" set out early on Tuesday morning to continue recruiting the slaves in the area. His group reached the home of Dr. Simon Blunt just before daybreak. Almost immediately, the rebels were fired on by a party of armed whites and by some of Blunt's slaves. Several of Turner's men were killed. The rest retreated to the home of Captain Harris, which earlier had been deserted. This time, another band of militia opened fire on the slaves from within the house. Most of the blacks fled into the woods, where they were quickly rounded up. Only two, Jacob and another slave named Nat, retreated to the woods with General Nat. They waited until evening, when Turner sent his last two followers in search of the rest of his original group. They never returned.

Sixty hours after the rebellion had begun, it was crushed. Nat

Also from the "Horrid Massacre" is this rendering of "Mr. Travis, cruelly murdered by his own slaves." Woodcuts like this satisfied the public taste for a visual record of sensational events, though they were usually far from accurate.

Turner was left alone with the shattered wreckage of his mission. According to Turner's own account, God had not promised him success — only that he would perform the "great work" of "carrying terror and devastation wherever we went." This he had done. In less than three days his men had killed fifty-five whites from Southampton County slaveholding families: eleven men, fourteen women, and thirty children. At least twice as many blacks were also killed during and after the revolt by white militiamen. These militiamen seldom knew whether their victims had actually taken part in the revolt.

As for Nat Turner himself, he proved more skillful in defeat than in battle. He managed to remain free, eluding thousands of whites, for almost two months. During that period, across the country, the black "Prophet" of Southampton County became both famous and infamous.

Just as Virginians of the seventeenth century had studied the omens that foreshadowed Bacon's Rebellion, so did most white Southerners see a train of alarming events leading up to Nat Turner's Revolt. Had not an even more widespread plot among slaves and free blacks been discovered in Charleston, South Carolina, a decade earlier? This conspiracy was led by a free black named Denmark Vesey. It was exposed in 1822, and its leaders were executed. But rumors of such plots cropped up regularly in the years before the Southampton revolt. Had not a militant free black in Boston, David Walker, published a widely distributed *Appeal* in 1829 calling for slave uprisings throughout the South? And, in that same city, had not a journalist and printer named William Lloyd Garrison begun publishing a notorious abolitionist newspaper called *The Liberator,* which demanded immediate and total emancipation of all slaves?

Although Boston was 500 miles from Southampton County, many Southerners blamed the abolitionist writings of Walker and Garrison for stimulating a desire for rebellion in blacks such as Nat Turner. Some even suspected antislavery Northerners of actually plotting the Southampton revolt. Almost every white Virginian, for example, would have agreed with the sentiments of the state's leading newspaper, the Richmond *Enquirer.* Only a few days after the slave rebellion had been crushed, it printed this comment:

> When an appeal is actually made through the press to this unfortunate class of our community, calculated to mislead them, and while it involves us in serious trouble, leads those unhappy creatures to destruction, it is time for us to arouse from an indifference to a conduct which is daily augmenting and becoming worse and worse. To attempt to excite discontent and revolt, or publish writings having this tendency, obstinately and perversely, among us, is outrageous — it ought not to be passed over with indifference. Our own safety — the good and happiness of our slaves, requires it.

This criticism came from a newspaper whose editor, Thomas Ritchie, believed in the gradual emancipation of slaves. Obviously, the reaction of proslavery Southerners was much more hysterical. Thinking about the

Nat Turner Revolt, supporters of the "peculiar institution"[2] may have remembered South Carolinian Edward D. Holland's warning at the time of the Vesey conspiracy:

> Let it never be forgotten, that "our NEGROES are truly the *Jacobins*[3] of the country; that they are the *anarchists* and the *domestic enemy*," the *common enemy of civilized society,* and the barbarians who would, IF THEY COULD, become the DESTROYERS of our race.

Southerners were fearful that Turner's insurrection would inspire other slaves to rebel. They began acting on these fears, often in an incredibly barbaric manner. An antislavery Northern observer, E. A. Andrews, wrote:

> In every town and village, an active and vigilant patrol is abroad at such hours of the night as they judge most expedient, and no Negro dares, after the prescribed hour, to be found at a distance from his quarter. Great cruelty is often practiced by the patrols toward unoffending slaves. The principal object of such visits is to terrify the slaves, and thus secure their good behavior, and especially to prevent their wandering about at night.

Andrews went south prepared to find such cruelties, and he might therefore be expected to exaggerate. But many similar accounts filled the Southern press itself. The editor of the Richmond *Whig*, a militiaman himself, wrote the following typical account:

> A party of horsemen started from Richmond with the intention of killing every colored person they saw in Southampton County. They stopped opposite the cabin of a free colored man, who was hoeing in his little field. They called out, "Is this Southampton County?" He replied, "Yes, Sir, you have crossed the line by yonder tree." They shot him dead and rode on.

Nowhere was the punishment of innocent slaves for Nat Turner's brief uprising more ruthless than in Southampton County itself. Nathaniel Bacon's men over a century earlier had consoled themselves for failing to find any marauding Indians by slaughtering villages of peaceful ones. In the same manner, roving companies of militiamen and vigilante slave patrols—often drinking from the same stocks that had nourished Nat Turner's band during its brief lifetime—butchered many innocent slaves unlucky enough to fall into their hands. The situation became so offensive to the commander of military forces at Southampton, General Eppes, that he issued an order on September 6 threatening to shoot any of his own men caught mistreating local blacks. Eppes cautioned against further "acts of barbarity and cruelty" on the part of his own troops; but numerous slaves in the area paid with their lives before the carnage ended.

---

[2]This term for slavery seems to have been used first by a South Carolina newspaper in the 1850s, which spoke of the dangers then threatening "the peculiar domestic institutions of the South."

[3]The Jacobins were a leftist political group of the French Revolution. Their name became synonymous with extreme and dangerous radicals.

Throughout the South, state legislatures reacted to the acute fear of uprisings by further limiting the already restricted lives of slaves. The Virginia assembly endorsed the widely proclaimed "lesson" of Southampton County (to quote the Richmond *Enquier*) that "no black man ought to be permitted to become a preacher" by passing a complete ban on "any assembly or meeting, for religious or other purposes" by either slaves or free blacks. Only whites could preach to black congregations, and slaves had to accompany their masters to church. Other new Virginia laws forbade free blacks to carry weapons, increased the penalties for blacks assaulting whites, prohibited the sale of liquor to slaves, and allowed whippings for blacks who expressed "seditious" thoughts.

In every other Southern state, within months after the Nat Turner Revolt, a flood of similar legislation tightened controls over both slaves and free blacks. These actions fulfilled the prediction made by Garrison's *Liberator* concerning the white Southerner's reaction to the Turner uprising. "In his fury against the revolters," wrote the abolitionist editor, "who will remember their wrongs?"

While Nat Turner remained free, the object of Southern fears and fury, forty-six other blacks were brought to trial in Jerusalem for taking part in the revolt. The militiamen had obviously cast their nets too wide, for five free blacks were included among the accused. Sixteen slaves and three freemen died on the gallows for their alleged role in the revolt. Seven more were sentenced to be deported to the harsher conditions of Deep South[4] slavery. The others were acquitted, although several slaves in nearby counties were also convicted as accomplices in the uprising.

Meanwhile, Nat Turner lived a hand-to-mouth existence as a fugitive. After his last supporters had scattered on August 23, he returned to the Travis home and collected some food. In a nearby field he scratched out a shelter under a pile of fence rails. There he remained undetected for six weeks, just a short distance from his former slave cabin. Every evening the hunted rebel would leave briefly to drink water from a nearby stream. As the days wore on, be began to spend the entire night prowling through the neighborhood "gathering little or no intelligence, afraid of speaking to any human being, and returning every morning to my cave before the dawn of day."

One time when he returned, Turner saw a dog leaving his hiding place carrying a piece of meat. His days were now numbered. A few evenings later, two slaves, hunting with the same dog, passed his hideaway. The animal spotted Turner walking nearby and began barking. Turner later recalled:

> Thinking myself discovered, I spoke to the Negroes to beg concealment. On making myself known they fled from me. Knowing then they would betray me, I immediately left my hiding place, and was pursued almost incessantly until I was taken a fortnight afterwards by Mr. Benjamin Phipps, in a little hole I had dug out with

---

[4]The term "Deep South" refers to the southeastern states, especially Georgia, Alabama, Mississippi, and Louisiana. The older Southern states such as Virginia and Maryland are often known as the Upper South.

After the revolt, Nat hid out in the woods for almost two months, settling at last in a cave near the Francis farm. He was captured by a local farmer who had come upon Nat by chance. Phipps tied Nat's hands and then fired his gun in the air to summon attention.

my sword, for the purpose of concealment, under the top of a falled tree. On Mr. Phipps' discovering the place of my concealment, he cocked his gun and aimed at me. I requested him not to shoot and I would give up, upon which he demanded my sword. I delivered it to him, and he brought me to prison.

Turner was captured on October 30. Once locked in his Jerusalem cell, he was questioned by a white lawyer named Thomas R. Gray. The black insurgent apparently agreed to tell Gray his own story of the revolt. Turner's narrative, edited by Gray, appeared as a pamphlet, *The Confessions of Nat Turner*, early in 1832. At Turner's trial he pleaded not guilty, "saying to his counsel that he did not feel so." His narrative, however, was read to the court and served to convict him. After finding him guilty on November 5, Judge Jeremiah Cobb pronounced the inevitable death sentence, though with added fervor. He sentenced Turner to "be hung by the neck until you are dead! dead! dead!"

In talking to Gray, Nat Turner denied the existence of any widespread slave conspiracy. When he saw the lawyer's skeptical expression he said: "I see, sir, you doubt my word; but can you not think the same ideas might prompt others, as well as myself, to this undertaking?" The prisoner apparently impressed Gray considerably. Despite the attorney's proslavery beliefs, he defended Nat Turner against charges being made in the Southern press that he was an ignorant and cowardly black who had rebelled only to secure enough money to escape northward. "For natural intelligence and quickness of apprehension," Gray wrote, Turner "is surpassed by few men I have ever seen." Furthermore, Turner's Revolt could be understood, the lawyer argued, only as the action of "a complete fanatic warped and perverted by the influence of early impressions." Gray was probably referring to the childhood religious visions "the Prophet" claimed to have had. But elsewhere in the *Confessions*, Gray evoked this fearful image of Turner:

> The calm, deliberate composure with which he spoke of his late deeds and intentions, the expression of his fiend-like face when excited by enthusiasm, still bearing the stains of the blood of helpless innocence about him; clothed with rags and covered with chains; yet daring to raise his manacled hands to heaven, with a spirit soaring above the attributes of man; I looked on him and my blood curdled in my veins.

Most accounts at the time agree on the dignity with which Turner spoke to questioners such as Gray and confronted his final days. "Do you not find yourself mistaken now?" Gray once asked him shortly before his death. "The Prophet" quietly responded, "Was not Christ crucified?" Calmly and without recorded last words, Nat Turner went to his death at noon on November 11, 1831.

Nat Turner was hanged from this tree. His death did not end white fears, though the savage reprisals against blacks —innocent as well as guilty—probably discouraged other slave uprisings.

One man who was intensely concerned with the whole episode of the Nat Turner Revolt and its aftermath was the governor of Virginia, John Floyd. His diary provides an interesting account of what the insurrection meant to a moderate white Southerner.

Floyd, born in Kentucky, had trained as a surgeon before going into Virginia politics. He had served as a Democratic congressman from 1817 to 1829. Although originally a supporter of Andrew Jackson, he felt increasingly drawn to the views of Jackson's pro-Southern Vice President, John C. Calhoun. Unlike Calhoun, however, he opposed slavery and advocated gradual emancipation.

Floyd had been governor for only a year when the Nat Turner Revolt occurred. He first heard of the rebellion on Tuesday, August 23, when the rider from Jerusalem reached Richmond. Floyd took immediate charge of preparations for quelling the uprising. Within hours he dispatched several companies of militia to Southampton County. By the end of the week the governor received definite news that the rebellion had been crushed. Yet, on August 29, his diary recorded a request from several other Virginia counties and from the town of Fredericksburg for militiamen to help quell other expected slave revolts. Virginians were obviously uneasy.

Governor Floyd insisted on being kept closely informed about the trials of those blacks accused of taking part in the rebellion. So completely did the Nat Turner Revolt obsess him that his diary in the following months mentions little else but the Jerusalem trials, rumors of other slave conspiracies, and reflections on their meaning. By mid-September, however, Floyd became suspicious of the many reports of black unrest that flowed into Richmond. None of them seemed to materialize once state militia were sent into the area. Of one such rumor he wrote: "I do not exactly believe the report. The slaves are quiet and evince no disposition to rebel."

On several occasions Floyd expressed concern over the fate of those blacks sentenced to be sent to the Deep South. The treatment of slaves was generally much harsher there. Floyd debated whether to commute the sentences rather than "endanger the lives of these Negroes." On other occasions he reprieved some slaves who had been sentenced to death in Jerusalem. Indeed, there is evidence that the governor reviewed personally almost every convicted rebel's trial record.

At the same time, Floyd could not contain his fury at those Northern abolitionists who, he believed, had encouraged the Nat Turner Revolt and similar conspiracies. On September 27 he wrote:

> I have received this day another number of the *Liberator*, a newspaper printed in Boston with the express intention of inciting the slaves and free Negroes in this and the other states to rebellion and to murder the men, women, and children of those states. Yet we are gravely told there is no law to punish such an offense. The amount of it then is this, a man in our states may plot treason in one state against another without fear of punishment, whilst the suffering state has no right to resist by the provisions of the federal Constitution. If this is not checked it must lead to a separation of these states.

When not complaining about the abolitionists, the governor's diary often denounced President Andrew Jackson. Floyd considered him dangerous to Southern interests, especially on such issues as a national tariff policy. After receiving South Carolinian guests returning from an antitariff meeting at Philadelphia, Floyd noted in his diary that the election of Calhoun would "turn out Jackson with all his unworthy officers, men not gentlemen, who lie and slander all men opposed to them to keep themselves in power."

A page of Govenor Floyd's journal from September 1831. The entry for the 27th, as well as attacking the *Liberator*, speaks of his willingness to recommend mercy in the case of three slaves sentenced in Southampton County, but being unable to do so because of "the forms of our infamous [state] constitution."

The governor had little time for national politics, however. Requests for men and arms to combat expected slave revolts continued to pour into Richmond from every section of Virginia. Floyd's diary spoke constantly about the "Northern conspirators" who he believed were planning fiendish schemes. As late as October 20, Floyd recorded hearing of a plot by "Northern fanatics" in Philadelphia to stir up a general insurrection throughout Virginia and massacre its white population. Floyd treated the rumors coming from outside his state more seriously than he did those concerning slave conspiracies within Virginia itself, and his diary cautioned that, if the North refused to check the activities of abolitionists, "this Union is at an end as we [in the South] cannot consent to be tied up by the confederacy from doing ourselves justice, when the authorities of those states refuse to check the evil."

Turner's capture and execution only reinforced the determination of antislavery Virginians like John Floyd to prevent such future uprisings, not simply by supervising blacks in the state more closely but also by eliminating the source of discontent itself—that is, slavery. "There are still demands for arms in the lower counties," Floyd's diary commented on November 21. "I could not have believed there was half the fear amongst the people of the lower counties in respect to their slaves."

The problem never seemed to die down, as the governor's subsequent November entries indicate:

> Twenty-third day. I have reprieved for sale and transportation southward several slaves.
> Twenty-sixth day. I have received more applications for arms.
> Twenty-eighth day. I am preparing a message to the General Assembly. It will be will be ultra states' rights.

By "ultra states' rights" Floyd meant that he would demand that Northern states begin controlling the activities of abolitionists; also he would denounce the federal government for raising tariff duties, in opposition to Southern desires for lower rates.

In his "message to the General Assembly" (the state legislature) the governor also planned to deal with the question of slavery itself. His diary notes: "Before I leave this government, I will have contrived to have a law passed gradually abolishing slavery in this state, or at all events to begin the work by prohibiting slavery on the west side of the Blue Ridge Mountains."

Floyd's plan may sound surprising to us today, but it had the support of many of his fellow Virginians. In large sections of the state slavery had never assumed great economic or social importance. Men like Floyd and Thomas Ritchie of the Richmond *Enquirer* spoke for many Virginians in supporting gradual freeing of the slaves. They favored compensated emancipation—that is, slaveholders would be paid for the slaves who were freed. Most of those who favored this type of emancipation also believed in colonization—resettling former slaves elsewhere. (Africa was the location most commonly thought of.)

Opposition to slavery was particularly strong in the hilly areas and lush valleys west of the Blue Ridge Mountains. There, blacks (whether slave or free) numbered less than 20 percent of the population. In the eastern sections of Virginia, plantation slavery was common and blacks numbered over 50 percent of the total population. Here, supporters of abolition were less numerous.

During the early decades of the nineteenth century, many antislavery voices such as John Floyd's were raised throughout the South. The leading organization devoted to gradual, compensated emancipation—the American Colonization Society—found many of its leaders, and followers, in the region.

When Floyd addressed the state legislature in December 1831, he urged its members to abolish slavery by gradual stages in Virginia. Debate began in January 1832. For three weeks Virginia's legislators wrestled with the problem of abolishing slavery. They engaged in the bluntest and most complete debate on this question ever to take place in the antebellum[5] South. Supporters and opponents of emancipation marshaled their arguments in long speeches detailing the benefits or dangers that would flow from such a policy. Even those who defended the institution did so mainly on the grounds that it was an unavoidable reality rather than a blessing.

A typical defense was that of a delegate named John T. Brown:

Govenor Floyd, though favoring gradual emancipation at the time of the 1831–1832 debate in Virginia, soon afterwood took a strong proslavery position.

> And is there, then, no apology for slavery? Is it a sin of so deep a die that none dare vindicate it? For my own part, I am not the advocate of slavery in the abstract, and if the question were upon introducing it, I should be the very last to agree to it. But I am yet to be convinced that slavery as it exists in Virginia is either criminal or immoral. It was cast upon us by the act of others. It is our lot, our destiny, and whether, in truth, it be right or wrong—whether it be a blessing or a curse—the moment has never yet been when it was possible for us to free ourselves from it. This is enough to satisfy my conscience, and I contend that the happiness of the slave does not call for his emancipation. His condition is better than that of four-fifths of the human family. He enjoys far more of the comforts of life, than the peasantry of many of the nations in Europe. The greater part of mankind must, in the nature of things, be poor and ignorant, toiling anxiously for their daily bread. All cannot be raised to the top of the scale. The Negro, of all others, is the least susceptible of elevation.

The debate ranged over many issues. What might be the economic effects of emancipation? How should colonization be handled? (Both supporters and opponents of abolition were in agreement on the need for this step if blacks were freed.) What was the morality of slaveholding? The specter of Nat Turner hung plainly over the entire proceedings. Few speakers, whatever their views on emancipation, bothered to disguise their anxiety over the prospect of future slave revolts. A typical antislavery speaker, for example, pleaded with his colleagues for support by reversing a standard proslavery argument. James McDowell observed:

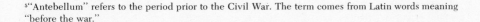

[5]"Antebellum" refers to the period prior to the Civil War. The term comes from Latin words meaning "before the war."

It is true to the letter that there is no laboring peasantry in any other part of the world who, in all external respects, are better situated than our slaves—who suffer less from want—who suffer less from hardship—who struggle less under the toils of life or who have a fuller supply of the comforts which mere physical nature demands. In all these respects the slave shares in the equalizing and benign spirit of our institutions and age.

But it is in this very circumstance, in this alleviated and improved condition, that we have a principal cause of apprehension from the slave. You raise his intelligence with his condition, and as he better understands his position in the world, he were not a man if it did not the more inflame his discontent. That it has this effect we all know. The truth is proverbial: that a slave is the more unhappy as he is the more indulged. He could not be otherwise; he follows but the impulse of human nature in being so.

Petitions for and against emancipation reached the legislature from all over Virginia. Debate was halted on January 25. Finally, the legislature voted on a mild measure providing for gradual emancipation over a period of many years. It was defeated by a vote of 73 to 58. The representatives had divided along distinct regional lines. Delegates from west of the Blue Ridge Mountains (who held only 102 slaves among them) supported abolition, 49 to 6. Representatives from the eastern areas (men who together owned 1,029 slaves) opposed emancipation by a margin of 67 to 9. The eastern counties were overrepresented in the legislature, as they had been since the time of Nathaniel Bacon. Thus they carried the day for slavery.

Antislavery Virginians such as Governor Floyd felt understandably disheartened. Floyd confided to his diary the thought that Virginia itself would split into two states on the question:

Goode, of Mecklenburgh [a slaveholder], said to me the day the debate closed upon the "slave question" that the eastern and western people were not all the same people, that they were essentially a different people, that they did not think alike, feel alike, and had no interests in common, that a separation of the state must ensue, and rather than have the subject of abolition again debated he would be glad for a separation. Both sides seem ready to separate the state if any one would propose it. I think that event from appearances highly probable.

Floyd was right, though the creation of a separate state—West Virginia—did not occur for another three decades.

As it turned out, the subject of abolition was never again debated anywhere in the antebellum South. Within months, antislavery Southerners like Governor Floyd shifted their attention to defending what they considered Southern rights over the question of tariff nullification. Yet the rebellion did force many white Southerners to confront their own deepest convictions about the relations between master and slave. Never again would this relationship seem as clear-cut as it had before the August rebellion in Southampton County.

The most lasting result of the Nat Turner Revolt turned out to be increasingly severe Southern control of both slaves and free blacks.

Many whites in the region apparently shared the fears (if not the conclusions) of the antislavery Virginia legislator who asked in January 1831:

> Was it the fear of Nat Turner and his deluded and drunken handful of followers which produced or could produce such effects? Was it this that induced distant counties, where the very name of Southampton was strange, to arm and equip for a struggle? No, it was the suspicion eternally attached to the slave himself, the suspicion that a Nat Turner might be in every family, that the same bloody deed could be acted over at any time in any place, that the materials for it were spread through the land and always ready for a like explosion.

A remarkable story was told by a black preacher who was in Virginia during the Nat Turner Revolt. Shortly after the rebellion a Southampton County slaveholder went hunting in the woods with a trusted slave, who carried his master's gun. The black had been with the slaveholder's family for many years, and he had led his master and his family to safety during the uprising. In the forest the bondsman handed the gun to his master, saying that he could no longer live as a slave. He asked his owner either to give him his freedom or to kill him. The white man hesitated for a moment, then took the gun and shot the black man through the heart.

Although this episode might never have occurred, it could be said that the choice it speaks of was given to white Virginians in the aftermath of the Nat Turner Revolt. Like the slaveholder in the story, they chose to kill the last promise of a peaceful emancipation.

18
SLAVERY IN THE UNITED STATES

A.W.

With the wisdom of hindsight, we can see that the issue of slavery was too complex to be resolved — even in one state — by a legislative debate such as that held in Virginia in 1832. The sons of these Virginians would go to war over the "peculiar institution." Their fathers and grandfathers had, after all, been wrestling with the problem unsuccessfully since the time of the Revolution.

When news of the Declaration of Independence reached England, even British supporters of the colonial cause complained about one aspect of the American Revolution. The "assigned cause and ground of the rebellion," wrote one Englishman, "is that every man hath an unalienable right to liberty and here the words, as it happens, are not nonsense, but then they are not true; slaves are there in America, and where there are slaves, there liberty is alienated." The practice of slavery in "republican" America seemed a glaring contradiction not only to Englishmen but to the revolutionaries themselves — many of whom owned black slaves. The Declaration of Independence opened with lofty phrases about equality. But the Second Continental Congress cautiously decided to omit a passage of the original draft that denounced human bondage. Some American leaders from Southern colonies, such as Thomas Jefferson and George Washington, expressed their concern over maintaining slavery within a democratic republic. But they did so privately.

The thirteen colonies contained about half a million slaves at the time of the Revolution. Every colony had some, but the great majority lived in the South. There were 200,000 in Virginia, 100,000 in South Carolina, and at least 70,000 each in Maryland and North Carolina. In some Southern colonies slaves composed 50 percent of the population. There were also slaves in the North. New York had 25,000 and New Jersey had about 10,000. Pennsylvania and Connecticut each had about 6,000 slaves. There were about 5,000 in Massachusetts and 4,000 in Rhode Island.

Fear of slave uprisings was common in eighteenth-century colonial America, despite the fact that only a few insurrections actually took place. Boston's Patriots were outraged by the presence of black troops among the occupying British army before the Boston Massacre. They were also angered by rumors that the redcoats were stirring up the city's small black population. Virginians were just as outraged in 1776 when the departing royal governor urged slaves to revolt against their masters and join the British in exchange for their freedom.

Along with fear of blacks went an equal measure of contempt. Most ordinary Americans of the Revolutionary era — even those who favored abolition — believed that blacks were innately inferior to whites. "Comparing them by their faculties of memory, reason and imagination," wrote Jefferson, "it appears to me that in memory they are equal to the whites, in reason much inferior, and in imagination dull and tasteless." Few people of Jefferson's time would have quarreled with his view (although some might have challenged the notion that a black person had a memory — or anything else — equal to a white's).

During the Confederation period, steps were taken to end slavery in large areas of the Republic. In the period between 1783 and 1786, Massachusetts, Connecticut, Rhode Island, New York, and New Jersey either abolished slavery outright or provided for its gradual disappearance. In Virginia the legislature passed an act in 1782 easing the process by which owners could emancipate their bondsmen. At Jefferson's direction the Northwest Ordinance of 1787 prohibited slavery in the Northwest Territory. And even though the Constitution made no provision for slavery as an institution, it did provide that the foreign slave trade be abolished after 1808.

Slave auctions were regarded as a necessary evil by many slaveowners. After turning some of his "people" over to an auctioneer, one Southerner grieved: "I did not know until the time came what pain it would give me." The auction pictured is at Richmond. The poster, from New Orleans, describes "choice Negroes" for sale.

But what would happen to slaves who were freed? Since even moderate whites feared blacks, or looked down on them, very few white Americans were prepared to accept a large free black population living among them. Most schemes for emancipation from the Revolutionary era up to the time of the Virginia legislative debate failed to resolve the problem of freed slaves. Most supporters of gradual emancipation, from Thomas Jefferson to John Floyd, believed in the need for colonization—a policy that was easier to agree on in principle than to achieve in practice.

The task of the North in emancipating its blacks after 1790 was relatively simple. The region contained only 40,000 slaves and 27,000 freed blacks; the white population totaled 1,900,000. Thus roughly 1 out of 28 people was a black. The situation was very different in the South, where there were 1,271,000 whites, 657,000 slaves, and 32,000 free blacks. In other words, over a third of the Southern population was black. By the time of the Nat Turner Revolt, through individual emancipation (a process known as manumission) and increases by birth, there were over 181,000 free blacks in the South.

Fears of an unstable free black population were obviously much greater among Southerners than among Northerners. Many white Southerners sincerely wanted to have slavery abolished. But Southern leaders from the time of the Founding Fathers until the Virginia legislative debate of 1832—and beyond—were afraid of even gradual emancipation. They thought it would pose a threat to the safety, stability, and "racial purity" of white society. Besides, slavery was profitable.

THE ECONOMICS OF SLAVERY

The antebellum South comprised a million square acres of territory. It stretched from Chesapeake Bay to western Texas and from the Ohio River south to the Gulf of Mexico. Although climate and terrain varied considerably in the South, most of the region had rainfall, temperature, and soil conditions adequate for producing a variety of staple cash crops.

During the colonial period, the major crops grown on Southern plantations were tobacco, rice, indigo, and (to a much lesser extent) cotton. In some areas more than one of these crops was important. In Southampton County, for example, farmers grew both rice and cotton on a large scale.

"King Cotton" Tobacco had been the South's leading export before the Revolution. But after 1800 the Southern economy came to center on cotton. The most important single factor in this change was the cotton gin. ("Gin" is short for "engine.") It was invented in 1793 by a New Englander named Eli Whitney. Before this time, separating cotton fiber from the seeds was done by hand and took a long time. But with Whitney's machine one person could do the work of fifty. At the same time, improvements in technology enabled England's textile industry to process raw cotton into cloth much more efficiently. Thus, early in the nineteenth century, growing cotton became truly profitable in the United States.

Cotton cultivation spread throughout older states such as Georgia and South Carolina. Even more important cotton-growing areas were the as yet sparsely settled regions that eventually became the states of Alabama, Mississippi, Louisiana, Texas, and Arkansas. The United States had exported only 3,000 bales of cotton in 1790. By the time of Nat Turner's Revolt this figure had grown to 805,000 bales. By 1859, on the eve of Civil War, the figure had skyrocketed to 4 1/2 million bales. Cotton alone accounted for almost two-thirds of the total export trade of the United States. And the United States—or, more particularly, the American South—had become the world's leading cotton producer. Along with this phenomenal growth went a continuing demand for more slaves to raise the crop.

Tobacco growing remained important in nineteenth-century Virginia, Kentucky, and North Carolina. Rice cultivation prospered along the South Carolina and Georgia seacoasts. Sugarcane production dominated Louisiana agriculture. Elsewhere in the South the main crop was cotton. Cotton alone accounted for almost two-thirds of the total export trade of the United States.

Who Owned Slaves The 1850 census showed that 1,815,000 slaves were employed in cotton production. Some 350,000 worked in the tobacco fields; 125,000 raised rice; 150,000 labored on sugar plantations; and 60,000 produced hemp. Smaller numbers worked as house servants and artisans on plantations. Several thousand labored as workers in the South's few mines and factories.

Throughout the nineteenth century, a constant flow of both white settlers and black slaves shifted millions of Southerners away from the older seaboard regions and into the newer regions of Alabama, Mississippi, Louisiana, Arkansas, and Texas. Older states such as Virginia and Maryland declined in economic importance in the South because they produced relatively little cotton (despite the output of scattered areas such as Southampton County). During the decades between Nat Turner's Revolt and the Civil War, more than 700,000 slaves were sold in the United States, mainly by owners in the Upper South to purchasers in the Deep South.

It would be incorrect to think of the South-

A mansion in Louisiana typifies the Greek Revival style favored by wealthy Southerners. Built in 1840, it was owned by a prominent sugar planter.

ern population as divided simply into two groups—white owners and black slaves. Most white Southerners owned no slaves at all. Most whites who owned slaves in Southampton County and other regions in the South, worked alongside their own bondsmen in the fields.

The entire white population of the South in 1860 numbered approximately 7 million, with the total of white families estimated at 1,400,000. There were 383,635 slaveholders. This meant that almost three out of every four families owned no slaves. Only 2,292 landowners owned more than 100 slaves. Some 46,000 slaveholders owned between 20 and 100. The great majority of slaveholders—those owning fewer than twenty slaves—were not owners of large plantations but simply moderately successful independent farmers, who worked alongside their own bondsmen in the fields. Except in the richest cotton-producing areas, slaveholders generally formed a minority of local landowners.

Before the 1830s, some slaveowners freed their own slaves. Like Governor Floyd, they expected that the policy of a colonized, gradual emancipation would be generally adopted throughout the South. But new laws made the practice of manumission more difficult after the Nat Turner Revolt. In any case, most nineteenth-century slaveholders did not consider the possibility of emancipation very seriously.

SOUTHERN SOCIETY

The social structure of the antebellum South resembled a pyramid. The region's few thousand large planters stood at the top. Beneath them was the larger group of slaveholding whites, who owned enough slaves to staff a small or medium-size plantation. Further down the pyramid stood the majority of slaveholders, who owned fewer than twenty slaves. Below them was the great mass of landowning but nonslaveholding white farmers. Toward the base of the pyramid were the lowest white Southerners, the landless and luckless "poor whites," who generally farmed the region's less fertile hill-country areas. At the base of the pyramid were, of course, the slaves themselves, on whose labor rested the South's entire social and economic structure.

Several groups in the South stood outside the central structure of plantation power and influence. There were professionals and businessmen, people like the journalist Thomas Ritchie or the physician (and governor) John Floyd. Such people were often absorbed into the plantation aristocracy by marriage, political alliance, or slave purchases. There were also free blacks—roughly 228,000 in 1860. Most of them lives in the cities of the Upper South or in New Orleans. Though better off than slaves, they were distrusted and discriminated against by Southern whites.

The plantation gentry were the elite of the South. They and their supporters dominated Southern politics up to the Civil War. Their social events, held in the larger cities and towns, set the tone for Southern society. Their impressive mansions often became centers of social life for the surrounding communities.

Though they might be compared to foreign aristocrats, Southern planters differed from them in at least two ways. (1) They were a working aristocracy. The business records of countless plantations show that the men and women who ran them were constantly concerned with the many problems of cash-crop agriculture. (2) They lived on their lands much of the time, rather than being absentee owners. This direct involvement helps account for the fact that slaveholders in the American South worked out a systematic proslavery argument to justify their holdings (see pages 331–333). They were the only "master class" in the Western Hemisphere to do so.

Susan Dabney Smedes, a planter's wife, once observed that "managing a plantation was something like managing a kingdom." A planter often found himself playing many roles within a brief space of time. He was an absolute ruler of his slaves. He was an aristocrat among fellow planters. He was a democratic politician among white men of all classes. He was a fellow Christian when conducting plantation religious services (often for a mixed audience of family members and slaves). The strains of moving back and forth quickly among such different roles produced anguish

Charleston in 1831

among some planters, at least according to their own diary accounts.

Planter Society The most typical of the South's few cities—as racially-mixed and tolerant New Orleans was atypical—was Charleston, South Carolina, the cultural center of the Old South. A prosperous seaport since colonial times, the planters of the area, together with the town merchants, supported concerts, lectures, plays, and libraries when such refinements were unknown elsewhere in the colonies. Charlestonians could point to the following "firsts": public library (1698), theater (1736), symphony orchestra (1762), city college (1770), and museum (1773).

The ebb and flow of social life was governed by the customs of the planters. From May to November, when the rice fields were under irrigation, they lived in the city to avoid the dangers of malaria. The Christmas holidays were usually spent in the countryside. By the end of January, the planters were back in town for a round of races, dinners, balls, and other entertainments.

Fully half the population of the city—the slaves—did not share in these pleasures. They were subject to many restrictions because of their numbers and fears of a revolt. In colonial times, slave uprisings that had broken out in Charleston had been crushed with great severity. In 1822 came the Denmark Vesey plot. Public gatherings of blacks were forbidden. Black sailors—free elsewhere—were jailed while their ships were in port. In 1815 Charleston was the leading port for the export of cotton and rice. But, as cotton growing spread into the Deep South, the city gradually lost its importance.

Conditions Favoring Slavery If so few Southerners actually owned slaves, why did the whole society support slavery so solidly from the Nat Turner Revolt to the South's secession in 1860? Probably a majority of the volunteer militiamen who had helped to quell Turner's uprising owned no slaves, yet they seemed passionately committed to maintaining slavery. Why? At least one answer suggests itself immediately in light of the Southampton County experience. Fear of slave insurrections was intense and constant among antebellum white Southerners. As whites rode their nightly slave patrols in the years after the 1831 uprising, many of them must have remembered that Nat Turner's band slaughtered slaveholders and nonslaveholding whites alike. Thus concern for personal and family security helped bind together different economic classes in the South.

Southerners also favored slavery because of its psychological advantages. The existence of a slave class gave all whites—especially poor white landless farmers—some reassurance that they were superior. Black people like Nat Turner and his men had no status within Southern white society. Even the poorest, least educated white person meant more in the eyes of the law and in Southern society than a planter's brightest, most talented slave. Nat Turner acknowledged having received special treatment from his original owner. But Turner had few, if any, rights that any white person was bound to respect.

Slaves on sugar plantations were driven very hard. During the harvest season, many worked from sixteen to eighteen hours a day, seven days a week.

Belief in the inferiority of blacks was common among almost all Southern (and Northern) whites, whatever their class. This universal sense of white supremacy blurred the sharp contrast between the South's democratic political system and its rigid economic structure, controlled by a few. Planters and poor whites, if they shared nothing else, still felt a common concern for maintaining slavery and the white racial unity it represented.

Slavery influenced status in another way. Nonslaveholding white farmers could aspire to purchase slaves, and some managed to do so; a few even broke into the planter ranks. When this happened, it bolstered the prevailing belief among white Southerners that only an economy run by slave labor could ensure a broad range of economic opportunity.

Clearly, anxiety, outright fear, and ambition helped create a feeling among almost all Southerners that their "peculiar institution" should be retained and, if necessary, defended. One other factor reinforced the consensus. Southerners were subject to fewer outside influences and new ideas than other Americans. For one thing, most white Southerners were native-born and therefore used to the customs of their region. Only 4.4 percent of the Southern population in 1860 was foreign-born, compared to 18.7 percent elsewhere in the country. Also, there were fewer big cities in the South than in other regions. Even places like Norfolk and Richmond were little more than overgrown country towns. The vibrant, unsettling qualities of urban life affected only a small minority. Most white Southerners lived on farms, on plantations, or in small towns such as Jerusalem. The bulk of the South's free blacks, however, did live in towns and cities—where they were closely watched and their movements rigidly supervised. Cities thus remained the most obvious breeding ground of discontent with the slave system. And free blacks were clearly the most dangerous element within the closed world of slave society.

The Treatment of Slaves The conditions under which slaves lived varied considerably. They could be treated relatively mildly and with consideration. Nat Turner, for instance, said that he was well treated by both his original owner and Joseph Travis. But savagely harsh practices prevailed on rice and sugar plantations in the Deep South. Slaves from other regions of the South were sent there to be punished, as was the case after the Nat Turner Revolt.

Because slaves were valuable property, an owner seldom abused them so cruelly that they died. Short of this, however, a master treated his slaves pretty much as he pleased. In times of extreme social tension, whites subjected blacks to the most degrading punishment with little fear of legal action or social criticism. Most recent scholars agree, however, that, under ordinary circumstances, slaves in the United States were generally better fed, housed, and clothed than those in Latin America during the same period. The economic condition of many slaves probably did compare favorably with that of many industrial workers in the North and elsewhere—as proslavery people argued. (Even black rebels such as Nat Turner did not complain primarily about their *economic* conditions.) Some slaves were allowed to grow crops on private patches and to keep animals, for their own use or for sale. Almost every plantation had a weekly day of rest and special holidays as well. Nat Turner's companions were probably not

Although some owners provided good housing for their slaves, much of it was poor, like this ramshackle cabin. Southern physicians often warned planters that they had to provide flooring, windows, and adequate space in order to prevent illness and disease.

missed by their owners as they spent that final Sunday eating roast pig, drinking brandy, and scheming rebellion.

Yet, no matter how kindly a master might treat his slaves, the slavery system was brutal, for it rested ultimately on force. "The whole commerce between master and slave," wrote Thomas Jefferson from his own experience, "is a perpetual exercise of the most boisterous passions. The most unremitting despotism on the one part, and degrading submission on the other." Slave codes, such as those strengthened throughout the South following the Nat Turner uprising, gave whites almost unrestrained physical power over their slaves. A slave master had absolute authority to decide how long his slaves should work and under what conditions. The law permitted the whipping and beating of slaves. Southern newspapers and court records during the antebellum decades contained numerous accounts of how slaves had been

mutilated, hanged, shot, starved to death, or even burned alive. (Indeed, the Southern press was the abolitionists' major source for reports on the mistreatment of blacks.)

The law seldom imposed more than minor penalties on whites found guilty of deliberately injuring or killing blacks. Most often, the offenders escaped punishment completely—as did the white militiamen who committed hundreds of atrocities against Southampton County blacks in 1831. Blacks, whether slaves or freemen, were not allowed to testify against whites in Southern courts of law.

It was often impossible for slaves to keep their families together as units. Slave marriages had no legal status. Slave families were separated and the members were sold individually as a matter of course. How understandable, then, that the troops of "General Nat" broke ranks at the Parker plantation to collect their missing kinfolk!

ATTITUDES OF BLACKS

In spite of massive oppression, many slaves appeared to be devoted to their masters, whether from affection, loyalty, or outright fear. This attitude emerges not only from the narratives of slaveholders themselves but from other sources. The slaves who belonged to Dr. Blunt defended their master by firing upon Nat Turner's retreating band. In the Vesey plot and in an 1800 conspiracy in Virginia—led by a slave artisan named Gabriel Prosser—fellow blacks were prominent among those who betrayed the plotters. There are at least two ways of looking at this situation. On the one hand, trusted and indulged slaves such as house servants and artisans had most to lose in any slave uprising—namely, their privileged status. Therefore, they might be expected to place loyalty to their white overlords above any feeling of kinship with rebel slaves. On the other hand, an effective slave rebellion was conceivable only among well-treated bondsmen such as Prosser or Turner. Such people could move easily among other blacks in their areas without arousing the white community's suspicion.

Often in history, those in an oppressed group who have privileged status, but most conscious of their condition, are willing to risk all. So it was with the slave preachers, artisans, house servants, and freed blacks who joined the Prosser, Vesey, and Turner conspiracies. It was easy for Nat Turner's original band of supporters—Will, Hark, Henry, Sam, Nelson, and Jack—to meet with their leader. They plotted rebellion for several months while attending church services and weekend gatherings, and on slave holidays, before finally deciding to strike. Their long period of preparation shows how confident slaveholders in the region were about the loyalty of their most trusted bondsmen.

Slave revolts were relatively uncommon in the antebellum South. Yet blacks used a number of other ways to indicate how much they opposed the system. Many slaves tried to flee from bondage: Almost every plantation owner worried about runaways. Some slaves reached freedom in the North, especially after abolitionists organized the "underground railroad" (see page 404). Others simply took off and hid in the woods for a while (as Nat Turner had done), often returning voluntarily as a sign of independence. The huge number of runaways in the antebellum South showed that many slaves silently nursed a keen desire for freedom, despite all the efforts by slaveholders to break the will of their blacks. Sabotage was common, too. Blacks burned crops and stole supplies. They also pretended to be sick, loafed on the job, and found other, often ingenious, ways to express their hatred for the system.

The Role of Religion In all the efforts by blacks to undermine slavery, the black church and its preachers played a significant role. Most slaves followed the religion of their masters, evangelical Protestantism.[1] It was hardly accidental that, after the Nat Turner Revolt, the Virginia legislature placed a ban on blacks like Turner wandering freely through the countryside preaching the Gospel. Most Southern states tried to restrict the activities of black church meetings from the 1830s on—and with good reason. For one thing, slaves bent on rebellion could plot in safety at such gatherings. For another, the Bible itself—especially the Old Testament—offered to blacks prepared to interpret it that way an ideology that justified resistance. Southern whites may have regarded as strange Nat Turner's claim that a heavenly vision had instructed him to lead his people from bondage and to slaughter their oppressors. But most of his fellow slaves would have immediately understood what he meant.

The spirituals sung by slaves in their churches and elsewhere expressed a great deal. They dwelt on the belief blacks held of themselves as a "chosen" people. "We are the people of God," said one. Another proclaimed: "I'm a child of God, with my soul set free." Such images probably helped keep many slaves from adopting their masters' view of them as submissive chil-

---

[1] In general, evangelical Protestants stress the teachings of the Bible rather than the authority of organized church doctrine. They also emphasize the importance of an individual's personal conversion.

JOHN RANDOLPH

John Randolph once said that asking one of the states to surrender part of its sovereignty was like asking a woman to surrender part of her virtue. This quip is typical of his wit. It also neatly summarizes his passionate belief in the sanctity of states' rights. To this proud, eccentric member of the Randolph family of Virginia, only Republican (Antifederalist) principles could ensure personal liberty and freedom from the "tyranny" of strong central government. To the end of his life he espoused these principles, sacrificing political friendships and his own promising career for the often reckless role of congressional gadfly.

In 1799, at the age of twenty-six, Randolph was elected to the House from Charlotte County. For the next thirty years, except for three two-year intervals (a single defeat, sickness, and service as a senator), he represented this district. His appearances on the floor of the House commanded attention. Usually a bit late, he would swagger in, whip in hand, booted and spurred, with one or two of his favorite hunting dogs. He would speak off the cuff in a rambling and theatrical fashion, scattering epigrams right and left. One historian described him as "one of the most brilliant figures that ever strutted and fretted his hour upon the American public stage."

Randolph's high point was his leadership in gaining congressional approval for the Louisiana Purchase in 1803. He did this although he felt that Jefferson was stretching his constitutional powers. Randolph himself believed in a strict interpretation of the Constitution in order to limit the scope of federal power.

His low point came in 1805, when he bungled the politically inspired impeachment trial of a Federalist judge and quarreled with Jefferson. In 1806 Randolph declared himself independent of his party, accusing Jefferson of "pulling Federalism forward." His opposition to the War of 1812, which swelled the power and popularity of the federal government, cost him his congressional seat.

Randolph returned to Congress in 1815 and opposed on principle the Bank of the United States, the tariff, and other nationalistic measures. His eccentric behavior remained unchecked, but he was no longer a figure of influence. It was the Missouri Compromise of 1820 that brought him back to the limelight—as a spokesman for states' rights and for the Southern way of life. He first linked the ideas that John Calhoun later developed more fully. He also pitted himself against the architect of the compromise, Henry Clay. The two even fought a duel in 1826. According to Clay, Randolph's actions "came near shaking this Union to the center, and desolating this fair land."

Randolph's final position was not altogether congenial to him and to others of his generation who were uneasy about slavery. He regarded himself a friend to blacks. By the terms of his will he freed his 400 slaves. When once asked whom he considered the greatest orator he had ever known, Randolph replied, "A slave, Sir. She was a mother, and her rostrum was the auction-block."

dren. The spirituals were "sorrow songs," telling of all the troubles and suffering that slaves experienced. They rarely spoke of black inferiority, inadequacy, or unworthiness.

In their religious lives, slaves found more than simply the strength to endure suffering, certain of a reward in heaven. Often, as in the case of Nat Turner, they also discovered the power to resist actively the efforts of those in authority to brutalize and degrade them. Spirituals, and the sermons of black preachers, were often prophetic. They promised a proud vision of betterment, justice, freedom, and personal worth. They taught that slaves could rise above slavery—not only in the next world, but in this one as well. Nat Turner and his fellow black ministers preached that their people could escape from bondage, through their own efforts and with the help of God. Countless deeds of slave resistance were inspired by this vision. It was embedded in the spiritual life of Southern blacks. Nat Turner's Revolt, the most extreme act of resistance by antebellum blacks, can be understood only as the product of such intense religious belief.

JUSTIFYING THE SYSTEM

While blacks found in the Bible a means of enduring slavery, white Southerners turned increasingly to it, and other writings, for evidence to help justify the system. Earlier proslavery advocates—such as those in the 1832 Virginia legislative debate—had apologized for slavery as a "necessary evil" inherited from the past. In the 1830s Southern political figures, led by Calhoun, began aggressively defending their peculiar institution. Southerners were disturbed for several reasons. They were shaken by such episodes as the Vesey and Turner revolts. The growth of abolitionism in the North frightened them. So did South Carolina's lonely championing of Southern interests in the nullification crises of 1832–1833. In defense, they began arguing that their system of bondage was morally justified on all grounds. In 1837, Calhoun expressed this point of view: "Where two races of different origin, and distinguished by color and other physical differences, as well as intellectual, are brought together, the relation now existing in the slaveholding states between the two is, instead of an evil, a good—a positive good."

Slavery as a Positive Good The "positive good" argument dominated the thinking of white Southerners between 1832 and the Civil War. The region's leading thinkers went to enormous lengths to devise a rationale for slavery. In doing so, they supported a set of beliefs that differed from the basically optimistic and democratic attitudes held by other Americans elsewhere in the country.

An antislavery cartoon, published in 1840, mocks the idea, advanced by many Southerners, that blacks had to be treated like children. Depicting black people as competent and capable was part of the strategy of those who favored colonization.

Southerners argued that most men are naturally limited in their capacities. They said that human progress and achievement come only at the cost of enslaving peoples that are supposedly suited for such bondage. And they held that human society has always been characterized by class distinctions. Not even the extreme proslavery advocates during the 1831–1832 Virginia legislative debates would have accepted such propositions. Yet, within a decade, they had become the orthodox Southern view of its "peculiar institution."

Governor James H. Hammond of South Carolina insisted that "in all social systems there must be a class to do the menial duties, to perform the drudgery of life." Without such a class, Hammond argued, "you would not have that other class which leads progress, civilization, and refinement." Slavery, then, "constitutes the very mudsill of society and of political government." George Fitzhugh, a brilliant proslavery spokesman, put it in a livelier way. He declared that "some are born with saddles on their backs, and others booted and spurred to ride them—and the riding does them good." These writers argued that whites could not be expected to perform the backbreaking tasks associated with cotton, rice, and tobacco cultivation. Slaves, therefore, became an economic necessity.

Proslavery people used a number of arguments in attempting to prove the virtues of slavery. They found citations in the Bible that justified enslavement, especially instructions that slaves obey their masters. They pointed to the glories of ancient Greece and Rome—both slave societies. They compared, unfavorably, the working conditions of Northern industrial laborers with those of Southern slaves. And, arguing from the false "scientific" theories of their day, they accepted the notion of the innate inferiority of black people.

Proslavery advocates also glorified planters as an aristocracy of talent and grace. Southern gentlemen were pictured as chivalrous heroes, brave and quick to defend their honor. Southern ladies were portrayed as gentle noblewomen who devoted countless leisure-filled days to such "feminine" pastimes as needlework and music. These romantic images were highly unrealistic. Yet reality and myth agreed on at least one aspect of regional life. Even hostile accounts of the slave South usually acknowledged the longstanding planter traditions of hospitality and generosity toward friend and stranger alike.

Basic to the proslavery defense was a false image of black people. White Southerners insisted on describing blacks as submissive, contented happy-go-lucky children. "A merrier being does not exist on the face of the globe," wrote one Vir-

Proslavery Americans undoubtedly enjoyed this pictorial jibe at the sometimes overheated arguments of abolitionists. It appeared in *Harper's Weekly* in 1861.

UNCLE CLEM. "Say, Massa Jim, is I wan of them onfortunate Niggers as you was reading about?"
YOUNG GENTLEMAN. "Yes, Uncle Clem, you are one of them."
UNCLE CLEM. "Well, it's a great pity about me.—I'se berry badly off, I is."

SLAVE STATES, 1860—PROPORTION OF WHITE AND BLACK POPULATION

(Figures rounded off to nearest whole percentage point.)

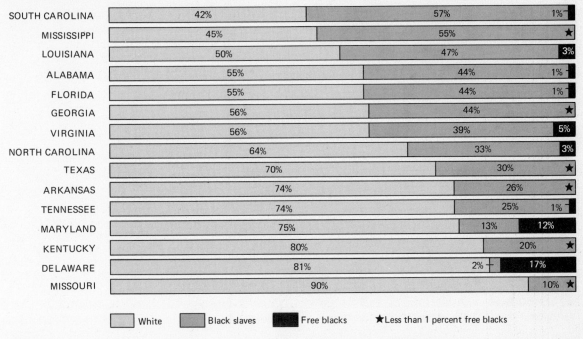

	White	Black slaves	Free blacks
SOUTH CAROLINA	42%	57%	1%
MISSISSIPPI	45%	55%	★
LOUISIANA	50%	47%	3%
ALABAMA	55%	44%	1%
FLORIDA	55%	44%	1%
GEORGIA	56%	44%	★
VIRGINIA	56%	39%	5%
NORTH CAROLINA	64%	33%	3%
TEXAS	70%	30%	★
ARKANSAS	74%	26%	★
TENNESSEE	74%	25%	1%
MARYLAND	75%	13%	12%
KENTUCKY	80%	20%	★
DELAWARE	81%	2%	17%
MISSOURI	90%	10%	★

White　■ Black slaves　■ Free blacks　★ Less than 1 percent free blacks

ginian, "than the Negro slave of the United States." This docile image fitted the hopes of Southern slaveholders better than it did the realities of their lives. But Southerners were concerned less with convincing outsiders than with persuading themselves that their proslavery arguments were true. So they convinced themselves of the happiness and essential docility of their slaves, despite all the evidence to the contrary.

The End of Moderation A frank and hard-hitting public debate in the South over the merits of slavery, like the one held in Virginia in 1832, would have been impossible a decade later. Even the idea of gradual emancipation, accompanied by colonization, could not be argued openly in the 1840s. By that time, no Southern state would have elected an emancipationist governor such as John Floyd. Opponents of slavery were driven from positions in Southern churches, universities, and newspapers. Freedom of speech and press on the slavery question no longer existed in the South during the decades before the Civil War. "South-

ern rights" were to be defended at all costs.

Even before this time, white fears and class tensions had made the South a notoriously violent region. The vengeance taken by militiamen against Southampton County blacks after the Nat Turner uprising did not appear excessive to most white Southerners. The antibellum South was noted for its expert brawlers, marksmen, and duelists. Most southerners owned guns or at least bowie knives (also known as "Arkansas toothpicks").

Once the "positive good" argument took hold during the 1830s, the level of militancy rose among white Southerners. Planters and their overseers armed themselves, and slave patrols rode regularly through the hot Southern nights. Many plantations became tiny military fortresses, their owners obsessed with thoughts of runaways and rebellions. Southern whites became "militarized," not only on their plantations but also in the cities, where militia and town guards watched free blacks closely. By the late 1840s most white Southerners had accepted a view that linked the defense of slavery to every other cherished virtue.

This 1850 drawing manages to be inaccurate about Southern slavery and British industrialism. Rarely did slaves have the time or energy (or heart) for carefree jollity. Nor did British workers die at forty or labor even fourteen hours a day.

The region's leading Presbyterian minister, the Reverend J. H. Thornwell, argued in 1850 that:

> the parties in this conflict are not merely abolitionists and slaveholders—they are atheists, socialists, communists, red republicans, jacobins on one side, and the friends of order and regulated freedom on the other. In a word, the world is the battleground—Christianity and atheism the combatants; and the progress of humanity the stake.

Thornwell probably spoke for the great majority of white Southerners.

The uncharitable, suspicious, and militant South of Thornwell's day seems light years away from the more leisurely, less fearful world of John Floyd and his fellow Virginians. Antislavery Southerners, of either Jefferson's generation or Floyd's, would have found little worth praising in the positive good argument. Yet leaders like Floyd had helped prepare the way for the more aggressive Southerners who followed.

Floyd, after all, supported John C. Calhoun. Like Calhoun, he managed to combine a strong nationalist fervor with an equally passionate belief in Southern rights. He had endorsed South Carolina's attempt at nullification. He opposed slavery, but he had denounced abolitionists and roused public opinion against the "menace" of Northern "agitators." Floyd's generation found it possible to believe strongly in gradual emancipation while at the same time nursing a violent hatred for Northern advocates of immediate abolition.

The next generation hardened its point of view. One Southerner who would have agreed with Thornwell was John Buchanan Floyd, son of the antislavery Virginia governor. John Buchanan Floyd believed wholeheartedly in slavery. Like his father, he went into politics. He served as secretary of war from 1857 to 1860 in the cabinet of President James Buchanan. While in this post, Floyd transferred an excessive number of arms from Northern to Southern arsenals. His aim was to stockpile military supplies for the sectional conflict everyone expected.

John Buchanan Floyd resigned from the Buchanan cabinet in December 1860, a convinced secessionist. After Virginia joined the Confederacy in May 1861, he volunteered his services to Virginia. Exactly three decades earlier, his father had unsuccessfully urged the Virginia legislature to abolish slavery. Now John Buchanan Floyd accepted a commission from the same legislature. He would become a major general in an army dedicated to preserve the South's "peculiar institution."

SUGGESTED READINGS – CHAPTERS 17-18

The Nat Turner Revolt

Herbert Aptheker, *American Negro Slave Revolts* (1943); William Styron, *The Confessions of Nat Turner* (1967); John B. Duff and Peter M. Mitchell, eds., *The Nat Turner Rebellion: The Historical Event and the Modern Controversy* (1971).

Slavery

John W. Blassingame, *The Slave Community* (1972); P. A. Davis, et al., *Reckoning with Slavery* (1976); Robert A. Fogel and Stanley L. Engerman, *Time on the Cross* (2 vols., 1974); John Hope Franklin, *From Slavery to Freedom* (1974); George M. Frederickson, *The Black Image in the White Mind: The Debate on Afro-American Character and Destiny, 1817–1914* (1971); Winthrop D. Jordan, *White Over Black* (1969); Kenneth M. Stampp, *The Peculiar Institution* (1956).

Slavery in America and Elsewhere

David B. Davis, *The Problem of Slavery in Western Culture* (1966); Carl Degler, *Neither Black Nor White: Slavery and Race Relations in Brazil and the United States* (1971); Stanley M. Elkins, *Slavery: A Problem in American Institutional and Intellectual Life* (1959); William Stanton, *The Leopard's Spots: Scientific Attitudes Toward Race in America, 1815–1859* (1960); Allen Weinstein and Frank Otto Gatell, eds., *American Negro Slavery: A Modern Reader* (3rd ed., 1978); Lawrence J. Levine, *Black Culture and Black Consciousness: Patterns of Afro-American Folk Thought in the United States* (1976).

The Negro in the North

Leon Litwack, *North of Slavery: The Negro in the Free States, 1790–1860* (1961); George Rawick, *From Sundown to Sunup: The Making of the Black Community* (1973); Richard Wade, *Slavery in the Cities* (1964).

The Negro in the South

Clement Eaton, *A History of the Old South* (1975) and *The Growth of Southern Civilization, 1790–1860* (1961); Eugene D. Genovese, *Roll, Jordan, Roll* (1974); Herbert G. Gutman, *The Black Family in Slavery and Freedom, 1750–1925* (1976); William Scarborough, *The Overseer: Plantation Management in the Old South* (1966); Robert Starobin, *Industrial Slavery in the Old South* (1970); Charles S. Sydnor, *The Development of Southern Sectionalism, 1819–1848* (1948); William R. Taylor, *Cavalier and Yankee: The Old South and American National Character* (1961).

19
CRISIS AND COMPROMISE IN 1850

A.W.

Potomac River breezes chilled the air as legislators returned to Washington, D.C., in December 1849 for the opening of Congress. Senators and representatives tramped through muddy streets past the city's boarding houses, hotels, and half-finished public buildings. An incomplete stone tower jutted out like a bruised silo; when completed several decades later, it would be a monument to George Washington. The Capitol, still topped by a temporary dome, was being repaired and enlarged to make room for the growing number of congressmen who crowded into its corridors with the admission of each new state into the Union.

The mood in Washington when a new Congress convenes is normally charged with excitement. There was special reason, though, for intense feeling in December 1849. Politicians from the North and South feared that the issue of slavery would wreck the approaching Thirty-first Congress. Some brooded anxiously over the possible collapse of the Union itself.

American politicans had deliberately suppressed the slavery question in national politics since the days of the Founding Fathers. No other issue could arouse Americans to such emotion. No other issue had such power to overcome party loyalties. Southerners were particularly troubled. Fearful of abolitionist attacks since the Nat Turner uprising a generation earlier, they warned that Northern interference with slavery could lead to a breakdown of the national party system.

A struggle to elect a Speaker of the House of Representatives began almost from the moment Congress opened on December 3. The difficulty confirmed the fears about sectional political warfare. The

Democratic party had dominated national politics since the days of Jackson. There were now 112 Democrats in the House and 109 Whigs. There were also 9 members of the newly formed Free Soil party.

Normally the majority party in the House agrees on its candidate for Speaker and then elects him at the opening session. But these were not normal times. The third party representatives held the balance of power, preventing either major party from having a majority.

Bitterness over slavery and sectional issues strained party lines, threatening to break them beyond repair. The Whigs nominated Robert C. Winthrop of Massachusetts, a descendant of the Puritan governor. He opposed the extension of slavery into the Western territories, but he was not an abolitionist. Still, eight Southern Whigs stormed out of the party's caucus. When the Democrats chose Howell Cobb of Georgia, a supporter of slavery, a small but significant minority of Northern Democrats balked at the choice. These defections meant that neither party could exercise control.

Vote followed vote for three weeks. After sixty-two ballots, the House had still failed to select a Speaker. Even the withdrawal of Cobb's and Winthrop's names on various ballots could not break the stalemate. This frustrating inaction immobilized the entire government. Congress was paralyzed. The Senate could not function without the House. President Zachary Taylor could not deliver his annual message.

On December 22 both sides finally recognized the dangers, and they agreed to change the election system itself. House members resolved that, in order to be elected, a Speaker would in future need only a plurality of votes, not a majority. On the sixty-third ballot they finally chose Cobb. Several Northern Democrats who had opposed Cobb voted for him in the end. Some doubtless hoped to ease the tension. Others were simply tired. "Many members," observed Senator Daniel Webster of Massachusetts, "wished to go home for the holidays."

The new Speaker was a moderate, genial man, popular with most

When this photograph of the Capitol was made in the 1840s, the building was still surmounted by a temporary iron dome. The permanent dome and the House and Senate wings, on either side of the central structure, were added between 1851 and 1865.

members. He tried to heal some of the wounds by carefully allotting committee chairmanships to members from all sections of the country. But other quarrels in Congress showed that tensions remained high. Because the Speaker was a Southerner, Northerners expected that someone from their section would be chosen clerk of the House, a position of some importance and profit for the holder. Two Northern Democrats in particular wanted the job. Several Democrats from the South broke party lines, however, to help elect a fellow Southerner (though a Whig) from Tennessee. One furious Northerner felt that this action taught a simple lesson. He wrote to his brother, stating angrily that if a Northerner:

> [does not] bow and humble and prostrate himself in the dust before their high mightinesses of the South, he must hope for nothing. My Yankee blood is fairly up in this matter, and I will see the South all d—to everlasting perdition before I will ever open my lips in its defense.

Even the President of the United States came under attack. Zachary Taylor, who owned a Mississippi plantation and dozens of slaves, should have presented no problem to the South. His career had been devoted entirely to military service. He had never held public office, nor had he even voted. Taylor had never expressed a hostile opinion on slavery—or anything else. During the campaign of 1848 the South had clearly seemed more content with Taylor, a Whig, than with his two opponents. One was Lewis Cass of Michigan, a Democrat. He favored popular sovereignty—that is, allowing people in the territories to decide the slavery question for themselves. Ex-President Martin Van Buren ran on the Free Soil ticket, opposing the extension of slavery into any territory.

Taylor had encouraged Southern hopes by straddling most embarrassing issues or remaining silent. Attacks on him from antislavery spokesmen in the North clinched the matter. The South supported Taylor, and he won the election by a narrow margin.

As President, however, Taylor seemed less acceptable to Southerners. In good Whig fashion he promised to relax the use of the presidential veto. This position caused concern among Southern Whigs who feared that he might allow passage of the Wilmot Proviso.[1] In November 1849 a prominent Southern Whig visited the White House to learn what Taylor intended to do if Congress adopted the proviso. The President claimed to be neutral on the matter. But he added ominously that "if Congress sees fit to pass it, I will not veto it." He opposed the "coercion of the veto" as undesirable. Taylor had already stated publicly that "the people of the North need have no apprehension of the further extension of slavery." In reaction, a group of Southern Whigs vowed once more to leave the Union before they would accept the Wilmot Proviso.

Two presidential statements in 1849 did little to reassure South-

---

[1]The Wilmot Proviso was first proposed in 1846. It stated that slavery should be prohibited in all of the lands acquired from Mexico. Congress did not adopt the proviso in 1846, but many Northern politicians were committed to its passage.

erners. Taylor's message to Congress in December urged all sides to avoid agitating "exciting topics of a sectional character." But Taylor did just that. He advised that, since Californians had already decided against slavery, a free California should become a state at once, bypassing entirely the territorial stage. Southerners found this idea unacceptable. They regarded as even worse Taylor's observation, in a later speech, that the New Mexico Territory (present-day New Mexico, Arizona, and part of Colorado) would probably follow California's lead in framing a state constitution prohibiting slavery. "A good Whig document," said Webster of the message, "written in a plain and simple style." But to the South it was evident that Taylor was biased against introducing slavery into newly acquired territories.

On January 21, 1850, Taylor again pleaded for action on California. His special message advised, in effect, that the people in California and New Mexico should enter the Union immediately as states. Avoid complicating the issue, Taylor seemed to say, by extending the Missouri Compromise line all the way to the Pacific Ocean. Let the territorial problem solve itself.

Unfortunately for Taylor's program, the slavery problem in the territories would not go away. Slavery had already reentered national politics to stay. In the summer of 1848, during debates over the Oregon Territory, Thomas Hart Benton, a Democratic senator from Missouri, had likened the slavery issue to the biblical plague of frogs:

> You could not look upon the table but there were frogs, you could not sit down at the banquet table but there were frogs, you could not go to the bridal couch and lift the sheets but there were frogs! We can see nothing, touch nothing, have no measures proposed, without having this pestilence thrust before us.

Ill feeling over slavery did indeed seem to crop up with every issue. As Congress got under way in 1850, debate in the House seldom rose above the level of name-calling. "For two years," accused Ohio Free-Soiler Joshua Giddings, "the people of the North have been defrauded, deceived, and imposed upon." Georgia's Robert Toombs countered: "I do not hesitate to avow before this House and the country that if by your legislation you seek to drive us from the territories of California and New Mexico and to abolish slavery in this District of Columbia, I am for disunion."

The problem of fugitive slaves brought further trouble. Some Northern states and many Northern citizens had been ignoring or flouting the existing fugitive slave law of 1791. Early in January, Senator James M. Mason of Virginia presented a bill to make the return of captured runaway slaves easier and more certain. William H. Seward, an antislavery Whig from New York and a man close to Taylor, warned that he would try to nullify the effect of a new law by adding a guarantee of trial by local jury for an alleged runaway. The Senate then exploded into a predictable outpouring of sectional complaints and threats. Mississippi's Henry S. Foote branded Seward a fanatic who wished to punish the

South. Mason himself, however, defended his proposed bill in reasonable language, and he even agreed to soften parts of it in a bid for Northern votes.

Within a few days two important Democratic senators, Daniel Dickinson of New York and Lewis Cass of Michigan, spoke in favor of milder language and sectional compromise. As tempers cooled, it became possible for someone to step forward and restore calm.

The man who took on this role was Henry Clay. He hoped to engineer the third major compromise of his long career. In 1820, while Speaker of the House, he had helped pass the Missouri Compromise. In 1833, together with John C. Calhoun, he had worked out a compromise tariff bill to lower import duties and thus ease the nullification crisis. The presidency had escaped him three times. But the seventy-three-year-old senator drew consolation from his reputation as a compromiser, and he gloried in the title of "the Great Pacificator" (peacemaker). Clay knew that the conflict of 1850 would be his last major political battle.

On January 29 Clay presented his program for compromise. It consisted of eight points, most of which would soon be joined in one comprehensive, or omnibus, bill. (1) Congress should accept California as a state with a free constitution. (2) In the New Mexico Territory—unfavorable ground for slavery, according to Clay and many others—there should be no congressional restriction or encouragement of slavery. (3) The slave trade should be abolished in Washington, D.C.

These were the pro-North points. Clay's additional proposals were designed to balance things sectionally. (4) The boundary between Texas and New Mexico should be established on a line favoring Texan claims. (5) The federal government should assume responsibility for the debts of Texas before it became a state. (6) Slavery itself was to be guaranteed in the District of Columbia. (7) Congress should pass a firmer fugitive slave law. (8) Congress should formally announce a policy of noninterference with the slave trade among the Southern states. (Clay's eighth and final suggestion, an attempt to sweeten the pill for the South as a whole, was later dropped.)

The North stood to gain more from Clay's proposals than the South. Admitting California as a free state would destroy the sectional balance—parity between free and slave states—that still existed in the Senate. (The House already had a Northern majority because the North had more people.) Giving the North a majority in the Senate as well as the House seemed suicidal to proslavery forces.

As for leaving the New Mexico Territory question undecided, Southern extremists feared, with good reason, that free states would eventually emerge from it. Why did this matter to a slaveholder in South Carolina? Because when such states joined the Union, they would elect antislavery congressmen who might vote to abolish slavery. The proposals regarding the Texas boundary and debt would not alter the sectional power balance. And enforcing a new fugitive slave law would depend on Northern cooperation, risky and uncertain at best.

Yet Clay made his appeal primarily to the North, asking for generosity, since the more powerful section had more to give. Northerners, he warned, must be especially understanding about slavery. Although the institution did not figure in their economy or society, slavery was woven into the fabric of Southern society. To talk of abolition threatened the South's "habits, safety, property, life—everything."

Clay expected no help from extremists on the slavery question, and he got none. Northern antislavery advocates had never liked him much, but they bided their time and let Southern extremists voice the first criticisms of his proposals. Eight Southern senators tore into "the Great Pacificator." One angry "fire-eater" (Southern proslavery extremist) denied that Clay had proposed a compromise at all. It was, he said, "cowardly capitulation" to the North.

On February 5 Clay responded with his major compromise

A cartoon of 1848 pokes fun at Taylor's unwillingness to commit himself on the issues of the day. The two disgruntled men at left have decided to turn to other candidates: John P. Hale, nominated by the Liberty party, and Van Buren ("Matty"), the Free Soil candidate.

speech. In an address lasting two and a half hours, he ignored the extremists and appealed to Northerners.

> What do you want? What do you want—you who reside in the free states? Do you want that there shall be no slavery introduced into the territories acquired by the war with Mexico? Have you not your desire in California? And in all human probability you will have it in New Mexico also. What more do you want? You have got what is worth more than a thousand Wilmot Provisos.

In the manner of a true compromiser Clay pleaded for moderation.

> Let me say to the North and to the South, what husband and wife say to each other. We have mutual faults; neither of us is perfect; nothing in the form of humanity is perfect; let us, then, be kind to each other—forbearing, forgiving each other's faults—and above all, let us live in happiness and peace together.

While Clay looked for votes and worked to generate "spontaneous" meetings, two leading Southerners, representing two generations of proslavery opinion, renewed the attack on his compromise proposals. Senator Jefferson Davis of Mississippi dismissed Clay's plan as misleading if not worthless. He pointed out what many congressmen perhaps chose to ignore in 1850—that no fugitive slave bill, no matter what its provisions, would work if the North chose to sabotage it. Even the Missouri Compromise line, which Davis hinted might be extended to the Pacific Ocean (thus satisfying the South), could not legally bind the states involved.

According to Davis, Northern aggression had caused the crisis. "I see nothing short of conquest on the one side, or submission on the other." He claimed that the North sought to degrade Southerners, to make them "an inferior class, a degraded caste in the Union." Unless this stopped, warned Davis, Southerners would follow the example of the thirteenth-century English barons who rose up and forced King John to sign the Magna Charta.

The other Southerner who spoke at this time was John C. Calhoun. In contrast to Davis's emotional oration, Calhoun's logical address demanded specific concessions for the South. The South Carolinian had long demanded Southern unity. A year earlier Calhoun had drafted a Southern Address, a strong document of grievance and warning that was signed by forty-eight congressmen.

By 1850 Calhoun was old and sick. He knew that his career and life were almost over. He had already fainted in the Senate lobby several times. On one of those occasions he was carried into the Vice President's office to recuperate. Another South Carolinian, Robert B. Rhett, rushed over. "Ah, Mr. Rhett," Calhoun sighed, "my career is nearly done. The great battle must be fought by you younger men. . . . the South—the poor South!" On March 4 Calhoun presented his speech to the Senate. He did not actually speak, however, because of his feeble health. Senator Mason read his address for him.

Calhoun in the early 1800s tried to avoid making an issue of slavery, but by 1836 he was declaring that abolition "strikes directly and fatally not only at our prosperity, but our existence as a people."

Though broken in body, Calhoun remained as firm and uncompromising as ever. He argued that an exact political balance between North and South had to be maintained. No temporary, patchwork solution would do. Compromisers might chant the word "Union!" till doomsday, but it would have no more effect than intoning the word "Health!" over a dying person. What could be done? As Calhoun saw it, the North had to give slaveholders a chance to settle the West. It had to return runaway slaves, to discourage them from fleeing. It had to agree to a constitutional amendment creating a precise balance between Northern and Southern political power in the national government (despite the fact that Northern whites outnumbered Southern whites by more than 2 to 1). If the North could not accept the South on these terms, he concluded, "tell us so, and let the states we both represent agree to separate and part in peace. If you are unwilling we should part in peace, tell us so, and we shall know what to do when you reduce the question to submission or resistance."

Calhoun's defiant stand might represent the views of a minority, but still it demanded some direct response. The South Carolinian had attacked Clay's proposals and momentarily upset the majority's impulse to compromise. The man who accepted Calhoun's challenge was Daniel Webster of Massachusetts.

Webster was a man of great eloquence in an age when long and polished speeches were more admired than they are today. For decades, American students were assigned his more famous speeches to memorize and recite.

Webster was scheduled to speak in the Senate on March 7. In those days, a major congressional address was a great public occasion. Congressmen worked for days carefully preparing lengthy speeches. Their fellow legislators sat through the speeches and actually listened. Others, too, wanted to hear. Notice of an important speech on the congressional calendar set off a stampede for seats in the gallery. Spectators would line up for admission to the chamber, even if it meant crowding in the aisles, close-packed with other standees, for four or five hours. The Senate presented just such a picture when Webster gave his famous "Seventh of March" speech.

The portly senator rose, pulled his vest down over his paunch, raised his head, and struck a theatrical pose. "I wish to speak today," Webster began, "not as a Massachusetts man, not as a Northern man, but as an American. I speak today for the preservation of the Union. Hear me for my cause."

Webster traced the history of North-South differences. First, he emphasized the contrast between the North's easy abolition of slavery after the Revolution and the South's commitment to the institution after the invention of the cotton gin and the spread of cotton culture. He did not go so far as to claim that only lack of economic dependence had made slavery seem wrong to the North. But he did argue that his listeners had to bear in mind slavery's significance to the white South. Why then had sectional conflict grown? Because, Webster said, too many radicals in the North now contended that right could be distinguished from wrong "with the precision of an algebraic equation."

Then, Webster denounced both Northern abolitionists and Southern secessionists as dangerous extremists. Abolitionism was harmful, he asserted. The Wilmot Proviso was offensive and unnecessary; no one need "reaffirm an ordinance of nature nor reenact the will of God" by prohibiting slavery in territories "naturally" hostile to its existence. He dismissed the idea of sectional disunion. Secession and peace were mutually exclusive. Finally, Webster argued that, although sectional tensions obviously existed, they could be eased, and major political problems could be settled. Taking Clay's cue, Webster called on the North to keep its part of the basic sectional bargain. It must not harass the South over slavery, however repugnant the slave system. It must obey the law regarding slavery and even approve a new federal law to ensure that Southerners could recapture their fugitive slaves.

When he attacked the secessionists, Webster included Calhoun, the man "who, I deeply regret, is prevented by serious illness from being in his seat today." But Calhoun was there that day, having shuffled into the Senate shortly after Webster started. Calhoun shot back: "The Senator from South Carolina is in his seat." Webster continued with hardly a pause, saying that "peaceable secession is an utter impossibility." When he had finished, the galleries broke into sustained applause. Calhoun tried for the final word: "I cannot agree that this Union cannot be dissolved. Am I to understand that no degree of oppression, no outrage, no broken faith, can produce the destruction of this Union? The Union *can* be broken." These were Calhoun's last words in the Senate.

Webster had more to worry about from Northern reaction to his speech than he did from Calhoun. Webster had opposed slavery, though he was not an abolitionist. Now his call for justice to the South, especially his support for capturing and returning fugitive slaves, infuriated Northern antislavery advocates. They responded predictably and savagely. Horace Greeley, editor of the influential New York *Tribune*, wrote that the speech was "unequal to the occasion and unworthy of its author." William Cullen Bryant wrote a poem about the "fallen angel," the "Godlike Daniel." Theodore Parker, an abolitionist Boston preacher, claimed that he knew "of no deed in American history done by a son of New England to which I can compare this but the act of Benedict Arnold."

Other Americans, however, hailed Webster's speech for what it was—a significant and eloquent statement urging both sides to stop agitating the slavery question. Conservatives, North and South, read it with approval; 120,000 copies had been rushed into print. Even the Charleston *Mercury*, unfriendly to the North and its politics, noted that "with such a spirit as Mr. Webster has shown, it no longer seems impossible to bring this sectional contest to a close." Businessmen overwhelmingly supported the Clay-Webster position. They worried that all the squabbling about slavery would interfere with trade. William W. Corcoran, an important Washington banker, went further. He sent Webster a letter of congratulation with a check for $1,000.

With Clay and Webster clearly speaking for an older generation, it remained for a different breed of politician to be heard from. While young Southern fire-eaters continued to regard Calhoun as their mentor (even after his death on March 31), a rising group of Northern politicians looked for new leadership. William H. Seward of New York, who had just arrived in the Senate, became their spokesman.

Seward, a little man of large ambition, had played the political game astutely since the middle 1820s, mainly in his home state. First an Anti-Mason, then a Whig, Seward broke the Albany Regency's monopoly on New York state government when he became governor in 1838. He knew the value of party organization and party discipline (even at the expense of party principles) far better than most older Whig leaders. He knew also that antislavery and anti-Southern feeling was rising in the North and would soon dominate American politics.

Seward addressed the Senate on March 11. His speech was clearly a reaction to Webster's effort of four days earlier, although there was little similarity between the two in structure, delivery, or content. Seward read a prepared text in a monotone to a sparsely filled chamber. Still, leading senators (even Calhoun) attended because they realized the importance of Seward's views and those for whom he presumably spoke.

In essence, Seward rejected all plans for compromise. Since no real threat of disunion existed, he insisted, why compromise? Slavery, a barbarous relic of earlier and less enlightened times, would die a peaceful and natural death. Why encourage it? Congress could legislate for the territories, and it should prohibit slavery there. "I shall vote for the admission of California directly, without conditions, without qualifications, and without compromise."

Most of Seward's speech followed a Northern hard line on territorial questions, not far removed from President Taylor's stand. But the New Yorker added some statements that made his speech notorious. Did the Constitution protect slavery? "There is a higher law than the Constitution," answered Seward. Slavery must go. A moral question had been raised that transcended the "too narrow creeds" of political parties. He dismissed slavery as "temporary, accidental, partial, and incongruous." Freedom, on the other hand, was "perpetual, organic, universal, and in harmony with the Constitution."

Southerners were outraged. Even many Northerners joined in attacking Seward's "higher law" doctrine as anarchy. President Taylor himself, previously close to Seward, ordered his administration newspaper to rap the New Yorker on the knuckles. These quick reactions revealed clearly that Seward, like Calhoun, spoke only for a congressional minority. But just as clearly, his stand could not be ignored.

On March 13 another Northerner, Stephen A. Douglas of Illinois, made an important speech. On the surface, Douglas was critical of Clay's proposals. Actually, however, he spent more time attacking Clay's enemies and upholding popular sovereignty, his preferred solution. Douglas regarded the will of local inhabitants in the territories as all-important. He felt that the Missouri Compromise restriction of 1820, which prohibited slavery in the Louisiana Territory north of 36° 30′ latitude,

Seward was somewhat vain and made his share of political enemies, but was well liked personally. A later historian has called him "lovable, cheerful, and generous."

Douglas, just over five feet tall, had a massive head and shoulders, and was called the "Little Giant." Though overshadowed by his fellow-Illinoisan, Abraham Lincoln, he was one of the ablest statemen of his era.

was no restriction at all. Politicians in Washington, he believed, could neither establish nor forbid slavery in a territory. Local laws would prevail. They would inevitably reflect local environment and attitudes. Douglas also added his opinion that slavery could not expand west of the Mississippi beyond where it already existed—that is, Missouri, Arkansas, Louisiana, and Texas. His statement made many Southerners suspicious of Douglas and other so-called National Democrats.

At this point, a Senate fracas indicated how deep the impasse had become. It involved Thomas Hart Benton of Missouri and Henry S. Foote of Mississippi. Both were Democrats, and both wanted a compromise. Beyond this they parted ways. Benton was tall and burly, a polished and often bombastic orator. He had been in the Senate for thirty years, as long as Missouri had been a state. Although he represented a slave state, Benton did not believe in the extension of slavery. Let California join as a free state, he urged, and then solve other disputed sectional matters one by one.

Foote was short, rotund, and animated. Other senators acknowledged his considerable talents yet regarded him as a bit eccentric. Previously, Foote had been close to the Southern extremists. But he now supported Clay's proposals for compromise and strongly urged combining them into an omnibus bill.

On April 17, Benton attacked Clay's omnibus approach as pandering to Southern hysteria. Foote labeled the charge a slander. Benton then rose and headed straight toward his adversary. No match for Benton at coining phrases, Foote decided on another equalizer. He pulled a gun. Other members of the world's greatest deliberative body—as the Senate likes to call itself—quickly moved to avoid catastrophe. Stopped by a friendly senator, Benton, who rarely let slip the opportunity to add drama to a situation, tore open his shirt front and shouted, "Let the assassin fire! I am not armed. I have no pistols. I disdain to carry arms. A pistol has been brought in to shoot me with—to assassinate me!"

"I brought it here to defend myself," Foote responded lamely, at the same time handing his gun to Senator Dickinson.

"Nothing of the kind, sir," Benton retorted. "It is a false imputation. I carry nothing of the kind, and no assassin has a right to draw a pistol on me."

Foote obviously did not want to shoot Benton, yet the outrageous incident could not be ignored altogether. A special Senate committee investigated. It reported two months later but declined to recommend any disciplinary action against Foote.[2]

Although congressional speechmaking played a more important role in 1850 than it does today, the real work of Congress—then as now—went on in committees. The day after the Benton-Foote confrontation, the Senate attended to more serious business. Foote moved that a select

Benton was no stranger to violence. During the War of 1812 he brawled with Andrew Jackson; a few years later he killed a district attorney in a duel. Yet he was always a moderate on slavery.

[2]As usual, Benton had the last word. Foote later tried to patch up the quarrel, announcing his intention to write a small book in which Senator Benton would figure prominently. Benton countered with an announcement that he would write a large book that would not even mention Senator Foote. Both men kept their word.

committee chaired by Clay work to resolve the sectional disputes. His resolution passed easily, 30 to 22. Thirteen senators would serve, seven Whigs and six Democrats. Seven were from slave states, and six were from free states. But only one senator from each section could be labeled an extremist.

For the next three weeks congressional activity creaked to a halt. Even the speechmakers were silent, waiting for Clay's committee to report. Its seven-point recommendation strongly resembled Clay's original plan. There was no minority report.

Few senators seemed satisfied with everything Clay's committee had proposed. When formal debate on the report began on May 13, almost every senator wanted to be heard, some several times.

Foote's life seemed to embody inconsistency. A Mississippian, he opposed secession. Then he served in the Confederate congress. Still later, he quarreled with Jefferson Davis, resigned his seat, and left the South.

The compromise faced another challenge—from outside Congress. The Mississippi legislature had called on representatives of the slave states to meet at Nashville, Tennessee, in June 1850 to adopt methods of "resistance to [Northern] aggressions." Calhoun had supported the Mississippi move enthusiastically. His spirit would certainly be present at Nashville. Daniel Webster predicted that if the Southern extremists actually convened at Nashville, Andrew Jackson's body would turn over in its nearby grave.

Nevertheless, the Nashville Convention did take place. But—like New England's Hartford Convention during the War of 1812—it proved a bit of a dud. Only nine of the slave states sent delegates, and not all of them were leaders in their own states. There was a great deal of heated talk. The meeting's final report, drafted by South Carolina fire-eater Robert B. Rhett, honored Calhoun's memory and most of his principles. Yet the convention kept cool. Delegates did not abandon their desire to defend Southern rights. But most still waited for a decision in Congress.

Most Americans observed the Nashville Convention fiasco with satisfaction, and none more so than President Taylor. The general was the nation's most important opponent of Clay's compromise, and he was angry. Clay and other Whig leaders had slighted him. Some had even made fun of him as lacking intelligence. Clay went so far as to heap praise on another general and would-be President, Winfield Scott—Taylor's rival for military glory during the war with Mexico. The President's anger boiled over whenever he heard talk of secession. At one point, a group of worried Southerners had trooped into the White House to ask Taylor if he really meant to maintain the Union at all cost. Eyes blazing (possibly thinking of Andrew Jackson's sternness at such moments), the President swore that he would blockade every Southern port if secessionists took over federal facilities. He promised to head an army of Northern and Western troops to put down any rebellion.

The situation had not yet come to a head, though. In the spring and summer of 1850 the legislative process still seemed the best solution. Yet it looked as if no compromise could jump the hurdle of a presidential veto. Taylor opposed the omnibus bill. When his own newspaper began speaking kindly of Clay, Taylor had the editor replaced by someone who would follow the administration line. Clay argued that his proposals would heal at least some, if not all, of the country's wounds on the slavery question, whereas Taylor's would heal only one, the status of California. The White House responded tartly that the original congressional resolution concerned only California and the New Mexico Territory, with no mention of such inflammatory side issues as fugitive slaves or Texan debts.

Throughout June procompromise forces made no progress. Opponents were trying to mutilate the select committee report with amendment after amendment and delay it with parliamentary obstruction. "We shall have a warm summer," Webster predicted. "The political atmosphere will be hot, however the natural may be. I am for it and shall fight it out." Arguments of "no earthly consequence start up from time to time," admitted Clay glumly, "to discourage the stoutest heart." The omnibus was stalled, perhaps permanently.

There matters stood, until Washington heat, gluttony, and divine Providence intervened. On the Fourth of July, President Taylor attended ceremonies at the base of the unfinished Washington monument. Under a broiling sun he dutifully heard the ever-present Henry S. Foote (presumably unarmed this time) deliver the Independence Day oration. As the President got up to leave, aides asked him to stay and witness yet another ceremony. A handful of dust from the tomb of Thaddeus Kosciusko, the Polish hero of the American Revolution, was to be deposited in the monument. Taylor waited, standing exposed to the summer sun for an additional hour.

Back at the White House at last, Taylor refreshed himself with huge quantities of fruits, vegetables, and iced liquids. "Cucumbers and cherries with mush and milk," runs the most bizarre of the many accounts of what he consumed.

Taylor loved to eat—heartily and often. He ignored all danger warnings, verbal or internal, even one that appeared in his own official newspaper: "Do not unnecessarily heat yourselves, but, when heated, drink cold water in moderation. Ice water, in small quantities, is an excellent tonic; but some persons flood the stomach till internal chemistry can no longer overcome its effects." The President's internal chemistry broke down. He was overcome with nausea, stomach cramps, and fever. Taylor lingered on until July 9, when he died of acute gastroenteritis.

Into the White House came Vice President Millard Fillmore. Like Seward, though always several rungs below him, Fillmore had climbed the ladder of New York Anti-Masonic and Whig politics. New Yorkers of all parties had a history of squabbling and splitting into factions. By 1850 Fillmore and Seward found themselves in warring camps. Taylor might have been on good terms with Seward, but Fillmore had no use for his fellow New Yorker. Where did Fillmore stand on the compromise? Most Southerners distrusted him, since he came from western New York, the most strongly antislavery part of the state. Fillmore's nomination and election to the vice-presidency in 1848 had caused an anxious stir in the slave states. But in that election the South had placed its faith and sectional interests in Taylor's hands.

As late as April 1850, Fillmore had indicated agreement with Taylor's policies. Sometime between April and early July, however, he became a supporter of Clay's compromise. He later claimed that, just before Taylor's death, he had told the President that if the Senate tied the vote on the compromise, he, as Vice President (and president of the Senate), would break the tie with a yes vote. Daniel Webster may have had something to do with Fillmore's conversion. As secretary of state, he emerged as the leading figure of the new administration. He exercised a strong influence over the conscientious but intellectually limited Fillmore. So did Clay, a semiofficial administration spokesman in Congress. Apparently all that remained was to push the omnibus bill through, have the new President sign it, and let peace reign. But this was not to be.

On July 31 the Senate was voting on a complicated series of amendments to the compromise. The omnibus was maneuvered by its opponents into a position where it could be killed. One by one, each of the bill's provisions was rejected by the Senate. The only part to be adopted was a bill granting territorial status to Utah. This passed easily, since the federal government wanted to reassert its authority over the Mormons (see page 288). Little else remained but disappointment for the procompromise forces and delight for Northern and Southern extremists. A reporter for a New York paper described the scene: "Jefferson Davis's face grinned with smiles. Old Bullion's [Thomas Hart Benton] few hairs actually bristled with delight. *He* had routed *Clay*! *He* had smashed his omnibus to atoms! Seward was dancing about like a little top." The reporter went on to describe other gleeful senators—a Northern supporter of Seward whose "thick sides shook with sporadic spasms"; a Southerner who "looked solemn in solitary glory"; and an Ohio abolitionist shaking hands with a Louisiana fire-eater.

Clay walked out of the Senate chamber humiliated. He had fumbled his last great compromise effort. He soon left Washington for the resort town of Newport, Rhode Island—probably in a huff and surely very tired.

Clay's failure created Douglas's opportunity. Since the omnibus package had fallen to pieces, the energetic Douglas took the logical course of action. He worked on one bill at a time. There were five altogether in addition to the Utah bill.

First was the bill settling the Texan boundary and debt. It passed on August 9. Next came the question of California. Southerners wanted to divide the region into two states—one free and the other undecided on slavery. Douglas, however, aimed to have the free-state California constitution adopted as it stood. Jeremiah Clemens of Alabama warned: "I do not know what Alabama may do, but if she determines to resist this bill by force, secession, by any means, I am at her service. If this be treason, I am a traitor—a traitor who glories in the name."

Despite talk of this kind, the Senate passed the California bill on

August 13. Next to clear the Senate was the New Mexico territorial bill.

The measure strengthening the fugitive slave laws, which would soon become the weakest link in the compromise chain, passed on August 26. In view of later reactions Northerners were surprisingly calm on the measure, perhaps because several leading antislavery figures had left Washington for cooler parts by that time. Still, twenty-one senators (fifteen of them Northerners) failed to vote on the fugitive slave bill. Had they all responded to the roll call, the bill would probably have been defeated. Douglas had applied strong and effective pressures on his Democratic colleagues in the Senate. The final bill of the compromise was one outlawing the slave trade in Washington, D.C. Clay himself came back to Washington in time to shepherd it through Congress on September 16.

The House of Representatives played second fiddle to the Senate throughout the dramatic 1850 session. Once the bills were through the Senate, the House passed them with little trouble early in September.

The Compromise of 1850 had initially been a Whig venture—or so Clay and Webster saw it, despite their nonpartisan appeals. But it became a reality through a series of bills shepherded through Congress by Stephen A. Douglas, a Democrat who relied largely on the votes of Democratic congressmen. Of eleven senators who supported at least five of the six compromise measures, nine were Democrats. Votes in the House of Representatives revealed the same Democratic concern for compromise. The Democrats, the party of Jefferson and Jackson, had clearly committed themselves to a new version of their old policy—keeping the slavery issue out of national politics.

In this bitter comment on the Fugitive Slave Act of 1850, Webster (center) helps a slave catcher chase a fleeing woman and child. In the accompanying caption, Webster is made to say: "Any man can perform an agreeable duty—it is not everyone that can perform a disagreeable duty."

20
A DEEPENING SECTIONAL CONFLICT

A. W.

Passage of the Compromise of 1850 and its acceptance by most Americans, North and South, seemed to close a dangerous chapter in United States history. Americans felt that they had achieved peace. Or at least they hoped so—with a fervor that showed how afraid they had been. If slavery took root as a national issue, the country itself might split apart. The apparent escape from this danger led to a feeling of elation in 1850. Yet if the past decade was a true indicator of the future, the years ahead would be anything but placid.

Indeed, slavery was already a national issue, even though people might wish to think otherwise. It had become so through its relationship to newly acquired territories in the West—the very question that had led to the Compromise of 1850. Throughout much of American history, disruptive political crises have often been involved with issues of geographic expansion. This was true of Bacon's Rebellion and the Burr conspiracy as well. The slavery controversy was no exception.

EXPANSION INTO THE FAR WEST

Americans have generally believed that they could move freely into unsettled territories wherever available. This belief was never more stoutly held than during the first half of the nineteenth century. In this period some Americans moved into land acquired through the Louisiana Purchase. Even more attractive, however, were Far West regions that did not belong to the United States. The most important of these were the Oregon Country, claimed by Great Britain, and the Mexican-held Southwest and California.

Americans had various reasons for wanting to expand westward. Merchants were attracted to trade possibilities. Oregon, for example, offered not only furs but also a possible base for commerce with Asia. Many Americans were looking for good farming or grazing land. Even those who stayed home in the East took pride in the idea of westward expansion.

Newspapermen and politicians wrote approvingly of national growth. The phrase that best expressed the current attitude was Manifest Destiny. The term was coined by John L. O'Sullivan, a Democratic editor from New York. He wrote in 1845 that it was the "manifest destiny [of the United States] to overspread and to possess the whole of the continent which Providence has given us for the development of the great experiment of liberty and federated self-government entrusted to us."[1]

In other words, it was manifest (obvious) that fate had destined the United States for an expansionist role. Americans had a God-given mission to establish the Protestant religion, a democratic political system, and a capitalist economy in all the lands from the Atlantic to the Pacific. Many Americans shared this imperial vision in some form.

The Oregon Country Since the late eighteenth century, many nations had shown an interest in the Oregon Country—the region between the Rockies and the Pacific coast extending from what is now California northward to Alaska. At various times Spain, Russia, Britain, and the United States had laid claim to all or part of the area.

American merchants en route to the Far East sailed along the Oregon coast. So did traders

---

[1]The term "Manifest Destiny" was first used in Congress by Robert C. Winthrop, the Whig nominee for Speaker of the House in 1849.

The artist who painted this *Emigrant Train Bedding Down for the Night* has somewhat idealized the westward movement of the 1840s and 1850s. It was more common—though perhaps less picturesque—for a wagon train to form a circle as protection against Indian attack.

in search of furs. In 1792 an American named Robert Gray explored and named the Columbia River. Lewis and Clark also explored the Oregon Country. In 1811 New York merchant John Jacob Astor founded a fur-trading post, Astoria, at the mouth of the Columbia River. When the War of 1812 broke out, however, he sold the post to a British company.

By 1825 both Spain and Russia had given up their claims to the Oregon Country. But British fur traders of the Hudson's Bay Company were quite active in the region. There was a spirited three-way rivalry between them, the American traders employed by the Rocky Mountain Fur Company, and Astor's American Fur Company. In 1818, Great Britain and the United States had agreed that the two countries would occupy Oregon jointly until 1827. When the agreement expired, it was extended for an indefinite period.

The settlement of American families in the Oregon Country was stimulated mainly by missionaries, who went to the area in the 1830s. Methodist minister Jason Lee opened a mission in the Willamette Valley near what is now Salem, Oregon. Marcus and Narcissa Whitman, backed by the Congregationalists and Presbyterians, established a mission on the Columbia River near present-day Walla Walla, Washington.

The missionaries' letters described in glowing terms Oregon's fertile soil, magnificent rivers, and excellent climate. Small groups of settlers moved westward in the early 1840s. The first major party of pioneers—a thousand strong—set out from Independence, Missouri, in 1843. The westward migration became so heavy in the late 1840s that it was known as the Oregon fever.

Pioneers made the trip to Oregon along the famous Oregon Trail. From Independence, the trail led northwest and then followed the Platte River, crossing the Rockies at South Pass. Travelers to Oregon proceeded northward through the valleys of the Snake and Columbia rivers.

In 1843, Americans in Oregon organized a provisional government and petitioned Congress for annexation. Settlers from the United States now far outnumbered those from Canada and Britain. The earlier arrangements for joint occupation of the region seemed unsatisfactory—at least to Americans.

Annexation of Oregon was one of the issues in the presidential campaign of 1844. The Whigs nominated Henry Clay, who tried to avoid the question of expansion. The Democrats chose James K. Polk, governor of Tennessee and former Speaker of the House of Representatives. Polk was an ardent expansionist, and the Democratic platform stressed "All of Oregon or none." In other words, said Polk, the United States should expand northward to the 54th parallel. The British insisted on the 49th parallel as a more reasonable dividing line, since it continued westward the already existing boundary that divided the rest of the United States from Canada.

After Polk was elected, some expansionists demanded war if the British refused to yield to American demands. Their slogan was "54° 40' or Fight!" But other Americans took a calmer view. In 1846 the Polk administration negotiated a settlement with Britain that established the 49th parallel as the boundary between the western United States and Canada.

An Independent Texas While American settle-ment in Oregon led to tension with Britain, expansion into Texas brought on conflict with Mexico. Spain had ceded Florida to the United States in 1819, and, as part of the bargain, Americans had given up their claim to Texas—a claim they had asserted since the purchase of Louisiana. Americans, however, were already moving into the region. In fact, traders and military adventurers from the United States had helped the Mexicans win independence from Spain in 1821. In return the new Mexican government had confirmed a large land grant previously made by the Spanish to Moses Austin.

Austin, a Missourian, had planned to colonize the Brazos River area with Americans. He died in 1821. Stephen Austin, his son, carried out the plan. In 1822 he planted a colony of 300 American families at Columbus, Texas. Most were Southerners, small slaveholders or nonslaveholding farmers. They were lured by the promise of practically free farmland for cotton cultivation.

During the next decade American settlers moved steadily into Texas. By 1830 there were at least 25,000 whites and 2,000 black slaves. Most of the newcomers remained Protestant despite the terms of the original Austin land grant, which committed American settlers to becoming Roman Catholics. Although Texas formed part of a state in the Mexican republic, the majority of its inhabitants were firmly committed to their American customs and beliefs.

U.S. GROWTH OF POPULATION, 1790–1860

U.S. FOREIGN TRADE, 1790–1860

The "invasion" of these American settlers frightened the Mexican government. Its leaders were afraid that the Texans would try to break away and join the United States. Mexico crushed one revolt in 1826. After this, Mexicans tried unsuccessfully to restrict further American immigration. They forbade the importation of slaves into Texas and placed heavy taxes on imported American goods. These efforts proved to be too little and too late. Americans in Texas were already encouraging their fellow countrymen to settle there. They were also agitating with the Mexicans for their own state government.

President Antonio López de Santa Anna decided to tighten Mexican control over Texas. Early in 1836 he led an army of 6,000 into the region. On March 2 the Texans met at Washington, Texas, and declared their independence from Mexico. They adopted a constitution legalizing slavery, and they set up a provisional government. As commander of the Texan army they named Samuel Houston, former governor of Tennessee and a friend of Andrew Jackson.

Meanwhile, Santa Anna had begun his siege of the Alamo, a former mission at San Antonio. For twelve days a garrison of 187 Texans led by William B. Travis withstood an attack force of 3,000. Finally, on March 6, the Alamo fell. Its defenders — including the famous frontiersman Davy Crockett — were massacred. Later in March 300 Texans were slaughtered in a similar fashion when they surrendered at Goliad. For several weeks Houston had to retreat before Santa Anna's army. Then, on April 21, he made a stand at San Jacinto. Shouting "Remember the Alamo!" and "Remember Goliad!" Houston's men defeated Santa Anna and took the Mexican general prisoner.

Santa Anna signed a treaty (which he later repudiated) recognizing the independence of Texas. In September 1836, Texas voters ratified their new constitution and elected Sam Houston president. At the same time, they indicated their desire for annexation to the United States.

Troubles Over Annexation The annexation of Texas became a controversial issue. Northern antislavery forces did not want to add another slave state to the Union. President Jackson, who wished to avoid a sectional split, refused to endorse the proposal. So did his successor, Van Buren.

Texans then began to turn to Europe for recognition and aid, showing particular interest in Britain. Southern expansionists were alarmed by the prospect of a close alliance between cotton-hungry Britain and the cotton-producing Republic of Texas. They pressed for a treaty of annexation. So did President Tyler (who had come into office after Harrison's death in April 1841) and Secretary of State John C. Calhoun. A treaty that they negotiated in 1844, however, was rejected overwhelmingly by the Senate.

Texas, like Oregon, was an issue in the presidential campaign of 1844. One of Polk's slogans was a demand for "the reoccupation of Oregon and the reannexation of Texas." (The "re" in each case cleverly implied that the United States had always owned the disputed territories.) After Polk won, but before he took office, President Tyler exploited the popular support for expansion. He pressed for a joint congressional resolution annexing Texas. Since it was not a treaty, the resolution did not require a two-thirds Senate vote, and thus it squeaked through. Texas ratified the resolution and joined the Union in December 1845.

The Mexican War When Texas became a state, Mexico broke off diplomatic relations with the United States. This was not the only sore point between the two nations. The United States claimed that the Texan boundary extended to the Rio Grande, whereas Mexico set it at the Nueces River. Another Mexican grievance was the growing number of Americans in California.

Early in 1846 Polk ordered General Zachary Taylor, commanding a force of 1,500, to take up a position along the Rio Grande. War fever grew among nationalists in both countries. The Mexicans refused to see John Slidell, an American diplomat sent to Mexico City to negotiate. A minor skirmish between Taylor's forces and Mexican troops along the Rio Grande gave the eager American President an excuse for war. Polk blamed Mexico for shedding American blood; Congress declared war on May 11; and the House author-

This print of the American army taking possession of the Mexican capital in 1847 appeared in a history of the war written by George W. Kendall of the New Orleans *Picayune*. Kendall was one of the first war correspondents ever to accompany an army on its campaigns.

ized the recruitment of an army of 50,000 volunteers.

The American troops, though fewer in number, were better supplied and better led than the Mexican forces. In fact, the Mexican War served as a training ground for many young officers who later commanded armies during the Civil War. Among them were Robert E. Lee, Ulysses S. Grant, J. E. B. Stuart, George B. McClellan, and "Stonewall" Jackson.

The United States won a series of victories on Mexican soil—at Monterrey, Buena Vista, and Veracruz. In September 1847, Americans took Mexico City itself. The United States also seized New Mexico and California with small military forces supported by American settlers. Mexico had to sue for peace.

The Treaty of Guadalupe Hidalgo ended the war. Mexico gave up California, New Mexico, and the disputed area east of the Rio Grande. In return it received $15 million and the Americans' promise to assume their own citizens' outstanding claims against Mexico. The United States acquired an additional 529,000 square miles of territory at a cost of 13,000 American lives, most of them lost as a result of disease. Mexican casualties totaled approximately 14,000 killed or missing in action.

Some rabid expansionists considered even these gains minor. They wanted the United States to obey its Manifest Destiny and seize all of Mexico. The Senate prudently disregarded these suggestions, however, and ratified the treaty of peace in March 1848.

In difficult terrain, American forces (left), attack the Mexicans (right) at the Battle of Buena Vista.

Americans in California Many Americans who trekked west from Independence, Missouri, had destinations other than Oregon. At about the same time that Stephen Austin led his settlers into Texas, merchants were opening up the Santa Fe Trail. Year after year their trade caravans left Independence and lumbered south, loaded with goods to be sold in New Mexico. Thousands of Americans started out on the Oregon Trail but turned off before reaching the Oregon Country. One group, the Mormons, went south into Utah (see page 288). Others pushed farther west on the California Trail; most of them went to either Sutter's Fort (Sacramento) or the Los Angeles area.

Like Texas, California originally belonged to Spain and, after 1821, to Mexico. In the early years of the nineteenth century it attracted relatively few Americans. There were only about 700 there in 1845.

Nevertheless, Polk had plans for California. Late in 1845 he wrote Thomas Larkin, the American consul at Monterey, asking him to stir up a revolt and encourage Americans in California to apply for annexation. Larkin received Polk's message in April 1846. At the same time, an explorer and military adventurer named John C. Frémont entered the picture. Moving south from Oregon, he helped lead a revolt of settlers in the Sacra-

mento Valley. On June 14, 1846, at Sonoma, they declared California an independent republic.[2]

Meanwhile, Mexico and the United States had gone to war. American naval forces led by Commodore John Sloat took Monterey on July 7. San Francisco was captured two days later. In August, Commodore Robert Stockton (who replaced the ailing Sloat) declared California annexed to the United States—with himself as governor.

The situation in California was clearly getting out of hand. Polk himself sent in Colonel Stephen Kearny, who had recently taken Santa Fe. When Kearney arrived with a small force in November, he found Stockton and Frémont bickering over who should be in control. Early in 1847 Kearny succeeded in quelling remaining Mexican resistance in the region and in establishing his own authority as governor. California was ceded to the United States in the Treaty of Guadalupe Hidalgo, which ended the Mexican War.

Even before the treaty was ratified, an event occurred that would soon transform California. This was the discovery of gold near Sutter's Fort in January 1848. When news reached the East, the Gold Rush was on, and in 1849, the "forty-niners" poured into California. By 1850 there were 100,000 people there, a figure that doubled in the next two years. Most of those who had joined the Gold Rush remained in California, although only a small proportion of them had struck it rich.

NATIONAL POLITICAL TENSIONS

During the 1830s and 1840s the United States had extended its boundaries to the Pacific Ocean. But these territorial gains brought major political headaches. They were the unwanted and unexpected consequences of Manifest Destiny. Were Northern or Southern patterns to dominate the

[2]This event is known as the Bear Flag Revolt because the home-made flag raised by the rebels was adorned with a picture of a grizzly bear.

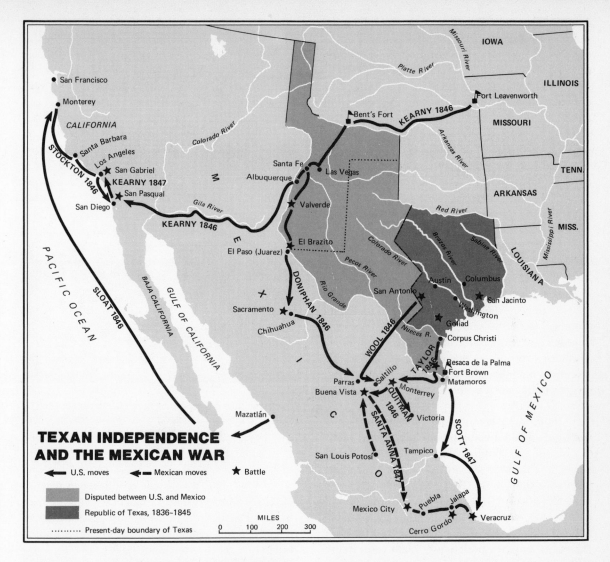

TEXAN INDEPENDENCE AND THE MEXICAN WAR

← U.S. moves   ◄--- Mexican moves   ★ Battle

Disputed between U.S. and Mexico

Republic of Texas, 1836–1845

.... Present-day boundary of Texas

MILES
0   100   200   300

In the spring of **1846**, before war was officially declared, Zachary Taylor engaged the Mexican army in two battles north of Fort Brown, Texas. After Palo Alto (May 8) and Resaca de la Palma (May 9), Taylor drove the Mexicans out of the disputed area between the Nueces River and the Rio Grande. He then crossed the lower Rio Grande and captured Matamoros (May 18) and Monterrey (Sept. 29). Before the end of the year Taylor, aided by John E. Wool, occupied Saltillo and, with General A. Quitman, went south to Victoria.

In the meantime Stephen W. Kearny led an expedition from Fort Leavenworth to Santa Fe (Aug. 15) and proclaimed New Mexico part of the United States. He left part of his army there, sent another detachment under Alexander W. Doniphan south to join Taylor, and proceeded to California. Doniphan, on his march from Santa Fe to Chihuahua, defeated the Mexicans at Valverde (Dec. 12) and El Brazito (Dec. 25). Meanwhile, Kearny had arrived in California, where John Sloat had already taken Monterey. After a temporary setback at San Pasqual (Dec. 6) Kearny joined Robert F. Stockton in San Diego.

In **1847** Kearny and Stockton were victorious at San Gabriel (Jan. 8-9). By February the Southwest was in American hands. Doniphan defeated the Mexicans at Sacramento (Feb. 28) and reached his goal, the provincial capital city of Chihuahua, on March 1. Taylor's army drove Mexican forces under Santa Anna out of a narrow mountain pass near the hacienda of Buena Vista (February 22-23).

In the winter of 1847 Winfield Scott led a force of about 10,000 with orders to take the fortified city of Veracruz. His men landed on the beaches outside the city on March 9, launching the first large-scale amphibious operation in United States military history. On March 29 he captured the city, and began an advance toward the Mexican capital. Near Jalapa, he stormed a mountain pass at Cerro Gordo (April 17-18), routing Santa Anna's army. He reached Puebla in May. Scott badly defeated Santa Anna at Contreras (Aug. 19) and Churubusco (Aug. 20), and captured the hilltop fortress of Chapultepec (Sept. 12). He smashed his way into Mexico City's last defenses on September 14, thus effectively ending the war.

new Western territories? Were the emerging new states to be slave or free? And who would decide the slavery question, Congress or the territories themselves?

National party politics in the 1840s underwent many shifts and changes reflecting the uncertainties of a rapidly growing country. The system in existence at this time is known as the second American national party system. (The first, which took shape during the early 1800s, pitted the Federalists against the Jeffersonian Republicans.) The second system had arisen in the 1820s out of the struggle for national power between the Jacksonians and the National Republicans. It resulted in two major national parties, the Democrats and the Whigs.

The Democratic party had supporters in both the North and South, and it specifically pledged to keep slavery out of politics. The Whigs promised to do the same. In general Whigs kept this promise. Still, they usually fared better in Northern states, a fact that made them more antislavery in tone than the Democrats. Thus an antislavery politician was more likely to be a Whig than a Democrat.

Some antislavery politicians preferred to work outside the two-party system. Radical abolitionists shunned political parties altogether. Other Americans decided on organized political effort through a third party. In 1840 a small group of moderate abolitionists organized the new Liberty party. They nominated a "reformed" ex-slaveholder and former Alabaman, James G. Birney, for President. But they polled only 7,000 votes in the 1840 election, which helped to place Harrison in the White House. Four years later the Liberty party again ran poorly. But this time, by taking votes away from Whig candidates in several important states, it helped swing the election in favor of Democrat James K. Polk.

The Wilmot Proviso Until the mid-1840s, party loyalties generally overcame American sectional differences. That is, a Southern Whig, for example, would consider himself a Whig first and a Southerner second, at least in matters in which party principle played a large role. But then things changed.

California gold miners pause for a photograph in 1852. In this type of sluice, water pushed gravel through, while heavier gold sank to the bottom of the trough.

One man who made a difference was an obscure Pennsylvania Democratic congressman named David Wilmot. In August 1846 he introduced a proviso (amendment) to an appropriation bill requested by President Polk to buy territory from Mexico. The Wilmot Proviso stated simply that slavery would be forbidden in any states formed out of territory acquired from Mexico.

Both of the major political parties tended to divide along sectional lines in the voting. Southerners—Whigs and Democrats alike—bitterly opposed the Wilmot Proviso. (The proslavery Whigs were sometimes known as "Cotton Whigs.") Some Northern Democrats also opposed the proviso. But many other Northerners—both Democrats and Whigs—favored it. (Northern antislavery Whigs called themselves "Conscience Whigs.")

One antislavery congressman from Illinois—a Whig named Abraham Lincoln—lost his

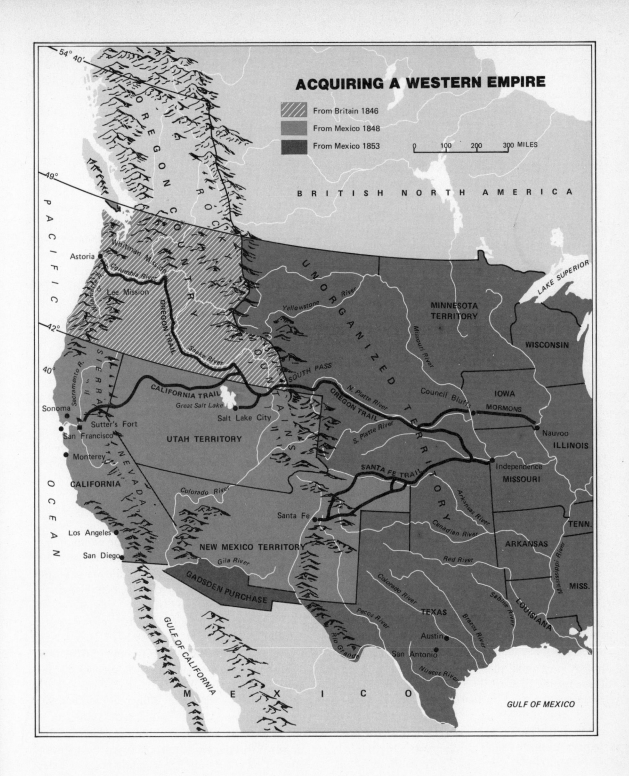

ACQUIRING A WESTERN EMPIRE

From Britain 1846
From Mexico 1848
From Mexico 1853

0   100   200   300 MILES

BRITISH NORTH AMERICA

OREGON COUNTRY

PACIFIC OCEAN

Astoria
Whitman Mission
Lee Mission
Columbia River
OREGON TRAIL
Snake River

54° 40'
49°
42°
40°

ROCKY MOUNTAINS

UNORGANIZED TERRITORY

Yellowstone River
Missouri River

MINNESOTA TERRITORY

LAKE SUPERIOR

WISCONSIN

SOUTH PASS
CALIFORNIA TRAIL
Great Salt Lake
Salt Lake City
OREGON TRAIL
N. Platte River
S. Platte River

Council Bluffs

IOWA
MORMONS

Sonoma
Sutter's Fort
San Francisco
Monterey

SIERRA NEVADA

UTAH TERRITORY

SANTA FE TRAIL

Nauvoo
ILLINOIS

Colorado River

Independence
MISSOURI

CALIFORNIA

Los Angeles
San Diego

NEW MEXICO TERRITORY

Santa Fe

Arkansas River
Canadian River

ARKANSAS

TENN.

Gila River

GADSDEN PURCHASE

Red River

MISS.

Colorado River
Pecos River
Rio Grande

TEXAS

Austin
San Antonio
Nueces River

Sabine River
Brazos River

LOUISIANA
Mississippi River

GULF OF CALIFORNIA

M E X I C O

GULF OF MEXICO

reelection bid in 1848 partly because of his support for the Wilmot Proviso. The growing strength of antislavery feeling in the North can be seen from the fact that the proviso passed the House twice. It was defeated only in the Senate, where Southerners enjoyed equal voting strength.

Effects of the Mexican War Another factor in the growth of sectionalism was the Mexican War. The war was understandably popular in the South, because proslavery people wanted the new territories. Northern opponents of slavery denounced the war and the prospect that the newly acquired territories might become slave states. Many Northerners saw the war as part of a conspiracy to extend the South's economic base and political power.

Even some thoughtful Southerners recognized the dangers. Calhoun supported the Mexican War, but he warned the Senate that "a deed has been done from which the country will not be able to recover for a long time, if ever. It has closed the first volume of our political history under the Constitution and opened the second."

The Election of 1848 Throughout the North many politicians seemed increasingly willing to sever old party loyalties in order to commit themselves more fully to the antislavery cause. A number of Liberty party abolitionists, antislavery Democrats, and Conscience Whigs banded together in 1848 to form the Free Soil party. They nominated ex-President Martin Van Buren as their candidate for the presidency.

The Free Soil platform cleverly appealed to many different segments of the population. It of course had an antislavery plank. It also included Whig economic demands, such as support for federally sponsored roads and other internal improvements. In addition it advocated Democratic social values, as in its demand for a federal homestead act that would provide free farms on public lands in the West. "Free Soil, Free Speech, Free Labor, and Free Men" ran the party's motto.

Southerners were now also banding into a party of their own, though it had no name. In Congress, bloc voting on slavery issues created a Solid South that cut across earlier party lines. Thus from 1848 to 1860 Southern Whigs and Democrats usually voted as Southerners on regional questions, particularly slavery.

Despite growing sectionalism, the Whig party managed to elect its 1848 presidential candidate, Mexican war hero Zachary Taylor. Although it had been only three months in existence, the Free Soil party did well. Its presidential candidate, Van Buren, received 290,000 votes, and the party elected nine congressmen and one senator.

Aftermath of the Compromise The country soon found itself involved in the crisis over slavery in the new territories that led to the Compromise of 1850. When the sectional crisis eased momentarily, tempers cooled. Public opinion in both North and South swung heavily behind such procompromise moderates as Stephen A. Douglas and the new President, Millard Fillmore.

Antislavery Northerners, however, continued to demand the exclusion of slavery from the new territories. Like Seward, they believed that "a higher law" had reserved the new lands for free labor. In 1851 Massachusetts sent Charles Sumner, a radical Conscience Whig, to the Senate. Everywhere in the North, abolitionists and their sympathizers denounced the new fugitive slave measure in the Compromise of 1850.

Southern fire-eaters found themselves badly undercut by the Compromise of 1850. Yet they did not give up. After passage of the compromise, a Georgia state convention warned that any further attempt by Congress to exclude slavery from the new territories or interfere with it elsewhere would lead to secession.

In 1852 the nation elected a Democratic President, Franklin Pierce of New Hampshire. Democrats also carried both houses of Congress. These victories were due partly to the fact that the Democrats, unlike the Whigs, had endorsed the Compromise of 1850. The Whig party lost in every section and never again ran a presidential candidate. Even the new Free Soil party suffered because of the general public support for compromise; it received only half as many votes as it had in 1848. In the South the Democrats took effective control of the region's political life. Except for the

SAM HOUSTON

When Sam Houston arrived in Washington, D.C., in 1846 as a senator from the new state of Texas, he was described as "a magnificent barbarian, somewhat tempered by civilization." He was a stately six-foot-three and had "a lion-like countenance capable of expressing fiercest passions." Flamboyant in speech and manner, he dressed in character. A favorite ensemble included a gold-headed cane, a panther-skin waistcoat, a large sombrero, and a Mexican blanket.

At age fifty-three, the freshman senator was a legend. A runaway youth on the Tennessee frontier, he lived for years with the Cherokees, who dubbed him "the Raven." He was a hero in the War of 1812. A long-time protégé of Andrew Jackson's, he became governor of Tennessee in his mid-thirties. His fame grew as the victorious commander in chief at the Battle of San Jacinto, which won independence for Texas. Twice president of the new republic, he was the prime mover in achieving annexation to the United States.

Texas was a slave state, and Sam Houston himself was a slaveholder. He was, as John F. Kennedy wrote, "a Southerner by birth, residence, loyalty, and philosophy." But he was also "one of the most independent, unique, popular, forceful, and dramatic individuals ever to enter the Senate chamber." He did not bind himself by sectional ties. As he said, "I know neither North nor South; I know only the Union." His was the only Southern vote for all five laws that made up the Compromise of 1850. He and a Tennessean were the only Southern senators to vote against the Kansas-Nebraska Bill.

Houston's staunch defense of the Union cost him his presidential ambitions in 1852 and again in 1856. He denounced "the mad fanaticism of the North" and "the mad ambition of the South," but he was caught between them. His vote against the Kansas-Nebraska Bill resulted in a formal censure by both the Texas legislature and the state Democrats. When he took his case to the people of Texas as an independent candidate for governor in 1857, he was defeated. But he served out his senatorial term and left the capital early in 1859. Still vigorous at age sixty-six, he was determined to make a comeback. By autumn he had done so, running again for governor and winning handily.

Houston's term of office was cut short, however. The presidential election of 1860 brought on a secessionist crisis in Texas. Pitted against a hostile legislature, Houston delayed—but could not prevent—withdrawal from the Union.

When he refused in March 1861 to take the oath of allegiance to the Confederacy, he was deposed. Gallantly, with sorrow, he bid his farewell: "I have seen patriots and statesmen of my youth one by one gathered to their fathers, and the government which they have reared rent in twain. I stand the last almost of my race, stricken down because I will not yield those principles which I have fought for."

short-lived Reconstruction period, they were to maintain this monopoly for over a century.

DANGER SIGNALS

Obviously, the nation wanted to bury the slavery question and exclude it from political debate. But factors still at work kept the issue alive.

Attempts to enforce the Fugitive Slave Act irritated and angered Northerners. The problem was more symbolic than real, though, since fewer than one in 5,000 slaves escaped annually. In 1859 over 500 of the 803 runaways came from border states,[3] where owners displayed little interest in recovering their lost property. Only a handful came from the Deep South, which had demanded the tough new law, and where feelings ran highest.

Most of the runaway slaves actually recaptured were caught in the border states and received little attention. But the few slave catchers who roamed New England and the Middle West stirred up a hornets' nest. Abolitionists who stymied the efforts of "slave-nappers" became heroes to their neighbors. Few Northerners objected to the presence of runaway slaves despite their otherwise racist treatment of black people.

Moreover, even Northern moderates who despised abolitionists and endorsed the 1850 compromise reacted emotionally to antislavery appeals. Thousands wept over *Uncle Tom's Cabin*, Harriet Beecher Stowe's best-selling novel. Published in 1851, the book portrayed the sufferings of the fictional Uncle Tom and other slaves at the hands of their masters. Tom, the novel's black hero, was martyred at the end. He represented for Mrs. Stowe the ultimate triumph of the Christian in an evil society. *Uncle Tom's Cabin* probably won hundreds of thousands of sympathizers to the antislavery cause. Translated into twenty languages, the book sold 300,000 copies within a year. Dramatized versions appeared in Northern theaters throughout the 1850s.

President Pierce tried to keep the slavery issue out of politics by pursuing an expansionist foreign policy. During his administration, American ships under Commodore Matthew C. Perry opened Japan to Western trade. The $10 million Gadsden Purchase of land from Mexico rounded out American continental borders in the Southwest. Pierce also pressured China for commercial privileges and agitated for American expansion into Cuba and Central America. Pierce, Douglas, and other Northern Democrats hoped that by stressing the national interests of Americans abroad they could destroy the virus of sectionalism at home. For a time, at least, their policies seemed effective.

But sectional bitterness intruded even into the conduct of foreign affairs. Pierce had directed the American minister to Spain, a Louisianan named Pierre Soulé, to offer Spain $130 million for the island of Cuba, whose purchase many favored both on strategic and on economic grounds. Soulé conferred on the matter with the American ambassadors to Great Britain and France (the former was James Buchanan, who himself became President in 1856). The three diplomats sent a confidential dispatch to the State Department after meeting at Ostend, Belgium, urging that—in the event Spain rejected America's offer—the United States should seize the island by force. After the "Ostend Manifesto" was leaked to Congress and the press, antislavery Northerners denounced this proposal as an outrageous bid by Southerners to extend slavery into yet another potential American territory. The controversy put an end to the possibility of acquiring Cuba peacefully.

The Kansas-Nebraska Act Stephen A. Douglas himself, however, helped to stoke sectional bitterness over slavery and destroy the very compromise he had so skillfully pushed through Congress. In 1854 he introduced a Senate bill to organize the territories of Kansas and Nebraska, a sparsely settled region at that time. Douglas hoped to prevent further congressional furor over the morality of slavery expansion through popular

---

[3]The border states—Delaware, Maryland, Kentucky, Tennessee, and Missouri—were slave states bordering the North that had more moderate views on controlling slaves (and, later, secession) than the rest of the South. West Virginia, which joined the Union in 1863, is usually considered a border state, too.

sovereignty, allowing settlers to decide the issue for themselves. Once again, however, as in President Taylor's solution regarding California, it proved easier to devise a practical approach to the slavery issue than to enforce it.

Congress soon found itself embroiled in another quarrel between antislavery and proslavery members. Since Kansas and Nebraska lay within the area of the Louisiana Purchase, the status of slavery there should have been governed by the Missouri Compromise of 1820. This agreement kept slavery out of land that far north. Passage of the Kansas-Nebraska Bill would in effect repeal the Missouri Compromise. This prospect infuriated antislavery Northerners.

Douglas sponsored his bill in order to encourage settlement in the region. This would enable a transcontinental railroad to move across it to the Pacific. The bill's final version included several concessions to Southerners, whose votes Douglas needed. With the support of President Pierce the bill passed in May 1854 after months of furious debate.

Debate over the Kansas-Nebraska Act broke the uneasy truce that had more or less silenced discussions about slavery since 1850. It aroused Northern public opinion against slavery as no previous congressional measure—not even the Fugitive Slave Law of 1850—had ever done. Douglas's concessions to Southerners during the long debate over his measure—and some changes he made to please this camp—were one factor offending the antislavery forces. Another was the possibility, slim, but (in theory) conceivable under the bill's terms, that territories *north* of the 1820 Missouri Compromise line might somehow adopt slavery. Primarily, the measure became a rallying point for (and a symbol of) Northern fears of Southern in-

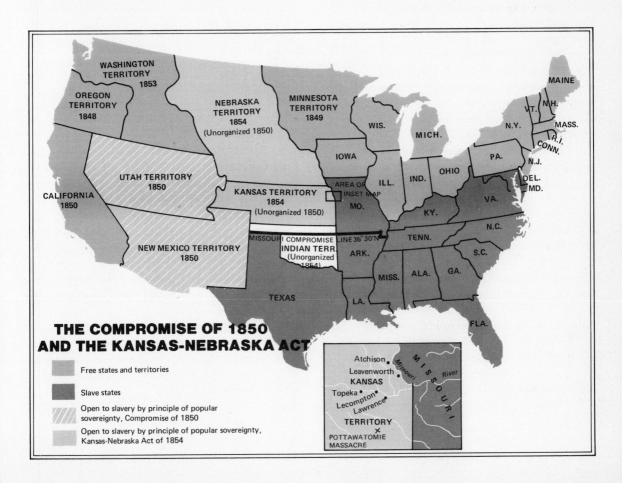

THE COMPROMISE OF 1850
AND THE KANSAS-NEBRASKA ACT

Free states and territories

Slave states

Open to slavery by principle of popular sovereignty, Compromise of 1850

Open to slavery by principle of popular sovereignty, Kansas-Nebraska Act of 1854 tentions on the question of slavery's expansion into the Western territories.

Two New Parties Northern outrage at passage of the Kansas-Nebraska Act took concrete form. Throughout the North in 1854 hundreds of thousands of people left the Democratic and Whig parties to join local anti-Nebraska political groups. In a few months these groups united to form the Republican party. It was a much broader coalition of Conscience Whigs, anti-Douglas Democrats, and abolitionists than the Free Soil party had been. The new party demanded complete exclusion of slavery from all remaining federal territories.

The Whig party was dying. Its members sought new political homes. While some became Republicans, others joined the recently formed American party. Members of the party were often called "Know-Nothings." Their platform was secret, and when asked about it, a party member would answer "I know nothing."

The Know-Nothings were nativists—that is, they felt that immigrants presented a threat to "native Americans." (By "native Americans" the Know-Nothings were referring, not to Indians, but to families who had been in America for two or three generations.)

Know-Nothings were particularly opposed to Roman Catholics. Hundreds of thousands of such newcomers, mainly Irish, had migrated to America in the 1840s after a potato famine in Ireland. Nativists feared the newcomers' religion, and they felt that the Catholics would not fit into American society.

Clearly, this was a time when many Americans were fearful of subversive elements in their society, elements plotting in secret to undermine democratic freedoms. Know-Nothings feared a Catholic conspiracy. Slaveholders were afraid of an abolitionist plot. And abolitionists were convinced of a slaveholders' intrigue.

"Bleeding Kansas" Many people moved to Kansas after passage of the Kansas-Nebraska Act. Most of them were farmers—from both the North and the South. Few seemed to care whether the state became slave or free. Unfortunately, this unconcern did not last.

Antislavery Northerners formed Emigrant Aid Societies, usually under the direction of abolitionists. These societies provided money, guns, and supplies for Northern settlers in Kansas—settlers who were determined that Kansas should be a free state. At the same time, a smaller group of proslavery settlers were backed by neighboring Missourians, who often crossed the border to vote and to fight.

Armed proslavery and antislavery forces clashed frequently and fiercely in what came to be called "Bleeding Kansas." Normal political processes broke down completely. Although a large majority of Kansas settlers voted for a free-state legislature, proslavery forces and Missourians elected their own assembly. Violence ruled the territory, and President Pierce could not maintain order.

The conflict reached Washington. In May 1856, Massachusetts Senator Charles Sumner delivered a fervent antislavery address, "the Crime against Kansas." His speech included an attack on Senator Andrew Butler of South Carolina. Butler's nephew was a hotheaded South Carolina congressman named Preston Brooks. Two days after Sumner's speech, Brooks—determined to avenge his family's honor—marched into the Senate chamber and beat the Massachusetts senator unconscious with a cane. Sumner was injured so severely that he did not reappear in Congress for three years.

As for "Bleeding Kansas," the fighting persisted between proslavery and antislavery irregulars for several more years. One of the antislavery militia leaders, the veteran abolitionist, John Brown, would become involved in a dramatic incident in 1859—far from Kansas—that would prove even more significant than the caning of Charles Sumner.

SUGGESTED READINGS– CHAPTERS 19-20

Crisis and Compromise in 1850
Holman Hamilton, *Prologue to Conflict: The Crisis and Compromise of 1850* (1964).

Expansion into the Far West
Ray A. Billington, *Westward Expansion* (1974) and *The Far Western Frontier, 1830–1860* (1956); Gene M. Brack, *Mexico Views Manifest Destiny* (1976); Frederick M. Merk, *Manifest Destiny and Mission in American History* (1963); John H. Schroeder, *Mr. Polk's War: American Opposition and Dissent, 1846–1848* (1973); Otis A. Singletary, *The Mexican War* (1960); George Rogers Taylor, *The Transportation Revolution, 1815–1860* (1951); Albert K. Weinberg, *Manifest Destiny* (1935).

National Political Tensions
Gerald M. Capers, *Stephen A. Douglas: Defender of the Union* (1959); Avery Craven, *The Growth of Southern Nationalism, 1848–1861* (1953) and *The Coming of the Civil War* (1963); Bernard DeVoto, *The Year of Decision, 1846* (1943); Eric Foner, *Free Soil, Free Labor, Free Men: The Ideology of the Republican Party Before the Civil War* (1970); Vincent C. Hopkins, *Dred Scott's Case* (1951); Robert W. Johannsen, *Stephen A. Douglas* (1973); Philip S. Klein, *President James Buchanan* (1962); Albert J. Kirwan, *John J. Crittenden* (1962); Allan Nevins, *The Emergence of Lincoln* (2 vols., 1950) and *Ordeal of the Union* (2 vols., 1947); Alice Nichols, *Bleeding Kansas* (1969); David M. Potter, *The Impending Crisis, 1848–1861* (1976); Joseph G. Rayback, *Free Soil: The Election of 1848* (1970); James A. Rawley, *Race and Politics: Bleeding Kansas and the Coming of the Civil War* (1969).

21
JOHN BROWN'S RAID

A.W.

The plot seemed so incredible that the secretary of war refused to believe it. John B. Floyd was relaxing at a Virginia resort late in August 1859 when he received an anonymous letter. It warned of a conspiracy to incite a slave uprising throughout the South. " 'Old John Brown,' late of Kansas," according to the writer, had stored a large quantity of arms in a Maryland hideaway. As the head of a "secret association," he planned to attack Virginia first, entering the state at Harpers Ferry, a northwestern border town.[1] The anonymous writer urged Floyd to send federal troops to the town.

The South had experienced no slave rebellion since the Nat Turner Revolt almost thirty years earlier. Floyd (the son of Virginia's governor at the time of the Turner uprising) was a fiery opponent of abolitionism. But he refused to believe that "a scheme of such wickedness and outrage could be entertained by any citizen of the United States." He took no action.

At this time John Brown was fifty-nine years old and a fugitive from justice. President Buchanan himself had authorized a $250 reward for his capture. Brown was wanted in connection with antislavery raids he had conducted in Kansas. It was partly because Brown's name was identified so closely with Kansas that Floyd did not take the Harpers Ferry plot seriously.

In Kansas, Brown had acquired some fame but little else. In fact, his life was marked by almost total failure. He had struggled constantly to achieve financial security (an understandable goal for the father of twenty children). Brown failed first during the 1830s as an Ohio land speculator. Then, in 1842, he went bankrupt as a sheep rancher. A later career as a wool merchant also ended in failure. In 1855 Brown and his family migrated to the newly opened Kansas Territory. Here Brown soon gained a reputation as a ferocious opponent of slavery.

John Brown had always been an abolitionist. Before he moved west, his house had been a station on the underground railroad. In Kan-

Gerrit Smith

---

[1] Harpers Ferry and other West Virginia towns mentioned in this chapter were still a part of Virginia at this time; West Virginia did not become a separate state until 1863.

sas the situation was violent, with proslavery and antislavery forces struggling for control of the territorial government. Brown and five of his sons took an active role in what was practically a guerrilla war.

Brown was best known for an incident that took place at Pottawatomie, Kansas, in 1856. He led a small band that murdered and mutilated five proslavery settlers. This raid was apparently in retaliation for the burning of Lawrence, Kansas (a free-state town), by slave-state advocates. None of Brown's victims owned slaves. The common thread linking them was their association with a local court that was soon to try a case in which Brown was the defendant.

Franklin B. Sanborn

In the fall of 1856 Brown went east with his sons. For the next three years he wandered across the North from Kansas to Massachusetts making speeches and holding private fund-raising meetings. Brown had long toyed with the notion of launching a direct assault on Southern slavery. He knew that this kind of action would frighten moderate abolitionists. So he usually described his aim as a simple raiding expedition southward to rescue a select handful of slaves. By early 1858, however, Brown began revealing his actual plan—"to overthrow slavery in a large part of the country."

Incredibly, Brown told about eighty Northern abolitionists of his scheme. Many had grave doubts about it. One such man was Frederick Douglass, the leading black abolitionist. Another dubious listener was an Iowa Quaker named David J. Gue. Gue had written the anonymous letter to Secretary of War Floyd. He hoped that, if Floyd ordered federal troops to Harpers Ferry, Brown would call off the raid before he and his men were all killed.

Thomas W. Higginson

Brown could not have gotten as far as he did without the aid of six leading abolitionists, known as the Secret Six. One was Gerrit Smith, a wealthy landowner in upstate New York. The other five were all from Massachusetts. Franklin B. Sanborn was a Boston schoolteacher. Thomas Wentworth Higginson and Theodore Parker were Unitarian ministers. George Luther Stearns was a prominent merchant and manufacturer of Boston. The sixth member of the group was a physician, Samuel Gridley Howe.

At first the Secret Six, like Brown's other abolitionist supporters, believed that their leader planned some new and dramatic strike against the proslavery forces in Kansas. But then Brown began to reveal his real intentions. Neither political action nor peaceful persuasion had settled the slavery question, he said. Only a slave uprising throughout the South would make slaveholders aware of their moral guilt. God had selected him, Brown continued, to organize and lead such an insurrection. The revolt would begin in Virginia. From there it would quickly spread like a raging brushfire across the entire South. Even if the plot failed, Brown believed that the hysteria that would then sweep the South would provoke a major sectional crisis, dividing a proslavery South and an antislavery North so that civil war might result.

Brown asked the Secret Six for financial help. He refused to dis-

Theodore Parker

George Luther Stearns

cuss any tactical and strategic objections they might have. He offered them, as Sanborn later remarked, "only the alternatives of betrayal, desertion, or support." Brown claimed that he now wanted "men of action." What he really wanted—and had in the Secret Six—was a group of people who would raise funds and thus fulfill their private dreams of being something more than mere talkers.

Though some of the six wavered, in the end they all cast their doubts aside and supported Brown. Why should a slave revolt be condemned, they probably reasoned, when the "slave power" had inflicted so much violence on the free states during the previous decade? Hadn't there been undeclared warfare in Kansas? Wasn't there a massive effort by slave catchers to hunt down fugitive slaves? And what about the physical assaults on abolitionists, not to mention the savage beating of Charles Sumner on the floor of the Senate?

By the late 1850s many abolitionists—not only the Secret Six— had become convinced that there could be no peaceful solution to the slavery question. Gerrit Smith wrote the Republican governor of Vermont:

> Hitherto I have opposed the bloody abolition of slavery, but now, when it begins to march its conquering bands into the free states, I and ten thousand other peace [movement] men are not only ready to have it repulsed with violence, but pursued even unto death, with violence.

Samuel Gridley Howe

John Brown represented, for Smith and the others among the Secret Six, the obvious instrument of what they believed to be justifiable violence. At the same time, Brown's supporters preferred being kept in the dark concerning his specific plans. They hoped to avoid being identified too closely with the scheme. "I have great faith in the wisdom, integrity, and bravery of Captain Brown," Gerrit Smith wrote Sanborn in July 1858. "Whenever he shall embark on another of his contests with the slave power, I shall again stand ready to help him." The limit on this support became clear only in the final sentences of Smith's note: "I do not wish to know Captain Brown's plans. I hope he will keep them to himself." Or, as Samuel Gridley Howe put it to Brown himself, "Don't tell me what you are about or where you are going."

Brown's ultimate destination was Harpers Ferry, Virginia. But as a base of operations he chose a farm across the Potomac River in Maryland. Brown, posing as a New York cattle buyer named Isaac Smith, had rented the farm from the Kennedy family in July 1859. He arrived with two of his sons, Owen and Oliver. A third son, Watson, joined them later.

By late August there were fifteen recruits living on the Kennedy farm. Oliver's wife, Martha, and a granddaughter of Brown's, Annie, were brought to the farm to keep house and quiet the suspicions of nosy neighbors. Most of the group were young. All but two of Brown's men were under thirty. The oldest, apart from the "commander in chief" himself, was a forty-eight-year-old free black named Dangerfield Newby. He had joined the company hoping to liberate his wife and seven children from a nearby Virginia plantation. As the group waited restlessly through the hot summer, hundreds of weapons reached the farm—200 revolvers, 198 rifles, and 950 iron-tipped pikes destined for use by insurgent slaves.

Several of the recruits still believed that they had come South to rescue a small group of slaves and escort them to safety in Canada. During the summer, though, Brown revealed his actual plan for a full-scale slave revolt that would spread quickly throughout the South.

Brown's men drilled, but their commander made few other preparations for the attack itself. He gathered almost no information about the slaves in the region. He did not even bother to scout the area's roads and hiding places. Nor did he develop a plan of escape in case the assault on Harpers Ferry failed.

The only preparation Brown made for possible failure was a curious effort to ensure that others besides himself would be blamed for the raid. Inside a trunk in the farmhouse, in plain view, Brown left letters that implicated his most prominent Northern supporters, among them the Secret Six.

A final handful of recruits drifted into the "Smith" farm in October. Brown decided to strike. He had already sent Martha and Annie back home and written last-minute notes to Northern relatives and friends.

There were now twenty-one "soldiers": five blacks and sixteen whites. On Sunday, October 16, Brown gathered them together for a final prayer service. He then explained his plan of attack to the newer recruits, three of whom had arrived only the previous day. First his men were to blockade the two bridges into Harpers Ferry. Then they would capture the armory buildings and a rifle factory. They would take hostages to use in the event of attack by federal troops or state militia. Once a sufficient number of blacks from the area had rallied to the invaders, the entire band would retreat toward the nearby mountains and regroup for their march southward.

At eight o'clock that moonless night Brown strode out of the farmhouse followed by eighteen of his men. He posted the remaining three as a rear guard. (One was to go to a nearby schoolhouse on Monday to await the escaping slaves who were expected to gather in the area.) Brown then climbed into a wagon filled with the weapons he had collected and rode toward a bridge that led into the silent, sleeping town across the Potomac.

Harpers Ferry was strategically located at the junction of the Potomac and Shenandoah rivers. Baltimore lay eighty miles east by rail and Washington fifty-seven miles by road. The town's main industry was arms manufacture. The federal government maintained a complex of buildings, including a fire-engine house, an armory, and an arsenal. There was also a private rifle works located on an island in the Shenandoah.

The town had a population of slightly more than 2,500. Of this total 1,251 were free blacks, and only 88 were slaves. Most of the white

HARPERS FERRY, 1859

residents were Northerners employed as skilled craftsmen or government officials in the armory-rifle works complex.

Harpers Ferry was not a typical Southern town. There were no large plantations in the area. Neither cotton nor tobacco was grown there. The few slaveholders in the area owned small farms. Most of the local slaves were house servants. There was no large pool of plantation field hands to be rallied in the immediate area.

Several of Brown's recruits stationed themselves at the two bridges leading into Harpers Ferry. Another group overpowered the single watchman at the government-owned properties and seized control of the armory, the arsenal, and the engine house. They also took over the private rifle works. The invaders herded a small group of prisoners into the engine house as hostages. Now that he controlled millions in government munitions, Brown grew increasingly confident of success. He ordered the telegraph wires cut and dispatched a raiding party to secure more hostages from the nearby countryside. This band returned in the early morning hours of Monday, October 17, with ten freed slaves and three prisoners. Among the latter was the great-grandnephew of George Washington, a minor slaveholder named Lewis W. Washington. Brown had particularly wanted Lewis Washington as a prisoner "for the moral effect it would give our cause having one of your name."

A train whistle signaled the beginning of danger for John Brown's plans. Shortly after midnight an express passenger train from Wheeling reached Harpers Ferry en route to Baltimore. Trainmen found the railroad bridge barricaded and a wounded night watchman shouting warnings of armed night raiders. Brown's raiders began firing, forcing the engineer to back up the train until it was safely out of gunshot range. Just then the Harpers Ferry baggage master, a free black named Hayward Shepherd, wandered down the track. When he tried to run in spite of a raider's command to halt, he was shot down. Shepherd died soon afterward, the first fatality in John Brown's private war against slavery.

By dawn the alarm had sounded throughout the countryside. The residents of Harpers Ferry, except for the handful Brown had taken as hostages or prisoners, armed themselves and fled in panic to a hilltop behind the town. Many of the town's blacks—both slave and free—fled with them. Church bells throughout northwestern Virginia and Maryland tolled the warning signal for slave insurrections. Militia companies began collecting their forces throughout the Blue Ridge towns that bordered on Harpers Ferry, preparing to march on the town.

Up to this point most Virginians who knew of the incident believed that *blacks* had begun a slave uprising at Harpers Ferry much like the one three decades earlier at Jerusalem. Only later in the day would the truth filter out. Brown, amazingly enough, had allowed the Baltimore express train to continue on its way. Thus he ensured that news of his invasion would pass instantly across the telegraph lines from Baltimore to Washington, Richmond, and elsewhere. It is difficult to know whether he was too dazed to act decisively or whether he deliberately wanted to publicize what he had done. In any case, by Monday noon, he and his men had clearly lost the initiative in Harpers Ferry.

Harpers Ferry at the time of the 1859 raid was a small town in a dramatic setting. In this view, looking southeast, the Potomac curves down from the left and into the far distance; the Shenandoah flows past the church at right. The government buildings are near the center, not far from the bridge over the Potomac.

Not only did Brown allow the train to proceed. He actually dawdled away the morning. Instead of collecting his hostages and making a dash for the nearby mountains, as several of his men urged him to do, he squandered time with his hostages at the engine house. He even ordered breakfast for all of them from a nearby hotel, the Wager House. He divided his already outnumbered forces, sending several raiders and a few freed slaves across the Potomac to join his rear guard at the schoolhouse.

In the morning, armed townspeople and men from nearby farms got the upper hand. Their rifle fire kept the raiders pinned down to their armory compound. Brown had obviously not expected his opponents to attack so quickly. Yet he remained in the town, either expecting slave reinforcements or perhaps simply making what he believed to be a divinely ordered last stand.

Brown's only means of escape, the two bridges, were retaken by militia late Monday morning. The militia dispersed the few raiders guarding the structures. One of them, the free black Dangerfield Newby, was the first of Brown's men to die in the assault. As he lay dead in the street, townspeople vented their fury at the raid on his body, beating it with sticks.

This tiny schoolhouse in Maryland was to be used as a gathering place for escaping slaves after Brown's raid. He had not intended to strike as soon as he did, but neighbors near the Kennedy farm were growing suspicious of the activity there.

Brown finally began searching for a way to get out. Some of his men were still across the river in Maryland. Others were trapped in the rifle works. He and most of his raiders, guarding about thirty hostages by now, could not link up with either group. Brown decided to offer an exchange. He would release the hostages in return for a guarantee that he and his men could go free. Will Thompson, the first raider who carried these terms to the militia under a flag of truce, was seized by the crowd and taken away at gunpoint. Brown recognized his predicament at last. He took his remaining men, his few slave recruits, and eleven of his most prominent hostages. They barricaded themselves in the engine house. He then sent out three more people—his son Watson, another raider, and one of the prisoners. They approached the militia under another flag of truce. The two raiders were shot down, although Watson managed to crawl back to the engine house.

The streets of Harpers Ferry were filled with drunken, hysterical townspeople and militiamen by late Monday afternoon. One group caught an escaping raider near the Potomac, killed him, and then spent hours puncturing his body with bullets. Brown's remaining three men in the rifle works received similar treatment when they were forced to flee toward the river. Two of them fell dead, riddled with bullets. The third, a black named John Anthony Copeland, was rescued from lynching by a local doctor, who protected him from a mob of captors until the arrival of slightly more sober militiamen.

Among the casualties on Monday afternoon was the mayor of Harpers Ferry, a gentle old man named Fontaine Beckham. (His will provided for the emancipation of a slave family owned by him.) He was shot by one of Brown's men. After Beckham's death the town went completely out of control. Residents and local farmers competed with frenzied militiamen in screaming at the raiders while senselessly firing their guns. A mob marched on the Wager House, where Will Thompson remained under guard. They dragged him down to the Potomac, as he shouted: "You may take my life, but eighty thousand will arise up to avenge me, and carry out my purpose of giving liberty to the slaves." The mob peppered his head with bullets before tossing the dead man into the shallow water.

The first word of the leader's identity came late Monday. He sent out yet another note from the engine house repeating his offer to exchange hostages for freedom. It was signed "John Brown." The offer was refused.

The night that followed must have been agonizing for Brown, as he struggled to retain some control over his future despite the obvious failure of his plan. Two of his sons, Oliver and Watson, lay dying. Brown and his four remaining able-bodied men took turns guarding their eleven hostages. Brown spent a good deal of time tending to his prisoners' comfort. Mainly, though, he strode quietly back and forth across the blood-spattered room, alone with his thoughts.

John Brown was fifty-six when this photograph was taken, early in 1857. (He soon grew a beard as a disguise.)

When Brown and his men peered out of their engine-house fortress at dawn on Tuesday, October 18, things had changed. They saw, not Monday's scruffy and jittery mob of local rabbit-shooting militia but a cool, well-dressed company of United States Marines. They were armed with rifles, bayonets, and sledge hammers for the siege that lay ahead. The marines were under the command of Colonel Robert E. Lee, accompanied by Lieutenant J. E. B. Stuart. Brown appeared neither shocked nor unhappy. One of his hostages, Lewis Washington, later observed:

> Brown was the coolest and firmest man I ever saw. With one son dead by his side, and another shot through, he felt the pulse of his dying son with one hand and held his rifle with the other, and commanded his men with the utmost composure, encouraging them to sell their lives as dearly as they could.

Lieutenant Stuart approached the engine house under a flag of truce. He handed a note to Brown demanding unconditional surrender and promising him and his men protection from vigilante justice. Brown refused. He insisted that he would surrender only when he and his men were promised their freedom. Stuart repeated Lee's surrender terms and then, without warning, leaped away from the door waving his cap. While thousands of excited spectators cheered wildly, a party of soldiers began battering at the oak doors of the engine house. Brown's men responded with a volley of shots. Within moments one of the doors had been broken down, and armed marines began dashing into the engine house. The first two were shot. But others swarmed in, overpowering Brown and his four remaining raiders.

Two of the four raiders were quickly bayoneted and died soon afterward. The remaining two, a Quaker youth named Edwin Coppoc and a free black named Shields Green, were captured without being seriously wounded. Brown himself knelt on the floor, his rifle cocked while

In this engine house Brown and his raiders took refuge on October 17. His small band pushed the fire engines up to the doors to impede entry, but Lee's troops broke in, using a heavy ladder as a battering ram.

awaiting the assault. Lieutenant Israel Green, the officer leading the attack on the engine house, entered the building and struck Brown with a light sword before the weary man could fire. Green then tried to run him through with his sword, practically lifting Brown off the ground. Somehow the sword struck either a bone or a belt buckle and failed to inflict a fatal wound. Nevertheless, as Brown collapsed on the gound, Lieutenant Green continued beating him over the head with his sword until his victim lost consciousness. Finally, the lieutenant regained his self-control. He ordered Brown and his men carried outside and placed on the grass, where their wounds were dressed.

Later that afternoon a detachment of militia confiscated boxes of revolvers and rifles from the Maryland schoolhouse where Brown's recruit had waited vainly for slaves to rally. Another patrol under J. E. B. Stuart occupied the Kennedy farm. By then the rest of Brown's rear guard had fled. They left behind not only hundreds of weapons but also the incriminating letters from the Secret Six and other abolitionists that Brown had abandoned so casually before the raid.

After his wounds had been dressed, Brown was taken to an office in the armory. He was guarded closely, for mobs in the streets of Harpers Ferry wanted to lynch him immediately.

On Tuesday afternoon Brown was visited by a group of politicians, military officers, and newspaper reporters who had just arrived in Harpers Ferry. Among them were Virginia Governor Henry A. Wise and Senator James M. Mason, also of Virginia. Brown did not shirk speaking to the visitors since, as he put it, he wanted "to make himself and his motives clearly understood." It was a new role for the militant man of action, who had often expressed his contempt for mere talkers. In Governor Wise's words Brown spoke "freely, fluently, and cheerfully." Whether he spoke truthfully, however, is questionable.

Senator Mason asked the old man how he had financed the raid. "I furnished most [of the money] myself," he answered. "I cannot implicate others. It is by my own folly that I have been taken." Brown insisted throughout the interview on accepting complete responsibility for the raid: "No man sent me here; it was my own prompting and that of my Maker, or that of the devil, whichever you please to ascribe it to." (If Brown had sincerely wished to avoid implicating his Northern supporters, though, he might have done so more effectively by not leaving their correspondence in plain view at the Kennedy farm.)

Brown departed most strikingly from the truth when he discussed his motives in attacking Harpers Ferry. He denied any intention of leading a violent slave revolt. He claimed that his purpose had been simply to liberate a group of slaves and lead them to freedom: "We came to free the slaves," he insisted, "and only that."

"Do you consider yourself an instrument in the hands of Providence?" one bystander asked. "I do," Brown replied. "I pity the poor in bondage that have none to help them; that is why I am here; not to gratify any personal animosity, revenge, or vindictive spirit." Brown claimed that only fear for his hostages' safety had prevented his fleeing earlier. He said too that his decision to allow the Baltimore train to proceed stemmed from his concern for the lives of its passengers.

Brown was clearly trying to suggest to his interviewers a change in his personality. His speech was free of the harsh and vindictive tone that he had used formerly in talking of Southern slaveholders. There now emerged the image of a gentle and rather sorrowful agent of Providence. To Senator Mason, he said:

> I think, my friend, [that Southerners] are guilty of a great wrong against God and humanity—I say it without wishing to be offensive. . . . I wish to say, furthermore, that you had better—all of you people at the South—prepare yourselves for a settlement of that question that must come up for settlement sooner than you are prepared for it. . . . You may dispose of me very easily; I am nearly disposed of now; but this question is still to be settled—this negro question I mean—the end of that is not yet.

Brown was directing his words more toward the northern audience that would read newspaper accounts of the interview than toward his southern questioners. He was trying to convey to northern readers the belief that had led him to Harpers Ferry—that slavery could no longer be fought by peaceful means but only by such methods as he had used in his unsuccessful raid.

By late Tuesday afternoon it was possible to tally the results of John Brown's invasion scheme. The slaves he had sent to the Maryland schoolhouse had deserted the previous night and returned to their masters. One unfortunate slave captured with Brown later died in a Charleston prison. Another of his reluctant slave recruits was later found drowned near Harpers Ferry.

Seventeen people were killed during the raid or died soon afterward: the two slaves, three townspeople, one slaveholder, and one marine; and ten of Brown's men, including two of his sons. Five raiders, including Brown, were captured, and the rest escaped into the Maryland mountains. Two others were caught in Pennsylvania a few days later, while five (including Brown's son Owen) fled to safety.

As a military effort, Brown's campaign failed miserably. Yet, even at its moment of failure, it began to trigger exactly the kind of sectional crisis that Brown had predicted.

Moderates in the North tried to minimize the raid's importance. They wrote John Brown off as a solitary madman whose efforts did not have support among respectable Americans of any section. "It is now well understood," editorialized *Harpers Weekly* in late October 1859, "that the insurrection was merely the work of a half-crazed white." Republican party politicians were especially eager to dissassociate their peaceful antislavery views from Brown's violent tactics. "John Brown was no Republican," insisted Abraham Lincoln, and not "a single Republican [has been implicated] in his Harpers Ferry enterprise."

On the other hand, Democrats in both the North and the South denounced the Brown plot as an extension of Republican antislavery agitation. In Virginia itself, a state legislative committee that later investigated the invasion probably spoke for most Southerners when it wrote:

> The whole argument against the *extension* of slavery is soon, by a very slight deflection, made to bear against the *existence* of slavery, and thus the anti-extension idea is merged in that of abolition. . . . The crimes of John Brown were neither more nor less than practical illustrations of the doctrines of the republican party.

Senator Stephen A. Douglas, the leading Democratic spokesman of the North, called the scheme a "natural, logical, inevitable result of the doctrines and teachings of the Republican party."

More directly concerned, of course, were the Secret Six and Brown's other Northern abolitionist backers. They faced possible arrest and prison terms for their role in the episode. Newspapers throughout the country began reprinting the incriminating letters found at the Kennedy farm. Within a week after Brown's capture Sanborn, Howe, and Stearns had fled to Canada to escape prosecution. Frederick Douglass, after writing an editorial defending the Harpers Ferry raid, sailed to England. Edwin Morton, another of Brown's abolitionist backers, also went to England. (Parker, dying of tuberculosis, had already gone to Europe.)

Gerrit Smith broke down completely. In November friends took him to an asylum for the insane, where he remained until late December, by which time he had "recovered his reason."

Higginson was the only member of the Secret Six to stand his ground. He did not try to deny involvement in the raid. But he did insist that Brown's "acquittal or rescue would do half as much good as being executed; so strong is the personal sympathy with him."

Higginson's view was shared by most abolitionists. They praised Brown for his actions—and they wanted the South to complete its work of immortalizing their hero. "Let no man pray that Brown be spared!" declared the Reverend Henry Ward Beecher. "Let Virginia make him a martyr!"

Virginia's Governor Wise seemed determined to oblige. Wise decided to charge Brown and his associates, under a Virginia statute, for treason against the state, rather than to hand over the men for trial in a federal court. The governor's position was legally questionable but politically shrewd. Brown's raid on the government arsenal and armory at Harpers Ferry had clearly broken federal laws. Nor did any of the raiders owe allegiance to Virginia. But Wise's action satisfied the general Southern clamor for swift (Southern) vengeance against the raiders. Virginia authorities, fearful that unruly mobs in Harpers Ferry might try to lynch Brown, shifted the trial and the prisoners to Charleston. On October 26 the grand jury indicted Brown and his four accomplices—two whites and two blacks—charging them with the murder of five people, conspiracy to provoke a slave revolt, and treason against the state of Virginia. All of the raiders pleaded not guilty. The judge agreed to separate trials, Brown's being the first.

The trial of John Brown began on October 27, with the defendant reclining on a cot confronting a packed courthouse. Brown's court-appointed lawyer, Virginian Lawson Botts, startled the courtroom audi-

At his trial for treason, the wounded Brown had to lie on a cot in the middle of the floor. Govenor Wise remarked that the prisoner reminded him of "a broken-winged hawk with talons set."

ence by immediately producing a telegram from a man in Akron, Ohio. He asserted that Brown and others in his family (which had lived in the Akron area for a number of years) were insane.

Botts felt that the only way to save his client's life was to have the jury commit him to an insane asylum. But Brown was not interested in saving his life. He wanted to use his trial as a national forum for preaching the antislavery gospel. He did not wish to wither away in obscurity. Finally, because of Brown's objections, his attorneys abandoned the insanity defense.

The trial came rapidly to a conclusion. On October 31, after deliberating only forty-five minutes, the jury found Brown guilty on all charges. Two days later he was carried back into court for sentencing. Before the judge could pronounce his sentence, the prisoner asked to speak. He talked for five minutes, addressing not the court so much as the country, which would read the text of his speech in newspapers the next day. He spoke slowly and eloquently, defending his actions at Harpers Ferry by distorting the facts and appealing directly and in the most emotional way for support from the antislavery North:

> In the first place, I deny everything but what I have all along admitted—the design on my part to free slaves. I intended to do as I did last winter, when I went into Missouri, and there took slaves without the snapping of a gun on either side, moved them through the country, and finally left them in Canada. I designed to have done the same thing again, on a larger scale. That was all I intended. I never did intend murder or treason, or the destruction of property, or to excite or incite slaves to rebellion, or to make insurrection. . . . I see a book kissed here, which I suppose to be the Bible, or at least the New Testament. That teaches me that all things whatsoever I would men should do to me, I should do even so to them. It teaches me further to "remember them that are in bonds, as bound with them." I endeavored to act up to that instruction.

Though Brown lied in his remarks about his plans for a slave revolt, he was truthful about his ultimate intention of liberating the slaves. This distinction was lost not only on many of Brown's Northern admirers but also on the judge, who sentenced him to die on the gallows on December 2. The four other captured raiders were also found guilty at their trials and, like Brown, were sentenced to hang.

In Brown's last month, he continued his efforts to replace his earlier image as a vengeful border fighter with that of a forgiving yet sternly moral Christian, one who endured his final days as a prisoner with simple dignity. Brown's lawyers worked furiously to collect sworn statements from the condemned man's family and friends testifying to his insanity, in the hope of persuading Governor Wise to commit the condemned man to an asylum. They gathered a large number of such statements, many doubtless from people who were trying to save Brown's life but did not really believe him mad.

At the same time, many people wrote Wise pleading with him to spare Brown and not create an antislavery martyr, thereby increasing sectional tensions. The governor finally rejected the many appeals for clemency, declaring Brown perfectly sane—"cool, collected, and indom-

A PREMATURE MOVEMENT.

JOHN BROWN. "Here! Take this, and follow me. My name's Brown."
CUFFEE. "Please God! Mr. Brown, dat is onpossible. We ain't done seedin' yit at our house."

Trying to recruit a less than enthusiastic disciple to his cause, Brown is ridiculed in this pro-Southern view of the raid.

itable." "He is a fanatic," Wise wrote, "but firm, truthful and intelligent." Brown could not have been more delighted at Wise's actions. He wrote: "I am worth inconceivably more to *hang* than for any other purpose."

Brown greeted a procession of visitors in his cell during his last month. Virginia officials also generously (perhaps foolishly) allowed their prisoner to receive and send a steady stream of letters to friends, family, and antislavery associates. These letters helped fix the image of Brown among Northerners as a Christian martyr for the abolitionist cause. The themes he dwelt on in his correspondence were constant: his "cheerful" resignation to death, comparisons of his own death with Christ's, his belief that his death would help achieve his aim of liberating the slaves, and his continued belief in his role as a messenger of God. In only one month's time Brown made his execution a national event. Thousands now saw him only as a brave Christian going to his death with calm nobility.

On December 1, the afternoon before his execution, Brown received a last visitor, his wife, Mary. She had traveled south, having received Governor Wise's permission to return the bodies of her husband and two sons to their New York farm for burial. Brown and his wife shared supper and discussed family matters. Before going to bed, Brown wrote a final letter to his brother Jeremiah in which he described himself as "quite cheerful and composed."

Brown rose at dawn on December 2, read his Bible briefly, and wrote a final note to Mary. He enclosed his will and gave instructions for his tombstone inscription—simply "John Brown born May 9th 1800 was executed at Charleston, Va, December 2d 1859." Soon afterward his jailers came for him and escorted him down the corridor.

A sentimental version of Brown on his way to his execution was painted by Thomas Hovenden in 1884. Just before, Brown had stopped by the cell of some of his fellow-raiders and spoken to them, parting with the words: "God bless you, my men. May we all meet in heaven."

Brown walked briskly down the corridor. Pausing by the cell where the two blacks, Copeland and Green, were being held, he advised them: "Stand up like men, and do not betray your friends." At the cell shared by Cook and Coppoc, the two captured white raiders, Brown engaged in a brief argument with the pair over whether they had made false statements at their trial concerning his conduct. Finally, he shook hands with them both and walked on, shouting: "God bless you, my men. May we all meet in heaven."

Brown stepped out into a street jammed with armed men, observing wryly to his guards: "I had no idea that Governor Wise considered my execution so important." Climbing into a wagon that would take him to the gallows, Brown sat down on his own coffin. He handed one of the guards a last message (punctuated in his own unique style). It was obviously addressed to Americans in every section of the country and read as clearly as a battle order:

> Charleston, Va, 2nd, December, 1859
> I John Brown am now quite *certain* that the crimes of this *guilty, land: will* never be purged *away;* but with Blood. I had *as I now think: vainly* flattered myself that without *very much* bloodshed; it might be done.

At the gallows site 1,500 federal troops and state militiamen waited, along with a huge crowd of onlookers. The day itself seemed much too pleasant for a hanging. Looking at the Blue Ridge Mountains in the

Brown maintained his usual calm to the very moment of his death. A few days earlier he had written to his wife: "I have been whiped, but am sure I can recover all the lost capital occasioned by that disaster; by only hanging a few moments by the neck."

distance and the cornfields that surrounded them, Brown observed: "This *is* a beautiful country. I never had the pleasure of seeing it before."

The prisoner walked quickly up the steps of the scaffold with no hesitation. For ten minutes the officials in charge stumbled about trying to take their assigned positions. Brown himself seemed the most calm and least worried person on the platform. Finally, the preparations were completed, and a hush fell over the spectators as the officials walked off the scaffold, leaving Brown alone and "as motionless as a statue." Moments later, John Brown hung dangling before the huge crowd.

Some of the Southerners present felt, like Edmund Ruffin (a pro-slavery Virginian), that Brown had gone to his death with "complete fearlessness." Others, like a young actor named John Wilkes Booth, remained too bitter toward the dead man to admire this courage. Several Southern military leaders were present, including "Stonewall" Jackson, later to be a Civil War hero. But it was Colonel J. T. L. Preston's voice that first broke the stillness after Brown's death. "So perish all such enemies of Virginia," Preston exclaimed. "All such enemies of the Union! All such foes of the human race!"

By the time Brown went to his death, he had become a symbol. In the North he had, of course, won the sympathies of convinced antislavery forces. But he had also captured the compassion of many who had previously been either indifferent or opposed to abolitionism. One such person was a prominent New York Democrat and conservative on the slavery issue named George Templeton Strong. A few days after the execution Strong wrote in his diary:

Old Brown's demeanor has undoubtedly made a great impression—his simplicity and consistency, the absence of fuss, parade and bravado, the strength and clearness of his letters, all indicate a depth of conviction that one does not expect in an abolitionist (who is apt to be a mere talker). Slavery has received no such blow in my time as Brown's strangulation. The supporters of any institution are apt to be staggered and startled when they find that any one man, wise or foolish, is so convinced of its wrong and injustices as to acquiesce in being hanged by way of protest against it. One's faith in anything is terribly shaken by anybody who is ready to go to the gallows condemning and denouncing it.

When Brown died, in fact, few Republicans and Democrats in the North were willing to denounce openly the character and aims of a man whom, only a month earlier, many had attacked as an insane fanatic.

In the South the image of John Brown was naturally a different one. Here he was not the Christian martyr who was becoming increasingly popular in the North. He was, instead, a grim, avenging devil figure who had tried to start a massive slave revolt. After November 1859, Northerners concentrated on the *words* that had come from John Brown's eloquent tongue and pen after his capture. But Southerners were more concerned with the *deeds* that he and his men had attempted at Harpers Ferry. After the raid several southern towns had called militia units and vigilante companies into service, declared martial law, and began hunting down conspirators—real or imagined—in their midst. A wave of hysteria sent thousands of fearful whites, many of whom did not own slaves, patrolling their neighborhoods, searching for abolitionist invaders and unruly slaves.

The South mobilized much more quickly and effectively after John Brown's assault than it had after Nat Turner's insurrection three decades earlier. After all, Southerners had been predicting such an assault from the North for more than a generation.

Southerners regarded John Brown even more harshly after election of Abraham Lincoln as President in November 1860. The impact of John Brown's raid was crucial in provoking what one historian has called a crisis of fear among southerners concerning northern-led efforts to stir up slave rebellions. It helped create the climate of intense sectional passion that led to secession and civil war.

Once the South had left the Union, John Brown provided a magnificent symbol for rallying a reluctant northern public to war. "Fifty years hence," George Templeton Strong confided to his diary in February 1862, "John Brown will be recognized as the Hero or Representative Man of this struggle." He added that "a queer rude song about him seems to be growing popular." The song to which Strong refers was set to the music of another northern tune, then also growing in popularity—"The Battle Hymn of the Republic"—whose eloquent verses were written by Samuel Gridley Howe's wife, Julia. But Brown would probably have enjoyed the "queer rude song," whose simplicity proved so appealing to the ordinary soldier:

John Brown's body lies a-mouldering in the grave,
John Brown's body lies a-mouldering in the grave,
John Brown's body lies a-mouldering in the grave,
But his soul goes marching on.

22 THE ROAD TO CIVIL WAR

A. W.

Had John Brown launched his raid thirty years earlier, in 1829 instead of 1859, almost all of the North would have joined the South in shock and condemnation. Although Northern states had abolished slavery, and many Northerners viewed the slave system with hostility, few shared the overriding desire of John Brown and the Secret Six to interfere with slavery's operation in the South. Most residents of New England, the Middle Atlantic states, and the Upper Midwest supported the Missouri Compromise, accepting the existence of slavery in the South as a political necessity, an essential compromise that cemented the Union of free and slave states.

But between the 1820s and the 1850s, Northern attitudes toward the South and slavery underwent a significant change. And a small group of antislavery men and women, stubborn and committed, intensely religious, often disagreeing violently with one another, could claim a good deal of the credit, and assume much of the responsibility, for bringing these changes about. At first, the agitators risked social ostracism and even physical injury. Several Southern states offered cash rewards for their arrest and extradition. But slowly these radical antislavery advocates, or abolitionists, gained a hearing for their belief—that slavery was morally wrong and should not be subject to political compromise.

The great majority of Northerners never accepted this concept entirely. As late as the eve of the Civil War, the term "abolitionist" was used to smear political opponents. Yet, for various reasons, even the majority of "moderates" in the North began to believe that although slavery could not be snuffed out at once, the institution should not be allowed to extend further, into the new Western territories. Both abolitionists and slaveholders believed that such a policy of restriction would inevitably lead to the end of slavery in the South. So, when the new Republican party won a national victory in 1860 on a slavery restriction platform, Southerners and abolitionists were in agreement on another point: national political compromise on the slavery question had become impossible.

THE ABOLITION MOVEMENT

A leading antislavery (but not abolitionist) organization of the early nineteenth century was the American Colonization Society, founded in 1817. But the Colonization Society, after a promising start, did not prosper. Everybody seemed to have a different notion as to what it stood for and what it might accomplish. Free blacks feared the society as a trap for expatriating them forcibly, and some antislavery people agreed. Thus the society would not end slavery but merely siphon off free blacks. Southerners from the Deep South did not cotton to colonization and took the society's antislavery professions much too seriously. Politicians from such states as South Carolina and Georgia consistently and insistently fought against giving a federal subsidy to the society, an idea opposed by many Northerners too. The shockwaves of fear that surged through all of the South in the aftermath of the Nat Turner Revolt in 1831 ended all realistic hopes for strong and widespread Southern support for colonization as a "solution" to the slavery question.

Garrison and His Followers Abolitionism as an independent movement began in the 1830s. Without doubt its leading figure was William Lloyd Garrison. Born in Massachusetts, he was influenced by a fanatically religious mother. For a time he edited the first temperance paper. Then he

Although Turner's revolt dampened the prospects of colonization as a viable solution to slavery, American blacks continued to emigrate to Africa throughout the nineteenth century. The ship drawn above, a Dutch steamer, left Savannah, Georgia in 1895 with 200 blacks bound for Liberia. Founded to provide an African homeland for freed American slaves, Liberia broke apart from the fading American Colonization Society in 1847 and established itself as an independent Republic.

turned to the antislavery cause and founded an abolitionist journal, the *Liberator*. It was first published in Boston in 1831. Two years later Garrison organized the American Antislavery Society.

Much of Garrison's support came from free blacks in the North. But the movement quickly grew among white sympathizers as well. By 1837 the American Antislavery Society had 145 local chapters in Massachusetts, 274 chapters in New York, and 213 in Ohio (the Middle Western center of antislavery activity). By 1843 the society had over 200,000 members.

Other abolitionist leaders included Frederick Douglass and Wendell Phillips, Garrison's Boston lieutenant. Prominent figures in New York

were Gerrit Smith and the Tappan brothers, Lewis and Arthur. Theodore Weld dominated the Middle West. Among the best-known speakers in the Northeast were Angelina Grimké and her sister, Sarah Grimké Weld.

Garrison and his followers broke deliberately with previous antislavery groups in several ways. First, they demanded the immediate rather than gradual abolition of slavery. Second, many of the abolitionists opposed the idea of colonization. They believed it was possible for black Americans to be absorbed into American society. Third, the "Garrisonians" abandoned the politeness of earlier antislavery groups. Instead they adopted a militant, aggressive style. Garrison set the tone

Travel in a Growing Nation

Almost from the beginning, Americans have been famous as travelers. (People used to say that the rocking chair was popular in the United States because, though a person might be sitting down, he could at least keep moving.) A vast continent bordered by vast oceans challenged American ingenuity. One response was the clipper ship (the one shown here was called *Lightning*)— in its time the fastest water transport known. Prince Maximilian of Wied, on his way home to Germany in 1834, wrote about the speed his ship made: ''The wind was favorable and, though very strong, even our topmost sails were spread. This is an experiment which other nations do not often venture upon, but the Americans are very bold seamen.'' This same boldness built the roads, dug the canals, and lay the rail lines that made American transportation the best in the world.

[For further information on the foreign observers quoted in this essay, see ''Notes on Sources.'']

An early railroad train meeting a steamboat at the dock

The American has a perfect passion for railroads. It is not merely because his supreme happiness consists in that speed which annihilates time and space, but also because he perceives that this mode of communication is admirably adapted to the vast extent of his country, to its great maritime plain, and to the level surface of the Mississippi Valley. This is the reason why railroads are multiplied in such profusion, competing not only with each other but entering into a rivalry with the rivers and canals.

[MICHEL CHEVALIER, 1834-35]

The Erie Canal near Little Falls, New York

I like traveling by the canal boats very much. Ours was not crowded, and the country through which we passed being delightful, the placid moderate gliding through it—at about four miles and a half an hour —seemed to me infinitely preferable to the noise of wheels, the rumble of a coach, and the jerking of bad roads. The only nuisances are the bridges over the canal, which are so very low that one is obliged to prostrate oneself on the deck of the boat to avoid being scraped off it. This humiliation occurs, upon an average, once every quarter of an hour.

[FANNY KEMBLE, 1838]

At Trenton we left our boat for the most detestable stagecoach that ever a Christian built to dislocate the joints of his fellow man. The change in our movement was not more remarkable than that which took place in the tempers and countenances of our fellow travelers. Gentlemen now looked more like victims than dandies armed for conquest. The pretty ladies too, with their expensive bonnets—how sad the change! As I looked into the altered eyes of my companions, I was tempted to ask, "Look I as cross as you?" Indeed, I believe that, if possible, I looked crosser still, for the roads and the vehicle together were quite too much for my calm.

[FRANCES TROLLOPE, 1830]

Stagecoach near Trenton, New Jersey

The steamboat was fitted for the twofold purpose of carrying as many bales of cotton as could be heaped upon it without sinking, and taking in as many passengers as could enjoy the luxuries which Southern manners and a hot climate require—especially spacious cabins, abundance of fresh air, and protection from the heat of the sun.

These steamers, notwithstanding their size, draw very little water. They cannot quite realize the boast of a Western captain that "he could sail wherever it was damp," but I was assured that some of them could float in two-foot water. The high-pressure steam escapes into the air by a succession of explosions alternately from the pipes of the two engines. It is a most unearthly sound, like that of some huge monster gasping for breath.

[SIR CHARLES LYELL, 1849]

A boatman on the Missouri River

Steamboat docked at New Orleans

Interior of a steamship

On the Great Lakes there is only one means of travel, and that is the steamship. The elegance of such a ship is quite remarkable. The vessel is equipped in every possible way for the convenience of the passengers. There is, for example, a barbershop. There is also a band. Its performance on brass instruments we found none too good, but in the evenings it won general approval by presenting comical Negro songs, accompanied by the guitar, and by playing dance music, to which the youthful Yankees executed their favorite cotillion, with many dainty skips and steps.

[OLE RAEDER, 1847]

Wooding Up on the Mississippi

In the evening we embarked on board the Philadelphia *and started up the Misssissippi. As the steamboats on this river burn nothing but wood, and as their engines are mostly high-pressure, the consumption of this bulky fuel is so considerable that they are obliged to call at least twice a day at the wooding stations on the banks of the stream. The* Philadelphia *used about one cord of wood an hour. When the supply on board began to run short, the pilot cast his eye round, and upon the first convenient opportunity, he steered the boat for one of the numerous piles of firewood which occurred every few miles along the way.*

[BASIL HALL, 1828]

The trail is a very remarkable piece of work. To rise 3,000 feet vertically about 4½ miles have to be traversed, and still the track is very steep. The ride up on our ponies was not absolutely free from danger, but, so long as the traveler does not lose nerve, the danger is slight. The ponies have the very sensible but slightly disquieting habit of walking to the very edge at the turns in order to make the inclined plane as easy as possible. But it was glorious! Every fresh turn, almost, introduced us to fresh views of this wonderful place. I affirm that, until I rode this trail and found myself looking down and around me from Glacier Point, I had no adequate idea of the beauty and grandeur of the Yosemite district.

[LORD RUSSELL OF KILLOWEN, 1883]

I was asleep when suddenly the coach stopped, which woke me up. I heard someone outside say, "Get out one at a time & throw up your hands." Then I knew in an instant that the coach was stopped by highwaymen. *The first thing I saw was a man with a double-barreled shotgun full cocked pointed at the driver and another behind the coach with 2 six-barreled pistols in his hands. When we were all out, the man with the pistols searched us. He began with me, he first took out my watch but he only looked at it & put it back & said he didn't want it. Then he searched the others. After they took our money, they handed round a bottle of whiskey for the passengers to drink. I took some just for the joke of it & because I was cold with standing out with my hands up.*

[SIDFORD HAMP, 1872]

I must take this occasion to say a word of the commodiousness and other advantages of the railroads in America, which I could well observe on my trip from Chicago westward. The possibility of covering long distances by rail in the United States under unfavorable climatic conditions depends on the use of materials and devices much superior to those that serve in Italy. The front of the locomotive is furnished with an apparatus capable of removing not only the little stones, but any objects that may obstruct the roadbed, especially animals and plants torn away from the sides. At the rear of the locomotive is a little glassed-in compartment designed to protect the engineer against the elements.

[GIOVANNI CAPELLINI, 1863]

Train stopped by buffalo on the Plains

Coach car on a train

Railroad car carrying emigrants westward

Railway traveling in America is not tiring; on the contrary, it is refreshing. A train on its way to San Francisco or to Mexico is a series of moving houses. The cars are divided into rooms, and are provided with all the necessaries of life. Spacious libraries, smoking rooms, and dining rooms open out of one another, and there are bathrooms and barbershops. In the anterooms are the servants, chiefly white-coated Negroes, who are there to carry out all orders.

[COUNT VAY DE VAYA UND LUSKOD, 1908]

I suppose the reader has some notion of an American railroad car, that long, narrow wooden box like a flat-roofed Noah's ark. Those destined for emigrants on the Union Pacific are remarkable only for their extreme plainness. The benches are too short for anything but a young child. Where there is scarce elbow room for two to sit, there will not be space enough for one to lie. In all other trains, a warning cry of "All aboard!" recalls the passengers to take their seats. But all the way to San Francisco, the train stole from the station without a note of warning, and you had to keep an eye upon it even while you ate.

[ROBERT LOUIS STEVENSON, 1879]

Garrison was stubborn, humorless, and courageous in his crusade for abolition. In 1854 he publicly burned a copy of the Constitution exclaiming, "So perish all compromises with tyranny!"

Their main objection to slavery was moral. Therefore, they thought, it was essential to convince the mass of Americans, North *and* South, that slavery was immoral and unjust. Abolitionists believed that personal recognition of this fact would result in nationwide demands for an immediate end to slavery. This technique was called moral suasion.

During the 1830s Garrison and his associates made a strong effort to reach slaveholders by mailing hundreds of thousands of abolitionist newspapers and tracts to the South. After the Nat Turner Revolt, the postmaster general, a Southerner, allowed Southern postmasters to refuse to deliver abolitionist propaganda. (His action clearly violated both the law and the senders' civil liberties.) Southerners held huge bonfires of antislavery material.

By the 1840s abolitionists recognized that moral suasion had failed to win over any significant number of slaveholders. They abandoned this tactic in the South, but they continued to use it in the North.

The abolitionists split into two separate wings—those who opposed Garrison and those who supported him. His opponents objected to him for several reasons. They resented his overbearing leadership. They also disapproved of his demand for equal status for women as abolitionist leaders, and for fusion of the woman's rights campaign with the antislavery movement. They disliked Garrison's constant attacks on the organized churches, many of whose leaders still opposed the drive for emancipation. And they wanted to involve the movement in practical political action. (Garrison wanted instead to focus on moral agitation.)

In 1840 the anti-Garrisonians withdrew from Garrison's organization and formed the American and Foreign Anti-Slavery Society. Both groups continued their propaganda campaigns to stir up Northern public opinion until the Civil War. But their major energies shifted during the 1840s into direct political agitation at the local, state, and national levels. Abolitionism was now the central concern of all American reformers, whatever their other interests.

himself in the first issue of the *Liberator:* "I *will* be as harsh as truth, and as uncompromising as justice. On this subject, I do not wish to think, or speak, or write with moderation. I am earnest—I will not equivocate—I will not excuse—I will not retreat a single inch—AND I WILL BE HEARD."

Changing Tactics The abolitionists' religious beliefs helped determine their strategy. Most were devout men and women. They believed that slavery was the country's greatest moral evil, a blot on the United States that had to be erased.

Reactions to the Abolitionists The abolitionists aroused intense feelings that often led to violence.

The murder of editor Elijah Lovejoy made him the first martyr of the abolitionist cause. He aroused controversy by his antislavery principles, first in St. Louis, where his printing office was destroyed, and then across the Mississippi in Alton. His murder by an anti-abolitionist mob sent a "shock wave as of an earthquake throughout this continent," according to John Quincy Adams.

It was dangerous during the 1830s to advocate immediate emancipation, even in the North. Anti-abolitionist mobs, often including prominent community leaders, disrupted abolitionist meetings and destroyed antislavery printing presses. When a leading English abolitionist came to New England in 1835, Bostonians rioted. Garrison was led through the city's streets with a rope around his waist, until police took him into protective custody. (This incident helped convert Wendell Phillips to the abolitionist movement.) That same year in New York City a mob destroyed Lewis Tappan's home, and throughout that stormy decade dozens of anti-abolitionist riots and mobbings took place. Henry B. Stanton, another militant antislavery figure, claimed to have been attacked personally over 200 times. The worst affray occured in Alton, Illinois, in 1837. There, Elijah Lovejoy, an abolitionist editor, was shot dead by a mob while defending his home and his press.

Those outside the South who opposed abolitionism feared the reformers almost as much as Southerners feared slave revolts. To conservative Northerners, the abolitionists seemed to threaten public order, national unity, and established institutions. In fact, race prejudice was as strong in the North as in the South. Certainly free blacks in the North suffered constant abuse and discrimination.

Even white abolitionists could not wholly shed their color prejudice. Only a few treated their black associates as complete equals. Garrison at one point urged the eloquent Frederick Douglass to use more "darky" mannerisms in his speeches. Such attitudes led Douglass to break with the Boston abolitionist.

Although Northerners did not lose their raending this flagrant violation of the abolitionists' right of petition in 1844.

THE MOVE INTO POLITICS

The abolitionists' earliest efforts in politics were limited to questioning major party candidates regarding slavery, and voting for the individual, if one could be found, whose answers were satisfactory—or the least unsatisfactory. Needless to say, this went on exclusively in the North. By this method, unpromising though it seemed, abolitionists hoped to hold the balance of power in some Northern districts and states. Only rarely did they succeed.

Many abolitionists yearned for bolder action. James G. Birney was an Alabama plantation owner and slaveholder who had become converted to abolitionism. Finding it unwise and unsafe to advocate abolition in the South, he left for Ohio to establish an antislavery newspaper. Birney had long differed with Garrison on the Boston editor's support for woman's rights and opposition to political action. In 1840, Birney ran for President as the candidate of the new Liberty party.

Both Harrison, the Whig candidate, and Van Buren, the Democrat, he argued, were totally unacceptable to abolitionists, and a new party had to be formed if abolitionists wished to cast a *moral* vote for President. But Garrisonians ridiculed the efforts of Birney and the Liberty party, and abolitionists found little more comfort in the slaveholding Harrison than in Andrew Jackson's handpicked successor, Van Buren. Of 2.5 million votes cast in 1840, Birney got only seven thousand.

The abolition movement had now split. Garrison maintained headquarters in Boston; the Liberty-ites were headquartered in New York City (where they generated most of their financial support). Although disappointed at their showing in 1840, Liberty party people decided to stay in business. "The fewer we have now," wrote one after the election, displaying strong faith but shaky logic, "the more we have to gain before we carry our point." They continued to work in local

Frederick Douglass, born in Maryland, escaped from slavery in 1838. He broke with Garrison, believing in a more political approach to abolition. During the Civil War he organized two black regiments from Massachusetts. Later he served as minister to Haiti.

cial prejudices, they gradually became more sympathetic to the abolitionists. Federal interference with antislavery mail to the South won many converts to the abolitionist cause. Even those who did not share abolitionist beliefs disliked the practice of suppressing ideas. A number of Americans who began by defending the abolitionists' civil liberties ended by joining the movement itself.

Other Northerners became aroused by the "gag rule." This resolution, passed by the House of Representatives in 1836, provided that no antislavery petitions would even be considered. Every year a small group of congressmen, led by former President John Quincy Adams, tried to repeal the gag rule. They finally succeeded in

A hotbed of antislavery activism in the 1830s and 40s, Boston was often the scene of abolitionist meetings and conventions, held in public halls or, as above, on the Boston Common. Although many Northerners viewed the abolitionist enthusiam with distaste, as demonstrated in the Boston riot of 1835 that almost took William Lloyd Garrison's life, the American Antislavery Society steadily gained affiliates through the Northeast and Midwest. By 1840, it claimed about 2,000 local Societies and almost 200,000 members.

and state elections in 1841 and 1842, and increased the party's vote slightly.

Garrison, meanwhile, expanded his antipolitical principles to new and broader dimensions. He had become a moral perfectionist, a pacifist, and a total nonresister, rejecting the use of force under any circumstances. In 1842, he proclaimed "it is morally and politically impossible for a just and equal union to be formed between Liberty and Slavery." By remaining in the Union, Northerners bore as much responsibility for slavery as the South. Only a break-up of the country could ease that guilt. Many who had remained loyal to Garrison up to then could not accept his new demand, nor his perfectionism, nor his commitment to various other reforms. Garrison for his part wanted no truck with such compromisers. He banished the doubters without a qualm, and forced the shrinking American Antislavery Society to accept his policy.

ABOLITIONIST ACTIVITIES

Despite the bitterness of their split, abolitionists from both wings of the movement engaged in many of the same activities. Both the Garrison and the Liberty party groups maintained newspapers, produced pamphlets, and organized public meetings. They cited the same books and stories detailing atrocities committed against blacks on Southern plantations. And all abolitionists were regarded as equally detestable by slaveholders and conservative Northerners.

Abolitionist orator Sojourner Truth, born a slave named Isabella in 1797 in upstate New York, traveled widely as a speaker for antislavery. An itinerant preacher, mystic, and former domestic, she drew great crowds with her statuesque bearing, resonant voice, and fervent denunciation of slavery.

Probably no single aspect of the abolitionists' work did more to gain sympathy for them than their efforts to assist fugitive slaves. Black abolitionists made daring raids into the South to rescue some of those in bondage. Other blacks took to podiums to denounce slavery. Outstanding were a famous pair of black women, Harriet Tubman (see p. 390) and Sojourner Truth. A large network of Northern sympathizers, both white and black, maintained the Underground Railroad. In its "stations"—safe havens such as barns and cellars—escaped slaves could hide until "conductors" led them onward to freedom in the North and in Canada.

Many abolitionists actively interfered with slave catchers who came North to recapture runaways. To those arguing that the Constitution gave slaveholders the legal right to reclaim their slave property, people like James Birney replied firmly, "Whatever pledges of noninterference may be given they will be disregarded—at least so long as our body has any life or humanity in it, or any greater fear of God than of man." Even a conventional major party politician like William H. Seward, the New York Whig, during the Compromise of 1850 debates, warned of a "higher law" than the Constitution—the law of freedom.

The abolitionist attack on slavery also included criticism of the deplorable condition of free blacks in the North. Few Northern states allowed blacks to vote, and the little schooling offered them was substandard and on a rigidly segregated basis. Although white abolitionists found it easier to attack Southern slavery than to rid themselves of prevailing anti-Negro prejudices or to imagine blacks living in equality with whites, the movement still fought against the worst forms of Northern racial discrimination. "No proposition is more true," admitted one Liberty party speaker, "than that the wrongs which the North has done, and continues to do, to its colored people . . . furnish the most influential argument in favor of Southern oppression."

Abolition and Expansionism By the time the Liberty party rallied for its second national campaign in 1844, the political abolitionists had acquired an issue with national appeal. The giant slaveholding republic of Texas, whose annexation to the United States (possibly as more than one state) the antislavery forces had steadily opposed, was about to be admitted by Congress. Once again, abolitionists organized meetings, printed anti-Texas petitions and newspapers, and tried to pressure Congress to refuse admission. This time, they began to gain support from other Northerners. Many of these did not care about slavery with the same moral intensity as the abolitionists, but they were leery of any action that would so greatly increase the South's size and national political power.

In the election of 1844, the Whigs' Henry Clay, making his last desperate stab at the office he wanted so badly, tried to keep Texas out of the campaign. James K. Polk, the Democratic candidate, openly favored the annexation of Texas and

HARRIET TUBMAN

The most famous "conductor" on the Underground Railroad was a former slave, Harriet Tubman. In the years 1850 to 1881, from the passage of the Fugitive Slave Act to the outbreak of the Civil War, she made nineteen secret trips into the South rescuing some 300 people. Offers of reward for her capture eventually totaled $40,000. But she eluded her enemies successfully and was never caught. In later years she claimed that "on my Underground Railroad, I never ran my train off the track, and I never lost a passenger."

Born in 1820 or 21 on a plantation in Dorchester County, on Maryland's eastern shore, Tubman knew only cruelty as a child. She was one of ten or eleven children born to Benjamin Ross and Harriet Greene. (Her grandparents on both sides had come in chains from Africa.) She received no schooling and thus could not read or write. Because she was found to be too awkward and clumsy for housework, she was made to work as a field hand. When she was about 13 years of age, an overseer struck her on the head with a two-pound weight and fractured her skull. This resulted in spells of somnolence that affected her for the rest of her life. In 1844, she married a free black named John Tubman, but the marriage was not a successful one, and Harriet never had any children.

In 1849, Harriet Tubman's master died and it was rumored that his slaves would be sold. The young woman decided that this was the time to make a break for freedom, which she did with the help of friendly Quakers. She reached Philadelphia and obtained employment in a hotel. There she met the black abolitionist, William Still, who recruited her for the Underground Railroad. He later said of her:

Harriet was a woman of no pretensions, indeed, a more ordinary specimen of humanity could hardly be found among the most unfortunate-looking farm hands of the South. Yet, in point of courage, shrewdness, and disinterested exertions to rescue her fellowmen, by making personal visits into Maryland among the slaves, she was without her equal.

In December 1850, this single-minded, deeply religious woman began the first of her many trips back into the South to bring out slaves. First, she brought out her brother and his family and later that same year a family of eleven. On one of her most difficult trips, she returned, in 1857, to the eastern shore and brought back her aged parents in a hired wagon. Many tales are told of her tenacity and ingenuity. To inform prospective fugitives that she would be arriving shortly, she sent messages in the "double-talk" that blacks had learned to use in their communications and even in the texts of their songs (spirituals).

Harriet Tubman became well known among abolitionists and sometimes addressed their conventions. But she preferred to remain a woman of mystery whose whereabouts were generally unknown. It was in St. Catharines, Ontario in April of 1858, however, that she counseled and encouraged John Brown in his plan to take action by force of arms. Only a flareup of her head injury kept her from joining him in his 1859 raid at Harpers Ferry.

When the Civil War broke out, "General Tubman" (as John Brown had called her) volunteered her services. For three years she worked for the "Union" forces securing information from black informants. She worked as a nurse and a cook, aiding freedmen who had joined the Union forces, supporting herself by selling chickens and eggs. After the war she returned to her farm in Auburn, taking in helpless old black people and black orphans as well. Her farm became the Harriet Tubman Home for Indigent Aged Negroes, which carried on even after her death in 1913.

westward expansion generally. Birney, running again on the Liberty party ticket, polled only 65,000 votes, a disappointing total. But had his 15,000 votes in New York gone to Clay, Whigs would have carried the state and the election. For the first time, the abolitionists had flexed a small but significant bit of political muscle.

Texas joined the Union shortly after the election, and a year later Polk went to war with Mexico to gain New Mexico and California. Abolitionists opposed the war passionately, first because most of them were pacifists, and second, because they feared that the new territories would be added to the roster of slave states. A few went so far as Henry David Thoreau, who refused to pay his local taxes and spent a night in jail to symbolize his protest. They began to charge that the country was being taken over by an "aggressive slavocracy" (the Slave Power), which intended to crush all criticism of slavery in the North and West, just as it had stamped out dissent in the South. The slavocracy would then embroil the nation in foreign wars to increase its own slave territory and wealth.

Thousands of individuals all over the North, up to now unmoved by the plight of the slaves, rallied to this standard of opposition. "The Mexican War and Slavery," predicted Charles Sumner, a Massachusetts antislavery Whig, "will derange all party calculations." The Whigs of his own Bay State were soon split over the slavery extension issue into "Cotton" and "Conscience" factions. Northern Democrats, unhappy over their party's control by Southerners and about always bowing to Southern demands, now supported the Wilmot Proviso (see Chapter 20). Many Westerners supported it, too; they wanted the land west of the Missouri River for small farms for white settlers, and wanted to keep both slavery and free blacks out of the area.

Although some Liberty men—and, of course, the Garrisonians—warned against accommodating these new allies, most of the party eagerly sought to construct antislavery coalitions. In 1846, New Hampshire Liberty-ites and independent Democrats elected John P. Hale to the U.S. Senate, and a growing number of congressmen openly declared themselves for slavery restriction. Whig Senator William Seward of New York was rapidly becoming the leader of a small group of national political figures committed to antislavery.

In August 1848, at a convention in Buffalo, the Free Soil Party emerged—a coalition of Barnburners (antislavery New York Democrats), Conscience Whigs, independent Democrats from the Midwest, and Liberty party members. Both major parties had nominated unacceptable candidates: the Whigs named General Zachary Taylor, a Louisiana slaveholder; and the Democrats, Lewis Cass, widely considered a "doughface"—a Northern man with Southern principles. The new antislavery party adopted a platform opposing the admission of *any* new slave states or allowing slavery to exist in the territories. Yet its presidential nominee was none other than Martin Van Buren, the Jacksonian Democrat who had been so important in forging the "doughface" coalition of Northern and Southern Democrats.

Many abolitionists felt that too much had been conceded. The Free Soil platform said nothing about abolition, nor about racial discrimination. Many recalled that only a decade before, Van Buren had been considered the worst of the doughfaces, a Northern President who would make no move to abolish slavery in the District of Columbia or speak out against the gag rule. Gerrit Smith, later of the Secret Six, led a small number of dissidents in forming the Liberty League to uphold the principles of the now disbanded Liberty party. Wendell Phillips, a close ally of Garrison, sneered at the "namby-pamby antislavery" of the Free Soilers.

THE GROWTH OF ANTISLAVERY SENTIMENT

The handful of antislavery men in the Senate, now including Seward, Hale, and a former Liberty-ite from Ohio, Salmon P. Chase, fought hard against the Compromise of 1850. Yet the Compromise, or rather one specific part of it, gave an enormous impetus to the antislavery movement.

WILLIAM N. TAYLOR.

Advertisements such as these proliferated after the passage of the Fugitive Slave Act of 1850. Despite the stronger law, slaves continued to seek freedom north of the Mason-Dixon line.

The Fugitive Slave Law of 1850 granted almost unlimited power to the federal commissioners appointed to enforce it, and to private slave catchers seeking to profit by it. The latter roamed the Northern states during the 1850s, collecting bounties from Southern planters for capturing and returning blacks who had allegedly escaped from slavery. Some of the victims were indeed runaways; others were not. But commissioners could decide as they pleased—there was little due process and no right of appeal. Northern legislatures, responding to public disgust over the slave catchers, passed what came to be know as "personal liberty laws," to counteract the fugitive slave law. Under the personal liberty laws, state and local officials might delay or withhold help in the distasteful process of returning alleged runaways. Southerners understandably fumed over this Northern betrayal of the Compromise, this Northern version of nullification.

Abolitionists went a step further and actively assisted fugitive slaves. It has been estimated that Boston alone sheltered a minimum of 600 runaway blacks at any given time. Abolitionists in that city even resorted to violence to keep Negroes out of the hands of slave catchers. Thomas Higginson, for example, led a Boston mob which prevented the return to slavery of a fugitive. Theodore Parker, who often hid runaways in his home, wrote sermons with a pistol within reach of his desk. But when the federal government decided to go into the slave-catching business seriously and with all its power, it usually had its way, as in the case of Anthony Burns of Boston, who was returned to slavery by a massive force of federal troops.

Still, the reaction to such activities showed how attitudes had changed. In the 1830s, Garrison had been led through the streets of Boston with a rope around his body (and placed under "protective custody") for opposing slavery. In the 1850s, when Anthony Burns was returned to the South through those same streets, thousands of protesters lined the streets, and church bells tolled the city's shame.

While persistently agitating the fugitive slave issue, Free Soilers sought to increase their political influence by forming coalitions with members of the major parties. The party might ally with Democrats in one Northern state, Whigs in another; and in yet a third state it might support a Democrat for one office and a Whig for another. Such tactics succeeded in some instances. In the early 1850s, when most Americans, North and South, wished to believe that the Compromise of 1850 had permanently settled the question of slavery, such "deals" may have been necessary to keep antislavery politics alive.

In 1852, both major parties endorsed the Compromise, and most of the Barnburners (Van

Fugitive Henry Box Brown attempted a most daring escape, after his master refused to purchase Brown's wife and prevent her sale to the South. In a specially constructed crate, 2 feet by 3 feet wide and 2½ feet high, complete with airholes, Brown had himself sent 350 miles by express to Philadelphia, where delighted abolitionists unpacked him. He had spent 27 hours in the box, much of the time upside down, awaiting his "resurrection from the grave of slavery."

This lithograph depicts why abolitionists were against the Fugitive Slave Act. The law gave unlimited power to slave owners and slave catchers seeking to profit from it. Quite often, however, escaped slaves were killed, rather than returned to their owners.

Buren included) returned to the Democratic party, their natural home. One result of this was to make the Free Soil party decidedly more radical than it had been four years before. Its platform now declared "that slavery is a sin against God and a crime against man . . . and that Christianity, humanity, and patriotism alike demand its abolition." John P. Hale, New Hampshire's non-Compromise senator, became the party's presidential nominee. A natural result of *this* was a falling off in votes. Hale polled about half of Van Buren's total of 1848. Yet the election in 1852 revealed a hard core of 150,000 antislavery votes, a seed for growth should the right issue appear.

That issue was not long in coming. When Stephen A. Douglas introduced the Kansas-Nebraska bill in 1854, reopening the possibility of forming slave states from those and other territories, the North exploded. Free Soilers and other restrictionists formed the new Republican party. "Our position is now rather enviable," wrote one Free Soil congressman, "We lead the hosts of free-

dom." "Anti-Nebraska" Democrats, as they were known, fielded their own tickets in many states. The American (or Know-Nothing) party, anti-immigrant and anti-Nebraska, made a strong showing. (The two issues did relate to each other, since many immigrants were deeply anti-Negro and also strongly opposed abolitionism.) With the existence of so many parties, shifting coalitions, and candidates with unclear partisan allegiances, finding the winners in the congressional elections of 1854 proved difficult. Despite doubt as to who had won, those who favored the *expansion* of slavery, under any formula or conditions, had clearly lost.

EMERGENCE OF THE REPUBLICAN PARTY

The Republican party, like most newly formed political organizations, was a mixed group. It en-

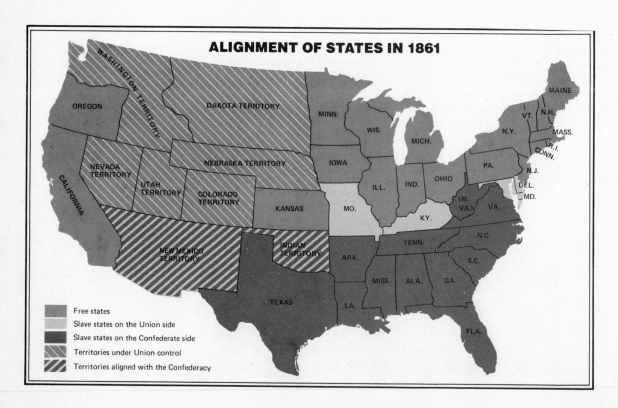

ALIGNMENT OF STATES IN 1861

Free states
Slave states on the Union side
Slave states on the Confederate side
Territories under Union control
Territories aligned with the Confederacy

rolled virtually all of the Free Soilers, most Northern Whigs (whose party had recently fallen apart), and a significant minority of Northern Democrats for whom the Kansas-Nebraska Act had been too much to swallow. All of these groups united, with varying degrees of commitment, on a single issue: slavery should not expand into the territories. Beyond that, they differed widely. "There are Republicans who are Abolitionists," explained Horace Greeley's New York *Tribune*, "there are others who anxiously desire and labor for the good of the slave, but there are many more whose main impulse is a desire to secure the territories for Free White Labor, with little or no regard for the interests of negroes, free or slave."

Yet, from the start, the party felt the heavy influence of the first group, the "political abolitionists," who regarded the prevention of slavery's spread as only a first step to total elimination of America's "national sin." They succeeded in getting through a strong antislavery platform at the 1856 Republican convention. But the party's presidential nominee, a professional Western explorer and amateur politician named John C. Frémont, left much to be desired. Even Garrison, however, admitted grudgingly that "as between the three rival parties, the sympathy of every friend of freedom must be with the Republican party, in spite of its lamentable shortcomings." Frederick Douglass led what little there was of the black vote into the new party, and even Gerrit Smith, running for President himself as the Abolition candidate, donated $500 to the "other" antislavery party.

After only two years of existence, the Republicans made a good run in 1856. Receiving virtually no votes in the slave states, the new party swept New England and carried New York, Ohio, and several other Western states. The Democratic candidate James Buchanan, another "doughface," carried only five Northern states, some of them only because Know-Nothings had voted for their own candidate, ex-President Millard Fillmore. "We are beaten," conceded a leading Republican, "but we frightened the rascals awfully."

Another Weak President By the time James Buchanan took office as President in March 1857,

political parties could no longer appeal to voters on a nationwide basis. Republicans now dominated the North, but they had no following in the South. The Know-Nothing party was dead; so were the Whigs. Southern Democrats generally voted as a bloc. Only Northern Democrats were still trying to bridge the widening gap between the sections. And only an extraordinary, national-minded President, one skilled in the political arts of bullying and compromise, would have stood a chance of repairing all of this political damage. James Buchanan, an elderly, fussy bachelor, quick to please, slow to offend, soon proved the obvious —he was *not* that kind of President.

The Dred Scott Decision Buchanan's first and only effort at sectional reconciliation produced immediate disaster. The Supreme Court, he stated blandly in his inaugural address, was about to decide the question of slaveholders' rights in the territories. The Court's decision, whatever it turned out to be, should be accepted by all sides, and the opinion should settle the dispute permanently. Dred Scott, a slave, had been taken from Missouri to Illinois and later to Wisconsin. Missouri was a slave state, Illinois a free state, and Wisconsin, at the time, a free territory according to the Missouri Compromise. In 1846, Scott sued for his liberty, claiming that residence in a free state and a free territory had put an end to his slave status. After passing through state courts and lower federal courts, the well-publicized case reached the U.S. Supreme Court.

Even before the decision, antislavery forces had rejected Buchanan's "offer." The Supreme Court of 1857 was controlled by slaveholders and doughfaces. Besides, slavery *did* enjoy protection from the Constitution and laws of the United States; Garrison and other radical abolitionists were right about that. In the twenty years before *Dred Scott* v. *Sandford*, the Supreme Court had upheld both the legality of the interstate slave trade and the rights of slaveowners to retrieve their property forcibly anywhere in the Union. In 1851, six years before *Dred Scott*, in *Strader* v. *Graham*, a case with very similar issues, the Court had ruled that a slave going from Kentucky to Ohio remained a slave under the laws of Ken-

Dred Scott was freed by his owner, despite the Supreme Court's decision in favor of the owner. Scott got a job as a hotel porter in St. Louis, but died of tuberculosis in 1858.

tucky, rather than becoming free under the laws of Ohio. Such decisions led John Hale to denounce the Court as "the very citadel of American slavery," an exaggerated but not preposterous allegation.

Moreover, Buchanan's offer of March 1857 was not so generous and open as the President wished people to think. While reading the speech, he already knew (through confidential contacts with one of the justices) how the Court would decide. He had in fact help persuade a justice from his own state, Pennsylvania, to join the five justices from slave states, so that the Court would not divide along totally sectional lines.

Chief Justice Roger Taney of Maryland, speaking for the majority, ruled against Scott, declaring that the plaintiff had no right to sue since a black could not be a citizen. Taney added gratuitously that white Americans had since colonial times considered blacks inferior human beings, possessing "no rights that a white man was bound to respect." Worst of all, from the North's point of view, Taney and the Court decided that slavery could not be excluded from *any* territory. Slaves, he explained, were property, and according to the Constitution's Fifth Amendment, persons could not be deprived of property without due process of law.

Opponents of slavery reacted furiously, charging that their warnings about the aggressions of the Slave Power had been confirmed. Not only was the South demanding the possibility of opening all new territories for slavery but the logic of the Court decision could be taken even further. "Does the Constitution make slaves property?" an irate Republican wanted to know. "If so, slavery exists in Ohio today, for the Constitution extends over Ohio, doesn't it?" Northerners, who had considered Kansas-Nebraska too favorable to the South, now felt some of that rage which characterized Southern grievances over nonenforcement of the fugitive slave law. The Buchanan administration, only a week old, was already doomed.

The Emergence of Lincoln Stephen A. Douglas had helped build the Compromise of 1850—and he had helped to destroy it with the Kansas-Nebraska Act. In 1858 he ran for reelection to the Senate from Illinois. His opponent was a popular former congressman, Abraham Lincoln.

Born in Kentucky in 1809 to poor parents, Abraham Lincoln had moved with his family first to Indiana and then to Illinois. During his early years in these frontier areas the young man educated himself through extensive reading. He managed a general store at New Salem, Illinois, served as a captain of volunteers during a brief Indian war in northern Illinois, and worked as New Salem's postmaster while studying law. Lincoln was admitted to the Illinois bar in 1836. The next year he moved to Springfield and opened a law office.

Lincoln served as a state legislator from 1834 to 1842 while engaged in a private law practice. He quickly acquired a reputation for his skill as a trial lawyer and his rough frontier humor. Elected in 1846 as a Whig, the young Illinois lawyer served one term in the House. He opposed the Mexican War but remained a member of the Whig party. Like many Northerners, Lincoln was pried loose from former party loyalties only by passage of the Kansas-Nebraska Act in 1854. He denounced the law and, in 1856, joined the newly formed Republican party.

Lincoln's views on slavery were typical of most Northern antislavery moderates. He believed that slavery was "a moral, social, and political wrong." But he denied having any intention of interfering with the institution in the Southern states. Like most Republicans, he felt that it would

die out gradually as an unprofitable labor system. He did insist, however, that slavery should be totally excluded from the Western territories.

During a statewide series of public debates Lincoln kept Douglas on the defensive with questions about how, in view of the Dred Scott decision, settlers could legally exclude slavery from a territory under popular sovereignty. Douglas was reduced to arguing that a free-soil majority could simply refuse to enact a slave code, a weak counter to Lincoln's basic point.

In the short run the Lincoln-Douglas debates of 1858 helped to reelect Douglas. But in the long run they damaged him as a national leader. His view that a territory could effectively exclude slavery in spite of the Dred Scott decision gained him votes in Illinois, but it offended Southerners.

Lincoln emerged as a major national figure in the Republican party. He had dramatized the differences between Douglas Democrats and the Buchanan-Southern Democratic coalition.

Kansas and Collapse President Buchanan scored no great successes. Perhaps his greatest failure was his Kansas policy, one inherited from fellow Democrat Franklin Pierce to deal with the civil war in Kansas. Pressured by Southerners in his cabinet, Buchanan submitted to Congress the "Lecompton Constitution," a document drafted by a proslavery minority in Kansas to serve as the basis for entry into the Union. The Lecompton Constitution legalized slavery, and prohibited agitation against the institution. Congress offered a huge land grant to Kansas if the state would ratify the document, but in 1858 free state settlers voted it down by a 9 to 1 margin. "Ever since the rendition [returning] of Anthony Burns," Thomas Higginson reported with pride, "I have been looking for *men*. I have found them in Kansas . . . . In Kansas, nobody talks of courage, for everyone is expected to exhibit it."

On the Lecompton issue, even Douglas, author of the Kansas-Nebraska Act, abandoned ship. Partly due to Lincoln's pressure in Illinois, partly due to obvious irregularities in the framing of the document, Douglas announced, "if this constitution is to be forced down our throats . . . I will resist it to the last." The Democratic party, the last national political institution, now broke in two: Southerners backed Buchanan; most Northerners supported Douglas.

THE FAILURE OF COMPROMISE

The reaction to John Brown's raid showed how fragile the political links between North and South had become. In the North even moderate antislavery advocates were outraged by the South's embittered defense of its "peculiar institution." They regarded President Buchanan as a turncoat. Though Brown was in fact and by right a federal prisoner, Buchanan had simply handed him over to a Virginia court.

In the South, moderates had lost control of public opinion. People there had already begun preparing for possible secession, if not war. To most Southerners, Buchanan's pro-Southern attitudes no longer seemed adequate protection against "aggressions" (such as the Harpers Ferry raid) that the South believed Northern Republicans were planning. By 1860 armed defense against Northern attack seemed as reasonable to most Southerners as did violent assaults against the slave system to the antislavery North.

What was left to negotiate? How could either section compromise, when each one felt its most vital interests at stake? Brown's raid came at the end of a decade of bitter argument and violent conflict over slavery. It hastened the collapse of normal political life, since democratic politics requires moderation—which no longer had many spokesmen.

Election and Secession The Democratic party split into sectional wings in 1860. Northern Democrats nominated Stephen A. Douglas for the presidency. The Southerners put forward their own candidate, John C. Breckinridge of Kentucky. He promised to sponsor federal laws that would protect slavery in the territories. The Republicans nominated Abraham Lincoln. A hodgepodge of former Whigs, Know-Nothings, and Democrats formed a new Constitutional Union party. They nominated a fourth candidate, John Bell, also of Kentucky. He pledged mainly to say and do nothing about the slavery question.

But a decade of agitation had worn away the basis for compromise solutions to the slavery question. It was no longer possible to wish away the issue by not talking about it. Douglas and Breckenridge split the Democratic vote. Bell carried three border states. Lincoln won the North. He became President with barely 40 percent of the popular vote, none at all from the Deep South.

Fear swept the South after Lincoln's election. "Secession fever" grew to epidemic proportions within days. South Carolina took the plunge first. Its legislature passed a secession ordinance on December 20, 1860, climaxing thirty years of leadership in defense of Southern nationalism. By February 1, 1861, six other states—Mississippi, Florida, Alabama, Georgia, Louisiana, and Texas—had adopted similar ordinances. Three days later, these seven states proclaimed the Confederate States of America in Montgomery, Alabama.

Five months separated the 1860 election and Lincoln's inauguration in March 1861. The "lame-duck" administration of James Buchanan did little to impede the course of secession. Buchanan condemned Southern actions and demanded obedience to federal laws. But neither he nor his government attempted to interfere as Southerners took control of federal forts, arsenals, and public property in their region.

There were various efforts to end the secession crisis by a political compromise in Congress, similar to the ones of 1820 and 1850. The most important of these was the Crittenden Compromise. It would have extended the Missouri Compromise line across the entire country, legalizing slavery south of it and prohibiting it to the north. By then, however, most Southerners were unprepared to accept any limitation, just as most Republicans opposed any extension of the system. Lincoln proposed that the North agree to enforce the Fugitive Slave Act and protect Southern slavery by constitutional amendments if necessary. But his suggestions seemed inadequate to the secessionists.

Both the Confederate states and the new Republican administration waited in March 1861 to see whether states in the Upper South would also secede. Fears about Republican intentions were widespread in states like Virginia and North Carolina, especially after John Brown's raid. But there were also more Unionists there than in the Deep South.

Lincoln's Inauguration Lincoln's inaugural address did little to calm the South. The new President promised not to invade the region or interfere with slavery where it already existed. But he made it clear that he believed the Union could not be dissolved at the whim of a state or group of states.

The earliest photograph of Lincoln was taken when he was a congressman—an obscure Whig and unpopular at home because of his opposition to the Mexican War.

He promised "to hold, occupy, and possess the property and places belonging to the federal government" throughout the country, including the South. And he pointed directly to the moral and political issue of slavery (and its extension) as the root of the conflict. "One section of our country," Lincoln said, "believes slavery is right, and ought to be extended, while the other believes it is wrong, and ought not to be extended. This is the only substantial dispute." Finally, he insisted that the question of war and peace was not in his hands but in those of his "dissatisfied fellow countrymen," the secessionists.

Lincoln's promise to maintain control of federal property in the South practically eliminated the possibility of a political compromise with the Confederate states. Lincoln was trapped between a desire for compromise and a need to maintain national authority, lest it collapse throughout the Upper South as well.

For weeks Lincoln and his cabinet debated their course of action toward the Confederacy. They worried especially about whether to send relief supplies and troops to the few remaining federal posts in the region, such as Fort Sumter in Charleston harbor.

Finally, on April 4, Lincoln dispatched a relief expedition to Sumter. It carried only fresh supplies for the garrison, not reinforcements. Lincoln wanted to avoid the charge that he was making a hostile move toward the Confederacy. He even went so far as to inform the governor of South Carolina about his desire to supply Sumter peacefully. The Confederate government demanded, however, that the fort be entirely evacuated or, if necessary, destroyed. Charleston's harbor batteries opened fire at Sumter on April 12. Within two days Confederate forces had captured the fort. Virginia, Arkansas, and North Carolina all joined the Confederacy within a few weeks. So did Tennessee. Elsewhere in the border states—especially Maryland, Missouri, and Kentucky—Lincoln took firm measures to maintain Union control. "Both parties deprecated war," Lincoln later wrote, "but one of them would *make* war rather than let the nation survive; and the other would *accept* war rather than let it perish. And the war came."

SUGGESTED READINGS–CHAPTERS 21-22

John Brown

R. O. Boyer, *The Legend of John Brown: A Biography and History* (1973); Stephen Oates, *To Purge This Land with Blood: A Biography of John Brown* (1970).

Abolitionism and the Antislavery Movement

Martin Duberman, ed., *The AntiSlavery Vanguard* (1969); Louis Filler, *The Crusade Against Slavery, 1830–1860* (1960); Larry Gara, *The Liberty Line: The Legend of the Underground Railroad* (1961); Aileen S. Kraditor, *Means and Ends in American Abolitionism . . . 1834–1860* (1967); Walter M. Merrill, *Against Wind and Tide: A Biography of William Lloyd Garrison* (1963); Russell B. Nye, *Fettered Freedom: Civil Liberties and the Slavery Controversy, 1830–1860* (rev. ed., 1963); Jane H. Pease and William H. Pease, *They Who Would Be Free: Blacks' Search for Freedom, 1830–1861* (1974); Gerald Sorin, *Abolitionism: A New Perspective* (1972); John L. Thomas, *The Liberator: William Lloyd Garrison* (1963).

Antislavery Politics

Eugene Berwanger, *The Frontier Against Slavery* (1967); F. J. Blue, *The Free Soilers: Third Party Politics, 1848–1854* (1973); S. W. Campbell, *The Slave Catchers* (1968); Avery O. Craven, *The Growth of Southern Nationalism, 1848–1861* (1953); David Donald, *Charles Sumner and the Coming of the Civil War* (1960); Don E. Fehrenbacher, *Prelude to Greatness: Lincoln in the 1850's* (1962); Eric Foner, *Free Soil, Free Labor, Free Men: The Ideology of the Republican Party Before the Civil War* (1970); Harry V. Jaffe, *Crisis of the House Divided: An Interpretation of the Issues of the Lincoln-Douglas Debates* (1959); Robert W. Johannsen, *Stephen A. Douglas* (1973); Roy F. Nichols, *The Disruption of the American Democracy* (1948); David M. Potter, *The Impending Crisis, 1848–1861* (1976); Richard H. Sewell, *Ballots for Freedom: AntiSlavery Politics in the United States, 1837–1860* (1976); Paul Sigelschiffer, *The American Conscience* (1973); Hans Trefousse, *The Radical Republicans* (1969).

The Secession Crisis

Steven A. Channing, *Crisis of Fear: Secession in South Carolina* (1970); David M. Potter, *Lincoln and His Party in the Secession Crisis* (1942); Kenneth M. Stampp, *And the War Came: The North and the Secession Crisis, 1860–1861* (1950).

23 SHERMAN'S MARCH TO THE SEA

A.W.

Early on the morning of November 16, 1864, the Union columns headed out of Atlanta, Georgia, bound southeast for the coastal city of Savannah. Northern troops, over 60,000 strong, with their horses, mules, and wagons, clogged the road. As they reached a hilltop, the soldiers turned to look back toward the town. Their commander, General William Tecumseh Sherman, recalled:

> Behind us lay Atlanta, smoldering and in ruins, the black smoke rising high in the air and hanging like a pall over the ruined city. Away off in the distance, on the McDonough road, was the rear of Howard's column, the gun-barrels glistening in the sun, the white-topped wagons stretching away to the south; and right before us the Fourteenth Corps, marching steadily and rapidly, with a cheery look and a swinging pace, that made light of the thousand miles that lay between us and Richmond. Some band, by accident, struck up the anthem of "John Brown's Body." The men caught up the strain, and never before have I heard the chorus of "Glory, glory, hallelujah!" done with more spirit, or in better harmony of time and place.

On that beautiful day of brilliant sunshine and clean, crisp air, the Civil War, already three and a half years old, seemed exhilarating, if not remote. Sherman later recalled experiencing a "feeling of something to come, vague and undefined, still full of venture and intense interest. Even the common soldiers caught the inspiration, and many a group called out to me—Uncle Billy, I guess Grant is waiting for us at Richmond!"

Although Richmond and victory for the Union were still five months away, Sherman had already made his mark in Georgia. The pall of smoke he and his troops saw above Atlanta came from the fires they had set in the town's railroad depot and machine shops. Flames soon swept into residential areas, destroying hundreds of dwellings. The general's reputation for toughness—"brutality" in the minds of most Southerners—took shape at Atlanta and on the subsequent campaign, his famous march to the sea. "We are not only fighting hostile armies," Sherman believed, "but a hostile people. We must make old and young, rich and poor, feel the hand of war."

Sherman, the tough-talking soldier, knew the South well. Born in Ohio in 1820, he attended West Point and, after graduation, spent most of his time on duty in military posts in the South. He resigned from the army in 1853. After working unsuccessfully as a bank manager in California and as a lawyer in Kansas, he tried to get back into the army. Rejected, he had to settle for the job of superintendent of a military academy in Louisiana. The school opened in 1859.

As the sectional crisis deepened, Sherman made it clear that, if Louisiana should secede from the Union, he would resign his post and do all he could to aid the national government. He kept his word when he heard of the Southern attack on Fort Sumter in April 1861. Secession, he thought, was "folly, madness, a crime against civilization." He immediately sought, and gained, reinstatement in the army. It was now more receptive to such applications, since so many regular officers had joined the Confederacy.

Sherman started as a colonel and rose rapidly in the Union high command. He served in the west as one of Grant's most trusted officers. By mid-1864, as a major general, he was assigned the mission of striking from Tennessee into Georgia and seizing Atlanta. The town, though relatively small, was an important railroad center. Confederate troops under General Joseph E. Johnston and, later, General John B. Hood fought hard to hold Sherman back. They were defeated in July at two crucial battles, those of Peachtree Creek and Atlanta. After a siege of several weeks, Atlanta fell.

Sherman's troops entered the city on September 2. Although Hood at first moved south toward safety, he later wheeled northwest

Union invasion of the South devastated the Confederate terrain as well as its morale. Marching through Georgia in 1864, General Sherman's troops occupied Atlanta and demolished much of the city—ripping up railroad tracks, destroying the depot, burning down homes, and evacuating the remainder of the residents. The fire-swept shambles behind them, Sherman's men moved on to Savannah.

toward Tennessee, hoping to harass Sherman's communications so badly that his forces would have to retreat. Inadvertently, Hood's actions may have influenced Sherman in his later decision to move to the sea without regard for communications or established supply lines.

For the time being, however, Sherman wanted to rest his troops and observe Hood's movements. He decided that Hood could be kept at bay by some detachments of his own army, plus Union troops in Tennessee.

Sherman meanwhile undertook some indirect negotiations with the governor of Georgia, Joseph E. Brown. His aim was to separate the state from the Confederacy. There was reason to hope that Georgia might pull out of the war. Brown had already withdrawn his state's militia from the rebel army. And, like many Southern politicians, he had come to detest Jefferson Davis, president of the Confederacy. Davis had stirred bitter reactions because of his insistent demands for troops and supplies from the hard-pressed Southern states. Nothing came of the negotiations; but they may have impressed on Sherman the need for bringing the hardships of war home to the Southern civilian population.

When the war started, Atlanta—not then the state capital—had only 12,000 inhabitants. Many of them had fled as the Union troops approached. Others followed when Hood abandoned the town. When Sherman entered, he ordered the rest of the civilians to leave, since he did not want them clogging the town and interfering with his lines of communication. He and Hood agreed to a 10-day truce so that these civilians could move out.

By late October, Sherman had decided to march to the sea. On November 2 Grant wired: "I do not really see that you can withdraw from where you are to follow Hood without giving up all we have gained in territory. I say, then, go as you propose."

Sherman's bold plan called for his army of 62,000 men (5,000 of them cavalry) to move the 300 miles to Savannah without supply lines and without communications until they reached the Atlantic coast. There the Union navy could provide cover and supplies. Sherman's troops carried enough provisions for twenty or thirty days, but those were considered emergency rations. Food on the march would be "provided" by the farms and plantations along the way—*not*, of course, on a voluntary basis. As a result, Georgia would be made to "howl."

Sherman's Special Field Order #120 detailed the procedure he hoped to establish. Brigade commanders were responsible for organizing foraging parties. Every morning, these would move out from the four main columns under the direction of one or two "discreet officers." Foragers—or "bummers," as they soon came to be called (even by the Yankees themselves)—could seize available livestock and food supplies. They were not supposed to enter houses. Only corps commanders had the authority to order destruction of buildings, and then only in areas of resistance. Foragers for artillery units could take all the animals and wagons they needed.

Tall, sharp-eyed, and red-haired, Sherman gained a reputation as a ruthless commander because of his march through the Confederacy.

If possible, foragers were to seize provisions from the rich plant- ers rather than poor farmers. The wealthy were presumed to be more in favor of the rebellion than their humbler fellow Southerners. (This as- sumption fitted Northern views of secession as a conspiracy of the elite. It did not square with the facts of Southern political life.)

Sherman's field order directed his men to "forage liberally." They obeyed with a will. Men would go out in the morning on foot, seize a wagon, and then load it with everything valuable and movable they could find. One of Sherman's aides, Major Henry Hitchcock, described a foraging expedition in his diary:

> Plenty of forage along road: corn, fodder, finest sweet potatoes, pigs, chickens, etc. Passed troops all day, some on march, some destroying railroad thoroughly. Two cotton gins on roadside burned, and pile of cotton with one, also burned. Houses in Conyers look comfortable for Georgia village, and sundry good ones along road. Soldiers foraging all along, but only for *forage*—no violence so far as I saw or heard. Laughable to see pigs in feed troughs behind wagons, chickens swinging in knapsacks. Saw some few men—Whites look sullen—darkies pleased.

Stories of Union brutality, supposedly encouraged by Sherman himself, began to circulate. (They continued to circulate for genera- tions.) But his march to the sea, devastating as it was, did not degenerate into an orgy of murder, rape, and arson. Sherman later acknowledged "acts of pillage, robbery, and violence" undoubtedly committed by some of his men. But, he argued, "these acts were exceptional and incidental. I have never heard of any cases of murder or rape; and no army could have carried along sufficient food and forage for a march of three hundred miles; so that foraging in some shape was necessary."

To Sherman, the march became just what he had ordered—harsh

A "bummer" goes his way, so loaded with booty that he cannot even hold the reins in his hands. For many of Sher- man's men, the march through Georgia vindicated their months or even years of difficult military life.

but, in the main, well-disciplined. The destruction of his "scorched-earth" policy centered on three main targets: railroads, the few factories on the route, and public buildings that could serve as temporary headquarters for military units.

Sherman marveled at the skill of his men in carrying out his order to "forage liberally." One fact among many proves how proficient they were: Sherman's army started the march driving 5,000 head of cattle; they ended it with over 10,000

Where were the Confederate forces during these agonizing weeks? Some small cavalry units of the Confederate army did appear from time to time to raid foraging parties. But they had little overall effect. Hood's army had marched northwest to Tennessee and defeat. Since most Georgians of fighting age were serving with the Southern forces, the state militia had been reduced to several thousand old men and young boys. They tried to make a stand at the state capital, Milledgeville, but the Union forces swept them aside. After viewing the casualties, a Northern officer wrote: "I was never so affected at the sight of dead and wounded before. I hope we will never have to shoot at such men again. They know nothing at all about fighting and I think their officers know as little."

Milledgeville fell on November 23. Georgia state officials had fled a short time before. The invading Yankee officers decided to mock the "sovereign state of Georgia." They pretended to hold a session of the state legislature, complete with resolutions and fire-eating oratory. Then they decided to repeal the ordinance of secession. When Sherman heard about these antics, he laughed. Meanwhile, his Milledgeville "legislators" ordered the burning of public buildings in the town.

Sherman's soldiers sliced a path forty to sixty miles wide through central Georgia. Every white family along the way underwent its own particular ordeal and emerged with its own sorrowful story. Tales of the devastation became commonplace: houses broken into and sacked, food and valuables hidden only to be found by the recurrent searches of intruding "bummers," treasured family possessions tossed into the flames, cotton gins and public buildings put to the torch. "Everything had been swept as with a storm of fire," wrote one Macon newspaper. "The whole country around is one wide waste of destruction."

Contrary to Sherman's conception of his foraging troops as skilled, most Southerners in their path regarded them as greedy marauders. The experiences of two Georgia women, a mother and daughter, typified the ordeal. Mary Jones, the widow of a Presbyterian minister, owned three plantations in Liberty County, not far from Savannah. At the time of Sherman's march she and her daughter, Mary Jones Mallard, were living at the plantation known as Montevideo. Their letters and journals vividly portray the impact of war.

Mary Mallard's husband was captured on December 13 by Union cavalry near Montevideo. (Mrs. Mallard was then pregnant and expecting to give birth within days.) The first groups of "bummers" reached the

Jones-Mallard household on December 15. They searched the house and made off with a number of family keepsakes. During the next two weeks, Union raiding parties—sometimes large detachments, sometimes only a few stragglers—arrived almost daily at the home. Each group searched the premises, insulted the two women, and took what food, supplies, or family items remained to be carted away.

Mary Mallard confided unhappily to her journal on December 17.

> The Yankees made the Negroes bring up the oxen and carts, and took off all the chickens and turkeys they could find. They carried off all the syrup from the smokehouse. We had one small pig, which was all the meat we had left; they took the whole of it. Mother saw everything like food stripped from her premises, without the power of uttering one word. Finally they rolled out the carriage and took that to carry off a load of chickens. They took everything they possibly could.

"Everything" included seven of the Jones family's slaves, who—like hundreds of blacks elsewhere along the army's line of march—were pressed into service as porters, laborers, or mule drivers. "So they were all carried off," Mary Mallard grieved, "carriages, wagons, carts, horses and mules and servants, with food and provisions of every kind—and, so far as they were concerned, leaving us to starvation."

Occasionally an officer would apologize for the behavior of his men. One friendly Union soldier, a Missourian, offered to show Mrs. Jones where to hide her things. Mary Mallard noted: "He said he had enlisted to fight for the *Constitution;* but since then the war had been turned into another thing, and he did not approve this abolitionism, for his wife's people all owned slaves." A few days later, a Virginian told Mrs. Jones that "there was great dissatisfaction in the army on account of the present object of the war, which now was to free the Negroes."

More often than not, however, the raiders stalked through the houses indifferent to its inhabitants. Never knowing whether soldiers coming to the door would behave politely or insolently, the two women lived in constant fear. Several times, "bummers" threatened to return and burn down their house. Yet on other occasions, Union commanders offered them protection and safe-conduct passes to Savannah, which was still in Confederate hands. The women declined to leave, partly because of Mary Mallard's pregnancy. On January 4, 1865, she gave birth to a daughter. Her mother noted in her journal:

> During these hours of agony the yard was filled with Yankees. They were all around the house; my poor child, calm and collected amid her agony of body, could hear their conversation and wild halloos and cursing beneath her windows. After a while they left, screaming and yelling in a most fiendish way as they rode from the house.

Mary Jones's journal makes it clear that Sherman had achieved his major purpose in marching through Georgia—to demoralize beyond repair what remained of the Deep South's fighting spirit. She wrote in January 1865:

Mary Jones was one of the Southerners who felt the brunt of Sherman's attack. She wrote: "The foundations of society are broken up; what hereafter is to be our social and civil status we cannot see."

A Confederate soldier returns to find his home a shambles in the midst of a devastated land. The artist who drew this scene was A. J. Volck, a German-born dentist who lived in Baltimore. He was the best-known satirist to interpret the Civil War from the Southern point of view.

As I stand and look at the desolating changes wrought by the hand of an inhuman foe in a few days, I can enter into the feelings of Job. All our pleasant things are laid low. We are prisoners in our own home. To obtain a mouthful of food we have been obliged to cook in what was formerly our drawing room; and I have to rise every morning by candlelight, before the dawn of day, that we may have it before the enemy arrives to take it from us. . . . For one month our homes and all we possess have been given up to lawless pillage. Officers and men have alike engaged in this work of degradation. I scarcely know how we have stood up under it. God alone has enabled us to "speak with the enemy in the gates," and calmly, without a tear, to see my house broken open, entered with false keys, threatened to be burned to ashes, refused food and ordered to be starved to death, told that I had no right even to wood or water, that I should be "humbled in the very dust I walked upon," a pistol and carbine presented to my breast, cursed and reviled as a rebel, a hypocrite, a devil.

Troubling Mrs. Jones almost as much as the behavior of Sherman's soldiers was the reaction of her slaves. During the first days of Union occupation, most of them stayed on the plantation, perhaps out of fear, perhaps out of loyalty. But when it became clear that the Northern army firmly controlled the area, a number of slaves left to join the Union columns marching on Savannah. "Many servants have proven faithful," Mrs. Jones wrote in January 1865, "others false and rebellious against all authority or restraint."

Sherman himself pursued an ambiguous policy toward the ex-slaves, who were known as "contraband." He did not want them as soldiers, despite the good record of black regiments in battle when they were allowed to fight. He rejected the suggestion of General Ulysses S. Grant (by now in charge of all Union forces) that blacks be armed. He felt that his troops would object. And he had another reason. "My aim then," he later wrote, "was to whip the rebels, to humble their pride and make them fear and dread us. I did not want them to cast in our teeth that we had to call on *their* slaves to help us to subdue them."

Nevertheless, Sherman did order the formation of black "pioneer battalions"—construction units—for each army corps. "Negroes who are able-bodied and can be of service to the several columns may be taken along," Sherman instructed, "but each army commander will bear in mind that the question of supplies is a very important one, and that his first duty is to see to those who bear arms." In other words, the army was to keep blacks at a distance, using labor as needed but refraining from becoming a relief organization for ex-slaves who had left their plantations.

Sherman's prejudice against blacks was a crucial factor in his military policy. His brother John was an important antislavery Republican politician from Ohio, but William did not share his views. When still in Louisiana, he had assured Southerners that slavery was best for blacks. "All the congresses on earth," he said, "can't make the Negro anything else than what he is"—namely a slave, or a second-class noncitizen. In a letter he stated:

> I would not if I could abolish or modify slavery. I don't know that I would material-ly change the actual political relation of master and slave. Negroes in the great numbers that exist here must of necessity be slaves. Theoretical notions of humani-ty and religion cannot shake the commercial fact that their labor is of great value and cannot be dispensed with.

Whatever Sherman's own attitudes, it was clear that, from the moment his troops left Atlanta, they sparked the imagination of Georgia's slaves. As Sherman rode through the town of Covington, a day's march from Atlanta, he found that "the Negroes were simply frantic with joy." He later recalled that "Whenever they heard my name, they clustered about my horse, shouted and prayed in their peculiar style, which had a natural eloquence that would have moved a stone."

During the following weeks, as Northern troops foraged their way across Georgia, Sherman witnessed "hundreds, if not thousands, of such scenes." He wrote later that he could still see "a poor girl, in the very ecstasy of the Methodist 'shout,' hugging the banner of one of the regiments."

Thousands of slaves did more than simply greet the liberating Northern army. They joined it, striding alongside or in back of the troop columns. Wrote Mary Jones: "Negroes in large numbers are flocking to them. Nearly all the house servants have left their homes; and from most of the plantations they have gone in a body." The ranks of contraband included strong young men and women in the prime of life, mothers carrying children, and the white-haired elderly.

More than 30,000 blacks joined Sherman's army at one time or another during its four-week march. Yet only 10,000 remained with its ranks as it entered Savannah. Many were actively discouraged from remaining with the soldiers. Neither Sherman nor most of his officers and

"Negroes leaving the plough" is the title given this drawing by Northern artist Alfred R. Waud, who reported the war for an illustrated journal.

men wished to add the task of foraging to feed a huge contraband population from the food collected each day.

Sherman later remembered personally telling an old black man at one plantation that:

> we wanted the slaves to remain where they were, and not to load us down with useless mouths. We could receive a few of their young, hearty men as pioneers. But if they followed us in swarms of old and young, feeble and helpless, it would simply load us down and cripple us in our great task. I believe that old man spread this message to the slaves, which was carried from mouth to mouth, to the very end of our journey, and that it in part saved us from the great danger we incurred of swelling our numbers so that famine would have attended our progress.

In any case, the thousands of slaves who remained with Sherman's forces did not all passively trudge along waiting to be fed and taken care of. Many played active roles. They carried supplies as porters and mule drivers. Some searched out food, animals, and equipment hidden by Confederates along the way. Others built roads or repaired bridges so that Sherman's men, equipment, and supply wagons could keep to their 10-mile-a-day pace across the swampy stretches of central Georgia. Still others helped the soldiers to destroy railroads and other

Black people followed Sherman's army on foot, on horseback, and in any kind of wheeled conveyance that could be found. No one in authority was well prepared to deal with the contraband situation, and many former slaves lacked adequate shelter, food, and clothing.

strategic targets. (A favorite trick was to heat the heavy iron rails and twist them into "Sherman's neckties.")

Local blacks also served as reliable guides behind Confederate lines. One of Sherman's officers, General Oliver O. Howard, ordered one of his men to reach the Union fleet anchored off Savannah. After safely rowing a canoe past enemy posts along the Ogeechee River, the officer and his patrol:

found some Negroes, who befriended him and his men and kept pretty well under cover until evening. Then they went ashore to get a Negro guide and some provisions [after which they passed through Confederate lines]. Soon after this they came to quite a sizable Negro house, went in, and were well treated and refreshed with provisions. When they were eating they were startled by hearing a party of Confederate cavalry riding toward the house. Of course they expected to be instantly captured, but the Negroes, coming quickly to their rescue, concealed them under the floor. The coolness and smartness of the Negroes surprised even Captain Duncan, though he had believed and trusted them. The cavalry stopped but remained only a short time, and the Negroes guided our men back to their boats.

Although few blacks aided the Union side quite so daringly during Sherman's march, the general himself acknowledged that the "large number employed as servants, teamsters and pioneers rendered admirable service."

Sherman's army marched into Savannah on December 21, along with the 10,000 black contraband. The general sent a playful telegram to "His Excellency," President Lincoln: "I beg to present you as a Christmas gift the city of Savannah, with one hundred and fifty heavy guns and plenty of ammunition, also about twenty-five thousand bales of cotton."

The message was quickly published throughout the North. Northerners had considered Sherman's army "lost" when the general had broken communication after leaving Atlanta. Sherman and his men instantly became popular heroes. "Our joy was irrepressible," said one high Washington official, "not only because of their safety, but because it was an assurance that the days of the Confederacy were numbered." Even to many Southerners, Savannah's capture seemed to foreshadow final defeat. Given the suffering that Confederate soldiers and civilians had undergone by then, the prospect seemed almost welcome.

Sherman did not order the city's residents to leave, as he had done at Atlanta. With Union ships in the harbor and his troops in control of the surrounding countryside, he felt no useful military purpose would be served by evacuating or burning the city. In fact, Sherman decided to govern Savannah's 20,000 inhabitants mildly—much to their amazement and that of other Georgians. He gave people the choice of remaining or leaving for other cities still under Confederate control.

Sherman placed one of his generals in overall command of Savannah, but the Confederate mayor and city council handled most day-to-day matters. Relations between Northerners and Southerners were polite, almost cordial. Only a few hundred citizens left the city. Most people calmly went about their business. Relief ships organized by private citizens in the North arrived regularly in January 1865, bringing much-needed food and clothing. Supplies were distributed to freed blacks and needy whites. Local markets selling meat, wood, and other necessities reopened under military supervision.

"No city was ever occupied with less disorder or more system than Savannah," Sherman wrote on December 31. "Though an army of 60,000 men lay camped around it, women and children of an hostile people walk its streets with as much security as they do in Philadelphia." Confederate newspapers raged about the alleged "barbarities" of Sherman's forces on their march from Atlanta, exaggerating the amount of property burned, and the numbers murdered or raped. Meantime the "barbarians" occupied Savannah with little friction.

In Savannah, as on the march from Atlanta, Sherman became a hero to the liberated blacks. He wrote to his wife on Christmas Day: "They flock to me, young and old. They pray and shout and mix up my name with that of Moses and Simon and other scriptural ones as well as 'Abram Linkom'." Hundreds of blacks hurried to see the general, wrote an aide. "There was a constant stream of them, old and young, men, women and children, black, yellow, and cream-colored, uncouth and well-bred, bashful and talkative—but always respectful and behaved—all day long."

It would have come as a great shock to the blacks of Savannah to learn that their hero was at that very moment being attacked in the North for his policy toward ex-slaves. Late in December General Henry W. Halleck wrote Sherman to congratulate him on the march through Georgia and his capture of Savannah. He also warned him that powerful individuals close to the President spoke critically of him, alleging that he "manifested an almost *criminal* dislike" to the Negro. "They say," added Halleck,

> that you are not willing to carry out the wishes of the government in regard to him, but repulse him with contempt! They say you might have brought with you to Savannah more than fifty thousand, thus stripping Georgia of that number of laborers, and opening a road by which as many more could have escaped from their masters; but that, instead of this, you drove them from your ranks, prevented their following you by cutting the bridges in your rear, and thus caused the massacre of large numbers by Wheeler's cavalry.

Sherman defended his decision to discourage slave runaways from joining the march on the grounds that their presence would have overburdened his army and hindered its military success. In responding to Halleck, however, he acknowledged that his sympathy for freed blacks was limited:

> Thank God I am not running for an office and am not concerned because the rising generation will believe that I burned 500 niggers[1] at one pop in Atlanta, or any such nonsense. The South deserves all she has got for her injustice to the Negro, but that is no reason why we should go to the other extreme.

It was no surprise to Sherman when Secretary of War Edwin M. Stanton arrived in Savannah on January 9, aboard the Union ship *Nevada*. Stanton was supposedly traveling on a vacation cruise and to supervise the disposition of captured Confederate cotton supplies. Actually he came to check on Sherman's handling of matters involving blacks. Stanton strongly supported Sherman's military strategy in Georgia. But he disapproved of the general's rumored hostility toward the ex-slave population, and of his refusal to use blacks as soldiers.

Sherman denied that any of his officers or troops had been hostile to slaves on their march from Atlanta. But Stanton wanted to hear about Sherman's behavior from the blacks themselves. At his request, therefore, Sherman invited "the most intelligent of the Negroes" in Savannah to come to his rooms to meet the secretary of war. Twenty black men attended the meeting with Sherman and Stanton on January 12, 1865.

Never before had any major American government official met with black leaders to ask what *they* wished for their people. Each man present began by introducing himself with a brief account of his life. The average age was fifty. Fifteen of the men were ministers—mainly Baptist and Methodist—and the other five were church officials of one kind or

---

[1]This term was considered only mildly discourteous in the 1860s. It was commonly used, even by anti-slavery Northerners.

another. Five of the leaders had been born free. Of the others, three had bought their freedom; most of the rest had been liberated by Sherman's army.

Secretary of War Stanton sat at a table facing the black visitors, making extensive notes on their remarks. Sherman, restless and uneasy over the interview, stood with two of his aides apart from the seated group. He watched the proceedings warily, pacing across the room from time to time during the exchange. The blacks had selected as their spokesman sixty-seven-year-old Garrison Frazier, a Baptist minister. He responded firmly to each of Stanton's questions.

Stanton asked first whether the men were aware of Lincoln's Emancipation Proclamation. Frazier replied that they were.

> STANTON: State what you understand by slavery, and the freedom that was to be given by the President's Proclamation.
> FRAZIER: Slavery is receiving by irresistible power the work of another man, and not by his consent. The freedom, as I understand it, promised by the Proclamation, is taking us from under the yoke of bondage, and placing us where we could reap the fruit of our own labor, and take care of ourselves, and assist the Government in maintaining our freedom.

Stanton then asked how black people could best maintain their new freedom. Frazier suggested that young men should be able to enlist in the army, and that other blacks ought to receive land to farm: "We want to be placed on land until we are able to buy it, and make it our own."

The secretary of war then asked whether the men believed that freed blacks "would rather live scattered among the whites, or in colonies by yourselves?" Frazier answered: "I would prefer to live by ourselves, for there is a prejudice against us in the South that will take years to get over; but I do not know that I can answer for my brethren."

Frazier and his black associates may have considered Stanton's next question offensive. The Secretary asked whether the ex-slaves of the South were intelligent enough to sustain their freedom while maintaining good relations with Southern whites. "I think there is sufficient intelligence among us to do so," Frazier replied simply.

The black minister was then asked what he believed were the causes and objectives of the Civil War, and whether blacks generally supported one or other side. He responded shrewdly and at length. Frazier told Stanton that blacks wished only to help the Union subdue the rebellious Confederacy. He acknowledged that the North's first war aim involved bringing the South back into the Union, that Lincoln had issued the Emancipation Proclamation mainly as a means toward achieving this end. Only the South's not freeing the slaves "has now made the freedom of the slaves a part of the war." Frazier pointed out that the thousands of runaways who had followed the Union armies, "leaving their homes and undergoing suffering," spoke clearly for the pro-Union sentiments of blacks.

Stanton then indicated that he wanted to ask a question about Sherman. The general—silently furious—left the room. In Sherman's absence, Stanton inquired about "the feeling of the colored people in regard to General Sherman" and whether Negroes regarded "his sentiments and actions as friendly to their rights and interests." Frazier's answer probably surprised Stanton, considering the rumors current in Washington:

> We looked upon General Sherman, prior to his arrival, as a man in the providence of God, specially set apart to accomplish this work, and we unanimously felt inexpressible gratitude to him. Some of us called upon him immediately upon his arrival [in Savannah], and it is probable he did not meet the Secretary with more courtesy than he met us. His conduct and deportment toward us characterized him as a friend and a gentleman. We have confidence in General Sherman, and think that what concerns us could not be under better hands.

The meeting soon ended, after Stanton had thanked his black visitors for their advice.

Stanton and Sherman spent the next three days discussing problems of policy toward the freedmen. They agreed that Sherman would issue a field order on January 16, the day after Stanton's departure from Savannah.

Special Field Order #15 set aside confiscated or abandoned land along rivers emptying into the Atlantic and on the Sea Islands—nearby islands that lie along the coast from Charleston, South Carolina, to Jacksonville, Florida. These lands were to be used exclusively for settlement by freed blacks. A freedman and his family taking up such land were to be given a "possessory title" to "not more than forty acres of tillable land" until Congress should regulate the title.

Sherman clearly viewed this scheme as a temporary one, in order to provide for freedmen and their families in the area during the rest of the war, or until Congress acted. "Mr. Stanton has been here," he confidently wrote his wife on the day of Stanton's departure, "and is cured of that Negro nonsense." By now Sherman was impatient to begin his march northward. He appointed General Rufus Saxton as Inspector of Settlements and Plantations for the entire area covered by his field order. On January 21 Sherman's army left Savannah, marching into South Carolina, the symbol of Confederate resistance.

Saxton energetically arranged to transport homeless blacks in Savannah to coastal farms. He wrote urgent letters to Northern sympathizers asking for food and supplies to help sustain the new agricultural settlements. By midsummer of 1865—with the war now over—Saxton and his aides had managed to settle more than 40,000 black people on lands covered in Sherman's order.

The people faced numerous hardships—neglected soil, old equipment (and little of it), poor seed, and shortage of supplies. But the hardworking freedmen, especially those on the Sea Islands of Georgia and South Carolina, successfully grew crops of cotton and various foodstuffs. They received support not only from Saxton and the military but also from Northern white teachers and missionaries, a number of whom traveled into the area to found schools.

Most of the planning and hard work, however, came from the freedmen themselves. Many started out with little more than the clothes on their backs. One party was led by Ulysses Houston, a minister who had been present at the interview with Stanton. Before leaving for Skidaway Island, he wrote a Northern reporter: "We shall build our cabins, and organize our town government for the maintenance of order and the settlement of all difficulties." The reporter later gave this account:

> He and his fellow-colonists selected their lots, laid out a village, numbered their lots, put the numbers in a hat, and drew them out. It was Plymouth colony repeating itself. They agreed if any others came to join them, they should have equal privileges. So blooms the Mayflower on the South Atlantic coast.

The impressive success of this resettlement led many Northerners to urge that Congress enact a general land distribution policy to help all freedmen. Landless ex-slaves also came to expect that, since 40,000 Deep South blacks had quickly and effectively settled new lands, others too would receive their forty acres in the near future. Such hopes were soon dashed.

Andrew Johnson became President after Lincoln was assassinated in April 1865. Many had believed that Johnson would be sympathetic to a generous land distribution policy once in the White House, since he had been sympathetic to black rights earlier as governor of Tennessee. But a proclamation of his in May 1865 completely shattered this belief. Johnson pardoned all former Confederates except those whose taxable property exceeded $20,000 and those who had held high military or civil positions. (Even these groups could apply for special presidential pardon.)

For the great majority of white Southerners. Johnson's proclamation not only restored civil and political rights. It also restored their property—except for slaves—even if previously confiscated as a result of temporary wartime orders such as Sherman's. Not only did the new President say nothing about the freedmen in his proclamation. He clearly intended them to resume their second-class economic status in the South, although no longer as slaves. Johnson made it plain that he intended landowning blacks such as those under Saxton's jurisdiction to surrender their newly acquired lands and return to their previous owners.

Saxton now administered the freedmen's new settlements in Georgia, South Carolina, and Florida as assistant director of the Freedmen's Bureau. This agency had been recently established by Congress to coordinate federal relief assistance to ex-slaves. Heading the bureau was Sherman's former subordinate, General Oliver O. Howard. He shared President Johnson's wish to conciliate the South. Unlike the President, though, he did not want to do so at the expense of the freedmen.

Both Saxton and Howard tried to resist and delay the restoration of black-occupied lands to their former white owners. They were support-

A Northern teacher reads to two of her pupils at a school on St. Helena, one of the Sea Islands off the coast of South Carolina. These former slaves were among those resettled by Sherman's Order #15.

ed by Stanton, who attempted various maneuvers to stave off the move. But Johnson was determined. Sherman's field order was revoked in June 1865. Saxton even traveled to Washington, but without success.

In September the former landholders of Edisto Island, then under Freedmen's Bureau control, petitioned Johnson for the return of their lands. The President directed Howard to visit the island and convince the freedmen to arrange a "mutually satisfactory solution." The President left little doubt that he wanted the blacks to pack up and leave.

Howard unhappily went to Edisto in late October. Trapped between his duty and his sympathies, he met with freed blacks in a local church. They crowded in, furious at the course of events. They refused to quiet down until a woman began the spiritual "Nobody Knows the Trouble I Seen."

The blacks then listened to Howard as he urged them to surrender their farms and return to work for the island's former white landholders. Angry shouts of "no, no" punctuated Howard's talk. One man in the gallery cried out: "Why, General Howard, why do you take away our lands? You take them from us who have always been true, always true to the government! You give them to our all-time enemies! That is not right!"

Howard patiently explained to his audience that their "possessory titles" to the land were not "absolute" or "legal." At his insistence, a committee was formed consisting of three freedmen, three white planters, and three Freedmen's Bureau representatives. It had authority to decide on the island's land ownership. (This practice was also adopted elsewhere on the Sea Islands.)

Howard still hoped to delay restoration of the property until Congress convened late in 1865. But the process of removing blacks from their assigned lands gathered momentum after he left the area to return North.

Saxton was still refusing to dispossess black landholders from the territories under his supervision, so Johnson removed him in January 1866. He was replaced by Davis Tillson, a Freedmen's Bureau official more sympathetic to presidential policy. Tillson issued an order allowing white owners to return to their former Sea Island farms and plantations. Tillson went so far as to charter a boat and accompany the first group, explaining personally to the blacks in residence that they would have to surrender their lands.

Blacks who were willing to sign contracts to work for white owners were allowed to remain. Others were driven from the islands either by Union troops or by white vigilante groups that began to terrorize black landholders throughout the Deep South during this period. One sympathetic New England schoolteacher later wrote of seeing all the freedmen on one Sea Island plantation leaving their newly acquired land with their hoes over their shoulders. "They told us that the guard had ordered them to leave the plantation if they would not work for the owners. We could only tell them to obey orders. After this many of the Sherman Negroes left the island."

For the moment, Howard's policy of delaying restoration had clearly failed. Yet shortly after Congress met in December 1865, the legislators debated the provisions of a new, postwar Freedmen's Bureau Bill designed to protect the rights of ex-slaves in peacetime. The final version of that bill was enacted by Congress over the President's veto in July 1866. It allowed freedmen deprived of their land by Johnson's restoration policy to lease twenty acres of government-owned land on the Sea Islands with an option to buy cheaply within six years. By then, however, almost all of the "Sherman Negroes" had lost their lands.

By this time, too, Congress and Johnson were struggling bitterly for the control of postwar policy toward the South. The outcome of that struggle would determine the nation's response to its millions of newly liberated blacks. Many of them probably shared the anguish of one Sea Island freedman who grieved shortly after his eviction: "They will make freedom a curse to us, for we have no home, no land, no oath, no vote, and consequently no country."

24
CIVIL WAR AND RECONSTRUCTION
A.W.

On February 23, 1861 (at a time when Sherman had just left his post at the Louisiana military academy), Abraham Lincoln slipped secretly into Washington after an all-night train ride. His aides had planned the night trip, fearing an assassination attempt at a previously scheduled stop in pro-Confederate Baltimore. On his special train the President-elect tried to sleep. But a drunken passenger kept singing the bouncy Southern melody "Dixie" over and over. Lincoln finally muttered to a companion, "No doubt there will be a great time in Dixie by and by." His concern over the impending showdown with the secessionist South was shared by most Northerners.

A thousand miles to the south, the Confederacy's president-elect took a different type of journey to his own inaugural. Lincoln had arrived in the nation's capital, according to one diplomat, "like a thief in the night." Jefferson Davis had traveled from his Mississippi plantation to Montgomery, Alabama — first capital of the rebellious states — like a conquering hero.

Davis was a moderate Southerner. Like others, he had opposed secession until after Lincoln's election. Now this group had taken charge of the South's new government, replacing many of the zealous fire-eaters who had spread the gospel of disunion during the 1850s. Southern moderates had selected Davis as their president largely because he had declared himself in favor of a peaceful settlement with the North. A West Point graduate, Davis had fought ably in the Mexican War, represented Mississippi in both the House and the Senate, and served as President Pierce's secretary of war.

FIRST STEPS

While Davis pondered his cabinet, the Montgomery convention that had chosen him president wrote a Confederate constitution. For the most part the document copied the provisions of the federal Constitution. It included a bill of rights, and it even prohibited the slave trade. Slavery was pronounced legal throughout the Confederacy, of course. In a significant speech at Savannah, the vice president-elect, Alexander Stephens of Georgia, spoke candidly of the new government: "Its foundations are laid, its cornerstone rests, upon the great truth that the Negro is not equal to the white man; that slavery, subordination to the superior race, is his natural and normal condition."

The new Confederate congress began its work by legalizing for the South all Union laws that did not conflict with its new constitution. For two months after Davis's selection as president, the Confederate government waited for some sign of how Lincoln intended to deal with the secession crisis. Then came Sumter — and war.

A "Brothers' War" When the Civil War began on April 12, 1861, Americans gave it various names. For secessionists it was a "War for Southern Independence" or "the War Between the States." Northerners, on the other hand, considered it "the War of the Rebellion" or simply "the War for the Union." Both sides agreed that, whatever else, it was a "brothers' war," severing links among families, personal friends, and public figures according to their sectional loyalties.

This deeply painful division reached even into Abraham Lincoln's family. A Kentucky officer named Ben Hardin Helm was the husband of Mary Todd Lincoln's sister. He spent several days at the White House talking to old West Point friends. Some of them were already preparing to head south and join the Confederate army. As Helm — still uncertain — concluded his visit, Lincoln gave him an envelope containing a major's commission in the Union army. The two men grasped hands warmly and exchanged good-byes. A few days later came the news that Helm had chosen the Confederacy.

But another Kentuckian, Fort Sumter's Robert Anderson, accepted Lincoln's promotion to brigadier general that same month. He then left for the Middle West to help keep his native state in the Union.

A third officer, a fervent Unionist, turned down Lincoln's offer to be commander of all Northern troops. Instead, he accepted command of the Confederacy's eastern force, the Army of Northern Virginia. "If Virginia stands by the old Union, so will I," Robert E. Lee declared. "But if she secedes (though I do not believe in secession as a constitutional right, nor that there is sufficient cause for revolution) then I will follow my native state with my sword and, if need be, with my life." When Virginia finally broke with the Union, Lee followed.

In many ways the Confederate struggle for independence resembled the American revolt against British rule two generations earlier. Some revolutions are a struggle for colonial independence from a ruling country. Such a revolution occurred in North America in the 1770s. Other revolutions result when one section of a country tries to break away from the whole, leading to an internal war between the nation and the break-away section. This type of separatist revolt may occur when the people of a particular region feel that their interests and values are directly threatened by those who control the national government. Such was the case in the South after Lincoln's election.[1]

National uprisings, such as the American Revolution, and separatist revolts, such as the Civil War, usually take place only after great soul-searching among those rebelling. The American people do not shift their loyalties easily. Washington, Franklin, and other Revolutionary leaders had served the British Empire faithfully for de-

[1]More recently, separatist revolts have taken place in Nigeria (where the Ibo province of Biafra revolted unsuccessfully) and in Pakistan (where the Bengali area formerly known as East Pakistan won its independence and became the new country of Bangladesh).

Abraham Lincoln, wrote George Templeton Strong, was "a most sensible, straightforward, honest old codger; the best President we have had since Jackson's time."

Jefferson Davis suffered from poor health throughout the war. Though he was strong-willed and irritable, his devotion to the South was unquestioned.

cades in war and peace. Lee, Davis, and other key Confederate leaders had served the American government before the South seceded. They finally revolted because they believed the Southern way of life—a culture based upon slavery—was directly threatened by Republican control of the central government.

Mobilization In the early months of the Civil War most Americans seemed to expect the conflict to be bloody but brief. Few realized what lay ahead. "No casualties yet, no real mourning, nobody hurt," wrote Mary Boykin Chesnut, the wife of a high Confederate officer, in June 1861. "It is all parade, fuss, and fine feathers."

A few leaders believed the situation was more serious. Among them were Lincoln and his generals and their counterparts behind the Southern lines. Mrs. Chesnut noted what Jefferson Davis had told her one evening: "Either way, he thinks it will be a long war, that before the end came we would have many a bitter experience. He said only fools doubted the courage of the Yankees, or their willingness to fight when they saw fit."

Nor did most Southerners underestimate the extent of Northern resources. In almost every respect—population, capital, and raw materials—the Union had the advantage over the Confederacy. Most important, the North could produce endless supplies of guns, ammunition, ships, and other war equipment. The South, on the other hand, had increasing difficulty in keeping its soldiers supplied.

Neither side began with much of an army. There were only 18,000 men in the regular army in 1860, with about 1,100 officers. Only a small number of these had significant combat experience, and most of them resigned to join the Confederate Army, so that the South's officer corps was initially better trained than the North's. These officers, Northern and Southern, prepared to fight a conflict far different, in strategy and tactics, from those for which they had been trained.

Both North and South started the war using a system of volunteer enlistments. At first they recruited men for only a few months, since both sides believed that the war would be short.

On April 15, the day after the surrender of Sumter, Lincoln issued a proclamation calling up "the militia of the several States of the Union, to the . . . number of seventy-five thousand, in order to supress [the rebellion] and to cause the laws to be duly executed." The initial news of Sumter's capture outraged Northerners of almost every political persuasion—Douglas Democrats, Constitutional Unionists, Whigs, and Republicans alike. Such unity would proved short-lived. But while it lasted, people as dissimilar as abolitionist ex-pacifists and formerly pro-Southern businessmen all hailed the President's call for troops. Patriotic meetings were held in towns and cities throughout the Union, demanding swift action against the rebellious states. Eager volunteers

RESOURCES OF THE UNION AND THE CONFEDERACY, 1861

	UNION	CONFEDERACY
Population	23,000,000	8,700,000*
Real and personal property	$11,000,000,000	$5,370,000,000
Banking capital	$330,000,000	$27,000,000
Capital investment	$850,000,000	$95,000,000
Manufacturing establishments	110,000	18,000
Value of production (annual)	$1,500,000,000	$155,000,000
Industrial workers	1,300,000	110,000
Locomotives	451,000	19,000
Railroad mileage	22,000	9,000

*Including 3,500,000 slaves

rushed to join military units in almost every Northern community.

"Before God it is the duty of every American citizen to rally around the flag of the country," shouted an ailing Stephen A. Douglas at a Chicago mass meeting. Douglas, still Lincoln's most influential Northern Democratic opponent, had gone to the White House immediately after Sumters's fall to pledge to Lincoln his complete support in restoring the Union.

As the fighting dragged on, however, it became apparent to both sides that volunteers would not provide enough manpower. Even the cash bounties offered to those who enlisted would not bring in enough volunteers. Casualties mounted in 1862. First the undermanned Confederacy and then the Union turned to drafting soldiers by lottery. Wealthy or influential young men, North and South, could, and often did, avoid going to war. They could provide a paid substitute, who might cost as much as $600. Or they could claim exemption on grounds that their civilian work was essential. (Slaveholders who grew cotton, for example, could avoid service this way.) By the end of the war, the South's troop shortage had become extreme. The Confederacy had by then begun drafting and training thousands of slaves.

FIGHTING THE CIVIL WAR

Late in May 1861 the Confederate government moved its capital to Richmond. This was done partly because the large Virginia city could accommodate the growing Confederate bureaucracy more easily than Montgomery could. The move also dramatized the Confederacy's promise to defend the Upper South. Besides, Richmond was an important rail and road center. With Northern and Southern capitals and armies now only a hundred miles apart, the area of Virginia and Maryland became, for obvious reasons, the war's pivotal theater of operations.

A thick layer of gloom spread over Washington as Lincoln and his generals prepared for a Southern attack. There was talk that, for the second time in half a century, an American President might be forced to flee the White House, pursued by an invading army.

Southern Strategy   Although a number of important battles were fought during the war, the Confederates generally used an overall guerrilla strategy that resembled Washington's in the American Revolution. A friend wrote Jefferson Davis

Lee was a vigorous fifty-five when the Civil War began. Like Washington, he fought against difficult odds and was much admired by his troops.

complaining of the Confederacy's "purely defensive" strategy and of its reluctance to launch a full-scale attack on the North. Davis replied: "Without military stores, without the workshops to create them, without the power to import them, necessity, not choice, has compelled us to occupy strong positions and everywhere—selecting the time and place of attack—to confront the enemy without reserves." In other words, the South chose to conduct an "offensive defense." It tried to select the time and place for major battles carefully. At other times Southerners harassed Northern armies with cavalry raids led by such intrepid commanders as "Stonewall" Jackson, J. E. B. Stuart, Nathan B. Forrest, and John S. Mosby.

Confederate army commanders realized that it was impossible to prevent Union invasions of the South. They knew too that they had neither the manpower nor the resources to mount a full-scale invasion of the North. So the Confederates worked instead to maintain their armies in the field while fighting back the Union troops thrown against them. They hoped that a war-weary Northern public would finally force Lincoln's government to negotiate a peaceful settlement. Lee and Davis recognized, as Washington did during the 1770s, that a revolutionary army wins by not losing —that is, by displaying the capacity to endure.

Northern Strategy Recognizing the Southern strategy, Lincoln and his generals committed Northern armies from the beginning to a policy of total war against the South. They were dedicated to the complete destruction of Confederate military power and civil authority by every necessary means. George Templeton Strong wrote in his diary in November 1861:

> Were I dictator at this time, my military policy would be: (1) to defend and hold Washington, Western Virginia, Kentucky, Missouri; (2) to support Unionists in North Carolina and in eastern Tennessee; (3) to recover and hold (or destroy with sunken ships) every port and inlet from Hatteras to Galveston.

Strong's proposals resembled the North's actual strategy during the war, which was three-fold: (1) to encircle the South in an ever-tighten-

ing military net by blockading its ports; (2) to divide the Confederacy in half by seizing control of the Mississippi and Tennessee rivers; (3) to capture Richmond and destroy the main Confederate armies in Virginia, where most Southern troops were concentrated. Strong believed, as did Lincoln and his officers, that if "the rebels of the South can be locked up and left to suffer and starve," victory would follow.

Grubby-looking but brilliant, Grant was modest and reticent about his feelings. Of him Lincoln said, "I can't spare this man—he fights."

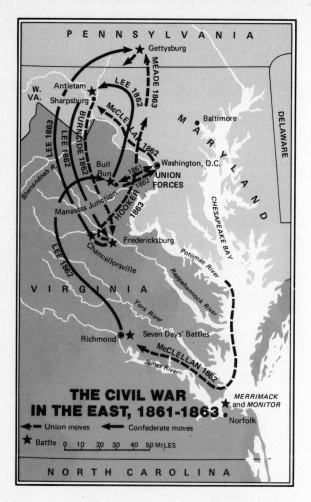

THE CIVIL WAR IN THE EAST, 1861-1863

← Union moves   ← Confederate moves

★ Battle   0   10   20   30   40   50 MILES

Fighting broke out on April 12, **1861**, when Confederate batteries opened fire on Fort Sumter in Charleston harbor. The Union quickly began a naval blockade of Confederate shipping. The first major engagement occurred on July 21, at Manassas Junction, Virginia. There an advancing Union army under Irvin McDowell was defeated in the first Battle of Bull Run and driven back to Washington, D.C.

The year **1862** witnessed the first naval battle between ironclads—the Union ship *Monitor* and the Confederate ship *Virginia* (formerly the *Merrimack*)—on March 9 near Norfolk, Virginia. The Union offensives of that year began in March with McClellan's Peninsula Campaign, an attempt to take Richmond from the southeast. He advanced slowly to within a few miles of the city. Confederate forces inflicted heavy casualties on his troops at the end of May. During the subsequent Seven Days' Battle (June 26-July 2) Lee and Jackson forced McClellan to retreat and abandon the campaign. The Confederate army moved northward to win the second Battle of Bull Run (August 29-30). From there Lee and Jackson advanced into Maryland. Near Sharpsburg, McClellan engaged the Confederates in the Battle of Antietam (September 17). Although militarily the battle was a draw, Lee withdrew to Virginia. McClellan was replaced as Union commander by Burnside, whose overwhelming force was shattered at Fredericksburg (December 13).

In **1863** Hooker took command of the Union army, only to be defeated at Chancellorsville (May 2-4). However, Confederate losses there included "Stonewall" Jackson. Lee marched into Pennsylvania and was defeated at Gettysburg by a Union army under Meade (July 1-3). Lee retreated to Virginia, his second offensive into Union territory a failure.

Superior to the South in its navy, the North was able to impose a blockade of Southern harbors. The Confederates counteracted with fast blockade runners, joined by a number of private merchantmen. In the early years of the war they managed to slip past Union vessels in five out of every six attempts. But the Union blockade became increasingly effective. By 1865 it had choked off Southern cotton exports to Europe, as well as imports of arms and supplies.

War in the East The outcome of the Civil War was decided not by naval encounters but by land battles. Northern armies began poorly but improved their performance every year. Confederate forces scored impressive victories at the first and second battles of Bull Run in July 1861 and August 1862. At Fredericksburg, Virginia, in December 1862, the North suffered a crushing defeat, with over 12,000 casualties.

In May 1863, at Chancellorsville, Maryland, outnumbered Southerners won another victory, though it cost them one of their best generals, "Stonewall" Jackson. They imposed a stalemate on the Virginia front and, several times, threatened to capture Washington itself.

Lincoln searched desperately for Union commanders capable of breaking the stalemate and executing major offensive operations. In the process he appointed a succession of commanding generals—George McClellan, John Pope, McClellan again, Ambrose Burnside, Joseph Hooker, and George Meade. One time, after McClellan had failed to pursue a retreating Confederate force, he received this letter: "My dear McClellan: If you don't want to use the Army of the Potomac, I should like to borrow it for a while. Yours respectfully, A. Lincoln."

The turning point of the Civil War in the East came in July 1863. Confederate troops under Lee marched into southern Pennsylvania, where they encountered a Union force near Gettysburg. After three days of costly fighting, Lee's invasion was repulsed decisively on July 3.

Each side had over 75,000 troops involved, and the South suffered almost 25,000 casualties. "The results of this victory are priceless," rejoiced the normally pessimistic Strong. "Philadelphia, Baltimore, and Washington are safe. The rebels are hunted out of the North, their best army is routed, and the charm of Robert Lee's invincibility broken."

War in the West The South's strategy of tying down and wearing out Union forces worked reasonably well in the East. Elsewhere, however, better-equipped and better-led Union troops won a series of important victories.

In February 1862 federal troops and a gunboat flotilla led by Ulysses S. Grant captured Fort Henry, on the Tennessee River, and Fort Donelson, on the Cumberland River. These moves forced Southern General Albert S. Johnston to abandon Kentucky and parts of Tennessee to the Union.

Admiral Farragut's capture of New Orleans in April 1862 and a series of Northern victories farther up the Mississippi—capped by defeat of the Confederate fleet at Memphis in June—brought most of the river under Union control. Arkansas, Louisiana, and Texas were thus isolated from the rest of the Confederacy.

In the West the decisive point was reached the day after Lee's defeat at Gettysburg. On July 4, 1863, Vicksburg fell. This key Confederate port surrendered after a six-week siege by Union troops. A final Confederate stronghold on the Mississippi—Port Hudson, Louisiana—fell later that same month.

Grant's remarkable success in this western campaign led to his appointment as Lincoln's seventh and last commanding general. Grant appealed to Lincoln for many of the same reasons he

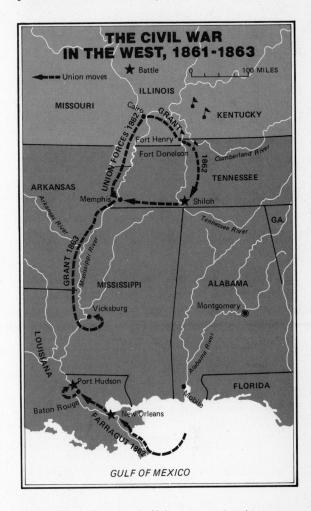

THE CIVIL WAR IN THE WEST, 1861-1863

Meanwhile, in the west, the Union won a series of important victories in **1862**. In February Grant captured Fort Henry on the Tennessee River and Fort Donelson on the Cumberland. Moving southward in Tennessee, he was attacked at Shiloh (April 6-7), but Union reinforcements forced the Confederates to withdraw into Mississippi. Union forces also made progress in their drive to gain control of the Mississippi River. Farragut bombarded and captured New Orleans in late April and proceeded up the river to Baton Rouge. To the north, a combined naval and land expedition defeated the Confederate fleet at Memphis on June 6 and captured the city.

In **1863** the Union continued its campaign to secure mastery of the Mississippi. Grant began attacking the Confederate stronghold of Vicksburg in May, and the city surrendered on July 4. With the fall of Port Hudson on July 9, the entire Mississippi was in Union hands and the Confederacy split in two.

did to most Northerners. Wrote one admirer of Grant: "He talks like an earnest businessman, prompt, clearheaded, and decisive, and utters no bosh."

Final Campaigns Grant took command of the Union forces in the spring of 1864. In May, he and Meade led a Northern force of 100,000 men against Lee's army, which had regrouped in Virginia after its Gettysburg defeat the previous year. It was in the same month that Union troops led by Sherman began their push to Atlanta.

For the remainder of the war Grant and Sherman pursued the same strategy of wearing down the enemy that Davis and Lee had hoped earlier would win for the Confederacy. No longer did Union forces concentrate on capturing Richmond or other Southern territory for its own sake. Instead, they struck directly at the remaining Confederate armies and resources—as Sherman did in Georgia. They aimed to inflict so heavy a price in casualties and physical devastation, that a war-weary South would be forced to surrender.

Beginning in June 1864, Grant's army tied down most of Lee's forces near Petersburg, Virginia. That fall Sherman led his famous march to the sea from Atlanta to Savannah. From Savannah, Sherman's forces turned north and extended their scorched-earth tactics into South Carolina and North Carolina.

Grant's troops, meanwhile, left their Petersburg trenches for frequent assaults on Lee's thinly manned lines. By early April 1865, Grant had blocked Lee's effort to retreat southward. Lee's army had by then been reduced by death and desertions from 54,000 to 30,000 men. Lee believed that further fighting was useless and that Confederate defeat was inevitable. He surrendered to Grant at Appomattox, Virginia, on April 9, 1865.

Despite pleas from Jefferson Davis for continued resistance, even if only by guerrilla bands in the Southern hills and forests, the rest of the Confederate armies still in the field surrendered by the end of May. Union troops had finally occupied Richmond after Davis and other Confederate officials had fled. For all practical purposes Southern resistance had ended by the time Jefferson Davis was captured on May 10.

A Summing Up The Civil War has been described as the "first modern war." A number of weapons and tactics associated with later military struggles were first used in its major campaigns. The basic **weapon** for the infantry, both Union and Confederate, **was the** single-shot, rifled musket, which had a range and accuracy two or three times greater than earlier, smoothbore guns. Troops could now engage in deadly fire from distances of a quarter to a half mile. Trench warfare, which later dominated much of World War I, came into being, and close-range or hand-to-hand combat was no longer inevitable.

This increased firepower of the infantry threatened both artillery and cavalry. A bank of cannon could no longer offer a solid defense; and the dash of a cavalry charge became mere vainglory when riders could easily be picked off, one by one, from a distance.

The American genius for creating new technology, shown earlier with such peaceful innovations as the cotton gin, was amply demonstrated during the Civil War, when Gatling guns (machine guns), repeating rifles, ironclad ships, and even submarines made their appearance (the latter were, for the most part, failures).

Civil War mortar

Railroads and telegraph lines revolutionized military communications, particularly for the Northern armies, who sent an estimated 6 million telegrams over 15,000 miles of wire set up by the Signal Corps. The most spectacular railroad supply system was that maintained for Sherman during the siege of Atlanta: 1,600 tons of supplies arrived daily in 16 trains from Union depots northwest of the city. European military observers flocked to the United States to study the lessons the New World's "internal war" had to offer the Old World's future struggles.

The Civil War was a modern war in the important sense that it required a break with traditional military thinking in order to achieve victory. Most Civil War generals on both sides regarded cities and territories—not enemy armies—as their objectives. They hoped to win by maneuvering rather than by fighting. By contrast, Lincoln's overall strategy was to move on all fronts simultaneously in order to crush the enemy's forces and gain control of his resources. This warfare of annihilation was a plan that tradition-bound generals scorned. Only in Grant and Sherman did Lincoln find generals who would employ his strategy successfully. They were willing to break the rules to play, and win, a new and deadly game.

Casualties on both sides in the four years of "internal war" totaled almost 40 percent of the armies; several hundred thousand soldiers gave their lives to battle. The South lost its separatist revolt for lack of manpower and equipment. "They are too many for us," Mary Boykin Chesnut despaired two days before Lee's surrender. "Nine tenths of our army are under ground!" she anguished in her diary. "Where is another to come from? Will they wait until we grow one?" Time had run out for the Confederacy, and its will to endure had been crushed.

LIFE ON THE HOME FRONTS

In the long run it would have been far cheaper to purchase the abolition of slavery, although such a course was unthinkable to both sides in 1861. Estimates of the war's total cost ran as high as $3 billion for the South and $5 billion for the North. This was three to four times the total estimated value of every slave in the Confederacy. Both the Union and the Confederacy had great difficulty in paying their enormous bills for war equipment, soldiers' salaries, and operating expenses. Both sides resorted to such financial measures as raising taxes, issuing various types of bonds, and printing vast quantities of paper money unsupported by gold or silver reserves.

Crisis in the South   The overriding desire for victory led to sweeping measures in the South. Some affected the master-slave relationship. Southern slaveholders had defended their right to absolute control over their bondsmen in antebellum days. When war came, they watched helplessly as the Confederate government and Southern state governments transferred hundreds of thousands of slaves from private plantations to more urgent labor in the war effort. Slaves even became Confederate soldiers shortly before Appomattox. And throughout the war Southerners relaxed their close supervision of slave movements and activities.

Normal political life also came to a halt in the South during the war. There was no two-party system (as in the North). There was only one all-inclusive ruling, but unruly, "government party." Within the Confederacy there were people who opposed Davis's conduct of the war. They spoke their minds freely. Yet the demands of fighting a separatist revolt prevented any change in government.

CIVIL WAR MANPOWER

	UNION	CONFEDERACY
Total serving in armed forces	1,556,678	1,082,119
Killed in battle or died from wounds	110,070	94,000
Died from illness	249,458	164,000
Wounded	275,175	100,000

Many a Civil War battle exacted enormous tolls in men. Above, Confederate dead lie in a shallow trench at Chancellorsville. Union forces, below, attack on the third day of the combat at Gettysburg. Watching a similarly dramatic panorama earlier in the war, Lee had remarked: "It is well that war is so terrible—we would grow too fond of it."

The major military actions of the fall of **1863** occurred in the west. On September 9 Union forces maneuvered the Confederates out of Chattanooga, Tennessee, without a battle. Moving south into Georgia, the Union army was stopped at Chickamauga (September 19-20) and driven back into Chattanooga. In October Grant was given command of all the Union's western armies. At the Battle of Chattanooga (November 23-25) he defeated the Confederates in engagements on Lookout Mountain and Missionary Ridge.

In **1864** Grant, now in supreme command of the Union armies, took charge of the Virginia front. He began a campaign to destroy Lee's army and take Richmond. Grant struck again and again: at the Battle of the Wilderness (May 5-6), at Spotsylvania (May 8-12), and at Cold Harbor (June 1-3). Lee parried Grant's blows, inflicting heavy casualties on his opponent. In this one-month period the Union army lost approximately 60,000 men, a number equal to Lee's total strength at the beginning of the campaign. But the North could provide reinforcements of men and supplies; the South lacked reserves of both. Grant pressed on, moving south to Petersburg. He failed to capture it in a bloody four-day battle (June 15-18). However, his subsequent nine-month siege of the town cut Richmond off from the Deep South.

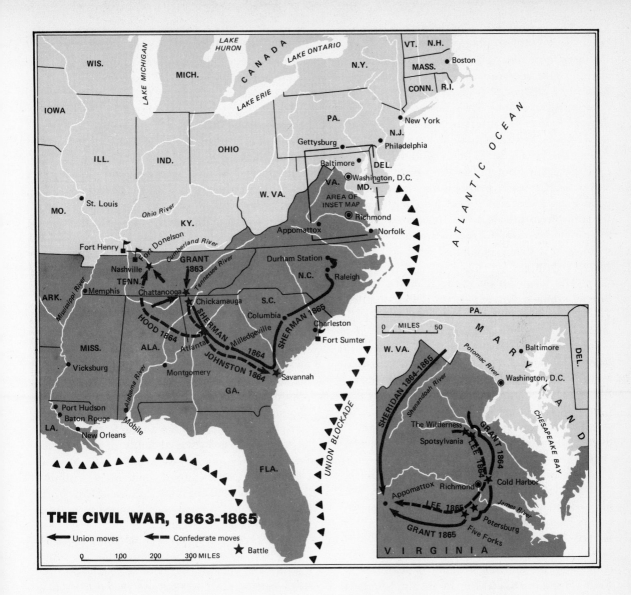

THE CIVIL WAR, 1863-1865

← Union moves   ←--- Confederate moves   ★ Battle

0   100   200   300 MILES

In the west, Union forces under Sherman moved out of Chattanooga in May 1864 to begin their invasion of Georgia. The opposing Confederate general, Joseph E. Johnston, fought a series of defensive actions but continued falling back toward Atlanta. John B. Hood, who replaced Johnston in July, suffered heavy losses in two pitched battles near Atlanta. It was occupied by Union forces on September 2. After the fall of Atlanta, Hood moved northwest to threaten Tennessee and the Union army's long lines of communication. Sherman sent part of his army to counter Hood's forces. He led the rest of his troops in a virtually unopposed march to the sea from Atlanta to Savannah, which fell on December 22. Meanwhile, Union forces shattered Hood's army at Nashville, Tennessee (December 15–16).

In 1865 Sherman continued his scorched-earth policy as he moved north from Savannah into North Carolina, where Johnston, restored to command, slowed his advance somewhat. In Virginia the Confederates, outnumbered more than two to one by Grant's reinforced army, were unable to lift the siege of Petersburg. On April 1, Lee's last attack (at Five Forks) was repulsed, and on April 2 he evacuated Petersburg and Richmond, moving westward. A Union army under Philip H. Sheridan, which had marched south through the Shenandoah Valley, blocked his path. Virtually surrounded by an overwhelming force, Lee surrendered to Grant at Appomattox on April 9. On April 18, Johnston surrendered to Sherman at Durham Station, North Carolina. Final Confederate capitulations occurred in Alabama (May 4) and Louisiana (May 26).

The war not only changed master-slave relations and Southern politics. It also altered the Southern economy. The cherished doctrine of states' rights received rough treatment at the hands of Confederate leaders. These men were determined to assume every power they needed to wage war. Davis centralized and nationalized the economy to a remarkable degree. If occasion demanded, he interfered freely with the rights of capitalists. The Confederacy did more than seize slaves for war work. It closely regulated foreign commerce. It confiscated food and equipment for the army from private farms. It created government-run industries to produce military equipment. And it tightly controlled what was left of private enterprise.

The Confederacy even created a Cotton Bureau, which took over planters' cotton supplies. The Cotton Bureau paid a set price for the entire crop. By running the Northern blockade, the government acted as the sole Southern salesman in Europe. Government supplies of cotton were used as security for the Confederacy's foreign loans. But the blockade grew daily more effective, and Confederate revenues from European cotton sales—its one important source of revenue—dwindled correspondingly during the war's final years.

In spite of truly heroic effort and sacrifice, the South was destitute by the end of the war. "We have no money, even for taxes, or for their confiscation," wrote Mrs. Chesnut in April 1865. "Our poverty is made a matter of laughing." Millions came close to starving. Confederate officials recommended the nutritional values of such fare as squirrels and rats to make up for the dire shortage of food. At the time of its surrender, Lee's army had enough ammunition to provide each man seventy-five rounds—but no food.

Southern economic devastation by 1865 could be measured in many ways. Compared to 1860, there were 32 percent fewer horses, 30 percent fewer mules, 35 percent fewer cattle, and 42 percent fewer pigs. Cotton crops were destroyed or rotted unpicked in the fields. Few factories remained in operation. There was almost no trade. Only a handful of banks were left, and they were nearly empty.

Prosperity in the North "We hear they have all grown rich," Mrs. Chesnut complained about Northerners in 1865. "Genuine Yankees can make a fortune trading jackknives!" Industrial growth in the North began before the Civil War, of course. But it was vastly accelerated by wartime demands to equip and supply the army. The number of Northern factories increased from fewer than 140,000 in 1860 to over 250,000 by 1870. Railroad mileage doubled during this decade. Growth in the North was aided not only by government contracts for arms and military supplies. It was helped also by wartime currency inflation, huge federal subsidies to railroads, and protective tariffs for industry.

The result was enormous inflation—high prices but also tremendous profits. There was rapid expansion in industries ranging from wool production to mining, from petroleum to iron manufacturing. Farmers prospered, too, because of the increased demand for every staple crop. Most merchants and shippers shared in the boom. Banking facilities were enlarged greatly after Congress passed several new banking acts. Senator John Sherman wrote his brother General William Sherman about the impact of the war on Northern capitalists: "They talk as confidently of millions as they formerly did of thousands." Aristocratic George Templeton Strong complained wistfully that the more sedate prewar culture of New York City was being "diluted and swamped by a great flood-tide of material wealth."

A shortage of manpower on Northern farms and in factories stimulated immigration from Europe. In 1865 alone, 180,000 new immigrants arrived on Union soil. In 1866 and 1867 the number spurted to 300,000 yearly.

Perhaps most important in the North, as in the Confederacy, was the role played by the government in stimulating economic growth. Southern Democrats had dominated Congress and the executive branch until the 1850s. They had blocked such measures as the protective tariff, a national banking system, and railroad subsidies. Now the Republicans were in control. They favored industrialization and economic growth. To further their aims, they adopted the Morrill Tariff of 1861, which raised duties. They passed the Na-

WALT WHITMAN

The poet who was best able to bring together the vitality and idealism of his generation was Walt Whitman. He was born in 1819 in Huntington, Long Island, the son of a carpenter-farmer father with leanings toward Quaker thought, and a sympathetic and understanding mother with very little education. He grew up in a family of nine children of whom both the oldest and the youngest were mentally retarded. Walter, as he was known in the family, left school early in his eleventh year and started a process of self-education that included moving from job to job—as printer's devil, compositor, carpenter, schoolteacher, newspaper writer, and editor.

Whitman's ideas were generated by his childhood in the farming and fishing community on Long Island—his associations with the haymakers and eel fishers, the baymen and pilots—and by the stimulating life of the city in which he worked. He roamed the streets, rode the ferries, and went regularly to the theater and the opera. Early in his life, books had become important to him. He read the Bible, Shakespeare, Ossian, the Greek tragic poets, the ancient Hindu poets, the Nibelungenlied, and the poems of Dante as well as Scott.

Politics were soon a consuming interest. The adult Whitman became an ardent Jacksonian and supporter of the Democratic party. Most of his newspaper jobs were with Democratic journals. The *Democratic Review* was one of the fine literary journals of the time and, through Whitman's work there, he met such literary figures as Hawthorne, Poe, Bryant, Longfellow, Thoreau, and others.

Whitman was especially imbued with the fire of Emerson's transcendentalist ideas. When *Leaves of Grass* appeared, Emerson wrote: "I am not blind to the worth of the wonderful gift of *Leaves of Grass*. I find it the most extraordinary piece of wit and wisdom that America has yet contributed . . . . I greet you at the beginning of a great career." But *Leaves of Grass*, in its first two printings in 1855 and 1856, was not a success. Some readers found it incomprehensible while others found the sexual implications shocking. With the mellowing of the author's language, finally in 1860 – 1861, the volume began to sell.

The Civil War became a critical influence in Whitman's life. Several of his articles at this time dealt with Broadway Hospital where he spent time helping the wounded. Then, in December 1862, he visited his wounded brother, George, a Union soldier, and suddenly realized that he had himself become a part of the war effort. With a part-time job for support, he spent the next three years serving the wounded in hospitals around the city of Washington and sometimes on the battlefields.

In 1865 Whitman published *Drum Taps*, the poems he had written during the war. Some poems are martial outbursts, describing the mobilization of the army. Others are quieter, describing a field hospital or his own lonely vigils with the dying and the dead.

Drum Taps was being printed when the news of Lincoln's assassination reached Whitman. He was inspired to write the dirge that many critics consider his masterpiece. The poem stresses that peace and beauty triumph in death, for death brings a joining of man and nature. It begins:

When lilacs last in the door-yard bloom'd
And the great star early droop'd
  in the western sky in the night,
I mourn'd — and yet shall mourn
  with ever-returning spring.
O ever-returning spring!
  trinity sure to me you bring;
Lilac blooming perennial
  and drooping star in the west,
And thought of him I love.

Richmond in April 1865. Only the shells of burned buildings surround the canal basin. Lee prepared to abandon the city on April 2, and mobs of its inhabitants set fire to the town on the eve of his evacuation.

tional Banking Acts of 1863 and 1864, which aided national banks at the expense of state banks. In addition, Congress awarded land-grant subsidies to transcontinental railroads and stimulated western settlement with the 1862 Homestead Act, which offered land to settlers for nominal sums.

The Republicans changed not only the economic habits of the North but its political life as well. Lincoln found it no easier than Davis did to govern a country at war. Throughout the conflict the President was attacked from all sides of his wartime government coalition, which was known as the Union party. Abolitionist Republicans (known as Radical Republicans) denounced him for moving slowly on the question of emancipation, while War Democrats denounced him for moving at all on the problem. Moderate Republicans criticized the slow military progress of the Northern armies.

Compared to the Confederacy, the North had a poor wartime record in the field of civil rights. In spite of Union victories, many Northerners opposed the war. Lincoln authorized a number of arbitrary military arrests of such civilians, especially Peace Democrats—called "Copperheads" by their enemies. He suspended the privi-

lege of habeas corpus[2] to keep pro-Confederate Northerners in jail once arrested.

In both sections, North and South, the war interfered with civil liberties, but in different ways. Northerners were more likely to be thrown in jail for opposing the war. Southerners were more likely to be punished for resisting government confiscation of their property. These interferences involved of course the civil rights of *white* people. Neither government troubled itself much about the rights of blacks, free or slave.

FREEDOM FOR BLACK PEOPLE

As soon as the war broke out, Northern black men tried to enlist in the Union army. They were not allowed to do so, however, until the fall of 1862. Eventually, over 186,000 blacks served as Union soldiers—almost 15 percent of all Northern troops.

[2]This privilege, guaranteed by the Constitution, provides that an arrested person can demand that legal authorities show why he or she has been imprisoned. A writ of habeas corpus (Latin words meaning "you have the body") thus protects a person against being held in jail without cause.

They were usually led by white officers and they were paid less than white troops. Union commanders were divided in their attitudes toward using black soldiers. Some welcomed them. Others, like Sherman, did not.

The Emancipation Proclamation Northern policy toward slavery changed during the war. Many Republicans in the government believed sincerely in emancipation. Lincoln, though, had always regarded it as secondary compared to the overriding importance of winning the war and reuniting the nation.

Like most Americans at the time, Lincoln believed that blacks were inferior. He never felt certain that 4 million ex-slaves could reach full equality with whites in the United States. Throughout the Civil War he tried unsuccessfully to link his moves toward emancipation with efforts to colonize freed blacks. None of these efforts worked out.

Lincoln had been elected on a platform that pledged to restrict slavery but not abolish it. He moved cautiously toward emancipation, mainly because of his military and political problems in conducting the war. Radical Republicans in Congress kept pressuring him for swift abolition. Even many moderate Northerners became fervent converts to emancipation as war casualties mounted, if only to punish the Confederacy. Such Unionists did not change their attitudes toward *black people* (and their supposed inferiority). They only changed their minds about *slavery*.

The situation was complicated by the fact that thousands of runaway slaves took refuge with the Union army. There, they were often treated— as with Sherman's army—as both a help and a hindrance. Thousands of blacks, however, did join Union army ranks. Lincoln, along with most Northerners, grew more sympathetic to emancipation.

Congress took the first step by abolishing slavery in the federal territories in June 1862. Then, in September 1862, Lincoln issued a preliminary proclamation. In it he stated that he would issue a final document on January 1, 1863, freeing the slaves in all states then in rebellion. This final document was the Emancipation Proclamation.

The Emancipation Proclamation actually freed very few people when it was issued. It did not apply to slaves in the border states fighting on the Union side. Nor did it affect slaves in Southern areas already under Union control. Naturally, the states in rebellion did not act on Lincoln's order. But the proclamation did show Americans, and the rest of the world, that the Civil War was now being fought to end slavery.

For all practical purposes the 3 1/2 million black slaves in the South found themselves free within days after Lee's surrender. It was only with final ratification of the Thirteenth Amendment, however, in December 1865, that slavery was ended completely throughout the United States.

Treatment in the North Though the Union— eventually, at least—fought to free black people, those who lived in the North faced many difficulties. In 1860 free Northern blacks numbered 225,000. Most of them were restricted to menial jobs. A rigid pattern of segregation in schools, hospitals, transportation, and other public facilities kept blacks and whites separated. Roughly 93 percent of Northern black people lived in states where they could not vote. (Only five New England states allowed blacks to cast ballots in 1865.)

Blacks were the victims of race riots throughout the North during the war. The most destructive took place in New York City in the summer of 1863. There, anger among the city's Irish working class at a new federal draft law exploded into violence during four days and nights of rioting. The new law allowed wealthy citizens to avoid the draft by buying the services of substitute soldiers—something poor laborers clearly could not afford.

Mobs of Irish workers rampaged over Manhattan Island from July 13 to July 16. They burned, looted, and killed. The rioters' main targets were free blacks and, to a lesser extent, white abolitionists and wealthy citizens. The city's outnumbered police force, also composed largely of Irishmen, fought the rioters with great bravery and discipline, finally putting down the rioting with the help of federal troops. By that time, some 1,200 persons, mostly black, had been killed.

Many thousands were injured. Property worth millions was damaged or destroyed. Other Northern cities, especially in the Middle West, experienced similar draft riots.

After the War The Thirteenth Amendment did not settle the basic questions about the future status of black Americans, especially in the postwar South. Former slaves were now free. But free to *do* what? Free to *be* what? What did freedom mean to someone raised in slavery?

Many ex-slaves simply stayed on their plantations, working for the same masters. Their old habits altered little at first, although now the whites were often as poor as their former bondsmen. "The Negroes seem unchanged," Mrs. Chesnut wrote, referring to her one-time slaves. Other former slaves left their old homes, usually for an uncertain future.

Whatever the fate of individual freed slaves, one characteristic of Southern emancipation was its peaceful nature. Despite the fears of

After General Lee surrendered the Army of Northern Virginia to General Grant at Appomatox on April 9, 1865, Confederate armies capitulated in North Carolina, Alabama, and Louisiana. Throughout the South, Confederate troops disbanded to return home, their ranks depleted by death and injury. In the days ahead, the returning veterans were to confront the desolation of a war-ravaged region: neglected fields, burned-out cities, and a worthless currency.

antebellum white Southerners, there were no bloodbaths, no vengeful attacks by ex-slaves on their former masters. Black people responded to their new freedom with dignity and grace.

Early in the twentieth century Benjamin Botkin and other folklorists traveled through the United States, recording the recollections of aged ex-slaves. One elderly man recalled:

> The end of the war, it come just like that—like you snap your fingers. Soldiers, all of a sudden, was everywhere—coming in bunches. Everyone was a-singing. We was all walking on golden clouds. Hallelujah! Everybody went wild! we was free. Just like that, we was free. It didn't seem to make the whites mad, either. They went right on giving us food just the same. Nobody took our homes away, but right off colored folks started on the move. They seemed to want to get closer to freedom, so they'd know what it was—like it was a place or a city.

The experience was exciting yet frightening for blacks, people like those who had joined Sherman's army on its march to Savannah. Many of them had never gone beyond the borders of their own farms. One ex-slave commented to Botkin:

> We knowed freedom was on us, but we didn't know what was to come with it. We thought we was going to be richer than the white folks, 'cause we was stronger and knowed how to work, and the whites didn't, and they didn't have us to work for them any more. But it didn't turn out that way. We soon found out that freedom could make folks proud, but it didn't make 'em rich.

As soon as the war was over, blacks began to organize and work for their own advancement. Historians sometimes overlook the fact that, even in 1860, there were 261,000 free blacks in the South. Tens of thousands of them were literate. These men and women—like the leaders who met with Stanton and Sherman—formed an important black leadership base at the end of the war. Many took part in black conventions held in a number of Southern cities in 1865 and 1866. They petitioned the federal government to assist freedom by granting them the franchise, protecting their civil rights, and providing land and other economic help.

THE FIRST YEAR OF RECONSTRUCTION

The basic dilemma of Reconstruction for all those who lived through it, black and white, Southerner and Northerner alike, was its revolutionary nature. Like the Civil War itself, the postwar period had no examples on which to model itself, no constitutional provisions by which policymakers might be guided.

Compared with reconstruction periods that have followed more recent civil wars in Russia, Spain, and China, the American experience was notably mild. Confederate leaders were neither shot nor driven into exile. Indeed, many resumed their careers in American politics. Only a few, such as Jefferson Davis, were imprisoned, and these only for a brief period. No Confederate property was confiscated. Nor was there any forced redistribution of wealth imposed on the defeated South by the victorious North.

Lincoln's Approach In Lincoln's Second Inaugural Address, delivered a month before his death, he called for a generous settlement with the defeated South: "With malice toward none, with charity for all . . . let us strive on to finish the work we are in, to bind up the nation's wounds."

As early as 1862 Lincoln had indicated his desire to restore a defeated Confederacy quickly and without revenge against either its leaders or its people. Lincoln suggested a basis for Reconstruction in December 1863. He called for amnesty[3] (except in the case of key leaders) for Southerners who pledged loyalty to the Union. Southern states in which 10 percent of the 1860 electorate took such a loyalty oath and accepted emancipation would be restored immediately to the Union.

Governments in Arkansas, Louisiana, and Tennessee met Lincoln's provisions in 1864. But Congress refused to seat their representatives.

---

[3]Amnesty is a form of pardon for offenses against the government—especially to a group of persons.

The problem was complicated by the fact that Lincoln believed that the executive branch should control Reconstruction, whereas Congress wanted this power for itself. Congressional attitudes were partly a reaction to the vast expansion of presidential authority under Lincoln during the Civil War.

Republicans in Congress were led by Radicals Thaddeus Stevens of Pennsylvania in the House and Charles Sumner of Massachusetts in the Senate. They were afraid that the Democratic party, led by Southern ex-Confederates, would quickly return to national power. So they offered a much tougher Reconstruction plan in a measure known as the Wade-Davis Bill. It provided that a majority of voters in each Southern state take an "ironclad oath" swearing to their *past* as well as to their *future* loyalty. Obviously, if the electorate were composed only of whites, no ex-Confederate state could honestly meet this provision. The bill also required that the Southern states abolish slavery in their constitutions, repudiate the Confederate war debt, and disfranchise Confederate leaders. Congress passed the Wade-Davis Bill on July 4, 1864. Lincoln killed the measure with a pocket veto. Then Congress passed the nonbinding Wade-Davis Manifesto, reasserting the provisions of the earlier bill.

Therefore, by mid-1864, the stage was set for a postwar confrontation between the President and Congress on Reconstruction policy. Was the

In September of 1862, President Lincoln visited with General McClellan and his officers at Antietam, where, as the Confederates advanced into Maryland, the Army of the Potomac had caught up with General Lee. After preliminary skirmishes, on September 17, McClellan defeated the Confederates in the bloodiest battle of the war. Lee retreated across the Potomac, where, to Lincoln's dismay, McClellan was reluctant to pursue him. Angered by his General's inability to exploit the Union victory, Lincoln removed McClellan from command.

South to be restored quickly, its new state governments falling into the hands of ex-Confederate whites with a minimum of federal interference? (This is what Lincoln wanted, though he did urge Southern whites to allow at least educated blacks to vote.) Or should the Southern states undergo fundamental political changes before they could rejoin the Union? Should they, for instance, allow blacks to vote and hold office, while disbarring ex-Confederate leaders and perhaps confiscating their land?

Assassination With the war almost over, Lincoln's thoughts had turned increasingly to the problem of reconstructing the South. After a trip to Richmond early in April 1865, he spent several days working out various programs.

On the night of April 14, Good Friday evening, President and Mrs. Lincoln went to Ford's Theater in Washington to see a popular play, *Our American Cousin*. Shortly after 10 P.M. a half-crazed Southern sympathizer named John Wilkes Booth shot Lincoln as he watched the play. Booth then stabbed another member of the President's party, leaped onto the stage, rushed from the theater, and rode away. (He was shot down on April 26 by Union troops that had pursued him into Virginia.)

The wounded Lincoln was taken from Ford's theater to a nearby house. There family, friends, and government officials kept an all-night vigil. The President remained unconscious until his death at 7:22 the following morning. "Now he belongs to the ages," said Secretary of War Stanton, one of those at his bedside.

Word of Lincoln's assassination spread quickly via the telegraph. The first reaction to the event, shared by most Northerners and even many Southerners, was one of profound shock: "I am stunned," wrote George Templeton Strong, "as by a fearful personal calamity."

For Lincoln was highly popular in the North at the time of his death, a result of Union military victories beginning in 1863 and culminating in Lee's surrender. During the war itself, Southerners—as one might expect—had little affection for "Uncle Abraham." Many Northerners felt the same way, especially in the early years.

One such person was Strong, an aristocrat and avowed snob. He never liked Lincoln's lack of polish and fondness for telling jokes. Yet these very qualities endeared the President to most other Americans. And even Strong, like other Unionists, responded to Lincoln's firm leadership and genuine anguish at the war's increasing toll in human suffering: "It must be referred to the Attorney General," Lincoln once told Strong about a request to pardon a criminal. "But I guess it will be all right, for me, and the Attorney General's very chicken-hearted."

By the war's end, most Northerners probably agreed with Strong's high estimate of Lincoln's wartime achievement. The President's "weaknesses are on the surface," Strong wrote on April 11, 1865. "His name will be of high account fifty years hence, and for many generations thereafter."

Johnson's Plan Lincoln's death placed the burden of reconstructing the South on the shoulders of his former Vice President, Andrew Johnson. Johnson was a War Democrat from Tennessee and a one-time Radical on the Reconstruction issue. Once in the White House, however, he soon adopted Lincoln's basic proposals. Unfortunately, Johnson completely lacked Lincoln's basic sympathy for the problems of freed blacks. Also, he was a dogmatic man. He showed almost none of Lincoln's tact in dealing with political opponents.

Johnson, like Lincoln, believed that Reconstruction was a matter to be handled by the President. His position was strengthened by the fact that Congress was not in session for several months after he took office. Johnson readmitted the states of Arkansas, Louisiana, and Tennessee. In May 1865 he issued his own Reconstruction plan. It provided that whites in each Southern state who pledged their future loyalty to the Union could elect delegates to a state convention. This convention had to revoke the ordinance of secession, abolish slavery, and repudiate the Confederate war debt. Then the state would be restored to the Union. Johnson granted amnesty to almost all Confederates who took the oath of allegiance. The exceptions were wealthy people and

Johnson was an honest but tactless man forced to cope with uniquely difficult circumstances. Born poor, he was a self-made man and touchy about it. Jefferson Davis said he had "the pride of having no pride."

high officials. Even they could apply for a presidential pardon. By late 1865 all the Southern states except Texas had complied with these provisions. (Texas did so early in 1866.)

Southern Regulation of Blacks Congress believed that the government had a duty to assist freedmen after the war. So in March 1865 it created the Freedmen's Bureau, a temporary federal assistance agency headed by Oliver O. Howard. The bureau distributed food and medicine to poor blacks (and whites), opened schools, supervised land distribution to freedmen, and tried to defend the civil rights of Southern blacks. (It exercised these functions in helping "Sherman's Negroes" in the resettlement program.)

The Freedmen's Bureau, however, could not protect the physical security of black South-

erners without the help of Union troops. This problem was clearly a most urgent one. Brutal riots against blacks occurred in Memphis and New Orleans in 1866.

After Appomattox, Union troops were mustered out of the army at a rapid rate. By the end of 1865 only 150,000 soldiers remained of the million serving six months earlier. Many of these were stationed on isolated western posts fighting Indians.

Under these conditions it was impossible for Union troops to offer the 4 million Southern blacks, most of them recently freed, any real protection. Most white Southerners had been raised to believe that blacks had no civil rights that whites were bound to respect. Killings, beatings, burnings, and other forms of physical terror directed against blacks — mostly to keep them out of politics — began soon after the war's end. Violence against blacks was often carried out by white secret societies. Several were formed after the war, primarily to keep blacks from voting. The most famous, the Ku Klux Klan, was founded in 1866. The turmoil increased during the 1870s.

Many whites in the South adopted other means to reduce black people to a state of virtual enslavement. In every Southern state new governments were elected by voters according to the provisions of Johnson's Reconstruction plan. But the Johnson state governments, as they were called, allowed no blacks to vote. They adopted so-called Black Codes to regulate the actions and behavior of freedmen. Southern whites claimed that such codes were necessary because of the threat of social disorder as a result of emancipation. There had been no major instance, however, of blacks rioting against whites anywhere in the region.

The Black Codes had some provisions to protect blacks. They legalized marriages between blacks, for instance. They also gave blacks the right to sue and testify in court. But the codes consisted mainly of restrictions. They supervised the movements of blacks, prevented them from carrying weapons, and forbade intermarriage between blacks and whites. Contracts, sometimes for life, forced black people to remain at their jobs. In some states, blacks could not own land or work at

Stern, intense, and militant, Thaddeus Stevens attacked Lincoln throughout the war for not punishing the South harshly enough.

Charles Sumner, once admonished during an argument, "But you forget the other side," thundered in reply: "There is no other side!"

any job other than farming without a special license. Black children were forced into certain job apprenticeships.

Reaction in the North Northern Republicans, both Radicals and moderates, attacked the Johnson state governments. They denounced the Black Codes and called for their immediate repeal. Most Radicals believed that the defeated Southern states should be treated, in Thaddeus Stevens's phrase, like "conquered provinces," until more repentant leaders emerged.

When Congress reconvened in December 1865, representatives and senators elected under the Johnson state governments applied for admission. Republicans in Congress refused to admit them. These Southerners who now claimed loyalty to the Union included fifty-eight former Confederate congressmen, six of Jefferson Davis's cabinet members, and four Southern generals. Most amazing of all was the presence of Alexander Stephens of Georgia, who eight months earlier had been vice president of the Confederacy!

The 1866 riots in Memphis and New Orleans gave Northerners additional evidence that the white South remained unrepentant. Thus it seemed inevitable that there would be a power struggle between Johnson and congressional

Republicans over who would control the Reconstruction process. Who was sovereign in the federal government, the President or Congress? Who could decide?

RADICAL RECONSTRUCTION

Congress answered these questions to its own satisfaction by taking the initiative completely out of Johnson's hands. By 1867 the legislature had won control. It dominated the government for the next ten years.

The Republicans who controlled Congress developed their strategy mainly through the Joint Committee on Reconstruction, which was dominated by the Radicals. This group asserted that Southern states could be readmitted only after meeting congressional requirements. The Joint Committee moved a series of measures through Congress between 1865 and 1867. Most of the bills were vetoed by the hapless Johnson, then repassed by a two-thirds majority.

First, in February 1866, came the new Freedmen's Bureau bill. It expanded the bureau's authority to protect Southern blacks, giving it the right to try in military courts persons accused of violating the civil rights of freedmen.

A Civil Rights Act of April 1866 granted to blacks the same civil rights as those enjoyed by whites. The measure also asserted the right of the federal government to interfere in state affairs to protect a citizen's civil rights.

In order to fortify their position, congressional Republicans in June 1866 adopted and sent to the states the Fourteenth Amendment. In effect, it gave blacks full citizenship. If a state denied the vote to blacks, its representation in the House would be reduced. The amendment also forbade ex-Confederate officials from holding federal or state office again without receiving congressional pardon. The Joint Committee declared that any Southern state wishing readmission would have to ratify the Fourteenth Amendment. The Johnson state governments in the South voted against ratification. (The amendment was eventually ratified in 1868.)

President Johnson hoped his Republican opponents would be defeated in the 1866 congressional election, and he campaigned personally against them. After a wild and bitterly fought campaign, however, anti-Johnson Republicans swept the election. They carried every Union state but three.

A Harsh Program   When Congress met after the election, Republicans enacted their program into law. They began with the First Reconstruction Act of March 1867. Significantly, the bill's final form came from a moderate, Republican John Sherman. By this time the moderates agreed with Radicals on most key issues of Reconstruction. This law abolished the existing Johnson state governments. It provided for universal male suffrage – that is, for black as well as white voting.

The First Reconstruction Act also authorized temporary military rule of the South. Ten former Confederate states were still outside the Union. (Tennessee had ratified the Fourteenth Amendment and had been readmitted.) These states were divided into five military districts. To rejoin the Union, a state had to call a constitutional convention elected by universal male suffrage. This body, in turn, had to create a new state government that would ratify the Fourteenth Amendment and guarantee black suffrage. Three subsequent congressional acts strengthened the powers of federal army commanders in the South.

The final act in the congressional drama of Radical Reconstruction involved the effort in 1868 to remove the President through impeachment. Congress had good reason to believe that Johnson would do everything in his power to sabotage the Reconstruction acts. From 1865 to 1868, he had worked to impede every major step Congress had taken to assist Southern blacks or to enforce a harsh settlement upon the white South. In the process, Johnson had systematically interfered with congressional statutes, practically crippling effective operation (for one thing) of the Freedmen's Bureau throughout the South (as in his interference with Sherman's land program) by presidential directives.

Johnson, moreover, had appointed as federal officials in the region (including even provision-

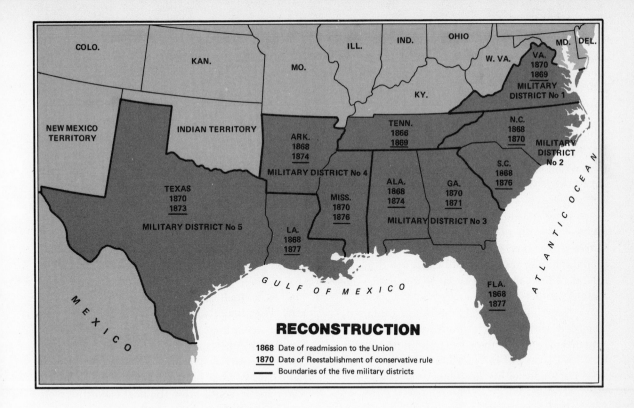

RECONSTRUCTION

1868 Date of readmission to the Union
<u>1870</u> Date of Reestablishment of conservative rule
— Boundaries of the five military districts

al governors) ex-Confederates who had not yet even taken the oath of allegiance to the Union. He used his presidential appointment powers ruthlessly to subvert congressional aims on Reconstruction, claiming for himself absolute direction of the process even after Congress had rejected his early effort to form state governments without first securing their approval. Johnson's view of presidential authority was a broad, almost modern one (as Lincoln's had been—but during the wartime emergency). At all times, Johnson lacked his predecessor's tact in dealing with those who disagreed with him—especially in Congress.

Johnson's recurrent efforts to undermine the program of congressional Reconstruction through issuing conflicting orders to federal officials (both military and civil) in the South provoked Republican moderates and radicals to combine in self-defense. An unprecedented special session was called which passed two measures on March 2, 1867.

One of the measures virtually deprived Johnson of command of the American army by requiring him to issue all military orders through the General of the Army, Ulysses S. Grant. The second was the Tenure of Office Act. It prohibited the President from removing those officials whose appointments had been made with Senate consent, without again securing Senate approval. This law meant that Johnson could not, for example, arbitrarily fire Secretary of War Stanton. This leading Radical was the man who—along with Saxton and Howard—had tried to block presidential interference with Sherman's land distribution policy. Johnson disregarded the measure and dismissed Stanton. Then the House passed a resolution impeaching Johnson on eleven charges, including alleged violations of the two March 2 bills.

After a Senate trial, the President was acquitted, although even some of his supporters acknowledged that they were less concerned with retaining Johnson—considering him an inept and insensitive chief executive—than they were with upholding the office of the presidency. If Johnson were successfully removed by impeachment, they felt, the process would rupture violently the normal relations between the three coordinate branches of national government. Both sides in the struggle argued from reasonable positions, and the entire impeachment process indicated the underlying strength of the constitutional mechanisms, even when tested in the midst of dire political crisis.

A two-thirds majority is needed to convict the President on an impeachment charge. Thirty-five senators voted for his conviction, while nineteen (including seven Republicans) voted for acquittal. Thus Johnson was saved by a one-vote margin.

After his acquittal, Johnson grudgingly complied with the tacit promises made by his supporters to secure the votes of borderline senators. No longer did he interfere actively—for the brief remainder of his presidency—with enforcement of duly passed congressional statutes on Southern Reconstruction or with those officials charged with enforcing these laws. For the moment, Congress controlled the Reconstruction process.

The effort to unseat Johnson was the most daring episode in the Radicals' Reconstruction plans. A few Radicals such as Stevens tried to push through bills confiscating 394 million acres of land owned by the 70,000 chief leaders of the Confederacy. (Charles Sumner called the antebellum plantations "nurseries of the Rebellion.") But such measures found little support among the party's moderate majority, and therefore they did not pass.

Most aims of the Radicals were fairly limited. They worked chiefly for Republican political control of the national government. They also hoped that coalitions of black voters and friendly whites would dominate Southern politics, thereby preventing national revival of the Democratic party.

But Republicans did not have any direct social or economic goals. Only a small number of Radicals were committed to complete equality for black Americans. There was no large-scale program to provide landless freedmen with an economic base. Many blacks had been promised "forty acres and a mule." But the thousands resettled on abandoned lands—such as "Sherman's Negroes" of the Deep South—were soon dispossessed.

After the attempt to impeach Johnson, Radicals left the problems of Reconstruction in the hands of federal commanders and new state governments in the South. The quarrel between legislative and executive branches over Southern policy ended in 1868, when Republican Ulysses S. Grant was elected President. By then the central drama of Reconstruction had shifted from Washington to the South itself.

The New Radical Governments Beginning in 1867, so-called Radical state governments were set up according to congressional regulations. New black voters made up a majority of the Radical electorate in five states—Alabama, Florida, Louisiana, Mississippi, and South Carolina. Elsewhere in the South, white Radical majorities were supported by black voters. By 1870 more than 700,000 blacks and 627,000 whites were registered as voters under the Radical state constitutions.[4]

Congress readmitted Louisiana and six other states to the Union under Radical rule in June 1868. By the end of 1870 all ten ex-Confederate states had been readmitted to the Union.

Throughout the South blacks filled public offices for the first time. These were not usually the highest offices, however. Nor did blacks hold office in proportion to their percentage of voters. Only one state legislature, that of South Carolina, ever had a black majority. No black ever became a Reconstruction Southern governor. (Some states, though, had black lieutenant governors.) There were two black United States senators and fifteen congressmen during the entire period of Radical rule.

---

[4]The Fifteenth Amendment, adopted in 1870, forbade any state from preventing citizens from voting because of race, color, or "previous condition of servitude." This was a clear effort to eliminate the hypocrisy of some Northern states that demanded suffrage for blacks in the South while continuing to deny it at home.

Congressional Reconstruction not only disfranchised many former Confederates but ensured the suffrage to black men throughout the South, who went to the polls for the first time. By 1867, black voters constituted a majority in half of the former Confederate states. Although during the course of Reconstruction blacks were elected to many public offices, at no time did they control the Governors' offices, state legislatures, or Reconstruction politics.

Many black political leaders were educated men. Some were among the most distinguished figures in the entire South. Francis L. Cardozo, for example, South Carolina's state treasurer, held degrees from the universities of London and Glasgow, making him perhaps the best-educated politician in the South of either race.

Who were the Radicals in the South? They included many different groups. Some were Southerners, most of whom had been prewar Whigs or secret Union sympathizers during the war. Many Southern businessmen and even a few planters joined the Radicals. They hoped that the new governments would have enough help from Northern capitalists and Republican politicians to rebuild the South's shattered economy. Radicals also included nonslaveholding farmers, who, while they disliked blacks, hated ex-Confederates even more for having led them into what they considered (at least after its loss) "a rich man's war and a poor man's fight." These Southern-born Radicals were called scalawags (an often undeserved term) by former Confederates.

Other Radicals were Northerners. Tens of thousands of them went south after the war for a variety of reasons. Hostile whites referred to them bitterly as carpetbaggers, whose only aim was to fill their luggage with ill-gotten Southern wealth. Yet many were teachers—their carpetbags stuffed only with McGuffey's Readers. Like the people who went to the Sea Islands, their aim was to set up schools for the freedmen. Northern soldiers returned to the South seeking good land; 5,000 went to Louisiana alone. Businessmen sought opportunities to invest capital and to profit from the region's economic reconstruction. A number of politically ambitious people did arrive to take part in the Radical governments. But they were by no means all opportunists.

Charges of Corruption   It has often been said that Radical state governments were corrupt. There is some truth to this charge. Legislators in South Carolina, for example, paid $200,000 for $18,000 worth of furniture for the state capitol. Louisiana's Radical governor H. C. Warmouth left the state with a personal fortune of half a million dollars, most of it acquired illegally. Similar fortunes were made throughout the South.

Several points should be noted in favor of the Radical governments, however. At this time scandals tainted the Grant administration and many Northern state and local governments. The historian John Hope Franklin has termed public dishonesty after the Civil War "bisectional, bipartisan, and biracial." (Actually, the blacks in Congress were not implicated in the Grant scandals, although many of their white colleagues were.) State governments everywhere ran up enormous debts. Postwar fortunes in the South were made by Radicals and ex-Confederates, Republicans and Democrats, alike. Given the level of immorality in American politics, North and South, during Reconstruction, it seems fair to say that the Radicals were no more corrupt than other politicians at the time.

In fact, most Radical state funds were spent rebuilding a ruined economy. Somehow, the Radicals managed to begin reconstructing Southern highways, railroads, hospitals, and orphanages. They also began building schools; many Southern states had had no public school system before the war. The rebuilding had to be done for an additional 3 1/2 million people. These were the ex-slaves, who were now citizens and entitled to the use of public facilities.

An Evaluation   Historians have long debated whether Radical state governments in the South ruled poorly or well. Opinions on this question depend in part on attitudes about whether (or when) blacks should have been allowed the franchise and a role in governing. We tend to forget how short a time Radical governments actually ruled. Tennessee never underwent this type of control. Virginia, North Carolina, and Georgia had returned to conservative hands by 1871. Arkansas, Alabama, and Texas had done so by 1874. And it was all over by 1877.

Some provisions of the Radical state constitutions found approval even among ex-Confederates. The documents ended imprisonment for debt, for example, and did away with property qualifications for voting. Basically, ex-Confederate whites objected less to the corruption of Radical state governments than to their very existence—especially to the presence of blacks on the political slate. Radical rule did not end because of its failure to meet the economic and social problems of the South. Radicals were driven from power because of their insistence on meeting these problems through biracial political cooperation.

THE END OF RADICAL RULE

Two trends put an end to Radical Reconstruction. One was the increasing hostility of white Southerners. The other was the growing indifference of its Northern Republican sponsors.

Southern hostility not only increased, but it grew more violent. Thousands of blacks and white Radicals lost their lives to armed bands of whites such as the Ku Klux Klan and local "rifle clubs" that roamed the South during the 1870s. Federal troops and black state militia could suppress only a small number of these groups. Congress passed several Force Bills, making it a national offense to interfere with any citizen's civil rights (including his right to vote). But they had little effect, since only a few thousand federal troops remained in the South to enforce the laws against guerrilla groups like the Klan. To compound the Radicals' problem, Congress repealed its ironclad oath in 1871. No longer did Southerners have to swear

Louisiana was one of five Southern states to have a majority of black voters. Between 1868 and 1896 the state had 133 black legislators—38 senators and 95 representatives. They were never numerous or strong enough to control political life in Louisiana, though Oscar Dunn (center) did lead a struggle against corruption and extravagance.

Reconstructionist efforts to ensure black civil and political rights were undercut economically by the rapid emergence of sharecropping. Devoid of financial resources to buy their own land, many freedmen began to work the farms of landowners, who, also short of cash, paid them for their labor with a "share" of the crop. Soon indebted to landowners for such costs as rent, provisions, and tools, sharecroppers often became tied down by debt, as securely as they had been held by slavery.

that they had always been loyal to the Union. In 1872 a general amnesty restored civil rights (including the right to hold office) to all but about 600 high Confederate officials.

As white terrorists harassed the remaining Radical state governments, Northerners became indifferent. Republicans in Washington grew increasingly weary of the struggle to protect black civil rights. "The whole public," complained President Grant, "is tired of these outbreaks in the South."

The death or retirement of such Radical leaders as Stevens and Sumner helped restore control of Congress to more conservative, business-minded Republicans. A combination of Democrats and reform-minded "Liberal Republicans" nearly won the presidency in 1872 on a platform pledging an end to federal support for Radical regimes in the South. In 1874 the Democrats regained control of the House for the first time since before the war.

Public attention strayed even further away from the South after 1873, when a major depression swept the country. The business slump threw hundreds of thousands out of work and shifted political attention from postwar Reconstruction to the problem of economic recovery.

The Compromise of 1877 In 1876 both presidential candidates, Republican Rutherford B. Hayes and Democrat Samuel B. Tilden, promised even before the election to restore "home rule" to the South. Both pledged to remove federal support for the three remaining Radical state governments — those of Louisiana, South Carolina, and Florida. They implied that Southern whites could now

The violence of new vigilante groups, such as the Knights of the Ku Klux Klan, contributed to the overthrow of Republican rule and the demise of Reconstruction. A secret, terrorist society, the Klan formed in 1867 to restore white supremacy by harassing Reconstructionists, intimidating black voters, forcing black officials into resignation, and depriving freedmen of their rights. The tactics of the Klan ranged from pressure, ostracism, and bribery, to arson, beatings, and murder.

handle all problems connected with blacks, including political rights.

The election ended in a unique stalemate. Two sets of returns arrived from the three states yet in Radical hands. The Radicals claimed that Hayes had won, while Democrats insisted on a Tilden majority. The nineteen doubtful electoral votes (including one disputed Oregon elector) meant the difference between a one-vote Hayes margin and a clear Tilden sweep. Congress finally accepted the recommendation of a specially appointed commission to award all the disputed votes to Hayes, thereby making him President. The South, in turn, received a pledge from Hayes that all remaining federal troops would be removed from the three Radical states, that federal subsidies would be provided for a Southern transcontinental railroad then under construction, and

that a Southerner would be appointed to the cabinet.

All these promises were met, and Radical rule promptly collapsed in the three remaining states. This so-called Compromise of 1877 marked the final surrender of the North's promise to defend black political and civil rights against the former white Confederates.

During the decades that followed, conservative governments defeated black efforts to participate in Southern politics. In every subsequent election fewer blacks voted.

Violence toward black people increased for the rest of the century. The great majority of Southern blacks farmed other people's lands as tenants or sharecroppers. They were forced into a subordinate place in Southern life, being neither slaves nor completely free men.

SUGGESTED READINGS-CHAPTERS 23-24

Sherman's March

T. H. Williams, *McClellan, Sherman, and Grant* (1962); K. P. Williams, *Lincoln Finds a General: A Military History of the Civil War* (4 vols., 1949–1956); Lloyd Lewis, *Sherman, Fighting Prophet* (1932).

The Civil War

Mark M. Boatner, III, *The Civil War Dictionary* (1959); Bruce Catton, *Centennial History of the Civil War* (3 vols., 1961–1963); David Donald, ed., *Why the North Won the Civil War* (1960); Clement Eaton, *A History of the Southern Confederacy* (1954); Shelby Foote, *The Civil War* (3 vols., 1958–1974); George Frederickson, *The Inner Civil War* (1965); Paul W. Gates, *Agriculture and the Civil War* (1965); David T. Gilchrust and W. David Lewis, eds., *Economic Change in the Civil War Era* (1965); Harold M. Hyman, *A More Perfect Union: The Impact of the Civil War and Reconstruction on the Constitution* (1973); Mary E. Massey, *Bonnet Brigades: American Women and the Civil War* (1966); James M. McPherson, *The Negro's Civil War* (1965) and *The Struggle for Equality:*
Abolitionists and the Negro in the Civil War and Reconstruction (1964); Allan Nevins, *The War for the Union* (4 vols., 1959–1971); Peter J. Parish, *The American Civil War* (1975); J. G. Randall and Richard Current, *Lincoln the President* (4 vols., 1945–1955); J. G. Randall and David Donald, *The Civil War and Reconstruction* (2nd ed., 1961); Benjamin P. Thomas, *Abraham Lincoln* (1952); Emory Thomas, *The Confederacy as a Revolutionary Experience* (1971); Frank Vandiver, *Their Tattered Flags* (1970); Kenneth P. Williams, *Lincoln Finds a General* (5 vols., 1949–1959).

Reconstruction

W. R. Brock, *An American Crisis* (1963); Robert Cruden, *The Negro in Reconstruction* (1969); John Hope Franklin, *Reconstruction After the Civil War* (1962); Rembert W. Patrick, *The Reconstruction of the Nation* (1964); Kenneth M. Stampp, *The Era of Reconstruction, 1865–1877* (1965); Hans L. Trefousse, *Impeachment of a President* (1975); C. Vann Woodward, *Reunion and Reaction: The Compromise of 1877 and the End of Reconstruction* (1951).

UNIT FIVE

INDUSTRIAL AMERICA

Americans thought about their Civil War in many different ways. But most of them agreed, North and South, that it was somehow a conservative war. Each side thought of itself as the conserving protector of an inherited social and political order. It was difficult for Americans to understand that what lay ahead was not a restoration of stability but a surprising burst of activity and change. The United States was transformed into a modern industrial nation in the last third of the nineteenth century. That transformation is the subject of Unit Five.

The examination, in Chapter 25, of the career of President James A. Garfield and of his assassination in 1881 by a crazed, disappointed office-seeker introduces the climate of political tensions. Chapter 26 then traces the conditions that made political careers such as Garfield's possible.

In an odd way, the people who could best have understood the revolutionary transformations of American society were those who had been most completely defeated by it: the American Indians. From the time of Jamestown, they had watched white society grow in size and power. Now, the forces of expansion increased dramatically. Railroads, miners, cattle ranchers, and farmers spilled out over the Great Plains to the Pacific Coast with fresh speed and energy.

One of the tribes that felt the forces of westward expansion most directly was the Sioux. By the close of the century, this determined people had been reduced from proud independence to reservation captivity. The destruction of their way of life reached a symbolic climax in 1890 in the battle involving Indians and United States soldiers in American American history—Wounded Knee. The defeat of the Sioux is the subject of Chapter 27. The following chapter discusses the larger process of white expansion that made their final conquest inevitable.

At the same time that postwar America was expanding geographically, a new economic landscape took shape. New inventions and manufacturing processes changed the ways that Americans earned their livings and made their goods. Giant factories in enormous cities with great immigrant and working-class populations arose. With them came the inevitable conflicts between rich and poor, employers and workers, immigrants and native Americans.

One of the most important examples of conflict was a series of events in Chicago in 1885 and 1886. It began with a labor strike at the McCormick Harvester Company, led to a famous bombing incident at Haymarket Square, and ended in the trial and execution of several immigrant German Americans.

Chapter 29 tells this story and Chapter 30 explores the background of industrialization that made the conflict possible.

Social and economic change created strains on political parties and governmental institutions, which resulted in a curious blend of politics. On the one hand the politics of the 1890s was intense in nature and characterized by close electoral contests, while on the other it was extraordinarily flat and lacking in any real economic or social significance. The emergence and failure of Populism is discussed in Chapters 31 and 32.

What comes through, then, from the late nineteenth century is a mixed picture of incredible industrial growth and geographical expansion alongside moments of crisis and bloodshed—with political leaders looking on as almost helpless and often confused spectators.

25
THE ASSASSINATION OF GARFIELD

A.W.

On the morning of July 2, 1881, the President of the United States, James Abram Garfield, was strolling toward a waiting train in a railroad depot in Washington. The train, scheduled to depart at 9:30 A.M., was to take him on the first leg of a trip to Williams College, his alma mater. There he was to address a class reunion and enroll his two sons. Walking alongside the President and chatting with him was the secretary of state, James G. Blaine, a close political associate and friend. Already inside the train were Garfield's two sons and other members of his cabinet.

The President and the secretary of state walked toward the train platform. Neither noticed a thin, bearded figure dressed in shabby and unpressed clothing, staring at them from a few feet away. The two men broke off their conversation for a moment and prepared to step aboard the train.

Suddenly the man who had been watching them drew a pistol from his pocket. He pointed it at the President and fired twice. Garfield fell to the ground, crying out only "My God!" before he fainted. Blood spurted onto his gray traveling suit.

At the sound of the shots, Blaine had lunged toward the assassin. But when he saw the President lying on the ground, he quickly returned to his side. Along with others who had reached the scene, Blaine raised the wounded man's head. Garfield regained consciousness almost immediately.

Garfield's two sons and the cabinet members rushed from the train to join the crowd of onlookers. Some railroad workers gently lifted the heavy-set man and placed him on a ragged mattress, brought hastily from a nearby room. The first physician to arrive was Dr. Smith Townsend, the District of Columbia health officer. The doctor assumed from Garfield's appearance that the chief executive was dying. Townsend

SHOT DOWN.

President Garfield Dangerously Wounded.

AN ASSASSIN'S WORK.

Fired at Entering the Railroad Depot at Washington.

THE SERIOUS HIP WOUND.

Carried in an Ambulance to the White House.

CHEERFUL IN THE FACE OF DEATH.

Grave Symptoms Succeeded by a More Hopeful Condition.

A STRONG MAN'S STRUGGLE

Arrest and Imprisonment of the Criminal.

CHARLES JULES GUITEAU.

An Erratic Creature of Low Antecedents—His Strange History.

MRS. GARFIELD'S SORROW

She Reaches Washington and Meets Her Husband.

INTENSE EXCITEMENT—WORLDWIDE SYMPATHY

SCENE OF THE ASSASSINATION.

Map of Washington Showing Location of the Baltimore and Potomac Railroad Depot.

After less than six months in office President Garfield was shot by a disgruntled office seeker, Charles Guiteau, as Secretary of State James G. Blaine looked on. Though the President was in a public place, he had no Secret Service protection.

gave the injured man aromatic spirits of ammonia and some brandy to ease his pain. Then he inspected the more serious of the two wounds Garfield had received—the one on the lower right side of his back. Garfield winced. The doctor's touch had reopened the wound. Townsend's face and manner remained grim but, somewhat mechanically, he assured Garfield that his back wound was not serious. "I thank you, doctor," replied Garfield in evident pain, "but I am a dead man."

After firing the shots, the assassin calmly returned the pistol to his pocket. Then, as anxious and curious spectators surrounded the bleeding President, he rushed toward a railway station exit. Just as he reached it, the exit's massive door burst open. The man who had shot the President found himself face to face with Patrick Kearney, a District of Columbia patrolman. Kearney had been running toward the sound of the shots. In an attempt to flee past the policeman, the slender, dark-complexioned figure mumbled in an excited voice, "I have a letter to send to General Sherman."[1]

Kearney, sensing that the agitated man was somehow connected with the earlier pistol cracks and the crowd now gathering on the platform, held onto him. Several railroad employees raced to the exit and reported that the President had been shot. The policeman then rushed his prisoner away from the scene. As they left the station, the man finally spoke, saying: "I did it. I will go to jail for it; [Vice President] Arthur is President."

When Kearney reached the police station, his fellow officers would not believe that Garfield had been shot. It took a few minutes before they accepted the patrolman's story. Kearney himself, still excited over having captured the man who had tried to kill the President, did not even take possession of the prisoner's gun until they had reached the stationhouse. For that matter, only then did the patrolman think to ask the assassin his name. The prisoner reached into his pocket, withdrew a small printed calling card, and handed it to Kearney, who stared at the name and address: Charles Guiteau, Chicago, Ill.

The President, meanwhile, had been carried to a police ambulance, which rushed him back to the White House. There he was placed in a second-floor bedroom. Dozens of physicians, family members, government officials, and well-wishers scurried about the sickroom for the remainder of the day. A horde of newspapermen also managed to reach the sickroom door. They pestered each visitor to the President's bedside for fresh news of his condition.

The physicians all agreed that Garfield's back wound was too serious to allow immediate removal of the bullet. They felt they could do nothing but give the President large doses of morphine to dull his pain. Their frequent bulletins to the waiting reporters seldom varied in con-

---

[1]William Tecumseh Sherman was then commanding general of the American army.

tent: "The President's wounds are grave. He remains pale, weak, and cold. Although he is not bleeding profusely *externally*, there is every chance of massive *internal* hemorrhaging."

To doctors and reporters alike, this meant only one thing: the President was dying. Several members of Garfield's cabinet joined his family and physicians in the sickroom. Together they waited for further developments throughout the long night. At one point the secretary of war walked out into the corridor for a breath of air. He turned to a reporter and said: "How many hours of sorrow I have passed in this town." With this remark, Robert Todd Lincoln, Abraham Lincoln's son, reentered the sickroom.

Garfield's spirits, and his condition, improved greatly once his wife reached his bedside. She had been recuperating in New Jersey, following a malarial infection, but hurried to rejoin her husband on receiving word of the shooting. A special train brought her to Washington. Arriving at the White House in the early evening, she spent a few minutes alone with Garfield. Then she stationed herself outside his sickroom, praying and waiting for news. The President, after being told that she had gone to bed, fell asleep himself.

An hour later Garfield awoke. He turned to the attending physician, D. W. Bliss, who had taken charge of his treatment, and asked about

The public's view of Garfield as a homespun, simple man was reinforced by the fact that he was "the last of the log cabin Presidents." This painting of his birthplace in Orange, Ohio, gives us a nostalgic view of the pure and pastoral life of Garfield's youth.

his chances for recovery. He told the physician, as Dr. Bliss later remembered, "that he desired a frank and full statement, that he was prepared to die and feared not to learn the worst." Dr. Bliss, somewhat less than frank, replied: "Mr. President, your injury is formidable [but] in my judgment you have a chance for recovery." Garfield smiled and, placing his hand upon the doctor's arm, answered simply: "Well, doctor, we will take that chance." The warmth, good humor, and optimism that had characterized James Abram Garfield throughout his rise to the presidency did not desert him during this final struggle for life.

Garfield's rise to the presidency parallels the success story of several other nineteenth-century American Presidents. He was a man of humble origins and, like President Lincoln before him, had the good sense to be born in a log cabin. The log cabin had become the American symbol of homespun integrity and was therefore very useful to budding politicians.

Garfield, who was born in Ohio in 1831, was a seventh-generation American. His ancestors came to Massachusetts Bay with John Winthrop. His father was a pioneer Ohio farmer who died when Garfield was two. His mother, Eliza, raised the future President and three other children in bitter rural poverty.

As a boy, Garfield worked at a variety of jobs, helping to support his mother while striving to earn an education. After graduating from a neighboring school called Western Reserve Eclectic Institute (later changed to Hiram Institute), Garfield worked his way through Williams College in Massachusetts. He graduated from there in 1856. Returning to Ohio, Garfield served first as a teacher and then—though still in his twenties—as principal of Hiram Institute. In 1858 he married Lucretia Rudolph, his childhood sweetheart.

Throughout the 1850s Garfield exhibited the talents that were later to win him high political office. In 1859 he ran for, and won, the Republican seat in the Ohio senate. He made friends easily, worked furiously, displayed great tact and an ability to compromise, took few extreme positions, and—above all—sought to please. When the Civil War began, the young state legislator organized a volunteer infantry regiment composed largely of his former students. Although he had no previous military experience, he mastered the appropriate army training manuals quickly and well.

Colonel Garfield's regiment was assigned to the Union army command in Kentucky. There it defeated a much larger force of Confederate soldiers at the Battle of Middle Creek in January 1862. This victory earned Garfield the rank of brigadier general. After fighting at the Battle of Shiloh, he had to leave the field because of poor health. When he returned to active duty in 1863, he served with distinction during the important Battle of Chickamauga. Garfield left the army in December of 1863 with the rank of major general. He had been elected to the House of Representatives that fall.

Garfield was then thirty-two and extremely popular in Ohio's

Western Reserve district. This area returned him to Congress seven more times. His skill as a legislative leader and orator quickly made him a leading Republican in the House. So great was his personal popularity that Ohio voters reelected him despite the fact that they did not agree with him on many issues.

Garfield, like all successful officeholders, quickly learned the skill of political survival: when to speak out on an important question, when to blur an issue, and when to remain silent. During Hayes's administration Garfield's talent for bringing together different viewpoints within the Republican party led to his selection as House minority leader. Early in 1880 he was elected by the Ohio legislature to a six-year Senate term. But he never filled this seat.

It was in that year that the Republicans held their convention to nominate a presidential candidate. They were bitterly divided among three leading contenders—former President Ulysses S. Grant, Senator John Sherman of Ohio, and Senator James G. Blaine of Maine. There was a three-way deadlock on thirty-four ballots. On the thirty-fifth a break occurred. Garfield's name was put forward as a compromise candidate. On the thirty-sixth, Garfield, who had gone to the convention as Sherman's campaign manager, emerged with his party's nomination for President.

Blaine quickly became a close political ally. Sherman remained cordial, if untrusting. Grant's managers (particularly the influential New York Senator Roscoe Conkling) never forgave Garfield, despite the fact that Chester A. Arthur, Conkling's colleague from New York, was chosen to be Garfield's running mate. Garfield and Conkling did eventually smooth over their differences, and the Republicans carried a close election with a popular plurality of only 10,000 votes. James Garfield, a mild-mannered and unforceful politician, became President of the United States.

During his years in Congress, Garfield and his family had lived modestly. When Congress was in session, they stayed in Washington. At other times they made their home in Mentor, Ohio, a small agricultural town on Lake Erie, twenty-five miles from Cleveland. They had a farm there, which they called Lawnfield. Garfield enjoyed the farm work and rural way of life. He left Mentor for the last time in 1881, for Washington and his inauguration. The letters he wrote during his few months as Chief Executive show that he often yearned to return to the peaceful isolation of Lawnfield.

Although Garfield had been a professional politican for more than twenty years, by the time he entered the White House, he retained an avid interest in cultural matters. This interest, no doubt, was a carry-over from his days as a student, teacher, and college principal. Throughout his adult life he corresponded with some of the country's leading men of letters and reformers.

But Garfield himself was not a reformer. Throughout his legislative career he allied himself with railroad, industrial, and other estab-

The Republicans' compromise candidate of 1880, dark-horse nominee James A. Garfield (shown here as a young man).

lished interests. He expressed skepticism about reforms dealing with woman suffrage, contempt for proposals to assist the Indians, and indifference toward efforts to aid blacks. Above all, Garfield was a party "regular"—a politician whose primary concern was advancing his own fortunes and those of his party.

Garfield did not know that one of the proposals he ignored would eventually mark him for an assassin's bullet. The issue was civil-service reform, which advocated filling government posts by qualifying tests rather than by political appointment. Some minor steps toward such reform were taken by Garfield's predecessor in the White House, Rutherford B. Hayes. But Garfield let the matter drop when he became President.

Instead, he put up with the hundreds who came weekly to the Executive Mansion in search of government jobs. True, they annoyed him. Daily he was besieged by a "band of disciplined office hunters who drew papers on me as highwaymen draw pistols."[2] One of these constant job-seeking visitors to the White House who "drew papers," on the President was a forty-year-old Chicago lawyer, bill collector, and itinerant preacher named Charles Julius Guiteau.

Charles Julius Guiteau's life was an interesting contrast to that of James Abram Garfield. Garfield had married happily and raised a family. His efforts as student, educator, soldier, and politican were all rewarded. The President remained secure in his early religious beliefs. He numbered among his friends and admirers not only the most powerful people in America but also many of its intellectuals. The road from log cabin to White House had been, by and large, a smooth one that he traveled with outer serenity and inner contentment. Garfield represented, for many of his generation, living proof of the continued American formula for achievement: personal integrity plus hard work plus trained intelligence yield success and happiness.

Both the personal life and public career of Charles Guiteau had been marked by frustration and failure. He was born the fourth of six children on September 8, 1841, in Freeport, Illinois. Jane Howe Guiteau, his mother, died when he was seven. The boy was raised by his father, Luther Wilson Guiteau, a Freeport bank official and religious disciple of John Humphrey Noyes.[3] Charles was usually cared for by his older sister, Frances, who maintained an interest in the boy's welfare even after her marriage to George Scoville, a Chicago lawyer.

Guiteau, like Garfield, worked extremely hard as a young man, helping his father at the bank and tending to family chores. Both young men were enthusiastic Republicans; both were physical- and mental-fitness buffs; and both dreamed of eventual success. But the quarrels between the young Guiteau and his domineering father were frequent

---

[2]White House security measures were not as strict then as they are now. Visitors were free to come and go, so that they might well run into the President as he was walking elsewhere in the Executive Mansion.

[3]John Humphrey Noyes was the founder of the Oneida Community, an experimental communal colony in upstate New York.

and stormy. In 1859, the same year that Garfield became principal of Hiram Institute, Guiteau decided to leave Freeport to seek his fortune.

The first goal he set for himself was that of obtaining a college education. Guiteau went to the university college at Ann Arbor, Michigan, where he attempted to register. But the teachers there asked that he first train for university work by enrolling at a Michigan preparatory school. Lonely, lacking funds, and keenly feeling his lack of academic preparation, Guiteau turned to religion for solace. Not surprisingly, he became interested in his zealous father's faith, the teachings of John Humphrey Noyes. In June of 1860, Guiteau left Ann Arbor to join the Oneida Community.

The Oneida Community, like other utopian settlements in mid-nineteenth-century America, was based upon religious fellowship and the principle that both work and worldly goods would be shared. Guiteau was no happier at Oneida than he had been in Ann Arbor. He was unpopular among other members of the community. Neither then, nor at any other point in Charles Guiteau's life, did he manage to keep a single close friend. A bad-tempered, solitary, and nervous figure, he often came under attack for selfishness and conceit at the community's important mutual-criticism sessions. In 1865 Guiteau left the community.

For the next fifteen years Guiteau's life consisted mainly of a series of career failures. He constantly borrowed from family members, was always in debt, and often ran away to escape arrest. He flitted back and forth between New York City and Chicago (where his sister lived). Hoping and expecting some great new career—which would be achieved instantly—Guiteau generally found himself teetering on the edge of despair.

Guiteau tried a succession of enterprises. After leaving the Oneida Community, he tried to found a religious newspaper. But he failed. He spent a short time in 1867 as a subscription and ad salesman for the Reverend Henry Ward Beecher's influential weekly paper, the *Independent*. He soon gave up the post. Then he spent a year threatening a lawsuit against Noyes and his other former brethren at the the Oneida Community. He tried to blackmail them into paying him $9,000. Otherwise, he threatened to publicize the colony's controversial sexual practices.[4] Guiteau's own father denounced his son publicly for this betrayal of Oneida. Guiteau finally stopped his abusive letters to Noyes after the latter threatened to prosecute him.

Guiteau next moved to Chicago, where he apprenticed in a law office. He was admitted to the Illinois bar in 1868. He made only one appearance as a trial lawyer. Inevitably, he lost the case. After this, his legal practice consisted almost entirely of bill collecting, a trade he followed with little success until 1875.

In 1869 Guiteau had married an eighteen-year-old girl, Anne Bunn. The union lasted five turbulent years, during which he often beat

---

[4]The community held that traditional marriage and family patterns bred selfishness and, thereby, many evils in society. Therefore, monogamy was banned, and children were cared for by the entire community.

his wife severely and sometimes even locked her in a closet overnight. In 1874 his wife divorced him.

By then, Guiteau had acquired a reputation as a sleazy and dishonest bill collector. He served a brief jail sentence in 1875 for petty fraud and abruptly, that same year, shifted his career plans once more. The penniless lawyer now announced plans to raise $200,000 in order to purchase a Chicago newspaper. Attempts to borrow the money failed miserably. Guiteau retreated to his family again. During a visit to his sister Frances, he threatened her with an ax. A physician who examined Guiteau after this incident recommended that he be placed in an insane asylum. Guiteau fled.

Now Guiteau adopted yet another vocation. He became an itinerant preacher and wandered across the country, selling religious pamphlets and preaching a version of John Humphrey Noyes's theology. Apparently Guiteau earned almost no money between 1875 and 1881. Yet somehow he managed to survive on the misplaced trust of creditors.

Charles Guiteau truly believed that Garfield's death was a necessity that would unite the Republican party and save the Republic. He claimed that the idea had come to him under "divine pressure."

In 1880 a new vision of success appeared to Guiteau. This time it was a political one. He wrote an incoherent pro-Garfield essay and had it privately printed. Then he attached himself to the Republicans' New York City campaign headquarters. There he became one of the many unwanted and unused hangers-on. Though he did nothing to bring it about, Guiteau viewed Garfield's election as a personal triumph. He immediately began making plans to apply for a high post in the diplomatic corps.

Guiteau wrote several letters to Garfield and other important Republican leaders, in pursuance of his plan. In them he asserted his importance in the party's New York victory and requested assignment to various foreign ministries. Eventually, he decided on the Paris consulship. He moved to Washington—one jump ahead of his creditors—to press this claim.

During the early months of Garfield's presidency, from March to June 1881, Guiteau became a familiar face at the White House and in the State Department corridors. He pestered Garfield and Blaine about the Paris post at every chance, by letter and even in person (when he managed to push his way through). "Never bother me again about the Paris consulship so long as you live," Blaine shouted at the pesky figure after one such May encounter. By then, Guiteau had decided that Blaine was a "wicked man." He demanded Blaine's dismissal in notes to Garfield that became increasingly intimate in tone. A new scheme for glory now began to hatch in Guiteau's crazed mind: a plan to murder the President.

Guiteau was not familiar with firearms. As his obsession grew more vivid, he purchased a revolver and practiced shooting on the banks of the Potomac. He took to following the President and observing his daily routine. On several occasions prior to the fateful day he came close to executing his scheme, only to back down at the last minute. By shooting Garfield, his odd reasoning ran, not only would his political friends be raised to power but he too would share in it.

Finally, on July 2, 1881, Charles Julius Guiteau, a man whose life had epitomized failure, managed to carry out the last of his innumerable schemes. He shot the President. Guiteau later acknowledged:

> I have had an idea [since my youth] that I should be President, and it has never left me. When I left Boston for New York, in June 1880 [to campaign for Garfield], I felt that I was on my way to the White House. My idea is that I shall be nominated and elected as Lincoln and Garfield were—that is, by the act of God.

Many blamed Garfield's opponents among the Republican party's Stalwart wing[5] (somewhat unfairly) for having allowed the assassin even a minor place within their ranks in New York during the 1880 campaign. Some even blamed Vice President Arthur. Until Garfield selected him as a running mate, Arthur had been a loyal associate of the country's leading Stalwart, Senator Roscoe Conkling of New York. Arthur remained loyal to Conkling despite his new responsibilities as Vice President.

In May 1881, Garfield insisted on appointing an anti-Conkling Republican to an important patronage post—Customs Collector for the Port of New York. Conkling and his New York Stalwart colleague, Thomas C. Platt, both resigned from the Senate. Arthur supported their decision. Conkling and Platt hoped, by resigning, to put pressure on their Senate colleagues to reject the President's nominee on the grounds of "senatorial courtesy." They planned to win Senate reelection from the New York state legislature and then to return to Washington with added power. This was the dispute between Garfield and the Stalwarts that Guiteau claimed had triggered his decision to kill the President.

In the end, Conkling and Platt lost the struggle—and their power. The two were brought down in July 1881 by Conkling's personal arrogance and an ill-timed peek over an Albany hotel transom by a political opponent, who found Platt in the company of a prostitute. Platt withdrew from the contest the same day that Garfield was shot, in order not to hurt Conkling's chances. It was no use. Neither man gained reelection. Thus, ironically, Garfield had begun to win his struggle against Conkling for control of the Republican party at the very moment he was cut down by a maddened office seeker claiming to be a Stalwart.

Garfield himself never blamed his political opponents for the shooting. Garfield also forgave his Vice President for supporting Conkling's reelection bid. During Garfield's struggle to recover from the shooting, Arthur remained at his New York City home, grief stricken and withdrawn from public notice. Garfield turned the daily management of government over to his cabinet. The rumors of a Stalwart conspiracy guiding Guiteau's hand quickly died away.

The wounded President lingered between life and death for seventy-nine days. He remained in his second-floor sickroom, only rarely

Roscoe Conkling, head of the Stalwarts, was a political boss who believed that "parties were not built by deportment or gush." He ruined his political career in an attempt to thwart Garfield's policies.

Senator Thomas C. Platt, a faithful political crony of Roscoe Conkling, followed his lead in resigning from the Senate. Promptly dubbed "Me Too" Platt, his loyalty cost him his Senate seat.

---

[5]The Stalwart wing was centered in New York. It actively opposed civil-service reform. Guiteau claimed to be a Stalwart, acting for the good of that faction in shooting Garfield.

A reproduction of a contemporary sketch shows two doctors attempting to discover the location of the bullet in Garfield's body through the use of a strange telegraphlike apparatus. They never succeeded in removing the bullet.

writing official dispatches or dealing with government business. Doctors, medical consultants, and free advice poured into the White House to assist in the President's treatment. But the bullet remained lodged in his back while physicians continued their painful probing. Nothing seemed to help.

At first the President's condition improved. But a mid-July rally turned into a late-July decline. In Washington's sweltering summer heat, Garfield ran a fever that only occasionally broke. His normally robust 200-pound frame had shrunk to 120 pounds by late August. When early September brought a record heat wave, the doctors decided to move Garfield to the cooler temperatures of his oceanside summer house at Elberon, New Jersey. He was carried there by special train on September 6, but his condition continued to deteriorate. Still, almost at the end, his spirits remained good. He even tried to cheer those around him.

On the night of September 19, with only an old friend, Captain D. G. Swain, and one servant attending him, Garfield's final agony began. He awoke suddenly, clutched his heart, and cried out, "How it hurts here!" Swain handed the President a glass of water, but it failed to help. The President cried: "Swain, can't you stop this?" Then Garfield fell into a coma. Within moments Dr. Bliss and Mrs. Garfield entered the room. Mrs. Garfield sat down calmly and held her husband's hand. But the strain was too much, and she had to leave the room. Dr. Bliss remained with his patient for a few minutes, then walked quietly to a nearby study and wrote in his medical log: "Applying my ear over the heart, I detected an indistinct fluttering that continued until 10:35 when he expired. The brave and heroic sufferer, the nation's patient, has passed away."

The waiting had ended; the grieving began. Garfield's seventy-nine days of suffering before death, borne with stoic dignity, made the slain President a hero in the eyes of his countrymen. His body was brought back to Washington on September 21 to lie in state in the Capitol rotunda. Thousands—Southerners and Northerners, Democrats and Republicans alike—filed past to pay their last respects. The world's rulers also mourned. The President's widow received condolence messages from Queen Victoria of England; the emperors of China, Russia, and Japan; the kings of Belgium, Italy, and Spain; the Pope; and the sultan of Turkey.

American advocates of civil-service reform found an obvious moral in Garfield's assassination by a disappointed office seeker. Throughout his long death agony, reformers organized countless meetings protesting the spoils system and demanding government appointments based on merit alone. "Garfield dead," one historian later wrote, "proved more valuable to reformers than Garfield alive."

The great majority of Americans, however, mourned Garfield's passing more sincerely. On September 23 a special train carried the President's casket from Washington to Cleveland for burial. Crowds lined the entire route to honor the dead President, just as sixteen years earlier throngs had wept as Lincoln's funeral train followed a similar route from the East back to Illinois. Some 250,000 people from throughout the Midwest jammed Cleveland's streets for Garfield's funeral ceremony. Thousands of tributes—sermons, memorial leaflets, and letters—reached his widow at their Mentor home. The nation's grief seemed remarkably intense, considering the fact that Garfield, unlike Lincoln, had not been a war leader. Moreover he had held the highest office in the nation for only a few months.

In New York, Walt Whitman heard of the President's death. In his journal he wrote some lines that expressed the genuine sorrow of most of his less eloquent countrymen:

The sobbing of the bells, the sudden death-news everywhere,
The slumberers rouse, the rapport of the People,
(Full well they know that message in the darkness,
Full well return, respond within their breasts, their brains, the sad
    reverberations,)
The passionate toll and clang—city to city, joining, sounding, passing,
Those heart-beats of a Nation in the night.

Another New Yorker also recoiled at the awful news that evening. At Chester Alan Arthur's house the bell rang at midnight. A reporter informed the servant who answered the door that Garfield had died. "Oh, no, it cannot be true," cried Arthur, who overheard the news. "It cannot be. I have heard nothing." His face was pale, and he was crying. When the reporter persisted, Arthur could say only "I hope—My God, I do hope it is a mistake."

The man who had just become President turned and walked back to his study, where a small group of silent friends now waited. The bell rang again, and a messenger handed Arthur a telegram sent by a number of Garfield's cabinet members. It confirmed the President's death and advised Arthur to take the oath of office immediately. Arthur's friends rushed out to find a judge who could administer the oath. Someone checked it for the exact wording. Within minutes a state supreme court justice, roused from his bed, administered the oath of office to the Vice President. The next morning President Chester A. Arthur left for Washington.

On September 20, two days after Garfield's death, his assassin sent a letter to Chester Arthur. He wrote, "My inspiration is a godsend to you, and I presume you appreciate it. It raises you from $8,000 to $50,000 a year. It raises you from a political cipher to President of the United States with all its power and honors. For the Cabinet I would suggest as follows. . . ." President Arthur never answered the letter. Instead, he ordered Guiteau tried promptly. He personally helped select the prosecuting attorneys.

Guiteau, however, still seemed convinced that the Stalwarts would somehow rescue and reward him. His confidence waned, though, as the trial date neared. He continued to deny responsibility for the killing. He insisted that divine inspiration made him pull the trigger. "I am here as God's man, and don't you forget it." No independent lawyer would touch the case, despite a newspaper appeal for such assistance. When the trial began on November 14, 1881, Guiteau's brother-in-law, George Scoville, served as defense counsel.

Lines between the defense and prosecution arguments were drawn clearly from the start. Scoville argued that his client was an insane

This caricature of Garfield's assassin shows some of his crazed intensity of purpose. We can easily believe that he wrote: "I presume the President was a Christian and that he will be happier in Paradise than here."

religious fanatic and therefore could not be held legally responsible for his actions. Furthermore, the defense insisted that Garfield's wounds were not necessarily mortal. The President had died, Scoville claimed, only because of incompetent medical treatment after the shooting.

Both defense arguments had merit, although the prosecution, of course, denied them. It insisted that Guiteau, although morally evil, had killed the President while in complete possession of his faculties. He had done so for calculated political motives—namely, as a malicious and disappointed job seeker.

The case against Guiteau, then, centered on the question of his sanity. Both prosecution and defense attorneys presented "expert" medical testimony to prove their respective contentions. A majority of the doctors who had examined Guiteau found the prisoner sane within the prevailing legal definitions of sanity, which were far broader than those of today. Guiteau demonstrated his unbalanced mental state by frequently interrupting the trial to shout abusive statements at everyone, including his own lawyer. He continued to claim divine inspiration.

The prosecution argued that such outbursts were merely a cynical act by Guiteau, who was trying to portray himself as mad. Apparently the jury also believed this. It took only a half-hour on January 25, 1882, to find Guiteau guilty of murder. The prisoner vented his anger by shrieking: "My blood will be upon the heads of [this] jury. God will avenge this outrage." One doctor who had observed the trial daily, George M. Beard, a noted psychologist, disagreed strongly with the jury's decision. Beard later wrote:

> The physicians called in to make a diagnosis mistook the symptoms of insanity for the symptoms of wickedness. [This] error is quite as natural for nonexperts in insanity in our time as that of the village physician of Salem, Dr. Griggs, in witchcraft times, in attributing insanity to possession by the devil.

Nevertheless, on February 3, Judge Walter Cox sentenced Guiteau to hang.

Before sentencing, Guiteau addressed the court a final time. He insisted again that Garfield's killing had been "God's act, not mine." He compared his fate to Christ's and threatened bloody divine vengeance on the United States if he hung. In the months before his execution the condemned man continued to believe that President Arthur would issue a last-minute reprieve or pardon.

Finally, Guiteau recognized the reality ahead of him. Four days before his death, while in his cell, he scrawled a "Scene between the Almighty and my murderers." In this imaginary scene God confronts Guiteau's persecutors, including President Arthur, and condemns them along with the entire American nation. A few days later, on June 30, 1882, Charles Guiteau was hung. He went to the scaffold, fighting back tears and singing a childlike hymn he had written especially for the occasion. Then he gave a final shout: "Glory hallelujah! I am with the Lord. Glory, ready, go!"

26 POLITICS IN TRANSITION

A.W.

The economic and social landscape of the United States in the nineteenth century underwent dramatic change. The period might best be termed a transitional one. It was characterized by the emergence of a new, industrial society. In the decades after the Civil War the preindustrial issues that dominated the antebellum era were overridden in importance by the realities of a rapidly maturing industrial society. New economic and social factors, some of them grim, were changing life. They included: transcontinental railroads, a truly national market for goods, a growing monopoly in oil, the factory system, and new technology in steel and other industries. In addition, there were deplorable urban living conditions, millions of new, non-English-speaking immigrants, rising labor violence, growing discontent among farmers, and brutal poverty among workers and farmers.

These factors were clearly visible. But both Republican and Democratic politicians managed to avoid confronting them. Not until a paralyzing business depression in the 1890s and the rise of a new third party, committed to reform, did politicians finally start to deal with the problems brought about by industrial development. Before then, in the 1870s and 1880s, political leaders were more concerned with traditional issues, particularly the currency and tariffs. They argued, for example, over whether the amount of currency in circulation should be expanded or reduced. And they debated whether the United States would benefit more from raised or from lowered tariffs.

Why did politicians avoid considering the problems of the new industrial society? Basically, they (and voters too) were unable to shift their attention from the intense issues arising out of the Civil War and Reconstruction. With the ending of war and the termination of Radical rule in the South, the old issues had disappeared. But this transitional generation of politicians, raised in the antislavery battles of the 1850s, was simply unprepared to face the new problems of an industrial nation.

Some steps were taken during this period to deal with elements in the changed economy, but these proved to be less than effective. Politicians of the era were themselves too deeply involved in the development of American industries to take an active role in helping to regulate them. Only in the face of the new political forces and new conditions of the 1890s did politicians begin to bring the unregulated corporate system under some measure of public supervision. It took more than two decades for them to realize that they could no longer ignore the urgent economic and social problems created by post-Civil War industrial growth.

A GENERATION OF ORDINARY MEN

Through the 1870s and 1880s, politics continued along at an unhurried pace. Leaders tried to avoid difficult issues. In large part the people who entered politics during this period were ordinary men, like Garfield, who displayed little achievement beyond their ability to win votes.

In *The American Commonwealth* (1888) James Bryce, an English historian, noted that in a country where all careers are open to those having talent and where "political life is unusually keen and political ambition widely diffused," the highest positions in the land are seldom "won by men of brilliant gifts."

Why did eminent figures usually not choose to run for political office in this period? First, for talented people American politics did not seem interesting or important. In European countries, officeholders in national governments generally held much more power over people's lives. First-rate men were attracted to vocations in which they felt they could make a significant impact. Politics in America was not one such vocation.

A second reason for the lack of brilliant people in politics was that success generally required a slow rise through the party ranks. The long apprenticeship in party loyalty necessary to achieve office discouraged ambitious people who wished to move quickly into positions of prominence. Also American voters, then as today, were distrustful of anyone who seemed overly eager for political power, however capable.

Finally, persons of outstanding ability may not have entered politics simply because the era seemed a quiet one, at least compared with the age preceding it. Profound ideological questions no longer separated the parties. The problems of slavery, sectional divisions, and civil war were settled. Few issues were significant enough to attract talented people into politics.

Small-Town Background   Given the lure of other fields, the slowness of the process of reaching the top, and the relative quietness of the times, the

President Garfield's home in Mentor, Ohio, was the kind of country setting most national politicians of this era preferred. Their living patterns represented a nostalgia for an older, simpler way of life in an increasingly complex industrial society.

quality of those who held high public office is hardly surprising. Nor is it surprising to find that those who did make politics their career shared very similar patterns of life. In fact, most successful figures in late nineteenth-century national politics, including the great majority of congressmen and senators, had backgrounds similar to that of Garfield. They came from small towns and cities like Garfield's Mentor, Ohio, rather than from large cities or predominantly rural areas. Furthermore, most began their careers in such professions as law, business, the ministry, or teaching.

During the 1860s and 1870s the number of politicians having business interests increased. But most politicians were nonetheless provincial in their values and outlook on life. They remained aloof and sheltered from the habits and problems of urban-industrial society. They brought to national affairs a viewpoint similar to that of their pre-Civil War counterparts. Most national elected officials, in fact, had little direct personal contact with the major new realities of a changed America—cities, industries, and immigrants.

As with most of the national politicians of this period, the Republican presidential candidates were men with roots in small cities and towns. And in 1884 all the Republican candidates but James G. Blaine came from the Midwest. Thus, even if Charles Guiteau had managed to build a successful career for himself in a city like New York, his urban and Eastern ties would probably have blocked his road to the White House.

Guiteau might have been more successful as a Democrat, however. The Democrats generally nominated presidential candidates from big cities during these years: Horatio Seymour (1868), Horace Greeley (1872), Samuel Tilden (1876), and Grover Cleveland (1884, 1888, 1892). But of this group only Cleveland succeeded in becoming President. Thus, while they controlled the big cities and even had respectable showings in congressional elections, the Democrats largely failed to take the biggest prize of all—the presidency.

Civil War Experience   As important as a small-town background seemed to be in achieving political success, there was another factor at least as important in advancing a politician's career—his

Civil War record. This was true at all levels in American politics but particularly in regard to seeking the presidency. Indeed, another reason why Guiteau could never have become President was that he had not served in the Union Army.

For many Northern voters, Republicanism was practically a family religion, sanctified by wartime sacrifices. (Most Northerners had lost at least one family member in the fighting.)

The Republican presidential candidates were usually Civil War generals. General Hayes succeeded General Grant in the presidency. He, in turn, was succeeded by General Garfield. As death and old age thinned out the number of high-ranking officers, Colonel Benjamin Harrison, and, finally, Major William McKinley entered the White House.

The Democrats, for their part, failed to choose nominees having a military background, at least on the national level. The single Democratic candidate who was a Union military man was General Winfield Scott Hancock. He lost to Garfield in 1880. It is understandable that Union officers were not nominated. The Democrats depended, for the most part, on Southern support for victory. In local and regional elections, of course, where Southern support was irrelevant, Democrats could play on old Civil War loyalties to win elections. But the presidential prize eluded them.

Codes of Personal Conduct   The victorious politicians of this period, besides sharing a small-town background and Civil War experience, were also strong believers in the strictest of moral codes. They usually presented themselves to the public as family men who lived their private lives according to the rigid ethical precepts of American middle-class culture. We do not know, of course, whether this was fact or sheer image building. The author of Garfield's semiofficial campaign biography wrote, for example: "No profane word, no unseemly jest is ever heard at Lawnfield [his home]. No wines sparkle on its table. The moral atmosphere is sweet, pure, and healthgiving to heart and soul. It is a Christian family—a Christian home."

Prior to the Civil War a politician's personal habits and morality had rarely influenced the suc-

James G. Blaine had been recently involved in an allegedly crooked railroad deal. He defended himself against the charge of corruption by reading selected portions of correspondence that was to prove his innocence. Many people were unconvinced. The so-called Mulligan letters hurt his chances for the presidency in 1876.

cess of his political career. Neither Andrew Jackson's background of frequent duels nor Henry Clay's inveterate gambling prevented these men from seeking the highest prize in American politics. During the middle of the nineteenth century, however, the American family adopted a stern moral code on such questions as sexual behavior, drinking, and gambling. Voters began to apply these standards to vote seekers as well.

Perhaps the only national politician of the era to overcome hostility toward "loose" morality successfully was Grover Cleveland. He won the presidency in 1884 despite the fact—brought out in the campaign—that in his youth he had fathered an illegitimate child. Ironically, voters that year were offered a choice between repudiating either Cleveland's single offense against private morality or James G. Blaine's questionable public morality. While a senator during the 1870s, Blaine had allegedly accepted money and stocks from railroad companies in return for political favors. When the returns were in, the electorate had registered its preference for a candidate with a single confessed private lapse to one probably tainted with several instances of political corruption.

ELECTING A PRESIDENT

National politics during the 1870s and 1880s was not oriented toward issues, although some of the older issues did play a part in the elections. Basically, politicians were concerned with party affiliation and moral, ethnic, and religious differences among the electorate. Three basic factors shaped presidential elections of the late nineteenth century: a close balance in voting strength between the two major parties, high voter turnout, and a stress on party loyalty.

The Closeness of Contests The statistics for every presidential election of the era show clearly that the parties were evenly matched. In the disputed 1876 election, Republican Rutherford B. Hayes was elected by one electoral vote, although he had received almost 250,000 fewer votes than his Democratic opponent, Samuel J. Tilden. In 1880 Garfield defeated the Democratic candidate, Winfield Scott Hancock, by a comfortable electoral majority. But his nationwide popular margin was a mere 7,368 votes. Actually, Garfield received only a plurality of the votes—48 percent; a third-party candidate, James B. Weaver of the Greenback-Labor party, cut into the major parties' totals.

Democrat Grover Cleveland's presidential election history is an interesting one, for he crossed and recrossed the narrow line between victory and defeat. In 1884 Cleveland won with less than 49 percent of the popular vote. His margin in the popular vote was only 63,000. When he was defeated by Republican Benjamin Harrison in the 1888 election, Harrison received the majority of electoral votes despite receiving 96,000 fewer popular votes. Cleveland again became President in 1892 when he received 360,000 more votes than

Election night, 1892, in New York City is typical of voter enthusiasm in this era. Despite political corruption and the lack of great issues, excitement over politics ran high.

Harrison. In this race a new third party, the Populists, received over one million votes. Thus a presidential candidate once more won with only a plurality, not a majority, of the popular vote.

The closeness of these presidential contests helps to explain the efforts usually made by both Republicans and Democrats to blur their basic differences over issues at the national level. Although the Republicans supported high protective tariffs, for example, there were many in the party, including Garfield, who favored much lower rates. Similarly, the Democrats were a low-tariff party. But Cleveland's decision to press the tariff-reduction issue during his first term cost the party support from many high-tariff Democrats and independents who might otherwise have voted for him when he ran again. In order to make its position seem close to that of the other party, and hoping thereby to gain votes, each party had to muffle its internal conflicts and contradictions on such issues as the tariff.

Because of the narrow margins of victory in each presidential election, both Republicans and Democrats were essentially in competition for the support of a small group of swing voters in a few doubtful states. These voters shifted back and forth between the major parties throughout this period. Business help was often invaluable in swinging the key votes and deciding the outcome of the election. Garfield's election in 1880 owed much to the fact that John D. Rockefeller instructed his thousands of salesmen in various states in the Midwest to work actively for the Republican ticket. Similarly, in 1888, Harrison's victory was due in part to corporate money that helped finance intensive drives for votes in a few key states.

Turnout of Voters   Another basic factor in presidential elections in the late nineteenth century was a surprisingly high voter turnout. This phenomenon is somewhat more difficult to explain. There were no dramatic public issues bitterly dividing the two parties as there had been earlier—and would be in the near future. Part of the explanation, however, can be found in the popular view of elections as spectacles.

Both parties waged furious campaigns. Republicans "waved the bloody shirt"—that is,

they reminded the voters of Southern Democratic disloyalty during the Civil War. Democrats, in turn, pointed to the corrupting influence of business on the Republican party.

Political campaigns were often the greatest show in town. Huge numbers of voters marched in torchlight parades. They listened for hours to familiar but rousing partisan oratory. As participants in and spectators of such grand displays, voters reaffirmed their strong allegiance to and identification with their party.

Importance of Party Loyalty   Political loyalties among politicians and voters were clear and strong during this period. However blurred the political issues might be, this kind of loyalty strengthened the parties as an institution in American life.

Among politicians, party loyalty, or regularity, was extremely important at the national level. Presidential power, which had reached a high point with Lincoln's wartime authority, declined after the crisis of civil war ended. Presidents were largely at the mercy of Congress to achieve their programs. The President's political task was two-fold: (1) to "carry" enough congressmen of his own party into office when he was elected and (2) to hold their loyalty once he was President.

Concerning the former, Presidents were not too successful. No President during this entire era governed for his entire term with a majority of his own party in control of Congress. The Democrats, for example, won control of the House in 1874, lost it in 1880, regained it in 1882, lost it in 1888, and won it back in 1890. Although Republicans controlled the Senate throughout this period, except for the 1879–1881 session, for all but two years they held no more than a slim three-vote Senate majority. There was considerable turnover in congressional membership during the 1870s and 1880s, particularly in the House.

It was even more difficult for a President to hold the party loyalty of congressmen after election. There were numerous factions in both parties. Various means of keeping the party together seemed to work, however. By the end of the era, congressional caucuses were a device used in both parties. They generally decided the legislative policies that all members were expected to, and usually did, abide by. A congressman who did not support the party could be disciplined in a number of ways. Leaders might deny him important committee assignments. They might refuse to help him in the passage of the numerous private bills that every congressman introduces yearly on behalf of his constituents. If necessary they would oppose his renomination. In these circumstances, most congressmen, of course, obeyed the dictates of their party's leaders.

Party loyalty among American voters was more easily assured. American voters adhered as firmly to their party allegiance as they did to their religious faith. If one was raised as a Democrat (or Republican), one usually remained a Democrat (or Republican) for life.

Recent studies point to the importance of ethnic backgrounds and religion as factors in the political behavior of most Americans in the period following the Civil War. A voter's ethnic, cultural, and religious ties shaped his party loyalty as much as it did his attitudes on specific economic or political issues. For example, in order to help capture the votes of the immigrants, who badly needed employment, civil-service reformers in each party complained about the use of the spoils system by urban political machines in the other party. Although jobs were dispensed through political patronage under the spoils system, and recent immigrants were thus unlikely to get them, few of these immigrants favored introducing a merit system. This, they felt, might result in jobs being awarded mainly to native-born Americans who had had greater opportunity to receive education and training.

Religious beliefs were also a factor in determining political affiliation. Recent voting studies have shown that during this period the more an individual's religion stressed correct behavior rather than strict adherence to doctrine alone, the more likely he was to vote Republican. Some Protestant religious denominations viewed politics as a moral battleground, in which state power should be used to regulate ethical behavior. For example, they supported laws prohibiting the sale of alcohol. Members of these denominations tended to support Republicans for office, whether in the

1850s or the 1890s. Certainly, Republican opposition at the state level to using public funds for parochial schools (schools particularly important for many new immigrant families) and the party's support for prohibition (viewed as an assault on Democratic-voting Catholic immigrant "drinkers") attracted large numbers of native-born Episcopalian, Congregationalist, Presbyterian, and other similar voters.

This does not mean that immigrant groups and church members voted in blocs for a single party. Nonetheless, ethnic and cultural ties did indeed influence political loyalties in the period of the 1870s and 1880s.

THE REPUBLICANS IN POWER

For three decades, from 1861 to 1892, the Republicans (except for Democrat Cleveland's 1885–1889 term) governed nationally, despite the close political balance between the parties. During this period, as already stated, the President was extremely dependent on Congress. In fact, more often than not, Congress—not the President—determined party policies and the legislation that emerged from Washington.

Americans did not seem to want strong Presidents during this period. Certainly they did not appear to need them, because of the relative quietness of the times. So, none of the Republican Presidents—Grant, Hayes, Garfield, Arthur, or Harrison—managed to wrest control of Republican policies from the Senate and House leaders.

Men like Blaine and Conkling remained the party's most influential national spokesmen throughout the period. They largely shaped national legislation during the era. Since they were Republicans, they believed in an effective and energetic national economic policy. In general, the purpose of this policy was to encourage industrial expansion. For this they were often criticized by Democratic politicians who retained their party's traditional faith—that government should not meddle actively in the economic lives of Americans.

But the Republican party, founded in an era when the national government had to expand its powers to preserve the Union, saw nothing wrong with continuing this trend at the war's end. To encourage economic development, party leaders aided business in every possible way. In accomplishing this purpose, they forged an informal alliance between the national government and the great majority of businessmen—bankers, industrialists, and merchants in foreign trade. While this alliance did further economic growth, it had other less fortunate consequences as well. It gave the era a reputation for corruption unparalleled in American history until then.

Corruption under Grant It is ironic that people who lived by strict small-town moral codes in their private lives found it difficult to maintain the same kind of integrity in public affairs. Political corruption was widespread in this period. The Grant years in particular saw some of the worst offenses against honest government in the nation's history.

A series of cabinet scandals during Grant's administration involved many people close to the President himself. His secretary of the navy sold work to contractors rather than taking honest bids. His secretary of war sold extremely profitable traderships on Indian reservations. Department of the Interior officials worked hand in hand with dishonest land speculators.

Some of the worst scandals involved the Department of the Treasury. Grant's secretary of the Treasury farmed out the collection of unpaid taxes to a private contractor who kept half of the money collected. The President's own private secretary protected a Whiskey Ring of corrupt Treasury inspectors. These officials received millions of dollars in bribes from liquor distillers to avoid payment of federal taxes. Through Grant's personal bungling, the Department of the Treasury cooperated with two New York stock speculators, James Fisk and Jay Gould, to manipulate the government selling of bullion. The two men cornered the gold market briefly in September 1869, forcing anyone else who needed gold to pay an exorbitant price for it. Although they caused a panic in the money market, Fisk and Gould made a fortune on the deal. Once they were exposed, Grant did little to punish the guilty parties in his administration.

The opportunities for politicians to profit through corrupt practices increased vastly as a result of the economic boom of the 1860s and 1870s. Many national leaders like Garfield had carefully watched their money while young, to further their education and careers. Suddenly they were responsible for handling millions of dollars in government funds. Politicians found themselves able to reap tidy sums (and benefit the country) simply by helping businessmen with government funds or favorable legislation.

The railroads were notorious seekers after these government favors. Railroad owners paid millions in bribes to public officials each year to secure cash subsidies, gifts of government land, and favorable legislation. Both Garfield and Blaine were linked to such transactions, although no specific criminal charges were ever made against either of them.

During Grant's administration, Garfield apparently profited, along with numerous other public officials, from a shady company known as the Crédit Mobilier. This was a purchasing and construction corporation organized by a few stockholders of the Union Pacific Railroad in the late 1860s. The Union Pacific stockholders retained control the Crédit Mobilier, to which they awarded huge and fraudulent contracts connected with building the railroad. Congressmen of both parties, including Garfield, were bribed with money and stocks in the Crédit Mobilier to avoid congressional inquiry into these transactions. Before the affair was exposed in 1873, the Crédit Mobilier (despite the Union Pacific's virtual bankruptcy) had paid yearly dividends to stockholders that often exceeded 300 percent of the original investment. Moreover, sometimes these excessive profits went to congressmen who had paid nothing for the stock in the first place!

Although the Grant administration provides the most famous instances of scandal, governmental corruption was not limited to the national level or to Republicans alone. In fact, some of the worst instances of corruption took place at the city level, where Democrats were more likely to be in con-

WILLIAM MARCY TWEED

From one perspective, William Marcy Tweed was three hundred pounds of grand larceny. From another, he was a major figure in the development of American city government. He was appropriately named after the New York Democratic politician, William Marcy, who had openly boasted that victors were entitled to spoils. As the boss of post-Civil War New York City, Tweed devised a method of dealing with an altered city. Most "respectable" New Yorkers wanted no part of it. If Tweed made himself a substantial profit, he could say, "I seen my opportunities and I took 'em."

By 1870, nearly a million people were crowded into the southern half of Manhattan Island, almost half of them immigrants. The city's startling growth had put enormous strains on its housing, public transportation, sanitation, and health facilities. The financial and social leaders of the city regarded the new residents with a mixture of disdain, foreboding, and bewilderment.

Tammany Hall, New York City's Democratic organization, had been working with immigrants, especially the Irish Catholics, for nearly seven decades before Tweed took over in the mid-1860s. Tweed and other leaders now increased their efforts to meet (and profit from) the incoming flood. Tammany Hall members greeted newcomers from Europe at the docks, helped them get settled, and assisted them in becoming voting American citizens.

With such support, the Tweed Ring controlled city politics. Close associates of Tweed held office as mayor and controller. The Boss himself served the public as chairman of the General Committee of Tammany Hall, president of the Board of Supervisors, deputy street commissioner, and state senator. He was grooming his close ally, Governor John T. Hoffman, for the Democratic nomination for the presidency of the United States.

The Ring, however, was interested in public office less for its own sake than as a lever on the door to the public treasury. During five years of almost uncontested power, the Tweed Ring stole between $30 and $200 million. By one estimate, only 15 cents of every tax dollar went for legitimate purposes. The Ring's classic achievement was a courthouse that cost $12 million to build, when $3 million would have been enough. Its costs included $179,729.60 for three tables and forty chairs.

Graft on such a scale could not and did not go unnoticed. Yet Tweed, sure of his power, responded to all charges with a sneering, "Well, what are you going to do about it?" Tammany's immigrant voters remained loyal, and Tweed even survived an investigation. But when, in 1871, two high-level Ring members began turning over evidence to the New York *Times*, the end came with startling swiftness. Tweed, in a desperate move, offered the *Times* $500,000 to abandon its probe, and a similar sum to *Harper's Weekly* cartoonist Thomas Nast, suggesting that he might like to study art in Europe. Neither accepted the bribes, and soon the Tweed Ring was shattered both at the polls and in the courts. Tweed was in and out of prison for the next five years; he died in jail at age fifty-five.

Twice voted into office, in 1868 and 1872, Ulysses S. Grant was the first professional soldier to become President since Zachary Taylor and the last until 1952. A West Point graduate, Grant had a lacklustre career until his rise to fame as General of the U.S. Army under Lincoln. As President, he was hampered by a lack of political sophistication, inept appointments, and opposition within his own party. His troubles were compounded by the scandals that pervaded his administration, most notably the Credit Mobilier of 1874.

Grant's successor, Rutherford B. Hayes, ordered that officeholders not be asked to make political contributions or be required to do political campaigning. But these orders were largely ignored. Garfield, as noted in the previous chapter, backed away from Hayes's civil-service commitment. With Garfield's death, public attention focused on Guiteau not merely as his assassin but as a symbol of the various evils that Americans identified with the spoils system of selecting officeholders.

Although the most blatant instances of national corruption had taken place a decade or more earlier, in 1883 Congress responded to the public outcry by passing the Pendleton Act. President Arthur, himself a one-time spoilsman, had lobbied hard for the bill. The act established a bipartisan Civil Service Commission, appointed by the President. Its purpose was to conduct competitive examinations to choose officeholders on the basis of merit. Arthur appointed three solid reformers as civil-service commissioners.

The original measure did not solve the entire problem, however, for the merit system affected only about one of every ten federal jobs. The others were to be filled as political appointments. Nonetheless, the Pendleton Act gave the President the authority to expand the number of positions classified as merit jobs. By 1900 over 40 percent of federal posts had been brought under the civil-service heading. This percentage has expanded in every decade since.

CONTINUING BUSINESS INFLUENCE

The assault on the spoils system did not have much effect on business influence within the national government. Businessmen tried less often to buy favors from individual politicians. Instead, increasing numbers of them began either running for office themselves or supporting politicians committed to business policies, through legal campaign contributions. Industrialists and bankers poured millions into Republican campaign treasuries.

trol. New York City, for instance, was run by a Democratic political organization, or "machine," known as the Tweed Ring (see page 473). Its political leader, "Boss" William Marcy Tweed, and members of his machine stole over $100 million in public revenues ($14 million in one profitable day).

Civil-Service Reform An important source of Tweed's money was from kickbacks forced from people who wanted city jobs. Once in office, the machine politicians had the power to distribute jobs. Many reformers of the era thought that this spoils system for filling political posts should be eliminated and replaced with a merit system. This, they thought, would do away with much of the corruption that had plagued the country at all levels.

Thomas Nast's cartoons exposed the unsavory Tweed Ring.

Even more important than business involvement in presidential contests, however, was the growing importance of senators who represented large corporate interests. By 1900 such businessmen, most of them Republicans, comprised a third of the Senate. Fifteen senators were involved in railroads; fifteen in extractive industries—minerals, oil, and lumber; nine in banking and finance; six in commerce; and three in manufacturing. Wealthy members of the House or Senate were not captives or "puppets" of the business interests with which they held close ties. But, on issues affecting the national economic life, their policies tended to favor businessmen and monied interests rather than farmers, laborers, and the poor. And they made only token efforts to regulate American industry or finance.

Currency Expansion Favoritism toward business interests is shown clearly in the monetary programs enacted by Congress in the era. The debate involved the amount of currency in circulation. Farmers and most other debtors favored an increase in the amount of money issued by the government. Businesses, on the other hand, especially banking interests, wanted the opposite.

To understand the farmers' demands, it is important to keep in mind that this group was experiencing especially hard times during this period. The mechanization of agriculture was a mixed blessing to farmers. It greatly added to their efficiency; but it helped create vast surpluses and consequent falling prices. Wheat, for example, which had sold for $2.50 a bushel in 1868 dropped to an average of 78 cents a bushel in the late 1880s.

While prices continued dropping, the cost of running farms remained high. Many farmers, for instance, were at the mercy of railroads that held a monopoly on transportation in their areas. These railroads often charged excessively high rates for carrying agricultural products to markets. Besides the cost of transportation, the cost of land, machinery, and tools was also quite high.

Faced with high costs and declining prices for their own products, farmers usually went into debt by mortgaging their land and goods. In the 1880s the number of mortgages soared. Of the total number of farms in the country, over 40 percent

This pro-Greenback cartoon portrays a gold-nosed government octopus linking itself to big business with its tentacles while strangling labor, farmers, and small business.

were mortgaged. In some areas, like Kansas, the figure was closer to 60 percent. Interest rates on these mortgages were high—6 to 15 percent on land and 10 to 18 percent on goods.

Farmers felt that government could relieve their distress by pumping more money into the economy. The government had increased the amount of paper money—greenbacks—in circulation during the Civil War in order to finance the war effort. After the war the government began to withdraw these greenbacks from circulation. This cutback in currency was hitting the indebted farmer particularly hard because he had borrowed when money was "cheap" or plentiful. Now he had to pay his debts in currency worth much more than its original value.

From the bankers' point of view, of course, the situation was ideal. They had a stake in seeing that money became scarcer. They would profit more on the repayment of loans, since the value of a dollar increases as its supply decreases. The government agreed with this viewpoint.

During the Hayes administration, the Specie Resumption Act of 1875 was passed, committing the United States to returning to a gold standard by 1879. The Treasury Department, to help ensure the successful "resumption of specie payments" (as it was called) in 1879, began to reduce the number of greenbacks in circulation. This policy (and the Treasury's refusal to print additional issues of greenbacks) combined with an increase in overall productive output during the 1875–1879 period to cause a total decline in the money stock. This was a direct slap at debtor interests, particularly farmers, coming as it did during the worst depression in American history up to that point.

The financial community benefited greatly, not only from the 1875 Resumption Act but from an earlier statute, in 1869, which provided that bonds issued during the Civil War should be paid off in gold. The banking community, of course, held most of these bonds. The provision meant that war bonds that had been bought with greenbacks worth less than 40 cents to the dollar could now be turned in for currency worth 100 cents to the dollar.

The resumption of specie payments (payment in gold alone) so enraged some farmers

that they banded together to form a third party. They were joined by many recruits from labor and became the Greenback-Labor party in 1878. In the short run the movement was unsuccessful, since it failed to win many votes or to change the government's policy in currency. In the long run, however, it was significant in laying the basis for a far more powerful agrarian movement during the 1890s.

Agitation for expanding the currency did not stop after the initial failure of the Greenback movement. In fact, a new strategy was tried—a demand that silver be coined into dollars. In 1873 the government had stopped coining silver and put the country back on the gold standard—that is, backed money with gold alone. But in the 1870s the supply of silver increased tremendously because of the discovery of new silver deposits in the West. Many charged that silver had been demonetized illegally. By the 1880s farmers and other debtor groups saw in the "remonetizing" of silver a way of getting cheaper money. This in turn would raise crop prices and secure them relief from their debts.

Those who agitated for silver were partially successful during the 1870s. The Bland-Allison Act of 1878 required the Department of the Treasury to buy not less than $2 million and not more than $4 million worth of silver each month to back the dollar. Unfortunately, the government continuously bought the lesser amount. Though the silver interests were placated, farmers did not get much relief.

The Tariff Issue Another government policy that tended to favor business interests at the expense of other segments of society involved the tariff. The tariff debate, as old as the country itself, took on new importance with the coming of the industrial age. The original justification for a tax on imports was to protect infant industries from the competition of foreign manufacturers. But long after competition from abroad ceased to be a threat, the tariff still remained high on most goods. And it was going higher.

Again those particularly hurt by the tariff were the farmers. They complained that they had to sell their goods competitively on an open world

An antitariff cartoon of the 1880s shows the spiraling bad effects of a high tariff. The tariff wall results in a glut of products on the home market, consequent cuts in production, and then widespread unemployment, at least in this hostile cartoon.

market. But they had to purchase tariff-protected manufactured and processed goods such as farm machinery and oil. In fact, consumers in general suffered from the imposition of high tariffs. Without the competition of cheaper imported goods, they paid whatever prices domestic manufacturers set—prices that were often determined by monopolistic practices.

Republicans were by no means the only supporters of high protective tariffs. Factions in both parties backed business interests (or farmer interests) on this matter. But it was not until a

Democrat, Grover Cleveland, took office that there was a serious challenge to high tariffs. Cleveland's advocacy of a lowered tariff provided the leading issue in his reelection bid in 1888. He was defeated, as was noted earlier, partly because he had alienated the pro-tariff faction in his own party. But his downfall came mostly because businessmen poured millions of dollars into the campaign of the Republican candidate, Benjamin Harrison.

Harrison repaid his business backers by supporting the highest tariff in the nation's history. The McKinley Tariff of 1890—named after its sponsor, William McKinley—aimed not just at discouraging competition but at eliminating it altogether. It raised rates from an average of 38 percent to an average of almost 50 percent. It clearly marked a triumph for American industrialists.

Token Reform Although business influence was at its height, the government could not afford to ignore the public altogether. Some steps were taken in this period to deal with elements in the changed economy. But these proved to be less than effective. Congressmen from both parties joined in passing two basically mild bills to regulate the new giant industries.

The Interstate Commerce Act in 1887 set up a federal commission (the ICC) to oversee "reasonable and just" rates on the nation's railroads. Congress did not provide the commission with any strong enforcement powers, however. Its only avenue was the courts, and these generally consisted of pro-business conservatives. Moreover, the persons who were appointed as commissioners during the 1890s were sympathetic to the railroads. This, of course, further prevented the ICC from making any serious efforts to regulate the lines in order to ensure fair and equal treatment for all shippers.

A second law, the Sherman Antitrust Act of 1890, was also supposed to curb big business. Anticipating public reaction to the high McKinley Tariff, congressmen hoped that the Sherman Act would quiet agitation. Unfortunately, the act provided only mild and ineffective penalties against companies that formed combinations in restraint of trade. Furthermore, it was rarely applied during the 1890s. Only five years after the law was passed, the Supreme Court handed down a decision in *U.S.* v. *Knight* that exempted most industries from its provision. A monopoly, according to the Court, was not itself illegal. It became so only when it served to restrain interstate trade.

The immediate effect of such token efforts was to prevent a massive public outcry. In the long run, though, they only added further grievances to the growing list of problems confronting the country. The nation had lived through more than two decades of conservative rule resulting from the informal alliance of business and government. The public was ready for reform, and pressure was mounting in various parts of society to bring that about.

SUGGESTED READINGS – CHAPTERS 25-26

Garfield

Charles E. Rosenberg, *The Trial of the Assassin Guiteau* (1968); Robert G. Caldwell, *James A. Garfield: Party Chieftain* (1931); Theodore C. Smith, *Life and Letters of James Abram Garfield*, 2 vols. (1925); David M. Jordan, *Roscoe Conkling* (1971); Thomas C. Reeves, *Gentleman Boss: Chester A. Arthur* (1975).

Politics in Transition

Irwin Unger, *The Greenback Era* (1964); Allen Weinstein, *Prelude to Populism* (1970); John G. Sproat, *"The Best Men": Liberal Reformers in the Gilded Age* (1968); H. Wayne Morgan, *From Hayes to McKinley* (1969); Ari A. Hoogenboom, *Outlawing the Spoils* (1961); John A. Garraty, *The New Commonwealth, 1877–1890* (1968); Robert D. Marcus, *Grand Old Party: Political Structure in the Gilded Age* (1971); David J. Rothman, *Politics and Power: The U.S. Senate, 1869–1901* (1966); Matthew Josephson, *The Politicos, 1865–1896* (1938); Daniel J. Elazar, *The American Partnership* (1962).

Republican Politics

C. Vann Woodward, *Origins of the New South* (1951); Robert H. Wiebe, *The Search for Order: 1877–1920* (1968); Leonard D. White, *The Republican Era, 1869–1901* (1958); Stanley P. Hirshon, *Farewell to the Bloody Shirt: Northern Republicans and the Southern Negro, 1877–1893* (1962); Vincent P. DeSantis, *Republicans Face the Southern Question* (1959).

Cleveland and the Democrats

Horace Samuel Merrill, *Bourbon Democracy of the Middle West, 1865–1896* (1969) and *Bourbon Leader: Grover Cleveland and the Democratic Party* (1957).

The Tweed Ring

Alexander B. Callow, Jr., *The Tweed Ring* (1966); Seymour Mandelbaum, *Boss Tweed's New York* (1965).

27 MASSACRE AT WOUNDED KNEE

R.J.W.

There was a confusion about names—there almost always was when Indians were involved. Most whites called the tribe the Sioux. But this name was just a French abbreviation of what some of the tribe's enemies had called them. They called themselves Dakota.

There was more than one Indian name for what the whites called Wounded Knee Creek, on the Pine Ridge Reservation in South Dakota. Also, whereas some people called what had happened at Wounded Knee Creek a battle, others called it a massacre. Even the man who rode out from reservation headquarters to Wounded Knee had two names. One was an Indian name, Ohiyesa. One was a white man's name, Charles Eastman. He was a Sioux, but he had been educated in white schools in New England. In fact, he was a doctor of medicine.

But there was no confusion about what Charles Eastman saw on that bright New Year's Day morning in 1891:

> On the day following the Wounded Knee massacre, there was a blizzard. On the third day it cleared, and the ground was covered with fresh snow. We had feared that some of the wounded Indians had been left on the field, and a number of us volunteered to go and see.
>
> Fully three miles from the scene of the massacre, we found the body of a woman completely covered with a blanket of snow, and from this point on we found them scattered along as they had been hunted down and slaughtered. When we reached the spot where the Indian camp had stood, among the fragments of burned tents and other belongings, we saw the frozen bodies lying close together or piled one upon another. I counted eighty bodies of men, who were almost as helpless as the women and babes when the deadly [gun] fire began, for nearly all their guns had been taken from them.
>
> Although they had been lying in the snow and cold for two days and nights, a number had survived. Among them I found a baby of about a year old, warmly wrapped and entirely unhurt. Under a wagon, I discovered an old woman, totally blind and helpless.

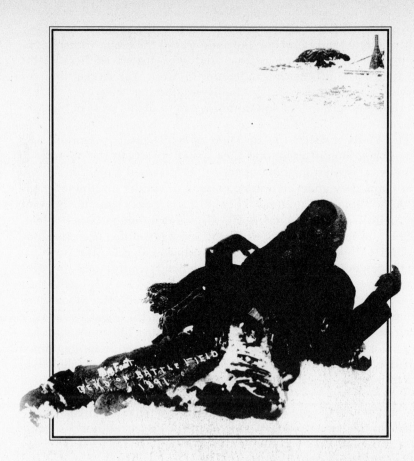

Big Foot, seventy-year-old chief of the Sioux, was one of 146 Indians killed by the U. S. Seventh Cavalry at Wounded Knee. He was found dead three days later, frozen grotesquely where he had fallen.

Eastman began to load the few survivors into wagons to return to the agency (reservation headquarters), where he had set up a small hospital. Two groups of white men stayed behind at Wounded Knee. One was a troop of the U.S. Seventh Cavalry. The other was a group of about thirty white civilians who had agreed to bury the dead, at a charge of two dollars a body. They found the body of the chief of the Indians, an old man named Big Foot, frozen half sitting, half lying down. Ill with pneumonia, he had been lying on a blanket on the winter ground when the shooting started.

It took until the next day to dig a big, open grave. Then the bodies were gathered. Under an unusually strong January sun, the grave diggers sweated; many worked in their shirtsleeves. They stacked 146 dead Indians — 128 men and women and 18 children — in the pit. Then, while the cavalrymen stayed out of sight, the civilians gathered in a half-circle around the grave to have their photograph taken. For the photographer, they held their rifles, not shovels. Then they shoveled dirt in over the bodies. When the diggers and the cavalry rode away, nothing was left at Wounded Knee but the fresh dirt of the grave and the charred poles of the Indian tepees that had been put up only a few days before. The battle, or massacre (it was really some of both), was over.

Wounded Knee was the last and most tragic moment in a long, difficult, and often ugly process: the conquest of the Sioux Indians. The conquerors were the white citizens and blue-coated soldiers of the United States. The process began before the Civil War. At that time the Sioux were a powerful tribe, probably numbering well over 20,000. They hunted on millions of square miles of the plains west of the Missouri River.

The Sioux resisted the invasion of white miners, farmers, and ranchers. They fought often, and they usually won. In the summer of 1876 they won two astonishing victories. At Rosebud Creek, in what is now Montana, they attacked a large column of cavalry and infantry and forced the soldiers into a retreat. Then, just a few days later, the Seventh Cavalry, with General George A. Custer commanding, attacked a large Sioux camp on the Little Bighorn River, just a few miles from Rosebud Creek. Custer divided his force, and the Indians killed Custer as well as most of the Seventh, one of the most experienced cavalry units operating in the West.

But there were too many other soldiers. Though the Sioux were never defeated, their surrender was inevitable. In 1877, just a year after "Custer's last stand," the great war chief Crazy Horse led many of his followers onto a reservation that had been recently set aside for the Sioux. Crazy Horse was murdered a short time later. Some of his people fled to Canada to join the other outstanding Sioux leader, Sitting Bull. About 2,500 Sioux then tried to survive in Canada. But hunger and cold—and the fact that white people had slain most of the buffalo—finally drove them back to the reservation. In 1881 Sitting Bull surrendered—"came in," as it was said. This was the end of a golden age for the Sioux, one that had lasted more than a century.

Originally, before white Europeans had come to North America, the Sioux had lived very much like the Indians of the eastern seaboard. Their territory was not the open plains of the Dakotas, but the woods and lakes of Minnesota and Wisconsin. There, they had built permanent bark

The Sioux moved onto reservations such as this one at Pine Ridge, South Dakota, in 1877. This traditional form of tribal encampment in tepees was one of the Sioux practices that disturbed the whites. Reservation policy encouraged separate and permanent houses for each Sioux family.

houses, used canoes, and hunted only small game. They had also farmed. This life was disturbed by indirect contact with white civilization. The Sioux were driven out of their woodlands and onto the Great Plains by another tribe, the Chippewas. The Chippewas had come into contact with the French in Canada and had obtained guns in trade for furs. The guns gave the Chippewas an overwhelming advantage, and the Sioux had had to retreat to the west and south, out onto the great Plains.

But what began as a painful retreat soon turned into a triumphant new life. Gradually, the Sioux themselves obtained guns. They also discovered another European "import," the horses descended from the mounts the Spanish had brought into Mexico and the southwest. Together, these European tools—the horse and the rifle—transformed Sioux culture. For the first time, they could hunt buffalo. The plains were transformed from a barren, hostile environment into a hunting paradise. The buffalo herds became a source of meat, clothing, and shelter. The old bark houses gave way to hide-covered tepees that could be moved from one hunting area to another. This nomadic life brought the Sioux into contact (and conflict) with other Plains tribes. Hunting and warfare became the central focus of the Sioux economy and culture. For men, status in the tribe became dependent on skill and bravery in hunts and skirmishes. To a Sioux man, the tools of the hunt—his ponies, his rifle, his bow and arrows—were everything. The rituals of hunting and warfare gave meaning to his life. Any work that was not part of hunting, like preparing hides or drying meat or gathering berries, belonged to women. By the early part of the nineteenth century, the new society the Sioux had built on the plains was confident, prosperous, and expanding. They hunted all the way from the Missouri River to the valleys of the Little Big Horn Mountains on the eastern edge of the Rockies.

But, almost as soon as this civilization was established, it was challenged. The whites, with their cannon, their railroads, their plows, and their reservations, eventually destroyed the Sioux way of life. The whites slaughtered buffalo by the thousands, until practically none were left. Then the whites insisted that the Sioux live again in permanent houses. Government rations of beef, flour, and beans substituted for the hunt. It did not help much if a kindly agent sometimes allowed the men to "hunt" their twice-monthly ration of cattle. Games like this could not replace the old life. The authority of warriors and chiefs had depended on their skill in violent and dangerous activities. Reservation life was, above all, peaceful. The white agents even forbade the most holy annual ritual of the Sioux, the Sun Dance. And they insisted, too, that the men of the tribe could have only one wife.

What was happening was simple, and, from the Sioux point of view, tragic. They had been defeated by a much more powerful and complex society. Some of them—the "nonprogressives"—might resist in a few ways. They could reject the cotton shirts and trousers of the white man and continue to wear Indian clothing. They could insist on wearing their hair in the traditional long braid. But resistance could not revive the old life. They had long ago accepted some of the white man's ways

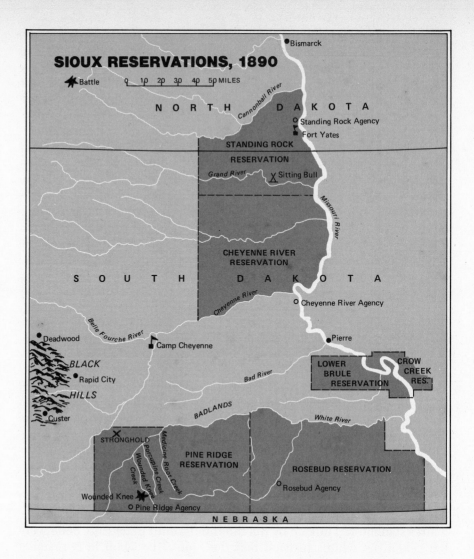

SIOUX RESERVATIONS, 1890

and tools. The horse and the rifle had been useful in the old life. But the government, with the "Great Father" President at its head, had plans for the Sioux that were utterly at odds with the old ways.

American policy was aimed at one long-range goal — to make each Indian family into a self-supporting, farming unit. In the old life, the tribal band, not the family, had been the basic social unit. The band moved, hunted, ate, and worshipped together, and families tended to merge imperceptibly with the common life of the band. The white vision saw each family gathered in its own log house, wearing white men's clothes, gathered around its own, private fire in a white man's stove, and, preferably, worshipping the white man's God instead of the old Sioux god, Wakan Tanka. To well-intentioned reformers in the East, this meant "raising the Indian to civilization." To whites in the West, it meant a final end to the Indian as a barrier to westward expansion.

For the Sioux, all of this meant a divided world. Even those who wanted to cooperate most, the so-called "progressives," lived a double life. A man might put on white clothes; he might plow and harvest, have only one wife, and send his children to white men's schools. But still there was the old life, alive in memory but dead in fact. George Sword, for example, was a progressive. He was even a member of the Indian police force the agents used to help keep order. But George Sword's description of his religious beliefs captures the painful division of loyalty that existed in the minds of even the most "civilized" Sioux:

> When I believed that Wakan Tanka was right, I served him with all my powers. In war with the white people, I found their Wakan Tanka superior. I then took the name of Sword, and have served their Wakan Tanka according to the white people's manner.
> I became chief of the United States Indian police, and held the office until there was no trouble between the Sioux and the white people. I joined the church and am a deacon in it and shall be until I die.

But all this Christianity and "progress" has not erased the old ways in George Sword. He was still a member of the Oglala band of the Dakota tribe, and his spirit might find itself in the Sioux's heaven, not the white man's:

> I still have my Wasicun [ceremonial pouch] and I am afraid to offend it, because the spirit of an Oglala may go to the spirit land of the Dakota.

This divided consciousness, unable to choose finally between the old and the new, the Indian and the white, touched every area of life for the reservation Indians. To the whites who watched them, the Indians seemed almost like children in their confusion. In fact, the Sioux men, especially, had been deprived of their adult roles in the hunt and battle. So their maturity *was* at stake.

One of the whites' main hopes for destroying the old Sioux culture was to educate a new generation in white schools. They took numbers of Sioux children away from their parents and put them in distant boarding schools. The Sioux reaction was mixed. They could hope that this process would make their childrens' lives better. But there was the inevitable resentment, too, the feeling that their children had been, in effect, kidnapped by the whites.

Even when the white schools were close to home, the Sioux sent their children to them reluctantly. When a new school was opened at Pine Ridge, Sioux parents brought their children in on the first day, but stayed outside the building, milling about, curious and frightened. Their fears were increased when the white teachers pulled down the shades, so no one could see what was happening inside. Suddenly, a gust of wind blew one of the blinds aside for a moment. The Indians got a glimpse of something that filled them with horror. A white woman was holding one Sioux boy while another woman cut his hair. The whole meaning of the reservation experience came quickly into the focus. In the old life, a Sioux male's long braids were a symbol of his manhood.

Here were white women scissoring away, symbolically, the tribal badge of masculinity. The Sioux parents, alarmed and outraged, charged into the school and took their children out.

Only at odd moments and in ineffective ways did the Sioux resist the relentless white pressure on their old ways. The whites controlled the Indians' sources of food, blankets, fuel, housing. The whites even controlled the ownership of an Indian's individual plot of land. The Sioux, like other American Indians, did not have a clearly defined concept of private property — especially private property in land. But they could see plainly that their survival depended on the white man's mysterious concept of land ownership. To lose the land would be to lose everything. Finally, the whites had one ultimate threat: the cavalry that was still stationed in forts scattered all around the Great Plains.

The deep conflict between Indian and white ways came to the surface in 1883, when a Senate investigating committee visited the Sioux. Sitting Bull, who had been one of the Sioux leaders at the Battle of the Little Bighorn, came to testify. But the chairman would not recognize Sitting Bull as chief. Sitting Bull got up and left. All the Indians followed him. But several of the progressive Indians returned to plead with the committee to use its influence with the Great Father to get better treatment for the Indians. Soon even Sitting Bull swallowed his hurt pride and returned to apologize.

Then Sitting Bull gave a remarkable account of what defeat had meant to the Sioux. They had been wealthy in their own terms, with land, ponies, and buffalo aplenty. In one lifetime the white man had reduced them to poverty.

> Whatever you wanted of me I have obeyed. The Great Father sent me word that whatever he had against me in the past had been forgiven and thrown aside, and I accepted his promises and came in. And he told me not to step aside from the white man's path, and I am doing my best to travel in that path. I sit here and look around me now, and I see my people starving. We want cattle to butcher. That is the way you live, and we want to live the same way. When the Great Father told me to live like his people, I told him to send me six teams of mules, because that is the way the white people make a living. I asked for a horse and buggy for my children; I was advised to follow the ways of the white man, and that is why I asked for those things.

Sitting Bull's ideas were a little confused, at least by white standards. But he summed up neatly the dilemma of the Sioux. He was still proud of himself and his tribal ways. He resented the whites' failure to understand this pride. But another side of him recognized defeat and was prepared to plead with the whites not for less civilization but for more. In Sitting Bull, and in almost all the other reservation Indians, pride, resentment, hunger, and begging were so intermixed that a meaningful pattern of life was almost impossible.

The situation was the same among all the Sioux. During the 1880s the Indians were gradually becoming "civilized." But the hunger and anger were just below the surface. Some crucial event or idea was all that was needed to bring the conflict with the whites back into the open, tip the scales one way or the other, and offer the Indians a clear choice between the old life and the new.

A new idea did come, and from an unpredictable direction. In the summer of 1889—about a dozen years after Crazy Horse had surrendered his band of hostiles—the Sioux began to hear rumors of an Indian messiah (or savior) who had come to earth in the West. They had learned enough of Christianity on the reservation to understand the alien notion of a messiah. If it were true that a messiah had come to save the Indians from the whites, surely it was worth investigating, they thought.

The Messiah was said to be at the Paiute reservation at Walker Lake, Nevada. Three of the six Sioux reservations[1] selected important men to make the trip west. It was about a thousand miles away—farther than almost any of the Sioux had ever traveled. Pine Ridge Reservation sent eight men, including Kicking Bear, who was to become the most effective disciple of the new Messiah. One of the men from Rosebud was Short Bull. The Cheyenne River Reservation, with a smaller population than either Pine Ridge or Rosebud, sent one man.

The eleven Sioux started west by train. Railroads had by then penetrated all the major western areas, and Indians hopped freight cars with little or no opposition from the white railroad men. When the Sioux reached Wyoming, they found that other tribes—Cheyennes, Arapahoes, Bannocks, and Shoshonis—had also sent wise men to seek the Messiah. The whole group then traveled south to Walker Lake. There the Paiutes gave them wagons to complete the pilgrimage. Soon they were in the presence of the Messiah.

His Indian name was Wovoka, his white name Jackson Wilson. He was about thirty-five years old. He was Paiute, but he had grown up close to a white ranching family named Wilson. (They gave him his English name.) The Wilsons were a religious family. From them Wovoka had learned in some detail how Jesus had controlled the wind and the seas, how he had promised eternal life to his followers, and how other whites had crucified him. Wovoka was apparently the son of a Paiute shaman, or medicine man.[2] One day in 1889, when he was ill (and perhaps delirious) with a high fever, there was an eclipse of the sun. This led him to believe that he had been taken up to heaven. After talking with God, he had been returned to earth to bring salvation to the Indians.

Wovoka's doctrines were a fairly straightforward Indian version of some of the basic teachings of the New Testament. In a sermon to some visiting Cheyennes he summarized his new faith:

Wovoka, the Messiah, claimed to be sent by God to save his people. He preached nonviolence and brotherly love. He demanded of his followers only that they dance the Ghost Dance and await the resurrection of their dead.

[1] One so-called Great Sioux Reservation had been created in 1868. It consisted of about 43,000 square miles in what is now South Dakota, and it was administered from several agencies on or near the land. In 1889 the Sioux territory, much reduced in size, was broken up into six separate reservations—Pine Ridge, Rosebud, Lower Brule, Crow Creek, Cheyenne River, and Standing Rock.

[2] Almost all American Indians relied on shamans, men or women who were thought to have supernatural powers such as being able to foretell the future or cure the sick.

You must not hurt anybody, or do harm to anyone. You must not fight. Do right always.

Do not tell the white people about this. Jesus is now upon the earth. The dead are all alive again. I do not know when they will be here; maybe this fall or in the spring. When the time comes there will be no more sickness and everyone will be young again.

In a simplified way Wovoka was telling his disciples that the dead would be resurrected soon. The earth would tremble; a new earth would cover the old. But true believers need not be afraid, because they would soon enjoy perfect life, youth, and health. In the meantime, the Indians should live in peace with the whites.

Do not refuse to work for the whites, and do not make any trouble with them until you leave them. When the earth shakes, do not be afraid, it will not hurt you. That is all. You will receive good words from me again some time. Do not tell lies.

Wovoka gave the visiting Cheyennes some clay for making the sacred red paint of the Paiutes. Symbols drawn with it were signs of their salvation. Then he advised them: "When you get home, you must make a dance to continue five days. You must all do it in the same way."

This was the famous Ghost Dance from which Wovoka's new religion soon took its name. During the five days it lasted, men and women sang certain songs and went into hypnotic trances. It was during the dance that Indians were supposed to be able to visit their departed relatives in heaven.

When Short Bull returned to South Dakota, he gave his version of the Ghost Dance religion to his excited Sioux audience. The tone was much more militant than Wovoka's. Short Bull promised punishment for those who refused to be converted—just as the Christian missionaries promised damnation for those who rejected their Messiah. He also promised victory over the hated and feared soldiers for those who wore holy shirts into battle. The shirts were supposed to protect wearers from the bullets of the whites.

If the soldiers surround you, three of you, on whom I have put holy shirts, will sing a song around them, then some of them will drop dead. Then the rest will start to run, but their horses will sink into the earth. The riders will jump from their horses, but they will sink into the earth also. Then you can do as you desire with them. Now, you must know this, that all the soldiers and that race will be dead. There will be only five thousand of them left living on the earth. The guns are the only things we are afraid of, but they belong to our father in heaven. He will see that they do no harm.

It was not only Short Bull who brought back this interpretation from the visit to Wovoka. A similar version of the Ghost Dance faith emerged on all the Sioux reservations during the summer of 1890. The Sioux were offered a new ritual, the Ghost Dance, and a new faith, which held that the whites would soon be buried in the earth and the Indians would once again own the plains. There is no way of knowing how sincere Short Bull was. Nor is there any way of knowing whether Sitting Bull—who soon became a disciple of the Ghost Dance—really be-

Ghost shirts, emblazoned with brightly colored thunderbirds and buffaloes, were supposed to protect Indians from the white man's weapons in battle.

During the Ghost Dance, which went on for five days, the Sioux worked themselves into a trance. Believers thought they could visit their dead while in this state.

lieved in the coming resurrection. Most of the Sioux probably rejected the Ghost Dance and decided to continue along the white man's path. For many, though, the religion of Wovoka offered great hope for the return of the old life and the end of their humiliating captivity. There can be no doubt that large groups of Sioux did accept the Ghost Dance.

Agents on all the reservations tried to stop the dances, using Indian police. But, time and again, the dancing Sioux refused to be cowed. They threatened their own police with rifles, insulted the agents, and began to behave like the Sioux of the 1870s. The agents reacted in various ways. When the police failed to make the Sioux obey, some of the agents refused to issue rations to those Indians who were active Ghost Dancers. At least two of the agents asked for federal troops. One, a new agent at Pine Ridge, was so incompetent that the Indians named him Young-Man-Afraid-of-Indians. White newspapermen, always hungry for a sensational news story, began to write about "hostile" Sioux. And white settlers in the Dakotas began to demand protection from the government.

Finally, after a tug of war between the Department of the Interior and the Department of War in Washington, the government authorized the army to send infantry and cavalry onto the reservations. This move brought about the first real confrontation since 1876 between the Sioux and the dreaded bluecoats. On November 20, 1890, cavalry and infantry units occupied Pine Ridge and Rosebud. A few days later the entire Seventh Cavalry arrived at Pine Ridge. This was Custer's unit, and it included many veterans of the Little Bighorn.

The effect on the Sioux of the appearance of the troops was overpowering. Instead of retreating to the outer edges of the reservations,

Kicking Bear spread the doctrines of the Messiah to Sitting Bull and the Standing Rock Reservation. But he gave the new faith a militant interpretation that caused a white reaction.

most of the Indians at Pine Ridge and Rosebud immediately left their cabins and camps and gathered around the agency buildings. They pitched their tepees in rambling confusion and hoped that they would not be suspected of any wrongdoing. It was as though the only way to safe from the rifles and cannon of the army was to be right under the noses of the officers and agents.

Thus the arrival of the army segregated the Indians. Those who wanted peace with the whites—those who had the good sense to be afraid—had gathered at the agencies. Only the most militant of the Ghost Dancers, led by Kicking Bear and Short Bull, decided to hold out. They were gathered along the creeks not far from the Pine Ridge Agency— at Medicine Root, Porcupine, and Wounded Knee.

About a week after the cavalry's arrival, several hundred of the militant Indians broke for open country. They plundered the farms of the peaceful Indians who had fled to the agencies, and they raided the agency cattle herds for beef. Then about 600 warriors and their families struck out for a low plateau at the northwest corner of Pine Ridge. This area was known as the Stronghold. Here the Indians had grass, water, cattle, ponies in large numbers, and plenty of guns and ammunition. They announced that they intended to stay all winter, dancing, and then see what the spring brought.

Fortunately, the officer in command at Pine Ridge decided to be cautious. He sent one messenger after another to the Stronghold, promising that there would be no punishment if the Indians surrendered and returned to the agency. In turn the Indians had to agree to give up the Ghost Dance and return the cattle and other things they had taken. The messengers were badly treated, but some of the men at the Stronghold wanted to surrender. It seemed clear that sooner or later the Indians would disagree among themselves and the threat of uprising would be broken. The situation at Pine Ridge settled into a stalemate, with neither side ready to force a confrontation.

Now the scene of the action shifted north to Standing Rock Reservation, where Sitting Bull kept his camp. The nonprogressive Indians regarded Sitting Bull almost reverently. He was probably not as great a war chief as Crazy Horse had been. But Sitting Bull had held out against the whites longer than any other Sioux leader. And his people believed that he had extraordinary powers as a medicine man.

The agent at Standing Rock was James McLaughlin, a tough, fair, and experienced agent. For years he had struggled to gain moral leadership of the Indians, and for years Sitting Bull had stood in his way. McLaughlin had been looking for a way to break Sitting Bull's hold over the nonprogressive Indians at Standing Rock. When Sitting Bull took up the forbidden Ghost Dance, McLaughlin decided that arresting him would be the best course. McLaughlin wanted to delay the arrest until winter, when the Indians stayed indoors to avoid the bitter cold and to rest. The agent also believed that the arrest should be made by the Sioux Indian police, not by the cavalry units stationed near the agency at Fort Yates.

When the Sioux faced the white men's cameras, they either dressed in their most formal clothing and struck stiff poses or they presented themselves the way Sitting Bull and some of his family did in this photograph—modest, uncertain, and huddled together. Most whites faced the new experience of being photographed in exactly the same two ways, of course.

In November 1890, McLaughlin began to enlarge his Indian police force. He ordered them to keep a close watch on Sitting Bull's camp and make certain that the old chief did not leave.

In mid-December McLaughlin learned that Sitting Bull had been invited to the Stronghold, where he would join the Pine Ridge and Rosebud Sioux under Short Bull and Kicking Bear. The agent was determined to stop Sitting Bull from taking his group to Pine Ridge. He knew that a stalemate had developed there, and he felt that Sitting Bull's presence might be enough to tip the scales toward open warfare between the Sioux and the cavalry. So McLaughlin ordered Sitting Bull's arrest. He commanded the Indian police, who were led by an experienced lieutenant, Bull Head, to sneak into Sitting Bull's camp at dawn on December 15. They were to arrest the chief and bring him into the agency.

Bull Head and the police met the command with mixed feelings. Most of them were progressives. They prayed to the white man's God before starting their mission. But the thought of Sitting Bull still brought back memories of the great days of the Sioux. One of the police, He Alone, whose white name was John Lone Man, later remembered the way he felt when the orders were read and translated to the police. (The English here is the work of an educated relative of his.)

I'm simply expressing my viewpoint as one who had reformed from all the heathenish ways, formerly one of the loyal followers of Chief Sitting Bull. But ever since I was about ten years of age, I had participated in a good many buffalo hunts and fought under Sitting Bull. But the most important fight I took part in was the Custer fight. After this fight I still went with Sitting Bull's band to Canada. Even after Sitting Bull was returned to Standing Rock Reservation, I remained in his camp, where I tamed down somewhat. We all felt sad.

The police gathered in the early evening of December 14 and passed the night telling war stories. Then, just before dawn, Bull Head ordered He Alone and the thirty or so other police to get ready.

Sitting Bull's camp stood on the north bank of the Grand River. The police, circling from the east, crossed the river to cut off any possible excape southward toward Pine Ridge. Soon they could see Sitting Bull's log cabin. In front of it stood the very tall tepee that was the headquarters for the Ghost Dance. Sitting Bull's two wives, his son Crow Foot, and several other children and relatives lived in the cabin. Other tepees were scattered around it. The police paused for a moment, then crossed the river again. He Alone recalled:

> We rode up as if we attacked the camp. We quickly dismounted, and while our officers went inside we all scattered around the cabin. It was still dark, and everybody was asleep, and only dogs greeted us.
>
> Bull Head knocked at the door, and the Chief answered, *"How, timahel hiyu you."* [All right, come in.]
>
> Bull Head said, "I come to arrest you. You are under arrest."
>
> Sitting Bull said, "How. Let me put on my clothes and go with you."
>
> When Sitting Bull started to go with the police, one of Sitting Bull's wives burst into a loud cry which drew attention. No sooner had this started, when several leaders were rapidly making their way toward Sitting Bull's cabin. Bear That Catches, particularly, came up close saying, "Now, here are the metal breasts[3] just as we had expected. You think you are going to take him. You shall not do it."

By now the entire camp was up and angry. The police might still have been able to arrest the sleepy Sitting Bull if Crow Foot, his seventeen-year-old son, had not intervened. Sitting Bull had been grooming Crow Foot to be a chief, filling his youthful head with tales of courage in battle. As He Alone described it, Crow Foot upset the delicate balance of fear and anger:

> Just about this time, Crow Foot got up, moved by the wailing of his mother and the remarks of Bear That Catches, and said to Sitting Bull, "Well, you always called yourself a brave chief. Now you are allowing yourself to be taken by the metal breasts."
>
> Sitting Bull then changed his mind, and said, *"Ho ca mni kte sni yelo."* [Then I will not go.]
>
> Lieutenant Bull Head said to the chief, "Come now, do not listen to any one."
>
> I said to Sitting Bull, "Uncle,[4] nobody is going to harm you. Please do not let others lead you into any trouble.
>
> But the chief's mind was made up not to go, so the three head officers laid their hands on him, pulling him outside. By this time, the whole camp was in commotion. Bear That Catches pulled out a gun from under his blanket and fired into Lieutenant Bull Head, wounding him. I ran up toward where they were holding the chief, when Bear That Catches raised his gun. He pointed and fired at me, but it snapped [misfired]. I jerked the gun away from his hands and laid him out. It was about this moment that Lieutenant Bull Head fired into Sitting Bull while still holding him, and Red Tomahawk followed with another shot which finished the chief.

---

[3]"Metal breasts" was a reference to the policemen's badges.
[4]Indians often used words like "Uncle" and "Father" as terms of respect.

There was more shooting, and soon the Ghost Dancers ran for a line of trees. After a time the police took shelter in Sitting Bull's cabin. The inner walls of the cabin were unfinished but hung with strips of brightly colored sheeting, sewn together and tacked to the walls. Suddenly, one of the policemen noticed a movement in a corner, behind the sheeting. He Alone raised the curtain:

> There stood Crow Foot, and as soon as he was exposed to view, he cried out, "My uncles, do not kill me. I do not wish to die." Lieutenant Bull Head said, "Do what you like with him. He is the one that has caused this trouble." I do not remember who fired the shot that killed Crow Foot—several fired at once.

Just after Crow Foot was killed, the cavalry units from Fort Yates arrived. The remaining members of Sitting Bull's band scattered toward the south.

He Alone and the rest of the Indian police went home filled with the confusion that was so much a part of reservation life. He Alone performed a Sioux ritual. He built a small shelter and dropped hot stones into water to create a steam bath "that I might cleanse myself for participating in a bloody fight with my fellow men." Then he burned all the clothes he had worn to Sitting Bull's camp. Next, He Alone set out to perform a white man's ritual:

> The next day, I took my family into the agency. I reported to Major McLaughlin. He laid his hand on my shoulders, and said, 'He Alone is a man. I feel very proud of you for the way you have carried out your part in the fight with the Ghost Dancers.' I was not very brave right at that moment. His comment nearly set me a-crying.

Four Indian policemen died at Sitting Bull's camp. Two more (including Lieutenant Bull Head) would soon be dead of their wounds. One of them, Shave Head, asked McLaughlin, "Did I do well, father?" McLaughlin nodded. Shave Head went on:

> Then I will die in the faith of the white man, to which my five children already belong. Send for my wife, that we may be married by the Black Gown [priest] before I die.

Shave Head's wife came, but too late. The next day, the six dead Indian police were buried. A squad of bluecoats fired honorary volleys over the graves, and taps were blown.

At least eight of Sitting Bull's followers had died. Their bodies were left where they had fallen. Only Sitting Bull was buried. A few moments after completion of the ceremonies for the Indian police, Sitting Bull's body, in a plain coffin, was lowered into a grave in the Fort Yates cemetery. The only people who watched were three officers, serving as official witnesses, and the four guardhouse gravediggers.

None of Sitting Bull's followers was present at his burial. Most of them—about 400—had fled south and west from the Grand River camp. The authorities at Standing Rock had a number of nightmarish ideas about what might happen next. The Standing Rock Ghost Dancers might join Chief Big Foot on the Cheyenne River, where the dance had been in full swing for weeks. On the other hand, the frightened Sitting Bull group might strike out for the Stronghold, where Short Bull and Kicking Bear still held out. Or they might set Big Foot in motion toward the Stronghold too, with terrible results. News of the death of Sitting Bull, likely to spread like prairie fire, could ignite the entire Sioux reservation system.

Agent McLaughlin immediately sent friendly scouts to find Sitting Bull's band. Upon finding them, the scouts were able to persuade over half to return to the Standing Rock Reservation. Some of those who simply scattered sooner or later also went back to their homes around Grand River. The rest—fewer than a hundred—headed south to join Big Foot.

They reached a camp that was already nervous and confused. Big Foot had been a great chief. But he was old now, in his seventies, and his control over his band was slipping. The band's medicine man, Yellow Bird, was a fanatical Ghost Dancer. Many of the young braves were ready to bring about their hoped-for victory over the whites. There were about 200 in the band, and all of them were aware of mounting pressure from the white soldiers.

The War Department had ordered Big Foot's arrest, on the false theory that he was almost as large a source of potential trouble as Sitting Bull had been. An observation camp, Camp Cheyenne, had been established by the cavalry just a few miles up the Cheyenne River. Infantry units from the east were trying to cross the Missouri River, which was partially ice-covered.

For several days Big Foot wavered among various alternatives. At one point he was convinced by messengers from the cavalry to go to the Cheyenne River Agency. But many of his young men wanted to go to the Stronghold instead. Big Foot had also been invited by the Pine Ridge chiefs to go there to settle the troubles. He had a great reputation as a diplomat, and he was offered a hundred ponies to heal the split between the "friendly" Sioux and the Ghost Dancers at Pine Ridge. Most of the time, however, Big Foot seemed to want only to stay put at his own camp and wait.

Finally, for reasons that are difficult to guess, Big Foot made his decision. He would go to Pine Ridge, make peace, and accept the gift of ponies. What he did not realize was that leaving his reservation when the whites were so frightened of a Sioux "uprising" would make him a fugitive "hostile" in the eyes of the military. Almost immediately, new orders went out for Big Foot's arrest. His band was to be disarmed and their horses taken. Then they would be marched to the railroad and sent to Omaha—far away from their own reservation lands. Big Foot never understood that this was the army's plan. He assumed that he was going to Pine Ridge on a mission of peace.

Big Foot's band left camp on December 23, under the cover of night. As soon as the officers at Camp Cheyenne realized that the old chief had gone, a desperate series of cavalry units started patrolling the line between Big Foot's camp and the Stronghold. But the chief passed east of the patrols. The band moved very slowly, for Big Foot had caught pneumonia. He rode in a wagon without springs. Soon Big Foot was bleeding from his nose. And it was bitterly cold for the old man. At one point, in a pass through a steep wall along the Bad River, Big Foot's men had to dig out a road for the wagon. Big Foot managed to reach Porcupine Creek, only about thirty miles from the Pine Ridge Agency, without being sighted by the army. He sent men ahead to tell the Sioux he was coming.

On December 28, five days after starting south, Big Foot's band was finally "captured" by the Seventh Cavalry. When the Indians and cavalry met, there was a tense moment. The cavalry formed a skirmish line and brought up cannon. Big Foot's braves formed a battle line in front of his wagon. But then the cavalry commander came forward. He and Big Foot shook hands, and the chief accepted an "escort"—going, he thought, to Pine Ridge. Together, the cavalry and the Indians made their way to a trading post at Wounded Knee Creek.

The officer in charge had wisely not tried to disarm the Sioux, and he let them keep their horses for the trip. He even transferred Big Foot into an ambulance wagon. When the two groups reached Wounded Knee, the Indians were issued rations. The rest of the Seventh Cavalry came from Pine Ridge to join the patrol. The Indians pitched their tepees in a low hollow near a ravine that led into the creek. There were 102 men and 230 women and children. The soldiers—a total of about 500—camped on a rise just to the north. Armed sentries surrounded the Indians, but on the whole everything seemed peaceful enough.

Soon the Indians settled down and the cavalry—except for the ring of sentries around the Indian camp—went to sleep. Only a few officers, veterans of the Little Bighorn disaster, stayed up late. They celebrated over a keg of whiskey someone had brought from the agency.

The next morning Colonel James Forsyth, commander of the Seventh Cavalry, asked all the men of Big Foot's group to gather in a council between the tepees and the cavalry encampment. The sentries remained in place. The rest of the cavalry units drew up, mounted, around the Sioux men and their camp. Forsyth asked the Indians for their weapons.

Big Foot tried diplomacy. From his ambulance bed he quietly advised his men to give up the bad guns but hide the good ones. Soon Forsyth sent twenty of the Indians to the tepees to bring the guns. Meanwhile, however, the Sioux women (who understood the value of a weapon) had hidden the rifles that the Sioux had bought, stolen, or taken in battle. The Indians returned to the council with only two old, broken cavalry carbines.

Forsyth heightened his search. He placed a line of troops between the Sioux braves and their camp and sent his own men into the tepees. But this search uncovered only thirty rifles, most of them old and useless. This left one other real possibility: the Sioux were hiding their rifles under the blankets they kept draped over their shoulders against the cold.

By now the situation was very delicate. Forsyth ordered Big Foot brought out on his blanket. The medicine man, Yellow Bird, was dancing around, chanting Ghost Dance songs, urging the young braves to be firm. In the tepees women were hastily packing, ready to run.

Suddenly, one Indian, Black Coyote, pulled a rifle from his blanket and began to shout, holding the weapon over his head. He was probably deaf and, by the Indians' own testimony, a little insane. Two soldiers grabbed him and struggled for the rifle. It went off, firing overhead. In what may have been a signal, Yellow Bird threw a handful of dust into the air. Several braves pulled rifles from their blankets and aimed at the cavalry. "By God, they have broken," an officer shouted. The Indians fired, and at about the same moment came the command "Fire! Fire on them!"

No one could stop what happened next. Big Foot was quickly killed. Cavalry carbines ripped into the group of Sioux men. The bullets that did not find a Sioux body passed on across the ravine into the tepees. Women ran this way and that, followed by children. Some of the Indians broke toward the creek, where they were cut down by waiting cavalrymen. Others ran into the ravine.

Corporal Paul Weinert manned one of the Seventh Cavalry's small, rapid-fire cannon on the hill. Like the other cavalrymen, he was surprised when the firing started. But within a moment or two, he was caught up in the battle, pumping shots angrily wherever he saw moving Sioux:

> All of the Indians opened fire on us. Lieutenant Hawthorne ran toward me and was calling, when suddenly I heard him say, "Oh, my God!" and then I knew he had been hit. I said: "By God! I'll make 'em pay for that," and ran the gun into the opening of the ravine. They kept yelling for me to come back. Bullets were coming like hail from the Indians' Winchesters. I kept going in farther, and pretty soon everything was quiet at the other end of the line.

Corporal Weinert was a soldier with a sophisticated weapon. The experience of Catching Spirit Elk, a Sioux who had surrendered his rifle, was almost the opposite of Weinert's:

> Then followed firing from all sides. I threw myself on the ground. I then jumped up to run toward the Indian camp, but was then and there shot down, being hit on my right leg, and soon after was shot again on the other leg. When the general firing ceased, I heard an interpreter calling out, saying the wounded would be kindly treated. I opened my eyes and looked about and saw the dead and wounded all around me.

Some officers did what they could to prevent women and children from being shot down. But the Indians (at least those who still had weapons) were fast and accurate with their repeating rifles, and the soldiers

The Sioux who died at Wounded Knee were buried in a mass grave. With them died the last remnants of Indian resistance on the Western plains.

sometimes fired at anything that moved. When the artillery on the hill opened up on the Indians in the ravine, the shells exploded on all without regard to age or sex. Apparently, too, some of the soldiers broke ranks and chased down fleeing Indians. These were the bodies Charles Eastman found miles away from Wounded Knee.

The actual battle lasted only a few minutes and the cavalry's mopping-up only a short time longer. About 150 braves rode out from Pine Ridge, too late and too few to help their comrades. The cavalry gathered their own dead (25) and wounded (39) and returned to the Pine Ridge Agency. They took some of the wounded Sioux with them and left the rest on the field. There were at least 146 Indian dead—about half of them men. Some bodies were probably taken away during the next two days, before Eastman's party arrived to rescue the living and bury the rest. All in all, probably 200 Sioux and whites had died.

Wounded Knee was followed by a few small skirmishes. But soon Pine Ridge was pacified. The Stronghold Indians had given up while Big Foot's band was on the march. The Ghost Dance was over. Spring came and went, but the earth did not cover the white man, as the Messiah had promised. Paul Weinert, the cannoneer, received a Congressional Medal of Honor for his part in the action at the edge of the ravine.

A small white church was later built at the Sioux mass grave, on what came to be called Cemetery Hill. In 1903, with the help of missionaries, the Indians put up their own small monument, burying Wounded Knee in the past.

This monument is erected by surviving relatives and other Ogalalla and Cheyenne River Sioux Indians in memory of the Chief Big Foot Massacre, Dec. 29, 1890. Col. Forsyth in command of U.S. troops. Big Foot was a great chief of the Sioux Indians. He often said, "I will stand in peace till my last day comes." He did many good and brave deeds for the white man and the red man. Many innocent women and children who knew no wrong died here.

28

SETTLING THE LAST FRONTIER

R.J.W.

There is nothing unique about the history of the Sioux. It is true they resisted the whites longer and more ferociously than most other Indians, east or west. And they were the only tribe that, inspired by the Messiah's new religion, developed a militant resistance to reservation life. But, despite these differences, they were finally defeated in a manner typical of the way in which white Americans subdued all the Indians.

The defeat of the Sioux and the other Plains Indians was just one part of the history of continental expansion. White Americans had begun moving west in the 1830s. In decades after the Civil War, this movement increased in speed and recklessness.

THE LAST WEST

Until the 1840s, America had a clearly drawn frontier. It was possible at each census before then to draw a zigzag line from north to south showing how far settlement had advanced in each decade. But after the Mexican War this was no longer true. The drift of pioneers into Oregon, the settlement of Texas and Utah, and the discovery of gold in California created isolated pockets of white settlement thousands of miles beyond the old frontier line near the Mississippi. By the early 1850s it was evident that the Pacific Coast would be settled fairly quickly, organized into territories, and carved into states. California had already been admitted

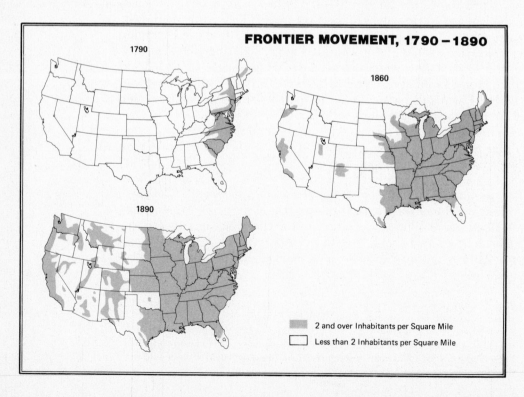

FRONTIER MOVEMENT, 1790–1890

1790

1860

1890

▨ 2 and over Inhabitants per Square Mile

☐ Less than 2 Inhabitants per Square Mile

to statehood as part of the Compromise of 1850. Oregon entered the Union nine years later.

Between the Pacific Coast and the old frontier in eastern Kansas and Nebraska lay a vast stretch of plains and mountains. It formed an area larger than the whole territory over which Washington governed as President. This region was the last frontier, the last region to be settled by white Americans.

The Great Plains begin in the first tier of states west of the Mississippi River, and extend west to the Rockies. In 1836 the Senate Committee for Indian Affairs declared that the Great Plains were an "uninhabitable region." The Indians there "are on the outside of us, and in a place which will forever remain on the outside." In fact the plains were given an official name, "The Great American Desert." The weather there is dry. There is no water in many of the rivers during most of the year. The land is not covered with trees but with stubborn grass. Only the Indian and the buffalo seemed able to thrive. The Rocky Mountain region also seemed to offer little to encourage settlement. For many years its great peaks and high valleys were the home of only small Indian bands and a few American fur traders.

There were many reasons why this myth that the West could not be settled came to an end. Three of the earliest and most important factors were gold, railroads, and cattle. As miners, railroad men, and ranchers moved into the region, they systematically seized Indian lands. Then came the final pioneers of the last West, the farmers. In 1890 the Census Bureau announced that the frontier no longer existed.

THE MINING FRONTIER

The discovery of gold and silver had been responsible for the rapid development of California. Miners who reached the Pacific Coast too late to find gold easily soon began to drift east over the mountains, looking for new bonanzas. In 1858 prospectors found gold near Pike's Peak in Colorado. Soon people were pouring into new, ramshackle towns like Denver, Pueblo, and Boulder.

Their covered wagons proclaimed "Pike's Peak or Bust!" A year after the first strike about 100,000 people—mostly men without their families—had moved into the area. Like most other Western gold and silver strikes, the Pike's Peak boom did not last. The earliest prospectors soon raked off the surface gold. The remaining precious metal was buried deep in the mountains, where it could be mined only with expensive machinery that individual miners could not afford. Within three months in 1859 the population of the Colorado goldfields dwindled to about 50,000. But enough men stayed to create a pocket of white settlement in the mountains.

A similar process was under way farther west, in what is now Nevada. Miners from California found gold near the western border of the region in the late 1850s. In 1859 they discovered the famous Comstock Lode. One of the richest single mines in America, it produced over $200 million worth of gold and silver in the thirty years following its discovery. Thousands of men rushed over the mountains from Sacramento to build nearby Virginia City. Soon the town had five newspapers, a miniature stock exchange, and a horde of prospectors, saloonkeepers, prostitutes, and gamblers. A few men became enormously wealthy. Most of the prospectors, however, went away disappointed.

Some miners who stayed found small pockets of loose gold that could be mined with a pan or a sluice, a simple trough that runs water downhill over dirt and loose rocks, washing out the heavy gold dust. This kind of mining, called placer mining, soon washed off the free metal near the surface. The only way to make the goldfields pay off on a large scale over a long period was to invest money in machinery that could dig out hard rock below the surface. This meant that the miner's frontier quickly became a corporate frontier, exploited by mining companies owned by Eastern investors. Within a few years any successful field soon became an industrial development. And the prospectors scattered again in search of a new discovery and easy pickings elsewhere.

The California Gold Rush that had excited so many thousands of Americans in 1849 was repeated over and over again throughout the West.

Virginia City, Nevada, sprang up after the discovery of silver nearby in 1859. Mark Twain described it as "the liveliest town that America ever produced" in its early years. Schools, churches, and "respectable" businesses replaced saloons and gambling halls after the initial excitement of silver fever had died down.

Open-pit mining, utilizing expensive heavy machinery to dig through the surface of hard rock to the ores below, helped turn the miner's frontier into a corporate frontier.

In the late 1850s a small strike was made in eastern Washington, but it seen petered out. Restless miners headed farther east, up the Snake and Salmon rivers into Idaho. There they built Boise, Silver City, and other new mining towns. By 1861, the start of the Civil War, there were probably 30,000 white men in Idaho.

During the Civil War—while their countrymen were battling at Bull Run and Chickamauga—white miners moved from Idaho into Montana. There they struck gold and silver at Last Chance Gulch (which later became the city of Helena) and Alder Gulch (Virginia City). By 1863 Idaho had enough citizens to organize as a territory, and Montana followed a year later.

The last Western gold rush occurred in 1874. In the Black Hills of South Dakota, in the heart of the Great Sioux reservation, an army expedition commanded by General Custer found traces of gold. According to a treaty between the United States and the Indians, the hills belonged to the Sioux "forever." For a short time the government tried to prevent white men from entering the Black Hills. But the pressure to find gold was too great. Within two years about 7,000 whites had built Deadwood and Custer City. The Sioux lands had been decisively invaded.

TRANSPORTATION WEST

The influx of miners, together with the settlement of Oregon and California, led to demands for quick, safe, and economical land transportation between the settled East and the Far West. Every new mining town wanted to be linked to the rest of the country. People who lived on the west coast wanted an overland route as an alternate to the long sea voyage around South America.

Trail, Stage, and Pony The Oregon Trail, Santa Fe Trail, and other routes followed by pioneers in the 1840s and early 1850s were more or less protected by army posts along the way. But they were far from being real roads. Something else seemed necessary.

In 1858 the first stage road was finally cut through the countryside for the Butterfield Overland Express. Its route ran 2,000 miles, from St. Louis south through Indian Territory,[1] then across

[1]This region—corresponding roughly to the present state of Oklahoma—was set aside in 1834 for Indians removed from east of the Mississippi. Later, parts of it were reserved for Western Indians, too.

This 1859 sketch shows a stage near Tucson, Arizona, on the Butterfield Overland Express route. Passengers had to endure the rough ride through desert lands on springless seats.

Texas, New Mexico, and Arizona. The ride was rough and usually very hot; although it took twenty-four days, the overland trip was faster than the sea voyage. Soon other stage and freighting companies were opening additional roads across Colorado and Utah to California.

In 1860 businessmen set up a mail service known as the pony express. Small, lightweight boys, like jockeys, rode big horses (not ponies) in relays between St. Joseph, Missouri, and Sacramento, California. The young riders were able to carry a message across the country in ten days. The pony express prospered for only about a year, however. In 1861 the first telegraph line was put through to the west coast. The time for sending and receiving cross-country messages was then cut to a split second.

A Transcontinental Railroad All these ways of getting people, goods, and information across the country were only preludes to the most dramatic and successful method of all, the railroad. A transcontinental railroad had been a dream since the 1840s — to move people through the West to California. The North and the South, however, had not been able to agree on the western part of the route. The North wanted a line to run from Chicago to San Francisco. The South insisted on a route through Texas to southern California.

The Civil War ended this competition. By seceding, the South lost its right to participate in the decision making. In 1862 Congress settled on a route between Council Bluffs, Iowa, and San Francisco. The same law provided for enormous financial support from the federal government. There would be two companies. The Central Pacific would build east from San Francisco. The Union Pacfic (a patriotic name suited to wartime) would go west across Nebraska and Colorado. They were to meet somewhere in the middle.

A railroad line spanning the continent would not have been possible without the help of thousands of Chinese laborers, who did much of the work on the Central Pacific.

Each railroad would be given a right of way 400 feet wide. In addition, the government would lend the railroads up to $48,000 for each mile of track laid—less for flat country, more for mountain track. Most important, the railroads would be given 6,400 acres for every mile of track completed. In 1864 this land allowance was doubled.

The Central Pacific started building toward the east slowly. The company lacked funds, and labor was scarce. But gradually these problems were resolved. The Lincoln administration cooperated by allowing the railroad to claim flat-country miles as mountain miles, thus entitling the companies to the largest possible federal loans. The labor problem was solved by importing thousands of Chinese. In 1864 the railroad laid only about 20 miles of track, but by 1867 the pace was up to 20 miles a month.

At the other end of the proposed route the Union Pacific also built slowly, at first. But it picked up speed by bringing in thousands of Irish immigrants to lay rails. In 1868 alone the Union Pacific laid 425 miles of track.

In May 1869, after only five years of construction, the two work gangs met at Promontory Point, Utah, just east of the Great Salt Lake. The last tie put down was coated with silver; the last spike was gold. A telegraph operator cabled east and west: "Hats off—prayer is being offered." Then there was a wait of almost fifteen minutes. Again the telegraph clicked: "We have got done praying. The spike is about to be presented." Railroad officials took turns with the hammer; the first blow was a bad miss, but the work was done. The two locomotives eased forward until they touched. The nation celebrated almost as wildly as it had at the end of the Civil War. Chicago's parade was seven miles long. The nation was joined, east to west, across a desert that an earlier generation had believed would never be settled.

During the next fifteen years three more routes were opened across the Rockies. Iowa, Missouri, Kansas, and Nebraska were criss-crossed by rails. In the process the government gave the railroad companies almost 180 million acres of public land, and it lent them over $100 million. Because of complicated regulations that allowed railroads to delay choosing the land they

wanted to keep along their rights of way, they were able to keep great stretches of land for years. At one point the railroads controlled—at least on paper—almost all of Iowa and Wisconsin. The Northern Pacific, whose route crossed the northern tier of states between Lake Superior and the Pacific, controlled a strip of land larger in area than many European nations. The same kind of situation developed in Arizona and New Mexico. By 1885 the railroads held land totaling almost a sixth of the entire country.

Many of the congressmen and senators who voted these huge grants to the railroads did so in the belief that most of the land in the "Great American Desert" was of little value. The motive behind the first transcontinental lines was not to build a transportation network for the Great Plains and the Rockies but to build a link to the Pacific Coast. It took a generation's experience to make clear that the intervening territory was valuable, that it would be settled and farmed. As things turned out, the railroads may have been a very efficient mechanism for disposing of the public lands, at least in some areas. The government's own land policy was confused and often corrupt, and the public interest may, on balance, have been served about as well by the railroad grants as by the government's direct land grant practices.

FROM BUFFALO TO CATTLE

In any case, the first important effects of the railroads on the Great Plains had less to do with land ownership and cultivation than with animals. The railroads created a new industry on the plains—ranching. Building the railroads not only hastened the destruction of the buffalo herds, it also made possible the systematic exploitation of another set of resources: grass and cows.

Early in the sixteenth century the Spanish had begun importing European cattle into America. Over the years the cattle had multiplied. Some had escaped and become wild, especially in southern Texas around the Nueces River. These were the famous Texas longhorns—lanky, tough, long-horned, and too dangerous to be captured or

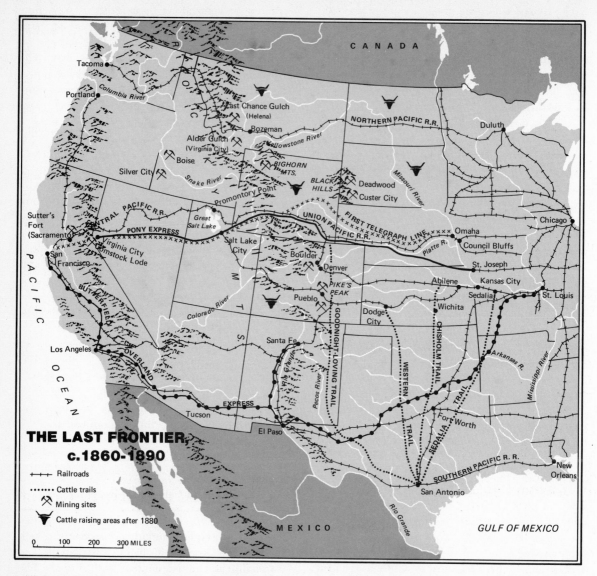

THE LAST FRONTIER
c.1860-1890

+++ Railroads
····· Cattle trails
⚒ Mining sites
🐂 Cattle raising areas after 1880

0   100   200   300 MILES

herded on foot. They roamed at will over the open range, a huge expanse of grass that was part of the public domain. By 1860, there were probably 5 million head of longhorns in Texas.

The Mexicans had learned to rope, brand, and even herd longhorns. In fact, it was Mexicans and not Americans who were the first cowboys. They originated almost all of the tools of the cowboy's trade, from his big hat and kerchief to his tooled leather saddle and boots. Mexico, however, had no real market for beef. The situation was different in the United States.

The Civil War sent beef prices soaring in both the North and the South. The beef herd in the Northern states was smaller at the end of the war than it had been at the beginning. At the same time, the population had grown by more than 20 percent. Thus the demand and price for beef had increased. A man could buy a longhorn steer in Texas for as little as three dollars. The same steer in Chicago was worth ten times as much.

The Long Drive By 1866 the Missouri Pacific Railroad had pushed its line west to Sedalia, Missouri, just east of Kansas City. That same year the first large group of Texans drove enormous herds north across Indian Territory to reach the rail line. The men ran into many difficulties. Part of the route passed through dense forests. The long-horns, unaccustomed to woods, panicked and refused to be driven through the trees. The Indians (whose treaty gave them control of all white travel across their land) harassed the cowboys. This early attempt showed, however, that it was possible to herd cattle safely over hundreds of miles to the railroad—and thus to Eastern markets.

Thus began the twenty-year era of the "long drive." As the years passed, the railroads extended farther west. New cattle towns replaced Sedalia. Among them were Abilene (probably the most successful), Wichita, and Dodge City. Between 1866 and 1888, Texans drove as many as 6 million head of cattle over the grasslands to Kansas.

For those who succeeded, the profits of the long drive were enormous. Cattlemen claimed that as much as 40 percent profit per year was not unusual. Like the miner's frontier, the cattleman's bonanza soon attracted thousands of eager Easterners. Each usually had a few hundred dollars and a dream of running a vast ranch. Like the prospectors, most of the would-be ranchers were disappointed. Many of them either returned home or switched to another line of work such as running a store or saloon.

The long drive, despite the romantic myth of the cowboy it fostered, was a business. It required capital if it was to succeed on a big scale. In the end only the lucky few who had been there first (like the prospectors in California or Nevada) became "cattle barons." In the long run, it was Eastern and European investors, with enough capital to buy and move large herds, who controlled most of the industry.

The long drives of cattle from the rich grasslands of the Southwest to Northern markets lasted through the 1880s. They created vast fortunes for a few fortunate cattle barons and gave the country the legend of the cowboy.

The End of the Open Range The long drive had a brief existence. Gradually, people north of Texas realized that, as the railroads came closer, it made sense to breed and feed cattle nearby instead of driving them up from Texas. During the 1880s the long drive from Texas was replaced by an even wilder cattle bonanza in other plains territories to the north. In 1860 there were no cattle at all in the northwestern plains, and there were only a few in Kansas and Nebraska. By 1880 Montana, the Dakota Territory, Wyoming, and Colorado had great herds, totaling almost 4 million head.

But the days of the open range, when cattle wandered on public land from one spring to the next, could not last long. The cattle industry soon found itself in a situation faced earlier by tobacco and cotton growers—overproduction. Rapid expansion led to an overstocked range. The grass could not support so many cattle. The increased supply also caused prices to fall. Between 1885 and 1886 the price of a steer dropped from thirty dollars to ten dollars. The following winter on the plains was the bitterest in memory. Thousands of cattle starved and froze to death. The cattle bonanza was over.

THE DEFEAT OF THE WESTERN INDIANS

The miners, railroaders, and cattlemen brought about the final chapter in the conflict between whites and Indians. It was a conflict older than Jamestown and as dark as any aspect of American history. The whites cloaked their actions with high-sounding expressions like "civilization against savagery" or "Manifest Destiny." But the facts were very simple: the white men came and took the Indians' lands.

White people in the New World had always regarded the Indians as a "problem." For most whites—whether they were French, Spanish, or English—the Indians were seen either as a people to be exploited through trade or slavery or as a barrier to westward expansion. A few whites sympa-

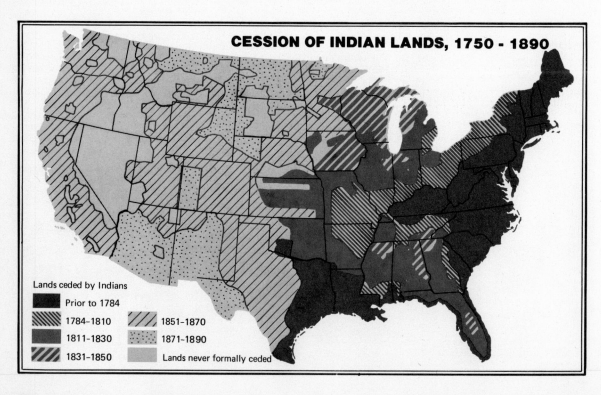

CESSION OF INDIAN LANDS, 1750 - 1890

Lands ceded by Indians

- Prior to 1784
- 1784–1810
- 1811–1830
- 1831–1850
- 1851–1870
- 1871–1890
- Lands never formally ceded

thized with the Indians and did what they could to protect them from the worst aspects of white civilization. But even to those who were sympathetic, helping meant teaching the Indians to "adjust to civilization."

The Indians might be a "problem" for the whites, but for the Indians the whites meant disaster. At stake for the whites was only the delay of continental expansion for a generation or so. The stakes for the Indians were much higher. They were in danger of losing their culture, their freedom, their identity as human beings, and, in many cases, their lives. This was true from the time Cortes invaded Mexico, through Bacon's Rebellion and the removal of the Cherokee and other tribes westward,[2] down to the final conquest of the tribes of the West.

Advantages of the Whites White people's ways were overpowering to the Indians. In the first place, the whites' methods of dealing with the environment were totally unlike those of the Indians. Some Indians farmed a little. But the whites were able to cultivate vast stretches of land, first with teams of mules or oxen, then with machinery. Some Indians, like the Navajos, made ornaments out of silver or gold. But the whites came for gold and silver in droves. Big new towns and frightening machines and explosives changed the face of the mountains and valleys of the Rockies. The Indians hunted wild animals, which seemed numerous enough to last forever. But the whites killed off the wild animals, fenced in the range, and raised great herds of cattle instead.

These were the main weapons of the whites—farming, mining, and ranching. Along with these the whites brought strange powers and "medicine" that made the Indians' situation hopeless indeed—the railroad, soldiers' machine guns and cannons, and the telegraph.

Another weapon of the whites against the Indians was something they did not use on purpose—indeed, the whites feared it themselves.

[2]In the 1830s the federal government forced the so-called Five Civilized Tribes—the Cherokees, Chickasaws, Choctaws, Creeks, and Seminoles—to move from the Southeast to Indian Territory. The Indians suffered so much on the trip west that the journey became known as the trail of tears.

These Mandan Indians survived a smallpox epidemic in 1872. Indians had no immunity to white men's diseases like smallpox and therefore died by the thousands when exposed to them.

This was disease. Smallpox, measles, and other sicknesses may have wiped out as many as half the Western Indians before any significant number of whites even arrived in their territory. The germs traveled with traders and so preceded actual white migrations by decades. The Indians had no inherited resistance or immunity to many diseases of the whites, since the germs had been "imported" from Europe. Indians died by the band and even by the tribe from sicknesses that only made most whites uncomfortable.

Finally, the whites had an advantage that probably counted more than anything else—numbers. They poured west by the thousands. In one change of seasons, between one Sun Dance and another, the whites seemed able to throw up towns like San Francisco, Denver, or Deadwood—towns with populations larger than the whole Sioux nation.

One by one, the tribes of the Great Plains, the California-Intermountain area, and the Northwest Coast were made to realize that the whites were a force they could neither understand nor control. Some groups, like the Sioux, the Kiowas, and the Apaches, fought back. They were sustained by their myths, their magic, and their hatred of the cavalry that invaded their villages, shooting men, women, and children. But, in the end, all the tribes were defeated. Only something as unusual as the Messiah's Ghost Dance could convince the Indians—and only a few at that—that there was any way to combat the enveloping white civilization.

Dealing with the Tribes From the beginning, United States policy toward the Indians had been contradictory. On the one hand, the government treated tribes as independent nations with whom it could make treaties. On the other hand, Indians were not citizens but wards of the government, subject to federal control. In addition, the American nation was growing with incredible speed. Again and again, government aims that seemed practical in one decade were obsolete ten years later.

In California and Oregon, and in the frontier regions of the Rockies, relations between whites and Indians were poorly controlled by the government. Groups of whites simply drove the Indians out, murdering many of them in the process. The Indians of California suffered especially. They had settled around Spanish missions and learned farming and various crafts. After the Spanish missions were closed down in the 1830s, the Indians were defenseless against the greedy whites. In the ten years after the Gold Rush of 1849, some 70,000 of these mission Indians died from starvation, disease, and outright murder.

On the Great Plains, whites might band together to attack Indians. But the government and its army played a much larger role in keeping the peace there than it did farther west. After 1850 the history of Indian-white relations settled down to a fairly steady rhythm of treaties, uprisings, war, and new treaties. The Indians were always the losers. Even when they won the battles, they lost in the making of the treaties.

This process began in 1851 at Fort Laramie on the Oregon Trail. To protect the trail, the government called hundreds of Indian leaders together and persuaded them to agree not to bother the wagon trains crossing their territory. Each tribe accepted boundaries to its hunting grounds. In return, the government promised to leave them in peace.

These agreements left the Indians in possession of almost all of the Great Plains. But, accepting boundaries laid out by Washington opened the door to a new government tactic—getting each tribe, by a separate treaty, to give up part of its lands. By 1865 the Indians had given up all of Kansas, most of Nebraska, the central half of Utah, and almost all of Texas.

The Sand Creek Massacre Much Indian land was surrendered peacefully, in return for promises of peace and annual shipments of government supplies, called annuities. But in 1861 in Colorado, a government attempt to move Cheyennes and Arapahoes onto a small reservation at Sand Creek resulted in the Indians waging a three-year guerrilla war. In 1864 the leader of the warring Indians, Black Kettle, tried to make peace with the whites. The army and the territorial government refused. The unyielding commander of the Colorado militia, Colonel John Chivington, told Black Kettle: "My rule for fighting white men or Indians is to fight them until they lay down their arms and surrender."

Black Kettle led his people to a camp at Sand Creek, where he hoped to be left in peace. But the Indians woke on November 29, 1864, to find 1,000 of Chivington's militia surrounding them. The militia rushed the camp, shooting at everything that moved. When the "fight" was over, 450 Indians were dead. Only about 50 had escaped the massacre. The next year the Cheyennes and Arapahoes had to sign a new treaty. It forced them to leave their Colorado plains for a barren corner of Indian Territory.

Negotiations with the Sioux The Sioux fared better, at least for a time. Their agreement at Fort Laramie in 1851 gave them one of the largest hunting areas in the West—most of the Dakota

CHIEF JOSEPH

Hinmaton-Yalaktit was his name—"thunder coming out of the water and over the land." He was a chief in the tribe the whites called Nez Percé—"pierced nose"—because of their habit of wearing nose ornaments made of shells. Joseph was his white man's name, and, like his biblical namesake, he was taken as a captive into a distant and hostile land. Before he went, however, he did two things. He fought the most brilliant and sustained military campaign against the United States Army ever waged by any American Indian leader. And he made the most poignant and famous surrender speech any American Indian ever delivered.

The surrender and the speech were the outcome of a long train of events that parallel very closely what happened to the Sioux and the other tribes of the West. In 1863, the Nez Percé ceded most of their lands to the United States and agreed to live on a small reservation in Idaho. A portion of the tribe, however, refused to recognize the treaty and became renegades. For ten years, the government did not try to enforce the treaty, and all the Nez Percé had to do was fend off the aggressive behavior of individual white squatters. This was the situation when Joseph, at age thirty-three, became chief after his father's death in 1873.

In 1876 (the year of Custer's expedition against the Sioux), the government decided to enforce the treaty and move the "renegade" Nez Percé onto the Idaho reservation. A group of Joseph's warriors, almost certainly without his blessing, went on a rampage and killed twenty or so white settlers. Reluctantly, Joseph was drawn into a situation in which he knew final victory was impossible. He decided to strike out for Canada.

The force Joseph led into the mountains was an impractical one. It contained fewer than 200 fighting men, who had to protect and care for about 600 women and children. But Joseph was able to lead this group on a superb fighting retreat that covered more than a thousand miles of difficult wilderness. He ran when he could and fought when he had to. In August 1877, he defeated the cavalry in a desperate struggle on the Big Hole River in Montana. Finally, Joseph got his people into the Bear Paw mountains, only thirty miles from Canada.

At this point, the thirty-seven-year-old chief thought he had won, and stopped to allow his dozens of wounded and helpless followers to rest. But he was overtaken by a force of cavalry, and had to decide, and quickly, whether to run, to surrender, or to fight. He chose to fight, and kept the cavalry at bay for five days. On October 5, he surrendered his beaten force: eighty-seven men, almost half of them wounded, and about 350 women and children. To this broken remnant of the Nez Percé, Joseph made his speech:

I am tired of fighting. The old men are all dead. [My brother] who led the young men is dead. It is cold, and we have no blankets. The little children are freezing to death. My people, some of them, have run away to the hills. No one knows where they are. I want to have some time to look for my children and see how many I can find. Maybe I shall find them among the dead.
Hear me, my chiefs. From where the sun now stands, I will fight no more forever.

Joseph and his people were taken first to Kansas and then to Indian Territory, where many of them died of disease. A small group was eventually returned to Idaho. But Joseph never went home. He was transferred to a reservation in Washington state, and he lived to visit a new "Great Father" in Washington, D.C., Theodore Roosevelt, in 1903. Joseph died in 1904, at the age of sixty-four. The official cause of death was entered as a broken heart.

Territory and the region around the Powder River in eastern Wyoming and southern Montana. But by 1865 miners had crowded into Montana at Bozeman, Virginia City, and Helena. These towns soon demanded a road connecting them with the Oregon Trail. This road would cross the Yellowstone River, skirt the Sioux hunting areas around the Big Horn Mountains, and cross directly over the valley of the Powder River.

In the summer of 1865 the cavalry moved into the area to construct forts and begin work on the road. A Sioux chief, Red Cloud, led his people in a two-year attack on the road and the forts. And in 1868 the government made a new treaty that seemed to give the victory to Red Cloud. The road was abandoned. But the Sioux, in return, had to agree to a reservation that included only the Dakotas west of the Missouri—the so-called Great Sioux Reservation. According to the treaty, they could still hunt in the Powder River country. For the first time, however, they had accepted a reservation to replace the large domain that their 1851 treaty had recognized.

The same commission that made the 1868 agreement with the Sioux dealt with other Plains tribes in the same way. Reservations were created in Indian Territory for the southern groups—the Kiowa, Comanche, Arapaho, Cheyenne, Osage, and Pawnee tribes. Between 1868 and 1874 the northern tribes—Crow and Blackfoot, Shoshoni and Mandan—also accepted new, restricted reservations. By 1876 the Plains Indians had given up over three-fourths of the land they had held under the Fort Laramie Treaty.

The Battle of the Little Bighorn The policy of concentrating Indians on reservations was applied once again in the Black Hills area of South Dakota. The treaty of 1868 guaranteed the Tetons complete possession of the Black Hills. But in 1874 rumors of gold led to a reconnaissance of the area by a military column of the Seventh Cavalry under Colonel George Custer. Custer's men found gold, and the resulting rush into Deadwood and other mining towns made conflict between the Sioux and the whites inevitable.

The Grant administration tried for a time to hold the prospectors back. The army even re-

moved some of them. But finally the government gave in and allowed the prospectors to enter the Black Hills "at their own risk." The next step was as cruel and illegal as any the government ever took against the Sioux. To prevent clashes between the miners and the Indians, Washington ordered all the Sioux to report to reservation agen-

A wagon train expedition, protected by Colonel George Custer's cavalry, entered the Black Hills of South Dakota in search of gold in 1874. Within three years the Sioux were forced off their lands and onto reservations.

cies. Any who remained outside would be considered automatically "hostile" and liable to attack. Many of the Sioux obeyed the order. But about 8,000 of them defied the government and gathered in the area of the Big Horn Mountains for their annual summer encampment and Sun Dance.

In June 1876 the army launched powerful forces of infantry, cavalry, and artillery against these Indians. One column, marching north from the Platte River, met Crazy Horse at Rosebud Creek on June 17. The army was beaten back in fierce fighting. Crazy Horse returned to the Sioux camp at the Little Bighorn River, where 8,000 Teton Sioux had gathered—the most powerful single force of Indians the army would ever face. Another army column advanced from the east. On June 25 the Seventh Cavalry, again under Custer's command, rode foolishly to the attack. The Sioux killed almost all of Custer's force in the most famous (and, from the white point of view, perhaps the most stupid) Indian battle in American history.

Another cycle of treaty, war, and new treaty was about to be completed. Within a year the Sioux were forced to give up their important Black Hills area. They were now forced onto a reservation covering only the central part of South Dakota, between the Missouri River and the Black Hills. But their troubles were not over. A railroad was pushing toward the reservation, and the remaining Sioux stood in its path. Farmers and ranchers were also beginning to look longingly at the land that the Sioux still held.

A Changing Indian Policy The idea of private property is so deeply rooted in white society that it is sometimes difficult to grasp the native Americans' concept of land "ownership." Most tribes looked on the land in more or less the same way that fisherman look on the sea—as a place to hunt. No Indian thought of himself as owning a piece of the land. He might own his horses, his weapons, his tepee. But the land itself was the "property" of the whole tribe, to be used communally and protected from other tribes.

When the various tribes of the plains agreed to give up their land, they did so as tribal units, not as individuals. When they accepted their "reser-vations," too, they accepted them as tribes, not as individual property owners.

Reformers, most of whom lived in the East, believed that private property was an essential feature of "civilization." To break the Indians' old, communal concept of land, the reformers proposed that the reservations be divided into lots and given to the Indians in "severalty"—that the Indians be treated as "several" or separate individuals. Westerners, anxious to exploit the Indians, agreed with this proposal. Their enthusiasm was a result of some simple arithmetic. If every Indian family was given an individual farm, a lot of reservation land would be left over. There simply were not enough Indians, in most tribes, to "fill" the reservations. The remaining land could become available to whites.

This new policy became law in 1887 in the Dawes Severalty Act. The next year, after much argument, some trickery, and probably some bribery, the whites persuaded the Sioux to accept the new plan. The one big Sioux reservation could then be broken down into five smaller ones that were, all together, less than half as large in area as the original. The same policy was applied to the other Plains Indians. One after another, the tribes settled for 160 acres per family. One after another, they realized that this meant giving up about half their tribal lands. The resulting demoralization provided a fertile ground for the new Ghost Dance religion. No matter what the intentions of the whites who wrote and supported the Dawes Severalty Act, it was a disaster for the Indians. In 1887, Indians held about 130 million acres of land in the United States; by 1930, after forty years of the Dawes Act, the total had been reduced to less than 50 million acres.

With the new policy came even stronger efforts to convert the Indians to white civilization—to make them "walk the white man's road," as Sitting Bull put it. These efforts hardened the conflict in attitudes between the progressive Indians, who accepted the new ways, and the nonprogressives, who clung to the old ones. The division was dramatized when Sitting Bull was arrested by Indian police from his own tribe. Even after the "reforms" of the 1880s, American policy toward the Indians was a calamity. They were reduced to a condition in some ways worse than that of the freed slaves in the South.

FARMING ON THE PLAINS

Mining, railroads, and cattle ranching had created a scattered pattern of settlement on the Great Plains and in the Rockies. Miners gathered in towns that were separated by hundreds of miles. Railroads created towns but only along their rights of way. And ranchers needed only a few cowhands to handle even very large herds. The actual white settlement of the plains had to await the slower migrations of farmers away from the Mississippi and onto the dry grasslands.

The Homestead Act The pace and pattern of settlement depended very much on government encouragement. In its youth, the Republican party had been the party of "free soil," which meant both agriculture without slavery and free land for any American. One of the first measures promoted by the Lincoln administration was the Homestead Act of 1862. According to this law, any citizen (or any immigrant who had taken the first step toward becoming a citizen) could claim 160 acres of public land, just by paying a fee of $26–34. If he "lived upon or cultivated" the land for five years, the land became his, free and forever. If the homesteader did not want to wait five years, he could pay for the land at $1.25 an acre and own it after six months.

The Homestead Act resulted in over half a million claims, totaling 80 million acres. But if its purpose was to award most of the public lands of the West to simple farmers, it was a failure. Much more land was given to railroads and states or sold directly to speculators than was ever acquired by small farmers.

Moreover, many of the homestead claims were phony. By law it was possible to transfer ownership at any time to any other person or corporation. So, for example, a rancher could have each of his hands claim a homestead and then (for a small bribe) transfer ownership to the ranch. Any

land speculator could do the same, just by paying a bribe to a stranger passing through.

Other Land Acts Congress made the situation worse by passing several more laws that promoted corruption and the robbery of public land. First, in 1873, came the Timber Culture Act, which allowed a homesteader (or a rancher or speculator) to claim an additional 160 acres if he would plant trees on 40 of the acres. In 1877 Congress passed the Desert Land Act, which allowed an individual to claim 640 acres of land if he would begin irrigation. Under the law, ranchers took up section after section of land, especially in the Southwest, since they needed it for grazing cattle. They had their friends swear that it was irrigated (even if they had only poured a bucket of water on it in the presence of their "witnesses").

Even more corruption resulted from the Timber and Stone Act of 1878. This law applied to forest land that could not be farmed but that was highly profitable for timber. Under this law any citizen or immigrant could purchase up to 160 acres of Western forest for $2.50 an acre. Lumbermen used the same tricks that ranchers and other speculators used. They imported sailors, prospectors, and others to buy land and then sign it over to a company for a small fee. And, since one good log sold for about $2.50, every tree but the first from any acre of land was pure profit. Under these laws over 20 million more acres of potentially valuable public land fell into the hands of corporations and speculators.

Hardships and Solutions Despite the fact that many of the profits went to land speculators and big corporations, Western lands were opened to the American people. Though they might have to pay $10 an acre to a speculator instead of getting homestead land virtually free from the government, farmers moved out onto the plains anyway. The majority came from the states bordering the Mississippi. Most of the rest were immigrants. Almost no workers from Eastern cities made the trip west. But the men and women who did settle on the plains performed a monumental task. In the thirty years after 1870 they brought more land under cultivation than had been cleared and

From the 1860s through the 1880s settlers rolled across the plains in prairie schooners like these, conquering one frontier after another. Hardships endured along the way paled in comparison with those met in taming the land.

plowed by all the generations of farmers from the settlement of Jamestown to the Civil War.

These farmers confronted problems that they had not met farther east. They found that their old ways of plowing and planting would not work. For one thing, rainfall was scarce, rivers often ran dry, and the water table[3] was low. Farmers had to haul water from long distances or collect it in holes when it did rain. New well-digging machinery, invented in the 1880s and 1890s, however, enabled people to dig deeper wells. And

steel windmills made it easier to pump the water up. Plains dwellers also developed dry farming. This technique—by which a farmer covers a plowed field with a blanket of dust—conserves the moisture in the soil.

Another problem on the plains was lack of wood. Farmers living there often made their first homes from cakes of sod. For fuel they burned old hay or dried cow dung. Fencing was a special problem until the invention of barbed wire in the 1870s.

A farm family soon learned that, while sixty acres of land could support them farther east, five times as much was needed on the plains. Plowing,

---

[3]The water table of an area is the supply of water within the ground.

Homesteaders like this Montana farmer took advantage of the government offer of cheap land in the West. Many failed, but those who mastered the harsh climate turned the Great Plains into the bread basket of America.

planting, and harvesting extensive acreage were greatly aided by the invention of mechanized farm equipment (see Chapter 30).

Nature seemed to do things on a grand scale on the plains. In summer the wind blew hot, and twice as hard as in the East. In winter blizzards howled down out of the mountains, burying homes and killing livestock. Tornadoes, dust storms, and plagues of locusts and grasshoppers were frequent.

Dry years drove thousands of farmers back east. Many of those who stayed barely survived. In the end, though, farmers turned the plains into the world's most efficient area for producing wheat, corn, and other grains. By 1880 American flour—like American beef and pork from the same area—was being exported in great quantities all over the world.

In all this the Indian was, of course, the great loser. The whites' successes on the plains did seem to prove what white Americans had always believed—that the Indians could not make "proper" use of their environment because they lived too much with it and not enough from it. White men were able to exploit even the tough plains environment, to draw from it enough food to feed not only most of the United States but part of the rest of the world, too. The Indian, in contrast, had been willing to settle for the little he needed to maintain his way of life. A full century was to pass before white Americans began to ask themselves seriously whether the Indian's way was not somehow at least as good as theirs. Only one thing was certain: in his "primitive" way the Indian had respected nature more. He had never viewed his world as an object to be owned, changed, and exploited. This, at least in part, was what the battle at Wounded Knee was all about.

SUGGESTED READINGS—CHAPTERS 27-28

Wounded Knee

Stanley Vestal, *Sitting Bull* (1957); C. M. Oehler, *The Great Sioux Uprising* (1959); Robert M. Utley, *The Last Days of the Sioux Nation* (1963); James Mooney, *The Ghost Dance Religion and the Sioux Uprising of 1890* (1965).

General

Frederick Jackson Turner, *The Frontier in American History* (1929); Walter P. Webb, *The Great Plains* (1931); Henry Nash Smith, *Virgin Land: The American West as Symbol and Myth* (1950); Thomas D. Clark, *Frontier America* (1959); R. A. Billington, *Westward Expansion* (1960).

The Plains Indians

F. G. Roe, *The Indian and the Horse* (1955); R. K. Andrist, *The Long Death: The Last Days of the Plains Indians* (1964); Dee Brown, *Bury My Heart at Wounded Knee* (1971).

Land Policy

B. J. Hibbard, *A History of the Public Land Policies* (1924); R. M. Robbins, *Our Landed Heritage* (1942).

The Mining Frontier

Mark Twain, *Roughing It* (1872); G. C. Quiett, *Pay Dirt: A Panorama of American Gold Rushes* (1936); R. W. Paul, *Mining Frontiers of the Far West* (1963).

The Cattle Frontier

E. E. Dale, *The Range Cattle Industry* (1930); J. B. Frantz and J. E. Choate, *The American Cowboy, Myth and Reality* (1955); Lewis Atherton, *The Cattle Kings* (1961).

The Farming Frontier

Everett Dick, *The Sod-House Frontier* (1937); F. A. Shannon, *The Farmer's Last Frontier* (1945); J. A. Malin, *The Grasslands Agriculture of North America* (1947); Gilbert C. Fite, *The Farmer's Frontier* (1966).

29 STRIKE AND VIOLENCE IN CHICAGO

R.J.W.

April 15, 1885

My Dear Virginia,

    We have had a week of trial and anxiety on the great subject of disturbances in our main factory—the serious labor troubles we have encountered—a great "strike," and all the resulting derangement of our relations—old and pleasant as they were—with our workmen.

    Trouble has come to hundreds of families in consequence; hatred and fierce passions have been aroused; and an injury has resulted to our good name.

    It began with a few molders and went on, one force operating on another, until 1,200 men went out, part of them by intimidation and part of them led by ignorant and blind passion. It ended by our conceding the terms demanded.

    What a sore heart I have carried these days!

Your Devoted Mother

This letter was written by a bewildered woman in her early seventies to her daughter. The writer, Nettie Fowler McCormick, was the widow of Cyrus Hall McCormick. An ambitious and ingenious Virginia farm boy, McCormick had made millions of dollars from the invention and manufacture of the reaper, a machine that harvested crops mechanically. He opened his Chicago factory, the McCormick Harvester Works, in the 1840s. It was the largest producer of harvesting machines in the world.

Nettie McCormick had always paid close attention to the family business. Now, just a year after her husband's death, a stable and profitable enterprise seemed to be falling to pieces before her eyes. At first, she remembered, her husband had known all of the original twenty-three workmen by name. He had worked alongside them in the little Chicago factory. Even when, after a few years, there were about 200 workers producing over 1,000 reapers a year, he could still name those who had been with the company for any length of time.

As the business grew, relations with the workers had become more difficult. During the Civil War, when labor had been scarce and prices had jumped every week, there had been many strikes or threats of strikes. McCormick had been forced to agree to one wage increase after another. But after the war ended, McCormick was able to cut wages in the plant five times in five years.

During the two decades after the Civil War, the McCormick company had grown rapidly. In 1884, when Cyrus McCormick died, the main factory covered dozens of acres. Its modern machinery, including two huge steam engines that supplied power for the whole factory, covered 12 acres of floor space. On these floors, about 1,300 men — 100 per acre — put in six 10-hour days a week. They turned 10 million feet of lumber and thousands of tons of iron into about 50,000 reapers a year. And these machines were making possible an agricultural miracle in the United States.

For the McCormicks, the result was money and status. In 1884, the company showed a profit of 71 percent. The family lived in a great mansion staffed with servants. They had invitations to the "best" Chicago homes, counted other wealthy people among their friends, sent their sons to Princeton, traveled luxuriously, and supported carefully selected philanthropies. Nettie Fowler McCormick had ample reason to be concerned about "our good name."

She had some reason to carry a "sore heart," too. The McCormick workers had always seemed contented enough. Nine out of ten of them were Germans, Norwegians, or Swedes, and most lived in the neighborhoods just west of the factory — neighborhoods built by the McCormicks — with Swedish and German street names. All this made the strike of 1885 difficult for Nettie Fowler McCormick to understand. Perhaps her husband's death was part of the problem. But McCormick's was still a family business. Her son, Cyrus McCormick II, had taken over the presidency, and other members of the family had always held important positions in the company. What had happened, then, to the "old and pleasant" relations with the workmen?

The problem had to lie, the McCormicks believed, with some small, misguided minority within the plant. And the most likely candidates for this role were clearly the molders. Ethnically, the molders were a distinct group. Almost all of them were Irish — "fighting Irish," as one plant official called them. And they had a tight, successful craft union, Molders Local No. 233. This union had been making trouble for the McCormicks for twenty years. There were only about ninety molders,

Cyrus Hall McCormick invented the first successful reaping machine in 1834. He turned his invention into a booming business, employing new sales methods such as installment buying.

Nettie Fowler McCormick, wife of the founder of the McCormick Works, understood little of the underlying causes of worker discontent at the plant in 1885.

Prior to the mechanization of the molding floor at the McCormick Works, much of the labor was done by unskilled and semiskilled workers. Pouring the molten metal into molds was the job of the common laborer, but working the metal into shape required more skill and was more highly paid.

but their operation was crucial to the manufacture of reapers. They could bring production to a complete standstill, and they had successfully used the power of this threat several times. Every time old Cyrus McCormick had tried to cut wages, the molders had been the first to resist.

The strike of 1885 had its origins in a decision by the new young president of the company to cut wages again. In December 1884, he had announced a 10 percent pay cut throughout the work force—except for the molders, who were to be cut by 15 percent. At first, there was quiet. Even the molders appeared to accept the reduction. But they were only biding their time until production reached its annual peak in the spring. In March of 1885, the molders demanded that the wage cut be restored to them. When McCormick refused, the molders came out on strike. And, to the McCormicks' alarm, some of the other workers followed them out.

McCormick was anxious to prove himself. To break the strike, he sent telegrams to McCormick salesmen all over the Midwest, asking them to send strikebreaking molders to Chicago. He even had these workers listed on the company payroll as "scabs"—the union term of insult for nonunion workmen who replaced striking members. The newcomers were housed inside the plant in a barracks listed in the company records as "scab house."

But McCormick's efforts to break the strike did not work. The "scabs" could not be trusted. Early in April, these two revealing telegrams were sent from company headquarters to salesmen in Iowa and Illinois:

To Tom Braden, Agent, Des Moines, Iowa: Out of the lot of men you sent us yesterday, but two of them showed up in Chicago. We find it not safe to ship these critters at our expense unless nailed up in a box car or chained.

> To J. F. Utley, Agent, Sterling, Illinois: The gentleman you sent to us as a molder did not remain over an hour or two until he packed his valise and skipped. We took special pains to get him into the Works by his riding with Mr. McCormick in his buggy. If you are able to do so, try and collect back his Rail Road fare.

Just a week after Cyrus McCormick had sneaked this unreliable scab into the plant, hidden in the president's own buggy, the strike reached a climax. On April 14, with the police scattered all over the city to patrol a local election, strikers had attacked McCormick workers outside the plant. McCormick—like many other companies of the period—had hired a small private army of the Pinkerton "detective" agency to maintain peace. A wagon loaded with Pinkerton men with a case of Winchester repeating rifles tried to enter the plant gate. The strikers set upon the wagon and burned it, and the rifles disappeared into the crowd. The captain in charge of the few Chicago police still in the area did nothing. His name—O'Donnell—was as obviously Irish as that of any molder.

The violence confirmed the McCormick family's opinion of the "fighting Irish" molders. If twenty years' experience were not enough, the Pinkerton agents' secret reports confirmed what the family had long suspected: They were the victims of an ethnic conspiracy. Just after the violent episode of April 14, one Pinkerton "detective" had submitted this report.

> The assault on the Pinkerton police during the strike of last week was urged by Irishmen, who are employed at McCormick's as molders and helpers. These Irishmen are nearly all members of the Ancient Order of Hibernians [an Irish social fraternity] who have a bitter enmity against the agency.

To the Pinkertons, it seemed clear that the molders were actually supported by their fellow Irishmen on the police force:

> It looks somewhat strange that these men at McCormick's could have police protection. On each occasion, the police stood by during the assaults and made no effort to stop the outrage.

Once, during the strike, a group of molders had attacked a group of non-union workers outside the plant gate. The police, according to Pinkerton reports, had this time not merely stood by but had actually chased and arrested the Pinkerton men who were trying to restrain the molders:

> The police made the utmost speed in calling a patrol wagon, which followed the Pinkerton men and arrested them! The men who made the arrests were treated by the strikers in saloons, and from their talk and insinuations, the police urged the mob to more violence by saying the Pinkerton men were sons of bitches, no better than scabs, there to take the bread out of women and children's mouths.

After the molders' triumphant April 14 attack on the Pinkertons, Cyrus McCormick went looking for help and advice. He appealed first to the mayor, Carter Harrison. But Harrison remembered full well that the McCormicks had consistently opposed him in local politics. He politely advised the young industrialist to give in to the molders' demands.

McCormick then turned to what he hoped would be a more sympathetic listener, old Philip Armour, head of a large meat-packing company and a veteran of many labor troubles. But even Armour told McCormick that the molders had won. There seemed to be no choice. McCormick offered to give back to the molders 5 percent out of their original 15 percent pay cut. But they refused this, and he ended by restoring the whole 15 percent.

To both Cyrus McCormick and his mother, their defeat at the hands of a few Irishmen was a painful mystery. But it was a mystery that had to be solved. Cyrus wrote to his mother as he mulled over the problem:

> The whole question of these labor troubles is vast and important and throws more new light on a department of our manufacturing interests which we have not hitherto studied with sufficient depth and understanding.

But to this twenty-five-year-old, who had only two years earlier been taken out of Princeton to run the plant, "depth and understanding" were limited to one fact and one conclusion. The fact was that a handful of disaffected molders could bring the entire McCormick enterprise to a standstill. The conclusion was that such a situation must be avoided in the future by making the skills of the molders unnecessary. He wrote his mother:

> I do not think we will have a similar trouble again because we will take measures to prevent it. I do not think we will be troubled if we take proper steps to weed out the bad element among the men.

McCormick went to work at once to "weed out" the offending Irish molders. He focused his efforts on a daring technological gamble. During the summer of 1885, the summer following the strike, the McCormick Company bought a dozen new pneumatic molding machines. They were supposed to perform mechanically most of the foundry tasks that the skilled molders had always done by hand. The machines were expensive, and they were experimental. No one knew whether they would work. McCormick hoped that they would enable the company to rid itself once and for all of the troublesome molders.

In August the McCormick foundry was closed for two months so that the machines could be installed. The closing was not unusual, since reapers were manufactured seasonally—much like automobiles are today, with a new model season every fall. August and September were always light months at the harvester works. But when the foundry reopened for full production, not one molder who had participated in the spring strike was back on the payroll.

McCormick seemed to have won a complete victory. All he had done was spend a vast sum of money on the new machinery. A few months after the machines went into operation, he wrote his mother triumphantly that the machines:

are working even beyond our expectations and everybody is very much pleased with the result. Two men with one of these machines can do an average of about three days work in one. Add to this fact that we have only nine molders in the whole foundry (the rest are all laborers), and you can see what a great gain this will be to us.

But McCormick was being more optimistic than he should have been—probably to reassure his anxious mother. Actually, there were troubles with the machines. In October the McCormick Company complained to the manufacturer that the castings turned out by the pneumatic molding device were too brittle to use. And in November Cyrus McCormick was called home from a trip to New York because of a crisis in the foundry. He wrote in his diary for Wednesday, November 11: "Telegram from mother urging come home at once about molding machines—probably failure. Critical situation."

The machines were fixed, but even when they worked they seemed to require an endless amount of labor to keep them functioning. Before the machines were installed, the total wage bill in the foundry was about $3,000 a week. After the machines had been in operation for about six months, foundry wages totaled $8,000 a week. Most of the labor was common, unskilled work. But gradually the company had to hire additional new molders to supervise the work. Economically, the machines were a complete failure.

Still, the new technology had broken the molders union at McCormick. And the union was unhappy. The leader of the molders was a veteran union man named Myles McPadden. He devised a new scheme that was much more dangerous to the McCormicks than the old union, with only ninety members. If there was to be no molders union, then McPadden would simply organize all the other workers in the plant into one union or another. The workers were discontented, so the time was ripe. By February of 1886, he had succeeded in organizing every major group of workers in the plant. The skilled workers—blacksmiths, machinists, and so on—joined the Metalworkers Union. McPadden encouraged the others to join the Knights of Labor, a general, nationwide union. Only 300 of the 1,400 McCormick workers remained nonunion. The lines of a new strike battle were shaping up clearly.

During this time McCormick, too, was busy. After his frustrated attempt to enlist Mayor Harrison's help, McCormick had gone to some lengths to make peace with the powerful political leader of the city. In every election before 1885 the McCormicks had opposed Harrison. After that year they supported him. As a result, Captain O'Donnell, the Irish police official who had been sympathetic to the workers in the spring of 1885, was replaced. The new man in charge of the area where the works were located was Police Inspector John Bonfield.

Bonfield had a reputation as a tough antilabor cop. He had once literally beaten his way through a crowd of strikers, shouting a slogan for which he became famous: "Clubs today spare bullets tomorrow." If there was going to be trouble in 1886, McCormick could count on the police in a way impossible a year before.

In mid-February 1886, a union committee representing all three unions—the Knights of Labor, the Metalworkers, and the Molders—presented McCormick with a series of demands:

> First, that all wages of laboring men be advanced from $1.25 to $1.50 a day. Second, that all vise hands[1] be advanced to $2.00 a day, and that blacksmith helpers be advanced to $1.75. Third, that time the men spend in the water closet [the toilet] not be limited as heretofore. Fourth, that, inasmuch as the molding machines are a failure, the preference should be given the old hands. The scabs in the foundry must be discharged, and a pledge given that no man would be discharged for taking part in a strike.

The company offered to meet some of the demands, but not the fourth, which must have made Cyrus McCormick furious. The unions rejected the offer and called a strike.

Before the strike was scheduled to begin, however, the company announced a complete shutdown of the plant for an indefinite period of time. Union pickets started marching near the plant, but they were kept away by 400 city policemen, now under Bonfield's command. To show its gratitude, the company served free hot meals to the police, with Cyrus McCormick sometimes personally pouring the coffee.

After two weeks the works were reopened, but only to nonunion employees. There was a loyal holdover force of only eighty-two men. The company furnished them with pistols. McCormick hoped they would lead an enthusiastic rush for jobs. But only 161 men showed up the first day. The second day was not much better. Once again the company's agents scoured the region for workers. Gradually, the company's situation improved a little. McCormick was willing to sacrifice almost half a year's production in order to settle the union question once and for all.

For the men on strike the situation was just as important. If they lost, their future at McCormick (or any other manufacturing plant in the city) was dim. As March turned into April, families got hungrier and tempers hotter. The explosion McCormick had avoided the year before by giving in to union demands now looked inevitable.

The situation at McCormick was complicated by the fact that during the spring of 1886 there were strikes all over Chicago. On May 1 all the unions in the city began a general strike for the eight-hour day. This was one of the largest and most heated labor actions in American history. The strike at McCormick merged with the more general agitation, involving thousands of skilled and unskilled workers from plants all over the city.

Then, on May 3, two days into the strike for an eight-hour day, a lumber workers union held a mass meeting to hear an address by August Spies, a radical labor agitator. The meeting took place on Black Road,

---

[1]"Vise hands" refers to workers who used a vise, a tool for holding metal being worked. They had a skill and were, therefore, to receive higher wages than the "laboring men," who were unskilled workers.

just a short distance from the McCormick factory. Some McCormick men were at the meeting, even though none was a lumber worker.

The McCormicks had been so desperate for workers that they had already granted the eight-hour day (with ten hours' pay) to their scab workers. So, at 3:30, two hours before the former 5:30 closing, the bell at the plant rang, and the strikebreaking workers streamed out of the plant. The striking union men at the meeting watched the strikebreaking workers leave the plant on their new short schedule.

The sight proved too much. Several hundred men, some of them McCormick strikers and some of them lumber workers, mobbed the scabs leaving the plant, driving them back inside the gate. The strikers began to smash windows, unleashing anger that had been building for months. About 200 policemen, under Inspector Bonfield, were there. Suddenly, they began firing their revolvers into the crowd, forgetting Bonfield's slogan about using clubs to spare bullets. When the noise died away, two workers lay dead and several others had been wounded.

August Spies, who had been addressing the meeting of lumber workers near the McCormick Works, followed the crowd and witnessed the violence that occurred. The next day, in the newspaper office where he worked, he heard that a mass meeting was scheduled at Haymarket Square to protest the shootings at McCormick. A circular announcing the meeting was being printed in both German and English when Spies arrived at the paper:

Attention Workingmen!

GREAT

MASS-MEETING

TO-NIGHT, at 7.30 o'clock,

AT THE

HAYMARKET, Randolph St., Bet. Desplaines and Halsted.

Good Speakers will be present to denounce the latest atrocious act of the police, the shooting of our fellow-workmen yesterday afternoon.

Workingmen Arm Yourselves and Appear in Full Force!

THE EXECUTIVE COMMITTEE.

Spies agreed to address the meeting, but he insisted that the final line in the circular be omitted. About 200 of the circulars had already been printed, but the line was removed from the rest. Few of the 20,000 circulars that were finally distributed on the streets of Chicago contained the threatening reference to arms.

August Spies was not, strictly speaking, a workingman. He might best be described as a radical journalist. At the time of the Chicago troubles he was thirty years old and the editor of the *Arbeiter-Zeitung*, a German-language newspaper with a radical viewpoint. He was also the business manager of an organization called the Socialistic Publishing Society, a propaganda organization of a small political party known as the Socialist Labor Party.

From time to time Spies had been in trouble with the police. Only a year before, during the McCormick strike of 1885, he had angered the police by intervening in the case of a poor German servant girl. She had been arrested by the police and held in jail for several days. When Spies and the girl's mother went to the jail, they discovered that the girl had been molested repeatedly. Rather than keep quiet, Spies swore out a warrant for the police sergeant in charge of the jail. He lost the case for lack of evidence, but he became well known to the Chicago police.

Spies was, in short, a politically active radical who did not hesitate to condemn people in positions of authority. He was also a committed

Workers gathered in Haymarket Square to protest police treatment of striking workers. The speakers' oratories were fiery and the police ordered the crowd's dispersal, leading to violence that was to set back the labor cause for some time.

socialist politician. Furthermore, he hoped that the rally at Haymarket would attract enough people to fill the square, which could hold about 20,000.

Spies reached Haymarket Square late, at about 8:30 on the night of May 4. He must have felt disappointed. No meeting was in progress, and there were only about a thousand people scattered around the square. The other main speaker, a socialist named Albert R. Parsons, was nowhere in sight. Spies climbed on a wagon, sent someone to look for Parsons, and began his talk. He was a good speaker, and soon the small crowd became enthusiastic:

> The fight is going on. Now is the chance to strike for the oppressed classes. The oppressors want us to be content. They will kill us. The day is not far distant when we will resort to hanging these men. [Applause, and shouts of "Hang them now" came from the crowd.] McCormick is the man who created the row on Monday, and he must be held responsible for the murder of our brothers! [More shouts of "Hang him!"]

Spies went on in the same vein for about an hour, trying to rouse his working-class audience to anger and a sense of solidarity against their "oppressors." Then someone announced that Albert R. Parsons had been found. Spies turned over his wagon rostrum to the second speaker.

The crowd had been waiting for Parsons, for he had a reputation as a spellbinder. Unlike Spies and many other Chicago socialists, he was a native American. Born in Alabama in 1848, Parsons came from a family whose ancestry went back to 1632 in New England. He was a self-trained printer in Texas before the Civil War. During the war he fought for the Confederacy in a Texas artillery company. After the war Parsons became converted to socialism and moved to Chicago, the center of working-class politics in the United States.

Like Spies, Parsons was not a worker at all but a political journalist. He edited a radical workingmen's paper called the *Alarm*. The Haymarket rally was just one more in a long series of political speeches for him. His speech was much like that of Spies but slightly stronger in tone:

> I am not here for the purpose of inciting anybody, but to speak out, to tell the facts as they exist, even though it shall cost me my life before morning. It behooves you, as you love your wife and children—if you don't want to see them perish with hunger, killed or cut down like dogs in the street—Americans, in the interest of your liberty and independence, to *arm*, to *arm* yourselves!

Here again there was applause from the crowd and shouts of "We'll do it! We're ready!"

What Parsons and Spies did not know was that the crowd was full of police detectives. Every few minutes one or another ran back to a nearby station house to report what the speakers were saying. Waiting in the station were almost 200 policemen, fully armed, and under the command of none other than John Bonfield.

Parsons and Spies probably did not notice Mayor Carter Harrison in the crowd, either. Only the mayor's presence had kept Bonfield from breaking up the meeting. As Parsons finished, the mayor left; it was obvious to him that everything was peaceful. It was almost ten o'clock and rain was in the air. Most of the crowd, too, began to drift off as the third speaker, Samuel Fielden, began to talk.

Suddenly, 180 policemen (a group almost as large as the crowd itself) marched into the square and up to the wagon where Fielden was speaking. One of the captains turned to the crowd and said: "In the name of the people of the State of Illinois, I command this meeting immediately and peaceably to disperse." After a moment the police captain repeated his order. The crowd was already starting to melt away (it was almost 10:30 by now). Fielden had stopped speaking and was climbing down from the wagon platform. "We are peaceable," Fielden said to Bonfield.

At that moment, without any warning, a dynamite bomb was thrown (it is not known from where or by whom) at the police. The fuse burned for a second or two after the bomb struck the ground. Then it went off with a deafening roar. Screams split the air as people ran in all directions. A number of policemen lay on the ground, one dead and the others wounded. Quickly, the police re-formed their ranks, and some of them began to fire into the crowd. Other policemen waded into the confusion swinging their clubs. The uproar lasted only a minute or two. Then suddenly the square was empty.

In addition to the dead policeman there were seventy-three wounded, six of whom died later. Four civilians were killed, and the official reports listed twelve as wounded. The twelve were those who had been too badly hurt to leave the square. Probably several times as many limped or struggled home and never became official statistics.

Like most riots, the Haymarket affair had been short. And, considering what could have happened, very few people were hurt. But the incident occurred on the heels of trouble at the McCormick plant, in the midst of the strike for an eight-hour day, with 80,000 Chicago working-

A contemporary sketch of what happened after a bomb exploded in Haymarket Square shows workers as well armed as police in battlelike poses. Pictures such as this fed the popular notion of union men as anarchists.

men off the job. Thus the Haymarket bomb touched off a near panic in the city and much of the rest of the nation. Thousands of respectable citizens convinced themselves that a dangerous conspiracy of anarchists, socialists, and communists was at work to overthrow the government and carry out a bloody revolution. One of the leading business magazines of the day, *Bradstreets'*, spoke for thousands of Americans when it said of the Haymarket incident:

> This week's happenings at Chicago go to show that the threats of the anarchists against the existing order are not idle. In a time of disturbance, desperate men have a power for evil out of proportion to their numbers. They are desperate fanatics who are opposed to all laws. There is no room for anarchy in the political system of the United States.

Also important was the fact that many people had been frightened and angered by a recent flood of immigration from Europe to America—and many of the "anarchists" were also foreigners. Not only in Chicago, but all over the nation, newspaper editorialists and public speakers demanded the immediate arrest and conviction of the alien radicals who had conspired to murder honest policemen and subvert law and order. The result was a swift and efficient series of illegal raids by the Chicago police. They searched property without warrants. They imprisoned people without charging them and threatened potential witnesses. All in all, the authorities arrested and questioned about 200 "suspects"—probably none of whom had anything at all to do with the bombing.

In this heated atmosphere, fueled by journalists who whipped up unreasonable fears of an anarchist conspiracy, a jury met to determine if indictments could be brought against anyone for the violence. It decided that, although the specific person who threw the bomb could not be determined, anyone who urged violence was a "conspirator" and as guilty of murder as the bomb thrower. On the basis of this decision another jury met and indicted thirty-one persons on counts of murder. Of the thirty-one, eight were eventually tried, all of them political radicals. Most had not even been present at the Haymarket bombing.

The effect of the Haymarket Affair had now become clear. What had begun weeks before as an ordinary strike at the McCormick Works had been transformed into a crusade against political radicalism, most of which was said to be foreign in origin. Only Parsons and Samuel Fielden were not German or of German descent. The names of the other six would have been as natural in Berlin or Hamburg as in Chicago: August Spies, Michael Schwab, Adolph Fischer, George Engel, Louis Lingg, and Oscar Neebe.

In one way or another, all the defendants had some connection with the labor movement and with political agitation for revolution. Several of them were anarchists, though their ideas about anarchism as a philosophy were vague. They might as well have called themselves socialists, as several of them did at one time or another. In general, they were intellectuals. Their jobs were connected with radical journalism in either the English- or German-language press. They did not all know one another, but by the time their trial was over, most of them were probably "comrades," a word they used more and more in the months ahead.

On the other side of the battle were all the forces of law, order, and authority. True, some agreed with Mayor Harrison that the Haymarket meeting had been peaceful, that the whole idea of a conspiracy was a false and legally incorrect notion. But most of Chicago society (including even many elements of the labor movement) favored a quick conviction and the hanging of all eight defendants. The judge who tried the case, the prosecuting attorney, most business leaders, almost all the local clergymen — almost everyone who had anything to say in Chicago — were convinced even before the trial began that the defendants were guilty. Moreover, most of Chicago's leading citizens, and their counterparts in the rest of the country, agreed that the trial was a struggle to the death between American republicanism and foreign anarchism. The entire established order of American society, with very few exceptions, was determined to make an example of the "conspirators."

The Haymarket trial began on June 21, 1886. The first three weeks of the seven-week trial were spent selecting a jury. Under Illinois law the defense had the right to reject a total of 160 jurors on peremptory challenges — that is, without having to discuss a juror's qualifications and abide by the judge's decision. As one prospective juror after another was called, it became clear that most of them were extremely prejudiced against the defendants. The defense attorneys quickly used up their 160 challenges. They then had to show cause for turning down a juror and depend on the judge, Joseph Gary, to rule fairly. Again and again, plainly biased jurors were accepted by the judge — whose own prejudice against the defendants became apparent as the process went on. The result was a jury composed of twelve citizens who obviously wished to hang the defendants.

In his opening statement, prosecuting attorney Julius Grinnell set the tone of the entire trial:

> Gentlemen, for the first time in the history of our country people are on trial for endeavoring to make anarchy the rule. I hope that while the youngest of us lives this will be the last and only time when such a trial shall take place. In the light of the 4th of May, we now know that the preachings of anarchy by these defendants, hourly and daily for years, have been sapping our institutions. Where they have cried murder, bloodshed, anarchy, and dynamite, they have meant what they said. The firing on Fort Sumter was a terrible thing to our country, but it was open warfare. I think it was nothing compared with this insidious, infamous plot to ruin our laws and our country.

It was obvious that this would not be an ordinary murder trial. The defendants would be judged by their words and beliefs. A ninth "conspirator," Rudolph Schnaubelt, had fled. The prosecution would try to prove that he had thrown the bomb. The next step would be to convict the other eight of conspiracy, which would carry the same penalty as murder itself. And they would be convicted by the fact that they had made speeches and written newspaper articles urging violent revolution. Day after day the prosecution offered evidence about the defendants' beliefs, their writings, and even pamphlets they had supposedly helped to sell.

The prosecution had weak cases against the individual defendants. They were able to prove that one of the defendants, Lingg, had actually made bombs. But Lingg was a stranger to most of the others, and he had not even been at Haymarket Square. Parsons, Spies, Fischer, and Schwab had left the square before the bomb was thrown. George Engel proved that he had been home drinking a glass of beer with his wife. In the end the prosecution's case rested on a theory of "general conspiracy to promote violence." No evidence of a single violent act was brought into court that could withstand even the mildest cross-examination by the frustrated defense attorneys.

After four weeks of testimony the jury retired. The jury members had been instructed by Judge Gary in such a way as to make conviction almost inevitable, and they needed only three hours to discuss the matter. After this short deliberation the jury filed solemnly back into the courtroom. It was ten o'clock, August 19, 1886, when the foreman read the verdict.

> We the jury find the defendants Spies, Schwab, Fielden, Parsons, Fischer, Engel, and Lingg guilty of murder in the manner and form as charged, and fix the penalty at death. We find Oscar Neebe[2] guilty of murder in the manner and form as charged, and fix the penalty at imprisonment in the penitentiary for fifteen years.

Years later Judge Gary recalled that "the verdict was received by the friends of social order with a roar of almost universal approval."

Before they were sentenced, each of the defendants made a speech to the court. Spies spoke for all of them when he said, in a German accent that he had never lost:

> There was not a syllable said about anarchism at the Haymarket meeting. But "anarchism is on trial," foams Mr. Grinnell. If that is the case, your honor, very well; you may sentence me, for I am an anarchist. I believe that the state of classes—the state where one class dominates and lives upon the labor of another class—is doomed to die, to make room for a free society, voluntary association, or universal brotherhood, if you like. You may pronounce the sentence upon me, honorable judge, but let the world know that in A.D. 1886, in the state of Illinois, eight men were sentenced to death because they believed in a better future.

There were appeals, of course, first to state courts and then to the Supreme Court of the United States. One by one the appeals failed. Then there were pleas to the governor of Illinois for mercy, and the sentences of Fielden and Schwab were commuted to life. Lingg, the bomb maker, who was probably half mad, committed suicide in jail—using dynamite set off by a fuse that he lit with his jail-cell candle. The other

---

[2]Oscar Neebe was the youngest defendant; almost no evidence had been presented against him. Most of the jury's three-hour deliberation was devoted to this case.

Albert Parsons, August Spies, George Engel, and Adolph Fischer were hanged on November 11, 1886, after one of the most unfair trials in American history.

four condemned men — Engel, Spies, Parsons, and Fischer — were hanged on November 11.

As the four stood on the scaffold, ropes around their necks and hoods over their heads, Spies broke the deep silence by shouting: "There will come a time when our silence will be more powerful than the voices you strangle today!"

At the McCormick Works the situation had returned to normal months earlier. On May 7, 1886, three days after the Haymarket bombing, Cyrus McCormick was able to write in his diary: "A good force of men at the works today, and things are resuming their former appearance." Three days later, taking full advantage of the public outrage over the "devilish plot," as McCormick called it, at Haymarket Square, the McCormick Works quietly resumed the ten-hour day. On Monday, May 10, McCormick wrote: "Things going smoothly. We returned to 5:30 closing hour today, instead of 3:30."

30 FACTORIES, CITIES, AND IMMIGRANTS

R.J.W.

This chapter examines the creation of a new social and economic setup in the United States: the industrial order. In some sense industry is as old as human society. People have always made things — tools, weapons, clothing, and so on. But, beginning in the eighteenth century, their ability to make goods began to increase rapidly. The so-called industrial revolution that resulted originated in England and spread quickly to the rest of Western Europe and to the United States. By the time of the Civil War this revolution was well under way in North America, fed by inventions like the steam engine, the cotton gin, and the reaper. After the war, industrialization drastically altered the basic patterns of life in the United States.

Everything had to be changed, since every element of this new system had to hang together. Raw materials, like coal and iron for making steel, had to be found and developed. Cheap transportation, like railroads, had to be available to bring these materials to factories and to take finished products from them. Workers had to be hired to operate the factories. And agriculture had to be improved so that fewer and fewer people would be needed to grow more and more food. More and more machines were needed to provide a livelihood for more and more factory workers, who would in turn make still more machines. Nothing could happen at all unless everything else happened — and in the proper order, too. Every factory functioned as part of a chain of invention, materials, transportation, and workers.

The McCormick Harvester Company, for example, was only one part of a complicated series of events and machines. The reapers made at the McCormick Works enabled farmers on the Great Plains to produce unheard-of quantities of grain. Some of this grain was milled into flour, for bread eaten by people like McCormick's molders. Other farm products fed cattle, which were slaughtered in big cities at factories owned by men like Philip Armour.

The new transcontinental railroads were necessary to take the reapers west and bring the flour and beef east. Since there were not enough workers to lay the new rails, Irish and Chinese were encouraged to immigrate. The McCormick plant, too, was tended by immigrants, and it was German immigrants who were the main victims of the Haymarket Riot. The city of Chicago itself was a new kind of city, built around railroads and factories, in a way that no other American city had ever been built — a great barracks for the workmen at dozens of factories like the McCormick Works.

In achieving its own industrial system, the United States was transformed. It had once been a nation in which nine out of every ten people lived on farms or in rural communities. By the end of the nineteenth century it was the world's most productive industrial nation. The landscape had been remade. The people had been changed, too. There had always been immigrants to the United States. But new industries attracted different types of immigrants in great numbers. In the end the daily lives and even the language of Americans were changed. New words like "telephone," "subway," "scab," and "millionaire" became common speech. They signaled just how deep and complete the change had been.

TECHNOLOGICAL CHANGE

Few of the men and women who made or watched the industrial revolution understood its complexity. Most of them probably regarded it as a product of technological change — the invention of new types of machines or the improvement of existing ones. Certainly one of the most obvious changes of the nineteenth century was that many things that had once been done slowly by hand were now being done rapidly by machine.

An Agricultural Revolution Agriculture was a prime example of the replacement of hand labor by machine power. The most rapid and striking introduction of new agricultural technology took place on the Great Plains. On these flat and treeless expanses, plowing, planting, and harvesting could be done on a scale that would have stunned colonial settlers and even most plantation owners of the Old South. But what happened on the plains was just an exaggerated version of what went on in all areas of American agriculture: the industrialization of the farm.

At first, the new machinery was fairly simple. McCormick's earliest reapers, built before the Civil War, were small. They were drawn by one horse and worked by one or two men. Another invention—a steel plow that could cut deeper and faster than the old iron plow—was a further small step. But gradually the new technology gained force and speed. Reapers were soon equipped with automatic binders that could fasten grain into bunches mechanically. The single steel plow was soon modified into a multiple, or gang, plow that could cut three or four furrows at one time.

Soon other new machines appeared. One could plow and plant at the same time. Another, the combine, added to the reaper a mechanical thresher, which could separate grain from stalks. A combine could move quickly through a wheatfield, gathering wheat and leaving behind only waste to be plowed under in the spring. The machine accomplished its work without a single human hand touching either the earth or the wheat plants.

During most of the nineteenth century new machinery was still driven primarily by animals. Some steam engines were used, but the final mechanization of farms had to await the gasoline-driven tractor in the twentieth century. Still, even before the tractor, the life of the American farmer had been fundamentally altered by technology.

Farming gradually came to resemble the running of factories, in which a product for sale was processed and made ready by machinery. Sooner or later, almost every step in all but a few kinds of agriculture was mechanized.

The result of the mechanical changes in agriculture was to double and redouble the volume and pace of food production. In 1840 it took more than three hours of human work time to produce a bushel of wheat. In the 1890s the time had been cut to ten minutes. In 1840 a bushel of corn required almost five hours of labor, from planting to final processing. In the 1890s the time had been cut to forty minutes.

Hand in hand with the reduction of hours was a marked decrease in the number of farmers needed to produce food. Mechanization made it possible for a tiny minority of Americans to feed the large majority. Those who left farms were then free to work for the railroads and in oil fields, iron mines, factories, and offices—thereby aiding the process of rapid industrialization.

The amount of land under cultivation doubled between the Civil War and 1900. The net result of the agricultural revolution was an enormous abundance of food.

Improving Rail Transport The agricultural revolution depended not only on new technology on the farms but also on new methods of carrying food from the farms to the cities—that is, railroads. It was railroads that brought Wyoming beef, Kansas wheat, and Louisiana rice to the table of a McCormick molder. Without the new railroad network built after the Civil War, the mechanization of agriculture would have had small effect.

Railroads, like farms, benefited from new technological developments. The principle of the steam engine remained the same. But almost every other mechanical aspect of railroading changed drastically during the generation after Appomattox.

The old railroads had used iron rails, small and dangerous wood-burning engines, and tiny, rickety coaches and freight cars. The new lines used steel rails that would last for many years without cracking or rusting. Because they could support almost twenty times as much weight as iron rails, larger engines and cars could be built. The typical pre-Civil War engine had weighed about 20 tons. By 1900 some engines weighed as much as 300 tons. The coal-burning locomotive became a giant source of power that could pull huge freights over the most difficult grades efficiently and safely. Freight cars increased in weight from 10 tons to over 100 tons.

Railroad mileage increased, too. In 1870 — even after the completion of the first transcontinental line — there were only about 60,000 miles of track in the United States. By 1900 there were over 250,000 miles. This total was greater than the entire railroad mileage of Europe, including Russia. Other inventions like the telegraph and the electric signal made it possible to control complicated traffic patterns and freight yards. The trains and tracks of 1900 were as dramatically different from those of 1850 as the jet plane is from the first wobbly aircraft of the 1920s. These new giants of the landscape transformed the process of moving food, objects, and people from one place to another.

MANUFACTURING

Taken by themselves, the technological changes in agriculture and the railroads would have meant little. They were important only in their relation to other parts of the new industrial system. In this system it was manufacturing that was crucial.

By 1900 — a little more than a century after Washington had taken the oath of office — the United States was the leading manufacturing nation in the world. Many factors made this growth possible. Americans found new beds of coal. They discovered iron ore in Michigan and Minnesota. They opened oil fields in Pennsylvania, the Ohio Valley, and the southern Great Plains. These raw materials and energy sources fed in turn the new factories of Pittsburgh, Chicago, and dozens of other cities. Mechanized agriculture made it possible for millions of people to move to cities to work in industrial plants. A high tariff kept down competition from foreign manufactured goods.

Alabama, rich in iron ore and coal, became a center of the steel industry. Steel was produced in giant blast furnaces, like these of the Tennessee Coal, Iron, and Railroad Company of Ensley, Alabama, and transported by rail to other centers.

Most important of all were the new machines and processes that enabled Americans to produce so much so quickly.

The Steel Industry Steel was (and still is) very close to the heart of the new economy. It is stronger than iron, more resistant to rust, and easier to shape or mold. People had been making small quantities of steel for centuries, but the process was slow and difficult, since it depended on hand labor. In the 1850s an Englishman named Henry Bessemer invented a converter that could turn iron into steel by blowing a blast of hot air through the molten iron. The process was spectacular to watch, sending a brilliant shaft of sparks and smoke skyward. The economic results were just as startling. For the first time it became possible to produce steel in massive quantities.

The combination of the Bessemer converter, the demand for steel from the railroads and other industries, and the discovery of additional sources of iron ore and coal created a new industry. In 1870 the United States produced only about 77,000 tons of steel. By 1900, steel production had increased to over 11 million tons a year—an increase of almost 2,000 percent. Pittsburgh became the first (and is still the largest) of the steel towns. But eventually cities like Birmingham, Alabama, and Gary, Indiana—built almost entirely around the steel industry—sprang up in what had until then been open countryside.

Other Industries What happened in steel was repeated in dozens of other industries. The sewing machine and other inventions made it possible to manufacture shoes and clothing on a mass scale. Steam-powered mills using steel equipment could cut lumber or grind wheat or print newspapers with a speed and efficiency no one had dreamed of earlier (see chart, page 665).

Another new industry grew up based on electricity. The foremost American in this field was the versatile Thomas A. Edison. Throughout the late nineteenth century a stream of inventions poured from his laboratories. These included the phonograph, the first practical electric light bulb, the storage battery, the dynamo, the electric voting machine, and the motion picture.

An industry also developed rapidly around the discovery of oil and new ways of refining it. It yielded kerosene to light lamps and fuel stoves. Heavier oils lubricated the motors of the new technology. Beginning around 1900, it became important as a source of gasoline for the internal combustion engine (see Chapter 38). This vast industry had simply not existed in 1800.

A revolution in communications began in 1876, on the hundredth anniversary of the Declaration of Independence. In that year a young inventor named Alexander Graham Bell exhibited the first working model of the telephone. At first the telephone was purchased only by individuals

In 1877 the telephone was the subject of a humorous song. By the turn of the century it had revolutionized communications in every major city in the United States. Just fifty years after its invention almost every middle-class American home had its own telephone.

who wanted to communicate between two specific locations, like a house and a factory or office. But soon there were enough phones in use to create the first telephone exchange. It was opened at New Haven, Connecticut, in 1878. Other cities and towns followed suit.

Soon cities began to link up with one another. The first connection linked New York and Boston in 1884. New York and Chicago were joined in 1892. By 1915, when lines connected New York and San Francisco, it was possible to place calls between any two cities in the nation.

The only way to measure the magnitude of what was happening to the United States is to use statistics. In 1869 the value of American manufactured goods was about $1.5 billion. By the end of the century the figure was more than $4.5 billion. In 1869 about 2 million workers ran American shops, mills, and factories and the market value of the average person's yearly work was only about $940. By 1900, when almost 5 million men and women worked in industry, the market value of their average yearly effort was almost doubled, to nearly $1,800.

By the 1890s the United States had more steel, more rails, more electric trolleys, more telephones, and more electric lights than any other nation in the world. To accomplish all this, Americans mined more metal, cut more lumber, dug more iron ore, and pumped more oil than any other country.

THE GROWTH OF "BIG BUSINESS"

Technology and manufacturing were crucial in making the United States an industrial nation. Equally vital were new methods of organizing industry and business.

The Factory System At the beginning of the Civil War, the majority of Americans who worked in industry were employed in small shops and mills—a tailor shop, for example, or a blacksmith's or harnessmakers. In 1870, when the revolution in industry was already well under way, the average industrial plant had only eight employees. A median plant (one halfway between the largest and the smallest) had thirty workers. By 1914 the average plant had twenty-eight workers, and the median 270. In 1870 no factory in America employed over 1,000 workers. By 1914 several had over 10,000 workers.

What was occurring, in other words, was a change that went beyond the technology of production and the rate of manufacturing. It was nothing less than a parallel revolution. The factory was replacing the traditional small shop.

In a traditional shop (or in the home manufacture of items like cloth or soap), work centers on the person. Power is supplied mainly through human toil. The same worker is involved in all stages of production, from spinning thread, for example, to weaving the final cloth.

The idea behind a factory (first introduced into England in the late eighteenth century) is very different. Work in a factory centers on a machine. Power is mechanical, not human. Parts are nearly identical, and so they are interchangeable. Most important is the division of labor. Each worker specializes, performing only one step in a chain. He or she may never touch or see the raw material. He or she may never look at or handle the final product. The result is mass production—manufacturing large numbers of articles in standard shapes and sizes.

Changes in Organization Factories were inevitably larger than shops. They cost more money to build and equip with machinery. More and more capital was needed in order to enter and compete in almost any line of business. As the factory system grew; so did the size of companies.

Growth in turn demanded changes in the organization of business. Mass production required a sizable investment. This made it difficult for family firms and partnerships to be truly competitive. So, large corporations gradually replaced companies owned by one family or a few partners.

The corporation is an old idea. The Virginia Company and the Massachusetts Bay Company were both corporations. The idea is as simple as it is old. If many people invest in an enterprise by buying stock in it, the company can grow much

ANDREW CARNEGIE

One of the dominant myths of the late nineteenth century was the rags-to-riches notion. In fact, most successful businessmen of the period were not born to rags at all, but came into the world with at least modest advantages. But, regardless of the facts, the most captivating idea in American culture was the image of the "self-made man." And, of all the industrial magnates of the day, the man who best fitted the picture was Andrew Carnegie. His life contained all the right ingredients: poor but honest parents, a daring willingness to gamble on innovations, and an almost blinding financial success.

The real picture, of course, was a little more complicated. Carnegie was the son of poor Scottish immigrants, yes. But his parents were poor because the skilled trade of weaving they had practiced in Dunfermline, Scotland, was a craft already being destroyed by technological innovation when Carnegie was born in 1835.

This family of skilled craftsmen had for generations been articulate and politically active. When his parents immigrated to the United States in 1848, Carnegie already had the fair beginnings of an education in literature and politics.

Carnegie started as a bobbin boy in a cotton factory in Allegheny, Pennsylvania, where his parents settled. By the time he was thirty years old, he had made what, by the standards of the day, was already classed as a great fortune: $400,000. The fortune derived from hard work, yes; but it was helped along by a powerful patron who was president of the Pennsylvania Railroad. When this patron was appointed assistant secretary of war in the Lincoln administration, Carnegie accompanied him to Washington as an aide. There, he was in a superb position to learn the crucial role that railroads and iron and steel would play in the new, industrialized economy.

Carnegie's first fortune came from railroading, bridge building, oil, and a series of clever speculations. He had, always, a somewhat ambiguous attitude toward his own material success. In fact, he sometimes seemed to *fear* money, as though it might destroy his character. In 1868, in a remarkable memorandum to himself, he listed his assets and the income they could produce:

An income of $50,000 per annum! . . . Beyond this, make no effort to increase fortune . . . . Man must have an idol—the amassing of wealth is one of the worst species of idolatry—no idol more debasing than the worship of money . . . . To continue much longer overwhelmed by business cares and with most of my thoughts wholly upon the way to make more money in the shortest time, must degrade me beyond hope of permanent recovery.

Such thoughts had only a limited effect on Carnegie's career. Within five years, he was embarked on the creation of Carnegie Steel, which he made into a model of vertical integration and efficiency. When he finally sold his interest in the company to the new trust, United States Steel, in 1901, it was worth $250,000,000.

But Carnegie did try to rescue himself from "idolatry" in a variety of other ways. For one thing, he wrote—five volumes of books and essays, a remarkable accomplishment for a man of affairs. For another, he engaged in the systematic cultivation of literary and philosophical friends in both England and America. He also embarked on a progam of "scientific philanthropy" that eventually totaled about $350 million, dotting the landscape with what came to be called "Carnegie libraries." Carnegie was not at all typical of the entrepreneurs of the period. But his articulateness and his rhetoric of benevolence combined to make him a model for the popular cult of individual struggle, success through fair competition, and enlightened capitalism as the economic basis of American democracy.

larger than if it is funded by only a few individuals. If the company fails, each investor has lost only the value of his stock. He cannot be held responsible for any of the corporation's debts.

Just as there had been American factories before the Civil War, so had there been corporations. But their number increased greatly after the war. The corporation became the standard way of organizing business, just as the factory became the characteristic method of organizing production.

Mass production required not only corporate investment. It also demanded that each firm market its product efficiently on a broad national scale, instead of selling just locally. To remain in business, a corporation had to create effective distributing and selling divisions. It had to buy raw materials on a large scale. Ideally, in fact, it would purchase its own source of raw materials—for example, a forest for a paper company or cotton plantations for a textile mill.

In other words, mass production made it profitable for a company to invest money in all the stages of its industry, from original materials to final sales. Economists call this phenomenon vertical integration. It involves a business firm not only in manufacturing but in all the other stages and phases relating to the business. An oil company that owned wells, pipelines, and refineries and had its own sales force would be almost perfectly integrated. It would be freed from dependence on any other economic unit—except, of course, customers.

Competition and Consolidation The new industrial order brought a new kind of competition into the American economy. Before mass production, small shops and mills had catered to limited territories. They competed only where one territory bordered on another. But large corporations needed large markets to absorb their massive outputs. Thus a number of companies might find themselves competing for the same customers.

To win a big market, a corporation might advertise heavily. It might hire high-pressure salesmen and reward them with big commissions. But the most obvious way to win a market was to cut prices. A large company with efficient factories and lower production costs could force its competitors into bankruptcy simply by lowering prices beyond the point where the smaller firms could stay in business.

In one industry after another a few corporations gradually emerged as the leading firms. Each was too large and powerful to be driven out of business by the others. Each was too small to be able to control the whole market. Whenever this happened—and it happened sooner or later in most industries—the firms entered a period of cutthroat competition.

Most American businesses did not welcome such competition. In the 1880s and 1890s they tried to find ways to avoid it. The railroads led the way. Railroad owners had witnessed the havoc and ruin that could be created when one railroad waged a price war with another. By a process of trial and error the railroads worked out private agreements among themselves to control freight rates. Railroads also developed a system of grouping their customers in "pools"; each line was entitled to a certain share of the market. Gradually, too, the railroads had become consolidated into a few major lines, each one absorbing dozens of smaller companies. The Pennsylvania and New York Central railroads dominated the Northeast. The Southern Railway controlled much of the South. The Louisville and Nashville line was supreme in the Ohio Valley.

By agreements and consolidations the railroads had become the models for big business. Other industries soon copied what railroad leaders had learned and used the economic devices they had developed. Consolidation became the order of the day.

No matter what industry was involved, the process was the same. First, a few large competing firms would emerge. A period of intense and costly competition would follow. Then firms would consolidate as a way of avoiding competition. During its period of rapid growth the McCormick Harvester Company was competing with a handful of other large manufacturers of agricultural machinery. In the years after the Haymarket Affair, however, the McCormicks began to realize that competition was wasteful and unnecessary. Early in the twentieth century McCormick merged with its competition to form the huge International

Harvester Company. Since then, it has produced practically all the harvesting machinery manufactured in the United States.

A similar development occurred in the steel industry, which was dominated for almost half a century by a Scotch immigrant, Andrew Carnegie. Carnegie was a classic example of the "rags-to-riches" success story. At thirteen he came to America with his family and immediately went to work. At eighteen he was a telegraph clerk for the Pennsylvania Railroad. During the quick railroad expansion of the Civil War years, Carnegie realized that iron and steel for rails and bridges were the key to the railroads' future, and that railroads, in turn, were the key to an expanding economy. He saved every cent and invested daringly but successfully. By 1872 he was able to build his own steel plant near Pittsburgh.

Carnegie's company grew with the industry. By 1890 he was producing almost a third of a million tons of steel. By 1900 this amount had nearly tripled. At the same time, Carnegie worked to achieve vertical integration. He bought iron ore deposits, steamers to transport ore on the Great Lakes, and railroad cars to carry it overland—in fact, everything that he needed for making steel.

In the meantime the process of competition had eliminated all but a few other steel companies. In 1892 the Carnegie Company was reorganized to combine seven other corporations in which Carnegie had acquired a controlling interest. In 1901 the largest steel concerns in the nation were all merged into one great new corporation, the United States Steel Corporation. The power behind this consolidation was another dominant figure of the period, J. Pierpont Morgan, a New York banker and financier. Morgan spent nearly half a billion dollars to buy out Carnegie and set up this supercorporation. Like International Harvester, the giant company dominated its industry. It produced almost all of some forms of steel and three-fifths of the total steel made in the United States.

The Trust An even more stunning example of consolidation brought John D. Rockefeller into control of the oil industry. Rockefeller started out as a poor boy, like Carnegie. He too saved every

cent (except for the 10 percent tithe he regularly gave to the Baptist Church). Starting with one refinery in Cleveland, Rockefeller by 1872 had created the giant Standard Oil Company.

Rockefeller also created a new device that made it even easier to consolidate an industry—the trust. A trust in industry is an arrangement in which several companies sell themselves to a group of trustees. The companies are paid for with shares in the new trust itself. Only paper changes hands, but the result is a group of directors who control the operations of several companies.

Through the Standard Oil Trust the Rockefeller interests acquired almost total control of the oil industry. The trust could phase out unnecessary plants. It could take full advantage of mass production and distribution techniques to provide most of the kerosene that lighted American lamps and the oil that lubricated American machines. Rockefeller himself summed up adequately the reasons for the trust:

> It has revolutionized the way of doing business all over the world. The time was ripe for it. It had to come, though all we saw at the moment was the need to save ourselves from wasteful conditions [of competition]. The day of combination is here to stay. Individualism has gone, never to return.

One by one the main American industries passed from competition to consolidation. It might occur through giant corporations created by mergers, like International Harvester or United States Steel. Or it might result from the formation of trusts—which involved everything from cottonseed oil to sugar to whiskey. By 1900 a few large concerns controlled almost all the major facilities of production and distribution in the United States.

THE NEW AMERICANS

Industry has always needed people, and the new industrial order was no exception in this respect. The growth in agriculture, railroads, and industry demanded millions of people, both as workers and as consumers.

U.S. GROWTH OF POPULATION, 1870-1910

The American population kept pace with the growing industrial order. For every 100 persons living in the United States in 1870, there were 126 in 1880, 158 in 1890, 190 in 1900 — and in 1910 a surprising 230! In one generation the population had more than doubled, from about 40 million in 1870 to over 90 million forty years later.

These were the millions who moved into the Great Plains and the Rockies, bringing about the final collapse of the Western Indians. These were the millions that bought McCormick's harvesters, worked in his factory, and built the railroads that carried his reapers into every flat corner of the country where grain could be planted and harvested by machine.

These millions, however, were not just more of the same kinds of Americans who had lived here in Jacksonian times. They were a new people, with different languages, different religions, and different ways of life. Andrew Jackson's common man was almost certain to be "native" American, white, Protestant, and a farmer. His parents or grandparents might have immigrated to the United States, but they would probably have come from England or Scotland. When they arrived here, they would have found the language, the way of worshiping God, and the customs familiar and comfortable.

The common man in New York in 1900 was more likely to be a Jew from Poland or a Roman Catholic from Italy. He lived in a city and proba-

bly had a job in a factory. His English might be poor, his memories of the "old country" at least as important to him as his hopes for the new. He represented a social revolution that had accompanied the revolutions in technology, industry, and business — the creation of an urban immigrant working class.

Shifting Trends in Immigration There have always been immigrants in America, at least from the time when the Indians began to cross over from Asia into Alaska. In the years since the American Revolution, the actual proportion of immigrants to the total population did not change much. Two other things happened instead: (1) the nature of the immigrant population changed; and (2) the immigrants (along with other Americans) began to congregate in urban centers. These two changes made factory cities like Chicago the gathering places for a new kind of American: the poor immigrant from a country where English was not spoken and where an Anglo-Saxon Protestant was rare.

In 1790, when the United States took its first census under the new Constitution, nine out of ten Americans (except for the black slaves in the South) had English or Scotch ancestors. This pattern changed somewhat with the "old immigration" of the 1840s and 1850s, when large numbers of Germans, Scandinavians, and Irish began to immigrate. However, most of the Germans and Scandinavians were Protestants, though their languages were strange to American ears. And though many native-born Americans resented the Catholicism of the Irish, these immigrants at least spoke English. In 1865 the United States had only about 200,000 inhabitants who had been born in Southern or Eastern Europe. They were easily absorbed by a total population of about 40 million.

By 1914 this picture had changed dramatically. A "new immigration" — mainly from Italy, Russia, and Austria-Hungary — flooded into the United States. Poverty drove many of these people from their home countries. Some men left to avoid the military draft, which discriminated against the poor. Jews wanted to escape the official anti-Semitism of Russia and Poland. Armenians fled from persecutions carried out by the

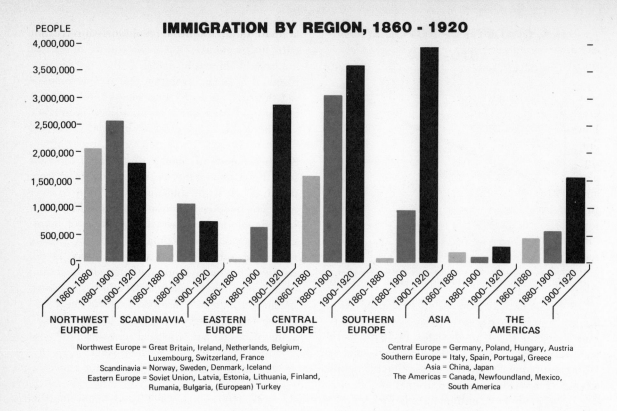

IMMIGRATION BY REGION, 1860 - 1920

PEOPLE

4,000,000 –
3,500,000 –
3,000,000 –
2,500,000 –
2,000,000 –
1,500,000 –
1,000,000 –
500,000 –
0 –

1860-1880 1880-1900 1900-1920 (repeated across each region)

NORTHWEST EUROPE · SCANDINAVIA · EASTERN EUROPE · CENTRAL EUROPE · SOUTHERN EUROPE · ASIA · THE AMERICAS

Northwest Europe = Great Britain, Ireland, Netherlands, Belgium, Luxembourg, Switzerland, France
Scandinavia = Norway, Sweden, Denmark, Iceland
Eastern Europe = Soviet Union, Latvia, Estonia, Lithuania, Finland, Rumania, Bulgaria, (European) Turkey

Central Europe = Germany, Poland, Hungary, Austria
Southern Europe = Italy, Spain, Portugal, Greece
Asia = China, Japan
The Americas = Canada, Newfoundland, Mexico, South America

Turkish government. The new immigrants were drawn to the United States by advertisements of cheap steamship transportation, by rumors of free land and golden opportunity, and by a massive propaganda campaign conducted by railroads anxious for workers and for customers to buy up their lands.

Immigration from Southern and Eastern Europe amounted to only a trickle in the 1860s and 1870s. But by the 1890s over half the immigrants to America were from Southern and Eastern Europe. In the next decade – the peak decade for immigration in the history of the United States – the proportion of new immigrants rose to over 75 percent. In simple terms this means that over 6 million Italians, Russian Jews, Hungarians, and other immigrants from Southern and Eastern Europe came here between 1901 and 1910.

Reactions to the Newcomers The strike at McCormick and the Haymarket Affair occurred just before the new immigration reached its peak in

the United States. But prejudice had already been aroused by the entry of Irish and Germans and by the beginnings of the influx from Eastern and Southern Europe. Both the McCormick strike and the trial of the so-called Haymarket radicals occurred in an atmosphere of fear and bigotry. The Pinkerton report on the "fighting Irish" molders and the newspaper comments on foreign "anarchists" make it clear that events in Chicago would have been different had they not taken place at the time of this bewildering flood of immigration.

The new immigrants were not only different in culture, language, and religion. They also behaved in a different way from those who had preceded them. They moved into a society that was no longer predominantly agricultural and rural, but urban. So they did not fan out onto farms as most of the old immigrants had done. Instead, they followed the lead of millions of other Americans and settled in cities. Two-thirds of foreign-born residents in the United States lived in towns or cities by 1900.

Bewildered and often victimized in America, new immigrants clustered together in their own city neighborhoods, or ghettos.[1] People from a particular province or even a particular village would move into buildings on the same block, re-creating much of the culture of their Old World homes. As the new immigration increased, so did antiforeign sentiment. Ghetto dwellers earned a reputation among "native" Americans for being clannish, dirty, superstitious, and generally undesirable. They were considered strange, chattering in their odd languages, and somehow suited only for city life. Actually, of course, they were no more "natural" city dwellers than were the English who had come to Virginia and Massachusetts in the seventeenth century. They were simply caught in

a phase of the industrial revolution—the creation of an urban society.

Becoming "American" In the era of the new immigration the goal was assimilation—taking on the traits of the new society so as to blend with it. But becoming an "American" was not an easy process for most Europeans who migrated to this country in the late nineteenth century. Foremost was the problem of language. Real assimilation meant being able to take advantage of American economic and political opportunities. And this in turn depended upon knowing the language.

Since a knowledge of English brought with it an almost immediate economic advantage over those who could not speak or write the language, most immigrant parents sacrificed the income they would have received from their children's labor to send their children to the free public schools. Workers often attended special night school class-

---

[1]The word "ghetto" dates back to the Middle Ages. It is Italian and may come from *borghetto*, meaning a small settlement outside the town. The term originally applied to the Jewish quarter of a city.

The new immigrants from Southern and Eastern Europe fueled the industrial machine by their labor. Forced to live in cities where the jobs were, they clustered in crowded and unsanitary ghetto areas like New York's Lower East Side.

es after their exhausting days in the factories. A Jewish immigrant, Mary Antin, recalls:

> Education was free. It was the one thing that my father was able to promise us when he sent for us; surer, safer than bread or shelter. On our second day in the country a little girl from across the alley came and offered to conduct us to school. We five children between us had a few words of English by this time. We knew the word "school." We understood. This child, who had never seen us till yesterday, who could not pronounce our names, who was not much better dressed than we were, still was able to offer us the freedom of the schools of Boston!

Countless immigrants must have felt similar emotions at the discovery that schooling—so restricted in Europe—was so readily available in the United States. In the words of Mary Antin, "No application made; no questions asked; no examinations, rulings, exclusions; no fees."

Learning English was the first step in assimilation. After that many immigrants joined some form of voluntary association that would put them in contact with native-born Americans. For city dwellers, the most available of such groups were the political parties. They provided favors, food, and jobs for poor and needly immigrants (see page 474). They also helped "Americanize" them.

"Boss" Richard Croker of Tammany Hall in New York described the function of his political machine as taking the city's newcomers, who "do not speak our language and do not know our laws, yet are the raw material with which we have to build up the state," and turning them into Americans. He asserted that a political machine like Tammany "looks after them for the sake of their vote, grafts them upon the Republic, makes citizens of them, in short; and although you may not like our motives or our methods, what other agency is there by which so long a row could have been hoed so quickly or so well?"

Another strong influence on the new immigrants was a small number of "old" immigrants—those who had arrived before the great influx.

Children old enough to work in factories did so by day and attended school at night. The goal was assimilation: shedding enough of the old folkways to enter "native" American society.

They had learned English and then helped recruit workers from Europe for factory labor in the United States. They often paid the newcomers' transportation and helped them settle in the ghettos of American cities.

Such men were sometimes called *padrones* (an Italian word meaning "patrons"). They might be paid by three different groups: (1) employers, for supplying cheap labor; (2) political machines, for delivering the votes of immigrants once they became citizens; and (3) the immigrants themselves, for favors received. Often the *padrones*—who existed among Jewish, Greek, Armenian, Polish, and other immigrant groups, as well as among the Italians—were ward leaders in political organizations. They provided a link between the concerns of the ghetto newcomers and those of the citywide machine.

URBANIZATION

In the ancient world, only two great cities—Rome and Alexandria—had populations of over half a million people. By the time George Washington was born, Rome and Alexandria had long ago declined. The only cities to have reached a comparable size since were London and Paris. At the time of the Haymarket Affair, however, Chicago had become a great city. In fact, by 1900 the United States had six cities with more than half a million inhabitants.

The process of urbanization was not confined to the United States. All the industrializing nations of Western Europe experienced it, too. The factory system demanded high concentrations of workers, and the agricultural revolution made it possible for millions of people to leave their farms—whether in Germany or in Maine—and move to towns.

The United States experienced three great migrations in the generation after the Civil War. One was from the East to the Great Plains and the Far West. Another was from Europe to America. The third was from the country to the city. Of the three, the movement from farm to city was easily the most extensive.

In 1800 only about three Americans out of every hundred lived in towns larger than 8,000. By 1900 this proportion had grown 1,000 percent; almost a third of the nation lived in cities of over 8,000. In 1800 there had been only six cities larger than 8,000; in 1900 there were over 400.

This increase was not gradual and smooth. Most of it came in the half-century after the end of the Civil War. During this period at least 15 million "native" Americans moved out of farming areas and into cities, and their number was swelled by an almost equal number of new immigrants who settled in cities instead of on farms. Statistics tell the story. Between 1870 and 1900 the population of the United States increased by about 35 million people. During the same period the urban population increased by about 24 million. The cities, which cover such a small proportion of the land, had absorbed more than two thirds of the total increase.

Technological Factors A city is not just a collection of people in a small area. Like industry, modern cities were made possible by technological change. In the centuries before the industrial revolution the size of a city had been determined mainly by the transportation available. It could not be too big, because a person had to be able to walk or travel by wagon or carriage to a marketplace or job and back home again. After about 1880, however, cities began to experience a transportation revolution. The introduction of electricity made it possible to replace slow and awkward horse-drawn transport with fast, clean trolleys, elevated trains, and subways. These improvements meant that people could live many miles from their place of work and still be part of a vast city.

Electricity also made it possible to light city streets. Cleveland, in 1879, became the first city to have electric street lighting. Similarly, the introduction of the telephone in the 1880s meant that homes, offices, and factories could be tied together in an almost instantaneous communications network.

At first, city buildings themselves were a limiting factor. Even with the thickest walls, a stone or brick building could not extend higher

A turn-of-the-century view of a typical Midwestern city, Kansas City, Missouri, shows that the pulse of American life had quickened and taken on an increasingly urban character. The city itself was being transformed—trolleys transported people as once horses had done.

than fifteen stories. To build a structure even this high, builders had to make windows smaller and smaller because glass could not support the weight. A second problem was that human legs could tolerate only so many stairs. The first problem was solved by the invention of the skyscraper in the 1880s. This development was pioneered by a Chicago architect, Louis Sullivan. Skyscraper construction—in which walls were hung on steel frames—made possible structures as tall as a hundred stories. Thus even more people could be concentrated, level upon level, on smaller parcels of land. The second problem was solved at about the same time by the invention of the electric elevator.

INDUSTRY AND CULTURE

Economically and socially, the most important facts about American society in the period following the Civil War were industrialization, urbanization, and immigration. These facts together brought about a change in the landscape that was almost brutally obvious—the crowded, dirty, smoky city, with its alien working class. But people very often do not or *will* not see and acknowledge what is most plain. In their art and architecture, their novels and magazines—in all the areas

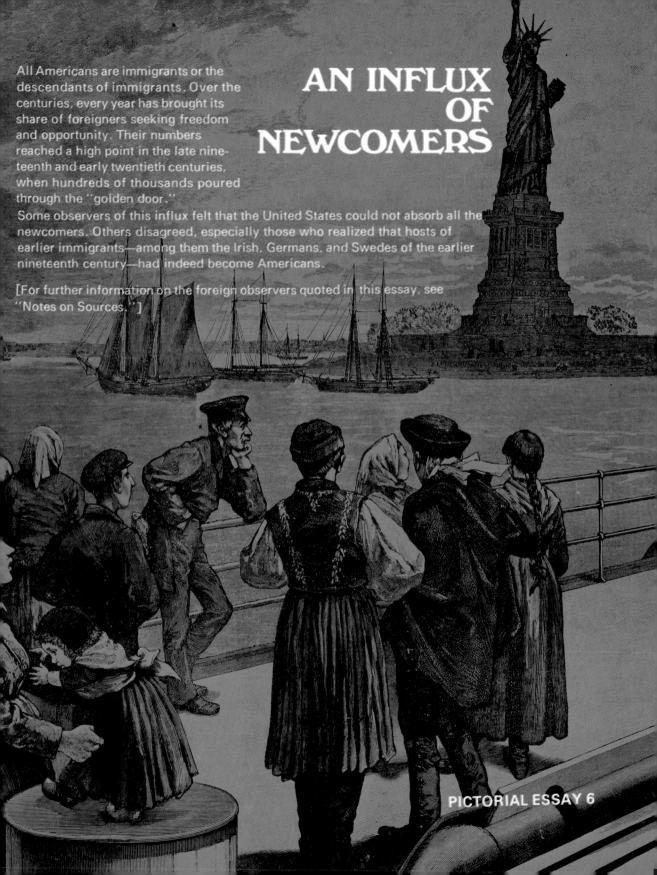

AN INFLUX OF NEWCOMERS

All Americans are immigrants or the descendants of immigrants. Over the centuries, every year has brought its share of foreigners seeking freedom and opportunity. Their numbers reached a high point in the late nineteenth and early twentieth centuries, when hundreds of thousands poured through the "golden door."

Some observers of this influx felt that the United States could not absorb all the newcomers. Others disagreed, especially those who realized that hosts of earlier immigrants—among them the Irish, Germans, and Swedes of the earlier nineteenth century—had indeed become Americans.

[For further information on the foreign observers quoted in this essay, see "Notes on Sources."]

PICTORIAL ESSAY 6

PE 6–2/ *My uncle Olaf, a seaman, used to come to us between voyages, and he was all the time talking about America; what a fine place it was to make money in. The school-master told us one day about the great things that poor Swedes had done in America. A man who had lived in America once came to visit near our cottage. He said that food was cheap in America and that a man could earn nearly ten times there as in Sweden. So at last it was decided that my brother was to go to America.*

[AXEL JARLSON, 1903]

Railroad poster soliciting immigrants

The emigrants flocked into the mess-room from the four doors to twenty immense tables spread with knives and forks and toppling platters of bread. Nearly all the men came in in their hats—in black glistening ringlety sheepskin hats, in fur caps, in bowlers, in sombreros, in felt hats with high crowns, in Austrian cloth hats, in caps so green that the wearer could only be Irish. A strange gathering of seekers, despairers, wanderers, pioneers, criminals, scapegoats.

[STEPHEN GRAHAM, 1913]

Between Decks in an Emigrant Ship

We carried our luggage out at eight, and in a pushing crowd prepared to disembark. At 8:30 we were quick-marched out of the ship to the Customs Wharf and there ranged in six or seven long lines. All the officials were running and hustling, shouting out "Come on!" "Hurry!" "Move along!" and clapping their hands. Our trunks were examined and chalk-marked on the run—no delving for diamonds—and then we were quick-marched further to a waiting ferry-boat [for Ellis Island].

[STEPHEN GRAHAM, 1913]

Immigrants disembarking in New York City

A doctor examining boys at Ellis Island

I visited Ellis Island yesterday. The central hall is the key. All day long, through an intricate series of metal pens, the long procession files, step by step, bearing bundles and trunks and boxes, past this examiner and that, past the quick, alert medical officers, the tallymen and the clerks. On they go, from this pen to that, pen by pen, toward a desk at a little metal wicket—the gate of America. Ellis Island is quietly immense. It gives one a visible image of one aspect at least of this world-large process of filling and growing and synthesis which is America.

[H. G. WELLS, 1906]

Waiting for processing at Ellis Island

We were carefully examined, and when my turn came the examining officials shook their heads and seemed to find me wanting. I confessed that I had only five cents in my pocket and had no relatives here, and that I knew of nobody in this country except Franklin, Lincoln, and Harriet Beecher Stowe, whose Uncle Tom's Cabin I had read in a translation. One of the officials, who had one leg only and walked with a crutch, with a merry twinkle in his eye said in German: "You showed good taste when you picked your American acquaintances." I learned later that he was a Swiss who had served in the Union army during the Civil War.

[MICHAEL PUPIN, 1874]

George Bellows, *Cliff Dwellers*

Italian saw sharpener at work on the sidewalk

There was a bootblack named Michael on the corner. When I had time I helped him and learned the business. Francisco, too, worked for the bootblack, and we were soon able to make the best polishes. Then we thought we would go into business.

We had said that when we saved $1000 each we would go back to Italy and buy a farm, but now that the time is coming we are so busy and making so much money that we think we will stay. We meet many people and are learning new things all the time. We were very ignorant when we came here, but now we have learned much.

[ROCCO CORRESCA, 1902]

Immigrant iron workers in Pennsylvania

The work given to the new arrivals is generally of a rudimentary nature, but it teaches them to work, and the wages, although low, at least enable them to live, besides giving them the chance of joining the great labor unions of the country and taking if ever so small a part in the industrial pursuits of the people among whom they have come to live.

[COUNT VAY DE VAYA
UND LUSKOD, 1908]

←*The inhabitants seem to have come from all quarters of the globe and to represent every known type. The streets, wide as they are, are yet too narrow to hold the masses of people who surge to and fro in them. Everyone is busy; everyone carries a parcel containing articles of clothing or food. Bargaining goes on in all the languages imaginable, and one hears an Italian praising his oranges as in the piazza of St. Lucia; a German discussing sausages of doubtful origin with a French urchin, who plays the part of a chef at the corner of the street; and Russian emigrants share their vodka, as a token of friendship, with Polish Jews.*

[COUNT VAY DE VAYA UND LUSKOD, 1908]

In the evening my sister and I took a walk; she went shopping and asked me to go with her. I saw a Jewish sign (in Hebrew letters) in a window reading "Kosher Butcher." I stopped and admired it very much and said to my sister, "This is the first time I see Hebrew letters in a window." In Rumania it is not allowed. Then I started to realize what anti-Semitism really meant and what an anti-Semitic country Rumania was.

[ROBERT MYERS, 1913]

Jewish hot potato vendor, New York City

Program for festivities at a Milwaukee *Turnverein* (German social and athletic club)

German band, Cincinnati

The German in America is badly off. Where in the world can he find a wife? He has little opportunity for family life. So the young people get acquainted only in public places, in restaurants, concerts, the theater, balls. But what can they learn of each other there? Everything, except that which relates to a wife and her duties.

[KARL GRIESINGER, 1858]

Polish store, Chicago

Those who are Americanized are American, and very patriotically American. Those who are not thus nationalized are not in the least inter-nationalized. They simply continue to be themselves; the Irish are Irish; the Jews are Jewish; and all sorts of other tribes carry on the traditions of remote European valleys almost untouched. Very often these exiles bring with them not only rooted traditions, but rooted truths.

[G. K. CHESTERTON, 1921]

Returning to the log house, we spent the evening—twenty-one Swedes altogether—in games, songs, and dancing, exactly as if in Sweden. I felt myself happy in being with my countrymen, happy to find them so agreeable and so Swedish still in the midst of a foreign land.

[FREDRIKA BREMER, 1850]

Harvesting, by the Swedish American painter Olaf Krans

Irish politicians, Chicago

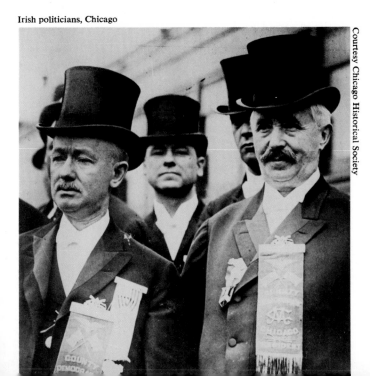

Courtesy Chicago Historical Society

I made the acquaintance of two local celebrities (Irish), namely Paddy Ryan and Michael McDonald. Paddy is a fighting man lately defeated in the twenty-four-foot ring by a compatriot, Sullivan. Michael McDonald runs a granite quarry. But his principal importance arises from his political position. He is supposed to direct and control what is called the rowdy element in Chicago—largely made up of our countrymen—and this gives him very great local influence. He is a rough diamond, with a decisive, masterful way about him, which clearly marks him out as a leader of men. His friends claim for him that he returned the present mayor of Chicago—the first Democratic mayor returned for Chicago for thirty years.

[LORD RUSSELL OF KILLOWEN, 1883]

PE 6–8 /   *The Chinese have built a great part of the Northern Pacific from the Continental Divide to the Pacific. As we sped along, we came upon their encampments again and again in forest glades, by the shores of the rivers and lakes, on the outskirts of the cities— always a community apart. It is said to their credit that they insist, when they can, on being located near water for purposes of personal cleanliness.*

[LORD RUSSELL OF KILLOWEN, 1883]

Chinese workmen on a Western railroad

In a place so exclusively Mexican as Monterey, you saw not only Mexican saddles but true vaquero riding—men always at the gallop up hill and down dale, and round the sharpest corner, urging their horses with cries and gesticulations and cruel spurs, checking them dead with a touch, or wheeling them right-about-face in a square yard. In dress they ran to color and bright sashes. Not even the most Americanized could always resist the temptation to stick a red rose into his hatband.

[ROBERT LOUIS STEVENSON, 1879]

Mexican horseman in California

The growth of New York City depended upon improved transportation facilities like the Brooklyn Bridge. The bridge's completion in 1883 made it possible to live outside Manhattan and commute to work by steam car, by carriage, or on foot.

of their culture—native, white, middle-class Americans seemed determined to ignore the realities of their age. At both the popular and the sophisticated level, middle-class culture seemed almost serene in its lack of awareness of industrial capitalism and its social consequences. To some extent, of course, the practice of ignoring, evading, or denying "reality" is a characteristic of culture in any society. But Americans in the 1870s and 1880s were abnormally, almost absurdly consistent in their unwillingness to come to terms culturally with the actualities around them.

This characteristic of American culture was not confined to the sentimental and quaint books and essays published for a middle-class, primarily female, readership. It was evident in the most talented and sophisticated intellectuals, too. Henry James wrote great novels and stories, as great as any ever published in English. But his subject matter was the elegant and complicated lives of wealthy Americans, usually set in Europe. And even when one of James's heroes was a businessman, as in *The American* (1876), he appeared in the novel only *after* he had made his fortune and arrived in Europe in pursuit of "culture" and an aristocratic French bride.

Henry James was born to wealth, cultivated society, and European travel. Samuel Clemens was born in Missouri into a modestly well-to-do family and spent much of his life scratching for a living as a journalist. As "Mark Twain," he wrote about plain people. But his plain people were not immigrants or factory workers. And his settings were the small towns of the Mississippi, where boyish and innocent characters like Huckleberry Finn and Tom Sawyer had their "adventures." *Huckleberry Finn* (1885) was a great novel by almost any standard. But it was hardly a novel that confronted American realities. Samuel Clemens lived in Hartford, Connecticut, a modern city; he was married to the daughter of a coal baron. But the closest he came to an examination of such realities was when he fantasized about the experience a technologically inventive Yankee might have if he suddenly woke up in medieval England, as in *A Connecticut Yankee in King Arthur's Court* (1887).

What was true of Mark Twain and Henry James was equally true of lesser talents. Even when novels were about businessmen—as in William Dean Howells's *The Rise of Silas Lapham* (1884)—the real subject seemed to be not business but society and romance, and the action occurred after the fortune was acquired. One of the most popular novels of the period was, on the surface at least, about industry, technology, and the city. Edward Bellamy's *Looking Backward* (1886) was a utopian romance about Boston in the year 2000. The utopia was, in theory at least, highly industrialized, urbanized, and socialistic. And the response of middle-class readers was enthusiastic. But, beneath its appearance of relevance to nineteenth-century realities, *Looking Backward* really described a pleasant, small Boston in which the factories, the poor, and the immigrants had disappeared as though by magic.

In the 1890s, a few books did try to deal with the more sordid aspects of factory and slum life. Jacob Riis's *How the Other Half Lives* (1890) described a slum in vivid language that alarmed his primarily middle-class, native audience:

> Cherry Street. Be a little careful, please! The hall is dark and you might stumble over the children pitching pennies back there. Not that it would hurt them: kicks and cuffs are their daily diet. They have little else. Here where the hall turns and dives into utter darkness is a step, and another, another. A flight of stairs. You can feel your way, if you cannot see it. Close? Yes! What would you have? All the fresh air that ever enters these stairs comes from the hall-door that is forever slamming, and from the windows of dark bedrooms.

Stephen Crane's *Maggie: A Girl of the Streets* (1893) was a darkly realistic account of the way that slum poverty turned innocent girls to sordid lives. But such books came only after decades of industrialization. And they created almost as much scandal as if they had been about sexual perversions. For the most part, writers and other intellectuals provided no insight whatever into the lives and difficulties of the new, alien, urban working class.

On the level of popular culture, the picture was much the same. A revolution in printing technology had made inexpensive books and magazines easily available, and a flood of popular fiction poured off the new steam-driven presses. But most of the stories and books dealt with rural life or the doings of chaste and sentimental small-town girls; or they had as their heroes idealized Western cowboys, romantic sailors, or heroic figures from ancient history.

A new type of popular fiction did emerge after the Civil War, the tale of business success. The most successful promoter of the rags-to-riches formula was a Harvard-educated former clergyman, Horatio Alger. His *Ragged Dick: Or, Street Life in New York* (1867) was a sensational sales success. For the next thirty years, under titles like *Jed the Poorhouse Boy* and *Struggling Upward,* Alger sold over 200 million copies of his stories.

Superficially, at least, the Alger stories reflected important economic realities. But the reflection was indirect and distorted. Alger did not deal with the adult, business careers of his heroes. Instead, he wrote coy exercises in moralism, designed to show how Ragged Dick, or Tattered Tom, or Poorhouse Jed overcame orphanhood and poverty by saving the drowning daughter of a wealthy, sonless merchant. The books always ended just as their heroes were about to embark on adult careers in commerce. The reader was left to assume that, in their adult lives, Alger's heroes would continue to thrive through a steady application of "pluck."

The practice of turning away from economic and social realities that was so central to the literature of the 1870s and 1880s was equally characteristic of the art and architecture of those decades. The greatest American artist of the period, James McNeill Whistler, painted mostly portraits and nocturnal landscapes. When Whistler did depict a scene of contemporary social or economic activity, the subject was more likely to be European than American (as in *The Last of Old Westminster*, PE 7-2).

Most artists confined themselves to painting scenes of nature or of domestic life—as in Mary Cassatt's *The Bath* (PE 7-3); or portraits of the wealthy in which the sources of wealth were carefully ignored—as in John Singer Sargent's 1897 study of *Mr. and Mrs. Isaac Newton Phelps Stokes* (PE 7-3). Winslow Homer, who probably was the second most talented American painter of the period, used his muscular and vivid style primarily on seascapes. When he did paint men at work, they were almost always fishermen in aged boats—an ardently preindustrial subject matter.

Architecture was even more flagrantly systematic in denying the actualities of industrialism. The expanding society of the period required an enormous number of new buildings—campuses for colleges and universities, building for banks and corporations, homes and summer houses for new millionaires, railroad stations, and so on. But even the most talented architects were mired in a contest to restore ancient styles. The familiar, reliable Greek and Roman styles that had been so popular since the Revolution were pressed into service again. There was an astonishing revival of Gothic and Georgian, especially in campus architecture. And anyone could stare for days at the largest of the new railroad stations, with their Greek columns or baroque decorations, without gaining any clue as to what the function of the building actually was.

In 1893, to celebrate Columbus's "discovery" of America, the industrial city of Chicago spent two years and about $15 million to create the World's Columbian Exposition. About 700 acres of Lake Michigan shoreline were transformed into a remarkable "White City." The exposition was a climactic moment in the long attempt to disguise the realities of the industrial system, with the newest inventions of the industrial era housed in wood-and-cardboard imitations of the buildings of ancient Greece and Rome. A seductive network of broad, tree-lined walks and lagoons made the buildings look like a virginal "congregation of brides."

New sources of power like the dynamo had to compete with the most sentimental and anti-industrial kinds of displays—a solid silver statue of a woman, sent by Montana; a statue of a knight sent by California, with armor made entirely of prunes; a full-sized model of the *Santa Maria*, sent over by Spain; a replica of the great hall at Versailles, built by the French; a "hootchy-kootchy" dancer with the archaic stage name of "Little Egypt." It all lived up to the description published by the Chicago *Tribune:* "a splendid fantasy of the artist and architect." American culture, it seemed, was not yet ready to acknowledge the staggering changes wrought by the new industrial order.

SUGGESTED READINGS– CHAPTERS 29-30

Haymarket

Henry David, *History of the Haymarket Affair* (1936).

General

T. C. Cochran and William Miller, *The Age of Enterprise* (1942); Samuel P. Hays, *The Response to Industrialism, 1885–1914* (1957); E. C. Kirkland, *Industry Comes of Age: Business, Labor and Public Policy, 1860–1897* (1961); Robert Wiebe, *The Search for Order, 1887–1920* (1968).

Industrialization

Lewis Mumford, *Technics and Civilization* (1934); Roger Burlingame, *Engines of Democracy* (1940); T. C. Cochran, *Railroad Leaders, 1845–1890* (1953); G. R. Taylor and I. D. Neu, *The American Railroad Network* (1956); Charles Singer, ed., *A History of Technology: The Late Nineteenth Century* (1958).

Business Organization and Leaders

Andrew Carnegie, *The Autobiography of Andrew Carnegie* (1920); Matthew Josephson, *The Robber Barons* (1934); Allan Nevins, *A Study in Power: Rockefeller* (1953); E. C. Kirkland, *Dream and Thought in the Business Community, 1860–1900* (1956); R. G. McCloskey, *American Conservatism in the Age of Enterprise* (1957); Alfred D. Chandler, *Strategy and Structure: Chapters in the History of the Industrial Enterprise* (1962); J. F. Wall, *Andrew Carnegie* (1971).

Immigration

Jacob Riis, *How the Other Half Lives* (1890); John Higham, *Strangers in the Land* (1955); Barbara Solomon, *Ancestors and Immigrants* (1956); Leonard Dinnerstein and F. C. Jaher, eds., *The Aliens: A History of Ethnic Minorities in America* (1970); David Ward, *Cities and Immigrants: A Geography of Change in Nineteenth-Century America* (1971).

The City

Arthur M. Schlesinger, *The Rise of the City, 1878–1898* (1933); Robert H. Bremner, *From the Depths: The Discovery of Poverty in America* (1964); Constance M. Green, *The Rise of Urban America* (1965); Stephan Thernstrom, *The Other Bostonians: Poverty and Progress in the American Metropolis, 1880–1970* (1973); Samuel B. Warner, *The Urban Wilderness: A History of the American City* (1973).

Culture

Warner Berthoff, *The Ferment of Realism, 1884–1919* (1965); Robert G. McCloskey, *American Conservatism in the Age of Enterprise* (1961); Irvin G. Wyllie, *The Self-Made Man in America* (1954); Barbara Novak, *American Painting of the Nineteenth Century* (1969).

31 THE ELECTION OF 1896

A. W.

For a week, arguments had raged through the lobby and corridors of Chicago's Palmer House hotel. Bellboys no longer looked up when a long-haired Southerner or a flat-voiced Midwestern farmer loudly debated a well-dressed Eastern delegate, or when reinforcements for both sides rushed to join the verbal melee. Only when it seemed the discussion would turn into a fistfight did hotel employees quietly suggest that the gentlemen might like to continue their chat elsewhere.

Since delegates to the Democratic National Convention had begun pouring into Chicago, these employees had heard the same argument many times. At its most basic level, it seemed dull, a technical question of economics. The United States government, in this year of 1896, promised to pay to each holder of a dollar bill one dollar in gold. Overexcited Democrats from the South and the West now demanded that the government be empowered to redeem its paper money in silver as well as gold. Equally aroused politicians from New York, Pennsylvania, and Massachusetts angrily retorted that such a policy would destroy the credit of the government.

Chicagoans grown sick of the nonstop bellowing over the currency issue in most of their downtown hotels, restaurants, and bars, could find no relief outside. Marching, shouting, prosilver convention delegates filled the sidewalks and streets, singing along with the marching bands imported by each presidential candidate to improve his chances.

If there was an eye to this emotional storm, it was probably an upstairs corridor at the Sherman House, the hotel where a small, "foreign-looking" politico held court. He would beckon to a waiting silverite, hold a short, animated conversation in which he did most of the talking, and dismiss his auditor and summon another in the same gesture. The next man would then scuttle forward to talk to John Peter Altgeld, gover-

Independent-minded John Peter Altgeld, the first Democratic Governor of Illinois in 36 years, had been a German immigrant, Civil War soldier, Chicago lawyer, and Judge, before winning the highest state office in 1893.

nor of Illinois and the closest thing at the moment to a leader of the silver forces.

Altgeld had been through controversy before. Two years earlier, when a railroad strike paralyzed Chicago, he had refused to call in federal troops, arguing that local forces were adequate to maintain order. When President Grover Cleveland, less interested in maintaining order than in breaking the strike, sent in troops anyway, Altgeld berated his party's leader. He was in turn attacked by conservatives all over the country, the Chicago *Tribune* calling him "the lying, hypocritical, demagogical, sniveling Governor of Illinois."

Earlier, Altgeld, realizing that the move might make him a "dead man politically," had pardoned the three Haymarket anarchists still in prison. He had long been troubled by charges of prejudice from the judge and jury and by the inadequacy of the evidence against the accused. This action caused the more conservative elements of the press to conclude that Altgeld was an anarchist himself.

Neither of these acts, however, bothered the silver forces who looked to him for leadership. Many of the Southern and Western farmers now thronging Chicago had risen up and in Alabama schoolhouse meetings and Kansas county conventions taken the Democratic party away from its astonished former owners.

The silver Democrats had swept state after state, and now they came to Chicago with a clear majority of the delegates. But the more perceptive among them would have traded any one of the marching bands for a strong presidential candidate. Altgeld, the most important figure in the movement, was disqualified because he was German born, although he had come to America at the age of three months. With the silver forces divided among several weak candidates, silverites feared a compromise that would allow the outnumbered gold men to name the candidate.

They feared one gold man in particular. In ability and intellect, William Collins Whitney was the only man in Chicago comparable to Altgeld. Both were farm boys who had become city lawyers—Altgeld in Chicago, Whitney in New York. But whereas Altgeld had gone into labor law and politics, Whitney had worked for the Vanderbilts, the railroad magnates, and moved on rapidly to build his own future. With the same brilliance and ruthlessness that had amassed him $40 million, he had engineered Cleveland's nomination and election in 1892 and gained a reputation as the most effective organizer in American politics.

Whitney rolled into Chicago as the brains of the "gold train," carrying the elite of the Eastern Democrats to the convention. The train, stocked with choice food and wines, carried cabinet officers, United States senators, and state party bosses. In previous years, this group had controlled the Democratic party; six of the last seven Democratic candidates for President had come from New York, and the seventh from Pennsylvania. Now they journeyed nervously, hoping that Whitney could work his magic and save them from humiliation.

Whether Whitney could do it, or whether the silver forces could agree on a candidate, remained in doubt when the convention opened.

Fifteen thousand people jammed Chicago's Coliseum, facing giant portraits of Jackson, Jefferson, and James Buchanan, with galleries rising in rows above the convention floor.

William Jennings Bryan, a thirty-six-year-old former congressman from Nebraska, owed loyalty to neither Whitney nor Altgeld. A strong silverite, he had his own ideas about who should lead the movement. On the convention's second night, before returning to his modest, two-dollar-a-day hotel room, Bryan uttered the following words to his wife and a friend: "So that you both may sleep well tonight, I am going to tell you something. I am the only man who can be nominated. I am what they call the logic of the situation."

The next day, the delegates waited expectantly as Bryan, famous as an orator but hardly considered a serious candidate, approached the stage to close the debate over the platform. Bryan began by warning that farmers were through with meekly asking the East for assistance. He reviewed the previous year's steady growth of silverite protest and challenged those Eastern gold Democrats who argued that returning to a dual monetary standard—gold *and* silver—would "disturb" the country's business interests.

New York financier William C. Whitney, a lifelong Democrat despite his substantial wealth, had supported Grover Cleveland in 1884 and 1892, and served as Cleveland's Secretary of the Navy.

The petitions of farmers had been scorned by Eastern men of wealth, Bryan shouted. Their entreaties had been disregarded, and— "when our calamity [the depression] came"—their begging had been mocked. "We beg no longer," he cried, "we entreat no more; we petition no more. We defy them!" From that moment, Bryan held most of his 15,000 listeners in his hands. Their cheers interrupted him constantly as he heaped scorn upon the Eastern gold Democrats and their arguments. The audience's enthusiasm reached its height as Bryan's speech drew to a close. Even the most hostile listener would be forced to acknowledge that Bryan had transformed the convention briefly into a sort of revival meeting.

"You shall not press upon the brow of labor this crown of thorns," cried Bryan, in one of the most famous perorations in American history. "You shall not crucify mankind upon a cross of gold!" For five seconds Bryan stood in dead silence, his arms outstretched in a Christlike pose.

Then the convention went mad. Dignified judges and legislators screamed and danced in the aisles. Silverites carried Bryan on their shoulders. State after state dipped its standard in front of Nebraska's, while silver politicians fought through the crowd to pledge Bryan their votes. One gold delegate grabbed a nearby newsman, hauled him to his feet, and bellowed, "Yell, damn you, yell!"

"I have enjoyed a great many addresses, some of which I have delivered myself," remembered Clarence Darrow, who would one day debate the Creation with Bryan in a Tennessee court, "but I never listened to one that affected and moved an audience as did that. Men and women cheered and laughed and cried. They listened with desires and hopes and finally with absolute confidence and trust. When he had finished his speech, amidst the greatest ovation I have ever witnessed, there was no longer any doubt as to the name of the nominee."

The thirty-six-year-old "boy orator," Nebraska Congressman William Jennings Bryan, was hoisted onto the shoulders of supporters, following his powerful "Cross of Gold" speech at the Democratic Convention in 1896.

Bryan's nomination on a silver platform delighted the South and the West. Two people less enthralled were the kingmakers of the convention, Whitney and Altgeld. Whitney, along with much of the stunned Eastern democracy, immediately announced that he would neither support nor vote for the ticket. Altgeld, despite the triumph of silver, was also disappointed. "It takes more than speeches to win victories," he told a friend the day after Bryan's triumph. "I have been thinking over Bryan's speech. What did he say, anyhow?"

Three weeks before, down the river in St. Louis, the Republicans had named Bryan's opponent. Their convention contrasted sharply with the hubbub and activity of the Democrats'. It was, one newspaper noted mournfully, the dullest convention anyone could remember.

Which was exactly how Marcus Alonzo Hanna wanted it. Hanna had worked for three years to lock the convention up for his friend Wil-

William Jennings Bryan's "Cross of Gold" metaphor had little appeal to his opponents in the business and industrial communities, no more than the candidate himself or his proposals for economic reform. The cartoon above, depicting Bryan as a trampler of scripture and vendor of sacrilegious souvenirs, accuses him of dragging Christian symbols into the dust.

liam McKinley of Ohio, and he wanted no disturbance that might unlock it. Although Eastern Republicans demanded a flat statement in support of gold and Republicans from Rocky Mountain silver-mining states wanted *their* metal endorsed, Hanna determined that the issue would not get out of hand.

McKinley had followed the path of the ambitious small-town Ohioan to success in Republican politics, the same trail that had led James Garfield to the White House. A former congressman and governor, McKinley had written the party's last tariff bill in 1890, a high tariff measure to "protect" American industries. If, as a friend admitted, "McKinley was no intellectual giant," he nevertheless understood politics, made friends easily, and came from the right state for a Republican candidate.

McKinley had every asset for political success except money. And while he did not possess much of that himself, he had the next best thing: an extremely wealthy friend and political backer. Mark Hanna, though he owned a shipping company, a bank, a street railway, an opera house, and much of the Cleveland area's Republican party, was more than just rich. He had been born to money, and he married much more of it, but he had then made a great deal more for himself and had thoroughly mastered all his businesses. Hanna believed in the durability of the

Mark Hanna, McKinley's campaign manager in the 1896 election, boss of the Ohio Republican machine and later of the national one, was a wealthy industrialist anxious for political power.

new industrial system. If the system could weather violent strikes, surely it could also withstand the threat of free silver. He had informed the panicky members of the Cleveland Union League Club, "There isn't going to be any revolution. You're all a lot of damned fools."

Over the years, Hanna had mastered national politics with McKinley as he had mastered his own shipping empire. With negotiating skill and with a personal expenditure of $100,000, Hanna won most of the delegates west and south of Pennsylvania for his candidate and brought him to St. Louis in possession of a clear majority of convention delegates.

Only the money question provided any interest. McKinley himself, now under pressure from both sides, had during his congressional career supported both gold and silver at different times. "McKinley isn't a gold-bug, McKinley isn't a silver-bug," mocked Speaker of the House Thomas Reed, who was his only real rival. "McKinley is a straddle-bug." Throughout the preconvention campaign, the candidate simply refused to answer letters asking his views on currency. When Easterners complained, Mark Hanna roared, "I don't give a damn what Wall Street thinks of McKinley's silence; they can go to hell down there. We are not going to nominate McKinley on a Wall Street platform."

Hanna now skillfully allowed the Eastern Republican bosses to push him into a flat declaration for gold, thus easing their resentment over McKinley's nomination. A handful of silver Republicans walked out, eventually to support Bryan. Hanna, wearing a blue shirt with white polka dots and an enormous diamond in his tie, watched happily as the convention overwhelmingly nominated his friend.

The nominee, who had fought for thirty years for the protective tariff, did not believe that currency could really decide the election. "Thirty days from now," McKinley told a friend, "you won't hear anything about silver."

William McKinley, Republican Governor of Ohio and protege of Mark Hanna, was the last Union army officer to reach the White House.

The friend disagreed. "Thirty days from now," he told McKinley, "you won't hear about anything else."

In this extraordinary election year, one more party had to meet in convention. The wave of rural anger and desperation that had rolled over the Democrats had also created an entirely new party, the Populists, also known as the People's party. Growing steadily in strength since its first appearance in 1890, the Populist party increasingly stressed silver as the answer to the farmer's problems. If the Populists now joined with the Democrats, who had declared for other reforms as well as silver, the combined ticket might sweep the country. But with two separate silver tickets, Hanna's Republicans would enjoy an easy victory.

The Populist delegates who now marched into St. Louis bore little resemblance to the Republicans who had preceded them. Populists were a ragtag collection of veterans from earlier third parties, like the Grangers and the Greenbackers, and bankrupt farmers hoping desperately for help from the movement, with a scattering of urban radicals, including some Socialists and a few labor people. It was not the usual free-spending convention crowd; many in it were poor, and some had walked to St. Louis or skipped meals to get there. To complete the bucolic atmosphere, the Populists presented awed Eastern reporters with a dazzling array of beards and whiskers, a sight rarely seen among urbane men of fashion.

On the key issue of endorsing Bryan, the Populists split along sectional lines. Midwestern and Western Populists, accustomed to cooperate with Democrats and encouraged by Democratic National Chairman James K. Jones, favored fusion with the Chicago ticket. Gaily singing, "We'll shoot the gold-bugs, every one," they were willing to join every effort to help boost the chances of silver. "I care not for party names," declared "Sockless Jerry" Simpson of Kansas. "It is the substance we are after, and we have it in William J. Bryan."

For Southern Populists, fusion with the Democrats was more distasteful. Like all political questions below the Mason-Dixon line, the Populist movement had become entangled in the race issue. Southern party members had declared racism to be a tool of the wealthy in oppressing the farmers and had welcomed blacks into the party. Hundreds of thousands of black farmers had joined the Colored Farmers' Alliance, working closely with the Southern Farmers' Alliance. In Georgia, Populist leader Tom Watson had called out dozens of white party members to stand guard over the house of a black leader who had been threatened. In North Carolina, white Democrats were stunned when a Populist legislature with black members adjourned for a day after the death of Frederick Douglass.

Because of such policies, Southern Populists had been beaten, shot at, and defrauded by the ruling Democratic machines. They would not now support a Democratic candidate. "Avoid fusion as you would the devil," wired Watson from Georgia. "Texas is here to hold a Populist

The delegates to Populist conventions, such as this one (held in a huge tent), were an amalgam of alliance leaders, politicos, visionaries, and other enthusiasts. In 1896 their ranks were divided over the presidential nomination, since free silverites and fusionists favored the Democratic candidate, young Nebraska Congressman William Jennings Bryan, who was to win the Populist nomination as well. The third party rejected the Democrats' vice presidential nominee in favor of Georgia Populist Tom Watson, a concession to those who wanted an independent Populist slate.

convention," cried one Southerner, "and we're going to do it before we go home."

Although the Populists lacked the organization of the older parties, making high-level wheeling and dealing difficult, a compromise did emerge. The party would nominate Watson for Vice-President. To assure the Southerners that the more numerous fusionists planned no betrayal, the Vice-Presidential ballot was held first. Only after Watson had been put on the ticket did the Populists name Bryan for President. The pro-fusion convention chairman did not bother to inform delegates of the telegram he had received saying that Bryan did not want the nomination without Sewall.

Now that he was the candidate of two major parties, not to mention the National Silver party, the Single-Taxers, the Christian Socialists, and a faction of the Prohibitionists, Bryan offered himself and his remedies to a stricken country. The unrest in American politics only reflected a greater instability in the American economy, as the United States entered the fourth year of the most severe depression in its history.

At its worst point, the depression of the nineties left two and a half million workers unemployed. Some Americans were reported to have starved to death. Many employers responded to depression (and the labor surplus) by cutting wages. In response, strikes exploded across the land. Half a million workers walked out, and the disputes prevented another two-thirds of a million persons from working. The Pullman strike centered in the Chicago railyards, and Altgeld had tried unsuccessfully to keep Cleveland from intervening. It was only one of a series of bitter struggles.

A single pathetic protest best reflects the desperation of the depression of the 1890s. A small businessman from Ohio, Jacob Coxey, vowed to send "a petition in boots" to Congress, asking for a $500 million public-works program to help the unemployed. "Coxey's Army," as it was derisively dubbed, never numbered more than 600, but it was reported by newspapers as if it were a vast horde come to sack the Capitol and lay waste the District of Columbia. Correspondents dogged the "army" on its slow journey through Pennsylvania, writing about the half-dozen comic-opera figures capering on elderly horses, ignoring the ragged unemployed marching with something like hope in their eyes. Only a few hundred reached Washington, where Congress ignored them and Coxey was arrested for walking on the Capitol lawn.

Despair ran even deeper on American farms throughout the Great Plains and down into the cotton fields of the South. There, the depression only intensified the crisis that began in the late 1880s. Overproduction was crushing the army of wheat, corn, and cotton growers. The more the farmer produced, the lower prices fell, forced downward by the law of supply and demand. Many gave up, and thousands of covered wagons rolled East across the Mississippi, bearing signs reading, "In God We Trusted, In Kansas We Busted."

Farmers reacted to this situation with stunned anger, believing that *they*, and not the railroad owners or the farm-machinery producers

"Coxey's Army" of unemployed, shown on their way to Washington in 1894, wanted to petition Congress for work relief. While not driven out at bayonet point (as was to be the case with the "Bonus Army" of 1932), the 500 or so of Coxey's troops who arrived at the Capitol were confronted by police and placed in custody for endangering the public health. General Coxey was arrested for walking on the grass and put in jail.

Jacob S. Coxey, on the right, upon his release from jail in Washington, D. C. in 1894, after serving 20 days. An Ohio businessman and Populist, Coxey proposed public works and federal relief to combat depression and, with his "Army" of the unemployed, marched on Washington to demand Congressional action. In the center is Carl Browne and on the left, with silk hat, Christopher Columbus Jones.

or the meat packers, formed the backbone of the country. Yet debts piled higher and higher, while middlemen profited handsomely. There was something wrong somewhere, probably a calculated conspiracy to defraud farmers of their rightful share of national wealth.

In a thousand sun-baked courthouse squares, farmers cheered orators who demanded action. "What you farmers have to do," declared Mary Lease, a fiery woman known affectionately as "Mary Yellin," "is raise less corn and more hell!" In 1890, several farm groups had organized the Populist party to do just that. The Populists had elected three senators and twenty-five congressmen that year, and in 1892 its presidential candidate had carried four states and polled over a million votes. The party also elected governors and state officials, sometimes allying with an older party on a combined ticket.

The Populist showing in 1892 startled most the country—and shocked the East. Populists demanded government ownership of railroads and telegraphs. Their platform also demanded an end to gambling in stocks, the direct election of the President and United States senators, and the secret ballot. And in a direct attempt to aid the mortgaged farmers, the Populists asked for no limit on the coinage of silver.

Requiring money to be backed only by gold, reasoned the Populists, greatly limited the amount in circulation. If the government could print money based on silver as well, and bought all silver mined in the country for that purpose, the resulting inflation would make mortgages easier to pay off and would raise farm prices. They spurned the arguments of bankers and industrialists that Europe would not accept money based on silver and that such a program would produce financial chaos. The Populists saw the issue as a battle of Eastern greed against Southern and Western sweat. "It is a struggle," explained "Sockless Jerry" Simpson, "between the robbers and the robbed."

The story of most presidential elections begins with the congressional election two years earlier. In the fall of 1894, in the midst of a depression and a farm crisis, the voters emphatically rebuked Cleveland and the Democrats. "The Democratic losses will be so great," predicted Thomas Reed, "that their dead will have to be buried in trenches labeled 'Unknown.'" The morning after the election, the trenches contained 113 of the 218 Democrats in the House. Cleveland's policies had shattered his party. Under intense pressure from their constituents, and with no reason to remain loyal to the administration, Democrats from the South and the West now rushed to embrace "free" silver.

Now the Democrats and the Populists had a candidate to go with the issue. Bryan, having captured the nomination with his stirring oration, now embarked upon a radically different kind of campaign. Presidential candidates, by tradition, remained at home, pleased and flattered by the efforts their friends were making on their behalf, but pretending to be far too modest to campaign for themselves. In the four months between convention and election, Bryan altered this pattern, traveling 18,000 miles, making 600 speeches, and addressing approximately five million persons. Republicans mocked his nickname, "the Boy Orator of the Platte," pointing out that the Platte River was six inches deep and a mile wide at the mouth; but Bryan's entranced audiences had apparently not heard the quip.

Across the nation, even in the supposedly hostile East, they yelled as the Democratic convention had yelled. After Bryan's triumphant tour of New England, a friend told him that he had never seen such a response. "You ought to come with me to Ohio, Indiana, and Kansas," smiled the confident nominee. "These people have given us a great reception in the East, but the West is on fire."

A Bryan speech in the West resembled a revival meeting more than a political rally. The crowd listened not with the skepticism usually accorded politicians, but with total trust and belief, cheering and responding at all the right moments. Before crowds so thick he sometimes could not reach the speaker's platform, Bryan painted a picture of a new America—a country whose abundant wealth would not be controlled by a small group, a country in which farmers would have their rightful place, in which the land across the Mississippi would not be an exploited colony of the East. Young and good-looking, Bryan appeared "every inch an Apollo," and farm wives as well as farmers were swept along in the spell of the new champion of the West.

Conservatives and Republicans, on the other hand, feared for their ticket. Hanna, panicked at the reception Bryan received that summer, went to McKinley, who was observing political tradition in his hometown of Canton. Hanna insisted that McKinley must campaign. The GOP candidate shook his head. "I might just as well put up a trapeze on my front lawn and compete with some professional athlete as go out speaking against Bryan," he reasoned. Hanna, reconsidering, agreed, and went off to New York to start his own campaign.

Joined by James J. Hill, railroad magnate of the Northwest, Hanna began visiting corporation offices. "I wish that Hanna would not talk so freely about money," complained one insurance company president, but the Ohio industrialist refused to play the hypocrite. He never denied that he proposed to beat Bryan by getting and spending more money than had ever been seen in an American election. Hanna extracted a quarter of a million each from John D. Rockefeller and J. P. Morgan. Four Chicago meat packers gave $100,000 apiece, and Hanna assessed banks and insurance companies one-quarter of 1 percent of their assets. The books of the Republican National Committee showed collections of $3.5 million, twice those of any previous campaign, but other estimates ranged from $10 million to $16 million being spent to beat silver. Cartoons in Democratic newspapers depicted Hanna in a suit checked with dollar signs.

With the money, Hanna sent out hundreds of speakers, preceding and following Bryan, including many converted Democrats. (He caused a furor at one luncheon by growling that some of the turncoat Democrats were not worth what it had cost to convert them.) Hanna's funds also enabled Republican headquarters to send out 250 million pieces of mail, including 120 million pamphlets, many of them in German, Swedish, Polish, Italian, Yiddish, and other languages. "He has advertised McKinley," complained the young Theodore Roosevelt, "as if he were a patent medicine!"

Bryan meanwhile had enough problems with his own party. Most major Democratic newspapers in the East refused to support the ticket. Immediately after Bryan's nomination, while gold Democrats were still stunned, Henry Watterson, editor of the influential and conservative Louisville *Courier-Journal*, wired from Europe, "Another ticket our only hope. No Compromise with Dishonor."

Taking that for their slogan, gold Democrats met in Indianapolis and nominated Senator John M. Palmer of Illinois, former Union Army general, for President, and former Confederate general Simon Bolivar Buckner of Kentucky for Vice President. The two old campaigners stumped actively, less for themselves than just to shake Democrats loose from Bryan. "Fellow Democrats," invited Palmer toward the end of the campaign, "I will not consider it any great fault if you decide to cast your vote for William McKinley." The Cleveland administration supported Palmer; when the secretary of the interior endorsed Bryan in August, Cleveland promptly fired him.

Bryan had also been unable to deal with the Populists' gift of a second running mate. Watson had accepted under the impression that the Democratic nominee, Arthur Sewall would retire, making Watson the candidate of both Democratic and Populist parties. Democratic chairman Jones, no longer the eager seeker of Populist support, replied coolly, "Mr. Sewall will, of course, remain on the ticket, and Mr. Watson can do what he likes." What Watson did was to campaign through the

West, urging Populists to vote for Bryan-Watson instead of Bryan-Sewall. (In most states, the slates combined on a single ticket of electors, with the vote to be cast for the vice-presidential candidate who led in the state's popular vote.) This policy was suicidal, since in the event of a Bryan victory neither Watson nor Sewall would share his majority and the Republican Senate would elect a Vice President. In the Democrats' idea of fusion, charged Watson, "We play Jonah while they play whale." Bryan dealt with the problem after a fashion by never formally accepting the Populist nomination.

A few Populists would never have supported Bryan anyway. "The Free Silver movement is a fake," sneered Henry Demarest Lloyd, one of the movement's few intellectuals. "Free silver is the cow-bird of the reform movement. It waited until the nest had been built by the sacrifice and labor of others, and then it laid its eggs in it, pushing out the others which it smashed on the ground." So saying, Lloyd groused off to vote Socialist Labor.

Feeling that their entire way of life was threatened, however, Republicans and conservatives intensified their attacks on Bryan. "Anarchists, Socialists, and destructives in society" supported Bryan, according to a Republican senator; *Harper's Weekly* compared Bryan and Altgeld to leaders of the French Revolution. But despite such invective, or perhaps because of it, the Republican New York *Herald* predicted in October that Bryan would get 237 electoral votes, thirteen more than needed for victory.

Hanna, however, had spotted the Nebraskan's weakness. "He's talking silver all the time," noted the Republican national chairman, "and that's where we've got him." The Chicago platform, with many planks favorable to labor, had gained Bryan the endorsement of Socialist leader Eugene V. Debs and J. K. Sovereign of the Knights of Labor, as well as the indirect support of Samuel Gompers of the American Federation of Labor. But even when speaking to workers, Bryan never stressed those planks, preferring to concentrate on currency. However attractive inflation appeared to a farmer with a heavy mortgage, it looked far different to a steelworker working twelve hours for a dollar a day. Bryan apparently saw no reason to broaden his appeal; as one observer commented, Bryan led a revolution without understanding it.

The Nebraskan would have had problems with urban workers, who were largely immigrants, anyway. He neither drank nor smoked nor gambled, and he always wore about him an aura of rural, prudish evangelism. This cultural difference could not but make segments of the urban labor force uneasy. Their apprehensions about the Boy Orator of the Platte increased when Monsignor John Ireland, a ranking Catholic leader, came out against free silver.

Both McKinley and Hanna had excellent reputations among labor groups. McKinley had signed several prolabor bills as governor of Ohio, and his refusal to send troops to break a strike had once led the Chicago *Herald* to compare him with Altgeld. Hanna had rarely suffered any labor trouble in his far-flung enterprises, and was known to have bellowed during one major strike: "Any [business] man who won't meet his men halfway is a goddamn fool!"

McKinley proved to be a formidable campaigner in his own way. Although he would not go to an audience, audiences came to him, to sit on his front lawn and listen to him speak from the porch. Seven hundred and fifty thousand people came to Canton that fall, encouraged by the special rates provided by friendly railroads. The reduced fares, a Democratic newspaper commented sourly, made it cheaper to visit McKinley than to stay home.

Many industrialists now decided to aid McKinley in their own way. "You may vote any way you wish," some factory owners were reputed to have informed their workers, "but if Bryan is elected on Tuesday the whistle will not blow on Wednesday." The idea spread rapidly, and a number of workers claimed to have received such warnings at factory gates or in their pay envelopes. "Boys," said a Bryan adviser, "I am afraid this beats us."

Possibly it did, although it was more likely that Hanna's efforts had decided the outcome. On November 3, Bryan came up half a million votes short. He carried no state north of the Mason-Dixon line nor east of the Mississippi. He still might have won, but he lost four Democratic border states as well as California, Oregon, Iowa, Minnesota, and North Dakota in the West. In several of these states the vote was close, with the Palmer Democrats holding the balance. Bryan's rural stalwarts managed to win mainly the agrarian strongholds of the South and most of the prairie states for their eloquent standard-bearer.

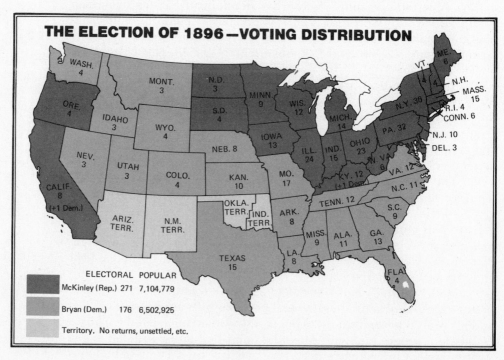

THE ELECTION OF 1896—VOTING DISTRIBUTION

	ELECTORAL	POPULAR
McKinley (Rep.)	271	7,104,779
Bryan (Dem.)	176	6,502,925
Territory. No returns, unsettled, etc.		

Democrats charged that the Republicans had simply bought the election. The Democratic party, said Altgeld bitterly, was "confronted by all the banks, all the trusts, all the syndicates, all the corporations, all the great papers. It was confronted by everything that money could buy, that boodle could debauch, that fear of starvation could coerce."

The returns outlined the voters who decided the election. Bryan had failed to break through labor's fears, carefully fostered by Republican propaganda. He had failed to persuade dairy farmers that silver would help them, and he lost every dairy state, from Ohio to Wisconsin. Although he had repudiated the Democratic administration, the party could not escape the nation's bitterness over the depression. "I have borne the sins of Grover Cleveland," explained the candidate who most strongly opposed Cleveland's "Bourbon Democracy."

Republicans rejoiced at the election result. Hanna had saved the gold standard; the forces of "anarchism" (as conservatives fearfully viewed Bryan's Democratic and Populist supporters) had been beaten back. McKinley could be expected to offer the country a "safe" administration, by which it was understood that he would retain the gold standard, raise tariff rates still higher, and avoid reforms. Thus it was that McKinley went to the White House.

Bryan cushioned his disappointment somewhat by writing a book on the campaign. In deference to both his beliefs and his own career, he called it *The First Battle*. He was certain that during his lifetime the forces favoring reforms in America would regroup for future political campaigns. The 1896 election result, therefore, saddened him less than it did many of his agrarian supporters, about whose frustrations Vachel Lindsay wrote in an elegy to the campaign:

Election night at midnight:
Boy Bryan's defeat.
Defeat of western silver.
Defeat of the wheat.
Victory of letterfiles
And plutocrats in miles
With dollar signs upon their coats,
Diamond watchchains on their vests
And spats on their feet . . .
Victory of the neat.
Defeat of the aspen groves of Colorado valleys,
The blue bells of the Rockies,
And blue bonnets of old Texas,
By the Pittsburg alleys.
Defeat of alfalfa and the Mariposa lily.
Defeat of the Pacific and the long Mississippi.
Defeat of the young by the old and silly.
Defeat of tornadoes by the poison vats supreme.
Defeat of my boyhood, defeat of my dream.

32 THE CRISIS OF THE 1890s

A. W.

The political turbulence of the 1896 election followed a long history of farm protest against the new industrial America. Jefferson, Jackson, and other great leaders in the past had assured the small farmer, armed with the vote, that he was the backbone of America. The Populists were only the last of a series of farm organizations to reflect the farmer's growing belief that since the Civil War the balance of power and wealth had shifted to the corporations—and that the balance must be redressed.

Although the thrust of the farmer's complaints remained the same, issues varied over the last three decades of the nineteenth century. Originally, farmers had demanded stricter control of the railroads. Then, in two separate movements, currency reform seemed the root of the problem. Finally, the Populists focused on the process of government corruption and demanded a change in the selection of leaders; they wanted direct election of senators, primary elections, and secret ballots.

The Populist party achieved some significant gains in state government, but after 1896 it never posed a national threat. Some farmers would be swayed by the reformist rhetoric of Theodore Roosevelt; others, as we saw, remained with Bryan and the Democrats. A few would take a different path; when Oklahoma was admitted to the union in 1907, it contained more Socialists than any other state in the nation. But with the rise of the cities, whatever the farmers did would matter less and less politically. The failure of the farmers' movement was written not in election returns, but in census figures.

SETTLING THE WEST

Even after the passage of the Homestead Act during the Civil War, and despite subsequent government actions to make settlement of the plains attractive, Americans were reluctant to farm much past the Mississippi Valley. The notion of the Great American Desert, where nothing would grow and Indians abounded, died hard. Settlers heading west would rather go all the way to California or Oregon than stop in between in Kansas, Nebraska, or the Dakota territory.

Almost immediately after the war, heavy government subsidies helped to crisscross the plains with new railroad track. Roads like the Kansas Pacific, the Southern Pacific, and the Santa Fe now appeared out of nowhere. Only heavy settlement of the area could make these roads profitable. The railroads, along with Western newspapers and local boosters, set out to recruit the needed settlers.

There was enough land for all of them. Not only did the government provide land virtually free to settlers under the Homestead Act, but the railroads had received millions of acres of public land in subsidies. They now used this land to lure farmers, selling it as cheaply as twenty-five cents an acre, and offering easy credit terms.

As a result of this effort, a tremendous boom in Western land took place. The population of the Dakota territory soared 853 percent between 1870 and 1880, and that of Kansas and Nebraska tripled. Some settlers mortgaged their homesteads to buy more land. Eastern and European money eagerly bought up Kansas mortgages, confident that prices would continue to rise. Not only settlers, but towns and cities went deeply into debt with the expectation that the boom would last forever. Well into the 1880s, bumper crops and financial boom flourished together, and farmers deeply in debt to banks and agricultural machinery companies considered themselves rich because of the book value of their heavily mortgaged land holdings.

Between 1860 and the turn of the century, the mileage of railroad tracks increased by the thousands each decade, criss-crossing the plains. Heavily subsidized by state and federal governments, the railroad companies preceded and stimulated settlement, expanded, and overexpanded. By the 1890s, many overextended companies had fallen into bankruptcy, and others into the hands of eastern banks and financiers.

More than any other industry, the railroads were anxious to stimulate western settlement, populate the plains, and reap the profits therefrom. Through advertisements such as this one, setting forth the delights of cheap land in Kansas, the railroad company hoped to profit from the sale of its excess acreage, the transportation of migrants to it, and, eventually, from the freight rates the settlers would pay for transportation of their produce. By the end of the century, the Atchison, Topeka, and Sante Fe line, running from Kansas to California, was one of the five major transcontinental railroads.

THE GRANGERS

Having come out to the West through the benevolence of the railroads, Plains settlers slowly learned how completely they had fallen into the power of the railroad barons. Only by the railroad could they send their produce to Chicago and New York, and only by the railroad could they bring out the farm machinery and barbed wire necessary to farm the plains. Towns flourished or went bankrupt depending on the route of the road.

But even as new settlers rode the Rock Island Line out to the plains, farmers further east were learning how helpless they too were against the railroad. From Ohio to Minnesota, farmers had united into the Patrons of Husbandry, also known as the Grange. The Grange was partially a social institution, but also a cooperative alliance with some political interests. By the early 1870s, it had taken over several legislatures and had passed bills regulating railroad freight and storage rates. The railroads immediately attacked the new laws in the federal courts.

In the first decision, *Munn* v. *Illinois* (1877), the Supreme Court upheld an Illinois Granger law regulating Chicago grain storage companies. But over the next ten years, as Presidents Hayes, Arthur, Cleveland, and Harrison appointed a series of corporation lawyers as Supreme Court justices,

The National Grange of the Patrons of Husbandry, founded in 1867, fostered cultural progress, agricultural improvement, and community spirit. Due to gains in membership during the 1873 depression, the Grange could soon claim 20,000 local lodges, mainly in the midwest and south. On Independence Day, 1873, proclaimed as the "Farmers' Fourth of July," the Illinois lodge shown convened at an outdoor rally to denounce the railroads, plan collective action, and read "The Farmers' Declaration of Independence," which demanded freedom from the tyranny of monopoly.

the Court slowly whittled away at *Munn* v. *Illinois*. By 1890, in *Chicago, Milwaukee, and St. Paul Railway Company* v. *Minnesota*, it practically prohibited the states from regulating any railroad engaged in interstate commerce. The Grangers rapidly faded from political significance.

CRISIS ON THE PLAINS

Two blows—one a sudden act of nature, the other a steady process of technical advance and hard work—broke the speculative bubble on the plains. In 1886 and 1887, the weather turned on the homesteaders. Blistering summers with little rain were followed by miserable winters. Thousands of settlers were at once wiped out financially and began the slow, painful trek back east of the Mississippi. The inflated prices of land collapsed, and investors no longer clamored for Plains mortgages.

The settlers who survived, when the rains returned and their corn again grew high, faced a worse problem. East of the Mississippi and in much of the West as well, advances in farming technology and efficient use of chemical fertilizers had tremendously increased American agricultural production. This increase sent the prices of wheat, corn, and hogs skidding downward. If, in a frantic attempt to catch up, farmers increased production, further price drops resulted. A bushel of wheat had plummeted from $1.19 in 1881 to 49 cents in 1894. The American farmer, whose productivity using indifferent soil had astounded the world, was being destroyed by his own success. Farmers now found it more profitable to burn corn for fuel than to sell it at current prices.

Farmers could blame themselves for creating part of the predicament. Many, out of greed, had dangerously overextended themselves. Before giving up entirely, farmers would mortgage virtually everything they owned. In Kansas and North Dakota, for example, the number of mortgages declared in 1890 amounted to one for every two citizens. Many farmers, having mortgaged their horses and wagons, did not even have the option of fleeing to the East. A steady deflation

since the Civil War, with less and less money in circulation, had crippled the mortgaged farmer. He had to pay back his loan in dollars that had doubled in value since he borrowed them.

Yet farmers had also worked hard, and they now felt bitterly that the rules had been changed on them. They had no difficulty in coming up with people and institutions to blame. Somewhere, the farmers knew, someone was getting rich from their labor.

Railroads stood at the top of the list of indictments. There was little competition among the roads servicing the plains. Generally, only one ran into an area, and the farmer had no choice as to how to ship crops to market. Even when two railroads were within traveling distance, they had generally agreed upon rates beforehand, and the farmer again had little or no choice. Large growers received preferential rates, a practice justified by the railroads' claim that they must turn a profit on their investment. Farmers retorted that the railroads now had far more stock outstanding than the road was worth.

Even without considering the Granger cases, farmers expected little help from their state governments. The railroads exerted great power in the governments of many states.

Farmers also denounced other businesses that they felt were exploiting them. They charged that the farm machinery companies had formed a trust to keep the prices of their equipment high. Livestock raisers attacked the Chicago meat packers for making huge profits.

The Plains farmers also stressed the need for a remonetization of silver, a cause they had adopted from the Greenbackers. Since the time of the earlier reform movement, in the late 1870s, the situation had worsened for debtors. A dollar, worth twice its 1865 value in 1877, was worth three times its 1865 value by 1895. To heavily mortgaged farmers, this meant a financial war of attrition that they were bound to lose. Behind the country's virtual abandonment of silver money— "the Crime of '73"—they saw an alliance of their enemies: railroads, grain storage companies, money lenders, Wall Street, and foreign bankers.

This bitterness was fed by the intensity of the farmers' outrage, which had roots far deeper than economics. The center of American life was shifting rapidly to the city, and the farmer felt abandoned and despised. National magazines began carrying more and more stories and articles about city life, and the farmer saw his children deserting farm areas for the more exciting cities. Worst of all, a deep and justified suspicion existed that the new urbanites laughed at farm folk and looked down on them as "hicks." The conditions of farm life, especially in the West, were not such as to foster tolerance toward critics or opponents. Existence on a plains homestead was a constant round of hard physical labor and mind-numbing chores, with little contact with the outside world.

SOUTHERN AGRICULTURAL PROBLEMS

Although the problems of the Southern farmer differed from those of the Plains homesteader, the two were partners in misery. When the plantation

Dry, dusty, deficient in rainfall and timber, the Great Plains had once been an unpleasant obstacle for westward bound pioneers. After the Civil War, both the railroads and the federal government stimulated western settlement, through favorable land acts and land sales, but the migrants to the plains still had to confront an inhospitable terrain, in which large acreage and expensive mechanized equipment was needed for success. Although many families failed, those who remained transformed the unpromising flatlands into a fertile source of grains and livestock.

system collapsed at the end of the Civil War, millions of acres became available for land-hungry poor whites and freed slaves. Few of them, however, could afford to buy the land outright, and investors eager to buy up Nebraska mortgages showed no interest in investing in Alabama cotton land.

Poor farmers in the South, therefore, were compelled to obligate themselves heavily to use the land. Most farmers, including the great majority of blacks, became sharecroppers, farming someone else's land and turning over a large portion of the crop to the owner. Generally, the southern farmer kept no more than half of the harvest. Many kept only one-third.

To support themselves while the crops were growing, farmers mortgaged themselves again, this time to local storekeepers. (And very often now, moreover, the landowner and the storekeeper tended to be the same person.) In exchange for supplies, the storekeeper received a lien on the farmer's crops. The crops, when they came in, rarely amounted to enough to wipe out the standing debt. Year by year, the debt increased, obligations to the storekeeper/landowner preventing the sharecropper from leaving the land. The result was a system of peonage. For black farmers, it was not much better than slavery, and, as the twentieth century approached, more and more white farmers became "croppers."

Further, the landowners and storekeepers demanded that the farmer grow the crop that could be most easily turned into cash—namely, cotton. This prevented Southern farmers from growing enough food crops to maintain their families, and took a heavy toll on Southern soil, which now required large doses of fertilizer. To make matters worse, the price of cotton was rapidly declining; from 1870 to 1890 it was cut almost in half.

Moreover, Southern farmers shared with the plains settlers the problems of currency appreciation and the railroads. In the South, railroads allied themselves with the Democratic rather than the Republican party, but they controlled state governments just as effectively. Southern farmers came to share their Western compatriots' interest in railroad regulation, and, being as deeply in debt, shared also a growing enthusiasm for free silver.

THE COMING OF THE FARMERS' ALLIANCE

Throughout American history, farm organizations had sprung up, scored some temporary successes, and then faded away. But in the late 1880s, a group appeared and began to spread with astounding speed. Helped along by the able leadership of several remarkable personalities, Farmers' Alliances enrolled millions of members in the South and the West. By the end of the decade, the Southern Farmers' Alliance had enrolled three million members, with another million and a quarter in the Colored Farmers' Alliance. The Northern Farmers' Alliance, comprised overwhelmingly of farmers from states west of the Mississippi River, counted about another million. No previous farm organization had been able to come close to such numbers.

Like the Grange, the Alliance was partly social in its objectives, giving farmers a chance to get together occasionally. Also, like the Grange, it distributed pamphlets seeking to educate farmers about their condition and the reasons behind it. In many states, both in the West and the South, the Alliance took an active role in politics and managed to elect legislators favorable to its aims. In some states, it established railroad commissions, only to find, as the Grange had, that such controls turned out to be inadequate. The Alliance, however, had far greater numbers than the Grange had ever claimed, as well as a more impressive geographical distribution.

Political scientists and reformers in the 1870s and 1880s frequently complained that "Gilded Age" politics lacked meaning. They professed to find little difference between the parties, and charged that elections reflected not popular choices on issues, but only a sordid struggle for government offices and power. True or not, soon after the farmers' massive entry into politics, the

THE INCREASE OF FARM TENANCY IN THE SOUTH—1890

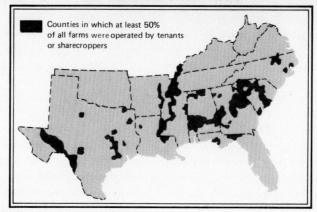

Counties in which at least 50% of all farms were operated by tenants or sharecroppers

parties indeed began to represent different ideas. This culminated in the bitter struggle of the 1896 campaign, when each side expected the destruction of the country should the other side win. It also culminated in the destruction of the balance between parties, leading to an unbroken, sixteen-year Republican rule in Washington.

While farmers gained strength, the tariff continued as the dominant surface issue in American politics. The farmers eventually came to oppose the tariff, seeing it as one more example of government aid to the rich and powerful, but they never felt as strongly about it as they did about silver and railroads. Republicans, however, saw the tariff as one of the keys to American (and their own party's) prosperity.

As Congress gathered in 1889, Republicans for the first time in fourteen years had working control of the presidency, the Senate, and the House. In 1890 they seized the opportunity, under the leadership of William McKinley, to pass the highest tariff in history. The McKinley bill flatly intended to protect as many American industries as possible from foreign competition.

The bill roused widespread opposition. Most Democrats attacked it; some were even known to send peddlers through the Midwest with items to sell at wildly inflated prices (which would be blamed on the tariff). When the votes were counted that November, Democrats had won an overwhelming victory, capturing heavy control of the House. Many senior Republican congressmen, including McKinley himself, lost their seats.

THE FOUNDING OF THE POPULIST PARTY

Alliance members in both the South and the West entered politics on a large scale in 1890. In the South, Alliance members won impressive victories within the Democratic party, running against railroads and their alliances with conservative, or "Bourbon" Democratic leaders. The Alliance elected three governors and claimed control of eight state legislatures. More than forty Southern Democratic congressmen announced that they favored the Alliance platform. The election also produced dramatic leaders for the Southern farmers, such as one-eyed "Pitchfork Ben" Tillman of South Carolina and slight but fiery Tom Watson of Georgia.

The plains farmers, however, had resolved to strike out for themselves. Angered by their lack of power within the existing party system, many farmers decided to bolt to the new party. From Minnesota to Colorado, farmers sang, "Good-bye, My Party, Good-bye," and named independent tickets. All across the plains, orators for the new party described Democrats and Republicans as nothing more than different fronts for the same railroad machine. A large number of the new agitators were women: Mary Elizabeth Lease, a lawyer with four children, became one of the most popular speakers on the Plains. Older reform protest figures joined in large numbers, and the Populists—although predominately agrarian in membership—also contained many Socialists, "Single Taxers" (followers of Henry George), "Nationalists" (disciples of Edward Bellamy), and Knights of Labor within their ranks.

From the 1890 returns, the new party seemed to make a promising start. It elected great numbers of state legislators, and two United States senators. Five Alliance congressmen were chosen from Kansas, and two more, along with a sympathetic Democrat named William Jennings Bryan, from Nebraska. Where the Alliance could not muster enough strength to win, it got the votes of enough normally Republican farmers to elect a large number of Democrats.

Both sides in the debate over a third party gained from the election. Westerners were now confident that a new party could succeed; the Southerners that they could gain control of the Democratic party. In a series of conventions over the next year, from Florida to Nebraska, they fought the issue out. Slowly the Southerners, unhappy at the conservatism of the national Democratic leadership, began to come around. At the organization of Congress, twenty Southern Democrats joined the Western Alliance men in supporting Tom Watson for Speaker of the House. Finally, in July 1892, delegates from the Northern and Southern Alliances and other organizations met in Omaha to take the final step, to nominate an independent Populist candidate for President of the United States.

Their candidate, and their platform, reflected the party more closely than convention products usually do. General James Baird Weaver, the candidate, was a veteran of the Civil War and of two decades of activism for reform and Prohibition. He had run for President as the Greenback candidate in 1880 and served three terms in Congress as a Greenback Democrat. As a new Populist and an old soldier, Weaver campaigned over the entire country.

"We meet in the midst of a nation brought to the verge of moral, political, and material ruin," warned the 1892 Populist platform. The time had come, the Populists announced, when either the railroads would own the people or the people would own the railroads. They demanded the end of national banks and the issuance of all money by the government, based on free coinage of silver. The program reflected the party's largely rural and agrarian base. Therefore, although there were planks that defended the right of unions to organize and denounced the oppression of factory workers, these were not central Populist concerns. And, although the platform also demanded a graduated federal income tax, direct election of senators, and other constitutional or political reforms, these were not central Populist concerns either.

What the new party wished, above all, was a series of reforms designed to help American farmers overcome what they felt were the unfair handicaps imposed upon agriculture in the United States by industrial growth. The most important of these demands was strict regulation or government ownership of the nation's railroads, which farmers believed discriminated against them. They also wanted an increase in the supply of money through remonetizing silver, since the Bland-Allison Act had been largely ineffective. Finally, they proposed establishing a government subtreasury warehouse system in which farmers could deposit their crops and receive loans up to 80 percent of the current market value of these crops. They would redeem the crops and sell them when open market prices had risen to acceptable levels. With this radical platform and a radical candidate, the Populists prepared to go before the nation.

THE ELECTION OF 1892

One reason for the willingness of some Southern Alliance members to leave the Democratic fold was the rapidly deteriorating condition of that party. Grover Cleveland, defeated for reelection in 1888, appeared to be the overwhelming favorite for his third nomination. Cleveland had never been much of an economic reformer. Since leaving the White House, he had practiced law in partnership with J. P. Morgan's attorney in Wall

Booker T. Washington

An ex-slave whose achievements in a thirty-five-year career spanned several important realms of national experience, Booker T. Washington may have been the single most influential American of his era in the field of race relations. His claim to greatness rests on his accomplishments as a teacher, educational pioneer, social theorist, fund raiser for philanthropic causes, advisor to Presidents, writer, politician and, most importantly, as the undeposed spokesman for black Americans.

Born on a Franklin County, Virginia plantation in 1856, Booker T. Washington lived in a slave cabin with his mother, sister, and brother until emancipation, when the family moved to West Virginia. In later years Washington credited his mother's "high ambitions for her children" as a dominant influence on his early years. He taught himself the alphabet using a Webster spelling book and, soon afterwards, he attended night school where he learned to read and write. In 1872, he entered Hampton Institute. He earned his board as a janitor while studying at Hampton, and graduated in 1875 after training as a brick-mason.

Most of Washington's adult life was spent in the South, first as a teacher in another Negro school before joining Hampton's staff in 1879 and then, two years later, becoming the head of a new Negro school being organized at Tuskegee, Alabama, which became world famous as the Tuskegee Institute.

During the 1880s, Washington addressed educational groups and public gatherings, in both the North and the South, covering such topics as race relations, the importance of education for black Americans, and the virtues of black-white harmony at almost any cost (including the temporary shelving of Negro demands for political rights and legal equality until a strong educational and economic base had been created).

Undoubtedly Washington's most famous statement of his central themes came during an 1893 speech at the Cotton States and International Exposition at Atlanta. At the Exposition, Washington called for friendship between the races while bluntly accepting the pattern of caste segregation then prevalent in every section of the country: "In all things that are purely social we can be as separate as the fingers, yet one as the hand in all things essential to mutual progress." Washington was praised by white moderates throughout the country. At the same time, many other black political leaders viewed the speech with dismay as an invitation to continued white interference with expressions of Negro militance.

Washington established rural extension programs at Tuskegee Institute designed to assist Southern farmers, helped found the National Negro Business League, and participated in many other activities intended to maximize black economic action and educational opportunity. In addition to these accomplishments, Washington wrote ten books and numerous articles. His most famous book, *Up From Slavery* (1901), further enhanced his extraordinary public reputation. Washington died while still maintaining his rigorous work schedule at the age of fifty-nine in November 1915. Even critics of his "accommodationist" philosophy have recognized that, within the pantheon of American black leaders, Booker T. Washington served as the monumental personal bridge who linked the tragic centuries of slavery with the long and continuing twentieth-century struggle of Negro Americans to achieve full equality and justice.

Street. He opposed free silver coinage even more strongly than the incumbent Republican President, Benjamin Harrison.

But even after Cleveland's nomination, the Southern Alliance split wide open over the question of leaving the Democrats. Regardless of any other issues, the Democrats were known in the South as "the white man's party." Joining the Populists meant public branding as a traitor to the white race. The South's best-known Alliance politicians were on opposite sides of the split. Tillman, governor of South Carolina and boss of the state Democratic party, refused to bolt, despite his well-known detestation of Cleveland; Watson led his Georgia followers into the Populist party and nominated a full state ticket to oppose the Democrats.

The Populists alarmed the white Southern establishment even more by openly appealing to the black vote. In many Southern states they allied closely with the Republicans, for whom blacks normally voted (when they were allowed to vote). In the campaign that followed, Southern Democrats used any weapon they could to smash the Populist-Republican-black alliance. Blacks were terrorized into staying away from the polls, or marched there by force to vote Democratic. When General Weaver campaigned in the South, Democrats broke up his rallies; Mary Lease claimed that in Georgia they made "a walking omelette" of the Populist candidate. Opponents shot at Populists, pressured them with economic threats, and if necessary stuffed the ballot boxes.

Without the race issue, Populist campaign-

Songs, revelry, and flag-waving characterized this election night crowd in 1892, as two U. S. Presidents contended for office. The Republican incumbent, Benjamin Harrison, and his Democratic challenger, former President Grover Cleveland, had few differences in policy, except on the tariff, but the Populist nominee, ex-Union General James B. Weaver, ran on a platform of economic reform that was to win him 22 electoral votes in the west.

ers faced little violence on the plains. There the Democrats, who were the minority party, established working arrangements with the Populists in most states. Democrats partially accepted the Populist platform, and Cleveland supporters, positive that they could not carry Kansas or Nebraska, planned to hurt Harrison by giving the states' votes to Weaver. The Democratic National Committee even supplied some under-the-table funds to the Populists for that purpose.

When the returns came in, Populists took a mixed view of the results. Cleveland won, but Weaver had polled a million votes (almost 10 percent) and carried five states, and the party claimed five senators and ten congressmen. Yet Populism had failed to make any serious inroads in the South, and had carried only Kansas on the plains.

The decline that had spurred the nation's farmers to take active steps for their own relief had no such effect on the rest of the country's workers. They failed to join the Populist movement. Several factors help to explain this. For one, the Populists never succeeded in breaking down the traditional political loyalties of most Americans, since party loyalty was extremely important to voters at this time. Even under the impact of economic depression, most people remained with their normal parties.

It was also true that the depression that began in 1893 occurred during a Democratic administration—Cleveland's second term. This resulted in political gains for the major opposition party even more impressive than those made by the Populists. In fact, Republicans almost doubled their number of House members in 1894—moving from 127 to 244—while the Democrats lost 113 seats. This was the most rapid major reversal of national political strength in American history, marking the first step in ending the close balance between the parties that had existed during the 1870s and 1880s.

Besides the depression working against them, there were other problems that the Populists could not overcome. The South presented the Populists with a unique set of problems that impeded their growth. There the new party attempted, for the first time since Reconstruction days, to create a biracial political coalition of black and white farmers against the business interests that still dominated most Southern state governments. For a time they made striking gains. But the political opponents of Southern Populism played upon such deeply felt racial fears and hostilities so effectively that, by the end of the decade, the new party had lost almost all its influence in the South. In that region, in fact, Populism had the ironic effect by 1900 of raising the race issue to an intensity and importance that it has maintained throughout most of the twentieth century.

Populist strength was sapped, especially in the industrial states, by internal tensions among its diverse sources of support. Such tensions between utopians and pragmatists often characterize reform movements. The Populists' agrarian leaders tended to be the movement's practical figures. Their overriding concern was for specific, immediate, and achievable goals such as free coinage of silver, the subtreasury plan, and other measures that would improve the economic bargaining position of most American farmers.

DEMOCRATS, DEPRESSION, DISASTER

Shortly after Cleveland took office for the second time, a business panic ushered in yet another of the series of depressions that had struck the nation at twenty-year intervals throughout the nineteenth century. Banks began to fail in 1893, and businesses laid off millions of workers in the cities and factory towns. By 1894, at the height of the depression, probably one out of every five workers was unemployed. Four out of five were living at subsistence level. As his first order of business, then, Cleveland would have to deal with a problem that had not figured in the campaign at all. At the same time, the price of farm products continued to decline disastrously on the world markets, while production costs skyrocketed.

Observers offered many explanations for the depression and suggested many ways to deal

Democrat Grover Cleveland, who had won the presidency in 1884 and lost it four years later, returned to challenge the Republican incumbent, Benjamin Harrison, in 1892. Cleveland also served as reform Governor of New York before becoming President.

with it. The conservative Cleveland accepted the prescription offered by big business. Confidence, he contended, had been shaken by the Sherman Silver Purchase Act, passed three years earlier by Congress as a sop to silver feeling. Cleveland claimed that the country had lost faith in its currency and noted the rush to exchange Treasury Department silver certificates for gold, a rush that was rapidly depleting the nation's gold reserves. In the midst of the depression, with sentiment for unlimited silver coinage sweeping the South and West, Cleveland called Congress into special session to repeal the law and silver coinage altogether. Using all his powers of patronage, Cleveland jammed repeal through Congress.

Worst of all, Cleveland's policies seemed to have no effect on the depression. Banks still closed their doors, workers remained unemployed, and gold continued to pour out of the

Treasury. By early 1895, the Treasury had only a three-week gold supply left. Cleveland and his secretary of the Treasury now arranged to buy $60 million in gold from a syndicate headed by J. P. Morgan and the Rothschilds, paying an extraordinarily high rate of interest. Cleveland's action may have saved the Treasury, but it did nothing for his popularity.

MCKINLEY AND PROSPERITY

The Republicans' comfortable though hard-fought victory over Bryan in 1896 appeared to put an end to the threats of radicalism and Populist agrarianism. Aided immensely by an economic upturn during the summer and fall of 1896, especially by a significant rise in farm prices, depression gave way to recession at an accelerating pace that soon produced recovery and helped to defuse agrarian protest. Mark Hanna had advertised McKinley as the "Advance Agent of Prosperity." Hanna appeared to be right, and Bryanism appeared to be doomed.

Perhaps the most striking feature of the 1896 election, however, was the Republicans' ability to put together a national majority that cut across class lines. McKinley won the votes not only of industrialists and the middle class, but also of a majority of urban workers. Bryan failed to capture the cities and the votes of most industrial laborers, despite prolabor planks in the Democratic platform. Many urban workers clearly felt that their economic interests were better protected by a probusiness Republican President than by a Democratic candidate who spoke (in the rich twang of Midwestern rural America no less) mainly about the problems of farmers. Moreover, Bryan had failed to hold together many of the Democratic party's traditional supporters in business, the middle class, and various ethnic groups. This failure may have been the single most important factor in his defeat.

But if Bryan failed in 1896 to create that farmer–laborer–small-businessman coalition that he believed could win national power and make needed political and economic reforms, he did lay the groundwork for such reformers, not only within the Democratic party but among Republicans as well. In the process, Bryan set a precedent for active presidential campaigning that almost all subsequent major party candidates followed in the twentieth century. In the end, therefore, the struggle for change in American society gathered momentum during the late 1890s despite Bryan's defeat, despite the disappearance of Populism, and even despite the country's return to economic prosperity.

McKinley's cabinet, even more conservative than the bimetallist President, wanted no tinkering with the financial machine. For his part, McKinley, who was not a reactionary on most issues, insisted on raising the tariff even beyond the demands of most conservatives. The resulting Dingley Tariff of 1897 pushed rates upward to an average of 52 percent.

Prosperity, not political enthusiasm, provided the key to the McKinley administration's success. The economic upturn of 1896–1897 continued full force, and even the strongest argument of the silverites—the contention that reliance on gold, a metal in short supply, strangled and would continue to strangle the nation's debtors—could no longer hold up. New discoveries of gold in Australia, Alaska, and South Africa dramatically increased supplies, and a strong inflationary trend accompanied the return to agricultural and industrial prosperity. In 1900, Congress and McKinley gave the country the Gold Standard Act, a law committing the federal government to a single monetary standard: gold. Another section of the law aimed at increasing the amount of national bank notes in circulation. Within a year, the dollar total of such notes almost doubled.

Nineteen hundred was also a presidential election year. From the start, McKinley had little to worry about. Bryan, again the Democratic candidate, had little hope, and his confusion over campaign strategies revealed his dilemma. Populism was dying during the late 1890s as rapidly as it had grown in the early years of the decade. Sensing this, Bryan tried to make antiimperialism his central campaign theme. A bored or even hostile response caused him to switch in midstream, and he gave primacy to the monopoly issue. Bryan did not abandon the free-silver stand (he insisted on a silver plank in the Democratic platform), but obviously his "second battle" would be no rerun of the first, except in the election returns. McKinley again won handily, and to conservative Republicans all things seemed right.

Prosperity's "advance agent" did not live to enjoy the fruits of this happy political situation. Within six months of his second inaugural, William McKinley was dead, victim of an assassin's bullet. In September 1901, McKinley journeyed to Buffalo, New York, to open the Pan-American Exposition of that year. Waiting for him amidst an almost adoring public was a young man named Leon Czolgosz. The Detroit-born son of Polish immigrant parents, Czolgosz was twenty-eight in 1901. He had survived, barely, the economic troubles of the nineties. He espoused the ideas of radical anarchists, though he had never joined any group in the movement. In 1901, he decided to kill the President. Without difficulty, Czolgosz joined the mass of people crowding around McKinley, who was "receiving" in one of the exposition buildings, shaking hands with all comers. Two shots rang out; one of them wounded McKinley mortally. A few days later the President died, and Theodore Roosevelt, a young New York Republican who had been chosen for the vice-presidency in order to slow down his political career, became the new President. Roosevelt differed from McKinley greatly in style and slightly in principles. It would be Roosevelt's job, first, to restore domestic tranquillity, which had been jolted by the third presidential assassination in almost as many decades. Then, he would be charged with maintaining prosperity, so recently returned, while consolidating America's new and enlarged role in the world. To these tasks, Roosevelt would add one of his own: the advocacy of reform in American society, at first cautiously but with growing boldness as his presidency progressed.

SUGGESTED READINGS– CHAPTERS 31-32

Election of 1896

Robert F. Durden, *Climax of Populism: The Election of 1896* (1964); Stanley Jones, *The Presidential Election of 1896* (1964); Paul W. Glad, *McKinley, Bryan and the People* (1964).

The Gilded Age

Harold U. Faulkner, *Politics, Reform and Expansion, 1890–1900* (1959); J. Rogers Hollingsworth, *The Whirligig of Politics* (1963); H. Wayne Morgan, *William McKinley and His America* (1963); Paul W. Glad, *The Trumpet Soundeth: William Jennings Bryan* (1959); Paolo E. Coletta, *William Jennings Bryan: Political Evangelist, 1860–1898* (1964); Arnold M. Paul, *Conservative Crisis and the Rule of Law, 1887–1895* (1960); Margaret Leech, *In the Days of McKinley* (1959); Richard J. Jensen, *The Winning of the Midwest* (1971); Morgan Kousser, *The Shaping of Southern Politics* (1974); Paul Kleppner, *The Cross of Culture* (1970); Ray Ginger, *The Bending Cross: A Biography of Eugene V. Debs* (1948); Edward C. Kirkland, *Industry Comes of Age* (1961); Lazar Ziff, *The American 1890s: Life and Times of a Lost Generation* (1966).

Populism

John D. Hicks, *The Populist Revolt* (1931); Norman Pollack, *The Populist Response to Industrial America* (1962); Walter T. K. Nugent, *The Tolerant Populists: Kansas Populism & Nativism* (1963); Lawrence Goodwyn, *Democratic Promise: The Populist Movement in America* (1976); Fred A. Shannon, *The Farmers' Last Frontier: Agriculture, 1860–1897* (1945); Allan G. Bogue, *Money at Interest* (1955); C. Vann Woodward, *Tom Watson: Agrarian Rebel* (1938); Francis B. Simkins, *Pitchfork Ben Tillman* (1944). Martin Ridge, *Ignatius Donnelly* (1962).

UNIT SIX

PROGRESSIVE AMERICA

The new century brought to Americans confidence in their own ability to control the nation's destiny. It also brought concern for the unresolved problems of industrial growth, urban squalor, and immigrant poverty. The business depression of the 1890s had ended by 1898, returning the country's middle and upper classes to full prosperity. A global empire had been won almost without cost or exertion.

The chapters that follow describe the decades of confidence, concern, and change within American society from 1900 through the Depression. The first of these chapters on the Triangle Fire dramatizes the lives of southern and eastern European immigrant workers in New York City garment factories. Underpaid and impoverished, they struggled to unionize the clothing industry. Only when a flash fire killed scores of young female workers at the Triangle Com-

pany did their appeal for better working conditions receive a hearing.

Chapter 34 then opens with a discussion of the urban world within which most of these recent immigrants lived. The chapter explores the varieties of industrial reform efforts. Since the political life of progressive America (1900–1917) often concerned the struggle for change, Chapter 34 also examines the connections between reform activities and partisan politics.

Popular confidence rose during these decades partly because of the ease with which the United States assumed a leading role in world affairs. Chapter 35 portrays one of the unhappier consequences of that new role— the unsuccessful revolt by Filipino nationalists against American takeover of their islands. The Philippine Revolt serves as the context for a general discussion in Chapter

36 of American foreign policy. The chapter traces developments from the country's brief involvement in the Spanish-American War to its costlier participation in the First World War. The connections between domestic concerns in progressive America and the nation's actions as a major global power emerge clearly.

One of the most widely publicized instances of American technological superiority was Charles Lindbergh's pioneering flight across the Atlantic in 1927. His feat captured the imagination of a machine-oriented world. Lindbergh's story unfolds in Chapter 37.

In the accompanying chapter the achievements, attitudes, and patterns of the optimistic, mechanically advanced America that produced Lindbergh's flight are examined. From the vantage point of the 1970s, the United States of the progressive era may seem, whatever its problems, a less complicated and perhaps even happier society. Certainly this country's leaders—even most of its critics—looked to the future with a measure of confidence that withstood involvement in a world war and collapsed only during the 1930s under the onslaught of the Great Depression.

The defeat of the Bonus Marchers in 1932, narrated in Chapter 39, symbolized the old order's inability to respond effectively to the vast human suffering of the times. Most of the marchers were unemployed World War I veterans who had come to Washington seeking aid. The accompanying chapter deals with the Depression and other social manifestations of the times: the "red scare," prohibition, Scopes, Sacco-Vanzetti, and the alarming popularity of the Ku Klux Klan.

33
THE TRIANGLE FIRE

A.W.

In September 1909, two hundred Jewish and Italian immigrant workers at New York City's Triangle Shirtwaist Company walked off their jobs. The previous year, Triangle's owners had organized an Employees Benevolent Association, a so-called company union, designed to head off unions organized by the workers themselves. But the tactic had not worked. Protesting miserable working conditions and poor pay, the workers at Triangle—most of them young women—sought to gain recognition of their union by their employers. They were led by officials from the recently organized International Ladies' Garment Workers' Union (ILGWU). They had also received the support of the Women's Trade Union League (WTUL).

The Triangle strikers and workers in other shirtwaist shops in the city had a number of complaints. They were forced to work in crowded, unclean factories. Fire hazards and unsanitary conditions presented a serious threat to their health. Windows and doors in the shops were often nailed shut. Rarely did the sun penetrate the factory lofts, which workers referred to as sweatshops.

Long hours and low wages added to the workers' discontent. Most employees in New York's garment factories worked a fifty-six-hour, six-day week. When a factory owner had a rush order, he could force employees to work overtime at night or on Sunday without pay. Wages in the shirtwaist industry were as low as $6 a week. Employers often deducted penalties from the workers' pay for mistakes made in sewing clothes. They charged the workers fees for "renting" the machines and using electricity. In addition, employees were subjected to a series of petty fines for talking, smoking, or singing on the job.

It was against such conditions and in the face of active opposition by the police, who were openly sympathetic to the factory owners, that the workers finally took a stand.

The Triangle Shirtwaist Company occupied the top three floors of the ten-story Asch Building in Lower Manhattan. A fire, which raged on those floors on March 25, 1911, ultimately affected the working conditions of a large segment of American laborers.

The strike dragged on into winter. Workers at nonstriking shirt-waist companies grew angrier as they watched police and hired thugs abuse the striking employees. On the evening of November 22 the city's shirtwaist workers held a mass meeting at Cooper Union to discuss the situation.

Within a few days between 10,000 and 20,000 workers, mainly young women, had walked off their jobs. The strike affected over 500 shirtwaist and dressmaking companies, including all the smaller shops and most of the big companies in the city. "The Uprising of the Twenty Thousand," as the ILGWU called the walkout, was the first industry-wide strike of immigrant workers in New York City. It was also the largest strike by women ever staged in the United States up to that time.

The shirtwaist[1] industry was a relatively recent one. The 1900 federal census described it as a "branch of the garment industry that has developed during the last decade." Before 1900 many of the garments produced in New York City and elsewhere came from workshops in ghetto slum apartments. Families were paid according to the number of garments produced. This piecework system proved inefficient. Clothing production gradually shifted to new loft buildings constructed especially for the trade.

---

[1]The shirtwaist was a tailored blouse for women usually made of sheer cotton and styled somewhat like a man's shirt.

Sweatshops like the one shown here were common to the garment industry. Unskilled women laborers usually worked under skilled male machine operators in crowded, poorly ventilated, and unsafe shops.

By 1910 New York had become the national center for the garment industry. The city's 600 shirtwaist and dress factories employed over 30,000 workers. They sold more than $50 million worth of clothing annually. In the new shops skilled machine operators, usually men, supervised crews of young women who performed simple, unskilled tasks. At large factories such as Triangle, the machine operators, called contractors, were paid by the owners not only for their own work but for the labor of their crews as well. The contractors, in turn, paid weekly salaries to their female assistants. This system was often abused by dishonest contractors, who cheated young women workers out of their proper wages.

Four out of every five workers in the garment trades were women. In the Uprising of the Twenty Thousand, 75 percent of the strikers were young women between the ages of sixteen and twenty-five. Almost all had been born abroad or to recently arrived immigrant families. Most of the workers were either Jewish or Italian. Most of the factory owners were Jews.

The 1909 garment trade's strike marked the first time that many of these immigrant workers managed to set aside their mutual fears and suspicions to work for common economic interests. The strike brought Jewish and Italian women together on the picket line and in the union. Thus it set a pattern for future cooperation in the labor movement among the city's ethnic communities. Jewish union organizers learned a smattering of Italian, while Italian leaders acquired enough Yiddish to make themselves understood. Political and community leaders from each ethnic group also worked together on behalf of the strikers. Meyer London, a socialist lawyer who later became the country's first Jewish congressman, cooperated with Fiorello La Guardia, a young state legislator who later became the country's first Italian congressman. La Guardia, the son of a Jewish mother and an Italian father, symbolized the alliance then being forged by the two groups.

Black workers were frequently hired as strikebreakers, or scabs, in the garment factories. Several hundred of them joined the Uprising of the Twenty Thousand. One black shirtwaist striker—a "real born American," as she described herself—kept a diary of the events. In it she recorded her shop's reaction to the November 22 call for a general strike:

> It's a good thing, this strike is. It makes you feel like a real grown-up person. . . . I simply can't get over the way little Ray Goldousky jumped on a chair and suddenly, without a minute's notice, stopped the electricity [in the shop]. Why, we were simply stunned. Before you could say Jack Robinson, we all rose, slipped on our duds, and marched down the stairs, shouting, yelling, and giggling about our walkout, as they called it.

Similar incidents in New York's garment factories that week shocked the industry's manufacturers into taking action against the strikers. Antistrike activities ranged from encouraging police brutality against strikers to organizing company unions among the minority of workers who did not support the strike. Employers also tried using "carrot-and-stick" tactics. They offered incentives to those who remained on the job and hired hoodlums to beat up workers on the picket line. The anonymous shirtwaist striker noted in her diary that the Triangle Company promised nonstrikers "from fifteen to twenty dollars weekly, free lunch, and dancing during the noon hour." These tactics, however, failed to break the morale and unity of the shirtwaist strikers. The Uprising of the Twenty Thousand continued throughout the bitterly cold winter of 1909–1910.

Somehow the tens of thousands of strikers managed to maintain orderly picket lines at each shop. Every day the police dragged away dozens of frozen, poorly clad young women from the lines. By Christmas Day, the arrests tallied 723. Yet those who were arrested and later bailed out of jail usually returned to the picket lines the next day.

The strike was an important event not only for women garment workers but also for woman suffrage reformers, ghetto community lead-

Strikers in the shirtwaist strike of 1909–10 sold copies of the *Call,* a New York socialist daily, in order to publicize their demands and raise money for their living expenses while on strike.

ers, labor officials, and socialist politicians. All these groups donated time and money to make the strike a success. The "uptown" supporters were joined by several of the city's most active reform groups: The Women's Trade Union League, the National Women's Suffrage Association, the Political Equality Association, and the National Civic Federation.

A host of muckraking reporters,[2] academics, social workers, and other professionals also worked on behalf of the strikers. Many of these middle- and upper-class reformers were German Jews whose ancestors had come to the United States during the mid-nineteenth century. The strike gave them an opportunity to display their solidarity with poorer Jews from the Lower East Side, most of whom had recently left Eastern Europe for the United States.

Everywhere on the Lower East Side community leaders worked in support of the strike. They included union officials from the United Hebrew Trades, Socialist party orators from both the Jewish and Italian communities, sympathetic rabbis and priests, and editors of Jewish newspapers. A number of other New York newspapers supported the striking workers, as did many of the city's residents. An open meeting held on December 5 drew over 8,000 pro-strike demonstrators. Pressure mounted on the garment trade employers to resolve the dispute.

A settlement was finally reached in February 1910. The agreement came in two stages. It represented a victory for the union, though

---

[2]Muckraking reporters were writers of the late nineteenth and early twentieth centuries who exposed corrupt conditions in business and government.

not a total triumph. At first the shirtwaist workers rejected several compromise offers arranged by arbitrators who brought the two sides together. Then a number of smaller manufacturers began settling privately with the ILGWU. In these agreements, however, neither the union nor the union shop was recognized.

By February 15, 1910, only 1,100 workers, from 13 shops, were still away from their jobs. The ILGWU officially declared the strike over. More than 300 firms had accepted the union's terms completely, and 19 shops (including Triangle and other large firms) had agreed to open-shop compromises, that is, to allow employers to continue hiring *non*union as well as union employees. The garment workers had made several important gains in the settlements: reduction of the workweek to 52 hours, a two-hour limit on night work, wage increases of 12 to 15 percent, and a promise by employers to end the contractor system of payment.

Later that year, prominent Jewish citizens of New York City helped to arrange a second agreement between employers and workers. Louis Brandeis, a Boston lawyer, served as chief arbitrator between union and management. Brandeis skillfully played on the common Jewish background of garment employees and garment employers. Many of the employers themselves had begun as poor workers.

On Labor Day evening both sides agreed to a "Protocol of Peace," which became a milestone in American industrial relations. Its provisions included a privately run Joint Board of Sanitary Control – representing union, management, and the public – set up to oversee health and safety conditions in garment factories. Although the agreement eventually broke down, the Protocol represented a significant victory for the ILGWU. Its membership skyrocketed from 400 to 60,000 workers in the months following the "uprising."

At the Triangle Company, however, the union remained unrecognized. Many strikers were not rehired, and most of the strikebreakers who had worked during the walkout were kept on the payroll. Some workers complained that the major effect of the settlement was to end the phonograph music and dancing contests that had been provided for nonstriking employees. Otherwise, work returned to normal at the country's largest shirtwaist shop, at least until the afternoon of March 25, 1911.

The Triangle Shirtwaist Company occupied the top three floors of a new loft structure, the Asch Building, in lower Manhattan. The ten-story building, constructed in 1901, was located on the northwest corner of Green Street and Washington Place. It stood next to New York University and a block east of Washington Square. Since the turn of the century, over $150 million had been spent on the construction of loft factories in lower Manhattan. The new buildings, made of brick or stone, were supposed to be fireproof, but they had wooden frame interiors that could easily catch fire. Few of the buildings had adequate fire escapes or staircases.

Using such buildings, manufacturers took advantage of cheap insurance rates, low operating costs, and a concentrated labor supply. State law required employers to allow 250 cubic feet of air per worker. But the law did not specify where the air space should be. Loft buildings, with their ten-foot-high ceilings, enabled owners to crowd hundreds of employees onto a floor and still meet the space requirements. (The extra space was above the worker's heads; it was not distributed among employees.) At Triangle about 500 people jammed the Asch Building's top three floors.

The Triangle employees never had a fire drill. Even though several small fires had occurred on the premises in 1909, no improved safety measures had been taken. There were only two narrow staircases leading down from the Triangle's three floors. All but one of the doors leading to the stairways were kept closed (often bolted) to prevent employees from loitering or stealing fabric. The single fire escape in the building went down only to the second floor, so that it was difficult to reach the street in case of emergencies. The only other means of descent were two small freight elevators, each above five feet square. Huge piles of cloth, tissue paper, rags, and cuttings covered the company's tables, shelves, and floors. The floors and machines were soaked with oil, and barrels of machine oil lined the walls. All these factors made the Triangle factory highly flammable.

As the day's work drew to a close on Saturday, March 25, 500 Triangle workers finished their chores and prepared to leave the building by the one open door on the eighth floor. A company guard stationed at the exit checked the women's handbags for cloth fragments. The time was 4:30 P.M. Saturday's weather was brisk and sunny—a perfect early spring afternoon.

Hardly had the guard rung the closing bell when a young woman employee on the eighth floor ran up to Samuel Bernstein, the company's production manager, and cried: "There is a fire, Mr. Bernstein." The manager and several other men, who had battled a small fire on the floor two weeks earlier, tried to put out the blaze with pails of water. But the flames shot up even higher. One of the men later remembered: "It was like there was kerosene in the water; it just seemed to spread it." Bernstein quickly realized that it would be impossible to stop the fast-spreading flames. He shouted to an assistant: "You can't do anything here. Try to get the girls out!" Bernstein and a few others tried to lead the stunned workers out in orderly fashion. But screams of "Fire!" soon filled the eighth floor.

Panic and confusion spread with the inferno. The 225 eighth-floor workers scurried across the smoke-filled room toward the various exits. As they ran, many called out the names of relatives—sisters and brothers, fathers and mothers—who also worked for Triangle. A young bookkeeper on the floor, Diana Lipschitz, sent an urgent message by interoffice teletype to the tenth floor: "The place is on fire. Run for your lives." The bookkeeper who received the message at first thought that Diana was joking. But the flames soon spurted through the tenth-floor windows, igniting bundles of cloth. Employees on that floor spread the alarm and hurried toward the exits. Because the Asch Building was supposedly fireproof, the blaze could not damage the walls or floors. But the flames curved in a swirling mass through the eighth-floor windows and engulfed the ninth and tenth floors within minutes.

On every floor workers pressed against one another in a desperate effort to reach the exits. The intense heat from the surrounding flames seared their bodies. Those on the eighth floor who had pushed their way down the congested stairway collapsed on lower floors, where firemen later found them.

Employees on the ninth floor, meanwhile, had not received even a teletype warning of the blaze. They learned of the danger only when the fire darted through the windows, bursting into pockets of flame. Most of the women dashed frantically toward exits. Others froze in fear and remained at their machines. When they discovered that the door next to the freight elevators was locked, the women rushed toward the other stairway. Over 150 workers fought for access to the twenty-inch passageway that led to the open stairway.

On the tenth floor those who did not excape via the roof crowded into the two freight elevators. Jammed with fleeing workers, the cars began their descent to the ground floor. Then, some workers still trapped on the top floors started jumping into the elevator shafts to land on top of the descending elevators. One elevator operator, Joseph Zito, recalled that so many girls hit the top of his car that it would not work: "It was jammed by the bodies." Nineteen bodies were later found wedged into one of the elevator shafts. The other elevator broke down when its power circuit became waterlogged by the spray of the fire hoses.

By 4:45 P.M. the top three floors of the Asch Building were engulfed in flames. Escape was no longer possible.

By this time, the fire on the top floors of the Asch Building was visible in the street below. Within minutes a crowd gathered around the

The sidewalk in front of the Triangle Company was strewn with the bodies of those who had jumped to their death at the height of the blaze. The fire department's safety nets were too weak to break the victims' falls.

building to watch the blaze. One policeman watching the scene observed: "It's mighty hard work burning one of those fireproof buildings, but I guess it's lucky it's Saturday afternoon. It looks as if everyone is out of the place." Suddenly, an object that looked like a bale of dress material dropped from an eighth-floor window.

The firemen's nets caught only a few of those who jumped. More often, as Fire Captain Howard C. Ruch recalled, the bodies—which struck the ground with a force almost a thousand times their actual weight—"didn't break through the nets; they just carried them to the sidewalk. The force was so great it took the men off their feet; they turned somersaults over onto the bodies." Sometimes, a group of girls would join hands before jumping from the ledge, soothing their fears in a joint death fall.

Fifteen minutes after the firemen arrived, the fire was brought under control. In those few minutes, 46 people jumped to their deaths. The charred remains of 100 workers were later recovered from inside the building. Most of those who perished were Jewish. All but 21 of the victims were women, and a dozen were so badly burned or disfigured that they were almost unrecognizable. In fact, 7 persons were never identified.

Hundreds of workers had managed to escape the flames. Those injured, stunned, and weeping survivors soon filled the hospitals and ghetto apartments of the Lower East Side. Police officials hurriedly tried to find coffins for the dead. On East Twenty-sixth Street a huge, enclosed pier was converted into a temporary morgue. The Triangle dead were piled up on sidewalks near the Asch Building while firemen watered down the smoldering building.

Police Department "death wagons" rode throughout the evening, bringing the dead to the temporary morgue. Policemen searched through personal belongings in an effort to identify victims. Fourteen engagement rings were later found on one floor alone of the Triangle factory. These and other rings collected at the morgue testified to a particularly bitter aspect of the tragedy, namely, the marital hopes and expectations of this young and largely female contingent of workers. Some of the victims had stuffed their skimpy pay envelopes inside their clothing. Others still had their wages clutched in their hands.

Many of the Jewish families on the Lower East Side had relatives or friends working at Triangle, and the community's grief was almost unbearable. Tens of thousands rushed to the East Twenty-sixth Street pier searching for missing friends or relatives. They were joined by numerous Italian and other immigrant families. The police finally let the frantic throng file through the pier a few dozen at a time. Inside the temporary morgue the bodies of the Triangle victims had been laid out in coffins in neat rows.

Heartbreaking scenes of recognition filled the night. A mother, discovering her daughter's body, would break down into uncontrollable wailing and have to be escorted out. A young woman, finding her sister's

Thousands of mourning relatives and friends filed through the temporary morgue on the East 26th Street pier to identify the victims. Some were never identified.

charred body, would simply faint. Some women completely lost control and tried to kill themselves, either by swallowing poison or by jumping off the pier. Police and onlookers stopped at least a dozen such attempts.

In the days following the fire, the Triangle victims were buried quietly by their families. Friends and relatives from the Lower East Side attended the funerals. They poured out their grief and sorrow. Reformers and community leaders arranged a series of memorial meetings to honor the victims. A fund-raising appeal conducted by the Red Cross, Jewish community groups, and the WTUL collected over $120,000 to assist needy families. Several of the victims had been the sole supports of their families, in either New York or "the old country." Half a dozen families had lost two sisters (one sister, a widow with five children); another had lost two brothers. In one Italian family a mother and two daughters were killed in the fire.

On April 5 a symbolic mass funeral was held in lower Manhattan. Over 100,000 people—mainly women who lived and worked on the Lower East Side—marched silently in the rain for five hours to honor the Triangle dead. As they approached the Asch Building, the women who marched gave way completely to their emotions. According to one paper's report, they uttered "one long-drawn-out, heart-piercing cry, the mingling of thousands of voices, a cry that was perhaps the most impressive expression of human grief ever heard in this city."

Who was to blame for the tragedy? This question haunted New Yorkers in the weeks that followed the Triangle disaster. "That a terrible mistake was made by somebody," *The New York Times* observed, "is easier to say now than to point out just where the blame for this destruction of human life may be placed."

The city's fire department bore a share of the responsibility, despite the bravery of those who fought the blaze. The department had failed to enforce even those few mild safety laws that were on the books. Moreover, its equipment was inadequate for fighting fires in the city's new loft buildings. The tallest fire ladders reached only to the sixth floor, although half the city's factory workers—more than 300,000—worked in lofts above this floor. Some of the department's safety nets were so weak that they broke under the force of falling bodies.

The City Buildings Department, too, had to accept a measure of the blame. The Asch Building, like most of New York City's garment shops, lacked adequate safety features. Several months earlier, a factory inspector had warned the owners of the Asch Building of such violations as insufficient exits and locked stairway doors. But the department made no effort to ensure that these conditions were corrected. There were only 47 inspectors in Manhattan to check over 50,000 buildings. Of these buildings 13,600 had been listed as dangerous by the fire department the previous month. Inspectors managed to visit 2,000 buildings in March, but the Asch Building was not among them.

Nor were the fire insurance companies innocent of blame. Insurance brokers in New York suffered heavy losses from the numerous fires that occurred in the city's loft buildings. Yet the insurance industry failed to insist on safety standards that might have reduced fire hazards. Rather, they preferred to pay off after a fire and then raise a company's premium costs. Higher policy rates also meant higher commissions for insurance brokers. During the 1890s a group of insurance companies attempted to offer cheaper rates to manufacturers who installed sprinkler systems in their factories. These companies were soon driven out of business by the city's powerful insurance industry. It was simply easier and more profitable to leave the "fireproof" firetraps alone and settle afterward.

At the time of the fire the Triangle Shirtwaist Company carried insurance policies totaling $199,750. The Triangle owners eventually collected full repayment for their losses in equipment and property damage. Under the terms of these insurance policies, they were also given an extra indemnity of $64,925, or $445 for each worker killed. The company's owners defended themselves against charges of responsibility for the fire by pointing out that building inspectors had never entered a complaint against the firm and that an employee carelessly dropping a cigarette might well have started the fire.

On April 11, a week after the public funeral for the Triangle victims, the company's owners, Isaac Harris and Max Blanck, were indicted by a grand jury and charged with manslaughter. Their trial began in New York eight months later, on December 4. Crowds of women gathered outside the courtroom each day screaming "Murderers! Murderers!" A heavy police guard was called in to protect the defendants. Harris and

Not much remained of the "fireproof" Asch Building once the fire had run its course. The Triangle owners collected insurance money for losses in equipment and property damages though their building had inadequate safety features.

Blanck—"the shirtwaist kings"—engaged as their defense counsel a well-known Jewish lawyer, Max D. Steuer.

In order to simplify the case, the state decided to try the pair only for responsibility in the death of a single worker, Margaret Schwartz, who died in the fire because of the locked ninth-floor door. Most testimony centered on three questions: (1) Was the ninth-floor door kept locked regularly? (2) Was it locked at the time of the fire? (3) Most importantly, did Blanck and Harris know it was locked?

The jury took less than two hours to find the shirtwaist kings not guilty. As one jury member later told a newsman: "I believed that the [door] was locked at the time of the fire. But I could not make myself feel certain that Harris and Blanck knew that it was locked."

One interesting sidelight to the tragedy emerged during the trial. The Triangle owners kept their exit doors locked for fear that employees would steal garments or pieces of fabric. At one point the prosecutor asked Isaac Harris: "How much in all the instances would you say was the value of all the goods that you found had been taken by these employees? You would say it was not over $25, wouldn't you?" Harris turned pale before responding: "No, it would not exceed that much."

If Harris and Blanck had been convicted, the Triangle fire might have been forgotten more easily. The public might have been satisfied that justice had been done. As it turned out, the acquittal of Blanck and Harris sparked a new effort to improve the conditions under which New

York City's laborers worked. Responding to public pressure, the state legislature created the New York Factory Investigating Commission in June 1911, to study working conditions in the state.

Among the commission's most active members were two politically powerful New York City Democrats, State Assembly Majority Leader Alfred E. Smith and State Senate Majority Leader Robert F. Wagner, Sr. They helped throw the Tammany machine's full support behind the commission's many proposals for reform. Other members included Samuel Gompers of the AFL and Mary Dreier of the WTUL. Many experts on factory safety and working conditions assisted the commission. Among them were progressive reformers such as Belle and Henry Moskowitz, and young social workers such as Frances Perkins, who later became the nation's first woman cabinet member as secretary of labor.

The Triangle Commission, as it was popularly called, went far beyond an investigation of fire hazards alone. It studied almost every type of labor problem in New York. In 1911 the group held public hearings in the state's major manufacturing cities and heard 222 witnesses. Staff field inspectors visited 1,836 factories in 20 industries. Smith, Wagner, and their associates talked with factory workers who had lost limbs because of unsafe machinery. They examined the "doctored" records kept by many companies on employees' wages and hours. Commission investigators watched hundreds of women leaving factories at 5 A.M., after working ten-hour shifts. They studied the horrible conditions in the disease-ridden tenements where workers lived.

On farms in upstate New York, commission members observed migrant women working alongside their children for eighteen hours and more a day. In canneries across the state they saw children of five working full time. The conditions wore no party label; the worst offenders among New York's manufacturers included both Republicans and Democrats. In a factory belonging to a leading upstate Democratic progressive, for example, Smith and Wagner found "the vilest and most uncivilized conditions of labor in the state."

By 1900 at least 1,700,000 children under the age of sixteen were in the labor market. One result of the Triangle fire was the passage of laws limiting child labor and improving working conditions for women and children.

Between 1911 and 1915, Smith and Wagner introduced over sixty bills based on their investigations. Despite much conservative opposition in the legislature, the two Tammany Democrats managed to pass fifty-six of their proposals by fusing the votes of Democratic regulars and antimachine reformers. The bills they passed called for the creation of a Bureau of Fire Prevention and the enforcement of strict fire safety codes (including compulsory fire drills and the installation of sprinklers in factories). Two other major bills provided for an increase in the number of factory inspectors and a strengthening of the supervisory authority of the state's Department of Labor.

One of the most hard-fought proposals in the legislature was a bill calling for a 54-hour workweek for women and minors. When cannery owners objected to the measure, Smith replied sarcastically that they wished to revise the Bible to read "Remember the Sabbath to keep it holy—except in canneries." The bill passed. Other laws forbade night factory work for women, prohibited smoking in factories, and called for better ventilation and sanitary facilities. Child labor was outlawed in tenement manufacturing and canneries. Sunday work was forbidden ("one day's rest in seven"), and insurance (workmen's compensation) was provided for employees injured in accidents. Other laws forbade employment of children under fourteen (*anywhere*) and required improved working facilities, rest periods, and minimum wages for women and children.

In the Triangle Commission's four years of existence, Smith and Wagner helped to pass the most enlightened code of industrial reform in the country. Their work served as a model for legislators in other states and foreshadowed many of the federal laws enacted under the New Deal. In the following decades, both men were to become leading Democratic progressives, and their concern for the improvement of working conditions in the state stemmed in large measure from their experiences on the Triangle Commission.

This sense of what Frances Perkins called "stricken conscience" was felt by Smith, Wagner, and Perkins—as well as by many of their colleagues in the legislature. Among them was a young, unknown Democratic senator from upstate who rose before the state senate one day to speak on behalf of a bill for a 54-hour workweek. The measure previously had been defeated by only one vote. Wagner had since rounded up an additional vote for the bill, and still another supporter—Manhattan's colorful East Side Democrat, "Big Tim" Sullivan—was now racing across Albany to cast the tie-breaking ballot.

The youthful Democratic senator began "filibustering" (speaking on irrelevant subjects—mainly, in this case, on birds) to stall for time until Sullivan could reach the senate floor. When Republican leaders opposing the bill complained that the subject of birds had nothing to do with the bill, the speaker responded that he was "trying to prove that nature demands shorter hours." His filibuster continued until Sullivan arrived. Only then, confident that the bill would now pass, did Senator Franklin Delano Roosevelt return to his seat.

34
NEW WAVES
OF REFORM

A.W.

The miserable working conditions that provoked the great shirtwaist-industry strike of 1909 were typical of American manufacturing in the half-century of industrial growth that followed the Civil War. Workers in manufacturing plants toiled an average of fifty-nine hours each week. They earned less than $10 per week for their backbreaking labor.

By contrast, most of their employers—the manufacturers, bankers, and merchants who directed the course of economic development in the United States—profited handsomely from the workers' long hours and low wage rates. Between 1860 and 1900 the country rose from fourth to first place among the world's industrial nations, producing more in 1900 than Britain, France, and Germany combined.

The rewards for business success during this period were high indeed. In 1890 an estimated 200,000 people owned 70 percent of the country's wealth. A survey taken in 1892 showed that close to 4,000 people had become millionaires since the Civil War. Almost all these individuals made their fortunes in manufacturing, railroads, trade, or finance. This great concentration of wealth among America's upper classes only added to the discontent of the nation's industrial laborers.

Union organization seemed to hold the only promise of changing the working conditions of American workers. But despite the efforts of union leaders and rank-and-file organizers throughout the period, no strong, united workingman's association emerged among the industrial labor force of the United States. Instead, in this era of eco-

nomic growth, industry-wide unions came and went. The ILGWU, for example, was only the latest in a line of unions attempting to organize the garment industry, the earlier ones having failed at the task.

At the turn of the century, 10 million men and women, over a third of the entire labor force, worked in factories. Yet the union movement had succeeded in organizing less than 4 percent of America's industrial workers. What was this union tradition? Why had it failed to mobilize the country's underpaid, overworked, and poorly treated laboring masses?

THE RISE OF ORGANIZED LABOR

Those who led or took part in the Uprising of the Twenty Thousand inherited a tradition of industrial union activity more than a half-century old. In Jacksonian America, factory workers and craftsmen attempted to form their own unions. Few of these trade organizations lasted beyond the Civil War. In the half-century afterwards a number of major unions were formed. Almost all these unions employed the strike weapon, though rarely with complete success. During the 1880s, for example, over 24,000 strikes occurred in the United States, involving over 6½ million workers.

During the turbulent depression years of the 1890s, 3 million people were thrown out of work, perhaps 15 to 20 percent of the country's work force. Over 7,000 strikes were called during this period. Between 1894 and 1896 numerous small armies of the unemployed marched on Washington demanding federal relief assistance.

By the early twentieth century the infant ILGWU, which was to lead the great shirtwaist strike of 1909, had counterparts in every other industry in the country. Like the garment union, most of these organizations were small and had to struggle for existence. The experience of the 1909 garment workers' strike demonstrates many of the difficulties unions encountered in organizing.

Difficulties in Union Organization For one

thing, few unions were as successful as the ILG-WU in persuading workers from different ethnic backgrounds to put aside their fierce hatreds and work for common goals. Indeed, the 1909–1910 strike was the first time that most of New York City's Jewish and Italian workers actually banded together in one union. More often, tensions among nationality groups, differences in language, and racial hostilities within the working class hampered union organization.

Employers skillfully exploited these ethnic and national hostilities to divide workers. When Jews went on strike, Italians would work, and vice versa. When both groups went on strike, blacks were called in to scab. Furthermore, the influx of Southern and Eastern European immigrants in the late nineteenth and early twentieth centuries kept wage rates down in most industries. More often than not, the labor supply greatly exceeded demand. Employers had little difficulty filling the unskilled and semiskilled positions at their plants.

Employers resorted to a variety of tactics to defeat the efforts of union organizers. These included the use of strikebreakers (such as the hoodlums who attacked ILGWU picketers), and the hiring of scabs (another tactic employed by Harris and Blanck). Employers also used blacklisting—the denial of work to union officials by all the firms in an industry—and lockouts of striking workers. Firms like the Triangle Company sometimes enlisted the aid of sympathetic policemen and judges who harassed strikers with arrests and court action. Another important weapon of management was the yellow-dog contract, in which new workers agreed not to join a union as a condition of their employment.

Attempts at Union Organization At the national level the union movement faced a number of difficulties in the half-century after the Civil War. Several national unions rose and fell because of unsuccessful strikes, the opposition of the middle class, and the inability of unions to hold the loyalty of most workers. The National Labor Union played a prominent role briefly during the depression of the 1870s. The Knights of Labor, under the leadership of Terence V. Powderly, became a major force in the labor movement in the following decade. These unions favored improvement of the American worker's economic state and a broad program of reform within American society.

The Knights had many self-employed or salaried middle-class Americans in its membership. During the 1880s it tried unsuccessfully to organize a series of strikes and to set up cooperative factories and stores—owned by the workers themselves—as an alternative to the privately run corporations. Leaders of the Knights were blamed for the Haymarket Affair of 1886 and were attacked as "anarchists." Actually, they had played no part in the bombing. Membership in the Knights of Labor nevertheless declined from 700,000 in 1886 to 74,000 by 1893. The union played an insignificant role in the labor movement during the 1890s, joining finally with the agrarian-led Populist party. By 1900 it had lapsed into obscurity.

American socialists were also influential in the union movement during these decades. Most of the leading figures in the ILGWU at the time of the garment strike, for example, held socialist beliefs or even positions within the immigrant wing of the American socialist movement. Similarly, socialists had been important in the Knights of Labor, the Western Federation of Miners, and other groups.

The leading force within American unionization during this period was the American Federation of Labor (AFL). It was a loose confederation of independent craft unions and semi-industrial affiliates such as the ILGWU. The AFL was formed in 1881 under the leadership of Samuel Gompers. A one-time socialist, Gompers criticized earlier union organizations such as the Knights for stressing general reforms in American society.

The labor movement, Gompers believed, should concentrate exclusively on winning economic gains for the working class. It should leave the tasks of reform to others. Union leaders should devote all their time and energy to raising workers' wages, reducing hours, and improving working conditions. Gompers also believed that unions should avoid independent political action, such as the affiliation of the Knights with the Populist party in the 1890s. Instead, labor should support its political friends and oppose its enemies,

Samuel Gompers, shown here at a meeting to organize the 1909 garment workers' strike, founded the American Federation of Labor around such craft unions. Using both the strike and collective bargaining, he forged a powerful national labor organization.

regardless of party. When asked at a congressional hearing what the unions wanted, Gompers replied simply: "More!"

By the time of the New York garment-industry strike, the AFL, under Gompers's leadership, had become the country's dominant national labor organization. It was also the most powerful union politically and economically up to that time.

REFORMERS IN THE LATE NINETEENTH CENTURY

Union leaders were not the only people concerned about the conditions of American workers. Socialists, middle- and upper-class reformers, and city politicians all worked to improve conditions for American laborers. Their suggested solutions to the problems posed by industrial society, though, were as different as the backgrounds from which these reformers emerged.

The Socialist Vision   In the late nineteenth century a group of socialist writers became the first generation of critics to tackle the dilemmas of ur-

ban-industrial America. They were grouped as socialists because they held in common the belief that ownership and control of industry, land, and so forth, should be shared by the community as a whole. These writers put forth a series of proposals for a complete overhaul of American institutions. In *Progress and Poverty* (1877–1879) Henry George attacked the inequities of the American economic system. Edward Bellamy's *Looking Backward* (1888) presents a vision of a socialist utopia. His book became a bestseller in the 1880s and 1890s. Henry Demarest Lloyd's *Wealth Against Commonwealth* (1894) attacked the corrupt business practices of the Standard Oil Company. Other influential critics of American industrial life included economist Richard Ely, "social gospel" minister Washington Gladden, and utopian writers Ignatius Donnelly and William Dean Howells.

Uppermost in the minds of these late nineteenth-century reformers was the notion that, if conditions in the nation's slums, factories, and farms were not improved quickly and drastically, the United States would explode into class warfare. Surely, they reasoned, abused workers would not tolerate such conditions indefinitely. They believed that a social catastrophe was close at hand. It could be prevented only by an immediate and total alteration in the nation's social and economic structure.

They offered no single remedy. Some, like Lloyd, Bellamy, and Howells, believed in a socialist commonwealth. They argued, though, over the details of Utopia and how to achieve it. Others, like George, felt that a single tax on unearned income from land would somehow provide enough money to solve the nation's problems. All these reformers were united in their belief that a single problem underlay all the social ills of the United States. Find and correct this overriding problem—"the root of our social difficulty," as George put it—and Americans could begin moving toward an era of moral and social perfection.

In this utopian vision of the United States these late nineteenth-century reformers resembled their pre-Civil War, preindustrial counterparts. Garrison, Emerson, and Fuller had also walked a thin line between social criticism and religious prophecy. However "practical" their remedies, therefore, people like George and Bellamy were basically seers. They preached a gospel of total reform, without which total catastrophe would result.

The Settlement House Movement The struggle to improve the lives of the immigrant poor, both in the factories and in the ghettos, was aided by a number of middle-class reformers and socially conscious members of the American upper classes. Women like Mrs. Belmont and other affluent leaders of the Women's Trade Union League who were active in the shirtwaist strike are representative of this trend.

During the 1880s and 1890s many college-educated women became concerned especially with the slum conditions under which immigrant workers lived. They helped to organize settlement houses in the ghettos of East Coast and Middle Western cities. There, foreign-born workers received food and shelter and learned how to speak English. They were given help in understanding and exercising their rights as Americans. In 1889 Lillian Wald founded the Henry Street Settlement in New York City. Jane Addams and Ellen Gates

Starr founded Chicago's Hull House that same year.

By 1910 over 400 settlement houses had been established in the country's slum districts. On New York's Lower East Side, settlement workers assisted the victims of the Triangle fire and their families. In the previous year they had provided money and support for the striking garment workers. As valuable instruments for Americanizing immigrant communities, the settlement houses helped immigrants to improve their working and living conditions at a time when most middle-class Americans remained indifferent or even hostile toward the foreign-born poor.

Municipal Reorganization For some reformers, however, the settlement-house movement seemed an inadequate response to the many problems of America's enlarged industrial cities. It was somewhat like putting bandages over a festering infection without treating the infection itself first. For such reformers the roots of the infection seemed clear: the inefficiency and corruption of urban political machines in alliance with equally corrupt business interests. Democratic politicians such as Al Smith and Robert Wagner, Sr., viewed New York's Tammany machine as the logical friend of the immigrants. But reformers such as Henry George and, later, Fiorello La Guardia believed that the machines merely exploited the immigrants, using their trust and votes to line the pockets of ward heelers, city officials, and local businessmen.

Reform groups such as the National Civic Federation (which later helped to organize the Triangle Fire Commission investigation) sparked a concern among voters for driving the political machines from office. These groups sought to run urban government more efficiently and less corruptly than the machines. They also tended to be dominated by wealthy citizens, leading businessmen, and other upper-middle-class or upper-class figures within their communities.

Municipal reformers, then as today, included businessmen, lawyers, ministers, and journalists—professionals concerned with the concentration of power in the hands of working-class-supported political machines and giant corpora-

JANE ADDAMS

"Even as a little child, she seemed inclined toward special work of some sort. In fact, she was anxious for a career." This is how, with some dismay, Mrs. John H. Addams described her stepdaughter Jane. After all, a girl born to a prosperous family in Cedarville, Illinois, in 1860 was not supposed to have such ambitions.

Jane's heart had been set on the newly opened Smith College for Women, but her father's wish was that she follow the path of her older sisters and enter the Rockford (Illinois) Seminary. She did as he asked and entered the seminary in 1877. Here, the foundations of her feminism were laid down, and, resisting pressure from Anna Sill, Rockford's indomitable head, to become a missionary, Jane decided to become a doctor. Accordingly, she enrolled in the Woman's Medical College of Pennsylvania. Unfortunately, never physically strong, her health broke and she was forced to withdraw.

For eight troubled years she traveled, read, and attended the social functions that suited Mrs. Addams's plans for her. It was a period of frustration, nervousness, and unhappiness. At long last, during a European tour with her friend Ellen Gates Starr, an idea began to take shape in Jane's mind. In London she witnessed a match-girls' strike and later she visited Toynbee Hall in London's East End, the University settlement that sought to alleviate the bitter human consequences of industrialization.

The two young women discussed these ideas and decided to return home to implement them. They searched for a suitable base of operations and found the decaying Hull mansion in the heart of one of the poorest districts in the city, a crowded area bursting with Greek, Italian, Russian, German, Sicilian, and other immigrants. In September of 1889, they moved in, and invited the neighbors to stop by.

Before long two things happened. First, neighbors, most of them immigrants, started coming—to attend lectures and to form clubs. Second, a number of talented men and women moved into Hull House. By 1893, Hull House was the center of some forty clubs, a day nursery, gymnasium, dispensary, and playground, cooking and sewing classes, courses in art, music, and language, a cooperative boardinghouse for working girls, and a little theater; each week 2,000 people entered its doors.

Under Jane Addams's leadership, Hull House took on another, more far-reaching task. It became a clearing house for various reform movements. The residents pressured legislators to act on such matters as child labor, factory inspection, recognition of labor unions, protection of immigrants, and industrial safety.

Jane Addams did not permit her energies to be siphoned off into the special enterprises sponsored by Hull House, but she remained the focus and center of the undertaking. She became sought after as a lecturer. Honors were bestowed upon her. She became the first woman president of the National Conference of Charities and Correction and in 1910 became the first woman to receive an honorary degree from Yale University. In 1931, sharing the award with Nicholas Murray Butler, she was given the Nobel Peace Prize.

A heart attack laid her low in 1933, and in 1935 she was stricken with cancer. She died at the age of seventy-four. She had been at Hull House for forty-six years and it stood as a monument to this remarkable woman who had devoted herself to humanitarian causes and had never swerved from what she conceived to be her duty.

tions. Many were native-born Protestants. Most had had little direct contact with foreign-born, largely Catholic and Jewish immigrants until they began a career of reform.

Quite often, these basic cultural differences between immigrants and reformers made it difficult, if not impossible, for the two groups to join successfully. Their interests were also often in direct conflict. New immigrants depended on the very political favors—jobs and other assistance from local political bosses—that the reformers wanted to eliminate. Moreover, the immigrant culture was more tolerant of gambling and drinking than the reformer's tradition of stern Protestant moralism. These differences over values certainly diluted the effect of municipal reformers in curing urban ills.

A NEW GENERATION OF REFORMERS

Many of those who had opposed unions and other reform movements prior to the 1890s gradually became convinced of the need for basic reforms in American society. They had been deeply affected by the tumultuous events of the nineties: the depression, the social unrest on farms and in factories, the deepening class conflict.

By the turn of the century many middle-class Americans saw the dangers. Conservative journalists such as William Allen White, "big business" lawyers such as Clarence Darrow and George Norris, and middle-of-the-road Republicans such as Theodore Roosevelt had all concluded that the future political and social health of the American republic depended on a variety of reforms. They sought improvements in the conditions under which the urban poor lived. They also wanted to bring giant trusts under governmental supervision in the public interest. These various reform interests came together in a movement that historians have labeled "progressivism."

The Progressive Movement However different progressive reformers were in their social and economic concerns, most shared certain fundamental beliefs. For one thing, unlike the Bellamys and Georges of the previous generation, they did not believe in imminent social catastrophe. Rather, they were highly nationalistic and optimistic about the future of the United States. Herbert Croly, one of their most influential writers, argued that this "promise of American life" consisted of "an improving popular economic condition, guaranteed by democratic political institutions, and resulting in moral and social [improvement]."

Nationalism and reform, then, went hand in hand. Both impulses were based on an idealistic faith in American potential. Most progressives believed that a decent society for all Americans could be created through gradual reform rather than through revolutionary changes. The reformers of the previous generation had not been so confident.

Progressive reformers harnessed their optimism about domestic affairs to a firm belief in the value of Christian morality. It was within this "ethical climate" that much reform legislation of the era took shape. To Frances Perkins the new climate was dominated by "the idea that poverty is preventable, that poverty is destructive, wasteful, demoralizing, and that poverty in the midst of potential plenty is morally unacceptable in a Christian and democratic society." An end to poverty, injustice, and unregulated economic power, the preservation of the nation's natural resources, a return to honest government—all this, the progressives believed, would follow from applying Christian ethics to reshaping the social environment.

Another belief shared by progressive thinkers was a confidence in the use of "experts" to manage public affairs. Professional advisers such as those who had assisted the Triangle Commission would provide rational, scientific measurement of the country's problems; they would also suggest efficient means for tackling social ills. Often this argument for "efficient" and "scientific" government cloaked the efforts of business groups and wealthier Americans to retain control of government—especially at the city and state level— and to deny power to the immigrant-supported urban political machines. In short, there was an important elitist, "antidemocratic" dimension to *certain* aspects of progressivism.

Progressive reformers called for the establishment of legislative investigating bodies at all levels of government, and the use of expert advisers—brain trusts—to help city and state governments develop programs of reform. They wanted to create regulatory agencies to supervise business practices. Progressives also favored the establishment of nonpartisan commissions or councils to eliminate machine corruption in city government. The independent commission form of city government originated in Galveston, Texas, in 1900. By 1914 it had spread to over 400 American cities, although not to most larger ones.

Finally, more reformers of the era believed strongly in the value of publicizing social problems as a first step toward solving them. As early as 1898 Congress had established a commission to study the giant business trusts. The commission eventually published nineteen volumes on American social and economic problems. In addition, many states set up investigatory groups to study business corruption. This technique of exposure was carried out most systematically under the reform governorship of Robert M. LaFollette in Wisconsin from 1901 to 1906. LaFollette's efforts to uncover business abuses and press for needed social legislation set a pattern for reform administrations in other states.

Newspapers and magazines provided a forum for investigations of social problems by muckraking journalists. Ida Tarbell wrote an explosive exposé of the Standard Oil Company. Lincoln Steffens studied corrupt city political machines. David Graham Phillips examined Senate corruption. Magazines such as *McClure's* and *Harper's Weekly* increased their circulation to the hundreds of thousands by becoming champions of reform.

New Politics for the Cities Nowhere was the belief in the need for "rational" government stronger than at the local level. Progressives were as appalled by corrupt city politics as they were by dirty tenements and unsafe factories. All three conditions came under the attack of municipal reformers. Beginning in the 1890s, reform groups won control of a number of cities and began deal-

Ida M. Tarbell's stunning exposés revealed the way giant corporations gained advantage over competitors by securing special rates (rebates) from railroads. Her landmark study of the oil industry appeared in *McClure's* magazine, which established it as the leading muckraking periodical.

Lincoln Steffens, one of the leading reformer journalists, wrote numerous articles exposing political corruption in city government. His autobiography gives an accurate account of the development of the muckraking movement.

Upton Sinclair is best remembered for his novel, *The Jungle*, which told of brutal and unsanitary conditions in Chicago's stockyards. The public revulsion it aroused resulted in the passage of the Meat Inspection Act of 1906.

ing with slum and factory conditions. In New York City, for example, after driving Tammany Hall from power in 1901, Mayor Seth Low worked closely with reformers to improve parks and playgrounds, tighten housing laws, and strengthen the city's health services to the poor. But, despite Mayor Seth's efforts, much remained to be done, as conditions in the city at the time of the Triangle fire demonstrated.

In other cities, too, the concern for social reform proved strong. During the 1890s and 1900s three remarkable Middle Western businessmen — all self-made millionaires — became pioneers in urban reform. Their cities served as models for social reformers throughout the country.

Hazen Pingree, mayor of Detroit, Michigan, from 1889 to 1896, and then governor of the state, fought corruption by politicians and local industrial groups, especially street railways and gas companies. Pingree authorized the construction of a city-owned electric lighting plant and urged public ownership of other such utilities. In Toledo, Ohio, Samuel M. "Golden Rule" Jones, mayor of the city from 1897 to 1904, established free kindergarten day-care facilities for working mothers, pressed for a minimum hourly wage and other social legislation, and supported public ownership of utilities.

Thomas Johnson, Cleveland's mayor from 1901 to 1909, became a social reformer after reading Henry George's *Progress and Poverty*. He, too, fought the private utility interests and urged public ownership. Johnson sponsored a number of social welfare projects, including the construction of municipal bathhouses (a crucial urban health measure, since many tenement houses did not have adequate bathroom facilities) and careful inspection of consumer meat and dairy products.

All three Middle Western mayors ran nonpartisan governments, dominated by professional administrators and reformers who took over the jobs that had formerly been filled by political appointees. Unfortunately, driving political machines from office did not always produce improvements in ghetto or factory conditions. Unlike Mayors Pingree, Jones, and Johnson, many municipal reformers were less interested in improving slum conditions than in eliminating the

Tom Johnson, Cleveland's reform mayor, instituted reforms, including city planning, that made that city one of America's best-governed. He had his own political machine, observing, "It all depends on whether a boss is a good one or a bad one."

power and corruption of immigrant-supported political machines. In Pittsburgh, for example, two-thirds of those involved in trying to revise the city's charter came from upper-class backgrounds and were closely tied to the city's leading banks and industries.

Changes at the State Level Many of the major reforms of this period were achieved at the state level. In a number of states progressive reformers were elected governors. Among them were Robert LaFollette in Wisconsin, Charles Evans Hughes in New York, Hoke Smith in Georgia, Hiram Johnson in California, and the Southern-born president of Princeton University, Woodrow Wilson, in New Jersey. Each state had its special problems, each its particular group of "entrenched interests." In Massachusetts, the railroads and insurance companies dominated; in California, it was the powerful and corrupt labor unions.

Almost all reform governors fought for stricter regulation of railroads, public utilities, and industries within their states. They tried to force corporations to pay a fair share of taxes and to conserve natural resources like forests and mines, which provided raw materials for industry. Finally, they fought to make state government more democratic through such reforms as the initiative, the referendum, and the recall.[1]

During the first two decades of the century, many states enacted broad programs of social legislation dealing with the wages and hours of factory workers, the employment of women and children, and safety conditions in tenements and factories. Maryland adopted the first statewide

workmen's compensation law in 1902. A year later Oregon passed a law restricting women's industrial work to ten hours per day. Illinois adopted the first measure providing public assistance to mothers with dependent children in 1911. And Massachusetts passed the first minimum wage law (applying to women and children) in 1912. All these measures were landmarks in the struggle of progressive reformers to achieve economic and social justice for all Americans.

Amending the Constitution Suffrage—the right to vote—had been a central concern of the woman's rights movement for several decades. In 1910 the American labor force included over 8 million women, many of them college-educated. During this period 36 percent of all professional jobs were held by women. Yet, prior to World War I only eleven states had granted women the right to vote.

Between 1914 and 1919 woman's rights advocates gave the suffrage issue national im-

---

[1]The initiative is a device by which a small number of citizens, sometimes as few as 5 percent, can bypass the legislature and force a vote upon measures at general elections. The referendum forces legislatures to return proposed laws to the electorate, who then approve or reject the proposals. The recall, perhaps the most controversial device, allows the electorate to remove an elected official from office. It requires a special election, called after a certain number of voters have signed a petition asking for the official's removal.

Women concentrated on making political gains in the early twentieth century. An intense campaign, and their increasing importance in the labor market, finally gained them full suffrage on a nationwide basis by constitutional amendment—the Nineteenth.

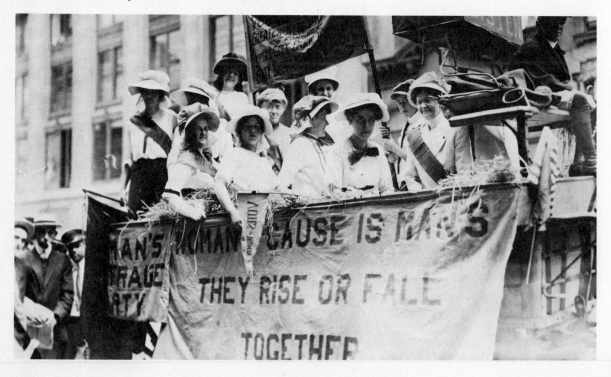

portance by conducting a massive campaign of petitions, lobbying, picketing, and nonviolent demonstrations. The campaign was sponsored by two national associations of woman suffrage advocates, led by Carrie Chapman Catt and Anna Howard Shaw. The picketing and demonstrations that had brought public sympathy for the demands of shirtwaist employees during the Triangle strike worked with similar effect for the suffragettes. The involvement of women in war work during World War I brought the movement increased public support. In June 1919 Congress responded by passing the Nineteenth Amendment, giving women the right to vote. The amendment received final state ratification in August 1920. Later that year, for the first time, American women in every state voted in a presidential election.

Another progressive interest, the temperance movement, had been a concern of reformers since before the Civil War. Municipal reformers joined the anti-alcohol drive for two major reasons. First, there was much political corruption associated with urban liquor dealers. Second, reformers felt that alcoholism was destroying the moral fiber and social well-being of many Americans.

The prohibitionists made their first gains at the local and state levels. A number of Southern and Western states voted themselves "dry." During World War I many of the same groups that later pushed the woman suffrage amendment through Congress secured passage of the Eighteenth Amendment, which forbade the sale and distribution of alcoholic beverages. Ratified by the states in January 1919, the amendment took effect the next year. It was considered the most impressive yet the most debatable triumph of progressive moralism.

In 1913 progressive reformers won two other important victories. The Sixteenth Amendment instituted a federal income tax. And the Seventeenth Amendment provided for direct election of senators instead of their election by state legislatures. An amendment prohibiting child labor passed Congress under intense reform pressure. It met strong opposition from the business community, however, and failed to win ratification by the states.

PROGRESSIVISM IN THE WHITE HOUSE

With the death of William McKinley on September 14, 1901, Theodore Roosevelt became the third man in less than forty years to succeed to the presidency because of an assassin's bullet. At forty-three, he was the nation's youngest President. Roosevelt came to the White House with a distinguished career in public service. He had served as state legislator, federal official, city police chief, army colonel, governor of New York, and Vice President. An energetic and impulsive man, Roosevelt responded candidly to McKinley's death: "It is a dreadful thing to come into the presidency this way; but it would be a far worse thing to be morbid about it."

Roosevelt's Square Deal for America Roosevelt moved cautiously during the next few years to take control of the Republican national machinery from McKinley's close friend Senator Mark Hanna of Ohio. In his first term he made few reform proposals. He did, however, publicize reform more and more, especially as his second term drew to a close. During this period no other American did as much as Theodore Roosevelt to educate his fellow citizens to the need for political and social change. He called the presidency "a bully pulpit." He often mounted its steps to criticize "malefactors of great wealth" and others—trusts, political bosses, destroyers of natural resources—who endangered his vision of a "square deal" for all Americans.

But Roosevelt did far more than simply publicize reform. Despite his strong party loyalties and keen appreciation of political patronage, he brought into government service a remarkable number of reformers. Roosevelt appointed William Howard Taft as secretary of war, conservationist Gifford Pinchot as chief of the Forest Service, James R. Garfield (the son of the former President and a dedicated conservationist) as secretary of the interior, and the great jurist Oliver Wendell Holmes, Jr., as Supreme Court justice.

Unlike his Republican predecessors in the White House, Roosevelt worked for the support of the black community. He employed Booker T. Washington, president of the Tuskegee Institute in Alabama, as his chief adviser on Southern Republican appointments. Washington's relationship to Roosevelt was perhaps the high point of the black leader's national influence during a long and distinguished public career.

Washington was born into slavery in 1856 and, after a difficult struggle for his own education, founded Tuskegee in 1881 with assistance from Northern white philanthropists. Tuskegee, under Washington's leadership, stressed vocational training, reflecting his belief that blacks in the South could advance only by concentrating on economic training and self-improvement. Washington's basic message seemed eminently reasonable to many blacks and whites in the region, especially considering the rise in violence directed toward blacks, the spread of caste segregation, and the overall white hostility toward black aspirations during the late nineteenth and early twentieth centuries in America.

Washington's reputation among Southerners, black and white, reached its apex in 1895 when he spoke in Atlanta, urging regional blacks to restrain their demands for political rights in favor of economic self-help, while pleading with whites for sympathy and assistance. Washington's speech became known as the "Atlanta Compromise," accepting as it did the "separate but equal" doctrines of the day. His views drew support also from Roosevelt and many other white progressives, who did not (for the most part) believe in a politically equal role for blacks. Washington came under increasing attack during his final years, however, from younger black leaders such as W. E. B. DuBois. The new breed—often Northern-born and well-educated professionals—demanded *immediate* action to achieve full political and civic equality for black Americans, and they condemned the Tuskegee educator for advocating patience and (or so they believed) accepting a subordinate role for blacks. Many of Washington's critics knew little, however, about his quiet, covert efforts to raise money needed to launch legal battles against segregation statutes, or of his efforts to ensure that (at least in the North) blacks were organized as an effective political voting block. It

was in this context that Washington interpreted his connection with Theodore Roosevelt as still another opportunity to secure influence and exercise patronage on behalf of his Southern black constituency and their white allies.

Underlying Roosevelt's actions and policies during his administration were certain firm beliefs shared by other progressives as well. Among them was the belief that government must begin to intervene in the economy to bring unregulated businesses under control. It was argued that such a move would reduce class tensions in American society as well. Toward this end Roosevelt lobbied actively to push several important reform measures through Congress. The Elkins Act of 1903 forbade railroads to give rebates[2] to large industrial companies. The Hepburn Act of 1906 strengthened the powers of the Interstate Commerce Commission (ICC) to regulate the nation's railroads.

Nevertheless, Roosevelt sometimes needed prodding from the public—for example, on the question of food and drug regulation. Americans were alerted to the vile conditions under which Chicago slaughterhouses and processed-meat plants operated by Upton Sinclair's 1906 novel, *The Jungle*. (Ironically, socialist Sinclair's portrayal in that same book of the horrendous living and working conditions among Chicago's immigrant community was ignored by many of its readers.) Pressure from muckrakers and from reformers such as Dr. Harvey W. Wiley of the Department of Agriculture forced passage in 1906 of both a Pure Food and Drug Act *and* a meat-inspection bill. The former banned the production or sale of fraudulently labeled or adulterated goods. Meat packers and other manufacturers managed to adulterate the measures themselves, however, so that the final versions provided, among other things, that the government and not business pay the costs of inspection. Still, the laws were milestones in their day.

---

[2]Rebates were special rates, lower than the published ones, granted secretly to users who accounted for a large share of freight traffic. Farmers felt especially cheated by these special rates, usually granted to industries.

Theodore Roosevelt surrounded himself with conservationists like John Muir who believed that the natural environment must be protected. Through Roosevelt's influence, 148,000,000 acres of forests were set aside for national parks like Yosemite, seen in the background.

In these and other regulatory measures, Roosevelt received much support from the business community. For many business leaders, federal action seemed the most rational response to the country's growing industrial problems. Thus the railroads favored tighter federal regulation to eliminate the rebate system and avoid even more rigid state regulation. Similarly, giant lumber corporations endorsed federal intervention to enforce a rational set of guidelines for the industry.

An energetic outdoorsman, Roosevelt did much to educate the American public to the need for environmental protection. The Newlands Act, passed in 1902, authorized federal funds for the construction of dams and reclamation projects in the West. In 1907 Roosevelt signed an executive order converting over 17 million acres of forest land in Western states to national reserves. He also withdrew from private sale many valuable natural resources, including coal and mineral lands, oil reserves, and water-power sites. In 1908 he summoned the nation's conservation experts to a White House National Conservation Congress. Its purpose was to plan future policies for the protection of natural resources.

Busting the Trusts In 1902 Roosevelt began a policy of "trust busting." He moved to break up many of the giant corporations that had been organized by industry mergers during the previous decade. At first Roosevelt sought only to regulate the trusts through appropriate legislative channels. He asked Congress to pass legislation authorizing the federal licensing of corporations, full disclosure of company earnings and profits, and other supervisory measures. But the conservative majority in Congress rejected these proposals. So Roosevelt took on the trusts himself, using the powers given to the President by the 1890 Sherman Antitrust Act.

The President's first target was the National Securities Company. This was a consolidation of three major railroad systems: the Northern Pacific, the Great Northern, and the Chicago, Burlington, and Quincy. New York banking houses, led by Rockefeller and J. P. Morgan, had organized the merger to put an end to damaging competition among the three lines. Roosevelt ordered his Attorney General, Philander C. Knox, to file suit against the Northern Securities Company for violating the Sherman Act. In 1903 the Supreme Court declared the merger illegal and ordered the Northern Securities Company dissolved.

Roosevelt brought similar antitrust actions against several other giant corporations. These included Standard Oil, the American Tobacco Company, and DuPont. In this policy, which proved highly popular politically, Roosevelt asserted the supremacy of federal authority over private economic interests.

In his antitrust campaign Roosevelt insisted that he opposed not large corporations as such, but corporate action against the public interest. The exact nature of that interest, Roosevelt felt, was something the President must judge. He wrote: "Our objection to a given corporation must be not that it is big, but that it behaves badly." In 1902 Roosevelt used his authority to force the settlement of a coal strike that threatened to deprive residents of the East Coast of fuel during the winter months. With the aid of Wall Street banker J. P. Morgan he forced coal company executives to accept a settlement favorable to the United Mine Workers. It was the first time that an American President had intervened in a labor dispute on behalf of the striking workers.

Roosevelt's actions toward big business were not always consistent, however. He came to private arrangements with U.S. Steel and other giant corporations to avoid invoking antitrust action. In some labor disputes he called in federal troops as strikebreakers. At heart, he believed that the federal government had to play the role of a neutral third party in resolving major disputes on industrial relations.

Roosevelt had been elected to the presidency in his own right in 1904, winning by the greatest landslide of any presidential contest since the pre-Civil War period. When he left the White House at the end of his second term in 1909, he bequeathed to his hand-picked successor, William Howard Taft, a well-formulated set of reform proposals for congressional action. These proposals included thorough governmental regulation of business, federal supervision of the stock market, a federal workmen's compensation law, and compulsory arbitration of labor disputes.

Taft and the Old Guard The new President showed little interest in carrying out Roosevelt's proposals. Not that Taft opposed reform completely. During his four years as President he supported the constitutional amendments providing for an income tax and for direct election of senators. In addition, Taft initiated twice as many antitrust actions as Roosevelt. But unlike his predecessor, he never acquired an image as a trust buster. Under Taft's administration Congress established the eight-hour day for government workers, widened the ICC's authority to include interstate communications systems, and extended a tax on corporate profits. Taft also gave genuine and vigorous support to the conservation movement.

In other areas, however, Taft remained a conservative, politically allied to the Republican Old Guard. In 1910 Taft's Interior Secretary, Richard Ballinger, made an agreement with private firms allowing them to develop valuable coal and water-power sites in Alaska. Chief Forester Gifford Pinchot objected to this decision, but Taft supported Ballinger and fired Pinchot. This move infuriated Roosevelt and marked the beginning of a political break between the two men

Taft also supported Republican conservatives in their battle for control of Congress against a coalition of reform Democrats and Republicans.

He worked actively for the defeat of leading Republican insurgents in the 1910 congressional election. Again Taft's actions angered Republican reformers, among them Senator Robert La-Follette, the party's most prominent progressive. Later that year Taft cooperated with the Republican Old Guard in helping to pass the Payne-Aldrich Tariff, a high-tariff measure beneficial to big business. The battle over the Payne bill split congressional Republicans into conservative and progressive wings. Roosevelt, usually more politcally astute than Taft, had dodged the issue. GOP reformers wished to lower the tariff, while most conservatives favored upward revision. Long before the close of his term in office, Taft had lost the support of most Republican reformers. They turned again to Teddy Roosevelt for leadership.

The Election of 1912 Roosevelt did not disappoint them. Beginning in 1910, he toured the country, supporting party insurgents against Taft and denouncing the Ballinger-Pinchot affair. He made it evident that he wished the Republican party's nomination for an unprecedented third term in the White House. Roosevelt's active campaigning helped him to capture the presidential primaries in six states. But in most states presidential nominations were made by party conventions rather than by primary elections. Taft had gained control of the party machinery during his four years in office. Thus in June 1912 the Republican national convention nominated Taft for a second term.

Republican progressives led by Roosevelt and LaFollette then split from party ranks. In August 1912 they organized the Progressive (or Bull Moose) party, which nominated Roosevelt for the presidency. The new party attracted the attention of the country's leading reformers. Its 1912 convention, held in Chicago, was attended by such figures as Jane Addams, William Allen White, and George W. Perkins—all activists in the era's various reform movements.

"We stand at Armageddon, and we battle for the Lord!"—Roosevelt shouted this rallying cry to Progressives at the Republican convention in June 1912. He was a man with a mission. He wanted to regain the presidency because

Many cartoons, such as this one, appeared during the 1912 presidential nominating conventions. Cartoonists had a field day depicting Roosevelt and the "Bull Moose" party.

he had a Progressive program, his "New Nationalism," that he wanted to see enacted into law. In his characteristic way he was ready to do battle. "I feel as fit as a bull moose," he told reporters.

When he lost the nomination, the Progressives would not accept the end of their dream. On August 5, 1912, they met as the newly formed Progressive, or "Bull Moose," party. Here in Chicago they would nominate Roosevelt as their presidential candidate.

The religious note that Roosevelt had sounded at the Republican convention seemed to find its real audience here. One historian has described the delegates as "a group of well-dressed, serious citizens with the respectability of Sunday School superintendents." The gathering seemed more like a religious revival meeting than a political convention. Speaker after speaker took the podium to deliver rousing, emotion-packed sermons on social justice. An already converted audience listened intently and often tearfully. Occasionally they would be moved to respond with hymns, feet stomping, and quotes from the Bible.

These were the men and women who for

years had sought reforms in their own communities. They were frequently isolated from the rest of society because of their beliefs. One writer described them as "men of character who had fought against local grafting politicians. College professors, social workers, businessmen of vision and independence, farmers tired of seeing agriculture on the cross—[all] were enlisting in a cause they loved for unselfish service."

On the second day of the convention Roosevelt rose to present his "Confession of Faith" in political and economic reform. Before he could speak, 15,000 people came to their feet to welcome him. They poured out all of the emotions that had been building in them since he was denied the Republican nomination.

Roosevelt did not disappoint them. His mood matched theirs. When it came time for him to accept their nomination, he launched the crusade in fervent, enthusiastic terms:

> Six weeks ago here in Chicago, I spoke to the honest representatives of a convention which was not dominated by honest men; a convention wherein sat, alas! a majority of men who, with sneering indifference to every principle of right, acted so as to bring to a shameful end a party which had been founded over half a century ago by men in whose souls burned the fire of lofty endeavor. Now to you men who, in your turn, have come together to spend and be spent in the endless crusade against wrong, to you who face the future resolute and confident, to you who strive in a spirit of brotherhood for the betterment of our nation, to you who gird yourselves for this great new fight in the never-ending warfare for the good of mankind, I say in closing what I said in that speech in closing: We stand at Armageddon and we battle for the Lord.

The Progressive party platform reflected a broad concern for major reforms in American life. It called for tighter governmental regulation of giant industries and financial companies, national presidential primaries, woman suffrage, and the initiative, referendum, and recall. Progressives also favored the prohibition of child labor, minimum wage standards for women, workmen's compensation, and a variety of banking and currency reforms.

On July 2, the Democrats nominated for the presidency a moderate reform candidate, Governor Woodrow Wilson of New Jersey. The Democratic platform favored collective bargaining for unions and revisions in the country's banking system. Unlike the Progressives, the Democrats sought the abolition of giant corporations rather than their regulation. Wilson called his program the New Freedom.

The Republicans, too, ran on a platform of moderate reform. They favored, among other legislation, tighter regulation of trusts and banking and currency changes. Thus, although Taft was more conservative than either Roosevelt or Wilson, he could hardly be considered an opponent of reform. A fourth candidate, Socialist Eugene V. Debs, ran on the most radical platform of all. Debs had led the American Railway Union during the Pullman Company strike of 1894. He served a jail term for his efforts, emerged from prison a confirmed socialist (largely the result of having read the works of other American socialists such as Edward Bellamy and Henry Demarest Lloyd). Debs ran for the presidency as the socialist candidate five times. He again served a jail sentence during Wilson's second term as President because of his opposition to American involvement in W.W. I. In this curious election of 1912, all four candidates were committed in varying degrees to reform.

In the end the Republican split sent Wilson to the White House. Roosevelt received 4,126,000 votes and Taft 3,483,000. Had these votes been combined, the Republicans could have retained control of the presidency. Wilson received 6,286,000 popular votes, less than 45 percent of the total. But he won enough state pluralities to capture a majority of electoral votes. For the first time since the depression of the 1890s, the presidency returned to Democratic hands. In the election the Democrats gained control of both houses of Congress. Thus the new President had a working majority to pass his legislative program.

Wilson and the New Freedom During his first term in office Wilson proceeded to enact his programs. Though he applied stern moral standards to the conduct of foreign relations, Wilson was a skillful realist about domestic affairs. He quickly tossed the notion of breaking up the trusts into the political ashcan. Instead, adopting Roosevelt's more moderate idea of regulating giant corporations, he helped push several bills through Congress to achieve this purpose.

The Federal Trade Commission Act of 1914 established a bipartisan body to supervise industry and prevent unfair methods of competition in interstate commerce. The Clayton Antitrust Act, passed that same year, strengthened the 1890 Sherman Act by spelling out specific business practices that violated the antitrust laws. The Clayton Act also restrained the government from using court injunctions against striking unions.[3] Though on paper the new law seemed a powerful weapon, it actually did little to regulate the behavior of giant corporations or aid organized labor.

One reason for this was that Wilson began permitting corporate leaders and their lobbyists to meet informally with administration officials and regulatory commission members in efforts to settle possible violations without penalty to industry. Businessmen quickly became adept at "co-opting" those nominally charged with overseeing them. In 1913 Wilson helped to steer through Congress the Underwood Tariff, the first downward revision in tariff rates since before the Civil War.

In December 1913 Congress passed the Federal Reserve Act, which created the present American banking system. The new law established twelve regional Federal Reserve banks, which were to serve member banks in their various geographic districts across the country. The Federal Reserve banks issued paper currency, supervised bank credit, and controlled other banking practices. The act also required existing national banks to become members of the Federal Reserve.

The financial "Panic of 1907," which severely disrupted the business community, had

persuaded even many conservative bankers and businessmen of the need for greater national coordination of the banking system. The Federal Reserve System's regulatory mechanisms, it was hoped, would prevent the recurrence of such massive runs on banks by depositors demanding immediate currency payments. The 1913 act also marked the acceptance of this new quasigovernmental institution as a means of both regulating the national banks and setting overall monetary policy for the United States.

Wilson was supported in all these measures by his close associations with Southern Democrats. Some historians have called his election "the revolution of 1912" because, for the first time since the Civil War, Southerners regained a large measure of national influence. Born and raised in the South, Wilson felt most comfortable with those from his native region, many of whom became his closest advisers. He appointed a number of Southerners ambassadors and awarded others with high-level government jobs. Several of his cabinet members came from the South; others, like Wilson himself, were of Southern background ("the South in exile," as some called it).

The Senate Majority Leader, Thomas Martin of Virginia, and the House Majority Leader, Oscar Underwood of Alabama, worked closely with the new President. During Wilson's administration fifteen out of seventeen Senate committees were led by Southern chairmen. These senators helped to formulate Wilson's domestic program and steer it through Congress. The Federal Reserve Act was largely the work of three Southerners, including Wilson's Secretary of the Treasury, Carter Glass of Virginia. The Clayton Antitrust Act was sponsored by Henry Clayton of Alabama, and House Majority Leader Underwood led the fight for the tariff-revision bill.

Protest and Progress Wilson's Southern background also had less fortunate consequences, however. Segregation officially came to Washington under Wilson's regime. Governmental offices and other public facilities in the city were ordered segregated by race. In doing this, Wilson was only following a practice that had become common af-

---

[3]An injunction is a court order requiring or forbidding certain activities. Business and government have sometimes used the injunction as an antiunion weapon to prevent strikes.

ter Reconstruction. In the late nineteenth century, "Jim Crow" laws[4]—that is, laws keeping blacks and whites apart in all public places—were enacted throughout the South (with little protest from the North). In 1896, in the case of *Plessy* v. *Ferguson,* the Supreme Court ruled that "separate but equal" facilities were constitutional. The decision was based to some extent on pseudoscientific assumptions of the day shared by many middle-class progressives in both the North and South. They believed that blacks (as well as Southern and Eastern Europeans) were essentially inferior. With the approval of the court, white supremacy asserted itself, in segregated railroad cars, restaurants, schools, and other public facilities and institutions.

In the early twentieth century the problems of black Americans were brought to the nation's attention by a group of young black businessmen and professionals under the leadership of the great scholar W. E. B. DuBois. In 1905 they founded the militant Niagara Movement to press for an end to Booker T. Washington's policy of "accommodation" with whites. The leaders of the Niagara group sought a return to active agitation for complete political and civil equality of blacks with whites—the earlier goals of Radical Reconstruction.

Four years later, members of the Niagara Movement and white supporters of black civil rights formed the National Association for the Advancement of Colored People (NAACP). DuBois was appointed editor of the NAACP's journal, *The Crisis.* Active in the new organization were several reformers who would support the garment workers' strike that same year: Lillian Wald, Jane Addams, and publisher Oswald Garrison Willard (William Lloyd Garrison's grandson). The NAACP grew rapidly in the next decade. It quickly took the lead in opposing the segregationist policies of the Wilson administration.

Wilson found himself under growing pressure from other groups of reformers as his first term drew to a close. There seemed little chance that he could again slip into the White House

---

[4]The laws got their name from a song sung by Thomas Rice in a Negro minstrel show.

W. E. B. DuBois, the first black to receive a Ph.D. from Harvard, founded the NAACP to agitate for black political rights. When he died in 1963, his goals were beginning to be realized, though he himself, disheartened, had moved to Africa.

through a split in Republican ranks. Roosevelt had rejoined his party, and most Progressives were unhappy with Wilson's refusal to support social welfare legislation. Concerned over the political situation, Wilson began a determined campaign to win over reform-minded voters by pushing several progressive measures through Congress.

The Federal Farm Loan Act, passed in May 1916, aided domestic agriculture by expanding the credit resources of American farmers. The Adamson Act, passed the same year, provided an eight-hour day for railroad workers. The Kern-McGillicudy Act created a model workmen's compensation program for federal employees. In August of 1916 Congress attempted to deal with the problems of child labor by passing the Keating-Owen Act, which outlawed the interstate shipment of products manufactured by children under fourteen. (Two years later the law was declared unconstitutional.) Wilson nominated progressive lawyer Louis Brandeis to the Supreme Court and fought for his confirmation in Congress against conservative opposition. Brandeis became the first Jewish Supreme Court justice.

During the election of 1916 Democrats stressed Wilson's skill at maintaining American neutrality during the growing war in Europe (see Chapter 36). But it was the President's energetic sponsorship of reform measures that won him the support of the labor movement and most middle-class reformers. In a hard-fought campaign against Republican Charles Evans Hughes, Wilson won reelection by narrow popular and electoral margins. In his second term he devoted most of his attention to the problems of fighting a war and winning the peace. Domestic reform took a back seat to world affairs during Woodrow Wilson's last four years in office.

SUGGESTED READINGS-CHAPTERS 33-34

Triangle Fire

Leon Stein, *The Triangle Fire* (1962); Daniel Aaron, *Men of Good Hope: A Story of American Progessives* (1951); Irving Howe, *World of Our Fathers: The Journey of the East European Jews to America* (1976); Moses Rischin, *The Promised City: New York's Jews, 1870–1914* (1960); Charles E. Zaretz, *The Amalgamated Clothing Workers* (1934).

Synthesis and Interpretations

Samuel P. Hays, *Response to Industrialism, 1885–1914* (1957); Richard Hofstadter, *The Age of Reform* (1955); Gabriel Kolko, *The Triumph of Conservatism* (1963); Christopher Lasch, *The New Radicalism in America* (1965); Henry F. May, *Protestant Churches and Industrial America* (1949) and *The End of American Innocence* (1959); Robert H. Wiebe, *The Search for Order, 1877–1920* (1968) and *Businessmen and Reform* (1962).

States and Cities

Robert H. Bremner, *From the Depths: The Discovery of Poverty in the United States* (1956); Roy Lubove, *The Progressives and the Slums: Tenement House Reform in New York City, 1890–1917* (1962); Zane L. Miller, *Boss Cox's Cincinnati* (1968); Irwin Yellowitz, *Labor and the Progressive Movement in New York* (1965).

Roosevelt, Taft, and Wilson

George E. Mowry, *The Era of Theodore Roosevelt, 1900–1912* (1958); John Blum, *The Republican Roosevelt* (1954); William H. Harbourgh, *The Life and Times of Theodore Roosevelt* (1961); Donald F. Anderson, *William Howard Taft* (1973); Arthur S. Link, *Woodrow Wilson and the Progressive Era* (1954) and *Wilson* (5 vols., 1947–1965).

The Progressive Movement

Samuel P. Hays, *Conservation and the Gospel of Efficiency* (1959); Philip Taft, *The A. F. of L. in the Time of Gompers* (1957); Gabriel Kolko, *Railroads and Regulation, 1877–1916* (1965); Richard Lowitt, George W. Norris, *Making of a Progressive* (1963); William O'Neill, *The Progressive Years* (1975) and *Divorce in the Progressive Era* (1967); David Thelen, *Robert La Follette and the Insurgent Spirit* (1976); Blake McKelvey, *The Urbanization of America 1860–1915* (1963).

Progressive Journalism

Richard Hofstadter, *The Progressive Historians* (1968); David W. Noble, *The Paradox of Progressive Thought* (1958); Charles Forcey, *Crossroads of Liberalism* (1961); Justin Kaplan, *Lincoln Steffens* (1974); David M. Chalmers, *Social and Political Ideas of the Muckrakers* (1964).

Reform Movements

Roy Lubove, *The Professional Altruist: The Emergence of Social Work as a Career, 1880–1930* (1965); James H. Timberlake, *Prohibition and the Progressive Movement* (1963); David Kennedy, *Birth Control in America: The Career of Margaret Sanger* (1970); Lawrence Cremin, *The Transformation of the School: Progressivism in American Education* (1961); Eleanor Flexner, *Century of Struggle: The Women's Rights Movement in the United States* (1974); Jeremy P. Felt, *Hostages of Fortune: Child Labor Reform* (1965).

35
THE PHILIPPINES REVOLT

A.W.

At age thirty, Emiliano Aguinaldo was a seasoned revolutionary. The son of a prosperous farmer from the island of Luzon, he was a member of the Katipunan, the Filipino movement for independence. In August 1896, Aguinaldo joined a revolt against Spain, which had held the Philippines as a colony since the sixteenth century. Two months later the rebels proclaimed the existence of the Tagal Republic. When the first president of the republic died, Aguinaldo became president and commander in chief of the insurgent forces.

But revolutionary organization and high-sounding titles alone could not defeat the Spanish in the field. Nor could Spain's colonial power crush the rebels. In December 1897, after more than a year of seesaw guerrilla warfare, both sides recognized the stalemate and signed a treaty.

Spain, apprehensive over the threats posed to its Caribbean empire by rebellion in Cuba and political unrest in Puerto Rico, agreed to consider reforms in the Philippines. In turn, Aguinaldo and other leaders of the rebellion agreed to leave their country for three years. They went to Hong Kong, a British colony on the southern coast of China. Meanwhile, the Spanish deposited 400,000 pesetas in a Hong Kong bank in the rebels' name. If Spain enacted the promised reforms, this trust fund would be used to educate Filipinos abroad. If Spain failed, the insurgents could use the money to buy arms and resume the war.

The Filipinos soon became convinced that they had been tricked. Spanish Governor-General Miguel Primo de Rivera did not declare a general amnesty, as expected. Reforms acceptable to the rebels did not come to pass. The trust fund that rested in Hong Kong now seemed to the rebels to be no more than hush money, a bribe to silence Filipino leaders. From their headquarters in the British colony, the insurgents began planning for future campaigns.

The American destruction of the Spanish fleet in Manila Bay on May 1, 1898, brought the United States into an era of overseas expansion. Gaining the Philippines from Spain proved easier than winning the loyalties of the Filipino people, as events of the next four years would show.

During this period, rebellion in Cuba brought on a crisis in Spanish-American relations. (Americans and their government were sympathetic to freedom movements in Latin America.) As Spain and the United States moved closer to war, the Filipino rebels thought about an alliance with the United States. Then, in April 1898, Aguinaldo was told that the American consul in Singapore, W. Spencer Pratt, wanted to discuss important matters of interest to both countries. The Filipino agreed to meet with Pratt in Singapore.

The Aguinaldo-Pratt talks took place in the Raffles Hotel, legendary center of "East Asian intrigue" and British colonial power at the turn of the century. Pratt claimed that Spain had broken the terms of the truce. He urged Aguinaldo to resume the rebellion. The consul added some important news: "As of the other day, Spain and America have been at war. Now is the time for you to strike. Ally yourselves with America, and you will surely defeat the Spaniards!"

Aguinaldo was clearly interested in this proposal, but he remained cautious: "What can we expect to gain from helping America?" Pratt assured him: "America will give you much greater liberty and many more material benefits than the Spanish ever promised you." When Aguinaldo asked whether such an arrangement could be put in writing, Pratt sidestepped. He obviously had no authority to speak for Washington. Yet he continued to offer verbal assurances.

Consul Pratt also told Aguinaldo that he would try to arrange for the rebels to be transported to Manila on American ships. Pratt contacted Commodore George Dewey, commander of the United States Pacific

Commodore George Dewey created the conditions for United States involvement in protracted guerrilla warfare in the Philippines. He needed Filipino help to defeat Spain but did not reckon with Filipino nationalist feelings after the conflict.

fleet in Hong Kong. The cable to Dewey read: "Aguinaldo, insurgent leader, here. Will come Hong Kong. Arrange with Commodore for general cooperation insurgents Manila if desired." The Yankee sailor answered quickly and tersely: "Tell Aguinaldo come as soon as possible." When informed of Dewey's okay, Aguinaldo promised that if his forces obtained sufficient arms the Filipino people would rise against the Spanish. Pratt, seldom at a loss for reassuring words, told him that Dewey felt that "the United States would at least recognize the independence of the Philippines under the protection of the United States Navy."

Commodore Dewey never met with Aguinaldo before the United States Pacific squadron sailed for Manila. A few years later he denied all knowledge of a political deal. Dewey dismissed Consul Pratt as a "busybody interfering with other people's business," a man whose letters he simply filed and ignored. Toward the Filipinos, Dewey adopted a paternal and disapproving stance. "They seemed to be all very young, earnest boys," he recalled. "I did not attach much importance to what they said or to themselves."

Certainly Dewey did not believe the rebels' boasts that they already had 30,000 armed men in the Philippines, with many more available. Why then did Dewey agree to take Aguinaldo and other Filipino leaders to Manila? By his own account, to get rid of them. "They were bothering me. I was very busy getting my squadron ready for battle, and these little men were coming aboard my ship at Hong Kong and taking a good deal of my time." So he consented to transport the rebels, though in the end only one Filipino went along.

Despite his denials, Dewey did want something from the Filipinos. He needed troops to occupy Manila and other parts of the Philippines if and when he defeated the Spanish navy. Aguinaldo and his followers might help Dewey accomplish the job.

On May 1, 1898, American forces defeated the Spanish navy in Manila Bay. The spectacular victory reaffirmed the rise of American military power on the world scene. The United States squadron blew the remnants of the decaying Spanish navy out of the water. (Some of Spain's ships were hulks, rotting at dockside, with guns that would not function.) Within a few hours it was over. Spain no longer ruled the Philippines. Yet Manila remained to be captured and occupied. The Spanish army had not been routed, nor had its commander indicated a willingness to surrender.

The victory at Manila Bay reopened the question of Dewey's need for Filipino support. From his ships Dewey could do nothing. Spanish artillerymen had allowed Dewey to anchor close to Manila's shore, but the commodore was reluctant to subject the city to a prolonged bombardment. Moreover, his small Marine battalion was an insufficient landing force. The commodore felt that with 5,000 troops he could end the war in one day. But he did not have 5,000 troops. Insurgent Filipinos were the only immediately available source of military manpower.

Early in May, Dewey sent for the rebel leader. Aguinaldo and a dozen of his associates arrived from Hong Kong in Manila on a United States Navy auxiliary vessel. Within a few days Dewey and Aguinaldo met for the first time. Their versions of the encounter are as different as the men themselves.

According to Aguinaldo, the American commander repeated the familiar assurances about American disdain for acquiring colonies and its support of Filipino independence. Dewey also requested that the insurgents resume fighting. He supplied them with sixty-two rifles and some abandoned Spanish naval guns. The United States commander stressed that all promises were guaranteed "by the word of honor of Americans." Finally, Aguinaldo claimed that Dewey instructed him to have a Filipino national flag prepared. It would be hoisted as soon as Spain surrendered.

Dewey presented an equally questionable account of the events. Shortly after meeting with Aguinaldo, Dewey claimed, the secretary of the navy instructed him to avoid entangling the United States in alliances with the Filipino insurgents. Dewey complied because he was bound by obedience and because he did not like the insurgents. He had little faith in their cause. He considered the soft-spoken Aguinaldo an "unimpressive little man," though he recognized the Filipino's enormous prestige among his people.

Dewey admitted that the insurgents might be of service in clearing the shoreline from the naval base of Cavite, which the Americans had now occupied, to Manila City. Thus he allowed the rebels to enter the Cavite arsenal. But he warned that Filipinos and Americans should keep at a distance from each other. The United States commander continued to maintain that Aguinaldo had been forced on him by the barrage of pleas from the American consuls in Hong Kong and Singapore. Dewey also insisted that he never believed the Filipinos wanted independence. How could they? Aguinaldo "considered me as his liberator, as his friend."

Friend would soon become foe, and Aguinaldo himself bore some of the blame for his later disillusionment with the United States. During his months of exile in Hong Kong and his first few weeks back in the Philippines, Aguinaldo seemed to accept everything the Americans promised. His proclamations and public letters of the time praised the United States in lavish terms.

The distance that Dewey sought to create between himself and Aguinaldo was quickly established. American officers had begun complaining about the many Filipinos inside the Cavite naval base. These "natives," they argued, might be friends or foes. So Dewey told Aguinaldo that he and his men must leave the arsenal but could remain in the town of Cavite. From its headquarters in the town, the Aguinaldo movement grew. Enlistees poured in, many of them armed with captured Spanish rifles.

On May 21 Aguinaldo felt militarily strong enough to issue a proclamation outlining his ultimate aims: "Everything appears favorable for attaining independence. The hour has arrived for the Philippines to be-

Emilio Aguinaldo was evaluated differently by his enemies and his own people. To Dewey he was at first a nuisance and later an "Oriental despot." To the Filipinos, however, he symbolized their hope for independence.

long to her sons." Aguinaldo advised his men to fight a "civilized" war, warning that "if we do not conduct ourselves thus, the Americans will decide to sell us or else divide up our territory, as they will hold us incapable of governing our land." Like it or not, Aguinaldo knew, the Filipinos would have to deal with the United States.

Throughout May, Manila remained in Spanish hands. The Americans had made no commitments to the rebels, but United States troops were on the way. In June the Filipino insurgents announced the establishment of a provisional government and issued a declaration of independence.

On June 23, Aguinaldo dissolved the dictatorship and declared himself president of the revolutionary government. In an effort to win support from the United States and other nations, the Filipinos promised to work for two primary goals: independence and the establishment of a representative, republican government.

By the time Aguinaldo formally declared independence, he and his forces controlled most of Cavite province and almost surrounded Manila. From the panic-stricken city, Dewey received requests from Spanish officials to help evacuate foreign and Spanish civilians, as well as wounded soldiers. Some were placed aboard foreign ships in the harbor. Aguinaldo, mindful of the need to wage war in a manner approved by Europeans, allowed civilians and wounded soldiers to pass through his lines. His cooperative spirit reached its height in mid-July when he helped pick the spot for a landing of United States soldiers. Thanks to the insurgents' advice, admitted Dewey, "we were able to land our troops within easy striking distance of their objective," a position more than halfway between Cavite and Manila.

But American gratitude did not mean acceptance of the Filipino forces as a political entity. According to Dewey, in fighting their way up the coast and surrounding Manila, the insurgents had merely prepared "a foothold for our troops when they should arrive." American army units, under General Wesley Merritt, entered Manila on June 30. From then on, the war against Spain became an exclusively American affair.

American soldiers quickly moved to replace the Filipinos in the trenches dug near the Manila fortifications. One of General Merritt's officers tried to convince the insurgents to pull out of the line and turn their trenches over to the Americans. In return he offered to supply the rebels with cannon and other artillery. The local Filipino commander consulted Aguinaldo. Aguinaldo would comply, but only if the request and the offer were put in writing. This concession demonstrated the Filipino leader's desperate desire for legal recognition of his government's standing. Pull out first—then we will furnish the paper, answered the Americans. Aguinaldo ordered his troops out of the trenches. But they never saw the cannon, nor did their commander receive written confirmation. Once again, as in Cavite, Aguinaldo had yielded to an American request under American pressure. This decision proved extremely costly to the rebel cause.

With insurgent forces neutralized and Aguinaldo's political status in doubt, the American capture of Manila proceeded swiftly and with little bloodshed. On August 13 the city capitulated. The United States now ruled the Philippines. On August 17 a War Department dispatch said that Filipino insurgents would not form part of the occupation forces:

> The United States, in possession of Manila City, Manila Bay and harbor, must preserve the peace and protect persons and property within the territory occupied by the military and naval forces. The insurgents and all others must recognize the military occupation and authority of the United States.

What was in store for the Philippines beyond the period of military occupation? In Washington, President McKinley began the process of reconciling the facts of conquest with the arguments of territorial expansionists. At first McKinley opposed taking all of the Philippines, though he held open the possibility that the situation might change. The President favored keeping Luzon, the large island in the northern part of the archipelago, and establishing a United States naval base at Manila. McKinley wished to show Europe that "a lofty spirit" guided American actions. But he also supported the "general principle of holding on to what we get."

These statements reflect McKinley's personality and his tactical approach to political decision making. The President worked hard to create the impression that he was forced to act. He wanted to make it appear that public opinion and the pressure of events directed the outcome of the Philippine conflict. In reality, as McKinley surely realized, the decision to take Manila made full-scale American involvement in the Philippines unavoidable.

The Treaty of Paris, which ended the Spanish-American War, was signed on December 10, 1898. Spain agreed to grant Cuba independence and to cede Puerto Rico and the tiny Pacific island of Guam to the United States. The United States also received the Philippine Islands, for which it paid Spain $20 million. "A goodly estate indeed!" crowed the head of the American delegation. He wrote President McKinley: "Perhaps the treaty may be an acceptable Christmas offering to you from the American commission."

During the negotiations between the United States and Spain, Aguinaldo tried desperately to gain legal standing for his revolutionary government. On August 6, shortly before Manila capitulated, he issued a memorandum to all foreign powers. It asked recognition of the belligerent status of the insurgents, a first step toward full diplomatic recognition. It also sought support for their ultimate aim of independence. Claiming to control fifteen provinces—an assertion not far from the truth at the time—and that the 9,000 Spanish prisoners in his hands were being treated with the "same consideration observed by cultured nations," Aguinaldo declared that the Philippines had "arrived at that state in which it can and ought to govern itself." But other countries refused to recognize the rebels. Nor did the United States indicate a willingness to consider Philippine independence seriously. Filipino insurgents were not America's allies, stated a directive from Washington. They had merely cooperated with Americans "against a common enemy."

Under these circumstances, tension between Americans and Filipinos mounted. In December 1898, President McKinley sent a message to the new military commander in the Philippines, General Elwell S. Otis. The President assured Otis that the United States wished to pursue a policy of "benevolent assimilation" in the islands and bestow the "blessings of good and stable government." But he warned Otis that all obstacles to achieving these ends were to be removed. Before publishing McKinley's message, General Otis cut out several sections critical of the Filipino rebels. When a junior United States officer in the city of Iloilo mistakenly printed the entire text, Filipino resentment grew.

The insurgents' reactions in January 1899 were firm but still friendly. Aguinaldo rejected the American claim to rule his country and accused the United States of betraying a loyal ally. In the United States another Filipino leader, Felipe Agconcillo, tried to reason with the new colonial power in terms of its own declared ideals: "I cannot believe that in any possible action on the part of the American republic toward my country there is an intention to ignore, as to the ten millions of human beings I represent, the right of free government." He concluded his memo with the warning that the accidental or impetuous act of one Filipino or American soldier might trigger a full-scale war.

On February 4, 1899, just such an act occurred. An American soldier on guard duty near Manila challenged a Filipino to halt. When the Filipino disobeyed, the sentry shot and killed him. Fighting between Americans and Filipinos, confined during the previous six months to isolated incidents, broke out all along the outskirts of Manila. The war was on. And as even Dewey had to admit: "Perhaps the insurrection was bound to break out."

Inevitably, each side circulated conflicting reports about the incident. The Filipinos accused the Americans of deliberate provocation. They denied that they had initiated the attack, adding that they were unprepared and that several of their leaders were on leave. They also asserted that Aguinaldo had believed the initial exchange of shots to be accidental. The day after the incident, the rebels claimed, one of their generals proposed an immediate cease-fire to General Otis. But Otis rejected the offer, and ordered the fighting to continue "to the grim end."

McKinley responded with an equally one-sided account. First, he brushed off the cease-fire claim: "There appears to have been no such application." Second, McKinley claimed, no American officer had promised the rebels independence.

Throughout the war, American military leaders tried to downgrade the enemy. American officials viewed Aguinaldo as a bandit, who robbed his own people and lived in luxury on the proceeds of his looting. Whatever Aguinaldo's shortcomings, he remained the leading Filipino insurgent for two years, the chief symbol of resistance to colonial power and of hope for independence.

General Otis, who predicted a quick and easy suppression of the rebellion, failed at the job. Otis boasted that his 21,000 troops would crush the insurgents in a few weeks. He repeated this promise with depressing regularity for the next twelve months. The gap between his fantasies and the realities of the Philippine war can be measured by the increased number of troops the general soon demanded. Shortly after the outbreak he had asked for 35,000. A year later he had 70,000 men and wanted 30,000 more.

In the spring of 1899, the United States Army drove northward from Manila to occupy—or pacify, as the government called it—the island of Luzon, center of Tagal resistance. In April, American forces captured the insurgent capital of Malolos. Aguinaldo and his followers fled farther north. But in mid-May they had to give up their provisional capital at San Isidro. Then, instead of mounting an all-out American attack, General Otis halted the advance. The rainy season had just begun, and many of the troops were scheduled for immediate return home. So Otis, a cautious field commander, suspended military operations.

Back in the White House McKinley remained optimistic. He assured Theodore Roosevelt that "Otis had things entirely in hand and that the insurrection would be speedily put down certainly after the opening of the dry season."

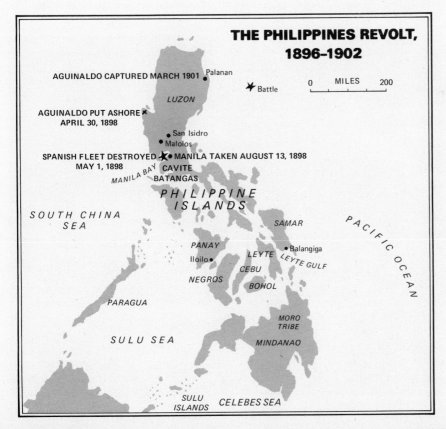

In the meantime, the Schurman Commission, a mixed civilian-military commission headed by the president of Cornell University, Jacob Schurman, was formed to investigate conditions in the Philippine Islands. A preliminary report, issued in the fall of 1899, found much to praise in the Filipinos. It expressed great interest in the islands' natural resources and potential for economic growth. But the report stressed that immediate self-government was out of the question and that the American presence must continue, to ensure peace and order. The commissioners concluded: "Whatever the future of the Philippines may be, there is no course open to us now except the prosecution of the war until the insurgents are reduced to submission." The report delighted McKinley.

Most Americans agreed that Filipinos were unprepared for self-government. Some, like Republican Senator George F. Hoar of Massachusetts, protested that Filipinos should be left to govern themselves, whatever the results. But the majority felt otherwise. They predicted that an American pullout would quickly produce internal wars and anarchy. This they were sure would be followed just as quickly by the intervention of other foreign powers. Theodore Roosevelt hoped that Filipinos might be able to govern themselves at some future, undeter-

Combat in the Philippines was particularly grueling. Fought in jungle terrain against twin unseen enemies—the guerrilla insurgents and disease—the war produced over 7,000 American casualties.

mined date. But he warned that the "consent-of-the-governed doctrine must not be pushed to an extent that would restore savagery."

William Howard Taft, at the time a federal judge, later went to the Philippines as the first American governor. He expounded on the theory of Filipino inferiority. In 1902 the Senate committee investigating the war asked Taft whether Filipinos were in fact so ignorant that a few leaders could easily misguide them. Taft replied: "That is quite possible, and that is one of the chief reasons why the Filipino people are utterly unfit for self-government." Americans had to lead the way, Taft asserted, for the Filipinos lacked any knowledge of how to carry on a government. The United States could not remain "blind to their serious defects, many of which are due to the environment, social and political, which has been presented by their history of three hundred years."

General Robert P. Hughes spoke more bluntly. In referring to one of the Filipino ethnic groups, he testified: "These people do not know what independence means. They probably think it is something to eat. They have no more idea what it means than a shepherd dog."

The suspension of American offensive operations in the spring of 1899 gave Aguinaldo and his followers time to regroup—and make a key decision. The insurgents knew they could not defeat the rapidly growing United States forces in conventional warfare. From then on, Aguinaldo and his staff decided, Filipino rebels would engage in guerrilla tactics. In order to succeed, they would have to depend on their own countrymen's support, voluntary or forced, and on their ability to blend in with the civilian population.

Aguinaldo's tactical switch posed new and serious problems for the United States Army. When a later American general, Arthur MacArthur, resumed his northward advance in Luzon in October 1899, his men had trouble distinguishing friend from foe among the Filipinos. The guerrillas tried to wear down the enemy by ambushing American patrols and firing at night into towns occupied by United States troops. Along the trails between villages, Filipino rebels set booby traps—pits lined with sharpened bamboo spears and covered with foliage. General Hughes complained: "As to actual engagements, there were very few. It was very hard to get an engagement of any kind. You could get what we would call a little skirmish, and probably there would be ten or twelve killed."

Though Americans denied that the Filipino army had any legal standing, guerrilla prisoners were not automatically executed as rebels. Instead, a generous American amnesty policy for the insurgents allowed for a decent gap between the official United States position and the actual treatment of those Filipinos who wished to surrender.

Many insurgents did surrender and swear allegiance to the United States. Some even joined American troops to crush the rebels. Combat reports often mentioned the Macabebe soldiers. They were Filipinos who fought with and supported the United States throughout the war. But American officials in the Philippines rejected the idea of forming an all-Filipino regiment. "To put in command of a Filipino a thousand men with a thousand rifles would not be wise," warned Taft. Still, many Filipinos cooperated with the Americans, and, as in most wars, the majority of the population remained uninvolved. These facts bolstered the American argument that Aguinaldo and his forces actually hurt the Filipinos more than anyone else.

Filipinos who continued to resist and rejected the American offer of amnesty received rough treatment. Captured insurgent leaders were shipped to Guam, and "enlisted men" were imprisoned. For a short while, Americans even set up security camps for Filipino civilians. (This same tactic, when employed by Spain in Cuba, had enraged the American public.) In the insurrectionary province of Batangas, American officials ordered a ban on all trade, hoping that wealthy Filipinos who supported the insurgents would yield to the pressure.

In the field, United States soldiers routinely burned Filipino villages. Sergeant Leroy Hallock testified that he had participated in the burning of a village of over 3,000 people. He claimed that he had heard of other burnings, including a town of 10,000 inhabitants. Another enlisted man recalled: "If a column was marching along and was fired upon, it was the practice to burn the buildings in that neighborhood. That impressed the natives with the fact that they could not fire upon us with

War atrocities committed by Americans, such as the burning of the native district of Manila in 1899, caused divisions of popular sentiment at home. Mark Twain suggested bitterly that the field of stars on the flag be "replaced by a skull and crossbones."

impunity, although they did not often do very great damage." No specific orders had been issued authorizing such indiscriminate reprisals, but they continued.

The issue that stirred the most controversy during the Philippine war, both in the islands and in the United States, was the "water cure." This was a method of torturing prisoners by forcing them to swallow enormous quantities of water. The water cure apparently became the standard means of obtaining information from rebel prisoners and civilians suspected of aiding the enemy. Charles S. Riley, an enlisted man from Massachusetts, described repeated attempts to question the *presidente*, or mayor, of a Filipino village:

> One of the men of the Eighteenth Infantry went to his saddle and took a syringe from the saddlebag, and another man was sent for a can of water . . . holding about five gallons. Then a syringe was inserted, one end in the water and the other end in his mouth. The water was forced into his mouth from the can, through the syringe. The syringe did not seem to have the desired effect, and the [army] doctor ordered a second one, and a handful of salt was thrown into the water. The interpreter stood over him in the meantime asking for information. Finally he gave in and gave the information.

When reports of such atrocities began to leak out in the American press, officials disavowed them. But William Howard Taft added the final irony in this unsuccessful attempt by American civil and military officials to deny the facts, unpleasant but true, of widespread torture: "There never was a war conducted," insisted Taft, "whether against inferior races or not, in which there was more compassion and more restraint and more generosity than there have been in the Philippine Islands."

Early in 1900 the superior military strength of the United States forces began to make itself felt. In May, General Otis resigned rather

Filipino guerrillas were not highly regarded as soldiers by the American military. General Arthur MacArthur claimed that they "could not hit a stack of barns" with their guns. But it took 70,000 American troops three years to defeat them.

Frederick Funston reaped most of the acclaim for the capture of Aguinaldo, including a Medal of Honor. But, although the plan was his, it was the Tagals and the Macabebes who actually captured the Filipino rebel leader.

than work under the all-civilian Taft Commission, which had been sent to Manila to set up a civil government. Otis's replacement, General Arthur MacArthur, already on the scene, harried the Filipino guerrillas whenever and wherever he could find them.

But the biggest setback for the insurgents' cause came with the capture of Aguinaldo himself. During late 1900 and early 1901, Aguinaldo's whereabouts remained a mystery. Some American military men and journalists began circulating rumors of his death. MacArthur knew better. In February 1901, United States troops captured an insurgent soldier carrying dispatches from Aguinaldo to rebel officers in the field. The messages did not pinpoint the location of rebel headquarters, but they indicated that the captive knew where to find Aguinaldo. Interrogation began, and before long the courier talked: Aguinaldo could be found in the village of Palanan, in the mountains of Luzon near the northeast coast.

But how could the Americans get to Aguinaldo? Thirty-six-year-old Brigadier General Frederick Funston, head of a volunteer regiment from Kansas, had a plan. The intercepted messages called for the movement of small groups of rebel reinforcements toward Aguinaldo's headquarters. Funston decided to use eighty Macabebe scouts pretending to be rebel reinforcements. He and four other American officers would go along, supposedly as prisoners. One additional and crucial element remained: several Tagals loyal to the United States would be needed to pose as leaders of the expedition. Funston found three such men; the messenger who had been captured was to be their guide. General MacArthur gave his approval to the plan, but with misgivings. Instead of wishing Funston well, he remarked: "I fear I shall never see you again."

The march to Palanan proved more difficult than the capture itself. The expeditionary force landed by gunboat on the east coast of Luzon, about a hundred miles from its objective. In heavy rain, the men had to struggle for several days across rough terrain near the shoreline and then through dense jungle. It had been decided, for reasons Funston never made clear, that the Tagal officers and the Macabebes would enter the village about an hour before the Americans.

On March 23, 1901, the Macabebes arrived in the rebel camp. They were relieved to find only a handful of insurgent soldiers to greet them. The Tagal officers entered rebel headquarters to confer with Aguinaldo and his staff. As the conversation wore on, all but two of the insurgent officers drifted out of the room. An expedition officer leaned out of the window to give the Macabebes the signal to open fire. Aguinaldo, thinking that his own men were firing in the air to welcome the fresh troops, rushed to the window to tell them to stop wasting ammunition. At that point one of the Tagal officers seized Aguinaldo. The others opened fire on the insurgent guards. It was all over before Funston and his American companions arrived.

At the sound of the firing, Funston had rushed to the rebel headquarters. Aguinaldo now asked if the "capture" was some kind of joke.

When Funston identified himself, Aguinaldo's shoulders drooped in resignation and defeat. On March 28 the group returned to Manila. Aguinaldo was imprisoned in the governor's mansion. When General MacArthur arrived, ever skeptical, he asked Funston: "Where is Aguinaldo?" Funston was able to reply triumphantly: "Right in this house."

Aguinaldo had sworn many times that he would never be taken alive. For several weeks American officers pressured him to swear an oath of allegiance to the United States. On April 19 he agreed to take the oath. He promised to issue a proclamation calling on Filipinos to lay down their arms in order to avoid further bloodshed. Aguinaldo's declaration suddenly made him a hero in American eyes. The *New York Times*, which had once described Aguinaldo as an "enslaver" and a "criminal aggressor," now found him to be "honest and sincere," a "natural leader of men with considerable shrewdness and ability."

On July 4, 1901, Taft took over as civil governor of the Philippines. He left a revealing account of his reception in Manila: "The populace that we expected to welcome us was not there, and I cannot describe the coldness of the army officers and the army men who received us any better than by saying that it somewhat exceeded the coldness of the populace."

Still, the rebellion—the ill-fated and barely understood war of national liberation—continued. Its center shifted southward to the island of Mindanao. The inhabitants of the island were Moros. They were Moslems who opposed the American presence but had never accepted the authority of the Tagals in Manila. Fire fights and armed conflict broke out. One fire fight in northern Mindanao left ten Americans dead and forty wounded. Fighting between American troops and Moro rebels continued off and on for another twelve years.

In the meantime, the "unfriendly" island of Samar exploded. Company C of the regular Ninth United States Infantry was stationed on the island in the fishing village of Balangiga. Hundreds of Filipino workmen, supposedly loyal to the United States, fell on the Americans with

More than 20,000 Filipino insurgents died in the three-year conflict—and independence was not achieved.

knives, bolos (machetes), and bare hands. A few soldiers escaped in a boat to another island. They were the only survivors. The massacre at Balangiga would not be forgotten. For the next six months American troops called for revenge, in the same way that a previous generation of American soldiers had sought to avenge Custer's defeat at the Little Bighorn.

Major Littleton Waller of the Marines received the punitive assignment. The area commander, General Jacob ("Hell-Roaring Jake") Smith, told Waller that he wanted the Samar rebellion ended quickly. Smith ordered Waller to remove all Filipino civilians from the island's interior and place them in stockades. Those who resisted, especially those capable of bearing arms, were to be considered enemies and shot. Waller asked what the cutoff point was. Anyone more than ten years old, replied Smith. Waller and his men did as they were told.

The pacification of Batangas province followed the same script. Miguel Malvar, head of the revolutionary government there, had 5,000 men and was better organized than the rebels on Samar. The American general, J. Franklin Bell, an ambitious young man who only three years before had been a lieutenant, saw his chance and took it. He waged an intense campaign, herding thousands of civilians into security camps. In April 1902, after several months of dodging and fighting on the run, Malvar surrendered. The last sustained pocket of armed Filipino resistance had been eliminated.

The war between American troops and Filipino rebels had lasted more than three years. Countless Filipinos had lost their homes in the burning of towns and villages. Thousands of rebel soldiers had been killed or wounded in the fighting. The United States had not gained an easy victory. Almost as many Americans died in the Philippine conflict as in the war with Spain. And the rebellion had cost the United States $160 million, or eight times the "indemnity" paid to Spain for the islands.

On July 4, 1902, the United States government declared the Philippine insurrection officially over. President Roosevelt then sent a special message to the Army.

The President praised American soldiers for the rapid accomplishment of their mission, despite great hardships in more than 2,000 skirmishes and battles. Teddy Roosevelt was still mentally fighting Indians, for he went on to say: "Utilizing the lessons of the Indian wars [the army] relentlessly followed the guerrilla bands to their footholds in mountains and jungle and crushed them." With surprisingly few exceptions, the President maintained, American troops had been humane and kind to both prisoners and civilians. They had fought bravely against "a general system of guerrilla warfare conducted among a people speaking unknown tongues, from whom it was almost impossible to obtain the information necessary for successful pursuit or to guard against surprise and ambush." The army, declared Roosevelt, had added honor to the flag.

36
BECOMING A WORLD POWER

A. W.

By 1900 many Americans came to question the presence of American soldiers in the Philippines. Wasn't the war with Spain fought to liberate Cuba, an island ninety miles off the coast of Florida? Then why was the United States involved in places halfway around the globe? Whose interests were served by such overseas commitments? Answers to these questions lay tangled in the history of late nineteenth-century America and in the international power struggles of an imperialist age.

For most of the nineteenth century, Americans had been more than content to search for and use the wealth of their own country. America was their Garden of Eden. And although many of its products were sold overseas (much cotton went to Britain, for example), the United States had avoided foreign political ties. America had allied itself with a foreign power only once in its history — during the Revolutionary War, when it signed an alliance with France. Concerned with domestic problems and opportunities, Americans had concentrated on developing their own continent.

GAINING AN OVERSEAS EMPIRE

Two major factors helped to change this attitude and promote American interests overseas. First, domestic industry grew at an astounding rate dur- ing the second half of the nineteenth century. A massive and efficient transportation network was constructed across the American continent. Much of the country's agriculture was mechanized, and heavy industries were established. By 1900 the United States was the world's leading economic power, one that could play an influential role beyond its own territorial borders.

Second, the major nations of Europe had been scrambling for empire in Asia and Africa. They were carving up these two continents into colonial dependencies, much as Spain had done three centuries earlier in the New World. As the nineteenth century ended, Americans entered into the same race. American power was to expand not only into the Caribbean and the rest of Latin America but into the Far East as well.

Arguments for Empire Basically, the United States shunned overseas political involvement. But many Americans argued for commercial expansion during the late nineteenth century. Why shouldn't the United States seek additional markets for its agricultural products and manufactured goods? The periodic recessions and depressions in the decades following the Civil War reinforced the argument for commercial expansion. Many business leaders had begun to feel that domestic markets were saturated. The new industrial complex seemed to be producing more goods than Americans could buy. Substantial cuts in production were out of the question. They would only put large numbers of American workers and farmers out of work. In turn, unemployment might cause political unrest and social instability. Perhaps the surplus from American factories and farms could be channeled into enlarged and more profitable markets overseas.

Other expansionists argued for American imperialism on strategic grounds. The chief spokesman for this point of view was Alfred T. Mahan, a naval officer and instructor at the Naval War College. In 1890 Mahan advanced his theory in a series of lectures, which he later published as *The Influence of Sea Power on World History.* Mahan asserted that, through the ages, naval power had been primarily responsible for national or imperial power. He also held that no country

In this illustration Uncle Sam looks longingly over the sea and says, "The world is my market; my customers are all mankind." Industrial and agricultural growth encouraged the late nineteenth-century belief in the necessity of overseas outlets to absorb American surpluses.

could maintain commercial expansion without a strong navy and overseas ports (bases, for example, such as the Philippines and other Pacific islands).

Mahan's ideas quickly gained favor with imperialists in every major European country. More important, they also influenced several American foreign policy makers at the turn of the century. Chief among the American advocates of a strong navy were Roosevelt, McKinley's assistant secretary of the navy, and John Hay, who served as secretary of state under McKinley and later under Roosevelt himself.

Expansionism also had its defenders outside the business and military communities. Many Americans prided themselves on the myth of Anglo-Saxon racial superiority and the dominance of

U.S. FOREIGN TRADE, 1870 - 1910

Western culture. For both selfish and humanitarian reasons, they argued that the United States had a moral duty to uplift and enlighten its less civilized neighbors. The culture and religion of the Anglo-Saxons should be exported to "heathen" lands for everyone's good. This spirit was captured in 1899 by the British poet of imperialism, Rudyard Kipling. His "White Man's Burden" was written and first published in the United States. It reflected the mood of many Americans who were then debating the virtues of keeping the Philippines.

Current theories of evolution seemed to support the claims of Anglo-Saxonists. In his book *Origin of Species* (1859) Charles Darwin argued that through the process of natural selection only the "fittest" would survive. Individual animal species might adapt and prosper while others declined and perhaps disappeared. So-called social Darwinists extended these generalizations to the domains of the social scientist, businessman, and politician. That is, individual nations and empires might attain greatness at the expense of their less fit neighbors. These ideas were powerful "scientific" supports for the missionary zeal of the expansionists.

Extending the Monroe Doctrine Although the United States moved cautiously and with uncertainty at first, it soon began to behave like a world power. Its debut on the world scene as a leading economic power provoked a great deal of controversy. But as the nineteenth century drew to a close, the prospect of increasing commercial activity abroad became highly attractive to American businessmen and politicians alike.

Even Grover Cleveland, who opposed acquiring new territories, supported commercial expansion. The severe depression that began during his second administration (1893–1897) gave the President added reason to seek foreign markets. Commercial expansion might cure some of America's economic ills. It might help the nation start its slow climb back to prosperity. But a drastic change would be needed in the pattern of America's overseas trading. Historically, farm products—not manufactured goods—had been the country's main export and source of foreign ex-

change. American business leaders began arguing for expanding the sale of industrial goods to non-industrialized countries such as China, the Philippines, and Latin American nations.

As early as 1889, Benjamin Harrison's secretary of state, James G. Blaine, had organized the first Pan American Congress, to promote American commerce in the Western Hemisphere and increase United States influence in Latin American affairs. During the 1890s a significant number of American businessmen responded to this opportunity by investing in Latin America. The United States thus began the process of replacing Britain as Latin America's major foreign investor. Both Harrison and Cleveland supported these efforts.

Cleveland's Latin American policy received a major test in 1895 when a crisis arose between Britain and Venezuela. The two nations disagreed over the boundary line between Venezuela and British Guiana. When the British threatened to use force against Venezuela, some Americans demanded that President Cleveland step in and apply the Monroe Doctrine to curb the European power. Stung by accusations of cowardice and beset by domestic problems, Cleveland decided to force a confrontation. He insisted that Britain submit to arbitration of the boundary dispute. Sensing that Cleveland was not bluffing, the British agreed.

The President's actions led to an important extension of the Monroe Doctrine: European powers could no longer resolve conflicts in the Western Hemisphere by military means. In a note to the British government, Secretary of State Richard Olney declared that the United States considered itself "practically sovereign" in this hemisphere. The will of the United States, Olney boasted, "is law." American industrial power and growing military and naval power made these phrases more than empty words.

The Problem of Cuba Another incidence of American expansionism concerned Cuba, the island ninety miles south of Florida. Americans have always been interested in Cuba. From the early decades of the republic, American politicians eyed the island with interest and greed. By the beginning of the nineteenth century, Spain had lost most of its overseas empire. The remnants of that empire—Cuba, Puerto Rico, and the Philippines—became all the more valuable to the Spanish as their power waned. During the second half of the nineteenth century, substantial American trade developed with the Spanish islands of the Caribbean. The situation appeared stable. But periodically groups of Americans called for absorbing Cuba, either by purchase or by force.

Cubans resented Spanish rule, which was repressive and corrupt. They had revolted unsuccessfully in the 1860s. By the 1890s they had had enough. At that time, the economic crisis in the United States had reduced the American sugar trade with Cuba. The Spanish island colony suffered sharply from the effects of the American depression. In 1895 a Cuban revolutionary movement called Cuba Libre ("Free Cuba") moved for independence. The Cuban rebels embarked on a new war of national liberation, a war similar to the revolution then under way against Spanish rule in the Philippines.

Neither Cuba Libre nor the Katipunan in the Philippines had sufficient strength to push out the Spanish without outside help. But Cuban rebels engaged in guerrilla warfare to wear down the Spanish soldiers. The Cubans also burned sugar plantations and anything else of value, hoping to drive out Spanish landowners. In response, Spanish officials set up *reconcentrados*, or "detention camps," for civilians suspected of helping the rebels. Thousands of Cubans died in the camps because of poor food, inadequate sanitation, and lack of medical attention.

The United States had been sympathetic but strictly neutral during the earlier Cuban revolution. But in the 1890s Americans gave increasing support to the Cuban rebels. A variety of factors led Americans toward direct intervention in Cuba. First, Americans had little sympathy for Spain and its culture. Many still believed in the "black legend."[1] Second, Spanish troops were committing atrocities. (Little did most Americans think that their own soldiers would shortly be acting in a similar manner to suppress the Filipino revolt.) Third, many American businessmen had investments in Cuba, though these investments were small. Finally, an increasing determination among Americans to become the dominant Caribbean power made events in Cuba of vital concern to Washington.

The Cuban question soon became a leading issue in United States politics. During the 1896 presidential election year, Congress passed a resolution calling for recognition of the belligerent status of the Cuban rebels. President Cleveland, a Democrat who opposed territorial expansion, rejected the resolution. Cleveland's successor in the White House, Republican William McKinley, also opposed intervention in Cuba. McKinley was apparently less eager for expansion than most other members of his party. The Republican platform of 1896 was openly proexpansionist and favored involvement in the Caribbean. McKinley remained firm.

But events in Cuba and America's desire to impose its will in the Caribbean won over McKinley's promises. "Jingoism"—boastful patriotism—soon took hold of the nation. Two sensationalist New York City papers, William Randolph Hearst's *Journal* and Joseph Pulitzer's *World*, helped to stir up the interventionist frenzy. Both Hearst and Pulitzer ran stories, some of them deliberate lies, attacking Spanish cruelty in Cuba and praising the rebels. The stories spread to other newspapers across the country. By early 1898 it had become clear that Spain could not put down the Cuban rebellion. Nor would the United States allow the stalemate to continue much longer.

On the night of February 15, 1898, an explosion aboard the U.S.S. *Maine* in Havana harbor settled the issue of United States intervention. The battleship had been sent to Cuba to demonstrate American concern for the Cuban situation. The explosion killed 260 American sailors. Spain, which had the most to lose from American intervention in Cuba, hastily sent notes of regret to Washington. The cause of the explosion was never determined. But public opinion in the United States placed the blame squarely on the Spanish. "Remember the *Maine*" became the slogan of

---

[1] This was the English notion—dating back to the days of Queen Elizabeth and the defeat of the Spanish Armada—that the Spanish were a particularly cruel and treacherous people.

WALTER REED

The year 1900 had been called the year of yellow fever in Cuba. The Spanish-American War had brought thousands of American troops there. Now, with the war over, hundreds of men lay near death from the disease in Columbia Barracks in Havana. Doctors and nurses worked untiringly to try to save the victims, frustrated by lack of knowledge as to what caused the disease and how it was transmitted. Among them was a dedicated army doctor, Major Walter Reed.

On his return from Cuba, Reed strode into the office of the surgeon general of the United States Army in Washington, D.C., and requested that he be sent back to Cuba with the equipment and personnel needed to conduct a full study of the dangerous, often fatal disease known as yellow fever.

Walter Reed, a practicing doctor and a research scientist, was peculiarly suited to the task he sought. Born 1851 in Farmville, Virginia, he showed as a boy the love of knowledge, force of character, self-control, and sense of honor that marked his whole life. At sixteen he entered the University of Virginia by special permission. In nine months he graduated, third in his class. He then went to Bellevue Hospital Medical College in New York and received the degree of M.D. a year later.

After hospital experience and work as an inspector of the Board of Health in Brooklyn, Reed decided to enter the army as a surgeon in 1874. He wanted a future that would be secure, so that he could carry on scientific research. The examinations for a commission in the Army Medical Corps were notoriously difficult, but he passed them brilliantly in 1875.

He was commissioned in February 1875, married on April 25, 1876, and left immediately for his station in Arizona. Thus began several years of garrison duty at army posts in the West. In 1890 he was assigned to duty in Baltimore and this gave him the opportunity for special studies in bacteriology at Johns Hopkins University. Up to the time he began his investigations into yellow fever, his most important work had been the study of typhoid fever in army camps during the Spanish-American War. One of the conclusions of this study was that the common house fly is a typhoid carrier.

Now he urgently wanted to discover how yellow fever was transmitted. The theory then accepted was that a person caught the disease upon coming into contact with the clothing or bedding of an infected person. Dr. Reed did not agree. Several clues had been uncovered leading to the possibility that a certain kind of mosquito carried the disease and infected people with its bite.

Soon his orders came through. He was to return to Cuba to organize and direct the work of three doctors. Reed and his group set up the experimental situation. In one building, volunteers slept on bedding that had been in contact with yellow fever victims. In another, volunteers lived in uncontaminated surroundings but were exposed to the suspected mosquitoes. Those bitten by the mosquitoes did contract yellow fever. The culprit was proved to be a mosquito of the species *Aedes aegypti.*

Armed with the knowledge that the mosquito was the culprit, United States sanitary engineers launched on the Herculean task of cleaning up the filth in and around Havana in which the mosquitoes bred. They were so successful that by 1902 there was not one case of yellow fever in Cuba. It was also eradicated from the United States, where epidemics had struck periodically on the eastern seaboard. And when work began on the Panama Canal, the mosquito-control measures taken there removed the workers from the peril of yellow fever.

American interventionists. The United States government began to pressure Spain to grant Cuba independence. But Madrid would not accept the loss of its Cuban colony.

On April 11, 1898, McKinley sent a message to Congress, asking for authority to use American troops in Cuba. The President described Americans as "a Christian, peace-loving people" who still hoped to achieve a just solution through diplomacy rather than war. But Spain would not modify its position, even with the certainty of American armed intervention. By late April the two nations were at war.

War with Spain The Spanish-American War of 1898 was over within a few months. American forces dominated Spanish military and naval power. Spanish soldiers and sailors fought brave-

---

Military action in the Spanish-American War of 1898 occurred largely on two fronts, the Philippines and Cuba, although a brief and almost bloodless American invasion of Puerto Rico led to rapid surrender of the island's Spanish garrison. Hostilities commenced in the Pacific. The United States Asiatic Squadron under Commodore George Dewey sailed from Hong Kong in late April to attack the Spanish Philippines. On May 1 Dewey destroyed the Spanish naval force in Manila Bay with no loss of American lives.

In the Caribbean theater, the Spanish fleet under Admiral Pascual Cervera arrived in Santiago Harbor in May and was blockaded there by an American naval squadron. The blockade was reinforced June 1 under the command of Rear Admiral William T. Sampson. In late June, United States troops under General William R. Shafter landed in Cuba at Daiquiri and Siboney and marched on Santiago. This force included the Rough

Riders, a volunteer cavalry regiment under Colonel Leonard Wood and Lieutenant Colonel Theodore Roosevelt. On July 1, the troops captured the heights north and east of Santiago in the battles of El Caney and San Juan Hill. They then began an artillery bombardment of Santiago.

On July 3, Admiral Cervera attempted to run the United States blockade and escape from Santiago harbor. But Sampson's force destroyed the entire Spanish fleet in a four-hour battle along the coast. The Spanish garrison of Santiago soon surrendered (July 17). Hostilities were ended in the Caribbean by July 25.

In the Pacific Dewey's naval squadron was reinforced in July by the arrival of American troops under General Wesley Merritt. On August 13, United States troops and Filipino guerrillas occupied the city of Manila.

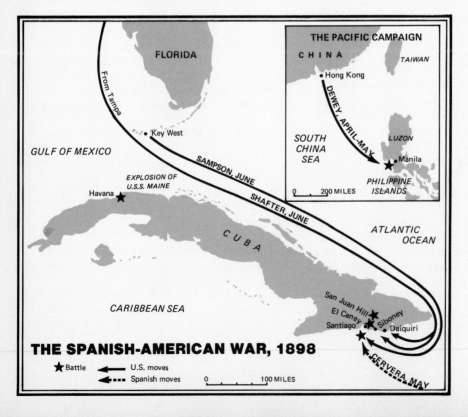

THE SPANISH-AMERICAN WAR, 1898

★ Battle ← U.S. moves ◄--- Spanish moves   0 ___ 100 MILES

ly, but they were hopelessly ill-equipped for war. Spain won no battles and suffered heavy losses. American casualties were light. Many more soldiers died from disease than from combat.

When the fighting ended in the summer of 1898, United States forces had won Cuba and Puerto Rico. In the Philippines, Dewey's squadron held Manila Bay while awaiting the arrival of American troops. Spanish officials reluctantly agreed to meet with American negotiators to hammer out a treaty that would end Spain's status as an imperial power.

During the short struggle, American expansionists achieved their longstanding wish of annexing Hawaii. In 1893 a revolutionary movement backed by American businessmen successfully overthrew the Hawaiian monarchy and sought annexation to the United States. But, like Texas between 1836 and 1845, Hawaii had to sit out a period of uneasy independence—five years—until United States politics entered into an expansionist phase. By mid-1898 annexationist forces had gained a majority in the House and the Senate. Congress passed a joint resolution declaring Hawaii a territory of the United States.

When Spanish and American negotiators met in Paris to work out the terms of a peace, the fate of the Philippines had not yet been established. But all signs pointed to a continued American presence on the islands. President McKinley's stance of indecision fooled few people—least of all Emilio Aguinaldo and other Filipino leaders. The President had clearly been drawn into the expansionist camp. For several months McKinley played a waiting game while expansionist forces in the Senate gathered support for a Spanish-American treaty.

In the end, McKinley demanded what he had perhaps had in mind all along. Determined to "educate the Filipinos, and uplift and civilize and Christianize them," McKinley asked Spain to give up all of the Philippines. The Spanish had to agree. The Treaty of Paris was signed in December 1898. The United States gained control of

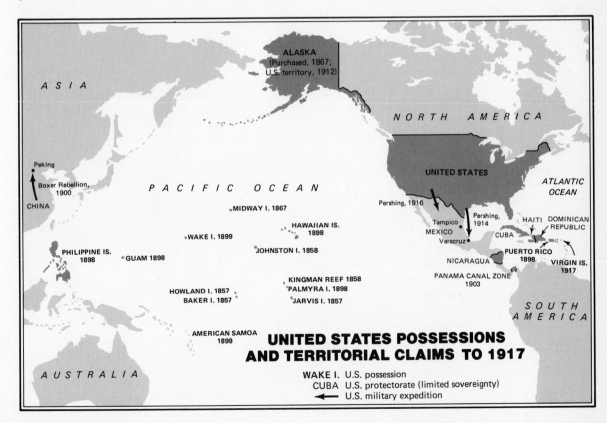

ASIA

PACIFIC OCEAN

ALASKA
(Purchased, 1867;
U.S. territory, 1912)

NORTH AMERICA

UNITED STATES

ATLANTIC OCEAN

Peking
Boxer Rebellion, 1900
CHINA

Pershing, 1916

MIDWAY I. 1867

Pershing, 1914

HAITI DOMINICAN REPUBLIC

Tampico
MEXICO
Veracruz

CUBA

HAWAIIAN IS. 1898

WAKE I. 1899

JOHNSTON I. 1858

PUERTO RICO 1898

PHILIPPINE IS. 1898

GUAM 1898

NICARAGUA

VIRGIN IS. 1917

KINGMAN REEF 1858

PANAMA CANAL ZONE 1903

PALMYRA I. 1898

HOWLAND I. 1857

JARVIS I. 1857

BAKER I. 1857

SOUTH AMERICA

AMERICAN SAMOA 1899

UNITED STATES POSSESSIONS AND TERRITORIAL CLAIMS TO 1917

AUSTRALIA

WAKE I. U.S. possession
CUBA U.S. protectorate (limited sovereignty)
← U.S. military expedition

Cuba, the Philippine Islands, Guam, and Puerto Rico.

Most Americans had supported the war with Spain. But the Treaty of Paris, which proposed immediate acquisition of an American overseas empire, ran into stiff opposition. Many Americans feared that imperialism would tarnish American democracy at home by imposing arbitrary rule abroad upon alien peoples who were, in addition, nonwhite. (Racism, in short, played an important role in the anti-imperialist movement at the time.) Others objected to imperialism on moral grounds. Nations or cultures, they argued, should not be taken over by larger nations merely because they were too weak to resist. An anti-imperialist movement organized to fight the peace treaty. In the Senate many Democrats and a minority of Republicans opposed imperialism. William Jennings Bryan, the Democratic presidential candidate of 1896, led the antitreaty forces.

But at the last minute Bryan changed his course. The day before the vote on the treaty, fighting broke out between American troops and Filipino rebels. Americans regarded the uprising as a show of ingratitude on the part of the Filipinos. Bryan announced that the challenge had to be met firmly. He threw his support to the treaty, though he declared that he would continue to oppose imperialism. The Senate ratified the Treaty of Paris in February 1899. Bryan, who again opposed McKinley in the election of 1900, attempted to make imperialism the central issue of the campaign. Bryan and the Democrats were defeated overwhelmingly. The American people had voted for empire.

The Search for Asian Markets   Early in the nineteenth century a few American businessmen had entered into a prosperous trade with China. But, even with the "opening" of Japan in the 1850s, the volume of United States trade in Asia never reached the proportions anticipated by American business leaders. By the end of the century, overproduction in America's factories generated new and powerful pressures for foreign trade. The lure of the China market made itself felt again.

But participation in the China market could not be accomplished without political involve-ment in Asia. The European powers had already carved up China into "economic spheres of influence."[2] American businessmen believed they could compete successfully in China if they were given a fair opportunity. In September 1899, Secretary of State John Hay sent a series of diplomatic notes to Japan and the major European powers. In the notes he asked them to support a new trade policy in China. This policy became known as the Open Door. Hay recognized the existence of foreign spheres of influence in China, but he asked the European nations to grant other countries free-

---

[2]A nation often established with other nations a world area where it would hold a dominant economic position. Once other countries agreed to accept this arrangement, the area in question would be free from the competition of other nations.

This Chinese Boxer, a member of the society whose official title was the Fist of Righteous Harmony, believed that his country's survival depended upon expulsion of foreign powers threatening to divide China for economic profit. The Boxer Rebellion nearly led to the extinction of China as a national entity.

trade privileges within these spheres—thus keeping the Chinese door open to all who wanted to
trade there. Hay also called on the European
powers to guarantee Chinese "territorial integrity"—that is, to avoid outright political partition of
the country. The European nations did not formally reject Hay's proposals, though some grumbled
about American interference. Hay announced
boldly that the Open Door was accepted by all,
although he was too sanguine in this judgment.

 While America was seeking support for its
Open Door policies, a group of Chinese nationalists, called Boxers, organized to drive foreigners
from their country. In 1900 they began killing foreign missionaries and diplomats. Survivors fled to
Peking and the temporary safety of the British le-
gation. There, they withstood a two-month siege
until troops from their own countries relieved
them. The United States participated by rushing
in troops from bases in the Philippine Islands.
The Boxer Rebellion was ended. Within a few
months peace—and imperialism—were reestab-
lished. In July, Hay issued a second series of diplomatic notes. In them he asked the victorious
European powers to preserve Chinese territorial
integrity. Hay reaffirmed America's desire to
"safeguard for the world the principle of equal
and impartial trade with all parts of the Chinese
Empire." Not wishing to risk a major war, the
imperialist powers agreed not to divide up China.
They accepted instead a sum of money from the
Chinese in payment for their losses.

 In comparison with other powers, the
United States had acted as a friend and protector
of China. But did the Open Door represent an
American willingness to guarantee Chinese territorial integrity? The United States had not signed
a formal agreement with China, or with any other
foreign nation, to enact its Open Door policy. Hay
quickly admitted that his country would not go to
war to enforce the Open Door—not in 1900 at any
rate. European imperialistic powers had battled to
a draw in China with the creation of economic
spheres of influence. Hay's Open Door declarations filled the partial vacuum created by this stalemate. The Open Door would work to America's
advantage only so long as no other major power
embarked on an all-out push to dominate China.

INTERVENTION IN LATIN AMERICA

The growth of United States industrial and military power, combined with America's interest in
the Caribbean, meant that Britain's position as the
leading Caribbean power would not last long. In
1895, during the first Venezuelan crisis, the
Cleveland administration had asserted America's
new role in the Western Hemisphere. The events
of the next decade confirmed this role.

Building a Canal to the Pacific A fifty-year-old
treaty between Britain and the United States became an early casualty of America's new attitude
of expansion. The 1850 treaty called for participation by both nations in the construction of any
canal across Central America. In February 1900,
Secretary Hay negotiated another accord with the
British ambassador, Lord Pauncefote. Under the
Hay-Pauncefote Treaty, Britain granted the United
States exclusive rights to build a canal. But the
American government was prohibited from fortify-

Roosevelt's famous boast that "I took the canal zone and
let Congress debate" is caricatured here. Roosevelt is
seen heaving his shovelful of Panamanian soil on
Bogota, capital of Colombia, the country from which
Panama was detached.

ing it. This compromise did not satisfy the United States Senate. The treaty was quickly rejected. Hay returned to the negotiating table, pulled a few teeth from the reluctant British lion, and produced a second agreement. The revised treaty placed no limitations on military fortification of the canal. The United States had only to promise that during peacetime all nations could use the canal on equal terms.

Americans next turned their attention to the question of where the Central American canal should be built. The shortest route was across the Isthmus of Panama, a province owned by Colombia. The Colombian government had sold the rights to the Panama site to a French company, headed by Ferdinand DeLesseps (builder of Egypt's Suez Canal). After several unsuccessful attempts to build a canal, the French offered to sell their rights for $109 million. Another proposed site, in Nicaragua, was a much longer route. But it was less expensive and free of foreign entanglements.

President Roosevelt and Congress argued the relative merits of both routes and initially favored the Nicaraguan site. Then, early in 1902, the French company lowered the price for sale of its rights to $40 million. Roosevelt quickly changed his mind in favor of the Panama site. Permission also had to be obtained from Colombia. In January 1903, Secretary Hay signed a treaty with Colombia agreeing to pay $10 million and an annual rent of $250,000 for a one-hundred-year lease on a canal zone in Panama.

But the Colombian senate, in a burst of patriotic pride and financial self-interest, rejected the canal treaty. President Roosevelt complained about the "bandits" of Colombia and their insistence on national honor. Roosevelt considered intervening in Panama under the terms of an 1846 treaty with Colombia. This granted the United States the right to maintain "free transit" across the isthmus. But United States troops were then busy fighting in the Philippines. Besides, the 1846 treaty required the agreement of Colombian authorities for the use of force in Panama.

In November 1903 a revolt in Panama settled the canal question. The revolt was organized by Philippe Bunau-Varilla, an agent of the French canal company. The Panamanian rebels received immediate United States aid. American ships were sent in to prevent Colombian forces from landing on the isthmus. Within a few days the new Panamanian government declared independence. Bunau-Varilla was appointed its chief representative to the United States. Bunau-Varilla and Secretary Hay quickly came to an agreement on an American-operated canal. Under the treaty the United States granted diplomatic recognition to Panama and obtained a perpetual lease on a canal zone.

Roosevelt's "big stick" diplomacy in Panama received sharp criticism from some Democrats in Congress. But the majority of Americans approved of the deeds and the bluster of their President. Some years later Roosevelt acknowledged with few apologies: "I took the canal zone and let Congress debate, and while the debate goes on, the canal does also."

In 1914 the Panama Canal opened to merchant shipping. The canal was acclaimed as a marvel of American engineering. It also put the finishing touch on a program for United States domination of the Caribbean and economic penetration of Latin America.

Policing the Caribbean While negotiations were being carried on in Panama, a second international crisis erupted in Venezuela. The dispute involved an attempt by European powers to collect debts owed their citizens by Venezuela. In December 1902, Britain, Germany, and Italy sent warships to blockade the Venezuelan port of La Guaira. An international court decided that the three nations that had blockaded Venezuela should be given priority in collecting their debts.

Roosevelt contested this decision. America could not permit European powers to use force to settle disputes in the Western Hemisphere. When a similar financial crisis arose in 1905 in the Dominican Republic, another Caribbean country, Roosevelt moved quickly to avoid European intervention. American officials took over the government and the financial affairs of the Dominicans.

In 1904 Roosevelt announced to Congress that the United States would not tolerate "chronic wrongdoing" by any Latin American country. If political or economic developments in Latin America invited the danger of European intervention, the United States could intervene first. The President's message, which became known as the Roosevelt Corollary to the Monroe Doctrine, asserted the role of the United States as an "international police power" in the Caribbean. The statement was actually a broad departure from the earlier doctrine.

Elsewhere in the world, Roosevelt also tried to project an American presence in global affairs in a variety of ways: by mediating (at Portsmouth, New Hampshire) an end to the Russo-Japanese War; by participating along with European heads of state in the Algeciras Conference of 1906 called to negotiate conflicting Great Power claims in Morocco; by sending the American fleet ("the Great White Fleet") on a "goodwill" tour of the world that had the effect of demonstrating America's growing naval might; and by pressing Congress for modernization of the armed forces.

Dollar Diplomacy   Theodore Roosevelt's successor, William Howard Taft, pursued Roosevelt's policies in Latin America. He favored economic penetration of foreign nations, a policy that became known as dollar diplomacy. Taft urged American capitalists to invest millions of dollars in overseas ventures, especially in the Caribbean. Such investments, he said, would bring Wall Street handsome profits. More important, they would serve the interests of American security. Also, American guardianship of the Western Hemisphere would benefit the people of Latin America. It would ensure them political stability and economic growth.

Nicaragua mounted the most serious challenge to the new American policy. Nicaraguan President José Zelaya, a strong opponent of the United States, tried to avoid the snares of dollar diplomacy. In 1909 he canceled special economic privileges granted to an American mining company. Zelaya's downfall came quickly. A revolutionary movement, supported by American businessmen, overthrew the Nicaraguan president. The United States granted diplomatic recognition to the new regime, took over the government's finances, and sent in the Marines to protect American interests. The pattern for implementing dollar diplomacy had been clearly established.

Idealism Versus Intervention in Mexico   In 1913 Woodrow Wilson, a Democrat, moved into the White House. In his campaign Wilson had promised a more liberal internationalism. He wanted a new foreign policy to curb the growing imperialist impulse. Wilson's choice for secretary of state, the anti-imperialist William Jennings Bryan, gave some indication that Republican policies would be modified or abandoned. Wilson stated that his aim in Latin America was to support "the orderly processes of just government based upon law, and not upon arbitrary or irregular force, and to cultivate the friendship of our sister republics of Central and South America."

But idealistic aims proved no match for big-power politics. As President, Wilson used military force in Latin America even more than his Republican predecessors. Seeking to bring peace and "constitutional liberty" to the unstable governments of Latin America, he sent troops into the Caribbean to put down a rebellion in Haiti. A year later, in 1916, the President ordered United States Marines into the Dominican Republic. There a military government was established under the Department of the Navy. Troops remained in both countries throughout Wilson's administration.

Wilson played his strongest and most controversial role as a moralist when he intervened in the Mexican revolution that had begun in 1910. The President at first refused to recognize the government of General Victoriano Huerta, who had risen to power in 1913. An unsavory politician, Huerta had ordered the murder of his predecessor, Francisco Madero, Mexico's first freely elected president in decades. Wilson wanted Huerta to resign and permit free elections in Mexico. Though such goals might have been welcomed by the Mexican people, they could hardly be imposed from outside by persuasion alone.

Huerta refused to budge from the presidential palace in Mexico City. But Wilson remained determined to "teach the South American republics to elect good men." Early in 1914 the President allowed ships to supply arms to Huerta's foes. In April, Huerta's forces arrested a group of American sailors who had landed at the port of Tampico. Washington demanded formal apologies. Huerta agreed but only on the condition that the United States support his government. Wilson and Bryan refused. When the President learned that an arms shipment from Germany—intended for Huerta's forces—was nearing the Mexican port of Veracruz, he decided to act.

In the meantime, Congress had granted Wilson permission to use armed force against Huerta. A message went out to the United States naval commander in the Caribbean: "Take Veracruz at once." American forces quickly seized Veracruz. Mexican opposition rose within a few days. Fighting broke out, and both sides suffered heavy casualties. Wilson, who had not anticipated bloodshed, found himself in an embarrassing position. Americans protested the involvement—and the death of United States soldiers. Withdrawal of troops had to be arranged by a mediating commission of three South American countries.

Wilson's problems regarding Mexico were not over, however, Huerta was overthrown in July 1914 by the Constitutionalist forces of Venustiano Carranza. As the new president tried to consolidate power, civil war again broke out in Mexico. In November 1915 Wilson gave unofficial support to Carranza's government. This move angered other pretenders to the Mexican presidency, particularly "Pancho" Villa. Operating in northern Mexico, Villa decided to teach the "gringos" a lesson. Early in 1916, Villa's forces stopped a train and killed sixteen American engineering students. Villa then crossed the border to raid the New Mexico town of Columbus, an act of revenge that cost seventeen American lives. The calculating and cold-blooded Villa hoped to lead America into military intervention in Mexico. Then, as the leading opponent of the United States, he would gain support from those people who supported Carranza.

Villa guessed correctly about United States intervention. But he misjudged its political consequences. Americans were enraged by Villa's actions. General John J. Pershing—soon to gain fame and glory as commander of the United States Army in France—led a "punitive" expedition

General John J. Pershing and his hastily mobilized American troops invaded Mexico in 1916 in pursuit of "Pancho" Villa. The mission was a failure and may even have convinced Germany of America's military unpreparedness.

deep into Mexico. Villa could not be found. Instead, American troops fought a bloody skirmish with Carranza forces. The battle was unwanted by both sides. The incident threatened another Veracruz. But anti-interventionists in Congress won out over those who wanted war. Early in 1917 Pershing's forces were withdrawn from Mexico. For most Americans it had become clear that Wilson's Mexican policy meant continuous trouble. By this time, too, the American people had become far more concerned with developments in Europe, where a devastating war had been raging since 1914.

THE UNITED STATES AND WORLD WAR I

Europe had enjoyed a period of relative peace during the century after Napoleon's defeat in

1815. International rivalries did not die down, and many short but limited wars broke out. Yet Europeans managed to avoid a general war. European leaders relied on the balance of power to maintain peace and political stability. But in 1914 the assassination of Archduke Franz Ferdinand, heir to the Austro-Hungarian throne, set off a chain reaction that resulted in World War I. Two powerful blocs emerged quickly once the war began: the Central powers (Germany, Austria-Hungary, and Turkey) and the Allies (Britain, France, Italy, and Russia).

The United States tried to stay out of the war. Whatever their personal opinions or sympathies, most Americans preferred neutrality. In 1914 Wilson issued a proclamation calling on all Americans to remain impartial "in thought as well as in action." But over the next three years a combination of factors edged the United States closer and closer to the side of the Allies and involvement in the European war.

The Road to War European powers violated America's rights as a neutral nation. American shippers tried to continue, and even expand, commerce with both sides. As in the case of the Napoleonic Wars a century before, American interests quickly clashed with those of Britain, the world's leading sea power. The British declared the North Sea a military zone. Before a neutral ship could pass through British waters, it had to enter a British port. There the ship's cargo was examined for war materials. British escorts would then lead the neutral ship through minefields to safety. Many Americans protested, and Wilson publicly condemned the British practice. But the United States clearly was not going to make the

EUROPE AT THE START OF WORLD WAR 1

Allies
Central Powers
Neutrals

issue a cause for war. No American lives were lost as a result of the British regulations. No American seamen were impressed into the British navy, as in the War of 1812.

The Germans knew that their navy was no match for British sea power. For the most part, German battleships and cruisers remained at anchor in home ports. Instead, the Germans turned to the submarine as a means of crippling their enemies. The British blockade of Continental Europe, launched soon after the war, threatened the German people with starvation. Germany fought back by declaring all-out submarine warfare. The Germans announced that any belligerent ships found in the waters surrounding the British Isles would be torpedoed without warning. Loss of life in such cases usually ran high.

Wilson denounced the German declaration as a violation of American neutral rights. Many Americans condemned submarine warfare as immoral. In the spring of 1915 the British passenger liner *Lusitania* was torpedoed by a German submarine off the Irish coast. Over 1,000 people died, including 128 Americans. Germany refused to accept responsibility for the incident or pay indemnities for American losses. The Germans pointed out that Americans had been publicly warned not to sail on British ships. Besides, the *Lusitania* carried arms as well as passengers. But Wilson drafted a strongly worded note to the Germans insisting that they end their surprise attacks. Secretary of State Bryan resigned rather than sign the message, which he believed was an ultimatum to Germany. When another British ship was torpedoed a few months later, Wilson threatened to cut off diplomatic relations with Germany. The Germans, fearful of drawing the United States into the war, gave in to Wilson's demands: German submarine commanders would no longer fire on British passenger liners without warning.

Economic factors also contributed to American intervention on the side of the Allies. The United States had always traded more with Britain than with Continental Europe. The onset of world war, combined with British domination of the seas, ensured an expanded trade with Britain and its allies. Americans might have to endure annoying British regulations, but at least most American ships could get through to Britain. Between 1914 and 1916 Allied purchases in America quadrupled. It soon became apparent that Britain and France would need loans in order to continue trading. Wall Street stood ready. Anti-interventionists, led by Secretary of State Bryan, argued that such loans were contraband and would inevitably drag the United States into the war. Again Wilson proclaimed strict neutrality. He did not move to prohibit credit to the Allies, however. The loans were, after all, big business, and the United States economy was booming.

Moreover, America was closely tied to Britain, both culturally and politically. Since the end of the nineteenth century, relations between Britain and the United States had improved dramatically, though the two nations had not entered into a formal alliance. Most Americans sympathized with Britain and its allies. German Americans, as well as Irish Americans who opposed Britain's policies in Ireland, were notable exceptions. One of the strongest supporters of Britain was Wilson himself. The President admired British culture and the parliamentary form of government. In contrast, Germany's image in America had suffered a complete change during recent decades. Americans had once viewed Germany as a country of poets and philosophers; they came to see it as a stark and frightening nation of militarists.

Within the context of these three factors—neutral rights, economic interdependence, and cultural ties—Wilson tried to maintain a course of neutrality. By 1916 the war had reached a stalemate. Neither side seemed capable of gathering enough strength to defeat the other. Hundreds of thousands of soldiers died in a series of brutal, inconclusive battles. Wilson attempted to use American prestige and the threat of use of American power to negotiate a European peace. His trusted adviser, Colonel Edward M. House, crossed the Atlantic several times to confer with foreign ministers and heads of state. European statesmen listened to House—America was too powerful to ignore—but they did not heed his message. They had fought too long and suffered too many losses to accept Wilson's "peace without victory." The British and French skillfully played along with Wilson and House, banking ultimately on American intervention to bring an Allied victory.

The war dragged on indecisively for three years. Early in 1917 Germany renewed unrestricted submarine warfare, cutting off food and supplies to the French and British. Germany knew that this action would bring the United States into the war. But Berlin hoped to smash the Allies before a large American force could be mobilized and sent to Europe.

Wilson acted. Early in 1917 Washington received news of a revolution in Russia and the establishment there of a constitutional government. The overthrow of the Russian czar removed many of the moral problems that Wilson faced in seeking support for American involvement on the side of the Allies. In April the President asked Congress to declare war on Germany. Wilson called upon Americans to embark on a great crusade, a "war to end all wars" and make the world safe for democracy. In his message to Congress Wilson noted: "It is a fearful thing to lead this great peaceful people into war. But the right is more precious than peace."

The Great Crusade When the United States entered World War I, the major European powers were nearly exhausted. On both sides men previously considered too old or too young for combat were pressed into military service. But after April 1917 the Allies suddenly had a great new reservoir of manpower to draw upon—the young manhood of the United States. The regular American army was small. Close to a million soldiers had to be recruited initially (over 4 million were eventually recruited). But America prepared willingly to meet the demands of Wilson's crusade. Military conscription was accepted by most Americans with fewer objections than during the Civil War or during the war in Vietnam.

The German submarine campaign achieved startling success during the first six months of 1917. But the Allied navies soon devised an effective countermeasure: the convoy system. A single ship crossing the Atlantic had little chance against the German submarine fleet. But a large group of troop ships and freighters traveling together could

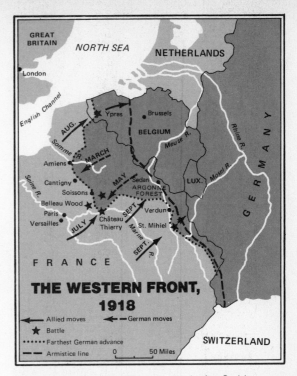

THE WESTERN FRONT, 1918

← Allied moves   ← German moves
★ Battle
••••• Farthest German advance
– – – Armistice line

0   50 Miles

War broke out in July 1914, one month after Serbian nationalists had assassinated Archduke Franz Ferdinand of Austria. Although the United States was neutral for the first three years of the conflict, its ships were at times boarded by the British and at other times threatened by the Germans. In early 1917, after the Germans renewed unrestricted submarine warfare against all shipping, the United States broke off diplomatic relations with Germany. Provoked by continued German submarine attacks, the United States declared war on Germany in April of that year. The United States entered the war on the side of the Allies as an associated power. In June an American Expeditionary Force under General John J. Pershing arrived in France.

In March 1918, after years of trench warfare, the Germans began an offensive with the Second Battle of the Somme, intending to reach the English Channel. The Allies (including the United States) later set up a unified command for the Western Front under French General Ferdinand Foch. In May, the German armies approached to within fifty miles of Paris. The turning point of the war came in July, when the German advance was stopped at the Second Battle of the Marne. Allied advances in the second half of 1918 were marked by major offensives at Belleau Wood in June–July, Ypres in August, St. Mihiel in September, and the Meuse-Argonne Forest drive of September–November.

The Military position of the central Powers deteriorated rapidly during the summer of 1918. On November 11, an armistice was signed, putting an end to the war.

The Meuse-Argonne offensive in World War I was noted for its vastness —1,200,000 American troops—and its human costliness—over 120,000 casualties. Sergeant Alvin York, the prewar conscientious objector, became famous here for his singlehanded capture of 132 Germans.

reach Europe in relative security. The rate of sinkings by German submarines fell rapidly. Most important, nearly all American soldiers completed the passage to France safely.

The large but still untested American army—General John J. Pershing's American Expeditionary Force—went into action late in 1917. French generals, hungry for more manpower, had originally called for small-sized American units, which they wished to integrate into their own commands. Pershing worked cooperatively with the French commanders and with the Allied commander in chief, Marshal Ferdinand Foch. But he and other senior American officers insisted that the Americans operate as an independent army.

American soldiers soon were allotted their own sector of the Western front to defend. American troops also helped the Allies hold their positions. Then they joined the Allied counteroffensive in the summer and fall of 1918. By November Germany was beaten. The Kaiser fled into exile in Holland. Worn out by four years of brutal warfare and beset by unrest at home, Germany asked for peace.

At home, America had organized its wartime economy as quickly and effectively as it had mobilized its soldiers. The United States had

begun to prepare for war as early as 1916. In that year Congress created the Council of National Defense, a mixed governmental and business commission. During the war the council supervised a network of agencies that controlled every aspect of the American economy. Under Bernard Baruch the War Industries Board supervised the allocation of raw materials and set production goals. The Food Administration controlled prices, and a War Trade Board regulated imports and exports. Congress established at least half a dozen other agencies, all of which reported to the President.

Wilson used his presidential war powers to the limit in waging a battle against dissent. Most Americans supported the war. But sizable minorities did not. German Americans opposed United States support of the Allies for ethnic reasons. Socialists and radicals condemned the war as a "capitalist" venture for profit. During the first months of American participation, German Americans suffered the abuse (and sometimes the assaults) of their fellow citizens. But when it became certain that Germany would have to yield to the Allies, radicalism came to be regarded as the prime threat to Wilsonian peace. In November 1917 Communist forces in Russia overthrew the new constitutional government and withdrew their nation from the war. With the new "Red scare," radical dissenters replaced German Americans as the nation's principal outcasts.

A government propaganda machine, the Committee on Public Information, was set up to publicize war efforts and to censor information or newspaper opinions unfavorable to the Allied cause. Congress enlarged the offensive against dissent by passing strict laws against treason. By the time the war ended, almost all Americans had been enlisted in the crusade.

Wilson the Peacemaker At the war's end Wilson turned his energies and ideals to the formidable task of obtaining a fair and lasting peace. The President had outlined his proposals for peace — the Fourteen Points — even before the armistice. The Germans surrendered in November 1918, hoping that Wilson's peace program would guide Allied policy.

The American President called for a new world order. It would help to eliminate worldwide political and economic rivalries. He sought to substitute international cooperation for the unstable and dangerous balance-of-power politics that had led the world to war. Wilson also proposed national self-determination for ethnic groups in the decaying European empires. Finally, Wilson called for a "general association of nations," a league of all the countries in the world. The league's members would cooperate actively to avoid future international conflicts.

In January 1919 Allied negotiators met at the palace of Versailles, a city a few miles from Paris. The peace conference was attended by Wilson and other Allied heads of state: Premier Georges Clemenceau of France, Prime Minister David Lloyd George of Britain, and Premier Vittorio Orlando of Italy. Clemenceau's overconcern with French security, though understandable, gave Wilson the most trouble. Lloyd George sought a middle ground, though he always kept the interests of the British Empire in mind. Orlando, junior partner of the Allies, did not participate in most of the "summit" deliberations.

The treaty that emerged from Versailles was a compromise. But it still remained compatible with Wilsonian goals. The President was de-

feated overwhelmingly on several issues. Despite Wilson's call for "open convenants of peace, openly arrived at," most of the treaty negotiations took shape in secret conferences among the Allied "Big Three" — Wilson, Lloyd George, and Clemenceau. Wilson compromised on national self-determination, allowing European leaders to redraw the political map of Europe. He agreed that Germany and its allies should pay staggering amounts in war damages. The Allied powers greedily divided up Germany's colonies, ignoring the wishes of the inhabitants of those areas. Nonetheless, some of the Fourteen Points were incorporated into the treaty. Perhaps most important for Wilson, the Treaty of Versailles called for the establishment of an international peacekeeping body, the League of Nations.

But dedication to ideals does not ensure success in politics, as Wilson quickly found out. Wilson brought the treaty and the League home to debate and disaster. A small group of isolationists in the Senate were opposed to any American participation in an international league. They feared that a headlong rush into internationalism would curb essential American rights and hurt American interests. Other American senators wanted to be convinced. If Wilson had confided in these senators and attempted to work out a compromise with them, the treaty and the League of Nations might have been saved.

The Fight Over the League On July 19, 1919, Woodrow Wilson submitted the Treaty of Versailles with its League of Nations covenant to the United States Senate. A poll taken earlier in the year showed that sixty-four senators — the necessary two-thirds majority — favored ratification. But time and events had reduced that figure. Everyone knew that trouble lay ahead.

One source of the trouble was Wilson himself. He had created hostility be neglecting to ask any leading Republican to accompany him on the peacemaking mission. Then, too, he was a stubborn man. Once he made a decision, he was certain that it was right. He refused to compromise.

Another source of trouble lay in the diverse reactions of the senators to the treaty and the League. Some thought the treaty dealt unfairly

Despite President Wilson's desire for "Open Diplomacy," The Treaty of Versailles, signed on June 28, 1919, was largely the work of the "Big Three." Shown here as they left the Palace of Versailles: French Premier Georges Clemenceau, to the left, hat in hand, followed by President Wilson, with British Prime Minister David Lloyd George on the right. Wilson's hopes for American approval of the Treaty, which included provisions for an international League of Nations as well as others of his 14 Points, were to be shattered by the Senate's rejection.

with various nations, but they favored the League of Nations. Others had no trouble with the treaty itself but feared that the League would take away American independence and possibly lead the United States into war again. And there were those who thought the treaty provisions were unjust and that the League would only uphold these injustices. Several Republicans objected to the League simply because they thought that members of both parties should have had a stake in its creation.

Battle lines were being drawn. There were forty-seven Democrats and forty-nine Republicans in the Senate, divided into three discernible groups. First there were those who were willing to ratify the treaty immediately—forty-three Democrats. Then there were the "reservationists" —about thirty-five Republicans and one Democrat —who wanted some of the provisions changed before they would agree to vote for ratification. Finally there were the "irreconcilables"—the remaining Republicans and three Democrats. This last group vowed never to sign the treaty under any circumstance.

At the center of this controversy was Senator Henry Cabot Lodge of Massachusetts, the new chairman of the Foreign Relations Committee.

Lodge disliked Wilson and objected to the treaty, which he thought was too easy on Germany. He was therefore, at heart, an irreconcilable. But he thought he knew a better way of defeating the treaty. As he said to one senatorial colleague, "I do not propose to beat it by direct frontal attack, but by the indirect method of reservations."

Before the treaty went to the Senate for a vote, it was stalled for two months in the unfriendly Foreign Relations Committee. When it emerged forty-nine revisions and amendments were attached to it. The disheartened Wilson was adamant. Democratic senators were not to vote for it with these "Lodge reservations." "Never! Never!" said Wilson. "I'll never consent to accept any policy with which that impossible name is so prominently identified."

He kept his word, and enough Senate Democrats stayed loyal to him to defeat the treaty with reservations. On November 19 it was all over. The Senate adjourned and the treaty that Wilson thought would be his crowning achievement would not be considered again. The United States would never join the League of Nations.

Wilson saw all Senate opposition to the treaty as betrayal of the highest trust, the cause of world peace. During the long debate, he had cracked the whip of party discipline over Democratic senators and had gone on the campaign trail seeking public support for his treaty. The trip ended tragically when Wilson suffered a stroke, which left him partially paralyzed. It was in this enfeebled state that Wilson watched the Senate reject the treaty and, with it, his dream of American leadership for world peace as a member of the League.

Wilson began looking ahead to the presidential election of 1920, which he hoped to turn into a "solemn referendum" on the League. The election became instead a referendum on Wilsonian politics. Republican Warren G. Harding, who promised Americans a retreat from internationalism and a return to "normalcy," won a landslide victory. All hope for American participation in the League of Nations vanished.

SUGGESTED READINGS— CHAPTERS 35-36

Philippines Revolt

Leon Wolff, *Little Brown Brother: America's Forgotten Bid for Empire* (1961); John M. Gates, *Schoolbooks and Krags: The U.S. Army in the Philippines, 1898–1902* (1972); Joseph L. Schott, *The Ordeal of Samar* (1964); Teodoro M. Kalaw, *The Philippine Revolution* (1969).

Becoming a World Power

William A. Williams, *The Roots of the Modern American Empire* (1969); Walter LaFeber, *The New Empire: An Interpretation of American Expansion, 1860–1898* (1963); Betty M. Unterberger, *America's Siberian Expedition* (1956); Christopher Lasch, *American Liberals and the Russian Revolution* (1962); H. Wayne Morgan, *America's Road to Empire* (1965); Robert E. Osgood, *Ideals and Self-Interest in America's Foreign Relations* (1962); Howard K. Beale, *Theodore Roosevelt and the Rise of America to World Power* (1956).

Imperialist Stirrings

Rubin F. Weston, *Racism in U.S. Imperialism* (1972); Foster R. Dulles, *The Imperial Years* (1956); Bradford Perkins, *The Great Raprochement: England and the United States, 1895–1914* (1968); Robert L. Beisner, *Twelve Against Empire: The Anti-Imperialists* (1968); David F. Healy, *The United States in Cuba, 1898–1902* (1963); Edward F. Berbusse, *The United States in Puerto Rico, 1898–1900* (1966); Thomas J. McCormick, *China Market: America's Quest for Informal Empire* (1967); Paul A. Varg, *Missionaries, Chinese, and Diplomats* (1958); Raymond A. Esthus, *Theodore Roosevelt and Japan* (1966); Clarence C. Clendenen, *The United States and Pancho Villa* (1961); P. Edward Haley, *Revolution and Intervention: The Diplomacy of Taft and Wilson with Mexico, 1910–1917* (1970).

War With Spain

Julius W. Pratt, *Expansionists of 1898* (1936); William A. Swanberg, *Citizen Hearst* (1961); Frank Freidel, *The Splendid Little War* (1958).

Wilson and Diplomacy

Ernest R. May, *Imperial Democracy* (1961); Arthur S. Link, *Wilson the Diplomatist* (1957); Dana G. Munro, *Intervention and Dollar Diplomacy in the Caribbean, 1900–1921* (1964); Edward H. Beuhrig, *Woodrow Wilson and the Balance of Power* (1955); N. Gordon Levin, *Woodrow Wilson and World Politics* (1968).

Wilson and War

John M. Cooper, Jr., *The Vanity of Power: American Isolationism and the First World War* (1970); Seward W. Livermore, *Politics is Adjourned: Woodrow Wilson and the War Congress* (1966); Horace C. Peterson and Gilbert C. Fite, *Opponents of War, 1917–1918* (1957); Robert K. Murray, *Red Scare* (1955); Thomas A. Bailey, *Woodrow Wilson and the Lost Peace* (1944) and *Woodrow Wilson and the Great Betrayal* (1945); John A. Garraty, *Henry Cabot Lodge* (1953).

37 LINDBERGH'S FLIGHT

R. J. W.

The captain was a little man, dapper and very French. But he sought a big prize: $25,000 for the first man to fly an airplane from New York to Paris. His name might sound somewhat strange—even funny—to American ears: René Fonck. But his reputation was formidable. He had been the youngest French air ace in the Great War of 1914 (as World War I was known until World War II). Without being seriously injured himself, he had shot down at least seventy-five German planes. In a war that had turned the new aviators into overnight heroes, Fonck's reputation for skill, courage, and "dash" was probably greater than that of any other pilot. Now, in the summer of 1926, he was preparing for a flight that could make him an even greater hero, both in France and in the United States.

Compared with any of the planes Fonck had flown during the war, his new silver-colored craft was huge. Like most of the other large aircraft of the day, it had three engines and two wings—a biplane, it was called. Its large cabin was equipped for a crew of four: a pilot, a copilot, a mechanic, and a radio operator. The problem that Fonck faced was simply getting the plane off the ground with enough fuel to fly the 3,600 miles to Paris. All summer he tested the plane in New York, gradually increasing the gasoline load for each test.

At daybreak on September 21 Fonck's plane was pulled onto the east-west runway at Roosevelt Field, a small airport on Long Island. The wind was blowing from the west, as it almost always does after dawn on Long Island. So Fonck would take off from east to west. To get the plane off the ground he and his crew would have to attain a speed of eighty miles an hour. One by one, the engines were turned up to their maximum power. The blocks were pulled away from the wheels, and the plane began to move. It lurched slightly, having over 2,000 gallons of gasoline aboard, and chased its own awkward shadow down the dirt runway.

When the plane passed the halfway point on the small airstrip, it did not have the speed needed for takeoff. The small crowd of onlookers waited for Fonck to cut power. But something had gone wrong, either with the pilot or with his controls. The plane simply roared on. The runway ended. The plane took a sharp, short drop into a gully, then exploded and burst into flames. Somehow Fonck got out, and so did his navigator. But the copilot and the radio operator burned to death.

Despite the crash, the man who had offered the $25,000 prize — Raymond Orteig, a Frenchman who managed two hotels in New York — announced that his offer still stood. For a while Fonck's crash made headlines and kept alive the idea of a New York — Paris flight. Late in February 1927 others began to announce that they would make the flight. It was soon obvious that a real contest was developing. It would not be merely a battle between one airplane and the ocean but a race among several aviators and their planes. The stage was set for what the public began to sense would be the greatest thrill of the decade.

By the end of March 1927 there were four serious contenders. One was the *America*, a plane piloted by Admiral Richard E. Byrd, who had gained fame as the first man to fly to the North Pole. Byrd was backed with over $100,000 from a wealthy New York merchant. His three-engined plane, with a wingspan of over seventy feet, was huge by the standards of the day. It seemed to have the best chance.

A second entry was another trimotored craft, the *American Legion*, named after and supported by the veterans' organization. It too was backed with $100,000. Unlike Fonck's plane and Byrd's *America* the *American Legion* carried only two men. A third entry was a plane known as the *Columbia*, a single-winged, single-engined craft. The *Columbia* would soon set the world endurance record by flying for over fifty hours. Finally, there was a French entry, a single-engined biplane called the *White Bird*. Its pilot and copilot, a pair of French aces from the Great War, planned to make the flight in reverse — from Paris to New York. The *White Bird* was said to have the most powerful gasoline engine ever put into an airplane.

By mid-April the weather had warmed up enough to make flight over the North Atlantic seem possible. On April 16 Commander Byrd took his *America* up from a New Jersey airport for its first test flight. Byrd and three crewmen tested the plane for a few hours and then brought it down for its first landing. The heavy landing gear touched ground smoothly. But almost at once there was a sound of splintering wood and wrenched metal. The *America* flipped over and skidded to a halt on its back. All four men managed to escape. Byrd had a broken wrist, and two of the other crewmen were badly hurt. They would not be able to fly again for weeks.

Ten days later the *American Legion* was in Langley Field, Virginia, undergoing its last test flight. The plane had flown well in earlier attempts. But both its designers and pilot knew it was too heavy. To find out whether the plane could make the Paris flight, the pilot and copilot decided to fly it from Virginia to New York with a full load of gasoline. The takeoff was slower than usual. For a moment it seemed as if the plane would not clear a line of trees at the end of the runway. To avoid them, the pilot banked to the right a few degrees. The slight turn was too much. It upset the delicate balance of the plane. The *American Legion* slid downward into a wet marsh and turned over. The pilot and copilot were trapped inside the cabin that filled first with gasoline fumes and then with water. By the time rescuers came wading through the marsh, the two men were dead.

Four men had been killed and three others hurt, and the race over the Atlantic had not yet begun. On both sides of the ocean, in America and in France, newspapers stirred public excitement to a high pitch. Surely one of the planes would make it sooner or later. But no one knew what might happen next or who might be injured or killed. The race to Paris had the competitive excitement of a World Series or a heavyweight championship fight. And it had the danger and drama of war. In the United States the race gained as much importance in the public's mind as had the war of 1898, the sinking of the *Lusitania,* or the declaration of war in 1917. In France the excitement was heightened by the memory of Fonck's crash. Moreover, the entry into the contest of two other young ace pilots from the Great War, Charles Nungesser and Francis Coli, held great promise. Both had been wounded a total of twenty-six times in air combat. Between them they had won almost every medal that their government could award.

At dawn on May 8 Nungesser and Coli took off for New York from Le Bourget airport near Paris. A great crowd gathered to watch the two heroes and their *White Bird.* Nungesser got the wheels off the ground, but too soon. The *White Bird* dropped back down on the runway with a thud. Finally, it gathered speed and left the ground almost two-thirds of a mile down the long strip.

The next morning, American newspapers reported that the plane had been sighted over Newfoundland. Paris celebrated with an excitement that almost matched that on the day of the armistice. Nungesser and Coli had dropped their landing gear over the ocean to save weight and lessen wind resistance. New Yorkers watched the harbor where the Frenchmen hoped to land and keep afloat until they could be reached by waiting boats. But the *White Bird* was never seen again. In France the celebrations quickly came to a shocked end.

The death toll in the New York—Paris race had reached six in less than a year. The world's most experienced pilots—backed by large sums of money, flying the best airplanes that modern technology could provide, with the most powerful motors ever developed—had all failed.

The man who was finally going to win the race to Paris had been reading every newspaper report he could find on all the airplane tests, takeoffs, and crashes. When Fonck's plane burned, Charles Lindbergh was flying airmail between Chicago and St. Louis. When Byrd and the others announced that they would enter the competition, Lindbergh was in San Diego supervising the construction of a new plane for himself. When Nungesser and Coli took off from Paris, he was waiting in San Diego for the weather to clear over the Rocky Mountains and the Great Plains, so he could fly east to St. Louis. From there he would go on to New York to make his attempt.

Lindbergh had only $2,000 of his own money, carefully kept for him by his mother in Detroit. He was only twenty-five years old. He looked even younger, so that almost everyone called him a boy. Worst of all, he decided on what struck everyone as a suicidal idea: to make the flight in a single-engine plane with only himself in the cockpit. He had been able to persuade some St. Louis businessmen to back him to the extent of $15,000. But this was a small sum compared to the support that Byrd's group and the *American Legion* had. Still, late in the summer of 1926, just before Fonck's crash, Lindbergh had come to an almost religious conviction that he could make the Paris flight.

At first Lindbergh tried to negotiate with several large aircraft companies. He was turned down. No one wanted to risk a company's reputation on an insane stunt like flying from New York to Paris alone. Then Lindbergh sent a plain but daring telegram to Ryan Airlines, a small, little known factory in California:

RYAN AIRLINES, INC.   FEB. 3, 1927
SAN DIEGO, CALIFORNIA

CAN YOU CONSTRUCT WHIRLWIND ENGINE PLANE
CAPABLE FLYING NONSTOP BETWEEN NEW YORK AND
PARIS. IF SO PLEASE STATE COST AND DELIVERY DATE.

Surprisingly, the answer came quickly. The small company could build the plane, and it could do so for the amount of money Lindbergh had at his disposal. But it would take three months, the telegram said. Lindbergh answered:

RYAN AIRLINES   FEB. 5, 1927
SAN DIEGO, CALIFORNIA

COMPETITION MAKES TIME ESSENTIAL. CAN YOU
CONSTRUCT PLANE IN LESS THAN THREE MONTHS.
PLEASE WIRE GENERAL SPECIFICATIONS.

Again the company answered quickly, making as much of a guess as a calculation. It could build a plane capable of carrying 380 gallons of gasoline at a cruising speed of 100 miles per hour, with an engine rated at only 200 horsepower. (This was less than half the power of the big engine that had taken the *White Bird* out over the Atlantic. It was also much less than the power supplied by the three engines of Byrd's great

This drawing shows the plane Ryan Airlines built for Lindbergh. Although the goal of the design was simplicity, sacrificing safety for the need to carry as much gasoline as possible, the plane was quite a sophisticated piece of machinery.

America.) Most important, the company promised to have the plane ready in time.

By the last week in February, Lindbergh was in San Diego working out the details on his plane. Neither Lindbergh nor the engineer who designed the plane knew how far it was to Paris. They drove to the San Diego public library to measure off the distance on a globe with a piece of string. Lindbergh remembered it this way:

> "It's 3,600 miles." The bit of white grocery string under my fingers stretches taut along the coast of North America, bends down over a faded blue ocean, and strikes the land mass of Europe. It isn't a very scientific way of finding the exact distance between two points on the earth's surface, but the answer is accurate enough for our first calculations. The designer was making quick calculations in pencil on the back of an envelope. "Maybe we'd better put in 400 gallons of gasoline instead of 380," he concludes.

Lindbergh's project was simple, almost amateurish: hastily drafted telegrams, bits of string stretched across a public-library globe, figures on the back of an envelope, and "maybe" calculations. But with no more detailed or expert plans, he decided to go ahead.

The mechanics and carpenters at Ryan started work at once on the plane that Lindbergh would call the *Spirit of St. Louis.* They built it almost literally around the pilot. The narrow, simple cockpit was just large enough to hold Lindbergh's tall, skinny body (and then only if the overhead ribs were hollowed out a little to make room for his head). In the end the plane would be only about three feet taller than Lindbergh

The cockpit of the *Spirit of St. Louis* was a model of stripped-down efficiency. The wicker seat was probably uncomfortable but lightweight. Only side windows were thought necessary since there was not much to see in flight. Leg room was limited by the controls.

himself. Moreover, it would have a smaller engine than any of the other planes in the race. But this was the secret of Lindbergh's plane—simplicity. He would build the smallest, simplest plane possible, a machine designed with only one purpose: to carry enough gasoline for the trip. Everything else—comfort, safety, complicated navigating equipment—would be sacrificed to save weight, weight that could be turned into gallons of gasoline.

On April 26, the day the two pilots of the *American Legion* were killed in Virginia, the *Spirit of St. Louis* was finished. Two days later Lindbergh was ready for his first test flight. He squeezed himself into his seat in the cockpit. He could touch the sides of the fuselage with his elbows. To the front the cockpit was blind. Shiny metal sloped all the way up from the engine to the top of the wing. There were only two side windows and a glassed-in skylight overhead. For takeoffs and landings he had to lean out of one of the side windows. But the plane was designed for only one important takeoff and landing. The rest of the time, over the Atlantic, there would be nothing to see but ocean, clouds, sun, and stars.

Directly in front of Lindbergh's face was a small cluster of instruments—an air-speed indicator, a turn-and-bank indicator, a fuel-flow meter, a compass, and one or two others. The plane carried a pitifully small survival kit containing a rubber raft, a flashlight, a canteen of water, some matches, and string. Surrounding the cockpit were nothing but gasoline tanks. One tank rested in the nose between the pilot and the engine. Another lay behind the cockpit in the fuselage. And there were more tanks in the wings overhead. There was no radio, no heater to provide warmth at freezing altitudes, no sextant for navigational sightings, not even a parachute. The *Spirit of St. Louis* was built to carry only gasoline—over a ton of it, as it turned out, weighing more than the plane and the pilot put together.

To Lindbergh, as he walked onto the sunny runway in San Diego, the *Spirit of St. Louis* was a thing of beauty and awe:

> What a beautiful machine it is, resting there on the field in front of the hangar, trim and slender, gleaming in its silver coat! All our ideas, all our calculations, all our hopes, lie there before me, waiting to undergo the acid test of flight. For me, it seems to contain the whole future of aviation.
> "Off! Throttle closed."
> I'm in the cockpit. The chief mechanic turns the propeller over several times.
> "Contact!"
> He swings his body away from the blade as he pulls it through. The engine catches, every cylinder hitting. This is different from any other cockpit I've been in before. The big fuel tank in front of me seems doubly large, now that I'm actually to fly behind it.
> I signal the chocks [blocks in front of the wheels of the plane] away. The *Spirit of St. Louis* rolls lightly over the baked-mud surface of the field.

The *Spirit of St. Louis* moved very quickly. Its tanks were almost empty for this first test flight.

> The tires are off the ground before they roll a hundred yards. The plane climbs quickly, even though I hold its nose down. There's a huge reserve of power. I spiral cautiously upward. I straighten out and check my instruments. I circle over the factory, watching little figures run outdoors to see the machine built actually flying overhead. I rock my wings and head across the bay.

During the next week Lindbergh tested the *Spirit of St. Louis* for speed, control, and, most important, takeoff under load. More and more gasoline was filtered by hand into the tanks for each run. With a load of slightly over 300 gallons the plane took off easily. But continued landings with large loads were dangerous. Lindbergh decided to stop the tests.

The *Spirit of St. Louis* had needed a little more than 1,000 feet of runway to take off with 300 gallons. From this and other data, the Ryan designers made a theoretical calculation that, fully loaded with 400 gallons, the plane would need 2,500 feet of hard runway. Rather than tempt fate, as the crew of the *American Legion* had done by testing with a full load, Lindbergh decided to trust the plane and the designer's arithmetic. He was ready. And he knew Byrd's *America* had been repaired and was undergoing final tests. The *Columbia*, too, was ready. Both planes were poised on Long Island. Time counted more than tests.

But time seemed to work against Lindbergh. A big storm blanketed the western United States, moving with painful slowness eastward. Lindbergh had to wait several days until the rain and clouds had moved east. On the evening of May 10 he began the first leg of his trip, from San Diego to St. Louis. He flew the 1,500 miles in record time. It was the longest nonstop solo flight ever made. Then, after a night's sleep, he headed for New York.

Lindbergh arrived on Long Island on May 12. He had set another record for the fastest transcontinental flight in history. The crews of Byrd's *America* and the *Columbia* came over to shake his hand and wish him luck. There was a crowd. Newspaper photographers and reporters pushed and shoved their way to Lindbergh, shouting for pictures and answers to their questions. A crowd of people climbed to the roof of a small building next to the hangar where Lindbergh parked the plane. Their weight caused a wall to collapse. Something new and strange was happening to Lindbergh. The newspapers and the public were making him into a hero, almost a myth.

Even without Lindbergh, the New York — Paris contest had all the elements of an exciting publicity event: death, drama, and competition. But Lindbergh's entry into the race added new elements. He was going alone, thus he could become an object of hero worship in ways that the crews of the other planes could not. He was tall, thin, blue-eyed, and handsome in a boyish way. And along with his youthful good looks went other personality traits that soon endeared him to the newspapers. Above all, he was modest, shy, and simple.

All these traits combined to present a picture of an innocent young man ready to dare the impossible, alone. Lindbergh was the honest, plain-spoken, cowboy-like young man from the West. He was a modern David challenging the Eastern Goliaths, with their money, their experience, their financial backers, and their head start. In short, he was an underdog. The *Spirit of St. Louis,* too, was simple and seemingly innocent compared with the other planes in the race. It was a sentimental favorite.

Lindbergh could not leave his hotel room without being mobbed by people anxious to touch him "just for luck." And the newspapers played his story for all it was worth. They nicknamed him "Lucky," "The Flyin' Fool," or just "Lindy." (He had always been "Slim" to his friends.) All the hero worship that the Americans of the 1920s usually reserved for baseball players like Babe Ruth or movie stars like Rudolf Valentino was now showered on the twenty-five-year-old airmail pilot. The worship was made more serious by the fact that "The Flyin' Fool" was doing something real and dangerous, not merely hitting baseballs or posing for motion picture cameras.

In most ways this public personality created for the new celebrity

What attracted the public to Lindbergh, besides his boyish good looks, was the power he had of symbolizing what was best about the country: not just daring, but moral courage and independence of spirit.

was only a myth. Lindbergh may not have had Byrd's $100,000, but he had finally obtained solid backing from St. Louis businessmen. And even if the *Spirit of St. Louis* was smaller than the other planes, it was still a sophisticated piece of machinery, created by advanced technology. It was a little silly for newspapers to write of Lindbergh and his plane as though they were a cowboy hero and his beloved horse.

Nor was Lindbergh's background as simple as the newspapers tried to make it appear. He came from a well-to-do, educated family. His father had been a congressman. Lindbergh had been to college for a time and held a commission as captain in the Army Air Service Reserve and the Missouri National Guard. He had been chief pilot for the airmail company in St. Louis. He was, despite his youth, an experienced professional pilot, flying an advanced aircraft.

But there was just enough truth to the mythical picture to make it stick. It probably infected Lindbergh somewhat, too. He had always been a bit wild, even though he was shy. Cars, motorcycles, ice boats—anything that involved speed—had always fascinated him. When he was just twenty he dropped out of college to learn to fly. He bought his first craft, a war-surplus plane, even before he had made a solo flight, and he almost crashed it on his first takeoff.

Lindbergh had barnstormed all over the West, crashing regularly and surviving only with luck. He had walked on airplane wings while in flight and done dangerous parachute jumps for one aerial circus after another. Four times he had been forced to parachute for his life from planes that had collided, run out of gas, or gotten lost at night.

All this—combined with Lindbergh's shyness and boyishness, his faith in himself and his plane—did smack of something supernatural and mythical. So the hero worship that began almost as soon as he reached Long Island was probably inevitable. At times the publicity and the public attention irritated Lindbergh. Reporters went so far as to burst into his hotel room without knocking to discover what kind of pajamas, if any, he wore to bed. But the irritation could not overcome the excitement. Lindbergh was becoming, even before takeoff, a national hero.

The *Columbia* was scheduled to take off on May 13, the day after Lindbergh reached Long Island. But the weather was closed in over New York and the North Atlantic. The same storm that had delayed Lindbergh in San Diego was making its slow progress north and east. So the *Columbia* had to wait. Lindbergh was able to test and tune his engine, to check and recheck every instrument. A noisy crowd that sometimes numbered over a thousand gathered around the hangar to watch him. By May 16 he was ready. As far as he could tell, Byrd was ready too. In the *Columbia* organization there was a legal quarrel over who would be the pilot. One of the men who had trained for the flight had secured a court order preventing the plane from taking off without him. But the court order could be lifted at any minute. So there seemed to be a real chance that two or possibly even three planes would take off from Roosevelt Field on the same morning.

The storm persisted for three more days. Then, on the evening of May 19, the forecast called for clearing skies. Though it was not clearing rapidly, Lindbergh made his decision. He would fly, even if it meant taking off into a rainy sky from a muddy field. He bought five sandwiches "to go." A few hours later the *Spirit of St. Louis* was towed to the west end of the Roosevelt Field runway. Lindbergh had decided to take off before dawn, while the wind was east to west. This was the opposite direction from the one Fonck had taken the preceding autumn. Not far behind the *Spirit of St. Louis* was the scorched area, marked by a bent propeller stuck into the ground as a tribute, where Fonck's plane had burned.

Slowly, carefully, mechanics strained five-gallon cans of gasoline into Lindbergh's plane. The tanks were oversized. They had a capacity of 450 gallons instead of the 400 that the designers had planned earlier. Lindbergh decided to fill them to the brim, even though it meant a dangerous overload for the takeoff. In the hangars of the *America* and the *Columbia*, there was only darkness and silence. No one else was going to fly.

As he looked over the situation, Lindbergh wondered whether he should go. He was overloaded with gasoline. The field was muddy. The wheels of the *Spirit of St. Louis* sank into the earth as though warning him that flight was out of the question. The wet weather affected the engine, which turned about thirty revolutions per minute slower than it should have at full power. Worst of all, the process of getting ready took so long that Lindbergh lost the night wind. By the time he was ready to fly, the breeze had shifted to his back, creating a tailwind of five or six miles per hour. This meant he would need even more speed on takeoff.

Lindbergh's only guidelines were the San Diego tests. They had demonstrated theoretically that he should be able to take off in 2,500 feet on a hard runway with no wind and with full engine power. At the end of the Roosevelt Field runway were a ditch, a tractor, some telephone wires and then a hill with a line of trees. He had to clear them all. He considered towing the *Spirit of St. Louis* through the misty rain and mud to the other end of the runway to get the help of the wind. He thought about postponing the flight altogether. But he decided to go.

Lindbergh looked around at the crowd that had gathered to watch. Nearby there were the mechanics, the engineers, several policemen, all looking into the dark cockpit at his pale face.

Their eyes are intently on mine. They've seen the planes crash before. I lean against the side of the cockpit and look ahead, through the idling blades of the propeller, over the runway's glistening surface. I study the telephone wires and the shallow pools of water through which my wheels must pass. A curtain of mist shuts off all trace of the horizon. Sitting in the cockpit, in seconds, minutes long, the conviction surges through me that the wheels *will* leave the ground, that the wings *will* rise above the wires, that it *is* time to start the flight.

I buckle my safety belt, pull goggles down over my eyes, turn to the men at the blocks, and nod. Frozen figures leap to action. I brace myself against the left side of the cockpit and ease the throttle wide open.

Moments before the takeoff: Lindbergh readies himself for the flight, while policemen guard and his backers inspect the plane that will carry him to Paris.

The *Spirit of St. Louis* feels more like an overloaded truck than an airplane. The tires rut through mud as though they really were on truck wheels. Even the breath of wind is pressing me down. The engine's snarl sounds inadequate and weak.

A hundred yards of runway passes. How long can the landing gear stand such strain? I keep my eyes fixed on the runway's edge. I *must* hold the plane straight. Pace quickens—the tail skid lifts off ground—I feel the load shifting from wheels to wings. The halfway mark is just ahead, and I have nothing like flying speed.

The halfway mark streaks past. Seconds now to decide. I pull the stick back firmly, and—*the wheels leave the ground!* The wheels touch again. I ease the stick forward. Almost flying speed and nearly 2,000 feet ahead. The entire plane trembles. Off again—right wing low—pull it up—ease back onto the runway. Another pool, water drumming on the fabric [covering the fuselage]. The next hop's longer. I could probably stay in the air, but I let the wheels touch once more.

The *Spirit of St. Louis* takes herself off next time. Full flying speed. The controls taut, alive, straining—and still a thousand feet to the telephone wires. If the engine can hold out one more minute. Five feet, twenty, forty. Wires flash by underneath. Twenty feet to spare!

Green grass below—a golf links. People looking up. A low, tree-covered hill ahead. The *Spirit of St. Louis* seems balanced on a pinpoint, as though the slightest movement of controls would cause it to topple over and fall. Five thousand pounds suspended from those little wings. Five thousand pounds on a blast of air.

Now I'm high enough to steal glances at the instrument board. The earth inductor compass needle leans steeply to the right. I bank cautiously northward until it rises to the center line—65 degrees—the compass heading for the first 100-mile segment of my great-circle route to France and Paris. It's 7:54 A.M. Eastern daylight time.

Back in San Diego, when Lindbergh and the designer of the *Spirit of St. Louis* had measured the distance of the flight across a library globe, the string had made a straight line between New York and Paris. But on a flat map, where the lines of latitude are straightened out into parallels, the route had to bend into an arc known as a great circle. The route Lindbergh would take curved north and east from New York, up the east coast over Cape Cod, then out over the ocean to Nova Scotia. Lindbergh planned to change his course every hundred miles (about one hour's flying time in the *Spirit of St. Louis*). He would head a few degrees farther south and east across the southern coast of Newfoundland and then out over the North Atlantic.

As Lindbergh flew up the coast on this route, people waited on streets and housetops to watch him pass. Despite the fact that his navigating equipment was primitive, he managed to reach the Nova Scotia coast only a few miles off course. Every hour excited messages were telephoned to New York giving details of his progress. In the twelfth hour of his flight, Lindbergh passed over St. John's, Newfoundland, then out over the ocean:

> I come upon it suddenly—the little city of St. John's, after skimming over the top of a granite summit. Farther ahead, the entrance to the harbor is a narrow gap with sides running up to the crest of a low coastal range. Twilight deepens as I plunge down into the valley. It takes only a moment, stick forward, engine throttled, to dive down over the wharves (men stop their after-supper chores to look upward) and out through the gap. North America and its islands are behind. Ireland is 2,000 miles ahead.

Throughout the flight Lindbergh faced the ever-present dangers of engine failure, storms, and the possibility of a structural weakness in the *Spirit of St. Louis* itself. But between Newfoundland and Ireland there were two additional dangers. The first was sleep. Lindbergh had not slept all the night before his takeoff. During the next night and the day after, as he flew over the ocean, he fought back the terrible temptation to close his eyes for just a few seconds of rest. Despite its virtues, the *Spirit of St. Louis* was not a very stable plane. Lindbergh knew that if he relaxed his hold on it for more than a moment, he might crash. He had to hold his eyes open with his hands. Once he even had to hit himself full force in the face to keep awake.

The second danger was ice. This hazard hit Lindbergh suddenly after he had climbed over 10,000 feet, trying to clear a bank of clouds about 200 miles east of Newfoundland. He was suddenly aware of being cold himself. (He had left the glass out of the side windows of the *Spirit of St. Louis,* hoping that the fresh air and engine noise would keep him alert.) Cold? He jerked himself wide awake. If *he* was cold, what about his plane?

> Good Lord! There are things to be considered outside the cockpit! How could I forget! I jerk off a leather mitten and thrust my arm out the window. My palm is covered with stinging pinpricks. I pull the flashlight from my pocket and throw its beam on a strut. The entering edge is irregular and shiny! *Ice!*
>
> I've got to turn around, get back to clear air—quickly!

Lindbergh fought the urge to turn quickly. He knew that if he did, the ice on the wings might cause the plane to go out of control. Instead, he eased the *Spirit of St. Louis* around in a long, slow curve back toward Newfoundland.

> I throw my flashlight [beam] onto the wing strut. Ice is thicker! Steady the plane. Everything depends on the turn indicator working till I get outside the cloud. Just two or three more minutes.
> My eyes sense a change in the blackness of my cockpit. I look out through the window. How bright! What safety have I reached! I was in the thunderhead for ten minutes at most, but it's one of those incidents that can't be measured by minutes. Such periods stand out like islands in a sea of time.

After this brief but dangerous encounter with the night sky, Lindbergh picked his way cautiously toward Ireland and dawn. (Since he was flying west to east, into the sunrise, he was experiencing the shortest night of any man before him in history.) He sipped cautiously at the quart canteen of water. For the rest of the time he just flew his plane, waiting for moonrise, then sunrise, then landfall. He later recalled the twenty-eighth hour of his flight.

> I keep scanning the horizon through breaks between squalls. Is that a cloud on the northeastern horizon, or a strip of low fog – or – *can it possibly be land?* It looks like land, but I don't intend to be tricked by another mirage. I'm only sixteen hours out of Newfoundland. I allowed eighteen and one-half hours to strike the Irish coast.
> But my mind is clear. I'm no longer half asleep. The temptation is too great. I can't hold my course any longer. The *Spirit of St. Louis* banks over toward the nearest point of land.
> I stare at it intently, not daring to believe my eyes, watching the shades and contours unfold into a coastline. Now I'm flying above the foam-lined coast, searching for prominent features to fit the chart on my knee. I've climbed to 2,000 feet so I can see the contours of the country better. Yes, there's a place on the chart where it all fits – Valentia and Dingle Bay, *on the southwestern coast of Ireland!* I can hardly believe it's true. I'm almost exactly on my route, closer than I hoped to come in my wildest dreams back in San Diego. What happened to all those detours of the night around the thunderheads? Where has the swinging compass error gone?
> Intuition must have been more accurate than reasoned navigation.
> The southern tip of Ireland! On course, over two hours ahead of schedule; the sun still well up in the sky, the weather clearing!

Now it was easy. So easy that Lindbergh himself fell into the temptation of making a myth out of his own achievement:

> I'm angling slowly back onto my great-circle route. I must have been within three miles of it when I sighted Ireland. An error of fifty miles would have been good dead reckoning under the most perfect conditions. Three miles was – well, what was it? Before I made this flight, I would have said carelessly that it was luck. Now, luck seems far too trivial a word, a term to be used only by those who've never seen the curtain drawn or looked on life from far away.

After Ireland the landmarks appeared rapidly – a lighthouse, the coast of England and the coast of France, "like an outstretched hand to

As the clock struck 10 P.M. the *Spirit of St. Louis* came to rest on the runway at Le Bourget airport. To the French, who had gathered by the thousands to celebrate the "Flyin' Fool's" success, Lindbergh was the epitome of "a real American."

meet me." For the first time Lindbergh felt hungry. He ate one of the sandwiches, stale and dry now, that he had bought in New York. He picked up a series of beacon lights marking the route between London and Paris. Then the city arose before him. He circled the brightly lit Eiffel Tower and then turned northeast to look for Le Bourget. "You can't miss it," he had been told. He was like a tourist.

It was almost ten o'clock at night in Paris. Lindbergh was confused by an incredible number of lights around the dark spot where the airport ought to be. A factory, he thought. He did not know that he had suddenly become the most famous man in the world. Thousands of Parisians had rushed out to the airport to greet the American flyer. The roads leading to Le Bourget were jammed with cars with headlights blazing.

Finally, Lindbergh was able to pick out floodlights showing the edge of a runway. He dragged the field once, flying low over it to check for obstructions—a tractor or maybe some sheep let out to crop the grass, he thought. He brought the plane in as carefully as possible, as though he were teaching a student to fly. The plane felt sluggish. By his own guess he still carried a lot of gasoline. His own reflexes seemed slow. Lindbergh had never landed the *Spirit of St. Louis* at night. He glided in at an angle so he could peer out of his side window.

It's only a hundred yards to the hangars now. I'm too high, too fast. Drop wing. Left rudder. Careful. Still too high. I push the stick over. Below the hangar roofs now. Straighten out. A short burst of the engine. Over the lighted areas. Sod coming up to meet me. Careful. Easy to bounce when you're tired. Still too fast. Tail too high. Hold off. Hold off. But the lights are far behind. Ahead, there's nothing but night. Give her the gun and climb for another try?

The wheels touch gently. Off again. No, I'll keep contact. Ease the stick forward. Back on the ground. Off. Back, the tail skid too. Not a bad landing, but I'm beyond the light. Can't see anything ahead. The field *must* be clear. Uncomfortable, though, jolting into blackness. Wish I had a wing light, but too heavy on the takeoff. Slower now, slow enough to ground-loop safely. Left rudder. Reverse it. The *Spirit of St. Louis* swings around and stops rolling, resting on the solidness of earth, in the center of Le Bourget.

I start to taxi back to the floodlights and hangars. But the entire field ahead is covered with running figures!

The American public was intoxicated by Lindbergh's adventure, a solo flight across the Atlantic. He was honored as a national hero in cities throughout the country —here in a parade in New York City.

38
A "NEW ERA"

R. J. W.

When Lindbergh completed his ground loop at Le Bourget, and turned to taxi back to the lighted area around the hangars, all he could see was a running crowd. About 100,000 Frenchmen had broken through police lines to rush onto the field, almost hysterical over this new hero. All day, the transatlantic cables, the newspapers, and radios had been full of news of the flight. And for hours before Lindbergh landed, Parisians had been fighting heavy traffic to drive out to Le Bourget to greet this "Flyin' Fool."

As soon as the *Spirit of Saint Louis* touched down, the crowd rushed the plane. Lindbergh was afraid (as he was to be for months, whenever he made announced landings anywhere in the world) that the people would lose their heads and run into his spinning propeller. When he tried to climb out of his cramped cockpit, the crowd grabbed him. For a long time, he could not even set foot on French soil, but was passed through the crowd, from shoulder to shoulder. In the din, he shouted for a mechanic, someone to protect the plane; but no one could hear or understand him.

In the log he kept of the flight, Lindbergh made this brief, slightly bitter entry: "May 20, Roosevelt Field, Long Island, New York, to Le Bourget Aerodrome, Paris, France. 33 hours. 20 min. Fuselage fabric badly torn by souvenir hunters." The first part of the entry, the flight, was what was significant to Lindbergh. But the second part, the half-crazed hero worship of the crowd, is just as important to understanding the full significance of what Lindbergh had done and become. In Paris, but even more in New York and dozens of other American cities, Lindbergh was adored.

From the time he landed at Le Bourget, his life was not his own. People crowded around wherever he went. They stole his hats in restaurants. He could not keep shirts, or even underwear, because laundry employees swiped them for souvenirs.

More than any other man of his generation, Lindbergh captured the imagination of his contemporaries. Newspapers printed more stories about him and his flight than they had about the death of President Wilson. More people—4 million the police said—turned out to see him in a New York parade than had ever come out to look at any President. Something about Lindbergh and his feat touched a deep and responsive chord in the America of the 1920s.

On the face of it, there was no overwhelming reason for Lindbergh's fantastic fame. As a matter of cold fact, his flight had proven nothing—except that a superb pilot, blessed by some luck, could fly a specially built airplane 3,600 miles. The *Spirit of Saint Louis* could carry no passengers and no cargo. In fact, Lindbergh had refused to carry even one pound of mail, though he was offered $1,000 to do so. Lindbergh was not even the first man to fly the Atlantic. Eight years earlier, in 1919, a British dirigible had done it *twice*. That year, too, an American seaplane had crossed from New York to England, landing several times on the ocean. And in the same year, two pilots had made it nonstop from Newfoundland to Ireland, to win a prize of $50,000—double Lindbergh's prize. For a variety of reasons, when Lindbergh made his flight in 1927, almost no one seemed to remember these earlier feats, while "Lucky Lindy" quickly became a household word.

The causes of Lindbergh's incredible celebrity have to be found outside his actual accomplishment. They lie in deep changes that had occurred in American society. Americans were excited about Lindbergh for reasons that had more to do with them than with him. They projected more significance into the event than it really had. When masses of people experience such excitement, they tend to see historical actors as demons or heroes. They oversimplify the world, and thus make some new kind of sense out of their own lives. This process often has very little to do with reality. Lindbergh became a symbol. His contemporaries saw in him what they wanted to see, making him into a sort of mirror for the technological and social changes that had transformed American society in the twentieth century.

REACHING A MASS AUDIENCE

One of the reasons for Lindbergh's rapid rise to fame was the publicity he received from the press and the radio. Since the 1890s the newspapers of the United States had been increasing in number and circulation. They competed fiercely for the attention of the public. This expansion of newspapers was only part of an important revolution in communications that began in the nineteenth century and still continues today.

One by one, new inventions brought people's lives closer together. These included the telegraph, the telephone, the phonograph, the camera, the radio, and the motion picture. They created a world in which whole nations and conti-

nents could share almost simultaneously in distant events. Lindbergh's flight was "covered" intensely by the press, which transmitted its stories over telegraph and telephone lines. Lindbergh was also photographed mercilessly. His activities were recorded both in newspaper photographs and in the newsreels that accompanied the early silent motion pictures. Hour-by-hour reports of his famous flight were transmitted on the radio—an invention that had come into use only a few years before. As soon as Lindbergh landed in Paris, the news was flashed back to the United States by transatlantic telegraph cable.

In many ways Lindbergh the hero was the creation of mass communications. He was the first celebrity to have the full advantage of every modern form of communication except television. (Television did not come into wide use until after World War II.)

The Communications Revolution The revolution in communications began with the telegraph, which linked California and New York more than half a century before Lindbergh's flight. During the same period, newspapers began to attract a

With the broadcast of the Harding-Cox election returns in November 1920, station KDKA in Pittsburgh gave birth to commercial radio. The broadcast opened a new era in communications.

mass audience. The telephone, too, contributed to the rapid and widespread circulation of information. In the first part of the twentieth century the number of telephones in use skyrocketed, from a little over 1 million in 1900 to more than 10 million in 1915. By the time Lindbergh took off for Paris, practically every middle-class American home had its own telephone.

But the communications revolution did not gather full speed until the invention of the radio. The principle of wireless transmission of sound was almost as old as the telephone. In 1887 a German scientist proved the existence of electrical waves in space. He speculated that they might be turned into signals. An Italian inventor, Guglielmo Marconi, applied the theory to wireless transmission of telegraph signals in 1896. From then on it was only a matter of assembling the appropriate tubes, transmitters, and receivers.

In 1920 Americans heard their first commercial radio broadcast. The station was KDKA in Pittsburgh, and the program was a news report on the 1920 presidential election. Soon after that, the winner of the election, Warren G. Harding, installed a radio set in the White House. Gradually Marconi's invention was transformed from a toy into a commercial reality. By the time Lindbergh made his flight to Paris, an estimated 10 million sets were in use in the United States, almost one for every telephone.

Two other inventions, the phonograph and the camera, furthered the revolution in mass communications. Thomas A. Edison found a way of capturing and recreating sound that was to make music available to millions at an instant. George Eastman's perfection of the camera made it possible for newspapers to include pictures on their pages.

All these changes allowed millions of people to participate indirectly in events they were not able to witness in person. In other words, these developing communications facilities had created a potential public that could take part in any happening, frown at any villain, worship any hero.

A Middle-class "Public" The new public that celebrated Lindbergh's flight with such enthusiasm should not be confused with the whole nation. Lindbergh's fame was primarily a middle-class phenomenon. He was, in some ways, a media creation; and the media that made him catered primarily to white, well-to-do citizens. Even newspapers catered mainly to a middle-class audience. Radios and telephones were still the property of the middle class almost exclusively. In 1927, the phonograph and the camera were still alien novelties to many millions of poor Americans. Whole great subpopulations — blacks, many poor white farmers, millions of immigrants in the cities — were practically excluded from the new "public" that the mass media helped create.

Eventually, of course, the new inventions (and the television sets that completed the communications revolution) would become the common property of almost every American, rich or poor. But in the 1920s, and for some time after, they were still middle-class conveniences. If Lindbergh was a symbol of popular values, they were not necessarily values that belonged to all of America. They were the beliefs and hopes of white, middle-class citizens. At the time, it was easy and tempting for the members of this restricted "public" to believe that they *were* America. Most of them would have agreed quickly with the American ambassador to France, who said that Lindbergh represented "the spirit of our people." Similarly, the *New Republic*, a magazine with a small, highly educated audience, could say confidently that Lindbergh "is US personified." But the ambassador and the *New Republic* spoke carelessly. The "people" and the "US" they referred to were in fact only the public defined by the media.

As for the others, the majority — the poor, the blacks, the immigrants — there is no way to know what (if anything) they thought about Lindbergh. In all likelihood, if they noticed Lindbergh at all, it was only for a moment, and with no special sense of identification with him or his feat. Like most of the cultural content of the "Roaring Twenties," the Lindbergh phenomenon occurred mainly within the very class from which he had come. In fact, one of the deepest needs he may have served was the need of this class to believe that it really did possess "the spirit" of the whole nation.

THE MACHINE AND THE MAVERICK
IN A TECHNOLOGICAL SOCIETY

Americans were fond of calling the period after World War I the New Era. Much of what they meant by the phrase was summed up symbolically in Lindbergh's airplane. The New Era was above all a machine age, a triumph of advanced technology. Compared with a modern jet or a moon rocket, the *Spirit of St. Louis* was a very primitive machine. But to millions of Americans of the 1920s it was the final and glistening outcome of the industrial and technological revolution that had begun in the preceding century. It symbolized what they believed was happening in the United States: the creation of a new kind of civilization, a miracle of progress in which every barrier to human comfort and achivement would be broken by industry and invention.

The United States of the mid-1920s was much more thoroughly industrialized than it had been at the turn of the century. Total steel production, for example, quadrupled during the period between the death of McKinley and Lindbergh's flight to Paris. The total value of all manufactured goods increased almost eight times in the same period. The number of people engaged in agriculture declined to about one-fourth of the total population. American cities grew at an astounding pace. By 1930, three years after Lindbergh's flight, 40 percent of the total population of the United States lived in twenty-five large metropolitan centers. In short, Lindbergh appealed to a society that was overwhelmingly industrial and urban, and fundamentally dependent on machines and factories.

Electric Power and Assembly Lines In some ways the New Era was an extension of the revolution in industry that had occurred after the Civil War (see Chapter 30). The factory system had continued to expand. New and more complex forms of machinery had been developed to produce more and more goods. But if the basic trends were the same, there were some new elements too. The New Era, to a far greater extent than the old, was powered by electricity and organized around assembly lines.

In 1870, when the industrial revolution was making its first powerful impact, steam and water were used equally to drive industry. Steam continued to be the main form of motor energy in industry until about 1917. But steam had its drawbacks, and the introduction of electricity made possible extraordinary advances in industry.

Again, the basic inventions belonged to the nineteenth century. Within the ten-year period from 1877 to 1887 the dynamo for generating electricity and the motor for converting it into motion were both perfected. This was largely the work of Thomas Edison. During these same years, Edison's incandescent light was introduced into homes and streets. In 1882 the first commerical electric power station, the Edison Illuminating Company, was built in New York.

While electric lighting brightened life in offices, houses, and streets, the electric motor helped transform industrial production. In 1900 electric motors provided only one-twentieth of the power used in American industrial plants. By World War I this figure had increased to about one-third. When Lindbergh flew to France, just ten years later, electricity provided almost two-thirds of the total industrial power in American factories and mills. Between 1870 and 1920 the amount of raw energy used by American industry, measured in horsepower, increased by well over 1,000 percent!

The development of the moving-belt assembly line also had far-reaching effects on industrial production. Assembly lines were first introduced on a large scale by Henry Ford at his automobile plant in Michigan in 1913. The principle was a simple one. Workers were placed in a row in the order of sequence of their jobs. As the product (in this case the automobile) moved past him, each man performed his assigned task. The idea might be simple, but the savings in time and motion were dramatic. Each worker, using a specialized tool to perform a small task, could now produce much more in a given day. Ford's assembly line was copied by dozens of other industries. By the middle of the 1920s it was a standard technique.

DEVELOPMENTS IN TECHNOLOGY, 1865–1930

(DATES REFER TO PATENT OR FIRST SUCCESSFUL USE)

YEAR	INVENTOR	CONTRIBUTION	IMPORTANCE/DESCRIPTION
1869	George Westinghouse	AIR BRAKE	Provided smoother and quicker braking action for railroad cars.
1874	Joseph Glidden	BARBED WIRE MANUFACTURE	Speeded the end of open grazing of cattle.
1876	Alexander Graham Bell	TELEPHONE	Made out of a cigar box, wire, and two toy magnets; revolutionized communication.
1877	Thomas Alva Edison	PHONOGRAPH	Extended availability of music to millions.
1879	Thomas Alva Edison	INCANDESCENT BULB	Made possible electric lighting.
1880	W. E. Sawyer	PRINCIPLE OF SCANNING	Established the possibility of using only a single wire or channel for transmission of a picture, thereby making television possible.
1888	George Eastman	HAND CAMERA	Revolutionized newspaper journalism.
1888	Nikola Tesla	FIRST MOTOR TO BE RUN BY ALTERNATING CURRENT	Made the transmission of electrical power over long distances possible.
1892	John Froelich	MOTORIZED TRACTOR	Powered by a 20-hp., single-cylinder gasoline engine; greatly increased agricultural efficiency.
1895	George B. Selden	INTERNAL COMBUSTION AUTOMOBILE ENGINE	Initiated a new mode of transportation.
1896	Guglielmo Marconi	WIRELESS TELEGRAPH	Formed the basis for radio transmissions.
1903	Orville & Wilbur Wright	FIRST FLIGHT OF A HEAVIER-THAN-AIR CRAFT	Marked the beginning of the air age.
1904	Thomas Alva Edison	SOUND MOTION PICTURE	Inaugurated a new entertainment/information medium.
1913	William M. Burton	CRACKING OIL-REFINING PROCESS	Made possible production of gasoline from kerosene.
1917	Ernst F. W. Alexanderson	HIGH-FREQUENCY ALTERNATOR	Made worldwide wireless transmission possible.
1918	Peter C. Hewitt F. B. Crocker	HELICOPTER	First helicopter to rise successfully from the ground.
1922	Herbert T. Kalmus	TECHNICOLOR PROCESS	Made possible color film.
1926	Robert Hutchings Goddard	ROCKET	First liquid-propellant rocket.

This photograph of a day's production of car chassis at a Detroit Ford plant vividly illustrates the increase in output made possible by the use of the assembly line. Mass-production methods cut assembly time from 12½ to 1½ hours.

Effects of Mechanization The industrial revolution continued. The changes brought about by the electric motor and the assembly line made the lives of most Americans in 1927 very different from their lives a generation or two earlier. More and more, the ways in which people lived and worked were determined by machines and technological innovations. More and more, mechanical devices replaced human energy and skill.

This process of mechanization had two deep effects on American society. First, it made modern Americans more conscious of the efficient use of time and effort than any other people in the history of the world. Second, it threatened to standardize life by reducing the area of imagination and individuality in peoples' daily working environment. The celebration of Lindbergh was connected to both these consequences.

In planning his flight, Lindbergh was almost ruthlessly efficient. The *Spirit of St. Louis* was a nearly perfect machine. It was designed to perform one simple task in the most effective way, with a minimum of wasted energy. Like a machine in a modern factory, the plane represented the harnessing of energy to a carefully designed instrument for the performance of a rigidly defined task. Much of what Americans admired in Lindbergh was precisely what they admired in their own society—his technological achievement.

But there was another side to Lindbergh. He was a maverick. Some of the pet names the newspapers gave him, like "The Flyin' Fool" and "Lucky," made his daring seem more important than his technical skill. Lindbergh seemed to go

against the trend toward standardization of life in the New Era. He represented individual imagination, as well as engineering and piloting skill. A large part of Lindbergh's fame probably rested on this contradiction. His flight was both a triumph of technology and a victory for individual daring.

WHEELS AND WINGS: THE MOTOR AGE

The development of electricity had a powerful effect not only on industry but also on American home life. New inventions like the electric washing machine and refrigerator (which utilized small, inexpensive motors) changed the working and eating habits of American families. And a dozen other smaller electric appliances—from toasters to thermostats for home furnaces—helped usher in the American consumer's vision of a New Era.

Perfecting the Automobile The largest change in American social life was brought about by the gasoline engine. The basic principle of the internal combustion engine was understood by the middle of the nineteenth century. The principle was simple. Instead of burning fuel externally to convert water into steam, the internal combustion engine burned fuel in an explosive way inside a chamber. The force of the explosion was then used to drive a piston or a rotor. The first internal combustion engine was built and operated in the 1860s in France. Power for the new engine was available in

HENRY FORD

As much as any other single factor, automobiles caused the dramatic change in American life in the twentieth century. Yet the man who did the most to put the nation on wheels, Henry Ford, disliked the change. The older he grew, the more fondly he looked back on the America of his youth. He valued its rural base, Puritan work ethic, and simple pleasures.

Life began for Henry Ford on a farm near Dearborn, Michigan, on July 30, 1863. Early in his life two traits became apparent: he loved machinery, and he hated farming. He was a born tinkerer. By the time he was thirteen, he could disassemble and reconstruct a watch. He was forever fixing his father's farm machinery and his mother's household appliances. When he ran out of things to repair at home, he repaired the watches, clocks, and machinery of neighbors.

As soon as he could, he left the farm for Detroit to become a machinist. He quickly learned his trade and was soon a well-paid, highly skilled workman. In his spare time he worked on a gasoline buggy in an old brick shed behind his home. By 1896 he was able to drive it through the hole he had knocked out of the shed wall. Mounted on four bicycle wheels was a two-cylinder, four-horsepower engine. Mounted on that was a buggy seat. To steer it he used a curved stick like the tiller on a boat.

From his awkward beginning Ford built a billion-dollar industry over the next fifty years. But as he grew from home-shop tinkerer to industrial tycoon, he never really changed his boyhood attitudes. They remained those of an agrarian Populist of the 1880s and 1890s.

As a result, Henry Ford was a mass of contradictions. While he professed a firm belief in the value of the individual workman and of hard and useful work, he developed an assembly-line process that was truly dehumanizing. He broke down each of the jobs involved in making a car into its tiniest steps. Consequently, a workman did only one thing — like tightening a single bolt — all day long. Ford was even proud of the fact that 43 percent of the jobs in his factories could be mastered in no more than one day.

While he was an expert businessman, as shown by his development of an enormous personal fortune and a vastly profitable corporation, Ford disliked many aspects of capitalism. He had an abiding mistrust of bankers and moneymen.

And while he continued to turn out millions of cars, making Americans a highly mobile and rootless society, he romanticized the stable, well-rooted small-town life. He so loved nineteenth-century rural America that he spent twenty years constructing a reproduction of the community he grew up in — Greenfield Village. There, skilled artisans worked at jobs that had long since been taken over by assembly lines.

Henry Ford died an old man of eighty-four, puzzled and unhappy with the people and the world he had done so much to transform.

the form of gasoline, a "waste" product in the making of kerosene, the basic fuel oil of the nineteenth century.

It was only a matter of time, then, until someone perfected the engine, mounted it on a "horseless carriage," and so created the automobile. No one, however, could have begun to guess at the end of the nineteenth century just how rapid the development of the automobile would be. Nor could they foresee the range of consequences it would have on the ways Americans lived.

The first man in the United States to build a workable automobile powered by a gasoline engine was probably Ransom E. Olds. (His rickety machine was the forerunner of the present-day Oldsmobile.) Five years later, in 1895, Henry Ford put together his first car. The new machine was noisy, unreliable, and expensive. Still, a few Americans were willing to pay the price and stop their ears against the noise. By 1900 there were about 8,000 of the curious new machines operating in the country.

But Ford was not so much an inventor of the automobile as the inventor of a style and a method of production. In the early years of the century Ford began simplifying the automobile. He cut away every fancy decoration and convenience that had been adapted from the luxurious carriages of the day. Moreover, he reduced costs by turning out standardized, mass-produced machines. The results were astonishing. In 1907 the average price of an automobile was over $2,000. The next year Ford introduced a model selling at only $850. By 1914 he was able to cut the price to a little over $500. By the mid-1920s Ford was selling his assembly-line Model T for less than $300. The car was similar in many ways to the *Spirit of St. Louis*. It was the simplest machine possible, designed to do a plain task in the most efficient way.

Other automobile makers began to imitate and compete with Ford. The result was an exploding new industry. By the 1920s the manufacture of automobiles was by far the largest consumer products industry in the United States. It employed tens of thousands of workers at large and growing factories centered in Detroit. The automobile had a remarkable impact on other industries, especially steel and rubber, which provided the raw prod-

ucts for the assembly lines. The oil industry also underwent a major expansion. The automobile turned gasoline into the main stock-in-trade of the petroleum companies.

Life in the Motor Age   The most obvious impact of the automobile was not on industry but on American social life. By 1927 Ford had made 15 million cars. About 20 million American families owned an automobile. The immediate result was that horses and other draft animals disappeared from the landscape and the streets.

But the automobile had other, less obvious and predictable effects. First, the automobile encouraged Americans to move farther and farther out of the cities, into the suburbs. From about the time of Lindbergh's trip to Paris, the "lure of the suburbs" attracted more and more middle-class Americans. Second, cars and buses transformed American education, especially in small towns and farm areas. The school bus made it possible to consolidate school districts into larger units. Gradually the simple one-room schoolhouse, with one or two teachers for all the grades, disappeared.

Finally, the automobile, the truck, and the bus began a process that would take another thirty years to complete: the near destruction of the railroads—the principal technological innovation of the nineteenth century. At first, in the 1920s and 1930s, the car and the bus cut mainly into the railroads' local traffic. But as roads and engines improved, the competition became more and more severe. As for freight, the trucking industry began to compete for what had been almost a railroad monopoly. The train, with its mighty steam engine, had been the great symbol of the industrial revolution up to the 1920s. By the middle of the twentieth century, much of the railroad industry was ailing and unprofitable, no longer able to survive as a private enterprise.

In the long run, the automobile proved to have unwanted as well as unpredicted consequences. Among these the modern decay of central cities was the most serious. Gradually, large sections of cities like New York, Boston, and Chicago became the slums of the poor, who could not afford suburban homes. Also, although no one in Lindbergh's day could have predicted it, the auto-

The automobile soon became a symbol of "the good life." Here a family enjoys a picnic on the grass with their Model T Ford parked behind them.

The prosperity in the 1920s that enabled millions of Americans to purchase automobiles gave rise to that most modern phenomenon—the traffic jam.

mobile caused a major problem of air pollution. Smog resulted from the exhausts of millions of cars and trucks burning hundreds of millions of gallons of gasoline every year.

To most Americans, though, the automobile was an unquestioned miracle. To those who could afford it, it meant freedom to move at will through the city or the countryside. It also provided status, as manufacturers introduced more elaborate models, some costing ten times as much as Ford's Model T. And the automobile meant adventure. Middle-class Americans could get behind the wheel of a powerful, complicated piece of machinery—just as Lindbergh climbed into the cockpit of his machine—and be off on an exciting journey of motion and speed every day. Like Lindbergh, too, Americans went beyond a concern with efficiency and practicality to a romantic affection for their machines. They polished them, paraded them, and gave them pet names like the "old bus," the "flivver," the "tin Lizzie," and the "merry Oldsmobile." Despite its defects, Americans loved the car.

Development of Air Transportation   For the first quarter of the twentieth century the automobile had the greatest social and economic impact on America. The development of the aircraft industry and airline passenger service did not become truly important until years after Lindbergh's flight. But the airplane was in many ways more thrilling than the automobile. (This was why Lindbergh and other pilots could make a living in the 1920s barnstorming across America in their aerial circuses.) Like the automobile, the airplane depended on the small, powerful, and efficient gasoline engine.

The first men to fly a real airplane were Orville and Wilbur Wright. In 1903, they camped at Kitty Hawk, North Carolina (a location they chose because it had strong and steady winds, plus a great expanse of beach), with a primitive biplane. It had a tiny gasoline engine, which turned two push-type propellers. The first successful test flight came in December, after a series of dangerous and frustrating failures. This first flight lasted a little less than a minute, and covered only about 800 feet. But the Wright brothers were soon experimenting with larger

planes and engines. In 1909, after six years of work, they sold the first plane to the United States Army.

World War I brought about a dramatic spurt in design sophistication, not only in the United States, but in Europe. The new planes had larger and better engines, and a much more rigid construction than the Wrights' original. The war also romanticized flight and created a new type of military hero, the "aviator." Lindbergh, then, was able to capitalize not only on advances in technology but on a new image of the heroic and daring "ace."

The main civilian use of the airplane was shipping mail. The government began service in 1918. Later, private companies (like the one Lindbergh worked for in St. Louis) took over the service. The operation was dangerous. A majority of the pilots were killed in crashes during the early years. But by the mid-1920s there was regular, all-weather airmail service between most major cities in America.

Lindbergh's flight, combined with the introduction of larger airplanes like Byrd's *America,* did more than any other single event to encourage the growth of air transportation. Lindbergh had faith in the future of aviation. Soon after his return to America in 1927, he began a flying tour of the country to promote airmail and air transportation. By 1930, just three years after his solo transatlantic flight, there were 43 domestic airline companies, operating over 30,000 miles of flying routes.

NEW MANNERS AND MORALS

All these changes—the development of mass communications, the expansion of industry, the introduction of a new technology—brought about another revolution. This revolution marked a dramatic difference in the manners and morals of the American people. Americans of the 1920s knew they were living in a time when the world was undergoing rapid change. They coined new words and phrases—like the "Roaring Twenties," the "lost generation," and "flaming youth"—to describe what was happening to them. Americans were adopting habits and moral standards that their parents found shocking and offensive.

A Revolution for Women At the center of the revolution in manners were women. The revolution that would change women's lives did not begin in the 1920s. During the first two decades of the twentieth century, many middle- and upper-class women had adopted new patterns of behavior (including divorce) that broke with the traditions of nineteenth-century Victorian America. But because of the impact of World War I and the influence of books, radio, and advertising, the trend started at the turn of the century began to affect ever-widening circles of women. By the 1920s the revolution was in full bloom.

Politically, women were new creatures. After decades of agitation, they finally won the right to vote, with passage of the Nineteenth Amendment in 1920. But this new political role was only a small part of the emancipation of women. The new woman of the 1920s wanted to do everything. "Everything" included more opportunities than her mother had had.

She was much more likely than her mother to attend college. She might go to work, too. By

The flapper symbolized the new woman's daring—her flouting of traditional social and moral restraints. Short, bobbed hairdos, knee-length skirts, and sheer silk stockings identify these four women as flappers, as do their nightclub surroundings.

1930, 10 million women were employed in the American labor force. This new experience of education and work increased the number of women who were likely to remain single, or, if they did marry, to get divorced. The divorce rate in 1930 was twice what it had been before the war. This did not mean that marriages were more unhappy. It meant, instead, that women were less likely to put up with a bad marital situation. They would demand their freedom instead.

There was an even more obvious revolution in the way women dressed. The ideal that gradually emerged in the decade of Lindbergh's flight was that of the "flapper." She wore her dress short—above the knees rather than at the ankle. And the dress was not only shorter, it was made of thin material, designed to move with her body as she walked or danced—designed, too, to give an occasional glimpse of thigh above the hemline. The flapper discarded the corsets that her mother had worn, and dispensed with the bustle, too. She put on much more make-up and perfume, and jangled with much more jewelry at her neck and wrists. In advertisements and in movies, and in real life, too, she was likely to pose with a cocktail in one hand and a cigarette in a long holder in the other—the essence of a new "sophistication."

Like Lindbergh, though, the flapper and the "liberation" she symbolized was a middle-class phenomenon primarily. College, careers, divorce, and emancipated dress still touched only a minority of American women. Even though the suffrage now belonged to every woman, in practice, voting was primarily confined to middle-class women. For the rest, life continued to be quite confining. And when women did leave the home to take jobs, they still suffered from a systematic discrimination in wages and opportunities. In the final analysis, the flapper, like Lindbergh, had a significance that was more symbolic than real.

The Jazz Age The new woman was part of a changing culture. A freedom of action and belief unheard of before seemed to go hand in hand with the triumph of industrial technology, with its prosperity and sense of unlimited possibilities for life. Both men and women listened to new music—jazz—and danced new steps. Instead of formal

The "Jazz Age" gave birth to the blues, an especially plaintive, bittersweet music of black American origin. Bessie Smith, one of the best American jazz artists, made the singing of the blues uniquely her own.

The Maturing of American Culture

Generations of foreigners, while admiring American achievements in other fields, criticized the nation's artistic backwardness. Even Americans who patronized the arts— like this eager visitor in Frank Waller's 1881 painting of the Metropolitan Museum—were said to appreciate money more than merit. Such views were exaggerated, yet held some truth. Until the late nineteenth century, a distinctive American culture was slow to emerge. But the situation changed in the next few decades. By the 1920s foreigners were admiring American literature, painting, architecture, and music. The United States had found a cultural voice of its own.

[For further information on the foreign observers quoted in this essay, see "Notes on Sources."]

PICTORIAL ESSAY 7

American art is still in a stage of evolution; the painters of today are the precursors of those who shall adorn the Golden Age which is to come. Though there have been, and are, individual artists of distinguished merit and ability, art itself is not yet fully developed nor understood. The nation has had hitherto neither time, opportunity, nor inclination to interest itself intelligently in the fine arts.

[COUNT VAY DE VAYA UND LUSKOD, 1908]

Behold! Mark Twain had curled himself up in the big armchair, and I was smoking reverently, as befits one in the presence of his superior. The thing that struck me first was that he was an elderly man; yet, after a minute's thought, I perceived that it was otherwise, and in five minutes, the eyes looking at me, I saw that the gray hair was an accident of the most trivial. He was quite young. I was shaking his hand, I was smoking his cigar, and I was hearing him talk—this man I had learned to love and admire fourteen thousand miles away.

[RUDYARD KIPLING, 1889]

Mark Twain in 1907. By this time the writer had gained world-wide acclaim for such books as *The Adventures of Tom Sawyer* (1876), *Life on the Mississippi* (1883), and *The Adventures of Huckleberry Finn* (1885).

American paintings are no longer strange to Europe. In the art division of the last Paris Exposition, Americans took their share of the honors, and they are highly appreciated at most of the Berlin and Munich picture shows. Sargent and Whistler are the best known. Sargent, as the painter of elegant ladies, prosperous men, and interesting children, has undoubtedly the surest and most refined gift with his brush of any son of the New World. Whistler is doubtless the greater, the real sovereign. He fathoms each human riddle, and expresses it intangibly, mysteriously. Everything is mood and suggestion, the dull and heavy is lightened, the whole is rendered in rich twilight zones.

[HUGO MÜNSTERBERG, 1904]

The Last of Old Westminster, painted by James Abbott McNeill Whistler in 1862. The scene is London, where Whistler lived for much of his life. This work was followed by a number of outstanding portraits, including the famous one of his mother (which he actually titled *An Arrangement in Grey and Black*).

Miss Cassatt is a true phenomenon. In more than one of her canvases she is on the verge of becoming a notable artist with unparalleled natural feeling, penetrating observation, and a welcome subjection before the model which is the accomplishment of peerless artists.

[ALBERT WOLFF, 1881]

The Bath, by Mary Cassatt, dates from about 1891. The artist—who lived most of her adult life in Paris—liked to paint mothers and children. She communicated feelings of warmth and tenderness without sentimentality.

The taste for plastic art [in the United States] has slowly worked upward. Recent movements have left many beautiful examples of sculpture. Cities are jealously watchful now that only real works of art shall be erected, and that monuments which are to be seen by millions of people shall be really characteristic examples of good art. More than anything else, sculpture has at length come into a closer sympathy with architecture than perhaps it has in any other country. Such a work as Saint-Gaudens' Shaw Memorial in Boston is among the most beautiful examples of modern sculpture. Vigorous and mature is the American, in plastic art as well as in poetry.

[HUGO MÜNSTERBERG, 1904]

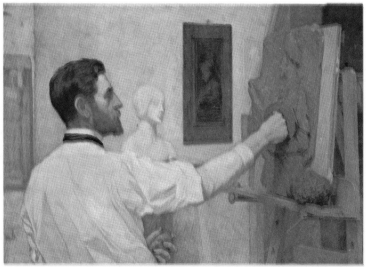

This work, showing Augustus Saint-Gaudens in his studio, was painted by Kenyon Cox in 1908. The sculptor was known for his public statuary, including Lincoln, in Lincoln Park, Chicago; General Sherman, near Central Park in New York City; and the Shaw Memorial on Boston Common.

Mr. and Mrs. Isaac Newton Phelps Stokes, portrayed by John Singer Sargent in 1897. These prominent New Yorkers, though pictured in informal dress, epitomize the wealth and refinement typical of Sargent's subjects.

People are inclined to smile at me when I suggest that you in America are at the commencement of a period of fine and vigorous art. The signs, they say, are all the other way. Of course you ought to know best. All the same, I stick to my opinion with British obstinacy, and believe I shall see it justified.

[JOHN GALSWORTHY, 1919]

Willa Cather builds her imagined world almost as solidly as our five senses build the universe around us. She has within herself a sensitivity that constantly presents her with a body of material which would overwhelm most of us. She has also a quality of mountain-pony sturdiness that makes her push on unfatigued under her load and give an accurate account of every part of it.

[REBECCA WEST, 1927]

On the threshold of her career, in 1902, Willa Cather had yet to gain a name for herself. She became noted for such novels as *O Pioneers!* (1913) and *My Antonia* (1918).

Sloan's canvas of girls under the elevated has more of New York in it than anything else I know.

[DIEGO RIVERA, 1942]

Six O'Clock was painted by John Sloan in 1912. He was one of a group called The Eight. They were known more familiarly as the Ashcan School because they depicted scenes of everyday city life rather than the more formal and traditional subjects favored by academic artists.

Characteristic of Frank Lloyd Wright's so-called "prairie houses" is this home in River Forest, Illinois. It was built in 1908. Wright's later works, noted for their daring innovation, included the Imperial Hotel in Tokyo, the Johnson administration building in Racine, Wisconsin, and the Guggenheim Museum in New York City.

Most of Wright's country houses, fitted into the oceanlike endlessness of the prairie, are very low, joined with, indeed pressed down toward, the earth. As a consequence the interior rooms spread out horizontally from one another. Therefore these houses do not seem like some grotesque thing which has grown out of the earth; they appear native to the soil and fitted to it, like the farmhouse.

[LUDWIG HILBERSHEIMER AND UDO RUKSER, 1920]

The chances are that Robert Frost will become a national figure, a sage, a Yankee sage. He has personal thought; he has wisdom; he has a basic conception from which he can speak. He likes the nation, every nation, and he dislikes the state, every state. He is a puritan, but he goes by the dictates of the heart.

[PADRAIC COLUM, 1936]

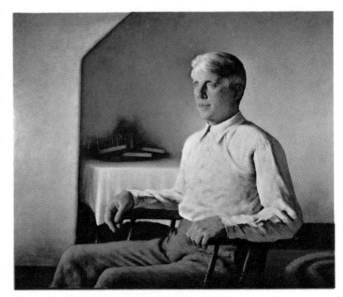

Robert Frost, as seen by artist James Chapin in 1929. The New England writer had by this time published some of his best-known poems, among them "Mending Wall," "Birches," and "Stopping by Woods on a Snowy Evening."

The mission which this land has, like all others, is to discover it s own being, to fulfill it s task of representing itself. And if one puts his ear to the ground, then one hears millions of forces at work to forge and shape this individual being.

[ANTON ERKELENZ, 1927]

Eugene O'Neill is one of the really great figures in modern drama. O'Neill is an example of what I mean when I say America is producing, and will produce in ever greater quantities, an art I feel is indigenous; it belongs to the American soil. No European dramatist could possibly have written those plays. The drama, under him, has found a new type of artistic expression.

[GERHART HAUPTMANN, 1932]

Eugene O'Neill in 1921, at the start of his career. His greatest plays came later: *Desire Under the Elms* (1924), *Mourning Becomes Electra* (1931), and *The Iceman Cometh* (1946). In 1936 he became the first American playwright to win the Nobel prize.

A scene from *Beyond the Horizon*, by O'Neill. Produced in 1920, it was the first full-length play by the dramatist to be acted.

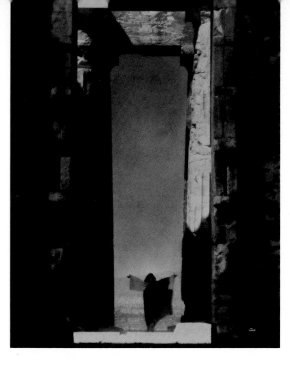

What she gives us is a sort of sculpture in transition.
*Imagine a dozen statues expressive, say, of the
cardinal phases of despair—the poses and gestures
and facial expressions of the moment in which
each of these phases reaches its maximum of
intensity. Then imagine some hundreds of statues
that represent, in faultless beauty, every one of the
moments of slow transition between these cardinal
phases, and you get the art of Isadora Duncan.*

[ERNEST NEWMAN, 1921]

The great American photographer Edward Steichen captured some
of the magic of dancer Isadora Duncan in this 1921 photo, taken at
the Parthenon. Her flowing Grecian costumes and striking interpretive power transformed modern dance.

*Gershwin's Rhapsody [in Blue] is by far the most interesting thing of its kind I have yet met with. It really has
ideas and they work themselves out in a way that interests the musical hearer. Perhaps it is better not to
prophesy. What is at present certain is that Gershwin has written something for a jazz orchestra that is really
music, not a mechanical box of tricks.*

[ERNEST NEWMAN, 1924]

Mexican artist David Siqueiros painted this *Portrait in a Concert Hall* (George Gershwin) in 1936. The composer, who died the
following year, had followed his *Rhapsody in Blue* (1923) with *An American in Paris* (1928) and *Porgy and Bess* (1935).

The outstanding achievement of American literature is the swiftness with which it strode from provincialism to half-acknowledged universality. Before 1800 there is nothing, save in the field of politics, which could command, or even deserve to command, a European audience; by 1900 it is true to say that there were few forms of creative effort in which Americans had not done work of the highest quality. America had moved to the very front of the cosmic stage. Henceforth it might be disliked; it could not be neglected.

[HAROLD LASKI, 1948]

It is hardly an exaggeration to say that Ernest Hemingway, more than any of his American colleagues, makes us feel we are confronted by a still young nation which seeks and finds its exact form of expression.

[NOBEL PRIZE CITATION, 1954]

The young Ernest Hemingway was painted by Henry Strater in 1922. His best work, yet to come, included *The Sun Also Rises* (1926), *A Farewell to Arms* (1929), and *For Whom the Bell Tolls* (1940).

Lunched with Sinclair Lewis. He is full of imagination. He tells me he wrote four or five novels before he wrote Main Street, *but they were not successes. I asked him why that had not discouraged him. He laughed, he said it was no use being discouraged, that writing novels was all he could do, he might starve at it, but he was incapable of any other form of work. (Truly an artist!)*

[CLARE SHERIDAN, 1921]

Sinclair Lewis, photographed with his wife in 1916. A year after his meeting with Clare Sheridan, he published one of his best-known novels, *Babbitt*. In 1930 he became the first American to win the Nobel prize for literature.

waltzes and other Victorian dances, they moved to the fast Charleston and the Black Bottom. They also danced close together in the slow fox trot. Many older Americans were shocked by these changes. But these dances became part of the new culture, sweeping their way through high-school gymnasiums and college campuses across the country.

The sexual ideas of Americans were changing, too. The ideas of the Austrian psychologist Sigmund Freud on sex began to be discussed at the dinner table and in the polite magazines of the middle class. Words like "bitch" appeared in novels published by respectable publishers and read by respectable people. "Petting" and "necking" became part of the everyday vocabulary of magazine readers and even ministers. In the movies, sex became a major box-office attraction. Stars like Theda Bara and Clara Bow appeared on the screen in thin clothing, locked in long, passionate embraces with their leading men. When Clara Bow was advertised as the "It" girl, hardly anyone needed to ask what "It" meant.

Americans drank more too. Despite prohibition (see page 694) liquor was easy to obtain. And since liquor was illegal, millions of Americans became technically criminals on an almost daily basis. Probably half of the respectable, middle-class families in the nation had their regular bootlegger. Terms like "bathtub gin" and "speakeasy" became part of the national language. Especially in colleges, drinking became a regular pastime of the "flaming youth" of the decade.

The Search for Innocence As their own lives became more and more confused, Americans began to celebrate innocence. In their movies and sports they created simple, naive heroes who were guided by straightforward codes of justice and virtue. The most popular type of movie hero of the decade was the cowboy, a symbol of innocent, preindustrial man. And the most popular movie star of the period, Rudolph Valentino, played roles that put him on horseback in a country far removed from Fords and factories and modernity. It was no accident, too, that the greatest sports hero of the decade, George Herman Ruth, was nicknamed "Babe."

Lindbergh stirred the deep urge of people to believe in innocence. His youth, honesty, and simple determination made him seem much purer than the public that worshipped him. Lindbergh did not smoke or drink. He displayed no interest in women, at least at the time of his flight. And his boyish face looked out at the world through clear blue eyes. They seemed to say that everything was still the same, that the world had not lost its innocence after all.

Illusions of Disillusionment In the midst of all this change and confusion, intellectuals offered very little help. Beginning in the 1890s, intellectuals in America had produced a remarkable body of literature on the workings of society. In the 1920s, a new generation of intellectuals began to turn out a profusion of superb novels, plays, and essays—as rich a cultural flowering as the country had ever produced. But their work embodied a marked shift away from a concern with social and political problems. With a few exceptions, the new writers either ignored society altogether or viewed it as the enemy, to be mocked or damned.

All in all, the viewpoint of the writers of the 1920s fits Malcolm Cowley's description quite well: "Society was something quite alien . . . a sort of parlor car in which we rode, over smooth tracks, toward a destination we should never have chosen for ourselves." This self-conscious sense of alienation from social structures and purposes governed the literary culture of the decade. It was what prompted the idea that the writers of the period belonged to a "lost generation." The result was a rush of great art that pointed in no particular social direction whatever.

The dominant theme of the writers of the 1920s was disillusionment. Their heroes and heroines usually entered their novels, plays, and stories caught up in some sort of innocent faith—in religion, civilization, progress, freedom, or the like. But, typically, this faith was broken by experience, and the outcome was a ripping away of old illusions. In the typical novel of the decade, the illusions were not replaced by any working new beliefs, but instead by a brooding sense of mistrust and disappointment, and a curious kind of boredom with the world.

The first great subject for disillusionment was the war and the mistaken peace that followed. Several of the best young writers cut their teeth on the war experience—William Faulkner, Ernest Hemingway, John Dos Passos—and for most of them, the conclusion was simple: the war had proved the bankruptcy of what people called "civilization." Hemingway summed up the experience in a story called "Soldier's Home," about the shattered illusions of a veteran named Krebs: "Krebs acquired the nausea in regard to experience that is the result of untruth or exaggeration." The same logic governed Maxwell Anderson's popular *What Price Glory*, E. E. Cummings's *The Enormous Room*—a hilarious book on his arrest and imprisonment in France—and the two war novels of Dos Passos, *One Man's Initiation* and *Three Soldiers*. The only way to escape the "nausea" brought on by the war was to make what Hemingway called "a separate peace."

Actually, when they are looked at carefully, the American war novels were not so much about the war at all, but about what the writers thought lay behind the war: technology, bureaucracy, and propaganda. For people like Faulkner or Dos Passos, the war was not so much a subject as a dramatic metaphor. In many of Hemingway's books and stories of the 1920s—*A Farewell to Arms* (1925) and *The Sun Also Rises* (1926) among them—the war was only the most violent phase of modern civilization. It merely brought into sharper focus the cruelty and inhumanity that were an inherent feature of contemporary social life.

When the writers looked at peacetime subjects, the result was much the same. Sinclair Lewis's riotous parody of the consciousness of a midwestern businessman, in his novel *Babbit,* was just as "disillusioned" as any war novel. In *Winesburg, Ohio*, Sherwood Anderson looked behind the drawn blinds of a small town with exactly the same sense of alienation and distaste. Dos Passos's voluminous novel, *1919*, made little or no distinction between war and peace. All in all, the writers of the decade agreed with the judgment of the poet Ezra Pound that Western civilization was "an old bitch gone in the teeth." Another poet, T. S. Eliot, summed up the attitude in the title of his most popular work of the period, *The Waste Land.*

For many the only solution seemed to be expatriation. In *The Sun Also Rises*, Hemingway portrayed the aimless confusion of American and British intellectuals in Paris. And for those who did not actually leave the country, there were other forms of withdrawal. William Faulkner—probably the best writer of the period—technically, stayed stubbornly in Mississippi. From that vantage point, he wrote social novels, but they were novels about a rural society whose problems were hardly those of an industrial and urban society. In novels like *The Sound and the Fury* (1929), Faulkner resorted to disarmingly traditional and innocent solutions to human problems—honesty, decency, and even simple modesty. At times, he even seemed to propose religious faith as the only authentic alternative to meaninglessness in modern life.

The writer who best caught the spirit of the "Jazz Age"—as he called it—was F. Scott Fitzgerald. *This Side of Paradise* (1920) rocketed him to a precocious fame. But his reputation was quickly confirmed by *The Great Gatsby* (1925). Fitzgerald's characters inhabited a world of money and sophistication. They were literate and articulate, young and dashing. They drank and smoked and danced their way toward disaster. They were a curious mixture of innocence and disillusionment.

Jay Gatsby, easily Fitzgerald's most characteristic hero, was in some ways a cynical man. He was a criminal who had become extraordinarily wealthy and had invented a false and cultured identity for himself, complete with a great mansion on Long Island. But there was another side to Gatsby, very like Lindbergh. He was a boy from the Midwest who had read Benjamin Franklin, worked hard for "success," and dreamed an innocent dream—that he might find and marry the girl he had loved as a youth. It was this dream, this "romantic readiness," that made Gatsby "great." And if the naive dream led only to corruption and murder, that seemed to Fitzgerald to capture the inner meaning of his generation's experience.

In a sense, Gatsby and Lindbergh were opposite manifestations of the same heroic figure.

Both were simple in the midst of complexity, daring in a world that had become increasingly routine and bureaucratic. Both were driven by a private conviction that had little or no social significance. The difference was that Fitzgerald's hero ended in failure and death; Lindbergh won success and fame and married the daughter of a wealthy financier.

SUGGESTED READINGS— CHAPTERS 37-38

Lindbergh

Charles A. Lindbergh, *The Spirit of Saint Louis* (1953); Kenneth S. Davis, *The Hero: Charles A. Lindbergh* (1959); Walter S. Ross, *The Last Hero: Charles A. Lindbergh* (1968).

General

John D. Hicks, *The Republican Ascendancy, 1921–1933* (1960); David A. Shannon, *Between the Wars, 1919–1941* (1965); John Braeman, R. H. Bremner, David Brody, eds., *Change and Continuity in America: The 1920s* (1968); William E. Leuchtenburg, *The Perils of Prosperity, 1914–1932* (1958).

Communications

Ronald Gellatt, *The Fabulous Phonograph* (1965); Beaumont Newhall, *The History of Photography* (1964); Erik Bernouw, *A Tower in Babel: A History of Broadcasting in the United States to 1933* (1966); F. L. Mott, *American Journalism* (1962).

Technology

Sigfried Giedion, *Mechanization Takes Command* (1948); Henry Ford, *My Life and Work* (1922); Allan Nevins and Frank E. Hill, *Ford* (3 vols., 1954–1962); F. C. Kelly, *The Wright Brothers: Fathers of Flight* (1943); Wilbur and Orville Wright, *Papers* (1953).

Popular Culture

J. W. Krutch, *The Modern Temper* (1929); F. L. Allen, *Only Yesterday* (1931); R. S. and H. N. Lynd, *Middletown* (1929); Arthur Knight, *The Liveliest Art* (1957); Andrew Sinclair, *The Other Half: The Emancipation of the American Woman* (1962); Harold Seymour, *Baseball* (2 vols., 1960–1971); Marshall and Jean Sterns, *Jazz Dance* (1968); Edward Wagenknecht, *Movies in the Age of Innocence* (1962).

Intellectuals

Malcolm Cowley, *Exile's Return* (1934); Edmund Wilson, *Axle's Castle* (1931); Alfred Kazin, *On Native Grounds* (1942); W. B. Rideout, *The Radical Novel in the United States, 1900–1954* (1956); Frederick Hoffmann, *The Twenties* (1955).

39
DEFEAT OF THE BONUS MARCHERS

R. J. W.

The witness shifted nervously but stood his ground. Having waited a long time to testify, he was not going to be put off. Without formally addressing the committee or saying so much as a polite "Gentlemen," he began: "My comrade and I hiked here from nine o'clock Sunday morning, when we left Camden. I done it all by my feet—shoe leather. I come to show you people that we need our bonus. We wouldn't want it if we didn't need it."

The witness was Joseph T. Angelo, veteran of World War I. He was addressing a committee of the House of Representatives of the United States Congress in 1931. The committee was hearing witnesses testify about a controversial matter: the immediate payment of a "bonus" to all the veterans of the war. The country was in the third year of a depression, and the bonus would pay about $1,000 each to over 3 million veterans and their families.[1] It would, in fact, be the greatest program of direct relief for the poor ever undertaken by the federal government.

For six days officials of the Republican administration testified. President Herbert Hoover was opposed to the bonus. The testimony of government officials reflected this opposition. A few congressmen and one or two officials of veterans' organizations spoke out for the bonus. But they were outnumbered by a long string of bank vice presidents, insurance executives, and other businessmen. The testimony was dull. It was full of statistics designed to prove that the bonus would bankrupt the federal treasury and bring about a dangerous inflation.

But now for the first time an ordinary veteran, with no job, a hungry family, and a plain man's English, was testifying. Before Angelo fin-

[1]Congress had set up the bonus (a combination of life insurance and a pension) in 1924. It was not due to be paid until 1945, except to the heirs of veterans who died earlier.

Disciplined regiments of World War I veterans marched silently and gravely to the Capitol in June 1932. This was a veterans' parade with a difference—the men did not want the people's gratitude now, but a bonus that would help them through hard times.

ished, the committee and the audience were stirred to a mixture of laughter, admiration, and stunned confusion.

> I have got a little home back there [in Camden, New Jersey] that I built with my own hands after I came home from France. Now, I expect to lose that little place. Last week I went to our town committee and they gave me $4 for rations. That is to keep my wife and child and myself and clothe us; and also I cannot put no coal in my cellar.

Here, in the poor grammar and tired face of the witness, was the whole meaning of the depression that had begun in 1929. Angelo said he spoke for hundreds like himself in New Jersey. But he spoke, too, for millions all over the country who had not worked for a long time, who stood in bread lines, and who built the shacks in the shabby little towns they wryly called Hoovervilles.

But Angelo was also a veteran. So he spoke from his experience of the two most important events in his time—the war that people still called the Great War and the depression they were beginning to call the Great Depression. There was no economic theory or political philosophy in his testimony. He was just a hungry man who had fought in France.

> All I ask of you, brothers, is to help us. We helped you, now you help us. My partner here has a wife and five children, and he is just the same as I am. He hiked down here at the same time with me, and our feet are blistered. That is all I have to say. And I hope you folks can help us and that we can go through with the bonus.

We don't want charity; we don't need it. All we ask for is what belongs to us, and that is all we want.

Some of the congressmen were confused. Others were curious. Following the custom of congressional committees, they began to question the witness:

MR. FREAR: What is your business?

MR. ANGELO: Nothing. I am nothing but a bum.

MR. FREAR: You say you have not worked for two years?

MR. ANGELO: I have not worked for a year and a half. But there is no work in my home town.

MR. RAINEY: You are wearing some medal. What is it?

MR. ANGELO: I carry the highest medal in America for enlisted men, the Distinguished Service Cross.

MR. RAINEY: You have a Distinguished Service Cross? What is that for?

MR. ANGELO: That is for saving Colonel Patton.

George S. Patton was already a well-known army officer. (In World War II he would become one of the most famous and controversial of America's generals.) Congressman Rainey continued the questioning and pressed Angelo for details. Angelo responded with a startling tale. He had been part of a 305-man unit attacked by German machine guns in the Argonne Forest in 1918. When the battle was over, he said, most of the men were dead. Colonel Patton was wounded, and only he—Angelo—was left standing. Then Angelo showed the committee a tiepin made from a bullet he said was taken from Patton's leg in France. Neither the watch nor the medal had ever gone to "Uncle," Angelo's pet name for the pawnshop that had swallowed up most of his other possessions.

The afternoon was wearing on, but Angelo had roused the attention of the committee members and the audience as none of the other witnesses had. So the congressmen began to ask about his life. As Angelo answered, the audience sometimes laughed, sometimes applauded. He told them of working in a DuPont plant, making munitions for the British before the United States entered the war. When Congress declared war in 1917, he enlisted at once. But he was almost rejected because he weighed a mere 107 pounds. Only after ten doctors had examined him and a general had watched him do a handspring and jump a table was he accepted.

Then, obviously agitated, Angelo wound up with another statement:

I can make money. I can make lots of money. Now, I could go bootlegging. It is just the same way I could have went to France and I could have run out on my outfit. Which is the best, to be a live coward or a dead hero?

When this was put on me, brothers, I wasn't worried when I went through. I don't have nothing to worry about. I wasn't married, and I got a wonderful sendoff when I went to France. My father throwed me out. [Laughter.] And when I came back, I went home to my father. I saw a big, fat woman sitting in the seat. I knowed her from next door. I said, "She is the last woman you want on earth. Pop, what is she doing here?" He says, "That is my wife." I says, "Oh, My God!" She says, "Get out of here," and that was my welcome home, and I got out. [Laughter.]

So, folks, I tell you all I will say to you is, help us through with the bonus. That is the best answer for you folks to give to the fellow at home. Don't forget me for a job. [Applause.]

Joe Angelo was three things: a veteran, a bum, and a victim of the most serious economic depression in American history. In each of these roles he was not just an individual grappling with purely personal problems. He represented over 4½ million soldiers (about half of whom had actually been sent to Europe) suddenly discharged into civilian life in 1918 and 1919. These veterans organized—like other veterans in America's previous wars. More than a million joined the new American Legion and the Veterans of Foreign Wars. They thought of themselves as a special type of citizen, with a special claim on their country's gratitude.

As a bum, Angelo also spoke for countless people, many of them veterans, who had worked unsuccessfully at one job or another but mostly drifted through the 1920s. Naturally, the depression added millions of new "bums." Angelo, who had not been able to find work for a year and a half, was only one of a great, restless mass of unemployed. When he appeared before the congressional committee, at least 5 million men and women were classed as unemployed. Probably another 5 million were able to find only part-time work. Almost every other worker in America had his wages cut after the stock market crash of 1929. Few people could

A group of New York veterans gathered in the yards of the Baltimore and Ohio Railroad at Jersey City, New Jersey, on June 4, 1932. These angry, frustrated men were hoping to seize a train and head for Washington where they would demand payment of their bonus.

doubt in 1931 that unemployment was one of the most serious problems the United States had ever faced.

Joe Angelo's instinct was to turn to Washington for help. On his walk from Camden he had met other small groups of veterans with the same idea. The unemployed, the veterans, and the bums (often one man, like Angelo, was all three) were looking more and more to the federal government for relief. They had one fairly good chance of getting help from a reluctant Congress and a stubborn President—payment of the bonus. This, in Angelo's words, was "the best answer for you folks to give."

Angelo wanted $1,000 immediately, instead of waiting until 1945 to collect a larger amount. This was the heart of an issue that was about to create the most dramatic crisis of the depression—the massing in Washington of a "Bonus Army." Behind the crisis lay the old task of writing a final chapter to the World War and the new, complicated task of dealing with the depression. But for the marchers in the Bonus Army, the problem was quite simple: When and how would they be able to collect their bonus in full?

Veterans could already borrow money against the promise of the government to pay. Over 2 million had taken out loans that averaged $100 each—just enough to pay a back grocery bill, buy some coal for winter, or meet a medical emergency. But veterans everywhere were beginning to ask for ten times more, the payment of the entire bonus. And they found some sympathetic ears in Congress. Representative Wright Patman of Texas introduced a bill to authorize printing almost $2½ billion in new paper money to pay the bonus. As time passed there was more and more talk of the bonus, not only in Washington but wherever knots of hungry veterans gathered.

In November 1931 a group of veterans left Seattle to ride freights to the capital. All over the country others were doing likewise. A movement began that would shake the Hoover administration.

For two years the President had been telling the nation that the depression was not so serious and would soon end. Administration officials had always played down unemployment statistics. They portrayed the crisis as a temporary economic slump that would cure itself. Meanwhile, Hoover kept to his principle that the federal government should not provide direct relief to poor individuals. The veterans who were hitchhiking and jumping freight trains headed toward the capital were not so sure of their principles. Certainly they lacked the President's political experience and skills. But they knew that they needed the bonus.

By May 1932, 300 men from Portland, Oregon, left for Washington in a group. They called themselves the Bonus Expeditionary Force—a play on the name of the American army in France, the American Expeditionary Force. They elected a leader, Walter F. Waters, once an army sergeant, then foreman in a fruit cannery, now unemployed. They rode freight cars east and, by late May, reached East St. Louis, Illinois. There they tried to hop new trains going farther east. When railroad police told them to leave, they began to break up trains by uncoupling cars. They also soaped the rails in some places, making it impossible for engines to move.

The state called for its national guard to drive the veterans away. A scuffle occurred, but no one was hurt badly. The marchers were soon on their way again — in national guard trucks that Illinois had provided in return for their promise to leave the state peacefully. But, most important, for the first time, the Bonus Army won the attention of the newspapers and the public. Other veterans soon followed suit.

The scene was repeated everywhere. Merchants and mayors, railroad officials and governors, found it easier to supply trucks or boxcars than to stop the veterans. Thus a steady stream of Bonus Marchers was pouring into Washington. Each group had a leader or two, and their purpose was the same. They were in Washington to demand their bonus, even if they had to wait there until 1945 to get it.

One man deeply interested in the veterans' cause was Pelham D. Glassford, a West Point graduate and the youngest American in the World War to become a brigadier general. In 1931 Hoover appointed Glassford superintendent of Washington's police force. So he would have to deal with the Bonus Expeditionary Force in the capital.

Glassford hoped that the Bonus Army either would not come or would go home quickly. But, when the marchers arrived, he became sympathetic and helpful. He regarded them as "his boys." He assigned them quarters in abandoned buildings on Pennsylvania Avenue. The location was at the heart of official Washington, between the White House and the Capitol.

At Glassford's suggestion, also, the marchers made a "muster," or list of their groups, to make it easier to track down criminals and keep out the "Reds" and radicals. Gradually the marchers formed companies and then regiments. They elected Walter Waters, leader of the Portland group, as commander of the Bonus Expeditionary Force. He appointed junior officers and divided the men into companies named after states. Soon, the Bonus Army had a structure of command like the regular army.

General Pelham D. Glassford here watches some men at Anacostia Flats prepare a stew for their dinner. Although as chief of police he was responsible for dealing with the alarming number of veterans arriving in the capital, Glassford was sympathetic to the Bonus Marchers' cause.

Glassford's original decision to let the marchers camp along Pennsylvania Avenue was based on his hope that few would come. Soon it was obvious that the Bonus Army was much too large and dangerous (and embarrassing to the administration) to be in the center of things. Glassford sent most of the marchers to a new campsite a few miles southeast of Capitol Hill. The place was Anacostia Flats, a muddy landfill near the forks of the Potomac and Anacostia rivers. There, about 6,000 veterans built a shabby but orderly camp, with shacks and tents arranged in winding rows.

At Anacostia Flats the veterans tried to recreate their old army life. They woke to bugles, conducted roll calls, and had inspections. A company of men was assigned every day to "KP." Waters exercised strict discipline.

Other aspects of camp life were more relaxed. Some men had

brought their wives and children. The Salvation Army set up a post office, a library, and a recreation room. Glassford managed to borrow some field kitchens and other equipment. He supervised the distribution of food donated by Washington citizens, American Legion posts, and others. At one point Glassford gave several hundred dollars of his own money to buy food. There was even a newspaper to keep the veterans informed about the progress of bonus legislation in Congress.

By June 6, 1932, the veterans were ready for their first direct action. About 7,000 left their separate camps around the city and lined up neatly in six "regiments" to parade through Washington. The men felt fairly hopeful as they moved along. The Patman bill, which was in the House, seemed as if it would pass soon. The rumors that they were controlled by communists, spread by some politicians to smear the Bonus Army, were not given much credit. Best of all, their parade had drawn a crowd of about 100,000; mostly Washington clerical workers. Every time another company with its American flag passed, the crowd applauded.

Shortly after dark the long line of march reached a monument circle near the Capitol. (They were forbidden to pass the White House or go to the Capitol itself.) Orders were given to fall out, and the marchers broke ranks to walk quietly back to Anacostia. They had heard that in less than a week the House would vote on the bonus bill. If it passed both the House and Senate and was signed by Hoover, most of the veterans could collect the thousand dollars needed to get their hungry families through another depression year.

The parade was simply a beginning. Veterans kept coming to Washington—the police estimated a hundred every hour. On June 15, when the House passed the bill, there were probably 15,000 veterans, plus some of their wives and children, scattered around Washington. Anacostia Flats was crowded, but new shacks kept going up. By now the ex-soldiers had stripped half the city of every stray board or door, every spare piece of tin or canvas. One man moved a burial vault onto the flats and took up residence in it. The camp was about level with the river, and had to be protected by a levee. When it rained, mud was a foot deep. But the Bonus Army kept building.

Obviously some kind of crisis might soon develop. Health officials predicted a typhoid epidemic. Waters predicted victory when 100,000 more veterans arrived. Hoover's advisers predicted that communists would take over the Bonus Force.

The Bonus Army and the administration were both waiting for the Senate to vote on the Patman bill. Hoover was sure he would win. The House elected in 1930 was Democratic. Since it was the first body of politicians to graduate from the depression, it was full of representatives who had recently promised their constituents direct action. But only a third of the Senate had been elected in 1930. The majority were still firmly Republican and loyal to the President. Both houses were striving for a July adjournment. (It was an election year, and everyone wanted to get home to campaign.) The administration hoped that the Bonus Army would simply disappear after the Senate voted and Congress adjourned.

On June 17 the Senate would debate and vote on the bonus. Waters commanded his marchers to go to the Capitol and fill the galleries, steps, and grounds. By noon, there were 10,000 marchers in and around the Capitol.

Inside, the Senate debated. Men would leave the galleries every few minutes to report to the marchers out on the steps. Opponents of the bill argued Hoover's position on what should be done about the depression: the government ought to cut spending, not spend more. Direct relief to individuals was not a federal responsibility. Recovery would come as large banks, businesses, and railroads regained their health. Then jobs would become available, and the economy would escape from radical tinkering.

Many senators supporting the bill argued that since the veterans were hungry and would be able to collect the bonus in thirteen years anyway, they should have it now. But one or two senators gave a more complicated justification for the bonus. In a depression, they insisted, the government should spend money, not save it. If the government printed 2 ½ billion new dollars for the bonus, the money would swiftly circulate. The veterans would be only the first to gain. The stores where they spent their payments would get the money. These stores, in turn, would order more goods from wholesalers and manufacturers. So every bonus dollar would become a dollar in motion, moving through the economy and stimulating all business. Naturally, when the depression was cured, the government would stop deficit spending—that is, spending more than it raised in taxes. The economy would return to normal. The government would only "prime the pump" with its paper dollars. The happy results would then be automatic.

Though the argument went on, it soon became clear that only a political miracle could save the bonus. The Senate was much too conservative to experiment with such legislation. Even some of the liberal sen-

Thousands of veterans waited tensely on the steps of the Capitol, as the Senate debated the fate of their bonus. The eventual defeat of the Patman bill that would have made their dream a reality nearly triggered a violent confrontation between them and the marines.

ators who usually opposed Hoover questioned the bill. What was needed, they said, was a general bill for relief of all the unemployed. Veterans should receive no special favors.

Finally, after eight o'clock, someone came from the galleries and whispered to Waters. The bill had lost decisively, 62 to 18. Waters climbed the steps and turned to face the largest body ever gathered in Washington to demonstrate for a cause. The marchers had been waiting for hours, and for a moment it seemed as if they might riot. Marines were stationed nearby, just in case. Members of the administration wanted to ready machine guns, but Glassford persuaded them not to. Waters shouted: "Comrades![2] I have bad news. Let us show them we can take it on the chin. Let us show them we are patriotic Americans." There was a muttering from the crowd. Then a gigantic roar came from 10,000 throats. Waters pleaded for calm:

> We are not telling you to go home. Go back to your camps. We are going to stay in Washington until we get the bonus, no matter how long it takes. And we are one hundred times as good Americans as those men in there who voted against it. But there is nothing more to be done tonight.

The situation was tenser than any in the capital since the Civil War. Ten thousand disappointed people, who had kept good discipline for weeks, were ready to break and mob the Senate. Waters played a final card to keep order: "I call on you to sing 'America,'" he shouted. After a few false starts, the men obeyed. Gradually, the song gathered strength.

The emergency was over, at least for the moment. The singing died out, and bugles sounded assembly. The men milled about, looking for their outfits for the march back to camp. It was dark now, and the nervous men waiting in the White House and the Capitol could take a deep breath. The bonus was dead, at least until Congress reconvened in December, after the presidential elections.

But the Bonus Army did not disappear. The government issued reports that the men were leaving. The Bonus Force and the police reported, however, that new recruits were arriving about as fast as old ones left. Estimates of the size of the force issued by the government, the police, the newspapers, and the Bonus Army itself varied widely. At its largest, the Bonus Army probably numbered just under 20,000 men. Membership shifted constantly; perhaps as many as 50,000 veterans were in Washington at one time or another during June and July of 1932.

The government offered to lend the marchers train fare or gas money to leave town, plus seventy-five cents a day for other expenses. Many veterans simply took the money and stayed in town. Others used it to recruit new members. Thus, a month after the Senate had defeated the Patman bill, there were about as many marchers as ever. The police

---

[2]This was an old term from the war, not a communist greeting.

Veterans inhabited eyesores such as these, located on government property close to the Capitol. In an election year, the government felt especially threatened by their well-publicized presence.

estimated 15,000 people, two-thirds of them now crowded into Anacostia Flats.

By July, with no hope of a bonus from Congress, the veterans' mood soured. Their newspaper published more militant calls for action. Waters began to allow the small group of about 150 communists to eat occasionally at the Anacostia mess. (He had always thrown them out before.) He even began to talk about a permanent organization of veterans in politics, which he would call "Khaki Shirts," in imitation of the "Brown Shirts" that Adolf Hitler had organized.

In the White House, too, opinions were getting stronger. After the Senate defeated the bonus, the President decided the marchers had no business squatting on government land. He also decided they were not truly patriotic veterans asking for relief. Instead he believed they had been:

> organized and promoted by the communists, and included a large number of hoodlums and ex-convicts determined to raise a public disturbance. They were frequently addressed by Democratic congressmen, seeking to inflame them against me.

The differences grew sharper, the summer hotter, and tempers shorter. On July 16 the most serious incident so far broke out at the Capitol. Congress was about to adjourn. Waters ordered his men to make one last symbolic demonstration. By midday nearly 7,000 Bonus Marchers were at the Capitol. Their mood was much uglier than a month before. Senators and congressmen crowded near every window to watch. Even Glassford lost his nerve.

Glassford ordered Waters taken into custody and moved to the basement of the Capitol. When the veterans saw what was happening, they stopped cheering Glassford and began to boo and jeer. "Waters! Waters!" they shouted. Glassford was forced to bring the Bonus Army's commander onto the platform. After a short, harsh exchange with Glassford, Waters tried to calm his people. Then he ordered them to move to the middle: "Use the center steps. But I want you to keep a lane open for the white-collared birds, so they won't rub into us lousy rats. We're going to stay here until I see Hoover!"

The demonstration was clearly dangerous. Several congressmen came out of the Capitol to speak to the demonstrators, trying to cool them off. Finally the Speaker of the House, John Nance Garner, agreed to meet with Waters and a committee of his aides inside the building. Garner handled the situation well. He made a few empty promises of help and was photographed with Waters. When the conference was over, Waters went back outside and ordered his followers to their camps. For a second time an extremely touchy and potentially violent situation had been controlled.

In the White House, however, tempers were also growing shorter. Hoover had just been renominated by the Republicans to run for a second term. The Democrats would meet soon to nominate Franklin D. Roosevelt, then governor of New York. Hoover knew the campaign would be rough. But he knew he would win if he could overcome the widespread idea that he was responsible for the depression.

A favorite tactic of Hoover's closest associates was to picture him as the firm opponent of all kinds of radicalism. Unfortunately, the Bonus Army was the most visible kind of radicalism. Hoover had always opposed the bonus. Now he and his advisers decided to move firmly against the veterans. Some even hoped for an incident. Then it would appear that the government had to defend its very life against a radical insurrection.

A few days after Congress adjourned, the administration decided to move. The tensest point in Washington was the two square blocks on the south side of Pennsylvania Avenue, just a block from the Capitol and a mile from the White House. The buildings here were part of a triangle of structures that had been condemned to make way for a government building program. All over the triangle, veterans had camped in and around vacant and half-demolished structures, eyesores that embarrassed the administration. On July 21, on instructions from the Treasury Department, the commissioners who governed the District of Columbia (and were directly responsible to the administration) ordered the veterans to evacuate the two blocks. For various reasons the order was not carried out at once. But Waters told his people to be ready to leave. Glassford was locating another site farther away, where they could take their few possessions and settle again.

Finally, at about 10 A.M. on July 28, Treasury officials accompanied by Glassford and his police entered the area. The veterans began to evacuate the buildings and their makeshift shanties, leaving behind everything that they could not carry or push along in small carts or baby carriages. Everything went peacefully, though a few veterans had to be taken out under arrest. Before noon the first building was empty. In the meantime, a large crowd of Washington citizens had gathered to watch. Their sympathies were divided between the police and the veterans.

Then, a little past noon, veterans from other camps filtered into the area, mixing with the crowd. One group came to stage a formal demonstration. Paul Anderson, a journalist, described what happened next:

> At noon, three bonus men, one carrying a large American flag, started across the block, followed by several hundred. When the leaders encountered a policeman, he grabbed the flag. There was a scuffle, and one of the marchers was hit on the head with a night stick. He wrested it from the officer and struck the cop, and there was a shower of bricks from the buddies in the rear. It looked like an ugly mess, but the cops kept their heads, and no shots were fired.
>
> Glassford dashed into the heart of the melee, smiled when a brickbat hit him on the chest, and stopped the fighting. Within two minutes, the veterans were cheering Glassford.

For another half hour the police continued their work. The veterans were leaving the buildings, but they stood around outside, many on big piles of bricks. No one is certain what happened next. Some witnesses said a policeman tried to clear veterans out of a building that had not even been ordered vacated. They resisted. Another observer said that a policeman started climbing some makeshift stairs, lost his balance, and fell. In a panic he pulled his revolver and began to fire wildly into a crowd near him. General Glassford gave what may be the most accurate account:

> I was about twenty yards away from the building when I heard a commotion. I went to the second floor. One officer had started up the steps, and near the rear, I heard some say, "Let's get him!"
> As he started up the steps, bricks started falling on him [Glassford was not certain whether the bricks were being thrown or were just falling], and as I leaned over the railing above, I saw him fall and draw his gun, firing two shots.

Other policemen also started shooting. Then veterans began to throw bricks at every policeman in sight. Again Glassford acted quickly to prevent a vicious riot. He ran outside, shouting, "Stop that shooting!" The firing ended, and the bricks stopped flying. Ambulances rushed to take away the injured. One policeman was hurt seriously by a brick. One Bonus Marcher was dead; another died later of gunshot wounds.

The battle of the Bonus Army might have ended here. Glassford had the situation in hand. The veterans were moving out of the buildings as they had been ordered. On the whole they were reluctant but still willing to cooperate. Waters had supported Glassford every step of the way. Within another hour or two the evacuation of the two blocks would have been complete. But the administration also had decided to act. Hoover had ordered the Chief of Staff of the Army, General MacArthur, to bring troops into the city to restore civil peace.

When the Bonus Marchers were ordered to clear the federal property on which they had been squatting, fights broke out between them and the police that led to a larger battle.

The troops—about 500 at first, then later over 1,000—formed up behind the White House. They came armed with bayoneted rifles and heavy blue canisters of tear gas. There were cavalry with sabers, a machine-gun squadron, several infantry companies, and even a half-dozen tanks. MacArthur put the troops under the command of General Perry L. Miles. But he later wrote, "In accordance with the President's request, I accompanied General Miles." With MacArthur was his aide, Major Dwight David Eisenhower. And in the cavalry was George S. Patton (who had no way of knowing that Joe Angelo had come back to Washington and was out in the troubled city with about 12,000 of his buddies, waiting).

At about four o'clock the cavalry led the way, the iron shoes of their horses clattering on the asphalt of Pennsylvania Avenue. Then came tanks, more cavalry, the infantry, and the mounted machine gunners. They rode, walked, and rumbled up to the triangle, pushing the crowds back and surrounding the buildings. Without any conference or hesitation the troops (who wore gas masks and carried fixed bayonets) began to throw tear-gas bombs into the buildings. They were going to clear the entire area.

The veterans did not resist. A few hung back, and had to be jabbed at with bayonets. Mostly they stumbled out of the area and toward Anacostia. MacArthur, who also had tears streaming down his face from the tear gas, ordered most of his men to herd the veterans south. Another detachment moved west, to attack the small, separate camp of the communist group.[3] Suddenly, it became clear that the general intended to clear the entire District. In the triangle, smoke began to rise. There, the troops had set fire to the shacks, tents, and scattered belongings of the Bonus Army.

MacArthur's forces kept pushing the straggling veterans before them with bayonets and sabers. The sun was going down behind them. Ahead lay the drawbridge to Anacostia. The Bonus Army's rear guard hurried across the bridge at about sunset. Waters had already given the order to evacuate Anacostia and had sent word to MacArthur asking for time to move women and children out of the camp. On the flats about 7,000 men were scurrying around, trying to keep order in a forced retreat.

From the time the troops first appeared, the Bonus Marchers gave no resistance. They booed, they swore—but they moved. MacArthur left his tanks north of the river and paused before Anacostia Flats for an hour before sending the infantry. But when they went onto the flats, the soldiers threw tear gas everywhere. Stragglers were treated very roughly. The soldiers then set fire to the camp. (Many of the veterans had already put matches to their borrowed army tents.) Next they moved out of the camp to the nearby area where many of the veterans still stood watching

General Douglas MacArthur with his aide, Dwight David Eisenhower, led the forces that finally cleared Washington of Bonus Marchers. MacArthur later claimed that if the situation had continued, the institutions of government would have been threatened.

---

[3]Communists in this camp included James Ford, their candidate for Vice President. On July 31 the New York *Times* ran a front-page article quoting the communists. "We agitated for the bonus and led the demonstration of the veterans in Washington." However, the communists were never the Bonus Force's prime movers.

Troopers used tear gas in a final effort to clear the Bonus Marchers out of Washington. The veterans were forced to retreat and in the main did not resist.

their shacks burn. As the troops rushed up the hill, which was not federal property, they continued to throw tear gas. One woman, whose baby had actually been born since the Bonus Army's arrival, told this story:

> The troops came up the hill, driving the people ahead of them. As they passed by the house [where the woman was staying], one of them threw a tear-gas bomb over the fence into the front yard. The house was filled with gas, and we all began to cry. We got wet towels and put them over the faces of the children. About a half an hour later, my baby began to vomit. I took her outside in the air and she vomited again. Next day, she began to turn black and blue.

A few days later the baby died—the third and last fatality of the battle of the Bonus Army.

The day after the action was a time for summing up. The White House and other administration officials issued statements. MacArthur gave his version in a press conference:

> That mob was a bad-looking mob. It was animated by the essence of revolution. They had come to the conclusion, beyond the shadow of a doubt, that they were about to take over either the direct control of the government, or else to control it by indirect methods. It is my belief that had the President not acted today, he would have been faced with a grave situation. Had he let it go on another week, I believe that the institutions of our government would have been severely threatened.

To this version of the threat posed by the Bonus Force, MacArthur added a simple lie—that it was the veterans who had burned their shacks in the triangle.

On July 29, 1932, in a blazing finale that brought the battle of the Bonus Army to an end, the camps at Anacostia Flats went up in flames.

Another kind of summing up came from Joe Angelo, who told a newspaper reporter his story. He was at Anacostia Flats, watching a group of infantrymen in gas masks overrun the shack he had been living in. They were urged on by a tough, confident cavalry officer. Angelo blinked the burning tear gas out of his eyes and recognized George S. Patton. Then like the rest of the Bonus Army, he ran. Soon he was back home in Camden, from where he had started his long hike to Washington a year and a half before.

40
PROSPERITY AND DEPRESSION

R. J. W.

Most of the Bonus March veterans who went to Washington were as politically innocent as Joe Angelo. Some of their leaders had a little political knowledge—and the tiny fraction who were communists thought they understood the basic problems of American society and sought a revolutionary solution. But the great rank and file of the marchers were simply caught in a web of circumstances they did not understand or want.

The marchers' experience was defined by the two great events they had participated in, the Great War and the Great Depression. Between lay the decade of the 1920s, the "Jazz Age." But most of the marchers had experienced only a little jazz. Like most Americans, they had passed through a curiously contradictory decade. On the one hand, American society of the 1920s was characterized by tremendous innovations—some technological, other social. But, alongside all the newness and experimentation, the 1920s had been a decade of profound, sometimes violent conservatism. Both in formal politics, centered in Washington, and in informal politics of organized movements, the keynote had not been innovation but restoration.

Conservatism in politics received a kind of endorsement from the economy. The 1920s was a period of apparent prosperity. In some sectors, in fact, the economy virtually underwent a "boom." And this prosperity made it appear to many Americans that the country had returned from the distortions of progressive reform and war to "normalcy." It took the Depression to show that normalcy was

an illusion, and that the 1920s had contained profound distortions of its own.

A TIDE OF REACTION

For millions of Americans, the uncertainties of modernity, the wave of progressive reforms, and the moral crusade of the war were all extremely unsettling. Even before the war was over, millions of people had already decided that change had gone too far, that the republic was in desperate danger of losing its stability and virtue. For some, the threat was simple: the country was being overrun by foreigners and by "foreign" political ideas. For others, the problem was alcohol, and the loose life associated with it. Still others viewed blacks as the principal threat. For many, the danger lay in the growing number and power of Jews and Catholics. Some complained about the inroads new scientific ideas were making on "traditional" values and beliefs.

Not every American participated, by any means, but a large and very active segment of society—especially in the South and the Midwest—joined in a series of movements and organizations to save their country from what were seen by them as the perils of change. Sometimes, the results were merely quaint—as when the sale of alcohol was forbidden by an amendment to the Constitution. Or when schoolteachers were prosecuted for explaining Charles Darwin's theory of evolution in their classrooms. At other times, however, the results were more serious, even tragic, as when dozens of blacks were lynched by mobs, or hundreds of immigrant "radicals" were hounded in court and even sentenced to die for their supposed crimes. This was part of the character of "normalcy," the opposite and darker face of the "Jazz Age."

The Red Scare The conservative reaction focused sharply on radicalism. The Russian Revolution, which had brought the communist government of the Bolsheviks to power, was followed by communist uprisings in Germany and Hungary. These developments created an atmosphere of fear in the United States. Many people, including a number of powerful leaders in federal and state governments, believed that a communist conspiracy was at work among them, ready to "radicalize" the country.

In 1919 a series of spectacular strikes and the outbreak of political sabotage fed the fear. In the spring of that year, two small groups of anarchists attempted to bomb the homes and offices of a number of government officials and businessmen. The bombs, most of which were sent through the mails, were probably the work of mentally unstable persons. Certainly they had nothing to do with the tiny organized Socialist and Communist parties of the country.

In fact, the bombers were incompetent. Most of the bombs were never delivered because they did not have enough postage. Another bomb only damaged the house of its intended victim, but it blew the bomber himself—an Italian anarchist—to bits. Another, addressed to a Georgia politician, was opened by his maid (a black worker, not a capitalist). She lost her hands as a result. But the bombings did convince many people that revolution was at hand.

One of the people who was most convinced was Woodrow Wilson's attorney general, A. Mitchell Palmer. Like Wilson, Palmer was a liberal and a strong antiradical. The attorney general also had his eye on the Democratic nomination of 1920. So he used the "red scare" to make his department the center of the action. He obtained a special appropriation for hunting down radicals. With the money he formed a new antisubversive division of the Justice Department, headed by J. Edgar Hoover.

Beginning in November of 1919 the Justice Department conducted a series of raids against radical groups, seeking out suspected communists at union meetings, at Communist party headquarters, and in their homes. The most spectacular of the raids, which came on New Year's Day 1920, resulted in the arrest of 6,000 people. In the end the Palmer raids led to the conviction of only a handful of citizens, most of them for minor crimes. Immigrant aliens, who were Palmer's main target,

suffered more; about 600 were eventually deported, mostly to the Soviet Union.

Palmer's campaign created an atmosphere of near hysteria among many Americans. It led to one tragedy that did more than any other single event of the 1920s to divide Americans of different political beliefs. In 1920 two Italian anarchists were arrested in Boston on a charge of robbing a shoe company and murdering two of its employees. Their trial soon became a political event, a test of the established authority against political radicalism. The trial was unfair. Even the judge privately referred to the defendants, Nicola Sacco and Bartolomeo Vanzetti, as anarchists.

But in the political climate of the red scare, Sacco and Vanzetti were convicted and sentenced to death. The process of appeals was long and unsuccessful. Finally, in 1927, the year of Lindbergh's flight, both men were executed in the electric chair. To the small number of American liberals and radicals of the 1920s, Sacco and Vanzetti were the century's greatest martyrs. They were modern counterparts of the victims of the Salem witch trials and the Haymarket Affair. But to most Americans, they were just Italian radicals who had been properly punished.

The Bonus Marchers of 1932 had to contend with the lingering effects of the red scare. They were accused of being communists, and of serving as tools in a foreign conspiracy. When Douglas MacArthur marched on their camp at Anacostia, he did so in the belief that he was protecting the country from a powerful revolutionary movement. The irony was, however, that the marchers themselves accepted much of the ideology of "Americanism" that underlay the red scare. Their response to the charge that they were communists was to insist on their own patriotism, and to point proudly to their record of military service. Most of the marchers were probably just as devoutly anticommunist, just as insistent on their own "100 percent Americanism" as their critics.

The red scare also made it possible for those Americans who feared immigrants and their ethnic and religious differences to restrict immigration. In February 1921 (over the veto of President Wilson) Congress passed a law that limited immigration, especially from countries in South-

Nicola Sacco and Bartolomeo Vanzetti entered a courthouse to make their final appeal in 1927. They were convicted essentially because they were Italians at a time when hatred of aliens ran high, and because they were anarchists in a politically conservative era.

ern and Eastern Europe. According to the law, the number of immigrants from a country in any given year could not exceed 3 percent of the number of people of that nationality who were already in the United States in 1910. In 1924 the law was made even more restrictive. Quotas would now be based on resident population in 1890, immigration limited to 150,000 a year after 1927, and Asians totally excluded. The effect of the laws was to end, almost at once, the flow of immigration.

Prohibition and Reaction Like the red scare and the movement for immigration restriction, the prohibition of alcohol in the 1920s had its roots in the progressive period. In 1919 the states had passed the Eighteenth Amendment, which empowered Congress to prohibit the sale of alcoholic beverages. The amendment marked the victory of a long campaign of temperance. It provided anoth-

er rallying point for conservative, small-town Americans. They divided society into the "drys" and the "wets" and opposed any politician who did not favor prohibition.

The prohibition movement failed to stop Americans from drinking. In most cities people continued to drink whiskey in speakeasies. The sale of bootleg whiskey was controlled largely by organized gangs of criminals. Gangs like the one led by Al Capone in Chicago bribed public officials and policemen to cover up their operations. But for most conservative Americans prohibition was above all a moral crusade. It was an issue they could use to split their countrymen into two camps: one composed of decent people, the other of riffraff.

Another conservative campaign of the 1920s was the attempt of many Protestant Americans—again, especially in the South and the Midwest—to prevent schools from teaching dangerous or "un-American" ideas. In several Southern states this crusade was aimed mainly at the idea of evolution. The notion of biological evolution was an old one. It became scientifically respected in the nineteenth century through the work of Charles Darwin. By the 1920s practically every scientist in the world believed that animals, including man, had evolved over a long period of time. But this seemed to many people to go against the fundamentals of their religion. They saw it as a challenge to the biblical story of creation.

Several state legislatures forbade their schools to teach the doctrine of evolution. In 1925 John Scopes, a schoolteacher in Dayton, Tennessee, decided to challenge the law. He was arrested, and his trial became almost as much a spectacle as the trial of Sacco and Vanzetti.

Scopes was defended by the most famous criminal lawyer in the United States, Clarence Darrow of Chicago. William Jennings Bryan led the prosecution. Bryan, an aging but still powerful leader of millions of fundamentalists, stood ready to smite the forces of modernism. He was humiliated on the witness stand by Darrow. Reporters from every major American newspaper—and several European papers—covered the trial.

Scopes lost the case and was fined $100. The Tennessee law stayed on the books. But after the Scopes trial the direction of education in the South and elsewhere shifted away from Bryan's intellectual conservatism toward the acceptance of modern science. Bryan's crusade, like many other conservative movements of the 1920s, was only a temporary victory over twentieth-century ideas and social habits.

The Ku Klux Klan The most spectacular conservative movement of the 1920s was the Ku Klux Klan. The Klan, which had all but disappeared after Reconstruction, was reorganized in 1915 in Georgia. Its membership grew slowly until the war was over. Then, taking many of its cues from the red scare, the Klan began to gain support. Much of its strength still lay in the rural South and Southwest. But there was a new element in this second growth: now, millions in the Northern

states, many of them city dwellers, joined this bizarre organization. At one time or another, about five million Americans took up membership and donned the white sheets that were the uniform of the Klan. The strongest Klan state was not in the South at all, but in Indiana, where the organization appeared for a time to control even the state government.

The Ku Klux Klan was a marginal, fringe organization. It attracted only the most conservative citizens. The white robes and hoods, the secrecy and the rituals, the burning of crosses in the night, demanded considerable dedication from its members. They had to be able to stomach a good deal of violence and torture. And they had to be able to tolerate a large element of the ridiculous—as in the titles of Klan officers, like Dragon, Kleagal, or Kludd. Nevertheless, the Klan was still able to elect one of its Dragons governor of Indiana, able to march openly in Washington in 1925, and able to control the Democratic presidential nomination in 1924.

In the long run, the Klan—like the prohibitionist movement and the fundamentalist attempt to prevent the teaching of evolution—was destined to lose. Blacks would not be lynched in great numbers forever, the freedom to drink alcohol would return, new scientific theories would get taught, eventually. But in the political atmosphere of the 1920s, it was possible for millions of Klansmen, and millions of other conservatives who did not join the organization, to convince themselves that their victory was close at hand, that the country would be saved, after all.

THE POLITICS OF CONSERVATISM

The political instrument of salvation, restoration, and "normalcy" was to be the Republican Party. As the war ended, the Republicans could see as plainly as anyone else that there was a change in the atmosphere. The policies of reform and military crusade, on which Woodrow Wilson and the Democrats had built their success in national poli-

The lunatic fringe of the 1920s had considerable strength, as this parade of Klansmen in the nation's capital in 1925 indicates. Terror was the Klan's chief method of warding off members' own fears of a rapidly changing America.

tics, were clearly going to fall into disrepute. The Republicans met at Chicago in their national convention of 1920 full of hope. They were still the majority party, they knew. And no Democrat on the horizon represented a real threat to the election of a Republican President. Wilson's illness, the failure of the League of Nations, the doings of A. Mitchell Palmer—all had helped to disorganize the Democrats.

The only question seemed to be whether the Republicans could unite on a candidate. The convention deadlocked for six ballots. Then, a few party leaders huddled in one of the most famous "smoke-filled rooms" in American history and chose a surprise candidate—Warren Gamaliel Harding, senator from Ohio.

Harding Harding was a small-town newspaper publisher and politician, reminiscent of the Republican style of the late nineteenth century. He had risen carefully through the party system in Ohio to become a senator. His political virtues were, primarily, loyalty to the organization and a discreet silence on most issues. A handsome but simple man, he was puzzled by complicated issues like taxation, the tariff, and foreign affairs. He was "one of the boys," who enjoyed a night of whiskey and poker with his cronies. He had never proposed an important law or policy, nor made an important speech, in his whole career. But he had a face that voters wanted to trust. And the people who ran the party knew they could trust him, too. He was a party regular. He would not have any strange ideas about regulating business or supporting labor unions; nor would he propose any odd reforms. He was, in a word, conservative.

Warren Harding, who won the presidency by being "one of the boys," was aware of his limitations. About his search for a capable economic adviser he said: "I don't know where to find him and haven't the sense to trust him when I find him." His candor was winning but, unfortunately, prophetic.

For Vice President, the Republicans nominated Calvin Coolidge, another small-town politician. Coolidge had first won a national reputation as a tough antilabor man during the strikes of 1919. When Boston's police organized as an AFL local, and went out on strike, Coolidge was governor of Massachusetts. Without attempting to settle the strike peacefully, he sent armed troops into Boston. The protest of Samuel Gompers, the AFL president, was met with one of Collidge's most famous quasi-grammatical retorts: "There is no right to strike against the public safety, anywhere, anytime."

Coolidge was less a party regular than Harding, but he was even more conservative in matters of policy. Except for his odd flair for terse statements, he was a lackluster man with a crabbed countenance, a striking contrast to Harding's open handsomeness. In any case, no one at the Republican convention thought that they were choosing anything but a Vice President.

The Democrats nominated a lackluster candidate of their own, James M. Cox. However, they tried to spice up the ticket with a dashing young New Yorker, Franklin D. Roosevelt. Roosevelt had served as assistant secretary of the navy under Wilson. The convention hoped the Roosevelt name would attract voters who remembered his cousin Theodore. But probably no Democratic ticket could have won in 1920. The voters wanted a change. Sixty percent of them voted for Harding. They also sent large Republican majorities to both the House and Senate, making it one of the most complete victories in the history of American national politics. Harding carried every state outside the Democrats' solid South and cracked even that by winning Tennessee. The repudiation of Wilson's New Freedom seemed complete.

Return to Normalcy Harding took office with a slogan that coined a new word. He said the country needed a "return to normalcy." No dictionary defined "normalcy," but almost every American probably knew what the President meant. Harding believed that there had been too much experimentation, too many attempts to regulate the economy and the working lives of Americans, too much speculation about new diplomatic arrangements such as the League of Nations. Normalcy meant letting things take their natural course—not interfering in the decisions of businessmen or in the complex affairs of other nations. Normalcy meant, in short, a return to simpler times and uncomplicated politics.

Harding's relaxed conservatism was not a well-defined policy. Rather, it was a wish for fewer policies and less activity by the government. For his cabinet, the President chose people sympathetic to the practices of industrial and business leaders. His most important appointment, in fact, was Secretary of the Treasury Andrew Mellon, a Pennsylvania industrialist who owned the only important company then making aluminum in the United States.

W.E.B. DU BOIS

William Edward Burghardt Du Bois had one of the most extraordinary and creative careers of any modern American writer or intellectual. It spanned from his birth just two years after the assassination of Lincoln to his death just a year before the assassination of Martin Luther King.

During those ninety-six years, Du Bois was a black student at Harvard, a poet, a novelist, a journalist, a reformer, a New York intellectual, a founder of the Pan-African movement, and, at the end, a communist and an expatriate citizen of Ghana.

Du Bois began his life in Massachusetts. Intellectually talented, he made his way through Harvard and did some graduate work in Germany to earn a prestigious Harvard Ph.D. His initial career choice was to be an academic. He taught at Wilberforce College in Ohio, at the University of Pennsylvania, and then at Atlanta University.

But his writing and his move to the South drew him gradually away from academic life and into the politics of race. His first book, *The Philadelphia Negro* (1899), was not only a superb exercise in academic sociology, but a passionate recognition that the "Negro problem" could be solved only when blacks chose no longer to merely imitate whites, but instead to cultivate a new attitude of respect for what they were as blacks.

In *The Souls of Black Folk* (1903), Du Bois pressed the point further. The prevailing program of reform among blacks had been devised by Booker T. Washington. But Washington's plan, as Du Bois saw it, proposed only that blacks should accept white society as they found it and seek gradually to work their way into it, from the bottom up. Du Bois believed this plan would not work partly because of white resistance, which he viewed as determined and even violent. Washington's program was flawed in other ways also. It did not recognize that blacks were different, that many of the black "souls" of which he wrote were kindly, gentle, submissive, and generous, and that it would be fatal merely to toss such souls into the white world of competition, materialism, and greed.

These ideas, combined with an increasing number of violent riots against blacks in all parts of the United States, eventually led Du Bois away from teaching and into political activism. He was one of the founders of an organization called the Niagara Movement, dedicated to a more militant defense of black rights. Du Bois wrote a series of resolutions that voiced the sense of crisis that gave form to the movement, a sense of no "progress" being made. "Stripped of verbose subterfuge and in its naked nastiness, the new American creed says: fear to let black men even try to rise lest they become the equals of the white. And that in the land that professes to follow Jesus Christ. The blasphemy of such a course is only matched by its cowardice."

In 1910, in league with a large number of white reformers and intellectuals, Du Bois formed the Niagara Movement into a new organization, the National Association for the Advancement of Colored People. He was for many years the editor of the Association's magazine, The Crisis. But Du Bois had been losing faith in the capacity of white society ever to accept blacks as blacks. He left teaching and moved into Harlem. He helped found the Pan-African Congress during the peace talks in Paris in 1918. And eventually, at the age of 96, he renounced his United States citizenship, announced his membership in the Communist Party, and moved to the new African state of Ghana, where he died.

Mellon helped to shape the small amount of legislation that the Harding administration presented to Congress. His pet bill was one cutting the maximum income tax on the wealthy from 65 percent to 25 percent. (Congress at first reduced the limit to only 50 percent, but Mellon later got most of what he wanted.) He also proposed, and got from Congress, much higher tariffs on imports, a policy that benefited American business and industry by limiting foreign competition.

The Ohio Gang Specific legislation was less important in Harding's conservative administration than its general relaxation of federal controls over business. Harding did not try to tear down the established regulatory agencies, like the Interstate Commerce Commission or the Federal Reserve Board. Instead, he merely appointed persons to these agencies who were so friendly toward corporations that they administered the law gently or not at all. And Harding named as his Secretary of Commerce Herbert Hoover, who had made a fortune as a mining engineer and investor.

Hoover was clearly the most distinguished of Harding's appointments. He had made an enormous reputation during the war as head of the federal Food Administration. Unlike most of his colleagues in the Harding administration, Hoover was a thoughtful man, with a fairly clear-cut ideological position. He was a promoter of what he called "individualism." His central faith was that private enterprise, left to its own devices, could end poverty and usher in a "new era" of prosperity and progress.

To Hoover, the modern corporation was, ultimately, an instrument of social justice. Capitalism had, he believed, emerged from its nineteenth-century youth into a mature period of development. In this new maturity, corporations would be less concerned with sheer competition for profits and more determined to produce goods efficiently. In the process, the corporations would also contribute a great deal of what Hoover called "service" to society—technological innovation, education, the redistribution of income, and so on, until ignorance, poverty, and disease were banished.

The role of government, Hoover believed, should be to help this process along by providing information and assistance to businesses, not to hinder them through wasteful and inefficient regulation. This was the logic that Hoover applied as secretary of commerce. And this was the logic he would later bring to the White House.

Unfortunately, Harding also brought to Washington a group of friends who soon became known as the Ohio Gang. Some held seemingly harmless positions, like Old Doc Sawyer, a doctor in less than good standing with the medical profession. Old Doc became the White House physician, with the rank of army brigadier general. Other Ohio Gang members were given more important positions, such as attorney general and secretary of the interior.

After two years in office, Harding, who was personally honest about money, begain to realize that his appointees were stealing and peddling influence. In the spring and summer of 1923 two administration officials committed suicide while being investigated. In June, Harding began a

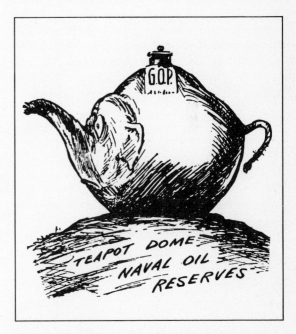

When the Teapot Dome scandal, involving the bribing of Republican officials, broke, a Memphis newspaper published this cartoon entitled, "Assuming Definite Shape."

long vacation in the West. As he left, he complained to a journalist, "My God, this is a hell of a job. I have no trouble with my enemies. But my friends! They're the ones that keep me walking the floor nights!"

Two months later, in California after a trip to Alaska, Harding suffered what Old Doc Sawyer called food poisoning. Harding now had to pay in person for this political appointment, for Sawyer was wrong. The President had suffered a heart attack instead; on August 2 he died. In a way, Harding was lucky. He was mourned by his countrymen almost as much as Lincoln had been. He was spared the knowledge of a new scandal that would later become almost synonymous with his name.

Albert Fall, Harding's secretary of the interior, had finagled Interior Department control of oil reserves set aside for the navy. There were two large reserves, at Elk Hill in California and at Teapot Dome in Wyoming. Private oil interests were willing to pay almost any price to drill the land. And they did.

Two oil company executives, Edward L. Doheny and Harry F. Sinclair, gave and "lent" Fall almost a half million dollars in return for secret leases allowing them to drill on the reserves. The secret leaked out faster than the oil. The government managed to cancel the leases, but Fall went to prison for a year. He was the first cabinet officer in American history to be put behind bars.

COOLIDGE AND BUSINESS

When Harding died, Vice President Calvin Coolidge became President. Though privately a talkative man, "Silent Cal" as Coolidge was called, spoke very little in public. He kept most of Harding's appointees and basically followed his predecessor's policies for the rest of the term. As the 1924 election approached, there was little doubt about what the Republicans would do. Their convention enthusiastically nominated Coolidge.

The Democrats experienced a struggle between two wings of their party. One represented the rural South and West, the old Bryan

supporters. They were at least as conservative as the Republicans. The other wing was newer and based in the Northern cities. It was made up mostly of "wets" (opponents of prohibition) and depended heavily on the support of immigrants (many of them Catholics or Jews). After 103 ballots the convention settled on a compromise candidate, John W. Davis.

Coolidge was conservative. But so was Davis, who was associated with the firm of J. P. Morgan. Once more the time seemed right, as in 1912, to try a third party. The Progressive candidate was Robert La Follette, now nearly seventy but still a fiery opponent of business interests. He did well. Although Coolidge won the election easily with 15 million votes, La Follette managed to get almost 5 million votes, and he carried Wisconsin's electoral vote. Davis and his badly split party could muster only 8½ million votes, less than a third of the total.

Coolidge's second term in office was a continuation of the conservative policies of the earlier years, but without the scandals of 1921-1923. Mellon and Hoover still exercised great influence. The new administration went on supporting high tariffs, low taxes on corporations and the wealthy, and a hands-off policy on trusts. It had an essentially do-nothing approach to farm problems and a negative attitude toward labor as well. The entire conservative politics of the 1920s was summed up in Coolidge's most famous sentence: "The business of America is business."

Still, the President was popular, and doubtless he could have been nominated for a second full term and won. But his second most famous sentence was: "I do not choose to run." Coolidge may have meant simply that he would accept a draft. Still, for once, "Silent Cal" had spoken too soon and said too much. The Republicans took him literally and turned to Herbert Hoover, the most prestigious official in the administration.

The Democratic Challenge of 1928 The Democrats partially healed their old split, hoping for victory. Governor Alfred E. Smith of New York won the nomination easily. Smith and Hoover were almost perfect contrasts. Hoover was conservative, even gloomy. He dressed in neat blue suits and was the perfect representative of stability and efficiency. Above all he opposed any extension of federal power over private enterprise (unless, as with tariffs, federal power could be used to help business).

Smith, on the other hand, was a happy, talkative, cigar-chomping Irish American politician. He wore a brown derby and checked suits and talked with an urban twang. During the campaign, Hoover accused Smith of socialism because the New Yorker favored federal ownership of electric power generating facilities.

However different their personalities and political backgrounds may have been, Smith and Hoover actually ran on very similar platforms. To head his campaign, Smith chose a Republican executive from General Motors, a man who had in fact voted for Coolidge in 1924. And, in a variety of other ways, the Democrats strained to capture the political center by hewing to a very conservative policy line. On the surface, at least, the election was a contest between personal styles and religious convictions.

Smith's Catholicism got most of the publicity. Some of the charges were merely nasty, as when the Methodist bishop of Virginia referred to Smith as "this wet Roman Catholic chamberlain of the Pope of Rome." But even literate, liberal Protestant newspapers and magazines were concerned. The *Christian Century*, one of the most popular Protestant journals, said that Smith's victory would be the victory "of an alien culture, of a mediaeval Latin mentality, of an undemocratic hierarchy and of a foreign potentate."

Smith's stand on prohibition also alarmed many voters. Hoover called prohibition a "noble experiment," and it may have been this stand, not Smith's religion, that won Hoover powerful support in the South and Southwest. Smith, on the other hand, was a publicly announced "wet," who believed that prohibition was not only a failure, but an act that unfairly deprived urban workers of their modest pleasures.

In the end, Hoover won what appeared to be a landslide. With 58 percent of the popular vote, he almost equaled Harding's record. In fact, because the turnout was unusually heavy, Hoover amassed 21 million votes—more than the combined votes of Coolidge and La Follette in 1924. In the process, Hoover cut deeply into the traditionally Democratic South, where he carried Virginia, Tennessee, North Carolina, Florida, and Texas.

But there was another side to the election, an aspect that was almost lost in the apparent landslide. Smith had made some gains, too. Although he had won fewer electoral votes than any Democrat since 1872, Smith had succeeded in taking two Eastern states, Massachusetts and Rhode Island. This was an indication of a powerful new source of support that the Democrats might be able to capitalize on later—support from immigrants and the children of immigrants in Eastern cities. In 1924, Coolidge had swept all twelve of the largest cities in the nation, and by a large margin. In 1928, Smith won more urban votes than Hoover.

Despite this straw in the wind, however, the Republican ascendancy was still in full swing. Hoover could look toward the inauguration and the future with confidence. The powerful and profitable industrial system, watched over at a discreet distance by a sympathetic government, did seem to be ushering in an era of unprecedented prosperity for millions. So it looked in the winter of 1928–1929.

BOOM AND BUST

On the surface, at least, the 1920s was a decade of great prosperity. Progress seemed inevitable as more and more cars, radios, washing machines, and other goods poured off assembly lines. More workers were producing more goods than ever before. The United States seemed to have created an economic miracle.

American buyers and investors were confident. The New York Stock Exchange, where the economy's pulse seemed most vital, enjoyed an amazing boom period after 1923. Sales on the Exchange quadrupled between 1923 and 1930. As sales increased, so did the prices of stocks. Americans were on an investment binge. The total amount of money kept in stocks and bonds increased faster than any other economic factor during the period (much faster, for example, than the actual production or sale of goods).

Much of the new investment was made on credit. According to the rules of the New York Stock Exchange, investors could buy stock by putting some money down and owing the rest to their brokers. These "brokers' loans" showed how little of the investment rush was real money and how much was pure speculation. By 1927 almost $4 billion was still owed on such loans. The whole structure of the stock market was rickety.

Such investment was really a form of gambling. If a stock cost $10 a share and an investor expected it to go up, he could buy a share and wait for the price to rise. In fact, for his $10 he could buy ten shares, one for cash and the other nine on loan. When the stock went up, he could sell his shares at the new price, pay off his broker, and pocket the difference in cash. There would be a problem though if the stock went down. Then, when the broker's loan was due, the investor might have to sell not only his ten shares of stock but other assets as well. If the stock market fell too low, he could be ruined.

Year after year, the gambles paid off. More and more ordinary people, with only small amounts of money to invest, began to play the market. The prospering economy appeared to justify their confidence.

A Warped Economy But this prosperity was very unevenly distributed through the population. There were large pockets of people throughout the country who did not share it at all. Blacks in both the South and the North did not benefit much. Nor did most farmers, whose lives had long been difficult.

The problems of farmers were especially difficult. In the second half of the nineteenth century, an agricultural revolution had provided the foundation for industrial expansion. Then, during the war, farmers had prospered because of high demand and government supports. The end of the war brought a sharp drop in the demand for exports, and an end to federal aid. At the same time, something odd happened in the domestic market. Improvements in diet slightly increased the demand for vegetables and fruit. But, at the same time, the demand for cereal grains dropped, partly because men released from heavy labor by ma-

One of every four farms was sold for debt or taxes from 1920 to 1932. Farm machinery proved costly not only in its purchase price but in the overproduction and falling prices it caused. Dust storms on the plains in the thirties proved the final blow to many more farms, like the one pictured here.

chines needed fewer calories. In addition, the prevailing Victorian ideal of a sturdy, almost fat figure for men and women had given way to a new slender image of the ideal American male and female.

At the same time, farmers were trapped by the high-volume, technologically sophisticated agriculture that had made many of them successful during the preceding two generations. In wartime, especially, the invested heavily in expensive machines, and they continued to do so even after the demand for their crops had fallen off. In the 1920s, in fact, the number of working tractors on American farms quadrupled.

The effect of these changes was to cause farm prices to drop and production to increase. In 1920, the income of farmers represented about 15 percent of the total national income. By 1929, this proportion had fallen to only about 9 percent. Several million farmers were driven off the land. They drifted to the cities or joined the ranks of the bums who made up a portion of the Bonus Army. Those who stayed in farming very often lost ownership of their land and had to become either tenant farmers or hired hands.

One solution to the problem was government intervention. Grain farmers, especially, supported a scheme that would guarantee farmers a "fair" price for their crop. The scheme involved two things. First, a tariff on imported foodstuffs was needed to prevent foreign producers from taking advantage of an "artificially" high price on the American market. Second, the domestic price of grain needed to be set at a level that was the average for the ten years preceding 1914. The result would be "parity," or a kind of rough equality of agricultural prices and other prices. Under the sponsorship of a senator from Oregon, Charles McNary, and a congressman from Iowa, Gilbert Haugen, a bill providing for parity for grain crops was introduced in the 1924 Congress, but it was defeated in the House.

Two years later, in a bid for Southern support, the McNary-Haugen bill was broadened to include cotton, tobacco, and rice. In 1927, it passed both houses of Congress but was turned back by a Coolidge veto that could not be overridden. The next year, 1928, Congress again passed the act, but President Coolidge once more exercised his veto power. The principle of parity would have to wait until well after the crash of 1929.

For industrial workers, the situation was a little better. Real wages—the actual purchasing power of earned dollars—rose during the decade by over 20 percent. And some corporations began to behave a little like Herbert Hoover's model, with programs of "enlightened" capitalism. Sanitary and safety conditions were improved in some of the more modern factories. Some companies started pension funds that gave workers a tiny share in the stock of the corporations that employed them. But the major purpose behind these "progressive" practices was to undercut the growth of industrial unionism. The AFL, meantime, pursued a very cautious policy throughout the decade. The failure of strikes in 1919 and several succeeding years made many workers hesitate to join even a conservative union like the AFL. The outcome was a decline of about 15 percent in union membership, despite an increase in the total number of factory workers.

Those at the outer edges of the industrial system—blacks, most women, the many underemployed recent immigrants in the cities—simply did not participate in the prosperity of the decade. Such "soft" spots in the economy led to a very serious distortion. Technological innovation increased productivity rapidly. The question was, simply, how would the increased production be absorbed? Who would buy the washing machines, the cars, the clothes, all the products of a sophisticated industrial system? The total quantity of goods for sale was increasing much faster than the population. Either wages would have to rise dramatically, so that workers would have more money to spend on all the things being made, or prices would have to fall, so that everyone could afford more. Otherwise, the gap between production and sales would grow until inventories were clogged with unsalable surpluses of consumer goods.

But businessmen generally raised wages less than they should have. They also kept prices high. In the short run, their measures meant higher profits—and higher profits for corporations meant the price of their stock rose. They could either invest the profits in still larger factories and produce still more goods. Or they could invest them in stock and heat up the stock market even more. Many corporations did both.

The result was a warped economy. The amount of goods being produced ran far ahead of the people's power to purchase them. Sooner or later an adjustment had to be made. Otherwise, factories would have to close until the surplus cars, clothes, tools, and other items could be bought. For a time the problem could be avoided in two ways. The surplus products could be sold, on credit, to people who could not really afford them. A family could pay for a car, for example, over two or three years. Or, the surplus could be exported to foreign countries. But both credit and exporting could help a distorted economic system only briefly.

The Stock Market Crash These facts were difficult to see. On the surface, the economy had never looked better, and Americans continued to bet on the future by speculating in stocks. In 1928 the average price of industrial stocks increased by about 25 percent. An investor who bought, say, $1,000 worth of stock in January could sell it in December for $1,250. He could then pocket the $250 profit or invest it in some new gamble. Most speculators did the latter.

Then, after a few rumblings and warnings, the bubble burst. The stock market was not a sure indicator of the country's economic health or disease. In 1929 reality finally caught up with it.

In September the most popular index of stock prices stood at 452. Two months later it was 234. What this meant, in plain terms, was that the market value of stocks on the Exchange had been halved. Most of the holders of the $4 billion in brokers' loans were ruined. So were many of the brokers. On the worst day of all, "Black Tuesday," October 29, the market index fell 43 points. Other days were almost as bleak and ruinous. Stock prices continued to slide. They reached bottom in 1932. Then most stocks were worth little more than a tenth of their cost in September 1929. The Great Depression had begun.

It was difficult then, and still is, for people to understand why the panic on Wall Street should have had any effect on the real economy. The factories were still there, ready to roll out goods. The farms were still there, ready to produce food. All the hands willing to work before Black Tuesday were still there, still willing to work.

But, month by month, the entire economic machine ground down. The stock market crash was the crucial link in the chain of events leading to this breakdown. It caused people to make the grim decision not to buy or invest. So storekeepers sold less. And factories produced less or closed down altogether. Many foreclosed on loans made to others because they needed money to pay off their own loans.

Farmers behind on their payments lost their farms as banks desperately tried to collect hard cash. The banks needed cash because millions of people with savings accounts, frightened now, lined up at tellers' windows to withdraw their money. The banks often could not produce the cash because they had invested or lent it. So even the banks began to fail.

Builders of houses and offices stopped construction because they could not borrow money to continue. Down at the bottom of this tangle were plain workers who, by the millions, received notices that they need not come to work anymore. Their jobs disappeared. Since they could not work, they could not buy; since they could not buy, others could not sell or make goods.

The jobless were not just the old-line poor. Many had been solid, middle-class citizens, such as bank tellers or factory foremen. Others were farmers, who had barely managed to survive throughout the decade. Now they had lost their farms forever. They moved to the cities, looking for food and work, or they began to drift, looking for migrant workers' jobs. People combed garbage heaps for food for their families. They made soup from dandelions. Mostly, however, they waited in a cold, gloomy fog of despair for something to happen.

Hoover's Optimism The question posed by the Depression and symbolized by the Bonus March was simple. Could the federal government be used as a tool for dealing with economic disaster? In the past the answer had been no. Other depres-

Amid the bright lights of Times Square hundreds of New York's hungry formed bread lines in 1932. Ironically, scarcity was not the problem. As Socialist Norman Thomas remarked: "It remained for us to invent bread lines knee-deep in wheat."

sions had been allowed to run their course without any federal attempt to bring early recovery or relieve human suffering. But the Great Depression was by far the worst ever. Now the industrial economy was so large and complicated that its collapse affected far more people. Countless millions were jobless; banks were failing by the thousands; tens of thousands needed food. Something had to be done.

At first the Hoover administration was optimistic. The stock market crash was called a needed adjustment. The economy, Hoover announced, was fundamentally sound. Recovery would be natural and would come soon. Meanwhile, no federal action of any kind was needed.

Surprisingly, most Democrats agreed. In the congressional elections of 1930, the Democrats made prohibition as big an issue as the de-

pression. Nor did the voters heavily punish the administration for its failure to bring about recovery. The Democrats won the House but the Senate stayed Republican. Hoover was still predicting that a return to prosperity was just around the corner.

But things kept getting worse. In 1929, over 600 banks shut down; in 1930, over 1,000; in 1931, 2,000. For farmers there seemed to be no bottom. Wheat in 1931 sold for $.36 a bushel, compared to $1.03 in 1929. No one even knew how many people were unemployed by 1932, but guesses ran as high as 15 million. For those who still had jobs, pay envelopes grew smaller. By 1932 wages in industry were less than half what they had been in 1928.

As he faced all these facts—or, sometimes, tried not to face them—the President grew gloomy and confused. He tried to stay optimistic in public, believing business confidence was crucial to recovery. In private, however, he was trapped between two different beliefs. A humane man, he did not like to see people suffer. But he still thought that government should not interefere in the economy. Free enterprise would bring the nation back to its feet.

Most important, Hoover believed that the federal government must never give direct relief to the poor, unemployed, and hungry. Direct federal welfare, he thought, would destroy people's moral character. It would make them dependent instead of healthy, strong personalities. This set of attitudes, which he referred to as individualism, made Hoover seem insensitive and cruel. He became the target of bitter jokes. People named their shantytowns Hoovervilles and called an empty pocket, turned inside out, a Hoover flag. Reluctantly, Hoover decided that the government must act.

New Federal Powers Early in 1932 Hoover signed a law creating a new federal agency, the Reconstruction Finance Corporation (RFC). It could lend up to $2 billion to banks, insurance companies, and railroads. These loans, the administration believed, would be used especially by the banks to make other loans to businesses. Businesses would in turn use the money for new construction or to reopen factories. Their moves would create new jobs and save old ones. Thus, eventually RFC loans would end up in the pockets of workers, who would then spend the money and create new demand, resulting in more new production, and so on, in a circle of recovery.

The President also went against his own beliefs by signing another law empowering the RFC to lend relief money to state governments. But the amount of the loans was too small to help much. Pennsylvania, for example, could borrow only enough to provide three cents a day to its unemployed workers. Also, the RFC loans to business were far too small to aid the economy effectively. Compared to previous government activity, Hoover's actions were bold experiments in the use of federal power. But, measured against what was actually needed, they were too little too late, as the Bonus Marchers recognized.

SUGGESTED READINGS— CHAPTERS 39-40

The Bonus March

Donald J. Lisio, *The President and Protest: Hoover, Conspiracy, and the Bonus Riot* (1974); Douglas MacArthur, *Reminiscences* (1964).

The Conservative Reaction

R. K. Murray, *The Red Scare* (1955); W. Preston, Jr., *Aliens and Dissenters: Federal Suppression of Radicals, 1903–1933* (1963); David Chalmers, *Hooded Americanism* (1965); K. T. Jackson, *The Ku Klux Klan in the City* (1967); A. S. Rice, *The Ku Klux Klan in American Politics* (1961); G. L. Jouglhin, *The Legacy of Sacco-Vanzetti* (1948); Francis Russell, *Tragedy in Dedham* (1962); N. F. Furniss, *The Fundamentalist Controversy* (1954); Ray Ginger, *Six Days or Forever* (1958); Herbert Asbury, *The Great Illusion* (1950); Andrew Sinclair, *Era of Excess: A Social History of the Prohibition Movement* (1962).

The Politics of the 1920s

William E. Leuchtenburg, *The Perils of Prosperity, 1914–1932* (1958); Arthur Schlesinger, Jr., *The Crisis of the Old Order* (1957); John D. Hicks, *The Republican Ascendancy* (1960); David Burner, *The Politics of Provincialism: The Democratic Party in Transition, 1918–1932* (1968); Andrew Sinclair, *The Available Man:*

Warren Gamaliel Harding (1965); D. R. McCoy, *Calvin Coolidge, The Quiet President* (1967); Oscar Handlin, *Al Smith and His America* (1958); A. U. Romasco, *The Poverty of Abundance: Hoover, the Nation and the Depression* (1965).

The Economy

George Soule, *Prosperity Decade: From War to Depression, 1917–1929* (1947); Alfred D. Chandler, *Strategy and Structure: Chapters in the History of American Industrial Enterprise* (1962); Allan Nevins and Frank Hill, *Ford: Expansion and Challenge, 1915–1932* (1957); James W. Prothro, *Dollar Decade: Business Ideas in the 1920s* (1954); John K. Galbraith, *The Great Crash, 1929* (1955); H. G. Warren, *Herbert Hoover and the Great Depression.* (1959).

UNIT SEVEN

MODERN AMERICA

Fifteen million Americans were unemployed on March 4, 1933, when the new President, Franklin Delano Roosevelt, was inaugurated. Roosevelt stirred his audience when he told his stricken countrymen: "Let me assert my firm belief that the only thing we have to fear is fear itself." A despairing nation responded eagerly to Roosevelt's determination to act quickly and boldly in confronting the emergency.

Twenty-eight years later another new President, John Fitzgerald Kennedy, also used his inaugural speech to proclaim new energy in national affairs. "Let the word go out," Kennedy intoned, "that the torch has been passed to a new generation of Americans [willing] to pay any price, bear any burden, to assure the survival and the success of liberty."

Roosevelt's address rallied Americans to begin the process of economic recovery. Kennedy's speech summoned Americans to leadership of the Western world. The three decades between these two orations saw the United States emerge from economic catastrophe to become the strongest and most prosperous country in world history. The following chapters trace the steps in this evolution.

The career of Eleanor Roosevelt, narrated in Chapter 41, portrays, through the experiences of America's most famous and influential twentieth-century woman, the country's transition from the relatively affluent Twenties into the era of the Great Depression (and beyond). The accompanying chapter on the New Deal years discusses both the social and economic impact of the Depression on the American people and the political world of

Franklin Roosevelt's pathbreaking Administration. Together, the two chapters offer an avenue into comprehending the formative years of our modern national experience.

The attack on Pearl Harbor, dramatized in Chapter 43, highlights the beginning of a shift in national attention from domestic to foreign concerns. Roosevelt and his successors, determined to avoid future "Pearl Harbors," led the country in a search for collective security through treaty alliances. The wartime "Grand Alliance" of the United States, Great Britain, and the Soviet Union rapidly deteriorated after World War II. A new era of Cold War between the Western allies and the Soviet communist camp began. Pearl Harbor thus vaulted the United States into a position of world leadership. Chapter

44 traces the development of that role from the 1930s to the Kennedy Administration.

Running parallel to Cold War developments in foreign affairs were anticommunist rumblings at home. The Alger Hiss case figured prominently in this. Hiss was a former high government official who was convicted in 1950 of having lied about involvement with Russian agents. His case came to symbolize for many the threat of communism to American society. The Red Scare that the incident helped trigger was central to many political, social, and economic developments that the next chapter discusses. Among those developments are the nation's return to affluence, the rise of a "military-industrial complex," and the evolution of social problems that would haunt the next decade.

41
ELEANOR ROOSEVELT: AN AMERICAN LIFE

A. W.

The coal miners were evidently a good distance beneath the surface. Only the lamps in their helmets illuminated the scene, and revealed the surprise on their faces. "For Gosh Sakes!" one exclaimed to the other, "It's Mrs. Roosevelt!"

Eleanor Roosevelt may never have actually gone down a coal mine, but the most famous cartoon of the 1930s showed that people found the idea plausible. During the worst of the Great Depression, Mrs. Roosevelt went to many places no First Lady had visited before, and she did things that the wife of no previous President had thought worth doing. She went to Appalachia, to the Gulf states' Black Belt, to Puerto Rico, and to just about everywhere else to see firsthand the worst poverty in a depression-stricken country. She explored the slums and alleys of the District of Columbia, which most politicians never saw during a lifetime in Washington. Driving with a friend, she visited one New Deal project after another, trying to see if they really helped the unemployed.

She also met people who had never before talked with a First Lady. Through the Women's Trade Union League she maintained ties with working women and their leaders. She considered herself a personal friend of the activists in the American Youth Congress, even after Communists surfaced in the organization. Mrs. Roosevelt provided the New Deal's most open ear to the problems of blacks and worked ceaselessly to protect their rights in government programs. Walter White, head of the National Association for the Advancement of Colored People (NAACP), remarked once that only the thought of Mrs. Roosevelt kept him from hating all white people.

Mrs. Roosevelt tried to keep her husband available to new ideas and often drove the points home herself. "No one," recalled one New

Dealer, "who ever saw Eleanor Roosevelt sit down facing her husband, and holding his eye firmly, say to him, 'Franklin, I think you should . . . .' or 'Franklin, surely you will not . . . .' will ever forget the experience." From her large correspondence she selected letters from people with ideas and from people needing help and laid them on his desk with the scrawled injunction, "F — read."

But, as First Lady, Eleanor Roosevelt was an individual personality, and not merely the wife of the President. She wrote a daily newspaper column, went on lecture tours, and spoke frequently on the radio. She held her own press conferences, the first President's wife to do so. She constantly tried to increase the role of women in the Democratic party and in government, and told a friend she considered that objective more important than any specific political issue.

Next to her husband, Mrs. Roosevelt was probably the best-known person in the country. Conservatives told each other "Eleanor stories," imitating her high-pitched voice and mocking her ungainly features. Friends remarked that her photographs did not do her justice. "My dear," she told one, "if you haven't any chin and your front teeth stick out, it's going to show on a camera plate."

People all over the United States knew Eleanor Roosevelt, and millions adored her. But her public life did not reflect her personal one. She agonized over a troubled marriage and suffered disappointing relationships with her children. Her private difficulties may have instilled in her the strength to sustain her public role; but they may also have caused her to seek among the poor and the disadvantaged the approval she could not find in her own family.

"My mother was one of the most beautiful women I have ever seen," runs the first sentence of Eleanor Roosevelt's autobiography. That beauty made a particular impression on her because she did not inherit it. Her mother and father were one of the most glamorous couples in New York society. In contrast, Eleanor remembered, "I was a solemn child, without beauty and painfully shy, and I seemed like a little old woman." Her exasperated mother called her "Granny."

Her early life did not tend to build either joy or self-confidence. The homely little Eleanor wore a back brace for two years to correct a curvature of the spine. She felt excluded from her mother's affections after the birth of her healthy, attractive, baby brother. Her father, Elliott (Theodore Roosevelt's younger brother), had begun the slow and painful process of drinking himself to death. He was away from home on one more effort to "dry out" when her mother died. Eleanor was eight years old when her mother's family decided that, because of her father's alcoholism, she and her brother should go to live with her maternal grandmother, a gloomy old lady in a gloomy old house in New York City, who hired governesses to deal with her unwelcome guests. The lonely Eleanor spent much time writing loving letters to her adored father. "He dominated my life for as long as he lived," she recalled, "and was the love of my life for many years after he died." Her father rarely answered

Eleanor, at age six, a shy, pensive child whom her mother addressed as "Granny."

her letters and more rarely saw her. He died two years after her mother. All her life Eleanor would be badly hurt when someone she loved disappointed her.

Eleanor was a good student, but—shy and awkward, dressed by her grandmother in children's clothes until she was fifteen—she made few friends when she was sent to school. And the few she made could not be invited to her house, because her maternal uncles were so often drunk. Her grandmother also severely limited Eleanor's visits to her uncle, Theodore Roosevelt, and his family. Theodore, then a rising young politician, had loved his brother and felt keenly for his daughter. On her rare visits to his house, he embraced Eleanor warmly and tried hard to include her in the rough activities of his own brood. "Poor little soul, she is very plain," noted Theodore's wife Edith. "Her mouth and teeth seem to have no future. But perhaps the ugly duckling will turn out to be a swan."

This situation, Eleanor remembered, "began to develop in me an almost exaggerated idea of the necessity of keeping all of one's desires under complete subjugation." It also taught her something about people, and their need to feel wanted. When she briefly visited a friend in the country, her hostess was surprised to find her writing to her young brother two days in a row. "I write him every day," Eleanor explained. "I want him to feel he belongs to somebody."

Her life improved dramatically when, at fifteen, she was sent to boarding school in England. The headmistress took an interest in the uneasy, gawky, but highly intelligent girl, and Eleanor, hungry for affection, responded happily to the attention. When she returned home, she had acquired enough self-confidence to enter New York society, although convinced that her appearance would keep her from achieving any great success. She soon limited her socializing and began teaching in a settlement house on the Lower East Side.

Yet Eleanor did not lack men who showed interest in her. She was soon seeing a good deal of her distant cousin, Franklin Delano Roosevelt. Their closest common ancestor had died in the seventeenth century. But the two Roosevelt families had always been friendly, although Theodore's Oyster Bay Roosevelts were Republicans and Franklin's Hyde Park Roosevelts were Democrats, Eleanor's father, Elliott Roosevelt, had been Franklin's godfather, and she had seen Franklin occasionally while she was growing up.

Franklin Roosevelt was then a popular and amiable Harvard student. He wrote editorials on school spirit for the *Harvard Crimson,* and was good-looking enough to make people wonder what he saw in the ungainly, strait-laced Eleanor. His father, much older than Franklin's mother, had died when his son was at prep school, and Franklin's mother, Sara, now centered her life around her only child. For two winters she had taken a house in Boston to be near him at college. She bent every effort to break up his relationship with Eleanor, a romance she considered both premature and unsuitable. Nevertheless, they became engaged.

A tall, stately, and elegant bride, Eleanor was married to Franklin on March 17, 1905, in a society wedding at a New York townhouse. Wearing the long satin gown covered with brussels lace in which her mother had been married, Eleanor, at twenty, appeared beautiful. She was given away by her uncle, Theodore Roosevelt, who had just been inaugurated as President, and whose daughter, cousin Alice, was one of the bridesmaids.

Uncle Theodore, now President of the United States, offered use of the White House for the marriage. But Eleanor chose her grandmother's house, selecting a day when the President would be in New York for the St. Patrick's Day parade. It was the outgoing TR—who, in the words of his acid-tongued daughter Alice, "wanted to be the bride at every wedding and the corpse at every funeral"—who stole the show, although, in her wedding gown, Eleanor for once looked almost beautiful.

The couple returned to New York from a European honeymoon to find that Sara had rented them a house three blocks from her own. They spent weekends at Sara's country house at Hyde Park, a hundred miles up the Hudson River, and summers at Sara's house on Campobello Island off the coast of Maine. While Franklin began his law career, Eleanor settled down to bearing children, and Sara to telling her how. Sara had no qualms about being an interfering mother-in-law, and Eleanor lacked the self-confidence to decline her advice. "Franklin's children," she said later, "were much more my mother-in-law's than they were mine."

Sara used her money to control her son and daughter-in-law's lives, doling it out according to her own interests and whims. In 1908, she built a new house for Eleanor and Franklin, at 49 East 65th Street. She also built herself a new house—at 47 East 65th Street. Eleanor normally bore up well under the strain, but Franklin came home once to find her in tears. She had no feeling for her house, she sobbed; her mother-in-law had bought the land, selected the architect, and decorated the rooms. Franklin succeeded in calming her, but he did not really understand.

Soon, other interests provided some diversion for them. Legal business bored Franklin; in 1910 he received the Democratic nomination for state senator from the Hyde Park district. Aided by a national Democratic landslide and a good deal of Sara's money, he won the election. Eleanor had encouraged him to enter politics, but the prospect of meeting new people terrified her, and she found their two years in Albany painfully difficult.

Franklin's political career prospered swiftly. He became an early and active backer of the presidential hopes of Woodrow Wilson, then governor of neighboring New Jersey. When Wilson won in 1912, Franklin snared the job of assistant secretary of the Navy, the same position that had propelled Theodore Roosevelt to national prominence.

Washington seemed no warmer to Eleanor than Albany had, but she doggedly made the effort to fit in. To help with her social obligations, she hired a secretary who knew Washington, Lucy Mercer. Lucy, the twenty-two-year-old daughter of impoverished Maryland aristocracy, had all the social graces that Eleanor lacked. She also had a pretty face, a dazzling figure, and a velvety voice. When Eleanor and the children went to Campobello for summers, Lucy remained in Washington to look after the house and Franklin.

Franklin's association with Lucy soon turned into a love affair that was common knowledge among Washingtonians. The two often appeared together when Eleanor was away, and Lucy became a secretary in the Navy Department. Eleanor's cousin, TR's daughter Alice Roosevelt Longworth, assisted the lovers, inviting them both to her house. "Franklin deserved a good time," explained Mrs. Longworth. "He was married to Eleanor." Not surprisingly, Eleanor did not take this tolerant view when she came across revealing letters from Lucy. Furious, she offered her husband a choice: He must never see Lucy again, or Eleanor would sue for divorce.

The situation really offered Franklin no choice at all. He and Eleanor had five children whom he loved and enjoyed. And a divorce would destroy his political aspirations. For once his mother took Eleanor's side, threatening to cut him off financially. Franklin gave up his mistress. From that point on, however, his wife's bedroom door was closed to him. "I have the memory of an elephant," Eleanor quietly told a friend years later. "I can forgive but I cannot forget."

The episode had a profound effect on Eleanor's attitudes about life. "The bottom dropped out of my own particular world," she remembered later, "and I faced myself, my surroundings, my world honestly for the first time. I really grew up that year." Her attempt to build a life around husband and children had failed. As her children grew, she sought more and more to create a satisfying existence for herself outside her home.

In 1920 the Democratic party, seeking to capitalize on the Roosevelt name, nominated Franklin for Vice President. "I am sure that I was glad for my husband," Eleanor wrote later, "but it never occurred to me to be much excited." Nevertheless, she dutifully went on the campaign trail. At first she hated it, writing home: "I really don't see that I'm of the least use on this trip." But she soon became friendly with the reporters and drew close to Louis Howe, the wizened, coughing little man who managed her husband's political fortunes. Harding's landslide victory buried the Democratic ticket, but Eleanor emerged with an interest in politics. After the election, she joined the board of the New York State League of Women Voters.

Eleanor's long career as a politician's wife exposed her to the demands of public life and to the public eye. During the campaign of 1920, when Franklin ran for Vice President, Eleanor joined Mrs. James Cox, wife of the Democratic Presidential nominee, on a reviewing stand in Ohio to watch a parade in honor of the candidates. On this occasion, the candidates were to be officially informed of their nomination, since it was not the custom at that time for them to appear in person at the national conventions.

The summer after Franklin's defeat the family went to Campobello as usual. He felt particularly tired one afternoon and went for a swim in the icy bay. When that did nothing to revive him, he went to bed early. He awoke the next morning to find both his legs paralyzed. Weeks later, the Roosevelts received a definite diagnosis: At thirty-nine, Franklin had contracted polio.

For two weeks, Eleanor nursed Franklin constantly, sleeping on a couch in his room. "You will surely break down if you do not have immediate relief," the doctor warned. But she and Franklin managed to present to the world an image of cheerfulness, of confidence that he would recover and resume his political career. In the months of agony that followed, the world saw Franklin's courage; only Eleanor saw his desperation.

Eleanor now needed all of her own stamina in a struggle with her mother-in-law. Sara had never liked the strange people with whom her son had to associate in politics, and she felt that he should now retire to Hyde Park and become a gentleman farmer. Eleanor, equally determined, insisted that her husband should continue to lead an active life and not die slowly among his trees. She refused to allow people to treat him as an invalid, and she found a tireless ally in campaign manager Louis Howe, who now moved into the Sixty-fifth Street house.

With Franklin largely confined indoors, Howe trained Eleanor to keep her husband's name before the public. He attended meetings at which she spoke and by pointed criticism managed to eliminate her nervous giggle. She chaired the Finance Committee of the Women's Division of the Democratic State Committee and joined the Women's Trade Union League. With growing confidence, she accepted invitations to speak on the radio and to write for magazines. She was becoming, to her own amazement, a prominent public figure.

Together, she and Louis Howe salvaged Franklin's career. But they did no less for Eleanor. Not only did she know that Franklin needed her; she was also creating a role for herself. When their youngest child went off to prep school, she broadened her activities to include full-time teaching at a New York private school. "I suppose," she once told an interviewer, "that if I were asked what is the best thing one can expect in life, I would say—the privilege of being useful."

But despite Eleanor's success and newly gained confidence, she could not withstand Sara's guerilla warfare on the home front. With Franklin often away in the South, where the good weather and warm water assisted his therapy, Sara and Eleanor shared the responsibility of the children. With Sara's encouragement they soon learned to compare their busy mother, who had never been close to them and who now tried to teach them discipline and self-control, with their generous, available grandmother.

The political careers of the two Roosevelts meshed perfectly in 1928, when Governor Al Smith of New York won the Democratic presidential nomination. At the 1924 national convention, Franklin, in a stirring demonstration of his triumph over polio, had risen from his wheelchair and walked without assistance to the podium, where he gave the speech placing Smith's name in nomination. Four years later, Smith asked Franklin to nominate him again. The candidate also asked Eleanor, whose effectiveness in the New York party he had noted, to run national women's activities in his campaign.

Smith soon requested even more. A New York City Catholic himself, he wanted Franklin, as a well-known upstate Protestant, to run for governor. Roosevelt was reluctant—he had just invested most of his capital in a resort in Warm Springs, Georgia, where he thought the waters would help his legs. Eleanor refused to advise Franklin either way, and Smith wore him down. To critics who questioned Roosevelt's physical ability, Smith snapped, "The Governor of New York does not have to be an acrobat!"

Eleanor exerted herself more actively in Smith's presidential

While FDR was Governor of New York, the Roosevelt family gathered for a portrait, with Franklin's mother, the imposing Mrs. James Roosevelt, seated at the far right. Eleanor and her daughter Anna, then married to stockbroker Curtis Dall, held the grandchildren. During these Albany years, Eleanor was commuting by train to New York every week to teach at the Todhunter School, where she served as vice-principal.

campaign than in her husband's. When the final returns buried Smith in defeat but gave Franklin a narrow win, she seemed more disappointed than elated. Nevertheless, she made preparations to assume new duties in Albany. "When I found I had something to do," she told a reporter once, "I just did it."

But things had changed in eight years. Eleanor would not—and indeed could not—again be merely a supportive wife. She spent only four days a week in the state capital; Monday through Wednesday she was in New York City to teach her classes. Her work for the Democratic State Committee also continued, although she removed her name from the organization's stationery. Even when present in the governor's mansion, Mrs. Roosevelt's approach to her role differed greatly from that of her predecessors.

Women's groups, which previously had met with hostility from the state government, now found an unaccustomed welcome in Albany, where Eleanor tried to advance their social programs with Franklin and the legislature. She also helped her husband by making unannounced inspection tours of state institutions and reporting directly to him. During train rides between New York and Albany she handled an enormous load of letters from people who had problems with the state government. She also managed to keep the mansion going. Although the wall between Franklin and Eleanor had not come down, they functioned as a team. "We are really very dependent on each other," she once wrote him wistfully, "though we do see so little of each other."

Eleanor had adjusted to being the governor's wife, but she did not look forward to the next step. Franklin now led the field of Democratic candidates for President, and the Great Depression made his election a strong probability. But he had acquired a new group of advisers, who found Eleanor too idealistic for serious politics. Their first job, one of them told a new recruit, was "to get the pants off Eleanor and on to Frank." But Eleanor still tried to keep her influence with her husband; when, for political reasons, he came out against the United States joining the League of Nations, she refused to speak to him for three days.

When it became clear, by 23 million Democratic votes to 15 million Republican, that the Roosevelts were going to Washington, Eleanor made plans to keep herself busy. Just before the inauguration, she published a book entitled *It's Up to the Women,* and accepted an offer to edit a magazine called *Babies—Just Babies.* She intended to continue her New York interests and remain active in women's causes. Riding to the inaugural ceremony with Mrs. Hoover, Eleanor asked her what she would miss most about the White House. Being taken care of, the outgoing First Lady answered; not having to worry about anything. Eleanor silently promised herself that she would never adopt that attitude.

She was now confident enough to lend a little self-assurance to the wife of Roosevelt's Vice President. Despite her husband's long career in the House of Representatives, Mrs. John Nance Garner of Uvalde, Texas, feared the publicity of her new role and stood somewhat in awe of the famous personage who was now First Lady. "If you see me making any mistakes, Mrs. Roosevelt," she asked uncertainly, "will you please tell me?" "Of course," Eleanor replied. "If you see *me* making any mistakes, will you please tell *me*?"

The country began to learn more about Eleanor when she beame the first President's wife to hold her own press conferences—which were for women only. The male White House correspondents scorned the idea at first; as the conferences began to produce news, however, they too wanted to attend. But Eleanor refused, wanting to help the newspaperwomen, who were then barred from membership in the National Press Club. "So few women writers," she once complained, "many of whom are just as capable of handling the big stories as the men, get a chance to be front-page writers."

Eleanor followed this policy in other ways as well. The Gridiron Club of Washington correspondents traditionally gave an all-male dinner, inviting most of official Washington and visiting politicos. Eleanor began holding a Gridiron Widows Dinner the same night, inviting woman reporters, cabinet wives, and women bureaucrats. She took a

In the early decades of the twentieth century, Eleanor strongly opposed woman suffrage, but once women had won the vote, she joined the Board of the League of Women Voters and began an intensive apprenticeship in public affairs. In her subsequent career, she became a staunch supporter of women's causes, a leader of women in the Democratic Party, and the most prominent woman in American political life. Eleanor is shown here at the 1952 New York Historical Society exhibit, sponsored by the League of Women Voters, that traced the campaign for woman suffrage.

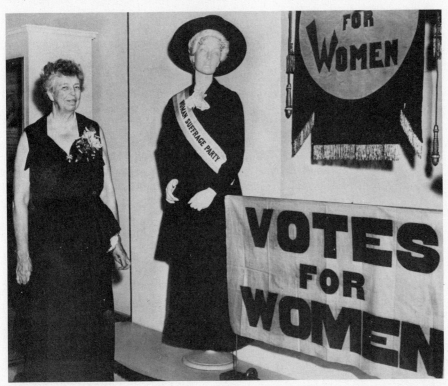

special interest in increasing the role of women in government and in the Democratic party, frequently inviting the handful of female office-holders to the White House. As a result of her efforts, she had the satisfaction of seeing, for the first time ever, women alternates chosen for the (all male) members of the Resolutions Committee at the 1936 Democratic convention.

Two months after Roosevelt's inauguration in March 1933, a new Bonus Army besieged Washington. Eleanor drove down to the camp-grounds with Louis Howe. What should they do? "Well," answered Howe, "you're going out there and I'm going to take a nap." Eleanor walked alone into the tent city and talked to the men, telling them of her own volunteer work during World War I and promising to do what she could to help them. The unemployed veterans cheered as she left. Said one, in words that became famous, "Hoover sent the Army. Roosevelt sent his wife."

The President "sent his wife" to many other strange places. She continued the inspection tours she had started in New York, often arriving unannounced and virtually alone. (She flatly refused to have the Secret Service follow her around, although they finally forced her to carry a pistol in the glove compartment of her car.) She visited the poorest parts of the country and ate a five-cent meal with welfare mothers. She tried to get something done about the slums of Washington and once took two carloads of cabinet wives down into the tenements, trying to awaken their interest in the city. They thanked her, but explained that their husbands took up most of their time.

As First Lady, and as a First Lady known to care about people, Mrs. Roosevelt received a flood of mail. The first year, 300,000 letters addressed to her poured into the White House. Eleanor, her secretary, and her staff read them all. If the problem lay with a federal agency, she got in touch with the agency head; if the problem was personal, she tried to counsel the writer or obtain assistance, using her friends in the Women's Trade Union League to check out the story.

Americans wanted to know more about this Mrs. Roosevelt, already known as the Conscience of the New Deal. She went on two lecture tours a year. Often, she surprised her audience: speaking to the conservative Daughters of the American Revolution (DAR), she called on a new idea of patriotism, one "that will mean living for the interests of everyone in our country, and the world at large, rather than simply preparing to die for our country." She spoke often on the radio, and in 1935 earned fees totaling $72,000. She gave the money earned directly to the American Friends Service Committee (AFSC), until a Republican congressman charged her with tax evasion. She then began accepting the money, paying the tax on it, and giving the rest to the AFSC.

In 1936, Eleanor Roosevelt took the unprecedented step of agreeing to write a daily syndicated newspaper column. "My Day," largely a diary of happenings in her life and her thoughts on them, became widely read. Columns that might be controversial she cleared with her husband, who sometimes used them to test public reaction. Her topics were wide-ranging: in one column she might disagree with the idea that women could not be great playwrights; in another discuss her opposition to war toys; in yet a third express her sympathy for children of both sides in the Spanish Civil War. After speaking at an exclusive prep school, she wrote, "Several of the boys asked me about the unemployed as though the unemployed were some strange species of animal. . . . We should realize that the unemployed are individuals, human beings with all the tastes, likes, dislikes, and passions we have ourselves."

The column gave Eleanor, a long-time supporter of organized labor, the chance to join a union herself. She became a loyal and working member of the Newspaper Guild, although she declined an offer to become its president. Eleanor had usually backed unions. Her interest in the Women's Trade Union League provided preparation for the White House years, during which she clearly stood on the side of workers against management. She tried to proceed as unabrasively as possible, but her bias in favor of such unions as the New York–based Ladies' Garment Workers Union was clear. Sometimes, it must be said, she acted in a labor dispute, writing letters pleading the workers' case or expressing her views in print, without full knowledge of the facts. Eleanor would not cross a picket line, even for a polio benefit meeting; she once canceled an appointment with a dressmaker at a fashionable Fifth Avenue store whose employees were on strike. "I will have to wait before coming to see you again," she explained to the store owner, "until you have some agreement with your people which is satisfactory to both sides." Such New Deal measures as emergency relief, the prolabor section of the National Industrial Recovery Act, social security, and the Wagner labor relations law received Mrs. Roosevelt's enthusiastic support.

Nor did she neglect the even more thorny problem of farm labor. She fostered New Deal agencies to deal with displaced farm laborers and to help those trying to continue in their farm work, and she became involved in a crisis in Arkansas over efforts by sharecroppers to join the Southern Tenant Farmers Union. Attempts to have evicted sharecroppers resettled by the federal government ran into stiff opposition from Arkansas growers and their political allies. Hoping to benefit from a personal acquaintance with Arkansas Senator Joseph Robinson, Eleanor told him the story as she understood it. Robinson remained unconvinced, blaming all the trouble on a "group of agitators." In the face of such stonewalling, Eleanor dropped the correspondence and worked behind the scenes to get immediate relief payments to the evicted sharecroppers.

The White House had brought Eleanor the feeling she most treasured—that of being useful. But although she clearly represented a major political asset to her husband, relations between them did not improve. Even apart from past hurts, their personalities differed too radically. Franklin found it essential to forget all his problems from time to time (exchanging banter with reporters or puttering with his stamp collection). But it seemed that Eleanor never could relax. Asked what she wanted for Christmas, she would answer, towels, sheets, pillowcases; at an election night celebration, she "worried about whether anybody was being neglected and whether there was enough food." These very different traits, which enabled them to complement each other as a political team, kept them from taking any real joy in each other's company. Eleanor saw Franklin filling his need for feminine companionship with his daughter, his daughters-in-law, and his long-time secretary, Missy LeHand. "Missy was young and pretty and loved a good time," wrote Eleanor in her autobiography; and "occasionally her social contacts got mixed with her work and made it difficult for herself and others." (Eleanor did not know that Franklin also looked elsewhere for companionship, to an attractive woman in her forties who was now Lucy Mercer Rutherford. The presidential train frequently stopped for two or three day in South Carolina near the Rutherford plantation on its way to Warm Springs. Lucy also had a house in Washington, and during Eleanor's frequent trips out of town Lucy often dined at the White House.)

Neither could Eleanor find much comfort in her children, whose marriages collapsed one after another. With the example of her mother-in-law always before her, Eleanor tried not to interfere: "I was almost obsessed with the idea that once the children were grown, they should not be subjected to the same kind of control that held such sway over me." But she could not create close relationships with them, although she tried. "We all turned out to have long memories," one of her sons wrote in 1973. "It was impossible to discount the coldness with which Mother treated us when we were young." Nor did her children inherit Eleanor's social conscience. "Mother!" cried her daughter once when she pressed Franklin on a reform issue at dinner, "Can't you see you are giving Father indigestion?"

The fact that she remained an outsider in her own family was perhaps what gave Eleanor such a strong interest in others who were outsiders—in the unemployed, in women, and, to a degree unique for an American national figure at the time, in blacks.

The latter interest created problems, since racial discrimination was everywhere around her, so ingrained as to seem beyond all remedy. Still, Mrs. Roosevelt labored. It was no surprise that blacks were being shortchanged in the distribution of New Deal aid, North and South. From the very start of the Roosevelt programs, Eleanor insisted on reminding the administrators of the National Recovery Administration (NRA) and of emergency relief that wage and benefit payment scales that set lower rates for Negroes should not be permitted. Harry Hopkins, Roosevelt's "Minister of Relief," responded sympathetically, but, all too often, edicts from the top proved no match for low-level bureaucracy and deeply ingrained prejudices.

Eleanor could only hope that New Deal programs would "spill over" and that blacks would get some appreciable share of the benefits. Certainly her husband had no intention of mounting a presidential crusade specifically in favor of blacks and their rights. FDR counted too much on the votes of Southern Democrats in Congress for that. Even

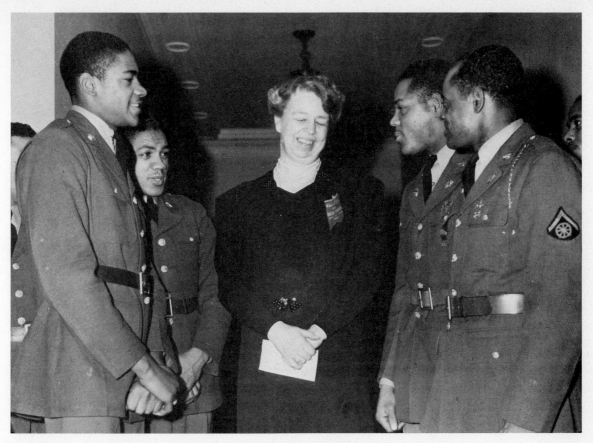

A pioneer in civil rights activism, Eleanor was well known for her public support of black interests. In addition to backing black appointments to federal civil service jobs and New Deal posts, the First Lady maintained contact with the NAACP, invited black organizations to visit the White House, appeared often as a speaker at Negro colleges, and consistently used her influence to combat bigotry. Here, during the War, she greeted black soldiers at a New York fund-raising event to establish recreation facilities for Negro troops; the U.S. Army and its facilities were not integrated until 1948.

though Roosevelt all but monopolized the Negro vote by 1940, no amount of prodding from his wife could induce the President to support an antilynching bill in Congress.

Eleanor battled on against the prevailing currents. Why should the U.S. Navy, she asked Secretary Swanson, enlist Negroes only as messmen—only as kitchen help? Swanson, who probably found the inquiry distasteful in itself (but, after all, it did come from the First Lady), responded firmly that during most of the 1920s blacks had not been allowed to enlist in the Navy at all. Their relegation to service in ship galleys was necessary, he argued, because otherwise they might rise to be petty officers and be placed in authority over whites; that "would create dissatisfaction, and would seriously handicap ship efficiency." The notion of black naval *officers* was not even broached. All Eleanor could do was to counsel, if not console, a Negro correspondent: "These things come slowly and patience is required in all great changes."

Not only did Eleanor try to get government assistance for blacks, she publicly identified herself with their cause. She urged the appointment of blacks to many New Deal agencies, and, for the first time since the days of Woodrow Wilson's "cleaning out of the Negroes" in the federal civil service, a small but noticeable number of blacks obtained middle-level government jobs. Eleanor refused to succumb to despair on the issue. She had frequent discussions with the head of the NAACP, Walter White, and even "forced" a meeting between White and FDR over the antilynching bill. She spoke at commencements and other ceremonies at black colleges. She praised and aided Richard Wright, the young novelist, as well as other Negro intellectuals. She received black sharecroppers at the White House and visited them in the fields.

In November 1938 Mrs. Roosevelt attended the first Southern Conference for Human Welfare, an interracial meeting of educators and social workers. Birmingham, Alabama, the site of the conference, strictly enforced its segregation ordinance, forcing whites to sit on one side of the aisle, blacks on the other. Eleanor entered the room with Mrs. Mary McLeod Bethune, a prominent civil rights advocate, and, chatting animatedly, sat down with her in the black section of the front row. Immediately a policeman appeared next to Eleanor and loudly cleared his throat. Although he was not about to arrest the First Lady, neither would he let her flout the law of the state of Alabama. Without looking up, Eleanor adjusted her chair slightly, so that she sat neither in the black nor in the white section. The policeman turned red, but left. "At a later meeting," Eleanor wrote, "word came to us that all the audience was to be arrested and taken to jail for breaking one of Birmingham's strongest laws against mixed audiences," but no police wagon appeared.

Early in 1939, Mrs. Roosevelt again had the chance to put preaching into practice. The DAR had barred the use of Washington's Constitution Hall to Marian Anderson, a black singer of international repute. Eleanor, herself a member of the DAR, decided to break with precedent. She had never thought much of resignation as a means of protest, considering it preferable to work for change within an organization But the DAR's refusal to budge on the issue caused her to resign and to express her reasons publicly. In April, Miss Anderson gave a triumphant open-air concert on federal property near the Lincoln Memorial, and a few months later, Mrs. Roosevelt presented her with the Spingarn Medal, the NAACP's award for achievement. "It is the little things that the Roosevelts do," observed a Negro newspaper, "which make them great and increases in the mind of the thinking Negro respect for the New Deal and most of what it represents."

Eleanor also had a particular interest in another powerless group. She was instrumental in starting the National Youth Administration, to aid the great numbers of young people made jobless by the Depression. She worked closely with leaders of the American Youth Congress (AYC), a left-wing organization demanding massive federal expenditures to provide employment for youth. In 1939, when the House Un-American Activities Committee subpoenaed the leaders of the AYC, Eleanor attended the hearings, sitting in the front row and knitting placidly like a benign Madame LaFarge. She had learned not to be frightened of names, perhaps because she had been called so many. (A friend once confessed to her of having voted in 1932 for the Socialist candidate for President. "So would I," Eleanor confided, "if I had not been married to Franklin.") After the student leaders had testified, she brought them back to the White House for dinner. In her column, she warned that if such witch-hunting continued, "It is really going to take quite a strong-minded person with a great indifference to what may be said about him to join an organization, even one with whose principles he is in agreement."

Even after Communist control of the AYC became clear, Eleanor spoke at their national convention, asking amidst angry heckling why they condemned Nazi aggression in Spain but not Soviet aggression against Finland. When her son commented that the AYC people obviously had bad manners she turned on him angrily. "And who are you to talk about their bad manners?" she blazed. "You were brought up in plenty, trained to good manners. You never had to worry about getting a job. Who are you to talk about the manners of young people who had to fight for everything they got, and didn't get much?"

The outburst showed both Eleanor's great empathy for those in need and her difficulties with her own family. Possibly her problems at home strengthened her interest in, and her commitment to, the outside world. For whatever reason, out of an unhappy childhood, a shattering disappointment in marriage, and her husband's paralysis, Eleanor forged a career that affected the history of her country and permanently changed the role of the American woman in public life.

Eleanor Roosevelt, from her particularly privileged vantage point, had done much to become a significant figure on the New Deal scene. With the outbreak of World War II in 1939, she adjusted to new conditions as the United States edged toward involvement in that struggle. The success of fascist totalitarian regimes in Europe caused her to drop her former pacifism in favor of a more "realistic" attitude of moral and material aid to the Western democracies. On that point, she and Franklin saw eye to eye. Eleanor became a leader in the Office of Civil Defense (OCD) during 1940 and 1941, working closely with a talented and flamboyant New Dealer, New York City's Mayor Fiorello La Guardia.

But when Japan attacked the United States in December 1941, Eleanor's course was set for wider horizons than those provided by OCD. She made a well-publicized trip to Britain in 1942 to visit Allied troops. The American buildup of armed forces overseas was proceeding at an astonishing pace, and even Eleanor's fabled stores of energy were hard pressed to keep up with all the war fronts. As a representative of the Red Cross and of the United Services Organization (USO), she became the First Gray Lady, earning the nickname the GI's Friend. A wartime tour of the South Pacific left Admiral William "Bull" Halsey decidedly impressed. During one twelve-hour stretch in New Caledonia, Mrs. Roosevelt inspected almost everything, including the many military hospitals. "When I say that she inspected those hospitals," Halsey reported, "I don't mean that she shook hands with the chief medical officer, glanced into a sun parlor, and left. I mean that she went into every ward, stopped at every bed, and spoke to every patient. . . . I marveled at her hardihood, both physical and mental, she walked for miles, and she saw patients who were grievously and gruesomely wounded. But I marveled most at their expressions as she leaned over them. It was a sight I will never forget."

The pace that both Roosevelts, Eleanor and Franklin, set for themselves during World War II was indeed killing. The President won his fourth presidential election in 1944, and was preparing for a summit meeting of Allied leaders at Yalta in Russia, but it was obvious by that time that his physical condition had deteriorated badly. He no longer wished to drive his car, and he had even surrendered his beloved ritual of cocktail mixing to others. After Yalta, Franklin went down to Warm Springs for rest and recuperation. Eleanor, still in Washington, seemed to convince herself that her husband would be all right. But on April 12, 1945, she learned that the President had died of a massive stroke. It was Eleanor who informed Harry Truman that he was the new President.

In Georgia, Eleanor had to bear the additional grief of learning that Lucy Mercer Rutherford had come to Warm Springs on April 9 and was with Franklin when he died three days later. Reflecting on her relationship with her husband as the funeral train moved toward Washington, Eleanor mused that Franklin "might have been happier with a wife who was completely uncritical. That I was never able to be, and he had

During World War II, Mrs. Roosevelt toured army bases and military hospitals wherever allied troops were stationed, from England to the South Pacific. Riding in jeeps, eating in mess halls, and visiting the wards, the President's wife displayed an energy and compassion that inspired the nation—and kept her in the news. "FIRST LADY DINES WITH DOUGHBOYS" cabled the United Press in 1943, as khaki-clad Eleanor appeared for lunch at an army camp in Australia.

The founding of the United Nations in 1945, after FDR's death, provided an appropriate opportunity for Eleanor to utilize her political and diplomatic talents and to remain active in public life. During her challenging years as United States delegate to the General Assembly, Eleanor served as Chairman of the Commission on Human Rights and was active in UNESCO. Here, she addresses the General Assembly on a human rights issue.

to find it in some other people. Nevertheless, I think I sometimes acted as a spur. . . .

Franklin was gone, but Eleanor never abandoned the conviction that one had to be *useful*. Too many things remained undone; too many desperate people around the world needed help. After the war, Mrs. Roosevelt went on to represent and to voice the best of the American humanitarian impulse. She served as a U.S. delegate to the United Nations from 1945 to 1953, earning worldwide respect and love. For another nine years she fought her version of the good fight as a lecturer and "spur" in support of causes she considered just. Her optimism, if not infectious, was certainly constant. She was, as her friend Adlai Stevenson expressed it following her death in 1962, a person who "would rather light a candle than curse the darkness."

Back in the early 1930s, when Soviet diplomat Maxim Litvinov made his first trip to the United States, President Roosevelt remarked that he regretted Madame Litvinov had not come with him. "Oh well, you know," answered the Russian, "very active woman, career of her own, constantly traveling, making speeches. Impossible to interrupt what she was doing. Came alone because she is individual in politics, just as I am."

Said Franklin Roosevelt, "I think I understand."

42
THE NEW DEAL ERA

A. W.

Eleanor Roosevelt assisted the New Deal in what was possibly its most important function — restoring the confidence of the American people in their government. Her husband, perhaps the country's master politician of the century, made the renewal of confidence a major objective, and in large measure he succeeded in achieving that goal. But Franklin Roosevelt also had to devise concrete policies, in legislation and in executive action, to deal with the crisis.

The Administration's responses followed no set pattern and derived from no single philosophical base. The New Deal was, instead, an extended improvisation in public policy — trying first one program to deal with a problem, then another if the first one failed, and sometimes returning to the original idea. Over six years, in this zig-zag pattern, Roosevelt and the New Dealers profoundly changed the face of American government and what the American people expected from it.

The New Deal did not end the Great Depression. It was World War II, with its massive government spending, that finally brought a full revival of production and an end to mass unemployment. By 1939, when foreign policy began to dominate his thinking, Roosevelt had shepherded the country from a crushing depression to a severe recession. Yet he could claim, for better or worse, to have preserved the American political and economic systems through a time when many expected that both would collapse.

ROOSEVELT

"The only thing we have to fear," declared the new President to a numbed nation, "is fear itself." Although the American people could search through the rest of his inaugural address without finding any reason not to be afraid and without learning what Roosevelt planned to do to ease their fears, they seemed to be comforted by his words as they had never been by Herbert Hoover's pronouncement of similar platitudes. Roosevelt's faculty for inspiring confidence by simple force of personality became one of his strongest weapons in the fight against chaos — as important as any bill he ever pushed through Congress.

Franklin Roosevelt was forty-seven when the stock market collapsed in 1929, fifty-one when he became President in 1933. His ideas about the world had already formed. There is no evidence that the Depression changed those ideas significantly. He was in many ways a traditionalist. He was, as we have seen, a wealthy aristocrat: educated in exclusive private schools, a graduate of Harvard, and owner of a country estate where he liked to play at being a gentleman farmer. FDR was a suave, smiling, confident man, who seemed to take the institutions and beliefs of his country very much for granted. A more unlikely candidate for leadership in a revolution is hard to imagine. Roosevelt, wrote a bemused columnist during the 1932 campaign, was a pleasant man, with no particular qualifications, who would like very much to be President.

On the other hand, Roosevelt's confidence opened his mind to experimentation. Because he had no serious doubts about American values and institutions, he could accept almost any specific suggestion for reform. Above all, he often said, the country demanded action. As long as the action was limited in its scope and possible consequences, he was willing to try almost anything.

Roosevelt appreciated fully the seriousness of the Depression. But he was nevertheless sure that, sooner or later, limited reforms would revive the economy. Then, all that would be needed would be a gentle system of laws and regulations to prevent a repetition of the worst mistakes of the 1920s.

SAVING THE BANKS

Yet, as Roosevelt took the oath of office, it appeared doubtful that he would get the chance to try his reforms. Since the fall of 1932, banks had been closing their doors, unable to pay depositors their money. In February, the governor of Michigan closed the state's banks for eight days to prevent collapse; state after state followed suit. By inauguration day on March 4, 1933, thirty-eight states had closed their banks; and before the sun rose on March 5, New York and Illinois had also closed theirs. The New York Stock Exchange and the Chicago Board of Trade shut down. "We are at the end of our rope," said Hoover in despair.

The day after inauguration, Roosevelt (with questionable legality) declared a national bank holiday. Four days later, he sent a mild banking reform and regulation bill to a special session of Congress. It went through both Houses in a day, although few congressmen knew what they were voting for. "The house is burning down," declared a Republican congressional leader, "and the President of the United States says this is the way to put out the fire." Roosevelt then spoke over the radio, in his first "fireside chat," assuring the nation that banks were now safe. When they reopened, bankers were astounded to find that deposits exceeded withdrawals.

Roosevelt's response to the situation clearly demonstrated his attitudes—and disappointed many radicals. A frightened Congress would have passed almost anything Roosevelt had asked for, up to and possibly including a bill nationalizing the banks. But the President clearly intended to preserve capitalism as well as to stimulate recovery. It would, on the other hand, be a controlled capitalism. Two months later Roosevelt signed the Glass-Steagall Act, which strengthened federal controls over banks and set up the Federal Deposit Insurance Corporation (FDIC) to guarantee bank deposits up to $10,000 (now up to $40,000).

The Emergency Banking Act of 1933, accompanied by a confident "Fireside Chat," began the legislative barrage of the First Hundred Days. With thousands of banks out of business and most of the remainder closed by the states, President Roosevelt proclaimed a bank holiday and proposed legislation to bolster the stronger banks with RFC loans and other assistance. When the banks opened their doors four days later, the nation responded by depositing billions in hoarded currency and gold. Above, FDR signs the Emergency Banking Act, and gold is returned to the vaults.

Bank failures ceased immediately. Roosevelt had bought some time.

THE HUNDRED DAYS

Congress and the people now awaited, with both eagerness and anxiety, a legislative program that Roosevelt had not quite worked out. During the campaign, he and other Democrats had called for a cut in spending and a balanced budget, and the Administration took a few halting steps in that

MAJOR NEW DEAL DOMESTIC LEGISLATION

YEAR	ACT/ADMINISTRATION	PURPOSE
REGULATION OF INDUSTRY AND AGRICULTURE		
1933	AGRICULTURAL ADJUSTMENT ACT	Set up the Agricultural Adjustment Administration to encourage stability in agriculture by attempting to control agricultural production.
	NATIONAL INDUSTRIAL RECOVERY ACT	Set up the National Recovery Administration to encourage corporations to create associations for planning production and controlling prices; created a blanket code of minimum wages and maximum hours.
1935	CONNALLY ACT	To prevent overproduction of oil.
	GUFFEY ACT	To control the coal industry.
	NATIONAL LABOR RELATIONS ACT (WAGNER ACT)	To give federal protection to the labor movement by making it illegal for an employer to refuse to recognize a labor union.
	PUBLIC UTILITIES HOLDING COMPANY ACT	To limit the development of holding companies and discourage financial concentration in public utilities.
1936	ROBINSON-PATMAN ACT	To prohibit wholesalers or manufacturers from giving preferential discounts or rebates to large buyers.
	WALSH-HEALY ACT	To set minimum wages and maximum hours for work done on federal contracts (enacted after NRA declared unconstitutional).
1938	AGRICULTURAL ADJUSTMENT ACT	To cut back farm production through marketing quotas, soil conservation payments, export subsidies, and crop loans. It began storage of surpluses.
	FAIR LABOR STANDARDS ACT	To establish minimum wages and maximum hours; forbade child labor.
REFORM		
1933	TENNESSEE VALLEY AUTHORITY	Set up the Tennessee Valley Authority to develop the nation's water resources and, therefore, provide cheap electric power.
1935	SOCIAL SECURITY ACT	To create a system of old-age insurance for Americans.
	WEALTH TAX ACT	To make the federal income tax more equitable.
MISCELLANEOUS		
1934	RECIPROCAL TRADE AGREEMENTS ACT	To lower tariff barriers in order to improve foreign trade.
1939	HATCH ACT	To remedy corrupt campaign practices by prohobiting active political campaigning and soliciting by federal officials.
	REORGANIZATION ACT	To reorganize the executive branch for greater efficiency.

MAJOR NEW DEAL DOMESTIC LEGISLATION

YEAR	ACT/ADMINSTRATION	PURPOSE
BANKING CURRENCY SECURITIES		
1933	EMERGENCY BANKING RELIEF ACT	To save failing banks by providing them with cash to pay their depositors.
	GLASS–STEAGALL ACT	To curb speculation by banks; set up the Federal Deposit Insurance Corporation to "insure" savings deposits up to $10,000.
	"TRUTH IN SECURITIES" ACT	To require corporations floating new securities to register them with the Federal Trade Commission.
1934	GOLD RESERVE ACT	To enable the President to fix the gold content of the dollar.
	SECURITIES EXCHANGE ACT	Set up the Securities and Exchange Commission to regulate the Stock Market.
1935	BANKING ACT	To reform and strengthen the Federal Reserve System by directing interest rates.
DIRECT RELIEF		
1933	FARM CREDIT ADMINISTRATION	To provide emergency relief to farmers in the form of mortgages.
	FEDERAL EMERGENCY RELIEF ACT	Set up the Federal Emergency Relief Administration to provide grants in aid to the states; also set up the Civil Works Administration to relieve unemployment by a temporary work relief program.
	FRAZIER-LEMKE FARM BANKRUPTCY ACT	To enable some farmers to regain their farms even after the foreclosure of mortgages.
	HOME OWNERS REFINANCING ACT	Set up the Home Owners' Loan Corporation to provide emergency relief to home owners in the form of government financed mortgage loans.
	NATIONAL INDUSTRIAL RECOVERY ACT	Set up the Public Works Administration to contract for heavy construction projects in order to increase employment.
	UNEMPLOYMENT RELIEF ACT	Set up the Civilian Conservation Corps to provide jobs for the unemployed on conservation projects.
1934	NATIONAL HOUSING ACT	Set up the Federal Housing Administration to insure mortgages for new construction and home repairs.
1935	WORKS PROGRESS ADMINISTRATION	To relieve unemployment by light public works projects.
1937	FARM SECURITY ADMINISTRATION	To make short-term loans for rehabilitation of farms, and long-term loans for purchase of farms.

direction. Awaiting the repeal of the prohibition amendment, it persuaded Congress to legalize beer, possibly to take people's minds off the Depression. Finally, the Administration produced comprehensive farm and industrial recovery bills.

Both the National Industrial Recovery Act (NIRA) and the Agricultural Adjustment Act (AAA) sought to regulate the economy without changing its private enterprise character. The NIRA also reflected Roosevelt's desire to maintain the broad support he had enjoyed when he assumed office—to move against the Depression at the head of a coalition of government, business, and labor. (His approach in some ways resembled Wilson's approach to fighting World War I—the last period in which Democrats had controlled the federal government.)

The National Industrial Recovery Act was, in essence, a repeal of parts of the old Sherman Anti-Trust Act (see page 730). Under a federal agency known as the National Recovery Administration (NRA), corporations were encouraged to create associations to plan production and control prices. Such a step meant the end of effective competition, but the Administration was prepared during the Depression to sacrifice competition to stability and recovery.

For workers, the act also proposed that employers agree on uniform standards for labor practices, wages, and hours. When some companies were slow to cooperate, the NRA created a blanket code of minimum wages and maximum hours. Companies that cooperated were awarded a flag with the NRA symbol—a blue eagle—to fly as evidence of their public spirit. Up to a point, it worked. Some workers—those who had jobs to begin with—began to work shorter days and take home fatter pay envelopes.

The Agricultural Adjustment Act was a similar but more radical attempt to alter prevailing economics. It recognized that the farmer had a peculiar problem. Manufacturers, when prices fell, could cut back production. The reduction in supply would, sooner or later, raise prices. But farmers had always met falling prices by trying to produce more, not less.

The law created an Agricultural Adjustment Administration (AAA) with the power to pay farm-

ers cash subsidies *not* to plant or harvest crops. The agency could also buy up agricultural products, such as cotton or wheat, and store them. This scheme would reduce supply and raise prices. In other words, a government body, with the cooperation of farmers, would try to control agricultural production. The goal was to enable farmers to earn as much (in real dollars, or purchasing power) as they had earned during the prosperous years from 1909 to 1914—a standard known as parity.

The AAA worked better than the NRA. Using its new powers, the agency in 1933 paid out $160 million to farmers who plowed under about 10 million acres of crops. That same year, farmers also withheld about 6 million pigs in return for $30 million in government money)—a controversial act, when millions of people did not have enough to eat. But these drastic measures worked—reinforced by drought in 1933 and 1934 that destroyed much of the wheat and corn crops. In 1933, farm prices were at 55 percent of parity; by 1936, at 90 percent. The act also had the indirect effect of forcing millions of tenant farmers and sharecroppers off the land, adding them to the unemployment rolls of the country's cities (and beginning a mass migration off the land that accelerated after World War II). Liberal New Dealers, including Mrs. Roosevelt, protested AAA contracts that allowed the eviction of farm tenants. But the group of liberal and radical lawyers that had fought the policy was "purged" from the agency by Secretary of Agriculture Wallace in 1935.

Wide ranging as they were, the NIRA and AAA were only a part of the legislative program achieved by FDR during the first months of his administration—the Hundred Days. He also demanded and received from Congress the Glass-Steagall Act, also known as the "Truth in Securities" Act, to regulate the stock market; and bills to provide emergency relief to farmers and homeowners in danger of losing their property. His advisers also persuaded Roosevelt to abandon his scruples over a balanced budget and set up the Federal Emergency Relief Agency to distribute half a billion welfare dollars to the states. Roosevelt, reversing the previous vetoes of two Republican Presidents, signed a bill creating the Tennessee Valley Authority (TVA), a massive government hydroelectric power development in the Upper South.

Nowhere was the Depression more severe than in the 40,000 square miles of territory spanning seven states known as the Tennessee River Valley. Each year the river swelled to flood stage with an average 52 inches of rain that washed out the area's meager crops. There was little industry and no hope of more, income being not even half the national average. The Tennessee Valley Authority was easily the most creative and far-reaching experiment in regional planning undertaken in American history. The TVA built a series of dams for flood control, thus making successful farming possible in the region and providing an abundance of hydroelectric power. It also made the rivers navigable. Cheap power and easy water transport, in turn, made the area appealing to industry. Schools, improved health facilities, recreational opportunities, reforestation, and other social benefits also flowed from the TVA, which, as the decade wore on, became a successful—if controversial—model for subsequent regional planning efforts in the United States. It marked the first time that government had attempted to mobilize the natural, economic, and human resources of a region to effect a rapid change in the overall conditions of life for most citizens of the area.

RESPONSE

Long before the success of Roosevelt's program could be gauged, it became clear that he had captured the American imagination. The President's picture appeared in homes across the country; journalists estimated his popularity at up to 90 percent. "How do you account for him?" asked William Allen White, a progressive Republican. "Was I just fooled in him before the election, or has he developed?" People now felt the country had begun to move again. "President Roosevelt has done his part, now you do something," read a sign posted in a factory. "Buy something—buy anything, anywhere; paint your kitchen, send a telegram, give a party, get a car, pay a bill, rent a

THE TENNESSEE VALLEY AUTHORITY · 1933

flat, fix your roof, get a haircut, see a show, build a house, take a trip, sing a song, get married."

Although Roosevelt's effect on music and marriage remains unclear, the economy did seem to respond to New Deal efforts. By spring of 1934, the crisis had eased. Unemployment dropped, and business indicators picked up a bit. But that was as far as it went. The NRA's program of voluntary regulation of everything, from the steel industry to show business, apparently could do no more.

Despite Roosevelt's personal popularity, his programs were beginning to draw criticism from both the left and the right. At the low point of the Depression, during Hoover's last two years, Americans had been too demoralized even for radicalism. With millions of people living in shantytowns, the Socialist party ran a disappointing race in 1932, winning less than 900,000 votes, while the Communists polled only 100,000 votes. Now, as vitality seemed to return to the country, the left began to stir as well. Strikes erupted throughout the country in 1934, including a general strike in San Francisco. The greatest radical challenge, however, came not from Marxian philosophers but from uniquely American demagogues—notably, Senator Huey Long of Louisiana (see page 435), who insisted that the New Deal had not been sufficiently reformist.

Wealthy businessmen argued, conversely, that Roosevelt had gone too far. In August 1934, the American Liberty League was organized. Originally financed by the Dupont family, the League soon gained enthusiastic support from leaders of such corporations as General Motors, Montgomery Ward, and General Foods. Calling itself nonpartisan, it could boast endorsement by the Democratic presidential candidates of 1924 and 1928—the conservative John W. Davis and the embittered progressive Al Smith. Smith felt that Roosevelt had cheated him out of the nomination and the presidency in 1932, and in his frustration he joined a group having little to do with his personal background or his political principles. "There can be only one capital," he warned appreciative Liberty Leaguers, "Washington or Moscow."

With such strident criticism apparently on the increase, New Dealers waited anxiously for the elections of 1934, hoping to hold their losses to under forty seats in Congress. The morning after election day, they were stunned and delighted to find Democratic gains in both houses, giving them the tightest control over Congress ever held by a party.

ENTER THE SUPREME COURT

With his massive electoral victories, Roosevelt controlled two of the three branches of government. Conservatives looked hopefully to the third, and the makeup of the Supreme Court seemed to justify their confidence. It would be almost two years before the legislation of the Hundred Days reached the Court, but when it did, it would find a Court roster that was unchanged, and probably unfriendly.

Of the nine men on the Court, seven had been named by conservative Republican Presidents. Although court decisions did not exactly follow a conservative pattern (two of the three liberal justices had been named by Republicans, while Justice McReynolds, possibly the most reactionary, had been nominated by Wilson, a Democrat), the Court did seem to bring the political and constitutional outlook of Calvin Coolidge to the judging of the New Deal. From early decisions, the Administration learned to count four justices as against the New Deal, three as tending to sustain it, and two, including Chief Justice Charles Evans Hughes, as holding the balance of power. For Roosevelt, a bad situation was compounded by simple bad luck; throughout his first term, he did not have a single Court vacancy to fill.

The Court's first decisions only prolonged the suspense. It threw out a section of the NIRA; but it upheld Roosevelt's financial policies by a series of 5 to 4 votes. Then, in May 1935, the Court unanimously ruled the National Recovery Administration unconstitutional. "Extraordinary conditions do not create or enlarge constitutional power," admonished Chief Justice Hughes, as he read the judicial obituary for NRA.

In a way, the Court had done Roosevelt a favor. The NRA, however useful it had been dur-

HUEY P. LONG

Because of an assassin's bullet, Americans will never know just how serious a threat Huey P. Long posed to their political institutions. Unquestioned master of his own state of Louisiana, the most potent demagogue of the Depression, Long attracted national support with a hazy program of redistributing wealth, and the seductive slogan "Every man a king." He was preparing to run for President when he was murdered, but probably not even so gifted a politician as Long could have outmaneuvered Franklin Roosevelt. Still, Long did make Roosevelt—and a great many other people—extremely uncomfortable.

Long grew up in a middle-class but radical-populist family in northern Louisiana. After a brief spell as a traveling salesman, he used his savings and a small loan to put himself through a three-year law course in eight months. But Long did not prosper in private practice and was more interested in finding a way into politics. In 1918, at age twenty-five, he won election to the State Railroad Commission. After six years of denouncing corporations (especially the oil interests), he ran for governor, but lost. The day after his loss in 1924, he declared himself a candidate for 1928, and campaigned hard for the next four years. That second time, he won.

As governor, Long pushed through a reform program that included free textbooks, a large state university, an expanded road system, and a tax on oil production. He also worked unceasingly to extend his own power, firing people throughout the state government and replacing them with his own henchmen. When one of his bills came up in the legislature, Long would go down to the floor of each house and bellow orders at the legislators he controlled.

During his second year as governor, Long tried to pass a bill taxing the refining of oil as well. Aghast, the legislature killed the measure, and impeached Long in a broad indictment covering virtually all impeachable offenses. Long barely managed to persuade, bribe, and threaten enough state senators to enable him to stay in office.

Tightening his control over the state, he began to develop a folksy image, calling himself "Kingfish" after a character in the radio program "Amos 'n Andy." The new nickname covered many activities; a U.S. Treasury agent reported to his superiors that "Long and his gang are stealing everything in the state." In 1930 he defeated an incumbent U.S. Senator and in 1932 played a large role in nominating Franklin D. Roosevelt for President. The Kingfish remained as governor for a year to ensure his control of the state before taking his seat in the Senate.

When he reached Washington, Long found the Democratic leadership too conservative for him, and within a year found he had problems working under President Roosevelt. Partly, the new President moved too slowly for Long; partly, Long was not born to follow.

From the second-best stage in the country (the U.S. Senate), the master showman began to assemble his own movement. He attacked the New Deal and offered his own program of Share Our Wealth. By 1935, he was receiving speaking invitations from all over the country and published a book modestly titled, *My First Years in the White House.* Roosevelt's advisers estimated he might poll several million votes as a third party candidate. Roosevelt showed his concern: he cut off federal patronage to the Long forces in Louisiana, and a small army of U.S. Treasury agents entered the state to examine Long's income tax returns.

In September 1935, the son-in-law of a Long opponent shot the Kingfish down in the lobby of the state capital. According to legend, Long's last words were "God, don't let me die. I have so much to do."

ing the crisis of 1933–1934, was collapsing, and many were charging, with some justice, that its industrial codes benefited big business at the expense of small producers. Clearly, the Administration would need to try a new approach, and the Court had saved FDR from having to admit failure. Nevertheless, the President denounced the justices for adhering to a "horse-and-buggy" definition of interstate commerce. For the next two years, the Administration would pass its bills looking uncomfortably over its shoulder at the Supreme Court.

THE SECOND NEW DEAL

Even before Black Monday, as the day of NRA's death came to be known for a while, Roosevelt had asked the new Congress to take bolder measures to deal with the Depression. The enactments of Roosevelt's second Congress differed greatly in philosophy from those of the first Hundred Days. Motivated by a combination of continuing economic hardship and the counsel of more liberal advisers (including Eleanor, who played a critical role at this time), and reacting to attacks from business and the Supreme Court, Roosevelt abandoned his earlier policy of stabilization and cooperation. He began to frame strategies for reforming the economic system that could bolster the poor and powerless and curb the power of business. The American Liberty League had not known when it was well off.

Faced by a stubborn persistence in the high rate of unemployment, Roosevelt shrugged off his hopes for a balanced budget and asked Congress for five billion dollars for work relief. To administer the agency charged with spending this money, Roosevelt selected a controversial former social worker named Harry Hopkins, the man who would eventually become the second most powerful figure in the Administration. Thin and pale, apparently existing on cigarettes and black coffee, Hopkins seemed perpetually on the point of death from tuberculosis. But he possessed an incredible

The WPA's immediate goal was to provide relief for the unemployed. But in its six-year life span it compiled a remarkable record of public construction, including more than 600,000 miles of road, like this one in Tennessee.

appetite for work and a keen social conscience. To those who suggested the economy would right itself in the long run without expensive government programs, he responded tartly, "People don't eat in the long run. They eat every day."

Hopkins' agency, the Works Progress Administration (WPA), soon employed three million people, paying a wage somewhere between relief and union wages. Careful not to take jobs away from workers already employed, WPA people worked on a wide range of projects, building or extending hospitals, schools, and playgrounds. The Federal Theater Project, Federal Writers' Project, and Federal Art Project subsidized unemployed hopefuls of varying talent and brought drama and art to many isolated communities. The National Youth Administration tried to deal with the enormous number of needy young people, giving part-time employment to help many stay in school, providing training to many who had left school.

Between 1935 and 1941, more than eight million Americans were employed by the WPA. It spent over $11 billion on 250,000 projects. Another $4 billion was spent by a similar agency, the Public Works Administration (PWA), which built large-scale public projects and employed union labor. Critics charged that the programs were involved in useless "make-work" tasks, that WPA stood for "We piddle around," and that the whole organization was a taxpayer-supported boondoggle and patronage plum to get Roosevelt and other Democrats elected. Others pointed out that WPA took care of only about one-third of the unemployed, and that most of the others had to rely on the states or private charity for subsistence.

Shortly after Black Monday, the President demanded immediate passage of five major Administration bills, terming them "must" legislative items. Included in the crash program were the two bills that became the New Deal's most significant legislative accomplishments. Despite the New Deal's reputation for innovation, however, neither of the two was really an Administration idea.

Older people had suffered more in the Depression than any other group. Since 1933, an elderly physician from Long Beach, California, Dr. Francis Townsend, had been promoting a plan to give everybody over sixty years of age a federal pension of two hundred dollars a month. The

During the depths of the depression, the 1934 street scene above was repeated in every city in the nation. The efforts of voluntary agencies and local governments were not enough to help the vast numbers of elderly and unemployed who, depleted of savings and broken in spirit, were reduced to destitution and hand-outs. The Social Security Act of 1935 not only provided immediate relief for the old and disabled, but also prospective annuities for those still at work — its most innovative feature.

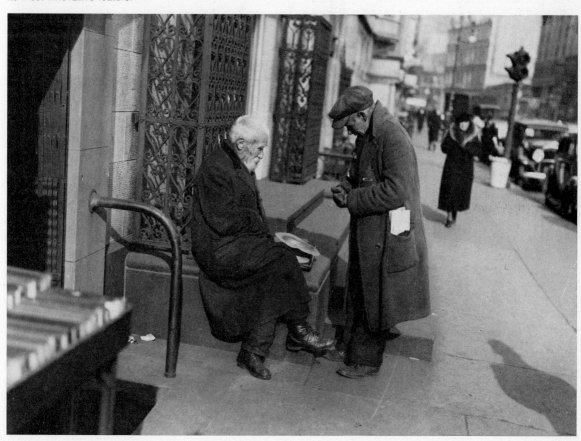

movement spread swiftly, and the impoverished elderly at last saw a chance for some dignity at the end of their lives. Several congressmen from both parties were elected with Townsendite backing in 1934, and although the House killed a Townsendite bill (avoiding a roll call, so that those against it would not be identified by name), both Houses saw the political necessity of doing something for the aged. By June, the Congress had passed Roosevelt's Social Security bill.

The bill provided that workers and their employers would contribute a small part of each year's earnings to a common fund. When a person reached retirement age (or could no longer work because of illness), he or she would receive a small pension from the fund. If a worker died, the survivors would receive benefits.

The Social Security Act of 1935 could in no way be considered radical. The pensions were much smaller than those suggested by Townsend, and payments would not start until 1942. Many who needed coverage most, including farm workers and domestics, did not come under its provisions. Finally, while most industrialized countries had instituted old-age pension systems decades earlier, none had tried to pay for them out of workers' current earnings. (Roosevelt himself maintained that workers were assessed for policy reasons: "With those taxes in there, no damn politician can ever scrap my social security program.") Social Security, however modestly begun, represented the longest step yet taken by the federal government toward becoming what Roosevelt's critics called a "welfare state," a government that involved itself directly in the financial security of its citizens.

Angered by the Court decision on NRA, convinced by business attacks on the Administration that his dream of cooperation had died, Roosevelt now insisted on passage of the bill that would have the New Deal's greatest effect on the American power structure. He declared himself a strong supporter of the National Labor Relations Act (or Wagner Act), a bill he had previously all but ignored.

The Wagner Act, the most significant piece of pro-labor legislation ever signed by an American President, became law at a time when organized labor had almost given up on Roosevelt. The act made it illegal for an employer to refuse to recognize a labor union favored by a majority of workers as their bargaining agent. The law also contained a list of "unfair labor practices"—an attempt to curb the power of employers in labor-management relations. And it set up the National Labor Relations Board (NLRB) to hear complaints and to supervise elections by workers who wished to unionize.

As a result of the act, labor unions tripled their membership, from a low of 3 million members in the early 1930s to about 9.5 million in 1941. Although this growth was marked by division between the craft unions of the American Federation of Labor (AFL) and a coalition of industrial unions formed in 1935 by the United Mine Workers' John L. Lewis, the Congress of Industrial Organizations (CIO), it raised organized labor to a new position of power. Unions could now tell prospective members, with some exaggeration, "The President wants you to join," and call in the NLRB to hold elections by secret ballot among workers to choose a union. Possibly exceeding Roosevelt's own desires, the Wagner Act would eventually make Big Labor a political and economic force capable of challenging Big Business.

Of Roosevelt's other legislative demands, for which he kept a reluctant Congress in session through the hot Washington summer, the most dramatic was the Wealth Tax. Throughout the 1920s, Secretary of the Treasury Andrew Mellon had steadily reduced taxes on the rich. Roosevelt now sought to reverse the trend, asking for higher tax rates on large personal incomes, a graduated corporate income tax, and federal inheritance taxes. Congress eliminated inheritance taxes but did institute the highest rates ever for the upper tax brackets: a 75 percent income tax, a 70 percent estate tax, and a 15 percent corporate income tax.

The Wealth Tax, a modest measure that Congress made even more modest, was as far as Roosevelt cared to go in the redistribution of America's wealth. Probably he only went that far under pressure from Senate liberals and a political need to ease criticism from the left. The bill had little real effect; by the end of the 1930s, the top one percent even held a slightly larger percentage of the diminished national wealth than it had before.

But more than any other New Deal measure, except perhaps the Wagner Act, the Wealth Tax infuriated business. A Chamber of Commerce poll in September 1935 revealed that member organizations opposed the New Deal thirty-five to one. Many businessmen could not bring themselves to speak Roosevelt's name, referring to him bitterly as "that man in the White House." They looked forward with eagerness to the election of 1936, when the country could be redeemed from bureaucracy and Bolshevism.

TRIUMPH OF THE NEW DEAL

Having finally abandoned his hopes for a cooperative policy, Roosevelt welcomed the opportunity to confront the rich. In his State of the Union message, he boasted of having "earned the hatred of entrenched greed." He drew a parallel between himself and Andrew Jackson, pointing out that in Jackson's fight with the Bank of the United States he had been opposed by the wealthy and most of the newspapers, and supported only by the people. "History," mused Roosevelt, "so often repeats itself."

Besides calling the New Deal socialistic and un-American, Roosevelt's opponents waged a whispering campaign against the President himself. His polio, they assured one another, had destroyed his mind; late at night, maniacal laughter was rumored to come from the Oval Office. The President was forcing on America a "Jew Deal"; his real name was Franklin Rosenfeld. A wealthy man, whose family money came from stocks, Roosevelt was "a traitor to his class."

To rid the country of this demon, Republicans selected as their candidate the mild-mannered governor of Kansas, Alfred M. Landon. Landon had a double claim to Republican admiration: he was the only Republican governor to win reelection in 1934, and he had balanced his state's budget. (Democrats pointed out that the state of

Father Charles Coughlin, whose national radio broadcasts combined support for the nationalization of banks, utilities, and natural resources with a persistent antisemitism, drew his support from the right.

Kansas had a budget roughly the size of New York City's Department of Sanitation.) Yet Landon was a weak choice to rally the fervid anti-New Dealers. He was a dull speaker, and he did not oppose all of the New Deal. His most forceful claim was that Republicans could provide a cheaper and more efficient federal government.

Riding the crest of an improved economy, Roosevelt compared business to the elderly gentleman who, having been saved from drowning, turns angrily on his rescuer because he has not also saved his top hat. He ignored Landon and focused his attack on the plutocrats of the Liberty League. His campaign staff set up separate organizations, so that Republican progressives and prolaborites could support Roosevelt without having to align themselves with the Democratic party.

Just before the election, a newspaper wire service asked William Allen White for a story to run in case Landon won. "You have a quaint sense of humor," White wired back. James Farley, the professional politician who ran the Democratic party and dispensed federal patronage for Roosevelt, predicted that the President would win every state but Maine and Vermont. Not even Roosevelt believed him.

But Farley was right. Carrying forty-six of the forty-eight states, Roosevelt beat Landon by twenty-seven million to sixteen million votes. He increased the already whopping Democratic majority in Congress, reducing the Republicans to

Republican candidate Alf Landon, former progressive Governor of Kansas, is shown here campaigning for the presidency in Ohio in October 1936. Despite Landon's promise to continue New Deal programs without running a deficit, FDR won an overwhelming victory, losing only two states to the Republicans. This impressive popular endorsement included a marked shift of black votes to the Democratic party.

sixteen votes in the Senate and less than a hundred in the House. The nation had overwhelmingly ratified the New Deal. "This," mourned the publisher of the Republican *New York Herald Tribune*, "is a great national disaster."

Roosevelt had done more than win an election and further depress the hearts of businessmen. He had redrawn the boundaries of American politics. From 1894 to 1930, Republicans had controlled every Congress except four during the Progressive Era. Roosevelt had changed the Democrats from the minority to the majority party in America.

Besides the Democratic South, the Roosevelt coalition found core support among the Catholic and immigrant voters in the large cities. Although many of these groups had previously voted Democratic, Roosevelt gave them, for the first time, heavy representation in top-level government positions. Of the 214 federal judges appointed by the three preceding Presidents, for example, only eight were Catholics. Roosevelt, on the other hand, named 51 Catholics among the 196 federal judges appointed during the New Deal era. The roll call of New Deal officials and advisers — including such names as Corcoran and Cohen, Frankfurter and Farley, Pecora and Bunche — symbolized this change for ethnic Americans. Big-city mayors, like La Guardia in New York and Curley in Boston, emphasized the point.

The third major factor in the coalition was organized labor, supporting Roosevelt in gratitude for the Wagner Act. Although labor had not yet gained the power and influence it was later to have in the Democratic party, it could supply a significant number of campaign workers. Furthermore, it could supply money, badly needed by a party that received few donations from business in 1936. The United Mine Workers became the largest single contributor to the Democratic war chest, giving $469,000.

Finally, for the first time ever, Roosevelt had drawn black voters into the Democratic party. In 1932, during the worst of a Depression that hurt blacks more than any other group, most black voters had clung to the GOP, the party of Lincoln. But in 1936 Roosevelt won most of the black vote. Remarkably, he effected this revolution while passing no civil rights legislation, while making no major black appointments, and while many New Deal programs existed in the South that were openly discriminatory. Yet relief, at least in the North and West, kept millions of blacks as well as other poor people alive; Roosevelt did appoint black advisers to many departments and agencies; and blacks deeply appreciated Eleanor Roosevelt's frequently expressed concern for their plight. "My friends, go turn Lincoln's picture to the wall," advised one publisher. "That debt has been paid in full."

ELECTION OF 1936

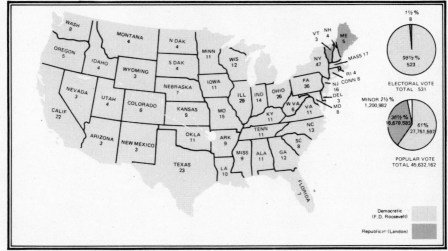

None of these groups had particularly strong feelings for the Democratic party. Their ties were to Roosevelt—and to Eleanor. Many of them idolized the couple. Yet they voted for Democratic governors, congressmen, and state legislators. Four times Roosevelt ran for President, and four times he was elected. By the time he died, the country had acquired the habit of voting Democratic.

THE COURT FIGHT

Roosevelt, with his massive congressional majorities, now contemplated a new round of reform. But all his plans might be frustrated by the Supreme Court. During 1936, the Court had killed the AAA, an Administration act to regulate the coal industry, and a state minimum wage bill. Soon the Wagner Act and the Social Security Act would be coming up before the tribunal.

Roosevelt felt he had to act quickly. He dismissed the notion of a constitutional amendment; the negative vote of only thirteen state legislatures was need to block passage, and he feared that the conservatives could "buy" those negative votes. He also declined to consider a simple bill to expand the size of the Court, something Congress had done before. FDR finally came up with a tricky plan based on the false premise that the Court could not keep up with its work. It would allow him to make a new appointment for every justice over seventy who did not retire, and it would extend this principle throughout the federal court system.

The members of Congress, including many dedicated New Dealers, were stunned by Roosevelt's scheme. The Democratic chairman of the

When FDR proposed his controversial Court Reform Bill in 1937, contending that the Justices were unable to cope with their workload, the *New Masses* supported his views by depicting the "Nine Old Men" dozing off on the bench. Although the size of the Supreme Court had been altered before, constitutionally, many felt that the President's "Court-Packing" bill was political trickery rather than legitimate reform. After Congress rejected the bill, a wave of retirements on the court enabled the President to make his own appointments.

House Judiciary Committee announced, "Boys, here's where I cash in my chips." Republicans hung back, allowing the many irate Democrats to take the lead in fighting against the bill.

Worse for Roosevelt, the same electorate that had ringingly endorsed him was plainly disturbed over the bill. Many asked themselves if Republican charges that Roosevelt dreamed of becoming a dictator had some truth in them. With the rise to supreme power of Hitler and Mussolini in Europe, Americans clung closer to the institutions that they saw as the protectors of their own freedoms, and the Supreme Court stood high on that list of respected institutions. Nevertheless, Roosevelt pushed hard for the plan.

The Court itself, in a variety of ways, actually killed the court-packing proposal. "If they want me to preside over a convention, I can do it," quipped Hughes publicly; but the chief justice, a skilled politician, led efforts by Court members to assure Congress that it could handle its work load. Louis Brandeis, at eighty the oldest and the most liberal man on the Court, lobbied personally against the bill.

Moreover, whether or not influenced by Roosevelt's attack, the Court seemed ready to take a friendlier view toward New Deal legislation. Within two months, it upheld both the Wagner Act and the Social Security Act by 5-to-4 decisions, and Roosevelt's supporters began to lose stomach for a fight. "Why run for a train after you've caught it?" asked one. Roosevelt's case seemed even less pressing when one of the conservative justices resigned.

But despite adverse public reaction and strong negative advice from congressional leaders, Roosevelt pressed for the bill even after it was obviously dead. One hundred sixty-eight days after the fight had begun, the bill was sent quietly back to committee. "Glory be to God!" proclaimed a senator who usually supported Roosevelt. The New Deal had sustained its first major legislative defeat.

A STRAIN ON THE NEW DEAL

Roosevelt's massive coalition of 1936, like any alliance of disparate groups, could not be maintained intact indefinitely. Its various elements had too many conflicting interests. The alliance began to break up shortly after the election. Industrial unionists of the CIO, newly armed with the Wagner Act, renounced the conservative leadership of the AFL and mounted a frontal attack on the most formidable anti-union forces—the steel and automobile industries. The nature of the campaign alarmed many people who had considered themselves liberals.

A half-century earlier, the McCormack Reaper Works in Chicago had been the site of the strike that spawned the Haymarket Riot of 1886. But in 1937, the strike scene at McCormick reflected the new activism of labor and the tripling of union membership that occurred during the New Deal. The Wagner Act of 1935, which insured union recognition by management and enumerated unfair labor practices, contributed greatly to union growth and also won labor support for FDR in the next three elections.

General Motors, as part of its campaign against the unions, paid out almost a million dollars to union-breaking private detectives between 1934 and 1936. Against such company spies and comparable tactics by management, normal union organization could hardly be expected to succeed. Early in 1937, workers occupied seventeen General Motors plants, refusing to come out until GM accepted the union. Thus began the "sit-downs." Strikers defied court orders; with wrenches and other makeshift weapons they turned back company attempts to oust them. They received support and reinforcements from other unionists. In February, the country's largest corporation surrendered.

Despite an early and surprising capitulation by U.S. Steel, the battles in the rest of the steel industry were even worse. Police killed ten strikers on Memorial Day, 1937, at the Republic Steel plant in South Chicago. (A Senate committee later discovered that the company was the largest private purchaser of tear gas in the country.) The unions lost their battle with steel in 1937, yet within a few years the steel industry and other holdouts had to give in, worn down by a combination of skillful union organizers (many radicals among them) and New Deal support for the new unions through the NLRB.

The strikes terrified millions of middle-class Americans, who were alarmed by the violence and by what they considered a threat to private property. Neither were they pleased with Roosevelt's response to the situation: Although he publicly denounced the sit-down strikes, he did not send troops to break them, as most of his predecessors would have done. Millions of Roosevelt voters began drifting back to the Republican party.

They received an even stronger impetus to do so when the fragile economic recovery collapsed in the fall. Although there were still eight million unemployed in 1937, other economic indicators had almost reached their pre-Depression level. Encouraged by those signs, Roosevelt, who had not accepted the idea of a permanent government role in the economy, tried to cut back and balance the budget. He sharply reduced expenditures in both the WPA and the PWA, bringing government "pump-priming" of the economy to a virtual halt. With startling suddenness, the bottom dropped out of the recovery. The Dow-Jones averages fell from 190 to 117 in two months. An additional four million people were thrown out of work. Republicans—and others—began to speak sarcastically of the "Roosevelt recession."

THE LAST NEW DEAL CONGRESS

Hurriedly, Roosevelt recalled the Congress. But he was still reluctant to resume heavy spending. "Everything will work out all right if we just sit tight and keep quiet," he explained, sounding a lot like the man he had replaced five years earlier.

As on so many other issues, New Dealers warred for influence over the President. His secretary of the Treasury, Henry Morgenthau, argued that the government could not support the economy forever; having done all it could, the government must now pull back and let the economy right itself. But Harry Hopkins and the liberal wing called for a final acceptance of the policies of John Maynard Keynes, a British economist who argued that only the government, by pumping money into the economy through deficit spending, could cure a recession. In April 1938, as the recession worsened and congressional elections approached, Roosevelt regretfully abandoned for the last time his hope of a balanced budget. When Congress voted him four billion dollars, he revitalized WPA and PWA, and slowly things began to improve.

Although the new Congress had the greatest Democratic majorities in history, Roosevelt could get little new legislation passed. He had weakened himself greatly in the Court fight, and conservative Southern Democrats, many of whom were alarmed by his popularity among blacks, now joined with Republicans to oppose his measures. Many anti-Roosevelt Southerners held positions of power in Congress, such as committee chairmanships won through seniority of congressional service. They could hurt the Administration badly. This conservative coalition, formed to frustrate Roosevelt, would continue to dominate Congress for years after his departure.

Roosevelt, after a fight lasting more than a year, did manage to get one more reform bill out of Congress. The Fair Labor Standards Act, although seriously weakened by congressional conservatives, established a national minimum wage of twenty-five cents an hour (to rise over eight years to forty cents) and a work week of forty-four hours (to drop to forty). It also prohibited child labor, something Wilson had tried to do twenty years earlier. Southerners, whose region paid the lowest wages in the country, fought hard against the bill. "Cotton Ed" Smith maintained that a man could live in his state of South Carolina for fifty cents a day and called the bill a measure to destroy the South. The opposition succeeded in attaching many exemptions to the bill. Still, it was a beginning.

Roosevelt's other innovation required no congressional endorsement. In previous years he had winked at evidence of business collusion and combination, feeling that such activities stabilized the economy. Now, half-convinced that business had conspired to prevent recovery in order to destroy him, he appointed a vigorous new assistant attorney general in charge of "trust busting," Thurman Arnold. Arnold more than quadrupled the size of the antitrust division of the Justice Department, raising its staff to 190 lawyers, and filed suits against such giant corporations as General Electric and Aluminum Company of America. Within five years, Arnold had filed almost half of the antitrust suits brought by the government since passage of the Sherman Act in 1890.

THE END OF THE NEW DEAL

In November 1938, Roosevelt reaped the fruits of middle-class alarm over sit-down strikes, court-packing bills, and the Roosevelt recession. The Republicans gained eighty-one seats in the House of Representatives, nearly doubling their numbers there. Although Democrats still had a large majority in both Houses, the Republican-Southern Democratic alliance now virtually controlled Congress.

Roosevelt probably had little new legislation to suggest anyway, having gone about as far as he wanted to go. He seems to have entertained no further plans to strengthen government control over business or to deal with the problems of poverty and chronic high-level unemployment.

Moreover, foreign affairs were claiming an increasing part of his time. Roosevelt early saw the threat to the United States posed by European fascist dictators, and he wanted to strengthen the country and take a more active role in foreign policy. Southern congressional leaders were willing to support him on this—if he would soft-pedal domestic reform plans.

From 1933 to 1939, Roosevelt tried to find cures for the Depression within the capitalist system. He never found a complete answer, and in the Roosevelt recession it became clear that he neither understood nor controlled the economy as much as he himself had thought. Certainly, little change in the functioning or power distribution of the economy occurred. The New Deal had not been a coherent body of reform thinking that the nation could adopt; it was mostly a strong belief in Roosevelt. People continued to cherish their old ideas about initiative and free enterprise.

But while Roosevelt may not have wrought deep changes in the American system, he had brought important changes to the American people. Workers saw their position in life anchored by strong unions. The elderly and the unemployed gained some hope. Blacks received some recognition from the national government. Farmers saw their position greatly strengthened. Moreover, if Roosevelt's achievements sometimes appear small next to the magnitude of the crisis, they clearly loom large next to the efforts of previous administrations.

Finally, Roosevelt could at least claim that through his efforts the country had survived a difficult and dangerous period. Millions of Americans had been saved from starvation, and American institutions had come through largely intact. His greatest achievement may have been the appearance of stability and peacefulness in American government and society in 1939, when contrasted with the deprivations and uncertainties so painfully evident in the winter of 1932–1933.

SUGGESTED READINGS— CHAPTERS 41-42

Eleanor Roosevelt

Tamara K. Hareven, *Eleanor Roosevelt: An American Conscience* (1968); James R. Kearney, *Anna Eleanor Roosevelt: The Evolution of a Reformer* (1968); Joseph P. Lash, *Eleanor and Franklin: The Story of Their Relationship Based on Eleanor Roosevelt's Private Papers* (1971) and *Eleanor: The Years Alone* (1972).

Franklin Delano Roosevelt

James M. Burns, *Roosevelt* (2 vols. 1956 and 1970); Frank Freidel, *Franklin D. Roosevelt* (4 vols. to date, 1952–1975); Alfred B. Rollins, *Roosevelt and Howe* (1962); Rexford G. Tugwell, *In Search of Roosevelt* (1972).

The New Deal

William E. Luchtenberg, *Franklin D. Roosevelt and the New Deal* (1963); Arthur M. Schlesinger, Jr., *The Age of Roosevelt* (3 vols. to date, 1957–1960); Daniel Fusfeld, *The Economic Thought of Franklin D. Roosevelt* (1955); Paul K. Conkin, *The New Deal* (rev. ed. 1975); Bernard Sternsher, *Rexford Tugwell and the New Deal* (1964); Sidney Fine, *Automobile Under the Blue Eagle: Labor Management, and the Automobile Manufacturing Code* (1963); Michael E. Parrish, *Securities Regulation and the New Deal* (1970); Charles F. Searle, *Minister of Relief: Harry Hopkins* (1963); Thomas K. McCraw, *TVA and the Power Fight* (1971); Roy Lubove, *The Struggle for Social Security* (1968); J. Joseph Huthmacher, *Senator Robert F. Wagner and the Rise of Urban Liberalism* (1968); Otis L. Graham, Jr., *Encore for Reform: The Old Progressives and the New Deal* (1967); Leonard Baker, *Back to Back: The Duel Between FDR and the Supreme Court* (1967); C. Herman Pritchett, *The Roosevelt Court* (1948); Ellis Hawley, *The New Deal and the Problem of Monopoly* (1966); James T. Patterson, *Congressional Conservatism and the New Deal: The Growth of the Conservative Coalition in Congress, 1933–1939* (1967); and *New Deal and the States: Federalism in Transition* (1969); Mario Eunaudi, *The Roosevelt Revolution* (1959); Jane D. Matthews, *The Federal Theater* (1967); Paul A. Kurzman, *Harry Hopkins* (1974); Bruce M. Stave, *The New Deal and the Last Hurrah: Pittsburgh Machine Politics* (1970); David E. Conrad, *Forgotten Farmers: Sharecroppers in the New Deal* (1965); Barry D. Karl, *Executive Reorganization and Reform in the New Deal* (1963); Richard Polenberg, *Reorganizing Roosevelt's Government: The Controversy Over Executive Reorganization, 1936–1939* (1966); Richard S. Kirkendall, *Social Scientists and Farm Policies in the Age of Roosevelt* (1966); John Braeman, *et al, The New Deal, I: The National Level* (1975) and *The New Deal, II: The State and Local Levels* (1975).

America In the Great Depression

Broadus Mitchell, *Depression Decade* (1947); Studs Terkel, *Hard Times: An Oral History of the Great Depression* (1970); Van L. Perkins, *Crisis In Agriculture* (1969); Charles Trout, *Boston, the Great Depression, and the New Deal* (1977); T. Harry Williams, *Huey Long* (1969); Charles J. Tull, *Father Coughlin and the New Deal* (1965); Abraham Holtzman, *The Townsend Movement* (1963); George Wolfskill, *The Revolt of the Conservatives* (1974); Irving Bernstein, *Turbulent Years: A History of the American Worker, 1933–1941* (1970); Walter Galenson, *The CIO Challenge to the AFL* (1960); Sidney Fine, *Sit-down: The General Motors Strike of 1936–1937* (1969); Lyle W. Dorsett, *The Pendergast Machine* (1968); David H. Bennett, *Demagogues in the Depression* (1969); Arthur Mann, *LaGuardia Comes to Power: 1933* (1965); Richard H. Pells, *Radical Visions and American Dreams: Culture and Social Thought in the Depression Years* (1973); William Stott, *Documentary Expression and Thirties America* (1973).

43
"REMEMBER PEARL HARBOR"

A.W.

On December 7, 1941, while negotiations to avoid war between the United States and Japan were proceeding in Washington, 353 Japanese planes attacked Pearl Harbor. This massive, audacious, and extremely successful attack on the Americans' principal—and supposedly impregnable—naval base in Hawaii came before Japan had even declared war. Grim-faced and resolved, President Roosevelt went before Congress to call it "unprovoked and dastardly" and "a day which will live in infamy."

Until this assault, Congress, like the country as a whole, had been sharply split between interventionists and isolationists. Now Congress and most Americans were furious at this shrewdly planned, superbly executed, and deadly raid. It dealt a staggering blow to American power in the Pacific. Congress swiftly and overwhelmingly voted to enter World War II. During the rest of the long, terrible conflict the single slogan that most readily aroused Americans to action was: "Remember Pearl Harbor!"

The attack on Pearl, referred to as Operation Z by the Japanese, had a history. A key figure in planning the attack was Admiral Isoruko Yamamoto, head of the Japanese Imperial Navy. If Japan's national interest called for war with the United States, the admiral reasoned, why not strike directly at the enemy fleet's Pacific home base? No mere "battleship admiral," the air-minded Yamamoto knew the possibilities of carrier-based warfare.

Yamamoto was neither a visionary nor overly optimistic. He was quite dubious about defeating the United States in war. He knew the country, having studied at Harvard and worked at the Japanese embassy in Washington during the 1920s. He had returned to Japan sobered by

Battleship Row, Pearl Harbor, is seen here from a Japanese bomber during the surprise attack. The Japanese commander of the air strike said of the sight: "Below me lay the U.S. Pacific Fleet in a formation which I would never have dared to imagine. A fleet should always be on alert since surprise attacks can never be discounted."

American industrial might. He harbored no illusions about *conquering* the United States. An invasion of the continental United States never figured seriously in Japanese war plans; Japan clearly lacked the resources for such a long-range, massive effort. "If I am told to fight regardless of the consequences," Yamamoto told the Japanese premier in 1940, "I shall run wild for the first six months, but I have utterly no confidence for the second or third years."

Others in the Japanese military shared Yamamoto's fears over the probable consequences of war with the United States. Then why venture such a dangerous policy, such a desperate gamble? By 1940 Japan was an authoritarian society ruled by a civilian-military government. Its leaders agreed on the country's basic needs. Most important was access to the raw materials vital for a modern industrial nation. Without them, heavily populated Japan would become a third- or fourth-rate power. Without expansion the Japanese would be forced to tighten their belts even to stay alive.

So Japan decided to expand. In 1931 it took Manchuria from a helpless China. American and Western Europe objected strongly but ineffectively. In 1937 Japan launched a full-scale invasion of the rest of China. Despite Western protests the Japanese captured the coastal portions and overran much of the Chinese interior. By mid-1940 Japan's ally, Hitler, had conquered France, the Netherlands, and much of the rest of Europe, isolating Great Britain. Therefore, Tokyo reasoned that it could now expand Japanese control into Southeast Asia. It planned to establish a massive sphere of influence, "the Greater East Asia Co-Prosperity Sphere."

Isoroku Yamamoto, commander in chief of the Japanese Imperial Fleet, was a strong advocate of the navy's use of air power. Responsible for planning naval operations, he was the mastermind of the audacious attack on Pearl Harbor.

Thus, by early 1941, Admiral Yamamoto was contemplating his strategy. Success hinged on two factors: the attackers must achieve total surprise; and the bulk of the American fleet, especially the capital ships (battleships and carriers), would have to be at their moorings the day of attack.

While Japanese and American diplomats in Washington were negotiating, naval aviators began months of intensive practice. When Yamamoto got wind of grumbling and possible footdragging, he threatened to resign if the plan was scrapped. Objections ceased. Yamamoto became for the moment the symbol of the Japanese navy. Under no condition would his fellow officers accept his resignation. Operation Z (named for the signal flag that Admiral Togo hoisted before trouncing the Russians) became a reality. If diplomacy failed, only the date of the attack on America remained to be fixed.

Meanwhile, political developments ominously paralleled the course of these military preparations. After France had fallen to Germany, Japan grabbed the northern half of French Indochina. It held back from the southern half—as well as from British Malaya and the Dutch East Indies (present-day Indonesia)—after the United States warned that action in these areas would have grave consequences. Roosevelt banned shipments of aviation gasoline and scrap metal to Japan, and increased American support to China. The American ambassador to Japan, Joseph C. Grew, noted: "We are getting ready, steadily, for the ultimate showdown."

By summer 1941 matters were even more tense. Hitler had invaded Russia; Japan could now pursue its Asian policy without fear of Stalin. Japan advanced, occupying southern Indochina in late July. The Americans, British, and Dutch responded by seizing all Japanese financial assets in their areas of jurisdiction. They also ended Japan's access to their raw materials. The United States gave an official warning that, if Japan took any further steps "by force or threat of force," the Americans would defend their "legitimate rights and interests."

In diplomacy's stilted language, these were strong words. The Japanese premier suggested that he and President Roosevelt hold a summit meeting, possibly in Hawaii. This could not be arranged. On October 16 a new premier, General Hideki Tojo, came to power. He was an all-out militarist.

Yet the national interests of both countries favored more negotiations. Further talks would hide Japanese war preparations—especially Operation Z, now in high gear. Washington would also benefit. It could use the extra time to reinforce its Pacific bases, particularly in the Philippines. In November 1941 Japan sent a veteran diplomat, Saburo Kurusu, to Washington to head a negotiating team. Diplomatic exchanges would obviously continue for at least a few more weeks.

At the same time, table-top maneuvers at the Japanese Naval War College demonstrated the most effective route for the Pearl Harbor attack force. The fleet would sail in a wide arc across the nearly deserted waters of the North Central Pacific. Then it would turn sharply south on reaching a point 500 miles north of Hawaii. Yamamoto thought that this route would give the best chance for surprise.

On November 5, while the Japanese and Americans negotiated in Washington, Yamamoto issued a secret order outlining the first phase of the Japanese offensive against Hawaii. The twenty-three attack ships included six carriers and two battleships under Admiral Chuichi Nagumo. He disliked the plan and still hoped the madcap attack would somehow be canceled.

The Japanese strike force sailed on November 26. The attack date had been set for December 7 (Sunday morning) in Hawaii. The American navy—even though on military alert because of the dangerous diplomatic situation—had weekends off. So its ships usually anchored in the harbor on Friday and stayed there until Monday. Nagumo's orders did contain one escape clause. If the Washington negotiations succeeded, the attack was off. The fleet would then wait in the North Pacific for new orders.

Yet, any chance that diplomacy could ease the crisis was now vanishing. On November 20 the negotiator Kurusu made Tokyo's final offer: Japan would leave southern Indochina but remain in the northern part, as well as in China. The United States must not only lift its ban on oil to Japan but also cut off aid to China. Secretary of State Cordell Hull immediately rejected these terms. Fearful of being called appeasers, Roosevelt and Hull would make no concessions. The American note of November 26—the very day the strike force set sail—stated that America's embargo would continue until Japan withdrew from both Indochina and China.

Roosevelt and Hull, along with their top civilian and military colleagues, had good reason to distrust the sincerity of Japanese negotiations. Operation Magic of American naval intelligence had cracked Japan's diplomatic codes. On November 22—two days after Kurusu's final offer and four days before the formal American reply to it—a cable intercepted from Tokyo read: "THIS TIME WE MEAN IT, THAT THE DEADLINE [November 29] CANNOT BE CHANGED! AFTER THAT THINGS ARE AUTOMATICALLY GOING TO HAPPEN."

What things? Most likely, reasoned the leaders in Washington, the Japanese planned to attack the Philippines and British and Dutch holdings in Asia. Hawaii seemed beyond the range of effective Japanese assault. So American short-sightedness was beginning to aid the future success of Operation Z. Knowledge of Magic was restricted to Washington's inner circle, to keep Tokyo from realizing its code had been broken. Thus American brass in Hawaii had no notion of Magic.

All the Pacific military commanders received some warning on November 27 to expect a hostile move by Japan. But Washington took no action during the next ten days. Only four Magic decoding machines existed then: two in Washington, one in the Philippines, and another in London. There were none in Hawaii. The commanders there, Admiral Husband E. Kimmel and General Walter C. Short, were not even told about Magic.

Admiral Kimmel had seriously considered, but then rejected, the idea of taking his fleet out of Pearl Harbor. In open water, he felt, the ships would be too vulnerable. His four carriers were not then available to provide air cover. (Three were bringing warplanes to American-held Pacific islands; the fourth was in San Diego for repairs.) Besides, moored safely in Pearl, his ships could be protected by the several hundred army planes stationed at Hawaiian bases. Still, Kimmel might well have sent most of the battleships out with the carriers to the other Pacific islands.

General Short reacted to the war warning by increasing the army's antisabotage defenses. Sabotage, he apparently thought, might come from Hawaii's large Japanese-American community. Instead of widely spacing his aircraft or protecting them in concrete shelters already constructed on the major fields, Short ordered the planes bunched together, wing tip to wing tip, so that fewer soldiers could then protect them against saboteurs. But Japanese Americans in Hawaii never aided Japan, although some Japanese diplomats were spies.

In short, Magic had been botched. Hawaiian commanders never received copies of important decoded messages. These messages piled up at the few overworked decoding centers. As far back as September, and with increasing frequency thereafter, Tokyo asked the Japanese consulate in Honolulu for details on the location of American warships in the harbor. By November such naval maps were being transmitted to Tokyo twice a week. Some of these Magic intercepts were not deciphered and translated for many days after reception. Especially revealing Japanese messages of November 29, for example, waited until December 5 to be deciphered. Even then, they received little attention.

Even key Washington officials, including Roosevelt and Hull, apparently did not take the Magic decodings very seriously.[1] But in Tokyo the die had been cast. Hull's note of November 26 refusing to lift the American embargo infuriated Premier Tojo. He thought it proved beyond all doubt American insincerity in the negotiations. Tojo persuaded Emperor Hirohito to let Operation Z proceed. A palace meeting ratified the decision for war. Hirohito did not attempt to intervene. He believed, as he later told an aide, that the United States was looking for nothing less than Japan's humiliation.

Should Kurusu continue negotiating or at least pretend to? Of course he should, Tojo decided; it would facilitate operations. In Wash-

If Admiral Kimmel had initiated adequate air reconnaissance of the seas around Pearl Harbor, Operation Z might have been discovered and foiled. But neither he nor anyone else in authority expected Japanese hostilities to begin there.

---

[1]There were, however, several notable exceptions. On November 25 Roosevelt told Secretary of War Henry L. Stimson of his fears that Japan would strike on December 1 without declaring war, "for the Japanese are notorious for making an attack without warning." Stimson wanted to bomb Japanese convoys if they moved farther south. Roosevelt rejected the notion because "we are a democracy."

Premier Tojo is shown in a respectful posture before Emperor Hirohito at a ceremony celebrating the Japanese Empire's 2,600th anniversary. Tojo's rise to power helped determine Japan's course toward war. Hirohito's role was largely symbolic, but he supported Tojo's militarism and anti-Americanism.

ington Kurusu asked a Japanese newspaperman rhetorically, "Am I being used as a smoke screen?" Indeed he was.

Kurusu had to help screen the task force then steaming across the North Pacific. After leaving port on November 26, the fleet enjoyed seven days of uneventful sailing. The weather cooperated. Light winds made refueling at sea relatively easy. Overcast conditions and generally poor visibility decreased chances of detection. Security precautions were rigidly enforced. No radio contact was made except within the fleet. At night a blackout was enforced. Most ships communicated by signal flags and blinkers. They did not even discard garbage, to avoid leaving a trail.

The fleet's passage north of the American base at Midway provided cause for some real concern. No American planes or ships spotted them, however. On December 6 there was the final fueling. Japanese intelligence from Hawaii reported the presence of many American warships there but no carriers or heavy cruisers. It was decided that the force would strike and destroy whatever was at hand.

A little past noon on December 6 all hands were summoned on deck. Their officers read them the emperor's war message. Yamamoto had also sent a statement: "The moment has arrived. The rise or fall of our empire is at stake." Then Admiral Togo's flag, the signal flag that gave its name to Operation Z, went up above the attack fleet's flagship. The crews shouted *"Banzai!"*—their battle cry—and turned the ships south toward Hawaii. All was ready for the great moment.

The launch itself was almost perfect. Pilots and flight crewmen were aroused at 3:30 A.M. The news that the Americans apparently had not adequately protected their ships encouraged the Japanese airmen. At zero hour (6 A.M.) the carriers were 200 miles from Oahu. As the ships rolled and pitched, the lead pilots waited eagerly for the order to take off. When it came, the first wave of 183 planes left the 6 carriers in 15 minutes, bettering their fastest practice runs. With Commander Mitsuo Fuchida in command, flying one of the high-level bombers, the air fleet headed for its target.

Overconfidence and negligence had made Americans complacent. Many viewed the Japanese as a society adept in imitating Western ways but with little creativity. Informed Americans knew that the Japanese had a history of attacking first and declaring war later. But most thought they would not dare attack the United States. In 1932 the American navy itself had successfully "attacked" the harbor during a mock raid. The event was quickly forgotten. The Navy Department filed the report in its archives as just another war-games exploit.

There were certainly some warnings during 1941. In January a Peruvian diplomat in Tokyo reported that a drunken Japanese official had boasted about Japan's plan to sink the American fleet and knock out Pearl Harbor. Ambassador Grew passed the "fantastic" rumor along to Washington. A few months later Grew noted that Japan was "capable of sudden and surprise action" with "a determination to risk all." In August, the chiefs of American naval and army aviation in Hawaii sent a gloomy memo noting Hawaii's vulnerability to air attack. They correctly predicted the use of six carriers in a dawn assault from the north.

The shortcomings of American defensive reactions were considerable, in view of what was known about Japanese intentions and how much could have been learned if the data from Magic had been properly exploited. One man who worried a great deal was Admiral Kimmel. After November 27 — the day Kimmel received the war warning from Washington — naval intelligence lost track of the Japanese fleet. Kimmel asked the head of his intelligence section at Pearl where the fleet was. The officer admitted he did not know. Not entirely in jest, Kimmel asked: "You mean to say that it could appear rounding Diamond Head [a famous high point close to Pearl Harbor] without our knowing it?" The intelligence officer answered: "I hope that it would be spotted before that."

Yamamoto had no intention of parading his ships past Diamond Head, impressive though the sight would have been. Instead, his planes crossed over Oahu's northern coast. At 7:49 A.M. Fuchida broke radio silence to signal Nagumo (and Yamamoto also, since Tokyo picked up the message). Attack by the first wave had begun, blessed with the key element of surprise. Fuchida's first signal was *"To-To-To,"* repeating the opening syllable of the Japanese word for "charge." Soon he sent an even more welcome message: *"Tora* [Tiger], *Tora, Tora,"* which meant that the Americans were almost completely unprepared.

They were unprepared. Yet that same morning warnings had come. Five full hours before the attack began, Magic in Washington had decoded the final Japanese message breaking off negotiations. The officer in charge took the intercept straight to Admiral Harold R. Stark, chief of naval operations. Though impressed, Stark did not phone Admiral Kimmel.

Yet another chance to prepare for the attack was missed. This occurred on Oahu's north coast, precisely where Fuchida's squadrons would penetrate American air space. The Army Signal Corps had installed a movable radar station there. At 6:45 Private George Elliott, the enlisted man on duty at the station, noted the presence of a single plane on the radar screen.

But at 7:06 Elliott noted much larger blips on the screen, again moving toward Oahu from the north, and rapidly growing larger. He asked the advice of another soldier. They decided to call signal headquarters at Fort Shafter. But the only officer on duty there, a pilot, told

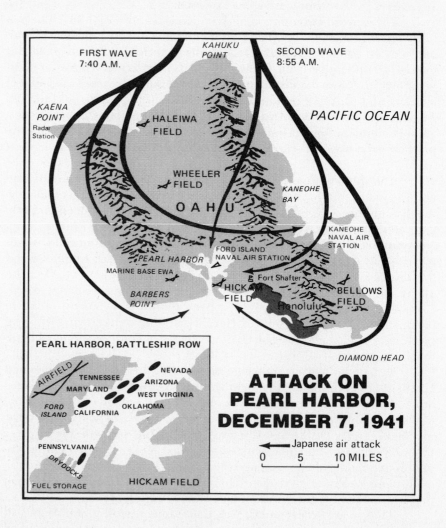

FIRST WAVE
7:40 A.M.

KAHUKU POINT

SECOND WAVE
8:55 A.M.

KAENA POINT
Radar Station

HALEIWA FIELD

PACIFIC OCEAN

WHEELER FIELD

KANEOHE BAY

O A H U

KANEOHE NAVAL AIR STATION

FORD ISLAND NAVAL AIR STATION

PEARL HARBOR

MARINE BASE EWA

Fort Shafter

BARBERS POINT

HICKAM FIELD

Honolulu

BELLOWS FIELD

DIAMOND HEAD

PEARL HARBOR, BATTLESHIP ROW

AIRFIELD

TENNESSEE
MARYLAND

NEVADA
ARIZONA
WEST VIRGINIA

FORD ISLAND
CALIFORNIA

OKLAHOMA

PENNSYLVANIA

DRYDOCKS

FUEL STORAGE

HICKAM FIELD

ATTACK ON PEARL HARBOR, DECEMBER 7, 1941

Japanese air attack

0   5   10 MILES

them to forget about it. He knew that a dozen American planes were scheduled to arrive from California that morning. Again the Japanese had benefited from a stroke of luck. Fuchida's first wave was confused with reinforcements from the States.

After sending the signal *"Tora, Tora, Tora,"* Fuchida fired a blue flare from his bomber. It informed pilots in planes without radios that surprise had been achieved. It would produce a prearranged pattern of attack, with the slow-flying but deadly torpedo bombers going in first. But apparently one group of pilots, their vision obscured by the cloud cover, had not seen the luminous signal. At least they did not wiggle their planes' wings in response. Fuchida then committed one of the few Japanese mistakes of the day. He fired a second flare.

This changed the flight plan. Two flares meant that dive bombers would attack first. Fighters and some dive bombers were to concentrate on American airfields and antiaircraft installations, rather than on the fleet. Happily for the Japanese, the commander of the torpedo bomber wing ignored the second flare. His forty heavy but superbly piloted aircraft peeled off and glided down to the prescribed low altitudes, heading straight for their principal targets, the battleships.

Meanwhile, in answer to the second signal, the faster planes went hunting for American aircraft at Wheeler, Hickam, Haleiwa, Bellows, and other fields. Wheeler housed most of the American fighter planes. These planes, already tested in combat, could hold their own against the more maneuverable Japanese fighters. But, owing to General Short's fear of ground sabotage, Wheeler's planes had been crowded together like sheep in a pen. The attackers quickly destroyed a third of the planes and damaged many more. Fires broke out in the hangars and storage buildings. One of them contained ammunition, which exploded, causing additional losses.

American military aviation tried to respond but it was useless. At Wheeler, for instance, most of the pilots were still sleeping. But Lieuten-

A special Japanese invention, the midget submarine operated by a crew of two, was used in the advance attack upon American battleships. The submarines failed in their mission that day and were not widely used in the war.

The devastation on the ground after the attack was extensive. By 10 A.M. Hickam Naval Air Station was in chaos and a smoking ruin.

ants George Welch and Ken Taylor, who were breakfasting at the officers' club, saw the dive bombers swoop. They rushed for a car and sped at a hundred miles an hour to an auxiliary airstrip unknown to the Japanese. There they took off, headed for a Japanese squadron, and shot down three planes before landing to refuel. During the dogfight one of the three machine guns in Welch's plane jammed. Taylor was wounded twice.

At Kaneohe Naval Air Station the commanding officer was drinking his morning coffee. When he heard planes, he glanced up. To his anger several V-formations of planes—all flying lower than regulations allowed—were turning toward the right into the bay where most of his thirty-three new flying boats were at anchor. He leaped to his feet shouting, "Those fools know there is a strict rule against making a right turn!" His young son, who was with him, exclaimed, "Look, red circles on the wings!" Realizing it was the Japanese rising-sun symbol, the commander rushed to his headquarters and set up a fierce antiaircraft fire against the invaders.

At the moment of attack only a fourth of the antiaircraft guns on the ships moored in the harbor were manned. Land-based antiaircraft guns could not respond immediately because ammunition had been stored to prevent deterioration. Their effectiveness increased as the morning wore on, however. Unluckily, the B-17s arrived from California about then. Weary after fourteen hours in the air, the American bomber pilots and crews thought they had flown into a nightmare. Columns of smoke rose from the ground. Airfields were ablaze, including the one the B-17s were supposed to use on Ford Island. Incredibly, not one Flying Fortress was shot out of the air. All landed at various fields, though some were shot at and destroyed after landing.

Ironically, Admiral Kimmel and General Short had arranged to play golf together that morning. Kimmel rose early. At about 7:30 he received a phone call from a staff officer. The destroyer *Ward* had sighted a submerged submarine and dropped depth charges. Kimmel headed for his office. Just as he was leaving, he received a second call adding some details about the *Ward* incident. Suddenly, the officer at the other end shouted that Japanese planes were attacking. Kimmel ran out to his garden, which overlooked the harbor. What he saw froze him. The carnage was under way. The sky over the bay seemed alive with attack planes. Kimmel knew his ships were doomed.

Kimmel got to his headquarters at 8:10, during the height of the first-wave attack. There was nothing he could do but stand at the window and watch his fleet and men under attack. A spent Japanese bullet crashed through the window and bounced off Kimmel's chest. He felt that "it would have been merciful had it killed me."

Fuchida's pilots wanted to destroy the American fleet. Disappointed over not finding carriers in port, they concentrated on the battleships. Seven of the eight were lined up on Battleship Row in the harbor. Five were moored to the docks, and two were on an "outside" parallel column. Thus the two inside battleships could not be attacked by torpedoes. The dive bombers went after them. Soon every battleship had been hit.

On the *Nevada*, at one end of the row, Bandmaster Oden McMillan stood with his musicians, ready to play morning colors at 8 A.M. As they began "The Star-Spangled Banner," a Japanese plane dropped its deadly burden on the nearby *Arizona*, then peeled off just feet above the band. The *Nevada's* deck officer, Ensign Joe Taussig, shouted over the public-address system: "All hands, general quarters. Air raid!" The *Nevada*, though damaged, tried to steam out to sea. The Japanese bore in, hoping to sink her at Pearl Harbor's mouth and thus close the port indefinitely. The *Nevada* took six bomb hits but made it to the other side of the bay, keeping the channel clear.

The *Oklahoma* took four torpedoes within one minute and began to capsize. The *California* sustained hits that caused her to settle slowly and finally sink. And so on down the row: *Tennessee, West Virginia, Maryland, Pennsylvania.* Fuchida, who was supervising the attack in his bomber overhead, frowned in disapproval as his pilots raced in. They were bunched up in their assault, instead of diving in stages as prearranged. But their formation no longer really mattered—every enemy ship was a sitting duck.

The worst blow for the Americans came when the *Arizona* blew apart and sank, trapping more than a thousand men inside. Later, it was claimed that a bomb had gone straight down her stack. But the probable cause of the disaster was the detonation of the ship's ammunition store. Whatever the cause, a gigantic pillar of fire and smoke rose 500 feet. The shock was so tremendous that, far above, Fuchida could feel his bomber tremble. Miraculously, many American seamen survived this searing blast. Some of these survivors tried to swim to shore and safety, but burning oil engulfed most of them.

The second wave, 170 additional planes, came in at 8:55. Fuchida and his pilots had taken more time than planned because of additional bomb runs. The fresh attackers went to work shortly after the first wave pulled out. They encountered considerably more opposition from heavy antiaircraft fire, and lost twenty-one planes. Towering columns of smoke cut visibility. Still, the second wave of bombers did considerable damage in its one-hour attack, knocking out some ships not previously hit. They withdrew at 9:45 to return to their carriers.

On Battleship Row the rescue effort began at once. Most of the giant ships were ablaze. One had overturned, while another had settled straight down into the mud. In the plotting room of the heavily damaged *West Virginia* Ensign Victor Delano watched smoke and oily water seep in. He and several others headed forward to another compartment. Just before closing a watertight door, they heard frantic calls from seamen, blown from the deck above them by the explosions, but had to go on. Delano then returned to the plotting room, risking his life to help a wounded sailor. Neither he nor his companion could get his footing on the oil-slick deck. The ship's angle compounded the problem.

The Japanese victory would have been more complete and would have had more serious consequences for the United States if American aircraft carriers had been in port. As it was, the Japanese had to be satisfied with destroying American battleships.

Luckily, one compartment wall was a switchboard. By grabbing its knobs, they were at last able to reach the door. As the men moved forward, they could hear the shouts and pleas of others, sealed off by the watertight doors in compartments that were rapidly filling with water. The damage-control officer had ordered the doors closed. He knew that this order condemned many men to death. But opening the doors would merely cause the ship to sink quickly and doubtless drown even more men. Many of the men did manage to make their way to the upper decks; others were able to swim to the surface by escaping through portholes. The harbor was filled with boats and launches rescuing the survivors.

The overturned *Oklahoma* posed special problems. Dozens of men, perhaps hundreds, were still alive in a crazy house where floors had become ceilings. Partial flooding meant that air pockets existed in most compartments. There, survivors could exist for awhile, if they treaded water or grasped whatever protruded from walls. About thirty men trapped in the dispensary waited an hour. Noting with alarm the decreasing amount of oxygen in the air, they decided to move. But where?

Diving into the water that covered most of the dispensary, they found a porthole. Though no one knew where it led, staying in the dispensary meant sure death. Those who were thin enough to squeeze through the porthole swam clear of the ship and were rescued. Others tried but could not squeeze through the porthole. They died in the dispensary.

Another group of sailors trapped near the *Oklahoma's* center seemed doomed beyond any hope. Amazingly, one of them dived downward through a funnel. He emerged directly under the capsized ship, reached topside, then swam clear of the wreckage and reached the surface. He led rescuers to his mates.

The rescue crews relied on this kind of information. Without it, they had no way of locating the living. Rescuers banged on ship hulls, and survivors lost no time in signaling back. Yet the sounds seemed to come from everywhere and nowhere. Several times crews laboriously cut holes in a hull, then found nobody.

Sometimes they unwittingly added to the tragedy. Acetylene torches consumed the oxygen in the air pockets once the hull had been punctured. Slower working pneumatic drills allowed precious air to escape as the water continued to rise in the compartments. Despite these dangers, inaction spelled sure doom for the trapped. So people worked through the night. They had surprisingly good results in the number of men saved.

The Japanese had fashioned a striking yet limited victory at Pearl Harbor. The casualty figures were all in their favor.[2] But, in the long run, Operation Z failed to cripple American power. First, no American carrier was in port; the war that followed showed conclusively that carriers were more vital than battleships. Second, American plane losses would soon be dwarfed by the huge air armadas that were already beginning to roll out of American factories. Third, the naval base itself had not suffered severe damage. Fouth, and possibly most significant, the Japanese—concentrating on ships and planes—had ignored the oil storage tanks. If Hawaii's fuel supply had been destroyed (as it easily could have been), Japan might have: (1) forced the carriers and other ships still functioning back to California for oil; (2) made Pearl useless as a base for several months and perhaps a year; and (3) thus given Japan freedom to expand in the Pacific without worrying about counterattacks. Instead, Pearl began to function right after December 7 as the staging area for a massive American build-up of military power.

By bombing the harbor, Japan gained some time—but little more. Even some of the sunken battleships came back to haunt their attackers. All but two were put back in service. But these consequences lay in the

---

[2]All 8 battleships in Pearl on December 7 were either sunk, capsized, or badly damaged. Ten other ships, including 3 cruisers and 3 destroyers, were also casualties. In military aviation 188 American planes were destroyed, and nearly all the others were damaged. About 100 civilians and 2,403 men in uniform died. Japan lost only 29 planes, 5 two-man submarines, and a total of 54 lives.

Secretary of State Cordell Hull and Japanese negotiators met several times to prevent a direct confrontation. But both sides took hard-line stands, so that the course of events was determined weeks before the final meeting at 2:00 P.M. on December 7.

future. December 7 was Japan's day. The assault on Hawaii was only part of a mighty Japanese drive. Simultaneous attacks took place on the Philippines and on British and Dutch colonies.

Some diplomatic strings remained to be tied. The final Japanese note to Secretary Hull was supposed to be delivered at 1 P.M.. But delay in decoding and typing the long document kept the Japanese diplomats from arriving at Hull's office until 2 P.M. In the meantime, Hull had read the Magic intercept of the note. Roosevelt got the news of the attack at 1:47 from Secretary of the Navy Knox.

Roosevelt called Hull at 2:05. The Japanese diplomats had just arrived and were in the waiting room. Roosevelt instructed Hull to receive them but say nothing about the attack. The Japanese ambassador, by way of apology, said he had been told by his government to hand over the note at 1 P.M. Hull pretended to read it (he knew its contents already) and handed it back saying it was "crowded with infamous falsehoods and distortions." With a disgusted shrug Hull dismissed the envoys.

In Tokyo, Ambassador Grew still hoped to achieve something positive. The day before the attack, Roosevelt had sent a personal appeal for peace to Emperor Hirohito. Grew asked for an audience with the emperor. At 7 A.M. Grew was awakened and told that the foreign minister wished to see him. Hoping to see Hirohito, Grew rushed to the ministry, only to be handed the note breaking off negotiations. Two hours later he heard that Japan had declared war on the United States and its European allies.

Japan greeted the news of war and victory at Pearl Harbor jubilantly. Newspaper extras appeared on the streets, and the radio alternated between martial music and patriotic slogans. At the end of December the fleet returned to Japan, and the government and people welcomed the heroes of Operation Z with celebrations and medals. Hirohito granted an audience to Nagumo and to Fuchida and several other task force leaders. The rising sun reached its zenith. But Yamamoto, clearheaded as usual, warned that "this war will give us many headaches in the future."

Roosevelt and most Americans never doubted this. On December 8, when the President asked Congress to declare war on Japan, he assured his listeners that, whatever the cost, Japan would be vanquished.

44
THE UNITED STATES AS A SUPERPOWER

A. W.

After Pearl Harbor anything seemed possible for the Japanese. Their plan for domination of Asia (the Greater East Asia Co-Prosperity Sphere) became a reality, at least temporarily. Japan had signed a mutual security treaty with Nazi Germany, and Hitler hastily declared war on the United States just after Pearl Harbor.

Only twenty-three years had elapsed since the end of World War I. Now another generation of American youth would have to fight overseas. Ironically, America's entry into the war came after a decade of intense isolationist feeling.

A profound disillusionment with World War I had spread throughout the United States. It no longer seemed a clean-cut crusade to "make the world safe for democracy." Instead, some regarded it as a capitalist war that the United States had fought to protect loans made to European Allies by American bankers. This in turn had benefited the arms manufacturers, the "merchants of death." Republican Senator Gerald P. Nye of North Dakota developed these themes in sensational congressional hearings during the mid-1930s. Nye's claims helped pressure Americans into favoring isolationism as a foreign policy.

THE NEUTRALITY ACTS

The Neutrality Act of 1935 limited Roosevelt's ability to respond effectively to overseas aggression, even if American interests were endangered.

This law attempted to close the gap between a President's control of foreign relations and Congress's right to declare war. Henceforth, if war broke out anywhere, the President had to issue a proclamation of neutrality. More important, the law forbade shipping arms to any nation at war, whether victim or aggressor. Roosevelt sought power to ban or "embargo" shipments to unfriendly or aggressor nations while permitting arms to go to the victims of aggression. Congress refused this request.

Yet isolationist hopes proved no match for events in the later 1930s. Italy invaded Ethiopia in October 1935. Roosevelt invoked the Neutrality Act, this time willingly, since an arms embargo would hinder Italy more than Ethiopia. He also asked American oil producers for a "moral embargo" on shipments to Italy, limiting amounts to prewar levels. Ethiopia fell to the Italian invaders.

Charles A. Lindbergh and Senator Gerald P. Nye stirred popular sentiment for isolationism. Americans had viewed World War I as a noble crusade. But Nye's munitions industry investigations uncovered less noble reasons for this country's entrance into the war, which led Lindbergh to campaign for nonintervention in future world power struggles.

Italy then quit the League of Nations, following the example of Japan and Germany. The foundations for the Axis alliance had been laid.

Further Triumphs for the Dictators The menace to the Western democracies increased in 1936. Hitler armed the Rhineland, which had been demilitarized after World War I. General Francisco Franco, leader of Spain's fascists, led a revolt—which was ultimately successful—against the Spanish government. Congress reacted by passing a second Neutrality Act, tightening the isolationist provisions of the first law.

So the first series of fascist moves, instead of weakening isolationism, strengthened it. Believing the Atlantic and Pacific oceans gave the United States ample security, isolationists argued that America should be a fortress prepared for any outside attack. But the United States should not meddle in foreign politics or wars. Yet isolationists were not pacifists. They favored American rearmament, particularly a larger, two-ocean navy.

Rise of the Interventionists In October 1937 Roosevelt sent up an anti-isolationist trial balloon, only to see it shot down quickly. In his "Quarantine Speech" he noted that an "epidemic of world lawlessness is spreading." Thus it was foolish to assume "that America will escape, that America may expect mercy, that this Western Hemisphere will not be attacked." To counter the threat, Roosevelt called for a quarantine of aggressor nations. Though some Americans agreed, the massive and negative outcry afterward caused Roosevelt to abandon his proposal.

A small but growing number of interventionists insisted, however, that the fascist Axis powers, if left unchecked, would eventually attack America. Like the isolationists, interventionists saw a world moving toward war. But, they also foresaw United States involvement—sooner or later. Better sooner, they thought, while Americans still had some overseas friends.

Events in 1938 and 1939 emphasized the failure of appeasement—the policy of buying off dictators with compromises. Compromises only brought new demands. France and Britain sold out part of Czechoslovakia to Germany at Munich

in September 1938. Not satisfied yet, Hitler merely kept on expanding. Having already absorbed Austria as part of the German Third Reich, in March 1939 he occupied all of Czechoslovakia. Then he threatened Poland.

Hitler took advantage of Russian weakness (and Stalin, in turn, of the apparent German willingness to turn elsewhere for immediate conquest) and the two totalitarian dictatorships negotiated a nonaggression pact in August 1939. The Nazi-Soviet Pact allowed Hitler to turn his undivided attention to the conquest of Poland without fearing Russian retaliation. (As it turned out, Stalin's armies helped Hitler to dismember and then divide Poland the following month.)

Roosevelt had approved of appeasement at Munich, but by 1939 he realized his mistake. He began a long campaign to repeal, or at least soften, the neutrality laws. He spoke of "many methods short of war" that might discourage aggression. But Congress would have to allow some presidential flexibility. Congress did not budge. No one can say to what extent American inertia and isolationism helped Hitler decide on war. Nevertheless, the American attitude surely encouraged him. On September 1, 1939, Germany invaded Poland. Britain and France declared war on Germany two days later, and World War II was under way.

GLOBAL CONFLICT

The start of World War II put American views on neutrality to a real test. Hitler quickly conquered Poland and divided it with Russia. Roosevelt was legally bound to issue a proclamation of neutrality. He was far from neutral, however. Nor did he try to hide his pro-Allied sentiments.

For Roosevelt, defeat of the Axis was basic. If American isolation meant defeat for Britain and France, American security would be disastrously, perhaps fatally, damaged. Thus, Roosevelt would go to war before letting the other Western democracies perish.

Since 1900, American foreign policy had increasingly involved British-American cooperation. Roosevelt developed a close friendship with Winston Churchill, Britain's prime minister.[1] Still, neither sentiment nor deep concern for the fate of democracy elsewhere in the world provided Roosevelt's chief motivation. He saw the savagery of dictators, especially Hitler. He concluded that, once Europe and Asia had been overrun by these "New Barbarians," America's turn would come.

Although Roosevelt accepted the risk of war, Congress would probably never have declared war prior to Pearl Harbor. Thus, Roosevelt's carefully worded pro-Allied efforts had to be made bit by bit. First, he asked Congress to repeal the arms embargo so that the United States might sell war goods to other Western powers. This passed with surprising ease. Now Britain and France might buy American arms but only on a "cash-and-carry" basis. Many Americans still hoped Hitler would be defeated without the necessity of making war loans to the Allies or placing American ships in Atlantic war zones.

These unreal hopes evaporated in the spring of 1940. Hitler launched a series of spectacular and successful campaigns that conquered much of Continental Europe. By May, five countries had been overrun — Denmark, Norway, Luxembourg, the Netherlands, and Belgium. In June the "impossible" happened: France collapsed before the Nazi onslaught and agreed to German occupation of half its territory, including Paris. This left Britain the only effective Axis opponent.

Steps toward Intervention These events profoundly disturbed Americans and shifted the isolationist-interventionist balance. Americans were shocked by the well-publicized picture of Hitler inspecting his new toy — the city of Paris — and dancing a little victory jig. What would come next? Americans might accept Allied defeats in limited wars, but this war seemed to have no limit.

Interventionists, who wanted massive aid for the battered Allies, grew bolder and better organized. Heroic British resistance to a German air assault on their homeland armed these inter-

ventionists with plenty of effective propaganda. The Committee to Defend America First, however, fought against any American involvement in the war. The America Firsters, like Charles Lindbergh, hero of the 1920s, argued that the war was simply none of our business. Many felt that a seemingly invincible Germany should not be stirred up unnecessarily.

Roosevelt moved shrewdly (1) to rearm America and (2) to aid Britain to the extent legally permissible and politically possible. Since 1940 was also a presidential election year, he had to be cautious. Meanwhile, Roosevelt broke the traditional ban on third-term Presidents by running again. Significantly, Republican isolationists could not nominate their man, Senator Robert A. Taft of Ohio. An internationalist named Wendell Willkie, a utilities executive with little political experience, won the nomination.

In the midst of the campaign Roosevelt made a daringly unneutral move. He transferred fifty World War I destroyers to the British navy. In exchange the United States received a dozen British air and naval bases in the Western Hemisphere. Churchill said of this: "It marked the passage of the United States from being neutral to being nonbelligerent [but involved]." Roosevelt won the election by a narrower margin than in 1936. Republican gains meant that Roosevelt had to take the views of the opposition party into greater account in facing the world crisis.

Every President who wins reelection regards it as a mandate for his policies. Now Roosevelt went even further than the destroyers-for-bases swap. He asked Congress for a Lend-Lease program. Under this law, passed in March 1941, the President could "lend" war material to countries whose security was deemed vital to American interests. The United States would become the "arsenal of democracy." By the end of World War II over $50 billion in Lend-Lease equipment and supplies had been distributed to America's allies.

Undeclared Naval Hostilities Further support for Britain soon materialized. The American navy patrolled the western half of the North Atlantic, freeing British ships for duty nearer Europe. American ships and planes fed data on Nazi sub-

---

[1]The Roosevelt-Churchill correspondence consisted chiefly of long, candid cables between the two men. Roosevelt ended one such message: "It is fun to be in the same decade as you."

marines to the Royal Navy. British ships used American ports freely, while this country kept sixty-five Axis ships tied up in its harbors. Some Americans joined the British or Canadian air forces, and British pilots trained at American airfields. The situation, as Germany knew, was not at all neutral. But Hitler was not yet ready to declare war on America; in the summer of 1941 he attacked Russia instead.

But American "nonbelligerence" soon provoked German countermeasures. When American warships began escorting Allied shipping halfway across the Atlantic, German submarines (or U-boats) responded. Several American destroyers were fired on; several merchant ships went down. In October a German submarine sank an American destroyer near Iceland. Congress then removed the last restriction of the neutrality laws: armed American ships could now take war supplies directly to Britain. An undeclared naval war raged in the Atlantic.

Some members of the Roosevelt cabinet wanted an immediate declaration of war against Germany. But Roosevelt preferred to continue active nonbelligerence. He would arm those fighting the Axis (including Soviet Russia). He would cement relations with Britain, as in the meeting with Churchill that produced the Atlantic Charter.[2] And he would let the Axis powers decide when to declare war.

THE UNITED STATES AT WAR

Japan, not Germany, made the decisive move. The assault on Pearl Harbor and other bases in the Pacific on December 7, 1941, ended the isolationist-interventionist debate. It also united the nation. Roosevelt's critics, including Lindbergh of America First, now pledged their hearty support for the war. One major isolationist, Michigan's Republican Senator Arthur H. Vandenberg, conceded that

[2]The Atlantic Charter stated common British and American beliefs: The right of people to choose their own form of government and the need for worldwide economic cooperation and an international security system to prevent future wars.

Pearl Harbor had opened his eyes: "That day ended isolationism for any realist."

Could the war with Japan have been avoided? Not unless one of the two nations, Japan or the United States, had been willing to change its basic policy. Japan was determined to expand in China and Southeast Asia. The United States was determined never to recognize Japan's partial conquest of China; it was equally opposed to any Japanese moves against Allied colonies like British Malaya or the Dutch East Indies. Neither side would budge. Japan's decision to expand by force made conflict with America almost inevitable.

Americans had a long job ahead. It was made even longer when Germany and Italy honored their Axis commitments by declaring war on the United States just after Pearl Harbor. In one way, however, this step simplified matters. American leaders believed that Hitler, the greatest threat to democracy, should be defeated first. Japan could not be ignored—Americans would indeed "Remember Pearl Harbor"—but the war in Europe against Germany, Italy, and their Axis allies received top priority. Hitler, then at the height of his power, relished the idea of smashing Franklin "Rosenfeld." (Hitler had the strange notion that Roosevelt, an Episcopalian since birth, was Jewish.)

Whatever his motives, Hitler's actions caused the creation of the Grand Alliance, a coalition of all nations fighting the Axis. America, Britain, and Russia were senior partners. Starting with a declaration by "United Nations," signed in January 1942 by twenty-six countries, the alliance grew to forty-seven members by 1945. This provided the basis for the United Nations (UN). Technically, all were equal. But in reality the great powers ran the war largely to suit themselves.

Joining the Allies was a new step for the United States. Even in World War I, America was only an "associated power" rather than an "ally." The difference went beyond hairsplitting over the meaning of words. World War II was unique; Americans felt their own security threatened. The world had indeed changed.

Big Three Relations Within the Grand Alliance, or United Nations, the closest cooperation existed between Britain and the United States. Churchill and Roosevelt met almost a dozen times to develop the partnership and sometimes to prepare a united strategy against Russia, the other major ally. It was not that the Soviet Union was an uncooperative ally. After withstanding the first German offensive of 1941 (a surprise attack by a supposed ally), the Russians fought the Germans tenaciously. The Nazi army was spending itself in Russia, winning many battles but nothing decisive. Churchill and Roosevelt hastened to assure Stalin, the Soviet dictator, of their esteem. They promised military aid as soon as possible.

But Stalin wanted immediate action by his allies in the West. Specifically, he called for an Anglo-American invasion of Western Europe launched across the English Channel in 1942. But instead of a dangerous, and probably disastrous, cross-channel invasion of occupied France that year, Western leaders settled for landings in North Africa. This move took little pressure off Russia. Stalin angrily rejected suggestions that this weak move represented a so-called second front against Germany.

Further friction developed during preliminary discussions of the postwar political settlements. Stalin, like Roosevelt and Churchill, never doubted his side would win. He wanted a hand in carving national boundaries after the war. Roosevelt conceded this point, but Churchill usually tried to pacify but contain Stalin. Roosevelt often urged the postponement of political decisions until later in the war.

Events in Asia and the Pacific The war was fought on many fronts. After the Japanese struck Pearl Harbor, they took over most of Southeast Asia. First they conquered the rest of French Indochina (Vietnam, Laos, and Cambodia). Then Malaya, Singapore, and Burma—all British colonies—fell. The Dutch East Indies were next. Australia was so sure its turn had come that it almost withdrew its troops from North Africa for a last-ditch homeland defense.

Meanwhile, the Japanese occupied most of America's colony, the Philippines. General Douglas MacArthur, the commander there when the

Philippines were attacked (on the same day as Pearl Harbor), was ordered to Australia. What remained of the American army—including Filipino units—held out bravely for several months on the Bataan peninsula near Manila until overwhelmed by superior force. Most Filipinos opposed the Japanese invasion. The islands had been promised independence; the war upset this timetable, forcing a postponement until 1946.

The Japanese drive of 1941–1942 was soon halted. Though a naval battle in the Coral Sea in May 1942 brought neither side victory, it removed the threat of a Japanese invasion of Australia. In June a key naval battle took place near Midway. Japanese strategy called for the capture of Midway, then a move against Hawaii. Japan probably should have made these two attacks right after Pearl Harbor. By mid-1942 things had changed. American aircraft carrier strength, though limited, was undamaged. Also, because Magic had broken the Japanese code, the American navy knew where to concentrate its forces.

Midway signaled the end of traditional naval warfare. Planes replaced guns and torpedoes as the most important offensive weapons. Enemy aircraft carriers were therefore the main target. Four Japanese carriers were sunk but only one American flat-top.[3] This gave the United States naval supremacy in the central Pacific, a factor of incalculable importance for the remainder of the Pacific war. Moreover, the troop transports had turned back toward Japan after the Coral Sea action. The Japanese never again made a serious thrust in the mid-Pacific.

Coral Sea and Midway set the stage for Allied offensive operations. In August 1942 Americans landed on Guadalcanal in the Solomon Islands. The battle there was long and fierce—a warning of what lay ahead. This "island hopping" followed a long and bloody course from Guadal-

---

[3]All four of the carriers Japan lost at Midway had been used to attack Pearl Harbor. Likewise lost at Midway—or during the harsh fighting that followed in the Solomon Islands—were nearly all the daring Japanese pilots of December 7. Neither the flat-tops nor the aviators were ever properly replaced. Admiral Nagumo, who had led the victory at Pearl and the defeat at Midway, survived until 1944. Then he died, evidently by suicide, during the American capture of Saipan.

WORLD WAR II IN THE PACIFIC

Japanese advances
Allied advances
Extent of Japanese conquest
Allied air operations
Battle or campaign

0   1000 MILES

The day after the Japanese surprise attack on Pearl Harbor on December 7, 1941, the United States declared war on Japan. On that same day, the Japanese invaded Thailand and Malaya. By late December they had captured Guam, Hong Kong, and Wake Island. The Japanese invasion of the Philippines began December 10; they took Manila on January 2, 1942. General Douglas MacArthur retreated to Australia.

In February 1942 the Japanese took Singapore and, by early March, most of the Dutch East Indies. In June they seized two of the Aleutian Islands. The Battle of the Coral Sea was fought between Japanese and Allied forces of May 7–8, which stopped Japan's advance on Australia. The air and naval battle of Midway (June 3–6) was a turning point in the Pacific war, and within two months the United States was for the first time on the offensive.

The first major Allied offensive, beginning in August 1942, was fought at Guadalcanal. The Japanese were driven from it in February 1943. During March–August the Japanese were driven from the Aleutians. In the second half of 1943 the South Pacific offensive took place. It gave the Allies control of the waters adjacent to the Solomon Islands. A Central Pacific offensive was launched in November under Admiral Chester Nimitz, during which

the Allies took the Solomons, Gilberts, Marshals, and Marianas. In December General Joseph W. Stilwell began a campaign in Burma; Burma was not completely retaken, however, until May 1945.

In June 1944 air attacks were opened against cities on the Japanese home islands. The Philippines campaign of June–December saw General MacArthur's return there. The naval Battle of Leyte Gulf (October 23–25), was a decisive defeat for Japan. It destroyed most of its remaining sea power. The Philippines campaign ended after the taking of Manila.

After heavy fighting, United States Marines took Iwo Jima in March 1945 and conquered Okinawa by late June. In May–August the greatest air offensive in the Pacific was launched against the Japanese home islands, culminating in the dropping of atomic bombs on Hiroshima (August 6) and Nagasaki (August 9). On August 8, the Soviet Union declared war on Japan and invaded Manchuria.

Japan surrendered and sued for peace on August 10. President Harry Truman announced August 14 as V-J Day. Japan's formal surrender took place September 2 in Tokyo Bay aboard the United States battleship *Missouri*.

The war in the Pacific was fought by island-hopping— retaking island by island territory captured by the Japanese. This marine landing in the Solomons in 1943 helped push Japanese forces back to the home islands.

canal in 1942 to Okinawa in 1945. In a series of landings on the various islands in between, United States troops fought for every bit of territory, notably the first few yards of each beachhead. Japanese resistance never let up. Even losing battle after battle did not diminish the enemy's will to fight.

After Midway, the Americans had sea and air superiority. The American fleet, especially the number of carriers, grew enormously. Even when the Japanese navy and air force came out in full strength (as when the United States recaptured the Philippines in 1944), Japan suffered staggering losses. On one day American pilots shot down nearly 500 Japanese planes. At Leyte Gulf, much of Japan's navy was destroyed.

American submarines (though less publicized than German U-boats) sank hundreds of Japanese ships. Many of them were carrying raw materials from Southeast Asia to Japan's factories. By early 1945 Japan had no hope for victory. The war in China ground on inconclusively. The Pacific, which three years before had seemed to belong to Japan, was now an American lake. The only way left to preserve Japanese martial honor or punish the American invaders was suicide assaults by *Kamikaze* pilots.[4]

Events in Europe and the Mediterranean The Allies mounted an equally relentless (and equally successful) effort in Europe and the Mediterranean. American and British forces overran North Africa and routed German General Erwin Rommel's *Afrika Korps*. In 1943 the Allies invaded Sicily and then mainland Italy. Meanwhile, massive preparations for invading France went on, with Britain as the staging area.

On another front the Russians took terrible losses. Yet they stopped the farthest German penetration at the Volga River in the Battle of Stalingrad. For the next two years the "Eastern Front" repeatedly saw Russian advances and German retreats.

The invasion of France on June 6, 1944, put Hitler's neck in the noose. Despite strong resis-

---

[4]*Kamikaze* pilots crashed their planes, loaded with bombs, into American ships.

Pleasures and Pastimes in a Mass Society

"The Americans are a queer people: they can't play. Americans rush to work as soon as they get up. They can't play. They try to, but they can't." Canadian humorist Stephen Leacock indulged in some poetic license when he described his neighbors to the south. Americans do play, of course. They enjoy light entertainment. They love competitive sports. And they find pleasure in the simple satisfactions of everyday life. (A happy man indeed is greeting *The New Television Set* in Norman Rockwell's 1949 painting.)

Foreign observers sometimes complain about the "canned" amusements of a mass society, but even French critic André Maurois commented favorably on them. He wrote, "Americans who never meet each other and who live under different skies come to have innumerable common memories and brotherly thoughts."

For further information on the foreign observers quoted in this essay, see "Notes on Sources."]

PICTORIAL ESSAY 8

Stronger than in various other countries, and perhaps also than in Turkey, seems to be the predilection in America for the lighter types of musical and theatrical entertainment—for jazz and operettas, or for comedies and thrillers rather than plays that have a pessimistic note or are centered around philosophical and social themes.

[ÖMER CELÂL SARC, 1959]

Broadcasting a radio drama, 1934

Scene from *Oklahoma!* (original production, 1943)

I could not agree that the creation of films is not an art at all, only an industry. It is actually a curiously mixed activity, coming into a new category, needing all the resources and organization of a large industry, but by no means devoid of genuine artistic impulses. The public looked to films for general entertainment, on a scale hitherto unknown, and accepted the moving pictures as a substitute for theaters, books, gossip, and dreams.

[J. B. PRIESTLEY, 1935-36]

A scene from *Gold Diggers of 1933*

Let's listen to Louis Armstrong on Broadway, the black Titan of the cry, of the apostrophe, of the burst of laughter, of thunder. An imperial figure, Armstrong makes his entrance. His voice is as deep as an abyss, it is a black cave. He bursts out laughing, he roars and puts the trumpet to his mouth. With it he is in turn demoniac, playful, and massive, from one second to another, in accordance with an astounding fantasy. The man is extravagantly skillful; he is a king.

[LE CORBUSIER, 1947]

Louis Armstrong

Elvis Presley and fans

Female teenagers are in the habit of greeting their heroes, the young crooners —the one best known being Elvis Presley, of the writhing hips and thighs—with a shrill yell that seems to issue from a single throat. The picture of young and well-dressed girls comporting themselves in this fashion is enough to send cold shivers down an adult's spine. Significantly, however, it has been observed that only the girls in the rows lit up by the stage lights break out in this yell; that is, only those who can be seen by the others. Moreover, they are looking not so much at the singer as at the other members of their own group.

[HERBERT VON BORCH, 1962]

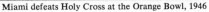

Miami defeats Holy Cross at the Orange Bowl, 1946

Willie Mays at second base, 1957

I do not pretend to understand even the coarser of the finer points of American college football, which must have been originally devised during an early revolutionary phase of American life, for like a revolution it is an odd mixture of secret plotting, with so many heads motionless and close together, and sudden violent action. When either side pressed towards goal, we all stood up. The danger over or the prize lost, we sat down again. The enormous clock ran off the seconds when the ball was actually in play. It stopped when the game stopped. And the game was always stopping.

[J. B. PRIESTLEY AND JACQUETTA HAWKES, 1954]

I have studied hundreds of photos of Louis in his big fights, of Louis preparing for his big fights, of Louis just after his big fights. His face almost never changes. The man is dignified, *in the toughest sport in the world, whether he's giving a licking or taking one. You cannot get away from this impression of the man being so superbly equipped to fight that he didn't need the window-dressing of a big grin of confidence, or glib phrases by the publicity boys. Louis wasn't just a great fighter. He was an admirable man.*

[HARRY CARPENTER, 1964]

The Brown Bomber, Louis and Schmeling Fight, by Robert Riggs

Robinson's character was the key. A fierce competitor, Jackie had in the early days to curb his angry pride. He ignored insults, and won recognition as a baseball player, on equal terms with others, whether white or black. Today ability is the key, not pigmentation. Some day Jackie's greatest honor will come when he is simply a name in a record book, when, because there was a Jackie Robinson and others like him, future generations have forgotten there was ever a need for a Jackie Robinson.

[CANADIAN SPORTSWRITER]

Cheerleaders at a high-school basketball game

To observe the North American in a large crowd within the United States—at a World Series game or a popular football game—is one of the most cheering spectacles in the world. Here we have an enormous mass of people, well balanced, attractive, determined to enjoy to the utmost an afternoon of relaxation, applauding their favorite team but wihout ill will or malevolence toward the adversary, on the contrary always disposed to recognize and applaud the courage and skill of the opposition.

[DANIEL COSÍO VILLEGAS, 1959]

We went into a bowling alley. It is the old game of skittles which the dwarfs of Rip Van Winkle played, but it has been brought up to date. Instead of a wild gully, I found a bar with tables and chairs: the bowling alleys, set side by side, are of varnished wood, and when the bowling ball has knocked over the ninepins, it falls through a trap door and is returned by an automatic device to the player. The game is so popular that the alleys are booked for days in advance. It is monotonous to watch.

[SIMONE DE BEAUVOIR, 1947]

Bowling at a fifty-six-lane alley, California

Father and son tossing a football, Newton, Iowa

Woman playing bingo in Muncie, Indiana

America is a modern land where technical ingenuity is apparent at every point, in the equipment of a kitchen as well as of a car, but at the same time a land of gardens, of flowers, of home activities, where a man, away from his office or his workplace, enjoys tinkering at his bench, making a piece of furniture, repainting his house, repairing a fence, or mowing his lawn. A land of luxury but also of simple pleasures. There is an America that strolls in the parks in its suburban Sunday clothes, or cavorts on the beaches, and plays baseball everywhere.

[JACQUES FREYMOND, 1959]

Teenagers at a "sock hop," Carlsbad, New Mexico

Wisconsin Farm Auction, by Joan Arend Kickbush

Girls jumping rope, Cleveland

The American smile, which has been so ridiculed by those who believe the intelligent thing is to know everything already—without, of course, knowing much of anything at all—seems to me to be the expression of love for one's fellow man, of the basic fact that in the United States it is firmly believed that living together is a blessing. This is derived, in my opinion, from the historical makeup of the United States and from the American spirit, from its loneliness and the fact that for so long the presence of other men was an occasion for joy.

[JULIAN MARIAS, 1959]

Children playing at an open water hydrant, New York City

WORLD WAR II IN EUROPE

Extent of Axis control

Neutral nations

Allies

← Allied offensives

✹ Battle

When Germany was at the height of its power, its armies had overrun much of European Russia, defeated France, occupied Norway and Denmark, and held much of North Africa. In December 1941 England and the Soviet Union were the only allies in Europe still undefeated by Germany.

The first United States troops for the European theater of the war arrived in northern Ireland in January 1942. Six months later in North Africa, the British checked the Axis advance at El Alamein. In November General Eisenhower's Allied forces landed in North Africa. By May 1943 the Germans had been defeated there. In Europe the Russians defeated the German armies, attacking Stalingrad in December 1942 after a four-month siege—a major turning point. Thereafter the Russians began to take the offensive.

The Allied invasion of Italy began in July 1943. Italy's unconditional surrender to the Allies in September was followed by stiff German resistance in northern Italy. The Germans were not finally defeated there until 1945.

The air offensive against Germany began in January 1944 in preparation for an Allied invasion. On June 6, D-Day, Allied armies invaded Normandy in northern France in a surprise attack. By August 10 this offensive was concluded and a second front in southern France was opened that began a drive up the Rhone Valley. All of France, Belgium, and Luxembourg was liberated by September. By this time the Russians had driven the Germans out of the Soviet Union and into Eastern Europe.

The battle for Germany began in September 1944. The first large German city to fall, Aachen, was taken in October. Within five months Belgrade, Budapest, and Warsaw had fallen.

A German counteroffensive in the west was launched in December 1944. The Germans almost succeeded in breaking through the American line in the Battle of the Bulge, but they were repulsed. Then a British offensive was launched in the Netherlands. By March United States troops had penetrated the Ruhr Valley and crossed the Rhine; a month later, they reached the Elbe. The Russians entered Berlin late in April. Berlin fell on May 2. The formal end of the war in Europe occurred on May 8. Germany surrendered unconditionally to the Allies.

tance, Allied invaders stormed the Normandy beaches. Happily, Hitler insisted that the Normandy invasion was unimportant. He refused to concentrate his available forces there. After several nerve-racking weeks American tank columns led by General George S. Patton pushed beyond Normandy and raced across France.

But the Nazi army could not be crushed in 1944. It withdrew toward the Rhine. Germany, as helpless now as Japan, was the target of massive air attacks. (Over 1,000 Allied planes participated in a single raid on Berlin.) Hitler still dreamed of victory, though he mistakenly believed his own people were betraying him. He forbade his generals to retreat. He hastened the murder of millions in concentration camps. Yet neither demoniac raving nor barbarous cruelty could produce military victories. Early in 1945 the Allies pushed ahead on all fronts.

The Big Three leaders — Roosevelt, Stalin, and Churchill — had long been preparing for victory. Stalin and Churchill met in Moscow in October 1944. There they began carving out spheres of influence. Roosevelt wanted to end the war first and then make such decisions. The Axis must accept defeat and unconditional surrender; the Allies should not squabble until they had won. Thus the 1943 Big Three meeting at Teheran, Iran, had dealt mainly with wartime strategy.

By early 1945 territorial questions could not be further postponed. Germany would surely surrender that year; Japan was next in line. Russian participation in the invasion of Japan could mean a shorter campaign, with fewer Western casualties. What price would Stalin demand, though, to bring Russia into the Pacific war? The answer emerged at the Yalta Conference of February 1945, a Big Three meeting at a Russian resort in the Crimea.

Stalin set a high though not outlandish price. He wanted Russian power in the Far East to equal its extent in 1904, before his country lost the Russo-Japanese War. Russia was to receive the northernmost islands of the Japanese chain, plus territorial and commercial rights in Manchuria and northern China. In return, Stalin would declare war against Japan within three months of the end of the war in Europe.

The Yalta discussions produced agreement on another subject, which later became a matter of grave contention between the Soviet Union and the Western powers: the fate of Poland. At Yalta, Roosevelt and Churchill agreed to allow the Soviet Union to annex large areas of Eastern Poland, presumably as a buffer region against any future German attack. Stalin, in turn, agreed to allow "free elections" to be held after the war, although the commitment was a meaningless one given his views on the "necessity" for a "friendly" (i.e., a Communist) regime in that country.

Polish-Americans and other opponents of the Yalta agreements would later denounce FDR for having "sold out" Poland and other Eastern European countries. Roosevelt, however, felt that he had exacted about as much as he could from Stalin on the question, given three elemental facts of international life: (1) the Russian armies would be controlling the country (as would American armies in Italy and a British one in Greece, countries where pro-Western governments were established); (2) Poland was clearly a security problem for the Soviet Union and not for the West; and (3) the issue was not of overriding importance to the United States compared to the future of Germany or securing Soviet entrance into the war with Japan.

Roosevelt's military advisers had warned that invading Japan without Russia might cost the United States a million casualties. The President had no wish for this. Nor could he count on the still untested atom bomb to end the war. Stalin's offer seemed the only reasonable choice.

The Yalta agreements included provisions for the dismemberment of Germany. The Allied powers (the Big Three and France) would each occupy a section. Germany must also pay reparations for the wartime destruction it had caused. Stalin wanted to weaken Germany so that the Germans might never again attack Russia. Reparations would keep Germany feeble. Moreover, splitting Germany into occupation zones assured Stalin that the eastern zone would remain firmly under Soviet control.

Within a half year of Yalta, the Axis was subdued. In April 1945 Hitler committed suicide in Berlin as the Allies overran Germany. Four

The strain of war was visible on FDR's face as he met with his allies, Churchill and Stalin, for the last time at Yalta. The concessions made to Stalin there to secure Russia's entrance into the Pacific war were denounced by some postwar critics as "appeasement."

months later the Pacific war ended spectacularly and ominously. In the meantime, Roosevelt had died and been succeeded as President by Vice President Harry S. Truman.

The Atomic Bomb Two American B-29s approached the southwestern tip of Japan on the morning of August 6, 1945. One of them was the *Enola Gay*. Its mission was to drop the first atomic bomb in the history of mankind. The target was the Japanese city of Hiroshima. At about 31,000 feet the doors of the bomb bay opened, and the bombardier released "Little Boy," a weapon that had twenty times the power of a ton of TNT. At 2,000 feet the bomb detonated.

A young Hiroshima girl who was riding a trolley gave this account.

At that moment my eyes were suddenly blinded by a flash of piercing light and the neighborhood was enveloped in dense smoke of a yellow color like poison gas. Instantly everything became pitch dark and you couldn't see an inch ahead. Then a heavy and tremendously loud roar. The inside of my mouth was gritty as though I had eaten sand, and my throat hurt. I looked toward the east, and I saw an enormous black pillar of cloud billowing upward. "It's all over now," I thought.

As the plane made a sharp turn to avoid the blast, the tail gunner looked down at the falling bomb. Within seconds he was looking directly into the center of the atomic detonation. He watched the shock wave approach the plane like a shimmering heat wave. The mushroom cloud started forming immediately. He described it as "a bubbling mass of purple-gray smoke, and you could see it had a red core to it and everything was burning inside."

Within an instant 70,000 people died. Another 30,000 would later die of radiation burns and

A mushroom-like cloud rose over Hiroshima—the first city ever to suffer the devastation of an atomic bomb.

a strange new disease, radiation sickness. Approximately 75 percent of the buildings in Hiroshima were destroyed. As another eyewitness said of those first few seconds. "Everything had crumbled away in that one moment and changed into streets of rubble, street after street of ruins."

What caused the decision to use this devastating weapon? President Truman had been told that if the Japanese fought to the end in defense of their own islands, as they vowed, the war would last more than another year, and an additional half million American lives would be lost. He thought a quick one-two punch—one atomic bomb dropped, followed swiftly by a second on another target—would force Japan to surrender.

Historians have conjectured that there may also have been other reasons. Soviet-American relations were strained. Truman may have wanted to show the Russians that American strength was superior. Or he may have wanted to end the war before the Soviet Union could occupy Asia as it had eastern Europe.

The atomic bomb did end the war. Three days after Hiroshima was bombed, Nagasaki suffered the same fate. The next day the Japanese asked for peace terms, though many Japanese still wished to fight to the death.

A HOT WAR TURNED COLD

History's greatest war ended with unconditional surrender by the Axis. Yet victory found the Grand Alliance anything but united. Differences over postwar policy produced visible strains, with the possibility of a new and dangerous confrontation. The United States and Russia were now superpowers. Their growing disagreements would soon be called a Cold War.

Soviet-American cooperation broke down completely after World War II. Eastern and central Europe came under Russian domination. The Baltic countries of Latvia, Lithuania, and Estonia ceased to be independent nations. Finland avoided the same fate by curbing its foreign policy in a treaty with Russia. The countries between Western-occupied Germany and the Soviet Union, plus the Balkan nations, became Soviet satellites. (Yugoslavia would later break away.) A Soviet empire emerged. Countries on its borders (Greece, Turkey, and Iran, for example) all felt the pressure of the new superpower.

The United States had hoped for cooperation, not conflict, among the major powers after the war. A return to the status quo and the isolationism of earlier periods was out of the question. Americans could not pull back as in 1919 and expect to maintain their interests in a vacuum. World War II had exhausted Britain and France. If North Atlantic leadership of the world were to continue, the United States had to step in. Thus Washington pushed for a new world organization, despite the League of Nations' failure and America's own sorry role in that failure.

Roosevelt had wanted a league. Unlike Wilson, though, he had made sure that Republicans participated in the sessions that preceded the founding of the United Nations in 1945 (soon after Roosevelt's death). The UN differed from the League in various ways. It was located in New York, not Geneva. More important, the great powers established a Security Council whose permanent members (the United States, Britain, France, Russia, and China) could defeat any proposal with a single negative vote. This big-power veto, a recognition of both national sovereignty and great-power interests, gravely limited UN effectiveness in crisis situations. Yet the veto was desired by all the large powers.

Containment in the Mediterranean American hopes for postwar stability suffered as a result of Roosevelt's death. The late President had not mapped a precise blueprint for peacetime policy; he had become increasingly disillusioned over Russian behavior. But he did possess enormous prestige. This was not true of President Truman, a man without experience in either high-level administration or foreign policy. Truman's baptism of fire in summit diplomacy—direct meetings by heads of government—came in July 1945, when he, Stalin, and Britain's new prime minister, Clement Attlee, met at Potsdam, Germany. Full agreement proved impossible. With Japan still undefeated, Truman accepted postponement of various pending issues.

Russia's expansionism and the weakness of America's allies soon ruled out further delay. By 1947 Western Europe seemed ready to collapse. Britain, France, Italy, and West Germany (not yet a separate country) were sliding downward, perhaps toward a chaos that could only benefit Russia. Britain had to give up its empire. The British move that most affected the United States was its decision to end aid to Greece and Turkey, Britain's anticommunist Mediterranean allies. The Russians and Turks had been at odds for centuries. The post-World War II period proved no exception. The Soviets tried to gain parts of eastern Turkey and establish bases at the Dardanelles—Turkey's (and Russia's) gateway to the Mediterranean.

The Greeks (unfriendly toward the Turks but now allied with them as another target of Russian expansionism) also needed help. A communist guerrilla movement was fighting the Greek government. Only active American intervention could keep Greece and Turkey out of the Soviet sphere. In March 1947 the President enunciated the Truman Doctrine "to help free peoples to maintain their free institutions" against the threat of "subjugation by armed minorities or by outside pressures." Congress appropriated $400 million to aid Greece and Turkey.

The congressional action and Truman's strong words were highly significant. They proved the Cold War had truly begun. The United States would, by threat of a third world war, contain Russia within the areas the Soviets had occupied or dominated in 1947. The support Truman received from Republicans in Congress signaled that the policy of containment had bipartisan support.

Containment in Western Europe After containing the Russian advance in the eastern Mediterranean, the United States turned to Western Europe. Secretary of State George C. Marshall announced in mid-1947 American willingness to contribute huge sums toward European reconstruction. All Europe was included; even Russia sent envoys to a preliminary conference. But the Russians quickly withdrew and kept their satellites from joining the European Recovery Program (ERP), better known as the Marshall Plan.

Congress moved more cautiously than on Greece and Turkey. But a communist takeover of Czechoslovakia in 1948 spurred it on. Billions of dollars flooded into Western Europe, stimulating the area's economic recovery. This also ended any early possibility that Communist parties there would reach power through elections.

The Western allies took an added step in containing communist advances in Europe by creating a formal military alliance in 1949. The North Atlantic Treaty Organization (NATO) included a dozen North Atlantic nations. They pledged to take any action necessary "including the use of armed force, to restore and maintain the security of the North Atlantic area." To implement the promise to defend any NATO country attacked by an outside power, large numbers of United States troops were sent to Germany. The American navy took over from Britain in the Mediterranean.

Through NATO the United States in effect became the policeman for the Western world, a break with American tradition. Not since the French alliance of 1778 had the United States linked itself formally in a military alliance with another power. NATO made the containment policy a firm one. Though the Soviets exploded their first nuclear weapon in 1949, they knew that further expansion to the west was unthinkable. NATO was soon functioning, with General Dwight D. Eisenhower (Supreme Allied Commander in Europe during World War II) heading NATO's forces. Obviously Washington would not allow a Russian "iron curtain" to fall over Western Europe.

The Struggle for Mainland China Unsettling events in Asia contrasted sharply with the success of containment in Europe. Events in postwar China were particularly disappointing for Americans. Civil war broke out there between the communists under Mao Tse-tung and the Nationalists under Chiang Kai-shek. Mao had fought for control of China long before the Japanese invasion. War with Japan temporarily united the two sides, but afterward, they returned to civil war.

By 1948 it became clear the Nationalists would lose. The next year Chiang fled to the island of Taiwan, while on the mainland Mao proclaimed his communist government, the People's Republic of China (often referred to as Red China). Massive American military intervention might

have prevented the communist takeover some American leaders thought, though few recommended it. And the history of later large-scale American involvement in Vietnam casts grave doubt on the wisdom of that course. In any case, two things were certain: by 1949 Red China possessed considerable power, and this power would increase.

The Korean Conflict The United States refused diplomatic recognition to Red China. Yet soon after the Chinese civil war ended, Americans were forced to recognize the Red Chinese army in combat. The scene was Korea, which had regained independence from Japan in 1945. But now Korea had been divided into communist-occupied North Korea and American-occupied South Korea. The communist North invaded the South in June 1950, perhaps because Washington had declared Korea outside the zone of American vital interest. (U.S. troops had been pulled back to Japan.)

When South Korea asked for American help, Truman quickly provided it. Available combat forces (two American divisions stationed in Japan) were sent at once to Korea. Also, a Soviet

Warfare in Korea was conventional in employing large numbers of men with standard weaponry in set battles. But since it was fought for limited aims —containing rather than destroying the enemy—it foreshadowed later combat in Vietnam.

mistake let Truman make the American response a United Nations venture. In June 1950 Russia was boycotting all UN meetings. The Security Council promptly branded North Korea an aggressor and authorized a UN military force to repel the attack. General Douglas MacArthur, leader of the occupation forces in Japan, also headed the UN army (mostly American soldiers) in Korea.

The Korean conflict was both a success and a failure for the United States. Two Koreas still exist. Thus the 1950–1953 military effort there did prevent a communist takeover. But this venture became a political liability for Democrats and a lasting frustration for all Americans. After a year of seesaw campaigns up and down the Korean peninsula, fighting ended close to the original dividing line.

Total victory was unattainable because the war had limited aims. And Washington permitted only limited means to achieve them. MacArthur, a great soldier and a great egotist, was especially frustrated. He had sent his troops to within sight of China's border in 1950, provoking full-scale Chinese intervention in Korea and an American retreat. Despite this—and the risk of bringing

Russia into combat also—MacArthur wanted to bomb China and fight the war more vigorously. Truman refused. When MacArthur aired his contrary views in public, Truman fired him.

REPUBLICANS BACK IN POWER

Truman fought the war his way; he and his party then paid the political price. When the Republicans regained the presidency in 1952, after twenty years, they promised changes in foreign policy. Dwight Eisenhower and his party came into power in part due to charges that the Democrats had not resisted communism as strongly as they could and should have. Containment, declared the Republican campaign platform, was "negative, futile, and immoral." Once in power, the Republicans assured the country, not only would they stop losing countries to communism, but, they hinted, countries already communist would be redeemed.

Eisenhower selected perhaps the ideal secretary of state to implement this policy. John Fos-

Secretary of State John Foster Dulles reporting on one of his many trips around the globe to President Eisenhower on May 17, 1955. Dulles had just returned from Europe where he signed a treaty restoring sovereignty to Austria and participated in the admission of West Germany to NATO. On several occasions, such as the one shown here, he briefed the President in informal public addresses that were broadcast to the nation from the White House.

GEORGE C. MARSHALL

One of George C. Marshall's biographers has described him as "the least typical of generals." He notes that what is remarkable in him is a "beautifully balanced mind thinking in terms of the dignity and integrity of the country which gave him birth."

Marshall was a soldier-statesman in the tradition of George Washington and Andrew Jackson. He was a military genius who turned diplomat, secretary of state, and secretary of defense after the close of his career as a professional soldier. His actions in war caused President Harry Truman to state in 1945: "In a war unparalleled in magnitude and horror, millions of Americans gave their country outstanding service. General of the Army George C. Marshall gave it victory." His actions in peace won him the Nobel Peace Prize in 1953. He was the first soldier ever to receive it.

Marshall was an absolute master of organization and military strategy. But he sometimes considered this talent a liability, for although his army career involved two world wars, he was never to lead troops in battle. He was considered too valuable a planner to be risked in field command.

In the 1930s Marshall had a tedious job as an instructor in the Illinois National Guard. But by 1936 his star began to rise. He was promoted to Chief of Staff of the Army on September 1, 1939, the opening day of World War II in Europe. Between that day and the end of the war Marshall built up the army and air corps from fewer than 200,000 men to over 8 million. Without his planning it has been estimated that the invasion of Europe would have come a full year later than it did in 1944.

At war's end Marshall wished to retire. But President Truman asked him to undertake a diplomatic mission to China to try to bring the warring Nationalist and communist forces together in a coalition government. The soldier hero's second career as a controversial statesman began.

After China Marshall was named secretary of state. He found himself in a new war—the Cold War with the Soviet Union. He helped to hammer out the Truman Doctrine and, of course, the Marshall Plan. Then he tried to retire again. This time, however, Truman wanted him to become secretary of defense.

In 1951 Senator Joseph McCarthy, whose crusade against communism became a witch hunt, lashed out at Marshall. He published a speech attacking Marshall's wartime strategy, his mission to China, and his actions as secretary of state. McCarthy accused this public servant of being "a man steeped in falsehood," who was guilty of "invariably serving the world policy of the Kremlin."

Marshall resigned soon after this vicious attack, because his effectiveness in office had been greatly reduced. It was a melancholy ending to a frequently brilliant and selfless career in the service of the nation. He was remembered by one of his colleagues in the State Department as "the image of the American gentleman at his best—honorable, courteous, devoid of arrogance, exacting of others, but even more of himself, intolerant only of cowardice, deviousness, and cynicism."

ter Dulles, a sixty-four-year-old Wall Street corporation lawyer, had long been one of the leading foreign policy spokesmen of the Republican party. Dulles's strong belief in the righteousness of the American system and the iniquity of communism appeared to have a great deal to do with the Christianity of the one and the atheism of the other.

Guided by this Manichaean view of the world, Dulles managed American foreign policy for six years, from 1953 to 1959. While retaining the final power of decision, Eisenhower believed strongly in delegating authority to cabinet members, and he reposed special trust in Dulles. Dulles became the most influential secretary of state of the postwar era, at least until the coming of Henry Kissinger. The secretary made diplomacy a personal affair, visiting forty-seven countries and flying half a million miles during his tenure.

Liberation The new Republican leaders proposed to differentiate themselves most dramatically from Truman with regard to the "captive nations" of Eastern Europe. The United States, said Dulles, should "make it publicly known that it wants and expects liberation to occur." During the election campaign, the policy had won the Republicans millions of votes from Americans of Polish, Hungarian, and other East European descent. Dulles quickly explained, once in office, that he meant that America should frequently restate its position that Eastern Europe should be free; he did not mean military action. Constant moral pressure, maintained Dulles, would lead to liberation.

Brinkmanship and Massive Retaliation Dulles labored hard and often to inform the world that the United States was not "scared to go to the brink," that it would not regard all-out war as unthinkable if its vital interests were threatened. As part of this strategy, Dulles purposely left unclear what situations would push the United States over the brink. Such a policy may have frightened America's enemies; it also discomfited America's allies.

Massive retaliation became a crucial corollary to brinkmanship. But it was partially forced on Dulles by the rest of the Eisenhower administration. As a result of the Korean War, defense spending had more than tripled, from $14 billion

in 1950 to $49 billion in 1953. The cabinet's fiscal conservatives hoped to reduce expenditures and balance the budget. To curb military expenses, they imposed on the armed forces a policy called the New Look.

The New Look became more popularly known as the policy of "more bang for a buck." Atomic weapons, its proponents argued, could most economically defend the country, far more so than large naval and land forces. By concentrating on American nuclear strength, especially the deterrent of the Strategic Air Command, the administration could prune the army and navy and cut the defense budget by 10 percent. Thus, when Dulles approached the brink, he threatened opponents with massive retaliation with nuclear weapons. The logic of the administration's fiscal policies dictated the all-or-nothing approach.

Ending the Korean War Eisenhower had pledged during his campaign, "I will go to Korea," to inspect battle lines and examine possibilities for peace. His visit, in December 1952, left him more than ever convinced of what he had believed from the start—Americans should not be fighting a land war in Asia.

The new President and his secretary of state rapidly began to test out their brinkmanship ideas. If the war did not end soon, Eisenhower proclaimed, the United States would take action "under circumstances of our own choosing." Chiang Kai-shek, driven by the Chinese communists to the island of Formosa, began bombing raids against the Chinese coast. Finally, Dulles sent a message to the Chinese through the government of India: If a Korean agreement was not reached soon, the United States would seriously consider using nuclear weapons. Within two weeks, the communists agreed to a settlement.

In its first innings, brinkmanship appeared to have scored a success. But some maintained that the war had ended largely because of stalemate on the battlefront and the death of Stalin two months earlier. In the next two years, Stalin's successors in Moscow appeared to be pursuing a more conciliatory role on several fronts, abandoning some territorial claims and improving relations with several countries. Eventually, the Soviets agreed to withdraw from their occupation zone in Austria, on condition that the reunited country follow a neutral foreign policy. The Soviets also indicated that they would be willing to solve the problem of German reunification the same way.

Dulles responded to all Soviet actions with deep suspicion. After the settlement of the Korean War, he explained, "This is the time to crowd the enemy—and maybe finish him, once and for all." Soviet overtures, he felt, reflected Soviet weakness, which the United States should exploit.

Problems in the Far East If Dulles distrusted Soviet policies and aims, part of his attitude stemmed from communist actions in the Far East, actions that the secretary interpreted as the direct work of the Kremlin. Since 1945, a dedicated Vietnamese nationalist and communist named Ho Chi Minh had been at the head of a rebellion to drive the French out of Indochina. France appealed for American aid against communism, and this valued ally received millions of American dollars to finance its colonial war. But by April 1954 France was through in that area. French troops had entrenched and trapped themselves in a fortress near Hanoi called Dien Bien Phu. In May, the Dien Bien Phu garrison surrendered.

Meanwhile, the communist insurgents and the French had begun negotiating in Geneva. After the fall of Dien Bien Phu they agreed to divide Vietnam temporarily, with Ho Chi Minh taking over the north and the French remaining in the south. Internationally supervised elections, aimed at reuniting the country, were supposed to be held by 1956. The elections never took place. In South Vietnam, an American-backed regime, headed by a Vietnamese Catholic named Diem, established a separate government in Saigon. The United States poured in support, and elections, which everyone knew Ho Chi Minh would win, were postponed. Dulles, who attended the Geneva sessions as an unhappy "observer" (the United States did not sign the final accords), had salvaged something: a noncommunist South Vietnam. On the list of American Pyrrhic victories, the 1956 Geneva Conference ranks at the top.

Dulles had been frustrated in Indochina by a lack of support from America's allies. He now

John Foster Dulles is the protective nurse guarding the "children" of Asia from the lure of the "Red Piper of Peking" by herding them around the SEATO carriage.

attempted to head off such embarrassments in the future by organizing the Southeast Asia Treaty Organization (SEATO) (ostensibly an Eastern NATO), comprising the United States, Britain, France, Australia, New Zealand, Thailand, Pakistan, and the Philippines. But many noncommunist states of Asia (India, Indonesia, Burma) refused to join or to align themselves with the United States. Nonetheless, Dulles believed he now had the means to repel future communist advances in the region.

Toward a European Settlement Neither Russians nor Americans expected substantive results from the Geneva conference of 1955. Neither side brought any new proposals to deal with the major East-West problem, the reunification of Germany. West Germany was being rearmed and had joined NATO, and the Soviet Union had organized its Iron Curtain satellites into the Warsaw Pact, which East Germany would join a few months later. Germany, like Europe, would remain divided for the forseeable future. The only positive result of the meeting was an intangible, rapidly dissolving "spirit of Geneva," which implied that the two countries would not seek to settle their differences by war.

This easing of tensions did not sit well with Dulles. It looked too much like American acceptance of the status quo, including permanent Soviet control of Eastern Europe. Accordingly, the United States continued to issue statements about "liberation" remaining a high-priority item in American foreign policy. Especially during the presidential election year of 1956, the administration would not forgo restating the crucial policy that differentiated it from the Truman administration.

But events soon demonstrated tragically the emptiness of these promises of liberation. In October 1956, discontent in Eastern Europe exploded in the streets of Hungary and forced changes in the government. Flushed with their success, Hungarians demanded the withdrawal of the Rus-

sian Army, which began evacuating the country, or at least pulled out of Budapest. Eisenhower had been careful not to urge on the "rebels," but CIA-sponsored Radio Free Europe offered encouragement, and Dulles mentioned the possibility of American economic aid.

Hungary maintained its independence for several days. But when the new premier announced that Hungary would withdraw from the Warsaw Pact, the Russians sent in their tanks. Hungarians resisted, pleading all the while for help from the West.

Given the realities of nuclear stalemate, Eisenhower never considered sending in Ameri-

Hungarian patriots hold an anti-Soviet demonstration on a torn-up Budapest street on October 24, 1956. In the week of bloody rebellion that followed, Soviet troops and tanks crushed the Hungarians' attempt to establish their own government. Although the United States joined in a U. N. resolution censuring the Soviets, and was to admit thousands of Hungarian refugees in the wake of the revolution, it did not intervene in Hungary.

can troops to Hungary. The Soviets would have construed such an action as an attack on them and would have responded, possibly with nuclear weapons. Despite the rhetoric of liberation, Eisenhower and Dulles had always known this. Now the East Europeans knew it too.

The Middle East Dulles's problems were just beginning. At the time of the Hungarian revolution, the secretary's ability to influence world events suffered another dramatic blow, as a crisis erupted in the Middle East involving America's closest allies. Without consulting the United States, Britain and France took military action against Egypt. Their joint expedition produced only frustration for both European nations, and further frayed the bonds of the Atlantic alliance.

The crisis arose, in part, from Dulles's own bumbling. He had attempted to improve America's standing with the Arab nations by agreeing to aid in building the Aswan Dam on Egypt's Nile River. But by 1956 the young nationalist Egyptian leader, Gamal Abdel Nasser, had moved to establish ties with communist countries as well. As a result, Dulles abruptly informed the Egyptians that the United States would not finance the dam (the Russians eventually did). Nasser, angered and humiliated, bolstered his prestige by nationalizing the Suez Canal.

This action infuriated the British and French, who considered control of the canal vital to their interests. When negotiations did not produce satisfaction, they allied with Israel in a combined attack on Egypt. (This development undoubtedly helped assure the Russians that they could move into Hungary without fear of Western reprisal.)

The United States reacted angrily, both at the invasion and at not having been consulted. Eisenhower immediately demanded that the British and French forces withdraw, before they had even reached the canal. Khrushchev, bidding for support among the Arabs, threatened Western Europe with nuclear weapons. Under pressure from both the Russians and the Americans, the British and French had no choice but to withdraw.

Dulles had ended the invasion, but he seemed to have accomplished little else. The af-

fair injured NATO prestige and allowed the Russians to ingratiate themselves with Nasser, gaining a base on the Mediterranean. To maintain the American position, the United States, in early 1957, proclaimed the Eisenhower Doctrine, affirming its intent to support established Arab governments against subversion. By the end of that year, Eisenhower had strengthened American ties with Jordan and Saudi Arabia. A year later, he committed American troops for the only time in his presidency, ordering a landing by United States Marines in Lebanon as a show of American strength. As on previous occasions, Eisenhower moved in a far more limited fashion than his military advisers or his secretary of state had wanted.

Problems with the Third World Eisenhower and Dulles presided over American foreign policy at a time when nationalism was rising throughout Asia, Africa, and Latin America. As shown by their difficulties in handling Egypt's Nasser, American policymakers had recurrent problems dealing with the new phenomenon. Although strongly opposed to old-style European colonialism, Americans did not know exactly what they wanted in its place.

Their major aim, to prevent the spread of communism, often lapsed into a policy of support for established regimes and opposition to virtually any insurgent movement, whether communist-led or not. While this did not restructure American policy, the Eisenhower-Dulles world view often clashed with the plans of emerging Third World countries to quicken their own development. The United States sought to strengthen existing governments, assist development, and turn the new nations from communism with offers of military and economic aid. By 1961, Eisenhower was asking $4.2 billion from Congress for such aid.

The United States faced a particular problem in Latin America, where it tried to maintain traditional hemispheric influence and safeguard nearly $10 billion of American investment. Strains developed in an area that many Americans regarded as their backyard. In 1954, after the Central American republic of Guatemala took a turn toward the left, Dulles denounced the existing government. But more than words were involved. The CIA helped finance Guatemalan groups opposed to the left-leaning government in a successful seizure of power. Dulles had seemed to pay little attention to Latin America. But when rock-throwing crowds later attacked Vice President Nixon in Venezuela, Washington began to worry about its position. For at least one country, Cuba, when Fidel Castro's guerillas overthrew a pro-American regime in 1958, this concern came too late.

Sputnik and U-2 In August 1957 the Soviet Union startled the United States, and the world, by orbiting its first space vehicle, Sputnik. Whatever the implications for interplanetary travel, Sputnik symbolized rapid advances by the Soviets in rocketry and atomic warhead delivery systems. The United States had also advanced in these directions, and had made great strides in developing nuclear submarines. More and more, international relations reflected a "balance of terror," with traditional considerations becoming less and less important.

Both sides now sought another summit conference to ease tensions and deal with international problems. But events seemed stalemated until Eisenhower decided to follow a more conciliatory policy. Dulles, terminally ill with cancer, had to retire in 1959. Ike invited Khrushchev to the United States, with an Eisenhower visit to Russia to follow. Khrushchev's visit passed pleasantly, including extensive conferences with the President at Camp David, the presidential retreat in Maryland. The two leaders agreed to hold a summit conference in Paris, in May 1960.

But, before the conference could take place, the Russians shot down an American U-2 spy plane over Sverdlovsk, deep in Soviet territory. (This was the same type of spy plane later used over Cuba.) The United States denied that the plane had been on a spy mission until the Russians produced the pilot, who had survived and confessed. Eisenhower then took personal responsibility for the flights, which had started in 1956, stating that he was obligated to keep a close watch on Russia for the sake of American security.

Khrushchev, possibly because of pressure from Kremlin hard-liners and from the Chinese,

The Khrushchev-Eisenhower meeting at Camp David, Maryland, in 1959 produced a temporary thaw in the Cold War. Khrushchev's new policy of peaceful coexistence with the West provided economic competition as an alternative to direct military confrontation in the world.

used the U-2 incident to torpedo the summit conference. He delivered a long anti-American tirade at a news conference and demanded an apology from Eisenhower. The President refused, the proposed meeting evaporated, and Khrushchev canceled Eisenhower's invitation to visit Russia.

Eisenhower thus concluded his foreign policy stewardship on an embarrassing note, although his popularity at home soared after the summit debacle. During Ike's eight years in office, no one had been liberated from the communist yoke—unless one can describe the creation of anticommunist dictatorships in South Vietnam and Guatemala as "liberation." Still, he had preserved peace and put some limits on defense spending. If he had not offered a daring or imaginative approach to the Third World, the Russians and later the Chinese would also learn the difficulty of maintaining relations between the "have" and the "have-not" nations.

Although Eisenhower was not active in the presidential campaign of 1960, his foreign policy came under attack. During his final presidential term, the United States had frequently seemed to be not acting but reacting, often too late, to Soviet initiatives. Democratic candidate John F. Kennedy made shrewd use of this issue in his campaign against Republican Vice President Richard M. Nixon. Kennedy's promise to get the country "moving again" won him a narrow election victory. Americans looked forward to the 1960s, keenly anticipating his fulfillment of that pledge. But when the turbulent sixties had become history, many looked back with nostalgia to the eight relatively quiet years of the Eisenhower era.

SUGGESTED READINGS— CHAPTERS 43-44

Pearl Harbor

Adolph A. Hoehling, *The Week Before Pearl Harbor* (1963); Walter Lord, *Day of Infamy* (1957); Roberta Wohlstetter, *Pearl Harbor: Warning and Decision* (1962).

Interventionists Versus Isolationists

Selig Adler, *The Isolationist Impulse* (1957); James M. Burns, *Roosevelt: The Soldier of Freedom* (1970); Mark Chadwin, *Hawks of World War II* (1968); Wayne S. Cole, *America First: The Battle Against Intervention, 1940–1941* (1953); Robert A. Divine, *The Reluctant Belligerent* (1965); Saul Friedlander, *Prelude to Downfall: Hitler and the United States, 1939–1941* (1967); Townsend Hoopes, *The Devil and John Foster Dulles* (1973); Manfred Jonas, *Isolationism in America, 1935–1941* (1966); Robert E. Osgood, *NATO, the Entangling Alliance* (1962); Martin J. Sherwin, *A World Destroyed: The Atomic Bomb and the Grand Alliance* (1975).

Depression Diplomacy

Dorothy Borg and Shupei Okamoto (eds.), *Pearl Harbor as History: Japanese-American Relations, 1931–1941* (1973); L. Ethan Ellis, *Republican Foreign Policy, 1921–1933* (1968); Lloyd C. Gardner, *Economic Aspects of New Deal Diplomacy* (1964) and *Architects of Illusion: Men and Ideas in American Foreign Policy, 1941–1949* (1970); David Green, *The Containment of Latin America* (1970); William L. Langer and S. Everett Gleason, *The World Crisis and American Foreign Policy* (2 vols., 1952–1953); Bryce Wood, *The Making of the Good Neighbor Policy* (1967); Allen Guttmann, *The Wound in the Heart: America and the Spanish Civil War* (1962); John E. Wiltz, *From Isolation to War, 1931–1941* (1968).

The Cold War

Selig Adler, *The Uncertain Giant: American Foreign Policy Between the Wars* (1965); Gar Alperovitz, *Atomic Diplomacy* (1965); Lynn E. Davis, *The Cold War Begins* (1973); John L. Gaddis, *The United States and the Origins of the Cold War* (1972); Akira Iriye, *The Cold War in Asia* (1974); Walter LaFeber, *America, Russia, and the Cold War* (1967); Joyce and Gabriel Kolko, *The Limits of Power: The World and United States Foreign Policy, 1945–1954* (1972); Gabriel Kolko, *The Politics of War* (1969); Robert J. Maddox, *The New Left and the Origins of the Cold War* (1974); Adam B. Ulam, *The Rivals: America and Russia Since World War II* (1972); Richard Walton, *Henry Wallace, Harry Truman and the Cold War* (1976); Daniel Yergin, *The Shattered Peace* (1977).

The Near East and the Far East

Dorothy Borg, *The United States and the Far Eastern Crisis of 1933–1938* (1964); Herman Finer, *Dulles Over Suez* (1964); Robert L. Neumann, *America Encounters Japan* (1963); John W. Spanier, *The Truman-MacArthur Controversy* (1965); Tang Tsou, *America's Failure in China, 1941–1950* (2 vols., 1963).

Wartime Diplomacy

A. Russell Buchanan, *The United States and World War II* (2 vols., 1964); Diane S. Clemens, *Yalta* (1971); Robert A. Divine, *Roosevelt and World War II* (1969); Herbert Feis, *Churchill, Roosevelt, Stalin*, 2nd edition (1967); Gaddis Smith, *American Diplomacy During the Second World War, 1941–1945* (1965).

45
THE ALGER HISS CASE

A.W.

Whittaker Chambers, star witness in the Hiss case, reflected on the importance of the case some years later and wrote to his children:

Beloved Children,

I am sitting in the kitchen of [our Maryland farm] writing a book. In it I am speaking to you. But I am also speaking to the world. To both I owe an accounting.

It is a terrible book—terrible in what it tells about men, more terrible in what it tells about the world in which you live. It is about what the world calls the Hiss-Chambers case, or even more simply, the Hiss case. It is about a spy case. All the props of an espionage case are there—foreign agents, household traitors, stolen documents, microfilm, furtive meetings, secret hideaways, phony names, an informer, investigations, trials, official justice.

But if the Hiss case were only this, it would not be worth my writing about or your reading about. It would not be what, at the very beginning, I was moved to call it: "a tragedy of history."

For it was more than human tragedy. Much more than Alger Hiss or Whittaker Chambers was on trial in the trials of Alger Hiss. Two faiths were on trial. Human societies, like human beings, live by faith and die when faith dies. At heart, the Great Case was this critical conflict of faiths; that is why it was a great case. On a scale personal enough to be felt by all, but big enough to be symbolic, the two irreconcilable faiths of our time—communism and freedom—came to grips in the persons of two conscious and resolute men. Both had been schooled in the same view of history (the Marxist view). Both were trained by the same party in the same selfless, semisoldierly discipline. Neither would nor could yield without betraying, not himself, but his faith [and] both knew, almost from the beginning, that the Great Case could end only in the destruction of one or both of the contending figures.

My children, as long as you live, the shadow of the Hiss case will brush you. In time you will ask yourselves the question: What was my father?

I will give you an answer: I was a witness. A witness, in the sense that I am using the word, is a man whose life and faith are so completely one that when the challenge comes to step out and testify for his faith, he does so, disregarding all risks, accepting all consequences.

Alger Hiss, chief among those high government officials accused of communist connections, related the circumstances surrounding his involvement in the investigation:

In August 1948 I was living in New York City. For the preceding year and a half I had been president of the Carnegie Endowment for International Peace. To accept that position I had resigned from the State Department, where I was director of the office responsible for proposing and carrying out our policies in the United Nations.

My new work was closely related to what I had been doing in Washington, for the Endowment had decided to concentrate its activities on support of the United Nations as the appropriate means of furthering Andrew Carnegie's aim "to hasten the abolition of international war, the foulest blot upon our civilization."

On Monday, August 2, 1948 a reporter reached me by telephone at my apartment. He told me that, according to information coming from the Committee on Un-American Activities of the House of Representatives, a man named Chambers was going to appear before the committee the next morning and call me a communist. The reporter asked whether I had any comment.

I did not. The untruthful charge of communism had been the lot of many who had been New Deal officials in the Washington of the 1930s and the early 1940s. I had not taken such charges seriously when made against others, and I saw no reason why I or anyone else should pay much attention to a similar fanciful charge that might now be made against me.

The next morning a witness named Whittaker Chambers appeared before the committee and said that years before he had been "attached" to "an underground organization of the United States Communist party" in Washington. He said that I had been a member of that group.

As I knew no one named Whittaker Chambers I chose to make my denials not only to the newspapers but in the same setting where the charges had been made. Therefore, I sent a telegram to the committee that same afternoon saying that I wanted to appear to deny Chambers's charges under oath.

Richard Nixon, then an obscure congressman from California, considered the case the first major crisis he would face while in public life:

My name, my reputation, and my career were ever to be linked with the decisions I made and the actions I took in that case, as a thirty-five-year-old freshman congressman in 1948. Yet, when I was telling my fifteen-year-old daughter, Tricia, one day about the [subject], she interrupted me to ask, "What was the Hiss case?"

I realized for the first time that a whole new generation of Americans was now growing up who had not even heard of the Hiss case. And now, in retrospect, I wonder how many of my own generation really knew the facts and implications of that emotional controversy that rocked the nation. I experienced [the case] not only as an acute personal crisis but as a vivid case study of the continuing crisis of our times, a crisis with which we shall be confronted as long as aggressive international communism is on the loose in the world.

The Hiss case began for me personally when David Whittaker Chambers appeared before the House Committee on Un-American Activities to testify on communist infiltration into the federal government. Never in the stormy history of the committee was a more sensational investigation started by a less impressive witness.

Chambers did not ask to come before the committee so that he could single out and attack Alger Hiss. The committee had subpoenaed him. Both in appearance and in what he had to say, he made very little impression on me or the other committee members. None of us thought his testimony was going to be especially important.

August 3, 1948. Six congressmen took their seats in a nearly empty House committee hearing room: Karl E. Mundt (South Dakota), John McDowell (New Jersey), John E. Rankin (Mississippi), J. Hardin Peterson (Florida), F. Edward Hébert (Louisiana), and Richard M. Nixon (California). Robert E. Stripling, chief investigator of the House Un-American Activities Committee (HUAC), called the sole witness waiting to testify—Whittaker Chambers. Chambers, not an impressive-looking witness, nevertheless had quite good credentials. He had combined two public careers over the previous twenty years, as a journalist and a gifted translator. Educated at Columbia College, he was fluent in several languages and had translated from German into English such popular works as the children's book *Bambi.*

Chambers had been subpoenaed the previous day. In answer to Stripling's questions Chambers said that in the 1920s and 1930s he had been a Communist party member "and a paid functionary of the party." He added:

> In 1937 I repudiated Marx's doctrines and Lenin's tactics. For a number of years I had served in the underground, chiefly in Washington, D.C. The underground group [included] Alger Hiss. The purpose of this group at that time was not primarily espionage. Its original purpose was the communist infiltration of the American government. But espionage was one of its eventual objectives.

On his role as star witness in the case against Alger Hiss, Chambers said, "I have testified against him with remorse and pity, but in the moment of history in which this nation now stands, so help me God, I could not do otherwise."

The committee members questioned Chambers at length about his charges. He pointed out that on several previous occasions in the past decade, he had given similar testimony to high State Department officials and to the FBI. No action, however, had ever been taken against any officials he had named as communists. The witness went on to suggest that he and Hiss had been particularly close:

> MR. STRIPLING: When you left the Communist party in 1937, did you approach any of these seven [alleged underground members] to break with you?
> MR. CHAMBERS: No. The only one of those people whom I approached was Alger Hiss. I went to the Hiss home one evening at what I considered considerable risk to myself and found Mrs. Hiss at home. Mrs. Hiss is also a member of the Communist party. Mr. Hiss came in shortly afterward, and we talked and I tried to break him away from the party. As a matter of fact, he cried when we separated; but when I left him, he absolutely refused to break. I was very fond of Mr. Hiss.

Despite repeated questions by committee members, Chambers stood by his charges and pointedly denied that the alleged communist underground group within the New Deal had ever committed espionage:

> These people were specifically not wanted to act as sources of information. These people were an elite group, which it was believed would rise to positions—as, indeed, some of them did—notably Mr. Hiss—in the government. Their position in the government would be of much more service to the Communist party.

Newsmen present promptly reported the hottest news item in the morning's testimony: a senior editor of *Time* magazine had accused the president of the Carnegie Endowment of being a secret Soviet agent!

August 5, 1948. It was now Alger Hiss's turn to appear before the committee. He offered a striking contrast to his stout and untidy accuser. His handsome face seemed cool and relaxed. His tall, lean body was fitted with elegant, carefully pressed clothes. Furthermore, he displayed none of Chambers's evident nervousness under questioning. Hiss began his testimony with a prepared statement.

> I am not and never have been a member of the Communist party. I do not and never have adhered to the tenets of the Communist party. I am not and never have been a member of any communist-front organization. I have never followed the Communist party line, directly or indirectly. To the best of my knowledge, none of my friends is a communist. To the best of my knowledge I never heard of Whittaker Chambers until 1947, when two representatives of the Federal Bureau of Investigation asked me if I knew him and various other people. I said I did not know Chambers. So far as I know, I have never laid eyes on him, and the statements made about me by Mr. Chambers are complete fabrications. I think my record in the government service speaks for itself.

Committee members questioned Hiss at length about his impressive government career. It included being secretary to the great Chief Justice Oliver Wendell Holmes and assistant counsel to the Senate's Nye Committee (see Chapter 44). He had also served with the solicitor general of the United States and then held high posts in the State Department until he left in 1947 to head the Carnegie Endowment.

Then HUAC members and Stripling questioned Hiss about Chambers's accusations:

> MR. MUNDT: I wonder what possible motive a man who edits *Time* magazine would have for mentioning Alger Hiss in connection with [communist involvement].
>
> MR. HISS: So do I, Mr. Chairman. I have no possible understanding of what could have motivated him.

The committee members recognized by this time that, in Stripling's words, there was "very sharp contradiction" between Hiss and Chambers. One of the two men was a monumental liar. Yet according to Mundt, both men were "witnesses whom normally one would assume to be perfectly reliable. They have high positions in American business or organizational work. They both appear to be honest. They both testify under oath [yet their] stories fail to jibe."

At this point Congressman Nixon suggested that Hiss and Chambers "be allowed to confront each other so that any possibility of a mistake in identity may be cleared up." The other HUAC members ignored Nixon's suggestion, and the questioning continued. After Hiss had concluded his testimony, a large crowd of spectators and reporters rushed up to congratulate him. Nixon later expressed the feelings of most of them—and of most members of HUAC—when he said that a terrible mistake had been made. The committee, he thought, should not have allowed Chambers to testify without first checking into the possibility of such a mistake.

A journalist confirmed this reaction when he asked Hiss: "How is the committee going to dig itself out of this hole?" HUAC was already being criticized widely for its careless handling of hearings. There was even a strong possibility that President Truman, if he won the upcoming 1948 election, would ask Congress to disband the committee. That same morning, while Hiss was denying Chambers's charges before the committee, Truman denounced HUAC's current spy investigation. He called it a red herring organized by the Republican-dominated committee to distract the public from the party's failure to pass an effective domestic economic program.

Thus, from the beginning, the Hiss-Chambers testimony was an issue in national politics, threatening Republican chances in the fall elections. "This case is going to kill the committee," one reporter told Nixon after the morning session had ended, "unless you can prove Chambers's story." The reporter did not know that this was exactly what Nixon intended to do.

Richard Milhous Nixon was then a freshman representative from Southern California. His family, like millions of others, had suffered during the depression. He had worked hard from his earliest years. After largely supporting himself through college and law school, Nixon worked briefly in Washington and then served as a naval officer during World War II. Returning to California, he ran for Congress. In his campaign he charged his Democratic opponent with being a radical and pro-communist. The tactic was successful, and he won the election. During his first year and a half in Congress, he had not acquired any wide reputation beyond his home district. Soon this would change.

Nixon later wrote that when HUAC met privately after Hiss testified, "it was in a virtual state of shock." For his part Nixon argued:

> While it would be virtually impossible to prove that Hiss was or was not a communist—for that would simply be his word against Chambers'—we should be able to establish whether or not the two men knew each other. If Hiss were lying about not knowing Chambers, then he might also be lying about whether or not he was a communist.

Nixon managed to persuade the acting committee chairman, Karl Mundt, to appoint him head of a subcommittee to question Chambers again. This time the session was to be private, with no spectators or press present.

August 7, 1948. The HUAC subcommittee headed by Nixon questioned Chambers secretly in New York City. Nixon asked in what period Chambers had known Hiss as a communist. The witness answered "roughly, between the years 1935 and 1937." Chambers said Hiss knew him not by his real name but "by the party name of Carl." He also asserted that he collected Communist party membership dues from Mr. and Mrs. Hiss. According to Chambers, therefore, Hiss was a member of the communist underground infiltrating the government. Moreover, he was also a dues-paying member of the party itself. At this point Nixon

Alger and Priscilla Hiss at first denied any knowledge of Chambers, then conceded that they knew him under another name when he exposed numerous details of their personal lives to the committee.

plunged into a detailed, rapid-fire series of questions testing whether Hiss had known Chambers. Specifically, Nixon noted, he wanted to know "What should one man know about another if he knew him as well as Chambers claimed to know Hiss?"

Chambers apparently remembered a great deal about Hisses, although as Nixon later admitted: "All of this information might have been obtained by studying Hiss's life without actually knowing him. But some of the answers had a personal ring of truth about them beyond the bare facts themselves." Chambers claimed he had seen the Hisses on numerous occasions. He had been a guest at their home several times. He also seemed to recall a great many details about the Hisses' private lives: nicknames for one another, eating and drinking habits, pets, personal mannerisms, relatives, the exteriors and furniture of their various homes.

Perhaps the most damaging details that Chambers provided about Hiss during the questioning concerned two episodes. One was the transfer of a car Hiss owned to another communist with Chambers or an associate acting as intermediary. The other impressed Nixon because it had a "personal ring of truth." It concerned a hobby the Hisses and Chambers had in common. Both were amateur ornithologists, bird watchers. Chambers testified, "I recall once they saw, to their great excitement, a prothonotary warbler." At this point Congressman McDowell, also a bird lover, interrupted to ask, "A very rare specimen?" Chambers replied. "I never saw one. I am also fond of birds."

The mass of detail concerning the Hisses' lives—birds, cars, homes, nicknames, and the like—restored a faith in Chambers's honesty among committee members.

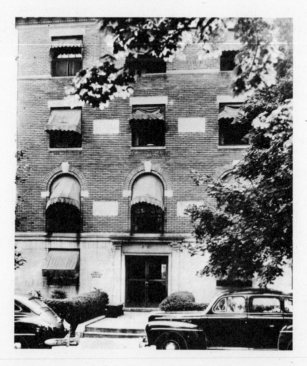

Alger Hiss lived in this apartment house in Washington, D.C., during the period 1934–1935. He admitted that he let Chambers sublet his apartment for a time in 1935.

August 16, 1948. At this closed session of HUAC Hiss seemed under severe strain. The cool composure of his earlier appearance before the committee had given way to a mixture of nervousness and anger. Nixon showed Hiss two pictures of Chambers and asked again whether he knew the man "either as Whittaker Chambers or as Carl or as any other individual." Hiss began to waver, admitting the "the face has a certain familiarity." Chief counsel Stripling and the committee members confronted Hiss with Chambers's detailed claims concerning their friendship. They probed for evidence confirming the *Time* editor's account.

Hiss repeatedly protested the committee's refusal to provide him with a transcript of Chambers's earlier testimony. He became increasingly hostile. He was angry that the committee found it difficult to decide whether truth was on the side of Chambers—"a confessed former communist" and "self-confessed traitor"—or himself, a highly respected man. Stripling, in turn, snapped back sharply that Chambers had "sat there and testified for hours. He said he spent a week in your house, and he just rattled off details like that. He has either made a study of your life in great detail or he knows you."

Moments after this exchange Hiss announced: "I have written a name on this pad in front of me of a person whom I knew in 1933 and 1934 who not only spent some time in my house but sublet my apartment." Hiss was not sure this person—a free-lance writer named George Crosley—was Chambers. He insisted that he had not seen Crosley since 1934. Hiss gave a detailed account of this relationship, claiming to have met Crosley while he was legal counsel to the Nye Committee in 1933.

Crosley, he said, wished to write several magazine articles about the Nye Committee's munitions-industry investigation. Hiss added that he took a liking to the young journalist. When moving his family to a new apartment, Hiss briefly sublet his old apartment to Crosley and his family. At the same time he gave the journalist "an old Ford we had kept for sentimental reasons." Crosley never paid the rent money, according to Hiss. As for the car, "I threw it in along with the rent" because of a desire to "get rid of it." Deciding that he "had been a sucker and [Crosley] was a sort of deadbeat using me for a soft touch," Hiss said he never saw the man again after 1935. (He later changed the date to mid-1936.)

Hiss also remembered taking several drives with Crosley and giving him "loans [he] never paid back." Once Crosley gave him "a rug he said some wealthy patron gave him. I have still got the damned thing." At one point Nixon asked Hiss about his hobbies. When the witness mentioned bird watching, Congressman McDowell asked: "Did you ever see a prothonotary warbler?" "I have right here on the Potomac," Hiss replied, unaware of Chambers's earlier testimony.

Several members of HUAC remarked during Hiss's testimony that either he or Chambers was obviously committing perjury. "Whichever one of you is lying is the greatest actor that America has ever produced," exclaimed Congressman Hébert. Before adjourning the bitterly tense executive session, the committee decided to have Chambers and Hiss

Alger Hiss and Whittaker Chambers silently confront each other before the House Un-American Activities Committee in August 1948. The case helped trigger a Red scare that was to have widespread effects in the fifties.

testify publicly, together, nine days later on August 25. Actually, the pair confronted one another the following day at a hurriedly arranged HUAC meeting in New York City.

August 17, 1948. The session was moved up, according to Nixon, to prevent Hiss from gaining "nine more days to make his story fit the facts." In fact there may have been another motive. The committee was uneasy over the death of Harry Dexter White, a former high Treasury Department official. He had died of a heart attack. White had appeared before a HUAC public hearing a few days earlier to deny charges leveled by Chambers that he had been either a party member or procommunist. He had asked for a postponement because of his bad heart but was refused. White had proved a good witness in his own defense despite the committee's attempt to browbeat him. Nixon and the other HUAC subcommittee members may have hoped to divert public outrage over White's untimely death following this grueling interrogation. They would shift attention to the still active Hiss-Chambers investigation.

Throughout the session, Hiss was extremely irritable, angry, and defensive. He observed that Harry Dexter White's death had upset him greatly, so that testifying would be difficult. He also protested that the committee (despite promises to the contrary) had leaked portions of his previous day's testimony to the press. (Both Nixon and Stripling denied this charge.) Finally Chambers, who had been waiting in an adjoining room, was brought in.

> MR. NIXON: Sit over here, Mr. Chambers. Mr. Chambers, will you please stand? And will you please stand, Mr. Hiss? Mr. Hiss, the man standing here is Mr. Whittaker Chambers. I ask you now if you have ever known that man before.
> MR. HISS: May I ask him to speak? Will you ask him to say something?
> MR. NIXON: Yes. Mr. Chambers, will you tell us your name and your business?
> MR. CHAMBERS: My name is Whittaker Chambers. [At this point, Hiss walked toward Chambers.] I am senior editor of *Time* magazine.
> MR. HISS: Are you George Crosley?
> MR. CHAMBERS: Not to my knowledge. You are Alger Hiss, I believe.
> MR. HISS: I certainly am.
> MR. CHAMBERS: That was my recollection. [Chambers read from a magazine so that Hiss could test his voice pattern.]

Hiss then announced that Chambers was probably the man he knew as Crosley. Nixon and Stripling began a lengthy series of questions comparing Hiss's version of the relationship with Crosley—apartment rental, car transfer, gift of a rug, and other details—with the facts previously supplied by Chambers. Hiss of course denied that Crosley had been more than a casual acquaintance, saying, "He meant nothing to me." Chambers again stressed their common bond, stating, "I was a communist, and you were a communist." At last Hiss acknowledged, "I am perfectly prepared to identify this man as George Crosley." But he denied knowing whether "Crosley" had ever been a communist and pointed out that "it was a quite different atmosphere in Washington then than today." He insisted he had known Crosley only as a journalist.

August 25, 1948. The hearing room was jammed with reporters and spectators. The hearing lasted nine hours. (Hiss testified for six, Chambers for three.) Not only Hiss but all seven other alleged members of the communist cell whom Chambers had named had meanwhile testified before HUAC. Except for Hiss's brother, Donald, who joined Alger in specifically denying any communist associations, the others refused to say whether they had been communists. In their refusals all invoked the Fifth Amendment, which provides protection from possible self-incrimination.

From the start Hiss, accompanied by his lawyer, treated the occasion as a kind of trial. He was convinced that HUAC believed Chambers and wished mainly to prepare evidence for a perjury charge against him. Therefore, Hiss was extremely guarded in responding. He qualified his answers with phrases such as "to the best of my recollection" more than 200 times. On several occasions he accused HUAC of believing Chambers largely for political reasons. The Republican-controlled committee, he claimed, wanted to expose a top civil servant closely identified with

Democratic-sponsored programs like the New Deal, the Yalta agreements, and the United Nations.

The day went badly for Hiss. At the start both Hiss and Chambers were directed to stand. Hiss again identified the *Time* editor as Crosley. Chambers again claimed to have known Hiss in the communist underground. Some of the most damaging passages for Hiss involved the Ford car. He had previously testified turning it over to Crosley along with his apartment.

> MR. NIXON: Did you give Crosley a car?
> MR. HISS: I gave Crosley, according to my best recollection . . .
> MR. NIXON: You certainly can testify yes or no as to whether you gave Crosley a car. How many cars have you given away in your life, Mr. Hiss?
> MR. HISS: I have had only one old car of a financial value of $25 in my life. That is the car I let Crosley use.
> MR. NIXON: My point now is, is your present testimony that you did or did not give Crosley a car?
> MR. HISS: Whether I transferred title to him in a legal, formal sense; whether I gave him the car outright; whether the car came back—I don't know.

Unfortunately for Hiss, a title search by HUAC agents produced evidence that Hiss had transferred the car on July 23, 1936, to William Rosen, the alleged communist about whom Chambers had testified earlier. The Hiss signature on the document had been notarized by W. Marvin Smith. He was a lawyer with the Justice Department. Smith told HUAC that he knew Hiss and that Hiss had personally signed the transfer in his presence. (Strangely, Smith fell or jumped to his death soon after he testified.)

Hiss now counterattacked. He denounced HUAC's investigation as a political attack on liberal Democrats. He reviewed his fifteen years of impressive public service and named as references for his achievements, personal character, and loyalty thirty-four prominent public figures. Nixon termed this an effort by Hiss to prove his "innocence by association," an ironic reference considering HUAC's past reputation for trying to show a witness' guilt by association.

During this day's testimony the two major witnesses reversed their previous roles completely. Chambers was now a cool, placid witness, calmly answering every question put to him. Hiss testified nervously and emotionally. But Hiss emphasized that some of Chambers's most obvious statements about him were incorrect. Thus the Hisses were not teetotalers and Hiss did attend church. Hiss's stepson was not a "puny little boy." Despite these and other errors about the Hisses, Chambers still displayed remarkable familiarity with their private life.

Hiss offered some explanation for this apparent familiarity. He claimed that Chambers, with access to *Time*'s excellent research records, could have discovered most of the personal material on Hiss in such publications as *Who's Who*. Congressman Hébert retorted: "Nobody could have read in *Who's Who* that you found a rare bird [the prothonotary warbler]." Hiss responded that he had "told many, many people." But this did not persuade the committee.

For his part, Chambers denied that he harbored any secret reason for wishing to ruin Hiss, as the latter charged. He went so far as to call Alger Hiss "the closest friend I ever had in the Communist party." Fighting back tears, he said softly:

> I am [not] working out some old grudge, or motives of revenge or hatred. I do not hate Mr. Hiss. We were close friends, but we are caught in a tragedy of history. Mr. Hiss represents the concealed enemy against which we are all fighting, and I am fighting.

By the time HUAC finally adjourned its August 25th session at 8 P.M., Alger Hiss had been placed on the defensive. Three days later HUAC issued an interim report. It called Hiss's testimony "vague and evasive," Chambers's "forthright and emphatic." In the committee's opinion "the verifiable portions of Chambers's testimony have stood up strongly; the verifiable portions of Hiss's testimony have been badly shaken."

The next act in this "tragedy of history" took place on a national radio show, *Meet the Press.* There, Chambers charged that "Alger Hiss was a communist and may be now." Several weeks passed without Hiss responding. His supporters grew impatient. "Mr. Hiss has created a situation," complained the liberal Washington *Post,* "in which he is obliged to put up or shut up." Finally, on September 27, Hiss brought suit against Chambers for slander. By then the election campaign was in full swing. HUAC members (including Nixon) had returned to their various states. An exciting four-way battle for the presidency crowded "the Hiss-Chambers case" off the front pages.

Nixon himself faced no reelection problem. He had won his district's Democratic *and* Republican nominations, then possible under California's cross-filing system that allowed candidates to enter both primaries. He did campaign for other Republicans, however, regaling crowds with a dramatic account of the Hiss investigation.

In the presidential election Truman ran against Governor Thomas E. Dewey of New York, who avoided the anticommunist issue because he believed no case could be made against Truman as "soft" on communism. After a hard-fought campaign Truman won a startling reelection victory. The Democrats, moreover, regained control of Congress.

Prospects for continuing the Hiss-Chambers inquiry looked bleak, since Truman still considered it a political red herring directed against his administration. After the election, many in Washington thought the President would try to abolish HUAC. The Hiss case itself dropped from public attention and went into its legal phase—a slander suit.

Deeply depressed by Truman's victory, Chambers even contemplated suicide (an action he considered at other critical points in the case). He also fretted at the possibility that a Justice Department controlled by Democrats might indict him, not Hiss, for perjury. Pressed for written proof of his charges and under severe emotional strain, Chambers (according to his own account) took a mid-November trip to Brook-

A smiling Alger Hiss shakes hands with President Truman at a conference to establish the United Nations. Because Hiss was a New Deal liberal, his fall from grace carried the implication that the government was permeated with communists.

lyn. There he visited a nephew with whom, he claimed, he had left a package ten years earlier. The nephew drew from a disused dumbwaiter shaft the "proof" Chambers needed—a dusty envelope containing papers and microfilms that (Chambers later insisted) he had forgotten about until the libel suit jogged his memory.

The papers were dated from early 1937 through April 1938. If genuine, they indicated that Hiss had lied in claiming not to have seen "Crosley" or Chambers after mid-1936. Furthermore, the papers had apparently been typed on an old Woodstock typewriter that belonged to the Hisses until 1937 or 1938. (The exact date that the Hisses got rid of the machine would later become a major point at issue.) Chambers hurried back to his farm with this evidence and hid the microfilms. On November 17, he submitted some of the material to Hiss's attorneys at a

Under pressure to provide HUAC with all the evidence against Hiss in his possession, Chambers led two HUAC investigators to the pumpkin patch on his farm (an arrow identifies the patch) and retrieved the microfilms from a hollowed-out pumpkin where he had hidden them earlier that day.

pretrial hearing—sixty-five pages of copied State Department documents, four memos in Alger Hiss's handwriting, and the envelope in which they had been hidden for a decade.

Chambers now claimed that he had tried until then to "shield" Alger and Priscilla Hiss from exposure as Soviet spies. But because of the pressures imposed by Hiss's libel suit, he had to reveal "that Alger Hiss had also committed espionage." Chambers then testified to Hiss's attorneys about a new claim. He alleged that he was a courier for Hiss while the latter stole secret State Department documents. Some of these Mrs. Hiss had retyped. The *Time* editor now asserted that he had actually left the party in April 1938 rather than in 1937, since some of the stolen documents dated from the later period. Hiss vigorously denied this new charge. His lawyers grilled both Chambers and his wife about the numerous contradictions between his previous and his new testimony.

The typed documents were explosive evidence. The Hiss and Chambers lawyers immediately turned them over to Alex Campbell, head of the Justice Department's Criminal Division. Campbell warned both parties to the slander suit not to discuss the envelope's contents (neither Campbell nor Hiss then knew of the microfilms) until the material had been investigated. But then a story in the pro-Hiss Washington

Post indicating that the Justice Department might drop its investigation of Hiss spurred Nixon into action. Before leaving for a Caribbean vacation, Nixon signed a subpoena ordering Chambers to provide HUAC with any further evidence he had relating to his charges against Hiss.

On December 2 HUAC staff members served the subpoena. A few days earlier, because of rumors that Hiss investigators were prowling around his farm, Chambers had taken the microfilms from his bedroom and hidden them in his pumpkin patch. Now he went to the hollowed-out pumpkin, removed the microfilms, and handed them to the HUAC representatives. "I think this is what you are looking for," he said. Within hours the press began headlining Chambers's mysterious "pumpkin papers" (actually not papers but microfilms). That same day Hiss confirmed that Chambers had turned over the typed stolen documents on November 17.

The Justice Department finally swung into action. Both Chambers and Hiss were called several times, beginning on December 6, to testify before a New York federal grand jury. After a hurried and well-publicized return from his Caribbean vacation, Nixon led HUAC in a new series of hearings. At one of these new sessions Assistant Secretary of State John Peurifoy (in charge of security matters) testified. He declared that the Soviet Union or any other foreign country possessing these microfilmed documents would have been able to break all the secret State Department codes then in use.

Clearly, the Republican-controlled HUAC, which had no legal authority to put Hiss on trial, was competing with the Democratic-controlled Justice Department for jurisdiction in what was now a criminal case. Nixon frankly stated that his committee "did not trust the Justice Department to prosecute the case with the vigor it deserved." On December 9 Truman again labeled the case a red herring. On December 10 Chambers resigned from *Time*.

On December 13 the FBI produced for the grand jury several old letters typed by Priscilla Hiss on the same machine that had typed the State Department documents. That day, Alger Hiss left the Carnegie Endowment on a three-month paid leave of absence. He never returned. The New York grand jury indicted Hiss on two counts of perjury on December 15. The first was for claiming he had not stolen State Department records and given them to Chambers. The second was for swearing he had not seen Chambers after January 1, 1937. Only the statute of limitations and the absence of witnesses who could back up the charge kept the grand jury from charging Hiss with espionage.

The former State Department official underwent two trials. The first ended on July 8, 1949, with a deadlocked jury that had voted 8 to 4 to convict Hiss. The prosecutor at both trials, Thomas Murphy, presented several types of evidence to prove the government's perjury charges. These included evidence that the two men knew one another more intimately (after 1936) than Hiss admitted, that Hiss had been a communist, and that Hiss had stolen the State Department documents. The weakest link in the government's case concerned Hiss's alleged communism. Only one witness, an ex-communist named Hede Massing, confirmed Chambers's claim that Hiss had been a party member. Her testimony was challenged, however, by a defense witness who swore that Mrs. Massing had been confused about the question of Hiss's involvement when discussing it at a party.

At both trials Chambers repeated the story he first told to Hiss's attorneys in November 1948 during pretrial hearings involving the libel suit. According to this story, Hiss had been recruited for espionage by Chambers's communist superior during the fall of 1936. Chambers said he served as Hiss's courier until April 1938. Then he broke from the party. (He previously testified to leaving the party months earlier.) At this point he turned the final batch of stolen documents over to his nephew in Brooklyn for safekeeping.

The microfilms and retyped State Department messages were at the heart of the case against Hiss. Prosecutor Murphy called them "immutable" witnesses, therefore presumably reliable ones. At neither trial did Hiss's attorneys challenge the testimony of an FBI expert who testified that a comparison of typing on the documents with letters written by Mrs. Hiss on the same machine established her as the typist. Nor did they challenge the argument that the documents had been typed on a Woodstock machine belonging to Hiss. Hiss did claim he had given the machine away sometime before the material was typed. But this claim was never proved conclusively in court, one way or the other. (Moreover, three defense experts confirmed that the stolen documents had been typed on the Hiss Woodstock.)

The jury at the second trial convicted Hiss of perjury on both counts. After that, Hiss's lawyers began arguing that the typewriter itself was a false piece of evidence constructed by either Chambers or the FBI. They also argued that the typed documents had been prepared only to implicate Hiss. (This argument, of course, did not affect the microfilmed documents or the handwritten Hiss memos.) Since the defense had actually located the typewriter in question prior to the first trial, Hiss's supporters began arguing that the FBI had somehow gained possession of the machine earlier, then "planted" it on the defense. This remains unproven even today, though those who argue that Alger Hiss was innocent tend to assume some degree of FBI involvement. The FBI files on the case, recently opened to researchers, failed to bear out this charge. They show that the FBI conducted a widespread, but unsuccessful, hunt for the Woodstock and that it was seriously embarrassed when the defense turned up the machine.

At the Hiss trials themselves, the defense paraded a distinguished group of Americans before the jury to testify to Hiss's outstanding career and good character. At the same time, they tried to throw doubt on Chambers's reliability. They placed a psychiatrist on the stand who labeled Chambers "a psychopathic personality" with irrational hostilities.

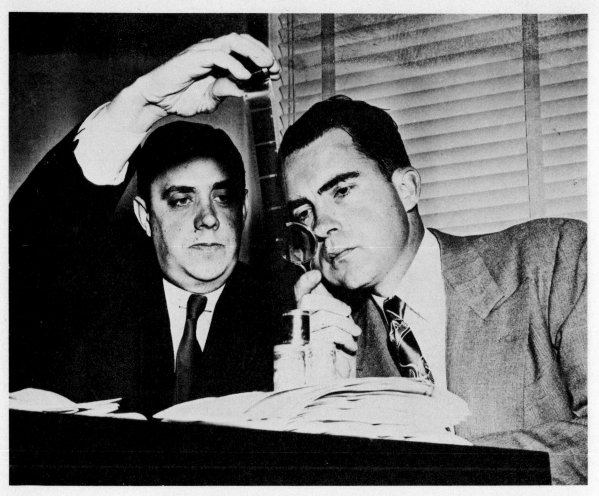

Richard Nixon and chief investigator Robert Stripling are shown examining microfilms of secret State Department documents, the most damaging evidence against Hiss.

Prosecutor Murphy ridiculed these defense efforts at both trials. He pointed repeatedly to the evidence that Hiss's lawyers could never adequately explain—the stolen government documents. The twelve jurors at the second trial, overlooking Chambers's minor inconsistencies, all believed Murphy. On January 21, 1950, they found Hiss guilty. Later appeals to overturn the verdict were rejected, and Hiss served forty-four months in prison. He emerged in November 1954, still proclaiming his innocence.

Hiss, now a convicted perjurer, did not return to the Carnegie Endowment, of course. He has had a series of obscure and ill-paying business jobs. He has written his version of the episode and worked continuously to revive public interest in the case. (The Watergate crisis revived attention in the episode because of its link to Richard Nixon.)

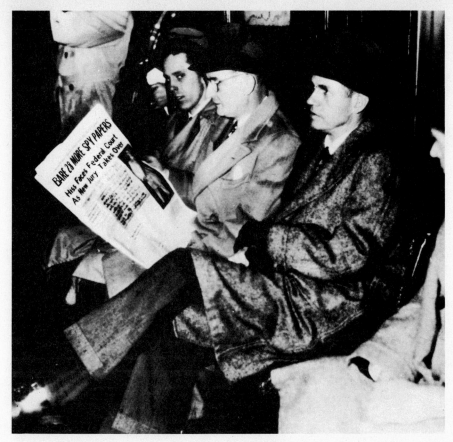

A withdrawn and beaten Alger Hiss sits on a New York subway trying to ignore headlines telling of his indictment the day before on perjury charges. He was eventually convicted.

Chambers returned to his Maryland farm, did special assignments as a journalist, and wrote his memoirs. In 1961 he died from a heart attack.

Nixon won a Senate seat in 1950, largely because of his efforts in the Hiss case. He went on to become Vice President in 1953. The House Committee on Un-American Activities temporarily regained its public prestige as a result of Hiss's conviction. Truman abandoned his effort to abolish it.

Less than three weeks after Hiss's conviction, a then obscure Wisconsin senator announced: "I have here in my hand a list of 205 known to be members of the Communist party and who, nevertheless are still working and shaping the policy of the State Department." With Joseph R. McCarthy's speech a new era of anticommunist politics in the United States acquired its leader—and its name.

46
AFFLUENCE AND ANTICOMMUNISM
A.W.

The depression ended—with a bang, not a whimper—when Japan attacked Pearl Harbor. The war years changed the lives of the people who were later to become key figures in the Hiss case very little. Alger Hiss remained a top official of the State Department, while Whittaker Chambers rose in importance on *Time* magazine. But Richard Nixon saw his life altered dramatically. Although reared as a Quaker, Nixon yearned for some role in the war effort. He first joined a new government agency, the Office of Price Administration (OPA), created to regulate wartime price levels. Then the young lawyer joined the navy and served on various Pacific islands, handling duties as a supply officer.

Nixon returned to a restless year of private practice in California before winning his first race for Congress in 1946. The war had clearly opened up significant career possibilities for Nixon, as it did for millions of his contemporaries. A nation still climbing uncertainly out of the depression in 1941 had regained, by war's end, most of its pre-1930 affluence and self-confidence.

THE WORLD WAR II HOME FRONT

Almost 4 million Americans were still unemployed on the eve of Pearl Harbor. Other millions still labored at government-sponsored jobs for such agencies as the WPA. Some 40 percent of America's families lived below the $1,500 annual minimum income needed for a family of four. (This amounted to only $30 a week to cover food, housing, clothing, and everything else!) Over 7½ million workers earned salaries below the legal minimum wage of 40 cents an hour.

Still, there were many signs of change by 1941. The economy, thanks largely to $8 billion spent on defense production, was now strong, almost booming. Of the country's 134 million people, one-third held civilian jobs while one-tenth worked on defense contracts at top wages. Farm prices had reached a new high in 1940, as had average hourly wages in the two dozen major defense-oriented industries.

Moreover, on the eve of war, most Americans supported the pro-Allied policies of the Roosevelt administration. But they did not expect a war to improve their condition much. Twelve years of depression had left the country somewhat doubtful of future prospects and skeptical of idealistic visions.

Bolstering Morale The government went to great lengths to counteract pessimism and ensure the cooperative involvement of most Americans in the war effort. The Office of Civilian Defense (OCD) sponsored various programs to stimulate patriotism. These included "town meetings" throughout the country. Their basic objective was "that of awakening all the elements of the community to their responsibilities for total participation for victory." Patriotic sentiments were also aroused by stage, screen, and radio productions, all of which tried to bolster national morale, particularly in the first year, when news from the fronts was often grim.

Usually such entertainment aimed at stirring up hatred toward the enemy, Germans and Japanese. Seldom did it assert any positive American war goals. Movie heroes such as John Wayne and radio idols like Jack Armstrong ("the all-American boy") battled tirelessly against Nazi saboteurs and Japan's "fanatical yellow hordes." American advertising encouraged sales of government war bonds or warned defense workers and soldiers to beware of possible spies in their midst. ("Loose lips sink ships!") Such efforts were remarkably successful in boosting home-front efforts.

Politically, the job of defending the country against attack had turned bipartisan even before the war began. A number of leading Republicans accepted Roosevelt's invitation in 1940 to help meet the impending emergency.

Mobilizing the Economy   Conversion to military preparedness had preceded Pearl Harbor. Total mobilization of both the American people and their economy, however, advanced swiftly after December 1941. An army of 1,600,000 existed then. By war's end the number of troops who had served or were serving in the army, navy, marines, air corps (then still part of the army), and coast guard exceeded 15 million—including 200,000 women.

The home front resembled one vast factory. A few statistics tell much of the story. Many Amer-

icans felt that Roosevelt was being unrealistic when in 1942 he called for an output of 60,000 planes, 45,000 tanks, and 8 million tons of shipping. Yet in 1944 the nation's factory workers—keeping plants open 24 hours daily on continuous shifts—produced over 96,000 planes. By 1945 the country's naval yards had turned out over 55 million tons of merchant shipping and 71,000 warships. Federal purchases grew from $6 billion in 1940 to $89 billion by 1944. During the first six months of the war alone, the government placed over $100 billion worth of war contracts with private industry.

Total federal spending during the three and a half years of war amounted to over $320 billion, an amount twice as large as the total of all previous spending from 1789 to 1941! The government financed this vast increase through higher taxes on both corporations and individuals. Even after taxes, though, corporate profits doubled between

Significant numbers of women belonged to the labor force that produced the winning margin in World War II, a continuous flow of planes from American factories.

1939 and 1944 (reaching $10 billion that year). War production clearly finished the job that the New Deal had begun of ending the country's economic depression. Much of the government's revenues came from taxes or public borrowing through war bonds. A still higher percentage came from running huge budget deficits throughout the war. The American national debt grew to $247 billion by 1945, nearly six times that of 1941.

Meanwhile, prosperity returned to the United States and unemployment vanished. Many women took full-time factory jobs to meet the shortage of labor created by the armed forces' need for men. Public confidence in the business community increased, replacing the widespread hostility apparent during the depression decade.

Rationing and Inflation Full employment during the war gave millions of Americans bigger bank accounts. It put more money in their pockets, though they had less to spend it on. "Disposable income" (income after taxes) increased from $67 billion in 1939 to $140 billion by 1945. Consumer spending alone rose from $62 billion in 1939 to $106 billion by 1945. Wartime rationing and shortages of consumer goods, as well as higher wages and profits, led to higher inflationary prices for those goods and services that were available.

The government tried to control inflation and regulate prices—which rose an average of 2 percent monthly during the war—by establishing official wage and price levels. It set ceilings on legal prices through OPA. Richard Nixon remembered his experiences in this agency as a time when he "became more conservative [and] greatly disillusioned about bureaucracy." Yet OPA did succeed in holding down runaway inflation throughout the war years, despite an enormous increase in the disposable income of most Americans.

On the nation's farms, conditions improved at this time, too. Farm income doubled during the war because of the insatiable demand for agricultural products by the armed forces and civilians alike. Despite a decline in the number of farm laborers, increased mechanization helped double farm output during the war years, 1941 to 1945. Legislation by powerful farm-bloc Democrats brought farmers' incomes to an all-time high.

Average weekly earnings among industrial workers also increased by 100 percent during the war years. Both the AFL and the CIO made "no-strike" pledges. But the number of strikes increased as prices and profits continued rising at a level greater than wage increases. Union membership increased from 10 to 15 million. The demand for factory workers led to a reduction of total unemployment from 5.6 percent of the work force in 1941 to 1 percent by war's end. More important, the war guaranteed the future of industrial unionism, which had grown with New Deal encouragement during the depression.

The wartime domestic economy lay in the hands of a triple alliance of big government, big business, and big labor. The three differed on specific policies. But each accepted the need for negotiated settlements with the other two. Wartime cooperation among union leaders, government officials, and corporation heads—all eager to maximize production for the war effort—shaped a new industrial state in America.

The Atomic Bomb The period's single most significant scientific and military achievement, which would notably affect postwar American policy, was the development of the atomic bomb. Wartime scientific research was placed in the hands of an Office of Scientific Research and Development (OSRD), headed by Vannevar Bush and James Conant. The United States benefited greatly from the work of refugee scientists, many of them Jews who had fled Nazi Germany or fascist Italy. Albert Einstein, Leo Szilard, and Enrico Fermi led this intellectual migration. It affected not only science but many other aspects of American life and culture.

At a cost of billions, a massively organized project was undertaken to develop an atomic bomb before the Germans, who were working on a similar project. The secret program, known as the Manhattan Project, involved scientists, technicians, and industrial workers. It included design laboratories at Columbia University, the University of Chicago, the University of California at Berkeley, and—most important—at a central headquarters near Los Alamos, New Mexico. There, under the leadership of physicist J. Robert Oppenheimer, the first atomic device was assembled. It was detonated on July 16, 1945, at Alamorgordo, New Mexico.

The bombs dropped subsequently at Hiroshima and Nagasaki led directly to Japan's defeat in August 1945. By then the United States had sent over $350 billion to achieve victory in World War II — apart from the tremendous cost in American casualties.

The Relocation Policy The country paid not only a high cost in human life but also a certain moral cost for its victory. For the Japanese attack on Pearl Harbor led to what the American Civil Liberties Union called "the worst single invasion of citizens' liberties" during the war. This was the confining in relocation centers of 112,000 Japanese Americans (more than half of them born in the United States). After Pearl Harbor, white residents of west coast states feared an internal threat from the Japanese Americans. They appealed to President Roosevelt to remove the entire community from the west coast.

Actually, there was no evidence whatsoever of sabotage. But officials such as California's attorney general Earl Warren (later a great civil libertarian as chief justice of the United States) urged their evacuation to protect the region's civil defense. Bowing to these pressures, President Roosevelt signed an executive order in February 1942 authorizing the relocation of Japanese Americans to nine inland centers. Driven from their homes into what were virtually an American version of concentration camps, these loyal Japanese Americans needlessly suffered loss of their freedom, homes, land, and dignity. This unfair treatment did not deter over 33,000 Japanese Americans from enlisting and fighting bravely for the United States. Although the Supreme Court upheld the relocation policy, the government later paid compensation to the displaced for their property losses.

Japanese American children are shown saluting the flag in their San Francisco elementary school two days before their relocation to internment camps.

THE TRUMAN YEARS

Franklin D. Roosevelt, reelected for an unprecedented fourth term in 1944, died in April 1945. He left to Vice President Harry S. Truman the responsibility for governing the world's most militarily powerful and economically prosperous nation. On learning of Roosevelt's death, Truman quite understandably felt "as though the moon and all the stars and all the planets have fallen on me."

Harry Truman was an accidental President. Roosevelt had chosen him for the vice-presidential nomination in 1944 almost as an afterthought. Truman had little formal preparation for holding the office. While Vice President, for example, he was not even told about the atomic bomb. Less than four months after taking office, he had to make the fateful decision whether to drop it on Japan.

A Missouri farm boy who served in World War I, Truman entered politics as a member of the notorious Pendergast machine that ran Kansas City politics. Although personally honest, he served this corrupt political machine loyally. Truman rose through its ranks and was first elected to the Senate in 1934.

Several factors helped Truman obtain the vice presidency in 1944. Hard-working and extremely liberal (by Missouri's border-state standards), he had fought the Ku Klux Klan in his home state, battled loyally for New Deal programs, and served with distinction as chairman of a Senate committee that investigated national defense spending.

Many of Truman's most pressing concerns during his first months in office were vitally important decisions on war policy and postwar settlements (see Chapter 44). Of immediate concern to the new President, once Japan surrendered, was the fact that the men overseas wanted to come home quickly. ("No Boats, No Votes," was the gist of GI mail.) Congress and President Truman responded by rapidly demobilizing (releasing from duty) the great bulk of American armed forces. By mid-1946 an army and air force that had numbered over 8 million troops the previous year was reduced to less than 2 million. A navy of almost 4 million was cut back to less than 1 million. Total military strength fell to 1½ million by mid-1947, and Congress had ordered even this number reduced to under 1 million by January 1948.

Postwar Economic Policy Congress allowed the 1940 draft to expire in mid-1947. Cold War military planning focused more and more on the defense shield provided by America's monopoly of nuclear weapons. Furthermore, the discharged servicemen found that Congress had provided more generously for them than for the Bonus Marchers. Under the Servicemen's Readjustment Act (which most people called the GI Bill of Rights), more than $13.5 billion was spent on veterans over the next decade. This money went not only for college educations and vocational training but also for special unemployment insurance (for a year) to smooth the return to civilian life. Funds were spent as well to provide medical services at veterans' hospitals and rehabilitation programs for the wounded. Finally, low-interest loans were made available to veterans to start businesses and to buy or build homes. This was particularly helpful because of the housing shortage at war's end.

There was widespread fear among the public, and many economists too, that without war spending the country would suffer a major postwar recession. A Council of Economic Advisers, created by Truman's Maximum Employment Act, committed Washington for the first time to using the nation's resources to ensure "maximum employment, production, and purchasing power." By mid-1946 Congress had also ended most wartime price and wage controls, cut taxes over $6 billion, and begun to tackle the massive problems of reconversion to a peacetime economy. These efforts were hindered by a wave of strikes and runaway inflation.

Auto workers struck for 113 days beginning in November 1945, and miners for a shorter period in mid-1946. Truman's decision to have the soft coal mines run by the government (control that continued until June 1947) lost him much support from businessmen. A railroad strike was settled the same month the mines were seized (May 1946) only when Truman threatened to take over the railroads, too. More strikes occurred in 1946 than in any other single year in American history. Over 4,750,000 workers were involved.

Truman faced a hostile congressional coalition of Republicans and antiadministration Southern Democrats in every area of his domestic program after Republicans won control of both Houses in the 1946 congressional election. This coalition responded to the strikes and general unrest among American unions with a tough law (passed over Truman's veto) regulating the labor movement. The Taft-Hartley Act of 1947 limited the President to seeking an eighty-day injunction to stop any strike that endangered "national health or safety" (rather than taking an extreme step like running an industry under government supervision). The new law also (1) required unions to accept a sixty-day "cooling-off" period before striking, (2) outlawed the closed shop, (3) restricted union involvement in political campaigns, and (4) required that union officials (but not company officers) take an oath that they were not communists.

Congress also passed the Twenty-second Amendment to the Constitution limiting future Presidents (although not Truman) to two full terms. This was a direct slap at FDR's four-term success. In various ways the Eightieth Congress prevented Truman from getting his own legislative program.

The Fair Deal The President called his program the Fair Deal. He viewed it essentially as an effort to continue the social welfare policies of Roosevelt's New Deal. Thus, soon after he took office, Truman had proposed to Congress legislation that would guarantee full employment, vastly expand public housing, and raise farm price supports. Other proposals were to continue a permanent Fair Employment Practices Committee (FEPC) to block discrimination against blacks and other minorities, nationalize atomic energy, and increase the minimum wage. A few parts of the program passed quickly. Congress approved a civilian Atomic Energy Commission in mid-1946 that took control of peaceful uses of atomic energy. Most of the program, however, was blocked by the same Republican–Southern Democratic coalition that opposed Truman on so many issues.

Truman went on the offensive in 1948. He proposed not only the enactment of his entire Fair Deal program but also a set of civil rights proposals to guarantee first-class citizenship for black Americans. These proposals included a permanent FEPC, measures against lynching and the poll tax, plus other laws that would ensure blacks full federal protection of their civil and political rights. After his renomination by a divided Democratic convention in 1948, Truman called Congress into special session to dramatize its opposition to his programs. He requested repeal of the Taft-Hartley Act and passage of civil rights, housing, health, and Social Security programs. Congress rejected it all.

This rejection allowed Truman to conduct his successful "whistle-stop" campaign (see Chapter 45) against what he called the "do-nothing Eightieth Congress." The public liked Truman's new stance as an aggressive, "give-em-hell" fighter. The Man from Independence scored the most smashing upset in American presidential history. The Democrats also recaptured both houses of Congress.

Still dominated in large measure by the Republican–Southern Democratic coalition, the new Eighty-first Congress blocked Truman's farm program and his request for a permanent FEPC.

The culmination of Harry Truman's 1948 whistle-stop campaign was this triumphant pose before a crowd at St. Louis's Union Station. He called the headline "one for the books."

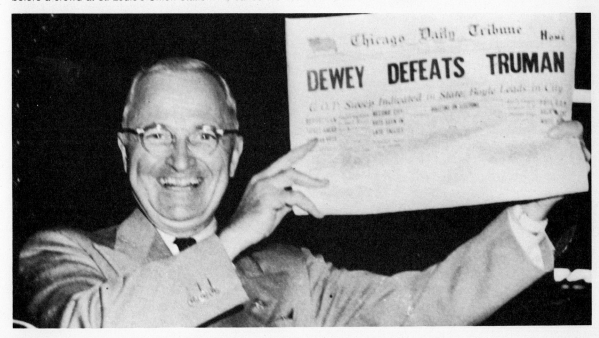

But it did pass a major low-income housing and urban-renewal program, raised the minimum wage, abolished segregation in the armed forces, and enlarged existing conservation programs. All in all, it enacted more liberal legislation than any Congress since that of 1937–1938.

The onset of the Korean War in June 1950, however, diverted the primary attention of Congress and the administration from home-front reforms to foreign policy. Little important domestic legislation passed in Truman's final two years in office. His energy between 1950 and 1952 was spent primarily fighting the Korean War and improving American security against communism abroad. Ironically, he also had to defend his administration against allegations of "softness" toward communism at home.

McCARTHYISM: "THE SECOND RED SCARE"

Truman reacted angrily whenever Republicans charged that his and Roosevelt's administration had "sold out" Eastern Europe and China to communist control. To Republican cries of "Twenty Years of Treason," Truman replied that he had welded the free nations of Western Europe into military and political alliances against the Soviet Union's expansionism. The Truman Doctrine, the Marshall Plan, and NATO had largely restored European stability. China had been lost—not for lack of American help—but through Chiang Kai-shek's political and military weakness.

Elsewhere, American troops (along with UN forces) defended South Korea against communist attack. Further, the Seventh Fleet prevented communist invasion of the Chinese Nationalists' last stronghold, the island of Taiwan. To achieve this global strategy of containment, the Truman administration had increased defense expenditures from $13 billion in 1949 to $22.5 billion the next year and $44 billion by 1951. Military expenses absorbed two-thirds of the federal budget in 1952, up from only one-third in 1950. In the process of increasing defense spending so swiftly and enormously, the country's gross national product

rose from $264 billion in 1950 to $339 billion by 1952. A continued high level of economic prosperity was almost assured.

None of these facts, however, silenced Republican critics. They continued to attack Truman and Secretary of State Dean Acheson. Nor were Republican anticommunist investigators like those on HUAC happy with Truman's efforts to rid the federal government of suspected subversives. The President, despite assurances from the FBI that the problem was under adequate control, had issued an executive order in May 1947 setting up a Loyalty Review Board. Its purpose was to check every federal employee and dismiss any found questionable "on reasonable grounds for belief in disloyalty." Over the next five years, such loyalty boards investigated over 6½ million government employees and their families. Of this number only 490 were dismissed on loyalty grounds. The boards uncovered no cases of espionage, but the investigations wrecked the careers of many loyal government officials accused without proof.

Prosecution of Leading Communists Under mounting pressure from Congress after Alger Hiss's indictment, Truman prosecuted the eleven leaders of the American Communist party under the 1940 Smith Act. They were indicted for organizing a group advocating the overthrow of the American government by force. The Communist party leaders were convicted in 1949, and other prosecutions of communists began, despite the fact that prosecutors never claimed they had uncovered an *actual* conspiracy to overthrow the government. The Supreme Court upheld the convictions in 1951. Through such actions Truman contributed to a growing climate of American fear over communism.

No single episode did more to spread this Red scare than the indictment and eventual conviction of Alger Hiss. The fact that Dean Acheson and other high administration officials testified on behalf of Hiss lent a touch of credibility to charges that the Democrats, under Roosevelt and Truman, were soft on left-wingers.

At this point Senator Joseph McCarthy began a series of speeches. It mattered little that McCarthy's figures for "known communists" in

To Senator Joseph McCarthy communism was a nationwide threat. He accused the Democrats of communist sympathies and also charged that the Protestant clergy had been infiltrated.

the State Department varied from speech to speech. Britain had just arrested communist Klaus Fuchs for atomic espionage; the new communist government had full control of the Chinese mainland; and Americans were jittery over possible new Russian moves against Berlin. Accordingly, many people were prepared to believe that something dire was about to befall the United States. McCarthy himself never actually located a single "known communist."

McCarthy's charges offended several Republicans in Congress, including Senators Margaret Chase Smith of Maine and Ralph Flanders of Vermont, who both denounced him publicly. Yet he was extremely useful to his party, despite his wild charges of disloyalty and communist activity in government. A significant number of Americans approved of McCarthy's relentless attacks. McCarthy's method, like that of most successful demagogues, was simple. He used "the multiple untruth," statements so complex and many-sided

that they were extremely difficult to deny intelligently.

Flow of Political Melodrama Among those McCarthy tried to smear were George Marshall (author of the Marshall Plan), Philip Jessup (later chief UN delegate under President Nixon), Secretary of State Dean Acheson, and even President Truman himself. In short, McCarthy turned this tactic of "red-baiting" against the Democrats. For a time, he had remarkable success. Little about his methods was new. He used the tactics of HUAC and even borrowed Nixon's files on the subject. From these he wrung a constant flow of political melodrama out of the noisy pursuit of "secret conspirators" and (occasionally) admitted communists. There were, after all, some American communists, even a few who had reached middle-level posts in the Roosevelt years.

The onset of the Korean War in June 1950 gave McCarthy and other Republican opponents of Truman additional ammunition. If communists were killing our soldiers in Korea, many Americans reasoned, why give possible reds the benefit of any doubt in this country? Loyalty oaths and security investigations soon involved millions of people in industries and labor unions, public schools and universities, as well as in government jobs at every level.

There is much irony in the fact that Truman spent his last two years in office using American and UN forces against communist aggression in Korea while trying to prove that he was not a dupe or agent of communism at home. Truman's attorney general carried on a vigorous prosecution of alleged communist agents. In April 1951 Julius and Ethel Rosenberg were convicted of having directed a spy ring that transmitted to the Russians diagrams and other data on the firing mechanism and internal structure of the atomic bomb. According to the Rosenbergs' accusers, this information had speeded up by years completion of the Soviet atomic bomb, first exploded in 1949. The Rosenbergs received the death sentence, while their accomplices were sentenced to long prison terms.

Such episodes persuaded Congress that tighter laws were needed to protect the country against domestic communists. So it passed the McCarran Internal Security Act in 1950. This law established a Subversive Activities Control Board to keep track of communist activities in America. The act made membership in the Communist party illegal and also ordered communist organizations to register with the attorney general. Other provisions barred former members of totalitarian groups from the United States and forbade communists to hold federal office or receive passports. Many of these provisions have since been declared unconstitutional by the Supreme Court. But the act passed by a two-thirds majority over Truman's veto, which showed how politically potent the anticommunist issue had become.

"Korea, Communism, and Corruption" The Democratic administration was very unpopular by 1952. Many voters accepted McCarthy's reckless charges against Truman and his associates, despite the Democrats' strong commitment to Cold War foreign policies. Truman's decision to seize the steel industry to prevent a nationwide strike in April 1952 (declared unconstitutional by the courts two months later) reminded Americans of his earlier troubles with labor and management. Several scandals involving big businessmen and some of Truman's associates had also come to light. So Republicans raised the issue of widespread government corruption. The Korean War dragged on, with American casualties mounting in a war that was increasingly unpopular.

The issues of "Korea, communism, and corruption" that Republicans stressed in 1952 would probably have brought about the election of any candidate after twenty years of Democratic rule. Still, the out-of-power party took no chances. At their 1952 convention the Republicans rejected the candidacy of the able conservative Senator Robert A. Taft of Ohio because they were not sure he could win. They nominated General Dwight David Eisenhower—World War II hero, university president, commander of American NATO forces, and easily the most popular public figure in the country. The party then reaffirmed its concern for the anticommunist issue by nominating Richard Nixon as Vice President.

The Democrats drafted Governor Adlai Stevenson of Illinois, a man who, though able, was assailed by Republicans as an "egghead" because of the intellectual quality of his campaigning. Stevenson's efforts to defend Democratic achievements and promise a continuation of Fair Deal reforms fell flat. Many voters were tired after two decades of depression, reform, world war, and Cold War. The public voted to make its grandfatherly first citizen, Dwight Eisenhower, President by an overwhelming 33 to 27 million popular vote margin and a 442 to 89 electoral majority. After two decades in the political wilderness the Republican party returned to full national power, winning not only the White House but also Congress.

THE EISENHOWER YEARS

With Eisenhower's inauguration in 1953, control of the federal government returned essentially—

JONAS SALK

Polio is a disease of civilization. It strikes hardest where sanitation is highest. It is also a disease that most frequently strikes children. It can keep a victim bedridden for weeks in intense pain; but, much worse, it can cause severe, life-long paralysis or even death. Since 1894, when the first cases of polio appeared in the Green Mountains of Vermont, epidemics of the disease had been a common and dreaded occurrence. And nothing could be done to prevent them until in 1953 a young researcher, Dr. Jonas Salk, announced the development of polio vaccine.

Dr. Salk's discovery was not one of medicine's happy accidents but rather the result of years of intensive research. Salk himself is said to have worked sixteen hours a day, six days a week over a long period of time before succeeding. His background had prepared him for such a test of endurance. Born in New York City on October 28, 1914, the son of an immigrant garment worker, he put himself through school largely by part-time jobs and scholarships. He entered New York University Medical School in 1934. There he met Thomas Francis, Jr., who was conducting a study on methods of killing influenza virus. In 1943, the two men field-tested a vaccine effective against both influenza A and influenza B.

In 1947, Salk joined the University of Pittsburgh School of Medicine as head of the Virus Research Laboratory. The polio vaccine that Salk finally developed was made by growing a representative strain of each of the three types of virus in a broth made with monkey kidney. The viruses were then killed with formaldehyde, which rendered them incapable of causing the disease. However, they did not lose the power to stimulate the human body to produce antibodies. These antibodies would give a person at least limited immunity to polio.

Salk, his wife, and their three sons were among the first to receive his vaccine. Then in the fall of 1954 a massive twelve-state test, sponsored by the National Foundation for Infantile Paralysis, was held. Almost one million school children in the primary grades participated. Half the children received the vaccine; the other half did not. The results were conclusive: in April 1955 the vaccine was pronounced safe and effective in preventing polio.

By the summer of 1961, there was a reduction by approximately 96 percent in the amount of polio in the United States as a whole compared to the five-year period before the introduction of vaccination, even though only 50 percent of the population had been vaccinated. Contributing to the eradication of polio, an oral vaccine was being developed and tested by another American researcher, Albert Sabin. In 1959 Sabin's oral vaccine had been accepted for use by the Soviet Union and in August of 1961 it was approved for use in the United States. One year later manufacture started, and the oral polio vaccine was licensed for general distribution.

Salk's discovery catapulted this shy, retiring man to instant and unwanted fame. He became a public figure deluged with offers to lecture and even to make his life into a movie. He was awarded a congressional gold medal for "great achievement in the field of medicine," and the people of San Diego voted to donate a tract of land on a bluff overlooking the Pacific on which to build an institute in his honor. The research center was dedicated in 1963. Under Dr. Salk's direction, it is now a leading center of research in immunology and cellular and molecular biology.

for the first time since Herbert Hoover—to businessmen. The new President's cabinet officers were either corporation executives or closely allied to the business community. Eisenhower was determined to run a less active presidency than either Truman or Roosevelt and was suspicious of the federal bureaucracy and New Deal–Fair Deal social welfare programs. He set himself the task of keeping the nation calm.

Eisenhower interfered less often than Roosevelt or Truman with his various department heads. Instead, he allowed each to make his own decisions with minimal overall supervision. Frequently, for example, Secretary of State John Foster Dulles and not Eisenhower made essential foreign policy decisions. Similarly Treasury Secretary George Humphrey slashed departmental budgets throughout the government—except for the military. Here the Joint Chiefs of Staff got many of the programs they wanted, especially those proposed by the air force and navy. The chain of command under Eisenhower thus often resembled that of a loosely organized corporation.

The Republican party's right-wingers became a real problem for Eisenhower. McCarthy, by his actions as head of the Senate's Government Operations Committee, posed a serious threat to Eisenhower's ability to rule. He publicly led the strong opposition to Eisenhower's nomination of career diplomat Charles E. Bohlen as ambassador to Russia because Bohlen had been Roosevelt's interpreter at Yalta! (However, Bohlen was eventually confirmed by the Senate.)

McCarthy's Fall Until 1954 the administration tried to compromise with the senator. In that year, however, McCarthy opened an investigation of subversion in an army base at Fort Monmouth, New Jersey. This attack on the military and on Eisenhower's army secretary, Robert Stevens, for "coddling" communists proved to be the last straw. It forced a reluctant Eisenhower to take a public stand against McCarthy and his tactics.

Senate hearings considered McCarthy's charges against the army. They reviewed the army's countercharges that the senator had sought special favors for an aide, David Schine, drafted into the Army. The hearings were watched on television by over 20 million Americans. McCarthy proved an adept television performer. But even more adept was the Army's counsel, Joseph N. Welch. He baited McCarthy into losing his temper, thus widely exposing the browbeating tactics that McCarthy had used so effectively against unfriendly witnesses before his committee in the past. McCarthy's influence began to decline.

In December 1954 the Senate (supported by the Eisenhower administration) "condemned" Senator McCarthy for "conduct unbecoming a member." After this censure he lost his remaining political influence. He died in May 1957. But "McCarthyism" lingered on.

The reckless hunt for possible communist subversives in American society, without proof of guilt or adequate safeguards for defense, continued to be a problem during the 1950s. Many thousands of Americans lost their jobs, suffered ruined careers because of blacklisting in their professions, and went to jail or even into exile because of it. The list of victims is long. It includes industrial workers and labor union officials, as well as prominent editors, broadcasters, and others in the arts.

"Peace, Progress, and Prosperity" The Eisenhower years signified far more than simply the tail end of McCarthyism. Eisenhower avoided tampering with New Deal–Fair Deal programs, even presiding over some extensions for them. He created the Department of Health, Education, and Welfare, approved a measure that added 7 million people to the Social Security rolls, signed another that raised the minimum wage, and supported a housing act that greatly increased urban-renewal projects. The decline of such public facilities as schools, hospitals, and public transport systems also received little attention in the 1950s.

Eisenhower avoided the type of scandal that had rocked Truman's second administration. His relations with the Democratic leaders who ran Congress were generally amicable, unlike Truman's with congressional Republicans. Eisenhower regularly consulted House Majority Leader Sam Rayburn and Senate Majority Leader Lyndon Johnson, the two Texans who dominated Congress during the 1950s.

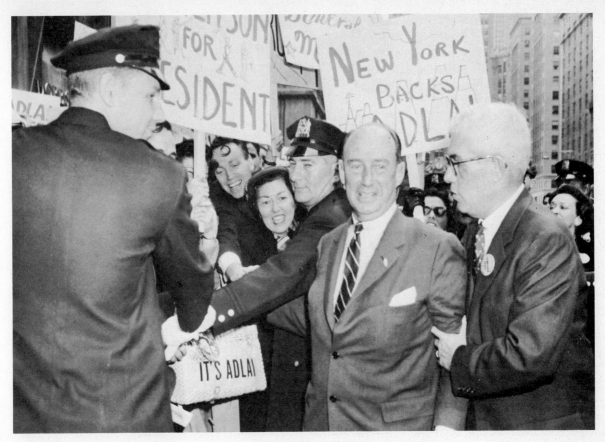

Adlai Stevenson, twice the Democratic nominee for President, was an eloquent and witty campaigner. But Eisenhower's image as a war hero and elder statesman proved unbeatable.

When the President decided to run for reelection in 1956, despite a serious heart attack in 1955, there were no issues that the Democrats could exploit. Eisenhower had negotiated peace in Korea, run a basically budget-conscious and honest administration, and toned down McCarthyism. Also, he had flown to Geneva in 1955 for a summit meeting on peaceful coexistence with Russia's post-Stalin leaders (the first such meeting since Potsdam). He kept the country out of major foreign involvements in the Indochina crisis of 1954 and the Hungarian and Suez crises of 1956. Not surprisingly, Eisenhower again whipped Adlai Stevenson, winning a landslide 58 percent of the popular vote.

There seemed little public interest during the 1950s in rocking a very prosperous national boat. Eisenhower provided an image of safe, solid leadership that appealed even to many Democrats.

Farm income in the 1950s netted more for farmers than even the thriving war years. Moreover, the much larger pie had to be divided among a smaller farm population. Median family income rose from $4,293 in 1950 to $5,904 in 1960. By 1956 white-collar workers outnumbered those in blue-collar jobs. Even for those in the latter group (particularly those unionized) real spendable income increased by 60 percent between 1940 and 1960. Much of this prosperity came in new industries—dealing with military weapons systems and space technology. These greatly expanded after the Russians sent the world's first missile, Sputnik I, into space in 1957. Suddenly, Americans found they had a lot of catching up to do if they were to equal the Russians in scientific pursuits. Many people realized that education had been lacking, and government funds were quickly demanded to inject the schools and universities with new monies for the expansion and updating of their facilities.

While *Brown* v. *Board of Education of Topeka* (1954) outlawed segregated education, the Supreme Court's Implementation Ruling of 1955, which called for "all deliberate speed" in school desegregation, actually paved the way for dilatory tactics, if not resistance. In some cases, federal intervention was eventually necessary to insure black children's rights to integrated education.

UNSETTLED PROBLEMS

Yet various social and economic problems of enormous scope remained during the Eisenhower era. These would haunt Americans in the 1960s. For one thing, the affluent society remained a myth in 1960 for the 42 million people (almost a third of America's families) with annual family income levels of less than $4,000. The "invisible poor," as Michael Harrington described them, were not "invisible" by their own choice. They were not so much unseen as ignored by those who had made dramatic ecomonic gains.

"Making it" often involved drawing firm barriers between oneself and those left behind. Groups heavily represented among the poor were the elderly, unskilled or nonunion workers, migrant farm laborers, blacks, and Spanish Americans. The average black family income in 1960, for example, was $3,838 compared with $6,508 for white families.

The wartime FEPC had opened thousands of jobs in Northern industries to blacks. President Truman's 1950 executive order desegregated the armed forces and barred discrimination in federal employment. The next great civil rights advance for blacks came in 1954. The Supreme Court, in the famous case of *Brown* v. *Board of Education of Topeka, Kansas*, ruled unanimously that segregation in public school education was illegal.

The case, *Brown* v. *Topeka Board of Education*, came before the Court on December 9, 1952.

It continued for over a year. The decision the Court handed down on May 17, 1954, presents the question the justices faced: "Does segregation of children in public schools solely on the basis of race, even though the physical facilities and other 'tangible' factors may be equal, deprive children of the minority group of equal educational opportunities?"

The Court answered this question with an affirmative: "We conclude that in the field of public education the doctrine of 'separate but equal' has no place. Separate educational facilities are inherently unequal." Later, the Supreme Court instructed schools to move "with all deliberate speed" to desegregate their facilities.

Although 792 of 2,985 biracial school districts had been integrated by 1959, none were in the Deep South or Virginia. There, massive resistance from leading politicians and local white citizens councils raised the level of racial tension to dangerous heights. In 1956 a hundred Southern congressmen promised to overturn the *Brown* decision by "all lawful means." Then in 1957 at

Little Rock, Arkansas—with white parents threatening violence against court-ordered desegregation—Governor Orval Faubus called out the National Guard to bar nine black students from a high school. After a court order removed the guard, a riot broke out. Eisenhower, himself a moderate on the segregation issue, sent federal paratroopers to help escort the nine children into the school. Elsewhere, one Virginia county even closed its public schools to avoid integration. The University of Alabama, after a riot on the campus, expelled a black student admitted under Supreme Court order.

Meanwhile, blacks in Montgomery, Alabama, led by an eloquent young minister, the Reverend Martin Luther King, Jr., organized a boycott against segregation on local buses in December 1955. Segregation on interstate buses had been banned the previous month. King's "direct action" tactics spread to other Southern cities. Soon he and other Southern black ministers formed the Southern Christian Leadership Conference (SCLC) to fight discrimination and all forms of bigotry.

In February 1960 a student wing of the SCLC held the first sit-in at a Greensboro, North Carolina, lunch counter to protest segregation in public eating places. Two mild civil rights acts in 1957 and 1960 somewhat strengthened federal authority against efforts to keep blacks from voting or exercising other rights. But as the sixties began, Americans knew that the major battles to secure full equality for blacks were still ahead.

Other critical problems faced the nation as Eisenhower's second term ended. He himself emphasized a major one in a January 17, 1961, farewell speech.

The conjunction of an immense military establishment and a permanent armaments industry of vast proportions is new in the American experience. The total influence—economic, political, even spiritual—is felt in every city, every state house, every office of the federal government. We must guard against the acquisition of unwarranted in-

In his inaugural address John Kennedy challenged a complacent citizenry with the words: "Ask not what your country can do for you; ask what you can do for your country."

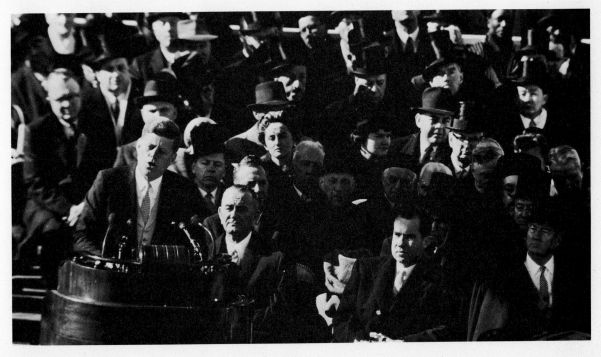

fluence, whether sought or unsought, by the military-industrial complex. We must never let the weight of this combination endanger our liberties or democratic processes.

A fair warning, but Eisenhower himself had speeded the growth of the "military-industrial complex." Militarists and industrialists became more powerful during the ten years following. Still, the checks of the American system have kept them from getting complete control of the nation's political or economic structure.

Return of the Democrats America faced still other unsolved problems, but it entered the 1960s in a confident mood, sure of its purposes and powers. Though this confidence would not long remain, both 1960 presidential candidates reflected this basic assurance about the American future.

Richard Nixon, while defending the Eisenhower record, promised progressive and dynamic new policies. John Kennedy urged Democrats to rally behind him for vigorous leadership. Little separated the two candidates in terms of issues, domestic or foreign, except that Kennedy attacked a presumed decline of American prestige abroad under Eisenhower and an alleged missile gap that threatened to make the Soviet Union dominant.

Kennedy benefited from a united party. His Texas Protestant running mate, Lyndon Johnson, helped keep much of the South Democratic for the Catholic Kennedy. He also profited from television debates with Nixon, which helped undercut the Republican charge of inexperience and youth. (Kennedy was forty-three, the youngest man ever elected President.) Most of all, his election resulted from the strong support he received among Catholics and blacks—who gave him over 70 percent of their votes. Nixon received only mild backing from Eisenhower. Nixon's earlier career as a "red hunter" haunted him and hurt him severely among Democratic and independent voters in 1960. Still, Kennedy won by only a tiny popular margin—113,000 votes out of 68,800,000 cast.

In his inaugural address Kennedy promised to lead the United States toward a New Frontier headed by young people: "The torch has been passed to a new generation of Americans, born in this century, tempered by war, [and] disciplined by a hard and bitter peace." The sense of promise and hope was strong among Americans that day, as the youthful new Chief Executive issued "a call to bear the burden of a long twilight struggle, year in and year out against the common enemies of man: tyranny, poverty, disease, and war itself." Few Americans doubted in 1961 that the country felt itself adequate to these great tasks.

SUGGESTED READINGS— CHAPTERS 45-46

Alger Hiss

Alistair Cooke, *A Generation on Trial: U.S.A. v. Alger Hiss* (1950); Meyer A. Zeligs, *Friendship and Fratricide: An Analysis of Whittaker Chambers and Alger Hiss* (1967); Allen Weinstein, *Perjury: The Hiss-Chambers Case* (1978).

The Truman Administration

William C. Berman, *The Politics of Civil Rights in the Truman Administration* (1970); Barton J.

Bernstein (ed.), *Politics and Policies of the Truman Administration* (1970); Richard M. Freeland, *The Truman Doctrine and the Origins of McCarthyism* (1972); Alonzo L. Hamby, *Beyond the New Deal: Harry S. Truman and American Liberalism* (1970); Earl Latham, *The Communist Controversy in Washington* (1966); Merle Miller, *Plain Speaking: An Oral Biography of Harry S. Truman* (1974); Cabell Phillips, *The Truman Presidency* (1966); Allen Yarnell, *Democrats and Progressives* (1974).

The Eisenhower Administration

Charles C. Alexander, *Holding the Line: The Eisenhower Era, 1952–1961* (1974); Richard Dalfiume, *Desegregation of the United States Armed Forces* (1969); Peter Lyon, *Eisenhower: Portrait of a Hero* (1974); Herbert S. Parmet, *Eisenhower and the American Crusades* (1975); James T. Patterson, *Mr. Republican* (1972); John B. Martin, *Adlai Stevenson of Illinois* (1976).

Communism and Anticommunism

William F. Buckley and L. Brent Bozell, *McCarthy and His Enemies* (1954); Richard Fried, *Men Against McCarthy* (1976); Walter Goodman, *The Committee* (1968); Robert Griffith, *The Politics of Fear* (1970); Robert Griffith and Athan Theoharis, *The Spectre* (1974); Alan D. Harper, *The Politics of Loyalty: The White House and the Communist Issue, 1946–1952* (1969); Louis Nizer, *The Implosion Conspiracy* (1975); Gary W. Reichard, *The Reaffirmation of Republicanism* (1975); Michael Paul Rogin, *McCarthy and the Intellectuals* (1967); Karl M. Schmidt, *Henry A. Wallace: Quixotic Crusader, 1948* (1960); Walter and Miriam Schneir, *Invitation to an Inquest* (1965); David A. Shannon, *The Decline of American Communism* (1959); Athan Theoharis, *Seeds of Repression* (1971).

Affluence

John K. Galbraith, *The Affluent Society* (1958); David M. Potter, *People of Plenty* (1954); Herbert Stein, *The Fiscal Revolution in America* (1969); Harold G. Vatter, *The United States Economy in the 1950's* (1963).

General Overview

Jacobus Broek, et al., *Prejudice, War and the Constitution* (1954); John M. Blum, *V Was for Victory: Politics and American Culture During World War II* (1976); Eric F. Goldman, *The Crucial Decade and After: America 1945–1960* (1960); Robert A. Garson, *The Democratic Party and the Politics of Sectionalism, 1941–1948* (1974); Douglas Miller and Marion Nowak, *The Fifties: The Way We Really Were* (1977); Richard Polenberg, *War and Society: The United States 1941–1945* (1972).

UNIT EIGHT

CONTEMPORARY AMERICA

The burst of optimism about the American future that marked the early 1960s barely survived the assassination of John Fitzgerald Kennedy in 1963. By mid-decade, the United States had been shaken by a series of domestic upheavals ranging from the Black Power protests to campus demonstrations and the beginnings of antiwar agitation. As the United States became more deeply involved in the Vietnamese War under Presidents Johnson and Nixon, national self-confidence disappeared—a casualty of bitter social unrest at home and battlefield stalemate abroad.

Older allies and enemies began to challenge their earlier acceptance of American dominance in the world, while a confused and divided American people reassessed their national values, grievances, problems, weaknesses, and strengths. The three pairs of chapters in Unit Eight describe milestones in the United States' fateful encounter with the vicissitudes of historical tragedy and loss during the past generation.

Chapter 47 portrays the 1962 drama of the Cuban missile crisis—the Soviet-American confrontation that nearly unleashed World War III. The accompanying chapter, 48, charts the complex "decline of *Pax Americana*"—the erosion of the United States' domination of international affairs under the impact of the Vietnamese War and other problems. Martin Luther King's stirring leadership of the black struggle for equality in the U.S. and his violent death form the subject of Chapter 49, while Chapter 50 sketches out the contours of political stalemate and social crises in the 1960s. Finally, the Watergate ordeal—the gravest political and constitu-tional crisis in American life since the Civil War—emerges in Chapter 51, accompanied by an analysis of American politics and society in the mid-1970s in Chapter 52. All six chapters relate part of the overall story of the United States in what may prove to be the formative years of a new society: more sober and restrained in the exercise of its global influence, more committed and fair-minded than ever to correcting the inequities of its own socio-economic order, and more faithful than in some earlier epochs to its noble, if imperfect, heritage of freedom and justice.

47 THE CUBAN MISSILE CRISIS

A. W.

For a week in October 1962 the United States and the Soviet Union, the two nuclear giants, stood facing each other in combat readiness. With the relatively "primitive" military weaponry of that time, probably no more than half a billion people were in actual danger. The year before, the Department of Defense had estimated a total of 120 million American casualties should crisis deepen from confrontation into all-out war. A like number of Soviets would probably die, along with most of the populations of Europe and Canada. If the war spread to China, of course, the final toll would run incalculably higher.

The crisis of 1962 began with strange markings on photographs taken from a U-2 spy plane flying ten miles above the island of Cuba. No one disputed the CIA's interpretation of the pictures: on an island ninety miles from Florida, the Soviet Union was installing medium-range guided missiles, capable of carrying nuclear bombs to the United States.

The United States had had many problems with Cuba since 1959, when Fidel Castro led his rebels out of the mountains and toppled the existing American-supported Batista dictatorship. The U.S. government was wary of Castro; the CIA had noted the presence of many Cuban communists in his government. When he began nationalizing extensive American holdings on Cuba, Washington refused his requests for loans. Just before leaving office in January 1961, Eisenhower decided to break diplomatic relations with Havana. Meanwhile, Castro was steadily strengthening his ties with the Soviets.

On October 14, 1962, two United States Air Force pilots, flying specially equipped U-2 planes borrowed from the CIA, revealed how close those ties had become. When the U-2 photographs reached Washington, analysts from the Defense Intelligence Agency agreed that the Cuban sites closely resembled missile bases in Russia. The head of the

DIA sent two officers to show the pictures to his superior, Roswell Gilpatric, the second-ranking civilian at the Pentagon, who relayed the news on to the President's special assistant for national security affairs, McGeorge Bundy.

In his twenty-one months as President, John F. Kennedy had dealt often with "the Cuban question." Campaigning in 1960 as a dynamic alternative to the bland do-nothingism of the Eisenhower years, Kennedy charged that Republican policies had created a communist state in Cuba. Once in office, Kennedy discovered that the Eisenhower Administration had been fostering a CIA-sponsored invasion of Cuba by anti-Castro Cubans living in the United States. Kennedy agreed to back the plan, which suffered a humiliating defeat in April 1961, when Castro's troops routed the invaders at the Bay of Pigs on Cuba's south shore.

Early on the morning of Tuesday, October 16, 1962, Kennedy learned about the missile site photos. The President immediately called a meeting for 11:45 that morning, summoning a group that would soon become known as ExComm, short for Executive Committee. Summonses went to Vice President Lyndon Johnson, Secretary of State Dean Rusk, Secretary of Defense Robert McNamara, Bundy, Gilpatric, Taylor, and a few other close advisors, notably the President's brother, Attorney General Robert Kennedy. "The President did not specify the problem over the telephone," recalled Robert Kennedy. "He said only that we were facing great trouble."

The news stunned the nation's highest councillors. Despite evidence of great Soviet shipping activity to Cuba, they had never concluded that the Russians were putting missiles there. Unlike the United States, which had established missile bases in Turkey, Italy, and Britain, the Soviets had never before placed missiles outside their own borders. According to one explanation, they distrusted the Poles, the East Germans, and other satellite allies. Moreover, Khrushchev and his envoys had gone out of their way in recent months to assure the American government that no major moves would be taken by Moscow before the U.S. election in November. In light of the new evidence, it was clear they had been trying to buy time until the missiles became operational.

Every one of the dozen men assembled in the Cabinet Room that morning agreed that the missiles must be sent back to Russia with haste. A missile base in Cuba would greatly improve the Russians' nuclear capability and would subvert the U.S. warning system. It could threaten Latin America, vastly increasing the Soviets' prestige and diminishing U.S. power in the area. On the basis of his new strength, Khrushchev might demand American concessions in other parts of the world, such as the withdrawal of troops from West Berlin.

ExComm deliberated all day, moving briefly to the State Department in the afternoon and returning to the White House that evening. Rather than planning specific responses, they spent the first day discussing the overall situation, evaluating the effect of the missiles, and speculating on why Khrushchev had tried this awesome gamble. That night they had reached only one conclusion: something had to be done.

OXIDIZER TRAILERS

2 MISSILE TRANSPORTERS

PROB IRBM PROPELLANT TRAILERS

OXIDIZER TRAILER

6 MISSILE TRANSPORTERS

ERECTOR

3 MISSILE TRANSPORTERS

An American reconnaissance plane photographed Soviet freighters, loaded with intermediate-range ballistic missile parts, in a Cuban port.

On Wednesday, October 17, ExComm met throughout the day in the State Department conference room to discuss policy options. No immediate consensus emerged; although these twelve men, scuttling in and out of the meeting from their other official duties, all served the same administration, they regarded the problem from a dozen different perspectives.

The group considered diplomatic options first: either to make a private demand to the Russians that they get the missiles out or to take the case to the United Nations. But swiftly, ExComm decided that diplomacy alone could not work. The Soviets would only stall for time while construction of the sites continued. Finally, the Soviets would demand a world conference on the missiles, further delaying any decisive decision.

The military men on ExComm proposed a straightforward response: send in B-52 bombers to blast the bases. According to evidence from stepped-up U-2 flights, between sixteen and thirty-two missiles would be ready for firing in a week. Bombing was the only strategy sure to eliminate the missiles before that point. This approach became known as "the fast track."

The most impassioned opposition to a military solution came from Robert Kennedy, the President's closest advisor, who rapidly emerged as a leading voice in the discussions. His intimate relationship with his brother added weight to his comments, and other cabinet officers tended to defer to RFK.

A surprise attack, argued Robert Kennedy, was not in the tradition of the United States. It would hurt the country in the eyes of the world and affront its conscience at home. The country that had been attacked without warning at Pearl Harbor would now seem to be following the Japanese example. "My brother," he warned the group, "is not going to be the Tojo of the 1960s." Furthermore, he doubted whether an air attack, even one referred to by the military as a "surgical strike," could be relied on to take out all the missiles. Very possibly, the United States would have to follow it up with an invasion, and would have to accept a heavy toll in Cuban and American lives.

The "slow track," advocated by most nonmilitary advisors, included a naval blockade of Cuba. This would prevent the Russians from sending more missiles in and could be maintained until they removed the weapons already there. With the United States Navy's total control of the Caribbean and the eastern Atlantic, the blockade could be made to work. But, according to international law, a blockade is an act of war.

Although the slow and fast tracks emerged as the major alternatives, the lines in the room did not harden during the Wednesday session. Most participants changed sides at least once. ExComm argued the alternatives throughout Thursday and Friday. McGeorge Bundy, who had originally stood with Stevenson for a diplomatic approach, now led the "surgical" air-strike faction. Llewellen Thompson, former Ambassador to the Soviet Union and the group's Kremlinologist, warned that bombing the missile bases was the worst course; Soviets would be killed, and Khrushchev's response to that could not be safely predicted. The Joint Chiefs unanimously argued for bombing; General Taylor suggested giving twenty-four hours' warning to minimize loss of life. McNamara argued that if the proposed blockade failed, the United States could then try bombing; but after bombing, the President could not go back to the blockade.

The discussions gave two new words to the American language—terms that would later be applied to hard-liners and soft-liners on Vietnam. Those favoring the air strike became known as "hawks," while supporters of the blockade were identified as "doves."

Slowly, a majority began to develop in favor of blockade. Treasury Secretary Douglas Dillon abandoned his support of the air strike, announcing himself convinced by the arguments of Robert Kennedy and McNamara. Former Secretary of State Dean Acheson, unable to support the blockade, left in a huff, "resigning" from the group.

On Saturday, ExComm made its report to the President. John Kennedy had campaigned in Chicago the day before but had cancelled Saturday's appearances because he had "a cold." He now sat at the cabinet table in a chair designed to ease the pain in his back and listened to the final recommendations of each side. Neither faction could maintain that their policy would be safe or easy.

The President came down on the side of the blockade. He did not wish to put Khrushchev totally into a corner. Although he wanted to speak again with tactical bombing specialists, he doubted that bombing could guarantee destruction of all the missiles. Aware of the possible consequences, Kennedy nevertheless ordered the blockade, instructing McNamara to ready all U.S. forces for the confrontation. "I guess," he had told Acheson the day before, "this is the week I earn my salary."

Fifty-one hours later, Kennedy planned to announce the blockade on television. He directed his top speechwriter, Theodore Sorenson, to prepare the address, and Sorenson retired to his office with copies of the speeches of Woodrow Wilson and Franklin Roosevelt in which they asked Congress to declare war.

The American military began moving well in advance of public announcements. Transport planes flew a thousand marines from Camp Pendleton, California, to reinforce the U.S. base at Guantánamo Bay, Cuba. The First Armored Division was loaded aboard special trains from Texas to Fort Stewart, Georgia, preparing its artillery for immediate use. One hundred eighty naval ships steamed toward blockade stations in the Atlantic, although their captains did not yet know their assignments.

The military was preparing for the possibility that the crisis would outgrow Cuba. Strategic Air Command planes began leaving their bases for civilian airports all over the country to guard against a sneak attack. B-52s loaded with atomic bombs were kept in the air at all times; as one landed, another would replace it in the sky. Crews tending ICBMs went on maximum alert. Warnings of an impending crisis went out to American military commanders all over the world.

Early Sunday morning, before going to church, President Kennedy reconfirmed his decision on the blockade by speaking to General Walter C. Sweeney, commander of the Tactical Air Force. Sweeney could pledge only 90 percent destruction of the missiles with an air strike. A few missiles would probably survive—and possibly be fired immediately at the United States. His mind now definitely made up, the President met with ExComm in the Oval Office at ten o'clock.

The Sunday morning session served to solidify the previous decisions and plans of operation. At the suggestion of Robert Kennedy, each participant brought his own ideas in writing. Assistant Secretary of Defense Paul Nitze's pocket contained a chilling but possible scenario: construction work on the missiles would continue, forcing a U.S. air strike; the remaining missiles would be fired at the United States, which would have to invade Cuba and launch a "purely compensatory" attack on the Soviet Union. Nitze's scenario did not say what would happen next.

As Sunday afternoon passed into Monday evening, the government prepared itself. Sorenson's draft of the President's speech was edited, rewritten, and edited again. American women and children were evacuated from Guantánamo Bay. Spanish-language stations in Florida were checked to make sure that Monday night's speech could be heard in Cuba. General Thomas S. Power, commander of the Strategic Air Command, issued his final orders from underground headquarters near Omaha.

One substantive alteration was made in the speech. Abram Chayes, the State Department's Legal Advisor, and his assistant Leonard Meeker, persuaded the President not to use the word "blockade," widely considered to be an act of war. Instead, they suggested that Kennedy announce that he was placing a "quarantine" around Cuba. The semantic change in no way altered the plan.

Kennedy had one more task before he made his public announcement. The presidential jet had hopped around the country Monday, rounding up nineteen Congressional leaders, most of whom were in their home states campaigning. They came to the White House at five o'clock Monday afternoon, to be briefed by Rusk, McNamara, and John McCone of the CIA, and then to meet with the President.

Their reaction stunned and angered Kennedy. He had expected Republicans to question his approach and oppose his policies, but two Democratic leaders, Chairmen Richard Russell of the Senate Armed Services Committee and William Fulbright of the Senate Foreign Relations Committee, dismissed a blockade as ineffective and insisted on an immediate invasion. For an hour, Kennedy angrily repeated all the arguments from the meetings of ExComm. The Congressmen were not convinced, so the President stormed out of the room to make final preparations for his speech.

Beginning with the traditional "My fellow citizens," Kennedy rapidly outlined the evidence of Soviet military activity on Cuba. The installation of missiles, he said flatly, "is a deliberately provocative and unjustified change in the status quo which cannot be accepted by this country."

To deal with the problem, Kennedy explained, a defensive quarantine would begin. "All ships of any kind bound for Cuba from whatever nation or port will, if found to contain cargoes of offensive weapons, be turned back." Later that evening, McNamara publicly confirmed what Kennedy had merely implied: ships that did not turn back would be seized or sunk.

The United States, Kennedy continued, wanted immediate emer-

When the Soviet Union began supplying Cuba with missiles, the Cold War reached crisis proportions. As the nation watched, President Kennedy announced a counteraction that brought the world perilously close to nuclear confrontation.

gency sessions of the U.N. Security Council and the OAS. But although he talked of negotiations, the President issued a warning: any missile launched from Cuba would be considered as coming from Russia "requiring a full retaliatory attack upon the Soviet Union."

A half hour after the President had begun speaking, the United States was in the middle of its most serious crisis since World War II.

"We have won a considerable victory," Dean Rusk told his undersecretary of state the next morning, waking him from his sleep on the couch in Rusk's office. "You and I are still alive." The absolute worst possibility—that Khrushchev would be so enraged he would immediately launch an attack on the United States, on Berlin, on the Turkish missile bases—had not occurred. But the next move still belonged to the Soviets; it would come when an American ship tried to stop one of their vessels heading for Cuba.

That morning, Tuesday, October 23, the OAS met to vote on the blockade issue. The United States needed fourteen votes, a two-thirds majority, and the assistant secretary of state for Inter-American Affairs estimated one chance in four of getting that many. Latin-American delegates listened to Rusk's speech and desperately called home for instructions. When a vote was taken, one by one the Latins rose and endorsed the position of the United States. The final vote was 19–0, with only Uruguay abstaining. The next day, when instructions came through from Uruguay, the vote became unanimous.

At the White House, the day passed in working out plans for the blockade to go into effect Wednesday morning at ten o'clock. If a vessel bound for Cuba refused to stop, the navy would attempt to cripple it by firing at the rudders and propellors—not to sink it. And rather than board the vessel by force, the Navy would attempt to tow it into Jacksonville or Charleston.

Cuban refugees gather in a Manhattan hotel to watch President Kennedy's televised address to the nation on October 22, 1962. In the Monday-night speech, the President outlined a 7-point program of American response to the missile crisis, including a limited "quarantine" of Cuba—in effect, a blockade. Calling the Soviet actions provocative, Kennedy threatened U.S. retaliation were any of the Cuban missiles to be launched at any nation in the Western Hemisphere.

ExComm worked out another contingency plan that day. To protect the missiles, the Russians had also installed SAMs (surface-to-air missiles) in Cuba. Since Tuesday, three U-2s a day had flown over Cuba. If a SAM destroyed a U-2, Kennedy and McNamara agreed that such an attack would require American bombers to destroy a SAM site, but that no action would be taken without the President's approval.

Still, the day brought no inkling of what the Russians might do. On the President's urging, his brother went to meet with Soviet Ambassador Anatoly Dobrynin, with whom he had developed a rapport. The meeting produced nothing, since Dobrynin denied that the missile bases even existed. Afterwards, the Ambassador attended a reception at his embassy for Lieutenant General Vladimir A. Dubovik. "We Russians are ready to defend ourselves against any acts of aggression, against ourselves or any of our allies," boasted the General. "Our ships will sail through."

The blockade would go into effect Wednesday morning, and Soviet ships were still steaming toward Cuba. Tuesday night, American intelligence picked up coded messages to the ships, but they were undecipherable.

Wednesday's regularly scheduled ten o'clock meeting of ExComm would coincide with the arrival of the first Russian ships at the blockade line. The President, sitting with his brother before the meeting, found some comfort in the thought that, had he not acted, he "would have been impeached." As the other members of ExComm gathered, the group quietly listened and waited. Some pored gloomily over the more recent U-2 photos, which showed that work on the missile sites was proceeding and that Soviet bombers were being uncrated and assembled. McNamara informed everyone that two merchant ships, the *Gagarin* and the *Komiles,* would reach the blockade line within minutes.

The next report ExComm received was not encouraging: a Russian submarine had joined the two ships. The group sat in frozen apprehension. The President held his hand over his mouth, but his eyes showed the strain. "We must expect that they will close down Berlin," he said, thinking ahead to the next step; "we must make the final preparations for that."

At 10:25, a CIA courier appeared at John McCone's elbow with a note. McCone read it rapidly and announced, "Mr. President, we have a preliminary report which seems to indicate that some of the Russian ships have stopped dead in the water."

Now information began to come in rapidly, confirming early reports. Twenty Russian ships near the line had indeed halted, and some had turned around and headed back across the Atlantic. "If the ships have orders to turn around," directed the President, eagerly grasping at the reprieve, "we want to give them every opportunity to do so."

A great burden seemed to have been lifted from the participants. Dean Rusk remarked bouncily: "We're eyeball to eyeball and I think the other fellow just blinked." In a more sober vein, Robert Kennedy reflected: "For a moment the world stood still, and now it was going around again."

The Soviets had not responded militarily, but the United States still did not know exactly what their next step would be. As ExComm had predicted, Khrushchev called for an international conference to discuss the problem. But his statement also struck a menacing note: "If the United States government carries out its program of piratical actions," he warned, "we shall have to resort to means of defense against the aggressor to protect our rights."

At 2:00 P.M. Wednesday, Acting U.N. Secretary-General U Thant of Burma, pressured by alarmed Asian and African nations, asked for an end to both the American quarantine and the Soviet weapons shipments. He urged a two-week cessation of both, during which the parties could

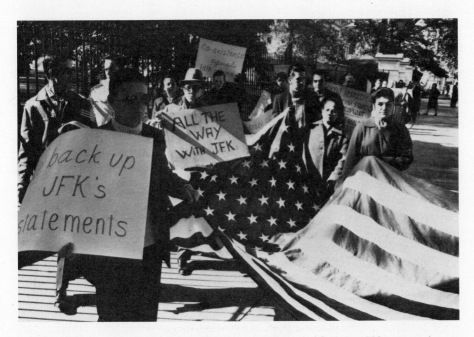

Opposing groups of pickets outside the White House at the end of October 1962 supported divergent strategies of retaliation against Soviet establishment of nuclear missile bases in Cuba, only 90 miles from the Florida coast. The "Hawks" wanted the U.S. to bomb the missile sites in Cuba before they could be completed. The "Doves" supported a naval blockade of Cuba that would continue until the missile bases were dismantled, a position endorsed by Attorney General Robert Kennedy and Secretary of Defense McNamara.

meet to resolve their differences. Khrushchev accepted the offer, but the United States did not. Time, ExComm felt, was essential; in two or three weeks, the missiles and bombers would be firmly established on Cuba. Before that happened, Khrushchev must be made to see the danger of keeping them there.

The Navy was letting ships with nonmilitary cargoes through the blockade. Among Soviet ships, these were mostly tankers, which clearly did not carry missiles. Yet a faction on ExComm strongly urged stopping and searching one of the tankers, to demonstrate American seriousness. After consideration, Kennedy rejected the idea as needlessly provocative.

Thursday, October 25, the United States presented its case to the U.N. Security Council. This day belonged to Adlai Stevenson, who had originally questioned the blockade and who was considered by some on ExComm to be too much of a dove. The Security Council meeting provided the most dramatic public moment of the crisis. Stevenson demanded of Soviet delegate Valerian Zorin whether the Russians had put missiles on Cuba.

> STEVENSON: Do you, Ambassador Zorin, deny that the USSR has placed and is placing medium- and intermediate-range missiles and sites in Cuba? Don't wait for the translation, answer yes or no.
> ZORIN: I am not in an American courtroom . . . . In due course, Sir, you will have your answer. . . .
> STEVENSON: I am prepared to wait for my answer until hell freezes over, if that's your decision. And I am also prepared to present the evidence in this room.

Stevenson then revealed blown-up photographs of the Cuban missile sites. Zorin refused to make any further statement, and the Security Council adjourned. The crisis was not resolved, but the exchange had focused world-wide attention on the photographic evidence.

Early Friday morning, October 26, the United States decided it was necessary to stop and search a ship. President Kennedy had personally selected the vessel, with great care. Although the *Marucla* was indeed sailing from Russia to Cuba, it was not a Soviet ship, but Panamanian-owned, registered in Lebanon, and chartered by the Soviets. Without incident, U.S. Navy men boarded the ship, inspected one of the holds, and then let it pass.

Still, depression and doubt reigned in ExComm on Friday as new evidence suggested that the Russians were speeding up construction. Even doves were coming to the conclusion that the United States would have to take more decisive action—an air strike against the missile sites, perhaps followed by an invasion.

McNamara warned that an invasion might entail forty to fifty thousand casualties. "They have a hell of a lot of equipment," CIA chief McCone warned. "And it will be damn tough to shoot them out of those hills." Nevertheless, the President ordered the State Department to prepare a program for civil government in Cuba after an invasion. That afternoon, ExComm developed plans for an air strike on the missiles.

THE RANGE OF CUBAN-BASED SOVIET MISSILES

The ranges of missiles shown on this map are only approximate

The administration strove to make the urgency of the situation clear to the Soviets. Officials and congressmen now talked publicly of American readiness. Robert Kennedy warned Dobrynin that there were at most two days left. Now ExComm could only wait to hear from Khrushchev.

The first intimations of a response came in a roundabout, totally unexpected fashion. John Scali, diplomatic correspondent from ABC-TV, received an unusual phone call early Friday afternoon. It came from Alexander Fomin, an official at the Soviet Embassy, who was rumored to be a colonel in the Soviet secret police. Could Scali meet him for lunch in ten minutes? To Scali's comment that he was busy, Fomin replied forcefully that it was urgent. Scali agreed to go.

Immediately after ordering his lunch, Fomin asked if the State Department would be interested in a three-part settlement: the missiles would return to the Soviet Union; the Russians would put no offensive weapons in Cuba in the future; and the United States would pledge not to invade Cuba. Scali said that he thought such a proposal showed promise. Upon the urging of Fomin, Scali went immediately to the State Department.

The Department's intelligence chief took Scali to seek Rusk. The Secretary, after consulting with the White House, sent Scali back with positive words of interest and a warning against delay. Scali and Fomin met again at 7:35 that evening in a coffee shop around the corner from the Soviet Embassy. After assuring himself that the statement came from the "highest circles," Fomin left to inform his superiors.

By that time, the White House teletype had already clacked out a strange letter from the American Embassy in Moscow. It was relaying a personal communication from Nikita Khrushchev to John Kennedy—a long, rambling letter, indicating a fear of war and a desperate search for a way out. Khrushchev wrote that he had seen war, and he detailed his experiences during two German invasions of his country. There were, he admitted, Soviet missiles in Cuba. But they were defensive, not offensive, weapons. (Khrushchev appeared to be playing the same semantic game with the word "defensive" that Kennedy had played in describing the "quarantine.") The missiles were there, Khrushchev said, because the United States had sponsored an invasion of Cuba, and Castro feared there might be another. The crisis must end before it spun out of control. If the United States would lift the quarantine and pledge not to invade Cuba, a solution might be possible. The Soviet Union would then have no further need to keep nuclear weapons in Cuba.

"Mr. President, you and we ought not now to pull on the ends of the rope in which you have tied the knot of war, because the more we pull, the tighter the knot will be tied," warned the Russian leader. "And a moment may come when the knot will be tied so tight that even he who tied it will not have the strength to untie it, and then it will be necessary to cut that knot . . . ."

ExComm went over the letter word-by-word, looking for traps and hoping not to find any. The group was not totally relieved: Khrushchev said nothing specific about withdrawing the missiles. But ExComm decided to treat Khrushchev's letter and Fomin's proposal as one single offer, an offer that the United States could accept.

Khrushchev's eagerness to extricate himself from the situation did not explain why the Soviets had put missiles in Cuba in the first place. Apparently, they wanted, first, to score a political victory and, second, to improve their country's military position. Khrushchev needed both in 1962. After four years of running his government's policy with a combination of probing, accommodation, and bluster, he had failed to gain ground. West Berlin remained in "enemy" hands, and the Soviets now faced opposition from the Chinese, who were beginning to chart a separate course from Moscow, one that threatened to flare into open hostility. In the end, Khrushchev suffered greatly from the crisis. The Chinese denounced him for adventurism in putting the missiles in—and for cowardice in taking them out. Within two years, he like Admiral Anderson, would be out of office.

Saturday, October 27, destroyed the fragile optimism of the night before. A new letter had arrived from the Kremlin, stripped of the rambling emotionalism of the first. The Soviet Union, Khrushchev wrote, would remove its missiles from Cuba when the United States removed *its* missiles from Turkey. Both major countries would pledge not to interfere in the affairs of their neighbors. Kennedy was not the only head of state who could issue an ultimatum.

ExComm studied the new note with perplexity. Had there been a *coup d'etat* in the Soviet Union? Did Khrushchev no longer control the government? Thompson, the Kremlinologist, had his doubts. He speculated that Khrushchev's new communiqué was in response to the feeling of the Soviet military and his other advisers that he was losing face in the way he was dealing with the crisis. For the first time, awareness of a Soviet ExComm pervaded the group.

The new offer contained a curious irony. The Turkish missiles were hardly essential to American defense and were, in any case, obsolete. Months before, Kennedy had given orders that they be removed. But the Turks, eager to retain the economic benefits of the bases, opposed removal, and the President's order had not been implemented. Now the President faced an unpleasant choice: risking a war over bases he no longer wanted, or giving European allies the impression that the United States would "sell them out" if its own security appeared in danger.

Other developments heightened the fragility of the situation. FBI Director J. Edgar Hoover notified Robert Kennedy that Soviet officials in New York were burning confidential documents, as though in preparation for war. McCone reported that construction of the bases on Cuba continued at a rapid pace. And the worst news was that Soviet missiles had downed an American U-2 in flight over Cuba. "There was the feeling," wrote Robert Kennedy, "that the noose was tightening on all of us, on Americans, on mankind, and that the bridges to escape were crumbling."

A decision to knock out the SAM bases could not be postponed much longer. Work continued on the bases, and they might be ready in a matter of hours. "It was generally agreed," remembered one member of ExComm, "that we couldn't go beyond Sunday without a further decision. At the very least . . . that would have been a decision to take out the missile sites by air attack." Invasion of Cuba would inevitably follow. McNamara stated that an air attack could be readied in forty-eight hours, but he would rather broaden the blockade to include petroleum.

Meanwhile, Khrushchev's letters remained unanswered. All Saturday afternoon, ExComm unsuccessfully tried to block out a way to remove the missiles from Turkey without giving the appearance of bowing to Soviet pressure. Rather, it drafted a series of responses refusing the terms offered by Khrushchev. Robert Kennedy found all of the drafts to be inadequate; they did not, in his opinion, sufficiently acknowledge the strong desire Khrushchev had shown for peace.

RFK then cut the knot brilliantly by suggesting that ExComm simply ignore Khrushchev's second letter and respond to the first—the one that offered withdrawal of Russian missiles but that did not mention the Turkish bases. He retired with Ted Sorenson to produce a draft. With some revisions, Robert Kennedy's letter went off to Khrushchev.

The same night, the Attorney General met with Dobrynin and told him of the letter going to Moscow. Regarding the problem of the Turkish missiles, he told the Ambassador that the United States could not re-

On October 31, 1962, President Kennedy met in his office with the U.S. Army Chief of Staff General Earle Wheeler, seated next to him, and two other key military officers to discuss American military preparedness. Fortunately for Kennedy, the Cuban Missile Crisis had ended three days earlier when Kruschev agreed to remove the missiles if the U.S. would end its naval "quarantine" and promise not to invade Cuba.

move them under threat. But Kennedy also told Dobrynin: "It was our judgment that, within a short time after this crisis was over, those missiles would be gone."

Dobrynin, however, was not optimistic, and neither were the Americans. ExComm met again at nine o'clock that evening to begin preparations for an attack not later than Tuesday. At 9:20 P.M., McNamara called twenty-four squadrons of the Air Force Reserve to active duty. Sixty thousand Army and Marine troops, the forces for the invasion, were ready in Florida and the Panama Canal Zone. "Now," said the President, utterly drained, "it can go either way."

Sunday morning, October 28, Kennedy was to meet at nine with McNamara and the generals to check details on the air strike. A few minutes before the meeting, Radio Moscow announced that at 9:00 A.M. (5:00 P.M. Moscow time) it would broadcast an important message. As the men in the White House listened, a Russian announcer read in English the Kremlin's response to the letter of the previous night. Khrushchev had agreed at last to dismantle and withdraw the missiles. The United States, in turn, would end the island's quarantine and pledge not to support any future invasion of Cuba. The crisis was over.

48

PAX AMERICANA IN DECLINE: THE KENNEDY-JOHNSON YEARS

A. W.

The Cuban missile crisis provides a convenient dividing line for American foreign policy in the postwar era. It ended one period of U.S.-Soviet relations and inaugurated another. Since the start of the Cold War, American diplomacy had consisted largely of responding to Soviet challenges (some real, some imaginary) with a counter-policy that in Eisenhower's time was called "brinkmanship." But in October 1962, the leaders of both superpowers peered into the abyss of thermonuclear war. What they saw frightened them as badly as many of their policies had frightened the world in the past.

The foreign policy pursued by Eisenhower in the 1950s, and continued by Kennedy in the early 1960s, perceived a world dominated mainly by the United States and the Soviet Union, in that order, and relied heavily on the threatened use of American atomic power to settle or deflect disputes between them. Although the two countries had never before come so close to an atomic exchange as during the Cuban missile crisis, public proclamations of their immediate readiness for mutual disaster, and the swollen size of nuclear

stockpiles, was, for both, evidence enough of such intention beyond reasonable doubt.

The United States and the Soviet Union did not resolve their differences after the Cuban missile crisis; they still pursued widely differing objectives in the world. But both countries, as if sobered by the experience, began to take steps to guard against a repetition of the terrifying days of October by improving communication and deemphasizing "nuclear diplomacy." Not since 1962 have the populations of the two superpowers waited desperately to hear whether they would live out the week.

THE "NEW FRONTIER" IN FOREIGN AFFAIRS

As Democrats before him had done throughout the Eisenhower years, the campaigning Senator John F. Kennedy claimed in 1960 that the President had not used the country's full power to maintain its position and prestige. He charged that Ike's cuts in the military budget had limited America's power to act, had narrowed its options, and had caused the United States to lose its status of world leadership. Kennedy singled out Cuba as one example of the Republicans' misdirected foreign policy, and he accused Eisenhower of not doing enough to topple Castro.

As President, Kennedy did not allow any one advisor to exercise the amount of power wielded by John Foster Dulles under Eisenhower; he made his own foreign policies. But in other areas he made a strong effort to attract capable and perceptive individuals, such as McNamara from Ford Motor Company and Bundy from Harvard University. Less than two years after his inauguration, Kennedy's "team" was to become ExComm during the missile crisis.

Kennedy also tried to bring new ideas to international policy. Regarding the Third World, he expressed greater willingness to work with nationalist leaders. He initiated the Peace Corps, sending thousands of young Americans overseas to teach and work in underdeveloped countries.

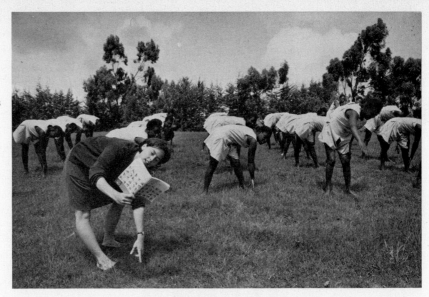

A Peace Corps volunteer from Baltimore conducts a gym class at a girls' secondary school in Chepkurio, Kenya. Established by President Kennedy in 1961, the Peace Corps trained thousands of volunteer workers, many of them young, and stationed them abroad, for two-year terms, in underdeveloped areas of the world.

But, like Truman and Eisenhower, Kennedy intended to prevent the spread of Communism, and to hold the line in Europe.

The sharpest break with Eisenhower's policies came in the area of defense. Kennedy downplayed "massive retaliation" in favor of a new policy called "flexible response," giving him more options in an emergency. One of Kennedy's favorite programs, the Army's Green Berets (specially trained counterinsurgency fighters), reflected both his wish to bolster military capability and his desire for a more imaginative approach to the problems of Communist power and the Third World.

THE BAY OF PIGS

Regardless of Kennedy's new ideas and his new advisors, within months he sustained one of America's most humiliating foreign policy defeats. Cuba proved to be as painful a problem for him as it had been for President Eisenhower, and the new President sought a way to deal with Castro on American terms. "Communist domination in this hemisphere," declared Kennedy, "can never be negotiated."

Once in office, Kennedy learned that the CIA, under Eisenhower's orders, was training anti-Castro Cuban exiles for an invasion of Cuba. Kennedy seemed to have advocated just this kind of action while a candidate, and he ordered the program continued. American planners calculated that when the exiles landed in Cuba, one-third of Castro's army would join them, another third would desert, and the rest would not be able to withstand the invaders. Hoping to achieve this aim, but with as little direct U.S. commitment as possible, Kennedy cancelled CIA air cover for the landing.

The invasion, in April 1961, failed miserably. Castro's forces remained loyal, fought well, and routed the invaders in two days. Moreover, the role of the United States in the fiasco could not be concealed. America had been caught intervening in the domestic affairs of another country—and in a clumsy and ineffectual fashion. Kennedy regained some prestige in the United States by taking on himself all responsibility for the action, but the American position in the world had suffered a serious setback.

VIENNA AND BERLIN

Two months after the Bay of Pigs, Kennedy met for the first time with Khrushchev in Vienna.

Skeptical of the new President's strength, Khrushchev apparently tried to bully him, demanding "adjustment" of the situation in West Berlin and Taiwan; neither of the two areas, he warned, could stay as they were indefinitely. Kennedy replied with a defense of existing conditions and warned that the United States could not watch more territory go Communist without taking action. Khrushchev answered that revolution was sweeping the world; the Soviet Union, he said, would assist the process. Kennedy left the meeting angry and shaken.

Khrushchev seemed most perturbed over the status of Berlin. The four wartime allied powers still governed the city, deep in the center of Communist East Germany. West Berlin—consisting of the British, French, and American sectors of the divided city—stood as an island of prosperity and democracy in the midst of the then drab Russian satellite. The contrast itself galled Khrushchev enough, but West Berlin's position as an escape hatch for fleeing East Germans presented a more tangible problem. Three million East Germans, mostly the young and educated, had escaped to the West since the war, and by the early 1960s they were leaving the German Democratic Republic at a rate of 300,000 a year.

Khrushchev continued to demand changes in the situation; Kennedy continued to decline to make any concessions. Tension increased, and the United States began to build strength for a confrontation. Kennedy tripled the draft call, called up 150,000 reserves, and sent another 40,000 troops to Europe. The president of East Germany threatened to cut West Berlin off from the rest of West Germany—to reinstitute the Berlin Blockade. "I hear it said that West Berlin is militarily untenable," Kennedy told Americans in a TV address. "Any dangerous spot is tenable if men—brave men—will make it so."

On August 13, 1960, Khrushchev and the East Germans responded to the crisis by building a barrier around West Berlin, (first barbed wire, later a brick wall), effectively cutting off further emigration. Although such an action violated the Four-Power treaty on Berlin, the United States took no action. The Russians had not touched West Berlin, and the United States would not go to war over a wall.

CONFLICTS WITH EUROPEAN ALLIES

From the start of Kennedy's term, American policymakers worried about a problem that the Cuban missile crisis—their greatest triumph—would only aggravate. The United States' relations with Western European nations, its closest world allies,

The foreign and economic ministers of Western Europe are shown conferring at a Common Market meeting in 1961. Since then, with its growing economic power, that bloc of nations has become an influential third force in world politics.

ROBERT F. KENNEDY

The life of Robert Kennedy, more so than most Americans of the 1960s, was profoundly shaken by the events of November 22, 1963. Before that day, he had operated as a satellite of his brother John, as his closest adviser, his campaign manager, and his attorney general. He had acquired a reputation for ruthlessness in pursuit of his brother's interests, often acting as "hatchet man" for JFK. After the day President Kennedy was shot down in Dallas, Robert Kennedy had almost to reassemble himself, to draw new strength from new people and things.

In 1960, Robert Kennedy would tell local Democratic leaders that he did not care what they thought of him, that he did not care what happened to him, that he wanted only to get his brother elected President. After John became the first President to name a brother to the cabinet, Robert still seemed to be characterized mostly by a driving intensity. As attorney general, he devoted a large part of his own and the Justice Department's time to putting Jimmy Hoffa of the Teamsters, a labor leader he considered corrupt, in prison. Realizing, once assuming office, the desperate situation of Southern blacks, he assisted them to an extent no previous attorney general had considered. Kennedy's response to situations tended to be visceral rather than intellectual, but he could also be the poised and effective advisor at the time of the Cuban missile crisis.

After the death of his brother, a friend described Robert Kennedy as "a kind of bruised animal." He wanted to be Lyndon Johnson's running mate in 1964, but the two men had long hated each other, and their respective positions now infused a strong element of mutual resentment. Since his brother Edward was already senator from Massachusetts, Robert Kennedy (RFK) ran for the Senate from New York. He won, with the help of the growing legend of his brother, family, wealth, and, ironically, a Lyndon Johnson landslide in the state.

Kennedy disliked both the routine of the Senate and the details of party leadership in New York. Although he made efforts to work in both directions, his real interest was developing and expanding his national constituency—Kennedy loyalists, minorities, liberals—for his eventual attempt to reclaim his brother's office.

After publicly attacking Johnson's Vietnam War policy, he faced demands that he run for President in 1968. Certain that it was not politically wise, he refused, and Senator Eugene McCarthy of Minnesota first carried the antiwar standard. Only when McCarthy ran strong in the New Hampshire primary did Kennedy announce he would run. The first month of the campaign held one more surprise; Johnson withdrew from the race.

Old New Frontiersmen hurried to the support of the second (but perhaps not the last), Kennedy to run for President. McCarthy now refused to withdraw, and Vice President Hubert Humphrey declined to challenge Kennedy in the primaries. Observers watched with awe—and foreboding—the intense emotion Kennedy evoked among widely differing groups. He won several primaries; but even after his June victory in the California primary, he faced a long and highly uncertain road to nomination at the convention. As he was leaving his victory party at a Los Angeles hotel, a young Palestinian-American named Sirhan Sirhan, shot and killed Robert Kennedy.

seemed to be fraying. Although Kennedy felt the United States had convincingly demonstrated its commitment to defend Western Europe in the Berlin crisis, many Western Europeans continued to express dissatisfaction with their role in the Atlantic Alliance and NATO.

Under Kennedy, the United States developed a two-part policy toward Europe. As an ultimate goal it urged a plan called the Grand Design, a united Western Europe (based on an expanded version of the European Common Market, the extremely successful economic alliance of France, West Germany, Italy, Belgium, Holland, and Luxemburg), which would share burdens and decisions with the United States. Until then, it urged Western Europeans to strengthen their conventional defenses while the United States controlled nuclear weapons.

Across both these plans fell the long shadow of France's President Charles de Gaulle. General de Gaulle wished to see France neither swallowed up in a greater Europe nor dependent upon the United States for its ultimate defense. He greatly distrusted both the Americans and the British, feeling that "the Anglo-Saxons" wished to control and divide the western world between them. Despite American objections, he decided that France, like Britain, must have its own nuclear weapons.

The Cuban missile crisis, with its proof that the United States would engage in nuclear diplomacy without consulting its allies, intensified de Gaulle's determination. In January 1963, he vetoed British entry into the Common Market, thus frustrating a long-time American policy aim. He also loosened France's ties with NATO, formed a close relationship with West Germany, and began to make his own overtures to Eastern Europe.

The United States tried to discourage France, and other European nations, from building their own bombs with a plan called the Multi-Lateral Force. This project called for ships carrying nuclear weapons to be manned by mixed crews representing all the NATO powers, but it stirred no interest outside Washington. Although Britain ultimately joined the Common Market, France continued to pursue a course independent of the United States, and eventually pulled out of NATO.

THE BEGINNINGS OF DETENTE

But if the Cuban missile crisis damaged America's relationship with its allies, it greatly improved relations with "the other side." Following the confrontation, both the United States and the Soviet Union looked for ways to lessen the probability of nuclear holocaust—intentional or accidental. Soon after the days of October, they cooperatively set up a two-way "hot-line" linking the White House and the Kremlin with a separate teletype system. The ability to communicate quickly would, they hoped, greatly lessen chances of nuclear war arising from misunderstandings.

The thaw in the Cold War yielded even more specific results in August 1963, when the two superpowers signed a treaty banning nuclear tests in the earth's atmosphere. The agreement reflected in part the fears of both nations about their allies—fears that proved well-founded when France, Communist China, and Cuba refused to ratify the document.

Further, both powers seemed more inclined to recognize the problems of the other, and to see the necessity of getting along. In June 1963, Kennedy expressed this growing tolerance in one of the best speeches of his career, declaring: "In the final analysis, our most basic common link is the fact that we all inherit this planet. We all breathe the same air. We all cherish our children's future. And we are all mortal."

ENTERING VIETNAM

Even with the nuclear pressures eased, major troubles loomed for the United States in a "fringe area." After the cancellation of the elections intended to unite Vietnam, America had supported Ngo Dinh Diem's government in South Vietnam.

Diem, a Catholic in a predominantly Buddhist country, had been having increasing problems with Communist Viet Cong guerrillas, and Kennedy chose to help him defeat the rebels. Much military and economic aid had already been sent to South Vietnam. And starting in 1961, Kennedy sent several thousand military personnel, including Green Berets, to aid Diem. Kennedy wanted to create a strong, pro-Western government in South Vietnam and to show that such a force, with American help, could defeat a Communist insurrection.

During 1961, Kennedy also dispatched both his Vice President, Lyndon Johnson, and General Maxwell Taylor of the Joint Chiefs of Staff to Vietnam to consult with Diem and examine the situation at first hand. Their reports to him, and his own reading of Mao Tse-tung and Che Guevara on guerrilla warfare, led Kennedy to increase the number of American soldiers and airmen in Vietnam. By November 1963, the U.S. presence had grown from a few hundred to 16,000, some of them combat troops. The South Vietnamese government, however, did not seem to be doing its part in holding off the rebellion.

Mounting discontent with Diem's government partly explained the ineffectiveness of the South Vietnamese effort. Buddhist leaders and others complained, justifiably, that the Saigon government was corrupt. Government officials gave favored treatment to their relatives, and they persecuted dissenters. Demonstrators demanded Diem's ouster, and several Buddhist monks gained international attention for their cause by publicly burning themselves to death. In Saigon, crisis piled upon crisis as Diem retreated to the temporary security and isolation of his palace. Then, probably with the covert support, and certainly with the knowledge of the American government, the South Vietnamese military took over the country on November 1, 1963. Diem and his

brother were executed. What Kennedy might have done next is speculation; he outlived Diem by only three weeks.

LYNDON JOHNSON's POLICY

In foreign affairs, as with domestic questions, Johnson was determined to continue Kennedy's example. This determination, plus his own reading of international conditions, made victory in Vietnam a priority issue for him. Retaining Kennedy's foreign-policy advisors, including Rusk, McNamara, and Bundy, Johnson hoped to win the war without greatly increasing American involvement.

In the election of 1964, Barry Goldwater, the Republican candidate, severely criticized Johnson's policy, charging that the United States was taking a "no-win" approach. He even talked vaguely about bringing nuclear weapons into

Senator Barry Goldwater of Arizona, Presidential hopeful and popular conservative, waves to supporters as he arrives in San Francisco for the Republican National Convention in July, 1964. In control of the convention throughout, Goldwater forces produced a conservative platform and jeered Nelson Rockefeller of New York, when the liberal Republican Governor proposed a strong Civil Rights plank.

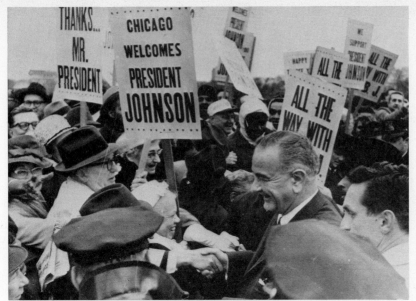

President Johnson, amidst supporters, arrives in Chicago in April, 1964, to address a Democratic fund-raising dinner. During the campaign for the presidency that fall, Republican nominee Goldwater criticized Johnson for not winning the war in Vietnam, while the incumbent President opposed enlarging the conflict or increasing American involvement. As the "peace" candidate, Johnson not only won the election handily but also received more votes, and a larger plurality, than any other presidential contender in American history.

play. Against such an attack, Johnson campaigned as an opponent of a wider war. "We don't want our American boys to do the fighting for Asian boys," he declared frequently.

But Johson also cultivated the image of toughness. In August 1964, American destroyers clashed with North Vietnamese torpedo boats in international waters. (Later, it was revealed that the American ships were convoying South Vietnamese raiders.) Denouncing the North Vietnamese action as piracy, Johnson ordered air strikes against their naval bases.

Shrewdly seizing the opportunity to enlarge the mandate for his Vietnam policy, he went to Congress for authority to "take all necessary measures to repel any armed attack against the forces of the United States, and to repel any further aggression." Johnson had apparently been waiting for a chance to present to Congress such a resolution, similar to Eisenhower's Formosa resolution. In the years that followed, the Johnson Administration would refer often to this Tonkin Gulf Resolution as the authority for all subsequent military actions. It passed unanimously in the House; and only two senators voted against it, warning that it probably would lead the nation into a wider war. Johnson, the peace candidate in 1964, easily won the election.

ESCALATION

Shortly after Johnson's inauguration in 1965, the Viet Cong attacked an American base in Vietnam. The President then ordered sustained bombing of North Vietnam, allegedly to bring the Hanoi communists to the peace table and force them to stop supplying the Viet Cong guerrillas in the South. But heavy American bombing produced the opposite result, steadily drawing the North Vietnamese deeper into the war and increasing the amount of supplies that came in from other communist powers. During this period, the U.S. government apparently rebuffed various North Vietnamese "peace feelers," fearing that the South Vietnamese government was too weak even to negotiate, since the removal of Diem had not brought stability to Saigon.

The weaknesses of successive South Vietnamese governments further complicated the American effort. For four years after the fall of Diem, governments came and went in Saigon. One of them lasted only eight days. No leader emerged strong enough to unite the non-communist elements in the country, to control corruption

When the Vietnamese War "escalated" under President Johnson in 1965, the U.S. intensified bombing raids on North Vietnam and increased by eight times, the number of American troops stationed in Vietnam. Here, soldiers from the U.S. 173rd Airborne brigade, who have just received supplies by helicopter, continue a "search and destroy" patrol through the jungle in Phuoc Tuy Province, in June 1966. This landing zone is guarded by an armored personnel carrier, in the rear.

in the South Vietnamese army, or to win the loyalty of the peasants. When a relatively stable government finally emerged, under two generals, it proved repressive and ineffectual, a creature spawned by U.S. aid and kept alive by the ever-increasing U.S. military commitment.

The worse the war went for Saigon, the deeper the United States became involved. Bombing raids intensified in the north and against communist positions in the south until American planes ultimately dropped more bombs on Vietnam than had been used during all of World War II. In 1965 American troop strength in Vietnam increased from 23,000 to 180,000. By the end of 1967 there were nearly half a million American soldiers in the country.

The failure of the American expedition in Vietnam and Washington's determination to seek military victory worried and alienated many American allies. The United States tried desperately to attract support for the war, to make Vietnam appear a joint action similar to the UN Command in Korea. A few Asian countries—Korea, the Philippines, and Australia—made token commitments. But no NATO ally would join the United States in Vietnam, and France (the previous West-

ern colonial power there) publicly derided American policy. The nature of the Vietnam war, the absence of a clearly defined front line, the inability to tell Vietnamese friend from foe—all these factors frustrated the U.S. effort. Indiscriminate use by American forces of napalm fire bombs and defoliant chemicals also weakened the moral position of the United States throughout the world.

Escalation of the war cost thousands of American lives and billions of dollars in equipment, divided public opinion at home, and strained foreign relations. Still, it did not lead to confrontation with the Soviets, who seemed content to let the United States sink deeper and deeper into the never-ending and costly Vietnam adventure. Soviet-American relations continued on fairly friendly terms during the period, although Russia supplied much of the arms used by the communist Vietnamese. In 1968, the United States, the Soviet Union, and sixty-six other nations signed a nuclear nonproliferation treaty, pledging not to assist additional countries in obtaining or developing nuclear weapons. President Johnson and Premier Kosygin met briefly, but amicably, during one trip by the Soviet leader to the United Nations headquarters in New York.

With the defeat of the French at Dienbienphu in 1954, Vietnam was, in effect, divided into two countries: North Vietnam with its capital at Hanoi, and South Vietnam with its capital at Saigon. Soon Communists and nationalists began guerrilla and terrorist activity against the Saigon government, which received support and increasing amounts of military aid from the United States. These guerrilla forces, formally titled the National Liberation Army, came to be known as the Viet Cong.

In August 1964 North Vietnamese torpedo boats reportedly fired on United States ships in the Gulf of Tonkin. President Johnson ordered the bombing of North Vietnamese naval bases in retaliation. The United States was soon bombing North Vietnam regularly and also areas in South Vietnam held by the Viet Cong. In turn, United States naval bases, such as the one at Danang, were attacked. American bombers then attacked eastern Laos in an attempt to stop the flow of men and supplies from North Vietnam over the Ho Chi Minh trails. United States military involvement increased until nearly 540,000 American troops were in Vietnam.

In early 1968 the Vietcong launched their Tet Offensive—simultaneous attacks on the major cities of South Vietnam. During an American counterattack, a massacre of Vietnamese civilians by American soldiers occurred at My Lai. In the same year President Johnson called a limited halt to the bombing of North Vietnam on March 31 and a full bombing halt on November 1. In 1970 occasional air attacks were resumed.

United States and South Vietnamese forces drove deep into Cambodia in April 1970 in an effort to locate and destroy Vietcong bases there. In February 1971 South Vietnamese troops, with United States air support, crossed the border into Laos in an unsuccessful attempt to cut the Ho Chi Minh trails.

In March of 1972 the Vietcong and North Vietnam launched a massive offensive, capturing the provincial capital of Quang Tri and scoring other successes; in May the United States began systematic bombing of all North Vietnam and mined North Vietnamese rivers, canals, and ports—including Haiphong Harbor.

Under President Nixon the number of American troops in Vietnam was drastically reduced—down to 65,000 in May 1972—and combat duties were transferred to South Vietnamese forces under a policy of "Vietnamization." In 1973 a cease-fire was concluded in Vietnam.

THE WAR IN SOUTHEAST ASIA

◄— United States and South Vietnamese troop moves
◄— National Liberation Army moves
◉ Capital cities
● Major U.S. Bases
— Friendship Highway

0 _ _ _ _ 100 MILES

SANTO DOMINGO

Early in his administration, Johnson became engaged in a policy that, although as unpopular internationally as Vietnam, appeared more successful. Since the violent death of its dictator, Rafael Trujillo, in 1961, the Dominican Republic had undergone several changes in government, and in 1965 a military dictatorship ruled the country. That year, a group of low-level officers and political radicals mounted what looked like a successful coup against the generals. The ruling junta appealed to the United States for help.

Johnson, acting on unconfirmed reports of communist and Castroite participation in the revolution, sent in 30,000 Marines. He announced, however, that he was acting to safeguard the lives of Americans in the country. But when all American civilians had been evacuated, American troops remained, and Johnson then warned of communist domination of the revolutionary forces.

Despite the resultant Latin American hostility, the Dominican intervention succeeded on one level. The left-wing revolution had been stopped, peace-keeping forces from the Organization of American States reinforced the Americans, and an election held in 1966 resulted in a pro-American president. But Johnson's action, like Kennedy's during the missile crisis, appeared to reconfirm in the minds of American leaders the effectiveness of armed intervention. Virtually all the members of ExComm were still holding top government posts during the Dominican intervention, and many remained to carry out further escalation in Vietnam.

JOHNSON STEPS DOWN

By early 1968, opposition to the Vietnam war echoed across the country. College students, in danger of being drafted and sent to fight in a war that was going nowhere, protested loudly. Some burned their draft cards or fled into exile. John-son's Vietnam schemes had all gone awry. Even Robert McNamara, a key architect in formulating war plans, the "Whiz Kid" of the Pentagon, became dove-ish and began questioning the military effort. He dropped out as secretary of defense. An antiwar candidate, Senator Eugene McCarthy of Minnesota, began to challenge Johnson in the Democratic primaries. Johnson rebuffed all his critics, declaring, "I'm the only President you've got." He would try to tough it out.

In January, battle reports from Vietnam shattered the President's apparent composure. During Tet, the lunar new year, the communists mounted their largest offensive of the war. They briefly captured Hué, South Vietnam's second-largest city, as well as parts of Saigon, besieging the American embassy for six hours. American forces counterattacked and recaptured the cities, but casualties were heavy on both sides. The Viet Cong and North Vietnamese seemed as strong as ever, despite a half million American troops and a steady barrage of optimistic public statements from the White House and the Pentagon. The Tet offensive revealed the obvious: the United States had failed to win the war in Vietnam.

Aided by the shockwaves from the Tet offensive, McCarthy nearly defeated President Johnson in the New Hampshire primary. This

Throughout the late 1960s, nationwide opposition mounted to U.S. involvement in Vietnam. On April 15, 1967, thousands of anti-war demonstrators attended a protest in New York's Central Park to demand an end to the fighting in Vietnam. Here, a twenty-three-year-old demonstrator in Green Beret Uniform, Gary Rader, burned his draft card in a ceremony at the start of the rally.

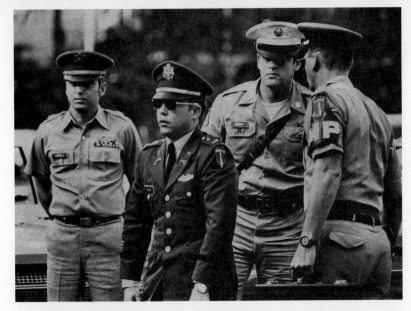

First Lieutenant William Calley, Jr., second from left, arriving at Fort McPherson, Georgia to take the stand as the first defense witness in the court-martial of Army Captain Ernest Medina in September 1971. Medina was being tried by the Army for his role in the My Lai Massacre of March 16, 1968, when South Vietnamese civilians were shot to death by American soldiers who occupied their village. Calley himself was convicted of unpremeditated murder during the massacre and was imprisoned.

By early 1968, opposition to the war in Vietnam and the popularity of anti-war candidates both altered President Johnson's policy and squelched his hopes for re-election. In a broadcast to the nation from the White House on March 31, 1968, Johnson dramatically announced that he would not be a candidate. In the same address, he revealed that he was halting the air attacks on North Vietnam.

strong antiwar showing led Robert Kennedy to enter the race as well. To add to Johnson's woes, his close friend Clark Clifford, the man who replaced McNamara, had also grown skeptical about the war. He began mobilizing sympathizers and amassing evidence in an effort to get the President and America off the Vietnam treadmill.

On March 31, Johnson announced an unconditional stop to the bombing of North Vietnam. This met North Vietnam's first-step requirement for negotiations. Johnson then added that to keep his action from being interpreted as a political gesture, he would not run for reelection. The Vietnam war had claimed yet another American casualty.

SUGGESTED READINGS– CHAPTERS 47-48

The Missile Crisis

Elie Abel, *The Missile Crisis* (1966); Graham T. Allison, *Essence of Decision: Explaining the Cuban Missile Crisis* (1971); Haynes B. Johnson, *The Bay of Pigs* (1964); Robert F. Kennedy, *Thirteen Days* (1969).

The Kennedy Years

Richard R. Fagen, *Cubans in Exile: Dissatisfaction and the Revolution* (1968); Maurice Halperin, *The Rise and Decline of Fidel Castro* (1972); John F. Heath, *John F. Kennedy and the Business Community* (1969); William Manchester, *The Death of a President* (1967); Lewis J. Paper, *The Promise and the Performance: The Leadership of John F. Kennedy* (1975); Jack M. Schick, *The Berlin Crisis, 1951-1952* (1971); Arthur M. Schlesinger, Jr., *A Thousand Days* (1965); Hugh Sidey, *John F. Kennedy, President* (1964); Theodore C. Sorenson, *Kennedy* (1965); Theodore H. White, *The Making of the President, 1960* (1961); David Halberstam, *The Best and the Brightest* (1972); Bruce Miroff, *Pragmatic Illusions: The Presidential Politics of John F. Kennedy* (1976).

The Johnson Years

Edward J. Epstein, *Inquest: The Warren Commission* (1966); Philip L. Geyelin, *Lyndon B. Johnson and the World* (1966); Herbert Y. Schandler, *The Unmaking of a President: Lyndon Johnson and Vietnam* (1977). (Additional biographies and studies of Johnson are cited in the "Suggested Readings to Chapters 49-50.)

The Cold War

Jerome Levinson and Juan de Onis, *The Alliance That Lost Its Way* (1970); James L. Sundquist, *Politics and Policy: The Eisenhower, Kennedy, and Johnson Years* (1968); Richard J. Walton, *Cold War and Counterrevolution* (1972).

Vietnam

John B. Martin, *Overtaken by Events* (1966); George M. Kahin and John W. Lewis, *The United States in Vietnam* (1967); Robert Shaplen, *The Lost Revolution: The U.S. in Vietnam* (1966); Theodore Draper, *Abuse of Power* (1967); Henry Brandon, *Anatomy of Error* (1969); Seymour M. Hersh, *My Lai 4* (1970); Bernard B. Fall, *Vietnam Witness, 1953-1966*.

49 MARTIN LUTHER KING: THE MAN AND THE DREAM

A.W.

The day had been long and hot. The interracial crowd of 250,000 that started August 28, 1963, in a jubilant, festive mood at the base of the Washington Monument and marched triumphantly to the steps of Lincoln Memorial had grown tired and restless in the heat of the late afternoon. They listened to freedom songs by Joan Baez, Bob Dylan, and Peter, Paul, and Mary. They heard demands for greater strides toward black equality from numerous civil rights leaders and celebrities. Exhausted marchers on the fringes of the crowd began to amble back toward the buses that had brought them. But Mahalia Jackson rose to the platform and sang most of the weary protestors back to life with her, "I Been 'Buked and I Been Scorned." Now came the last speaker of the day — Martin Luther King.

The band played "The Battle Hymn of the Republic" as King approached the microphone to give a speech that would become memorable in the annals of the struggle for black freedom. Combining Baptist oratory with civil rights rhetoric, Martin Luther King preached to the marchers and to America about his vision:

> I have a dream today.
>
> I have a dream that one day [in] the state of Alabama . . . little black boys and black girls will be able to join hands with little white boys and white girls and walk together as sisters and brothers.
>
> I have a dream today.
>
> I have a dream that one day every valley shall be exalted, every hill and mountain shall be made low, the rough places will be made plain, and the crooked

places will be made straight, and the glory of the Lord shall be revealed, and all flesh shall see it together.

This is our hope. This is the faith with which I return to the South. With this faith we will be able to hew out of the mountain of despair a stone of hope. With this faith we will be able to transform the jangling discords of our nation into a beautiful symphony of brotherhood. With this faith we will be able to work together, to pray together, to struggle together, to go to jail together, to stand up for freedom together, knowing that we will be free one day. . . .

And if America is to be a great nation, this must become true. So let freedom ring from the prodigious hilltops of New Hampshire! Let freedom ring from the mountains of New York! Let freedom ring from the heightening Alleghenies of Pennsylvania!

But not only that; let freedom ring from Stone Mountain of Georgia!

Let freedom ring from every hill and mole hill of Mississippi. From every mountainside, let freedom ring.

When we let freedom ring, when we let it ring from every village and every hamlet, from every state and every city, we will be able to speed up that day when all of God's children, black men and white men, Jews and Gentiles, Protestants and Catholics, will be able to join hands and sing, in the words of that old Negro spiritual, "Free at last! Free at last! Thank God Almighty, we are free at last!"

The response was deafening. People wept and cheered. Martin Luther King had put into words the great emotional cry of blacks who had been oppressed and ignored for three hundred years. The speech filled them with optimism: his dream would one day become a reality.

King triumphed that day. The minister himself probably believed that such dramatic changes were at hand; and there were reasons for his optimism. What had started eight years before in Montgomery, Alabama, as a campaign for desegregating a city bus line had grown into a national civil rights movement; and King, who had started his career as a minister in a small southern Baptist church, had become the nationally recognized leader of American Negroes.

Martin Luther King, Jr., was born in Atlanta, Georgia, on January 15, 1929, product of a complex inheritance. His maternal grandfather had founded the Ebenezer Baptist Church, and his father had nurtured it into one of the largest and most successful churches in the city. Martin inherited not only his father's name; it was also understood that he would be the next minister of the Ebenezer Church.

But King entered Morehouse College, an all-black male college in Atlanta, at the age of fifteen, still undecided about his future career. Despite his inheritance, he was then trying to choose between law and medicine. The ministry appeared to him as intellectually crude; he was too familiar with the image of the black pastor working his congregation into an evangelical fever. But by the end of his junior year, Martin announced his commitment to the church.

During his years at Morehouse, King began to develop the philosophical basis for his later stance on nonviolent protest against discrimination. Henry David Thoreau's justification for "Civil Disobedience" especially impressed the young man. "One has a moral responsibility to disobey unjust laws. . . . An unjust law is a code that is out of harmony with the moral law," wrote King later, much in the spirit of Thoreau.

Two hundred thousand people, black and white, filled the Washington Memorial mall in August 1963 to give a visible form to Martin Luther King's dream of racial harmony.

Martin Luther King, Jr., was the most eloquent spokesman for racial justice in the 1960s. For many, his passionate plea for nonviolence was undercut by his own violent death at the hands of an assassin.

King graduated from Morehouse at the age of nineteen. He could have moved directly into the ministry, as the assistant pastor of his father's church, but he chose instead to continue his education by attending, first, Crozer Theological Seminary in Chester, Pennsylvania, and later, Boston University. It was at Crozer that King first became acquainted with the writings of Mahatma Gandhi and became strongly attracted to the Indian leader's philosophy of pacifism.

While King pursued his graduate studies at Boston University, he was introduced to Coretta Scott, a graduate of Antioch College, whom he later married. The Kings stayed in Boston while Martin completed his dissertation and received his doctorate.

In May 1954, King accepted the pastorate of the Dexter Avenue Baptist Church in Montgomery, Alabama. That same month, the United States Supreme Court decided *Brown* v. *Board of Education of Topeka*. The unanimous Court opinion declared racially separate school systems unconstitutional. Neither the court nor the twenty-five-year-old minister realized it, but a revolution was about to begin.

It started without fanfare, and, as it turned out, had nothing to do with the schools. On Thursday, December 1, 1955, Rosa Parks entered her usual crowded bus and took a seat behind the vehicle's white section. Farther down the line more whites boarded, and Mrs. Parks was ordered by the driver to give up her seat to a white man. She refused. The bus driver called the police and she was arrested for violating the city's segregation code. Four similar episodes had occurred in Montgomery the previous year, but this time the black community responded.

The groundwork had been laid for concerted black action. Negro leaders had been active in NAACP (National Association for the Advancement of Colored People) programs, and many black women of the community had been working for equality of public facilities through their Women's Political Council. Jo Ann Robinson, head of the women's organization, had already formulated plans for a bus boycott by blacks; she had only been waiting for a defendant like Rosa Parks, a determined and respected member of the black community. When news of the arrest reached Mrs. Robinson, she approached various leaders to seek support for her plan. She first called Ed Nixon, an NAACP official who, in turn, telephoned the Reverend Ralph Abernathy and Martin Luther King, Jr. After King conferred with Abernathy, he decided to give the boycott his full support.

On Friday evening, December 2, black community leaders met at King's church and called a boycott for the following Monday, December 5. They spent the weekend getting news of the boycott to the rest of the black community. On Monday morning the bus boycott proved a total success. Blacks walked to work or used taxis driven by other blacks who had agreed to charge bus rates. Late that afternoon, the leaders met again. They decided, on the basis of this initial success, that the boycott would continue, and they founded the Montgomery Improvement Association (MIA) to superintend it. Martin Luther King, Jr., was elected President of the MIA, and blacks and whites alike recognized him as leader of the boycott. That evening, at a seven o'clock rally, King both challenged and inspired his audience with a call for community protest against the years of racial oppression. As the boycott continued throughout the next year, King was to find that not only were Montgomery blacks ready for protest but the nation itself was prepared to listen.

King and the MIA spent most of December attempting to negotiate with the city government. The city's lawyer warned that recognition of MIA's demands would destroy the social fabric of the South; the negotiations were doomed. By January 1956, the white establishment, frightened by the overwhelming success of the black boycott, began to fight back, legally and extralegally. Police harassment of private car pools among blacks became commonplace. On January 30 King was arrested for speeding. His short imprisonment added impetus to the black movement, and a crowd gathered at the jail to demand his release.

While in jail, King learned that his home had been dynamited. For a man less committed to nonviolence, this would have become a time to seek revenge. Instead, King pleaded for restraint. From the steps of his demolished porch, he spoke of love, not hate. "We want to love our enemies. We must love our white brothers no matter what they do to us." For the moment, violence was averted, and the crowd dispersed.

In February the city indicted the leaders of MIA for conspiring to interfere with normal business. By this time, the Montgomery bus boycott had become an issue of wider scope. King was fast becoming the national symbol of civil rights; his arrest and trial in March received national press coverage, and the majority reaction nationwide was overwhelmingly sympathetic. The local judge found the MIA leaders guilty. At a subsequent appeal, a higher court ruled the bus ordinance unconstitutional. The city appealed the ruling, and the case began a long journey through normal appelate channels that led eventually to the United States Supreme Court. King used the next three months to carry his message across the country, speaking at rallies from coast to coast.

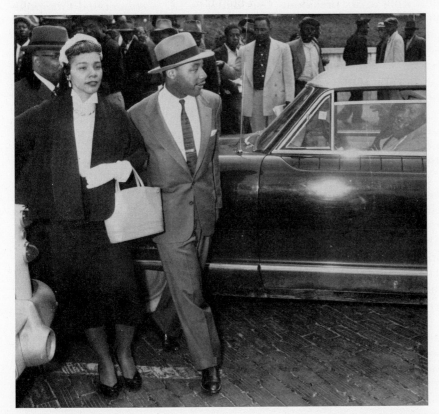

The first of ninety defendants to go on trial for illegal conspiracy in the Montgomery bus boycott, King left the Montgomery courthouse with his wife, Coretta, on March 19, 1956. Although found guilty, along with other MIA leaders, the defendants won the case on appeal, when the Montgomery bus ordinance was found unconstitutional.

Eleven months after the boycott began, MIA faced another crisis. In November the city issued an injunction against the carpool. Without the pool, the boycott would fail. On the morning of November 13, 1956, King and the other MIA leaders entered the Montgomery court in a gloomy frame of mind. And as their trial wore on, it gave them little cause for hope. Suddenly, during a recess, there was a news bulletin that the Supreme Court had reached its decision: segregated buses were indeed unconstitutional. Triumphantly, on the morning of December 21, 1956, King entered a bus and took a seat in one of the first ten rows. His success was marred, however, by the violence that followed. For a month, Montgomery experienced dynamitings and individual assaults, but eventually the city moved to establish peace. Seven white men were arrested and tried for participating in the violence, but they were acquitted.

King and his supporters felt, however, that their legal campaign in Montgomery had succeeded. They had won their court battle, and could now count the federal judiciary as an ally. More important, Montgomery had awakened the nation to the issue of civil rights for blacks in a specific, admirable, and dignified way.

In the years that followed, King devoted his energies to mobilizing his following and organizing his ideas. Meetings in early 1957 led to the formation of the Southern Christian Leadership Conference (SCLC), with King as its president. Originally, SCLC was intended to supplement the efforts of existing civil rights organizations such as the NAACP and the Urban League. But the leaders of these older, established groups opposed King's primary strategy of passive resistance. The NAACP felt that the best way to achieve racial equality was through the courts; Urban League leaders believed that black economic gains would provide the answer.

Not all of King's activities during these years were directed toward civil rights organizing. In February 1959, he and his family visited India, where he was received enthusiastically. King returned to America with an even deeper commitment to Gandhi's principles of nonviolence.

When King returned to America, his father offered him, for a second time, the co-pastorate of his Ebenezer Baptist Church in Atlanta. This time King accepted, for reasons that went beyond simply pleasing his father. By this time the SCLC had grown into a full-fledged organization, with headquarters in Atlanta. King believed that to put Gandhian principles into action, he would have to devote more time to the civil rights crusade. In January 1960 he moved his family to Atlanta and prepared to escalate his campaign with an antisegregation movement centered in that city.

Like the campaign in Montgomery, the Atlanta movement started quietly and simply. On February 1, 1960, in Greensboro, North Carolina, two black university students refused to leave a Woolworth's lunch counter when they were denied service. Within a week, their simple demonstration had sparked similar "sit-ins" in other major Southern cities. By March, the sit-in movement had reached Atlanta, where Atlanta

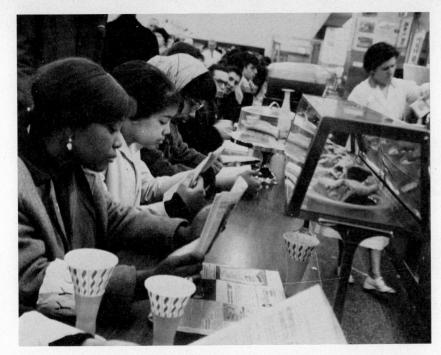

The lunchcounter sit-ins, started in 1960 in Greensboro, North Carolina, proved an effective technique of protest against racial discrimination in public places. The proliferation of sit-ins in the early 1960s, and the attention they drew, contributed to the passage of the 1964 Civil Rights Act.

University students issued a manifesto demanding an end to racial discrimination in education, housing, jobs, voting, law enforcement, hospitals, and entertainment facilities.

The Atlanta campaign operated under the careful guidance of King and the SCLC. In April, King called a civil rights student conference, advocating the establishment of a permanent student organization (later to become known as SNCC—Student Nonviolent Coordinating Committee), a campaign of selective economic boycott, and the establishment of a volunteer army of student demonstrators. King was facing pressure from both sides of the black community. The student movement's potential for violence had to be controlled, while the older civil rights groups—the NAACP and the Urban League, which opposed the new civil disobedience techniques—had to be won over. King moved quickly to maintain the momentum of protest and to retain control of the unfolding situation.

On October 19, he and thirty-six other demonstrators were arrested and charged with trespassing when they would not leave the lunch counter of Rich's department store after being denied service. King and the others refused to post bond. The judge proposed a two-month truce. Arrangements between the prisoners and the city government were being negotiated when an unexpected move by the DeKalb County authorities pushed King's case into headlines all over the nation. Six months earlier, the minister had been arrested in DeKalb County, Georgia, for driving with an invalid out-of-state license, and had been placed on probation for twelve months. The DeKalb authorities maintained that

King's October arrest violated his probation. The prisoner was transferred to DeKalb County and given a sentence of four months hard labor at Reidsville State Prison.

The imprisonment created national outrage, and demands poured into the White House for King's release. President Eisenhower declined to intervene in matters of local concern, however, and Vice-President Nixon, then embroiled in his presidential campaign against John F. Kennedy, refused to comment. But Kennedy showed no reluctance. After telephoning Mrs. King, the Democratic presidential nominee instructed his brother, Robert, to help get King out of jail. King himself was not especially impressed by Kennedy's move, which he saw as one primarily of political expedience, designed to win Kennedy black support at the polls in November.

In March 1961 the combined organizations of three civil rights groups—CORE (Congress of Racial Equality), SNCC, and King's SCLC—initiated a new program: the Freedom Rides. King was appointed chairman of the Freedom Rides Coordinating Committee. The rides were designed to "mobilize" the sit-in; the riders travelled from Washington, D.C., through the South to Montgomery, Alabama. Participants tested the segregation codes of each city enroute by staging sit-ins in public facilities such as bus station waiting rooms and lunch counters.

The results were damaging to King personally and to his philosophy of nonviolence. The first riders met with disaster in Anniston, Alabama, where one of the buses was attacked and set on fire. The second bus made it safely as far as Birmingham. There, the riders were brutally beaten by a mob of whites while police looked on. The riders continued to Montgomery, but many demonstrators were left bruised and bloodied on the highway. King and 700 special marshals appointed by Attorney General Robert Kennedy rushed to Montgomery, but the damage was irreparable.

King then decided to compromise: in May, SCLC suggested a "temporary lull" in the Freedom Rides. This suggestion was totally ignored by SNCC, and during the summer of 1961 more rides and more violence occurred throughout the South. King had been labelled a moderate, and he had lost much of his support among black youth. But there was more to come.

Albany, Georgia, typified many Southern black belt towns. The subordination of the black race was accepted and recognized as the socially correct way of life. The unwritten code provided that blacks were mildly tolerated as long as they kept to themselves. For the black community, Albany was not particularly better or worse than other Southern hamlets. But the events in Montgomery and other civil rights confrontation sites eventually had their impact on Albany.

SNCC decided to test the September 1961 Interstate Commerce Commission ruling that outlawed segregation in bus station waiting rooms. In October, nine students entered the white section of the Trailways bus depot in Albany and were arrested. When the ICC took no immediate action, black leaders decided to mobilize. The Albany Movement was born. Trial for the original "offenders" was set for December 11. That same day, five black and four white Freedom Riders arrived in Albany. They left their bus, entered the white waiting room of the station, and were arrested.

Their arrests touched off protest marches and more demonstrations. By December 15, many people were in jail. That day, King arrived in Albany to lead the campaign. The SNCC leaders reacted angrily to what they saw as a usurpation of their control. Their jealousy would seriously hamper the campaign's effectiveness.

Pitched battles between civil rights groups and city authorities continued. King and his followers staged sit-ins and marches. King was jailed twice, and the city refused to honor its December truce agreement, issuing injunctions against demonstrations of any kind. In July, news of an assault on a pregnant black woman touched off a battle involving several thousand blacks and the police. This appalled King, and he called for a one-day moratorium on demonstrations, which served to alienate further the SNCC. Moreover, black leaders of the conservative NAACP and Urban League continued to hold King's methods ultimately responsible for the outbreaks of violence.

The struggle continued throughout August. King attacked the Kennedy administration for its failure to act. The Albany city officials refused to yield to any of the Albany Movement's demands, and the white community stiffened its determination to retain supremacy. September was a month of white retaliation. Within one week, the Ku Klux Klan bombed four black churches.

King, meanwhile, had returned to Atlanta, where he turned his energies toward another and larger-scale campaign—this time in Birmingham, Alabama. Albany had taught him that future campaigns must be better organized and must be directed toward an assault on specific issues rather than an attack on racial discrimination in general.

The industrial metropolis of Birmingham, Alabama, was especially tough on blacks. Its police commissioner, Eugene "Bull" Connor, was an outspoken racist, and King was anxious to challenge its overbearing, white-dominated control. King had no major worries about divided leadership here; Fred Shuttlesworth, leader of the black Birmingham community, was a long-time personal friend.

Neither did the Birmingham venture suffer from lack of organization. Many meetings and much paramilitary planning went into the formulation of "Project C" (C for confrontation). On April 3, 1963, the campaign opened with the declaration of "B Day" (B for Birmingham). For two days, blacks staged sit-ins and picketed in front of white businesses. On April 6 the second stage of Project C began. Shuttlesworth led forty-five people on a march to city hall. Connor had them arrested and jailed. The next day, Palm Sunday, another group of marchers set out for city hall to join those in jail. Three days later city officials obtained an injunction against the black leaders.

Again King had decided to defy the court order. On the morning of Good Friday, he and Abernathy led fifty hymn-singing marchers toward city hall as black spectators lined the streets shouting encouragement. Soon after they had begun, Connor ordered their arrest. King was placed in solitary confinement. Disturbed by her inability to find out what might have happened to her husband, Coretta King phoned President Kennedy for help. On Monday the President returned the call, giving Mrs. King personal assurances concerning her husband's safety.

While King and Abernathy remained in jail, matters worsened in the city. King's brother was imprisoned for demonstrating without a permit, and his arrest touched off further street disturbances. Governor George Wallace, who had personally defied court orders to desegregate the University of Alabama, was meanwhile encouraging counterdemonstrations by whites. King and Abernathy were released on bail on April 20. The relatively mild sentences meted out to them six days later indicated that the white power structure feared the consequences of imprisoning King, and thus creating a black martyr.

Early May saw more marches and more violence. On May 2nd, 6,000 children marched and 959 were arrested. For the next four days, the nation watched with horror as police swung their clubs and unleashed their dogs. By May 7, open rioting flared in the streets. Kennedy could no longer remain inactive. The next day King was rearrested and Kennedy made his move.[1]

Behind the scenes, the President had already put pressure on Birmingham businessmen to negotiate, and a truce was beginning to take shape. When King was returned to jail, Robert Kennedy immediately called Birmingham city officials to warn them of imminent federal intervention unless the city agreed to black demands that public facilities be desegregated. That evening King was released; the next morning, white officials agreed to meet with black leaders.

The outcome of those meetings in Birmingham were disappointing. The pact between the civil rights leaders and the city was informal, and in the following months the city reneged on much of it. Certainly the pact had not put an end to white violence. In the week after the compromise, King's brother's home was bombed, and more violence ensued. But on the national scale, Birmingham seemed a "success." King's personal prestige soared, and blacks in Birmingham took pride in what they considered a tactical victory. On May 20 the United States Supreme Court upheld the constitutionality of sit-ins. King had succeeded in arousing the country to the issue of civil rights. In June, after several years of directly confronting the issue, Kennedy called for a comprehensive civil rights bill.

---

[1] Both President Kennedy and his successor, Lyndon Johnson, authorized FBI investigations into King's personal life. FBI Director Hoover, who was trying to find evidence that King's SCLC was "Communist-infiltrated," supervised an extensive probe of the black leader that included wiretaps and close surveillance of his activities. At one point, the FBI sent a note to King that threatened that if he did not commit suicide, compromising tape recordings of his personal life would be publicly released. The entire FBI probe continued right up to King's death; it never produced an iota of evidence that sustained the attacks on King's loyalty as an American. The entire episode—only recently revealed—was one of the most shameful abuses of governmental authority in recent American history.

After Birmingham, civil rights and Martin Luther King became truly national concerns. During 1963 and 1964, King received immense personal recognition; but he also suffered severe moral defeats, as the country rocked with violence. On June 12, 1963, Medgar Evers, the NAACP field secretary, was murdered in Jackson, Mississippi. The militancy of black youth, which had surfaced briefly in the Albany and Birmingham campaigns, was on the rise. King found it increasingly difficult to keep the black movement identified with nonviolence.

Throughout June 1963, King toured the nation giving speeches and leading marches in the major cities. But the teachings of the Muslim separatist Malcolm X and other black leaders were also being heard. King's national fame was now drawing criticism from persons who equated his efforts with publicity-seeking. He was seen as a creation of the media, as a peacefully protesting black man—an image more or less acceptable to the country's white majority. King had little control over his image, although he did try to reshape his program.

To gain more national support, King and the SCLC planned a March on Washington, to be held in August 1963. Though originally conceived in 1962, the plan took on special significance as the civil rights bill before Congress faced defeat by a Southern filibuster. In July, leaders from five civil rights organizations and representatives of many national organizations sympathetic to the movement met in New York to plan the march. Black militants censured the meeting, charging that a white conspiracy was seeking to moderate black demands by limiting the demonstration's objectives. Despite this internal discord, the march went on, and King's emotional speech moved the world.

In the South, in Birmingham and Atlanta and elsewhere, violence continued. On September 22, 1963, yet another church was dynamited, this time in Birmingham. Four little black girls were killed and in the ensuing confusion Birmingham police shot and killed two black youths near the scene. In Atlanta, where past demonstrations had been generally peaceful, violent battles raged between blacks and policemen. But neither King nor the nation was prepared for the events of November 22, 1963. John Kennedy's assassination threatened not only King's dream—it threatened the American dream as well. To King, Kennedy's murder reaffirmed the malignant role of violence in the American way of life: "We mourned a man who had become the pride of the nation, but we grieved as well for ourselves, because we knew we were sick."

The events of 1964, in both the North and the South, further dramatized the extent of the illness. A drive to desegregate beaches and other public facilities in St. Augustine, Florida, proved both bloody and frustrating. Promises extracted from the city were quickly retracted, and racial polarization bred more violence. The Mississippi Freedom Summer is remembered more for the brutal slaying of three young civil rights workers—one black, two white—than for the significant gains in registering black voters. In the North, the cities of Rochester, Detroit, and Philadelphia were rocked by racial rioting. These disturbances foreshadowed the even greater violence in Los Angeles, Chicago, Detroit, and Newark

CIVIL RIGHTS GROUPS

Year Founded	Group Name	Purpose
1909	National Association for the Advancement of Colored People (NAACP)	An association that aims to achieve equal citizenship rights for all American citizens, through peaceful and lawful means, by eliminating segregation and discrimination in housing, employment, voting, schools, the courts, transportation, and recreation.
1910	National Urban League	A community service agency that aims to eliminate racial segregation and discrimination in the United States and to help black citizens and other economically and socially disadvantaged groups to share equally in every aspect of American life.
1918	Southern Regional Council	A research and information center that seeks the improvement of economic, civic, and racial conditions in the South by providing community relations consultation and field services when requested by official and private agencies; distributing pamphlets that deal with desegregation of various public facilities, and fostering elimination of barriers to black voting registration.
1935	National Council of Negro Women	A coalition of twenty-five national organizations and concerned individuals that seeks to stimulate the development and utilization of the leadership of women in community, national, and international life.
1939	NAACP Legal Defense and Educational Fund	The legal arm of the civil rights movement that represents civil rights groups as well as individual citizens who have bona fide civil rights claims.
1942	Congress of Racial Equality (CORE)	A black nationalist organization that seeks the right of black people to govern themselves in those areas that are demographically and geographically defined as theirs.
1957	Southern Christian Leadership Conference	A coordinating and service agency for local organizations that aims to improve civic, religious, economic, and cultural conditions through nonviolent resistance to all forms of racial injustice,

in the summer of 1965. "Black Power," a slogan symbolizing violent retaliation to white oppression, became an increasingly popular rallying cry for militant black youth.

King feared that Johnson, Kennedy's successor, would oppose civil rights legislation. But his optimism was renewed in the early days of the new administration, as he and the President worked together amicably. On July 2, 1964, Johnson signed a new, tough Civil Rights Bill into law. During this period, King's emphasis shifted from desegregation to an attack on poverty and economic discrimination. Johnson's antipoverty program, launched in August 1964, complemented King's moves, and prospects for continued support from the White House looked good.

CIVIL RIGHTS GROUPS

Year Founded	Group Name	Purpose
1960	Student Nonviolent Coordinating Committee (SNCC)	including state and local laws and practices. Formerly: Student Nonviolent Coordinating Committee. A committee that sought to help poor people, eliminate slums, and reduce long working hours (now moribund).
1960	National Catholic Conference for Interracial Justice	A religious organization that initiates programs within and without the Catholic Church to end discrimination in community development, education, employment, health care, and housing.
1962	Scholarship, Education and Defense Fund for Racial Equality	An organization that creates programs to provide services in community development, including Eleanor Roosevelt scholarships for students who have demonstrated leadership in civil rights, leadership training programs, and technical assistance for newly elected black officials.
1962	Voter Education Project	A project created as part of the Southern Regional Council to investigate the causes and remedies of low political participation by southern blacks.
1963	Commission for Racial Justice	Commission's purpose is to make racial justice a reality in our national life.
1963	Law Students Civil Rights Research Council	An independent, civil rights legal organization that recruits, trains, and places law students in legal clerkship positions and aims to influence the attitudes of future lawyers about law and social change.
1964	A. Philip Randolph Institute	A nonmembership institution established to serve civil rights activists and promote cooperation between labor and the black community.
1964	Student Afro-American Society	A society that seeks to combat apathy toward the civil rights movement among black college students.
1970	Southern Poverty Law Center	An organization that seeks, through legal precedents it helps to establish via court decisions, to protect and guarantee the legal and civil rights of poor people of all races throughout the nation.

Adapted from *Gales Encyclopedia of Associations*

The results of the 1964 voter registration drive in Alabama were impressive. The number of registered blacks rose from 6,000 in 1947 to 110,000. But at the start of 1965, King returned to the South with plans for a new registration campaign. He singled out Selma, Alabama, as the campaign's focal point. On February 1, King, Abernathy, and 770 demonstrators marched on the courthouse and were promptly arrested. After being jailed for four days, and feeling the momentum dying, King organized a march from Selma to Montgomery to confront Governor Wallace. The marchers, however, threatened with violence, dispersed before reaching Montgomery. But in Selma, three white ministers sympathetic to the black movement were beaten, one of them fatally.

At this point, President Johnson made a historic move. Addressing Congress on March 15, he introduced a voting rights bill designed to guarantee black voting in the South. Johnson also called for a national drive to end racial discrimination. Thus he identified himself with the aspirations of blacks more strongly than had any other President: "Their cause is our cause, too. Because it is not just Negroes, but really all of us who must overcome the crippling legacy of bigotry and injustice. And we shall overcome." Two days later the Selma-to-Montgomery march received federal protection. On March 21 King and his supporters set out, triumphantly entering Montgomery four days later. Clearly, King had succeeded in rallying national support behind a voting rights bill.

And King's dream grew. Encouraged by his recent success, he decided the time had come to broaden his crusade: he began to express his opposition to the Vietnam war. In October 1964 he had won the Nobel Peace Prize. In keeping with his status as an international advocate of peace, he attacked the United States for waging war and for wasting federal funds sorely needed for domestic programs. This new stand cost him considerable support among many conservative black leaders. And it ended his chances of future support from President Johnson, whose administration had widened America's involvement in the war.

The King family moved North to Chicago in June 1966. There, King began a program of organizing black tenants to force their landlords to improve housing in the slums. The opposition to King's first assault on Northern abuses of the Negro was both sophisticated and well organized. Chicago's Mayor Richard Daley commanded one of the best-run municipal political machines in the history of American politics; also, the city's black leaders were disorganized and their political leader, Congressman William Dawson, owed his primary allegiance to Daley. Moreover, the problems of poverty and racism in an urban metropolis

A revolutionary manifestation of black militance, "black power," and separatism, the Black Panthers presented a threatening counterpoint to the nonviolent, integrationist spirit that had dominated the Civil Rights movement in the early 1960s. The Panthers' influence was eclipsed at the end of the decade by the murder of several of their leaders in Chicago.

were unfamiliar to the Southern minister. In the final analysis, they would prove to be more than he could control.

King's announcement of a June march drew only criticism from black militants. Black Power advocates Stokely Carmichael and Adam Clayton Powell both called for excluding whites from the black movement. The June rioting in Chicago's black ghetto postponed the march until July 10, and the turnout was disappointingly small. The aftermath was even worse. Three more terrible days of rioting followed, and King found himself and the SCLC on the defensive.

Faced with the indifference of Mayor Daley and President Johnson, as well as an injunction that limited the size of any further demonstrations, King played his full hand—by this time a weak one. He called for a march on Cicero, a Chicago suburb and the center of white resistance to black demands. Two days before the march was scheduled, black leaders and city officials announced a compromise, but its terms brought no real victory for King and his program. He had obviously ended his Chicago campaign without making clear gains for the city's black poor.

Reverend Martin Luther King, Sr., on June 12, 1977, at a press conference held before he spoke at a Baptist Church in Knoxville, Tennessee.

Although King failed in Chicago, he did not desert his aim of economic racial equality. Rather, in the months following that drive, he devoted even more energy to economic issues. But the rumblings of discord that had started in Albany and had increased over the years had by this time escalated into public attacks on King and the SCLC. Militant blacks characterized King's position as "tokenism"; conservative blacks condemned his anti-Vietnam pronouncements and held him personally responsible for black violence.

Although King continued to urge nonviolent resistance as the most effective way to minimize racial conflict, by 1967 he began to devote far more time and energy to the peace movement than to civil rights. In March and April he headed peace marches and spoke out against the war. Civil rights issues had become overshadowed by the growing national opposition to the war in Vietnam.

In April 1968 King began to plan a Poor People's March on Washington, D.C.—a two-barreled protest against poverty and military involvement overseas. While details were being worked out by the SCLC staff, he received word that his help was needed by black organizers in Memphis, Tennessee. After conferring with his staff, King agreed to go.

A strike of Memphis garbage workers, mostly blacks, had become the focal point for organizing black protest. The effort appealed to King. He believed that a victory in Memphis would provide badly needed momentum for the supporters of nonviolent protest elsewhere in the country. Therefore, he announced plans for a peaceful march to support the garbage workers. But March 28, 1968, the day of the demonstration, was anything but peaceful.

Shortly after the march began, a group of young blacks began breaking windows. The confusion that followed quickly escalated into a riot. Fifty persons were injured, and more than twice that number were arrested. The march was a personal defeat for King. His inability to control his own followers triggered vicious attacks from all sides, and the

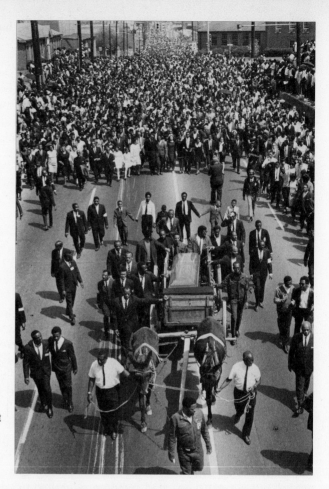

Dr. King's funeral, on April 9, 1968, was attended by 150,000 persons, who marched through the streets of Atlanta, after final ceremonies at the Ebenezer Baptist Church. King's murder, five days earlier, had been followed by riots in sixty-three cities across the nation. The riots, according to Dr. King's widow, were "an ironic tribute to the apostle of non-violence."

city obtained an injunction against further demonstrations. Once again, King announced his decision to defy the court order and to lead another march. That evening, King delivered one of his most fiery sermons to a group of followers in a Memphis church, pleading with them to remain nonviolent toward their enemies. "I have been to the mountain," he intoned, reminding his supporters that he had witnessed the triumphs and tragedies of their movement for over a decade.

King did not march again. The next day, Thursday, April 4, 1968, King was shot in the head as he leaned over the balcony railing of his Memphis motel room. He died before reaching the hospital.[2]

World leaders and thousands of Americans gathered in Atlanta to attend his funeral. Although many speakers eloquently lauded his contributions to racial justice, a simple inscription was carved on the slain minister's monument: "Free at Last, Free at Last, Thank God Almighty, I'm Free at Last."

---

[2]Several months later, an escaped convict, James Earl Ray, was arrested, and confessed the crime. Ray later recanted his confession, but still serves a life sentence for the crime.

50
AMERICA IN THE 1960s: CRISIS AND CHANGE

A. W.

On January 20, 1961, John F. Kennedy became the thirty-fifth President of the United States. Though he won narrowly over Richard M. Nixon, for many Americans of all races Kennedy symbolized the same hope for a better future that Martin Luther King symbolized for blacks. But, in the decade of the sixties, there were over 100,000 American casualties in the Vietnam war. At home, great masses of antiwar protestors spoke out. Black people vented their anger in the March on Washington and in violent riots in the ghettos. University students demonstrated their outrage at government defense research being conducted on their campuses. The voices of women loudly protested sexual inequality. The 1960s, in short, were characterized by an enormous release of energy both within the government and among groups seeking change within the society. What emerged was a mixture of achievement and anguish, confrontation and crisis, impressive social changes and the most depressing of national tragedies.

THE KENNEDY ANSWER: THE NEW FRONTIER

In his acceptance speech at the Democratic Convention in 1960, Kennedy summarized what *he*

hoped to do for his country under the banner of the New Frontier. His domestic program was designed to benefit everyone. He promised to strengthen the economy by reducing inflation and unemployment. To improve the lot of the poor, he intended to provide medical care and increased social security benefits. Blacks were assured that their civil rights would be federally protected. Education was to receive additional federal funding. And all Americans would see the age of consumerism replaced by the virtues of commitment.

Kennedy's Cold War program involved "out-gunning" the Russians. Using the "missile gap" argument in 1960 (the claim that Russia had a greater nuclear striking capacity than the United States), Kennedy supported defense spending designed to ensure that the existence of American arms superiority would deter Russia from initiating nuclear war. This type of thinking ignited a nuclear arms race with Russia in the early sixties, with ramifications evident at home. In 1961 and 1962, hundreds of Americans built nuclear fall-out shelters near or under their homes; millions of school children were drilled on where to go in case of an atomic war; a federal and civil defense bureaucracy plastered shelter signs and stored dehydrated emergency food rations in public buildings all over the country.

The shelters were not used, and the American people breathed sighs of proud relief after the Berlin and Cuban crises. But an important lesson had been learned. Although the Red Scare atmosphere of the fifties had not vanished completely, the outcome of the Cuban and Berlin crises definitely lessened perceived threats of Russian aggression. The Cold War produced a confusing set of circumstances. On the one hand, Americans were led to believe that nuclear war and Communist domination of the world were constant threats. On the other hand, when "eyeball-to-eyeball" crises occurred, the Russians backed down. Was Russia really an aggressive and powerful adversary?

Kennedy's domestic programs met with less success. The civil rights issue exploded in 1961 and 1962, and all Kennedy could do was to ask for a cooling-off period. Kennedy's social reform plans faced stiff resistance from Congress. He failed to win approval for his education, tax revision, and Medicare programs. But he did win moderate increases in federal spending, expanded trade, and stabilized interest rates, which brought the economy out of the recession of the Eisenhower years. These gains, however, did not decrease the 5.5 percent unemployment rate. Kennedy's biggest domestic triumph was the space program, but even that achievement had its drawbacks.

The space program was partially, if not entirely, initiated as another race with the Russians. Distressed that Russia got into space first in the 1950s with Sputnik, Kennedy decided that Ameri-

Neil Armstrong took this photograph of Edward Aldrin preparing a scientific experiment on the surface of the moon. Their successful lunar landing fulfilled John Kennedy's promise of 1961 to put Americans on the moon before 1970.

cans would be the first to land a man on the moon. On May 6, 1961, Alan Sheppard made the first American suborbital flight. Less than a year later, John Glenn circled the earth. Both flights were part of phase one, the Mercury project. Phase two, Gemini, involved two-man space trips. Apollo, the third phase, took men to the moon. This feat was first accomplished on July 20, 1969, when Neil Armstrong took his "giant step for mankind" on the moon.

Although few failed to be impressed by this major technological achievement, some wondered whether it was worth the cost. When three astronauts died on the launch pad in 1967, some scientists blamed their deaths on America's obsession to get to the moon first. Moreover, second to the defense budget, the moon shot proved to be the most expensive of Kennedy's programs. Many critics challenged this expenditure in light of other pressing domestic programs that were seeing their funding reduced or held to inadequate levels.

Despite the complaints and setbacks, Kennedy remained optimistic in 1963, and with some reason. The civil rights movement was gaining momentum. Kennedy's foreign policies won America prestige abroad and fostered American pride at home. In the summer of 1963, the Soviet Union and the United States agreed to ban aboveground nuclear testing. Although this agreement did not end the arms race, Kennedy reassured Americans that their air would no longer be polluted by radioactive materials. Kennedy's popularity began to soar. In the fall of 1963, the President planned a political tour to drum up support for his programs and for the Democratic party. The last stop planned was in Dallas. For Kennedy, it proved the final stop of his career. On November 22, 1963, Lee Harvey Oswald shot and killed the President. The assassin was himself gunned down the next day in the basement of the Dallas police headquarters. For the next week, the American people sat stunned while the events of Kennedy's life, death, and funeral filled the media. Few will forget the blood-stained clothes of Jacqueline Kennedy, or the traditional riderless horse of the funeral procession. John Kennedy passed from the presidency into mythology. His actual achievements and failures became blurred and the prom-

President Kennedy's funeral procession, with its riderless horse, is shown here at the Capitol. At the time he was assassinated, November 22, 1963, Kennedy had been visiting Dallas in quest of Southern support for the 1964 Presidential election. His successor, Lyndon Johnson, soon after being sworn into office, told Congress that he intended to memorialize Kennedy by enacting the legislative program of the New Frontier.

ise he symbolized took hold of the public imagination. His life became an emblem of honesty and peace; his death, in turn, symbolized the corruption and violence in American life.

A presidential commission, headed by Chief Justice Earl Warren, investigated the assassination but did little to alleviate American bitterness. Warren and his colleagues concluded that Oswald had acted alone. But since many questions remained unanswered, the Commission report only heightened public frustration and doubt. The understaffed Commission passed over conflicting data, which led many to believe that the whole truth had not been told. Conspiracy theories mushroomed, some more plausible than others, but distrust of the official explanation continues to disturb the American consciousness.

THE JOHNSON ANSWER: THE GREAT SOCIETY

If Kennedy symbolized a new breed of politicans, the man who inherited Kennedy's challenge stood for the old. Though Lyndon Johnson was only nine years older than Kennedy when he was sworn into office aboard Air Force 1, his style was quite different. Johnson's terms in Congress, including several years as Democratic leader of the Senate, had taught him the intricacies of power politics. Though this kind of political strength helped push his domestic programs through Congress, many Americans, especially younger ones, came to view this power as a corrupting force. And the formation of a "credibility gap" pointed up the distrust enveloping the nation.

In the first months after Kennedy's death, Johnson used his political might—and support from black leaders such as King—to ram through Congress a comprehensive Civil Rights Bill and to launch his antipoverty program. Other Kennedy bills that had bogged down also slid through Congress during Johnson's first year in office. Congress authorized federal funding for higher education, made appropriations for mass transit, and approved a tax cut. In May 1964, Johnson announced that this "drive" was part of his new program—the Great Society, "a place where men are more concerned with the quality of their goals than the quantity of their goods."

Johnson continued to press his domestic programs. In the fall of 1965, Congress passed an impressive number of domestic bills, many originating in or supported by the White House. Health care for the aged and indigent became law under Medicare and Medicaid. The Elementary and Secondary Education Act called for billions of dollars of assistance to low-income children, and private schools received federal assistance for the first time. A new Cabinet post, the Department of Housing and Urban Development (HUD) came into existence. And numerous other bills to combat disease, clean up the environment, make highways safer, equalize immigration quotas, and provide more money for the war on poverty passed easily. Johnson's accomplishments in domestic areas drew applause and even astonishment. Apparently he could do no wrong—until his magical political fingers were burned to a crisp on Vietnam.

The "credibility gap" in foreign affairs grew out of the 1964 election. Like Wilson, who in 1916 campaigned as the man who kept the United States out of war, Johnson promised in 1964 that American boys would not do the job of Asian boys in Vietnam. Johnson fashioned his image as a dove using fabricated cabinet and Pentagon reports on conditions in Vietnam. The South Vietnamese, Americans were told, had the war all but won; United States intervention would be discontinued. Voters believed the Democrats and returned Johnson to office in a landslide victory.

On February 7, 1965, Johnson approved air strikes on North Vietnam, and his image as a peacemaker was soon discarded. Explanations for the bombings did little to restore faith. Americans were told that in order for the war to be ended, it would have to be escalated. Debates on escalation raged across the country, but the Johnson administration wanted victory in Vietnam.

From then on, Johnson's main concern would be the war. Billions of dollars and thousands of lives were committed to the effort. Every night, Americans witnessed the atrocities of war on television screens and wondered which of their husbands, fathers, sons, or friends would die next. No other war in history was so graphically brought home to the nation. The impact of the media coverage of Vietnam, generally, was disastrous to Johnson. The administration's contention that the South Vietnamese supported the American-supported Saigon government was hard to reconcile with televised coverage of Buddhist riots and self-immolations.

But even harder to understand or believe was the notion that United States involvement truly aided the Vietnamese people. Night after night, Americans viewed the charred bodies of Vietnamese and their demolished villages—the aftermath of American air raids. And even if, somehow, Americans got used to hearing reports of napalm air strikes to burn out the Viet Cong, they were not ready to digest the slaughter of 347 Vietnamese men, women, and children by an American unit on a "search and destroy" mission at My Lai on March 19, 1968.

THE SUPREME COURT ANSWER: CIVIL LIBERTIES

The years of Vietnam involvement—and Vietnam disaster—were also years during which legislation broadening personal freedom was being passed at an intense rate. This expansion for civil liberties received support from the decisions of the Warren Court (named for Chief Justice Earl Warren, who presided over the court from 1953 to 1969). The majority of justices who served on the Supreme Court during these years believed strongly that individual freedoms must be preserved; they maintained that an active judiciary should protect these rights against local, state, and federal infringement. The impact of this judicial philosophy was felt in decisions on a wide range of cases, from the issue of civil rights to that of prayer in public schools.

The Warren Court dropped a major bombshell opinion in May 1954. In *Brown* v. *Board of Education of Topeka, Kansas,* Chief Justice Warren and all his colleagues maintained that separate education based on race, regardless of the "equality" of facilities offered to those separated, was inherently unequal. Segregation violated the equal protection clause of the Fourteenth Amendment.

The South, angered by the *Brown* decision, fought the ruling. In Arkansas, conflict over desegregation of a high school in Little Rock erupted into a confrontation between states' rights and federal power. The Arkansas governor attempted first to delay school integration and later to close the high school, but the federal courts were determined to fight school segregation. Ultimately, President Eisenhower had to send United States Army troops to Little Rock to enforce the court order. In subsequent cases involving school segregation, the Supreme Court has upheld the *Brown* ruling.

The Land Americans Have Shaped

How to describe the United States of today? Travelers use words like "size," "diversity," "achievement," "efficiency," "wealth." All are valid. But all seem somewhat abstract without a sense of the people who have worked to make America what it is. Their monuments may be as modest as a tiny New England village—this one in Vermont—or as vast as Boulder Dam. Clearly, they have transformed the land first explored by Europeans over 450 years ago. Wrote Mohamed Mehdevi of Iran: "My imagination could not keep pace with the trials and labors that must have gone into this spanning and building of a continent, an achievement of man. And it had been done not by heroes and great warriors, but everyone."

[For further information on the foreign observers quoted in this essay, see "Notes on Sources."]

PICTORIAL ESSAY 9

Skyscrapers, New York City

New York is a vertical city. It is a catastrophe with which a too hasty destiny has overwhelmed courageous and confident people, though a beautiful and worthy catastrophe. Nothing is lost. Faced with difficulties, New York falters. Still streaming with sweat from its exertions, wiping off its forehead, it sees what it has done and suddenly realizes: "Well, we didn't get it done properly. Let's start over again!" New York has such courage and enthusiasm that everything can be begun again, sent back to the building yard and made into something still greater, something mastered!

[LE CORBUSIER, 1947]

Levittown, Pennsylvania

Already, three out of every five American families own homes. The horizontal trend which has replaced the vertical trend of the skyscrapers is covering the great green spaces around the cities with the individual houses of suburbia. Suburbia is a way of life. In the family-centered society which America has become in recent years, suburbia is regarded as the ideal place to rear children. In this world of carefully mowed lawns there already lives one-third of the nation.

[HERBERT VON BORCH, 1962]

On the banks of the Mississippi stands a stately home with pillared porch, dappled oak alley and a spacious lawn, on which magnolias shed their heavy-lidded blossoms. The home is open to visitors on Sundays, though a family is in residence. There is a guide in the shape of an overpowering lady who waits until the number of visitors meets her approval. The lady praises the past in a voice that echoes in the marble halls.

[JAN DE HARTOG, 1961]

South Carolina plantation

The Americans are proud of their Lincoln and Jefferson Memorials, and they enjoy showing visitors their National Art Gallery, a splendid white Tennessee marble building which looks pink after a rain. Next we visited the Library of Congress. As we walked around the city this evening in the warm moist air filled with swirling leaves, we saw the dome of the Capitol illuminated against the dark sky. Washington is not a provincial city but a melting pot for people from every state who come to do business, petition, or simply visit.

[NIKOLAI MIKHAILOV AND ZINAIDA KOSSENKO, 1960]

Joint session of Congress

The Capitol, Washington, D.C.

Assembly line workers, Detroit

I became aware of the pace of work in North America, a pace that was not the international one but that of Uncle Sam. During the eight-hour day people really attended to their job, and it was taken for granted that the chiefs would set an example of punctuality and dedication. Among us Chileans, and I believe also in all the Latin countries, the boss enjoys the privilege of arriving late at the office and staying away whenever he feels like it, and the employees, by the same token, can refrain from showing too much devotion to their work. Compared with us, the North Americans strike me as a much more powerful and better run machine.

[AMANDA LABARCA H., 1959]

Steel works, Gary, Indiana

University of Chicago Law Library, designed by Eero Saarinen

American architecture has beauty, audacity, and a superb sense of scale, absorbing what is best in modern architecture in Western Europe, adapting itself to American needs, scenery, and wide horizons, and yet presenting what is exciting, new, and vital. The architect works in freedom and according to the needs he must satisfy and the function his building must perform.

[MORRIS BROUGHTON, 1959]

Then there are the cities, and especially those
small towns that hold the secret of the United
States—with their frame houses, their adjoining
gardens always open to the view, their grass
of a succulent and hospitable green, their tall,
powerful trees, their modest and silent
intimacy, softened in the whiteness of the
snow or expressed passionately in the floral
effusion of the springtime; their hospitable
and secluded churches, their bustling schools,
their solitary streets along which there shine
at night, among the trees, the lights of so many
open windows; and the business streets with the
bank, the gasoline station, the tempting and
ingeniously arranged shop windows.

[JULIAN MARIAS, 1959]

Parade at Taylor, Wisconsin

Wheat farm on the Great Plains

If you come from the Eastern states,
or farther east still, from Europe,
going west is a continuous journey of
suspense, from the moment you are
over the Appalachians and know that
the Atlantic has gone for good. In
the Midwest, the sky is a little wider,
and the prairie is a kind of sea all its
own; so much so that in the wheat-
lands of Kansas you get the illusion of
great heaving yellow swells, and the
silos float by like battleships on
the horizon.

[ALISTAIR COOKE, 1968]

Taos Pueblo, New Mexico

Taos is the most characteristic of all the reservations. We were struck at once by its beauty. On two sides of an open space, traversed by a stream, are enormous blocks of buildings, as high as they are long, in which adobe houses are encrusted and superimposed one above the other. The dominant color is a dull yellow, but red and violet cloths, hung up to dry on the flat roofs and fluttering in the breeze, light up the sombre background.

[SIMONE DE BEAUVOIR, 1947]

Hoover Dam (Boulder Dam), on the Arizona-Nevada border

Boulder Dam is something more than a vast utilitarian device, a super-gadget. Enchanted by its clean functional lines and at the same time awed by its colossal size, you might be tempted to call it a work of art; as if something that began with utility and civil engineering ended somewhere in the neighborhood of Beethoven's Ninth Symphony.

[J. B. PRIESTLEY, 1935-36]

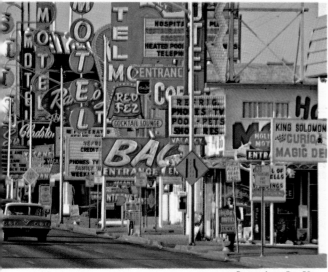

Street signs, Las Vegas

Harbor Freeway, Los Angeles

A feature of Las Vegas hotels is that there are no windows or clocks. Gamblers must not be reminded to go to bed. The less expensive gambling avenue caters for a poorer class of tourist and is known as Glitter Gulch. Its electric signs made it as bright as day. It is ridiculous to sneer at the lighted advertisements of the U.S. Romantic historians are always saying how wonderful Elizabethan London must have been "with all those painted inn signs swinging in the wind." Well, here you have it still alive. Why sneer? It is living, it is folk art, it is exquisite from an aircraft, and I personally like *to be saluted by an electric cowboy a hundred feet high who waves his arm in a gesture of Hi!*

[T. H. WHITE, 1964]

Just leaving my hotel [in Los Angeles] I feel lost —the distance to the nearest drugstore is the same as between two villages in France. One's helplessness in such vastness is paralyzing. In a car with a girl I said: "Let's go somewhere out of town...." "But where?" she asked. "Oh, no matter where...," I smiled, "...where the city ends." "Los Angeles never ends," she said firmly.

[LEOPOLD TYRMAND, 1966]

San Francisco at night

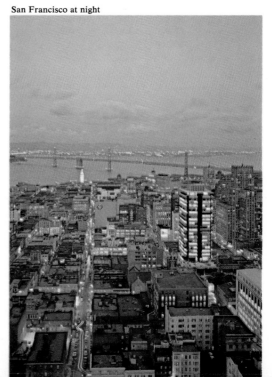

We sped toward the Mark Hopkins [and went to] the top floor. The walls were of glass, and we walked slowly around the room, looking at the myriad lights below; it was far more beautiful than Los Angeles at night, than even New York itself, because of the bay traced out in shining lines against a background of dark water and also those fiery ladders rising from the sea. We looked for a long time. There are, in such travels, moments which are promises and others which are only memories: this one was complete in itself.

[SIMONE DE BEAUVOIR, 1947]

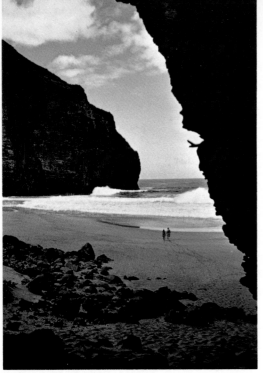

Beach and cliffs, Kauai Island, Hawaii

There is enough wilderness in the world to increase very greatly the number of national parks and to see to it that some of them are preserved in their original condition with access kept so strenuous that the solitary walker is most unlikely to be crowded out.

And this perhaps is the ultimate meaning of the wilderness and its preservation—to remind an increasingly urbanized humanity of the delicacy and vulnerability of all the living species—of tree and plant, of animal and insect —with which man has to share his shrinking planet. As he learns to observe their interdependence and their fragility, their variety and their complexity, he may remember that he, too, is a part of this single web and that if he breaks down too thoroughly the biological rhythms and needs of the natural universe, he may find he has destroyed the ultimate source of his own being. If somewhere in his community he leaves a place for silence, he may find the wilderness a great teacher of the kind of planetary modesty man most needs if his human order is to survive.

[BARBARA WARD AND RENÉ DUBOS, 1972]

Glacier Peak Wilderness, Washington

EARL WARREN

Of the three men generally considered great Chief Justices of the U.S. Supreme Court, Earl Warren served only about half as long as John Marshall or Roger Taney. He was over sixty when named to the Court and had never served as a judge before. Yet from 1953 to 1969, Chief Justice Warren stirred up as much controversy—and helped write as much new law—as most men do in life-long judicial careers. While millions of Americans hailed the bold initiatives of the Warren Court, others bought billboard space and bumper stickers demanding, "IMPEACH EARL WARREN."

The son of a Norwegian immigrant, Warren had slowly and painstakingly worked his way up in California politics, from Alameda County district attorney, to attorney general, to governor. Although a very private man, not given to backslapping, he rapidly became the most popular politician in the state, establishing a strong record as a liberal, effective administrator. Taking advantage of California's unique election laws of that era (laws that allowed "cross-filing"), he won both the Republican and Democratic nominations in 1946, and overwhelmingly won a third term in 1950.

Defeated as the Republican candidate for Vice President in 1948, Warren hoped for the presidential nomination in 1952. But instead, he helped Dwight Eisenhower win the prize. Shortly after the election, President Eisenhower, although himself a conservative, named his useful supporter chief justice. Ike—stung by Warren's liberal activism—later regretted the act, calling it the biggest mistake he had made during his presidency.

Less than a year after his appointment, on May 17, 1954, Warren spoke for a unanimous court in *Brown* v. *Board of Education*, declaring racial segregation in public schools to be unconstitutional. At least one Justice had been dubious about the ruling; the chief justice persuaded him that a decision of such importance had to be unanimous. *Brown* was the first of many decisions in which the Warren Court upheld the rights of minorities.

Not all of Warren's major decisions, however, received unanimous consent from Court members. In a long series of rulings on the rights of criminal suspects, the Chief Justice and four colleagues comprised the bare majority. In *Gideon*, they ruled that the state must provide a lawyer for any defendant unable to afford one; in *Escobedo*, that a suspect can have a lawyer present during questioning; in *Miranda*, that a suspect has the right to remain silent and refuse to answer questions.

In perhaps its most far-reaching decisions, the Warren Court ruled that legislative districts had to be drawn on the basis of population, rather than of county or township borders. These became known as the "one-man-one-vote" rulings, because they voided long-standing practices that gave rural voters greater political power than underrepresented city dwellers.

If such rulings caused right-wingers to hang Warren in effigy, he also earned the distrust of the left while presiding over the Warren Commission, which investigated the assassination of President Kennedy. Warren issued a controversial report which asserted that Lee Harvey Oswald had been the lone gunman. By the time Warren retired in 1969, at age seventy-eight, some but not all of the bitterness directed against him and his Court by extremists had died down.

Still the evasions continued. One technique to evade the ruling was to close public schools and subsidize all-white private schools with county funds. In *Griffin* v. *County Board of Prince Edward County* (1964), the Supreme Court ruled that this practice "denied petitioners the equal protection of the laws." The next assault on the *Brown* decision came through "freedom of choice" plans adopted by many Southern states. Under these, parents could choose the student's school, and local custom insured that black children attended black schools. The Supreme Court overturned this practice in subsequent rulings, which also held that the *Brown* decision required desegregation be accomplished as quickly as possible. These decisions did not achieve immediate desegregation, but more than simply deny the constitutionality of segregation, they required that measures be taken to ensure desegregation.

In a number of other cases involving racial discrimination heard from 1955 through 1966, the Warren Court invalidated segregation of public facilities and laws prohibiting racial intermarriages. It also confronted the legality of convictions growing out of "sit-ins." From 1961 through 1963, the Supreme Court concluded in several cases that demonstrators had lawfully exercised the right of free speech and that arrests had been based on illegal segregation codes. In cases involving housing, the Court ruled that discriminatory practices in sales and rentals were unconstitutional.

The judicial attack on discriminatory voter registration practices had ample precedent. As early as 1927, the Court invalidated Texas's "white primary" law. In 1949, an Alabama law requiring that voters understand and explain any articles of the state constitution was ruled "patently unconstitutional" under the Fifteenth Amendment. After passage of the Twenty-Fourth Amendment prohibiting poll taxes as a voting requirement, and the Voting Rights Act of 1965, the Supreme Court continued to rule against laws designed to deny blacks the right to vote. In a series of cases it upheld federal power to prohibit poll taxes, discrimination tests, and literacy tests as voting requirements.

While defending the rights of black people to equal protection of the law, the Warren Court also enunciated new procedures for guaranteeing the rights of political dissenters and accused criminals. With its attack on various acts designed to suppress political dissent, the Court undermined much of the legality of the McCarthy era assault on Communists, subversives, and political dissenters. In *Yates* v. *United States* (1957), the Warren Court held that, to be prosecuted under the Smith Act, it must be proven that an individual engaged in specific acts advocating revolution. Subsequent cases involving state prosecution of subversives resulted in Court declarations that states could not outlaw mere advocacy of the use of force, because to do so would deny freedom of speech. The requirement that government employees sign loyalty oaths was attacked by the Court in a number of cases from 1962 to 1967. In 1967, the Court held that the requirement of loyalty oaths "threatened the cherished freedom of association protected by the First Amendment." The right of persons to plead the Fifth Amendment to avoid self-incrimination was also reinforced by Warren Court rulings.

Perhaps the most revolutionary aspect of this civil liberties revolution came in cases involving the rights of suspected or accused criminals. In *Mapp* v. *Ohio* (1961), the Court applied an earlier ruling to invalidate the use in court of illegally obtained evidence. *Gideon* v. *Wainwright* (1963) obliged states to provide counsel for defendants who could not pay for their own attorneys. Confessions obtained under duress were declared a violation of due process. In *Escobedo* v. *Illinois* (1964) and *Miranda* v. *Arizona* (1966), the Court ruled out confessions obtained before defendants had been advised of the right to consult an attorney or the right to refuse to answer police questions. The right of the defendant to a jury trial was extended to include state criminal procedures in 1968.

Freedom of the press, protected under the First Amendment, posed difficulties for the Supreme Court in the 1960s. At issue was the constitutionality of censoring obscene or pornographic literature. As one writer expressed the problem, "obscenity, at bottom, is not crime; obscenity is sin." But the Warren Court tried to define obsceni-

DISTRIBUTION OF FAMILY INCOME 1936 AND 1962

1936
Total family income
(= 100%)

14.1%
20.9%
9.2%
4.1%
51.7%

1962
Total family income
(= 100%)

16.3%
22.7%
10.9%
4.6%
45.5%

| Poorest fifth of population | Second fifth of population | Middle fifth of population | Fourth fifth of population | Richest fifth of population |

In this chart, the first "pie" shows the percentages of the total income for 1936 received by the poorest fifth of the people, the richest fifth, and the three fifths in between. The second pie reflects the same data for 1962.

ty constitutionally. The Court tended to vacillate between declaring some censorship invalid as a violation of the First Amendment and, at the same time, upholding censorship as the prerogative of the local community. As a result, the issue became more confused than before.

The Court also threatened many established patterns in American politics by a revolutionary decision, neatly summed up as "one man, one vote." This ruling (*Baker* v. *Carr*, 1962) declared that electoral districts for Congress and state legislatures had to be drawn so that they contained almost equal numbers of people. For generations, cities had been underrepresented in both state and national legislatures. In contrast, rural areas had enjoyed disproportionately higher political representation. The Court ruling threatened this practice and shifted the balance of political power toward the cities.

But the Court provoked the most controversy in the 1960s by deciding against public school prayers. In 1962 the Court declared that the daily recitation of a nonsectarian prayer in New York schools violated the First Amendment injunction that "Congress shall make no law respecting an establishment of religion." One year later it de-

clared unconstitutional a Pennsylvania statute requiring the daily reading of ten Bible verses. These decisions elicited vehement criticism from congressmen and the public. Some irate Court critics wanted to impeach Earl Warren. Attempts were made to pass a "prayer amendment" to the Constitution to overrule the Court's decision, but the measure stalled in the Senate.

By the end of the 1960s the Supreme Court had established an unprecedented record for defending civil liberties in a wide variety of areas. But in the final years of the decade, it became increasingly apparent that this trend toward judicial libertarianism would slow down. The Nixon appointees to the Supreme Court, like Warren Burger, the man who replaced Earl Warren, began to shift the Court's balance toward a more conservative stand.

THE BLACK ANSWER: EQUALITY FOR ALL

The start of Martin Luther King's crusade in the late 1950s took most white Americans by surprise.

Many believed that blacks held inferior positions in society because they *were* inferior. They gave credence to the American work ethic—those who work hard get ahead, and those who fall behind have no one to blame but themselves—to rationalize the oppression of blacks. And King's new tactical program of civil disobedience, although the backbone of the Founding Fathers' opposition to George III, seemed decidedly alien. Still, King's actions forced thoughtful people to admit that perhaps racism *was* part of the American system. This proposition once accepted, King's nonviolent tactics could then be applauded. King merely asked for a fair share of the American dream; other militants who followed attacked the dream itself.

Although King's demonstrations were often accompanied by violence, it appeared that he was succeeding and improving American society's ability to cure its own ills. By 1965, several important federal measures put the seal of governmental approval on King's campaign. The Civil Rights Bill of 1964 outlawed racial discrimination in pub-lic facilities. The ratification of the Twenty-third Amendment in 1964 ended poll taxes in federal elections. In August 1965, Johnson signed the Voting Rights Act, ending literacy tests and authorizing voter registration by federal examiners.

But some blacks remained angry over what remained undone. Since Birmingham, a feeling of frustration had been mounting. In 1965, the first of four successive summers of racial rioting erupted in the ghettos of Watts, Detroit, and Newark. Black militancy was superceding civil disobedience. During a march to Jackson, Mississippi, Stokely Carmichael of SNCC heralded the new black image—Black Power. Many black leaders tried to tone down the implications of Carmichael's approach, but the primary message came through. "Black and white together" (a stanza from "We Shall Overcome") was no longer viable. Black Power meant white exclusion from the movement. Black Power also meant that black people would not wait for justice to be dispensed like welfare payments. The new organization that

Among those influenced by King's advocacy of nonviolent tactics was Cesar Chavez, leader of the Mexican American farm workers. Here he ends a twenty-three day fast in support of striking grape growers by breaking bread with Robert Kennedy.

promoted these ideals most truculently was the Black Panthers.

Even before this, another black, and much more radical than King, Malcolm Little (or Malcolm X as he was known after he joined the militant, but separatist, Black Muslims) had already presented a serious challenge to King's moderate leadership in New York and other Northern cities. Malcolm X himself was killed at a New York rally in 1965. His death—combined with King's and the killing of several Black Panther party leaders in Chicago in 1970—opened the way for a more and more splintered contest for public leadership of black Americans.

By the time Martin Luther King was assassinated in 1968, the crusade for black equality had been transformed into black separatism. Even followers of King's nonviolent philosophy began to question whether blacks would ever be integrated into American society on an equal basis; the Black Panthers and other black nationalist groups had already decided that they would not—nor did they want to be. Although the Panthers were not the only black nationalists, they did receive the most publicity, thus providing Americans with a fractured picture of what black nationalism meant. In the end, some Panthers were killed in police raids. Others were arrested on a variety of charges. Still others shifted to electoral politics and community action to achieve their goals.

During 1968 and 1969, the years of "nonnegotiable" demands, black militants confronted college and university administrations. They called for more black admissions, black faculty, and black studies programs. At many schools, the administration moved quickly to satisfy the blacks. At others, black students took over buildings and conducted teach-ins to apply pressure on

The nonviolent spirit of protest that characterized the early Civil Rights movement, as seen in the peaceful demonstration on the left, during the 1965 march from Selma to Montgomery, gave way within the decade, to a mood of strident militance. The shift in attitude reflected increasing internal division within the Civil Rights movement, the growth in influence of separatist and nationalist leaders, and a mounting sense of frustration, most manifest in the ghetto riots of the later 1960s.

the administration. The long-range effects are hard to assess. Colleges and universities did admit more black students and hire more black faculty, but the gap in educational equality is not so easily closed.

The black response to the 1960s had more to it than black nationalist separatism. All black groups, from the NAACP to the Black Panthers, shared at least a common opposition to racial oppression. What they achieved through their varied approaches and policies still cannot be accurately measured, but by the end of the sixties, the slogan, "I'm Black and I'm Proud" had become a "non-negotiable" reality.

THE STUDENT ANSWER: FREEDOM NOW

College life in the 1950s evokes images of football games, sorority and fraternity parties, and political apathy. But in the 1960s, a number of university students caught the public eye through political demonstrations, takeovers of school administration buildings, and antiwar protests. A variety of explanations have been offered for the new activism. Some maintain that it was the effect of keeping young people bottled up in institutions for the first two decades of their lives. Others contend that by the 1960s, universities had become so bureaucratic that students felt lost and alienated. Still others argue that the consumer culture of the 1950s provided no ideological goals for its youth. Whatever the explanation, students in the sixties demonstrated that they wanted their country to honor its commitments to free speech, equality of opportunity, world peace, and individual freedom. More often than not, the means they adopted to reach these goals defeated their purposes.

Many college and university students were introduced to the tactics of political activism in 1964, during the Freedom Summer and the Berkeley Free Speech Movement. Hundreds of students spent their summer vacation canvassing the back country of Alabama and Mississippi trying to get potential black voters registered. Others parti-cipated in the Freedom Rides. Many activist groups, such as the SDS (Students for a Democratic Society), became increasingly vocal in their opposition to the Vietnam War and to the anonymity of the university complex.

The first student movement to receive intensive national attention was the 1964 Free Speech Movement (FSM) at the University of California, Berkeley. Students and administrators disagreed over the use of a campus sidewalk for distributing student activist literature. When the university ordered the students' tables evacuated, they refused to leave. The confrontation escalated into an attack on the bureaucratic nature of the university itself. A student strike proved 50 percent effective. The next day, the faculty met and voted to remove all restrictions on speech. The FSM had won. Students learned that they had some power to change university policy.

The campus protests quickly spread. From 1965 through 1970, student disturbances rocked universities throughout the country. Many of these disturbances resulted in greater student participation in a university's management. But a backlash by conservatives, appalled at student militancy, was also taking hold. In California, these sentiments helped elect Ronald Reagan governor. Reagan appealed to the disaffected public with promises to discipline students and professors involved in the FSM.

This polarization increased when college campuses became the centers for antiwar demonstrations. Most of the participants and organizations in the antiwar movement had university or college connections. In 1965 numerous campus teach-ins took place; faculty and students discussed and debated American involvement in Vietnam, and most condemned the action. In September the SDS launched a campaign against the draft, declaring October 16–21 "Stop the Draft Week." Students responded with protest meetings and draft card burnings. Not all of the demonstrations were peaceful. A protest march from the University of Wisconsin on Dow Chemical Company (Dow had been selected because it manufactured napalm) ended in battles between the students and police. The week climaxed with a march on the Pentagon building itself. American

Antiwar demonstrators at Stanford University in May 1969, were rousted out of Encina Hall, a University administration building, after voicing their objections to U.S. policy in Vietnam. The array of protagonists typifies social protest confrontations of the 1960s: on one side, the helmeted forces of "law and order," and on the other, a taunting remnant of the counterculture, young and defiant.

TV viewers witnessed the spectacle of armed policemen beating off the protesters.

Organized student opposition grew, and so did violence. Another march on the Pentagon took place in October 1967. And again America witnessed bayoneted rifles confronting militant students.

Antiwar sentiment had been gathering momentum in other strata of society as well. Congress began expressing doubts about the war by the mid-1960s. In January 1966, Senators Mansfield and Fulbright began to hold committee hearings on the conduct of the war. In February, Mansfield announced that Americanization of the war had gained nothing. The Senate Foreign Relations Committee headed by Fulbright brought the congressional debate into American homes with televised hearing on American involvement. While these hearings did not appear to sway President Johnson, they gave some legitimacy to the antiwar movement.

The student movements in the 1960s left their mark, especially in attacking the university's paternalistic tradition. Administrators and regents had to pay more attention to student needs, and students gained a larger voice in shaping policy. Still, the impact of student representation on policy formulation remained minimal.

The antiwar movement was more than somewhat successful in demonstrating the need to reevaluate American foreign policy, but much public hostility toward students surfaced in response to splinter extremist groups that preached revolution. Organizations like the Black Panthers and the Weathermen, although small in numbers, alienated a significant portion of the adult population. To many Americans, the student movement of the 1960s seemed but one part of a widespread and threatening counter-culture.

THE COUNTER-CULTURE

The term "counter-culture" is a handy label for describing the social phenomenon of the 1960s. In simplest terms, the counter-culture represented an unorganized and varied attack by young people on the "Establishment." Student protest and antiwar activity were not the only elements of the movement. Nor were campuses the only settings for expressing counter-culture ideology or attitudes. The counter-culture "mind-set" defies succinct description. But in practice, the idea of a counter-culture implied a rejection of traditional cultural values.

American attitudes toward sexual experience underwent the greatest change. Sexual freedom became a national preoccupation—traditional sex roles were denounced. Young men rejected the time-honored outward manifestations of manhood by letting their hair grow long and adorning themselves with jewelry. Women rejected lace and frills, choosing blue jeans and workshirts instead. Young people of both sexes openly rejected the taboos against premarital sex. College dorms went coed, and the practice of living together replaced or preceded marriage for many couples.

The entertainment world responded to the new sense of personal liberation by exploiting and promoting it. Rock musicians sang about sexual openness. Theater groups produced plays like "Hair" and "Oh! Calcutta," displaying nudity and simulated sex acts. Movies became progressively more sexually explicit. Certainly the easy availability of contraceptives (especially birth control pills) contributed to this revolution and its underlying philosophy: that all middle-class inhibitions on sexual freedom must be repudiated.

In some cases, the general attack on sexual attitudes took organized forms. Many women began to denounce the repressiveness of sexual roles. A growing movement designed to eradicate male domination in American society, Women's Liberation, arose in the late 1960s. Schooled in the tactics of activism by earlier involvement in the black and antiwar movements, many women began to see their most pressing social problems in terms of gender, not class or race. "Male chauvinism" was added to "racism" and "imperialism" in describing American "repression."

Like other movements in the decade, Women's Liberation adopted varied means for ending male dominance. Some organizations like NOW (National Organization of Women) advocated political techniques. Hiring policies in businesses and college and university campuses were attacked for practicing sexual discrimination. Women demanded stronger penalties for rape. A number of women supported legalized abortion. The Women's groups lobbied for the passage of an Equal Rights Amendment, which they hoped would provide the same constitutional basis for

The movement for black civil rights inspired other movements like Women's Liberation. These demonstrators use the foremost symbol of freedom as the backdrop for their demands for political and economic equality.

woman's rights as the Fourteenth Amendment had for blacks, although a number of women fought the amendment as destructive of woman's special rights within American society.

Not all women involved in Women's Liberation saw politics as the correct or only path. Other women's organizations worked on issues closer to home. Female collectives and female consciousness-raising groups formed in most parts of the country. Other feminist groups rejected marriage, the traditional role of the mother as the primary parent, and the concept that the women's place was in the home. Some women extremists advocated an abandonment of heterosexuality. Many American women remained sympathetic to the movement's more immediate and practical demands for full equality in employment opportunities and pay scale, liberalized abortion laws, and expansion of day-care centers. Certainly the Women's Movement of the late 1960s and 1970s eroded the image that most women were content homemakers alone.

Another institution that found itself under attack by the counter-culture was the family. The Women's Movement gave strength to this assault by questioning traditional sex roles within the family, but other counter-culture groups posed more serious threats. One such group was the Gay Liberation League. During the sixties, homosexuals denounced society's legal and moral sanctions against them. They demanded an end to job discrimination and to legal prosecution of their members.

Another challenge to established definitions of family came from the commune movement. Some young people in the sixties started living together in groups, reviving a tradition of utopian communal living with roots that went back to the 1840s. Some of the communes survived, although many were plagued by economic pressures and internal conflicts.

Other counter-culturists challenged basic American traditions and values, questioning the work ethic and the idea that American technological growth guaranteed progress. Some young Americans declared that technology degraded and corrupted life. They decided to return to the rural environment. Organic farming—agriculture without chemical fertilizers or pesticides—became a popular symbol of their philosophy. Others found the answer in Timothy Leary, and the drug culture. Marijuana use skyrocketed in America. This, and other psychedelic drugs, became an integral part of the counter-culture.

The counter-culture thrived in the 1960s and the early 1970s. Though American traditions had been attacked, they were not toppled. Yet a new level of tolerance for alternative life styles was achieved. Nonconformity was tolerated to a far greater degree by the end of the 1960s than ever before.

THE MAJORITY ANSWER: A CONSERVATIVE PRESIDENT

Nineteen sixty-eight was a bad year for many Americans, and an especially bad one for Democrats. On January 31, the Viet Cong launched its Tet offensive in South Vietnam, illustrating a determination and ability to continue the war. The attack spelled disaster for President Johnson. After having assured the American people for more than four years that the United States was winning the war, he was forced to concede his overconfidence. In March, Johnson announced deescalation of the war and a drive for a negotiated peace. The second part of this televised message, however, stunned his audience. "I have concluded that I

Lyndon Johnson's legislative experience helped him get an impressive domestic program through Congress during his presidency. This same activism in foreign affairs, however, proved to be his downfall.

With the Democrats about to nominate Hubert Humphrey inside, the passions of demonstrators outside intensified—but so did the reaction of the police. Here police are shown dispersing demonstrators outside convention headquarters.

should not permit the presidency to become involved in the partisan divisions that are developing in this political year. Accordingly, I shall not seek, and I will not accept the nomination of my party for another term as your President." Johnson, the shoo-in victor of 1964, had dropped out.

Johnson's dramatic withdrawal came in part because he could not hold the Democratic party together. Senator Eugene McCarthy had already effectively demonstrated that fact by nearly beating Johnson in the New Hampshire primary. McCarthy's promise to end the war in Vietnam had won him the support of the student activists. His campaign in New Hampshire succeeded largely because of their volunteer efforts. After Johnson's withdrawal, Robert Kennedy, then holding a New York Senate seat, entered the presidential race. Vice President Hubert Humphrey appeared on a few primary ballots as a pro-administration surrogate candidate. But McCarthy won

some primaries and Kennedy others. Gradually, attention focused on the last primary, California. There, Kennedy won by a narrow margin. There, too, leaving a victory celebration in a Los Angeles hotel, Robert Kennedy was murdered by a young Palestinian immigrant, Sirhan Sirhan.

This assassination—Kennedy's removal from the political scene—turned the Democratic convention into a struggle between a liberal wing, led but not controlled by Eugene McCarthy, and the party regulars, who rallied behind Hubert Humphrey. The regulars held a sufficient number of delegate votes to nominate Humphrey. But while the party regulars were winning inside the convention hall, the actions of demonstrators in the streets outside were losing them votes in the election. Thousands of people, most of them young, had come to Chicago not to attend the convention but to protest the Johnson administration's domestic and foreign policy.

President Nixon and former President Johnson at the Nixon inauguration in January 1969, with Chief Justice Earl Warren, at the left. Nixon, who had refused to debate his opponent, Vice President Humphrey, during the campaign, had won the presidency by a narrow popular margin of about five hundred thousand votes out of seventy-three million. Neither he nor Humphrey had aroused overwhelming enthusiasm among the electorate, nor had the campaign reflected the vital issue of the day—U.S. policy in Vietnam.

On millions of television sets around the country, Americans watched the two simultaneous events: the convention went on with the cumbersome and traditional speeches and roll calls, while outside, the police broke discipline and began to attack the demonstrators. Some protestors fought back with rocks, bottles, fists, and feet. But the main battle ended quickly. The police assumed control, and the crowd scattered to other parts of the city.

The federal government eventually indicted eight protest march leaders on conspiracy charges. But a spectacular trial produced no convictions. And little or no disciplinary action was taken against the Chicago police.

The convention itself was bitterly split between anti-Johnson forces and Administration stalwarts. In that sense the battle almost assured the defeat of Hubert Humphrey, the presidential nominee and Johnson's Vice President, and the election of a Republican President that November. Richard Nixon easily won the Republican nomination at a much more peaceful convention in Miami, although the election itself proved close.

Nixon won a marginal victory. He received fewer votes than in 1960 and won by only seven-tenths of one percent of the popular vote. Both Nixon and Humphrey represented the old guard of politicians, the latter more liberal in his policies, but both urged on immediate end to street protests and a return to "law and order."

When Nixon took office, he promised to bring Americans into an era of retrenchment and tranquility. To accomplish this, he sought to buy off the right while undercutting the left. But this center-of-the-road plan often ran into difficulties. The first three years of the Nixon administration ran a decidedly zig-zag course. To appease moderate liberals, he advocated a sweeping reform of the welfare system that would set up a guaranteed minimum income for every family; but he ignored the issues of urban development and civil rights. In foreign policy, Nixon promised to end the Vietnam war, but to end it "with honor." His plan for accomplishing this surfaced slowly [see Chapter 52].

The economy presented even stickier problems. Nixon vowed allegiance to big business and big labor, whose support had been instrumental in getting him the presidency. In 1969 he promised no government interference and ridiculed the idea of economic controls. But rapid inflation and growing unemployment cut into his popularity. In August 1971 the President announced a three-month freeze on prices, wages, and rents, and after that he placed a ceiling on price and wage in-

U.S. GROWTH OF POPULATION, 1920–1970

creases. Neither big business nor the unemployed were pleased, but Nixon had demonstrated a surprising flexibility.

If the silent majority was happy with Nixon, a vocal minority was not. The war in Vietnam continued; and despite United States troop withdrawals, the end did not seem near. In April 1970 Nixon announced that American troops had entered Cambodia. The promise of peace had been betrayed. Within days, protests erupted on campuses across the country. Four days after Nixon's announcement, students at Ohio's Kent State University were battling police and National Guardsmen. This now-familiar scene escalated to an unfamiliar and tragic climax. In the middle of a May 4 demonstration, National Guardsmen, without warning, opened fire on the students. Four students were killed, eleven wounded. Some of the dead were bystanders. During the rest of the month, buildings were burned and more battles took place on major college campuses. By the end of the month, hundreds of universities and colleges had been shut down, either by student strikes or by administrators fearful of violence. The President's Committee on Campus Unrest reported that, although the use of live ammunition was unwarranted, the Kent State students shared the responsibility for the events of May 4, 1970. The Cambodia spring of 1970 provoked the last of the large campus demonstrations, but never before had student anger and frustration been displayed on such a massive scale.

SUGGESTED READINGS– CHAPTERS 49-50

Martin Luther King

Coretta Scott King, *My Life with Martin Luther King, Jr.* (1969); Martin Luther King, Jr., *Why We Can't Wait* (1964); David L. Lewis, *King: A Critical Biography* (1970); Lerone Bennett, *What Manner of Man* (1968).

Civil Rights and Civil Disorders

Richard Bardolph, *The Negro Vanguard* (1959); Numan V. Bartley, *The Rise of Massive Resistance* (1969); Harold Cruse, *The Crisis of the Negro Intellectual* (1967); James Forman, *The Making of Black Revolutionaries* (1972); Charles V. Hamilton and Stokely Carmichael, *Black Power* (1967); Marshall McLuhan, *Understanding Media* (1964); August Meier and Elliott Rudwick, *CORE* (1973); *The Autobiography of Malcolm X* (1965); Howard Zinn, *SNCC: The New Abolitionists* (1964).

The Supreme Court

Alexander M. Bickel *The Supreme Court and the Idea of Progress* (1970); Albert P. Blaustein and

Clarence P. Ferguson, Jr., *Desegregation and the Law* (rev. ed., 1962); Richard M. Dalfiume, *Desegregation of the U.S. Armed Forces, 1939–1953* (1969); Samuel Krislow, *The Negro in Federal Employment* (1967); Philip B. Kurland, *Politics, the Constitution, and the Warren Court* (1970); Clifford M. Lytle, *The Warren Court and Its Critics* (1968); Loren Miller, *The Petitioners . . . the Supreme Court . . . and the Negro* (1966).

J.F.K. and L.B.J.

Carl M. Brauer, *John F. Kennedy and the Second Reconstruction* (1977); Eric Goldman, *The Tragedy of Lyndon Johnson* (1969); Theodore H. White, *The Making of the President, 1964* (1965); Tom Wicker, *JFK and LBJ* (1968); Rowland Evans and Robert Novak, *Lyndon B. Johnson* (1966).

Protests of the 1960s

William Henry Chafe, *The American Woman* (1968); Robert M. Fogelson, *Violence as Protest* (1971); Betty Friedan, *The Feminine Mystique* (1963); Robin Morgan, ed., *Sisterhood is Powerful* (1970); Kate Millett, *Sexual Politics* (1970); William L. O'Neill, *Coming Apart* (1971); Theodore Roszak, *The Making of a Counter-Culture* (1969); Kirkpatrick Sale, *SDS* (1973); Doris Kearns, *Lyndon Johnson and the American Dream* (1976).

Prosperity and Poverty

Edward C. Banfield, *The Unheavenly City* (1970); Erik Barnouw, *The Image Empire: From 1950* (1970); Scott Donaldson, *The Suburban Myth* (1969); Jane Jacobs, *The Death and Life of Great American Cities* (1961); Charles E. Silberman, *Crisis In Black and White* (1964); Sam B. Warner, Jr., *The Urban Wilderness* (1972).

(For books on the United States in Vietnam, see the Suggested Readings for Chapters 47–48.)

51
WATERGATE

A. W.

The young man on the witness stand was in trouble. Federal prosecutors had enough evidence to put him away for a long time. He had obstructed justice, failed to report a crime, and helped destroy evidence. Like many other people in similar situations, he was trying to soften the coming blows by testifying against his associates. But John Wesley Dean III, former White House counsel, differed from most informers. He was testifying during the last week of June 1973, not in court, but before a U.S. Senate committee probing illegal presidential campaign activities, as millions of Americans watched on television. Under penalty of perjury, John Dean was calling the President of the United States a criminal.

Tensely awaiting Dean's disclosures, the White House was prepared to fight the accusations—the President's lawyer had already given the committee fifty questions designed to discredit Dean. Furthermore, the White House now claimed that Dean himself and former Attorney General John Mitchell had masterminded both the illegal activities and the attempt to cover them up.

Disowned by the White House and hopelessly ensnared by federal prosecutors, John Dean told his story for five suspense-filled days. Senators and committee lawyers questioned him closely, and journalists examined his account for contradictions. All the while the White House offered opposing evidence. Everyone, especially the large television audience, searched Dean's face for clues as to his truthfulness. But at the end of his testimony, the committee and the public knew only what they had known before—either John Dean or Richard Nixon was lying. If Dean was lying, the country had just witnessed a dramatically effective performance. If President Nixon was lying, he would have to pay for it with his office.

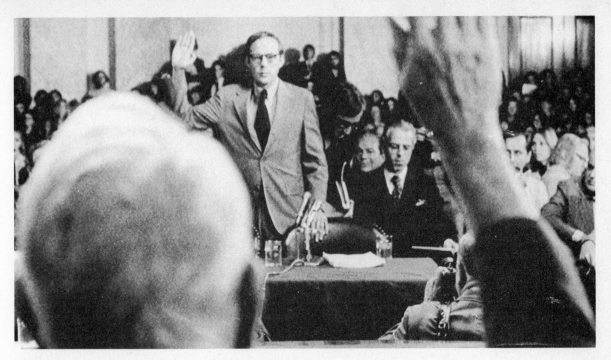

The Watergate hearings reached a dramatic climax with the testimony of John Dean, here being sworn in before the Senate investigating committee by its chairman, Sam Ervin. To test the truthfulness of Dean's testimony, Senate investigators subpeonaed presidential tapes, and a confrontation with the executive branch resulted.

On May 4, 1972, speaking at the funeral of J. Edgar Hoover, President Nixon said, "The American people are tired of disorder, disruption, and disrespect for law. America wants to come back to the law as a way of life."

One month and thirteen days later, a night watchman at Washington's fashionable Watergate office/apartment complex noticed a door handle taped so that it would not lock. Frank Wills removed the tape, but on his next rounds he found the door taped again. At 2:30 A.M., convinced of the presence of intruders, Wills called the police. Within minutes of Wills's call police cars arrived. On the sixth floor, in the offices of the Democratic National Committee (DNC) the police found five men and a large amount of electronic equipment. They appeared to be attaching wiretaps to the DNC telephones. The police took them all downtown in handcuffs.

That afternoon the five appeared at a preliminary hearing to set bail. The government prosecutor stated that the burglars were carrying $2,300, mostly in consecutively numbered hundred-dollar bills, plus elaborate and expensive electronic equipment. He asked the judge not to grant bail. When asked to state their occupations, one of the burglars (one of four Cuban-Americans in the group) answered "anticommu-

Former Attorney General John Mitchell went on trial in New York on February 19, 1974. The ex-cabinet officer was indicted for an attempt to get favorable treatment for millionaire Robert Vesco at the S.E.C. in exchange for a secret cash contribution to the Nixon reelection campaign in 1972.

G. Gordon Liddy, former counsel to the Committee for Re-election of the President, at court on January 30, 1973 for a session in the Watergate bugging trial. The enigmatic Liddy, who refused to testify, was found guilty.

nist." Their leader, James McCord, said that he was a security consultant recently retired from the Central Intelligence Agency.

The CIA connection and the presence of a reporter in the courtroom put the story on the front page of the next day's Washington *Post*. Then the Associated Press discovered for whom McCord worked as a security consultant—the Committee to Reelect the President (CRP), an independent group set up to run Richard Nixon's campaign and bypass the Republican National Committee. Contacted for a comment, John Mitchell, former attorney general, close friend of the President, and current director of CRP (popularly pronounced "CREEP"), said, "There is no place in our campaign or in the electoral process for this type of activity, and we will not permit or condone it."

Bob Woodward, the reporter who had happened to drop in on the hearing, found another lead. The *Post*'s police reporter had learned that one of the burglars carried an address book that included an entry: "E. Howard Hunt—W. House." Woodward called the White House and was given another number to call. When Woodward explained why he was calling, Hunt blurted, "Good God!" and then refused further comment. Although presidential press secretary Ron Ziegler dismissed the affair as "a third-rate burglary," the grand jury on September 15 brought in indictments against the five burglars as well as E. Howard Hunt and G. Gordon Liddy—McCord's boss at CRP. The prosecution indicated it would argue that these seven had planned and executed the Watergate break-in.

Despite its scoop, the Washington *Post* seemed to lose interest shortly after the arrests. Woodward and the other Watergate reporter, Carl Bernstein, were reassigned. The paper regained interest only in late July when the New York *Times*—the *Post*'s archrival—revealed that, before the break-in, fifteen phone calls had been made from the Miami home of one of the burglars to CRP. The *Post* now sent Bernstein to Miami. There, at the district attorney's office Bernstein found the bank records of the burglar, showing deposits of $114,000. Most of the checks came from Mexico.

Other evidence began to appear. The General Accounting Office found a large "slush fund of cash" kept at CRP. On a second trip to Miami, Bernstein learned of a practice called laundering—money was sent through a bank in Mexico so it could not be traced. The Mafia did it all the time, an aide to the Miami district attorney told him, and CRP had done it with $750,000 collected just before April 7 to beat the deadline established by a new law prohibiting secret political contributions. Bernstein also learned that Bernard Barker, one of the Watergate burglars, had told a friend, "I'm not worrying. They're paying for my attorney." Woodward and Bernstein now began digging in Washington, piecing bits of data together. The FBI was not pressing very hard on the case, they learned. Several people were known to have lied to investigators. Money was still going through the slush fund. Woodward also developed his own source—a high-ranking official whom he identified as "Deep Throat." Another source was Hugh Sloan, a young Republican who had

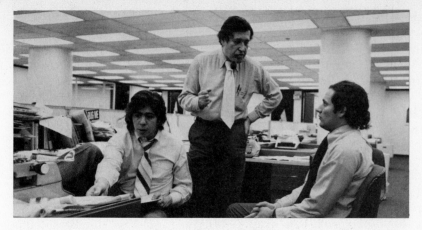

Investigative reporters Carl Bernstein (left) and Bob Woodward, (right) astounded the nation with their dogged inquiry into the Watergate burglary and their exposé of its ramifications in the Washington *Post*. Although their investigation drew intensive pressure from the White House, Woodward and Bernstein persisted with their phone calls, interviews, and diligent pursuit of all leads.

resigned as treasurer of CRP. Sloan would not talk for publication, on the advice of his attorneys. But he did confirm stories Woodward and Bernstein uncovered elsewhere.

Sloan's confirmation proved crucial for their next big story, the revelation that Mitchell, while still attorney general in 1971, had approved payments from the secret fund. The two reporters, armed also with confirmation from sources in the Justice Department, told the story to Benjamin Bradlee, Washington *Post* editor. Bradlee examined the evidence and, after considering the interests of the paper and of Katherine Graham, its publisher, decided to let them go ahead with the story.

Bernstein called Mitchell, who had since resigned from CRP, asking him to comment on the story so far. "Jeeesus!" said Mitchell, stunned. Then "All that crap, you're putting it in the paper? It's all been denied. Katie Graham's going to get her tit caught in a big fat wringer if that's published." The *Post* printed Mitchell's comments, and Mrs. Graham asked Bernstein if he had any further messages for her.

By October other newsmen—from *Time, Newsweek,* the Los Angeles *Times*—had picked up the story. On October 5 the Los Angeles *Times* printed a long interview with Alfred Baldwin, who on the night of the Watergate breakin had been in a nearby motel, linked to the burglars by walkie-talkie. Baldwin said he had delivered logs of wiretapped DNC conversations to somebody at the Committee to Reelect the President. Each new discovery spurred Woodward and Bernstein to dig deeper. Encouraged by Bradlee the two reporters now pushed to keep their advantage, but they could find only scattered fragments of evidence. Unwisely and illegally they tried to get to a member of the grand jury to find out what evidence the government was presenting. The grand juror reported it, and the judge issued a warning—but without naming the culprits.

As November and December passed, the *Post* faced worse problems than judicial disapproval or professional rivalry. "Deep Throat" had warned that the White House was about to move against the *Post*. Under administration pressure to remain silent, the *Post*'s information sources dried up. Bradlee warned Woodward and Bernstein to do noth-

H. R. "Bob" Haldeman, former top White House aide, during a pause in his testimony at the Senate Watergate Committee Hearings, on July 30, 1973. Throughout his testimony, Haldeman denied John Dean's allegations that he had been involved in the Watergate cover-up.

ing they did not want known, to be careful on the telephone, and to have a lawyer handle all their personal tax matters. The White House began to exclude *Post* reporters from social occasions and, more significantly, to give news leads to its competitor, the Washington *Star*. People (known to be friends of the President) challenged the broadcasting licenses of the *Post*'s two Florida television stations. "As soon as the election is over," proclaimed Charles Colson, a White House aide with a reputation for ruthlessness, "we're going to really shove it to the *Post*."

The White House gave another sign of what Nixon's second term would be like. A few days after his easy reelection the President gathered his cabinet, thanked them for their efforts, and announced that he planned major changes. He then turned the meeting over to H. R. Haldeman, his chief of staff, who liked to describe himself as "the President's son-of-a-bitch." "I'm not entirely sure you people understood what the President said," explained Haldeman to the secretaries of State, Defense, and the nine other departments. "When he said he wanted your resignations, *he meant he wanted your resignations.*"

Richard Nixon had often complained about lenient judges contributing to the breakdown of law and order in America. By anybody's standards John J. Sirica was a tough judge. The son of an Italian immigrant, he had worked his way through law school as a boxing coach, and his stern philosophy on sentencing earned him the nickname "Maximum John." Even before the trial began, he had jailed one reporter for refusing to give tapes of an interview to the court. In the pretrial hearing, Sirica made his intentions clear. "The jury is going to want to know: What did these men go into that headquarters for? Who hired them? Who started this?"

All seven defendants had entered preliminary pleas of not guilty. But, just before the trial opened in January, Hunt, who knew the four Cubans from his stint in the CIA, apparently persuaded them to plead guilty, as Hunt himself would. He promised that their families would be taken care of while they were in jail and that after a few months they would receive executive clemency. When the trial opened, all five pleaded guilty.

"Don't pull any punches—you give me straight answers," warned Sirica when the four burglars appeared before him to change their pleas. Who gave them their orders? Liddy, they answered, who was acting on his own. Had anyone mentioned executive clemency? No. Where had the $114,000 in the bank come from—the "hundred dollar bills floating around like coupons"? They didn't know—the money had arrived one day in the mail. "I'm sorry," said Sirica, "but I don't believe you."

The trial of Liddy and McCord lasted only two weeks. The prosecution argued that Liddy had received the money for legitimate security but had decided to use it for the break-in. Liddy refused to say anything; McCord insisted that he had bugged the Democrats to uncover plans for radical violence against the Republicans. Liddy was determined to keep his secret even in the face of repeated interrogation and a possibly long jail sentence. (He had earlier suggested to CRP a surefire way to guarantee his permanent silence—he would go to a specific place, and CRP could send somebody to shoot him.)

Day by day Judge Sirica grew angrier. As Theodore White wrote later, "Sirica's intelligence and dignity had been insulted by the testimony before him." Because he regarded the prosecution's questioning as inadequate, Sirica at one point dismissed the jury and asked one CRP witness forty-one questions of his own.

The jury took an hour and a half to find both Liddy and McCord guilty on all counts. After the verdict Sirica stated, "I have not been satisfied, and I am still not satisfied that all the pertinent facts have been produced before an American jury." And, he complained, "I don't think we should sit up here like nincompoops." He told all seven defendants that final sentencing would be based on their cooperation with investigators, including the Senate select committee that was then being formed to probe Watergate. Sirica put off sentencing until March 23. This would give the seven almost two months to ponder how much time they might spend in prison.

When John Sirica adjourned the trial on February 2, 1973, Watergate suspicions remained several steps away from the President. Little hard evidence implicated either the highest men at CRP or those closest to the President in the White House. In the next three months, one by one, the men between the scandal and the President went down.

On February 17, Nixon named L. Patrick Gray to head the FBI. As acting director, Gray had directed the bureau's investigation of Watergate, maintaining that the White House had not interfered. Although the President had so far refused to say whether administration officials would testify before the committee, Gray had no choice. Requiring confirmation by the Senate for his FBI appointment, he had to face the Judiciary Committee. On the first day of his confirmation hearings, Gray made a damaging admission without even being asked: While conducting the Watergate probe, he had met often with John Dean, counsel to the President, and shown all the evidence to him. But Gray denied that such action implied White House interference and offered to show the investigating files to the senators. Nevertheless, committee members were startled and disturbed by this admission.

Immediately the committee subpoenaed Dean. But the White House announced that Dean would not appear, citing "executive privilege" for the first though not the last time. Nixon also ordered Gray to keep his files confidential. That order came too late. On March 6 Gray released the FBI files, including one headed "Interview with Herbert Kalmbach" (the President's personal attorney). In the interview Kalmbach admitted that he had routed money for undercover political activities. The White House had been caught in an open lie, and now the scandal had reached a presidential aide. On the last day of Gray's doomed confirmation hearings he revealed that Dean had "probably" lied to agents during the investigation.

Thirty-four year old attorney John W. Dean III, former White House Counsel, was President Nixon's chief accuser at the nationally televised Senate Watergate hearings in June 1973.

John D. Ehrlichman, formerly the key White House aide in charge of domestic affairs, appeared before the Senate Watergate Committee on July 30, 1973, for his fifth day of testimony. Ehrlichman attempted to discredit John Dean's testimony, as well as to defend his own role in the break-in of the office of Daniel Ellsberg's psychiatrist.

Almost before the White House could absorb the impact of that assertion, John Sirica walked out of his chambers to find James McCord holding a letter for him. Three days later, on March 23, Sirica read the letter in open court. "Several members of my family have expressed fear for my life if I disclose knowledge of the facts in this matter," wrote the convicted burglar. But he wanted to talk. He said the defendants had been pressured to "plead guilty and remain silent"; also, that "others involved in the Watergate operation were not identified during the trial." Sirica postponed the sentencing of McCord. Hunt and the others who had pleaded guilty received "provisional" sentences of between thirty-five and forty years. Sirica told them that their final sentences would "depend primarily on whether or not you cooperate with the United States Senate."

Within days Washington knew that McCord, talking to Senate investigators, had blown the case wide open. McCord swore that Dean and Jeb Magruder, assistant director of CRP, had known beforehand of the break-in plan. He later added John Mitchell's name to the list. Hunt now testified before the grand jury. On April 2 Dean's lawyers told U.S. attorneys that he was willing to talk. Ten days later Magruder confessed having committed perjury in the Watergate trial.

It seemed that many in the administration were racing to reach the federal prosecutors first, to plead guilty and perhaps lighten their sentences. The prosecutors, of course, encouraged the panic atmosphere, telling Watergate figures that only early confession would count, that the government had virtually completed its cases. The confessional wave uncovered new issues. Why had the FBI not discovered the involvement of all these people earlier? Had there been, as McCord had indicated, a strong effort by the top government men to suppress the truth? Anyone involved in such efforts had committed a crime, obstruction of justice. Slowly interest shifted from the break-in to its aftermath—the coverup.

Dean held the key, since he had met regularly with the President and his closest aides, Haldeman and John D. Ehrlichman. Haldeman warned Dean in early April, "Once the toothpaste is out of the tube, it's going to be very difficult to get it back in." But Dean had no intention of imitating Liddy by going stoically and silently to jail. He announced publicly on April 19 that he would not be made a "scapegoat." He had already turned over to the prosecutors documents implicating Haldeman, Ehrlichman, and Mitchell.

Richard Nixon now saw only one choice. On April 30 he announced the resignation of Haldeman and Ehrlichman, "two of the finest public servants it has been my privilege to know." Speaking on television, flanked by a picture of his family and a bust of Abraham Lincoln, Nixon finished, "I must now turn my full attention to the large duties of this office. I owe it to this great office that I hold, and I owe it to you—to our country." Nixon also chose a new attorney general, Elliot Richardson, a man of unquestioned honesty, and Richardson in turn named a special Watergate prosecutor—Archibald Cox, a Harvard Law School professor and former U.S. solicitor general.

Less than three weeks later, the Senate hearings opened in Washington. Senator Sam Ervin of North Carolina, chairman of the Watergate committee, rejected the idea of calling in the higher-ups first. Instead the hearings started with the lesser fry, who confirmed what the committee already knew: authority for the break-in had come from the top echelons of the CRP, and the defendants had been paid off during the trial. As the hearings gained momentum, the committee members rapidly became a focus of public attention. But Sam Ervin, the seventy-six-year-old chairman, stole the show. A constitutional conservative and anti-civil rights senator in the 1950s, by the late 1960s Ervin showed increasing concern for civil liberties and the boundaries of presidential power. He quickly captivated the nation with his drawling rebukes to witnesses—when his jowls would bounce and his eyebrows waggle with indignation. Responding to a complaint that he was badgering a witness, he responded, "I'm just a country lawyer from North Carolina. I just have to do it my way." Then, Samuel J. Ervin, scholar and Harvard Law School graduate, would lean back and smile not-so-innocently.

Important new revelations came out of the dramatic hearings. Magruder implicated a dozen White House and/or CRP people in the break-in and coverup, including Haldeman, Ehrlichman, and Mitchell. Originally Liddy had suggested a program costing $1 million, involving electronic surveillance, kidnapping radical leaders and holding them in Mexico until after the Republican convention, and anchoring a yacht off the Miami coast during the Democratic convention that would be supplied with prostitutes and wired for sound and photographs. Magruder testified that when Liddy offered his plan in January 1972, Attorney General Mitchell balked—but mostly at the cost. Mitchell, however, later approved a cheaper plan to bug the DNC.

Magruder had named everyone but the President. John Dean completed the list. He had met with Nixon four times to discuss the coverup, Dean stated—once in September 1972 and three times in the spring of 1973. He had told the President details of the coverup and had conveyed the demands of the Watergate burglars of up to a million dollars in aid. The President had told Dean it could be raised. In their final meeting, which Dean suspected was being taped, Nixon had said his earlier statement had been a joke. Dean's account stood up under a full week of cross-examination.

So far no one had explained what had motivated the Watergate conspiracy. Dean said that the activities had arisen from an "insatiable appetite for all political intelligence, all coupled with a do-it-yourself White House staff, regardless of the law." Dean cited examples of White House paranoia, including the "enemies list"—a secret list of political opponents singled out to be given trouble by the Internal Revenue Service (IRS) and other arms of the government. This list included Democratic politicians, reporters, and liberal show business people, such as Paul Newman, as well as various figures whose presence was difficult to explain, such as Joe Namath, quarterback of the New York Jets. Many of those listed proclaimed their delight at being considered a Nixon enemy.

Over the next four weeks the committee heard from all but one of the men accused. Mitchell continued to deny that he had ordered the break-in or conspired with anyone in the coverup. He admitted only that he had kept information from the President in order to ensure Nixon's reelection. Mitchell proved himself a recalcitrant witness; at the end of his second day of testimony before the increasingly skeptical committee, he muttered sarcastically, "It's a great trial being conducted up here, isn't it?" Haldeman and Ehrlichman testified that John Dean had been the mastermind behind the coverup and had misled them. The President's men were stonewalling—not without success from their point of view.

Soon another astounding development overshadowed their testimony. A committee investigator, talking to former White House aide Alexander Butterfield, discovered almost accidentally that the President had been taping conversations in the Oval Office since 1971. Three days later Butterfield told his story publicly, saying that only Nixon, Haldeman, and he had known of the White House tapes. It was no longer John Dean's word against Richard Nixon's.

On August 1 at a state dinner for Japanese Prime Minister Kakuei Tanaka, President Nixon said, "Let others spend their time dealing with the murky, small, unimportant, vicious little things. We will spend our time building a better world."

Outside, bumper stickers read: "Honk if you think he's guilty."

On October 10, NBC News interrupted a baseball game to broadcast a bulletin. Vice President Spiro Agnew had resigned. While serving as Vice President, and earlier, as governor of Maryland, he had accepted cash bribes.

Over the summer of 1973, U.S. attorneys in Maryland had built a tight case against Agnew, but the evidence was not made public until August. Attorney General Elliot Richardson had watched the evidence accumulate since July and was now convinced that the Justice Department had a solid case against the Vice President. In September, before he was brought to trial, Agnew appealed to the House of Representatives, arguing that according to the Constitution a President or Vice President could not be indicted. However, the Democratic majority in the House showed little interest in helping Agnew out of his dilemma. Because Nixon too had maintained that the President was not subject to court action, he had a personal stake in the constitutional issues that would have to be decided if Agnew went to court. Richardson and the White House finally struck a compromise—over the protests of the Maryland prosecutors, who wanted to indict and convict Agnew.

The compromise was simple. Agnew resigned and pleaded no contest to one charge of income tax evasion. For this he received three years probation and a fine of $10,000. The judge announced that he would have sent Agnew to jail, given the evidence mounted against him.

After pleading no contest to a tax evasion charge at a Baltimore federal court, Vice President Spiro Agnew resigned his office. He claimed that he acted to avoid a divisive struggle in the courts.

But Richardson in making the compromise had reasoned that it was of prime importance to have Agnew removed, since he was first in line as presidential successor. After all, Watergate might topple Nixon, or Nixon's health might break down. A long bribery trial would leave the problem of presidential succession dangerously in suspense.

Even after the Justice Department had released the evidence against him, Agnew was not contrite. Five days after resigning, the former Vice President addressed the nation on television, complaining that he was merely the victim of "the new post-Watergate political morality."

On October 6 the Providence *Journal* revealed that President Nixon on a salary of $200,000 had paid income tax of only $792.81 for 1970 and $873.03 for 1971.

Once the existence of the tapes became known, Archibald Cox wanted them. Two days after Butterfield's testimony, Cox requested nine crucial tapes. When the White House refused to deliver, claiming the tapes were covered by executive privilege, Cox went to court, asking Judge Sirica to order the President to give him the tapes. Earlier, Sirica had ruled that the tapes should be delivered to him personally so that he could determine their relevance. The judge rejected the White House argument that the President had "absolute power" to withhold the tapes, and he denied that the constitutional doctrine of separation of powers protected the Executive Branch from court orders. Throughout September these issues were argued before the district court of appeals, with the White House, Cox, and Sirica himself submitting briefs.

On Friday, October 12, the court of appeals ruled 5 to 2 that Nixon had to deliver the tapes to the Senate. But it gave the President one week to work out an alternative arrangement with Cox. On the last day of the week Nixon announced a unilateral solution. He would make summaries of the tapes available to the court, and Senator John Stennis, a pro-Nixon Democrat from Mississippi, would verify the accuracy of the summaries. The President ordered Cox to cease court efforts to obtain the full tapes—or he would be fired.

The next day Cox held his own press conference. Almost apologetically, Cox said that the proposed arrangement ran counter to the pledges made when he became special prosecutor, and he would not stop seeking the tapes. He also stated that the President could not fire him—only the attorney general could.

At 8:31 that night the White House acted. Richardson had refused to fire Cox when ordered to do so and had resigned. William Ruckelshaus, deputy attorney general, had refused to fire Cox and had himself been fired. Solicitor General Robert Bork, convinced that someone had to carry out the President's orders, became acting attorney general and fired Cox. Reporters referred to the removals and resignations as the "Saturday Night Massacre."

Immediately after the announcement, callers jammed Western Union switchboards. In thirty-six hours 70,000 telegrams reached Washington, in four days 220,000, in ten days 450,000. Almost unanimously they denounced the President's action. Many newspapers called for Nixon's resignation. *Time* magazine, in its first editorial ever, asked that he quit. Nixon had badly misjudged the temper of the American people.

The White House held out for three days, then capitulated. On Wednesday Nixon's lawyer stood before Sirica to announce that the President would yield the tapes. "This President," he explained, "does not defy the law." Within two weeks the President named a new special prosecutor, Leon Jaworski of Texas, promising not to fire him without consulting congressional leaders.

But it all came too late. Congress had ample opportunity to gauge the widespread anger rising all across the country against Richard Nixon. Slowly the House leaders began moving toward impeachment. During the next eight months, while the House Judiciary Committee put its case together, the President's situation grew more and more desperate.

On November 17 Nixon spoke to a convention of newspaper editors at Disney World in Florida. He assured them, "I am not a crook."

On November 19 the President promised a group of Republican governors that there would be no more "bombshells" coming out of Watergate. The next day the White House told Sirica that one of the tapes—a conversation Nixon had with Haldeman three days after the break-in—had an eighteen-minute "gap" in it.

On December 20, Peter Rodino as chairman of the House Judiciary Committee named John Doar special counsel for the impeachment hearings. Doar was a Republican who had served in the civil rights division of the Justice Department. Congress rented space in a local hotel for Doar to carry out his work—he eventually filled it with a staff of 106 people. Soon the first partisan consequences of Watergate were being felt outside of Washington. After Congressman Gerald Ford had been appointed to succeed Agnew as Vice President, a Democrat won the special election to fill Ford's seat in the House—the first Democrat to be elected by the district in sixty-four years.

But the scandal had not played itself out yet. On March 1, 1974, the Watergate grand jury indicted seven people in the Watergate cover-up, including Haldeman, Ehrlichman, and Mitchell. The Washington *Post* calculated that twenty-eight persons formerly associated with the White House or CRP had been indicted. On April 3 the Congressional Joint Committee on Internal Revenue Taxation, to whom the President had given all of his tax materials, ruled that he owed $432,787.13 in back taxes. The President said he would pay it.

Finally, on April 29, Nixon made a stark attempt to quiet the scandal. He released to the public twelve hundred pages of transcripts from the tapes. In a television address he argued that he had had little control of the 1972 campaign, for he had spent the year pursuing peace in Moscow and Peking. Incredibly, the President's transcripts were the most damning evidence yet. When Dean said that the defendants might want a million dollars, the President replied, "I know where it could be gotten. It is not easy, but it could be done." The tapes revealed an almost total concentration on political expediency, as well as appalling indecision. And they were studded with the phrase "expletive deleted"—meaning that a profanity had been edited out. This made what was already bad seem even worse. Thus when Dean told the President that Hunt wanted $120,000 immediately, Nixon answered, "(Expletive deleted), get it." Instead of calming the storm, Nixon's release of the tapes touched off a new wave of demands for his resignation and seriously weakened his position as the Judiciary Committee hearings opened.

Unassuming Congressman Peter Rodino of Newark, New Jersey, would never be the folksy, Bible-quoting television star Sam Ervin had been. But in a methodical, cautious fashion, Rodino and Doar began organizing evidence, taking time to assemble every shred. In March, Rodino killed a move by committee liberals to subpoena Nixon. Instead Doar politely requested more tapes. In the spirit of fairness, Rodino's committee allowed the President's lawyer to participate in the hearings. Nevertheless, the White House attacked the committee's motivation and delayed in supplying material.

When Doar began presenting evidence to the committee in May, many politicians complained about his and Rodino's slow, careful style. Some Democrats on the committee were ready to vote right away, and some Republicans charged that the Democrats were prolonging the agony. By the end of June, as Doar continued to present evidence with no vote in sight, Majority Leader O'Neill exerted pressure. But Rodino refused to be hurried. His committee included three conservative Southern Democrats, and Rodino wanted to hold all of them; it had seventeen Republicans, and Rodino wanted at least five of their votes. He did not want his committee to recommend impeachment on a narrow or party-line vote.

Finally in July the situation began to crystallize. Dean and other witnesses appeared before the committee. Doar made his final argument, summarizing the evidence for impeachment. Rejecting the administration argument—that impeachment required proof of a criminal act—he urged the committee to look at the pattern of all the President's acts, which added up to "the terrible deed of subverting the Constitution." He recommended four articles of impeachment: the Watergate coverup; abuse of power, including using the CIA and IRS for political ends; failure to respond to committee subpoenas for the tapes; and the President's tax case.

At last the time had come for the committee members to make a decision. The thirty-eight members of Congress, barely known outside their own districts, had been readying themselves. The Southern Democrats had consulted with one another, as well as with Rodino and Doar. The half-dozen undecided Republicans had consulted with one another and with the Southern Democrats.

Meanwhile Leon Jaworski had been pressing for access to the tapes that had cost Cox his job—and the issue had reached the highest court in America. On the morning of July 24 the Supreme Court ruled that Richard Nixon must release the tapes. Speaking for a unanimous Court, Chief Justice Warren Burger, a Nixon appointee, declared that the courts, not the President, would decide what evidence was required by the courts: Nixon must hand over the tapes.

The President had run out of options. Defiance of the Supreme Court would precipitate impeachment by the committee and catapult the issue into the House and Senate. To avoid this, Nixon announced from San Clemente that he would surrender the tapes, although preparing them might take a little time. That same night the Judiciary Committee began its televised hearings. Each member opened with a fifteen-minute statement, which proved to be a fascinating preview of the issues

The House Judiciary Committee, headed by New Jersey Congressman Peter Rodino, opened debate on July 24, 1974 on whether to recommend impeachment of President Nixon. After months of inquiry, as well as several subpoenas of the damaging White House tapes, the politically divided committee assessed the evidence they had amassed. At the conclusion of their session, the House Committee voted to recommend three articles of impeachment.

at stake. "This is no ordinary set of speeches," wrote one reporter. "It is the most extraordinary political debate I have ever heard—perhaps the most extraordinary since the Constitutional Convention."

On the third day the committee began considering the first impeachment article—charging that the President and his agents had acted "to delay, impede, and obstruct the investigation" and listing the means used. The last sentence stunned the room, although everyone had known it was coming: "Wherefore, Richard M. Nixon, by such conduct, warrants impeachment and trial, and removal from office."

Charles Sandman, Republican of New Jersey, opened the attack on the article, demanding "specificity"—hard facts. Proponents of the article, stung by the challenge, prepared to present justification for each clause. If Sandman and others wanted specificity, specificity they would get. For two days Democrats and Republicans rehashed the entire story: the payments to Hunt and the burglars, proven on the tapes; Dean's monitoring of the FBI investigation; the President's lack of interest in finding out the facts about the break-in; his discussing the case with Haldeman and Ehrlichman when he knew both were under suspicion; his knowledge of perjury all around him; his refusal to supply the tapes; his firing of Cox. The pro-Nixon Republicans listened to the exposition bitterly, noting only that no one had yet produced the "smoking gun" that would indisputably establish Nixon's guilt.

On the night of July 27, 1974, the Judiciary Committee passed the first article, recommending that the House impeach the President. The roll call ran down twenty Democrats, all voting aye in soft voices. The first four Republicans voted no; then one voted aye, and another, until six Republicans of the seventeen had voted to remove the President, head of their own party. Rodino, casting the last vote, made the total 27 to 11 for impeachment.

Many of the congressmen tried to compose themselves as they left the committee room to talk to reporters. Several, including Rodino, could not—they went into the antechamber and wept. The margin was big enough to counter the charge of partisanship. During the next week the committee passed two additional articles and defeated two more.

Although John Doar had not been able to present it, the "smoking gun" did exist. The President's lawyer, James St. Clair, had found it while listening to the tapes about to be turned over to Judge Sirica. He showed the transcript to Alexander Haig, a general serving as the President's chief of staff. Haig, who had assumed almost the duties of "acting President" while Nixon concentrated on his impeachment troubles, showed it to a Nixon loyalist in the Senate. The senator told Haig that the Senate would convict Nixon with this information. On the afternoon of August 2 Haig called Nixon defender Congressman Charles Wiggins, who was busy organizing the President's defense on the House floor, to the White House and showed him the key transcript. Wiggins went back to the Capitol and tore up his defense notes.

Haig and Republican leaders now sought a quick resignation. They tried to nudge the President toward that decision. On the afternoon of August 5 the President—at Haig's insistence—released three of the tapes to the public, acknowledging that they "may further damage my case." The tapes he stated "are at variance with certain of my previous statements." Nevertheless, he did not believe that the new evidence justified impeachment.

Later that night the incriminating transcript reached the press. It was taken from the tapes for June 23, 1972—six days after the Watergate break-in. In it Haldeman informed Nixon that the FBI was pushing the investigation hard and would soon trace the burglars' cash back through Mexico to the CRP. The only way to avoid this, he told Nixon, was to direct the CIA to tell the FBI to back off for "national security" reasons. Nixon ordered Haldeman to do just that.

The next day, all ten Republicans who had supported the President on the Judiciary Committee announced that they would vote for impeachment. So did John Rhodes, the House minority leader. Senator Barry Goldwater, one of the Republican party's most respected politicians, told a group of senators, "You can only be lied to so often." Washington by now was discussing an Agnew-like deal: Nixon's resignation in exchange for immunity from prosecution. On Wednesday, August 7, Goldwater, Rhodes, and Senate Republican Leader Scott went to the White House. Impeachment by the House and conviction by the Senate would come, they told the President. Even they might have to vote to impeach on at least one article.

On Thursday evening Nixon became the first President of the United States to step down from office. His resignation took effect at noon of the next day, by which time Richard M. Nixon was already in an air force plane flying home to California.

Surrounded by his family, President Nixon gave a resignation speech to his staff in the East room of the White House, before a tearful departure for San Clemente. After a year of trials and convictions, hearings and debates, subpoenas and revelations, impeachment by the House and conviction by the Senate now seemed inevitable.

52
AMERICA IN
THE 1970s

A.W.

Many Americans considered Watergate as much a symptom as a cause of this country's troubles during the first half of the 1970s. The nation endured its final humiliation in Southeast Asia—the Communist takeover of all of Vietnam—and Americans began to question some of their longest-held assumptions about foreign policy. The racial violence of the sixties, while largely abated, had left a large residue of resentment on both sides, one that flared up hotly as school integration struggles moved North.

In the midst of these sobering realities, the country suffered its worst economic crisis since the Great Depression. Unemployment rose steadily, while at the same time—and in defiance of conventional theory—inflation also became a major problem. By the middle of the decade the rate of inflation had eased slightly; but prices continued upward, and government anti-inflationary monetary policies did little to curb the rise in unemployment.

Following on the heels of these social and economic crises, the forced resignations of the President and Vice President of the United States left the country stunned. Polls showed that Americans felt less confidence in politicians than in any other group or profession. The country tried to extract some comfort from the performance of other public institutions during Watergate— Congress, the courts, the press. Although Americans as they prepared for the bicentennial cele-

bration had by no means given up on their system, attitudes toward government contrasted disturbingly with the bouncing optimism that is supposed to animate such affairs.

THE NIXON ERA

Nixon Takes Over the War   When Richard Nixon entered the White House in 1969, his most urgent problem was the war in Vietnam. The issue had done much to destroy the previous administration and to get him elected. During the campaign he had announced—but refused to reveal details of— a plan to get the United States honorably out of Vietnam. As the futility of the Paris peace negotiations became apparent, Nixon's strategy assumed an even greater importance.

Gradually the President unveiled a policy of slow withdrawal of American troops with continued or increasing military and economic aid to the South Vietnamese government. This approach gained the name of "Vietnamization." Nixon broadened the idea to include future problems in Asia by proclaiming a "Nixon Doctrine"—that America would aid anticommunist governments in Asia but would avoid further land wars on that continent.

Although Nixon would not accept outright defeat in Vietnam, neither would he let the war interfere with his broader aims in foreign policy. He had a particular interest in foreign affairs and often remarked that the country could almost run itself domestically. For advice and assistance, Nixon bypassed the State Department and relied on his special assistant for national security, a Harvard professor named Henry Kissinger.

The Nixon Administration and Dissent   The upheaval following the Cambodian invasion, while it did little to alter his foreign policy, deeply impressed Nixon. It appeared, as Jeb Magruder later told the Watergate Committee, that radicals and dissenters were tearing the country apart. The government launched strong public and covert efforts to stop them, by devising a broad plan calling for a council of all American intelligence organizations, including the CIA and the FBI. This group would be authorized to open mail, tap telephones, and conduct illegal break-ins. Files of the Internal Revenue Service were considered especially valuable for use against critics. In July 1970, President Nixon approved this plan. But steady opposition by FBI chief J. Edgar Hoover, who wanted no reorganization that affected his bureau, prevented its implementation.

Nixon then carried his attack on dissenters into the political arena. During the congressional elections of 1970, Vice President Spiro Agnew, whose attacks on the media had already gained him a wide following, proclaimed that the President would not be intimidated by "a disruptive, radical, and militant minority—the pampered prodigies of the radical liberals in the United States Senate." Nixon himself campaigned actively, claiming that "creeping permissiveness" allowed violent dissenters to "increasingly terrorize decent citizens." But the 1970 election results proved disappointing. Republicans gained only two seats in the Senate while losing nine seats in the House and seven governorships.

Nixon also had problems with the courts. Attorney General John Mitchell had obtained a lower court injunction to prevent the *New York* *Times* from publishing the "Pentagon Papers," but by a 6-to-3 vote the Supreme Court ruled that the newspaper had acted within its First Amendment rights. A year later, on June 19, 1972, a unanimous Court that included three Nixon appointees rejected Mitchell's contention that the President possessed inherent power to wiretap without a court order. The decision came two days after the Watergate burglars' arrest.

Nixon and the Economy Nixon had originally intended to reduce federal spending and work toward a balanced budget—an aim piously invoked by many Presidents (including FDR) but seldom pursued. Nixon followed such a belt-tightening policy during his first year in power. By mid-1970 the country had entered a serious recession, and at the end of that year unemployment stood at 6.2 percent—almost twice the level under Johnson.

At the same time prices rose steadily. This unaccustomed combination of high unemployment, inflation, and limited economic growth soon acquired the name, "stagflation," although Democrats preferred the political label, "Nixonomics." Actually, the inflation was hardly Nixon's fault. It resulted largely from heavy spending for the Viet-

When the dollar was devalued in February 1973, brokers in international currency were deluged with calls. The dollar's weakness was a sign of the economy's illness.

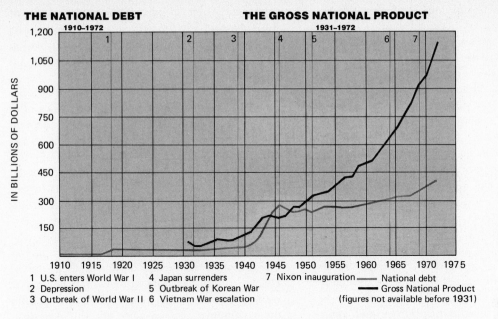

THE NATIONAL DEBT 1910–1972   **THE GROSS NATIONAL PRODUCT** 1931–1972

IN BILLIONS OF DOLLARS

1 U.S. enters World War I   4 Japan surrenders   7 Nixon inauguration ----- National debt
2 Depression   5 Outbreak of Korean War   ——— Gross National Product
3 Outbreak of World War II 6 Vietnam War escalation (figures not available before 1931)

It seems less disturbing in comparison with the even more rapid growth of the economy, as measured by the increase in the Gross National Product. The GNP for a given year represents the total value, at current prices, of all goods and services produced in the country during that year. The growth of the GNP reflects a rising price level as well as an increasing output of goods and services. The actual increase in output has been much less, therefore, than the graph seems to indicate.

nam War and expanded social programs, combined with Johnson's refusal, for political reasons, to raise taxes. By 1971 the state of the economy posed a potent threat to Nixon's reelection, causing him to make a turnaround on spending and taxes. By election time he had managed to force down the unemployment rate.

In August of 1971 Nixon made an even more startling turnaround. Throughout his career he had opposed government controls on wages and prices. But with little more than a year to go before the election, the President imposed a ninety-day freeze on wages and prices, which he labeled Phase I of a new economic plan. In the fall the economy entered Phase II, with limits on wage and price increases. Both phases worked fairly well, controlling inflation throughout 1972.

After the election Nixon began cutting back on government programs, especially social welfare programs. He inaugurated Phase III, a system of largely voluntary limits on increases. The removal of mandatory controls, combined with the

additional money the administration had pumped into the economy, produced the sharpest burst of inflation since World War II.

Détente with Russia and China   Phase I was not the only shock Nixon produced in the summer of 1971. The President, who had been perhaps the country's leading anticommunist for twenty years, announced that he would visit China—not what he used to call "Red China," the international outlaw, but the People's Republic of China. Henry Kissinger had already secretly visited Peking and made arrangements for Nixon's trip.

Only a politician like Nixon, possessing impeccable credentials as an anticommunist, could have altered American policy toward China. The President's visit early in 1972 provided a startling experience for Americans still thinking in Cold War stereotypes. There was Dick Nixon, the man who had talked down Nikita Khrushchev, cozying up to Mao Tse-tung and Chou En-lai while admiring the Great Wall as if viewing Hoover Dam on a campaign tour. By the time of Nixon's visit the United States had acquiesced in the admission of mainland China to the United Nations. Shortly after the President's visit, China and the United States established offices in each other's capitals, although continued American support for the Nationalist Chinese on Formosa ruled out full diplomatic relations.

Three months later, Nixon was traveling again, this time to the Soviet Union. Nixon and Kissinger were determined to build on the easing of Soviet-American relations (détente) that had begun during the Kennedy and Johnson years. Since 1969 the two superpowers had been engaged in the SALT (Stategic Arms Limitation Talks) negotiations, and Nixon and Soviet leader Brezhnev now signed SALT I, a temporary and limited agreement to cut back on some new weapons. The leaders also agreed to expand trade, beginning with a large Russian purchase of American wheat. The total sale amounted to a quarter of the American crop for 1972, at a price well below that of the American market. For Americans the first concrete result of détente was a sharp increase in the price of bread.

Nixon did not intend, however, that more relaxed relations should include an American defeat in Vietnam. Indeed, his dealings with two communist powers, Russia and China, who feared one another at least as much as each feared the United States, apparently enabled him to take bolder steps in Indochina. In March 1972, responding to expanded North Vietnamese activities in the south, Nixon first unleashed heavy American bombing on Hanoi and Haiphong (the largest cities of North Vietnam) and then mined the harbor of Haiphong, closing it to all ships. Despite rumblings from Moscow and Peking, as well as protests from many Americans, neither the communist superpowers nor the American people reacted strongly to Nixon's new military offensive. The U.S. effort in Vietnam had become an enormously expensive and costly bore—costly in human as well as in dollar terms.

The Election of 1972 Nixon had greatly strengthened his political position with his trips to China and Russia as well as some easing of the recession. He also gained strength from political floundering on the Democratic side. Originally, Senator Edmund Muskie of Maine seemed to have a good chance to unite the Democrats, still divided by the passions and violence of 1968. But Muskie's campaign fizzled. Senator Hubert Humphrey of Minnesota cut deeply into Muskie's support among moderates. George Wallace, former governor of Alabama, returning to the Democratic party after an independent race in 1968, ran strongly in many primaries, including a surprising victory in Michigan. Senator George McGovern of South Dakota led the forces of antiwar activists and students that had been symbolized by Eugene McCarthy and Robert Kennedy in 1968.

Benefiting from divided opposition and recent party reforms, McGovern won Democratic convention delegates faster than any other candidate. Finally he defeated Humphrey in a close California primary. To most of the Democratic

During President Nixon's visit to China in February 1972, he and Premier Chou En-lai reviewed the Chinese Red Guard. Televised scenes like this startled the American public, long accustomed to thinking in Cold War terms.

Governor George Wallace's third-party candidacy in 1968 siphoned off nearly ten million votes, making that election one of the closest in recent history.

political pros and to labor leaders allied with the party McGovern seemed too extreme. But he had enough delegates, barely enough, to win nomination, and he named Senator Thomas Eagleton of Missouri as his running mate.

McGovern's nomination did not heal the party division. Many Democratic politicians refused to rally behind him. He represented something novel on the American political scene. The "new politics" centered on youth, the rights of ethnic minorities, and the aspirations of women. McGovern proposed several controversial schemes—for example, that every family whose income fell below $10,000 should receive a yearly cash grant of $1,000. Ideas such as these, as well as the overall "too liberal" impression he and his campaigners created, alienated many normally reliable sources of Democratic political power.

McGovern's slim chances faded when reports began to circulate that Eagleton had been treated for psychiatric disorders. That posed a problem which McGovern's maladroit response turned into a crisis. McGovern at first announced that he supported Eagleton "one thousand percent." But soon he asked for the vice-presidential

candidate's resignation, an act interpreted by many as both vacillating and ruthless. After four Democrats had publicly rejected McGovern's offer, Sargent Shriver, a brother-in-law of John and Robert Kennedy, became Eagleton's replacement.

Nixon, meanwhile, campaigned by seeming to be above politics. He stayed in the White House while presidential surrogates took on McGovern. To separate himself from the Republican party organization, he set up CRP (Committee to Reelect the President), and he put an emphasis on "Democrats for Nixon," a group of Democrats alienated by McGovern. Aiming for the largest victory possible, he refused to associate his campaign with those of Republican congressional candidates.

Nixon's personal victory, or at least McGovern's defeat, was enormous. The President carried forty-nine states, losing only Massachusetts and the District of Columbia. But, while the President claimed a broad mandate, he had brought in only thirteen Republican congressmen, and his party had actually lost two seats in the

George McGovern, in attempting to open the Democratic party to groups shut out of the 1968 convention, alienated the traditional base of Democratic support—blue-collar workers. Richard Nixon capitalized on this to win in a landslide.

Senate. The "deadlock of democracy" (GOP control of the White House and Democratic control of Congress) would continue.

PREPARING FOR THE SECOND TERM

Shortly after the election Haldeman's demand for the resignation of cabinet members was echoed throughout the executive branch, and many high-level appointees were replaced by Nixon loyalists. Jeb Magruder, for example, became undersecretary of commerce. The actions reflected a long-standing Nixon desire to centralize control of the executive branch by the White House.

The President also tightened control over the cabinet. Congress had earlier rejected a reorganization plan, but Nixon now named Kissinger, Secretary of the Treasury George Schultz, and Roy Ash, director of the Nixon-created Office of Management and Budget, as a "supercabinet," to whom other cabinet members would report. The supercabinet, in turn, would report to Haldeman and Ehrlichman. With such a structure, Nixon made himself the most isolated President of modern times.

The President also claimed ever-widening powers for his office. He issued a broad definition of "executive privilege," limiting the information Congress could require the executive branch to supply. He also announced that he would impound funds appropriated by Congress that he felt should not be spent, refusing to release $6 billion appropriated by Congress for environmental programs. In March, vetoing a number of spending bills, the President announced that even if Congress overrode his vetoes he would impound the money.

Nixon also celebrated his reelection with a treaty in Vietnam. Kissinger had announced a few days before the election that "peace is at hand." But snags developed, and Nixon responded with the heaviest bombing of the war in December—a saturation "carpet bombing" of parts of Hanoi. Shortly after Nixon's inauguration, the two sides signed a treaty calling for a permanent cease-fire and removal of American troops. But despite American troop withdrawal, the war continued among the Vietnamese, and U.S. B-52 bombers continued to pound communist forces in Cambodia.

Government During Watergate Despite his ambitious plans, Watergate quickly closed in on Nixon. After McCord, Magruder, and Dean began talking, the President lost standing in the country, and what little influence he had retained over Congress evaporated. In August 1973 Congress forced Nixon to end the bombing in Cambodia. Shortly thereafter Congress passed the War Powers Act, stating that unless Congress approved an American military intervention within sixty days the President must withdraw troops. Nixon vetoed the bill, but both houses overrode his veto.

By then, Nixon's ability to govern was shaken. After the forced resignation of Agnew, Nixon hosted a White House extravaganza to announce his selection of House Minority Leader Gerald Ford as Vice President, the first exercise of a new presidential power under the 25th Amendment. A cabinet member remarked to House Majority Leader O'Neill that they might not see something like it again for a long time. "No," answered O'Neill, "not for about eight months."

Within certain limits, however, Nixon could still act decisively. In October, Egypt, Syria, and Iraq, with heavy Soviet arms support, attacked Israel. Nixon, in the midst of the Agnew and Watergate crises, launched a huge American airlift to the Israelis, possibly preventing a disastrous defeat for the Jewish state. America's European allies, heavily dependent on Arab oil, refused to assist and publicly expressed their anger.

Despite the strain on the NATO alliance, Nixon and Kissinger could claim success in preventing Israel's extinction and, later, in negotiating a Middle East cease-fire. But when Nixon, warning of the danger of Russian intervention in the area, put all American forces on a worldwide military alert, the effects of Watergate-inspired skepticism became obvious. Americans openly speculated on how much Nixon's political difficulties had influenced him in calling the alert.

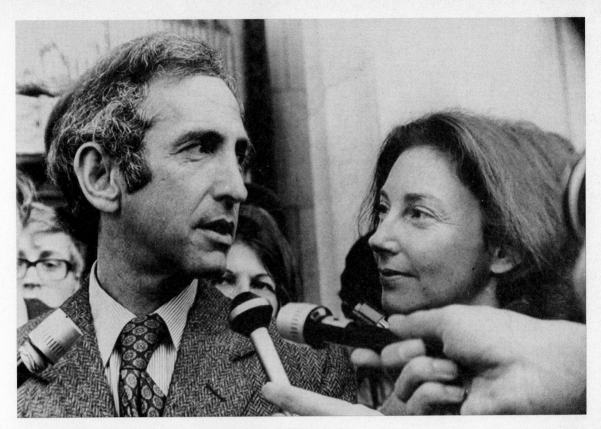

Daniel Ellsberg, with his wife Pat, talks to reporters before testifying for the second day at the "Pentagon Papers" trial in April 1973. Ellsberg had been responsible for leaking the secret Defense Department study of the Vietnam War. The court case was dismissed, however, after Nixon had Ehrlichman offer the Judge a position as Director of the FBI.

Even the President's success brought problems, as the Arab countries cut off petroleum exports to the United States. Long before the embargo, the country had faced the prospect of shortages. Fuel consumption had been increasing far more rapidly than domestic fuel production. Moreover, the country's output of polluting fuels such as coal was being cut back for environmental reasons.

The Arab embargo intensified the country's problems, with immediate and unpleasant results. The price of heating oil tripled, and gas prices doubled—when gas was available. Long lines of cars formed outside and around gas stations, which stayed open for limited hours each day.

What angered Americans most, however, were skyrocketing profits for oil companies.

The President refused to enforce controls on oil prices or profits, preferring to try to ease demand. A national speed limit of fifty-five miles an hour was adopted, Sunday gasoline sales were banned, and Nixon asked Americans to turn down their thermostats. With voluntary restrictions, and an unusually mild winter, the country came through the boycott.

During the winter, Kissinger, now secretary of state, made numerous trips to the Middle East, testing his hand at shuttle diplomacy. Since the Arabs refused to talk directly with the Israelis, he had to fly between the hostile capitals and suc-

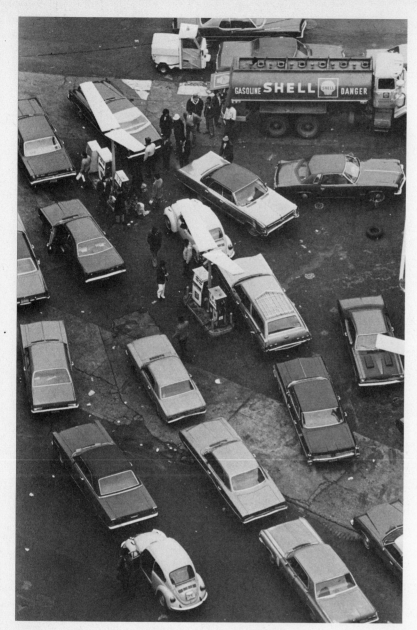

The Arab Oil Embargo of 1973 intensified an energy crisis that had just begun to be felt in the United States. Although the Arabs ended their boycott after a month, the impact of the crisis, the prospect of winter fuel shortages, and the endless lines of cars waiting for service at gas stations, made it clear that an energy policy was needed at home.

ceeded in working out a disengagement of opposing troops. By March the Arabs ended the oil boycott, and the situation ended. But the U.S. government had failed to establish a long-term answer to the problem of diminishing energy resources.

Henry Kissinger's accomplishments in the Middle East provided the one and only consola-

tion for Richard Nixon's administration in its last days. Through mid-1974, as Nixon approached his final reckoning, the White House became increasingly paralyzed. By the summer of that year, as the Judiciary Committee began its hearings, the President was almost entirely preoccupied with the unsuccessful efforts to clear his name and to remain in office.

Criss-crossing the globe for negotiations, Secretary of State Kissinger confers with Morocco's King Hassan II at Rabat in November 1973, while en route to China. Kissinger joined Nixon's staff as a special assistant for national security and became Secretary of State at the outset of Nixon's second term. Kissinger not only replaced "Containment" with "Detente," but also introduced his own brand of "shuttle diplomacy"—a one man patrol of the world's trouble spots.

THE FORD ADMINISTRATION

Gerald Ford's electorate had never been larger than the voters of Grand Rapids, Michigan. Still, President Ford received strong support when he assumed the office. His openness seemed a welcome change after Nixon's secretiveness; Americans relaxed when he announced, "Our long national nightmare is over." The comic strip *Doonesbury* showed a brick wall around the White House being demolished. A television crew went into the White House to show the new President making his own breakfast.

Some of the beatific aura faded, however, a month after the inauguration—when Ford pardoned Nixon for any criminal actions committed during his presidency. Ford had said during his confirmation hearings that he did not expect to take such an action, and his new press secretary resigned in protest. At a time when most of Nixon's White House associates faced prosecution and possible jail terms, many Americans objected to Ford's action as charity misplaced and presidential power misused.

The pardon played a large role in the congressional campaign of November 1974. Republicans had originally thought that Ford, by replacing Nixon, would save the party from heavy

The first man to reach the White House without ever winning a national election, Gerald R. Ford, shown here with his wife Betty, had entered the House of Representatives in 1948 as Congressman from Grand Rapids, Michigan. After twenty-five years in the House, ten of them as Minority Leader, Ford was appointed to the Vice Presidency when Spiro Agnew resigned in August 1973. He became President on August 9, 1974, upon Nixon's resignation.

congressional losses. Ford campaigned strenuously and tried to rally support for his policies with the slogan "WIN—Whip inflation now." But Democrats increased their already large majorities in both houses of Congress.

Ford and the New Congress With top-heavy majorities and in the new post-Watergate atmosphere, Democrats in Congress now sought to take policy initiative away from the White House.

Many journalists and political scientists had warned, after Vietnam and Watergate, that the presidency had become too powerful.

Congress and the President faced off over two major issues during the balance of Ford's term—the economy and the energy crisis. By early 1975 the economy appeared to be approaching disaster. Unemployment was running at levels near 10 percent, especially among auto workers and in the construction and aerospace industries.

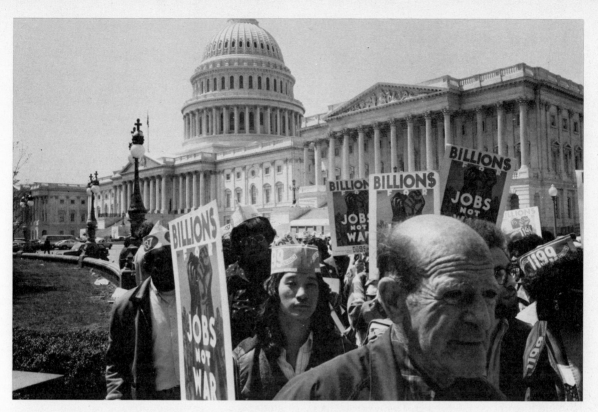

Demonstrators at the Capitol protest both the upswing in military expenditures in Vietnam and the spectre of rising unemployment at home. The advent of "stagflation," with its combination of rising prices, low economic growth, and consequent shortage of jobs, forced the Nixon Administration to confront an economy in which both unemployment and inflation were getting out of hand. A sequence of controls and decontrol, plus the dismantling of Johnson era social welfare programs, did little to lessen the rising tide of unemployment.

Although inflation had been brought under some control and the rate of price increases had slackened, economic growth had also declined.

Energy seemed to be at least as great a problem. The Arab nations and other Third World oil producers had formed a cartel—OPEC (Organization of Petroleum Exporting Countries)—and quadrupled oil prices within a short period. The United States' own supplies of oil could not last much longer, and intensive efforts to find and develop more, such as on the north slope of Alaska and off the Atlantic and Pacific coastlines, raised environmental questions and political controversy. The same problems applied to the development of America's huge supplies of coal; and widespread use of alternative fuel sources, such as solar and atomic energy, were decades and billions of dollars away.

Congressional militancy proved no match for problems of such magnitude. Democrats struggled in vain to produce an energy bill acceptable to one another, let alone strong enough to override a presidential veto. Congress did manage to produce a number of bills intended to boost the economy, but only one major bill—a compromise tax cut in the spring of 1975—became law. Most of the others were vetoed by Ford, and Democrats rarely managed to muster the two-thirds majority needed to override. Although the new Congress had restated some congressional prerogatives, it had again been shown that effective national government depended on strong presidential leadership.

RALPH NADER

Ralph Nader became America's best-known and most influential critic of corporate practices through the direct assistance of America's largest corporation, General Motors, in 1965. Nader was an obscure thirty-one-year-old graduate of Harvard Law School, researching the issue of automobile safety, and barely supporting himself with articles and lectures on the subject. That year, he had published a book called *Unsafe at Any Speed*, examining in particular the performance of the Corvair, a product of GM's Chevrolet Division. The Corvair, Nader charged, had a tendency to roll over even when driven carefully, and the car had been involved in a startlingly high number of serious accidents.

In 1966, at a Senate hearing on auto safety, General Motors admitted that its response to Nader's charges had been to send out private detectives to find some "dirt" on Nader. They had been instructed to keep Nader under surveillance, to investigate his drinking and sex habits (especially why he had never married), and to check whether Nader, the son of Lebanese immigrants, might be anti-Semitic. All "leads" checked out negative. Nader got wind of the snooping, and filed a $26 million lawsuit. GM's president tried to get off with a private apology to Nader. Four years later, Nader settled out of court for $425,000, declaring he would use the money to monitor General Motor's future business practices.

But by then Nader had already become a virtual legend. GM's action had made him famous, and focused attention on his investigations, which rapidly broadened to include new subjects. Young lawyers and researchers flocked to work for his Center for the Study of Responsive Law, and later his Corporate Accountability Research Group—groups known more popularly as "Nader's Raiders." They have issued critical reports on the workings of federal regulatory commissions, the criminal justice system, various corporate practices, and Congress itself. In a style somewhere between scholarship and journalism, the reports have helped pass legislation in several areas (motor vehicle safety, meat inspection, and safety in mining, for example), although the results have rarely been strong enough to satisfy Nader.

Besides running what has been called an investigative conglomerate, Nader is a congressional lobbyist, a publicist for his causes, and an untiring lecturer. He speaks to civic groups, professional bodies, and college students all over the country, demanding that all Americans become involved in local citizens' action groups. "We can't possibly have a democracy," he warns, "with two hundred million Americans and only a handful of citizens."

General Motors' investigators had discovered that Nader worked nonstop and seemed to have no other interests. This life style, widely reported by the media, is now a key aspect of the Nader legend. Nader puts in eighteen to twenty hours a day, sleeping only four to five hours in his $80-a-month room in a Washington boarding house. He expects lawyers working for him to keep up a similar pace, for salaries well below what they might earn elsewhere. He is rarely tolerant of lesser effort. "You go off on a trip for a week with some twenty-five-year-old lawyer," he once complained, "and when you come back *he wants the weekend off!*" But Nader's zeal, his small army of devoted and equally hard working associates, and his political skills have made him the most durable and effective single reformer in contemporary America.

Ford and Foreign Affairs Congress had some success in deflecting Ford's foreign policy proposals. In March 1975, North Vietnamese troops launched a major offensive, and the South Vietnamese retreat quickly turned into a rout. With the Saigon government on the verge of collapse, Ford requested $700 million in emergency aid for South Vietnam and a smaller amount for Cambodia, also threatened by a communist takeover.

At virtually the last moment in the fifteen-year Indochina War, Congress asserted itself and refused the request for aid, which would probably have come too late to change the outcome. By mid-April the communist armies had captured the capital of Cambodia, and by the end of the month Saigon had fallen. The war was over.

But its final scene would remain to haunt Americans. Thousands of Vietnamese who had cooperated with the American forces tried desperately to get aboard departing American helicopters and ships. Many had been promised passage out of the country and had remained at their jobs on the strength of those assurances. Now American marines fought off the thousands of terrified Vietnamese swarming over the walls of the American embassy, begging to be taken along. One American devised a simple, hard rule for the last days: "Don't look in their eyes."

Post-Vietnam Foreign Policy By mid-1975 it was becoming more and more difficult to see American foreign policy as an anticommunist crusade. Ford had retained both Nixon's secretary of state, Henry Kissinger, and his policy of détente with the Russians. America and the Soviet Union reached a new level of agreement in the SALT talks and, along with the European powers, signed a major agreement at Helsinki calling for peace and recognizing territorial changes made at the end of World War II.

But some Americans, including many liberals, upset with Russian policy on the Middle East and treatment of Soviet Jews, began to question the value of détente. They pointed out that parts of the Helsinki Agreement, such as those calling for respect for human rights and free travel from country to country had been ignored by the Soviet Union. Those opposed to détente also cited the large Soviet involvement in Angola, where a withdrawal of Portuguese colonial authority in that African state had led to a civil war between Marxist and pro-Western factions. With hundreds of millions of dollars in Russian military aid, and several thousand Cuban soldiers, the Marxists won easily. But if Angola showed the unchanged nature of Soviet policy, it also illustrated the different attitude of Congress, which refused President Ford's request for aid to the pro-Western Angolans and directed an immediate end to all American involvement.

Aid to Angola and congressional attitudes were also involved in another controversy related to foreign affairs. Congressional committees dug out large amounts of evidence of illegal and disturbing activities by the CIA, including aborted assassination plots against foreign leaders. Ford announced new controls on the agency. But neither Congress nor the public seemed to consider the new directive the final answer, possibly because neither seemed sure what actions would simultaneously serve the interests of American freedom *and* security.

Ford and the Economy By early 1976 the economy seemed to be making some improvement. The President declared the recession over. Unemployment although still high had come down somewhat, and the stock market was running surprisingly high. The White House pointed to the improvement as an argument against further bills passed by Congress to stimulate the economy.

In the midst of the improvement at least one highly disturbing situation boiled over. New York City was rapidly going bankrupt and would soon be unable to cover its debt obligations. Nobody knew exactly how far the effects of a default by the nation's largest city would extend, but many people felt that it would have an appalling effect on the sluggishly improving economy. Others argued that New York had brought the problem on itself through fiscal mismanagement and overgenerous welfare and employee benefits. President Ford, bidding for conservative support, delivered a speech so strong that the pro-Republican *New York Daily News* headlined the story, "FORD TO CITY: DROP DEAD."

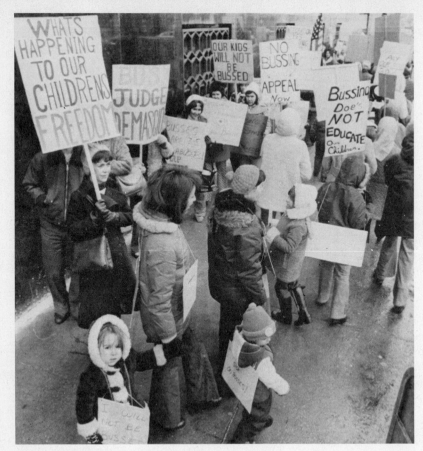

Antibusing parents and children demonstrate outside a federal building in downtown Detroit on January 22, 1976, four days before a court-ordered school integration program, affecting 22,000 public school students, was due to begin. By the mid-seventies, two decades after the Supreme Court's historic desegregation decision, the problem of school integration was no longer solely a Southern one. Court-ordered integration plans, requiring busing, now evoked controversy in big Northern cities.

In the end, Ford approved some federal aid to the city. But while New York's problem remained to some extent unique, it gave a foretaste of what might happen to many American cities. Since World War II, the middle and upper-middle classes and many businesses had fled the inner city, while welfare costs and the cities' low-income population stayed behind. New York's plight reminded Americans that the urban crisis, while no longer receiving the attention it had during the 1960s, had not been solved or even eased.

THE BICENTENNIAL ELECTION

When the two major presidential candidates gained their parties' first-ballot nominations at the party conventions, it would appear that the preconvention presidential battle was a cut-and-dried affair. Although the 1976 campaign produced first-ballot nominations, things were anything but predetermined.

First, Gerald Ford had to fashion for himself a credible image as a presidential candidate, something more than the caretaker role assigned him by the Watergate mess and the Nixon resignation. Second, Ford had to fight off a strong challenger.

To avoid becoming an interim president, an appointed lame duck, Ford announced early that he would run for President. He became less apologetic about his status, acting more like a chief executive and less like a political accident. He even took to the skies, emulating Nixon's eye-opening visits to China and Russia, but not necessarily reaping the same results. Ford also stripped himself of another lame duck, the man he had appointed Vice President, New York's ex-governor Nelson Rockefeller—a person who carried an aura of liberal Republicanism about him. GOP conservatives still viewed Rockefeller with suspicion and wanted his head. They got it.

In the wings (the right wing, to be precise) stood Ronald Reagan, ex-movie star, former two-term governor of California, and still a dashing figure in his mid-sixties. Reagan offered a fundamentalist Republican line, attacking the federal government, the welfare state, and the détente policy of cozying up to the Russians and the Chinese.

At first it appeared that Ford had nothing to worry about. The President scored handily over Reagan in the initial Republican primaries. But in North Carolina Reagan won his first primary. And during the spring primary season he and the President came closer and closer in delegate strength. At convention time it looked like a toss-up. Then Reagan took a daring, costly gamble. He broke tradition by announcing in advance who his vice-presidential running mate would be. That was novel. But Reagan chose a very liberal Republican senator from Pennsylvania. To GOP conservatives that was shocking. Some, including Barry Goldwater, the party's "conservative conscience," came out in support of Ford. It was no runaway, but the Republican convention nominated Ford on the first ballot.

In the enemy camp, the Democrats began the election year with more generals than buck privates. At least a dozen persons declared for the nomination. One of them, a Georgia politician with a permanent smile and an undistinguished

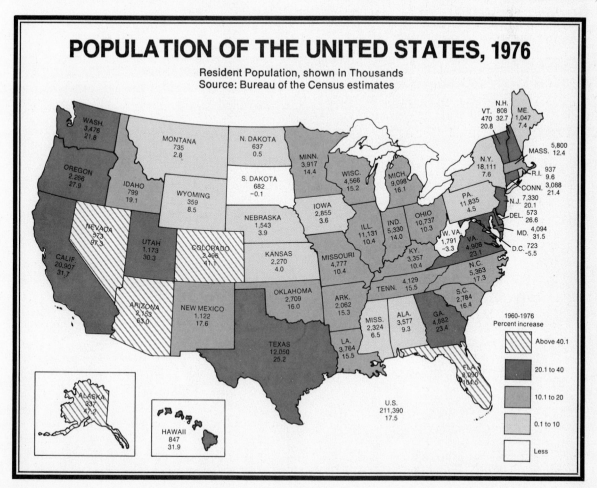

POPULATION OF THE UNITED STATES, 1976

Resident Population, shown in Thousands
Source: Bureau of the Census estimates

1960-1976 Percent increase

Above 40.1	
20.1 to 40	
10.1 to 20	
0.1 to 10	
Less	

WASH. 3,476 21.8
OREGON 2,266 27.9
IDAHO 799 19.1
MONTANA 735 2.8
WYOMING 359 8.5
N. DAKOTA 637 0.5
S. DAKOTA 682 -0.1
MINN. 3,917 14.4
WISC. 4,566 15.2
MICH. 9,098 16.1
N.Y. 18,111 7.6
VT. 470 20.8
N.H. 808 32.7
ME. 1,047 7.4
MASS. 5,800 12.4
R.I. 937 9.6
CONN. 3,088 21.4
NEVADA 573 97.3
UTAH 1,173 30.3
COLORADO 2,496 41.1
NEBRASKA 1,543 3.9
IOWA 2,855 3.6
ILL. 11,131 10.4
IND. 5,330 14.0
OHIO 10,737 10.3
PA. 11,835 4.5
N.J. 7,330 20.1
DEL. 573 26.6
MD. 4,094 31.5
D.C. 723 -5.5
CALIF. 20,907 31.7
ARIZONA 2,153 63.0
NEW MEXICO 1,122 17.6
KANSAS 2,270 4.0
MISSOURI 4,777 10.4
KY. 3,357 10.4
W. VA. 1,791 -3.3
VA. 4,908 23.1
N.C. 5,363 17.3
OKLAHOMA 2,709 16.0
ARK. 2,062 15.3
TENN. 4,129 15.5
S.C. 2,784 16.4
TEXAS 12,050 25.2
MISS. 2,324 6.5
ALA. 3,577 9.3
GA. 4,882 23.4
LA. 3,764 15.5
FLA. 8,090 104.5
ALASKA 337 47.2
HAWAII 847 31.9
U.S. 211,390 17.5

record in his state's politics seemed the least likely to succeed.

James Earl Carter, Jr. (he preferred to be called Jimmy) had announced in 1974 that he intended to become President. Those outside of his entourage thought Carter was as likely to walk on the moon. But Carter's persistence slowly changed his candidacy from something almost comic into something substantial. Though he was not taken too seriously before the primaries, Jimmy would not quit — soon enough his considerable political talents began to draw the public's attention.

In January 1976, Carter won Iowa delegates; a month later he repeated with a win in New Hampshire. He was moving away from the pack, a process accelerated greatly in subsequent Southern primaries, which included his rout of Alabama's perennial maverick George Wallace. Democratic leaders such as Senators Henry Jackson and Birch Bayh pulled out of the contest. A few more entered. But it was over by early June, when Carter won the Ohio primary and endorsements from most of the party's establishment poured in. So it was off to New York City for the Democratic convention in mid-July for this self-styled Georgia peanut farmer. (Actually the Carter family's wholesale peanut business and land holdings in Plains, Georgia, kept them moderately wealthy.)

Before the politicos got together, the country had an anniversary to face — July 4, 1976. Presi-

Former Georgia Governor Jimmy Carter, surrounded by his family, at the Democratic National Convention of 1976 in New York City. The front-runner in the primaries, Carter had stressed his role as a non-Washingtonian "outsider," at a time when the memory of Watergate put "insiders" under suspicion.

U. S. Ambassador to the United Nations, Andrew Young, one of the most prominent appointees of the new Carter Administration, visits Israeli Ambassador Chaim Herzog at the Israeli Mission on January 31, 1977. A former Democratic Congressman from Atlanta, the youthful Georgian soon drew world-wide attention by his outspoken comments and candor.

dent Ford spent the preceding days in Pennsylvania—at Valley Forge and then at Independence Hall in Philadelphia, where one million persons celebrated America's two hundredth birthday. Then on to New York. The city and its neighbors spent a festive, frolicsome Sunday on the Glorious Fourth, a day remarkably filled with good cheer. The highlight of this spectacular was the procession of hundreds of ships and boats up the Hudson River, featuring sixteen "tall ships"— beautiful high-masted sailing ships from naval academies around the world. Not since the moon

landing in 1969 had American morale received a greater boost.

New York's Fourth of July euphoria lingered on a bit. Democrats in convention there from July 12 through 15 took advantage of it. Carter knew he had the nomination, and to help re-cement the Democratic coalition he put a Northern, prolabor liberal—Walter Mondale of Minnesota—on the ticket. At that point it looked as if Carter would trounce Ford.

But midyear polls and November election results seldom jibe. The campaign, not nearly so exciting as the primary fights, narrowed the margin established by the pollsters. Carter's religiosity (a "born again" Southern Baptist) was always an issue, but a lessening problem for him as he became better known. Jimmy did gain unfavorable headlines because of an interview he granted *Playboy* magazine, in which he admitted harboring sexual impulses. Ford, meanwhile, had to fire his foot-in-mouth secretary of agriculture, Earl Butz, because of a tasteless and racist remark made by Butz.

Election year 1976 saw the return of direct presidential debates, a device used only once before, in 1960. This time the incumbent President, Ford, decided to gamble by debating with Carter three times. The debates were televised, and Carter later stated that it was his performances in the second and third debates that won him the election.

But in close elections any positive factor can be isolated as decisive. 1976 was close. Electoral vote counts usually show a good spread, but in 1976 it was only Carter 297 to Ford 241. Carter got 50.4% of the popular vote (to Ford's 48.5%), so he could at least claim to be a majority president. But neither he nor Ford had excited the voters — only 53 percent of Americans eligible to vote did so, a drop of 2 percent since 1972, and a considerable drop from the 63 percent of eligibles who had voted in 1960. Many Americans simply did not care. And among the least involved in the electoral process were those in the 18-to-21 age group granted voting rights in 1972. Despite the stay-at-homes, Carter had carried enough of the industrial Northeast, and his own near solid South to win election. It was virtually an East-West split, with Ford carrying most Western States.

Carter's inaugural day, January 20, 1977, was upbeat and informal. The address contained a characteristic biblical quotation and a plea that "we must again have faith in our country — and in one another." The President also issued an inaugural statement to the world, imprecise but reassuring, indicating that he appreciated both the extent and the limits of American power. Once installed, the President and Mrs. Carter walked from Capitol Hill to the White House, a distance normally traveled by a President in a glass-topped bullet-proof limousine. At night, inaugural parties replaced inaugural balls, and no one seemed to mind the informality.

All new Presidents want to begin afresh. They certainly want to bury old, divisive issues, those that can upset their administrations as badly as they did those of their predecessors. The day after assuming office, Carter pardoned Vietnam era draft evaders. The President wanted to heal that wound left from the past.

Too many pressing elements of the present had to be faced, and some might even have to be solved: the United States had become increasingly dependent on foreign oil in the 1970s, the welfare system had not been reformed, the urban crisis had not eased, environmentalists and those fighting stagflation could not agree, and America's relations with the rest of the world had to be worked out in a post-Vietnam context. So too did individual Americans have to ponder what their country meant to them and where they thought it was headed — no small task in view of the sobering events and many changes of the preceding decade.

SUGGESTED READINGS— CHAPTERS 51-52

Watergate

Carl Bernstein and Bob Woodward, *All the President's Men* (1974) and *The Final Days* (1976); John Dean, *Blind Ambition* (1976); William B. Dickinson, Jr., *Watergate: Chronology of a Crisis* (2 vols., 1974); Leon Jaworski, *The Right and the Power: The Prosecution of Watergate* (1976).

Politics: Nixon and Beyond

Marvin and Bernard Kalb, *Kissinger* (1974); Leonard W. Levy, *Against the Law: The Nixon Court and Criminal Justice* (1974); Earl Mazo and Stephen Hess, *Nixon: A Political Portrait* (1968); Joe McGinnis, *The Selling of the President, 1968* (1969); Arthur M. Schlesinger, Jr., *The Imperial Presidency* (1973); James F. Simon, *In His Own Image: The Supreme Court in Richard Nixon's America* (1973); Theodore H. White, *The Making of the President, 1968* (1969) and *Breach of Faith: The Fall of Richard Nixon* (1975); Gary Wills, *Nixon Agonistes* (1970); George B. Reedy, *The Twilight of the Presidency* (1970); R. Reeves, *A Ford Not A Lincoln* (1974); Samuel Huntington, *The Crisis of Democracy* (1977); Sumner Rosen, ed., *Economic Power Pailure* (1975).

Interpretations of Society

Jonathan Schell, *The Time of Illusion* (1975); Harland B. Moulton, *From Superiority to Parity: The United States and the Strategic Arms Race, 1966–1971* (1973); Otis L. Graham, Jr., *Toward a Planned Society: From Roosevelt to Nixon* (1976); Alexander M. Bickel, *The Supreme Court and the Idea of Progress* (1970); Robert L. Heilbroner, *An Inquiry into the Human Prospect* (1974); Andrew Hacker, *The End of the American Era* (1971); Daniel Bell, *The Coming of Post-Industrial Society* (1976).

THE DECLARATION OF INDEPENDENCE

In Congress, July 4, 1776. *The unanimous Declaration of the thirteen united States of America,*

When in the Course of human events, it becomes necessary for one people to dissolve the political bands which have connected them with another, and to assume among the powers of the earth, the separate and equal station to which the Laws of Nature and of Nature's God entitle them, a decent respect to the opinions of mankind requires that they should declare the causes which impel them to the separation.—

We hold these truths to be self-evident, that all men are created equal, that they are endowed by their Creator with certain unalienable Rights, that among these are Life, Liberty and the pursuit of Happiness.—

That to secure these rights, Governments are instituted among Men, deriving their just powers from the consent of the governed,—

That whenever any Form of Government becomes destructive of these ends, it is the Right of the People to alter or to abolish it, and to institute new Government, laying its foundation on such principles and organizing its powers in such form, as to them shall seem most likely to effect their Safety and Happiness. Prudence, indeed, will dictate that Governments long established should not be changed for light and transient causes; and accordingly all experience hath shown, that mankind are more disposed to suffer, while evils are sufferable, than to right themselves by abolishing the forms to which they are accustomed. But when a long train of abuses and usurpations, pursuing invariably the same Object evinces a design to reduce them under absolute Despotism, it is their right, it is their duty, to throw off such Government, and to provide new Guards for their future security.—

Such has been the patient sufferance of these Colonies; and such is now the necessity which constrains them to alter their former Systems of Government. The history of the present King of Great Britain is a history of repeated injuries and usurpations, all having in direct object the establishment of an absolute Tyranny over these States. To prove this, let Facts be submitted to a candid world.—

He has refused his Assent to Laws, the most wholesome and necessary for the public good.—

He has forbidden his Governors to pass Laws of immediate and pressing importance, unless suspended in their operation till his Assent should be obtained; and when so suspended, he has utterly neglected to attend to them.—

He has refused to pass other Laws for the accommodation of large districts of people, unless those people would relinquish the right of Representation in the Legislature, a right inestimable to them and formidable to tyrants only.—

He has called together legislative bodies at places unusual, uncomfortable, and distant from the depository of their public Records, for the sole purpose of fatiguing them into compliance with his measures.—

He has dissolved Representative Houses repeatedly, for opposing with manly firmness his invasions on the rights of the people.—

He has refused for a long time, after such dissolutions, to cause others to be elected; whereby the Legislative powers, incapable of Annihilation, have returned to the People at large for their exercise; the State remaining in the mean time exposed to all the dangers of invasion from without, and convulsions within.—

He has endeavoured to prevent the population of these States; for that purpose obstructing the Laws for Naturalization of Foreigners; refusing to pass others to encourage their migrations hither, and raising the conditions of new Appropriations of Lands.—

He has obstructed the Administration of Justice, by refusing his Assent to Laws for establishing Judiciary powers.—

He has made Judges dependent on his Will alone, for the tenure of their offices, and the amount and payment of their salaries.—

He has erected a multitude of New Offices, and sent hither swarms of Officers to harrass our people, and eat out their substance.—

He has kept among us in times of peace, Standing Armies without the Consent of our legislatures.—

He has affected to render the Military independent of and superior to the Civil power.—

He has combined with others to subject us to a jurisdiction foreign to our constitution, and unacknowledged by our laws; giving his Assent to their Acts of pretended Legislation:—

For quartering large bodies of armed troops among us:—

For protecting them, by a mock Trial, from punishment for any Murders which they should commit on the Inhabitants of these States:—

For cutting off our Trade with all parts of the world:—

For imposing Taxes on us without our Consent:—

For depriving us in many cases, of the benefits of Trial by Jury:—

For transporting us beyond Seas to be tried for pretended offences:—

For abolishing the free System of English Laws in a neighbouring Province, establishing therein an Arbitrary government, and enlarging its Boundaries so as to render it at once an example and fit instrument for introducing the same absolute rule in these Colonies:—

For taking away our Charters, abolishing our most valuable Laws, and altering fundamentally the Forms of our Governments:—

For suspending our own Legislatures, and declaring themselves invested with power to legislate for us in all cases whatsoever.—

He has abdicated Government here, by declaring us out of his Protection and waging War against us.—

He has plundered our seas, ravaged our Coasts, burnt our towns, and destroyed the lives of our people.—

He is at this time transporting large Armies of foreign Mercenaries to compleat the works of death, desolation and tyranny, already begun with circumstances of Cruelty & perfidy scarcely paralleled in the most barbarous ages, and totally unworthy the Head of a civilized nation.—

He has constrained our fellow Citizens taken Captive on the high Seas to bear Arms against their Country, to become the executioners of their friends and Brethren, or to fall themselves by their Hands.—

He has excited domestic insurrections amongst us, and has endeavoured to bring on the inhabitants of our frontiers, the merciless Indian Savages, whose known rule of warfare, is an undistinguished destruction of all ages, sexes and conditions.

In every stage of these Oppressions We have Petitioned for Redress in the most humble terms: Our repeated Petitions have been answered only by repeated injury. A Prince, whose character is thus marked by every act which may define a Tyrant, is unfit to be the ruler of a free people.

Nor have We been wanting in attentions to our British brethren. We have warned them from time to time of attempts by their legislature to extend an unwarrantable jurisdiction over us. We have reminded them of the circumstances of our emigration and settlement here. We have appealed to their native justice and magnanimity, and we have conjured them by the ties of our common kindred to disavow these usurpations, which, would inevitably interrupt our connections and correspondence. They too have been deaf to the voice of justice and of consanguinity. We must, therefore, acquiesce in the necessity, which denounces our Separation, and hold them, as we hold the rest of mankind, Enemies in War, in Peace Friends.—

We, therefore, the Representatives of the united States of America, in General Congress, Assembled, appealing to the Supreme Judge of the world for the rectitude of our intentions, do, in the Name, and by Authority of the good People of these Colonies, solemnly publish and declare, That these United Colonies are, and of Right ought to be, Free and Independent States; that they are absolved from all Allegiance to the British Crown, and that all political connection between them and the State of Great Britain, is and ought to be totally dissolved; and that as Free and Independent States they have full Power to levy War, conclude Peace, contract Alliances, establish Commerce, and to do all other Acts and Things which Independent States may of right do.—

And for the support of this Declaration, with a firm reliance on the protection of divine Providence, we mutually pledge to each other our Lives, our Fortunes and our sacred Honor.

John Hancock
(MASSACHUSETTS)

NEW HAMPSHIRE
Josiah Bartlett
William Whipple
Matthew Thornton

MASSACHUSETTS
Samuel Adams
John Adams
Robert Treat Paine
Elbridge Gerry

DELAWARE
Caesar Rodney
George Read
Thomas McKean

NEW YORK
William Floyd
Philip Livingston
Francis Lewis
Lewis Morris

NEW JERSEY
Richard Stockton
John Witherspoon
Francis Hopkinson
John Hart
Abraham Clark

NORTH CAROLINA
William Hooper
Joseph Hewes
John Penn

MARYLAND
Samuel Chase
William Paca
Thomas Stone
Charles Carroll
of Carrollton

SOUTH CAROLINA
Edward Rutledge
Thomas Heywood, Jr.
Thomas Lynch, Jr.
Arthur Middleton

RHODE ISLAND
Stephen Hopkins
William Ellery

CONNECTICUT
Roger Sherman
Samuel Huntington
William Williams
Oliver Wolcott

PENNSYLVANIA
Robert Morris
Benjamin Rush
Benjamin Franklin
John Morton
George Clymer
James Smith
George Taylor
James Wilson
George Ross

VIRGINIA
George Wythe
Richard Henry Lee
Thomas Jefferson
Benjamin Harrison
Thomas Nelson, Jr.
Francis Lightfoot Lee
Carter Braxton

GEORGIA
Button Gwinnett
Lyman Hall
George Walton

915

THE CONSTITUTION OF THE
UNITED STATES OF AMERICA

We the People of the United States, in Order to form a more perfect Union, establish Justice, insure domestic Tranquility, provide for the common defence, promote the general Welfare, and secure the Blessings of Liberty to ourselves and our Posterity, do ordain and establish this Constitution for the United States of America.

The preamble establishes the principle of government by the people, and lists the six basic purposes of the Constitution.

ARTICLE I • LEGISLATIVE DEPARTMENT

Section 1. All legislative Powers herein granted shall be vested in a Congress of the United States, which shall consist of a Senate and House of Representatives.

Section 2. The House of Representatives shall be composed of Members chosen every second Year by the People of the several States, and the Electors in each State shall have the Qualifications requisite for Electors of the most numerous Branch of the State Legislature.

Representatives serve two-year terms. They are chosen in each state by those electors (that is, voters) who are qualified to vote for members of the lower house of their own state legislature.

No Person shall be a Representative who shall not have attained to the Age of twenty-five Years, and been seven Years a Citizen of the United States, and who shall not, when elected, be an Inhabitant of that State in which he shall be chosen.

Representatives and direct Taxes shall be apportioned among the several States which may be included within this Union, according to their respective Numbers, which shall be determined by adding to the whole Number of free Persons, including those bound to Service for a Term of Years, and excluding Indians not taxed, three-fifths of all other Persons. The actual Enumeration shall be made within three Years after the first Meeting of the Congress of the United States, and within every subsequent Term of ten

The number of representatives allotted to a state is determined by the size of its population. The 14th Amendment has made obsolete the reference to "all other persons"—that is, slaves. A census must be taken every ten years to determine the number of representatives to which each state is entitled. There is now one representative for about every 470,000 persons.

Source: House Document #529. U.S. Government Printing Office, 1967.
[NOTE: *The Constitution and the amendments are reprinted here in their original form. Portions that have been amended or superseded are underlined.] The words printed in the margins explain some of the more difficult passages.*

Years, in such Manner as they shall by Law direct. The Number of Representatives shall not exceed one for every thirty Thousand, but each State shall have at Least one Representative; and until such enumeration shall be made, the State of New Hampshire shall be entitled to chuse three, Massachusetts eight, Rhode Island and Providence Plantations one, Connecticut five, New York six, New Jersey four, Pennsylvania eight, Delaware one, Maryland six, Virginia ten, North Carolina five, South Carolina five, and Georgia three.

"Executive authority" refers to the governor of a state.

When vacancies happen in the Representation from any State, the Executive Authority thereof shall issue Writs of Election to fill such Vacancies.

The Speaker, chosen by and from the majority party, presides over the House. Impeachment is the act of bringing formal charges against an official. (See also Section 3.)

The House of Representatives shall chuse their Speaker and other Officers; and shall have the sole Power of Impeachment.

Section 3. The Senate of the United States shall be composed of two Senators from each State, chosen by the Legislature thereof, for six Years; and each Senator shall have one Vote.

The 17th Amendment changed this method to direct election.

Immediately after they shall be assembled in Consequence of the first Election, they shall be divided as equally as may be into three Classes. The Seats of the Senators of the first Class shall be vacated at the Expiration of the second Year, of the second Class at the Expiration of the fourth Year, and of the third Class at the Expiration of the sixth Year, so that one third may be chosen every second Year; and if Vacancies happen by Resignation, or otherwise, during the Recess of the Legislature of any State, the Executive thereof may make temporary Appointments until the next Meeting of the Legislature, which shall then fill such Vacancies.

The 17th Amendment also provides that a state governor shall appoint a successor to fill a vacant Senate seat until a direct election is held.

No Person shall be a Senator who shall not have attained to the Age of thirty Years, and been nine Years a Citizen of the United States, and who shall not, when elected, be an Inhabitant of that State for which he shall be chosen.

The Vice President may cast a vote in the Senate only in order to break a tie.

The Vice President of the United States shall be President of the Senate, but shall have no Vote, unless they be equally divided.

The president *pro tempore* of the Senate is a temporary officer; the Latin words mean "for the time being."

The Senate shall chuse their other Officers, and also a President pro tempore, in the absence of the Vice President, or when he shall exercise the Office of President of the United States.

No President has ever been successfully impeached. In 1868 the Senate fell one vote short of the two-thirds majority needed to convict Andrew Johnson. Twelve other officials —ten federal judges, one senator, and one Secretary of War—have been impeached; four of the judges were convicted.

The Senate shall have the sole Power to try all Impeachments. When sitting for that Purpose, they shall be on Oath or Affirmation. When the President of the United States is tried, the Chief Justice shall preside: And no Person shall be convicted without the Concurrence of two thirds of the Members present.

Judgment in Cases of Impeachment shall not extend further than to removal from Office, and disqualification to hold and enjoy any Office of Honor, Trust or Profit under the United States: but the Party convicted shall nevertheless be liable and subject to Indictment, Trial, Judgment and Punishment, according to Law.

Elections for Congress are held on the first Tuesday after the first Monday in November in even-numbered years.

Section 4. The Times, Places and Manner of holding Elections for Senators and Representatives, shall be prescribed in each State by the Legislature thereof; but the Congress may at any time by Law make or alter such Regulations, except as to the Place of chusing Senators.

The 20th Amendment designates January 3 as the opening of the congressional session.

The Congress shall assemble at least once in every Year, and such Meeting shall be on the first Monday in December, unless they shall by Law appoint a different Day.

Section 5. Each House shall be the Judge of the Elections, Returns and Qualifications of its own Members, and a Majority of each shall constitute a Quorum to do Business; but a smaller number may adjourn from day to day, and may be authorized to compel the Attendance of absent Members, in such Manner, and under such Penalties as each House may provide.

Each House may determine the Rules of its Proceedings, punish its Members for disorderly Behavior, and, with the Concurrence of two thirds, expel a Member.

Each House shall keep a Journal of its Proceedings, and from time to time publish the same, excepting such Parts as may in their Judgment require Secrecy; and the Yeas and Nays of the Members of either House on any question shall, at the Desire of one fifth of those Present, be entered on the Journal.

Neither House, during the Session of Congress, shall, without the Consent of the other, adjourn for more than three days, nor to any other Place than that in which the two Houses shall be sitting.

> Each house of Congress decides whether a member has been elected properly and is qualified to be seated. (A quorum is the minimum number of persons required to be present in order to conduct business.) The House once refused admittance to an elected representative who had been guilty of a crime. The Senate did likewise in the case of a candidate whose election campaign lent itself to "fraud and corruption."

Section 6. The Senators and Representatives shall receive a Compensation for their Services, to be ascertained by Law, and paid out of the Treasury of the United States. They shall in all Cases, except Treason, Felony and Breach of the Peace, be privileged from Arrest during their Attendance at the Session of their respective Houses, and in going to and returning from the same; and for any Speech or Debate in either House, they shall not be questioned in any other Place.

No Senator or Representative shall, during the Time for which he was elected, be appointed to any civil Office under the Authority of the United States, which shall have been created, or the Emoluments whereof shall have been encreased during such time; and no Person holding any Office under the United States, shall be a Member of either House during his Continuance in Office.

> Congressmen have the power to fix their own salaries. Under the principle of *congressional immunity,* they cannot be sued or arrested for anything they say in a congressional debate. This provision enables them to speak freely.

> This clause reinforces the principle of separation of powers by stating that, during his term of office, a member of Congress may not be appointed to a position in another branch of government. Nor may he resign and accept a position created during his term.

Section 7. All Bills for raising Revenue shall originate in the House of Representatives; but the Senate may propose or concur with Amendments as on other Bills.

Every Bill which shall have passed the House of Representatives and the Senate, shall, before it become a Law, be presented to the President of the United States; If he approve he shall sign it, but if not he shall return it, with his Objections to that House in which it shall have originated, who shall enter the Objections at large on their Journal, and proceed to reconsider it. If after such Reconsideration two thirds of that House shall agree to pass the Bill, it shall be sent, together with the Objections, to the other House, by which it shall likewise be reconsidered, and if approved by two thirds of that House, it shall become a Law. But in all such Cases the Votes of both Houses shall be determined by Yeas and Nays, and the Names of the Persons voting for and against the Bill shall be entered on the Journal of each House respectively. If any Bill shall not be returned by the President within ten Days (Sundays excepted) after it shall have been presented to him, the Same shall be a Law, in like Manner as if he had signed it, unless the Congress by their Adjournment prevent its Return, in which Case it shall not be a Law.

Every Order, Resolution, or Vote to which the Concurrence of the Senate and House of Representatives may be necessary (except on a question of Adjournment) shall be presented to the President of the United States; and before the Same shall take Effect, shall be approved by him, or being disapproved by him, shall be repassed by two thirds of the Senate and House of Representatives, according to the Rules and Limitations prescribed in the Case of a Bill.

> The House initiates tax bills but the Senate may propose changes in them.

> By returning a bill unsigned to the house in which it originated, the President exercises a *veto.* A two-thirds majority in both houses can override the veto. If the President receives a bill within the last ten days of a session and does not sign it, the measure dies by *pocket veto.* Merely by keeping the bill in his pocket, so to speak, the president effects a veto.

> The same process of approval or disapproval by the President is applied to resolutions and other matters passed by both houses (except adjournment).

Section 8. The Congress shall have Power to lay and collect Taxes, Duties, Imposts and Excises, to pay the Debts and provide for the common Defence and general Welfare of the United States; but all Duties, Imposts and Excises shall be uniform throughout the United States;

To borrow money on the credit of the United States;

To regulate Commerce with foreign Nations, and among the several States, and with the Indian Tribes;

To establish an uniform Rule of Naturalization, and uniform Laws on the subject of Bankruptcies throughout the United States;

To coin Money, regulate the Value thereof, and of foreign Coin, and fix the Standard of Weights and Measures;

To provide for the Punishment of counterfeiting the Securities and current Coin of the United States;

To establish Post Offices and post Roads;

To promote the Progress of Science and useful Arts, by securing for limited Times to Authors and Inventors the exclusive Right to their respective Writings and Discoveries;

To constitute Tribunals inferior to the supreme Court;

To define and punish Piracies and Felonies committed on the high Seas, and Offenses against the Law of Nations;

To declare War, grant Letters of Marque and Reprisal, and make Rules concerning Captures on Land and Water;

To raise and support Armies, but no Appropriation of Money to that Use shall be for a longer Term than two Years;

To provide and maintain a Navy;

To make Rules for the Government and Regulation of the land and naval Forces;

To provide for calling forth the Militia to execute the Laws of the Union, suppress Insurrections and repel Invasions;

To provide for organizing, arming, and disciplining the Militia, and for governing such Part of them as may be employed in the Service of the United States, reserving to the States respectively, the Appointment of the Officers, and the Authority of training the Militia according to the discipline prescribed by Congress;

To exercise exclusive Legislation in all Cases whatsoever, over such District (not exceeding ten Miles square) as may, by Cession of particular States, and the acceptance of Congress, become the Seat of the Government of the United States, and to exercise like Authority over all Places purchased by the Consent of the Legislature of the State in which the Same shall be, for the Erection of Forts, Magazines, Arsenals, dock-Yards, and other needful Buildings;—And

To make all Laws which shall be necessary and proper for carrying into Execution the foregoing Powers, and all other Powers vested by this Constitution in the Government of the United States, or in any Department or Officer thereof.

Section 9. The Migration or Importation of such Persons as any of the States now existing shall think proper to admit, shall not be prohibited by the Congress prior to the Year one thousand eight hundred and eight, but a tax or duty may be imposed on such Importation, not exceeding ten dollars for each Person.

The privilege of the Writ of Habeas Corpus shall not be suspended unless when in Cases of Rebellion or Invasion the public Safety may require it.

No Bill of Attainder or ex post facto Law shall be passed.

No capitation, or other direct, Tax shall be laid, unless in Proportion to the Census or Enumeration herein before directed to be taken.

No Tax or Duty shall be laid on Articles exported from any State.

No Preference shall be given by any Regulation of Commerce or Revenue to the Ports of one State over those of another; nor shall Vessels bound to, or from, one State, be obliged to enter, clear, or pay Duties in another.

No Money shall be drawn from the Treasury, but in Consequence of Appropriations made by Law; and a regular Statement and Account of the Receipts and Expenditures of all public Money shall be published from time to time.

No Title of Nobility shall be granted by the United States: And no Person holding any Office of Profit or Trust under them, shall, without the Consent of the Congress, accept of any present, Emolument, Office, or Title, of any kind whatever, from any King, Prince, or foreign State.

A *bill of attainder* is an act of legislation that declares a person guilty of a crime and punishes him or her without a trial. An *ex post facto* law punishes a person for an act that was legal when performed but later declared illegal.

The object of Clause 4 was to bar direct (per person) taxation of slaves for the purpose of abolishing slavery. The 16th Amendment modified this provision by giving Congress the power to tax personal income.

Section 10. No State shall enter into any Treaty, Alliance, or Confederation; grant Letters of Marque and Reprisal; coin Money; emit Bills of Credit; make any Thing but gold and silver Coin a Tender in Payment of Debts; pass any Bill of Attainder, ex post facto Law, or Law impairing the Obligation of Contracts, or grant any Title of Nobility.

No State shall, without the Consent of the Congress, lay any Imposts or Duties on Imports or Exports, except what may be absolutely necessary for executing its inspection Laws: and the net Produce of all Duties and Imposts, laid by any State on Imports or Exports, shall be for the Use of the Treasury of the United States; and all such Laws shall be subject to the Revision and Controul of the Congress.

No State shall, without the Consent of Congress, lay any duty of Tonnage, keep Troops, or Ships of War in time of Peace, enter into any Agreement or Compact with another State, or with a foreign Power, or engage in War, unless actually invaded, or in such imminent Danger as will not admit of delay.

States are hereby forbidden to exercise certain powers. Some of these powers belong to Congress alone; others are considered undemocratic.

States cannot, without congressional authority, tax goods that enter or leave, except for a small inspection fee.

ARTICLE II • EXECUTIVE DEPARTMENT

Section 1. The executive Power shall be vested in a President of the United States of America. He shall hold his Office during the Term of four Years, and, together with the Vice President, chosen for the same Term, be elected, as follows.

Each State shall appoint, in such Manner as the Legislature thereof may direct, a Number of Electors, equal to the whole Number of Senators and Representatives to which the State may be entitled in the Congress: but no Senator or Representative, or Person holding an Office of Trust or Profit under the United States, shall be appointed an Elector.

The Electors shall meet in their respective States, and vote by Ballot for two persons, of whom one at least shall not be an Inhabitant of the same State with themselves. And they shall make a List of all the Persons voted for, and of the Number of Votes for each; which List they shall sign and certify, and transmit sealed to the Seat of the Government of the United States, directed to the President of the Senate. The President of the Senate shall, in the Presence of the Senate and House of Representatives, open all the Certificates, and the Votes shall then be counted. The Person having the greatest Number of Votes shall be the President, if such Number be a Majority of the whole Number of Electors appointed; and if there be more than one who have such Majority, and have an equal

Federal officials are ineligible to serve as presidential electors.

The 12th Amendment superseded this clause. The weakness of the original constitutional provision became apparent in the election of 1800, when Thomas Jefferson and Aaron Burr received the same number of electoral votes. The 12th Amendment avoids this possibility by requiring electors to cast separate ballots for President and Vice President.

Number of Votes, then the House of Representatives shall immediately chuse by Ballot one of them for President; and if no Person have a Majority, then from the five highest on the List the said House shall in like Manner chuse the President. But in chusing the President, the Votes shall be taken by States, the Representation from each State having cne Vote; a quorum for this Purpose shall consist of a Member or Members from two thirds of the States, and a Majority of all the States shall be necessary to a Choice. In every Case, after the Choice of the President, the Person having the greatest Number of Votes of the Electors shall be the Vice President. But if there should remain two or more who have equal Votes, the Senate shall chuse from them by Ballot the Vice President.

The Congress may determine the Time of chusing the Electors, and the Day on which they shall give their Votes; which Day shall be the same throughout the United States.

A naturalized citizen may not become President.

No person except a natural born Citizen, or a Citizen of the United States, at the time of the Adoption of this Constitution, shall be eligible to the Office of President; neither shall any Person be eligible to that Office who shall not have attained to the Age of Thirty-five Years, and been fourteen Years a Resident within the United States.

The Vice President is next in line for the presidency. A federal law passed in 1947 determined the order of presidential succession as follows: (1) Speaker of the House; (2) president *pro tempore* of the Senate; and (3) Cabinet officers in the order in which their departments were created. (So far, death has been the only circumstance under which a presidential term has been cut short.) This clause has been amplified by the 25th Amendment.

In Case of the Removal of the President from Office, or of his Death, Resignation, or Inability to discharge the Powers and Duties of the said Office, the same shall devolve cn the Vice-President, and the Congress may by Law provide for the Case of Removal, Death, Resignation or Inabiltiy, both of the President and the Vice President, declaring what Officer shall then act as President, and such Officer shall act accordingly, until the Disability be removed, or a President shall be elected.

The President shall, at stated Times, receive for his Services, a Compensation, which shall neither be encreased nor diminished during the Period for which he shall have been elected, and he shall not receive within that Period any other Emolument from the United States, or any of them.

Before he enter on the Execution of his Office, he shall take the following Oath or Affirmation:—"I do solemnly swear (or affirm) that I will faithfully execute the Office of the President of the United States, and will to the best of my Ability, preserve, protect and defend the Constitution of the United States."

This clause suggests written communication between the President and "the principal officer in each of the executive departments." As it developed, these officials comprise the Cabinet—whose members are chosen, and may be replaced, by the President.

Section 2. The President shall be Commander in Chief of the Army and Navy of the United States, and of the Militia of the several States, when called into the actual Service of the United States; he may require the Opinion in writing, of the principal Officer in each of the executive Departments, upon any subject relating to the Duties of their respective Offices, and he shall have Power to Grant Reprieves and Pardons for Offenses against the United States, except in Cases of Impeachment.

Senate approval is required for treaties and presidential appointments.

He shall have Power, by and with the Advice and Consent of the Senate, to make by and with the Advice and Consent of the Senate, shall appoint Ambassadors, other Treaties, provided two thirds of the Senators present concur; and he shall nominate, and public Ministers and Consuls, Judges of the supreme Court, and all other Officers of the United States, whose Appointments are not herein otherwise provided for, and which shall be established by Law: but the Congress may by Law vest the Appointment of such inferior Officers, as they think proper, in the President alone, in the Courts of Law, or in the Heads of Departments.

Without the consent of the Senate, the President may appoint officials only on a temporary basis.

The President shall have Power to fill up all Vacancies that may happen during the Recess of the Senate, by granting Commissions which shall expire at the End of their next Session.

Section 3. He shall from time to time give to the Congress Information of the State of the Union, and recommend to their Consideration such Measures as he shall judge necessary and expedient; he may, on extraordinary Occasions, convene both Houses, or either of them, and in Case of Disagreement between them, with Respect to the Time of Adjournment, he may adjourn them to such Time as he shall think proper; he shall receive Ambassadors and other public Ministers; he shall take Care that the Laws be faithfully executed, and shall Commission all the Officers of the United States.

The President delivers a "State of the Union" message at the opening of each session of Congress. Woodrow Wilson was the first President since John Adams to read his messages in person. Franklin D. Roosevelt and his successors followed Wilson's example.

Section 4. The President, Vice President and all civil Officers of the United States, shall be removed from Office on Impeachment for, and Conviction of, Treason, Bribery, or other high Crimes and Misdemeanors.

ARTICLE III • JUDICIAL DEPARTMENT

Section 1. The judicial Power of the United States, shall be vested in one supreme Court, and in such inferior Courts as the Congress may from time to time ordain and establish. The Judges, both of the supreme and inferior Courts, shall hold their Offices during good Behaviour, and shall, at stated Times, receive for their Services, a Compensation, which shall not be diminished during their Continuance in Office.

Federal judges hold office for life and may not have their salaries lowered while in office. These provisions are intended to keep the federal bench independent of political pressure.

Section 2. The judicial Power shall extend to all Cases, in Law and Equity, arising under this Constitution, the Laws of the United States, and Treaties made, or which shall be made, under their Authority;—to all Cases affecting Ambassadors, other public Ministers and Consuls;—to all Cases of admiralty and maritime Jurisdiction;—to Controversies to which the United States shall be a Party;—to Controversies between two or more States;—between a State and Citizens of another State;—between Citizens of different States;—between Citizens of the same State claiming Lands under Grants of different States, and between a State, or the Citizens thereof, and foreign States, Citizens or Subjects.

This clause describes the types of cases that may be heard in federal courts.

The 11th Amendment prevents a citizen from suing a state in a federal court.

In all Cases affecting Ambassadors, other public Ministers and Consuls, and those in which a State shall be Party, the supreme Court shall have original Jurisdiction. In all the other Cases before mentioned, the supreme Court shall have appellate Jurisdiction, both as to Law and Fact, with such Exceptions, and under such Regulations as the Congress shall make.

The Supreme Court handles certain cases directly. It may also review cases handled by lower courts, but Congress in some cases may withhold the right to appeal to the highest court, or limit appeal by setting various conditions.

The trial of all Crimes, except in Cases of Impeachment, shall be by Jury; and such Trial shall be held in the State where the said Crimes shall have been committed; but when not committed within any State, the Trial shall be at such Place or Places as the Congress may by Law have directed.

The 6th Amendment strengthens this clause on trial procedure.

Section 3. Treason against the United States, shall consist only in levying War against them, or in adhering to their Enemies, giving them Aid and Comfort. No Person shall be convicted of Treason unless on the Testimony of two Witnesses to the same overt Act, or on Confession in open Court.

Treason is rigorously defined. A person can be convicted only if two witnesses testify to the same obvious act, or if he confesses in court.

The Congress shall have Power to declare the Punishment of Treason, but no Attainder of Treason shall work Corruption of Blood, or Forfeiture except during the Life of the Person attainted.

Punishment for treason extends only to the person convicted, not to his or her descendants. ("Corruption of blood" means that the heirs of a convicted person are deprived of certain rights.)

ARTICLE IV • RELATIONS AMONG THE STATES

States must honor each other's laws, court decisions, and records (for example, birth, marriage, and death certificates).

Section 1. Full Faith and Credit shall be given in each State to the public Acts, Records, and judicial Proceedings of every other State. And the Congress may by general Laws prescribe the Manner in which such Acts, Records and Proceedings shall be proved, and the Effect thereof.

Each state must respect the rights of citizens of other states.

The process of returning a person accused of a crime to the governmental authority (in this case a state) from which he or she has fled is called *extradition.*

The 13th Amendment, which abolished slavery, makes this clause obsolete.

Section 2. The Citizens of each State shall be entitled to all Privileges and Immunities of Citizens in the several States.

A Person charged in any State with Treason, Felony, or other Crime, who shall flee from Justice, and be found in another State, shall on demand of the executive Authority of the State from which he fled, be delivered up, to be removed to the State having Jurisdiction of the Crime.

No Person held in Service or Labour in one State, under the Laws thereof, escaping into another, shall, in Consequence of any Law or Regulation therein, be discharged from such Service or Labour, but shall be delivered up on Claim of the Party to whom such Service or Labour may be due.

A new state may not be created by dividing or joining existing states unless approved by the legislatures of the states affected and by Congress. An exception to the provision forbidding the division of a state occurred during the Civil War. In 1863 West Virginia was formed out of the western region of Virginia.

Section 3. New States may be admitted by the Congress into this Union; but no new State shall be formed or erected within the Jurisdiction of any other State; nor any State be formed by the Junction of two or more States, or parts of States, without the Consent of the Legislatures of the States concerned as well as of the Congress.

The Congress shall have Power to dispose of and make all needful Rules and Regulations respecting the Territory or other Property belonging to the United States; and nothing in this Constitution shall be so construed as to Prejudice any Claims of the United States, or of any particular State.

A *republican* form of government is one in which citizens choose representatives to govern them. The federal government must protect a state against invasion and, if state authorities request it, against violence within a state.

Section 4. The United States shall guarantee to every State in this Union a Republican Form of Government, and shall protect each of them against Invasion; and on Application of the Legislature, or of the Executive (when the Legislature cannot be convened) against domestic Violence.

ARTICLE V • AMENDING THE CONSTITUTION

An amendment to the Constitution can be proposed (a) by Congress, with a two-thirds vote of both houses, or (b) by a convention called by Congress when two-thirds of the state legislatures request it. An amendment is ratified (a) by three-fourths of the state legislatures, or (b) by conventions in three-fourths of the states. The twofold procedure of proposal and ratification reflects the seriousness with which the framers of the Constitution regarded amendments. Over 6,900 amendments have been proposed; only 26 have been ratified.

The Congress, whenever two thirds of both Houses shall deem it necessary, shall propose Amendments to this Constitution, or, on the Application of the Legislatures of two thirds of the several States, shall call a Convention for proposing Amendments, which, in either Case, shall be valid to all Intents and Purposes, as part of this Constitution, when ratified by the Legislatures of three fourths of the several States, or by Conventions in three fourths thereof, as the one or the other Mode of Ratification may be proposed by the Congress: Provided that no Amendment which may be made prior to the Year One thousand eight hundred and eight shall in any Manner affect the first and fourth Clauses in the Ninth Section of the first Article; and that no State, without its Consent, shall be deprived of its equal Suffrage in the Senate.

ARTICLE VI • GENERAL PROVISIONS

All Debts contracted and Engagements entered into, before the Adoption of this Constitution, shall be as valid against the United States under this Constitution, as under the Confederation.

This Constitution, and the Laws of the United States which shall be made in Pursuance thereof; and all Treaties made, or which shall be made, under the Authority of the United States, shall be the supreme Law of the Land; and the Judges in every State shall be bound thereby, any Thing in the Constitution or Laws of any State to the Contrary notwithstanding.

The supremacy clause means that if a federal and a state law conflict, the federal law prevails.

The Senators and Representatives before mentioned, and the Members of the several State Legislatures, and all executive and judicial Officers, both of the United States and of the several States, shall be bound by Oath or Affirmation, to support this Constitution; but no religious Test shall ever be required as a Qualification to any Office or public Trust under the United States.

Religion may not be a condition for holding public office.

ARTICLE VII • RATIFICATION

The Ratification of the Conventions of nine States shall be sufficient for the Establishment of this Constitution between the States so ratifying the Same.

The Constitution would become the law of the land upon the approval of nine states.

DONE in Convention by the Unanimous Consent of the States present the Seventeenth Day of September in the Year of our Lord one thousand seven hundred and eighty-seven and of the Independence of the United States of America the Twelfth. In Witness whereof We have hereunto subscribed our Names.

G° WASHINGTON
Presid^t and deputy from
VIRGINIA

Attest: *William Jackson,* Secretary

DELAWARE
Geo: Read
Gunning Bedford, jun
John Dickinson
Richard Bassett
Jaco: Broom

MARYLAND
James McHenry
Dan: of St Thos Jenifer
Danl Carroll

VIRGINIA
John Blair
James Madison Jr.

NORTH CAROLINA
Wm Blount
Richd Dobbs Spaight
Hu Williamson

SOUTH CAROLINA
J. Rutledge
Charles Cotesworth
Pinckney
Charles Pinckney
Pierce Butler

GEORGIA
William Few
Abr Baldwin

NEW HAMPSHIRE
John Langdon
Nicholas Gilman

MASSACHUSETTS
Nathaniel Gorham
Rufus King

CONNECTICUT
Wm Saml Johnson
Roger Sherman

NEW YORK
Alexander Hamilton

NEW JERSEY
Wil: Livingston
David Brearley
Wm Paterson
Jona: Dayton

PENNSYLVANIA
B Franklin
Thomas Mifflin
Robt. Morris
Geo. Clymer
Thos. FitzSimons
Jared Ingersoll
James Wilson
Gouv Morris

AMENDMENTS

AMENDMENT I • (1791)

Establishes fredom of religion, speech, and the press; gives citizens the rights of assembly and petition.

Congress shall make no law respecting an establishment of religion, or prohibiting the free exercise thereof: or abridging the freedom of speech, or of the press; or the right of the people peaceably to assemble, and to petition the Government for a redress of grievances.

AMENDMENT II • (1791)

States have the right to maintain a militia.

A well regulated Militia, being necessary to the security of a free State, the right of the people to keep and bear Arms, shall not be infringed.

AMENDMENT III • (1791)

Limits the army's right to quarter soldiers in private homes.

No Soldier shall, in time of peace, be quartered in any house, without the consent of the Owner, nor in time of war, but in a manner to be prescribed by law.

AMENDMENT IV • (1791)

Search warrants are required as a guarantee of a citizen's right to privacy.

The right of the people to be secure in their persons, houses, papers, and effects, against unreasonable searches and seizures, shall not be violated, and no Warrants shall issue, but upon probable cause, supported by Oath or affirmation, and particularly describing the place to be searched, and the persons or things to be seized.

AMENDMENT V • (1791)

To be prosecuted for a serious crime, a person must first be accused (indicted) by a grand jury. No one can be tried twice for the same crime (double jeopardy). Nor can a person be forced into self-incrimination by testifying against himself or herself.

No person shall be held to answer for a capital, or otherwise infamous crime, unless on a presentment or indictment of a Grand Jury, except in cases arising in the land or naval forces, or in the Militia, when in actual service in time of War or public danger; nor shall any person be subject for the same offence to be twice put in jeopardy of life or limb; nor shall be compelled in any criminal case to be a witness against himself, nor be deprived of life, liberty, or property, without due process of law; nor shall private property be taken for public use, without just compensation.

AMENDMENT VI • (1791)

Guarantees a defendant's right to be tried without delay and to face witnesses testifying for the other side.

In all criminal prosecutions, the accused shall enjoy the right to a speedy and public trial, by an impartial jury of the State and district wherein the crime shall have been committed, which district shall have been previously ascertained by law, and to be informed of the nature and cause of the accusation; to be confronted with the witnesses against him; to have compulsory process for obtaining witnesses in his favor, and to have the Assistance of Counsel for his defence.

[The date following each amendment number is the year of ratification.]

AMENDMENT VII • (1791)

In suits at common law, where the value in controversy shall exceed twenty dollars, the right of trial by jury shall be preserved, and no fact tried by a jury, shall be otherwise reexamined in any Court of the United States, than according to the rules of the common law.

A jury trial is guaranteed in federal civil suits involving more than twenty dollars.

AMENDMENT VIII • (1791)

Excessive bail shall not be required, nor excessive fines imposed, nor cruel and unusual punishments inflicted.

AMENDMENT IX • (1791)

The enumeration in the Constitution, of certain rights, shall not be construed to deny or disparage others retained by the people.

The listing of specific rights in the Constitution does not mean that others are not protected.

AMENDMENT X • (1791)

The powers not delegated to the United States by the Constitution, nor prohibited by it to the States, are reserved to the States respectively, or to the people.

Limits the federal government to its specific powers. Powers not prohibited the states by the Constitution may be exercised by them.

AMENDMENT XI • (1798)

The Judicial power of the United States shall not be construed to extend to any suit in law or equity, commenced or prosecuted against one of the United States by Citizens of another State, or by Citizens or Subjects of any Foreign State.

A state cannot be sued by a citizen of another state in a federal court. Such a case can be tried only in the courts of the state being sued.

AMENDMENT XII • (1804)

The Electors shall meet in their respective states and vote by ballot for President and Vice-President, one of whom, at least, shall not be an inhabitant of the same state with themselves; they shall name in their ballots the person voted for as President, and in distinct ballots the person voted for as Vice-President, and they shall make distinct lists of all persons voted for as President, and of all persons voted for as Vice-President, and of the number of votes for each, which lists they shall sign and certify, and transmit sealed to the seat of the government of the United States, directed to the President of the Senate; —The President of the Senate shall, in presence of the Senate and House of Representatives, open all the certificates and the votes shall then be counted;—The person having the greatest number of votes for President, shall be the President, if such number be a majority of the whole number of Electors appointed; and if no person have such majority, then from the persons having the highest numbers not exceeding three on the list of those voted for as President, the House of Representatives shall choose immediately, by ballot, the President. But in choosing the President, the votes shall be taken by states, the representation from each state having one vote; a quorum for this purpose shall consist of a member or members from two-thirds of the states, and a majority of all the states shall be necessary to a choice. And if the House of Representatives shall not choose a President whenever the right of choice shall devolve upon them, before the fourth day of March next following, then the Vice-President shall act as President, as in the case of

Revises the process by which the President and Vice President were elected (see Article II, Section 1, Clause 3). The major change requires electors to cast separate ballots for President and Vice President. If none of the presidential candidates obtains a majority vote, the House of Representatives— with each state having one vote—chooses a President from the three candidates having the highest number of votes. If no vice presidential candidate wins a majority, the Senate chooses from the two candidates having the highest number of votes. The portion printed in color was superseded by Section 3 of the 20th Amendment.

the death or other constitutional disability of the President.— The person having the greatest number of votes as Vice-President, shall be the Vice-President, if such number be a majority of the whole number of Electors appointed, and if no person have a majority, then from the two highest numbers on the list, the Senate shall choose the Vice-President; a quorum for the purpose shall consist of two-thirds of the whole number of Senators, and a majority of the whole number shall be necessary to a choice. But no person constitutionally ineligible to the office of President shall be eligible to that of Vice-President of the United States.

AMENDMENT XIII • (1865)

Abolishes slavery.

Section 1. Neither slavery nor involuntary servitude, except as a punishment for crime whereof the party shall have been duly convicted, shall exist within the United States, or any place subject to their jurisdiction.

Section 2. Congress shall have power to enforce this article by appropriate legislation.

AMENDMENT XIV • (1868)

This section confers full civil rights on former slaves. Supreme Court decisions have interpreted the language of Section 1 to mean that the states, as well as the federal government, are bound by the Bill of Rights.

Section 1. All persons born or naturalized in the United States, and subject to the jurisdiction thereof, are citizens of the United States and of the State wherein they reside. No State shall make or enforce any law which shall abridge the privileges or immunities of citizens of the United States; nor shall any State deprive any person of life, liberty, or property, without due process of law; nor deny any person within its jurisdiction the equal protection of the laws.

A penalty of a reduction in congressional representation shall be applied to any state that refuses to give all adult male citizens the right to vote in federal elections. This section has never been applied. The portion printed in color was superseded by Section 1 of the 26th Amendment. (This section has also been amplified by the 19th Amendment.)

Section 2. Representatives shall be apportioned among the several States according to their respective numbers, counting the whole number of persons in each State, excluding Indians not taxed. But when the right to vote at any election for the choice of electors for President and Vice-President of the United States, Representatives in Congress, the Executive and Judicial officers of a State, or the members of the Legislature thereof, is denied to any of the male inhabitants of such State, being twenty-one years of age, and citizens of the United States, or in any way abridged, except for participation in rebellion, or other crime, the basis of representation therein shall be reduced in the proportion which the number of such male citizens shall bear to the whole number of male citizens twenty-one years of age in such State.

Any former federal or state official who served the Confederacy during the Civil War could not become a federal official again unless Congress voted otherwise.

Section 3. No person shall be a Senator or Representative in Congress, or elector of President and Vice-President, or hold any office, civil or military, under the United States, or under any State, who, having previously taken an oath, as a member of Congress, or as an officer of the United States, or as a member of any State legislature, or as an executive or judicial officer of any State, to support the Constitution of the United States, shall have engaged in insurrection or rebellion against the same, or given aid or comfort to the enemies thereof. But Congress may by a vote of two-thirds of each House, remove such disability.

Section 4. The validity of the public debt of the United States, authorized by law, including debts incurred for payment of pensions and bounties for services in suppressing insurrection or rebellion, shall not be questioned. But neither the United States nor any State shall assume or pay any debt or obligation incurred in aid of insurrection or rebellion against the United States, or any claim for the loss or emancipation of any slave; but all such debts, obligations and claims shall be held illegal and void.

Makes legal the federal Civil War debt, but at the same time voids all Confederate debts incurred in the war.

Section 5. The Congress shall have power to enforce, by appropriate legislation, the provisions of this article.

AMENDMENT XV • (1870)

Section 1. The right of citizens of the United States to vote shall not be denied or abridged by the United States or by any State on account of race, color, or previous condition of servitude.

Gives blacks the right to vote.

Section 2. The Congress shall have power to enforce this article by appropriate legislation.

AMENDMENT XVI • (1913)

The Congress shall have power to lay and collect taxes on incomes, from whatever source derived, without apportionment among the several States, and without regard to any census or enumeration.

Allows Congress to levy taxes on incomes.

AMENDMENT XVII • (1913)

The Senate of the United States shall be composed of two Senators from each State, elected by the people thereof, for six years; and each Senator shall have one vote. The electors in each State shall have the qualifications requisite for electors of the most numerous branch of the State legislature.

Provides for election of senators by the people of a state, rather than the state legislature.

When vacancies happen in the representation of any State in the Senate, the executive authority of such State shall issue writs of election to fill such vacancies: *Provided,* That the legislature of any State may empower the executive thereof to make temporary appointments until the people fill the vacancies by election as the legislature may direct.

This amendment shall not be so construed as to affect the election or term of any Senator chosen before it becomes valid as part of the Constitution.

AMENDMENT XVIII • (1919)

Section 1. After one year from the ratification of this article, the manufacture, sale, or transportation of intoxicating liquors within, the importation thereof into, or the exportation thereof from the United States and all territory subject to the jurisdiction thereof for beverage purposes is hereby prohibited.

Legalizes prohibition—that is, forbidding the making, selling, or transporting of intoxicating beverages. Superseded by the 21st Amendment.

Section 2. The Congress and the several States shall have concurrent power to enforce this article by appropriate legislation.

Section 3. This article shall be inoperative unless it shall have been ratified as an amendment to the Constitution by the legislatures of the several States, as provided in the Constitution, within seven years from the date of the submission hereof to the States by the Congress.

AMENDMENT XIX • (1920)

Gives women the right to vote.

The right of citizens of the United States to vote shall not be denied or abridged by the United States or by any State on account of sex.

Congress shall have power to enforce this article by appropriate legislation.

AMENDMENT XX • (1933)

Section 1. The terms of the President and Vice-President shall end at noon on the 20th day of January, and the terms of Senators and Representatives at noon on the 3d day of January, of the years in which such terms would have ended if this article had not been ratified; and the terms of their successors shall then begin.

The "lame duck" amendment allows the President to take office on January 20, and members of Congress on January 3. The purpose of the amendment is to reduce the term in office of defeated incumbents—known as "lame ducks."

Section 2. The Congress shall assemble at least once in every year, and such meeting shall begin at noon on the 3d day of January, unless they shall by law appoint a different day.

Section 3. If, at the time fixed for the beginning of the term of the President, the President elect shall have died, the Vice-President elect shall become President. If a President shall not have been chosen before the time fixed for the beginning of his term, or if the President elect shall have failed to qualify, then the Vice-President elect shall act as President until a President shall have qualified; and the Congress may by law provide for the case wherein neither a President elect nor a Vice-President elect shall have qualified, declaring who shall then act as President, or the manner in which one who is to act shall be selected, and such person shall act accordingly until a President or Vice-President shall have qualified.

Section 4. The Congress may by law provide for the case of the death of any of the persons from whom the House of Representatives may choose a President whenever the right of choice shall have devolved upon them, and for the case of the death of any of the persons from whom the Senate may choose a Vice-President whenever the right of choice shall have devolved upon them.

Section 5. Sections 1 and 2 shall take effect on the 15th day of October following the ratification of this article.

Section 6. This article shall be inoperative unless it shall have been ratified as an amendment to the Constitution by the legislatures of three-fourths of the several States within seven years from the date of its submission.

AMENDMENT XXI • (1933)

Section 1. The eighteenth article of amendment to the Constitution of the United States is hereby repealed.

Section 2. The transportation or importation into any State, Territory, or possession of the United States for delivery or use therein of intoxicating liquors, in violation of the laws thereof, is hereby prohibited.

Section 3. This article shall be inoperative unless it shall have been ratified as an amendment to the Constitution by conventions in the several States, as provided in the Constitution, within seven years from the date of the submission hereof to the States by the Congress.

AMENDMENT XXII • (1951)

Section 1. No person shall be elected to the office of the President more than twice, and no person who has held the office of President, or acted as President, for more than two years of a term to which some other person was elected President shall be elected to the office of the President more than once. But this Article shall not apply to any person holding the office of President when this Article was proposed by the Congress, and shall not prevent any person who may be holding the office of President, or acting as President, during the term within which this Article becomes operative from holding the office of President or acting as President during the remainder of such term.

Section 2. This article shall be inoperative unless it shall have been ratified as an amendment to the Constitution by the legislatures of three-fourths of the several States within seven years from the date of its submission to the States by the Congress.

AMENDMENT XXIII • (1961)

Section 1. The District constituting the seat of Government of the United States shall appoint in such manner as the Congress may direct:

A number of electors of President and Vice-President equal to the whole number of Senators and Representatives in Congress to which the District would be entitled if it were a State, but in no event more than the least populous State; they shall be in addition to those appointed by the States, but they shall be considered, for the purposes of the election of President and Vice-President, to be electors appointed by a State; and they shall meet in the District and perform such duties as provided by the twelfth article of amendment.

Section 2. The Congress shall have power to enforce this article by appropriate legislation.

AMENDMENT XXIV • (1964)

Section 1. The right of citizens of the United States to vote in any primary or other election for President or Vice-President, for electors for President or Vice-President, or for Senator or Representative in Congress, shall not be denied or abridged by the United States or any State by reason of failure to pay any poll tax or other tax.

Section 2. The Congress shall have power to enforce this article by appropriate legislation.

AMENDMENT XXV • (1967)

Outlines the procedure to be followed in case of presidential disability.

Section 1. In case of the removal of the President from office or of his death or resignation, the Vice-President shall become President.

Section 2. Whenever there is a vacancy in the office of the Vice-President, the President shall nominate a Vice-President who shall take office upon confirmation by a majority vote of both Houses of Congress.

Section 3. Whenever the President transmits to the President pro tempore of the Senate and the Speaker of the House of Representatives his written declaration that he is unable to discharge the powers and duties of his office, and until he transmits to them a written declaration to the contrary, such powers and duties shall be discharged by the Vice-President as Acting President.

Section 4. Whenever the Vice-President and a majority of either the principal officers of the executive departments or of such other body as Congress may by law provide, transmit to the President pro tempore of the Senate and the Speaker of the House of Representatives their written declaration that the President is unable to discharge the powers and duties of his office, the Vice-President shall immediately assume the powers and duties of the office as Acting President.

Thereafter, when the President transmits to the President pro tempore of the Senate and the Speaker of the House of Representatives his written declaration that no inability exists, he shall resume the powers and duties of his office unless the Vice-President and a majority of either the principal officers of the executive department or of such other body as Congress may by law provide, transmit within four days to the President pro tempore of the Senate and the Speaker of the House of Representatives their written declaration that the President is unable to discharge the powers and duties of his office. Thereupon Congress shall decide the issue, assembling within forty-eight hours for that purpose if not in session. If the Congress, within twenty-one days after receipt of the latter written declaration, or, if Congress is not in session, within twenty-one days after Congress is required to assemble, determines by two-thirds vote of both Houses that the President is unable to discharge the powers and duties of his office, the Vice-President shall continue to discharge the same as Acting President; otherwise, the President shall resume the powers and duties of his office.

AMENDMENT XXVI • (1971)

Lowers the voting age to eighteen.

Section 1. The right of citizens of the United States, who are eighteen years of age or older, to vote shall not be denied or abridged by the United States or any state on account of age.

Section 2. The Congress shall have the power to enforce this article by appropriate legislation.

NOTES ON SOURCES

Quotations by these foreign observers appear in the nine Pictorial Essays. Minor adaptations have been made in some quoted material, chiefly to modernize spelling and grammar. In the essays, the writer's name is followed by a date or dates. These represent the years in which the observations were made, if known. If the exact period is not known, the date represents the year in which the account was first published in the original language.

Anburey, Thomas *(Essay 2)* An officer in the British army during the Revolution, he journeyed through Canada and several of the colonies between 1776 and 1781. His *Travels Through the Interior Parts of America* was published in 1789.

Beaujour, Felix de *(Essay 2)* French consul-general in the United States from 1804 to 1816. His *Sketch of the United States at the Commencement of the Nineteenth Century* (1814) was highly critical of Americans as crude and money-grubbing.

Beauvoir, Simone de *(Essays 8, 9)* The noted French writer and philosopher made a nationwide tour of the United States between January and May 1947. *America Day by Day* (1953), based on her travels, shows her as an intelligent and sensitive reporter of the American scene.

Bernard, John *(Essays 3, 4)* This English actor made several professional tours in the United States between 1797 and 1811. Selections from his witty and gossipy *Retrospections of America* appeared at intervals later in the nineteenth century.

Birkbeck, Morris *(Essay 4)* An Englishman who relocated in southern Illinois in 1818. His writings greatly influenced other would-be settlers. The two quotations given here are from his *Letters From Illinois* (1818).

Blane, William *(Essay 4)* Little is known of this young Englishman other than that he lived from 1800 to 1825. His *Excursion Through the United States and Canada During the Years 1822-23* was published anonymously three years after his death.

Bremer, Fredrika *(Essays 4, 6)* A Swedish novelist well known in her day, who traveled in America from 1849 to 1851. Her impressions, in the form of letters to her sister, appeared in *Homes of the New World* (1853).

Broughton, Morris *(Essay 9)* A South African journalist and editor of *The Cape Argus*, he came to the United States in 1956 as a guest of the State Department. By his estimation, he traveled over 10,000 miles and visited over thirty states during his three-month stay here.

Burnaby, Andrew *(Essay 2)* A clergyman of the Church of England, Burnaby traveled in the colonies in 1759-60. His firm loyalty to the British crown is evident in his *Travels Through North America,* first published in 1775.

Cabeza de Vaca, Álvar Núñez *(Essay 1)* After his stay among the Indians in North America, the Spanish explorer led an expedition in South America and served as governor of Paraguay. He returned to Spain in 1544. His account of his years in North America, *Los Naufragios* ("The Shipwrecked") was published in 1542.

Capellini, Giovanni *(Essay 5)* An Italian professor of geology, Capellini toured the western United States in 1863. He recorded his scientific observations in a journal published in 1867.

Carpenter, Harry *(Essay 8)* An English sports expert, Carpenter was boxing and general sports columnist for *The London Daily Mail* from 1954 to 1962, as well as a full-time correspondent for the BBC. In his *Masters of Boxing* (1964) he spoke of Joe Louis as the "headmaster" of boxing.

Castañeda, Pedro de *(Essay 1)* This Spaniard—one of the 300 men who accompanied Coronado on his expedition in the 1540s—was the most famous chronicler of the journey. Little is known of him except his birthplace, Najera, Spain.

Champlain, Samuel de *(Essay 1)* The renowned French explorer was the chief founder of New France. He made a number of voyages to Canada in the early seventeenth century, and published several different accounts of them.

Chastellux, Marquis de (François-Jean de Beauvoir) *(Essay 3)* A French army officer, he served as aide to Rochambeau during the American Revolution. His *Travels in North America in the Years 1780, 1781, and 1782* (1786) is a vivid and generally accurate account.

Chateaubriand, François-René de *(Essay 4)* This French novelist visited the United States for four months in 1791, but did not publish his *Travels in America* until 1827. It is a romantic work devoted mainly to the Indian as a "noble savage" rather than to the author's own experiences.

Chesterton, G. K. *(Essay 6)* The English poet and novelist visited the United States on a lecture tour in 1921. His book, *What I Saw in America,* was published in London in 1922.

Chevalier, Michel *(Essay 5)* As a young French engineer, he was sent by his government in 1834-35 to study transportation and public works in the United States. He praised the country in *Letters on North America* (1836).

Cobbett, William *(Essay 3)* Opinionated and outspoken, this English journalist was twice forced to flee to the United States, where he lived from 1792 to 1800 and again from 1817 to 1819. The selection quoted is from *A Year's Residence in the United States of America* (1818).

Colum, Padraic *(Essay 7)* This Irish man of letters made his home in the United States after 1914. He was a friend of many writers, including Robert Frost.

Columbus, Christopher *(Essay 1)* The great explorer kept a journal account of his first voyage, which he presented to the Spanish monarchs. It has since been lost, but an abstract of it was made earlier by the Spanish missionary Bartolomé de Las Casas.

Cooke, Alistair *(Essay 9)* Of Anglo-Irish birth, this popular journalist and broadcaster has lived primarily in the United States since the 1930s, and became an American citizen in 1941. He is the author of many books on American culture. This selection comes from *Talk About America* (1968).

Corresca, Rocco *(Essay 6)* An Italian immigrant, he typified the penniless hopefuls who flocked to America to make their fortune. His "Biography of a Bootblack" appeared in a magazine, *The Independent,* in December 1902.

Dal Verme, Francesco *(Essay 2)* Member of a noble Milanese family. The journal and letters concerning his travels in 1783-84 were meant only for his relatives, but were published in 1969 as *Seeing America and Its Great Men.*

Danckaerts, Jaspar *(Essay 2)* A Dutchman, he belonged to a small Calvinist sect, the Labadists. He and Peter Sluyter spent thirteen months in America in 1679-80 looking for a place for the Labadists to settle (they chose Maryland). Danckaerts' journal was discovered in the nineteenth century by an American, and published in 1867.

Dickens, Charles *(Essay 4)* The famous English writer first toured the United States in 1842. His *American Notes,* published that same year, was highly critical of Americans. Out of this experience came his novel *Martin Chuzzlewit.*

Dubos, René—See Ward, Barbara

Erkelenz, Anton *(Essay 7)* A member of the German parliament, he wrote a book called *America Today* (1927), in which he expressed an optimistic belief that the United States would some day create a culture uniquely its own.

"A Fidalgo of Elvas" *(Essay 1)* Nothing is known of this chronicler of De Soto's expedition other than his nationality—Portuguese, the language of his narrative. He was clearly a modest man, since he mentioned himself only once in the entire account (first published in 1557).

Freymond, Jacques *(Essay 8)* On his first trip to the United States (1949–1950), Freymond, a Swiss historian, studied at Yale University and made an extended auto tour of the country. He returned for a two-month trip in 1955.

Galsworthy, John *(Essay 7)* The noted English writer gave a series of speeches in the United States that were published in a volume called *Addresses in America* (1919).

Gilbert, Bartholomew See Gosnold, Bartholomew.

Gosnold, Bartholomew *(Essay 1)* An Englishman, he led an expedition—including Bartholomew Gilbert as navigator—of the first Europeans to explore Cape Cod. They also visited Martha's Vineyard, which Gosnold named after his daughter and because of its lush growth of strawberries, grapes, and other fruit.

Graham, Stephen *(Essay 6)* A British traveler and journalist who visited the United States in 1913. These quotations are from his work *With Poor Immigrants to America* (1914).

Grassi, Giovanni *(Essay 3)* This Italian Jesuit priest spent the years 1810-17 in the United States. His report, emphasizing general characteristics rather than specific people or places, appeared in 1819.

Griesinger, Karl Theodor *(Essay 6)* This German historian spent five years in the United States, although he did not find the American form of democracy to his liking. His *Living Pictures from America*, published in 1858, is characterized by a cutting and ironical humor.

Grund, Francis J. *(Essay 4)* A Bohemian journalist who spent several years in the United States during the 1830s. His book of observations—*The Americans in Their Moral, Social, and Political Relations*—was published in 1837.

Hall, Basil *(Essays 4, 5)* A retired English naval officer, he visited the United States in 1820 and in 1827-28. His *Travels in North America* (1829) is a valuable description.

Hamp, Sidford *(Essay 5)* This English youth was only seventeen when his uncle—who had helped found Colorado Springs—arranged for him to travel to the United States on a scientific expedition. His diary reflects his youthful enthusiasm.

Hartog, Jan de *(Essay 9)* A Dutch author and playwright who made a leisurely voyage in 1958-61 from Houston to Nantucket, largely by inland waterways. He gives a charming account of his adventures in *Waters of the Western World*, published in 1961.

Hauptmann, Gerhart *(Essay 7)* In 1932 this German playwright, a Nobel prize winner, visited the United States. He remarked on leaving that the high points of his trip had been meeting O'Neill and attending *Mourning Becomes Electra*. The critique quoted here is from an interview the same year with an American correspondent.

Hawkes, Jacquetta—See Priestley, J. B.

Hawkins, John *(Essay 1)* The famous English naval commander visited America on many of his voyages. The excerpt quoted is from Richard Hakluyt's great compendium of travel accounts, *Principall Navigations, Voiages, and Discoveries of the English Nation.*

Heriot (or **Harriot**), **Thomas** *(Essay 1)* An English mathematician and astronomer, he traveled to Roanoke as a surveyor on Sir Richard Grenville's 1585 expedition (financed by Raleigh). His *Brief and True Report of the new-found Land of Virginia* appeared in 1588.

Hilbersheimer, Ludwig and **Udo Rukser** *(Essay 7)* These German architects praised the innovations of American architecture and especially the work of Frank Lloyd Wright. Their article appeared in a 1920 issue of the German journal, *Art and Artist.*

Jarlson, Axel *(Essay 6)* The story of this Swedish farmer's immigration to America illustrates how the members of a single family helped each other to settle in the United States. Jarlson's narrative was published in the January 8, 1903, issue of *The Independent.*

Josselyn, John *(Essay 2)* An English traveler who visited the American colonies in 1638-39 and again in 1663-71. This quotation is taken from the second of two books he wrote, *An Account of Two Voyages to New-England* (1674).

Kalm, Peter *(Essay 2)* A Swede who traveled in America from 1748 to 1751. As a botanist, he was interested mainly in plants and farming. (Mountain laurel is named after him—*Kalmia latifolia.*) His *Travels* appeared at intervals between 1753 and 1761.

Kemble, Fanny *(Essay 5)* A leading English actress, she first toured the United States in 1833-34, when she met and married a Philadelphian who owned cotton and rice plantations in Georgia. Her *Journal of a Residence on a Georgian Plantation in 1838-39* (1863) is an animated account.

Kipling, Rudyard *(Essay 7)* Between March and September 1889, the famous English writer (then only twenty-four) sent thirty-seven letters back to an Indian newspaper, as he traveled from India to England via the Far East and the United States. The last of his letters is titled "An Interview with Mark Twain." All this correspondence was published in *From Sea to Sea* (1890).

Klinkowström, Axel *(Essays 3, 4)* A member of an old Swedish family, Baron Klinkowström served as a naval officer, and visited the United States in 1818-20 primarily to investigate the practical workings of the steamboat. His *Letters on the United States* appeared in 1824.

Kossenko, Zinaida—See Mikhailov, Nikolai

Labarca H., Amanda *(Essay 9)* A distinguished Chilean educator, feminist, and public servant, she visited the United States ten times between 1911 and 1952. She represented Chile in the first General Assembly of the United Nations in 1946.

Lambert, John *(Essay 3)* Little is known of this Englishman's life except his trip to North America in 1806-09 to investigate the possibilities of hemp cultivation in Canada. The chief result was his *Travels Through Lower Canada and the United States of North America* (1810).

Lane, Ralph *(Essay 1)* This Englishman sailed on Grenville's 1585 expedition, and remained to become the first governor of Virginia. He and the rest of the colony, however, returned to England with Drake in 1586. The quotation is from Hakluyt's *Voyages*.

Laski, Harold *(Essay 7)* A noted British socialist, he taught history at Harvard University from 1916 to 1920. After returning to England, he devoted himself to teaching, writing, and journalism. His *American Democracy* was published in 1948.

Leacock, Stephen *(Essay 8)* The Canadian humorist and man of letters was also a distinguished political scientist and professor at McGill University. This quotation is from *Stephen Leacock's Laugh Parade*, published in 1940.

Le Corbusier (Charles Edouard Jeanneret) *(Essays 8, 9)* This Swiss-born French architect has been called "the voice and conscience of modern architecture." He visited the United States several times during his lifetime. His book *When the Cathedrals Were White* (1947) was devoted mostly to his impressions of America.

Lederer, John *(Essay 2)* This scholar and student of medicine explored the Piedmont and the Blue Ridge Mountains in 1669-70, the first European to do so. He then moved to New England, returning to his native Germany in 1675. His *Discoveries*, written in Latin, was translated and published in London in 1672.

Leigh, Charles *(Essay 1)* A merchant, he sailed from his native England in 1597 to trade and to plunder Spanish ships. His description of Newfoundland, from Hakluyt's *Voyages*, is one of the few accounts of his many travels to survive.

Lyell, Sir Charles *(Essay 5)* The leading English geologist of the nineteenth century, he made four trips to the United States. His steamboat description is from *A Second Visit to the United States of North America* (1849).

Marias, Julian *(Essays 8, 9)* A Spanish philosopher, he helped found Madrid's Institute of Humanities. In 1951–52 Marias was a visiting professor at Wellesley College.

Martineau, Harriet *(Essay 4)* A writer, she spent the years 1834-36 in the United States, returning to her native England an ardent abolitionist. Her *Society in America* was published in 1837.

Maurois, André *(Essay 8)* The noted French critic and novelist was a frequent visitor to the United States, where he was a popular lecturer. In 1939 he published *Thirty-Nine States, Journal of a Voyage to America,* from which this quote is taken.

Maximilian of Wied, Prince *(Essay 5)* This Prussian aristocrat traveled in the western United States in 1832-34. He was accompanied by a young Swiss artist, Charles Bodmer; the result of their stay was *Travels in the Interior of North America* (1839-41), with maps and illustrations by Bodmer.

Mehdevi, Mohamed *(Essay 9)* An Iranian journalist and diplomat, he first became acquainted with the United States as a foreign student in Florida. *Something Human* (1962) was the result of his adventures hitchhiking from Florida to the West Coast.

Mikhailov, Nikolai and Zinaida Kossenko *(Essay 9)* This Russian geographer and his wife, a psychiatrist, made a tour of America in 1960. Their account first appeared in a Moscow publication the same year and was later published in the United States as *Those Americans, a Travelogue* (1962).

Moreau de Saint-Méry, M. L. E. *(Essay 3)* A French judge, he fled to the United States in 1794 to escape the Revolution. He remained until 1798, an embittered critic of the American scene. His *Voyage to the United States* remained in manuscript form until it was published in 1913.

Münsterberg, Hugo *(Essay 7)* This German philosopher and professor at Harvard University wrote *The Americans* (1904) in order to dispel German prejudice against Americans.

Myers, Robert *(Essay 6)* A Jewish immigrant from Rumania, Myers came to the United States in 1913 and later became active in the labor movement. His recollections, *Stimmer* ["stutterer"]: *The Boy Who Couldn't Talk,* were published in 1959.

Newman, Ernest *(Essay 7)* From 1910 to 1940 he was the major British music critic. His review of Isadora Duncan quoted here was written in April 1921. Several years later, he moved to New York City, where he wrote music reviews for the *New York Evening Post.* The November 17, 1924, edition carried his appreciation of Gershwin's *Rhapsody in Blue.*

Oñate, Juan de *(Essay 1)* Born in the New World, he founded the province of New Mexico in 1598 and was its governor until 1609. Though convicted of misconduct in office, he was later pardoned.

Priestley, J. B. *(Essays 8, 9)* The English novelist and critic lived in the United States in 1935–36; *Midnight on the Desert* (1937) grew out of this experience. In 1954 he and his wife Jacquetta

Hawkes (an author and anthropologist) traveled in the American Southwest. Their wry and amusing collaboration, *Journey Down a Rainbow,* for which each wrote alternating chapters, was published in 1955.

Pupin, Michael Idvorsky *(Essay 6)* Born in Yugoslavia, the brilliant physicist sold all his belongings in order to come to America. In 1924 he won a Pulitzer Prize for *From Immigrant to Inventor* (1923), the story of his life.

Raeder, Ole *(Essay 5)* A leading Norwegian lawyer and judge, he was sent to the United States in 1847 to study the jury system. He regularly sent home newspaper dispatches, which were eventually published in 1929 as *America in the Forties.*

Rivera, Diego *(Essay 7)* In 1942 the celebrated Mexican artist spoke of his contemporary, John Sloan, to American art critic Walter Pach. Rivera himself had visited the United States in the 1930s, where he painted frescoes in Detroit, San Francisco, and New York. He was much impressed with American technology.

Ross, Alexander *(Essay 4)* A Scot, he worked for John Jacob Astor's Pacific Fur Company from 1810 to 1813, then for the Canadian North West Company until 1825. His *Fur-Hunters of the Far West* appeared in 1855.

Rukser, Udo—See Hilbersheimer, Ludwig

Russell of Killowen, Lord *(Essays 5, 6)* Born in Ireland, this lawyer first visited America in 1883 and wrote a *Diary of a Visit to the United States of America* (published in 1910). He served as lord chief justice of England from 1894 until his death in 1900.

Sarc, Omer Celâl *(Essay 8)* This Turkish economist has spent much time in the United States. In 1950 he visited universities across the country as a guest of the State Department. He also taught at Columbia University and worked for the United Nations.

Schoepf, Johann David *(Essay 3)* A German scientist, he came to America as a physician for Hessian troops in 1777, and remained in this country until 1784. His *Travels in the Confederation* appeared in 1788.

Settle, Dionise *(Essay 1)* A mariner who sailed on the second to Frobisher's three expeditions to North America. This account is from Hakluyt's *Voyages.*

Sheridan, Claire *(Essay 7)* A celebrated British sculptress, known for her busts of Lenin, Trotsky, and Gandhi. She met Sinclair Lewis in Washington, D.C., in April 1921. A vivid account of their meeting appeared in her book *My American Diary,* published the following year.

Stevenson, Robert Louis *(Essays 5, 6)* The Scottish writer crossed the United States in 1879 to visit an American woman he had met in Europe (and whom he eventually married). *Across the Plains* was published in 1892.

Tocqueville, Alexis de *(Essays 3, 4)* This French statesman and writer was sent to the United States in 1831 by his government in order to study American penitentiaries. He is best known, however, for his two-volume *Democracy in America* (1835, 1840), widely regarded as one of the most insightful commentaries ever written on the United States.

Trollope, Frances *(Essays 4, 5)* An English novelist (and the mother of novelist Anthony Trollope), she visited the United States in 1827-30, trying unsuccessfully to set up a store in Cincinnati. Her *Domestic Manners of the Americans* (1832) is a humorous critique that much offended Americans of the time.

Tyrmand, Leopold *(Essay 9)* A journalist born in Warsaw, Poland, he moved to the United States in the 1960s. Portions of his writings, dealing with his experiences as a European in America, appeared in *The New Yorker.* They were collected in *Notebooks of a Dilettante* (1967).

Vay de Vaya und Luskod, Count *(Essays 5, 6, 7)* A Hungarian nobleman, he traveled widely as a diplomat for the Roman Catholic Church. Visiting the United States several times between 1903 and 1906, he described his travels in *The Inner Life of the United States* (1908).

Verrazano, Giovanni da *(Essay 1)* The Italian navigator commissioned by France is believed to have been the first European to enter New York Harbor and sail up the Hudson River. Gilbert and Gosnold had his account with them when they explored Cape Cod.

Vizcaíno, Sebastián *(Essay 1)* A Spanish trader, he was commissioned by the viceroy to explore California, which he did in 1596 and again in 1602-03.

Von Borch, Herbert *(Essays 8, 9)* This German writer's book *The Unfinished Society* (1960) was based on notes he made while working in the United States as a newspaper correspondent.

Wansey, Henry *(Essay 2)* An English clothier who retired to take up scholarship, he visited the United States in 1794. His observations were published in 1796 under the title of *An Excursion to the United States of North America.*

Ward, Barbara and René Dubos *(Essay 9)* Barbara Ward, an English social scientist, lectured frequently in the United States in the period after World War II. *Only One Earth* (1972) was written with the Pulitzer-prize winning microbiologist, René Dubos, who was born in France but moved to the United States in 1924.

Wells, H. G. *(Essay 6)* The famous English novelist

visited Ellis Island during his first trip to the United States in 1905. He wrote of his impressions in *The Future of America* (1906).

West, Rebecca *(Essay 7)* Born in Ireland, she became known for her writings on history and politics. Her essay on Willa Cather was originally published by the *New York Herald Tribune* in September 1927, and was reprinted in *The Strange Necessity* (1928).

White, T. H. *(Essay 9)* Best known for his books on King Arthur, this English author kept a journal while on a lecture tour in the United States. It was later published as *America at Last, the American Journal of T. H. White* (1965).

Wolff, Albert *(Essay 7)* A French art critic, he wrote for the noted French newspaper, *Le Figaro*. This selection is quoted from his 1881 review of the Impressionists' sixth group exhibition.

ILLUSTRATION CREDITS

UNIT ONE
Page 3, N.Y.P.L. Picture Collection; 5, American Museum of Natural History; 6, Brown Brothers; 8, Culver Pictures, Inc.; 10, American Museum of Natural History; 12, Brown Brothers; 15, Culver Pictures, Inc.; 18, Culver Pictures, Inc.; 22(top left), American Museum of Natural History; (bottom left and right), George Holton/Photo Researchers; 23, George Holton/Photo Researchers; 24, Library of Congress; 25, American Museum of Natural History; 26(top left and bottom), Museum of Primitive Art; (top right), American Museum of Natural History; 27(top left), Bureau of Ethnology; (top right), American Museum of Natural History; (bottom), Museum of Primitive Art; 28, Metropolitan Museum of Art— Gift of J. Pierpont Morgan, 1900; 29, Culver Pictures, Inc.; 30, Brown Brothers; 31, Brown Brothers; PE 1-1, P. W. Grace/Photo Researchers; PE 1-2, Steven C. Wilson; PE 1-3(top), Robert E. Jackson; (bottom), Harold Sund; PE 1-4(top), Russ Kinne/Photo Researchers; (bottom), Ken Brate/Photo Researchers; PE 1-5(top), Bruce Roberts/Rapho/Photo Researchers; (bottom left), Shelley Grossman/Woodfin Camp, Inc.; (bottom right), Woodbridge Williams/Magnum; PE 1-6(top left), Yaeger & Kay/Photo Researchers; (top right), Van Bucher/Photo Researchers; (bottom), Bradley Smith/Photo Researchers; PE 1-7(top), Barbara Young/Photo Researchers; (center left, center right, and bottom), (Mark Catesby) *The Natural History of Carolina, Flordia and the Bahama Islands . . .* (London, 1754)—N.Y.P.L. Rare Book Collection; PE 1-8(top), Dennis Stock/Magnum; (bottom), (André Thevet) *Les Singularitez de la France Antarctique . . .* (Antwerp, 1558)—N.Y.P.L. Rare Book Collection; PE 1-9, Marvin B. Winter/Photo Researchers; 34, Hispanic Society of America; 38,

Colonial Williamsburg; 39(top), Culver Pictures, Inc.; (bottom), N.Y.P.L. Rare Book Collection; 40, N.Y.P.L. Picture Collection; 41, N.Y.P.L. Rare Book Collection; 42, N.Y.P.L. Picture Collection; 51, Berkeley Castle—Courtesy, Virginia Historical Society; 54, Photo by Thomas L. Williams, Mural by Sidney King—Jamestown Foundation; 55, Virginia Historical Society; 56, 57, 58, Details of engraving by Bry—N.Y.P.L. Prints Division; 61, Culver Pictures, Inc.; 66, (Bry) *America, Part XIII*—N.Y.P.L. Rare Book Collection/Astor, Lenox, and Tilden Foundations; 68, Virginia State Library; 70, N.Y.P.L. Picture Collection; 78, Culver Pictures, Inc.; 81, Metropolitan Museum of Art, Bequest of Charles Allen Munn, 1924; 83, Samuel Chamberlain; 92, Harvard University Portrait Collection; 94, (R. Gardiner) *England's Grievance Discovered . . .* (1655); 95, Essex Institute, Salem, Mass.; 96(top), Massachusetts Historical Society; (bottom), *Proceedings of the Massachusetts Historical Society,* 1884; PE 2-1, Carolina Art Association of Gibbes Art Gallery, Charleston, S.C.; PE 2-2(top), Maryland Historical Society; PE 2-3(top left), (Holm Campanius) *Kort Beskfrifnin om Provincien nya Swerige uti America* (Stockholm, 1702)—N.Y.P.L. Rare Book Collection; (top right), (Thomas Anburey) *Travels Through the Interior Parts of America* (London, 1784)—Smithsonian Institution; (bottom), N.Y. State Historical Association—Courtesy, American Heritage Publishing Co.; PE 2-4, Trustees of the Dorset Natural History and Archaeological Society —Courtesy, American Heritage Publishing Co.; PE 2-5(top), Essex Institute, Salem, Mass.; (bottom), Massachusetts Historical Society; PE 2-6(top), Painting by Ralph Earl from the Collection of Mrs. Cornelius Boardman—Courtesy, Metropolitan Museum of Art; (bottom), New-York Historical Society; PE 2-7(top), New-York

Historical Society; (bottom), American Antiquarian Society; PE 2-8 (top), New-York Historical Society; (center), Corning Museum of Glass, Corning, N.Y.; (bottom), Smithsonian Institution; 98, American Antiquarian Society; 103, Pilgrim Hall, Plymouth, Mass.; 105, N.Y.P.L. Picture Collection; 106, Culver Pictures, Inc.; 108, *Howard Pyle's Book of the American Spirit;* 111, New-York Historical Society; 116, Pennsylvania Academy of the Fine Arts .

UNIT TWO
Page 119, Library of Congress; 123, Henry Francis DuPont Winterthur Museum; 124, Massachusetts Historical Society; 131, Chamberlain Collection, Boston Public Library; 132, Museum of Fine Arts, Boston— Gift of Joseph W., William B., and Edward H. R. Revere; 133, N.Y.P.L. Picture Collection; 135, Massachusetts Historical Society; 139, Brown Brothers; 141, Brown Brothers; 143, N.Y.P.L. Picture Collection; 144, Colonial Williamsburg; 147, Metropolitan Museum of Art, Bequest of Charles Allen Munn, 1924; 149, Culver Pictures, Inc.; 152, John Carter Brown Library; 153, I. N. Phelps Stokes Collection, N.Y.P.L. Prints Division; 155, John Carter Brown Library; 156, Henry Francis DuPont Winterthur Museum; 159, Pierpont Morgan Library; PE 3-1, New-York Historical Society; PE 3-2(top), Daughters of the American Revolution Museum, Washington, D.C.; (bottom), Moravian Historical Society, Nazareth, Pa.; PE 3-3(top), Connecticut Historical Society; (bottom), Newport Historical Society; PE 3-4(top), N.Y.P.L. Rare Book Collection; (bottom), New-York Historical Society; PE 3-5(top left), Detail of "The Shop and Warehouse of Duncan Phyfe, 168-172 Fulton Street, N.Y.C."—Metropolitan Museum of Art, Rogers Fund, 1922; (top right), (N. Heideloff) *Gallery of Fashion* (London, 1794)—N.Y.P.L.; (bottom), "The Dinner Party" by

Henry Sargent, Museum of Fine Arts, Boston--Gift of Mrs. Horation A. Lamb in Memory of Mr. and Mrs. Winthrop Sargent; **PE 3-6(top)**, Abby Aldrich Rockefeller Folk Art Collection; **(bottom)**, Metropolitan Museum of Art, Rogers Fund, 1942; **PE 3-7**, National Gallery of Art—Gift of Edgar William and Bernice Chrysler Garbisch; **PE 3-8(top)**, Ann Parker; **(bottom)**, Firestone Library, Princeton University; **166**, National Gallery of Art, Gift of Edgar William and Bernice Chrysler Garbisch; **170**, N.Y.P.L. Manuscript Division; **171**, Virginia State Library; **178**, N.Y.P.L. Picture Collection; **181**, N.Y.P.L. Picture Collection; **184**, Peabody Museum of Salem; **185**, Historical Society of Pennsylvania; **186**, Thomas Gilcrease Institute; **187**, Culver Pictures, Inc.; **189**, American Antiquarian Society; **190**, New-York Historical Society; **191**, Yale University Art Gallery.

UNIT THREE
Page 195, Culver Pictures, Inc.; **197**, Museum of the City of New York; **199**, Independence National Historical Park Collection; **203**, Corcoran Gallery of Art; **204**, Newberry Library; **206**, Cincinnati Historical Society; **212**, New-York Historical Society; **215**, New-York Historical Society; **217**, Library of Congress; **219**, N.Y.P.L. Picture Collection; **220**, White House Collection; **226**, New-York Historical Society; **227**, New Orleans Museum of Art; **229(left)**, Granger Collection; **(center)**, Independence National Historical Park Collection; **(right)**, Missouri Historical Society; **237**, Culver Pictures, Inc.; **241**, Culver Pictures, Inc.; **243**, Culver Pictures, Inc.; **250**, Corcoran Gallery of Art; **254**, Historical Society of Pennsylvania; **255**, James Monroe Memorial House and Library; **PE 4-1**, (Maximilian, Prince of Wied) *Travels in the Interior of North America* (1833)—N.Y.P.L. Rare Book Collection; **PE 4-2(top)**, Museum of Fine Arts, Boston—Bequest of Henry L. Shattuck in Memory of the Late Ralph W. Gray; **(bottom)**, Missouri Historical Society; **PE 4-3(top)**, Northern Natural Gas Company Collection of the Joslyn Art Museum, Omaha, Neb.; **(bottom left)**, Granger Collection; **(bottom right)**, Culver Pictures, Inc.; **PE 4-4(top left)**,

Northern Natural Gas Company Collection of the Joslyn Art Museum, Omaha, Neb.; **(top right)**, (F. J. Meine) *The Crockett Almanacks* (Chicago, 1955)—N.Y.P.L. Rare Book Collection; **(bottom)**, Detail of "Spring Burning Up Fallen Leaves" by George Harvey—Brooklyn Museum; **PE 4-5(top)**, Collection of Mr. and Mrs. Leslie Cowan, Columbia, Mo.; **(center)**, New-York Historical Society; **(bottom)**, Glenbow-Alberta Institute— Courtesy, American Heritage Publishing Co.; **PE 4-6(top)**, "Flax Scutching Bee" by Linton Park— National Gallery of Art, Gift of Edgar William and Bernice Chrysler Garbisch (Courtesy, Time/Life Books, © Time, Inc.); **(bottom)**, Detail of "Shooting for the Beef" by George Caleb Bingham; **PE 4-7**, Boatmen's National Bank of St. Louis; **PE 4-8(top)**, Minnesota Historical Society; **(bottom)**, (Mrs. Frances Trollope) *Domestic Manners of the Americans* (Kiel, Germany, 1835); **259**, The Cooper Union; **260**, Library of Congress; **264**, Courtesy, Chicago Historical Society; **266**, Benjamin Harrison Home; **267**, Courtesy, Chicago Historical Society; **270**, Culver Pictures, Inc.; **271(top and bottom)**, Brown Brothers; **272**, Culver Pictures, Inc.; **280**, Culver Pictures, Inc.; **286**, Culver Pictures, Inc.; **288**, Brown Brothers; **289**, Brown Brothers; **295**, Culver Pictures, Inc.; **296**, Brown Brothers; **297(top)**, Brown Brothers; **(bottom)**, Culver Pictures, Inc.; **298**, Culver Pictures, Inc.; **301**, Culver Pictures, Inc.

UNIT FOUR
Page 305, Brown Brothers; **310**, Virginia State Library; **311**, Virginia State Library; **315**, N.Y.P.L. Picture Collection; **316**, N.Y.P.L. General Research and Humanities Division/ Astor, Lenox, and Tilden Foundations; **317**, Virginia State Library; **319**, Virginia State Library; **323(left and right)**, New-York Historical Society; **324**, Louisiana Tourist Development Commission; **326**, Yale University Art Gallery; **327**, Glenbow-Alberta Institute; **328**, Duke University Library; **330**, Virginia State Library; **331**, New-York Historical Society; **332**, Library of Congress; **334**, Library of Congress; **337**, Library of Congress;

341, Library of Congress; **342**, Library of Congress; **343**, Library of Congress; **345(top and bottom)**, Library of Congress; **346**, Library of Congress; **347**, Library of Congress; **350**, Worcester Art Museum; **352**, Corcoran Gallery of Art, Gift of Mr. and Mrs. Landsell K. Christie; **353**, Library of Congress; **355**, Library of Congress; **360**, California State Library Picture Collection; **361**, International Museum of Photography at George Eastman House; **366**, Library of Congress; **367(top)**, N.Y.P.L. Picture Collection; **(center)**, Boston Athenaeum; **(bottom)**, N.Y.P.L. Picture Collection; **368(top and bottom)**, Library of Congress; **371**, Baltimore and Ohio Railroad; **372**, Virginia State Library; **373**, Library of Congress; **374**, Baltimore and Ohio Railroad; **377**, New-York Historical Society; **379**, Library of Congress; **380**, MET, Gift of Mr. and Mrs. Carl Stoeckel, 1897; **381**, Virginia State Library; **384**, Culver Pictures, Inc.; **PE 5-1**, Permission of Frost and Reed, London—Courtesy, Mariners Museum, Newport News, Va.; **PE 5-2(top)**, Kennedy Galleries, Inc.; **(bottom)**, New-York Historical Society; **PE 5-3**, "Travel by Stagecoach Near Trenton, New Jersey" by Paul Svinin— Metropolitan Museum of Art, Rogers Fund, 1942; **PE 5-4(top)**, Thomas Gilcrease Institute, Tulsa, Okla.; **(bottom)**, Tulane University; **PE 5-5(top)**, Mariners Museum, Newport News, Va.; **(bottom)**, Boatmen's National Bank of St. Louis; **PE 5-6 (top)**, California Historical Society —San Francisco/San Marino; **(bottom)**, Thomas Gilcrease Institute, Tulsa, Okla.; **PE 5-7**, Smithsonian Institution; **PE 5-8(top)**, Library of Congress—Courtesy, American Heritage Publishing Co.; **(bottom)**, Granger Collection; **385**, Chicago Historical Society; **386**, Brown Brothers; **387**, Kansas State Historical Society, Topeka, Kansas; **388**, Brown Brothers; **389**, Brown Brothers; **390**, Library of Congress; **392**, N.Y.P.L. Picture Collection; **393(top and bottom)**, Library of Congress; **396**, Missouri Historical Society; **399**, Culver Pictures, Inc.; **402**, Culver Pictures, Inc.; **403**, Brady Collection, U.S. Signal Corps, National Archives; **404**, N.Y.P.L. Prints Division; **406**, Charles Colcock Jones Papers/Manuscript

Dept., Special Collections Division, Tulane University Library; **407**, N.Y.P.L. Prints Division; **409**, Library of Congress; **410**, Library of Congress; **416**, Penn Community Services Cultural Program; **420(top)**, Courtesy, Chicago Historical Society; **(bottom)**, Brady Collection, U.S. Signal Corps, National Archives; **422**, Valentine Museum, Richmond, Va.; **423**, Brady Collection, U.S. Signal Corps, National Archives; **426**, National Archives; **428(top and bottom)**, Library of Congress; **431**, Library of Congress; **432**, Library of Congress; **434**, Culver Pictures, Inc.; **436**, Brown Brothers; **438**, Library of Congress; **439(left and right)**, Library of Congress; **443**, Brown Brothers; **445**, Louisiana State Museum; **446**, Brown Brothers; **447**, Culver Pictures, Inc.

UNIT FIVE
Page 451, Culver Pictures, Inc.; **453**, Library of Congress; **455**, Library of Congress; **457**, Culver Pictures, Inc.; **460**, Library of Congress; **461 (top and bottom)**, Library of Congress; **462**, Culver Pictures, Inc.; **464**, Culver Pictures, Inc.; **467**, Library of Congress; **468**, Culver Pictures, Inc.; **469**, Culver Pictures, Inc.; **473**, United Press International; **474**, Culver Pictures, Inc.; **475**, Culver Pictures, Inc.; **476**, Culver Pictures, Inc.; **478**, Culver Pictures, Inc.; **481**, Smithsonian Institution/ National Anthropological Archives; **482**, U.S. Signal Corps/National Archives; **487**, Smithsonian Institution/National Anthropological Archives; **488**, Smithsonian Institution/National Anthropological Archives; **489**, Smithsonian Institution/National Anthropological Archives; **490**, U.S. Signal Corps/ National Archives; **491**, U.S. Signal Corps/National Archives; **497**, Nebraska State Historical Society; **500(top)**, Library of Congress; **(bottom)**, Minnesota Historical Society; **501**, Permission of Huntington Library, San Marino, Calif.; **502**, Southern Pacific Railroad; **505**, Library of Congress; **507**, Manitoba Archives; **509**, Smithsonian Institution/National Anthropological Archives; **510**, Naval Observatory/National Archives; **513**, Western History Dept., Denver Public Library; **514**,

Bureau of Reclamation/National Archives; **517(top and bottom)**, International Harvester Company Historical Archives; **518**, International Harvester Company Historical Archives; **524**, Library of Congress; **533**, Library of Congress; **534**, A.T.&T.; **536**, Library of Congress; **541**, International Museum of Photography at George Eastman House; **542**, Photo by Jacob A. Riis—Jacob A. Riis Collection, Museum of the City of New York; **544**, Kansas State Historical Society, Topeka, Kansas; **PE 6-1**, Culver Pictures, Inc.; **PE 6-2(top)**, New-York Historical Society; **(bottom)**, Metropolitan Museum of Art; **PE 6-3 (top and center)**, Bettmann Archive; **(bottom)**, N.Y.P.L. Picture Collection; **PE 6-4(top)**, Los Angeles County Museum of Art; **(bottom)**, Museum of the City of New York; **PE 6-5(top)**, Bettmann Archive; **(bottom)**, N.Y.P.L. Picture Collection; **PE 6-6(top left)**, Wisconsin State Historical Society; **(top right)**, Missouri Historical Society; **(bottom)**, Chicago Historical Society; **PE 6-7(top)**, Illinois Department of Conservation; **(bottom)**, Chicago Historical Society; **PE 6-8(top)**, Thomas Gilcrease Institute, Tulsa, Okla.; **(bottom)**, Franklin D. Roosevelt Library, Hyde Park, N.Y.; **545**, Museum of the City of New York; **550**, Brown Brothers; **551**, Culver Pictures, Inc.; **552**, Culver Pictures, Inc.; **553**, Culver Pictures, Inc.; **554(top)**, Culver Pictures, Inc.; **(bottom)**, Brown Brothers; **556**, Culver Pictures, Inc.; **557**, Culver Pictures, Inc.; **558**, United Press International; **565(top)**, Culver Pictures, Inc.; **(bottom)**, Brown Brothers; **566**, Culver Pictures, Inc.; **568**, Culver Pictures, Inc.; **572**, Culver Pictures, Inc.; **573**, Culver Pictures, Inc.

UNIT SIX
Page 579, Culver Pictures, Inc.; **581**, Brown Brothers; **582**, Brown Brothers; **584**, New-York Historical Society; **587**, Brown Brothers; **589**, Brown Brothers; **591**, Brown Brothers; **592**, Library of Congress; **596**, Brown Brothers; **600(top and center)**, Library of Congress; **(bottom)**, Culver Pictures, Inc.; **601**, Cleveland Public Library Picture Collection; **602**, Library of Congress; **605**, Library of Congress; **607**,

Library of Congress; **610**, Library of Congress; **613**, Bettmann Archive; **614**, Naval Photographic Center; **615**, U.S. Signal Corps/National Archives; **620**, Library of Congress; **622**, Library of Congress; **623**, U.S. Signal Corps/National Archives; **624**, U.S. Signal Corps/National Archives; **625**, Library of Congress; **628**, New-York Historical Society; **631**, Library of Congress; **634**, U.S. Signal Corps/ National Archives; **635**, Library of Congress; **638**, U.S. War Dept. General Staff—National Archives; **642**, U.S. Signal Corps/National Archives; **644**, Culver Pictures, Inc.; **650**, National Air and Space Museum, Smithsonian Institution; **651**, National Air and Space Museum, Smithsonian Institution; **653**, Brown Brothers; **656**, Brown Brothers; **659**, National Air and Space Museum, Smithsonian Institution; **660**, Culver Pictures, Inc.; **662**, Westinghouse Broadcasting Company; **666**, Ford Archives; **667**, Ford Archives; **669(top)**, Brown Brothers; **(bottom)**, Michigan History Division; **671**, Bettmann Archive; **672**, Bettmann Archive; **PE 7-1**, Painting of the Museum's Interior in 1881 by Frank Waller; Photo by Francis G. Mayer— Metropolitan Museum of Art; **PE 7-2 (top)**, Culver Pictures, Inc.; **(bottom)**, Museum of Fine Arts, Boston; **PE 7-3(top)**, Art Institute of Chicago; **(bottom left)**, Metropolitan Museum of Art; **(bottom right)**, Museum of Modern Art—Gift of Friends of the Sculptor in 1908; **PE 7-4 (top)**, N.Y.P.L. Picture Collection; **(bottom)**, Phillips Gallery; **PE 7-5(top)**, Hedrich-Blessing; **(bottom)**, Amherst College Collection; **PE 7-6 (top)**, Culver Pictures, Inc.; **(bottom)**, Museum of the City of New York; **PE 7-7(top)**, Edward Steichen; **(bottom)**, Courtesy of Mr. Ira Gershwin and The Humanities Research Center, University of Texas at Austin; **PE 7-8(top)**, Museum of Art at Ogunquit; **(bottom)**, Brown Brothers; **677**, United Press International; **679**, Wide World Photos; **681**, United Press International; **683**, Wide World Photos; **685**, Acme News-Pictures, Inc. (UPI); **688**, Wide World Photos; **689**, United Press International; **690**, Underwood and Underwood; **691**, Wide World Photos; **694**, United Press International; **696**, Wide World Photos; **697**, Wide World Photos;

698, Courtesy The Moorland-Spingarn Research Center, Howard University; 699, Cartoon by Alley—*Memphis Commercial Appeal;* 702, Wide World Photos; 705, Wide World Photos.

UNIT SEVEN

Page 709, Courtesy, United Nations; **712,** United Press International; **713,** United Press International; **715,** United Press International; **717,** Brown Brothers; **719,** United Press International; **723,** United Press International; **726,** United Press International; **727,** Culver Pictures, Inc.; **729,** United Press International; **735,** United Press International; **736,** Wide World Photos; **737,** United Press International; **739,** Culver Pictures, Inc.; **740,** United Press International; **742,** Brown Brothers; **743,** Brown Brothers; **748,** Navy Dept./National Archives; **749,** Naval Photographic Center; **751,** United Press International; **752,** U.S. Office of War Information/National Archives; **755(top and bottom),** Navy Dept./National Archives; **758,** Navy Dept./National Archives; **760,** United Press International; **762,** Acme Newspictures, Inc. (UPI); **768,** U.S. Information Agency/National Archives; **PE 8-1,** Detail of "The New Television Set" by Norman Rockwell—Permission, Los Angeles County Museum of Art; **PE 8-2(top left),** Culver Pictures, Inc.; **(top right),** Eileen Darby/Graphic House; **(bottom),** Brown Brothers; **PE 8-3 (top),** Globe Photos; **(bottom),** Time-Life Picture Agency; **PE 8-4(top left),** Acme News-Pictures, Inc. (UPI); **(top right),** Hy Peskin/Time-Life Picture Agency; **(bottom),** Capricorn Art Gallery; **PE 8-5(top),** Francis Miller/Time-Life Picture Agency; **(bottom),** Ralph Crane/Time-Life Picture Agency; **PE 8-6 (top),** Margaret Bourke-White/Time-Life Picture Agency; **(bottom),** Leonard McCombe/Time-Life Picture Agency; **PE 8-7(top),** Nina Leen/Time-Life Picture Agency; **(bottom),** University of Wisconsin Dept. of Photocinema; **PE 8-8(top),** Frank Scherschel/Time-Life Picture Agency; **(bottom),** Peter Stackpole/Life Magazine, © Time, Inc.; **771,** Acme Newspictures, Inc. (UPI); **772,** U.S. Office of War Information/National Archives; **774,** U.S. Information Agency/National Archives; **775,** United Press International; **776,** Wide World Photos; **778,** Estate of David Low; **779,** United Press International; **781,** Wide World Photos; **785,** Wide World Photos; **787,** United Press International; **788,** Wide World Photos; **790,** Wide World Photos; **794,** Wide World Photos; **795,** Wide World Photos; **798,** Wide World Photos; **799,** Wide World Photos; **801,** Wide World Photos; **803,** Dorothea Lange Collection—Oakland Museum; **805,** United Press International; **807,** Wide World Photos; **809,** Wide World Photos; **811,** Wide World Photos; **812,** Wide World Photos; **813,** Wide World Photos.

UNIT EIGHT

Page 817, CBS News Photo from UPI; **820,** United Press International; **823,** United Press International; **824,** United Press International; **827(top and bottom),** Dan Budnik/Woodfin Camp & Assoc.; **832,** United Press International; **834,** Marc & Evelyne Bernheim/Woodfin Camp & Assoc.; **835,** Wide World Photos; **836,** United Press International; **838,** United Press International; **839,** United Press International; **840,** United Press International; **842,** United Press International; **843(top and bottom),** United Press International; **847(left and right),** Wide World Photos; **849,** United Press International; **851,** United Press International; **859,** Stephen Shames/Magnum; **860,** Burk Uzzle/Magnum; **861,** United Press International; **862,** United Press International; **863,** United Press International; **PE 9-1,** Esther Henderson/Rapho/Photo Researchers; **PE 9-2(top),** Charles Moore/Black Star; **(bottom),** Van Bucher/Photo Researchers; **PE 9-3 (top),** Bruce Roberts/Rapho/Photo Researchers; **(bottom left),** Fred J. Maroon/Photo Researchers; **(bottom right),** Porterfield Chickering/Photo Researchers; **PE 9-4(top),** Ford Motor Company; **(center),** Charles E. Rotkin/Photography for Industry; **(bottom),** Hedrich-Blessing; **PE 9-5 (top),** Lucia Woods/Photo Researchers; **(bottom),** F. Hulnegle/Monkmeyer; **PE 9-6(top),** Myron Wood/Photo Researchers; **(bottom),** Ray Manley/Shostal Photos; **PE 9-7 (top),** Russ Kinne/Photo Researchers; **(center),** Tom McHugh/Photo Researchers; **(bottom),** Joe Munroe/Photo Researchers; **PE 9-8 (top),** Jack Fields/Photo Researchers; **(bottom),** Ray Ateson; **865,** United Press International; **868,** United Press International; **869(left),** Dan Budnik/Woodfin Camp & Assoc.; **(right),** United Press International; **871,** United Press International; **872,** United Press International; **873,** Wide World Photos; **874,** Wide World Photos; **875,** Elliott Erwitt/Magnum; **879,** United Press International; **880(top and bottom),** United Press International; **881,** Mark Godfrey/Magnum; **882,** United Press International; **884(top and bottom),** United Press International; **887,** United Press International; **890,** United Press International; **892,** Mark Godfrey/Magnum; **896,** United Press International; **897(top),** United Press International; **(bottom),** Wide World Photos; **899,** United Press International; **900,** Sepp Seitz/Magnum; **901,** United Press International; **902,** Mark Godfrey/Magnum; **903,** Alex Webb/Magnum; **904,** United Press International; **906,** United Press International; **908,** Elliott Erwitt/Magnum; **910,** United Press International.

INDEX

ABOUT THE AUTHORS

Allen Weinstein is a Professor of History at Smith College, where he directed American Studies for six years and teaches U.S. political and social history. Recently, he published *Perjury: The Hiss-Chambers Case*, and he is now writing two additional books on the Cold War Period. He also directs The Twentieth Century Fund's study on the impact of the Freedom of Information Act upon U.S. intelligence agencies. His previous books include *Prelude to Populism* and *American Negro Slavery: A Modern Reader*. Professor Weinstein's articles have appeared in *The Dictionary of American Biography*, *Esquire*, *The Journal of American History*, *The Journal of American Studies* (on whose Editorial Board he serves), *The New York Times*, *The New York Review of Books*, and in many other journals. He has lectured throughout Europe and Israel, twice served as Fulbright Lecturer in Australia, and has taught at Amherst College, Brown University, Hartford College for Women, Teacher's College (Columbia), and the University of Maryland.

R. Jackson Wilson is a Professor of History at Smith College, where he also teaches American Studies and Philosophy. His special field of interest is cultural history, and he is currently at work on a study of nineteenth-century American writers. His books include *In Quest of Community: Social Philosophy in the United States* and *Darwinism and the American Intellectual*. He has taught at an unusually wide range of institutions, including the University of Wisconsin, the University of Arizona, Columbia University, Yale University, Hartford College for Women, the University of Massachusetts, Amherst College, and Teacher's College (Columbia).